ISBN 978-0-266-02254-1
PIBN 10959953

1 MONTH OF
FREE
READING

at

www.ForgottenBooks.com

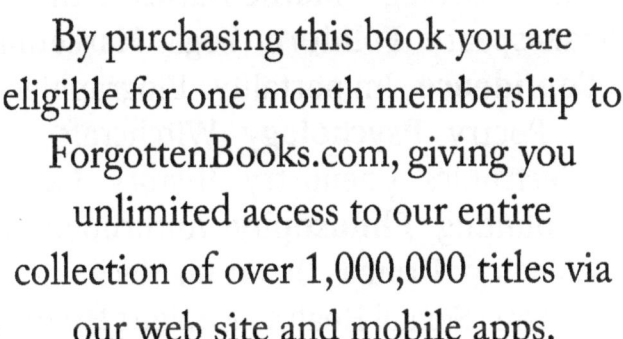

By purchasing this book you are eligible for one month membership to ForgottenBooks.com, giving you unlimited access to our entire collection of over 1,000,000 titles via our web site and mobile apps.

To claim your free month visit:

www.forgottenbooks.com/free959953

English
Français
Deutsche
Italiano
Español
Português

www.forgottenbooks.com

Mythology Photography **Fiction**
Fishing Christianity **Art** Cooking
Essays Buddhism Freemasonry
Medicine **Biology** Music **Ancient
Egypt** Evolution Carpentry Physics
Dance Geology **Mathematics** Fitness
Shakespeare **Folklore** Yoga Marketing
Confidence Immortality Biographies
Poetry **Psychology** Witchcraft
Electronics Chemistry History **Law**
Accounting **Philosophy** Anthropology
Alchemy Drama Quantum Mechanics
Atheism Sexual Health **Ancient History**
Entrepreneurship Languages Sport
Paleontology Needlework Islam
Metaphysics Investment Archaeology
Parenting Statistics Criminology
Motivational

JOURNAL OF THE UNITING CONFERENCE

JOURNAL

OF THE

UNITING CONFERENCE

OF THE

METHODIST EPISCOPAL CHURCH
METHODIST EPISCOPAL CHURCH, SOUTH
METHODIST PROTESTANT CHURCH

HELD AT

KANSAS CITY, MISSOURI
April 26 - May 10, 1939

★

EDITED BY

LUD H. ESTES, Secretary
EDGAR R. HECKMAN and CUTHBERT W. BATES
Associate Secretaries

THE METHODIST PUBLISHING HOUSE
(FOUNDED 1789)

NEW YORK	CINCINNATI	CHICAGO
NASHVILLE	DALLAS	RICHMOND
	PITTSBURGH	BALTIMORE

RESOLUTION FOR EDITING OF JOURNAL

RESOLVED, That the Secretary of the Uniting Conference, together with the Associate Secretaries, be authorized to edit the Journal of the Uniting Conference for publication; that they be authorized to make such verbal changes in the phraseology of the Journal as may be necessary to correctness and uniformity, but not so as to change the meaning of any action of the Uniting Conference; and that the published copy, properly certified by him, be the official Journal of this Conference.

RESOLVED FURTHER, That the Publishing Agents be authorized to publish the Journal of the Uniting Conference, and to send a copy to each delegate of the Uniting Conference, to each Bishop, and to each approved college, seminary, and theological school of The Methodist Church in the United States; the expense for publication and distribution to be charged to the Uniting Conference Expense Fund.

THE JOURNAL, May 5, 1939.

CONTENTS

8 *Contents*

PROCEDURE—UNITING CONFERENCE

Article I.—There shall be a Uniting Conference composed of 900 delegates, of whom 400 shall be from the Methodist Episcopal Church, 400 from the Methodist Episcopal Church, South, and 100 from the Methodist Protestant Church, chosen in such manner as may be determined by the respective General Conferences, provided that the ministerial and lay members shall be in equal number.

Article II.—The Uniting Conference shall be held within twelve months after the final approval and adoption of this Plan of Union by the three Churches, at the call of the Bishops of the two Churches and the President of the General Conference of the Methodist Protestant Church, and at a date fixed by them and at a place selected by a Joint Commission on Entertainment of five persons from each of the three Churches, this commission to be appointed by the Bishops of the two Churches and the President of the Methodist Protestant General Conference.

Article III.—The expenses of the Uniting Conference shall be borne by the three Churches in proportion to their respective representation.

Article IV.—The duties and powers of the Uniting Conference, subject to the provisions of this Plan of Union, shall be:

1. To harmonize and combine the rules and regulations as found in the *Disciplines* of the three Churches relating to membership, the Conferences, the ministry, judicial administration, and temporal economy.

2. To harmonize and combine the Rituals of the three Churches.

3. To provide for the unification, co-ordination, and correlation of the connectional missionary, educational, and benevolent boards and societies of the three Churches

4. To provide for the unification, co-ordination, and correlation of the publishing interests of the three Churches.

5. To provide a plan for the control and safeguarding of all permanent funds and other property interests of the three Churches and the interests of those persons and causes for which these funds were established.

Article V.—In order to facilitate the work of the Uniting Conference, the three General Conferences at the sessions wherein this Plan of Union is approved shall continue their

9

Commissions on Union with such changes in personnel as they may desire, and authorize the Joint Commission thus formed to make special preparation for the Uniting Conference by the appointment of proper committees to deal with (a) membership, Conferences, ministry, judicial administration, and temporal economy; (b) rituals; (c) connectional boards and societies; (d) publishing interests; (e) permanent and pension funds; and (f) such other matters as imperatively call for advance consideration.

Article VI.—All Annual Conferences of the three Churches shall retain their existing status until by the action of the Uniting Conference it shall be determined otherwise.

Article VII.—The legislative power of the Uniting Conference shall be confined to harmonizing and combining provisions now existing in the *Disciplines* of the three Churches, or one or more of these Churches.

Article VIII.—The boundaries and composition of the Annual Conferences within the several Jurisdictional Conferences as made up in this Plan of Union shall be adjusted at the time of the meeting of the Uniting Conference by the delegates from the Annual Conferences within the respective Jurisdictions, sitting apart for that purpose during the period of the Uniting Conference, provided that in the case of those Annual Conferences that may be divided by the Jurisdictional Conference lines, their delegates shall allocate themselves to the respective Jurisdictional Conferences upon the basis of church membership of their Conferences in the respective Jurisdictions.

Article IX.—The Uniting Conference shall fix the basis of representation of the Annual Conferences in the first General Conference and in the Jurisdictional and Central Conferences.

Article X.—Pending the meeting of the Uniting Conference each of the three uniting Churches shall be governed by the rules and regulations of its own *Discipline*.

THE DECLARATION OF UNION

WHEREAS, The Methodist Episcopal Church, The Methodist Episcopal Church, South, and The Methodist Protestant Church did through their respective General Conferences appoint Commissions on Interdenominational Relations and Church Union; and

WHEREAS, These Commissions acting jointly did produce, propose, and present to the three Churches a Plan of Union; and

WHEREAS, These three Churches, each acting separately for and in its own behalf, did by more than the constitutional majorities endorse and adopt this Plan of Union in accord with their respective constitutions and disciplines, and did effect the full consummation of union in accordance with the Plan of Union; and

WHEREAS, These three Churches in adopting this Plan of Union did authorize and provide for a Uniting Conference with certain powers and duties as therein set forth; and

WHEREAS, The Uniting Conference duly authorized and legally chosen in accordance with the Plan of Union is now in session in the city of Kansas City, Missouri:

Now, THEREFORE, We, the members of the Uniting Conference, the legal and authorized representatives of The Methodist Episcopal Church, The Methodist Episcopal Church, South, and The Methodist Protestant Church, in session here assembled on this the 10th day of May, 1939, do solemnly in the presence of God and before all the world make and publish the following Declarations of fact and principle:

I

The Methodist Episcopal Church, The Methodist Episcopal Church, South, and The Methodist Protestant Church are and shall be one United Church.

II

The Plan of Union as adopted is and shall be the constitution of this United Church, and of its three constituent bodies.

III

The Methodist Episcopal Church, The Methodist Episcopal Church, South, and The Methodist Protestant Church

11

had their common origin in the organization of the Methodist Episcopal Church in America in 1784, A.D., and have ever held, adhered to and preserved a common belief, spirit and purpose, as expressed in their common Articles of Religion.

IV

The Methodist Episcopal Church, The Methodist Episcopal Church, South, and The Methodist Protestant Church, in adopting the name "The Methodist Church" for the United Church, do not and will not surrender any right, interest or title in and to these respective names which, by long and honored use and association, have become dear to the ministry and membership of the three uniting Churches and have become enshrined in their history and records.

V

The Methodist Church is the ecclesiastical and lawful successor of the three uniting Churches, and through which the three churches as one United Church shall continue to live and have their existence, continue their institutions, and hold and enjoy their property, exercise and perform their several trusts under and in accord with the Plan of Union and *Discipline* of the United Church; and such trusts or corporate bodies as exist in the constituent churches shall be continued as long as legally necessary.

VI

To The Methodist Church thus established we do now solemnly declare our allegiance, and upon all its life and service we do reverently invoke the blessing of Almighty God. Amen.

BISHOPS OF THE METHODIST EPISCOPAL CHURCH

(Names of Retired Bishops in italics)

William F. Anderson, 960 East Park Ave., Winter Park, Fla.
John L. Nuelsen, Rue des Photographes, Geneva, Switzerland.
Edwin H. Hughes, 100 Maryland Ave., N. E., Washington, D. C.
Francis J. McConnell, 150 Fifth Ave., New York City.
Frederick D. Leete, 730 Cherokee Ave., DeLand, Fla.
~~Herbert~~ *Welch,* 420 Riverside Drive, New York City.
Thomas Nicholson, 812 Summit Ave., Mount Vernon, Iowa.
Adna W. Leonard, 1724 Koppers Building, Pittsburgh, Pa.
Charles B. Mitchell, 456 La Loma Road, Pasadena, Calif.
John W. Robinson, 37 Cantonments Road, Lucknow, India.
Eden S. Johnson, Route 6, Box 900A, Portland, Oreg.
Ernest L. Waldorf, 1609 Chicago Temple Building, Chicago, Ill.
Charles Edward Locke, 445 Georgia St., Santa Monica, Calif.
Ernest G. Richardson, 1701 Arch St., Philadelphia, Pa.
Edgar Blake, 1205 Kales Bldg., 74 W. Adams Ave., Detroit, Mich.
Frederick T. Keeney, 740 Rush St., Chicago, Ill.
H. Lester Smith, 420 Plum St., Cincinnati, Ohio.
Charles L. Mead, 1121 McGee St., Kansas City, Mo.
Robert E. Jones, 1375 East Long St., Columbus, Ohio.
Matthew W. Clair, 1040 Russell Ave., Covington, Ky.
George A. Miller, 1215 Pine Ave., San Jose, Calif.
Titus Lowe, 370 Pittock Block, 10th and Washington Sts., Portland, Oreg.
Brenton T. Badley, 12 Boulevard Road, Delhi, India.
Wallace E. Brown, Box 428, Chattanooga, Tenn.
Raymond J. Wade, 505 W. Franklin St., Elkhart, Ind.
James C. Baker, 83 McAllister St., San Francisco, Calif.
J. Ralph Magee, 32 South Snelling Ave., St. Paul, Minn.
Ralph S. Cushman, 312 Trinity Building, Denver, Colo.
Wilbur E. Hammaker, Nanking, China.
Charles W. Flint, Hotel Syracuse, Syracuse, N. Y.
Alexander P. Shaw, 631 Baronne St., New Orleans, La.
G. Bromley Oxnam, 870 Insurance Building, Omaha, Nebr.

Missionary Bishops

Edwin F. Lee, 5 Mount Sophia, Singapore, Straits Settlements, Malaya; 1265 Calle General Luna, Manila, Philippines.
John M. Springer, Umtali, Southern Rhodesia, Africa.

Central Conference Bishops

ELECTED BY THE EASTERN ASIA CENTRAL CONFERENCE
Ralph A. Ward, Chengtu, Szechuen, China.
John Gowdy, Foochow, China.

ELECTED BY THE SOUTHERN ASIA CENTRAL CONFERENCE
Jashwant R. Chitambar, Jubbulpore, C. P., India.
J. Waskom Pickett, Byculla, Bombay, India.

ELECTED BY THE LATIN AMERICA CENTRAL CONFERENCE
Juan E. Gattinoni, Rivadavia, 4044, Buenos Aires, Argentina.
Roberto Elphick, Gral, Korner 180, Santiago, Chile.

ELECTED BY THE CENTRAL CONFERENCE OF GERMANY, SEPTEMBER, 1936
F. H. Otto Melle, 30 Paulinen Strasse, Berlin-Lichterfelde, W., Germany.

13

BISHOPS OF THE METHODIST EPISCOPAL CHURCH, SOUTH

(Names of Retired Bishops in italics)

Warren A. Candler, 1663 North Decatur Road, Atlanta, Ga.
*Collins Denny,** 1619 Park Ave., Richmond, Va.
John M. Moore, 4311 Rawlins St., Dallas, Tex.
Urban V. W. Darlington, 524 Tenth Ave., Huntington, W. Va.
Horace M. Du Bose, Washington Apartments, Nashville, Tenn.
William N. Ainsworth, 379 College St., Macon, Ga.
Samuel R. Hay, 4004 Mount Vernon, Houston, Tex.
James Cannon, Jr., P. O. Box 605, Richmond, Va.
Hoyt M. Dobbs, Robert E. Lee Hotel, Jackson, Miss.
Hiram A. Boaz, 5037 Bryce Ave., Fort Worth, Tex.
Arthur J. Moore, 2146 W. Gramercy St., San Antonio, Tex.
Paul B. Kern, 810 Broadway, Nashville, Tenn.
A. Frank Smith, 2308 Southmore Blvd., Houston, Tex.
Ivan Lee Holt, 1910 Main St., Dallas, Tex.
William W. Peele, Jefferson Hotel, Richmond, Va.
Clare Purcell, Poplar Apartments, Charlotte, N. C.
Charles C. Selecman, 1901 N. Douglas, Oklahoma City, Okla.
J. Lloyd Decell, 120 Tuscaloosa Ave., Birmingham, Ala.
William C. Martin, 1254 N. Cedar St., Glendale, Calif.
William T. Watkins, Emory University, Ga.

---

* Bishop Denny has declined to become a Bishop of The Methodist Church.

PRESIDENT OF GENERAL CONFERENCE, METHODIST PROTESTANT CHURCH

James H. Straughn, D.D., 516 North Charles St., Baltimore, Md.

COMMISSIONS AND COMMITTEES

COMMISSIONS ON INTERDENOMINATIONAL RELATIONS AND CHURCH UNION

The Methodist Episcopal Church

Bishops: Edwin Holt Hughes (Chairman), Frederick D. Leete, Edgar Blake, Robert E. Jones, Ernest G. Richardson.

Ministers: J. S. Ladd Thomas, Philadelphia, Pa.; Edmund D. Soper, Evanston, Ill.; Edward Hislop, Kansas City, Mo.; F. W. Mueller, Philadelphia, Pa.; Edward Laird Mills, San Francisco, Calif.; Harry E. Woolever (Secretary), Washington, D. C.; E. J. Hammond, Atlanta, Ga.; Willis J. King, Atlanta, Ga.; Morris E. Swartz, Williamsport, Pa.; Robert B. Stansell, Milwaukee, Wis.

Lay Members: Ernest H. Cherrington, Washington, D. C.; James R. Joy, New York, N. Y.; Dean James A. James, Evanston, Ill.; Fred D. Parr, San Francisco, Calif.; Vincent P. Clarke, Boston, Mass.; William H. Spurgeon, Colorado Springs, Colo.; W. H. Wilcox, Stillwater, Okla.; W. W. Schwaninger, New Albany, Ind.; Clyde O. Law, Wheeling, W. Va.; F. H. Trotter, Chattanooga, Tenn.

The Methodist Episcopal Church, South

Bishops: John M. Moore (Chairman), Paul B. Kern, Arthur J. Moore, A. Frank Smith, Ivan Lee Holt. Alternates: J. Lloyd Decell, W. W. Peele.

Ministers: T. D. Ellis (Vice-Chairman), Louisville, Ky.; F. N. Parker, Atlanta, Ga.; Grover C. Emmons, Nashville, Tenn.; J. W. Moore, Newport News, Va.; Paul W. Quillian, Houston, Tex.; B. P. Taylor, Huntington, W. Va.; J. Emerson Ford (Secretary), Marion, S. C.; H. H. Sherman, Front Royal, Va.; Willard G. Cram, Nashville, Tenn.; W. M. Alexander, Nashville, Tenn. Alternates: W. L. Duren, New Orleans, La.; John W. Frazer, Mobile, Ala.; L. L. Evans, Tulsa, Okla.

Laymen: John S. Candler, Atlanta, Ga.; Percy D. Maddin, Nashville, Tenn.; H. H. White, Alexandria, La.; H. N. Snyder, Spartanburg, S. C.; J. H. Reynolds, Conway, Ark.; W. E. Brock, Chattanooga, Tenn.; John T. Scott, Houston, Tex.; Harry Denman, Nashville, Tenn.; W. P. Few, Durham, N. C.; Mrs. J. W. Perry, Abingdon, Va. Alternates: W. W. Parker, Cape Girardeau, Mo.; Harwell Wilson, Winter Haven, Fla.; Mrs. Homer Tatum, Alamo, Tenn.; S. G. Houston, New Albany, Miss.

The Methodist Protestant Church

Ministers: James H. Straughn (Chairman), Baltimore, Md.; John C. Broomfield, Fairmont, W. Va.; Leonard B. Smith (Secretary), Baltimore, Md.; J. C. Williams, Columbus, Ohio; E. A. Sexsmith, Baltimore, Md.; Roby F. Day, Inwood, Far Rockaway, N. Y.; L. E. Bee, Weston, W. Va.; F. W. Lineberry, Elkhart, Ind.; S. W. Taylor, Asheboro, N. C.; Charles S. Bragg, Clio, Mich.; J. S. Eddins, Birmingham, Ala.; G. C. Weaver, Rochester, N. Y.; F. B. Hanna, Cuba, Ill.; C. R. Green, Maxwell, Iowa.

Lay Members: Harry Shaw, Fairmont, W. Va.; J. H. Baker, Baltimore, Md.; Nate S. Williamson, Meridian, Miss,; P. M. Ellis, Reesville, Ohio; W. C. Perkins, Pittsburgh, Pa.; J. N. Wills, Greensboro, N. C.

15

PREPARATORY COMMITTEES APPOINTED BY THE JOINT COMMISSION

The Executive Committee

From the Commission of the Methodist Episcopal Church

Bishop Edwin Holt Hughes (Joint Chairman), Washington, D. C.; Edmund D. Soper, Evanston, Ill.; James R. Joy, New York, N. Y.; F. W. Mueller, Philadelphia, Pa.; James A. James, Evanston, Ill.; Bishop Robert E. Jones, Columbus, Ohio.

From the Commission of the Methodist Episcopal Church, South

Bishop John M. Moore (Joint Chairman), Dallas, Tex.; T. D. Ellis, Louisville, Ky.; Grover C. Emmons, Nashville, Tenn.; W. M. Alexander, Nashville, Tenn.; Harry Denman, Nashville, Tenn.; J. H. Reynolds, Conway, Ark.

From the Commission of the Methodist Protestant Church

James H. Straughn (Joint Chairman), Baltimore, Md.; J. C. Broomfield, Fairmont, W. Va.; J. H. Baker, Baltimore, Md.

Secretary of the Executive Committee

Harry E. Woolever, 3511 Rodman St., N. W., Washington, D. C.

Committee on Rules of Order and Plan of Organization

Methodist Episcopal

John M. Arters, Bangor, Me.; J. E. Skillington, Bloomsburg, Pa.

Methodist Episcopal, South

Bishop Charles C. Selecman, Oklahoma, City, Okla.; Lud H. Estes, Memphis, Tenn.

Methodist Protestant

Cuthbert W. Bates, Browns Summit, N. C.

Committee on Conferences

Methodist Episcopal

Bishop Ernest G. Richardson, Philadelphia, Pa.; L. O. Hartman, Boston, Mass.; W. A. C. Hughes, Philadelphia, Pa.; Edward Hislop, Kansas City, Mo.; Edward R. Carman, Jamaica, N. Y.; George W. Crabbe, Baltimore, Md.

Methodist Episcopal, South

Bishop W. W. Peele, Richmond, Va.; T. D. Ellis, Louisville, Ky.; B. P. Taylor, Huntington, W. Va.; F. N. Parker, Emory University, Ga.; J. F. Caskey, St. Louis, Mo.; Roy H. Short, Louisville, Ky.

Methodist Protestant

J. C. Williams, Columbus, Ohio; F. B. Hanna, Cuba, Ill.; Ely D. Miller, Columbus, Ohio.

Committee on the Ministry and Judicial Administration

Methodist Episcopal

Bishop Edgar Blake, Detroit, Mich.; O. W. Fifer, Cincinnati, Ohio; Francis R. Bayley, Baltimore, Md.; Willis J. King, Atlanta, Ga.; Charles F. Eggleston, Philadelphia, Pa.; W. H. Spurgeon, Colorado Springs, Colo.

Methodist Episcopal, South

Bishop Hoyt M. Dobbs, Jackson, Miss.; W. F. Dunkle; Orlando, Fla.; W. W. Holmes, New Orleans, La.; Foster K. Gamble, Birmingham, Ala.; Grover C. Emmons, Nashville, Tenn.; W. A. Shelton, Birmingham, Ala.

Methodist Protestant

Frank L. Shaffer, Clarksburg, W. Va.; J. E. Butler, Haynesville, La.; P. M. Ellis, Reesville, Ohio.

Committee on Membership and Temporal Economy

Methodist Episcopal

Bishop Frederick D. Leete, DeLand, Fla.; George W. Henson, Philadelphia, Pa.; William C. Hartinger, Indianapolis, Ind.; Edward Laird Mills, San Francisco, Calif.; Vincent P. Clarke, Boston, Mass.; Fred C. Huebner, Des Moines, Iowa.

Methodist Episcopal, South

Bishop A. Frank Smith, Houston, Tex.; Costen J. Harrell, Nashville, Tenn.; George L. Morelock, Nashville, Tenn.; Mrs. F. B. Godfrey, Orlando, Fla.; J. W. Mills, Tyler, Tex.; William R. Webb, Bell Buckle, Tenn.

Methodist Protestant

Leonard B. Smith, Baltimore, Md.; S. W. Taylor, Asheboro, N. C.; Nate S. Williamson, Meridian, Miss.

Committee on Missions, Church Extension, Hospitals, Homes, Orphanages, Evangelism, Deaconess Work, Temperance, and Social Service

Methodist Episcopal

Bishop Edwin H. Hughes, Washington, D. C.; Mrs. W. H. C. Goode, Sidney, Ohio; Mrs. Thomas Nicholson, Mount Vernon, Iowa; Howard C. Baldwin, Detroit, Mich.; Edgar T. Welch, Westfield, N. Y.; R. E. Diffendorfer, New York, N. Y.; Edward D. Kohlstedt, Philadelphia, Pa.; Roy L. Smith, Los Angeles, Calif.; Benjamin F. Smith, Chicago, Ill.; John G. Benson, Indianapolis, Ind.

Methodist Episcopal, South

Bishop Arthur J. Moore, San Antonio, Tex.; Willard G. Cram, Nashville, Tenn.; Mrs. J. W. Perry, Abingdon, Va.; T. D. Ellis, Louisville, Ky.; J. H. Groseclose, Dallas, Tex.; J. W. Moore, Newport News, Va.; W. E. Brock, Chattanooga, Tenn.; Silas Johnson, Macon, Ga.; J. D. Hammons, Little Rock, Ark.; Percy D. Maddin, Nashville, Tenn.

Methodist Protestant

J. W. Hawley, Pittsburgh, Pa.; G. W. Haddaway, Baltimore, Md.; G. C. Weaver, Rochester, N. Y.; Mrs. J. W. Shell, Pittsburgh, Pa.; Mrs. S. W. Rosenberger, Columbus, Ohio.

Committee on Education

Methodist Episcopal

Bishop G. Bromley Oxnam, Omaha, Nebr.; John L. Seaton, Albion, Mich.; Horace G. Smith, Evanston, Ill.; H. W. McPherson, Chicago, Ill.; Jesse Lee Corley, Los Angeles, Calif.; David D. Jones, Greensboro, N. C.; D. Stewart Patterson, Washington, D. C.

Methodist Episcopal, South

Bishop Paul B. Kern, Nashville, Tenn.; H. N. Snyder, Spartanburg, S. C.; Paul W. Quillian, Houston, Tex.; J. Emerson Ford, Marion,

S. C.; William F. Quillian, Nashville, Tenn.; William P. Few, Durham, N. C.; Miss Mabel K. Howell, Nashville, Tenn.

Methodist Protestant

E. A. Sexsmith, Baltimore, Md.; F. W. Stephenson, Pittsburgh, Pa.; J. Leas Green, Salisbury, Md.; Congressman Teague, High Point, N. C.

Committee on Publishing Interests

Methodist Episcopal

Bishop H. Lester Smith, Cincinnati, Ohio; Benjamin W. Meeks, Frederick, Md.; George C. Douglass, Cincinnati, Ohio; Matthew S. Davage, Atlanta, Ga.; Frank A. Horne (deceased), New York, N. Y.; John D. Crummey, San Jose, Calif.; Ernest H. Cherrington, Washington, D. C.

Methodist Episcopal, South

Bishop J. Lloyd Decell, Birmingham, Ala.; B. A. Whitmore, Nashville, Tenn.; W. Angie Smith, Dallas, Tex.; R. E. L. Morgan, Lawton, Okla.; H. H. Sherman, Front Royal, Va.; M. T. Plyler, Greensboro, N. C.; W. H. Swiggart, Nashville, Tenn.

Methodist Protestant

W. C. Perkins, Pittsburgh, Pa.; Roby F. Day, Inwood, Far Rockaway, N. Y.; R. L. Shipley, Baltimore, Md.; Mrs. W. C. Hammer, Asheboro, N. C.

Committee on Superannuate Support, Pensions, and Relief

Methodist Episcopal

Bishop Ernest Lynn Waldorf, Chicago, Ill.; Thomas H. Stafford, Chicago, Ill.; Thomas S. Brock, Trenton, N. J.; Henry L. Davis, Indianapolis, Ind.; Roy L. Sprague, Seattle, Wash.; E. J. Matthews, Waukesha, Wis.

Methodist Episcopal, South

Bishop U. V. W. Darlington, Huntington, W. Va.; Charles W. Tadlock, St. Louis, Mo.; C. W. Webdell, St. Louis, Mo.; B. R. Turnipseed, Rock Hill, S. C.; A. T. McIlwain, Greenwood, Miss.; S. H. C. Burgin, Corpus Christi, Tex.

Methodist Protestant

Eugene C. Makosky, Arlington, Va.; C. R. Green, Maxwell, Iowa; L. E. Bee, Weston, W. Va.

Committee on Rituals and Order of Worship

Methodist Episcopal

J. S. Ladd Thomas, Germantown, Philadelphia, Pa.; Oscar T. Olson, Cleveland, Ohio; Richard C. Raines, Minneapolis, Minn.

Methodist Episcopal, South

Bishop Ivan Lee Holt, Dallas, Tex.; R. W. Goodloe, Dallas, Tex.; Nolan B. Harmon, Jr., Roanoke, Va.

Methodist Protestant

C. E. Forlines, Westminster, Md.; Mrs. H. W. Maier, Toronto, Ohio.

Legal Committee on Permanent Funds

Methodist Episcopal

Benjamin A. Matthews, New York, N. Y.; H. R. Van Deusen, Scranton, Pa.; Charles O. Loucks, Chicago, Ill.; Vincent P. Clarke, Boston, Mass.

Methodist Episcopal, South

H. H. White, Alexandria, La.; J. Morgan Stevens, Jackson, Miss.; Walter McElreath, Atlanta, Ga.

Methodist Protestant

Harry Shaw, Fairmont, W. Va.; Henry Gilligan, Washington, D. C.

Committee on Enabling Acts

Methodist Episcopal

Bishop Edgar Blake, Detroit, Mich.; F. W. Mueller, Philadelphia, Pa.; Ernest H. Cherrington, Washington, D. C.

Methodist Episcopal, South

Bishop Paul B. Kern, Nashville, Tenn.; W. M. Alexander, Nashville, Tenn.; Harry Denman, Nashville, Tenn.

Methodist Protestant

J. C. Broomfield, Fairmont, W. Va.

Committee on Public Meetings

Methodist Episcopal

Bishop Charles L. Mead, Kansas City, Mo.; Fred D. Stone, Chicago, Ill.; H. R. Snavely, Marshall, Ill.

Methodist Episcopal, South

Bishop Ivan Lee Holt, Dallas, Tex.; W. F. Quillian, Nashville, Tenn.; J. M. Williams, Conway, Ark.

Methodist Protestant

Charles S. Bragg, Clio, Mich.

JOINT COMMISSION ON ENTERTAINMENT OF UNITING CONFERENCE

(Elected by the General Conferences)

Chairman—Dr. Isaac E. Miller, Cincinnati, Ohio.
Vice-Chairman—Dr. F. W. Lineberry, Elkhart, Ind.
Secretary-Treasurer—Dr. H. P. Myers, Nashville, Tenn.

Executive Committee

Isaac E. Miller, Cincinnati, Ohio; F. W. Lineberry, Elkhart, Ind.; H. P. Myers, Nashville, Tenn.; E. C. Watson, Clarksburg, W. Va.; L. J. Lyons, Kansas City, Mo.; Harry Shaw, Fairmont, W. Va.

Methodist Episcopal

L. J. Lyons, Kansas City, Mo.; John A. Rinkle, Minneapolis, Minn.; Aubrey S. Moore, Chicago, Ill.; T. W. Appleby, Cincinnati, Ohio; Isaac E. Miller, Cincinnati, Ohio.

Methodist Episcopal, South

H. P. Myers, Nashville, Tenn.; S. S. McKenney, Tyler, Tex.; E. C. Watson, Clarksburg, W. Va.; Miller S. Bell, Milledgeville, Ga.; C. W. Tadlock, St. Louis, Mo.

Methodist Protestant

Harry Shaw, Fairmont, W. Va.; F. Murray Benson, Baltimore, Md.; J. E. Pritchard, High Point, N. C.; J. S. Eddins, Birmingham, Ala.; F. W. Lineberry, Elkhart, Ind.

COMMITTEE ON ENTERTAINMENT OF THE UNITING CONFERENCE

(From Kansas City, Missouri)

Chairman—Bishop Charles L. Mead, 1121 McGee St.
Co-Chairman—Bishop W. T. Watkins, Emory University, Ga.
Executive Vice-President—Dr. Thomas B. Mather, 7434 Madison.
Secretary—Dr. C. E. Street, Linwood and Olive.
Treasurer—Mr. Kenneth Robertson, 1111 Grand Ave.

Executive Committee

Bishop Charles L. Mead, 1121 McGee St.; Bishop W. T. Watkins, Emory University, Ga.; Thomas B. Mather, 7434 Madison; Kenneth Robertson, 1111 Grand Ave.; R. S. Kenaston, 5116 Brookside; W. R. Clower, 804 LaFayette; G. F. Tipton, 2421 Brooklyn; R. Carter Tucker, Scarritt Building; A. W. Allen, 1938 N. 28th St.; Mrs. Dan B. Brummitt, 1010 W. 70 Terrace.

Committees—Chairmen

Finance—R. Carter Tucker, Scarritt Building.
Auditing, Budgeting, Expenditures—T. O. Cunningham, Independence, Mo.
Registrations-Hotels—J. E. Kulp, Chamber of Commerce.
Ushers-Pages—E. L. Hobbs, 506 Gladstone Boulevard.
Transportation—J. W. Miller, 4401 Charlotte.
Hospitality—W. C. Hanson, 1121 McGee St.
Women's Activities—Mrs. Fred A. Lamb, 6635 Edgevale Road.
Activities Among Negroes—Rev. G. F. Tipton, 2421 Brooklyn.
Pulpit Supply—S. B. Edmondson, 57th and Wornall.
Music—Powell Weaver, 107 Ward Parkway.
Radio—Rev. King D. Beach, Armour Boulevard and Kenwood.
Publicity—William C. Hanson, 1121 McGee St.
Restaurants—C. M. Hayman, Fidelity Bank Building.
Secretarial Help—Mrs. H. O. Boling, 5030 Wabash.
Press—Frank Rucker, Independence, Mo.
Exhibits—Rev. H. G. Conger, Chicago, Ill.
Decorations—Edwin J. Barnes, Jr., 4831 Liberty.
Information—George E. Ryder, 8001 Wayne.
Housing—Residential Homes—Rev. Mills M. Anderson, 406 W. 74th St.
Telephone-Telegraph—Mrs. J. W. Showalter, 2723 N. 10th St.
Post Office—A. A. McCullum, 2506 Northon.
Ex-Officio—L. E. Dixon, 1208 N. 25th St.; Edward Hislop, 1121 McGee St.; W. A. Keve, 1227 Rowland St.

COMMISSION ON ENTERTAINMENT OF THE 1940 GENERAL CONFERENCE

Chairman: Leslie J. Lyons, 1002 Walnut, Kansas City, Mo.
Vice-Chairman: E. C. Watson, 306 Altamont Apts., Birmingham, Ala.
Secretary: Dr. Aubrey S. Moore, 77 Washington St., Chicago, Ill.
Northeastern Jurisdiction: Dr. J. Edgar Washabaugh, J. H. Baker.
Southeastern Jurisdiction: Dr. Thomas D. Ellis, E. C. Watson.
North Central Jurisdiction: Dr. Aubrey S. Moore, Troy W. Appleby.
South Central Jurisdiction: Dr. C. M. Reves, Judge Leslie J. Lyons.
Western Jurisdiction: Dr. Roy O. Hills, Judge Nathan Newby,
Central Jurisdiction: Dr. Stanley E. Grannum, John A. Patton.

SECRETARIES OF THE GENERAL CONFERENCES

Methodist Episcopal—John M. Arters, Bangor, Me.
Methodist Episcopal, South—Lud H. Estes, Memphis, Tenn.
Methodist Protestant—Cuthbert W. Bates, Browns Summit, N. C.

THE ECUMENICAL COUNCIL

(Western Section)

The members of the Ecumenical Council of Methodism who live in the United States are: Bishop F. D. Leete, Chairman; Dr. A. J. Weeks, Secretary; Bishop A. W. Leonard, Bishop Herbert Welch, Bishop John M. Moore, Bishop Paul B. Kern, Bishop Ivan Lee Holt, Bishop C. C. Selecman, Bishop J. C. Broomfield, President H. W. Cox, Dr. T. D. Ellis, Judge M. E. Lawson, Mrs. J. W. Perry, Dr. W. F. Quillian, Dr. G. W. Haddaway, Judge Harry Shaw, Dr. W. T. Collfas, Dr. J. R. Edwards, President M. S. Davage, Dr. E. R. Lowther, Dr. D. L. Marsh, Mrs. F. C. Reynolds, Dr. R. C. Raines, Dr. O. T. Olson, Mr. C. C. Parlin, Dr. E. D. Soper, Mrs. H. E. Woolever.

CONSTITUTION OF THE METHODIST CHURCH

DIVISION ONE

Article I—Declaration of Union

The Methodist Episcopal Church, The Methodist Episcopal Church, South, and The Methodist Protestant Church shall be united in one Church.

Article II—Name

The name of the Church shall be The Methodist Church.

Article III—Articles of Religion

The Articles of Religion shall be those historically held in common by the three uniting Churches. (See *Disciplines.*)

DIVISION TWO—CONFERENCES

1. There shall be a General Conference for the entire Church with such powers, duties, and privileges as are hereinafter set forth.

2. There shall be Jurisdictional Conferences for the Church in the United States of America, with such powers, duties, and privileges as are hereinafter set forth.

3. There shall be Central Conferences for the Church outside the United States of America, with such powers, duties, and privileges as are hereinafter set forth.

4. There shall be Annual Conferences as the fundamental bodies in the Church, with such powers, duties, and privileges as are hereinafter set forth.

SECTION I—GENERAL CONFERENCE

Article I.—The General Conference shall be composed of not less than 600 nor more than 800 delegates, one-half of whom shall be ministers and one-half lay members, to be elected by the Annual Conferences.

Article II.—The General Conference shall meet in the month of April or May once in four years, beginning with such year and at such place as shall be fixed by the Uniting Conference, and thereafter at such time and in such place as shall be determined by the General Conference or by its duly authorized committees.

Article III.—The General Conference shall fix the ratio of representation in the General, Jurisdictional, and Central Conferences from the Annual Conferences, with the total ministerial membership in the Annual Conference as a basis, provided that each Annual Conference shall be entitled to at least one ministerial and one lay delegate in the General Conference and also in the Jurisdictional or Central Conference.

Article IV.—The General Conference shall have full legislative power over all matters distinctly connectional, and in the exercise of said power shall have authority as follows:

1. To define and fix the conditions, privileges, and duties of church membership.

2. To define and fix the qualifications and duties of Elders, Deacons, Supply Preachers, Local Preachers, Exhorters, and Deaconesses.

3. To define and fix the powers and duties of Annual Conferences, Mission Conferences, and Missions, and of District, Quarterly, and Church Conferences.

4. To provide for the organization, promotion, and administration of the work of the Church outside the United States of America.

5. To define and fix the powers, duties, and privileges of the Episcopacy; to adopt a plan for the support of the Bishops, to provide a uniform rule for their superannuation, and to provide for the discontinuance of a Bishop because of inefficiency or unacceptability.

6. To provide and revise the Hymnal and Ritual of the Church and to regulate all matters relating to the form and mode of worship, subject to the limitations of the First Restrictive Rule.

7. To provide a judicial system and a method of judicial procedure for the Church, except as herein otherwise prescribed.

8. To initiate and to direct all connectional enterprises of the Church, such as publishing, evangelistic, educational, missionary, and benevolent, and to provide boards for their promotion and administration.

9. To determine and provide for raising the funds necessary to carry on the connectional work of the Church.

10. To fix a uniform basis upon which Bishops shall be elected by the Jurisdictional Conferences and to determine the number of Bishops that may be elected by Central Conferences.

11. To select its presiding officers from the Bishops, through a committee, provided that the Bishops shall select from their own number the president for the opening session.

12. To change the number and the boundaries of Jurisdictional Conferences upon the consent of a majority of the

Annual Conferences in each Jurisdictional Conference involved.

13. To establish such commissions for the general work of the Church as may be deemed advisable.

14. To enact such other legislation as may be necessary, subject to the limitations and restrictions of the Constitution of the Church.

SECTION II—RESTRICTIVE RULES

1. The General Conference shall not revoke, alter, or change our Articles of Religion, or establish any new standards or rules of doctrine contrary to our present existing and established standards of doctrine.

2. The General Conference shall not change or alter any part or rule of our government so as to do away Episcopacy, or destroy the plan of our itinerant General Superintendency.

3. The General Conference shall not do away the privileges of our Ministers or Preachers of trial by a committee and of an appeal; neither shall it do away the privileges of our members of trial before the church, or by a committee, and of an appeal.

4. The General Conference shall not revoke or change the General Rules of the United Societies.

5. The General Conference shall not appropriate the produce of the Publishing House, the Book Concern, or the Chartered Fund to any purpose other than for the benefit of the traveling, supernumerary, superannuated, and worn-out preachers, their wives, widows, and children.

SECTION III—AMENDMENTS

1. Amendments to the Constitution may originate in either the General Conference or an Annual Conference.

2. Amendments to the Constitution shall be made upon a two-thirds majority of the General Conference present and voting and a two-thirds majority of all the members of the several Annual Conferences present and voting, except in the case of the First Restrictive Rule, which shall require a three-fourths majority of all the members of the Annual Conferences present and voting. The vote, after being completed, shall be canvassed by the Council of Bishops and the amendment voted upon shall become effective upon their announcement of its having received the required majority.

3. A Jurisdictional Conference may by a majority vote propose changes in the Constitution of the Church, and such proposed changes shall be submitted to the next General

Conference. If the General Conference adopt the measure by a two-thirds vote, it shall be submitted to the Annual Conferences according to the provision for amendments.

SECTION IV—JURISDICTIONAL CONFERENCES

Article I.—The Jurisdictional Conferences shall be composed of as many representatives from the Annual Conferences as shall be determined by a uniform basis established by the General Conference.

Article II.—All Jurisdictional Conferences shall have the same status and the same privileges of action within the limits fixed by the Constitution. The ratio of representation of the Annual Conferences in the General Conference shall be the same for all Jurisdictional Conferences.

Article III.—The General Conference shall fix the basis of representation in the Jurisdictional Conferences, provided that the Jurisdictional Conferences shall be composed of an equal number of ministerial and lay delegates, the ministerial to be elected by the ministerial members of the Annual Conferences and the lay delegates by the lay members.

Article IV.—Each Jurisdictional Conference shall meet within the twelve months succeeding the meeting of the General Conference at such time and place as shall have been determined by the preceding Jurisdictional Conference, or by its properly constituted committee. The first meeting of each Jurisdictional Conference after the General Conference shall be called by the Council of Bishops at a date fixed by them and at a place selected by a Committee on Entertainment appointed by them.

Article V.—The Jurisdictional Conferences shall have the following powers and duties and such others as may be conferred by the General Conference:

1. To promote the evangelistic, educational, missionary, and benevolent interests of the Church, and to provide for interests and institutions within their boundaries.

2. To elect Bishops and to co-operate in carrying out such plans for their support as may be determined by the General Conference.

3. To establish and constitute Jurisdictional Conference Boards as auxiliary to the General Boards of the Church as the need may appear, and to choose their representatives on the General Boards in such manner as the General Conference may determine.

4. To determine the boundaries of their Annual Conferences, provided that there shall be no Annual Conference with a membership of fewer than fifty ministers in full connection, except by the consent of the General Conference.

5. To make rules and regulations for the administration of the work of the Church within the Jurisdiction, subject to such powers as have been or shall be vested in the General Conference.

6. To appoint a Committee on Appeals to hear and determine the appeal of a traveling preacher of that Jurisdiction from the decision of a trial committee.

SECTION V.—CENTRAL CONFERENCES

Article I.—There shall be Central Conferences for the work of the Church outside the United States of America with such duties, powers, and privileges as are hereinafter set forth. The number and boundaries of the Central Conferences shall be determined by the Uniting Conference. Subsequently the General Conference shall have authority to change the number and boundaries of Central Conferences. The Central Conferences shall have the duties, powers, and privileges hereinafter set forth.

Article II.—The Central Conferences shall be composed of as many delegates as shall be determined by a basis established by the General Conference. The delegates shall be ministerial and lay in equal numbers, the ministerial delegates to be elected by the ministerial members and the lay delegates by the lay members of the Annual Conferences.

Article III.—The Central Conferences shall meet within the year succeeding the meeting of the General Conference at such times and places as shall have been determined by the preceding respective Central Conferences or by commissions appointed by them, or by the General Conference. The date and place of the first meeting succeeding the first General Conference shall be fixed by the Bishops of the respective Central Conferences, or in such manner as shall be determined by the General Conference.

Article IV.—The Central Conferences shall have the following powers and duties and such others as may be conferred by the General Conference:

1. To promote the evangelistic, educational, missionary, and benevolent interests and institutions of the Church within their own boundaries.

2. To elect the Bishops for the respective Central Conferences in number as may be determined from time to time, upon a basis fixed by the General Conference, and to cooperate in carrying out such plans for the support of their Bishops as may be determined by the General Conference.

3. To establish and constitute such Central Conference Boards as may be required and to elect their administrative officers.

4. To determine the boundaries of the Annual Conferences within their respective areas.

5. To make such rules and regulations for the administration of the work within their boundaries as the conditions in the respective areas may require, subject to the powers that have been or shall be vested in the General Conference.

6. To appoint a Committee on Appeals to hear and determine the appeal of a traveling preacher of that Central Conference from the decision of a Committee of Trial.

SECTION VI.—EPISCOPAL ADMINISTRATION IN CENTRAL CONFERENCES

1. The Bishops of the Central Conferences shall be elected and inducted into office by their respective Central Conferences.

2. The Bishops of the Central Conferences shall have membership in the Council of Bishops with vote limited to matters relating to their respective Central Conferences.

3. The Bishops of the Central Conferences shall preside in the sessions of their respective Central Conferences.

4. The Bishops of each Central Conference shall arrange the plan of Episcopal visitation within their Central Conference.

5. The Council of Bishops may assign one of their number to visit any Central Conference. When so assigned the Bishop shall be recognized as an accredited representative of the general Church; and when requested by a majority of the Bishops of a Central Conference may exercise therein the functions of the Episcopacy.

SECTION VII—ANNUAL CONFERENCES

Article I.—The Annual Conference shall be composed of all the Traveling Preachers in full connection with it, together with a lay member elected by each pastoral charge. The lay members shall be at least twenty-one (21) years of age and shall have been for the four years next preceding their election members of one of the constituent Churches forming this union, or of The Methodist Church.

Article II.—The Annual Conference is the basic body in the Church, and as such shall have reserved to it the right to vote on all constitutional amendments, on the election of ministerial and lay delegates to the General and the Jurisdictional or Central Conferences, on all matters relating to the character and conference relations of its ministerial members, and on the ordination of ministers, and such other rights as have not been delegated to the General Conference under the Constitution, with the exception that the lay members may not vote on matters of ordination, character, and conference relations of ministers. It shall discharge such duties and exercise such powers as the General Conference under the Constitution may determine.

Article III.—The Annual Conference shall elect ministerial and lay delegates to the General Conference and to its Jurisdictional or Central Conference in the manner provided in this section, Articles IV and V, at the session preceding the General Conference. The persons first elected up to the number determined by the ratio for representation in the General Conference shall be representatives in that body. Additional delegates shall be elected to complete the number determined by the ratio for representation in the Jurisdictional or Central Conference, who, together with those first elected as above, shall be delegates in the Jurisdictional or Central Conference. The additional delegates to the Jurisdictional or Central Conference shall in the order of their election be the reserve delegates to the General Conference. The Annual Conference shall also elect reserve ministerial and lay delegates to the Jurisdictional or Central Conference as it may deem desirable.

Article IV.—The ministerial delegates to the General Conference and to the Jurisdictional or Central Conference shall be elected by the ministerial members of the Annual Conference, provided that such delegates shall have been traveling preachers in the constituent Churches forming this union, or in The Methodist Church, for at least four years next preceding their election and are in full connection with the Annual Conference electing them when elected and at the time of holding the General and Jurisdictional or Central Conferences.

Article V.—The lay delegates to the General Conference and to the Jurisdictional or Central Conference shall be elected by the lay members of the Annual Conference, provided that such delegates be at least twenty-five (25) years of age and shall have been members of the constituent Churches forming this union, or of The Methodist Church, for at least four years next preceding their election, and are members thereof within the Annual Conference electing them at the time of holding the General and Jurisdictional or Central Conferences.

SECTION VIII—BOUNDARIES

Article I.—The Methodist Church in the United States of America shall have Jurisdictional Conferences made up as follows:

Northeastern—Maine, New Hampshire, Vermont, Massachusetts, Connecticut, Rhode Island, New York, Pennsylvania, New Jersey, Maryland, West Virginia, Delaware, District of Columbia, Porto Rico.

Southeastern—Virginia, North Carolina, South Carolina, Georgia, Florida, Alabama, Tennessee, Kentucky, Mississippi, Cuba.

Central—The Negro Annual Conferences, the Negro Mission Conferences and Missions in the United States of America.

North Central—Ohio, Indiana, Illinois, Michigan, Wisconsin, Minnesota, Iowa, North Dakota, South Dakota.

South Central—Missouri, Arkansas, Louisiana, Nebraska, Kansas, Oklahoma, Texas, New Mexico.

Western—Washington, Idaho, Oregon, California, Nevada, Utah, Arizona, Montana, Wyoming, Colorado, Alaska, Hawaiian Islands.

Article II.—The work of the Church outside the United States of America may be formed into Central Conferences, the number and boundaries of which shall be determined by the Uniting Conference, the General Conference having authority subsequently to make changes in the number and boundaries.

Article III.—Changes in the number, names, and boundaries of the Jurisdictional Conferences may be effected by the General Conference upon the consent of a majority of the Annual Conferences of each of the Jurisdictional Conferences involved.

Article IV.—Changes in the number, names, and boundaries of the Annual Conferences may be effected by the Jurisdictional Conferences in the United States of America and by the Central Conferences outside the United States of America, according to the provisions under the respective powers of the Jurisdictional and the Central Conferences.

SECTION IX—DISTRICT CONFERENCES

Article I.—There may be organized in an Annual Conference District Conferences composed of such persons and invested with such powers as the General Conference may determine.

SECTION X—QUARTERLY CONFERENCES

Article I.—There shall be organized in each pastoral charge a Quarterly Conference composed of such persons and invested with such powers as the General Conference shall provide.

Article II.—Election of Church Officers.—Unless the General Conference shall order otherwise the officers of the church or churches constituting a pastoral charge shall be elected by the Quarterly Conference or by the members of said church or churches at a meeting called for that purpose, as may be arranged by the Quarterly Conference, unless the election is otherwise required by local church charters or state laws.

SECTION XI—CHURCH CONFERENCES

There may be a Church Conference in each church, having such powers and duties as the General Conference may prescribe.

DIVISION THREE—EPISCOPACY

Article I.—There shall be an Episcopacy in The Methodist Church of like plan, powers, privileges, and duties as now exist in The Methodist Episcopal Church and The Methodist Episcopal Church, South.

Article II.—The Bishops shall be elected by the respective Jurisdictional and Central Conferences and ordained or consecrated in the historic manner of Episcopal Methodism at such time and place as may be fixed by the General Conference.

Article III.—There shall be a Council of Bishops composed of all the Bishops of all the Jurisdictional and Central Conferences. The Council shall meet at least once a year and plan for the general oversight and promotion of the temporal and spiritual interests of the entire Church and for carrying into effect the rules, regulations, and responsibilities prescribed and enjoined by the General Conference, and in accord with provisions set forth in this Plan of Union.

Article IV.—The Bishops of each Jurisdictional and Central Conference shall arrange the Plan of Episcopal Supervision of the Annual Conferences, Mission Conferences, and Missions within their respective territories.

Article V.—The Bishops shall have residential and presidential supervision in the Jurisdictional Conferences in which they are elected. A Bishop may be transferred from one Jurisdiction to another Jurisdiction for presidential and residential supervision by the Council of Bishops when such transfer is requested by the Jurisdictional Conference to which such proposed transfer is to be made.

A Bishop may be assigned by the Council of Bishops for presidential service or other temporary service not to exceed a year; in another Jurisdiction than that which elected him, provided request is made by a majority of the Bishops in the Jurisdiction of the proposed service.

. In the case of an emergency in any Jurisdiction through

the death or disability of its Bishops the Council of Bishops may assign one or more Bishops from other Jurisdictions to the work of the said Jurisdiction with the consent of a majority of the Bishops of that Jurisdiction.

Article VI.—The Bishops of The Methodist Episcopal Church and of The Methodist Episcopal Church, South, at the time union is consummated, shall be Bishops of The Methodist Church.

The delegates from the Annual Conferences of The Methodist Protestant Church in the Uniting Conference shall have the authority and power to elect to the office of Bishop two ministers of their Church who, upon ordination or consecration at the Uniting Conference by the Bishops of the other two Churches, shall become effective Bishops of The Methodist Church.

The effective Bishops shall be assigned for service to the various Jurisdictional Conferences by the Uniting Conference.

Article VII.—A Bishop presiding over a District, Annual, or Jurisdictional Conference shall decide all questions of law coming before him in the regular business of a session, provided that such questions be presented in writing and that his decisions be recorded in the Journal of the Conference.

Such an Episcopal decision shall not be authoritative except for the pending case until it shall have been passed upon by the Judicial Council. Each Bishop shall report in writing annually all his decisions of law, with a syllabus of the same, to the Judicial Council, which shall affirm, modify, or reverse them.

Article VIII.—The Bishops of the several Jurisdictional Conferences shall preside in the sessions of their respective Jurisdictional Conferences.

DIVISION FOUR—THE JUDICIARY

Article I.—There shall be a Judicial Council. The General Conference shall determine the number and qualifications of its members, their terms of office, and the method of election and the filling of vacancies.

Article II.—The Judicial Council shall have authority:

1. To determine the constitutionality of any act of the General Conference upon an appeal of a majority of the Council of Bishops, or one-fifth of the members of the General Conference; and to determine the constitutionality of any act of a Jurisdictional or Central Conference upon an appeal of a majority of the Bishops of that Jurisdictional or Central Conference or upon the appeal of one-fifth of the members of that Jurisdictional or Central Conference.

2. To hear and determine any appeal from a Bishop's decision on a question of law made in the Annual or District Conference when said appeal has been made by one-fifth of that Conference present and voting.

3. To pass upon decisions of law made by Bishops in Annual or District Conferences.

4. To hear and determine the legality of any action taken therein by any General Conference board or Jurisdictional or Central Conference board or body, upon appeal by one-third of the members thereof or upon request of the Council of Bishops, or a majority of the Bishops of a Jurisdictional or a Central Conference.

5. To have such other duties and powers as may be conferred upon it by the General Conference.

6. To provide its own methods of organization and procedure.

Article III.—All decisions of the Judicial Council shall be final. However, when the Judicial Council shall declare any act of the General Conference unconstitutional that decision shall be reported back to that General Conference immediately.

UNITING CONFERENCE OFFICERS

PRESIDING OFFICERS

EDWIN H. HUGHES	ERNEST L. WALDORF
JOHN M. MOORE	A. FRANK SMITH
JAMES H. STRAUGHN	H. LESTER SMITH
CHARLES L. MEAD	IVAN LEE HOLT
PAUL B. KERN	FRANCIS J. McCONNELL
ADNA W. LEONARD	JOHN C. BROOMFIELD
URBAN V. W. DARLINGTON	EDGAR BLAKE
ERNEST G. RICHARDSON	CHARLES C. SELECMAN
ARTHUR J. MOORE	TITUS LOWE

SECRETARIAL STAFF

Secretary-in-Chief
LUD H. ESTES

Associate Secretaries

EDGAR R. HECKMAN	CUTHBERT W. BATES

Standing Votes

CUTHBERT W. BATES	J. LEAS GREEN
ARTHUR J. CALLAGHAN	ALBERT G. JUDD
R. F. CURL	ASA J. KESTLE
JOHN C. GLENN	CHARLES S. KIRKPATRICK

CHARLES A. ROBBINS

Calendar

JOHN B. F. YOAK, JR.	D. STEWART PATTERSON

Non-Concurrent Calendar
ROBERT N. BROOKS

Daily Advocate
ROBERT S. SATTERFIELD

Ballots and Tellers
JOHN J. BUNTING

Telegrams
JOHN N. R. SCORE

Discipline

FRED B. NEWELL	T. LeROY HOOPER

GROVER C. EMMONS

General Assistants

CURTIS B. HALEY	THOMAS P. POTTER

33

TELLERS

Secretary of Ballots and Tellers

J. J. BUNTING

Ministers

CLEM BAKER
HENRY W. BLACKBURN
FRANK L. BROWN
CLYDE K. CAMPBELL
H. ALMON CHAFFEE
DANA DAWSON
J. S. EDDINS
GLENN ENGEBRETSEN
HOMER R. GETTLE

MISS IRMA HIGHBAUGH
REUBEN MCALLISTER
WALTER S. ROGERS
J. FISHER SIMPSON
FRANK H. TROTTER
EDWARD E. WHITE
PAUL P. WIANT
ERNEST L. WOOLF
JAMES D. WOOTEN

Reserves

MRS. W. H. DANGEL
JOHN C. GLENN
R. E. GREER

EARL G. HAMLETT
CHARLES A. JONES
JOHN A. PATTON

Laymen

FRED P. ADKINS
LAWRENCE M. BARNARD
W. O. BATTS
GEORGE W. BRIGHT
CLARENCE M. DANNELLY
PAUL S. HALEY
CLAUDE C. HALL
ALFRED F. HUGHES

GLENN C. JAMES
A. J. KOONCE
HARRY C. LEONARD
ELBERT M. MOFFATT
E. M. SWEET, JR.
CHARLES C. SHERROD
WILLIAM H. UTZ, JR.
MERLE T. WAGGONER

Reserves

RAYMOND L. ARCHER
THEODORE ARVIDSON
J. S. M. CANNON

CARL S. MCFALL
BOYCE MARTIN
W. H. WISEMAN

PERSONNEL OF THE UNITING CONFERENCE

Names of Delegates and Reserve Delegates, Ministerial and Lay, elected, appointed, or ex-officio, arranged alphabetically by Annual Conferences, with post-office addresses, appointments, or occupations.

HOW THE DELEGATES WERE ELECTED OR APPOINTED

Methodist Episcopal Church

Report No. 2—Commission on Interdenominational Relations Choosing the Membership of the Uniting Conference. *General Conference Journal*, 1936, page 568.

"1. Each Annual Conference in the United States shall elect one Ministerial Delegate for each one hundred members, but a fraction of two-thirds or more of one hundred members shall be entitled to an additional Delegate. Lay Delegates in like numbers shall be elected by the Lay Conference, provided strictly, that each Annual Conference and each Lay Conference shall be entitled to at least one Delegate. Annual Conferences and Lay Conferences may elect as many Reserve Delegates as they have Delegates.

"2. The Ministerial and Lay members of the Commission on Interdenominational Relations shall be ex-officio members of the Uniting Conference.

"3. The Bishops shall have authority to elect a sufficient number of Delegates-at-large to the Uniting Conference to complete the full number of four hundred Delegates fixed by the Plan of Union as the Methodist Episcopal quota.

"4. In carrying out the provision of Paragraph 3 as above given, the Bishops are requested to provide for an equitable representation in the Uniting Conference of our Conferences or Missions in foreign lands—if possible among such missionaries or nationals as may be in the United States on visitations or furloughs—this with a view to curtailing the expenses incident to holding the Uniting Conference, and also they shall have regard to the connectional agencies of the Methodist Episcopal Church, including The Woman's Home and The Woman's Foreign Missionary Societies."

Methodist Episcopal Church, South

Report No. 3—Committee on Church Relations and Bible Cause. *General Conference Journal*, 1938, page 150.

"5. That the four hundred members of the Uniting Conference allotted to the Methodist Episcopal Church, South, shall be chosen as follows:

"a. That the ten clerical members and the ten lay members of the Commission on Interdenominational Relations and Church Union elected by the General Conference be members of the Uniting Conference.

"b. That three hundred and eighty members of the Uniting Conference be elected by the several Annual Conferences upon a basis of a ratio determined by the number of clerical members and potential lay members of the several Annual Conferences as reported in the *General Minutes and Yearbook* of 1937-38, which computation results as follows (see first number in ( ) following name of each Annual Conference, ME,S in this section).

"6. That the Annual Conferences next succeeding this General Conference elect their Delegates to the Uniting Conference and Alternate Delegates, providing that the number of Alternate Delegates shall not exceed the number of Delegates."

Methodist Protestant Church

Report of Special Committee on Methodist Union. *Journal of General Conference*, 1936, page 96.

"4· That, in the event of the ratification of the Plan of Union by all three contracting parties, this Commission shall determine the ratio of representation by the various Annual Conferences to the Uniting Conference, based on the present ratio of representation in the General Conference, and shall so notify the Annual Conferences of their apportionment of representation, the Delegates to be elected by the Annual Conferences at their sessions immediately preceding the assembly of the Uniting Conference."

Key

Abbreviations used—ME, Methodist Episcopal Church; ME,S, Methodist Episcopal Church, South; MP, Methodist Protestant Church; C.M., Commission Member; R.C.M., Reserve Commission Member; D.L., appointed Delegate-at-large; R.D.L., appointed Reserve Delegate-at-large; Y.D.L., appointed Youth Delegate-at-large; R.Y.D. L., appointed Reserve Youth Delegate-at-large; D.L.O.C., appointed Delegate-at-large representing overseas Conferences of the Methodist Episcopal Church; W.M.S., Woman's Missionary Society.

Figures in ( ) following the name of each Annual Conference, designate the number of elected Delegates, Commission members, or appointed Delegates-at-large.

Underneath the name of each Annual Conference will be found the location in the Conference Hall where the delegation was seated, giving the Section, Row, and the seats allocated.

The names of Lay Delegates are preceded by (*).

DELEGATES BY CONFERENCES

(*Denotes Lay Delegate)

AFRICAN CONFERENCES—ME (2 D.L.O.C.)

Sec. D; Rows 6, 8 to 10; 7, 5 to 10; 8, 5 to 10; 9, 5 to 10
Roberts, G. A., 2709 Lincoln Way, Ames, Iowa.
*Stauffacher, C. J., Box 41, Inhambane, P. E., Africa.

Reserve

Gillett, I. E., Africa.

ALABAMA—ME (2)

Sec. D; Row 9, 3 and ·4
Brasher, J. L., Evangelist, Attalla, Ala.
*Peck, A. D., Businessman, Box 696, Birmingham, Ala.

Reserves

Bailey, T. M., Pastor, Cullman, Ala.
*Franke, W. F., Businessman, 501 Morris Blvd., Birmingham, Ala.

ALABAMA—ME,S (10)

Sec. B; Rows 12, 1 to 4; 13, 1 to 6
Andrews, H. M., Presiding Elder, 713 Church St., Selma, Ala.
Ellison, R. R., Presiding Elder, Pensacola, Fla.
Curtis, W. M., Pastor, 908 E. Jackson St., Pensacola, Fla.
Shafer, A. E., Presiding Elder, 407 E. Appletree St., Dothan, Ala.
Slaughter, D. P., Pastor, 220 N. Foster St., Dothan, Ala.
*Judd, Zebulon, College Professor, S. College St., Auburn, Ala.
*Dannelly, C. M., Superintendent Education, Montgomery, Ala.
*Ellison, Mrs. R. R., Conference President, W.M.S., Pensacola, Fla.
*Ellison, J. T., Attorney, Centerville, Ala.
*Tompkins, O. L., Attorney, Dothan, Ala.

Reserves
McLeod, J. F., Pastor, 100 Cervantes St., Pensacola, Fla.
Frazer, J. W. (R.C.M.; also Annual Conference Reserve), Presiding Elder, Mobile, Ala.
Calhoun, W. F., Presiding Elder, Montgomery, Ala.
Sledd, Andrew (deceased).
Moore, E. C., Presiding Elder, Marianna, Fla.
*Christenberry, W. B., Bookkeeper, Selma, Ala.
*Searcy, Hubert, College President, Montgomery, Ala.
*Cowart, Mrs. Bessie, Housewife, Troy, Ala.
*Malone, E. R., Banker, 18 W. Jackson St., Pensacola, Fla.
*Norton, E. B., Educator, Andalusia, Ala.

ALABAMA—MP (4)
Sec. D; Row 7, 1 to 4
Eddins, J. S., Conference President, Birmingham, Ala.
Casaday, T. C., Pastor, Box 575, Montgomery, Ala.
*Rogers, A C., Merchant, Speigner, Ala.
*Goddard, J. J., State Employee, Birmingham, Ala.

Reserves
Walton, C. W., Pastor, Notasulga, Ala.
Lynch, A. H., Pastor, Panola, Ala.
*Jones, L. L., Dairyman, New Merkel, Ala.
*Heustess, Mrs. Arthur, Housewife, Montgomery, Ala.

ARIZONA—ME,S (2)
Sec. A; Row 17, 1 and 2
Coleman, William H., Pastor, Phoenix, Ariz.
*Evans, J. H., Farmer, R.F.D. 4, Box 330, Phoenix, Ariz.

Reserves
Walker, O. L., Presiding Elder, Roosevelt St., Phoenix, Ariz.
*McGough, B. F., Restaurant Proprietor, Box 1523, Phoenix, Ariz.

ARKANSAS—MP (2)
Sec. A; Row 18, 3 and 4
Butler, J. E., Conference President, Haynesville, La.
*Sherman, L. L., Farmer, Haynesville, La.

Reserves
Lynch, W. O., Pastor, Haynesville, La.
Corn, A. R., Pastor, Bienville, La.
*Whitley, Henry, Magnolia, Ark.
*Nipper, Roy, Farmer, Magnolia, Ark.

ATLANTA—ME (2)
Sec. C; Row 2, 9 and 10
Stanton, D. H., Division Secretary, American Bible Society, 56 Gamman Ave., S. E., Atlanta, Ga.
*Brawley, J. P., Dean, Clark University, South Atlanta, Ga.

Reserves
Queen, J. W., District Superintendent, Atlanta, Ga.
*Brookes, E. L., Professor, Clark University, South Atlanta, Ga.

BALTIMORE—ME (4 and 1 D.L.)
Sec. D; Row 6, 1 to 7
Bayley, F. R., District Superintendent, Baltimore, Md.
Meeks, B. W., Pastor, Frederick, Md.
Edwards, J. R. (D.L.), Pastor, Washington, D. C.
*Patterson, D. S., Promotion Secretary, Board of Temperance, Prohibition, and Public Morals, Washington, D. C.
*Crabbe, G. W., Superintendent, Anti-Saloon League, Baltimore, Md.

Reserves

Burgan, H. W. (R.D.L.; also elected a Reserve), Pastor, 1206 Decatur St., N. W., Washington, D. C.
Williams, G. E., District Superintendent, Washington, D. C.
*Grace, J. H., Salesman, 2516 Hermosa Ave., Baltimore, Md.
*Beall, Bessy B., Housewife, 421 Prince George St., Laurel, Md.

BALTIMORE—ME,S (12 and 1 C.M.)

Sec. C; Rows 9, 5 to 9; 10, 5 to 12

Harmon, N. B., Jr., Pastor, 541 Washington St., Roanoke, Va.
Woolf, E. L., Pastor, 540 Prospect Walk, Clifton Forge, Va.
Canter, H. M., Superannuate, 235 Franklin St., Harrisonburg, Va.
Beery, E. C., Presiding Elder, Washington, D. C.
Sydenstricker, H., Presiding Elder, Roanoke, Va.
Cockrell, S. K., Pastor, Baltimore, Md.
Sherman, H. H. (C.M.), Conference Executive Secretary, Board of Christian Education, Front Royal, Va.
*Rosenberger, J. H., Merchant, Winchester, Va.
*Easter, J. E., Merchant, 141 Campbell Ave., Roanoke, Va.
*Canter, N. M., Physician, Harrisonburg, Va.
*Coffman, C. S., Dentist, Lewisburg, W. Va.
*Lamar, G. H., Attorney, 101 S. Washington St., Rockville, Md.
*Norman, J. R., Merchant, Elk Garden, W. Va.

Reserves

Brandt, C. E., Presiding Elder, Romney, W. Va.
Copenhaver, J. C., Pastor, 16 Church St., Staunton, Va.
Ray, C. K., Pastor, Washington, D. C.
Richardson, F. M., Editor, 122 E. Main St., Salem, Va.
*Dudley, A. H., Banker, Baltimore, Md.
*Ray, J. H., Broker, 5223 Reno Road, Washington, D. C.
*Ballengee, Mrs. W. H., Conference President, W.M.S., Edinburg, Va.
*Cross, W. R., Mayor, Salem, Va.

BELGIAN—ME,S (1)

Sec. D; Row 18, 9 and 10

Thonger, W. G., Presiding Elder, Brussels, Belgium.
(No Lay or Reserve Delegates elected.)

BLUE RIDGE-ATLANTIC—ME (2)

Sec. C; Row 4, 8 and 9

Fletcher, M. O., Pastor, Tayloe Hospital, Washington, N. C.
*Kennedy, Mrs. R. C., Housewife, Bessemer City, N. C.

Reserves

White, C. M., Pastor, Candler, N. C.
*Clayton, J. W., Industrial Worker, Kannapolis, N. C.

CALIFORNIA—ME (4 and 1 C.M.)

Sec. C; Row 22, 1 to 6

Knoles, T. C.; President, College of the Pacific, Stockton, Calif.
Richardson, C. A., Superintendent Department City Work, Board of Home Missions, Philadelphia, Pa.
Parr, F. D. (C.M.), 1 Drumm St., San Francisco Calif.
*Crummey, J. D., Businessman, San Jose, Calif.
*Tunnicliffe, John, Treasurer, San Francisco, Calif.

Reserves

Hamilton, H. K., Pastor, Lodi, Calif.
Rankin, W. P., Pastor, Box 272, Modesto, Calif.
*Rose, Mrs. H. D., Housewife, Sonora, Calif.
*Ferguson, A. P., Auditor, 108 N. First St., Turlock, Calif.
*Morris, P. F. (R.D.L.), Businessman, Berkeley, Calif.

The Methodist Church

CENTRAL ALABAMA—ME (2)
Sec. A; Row 7, 1 and 2
Jones, E. M., District Superintendent, Prattville, Ala.
*Lynn, L. W., Shipping Clerk, 547 S. 6th St., Gadsden, Ala.
Reserves
Turner, W. L., District Superintendent, Box 552, Gadsden, Ala.
*Sanks, L. W., Mortician, 12 S. 62d St., Birmingham, Ala.

CENTRAL NEW YORK—ME (4 and 1 C.M.)
Sec. D; Row 4, 1 to 5
Huse, R. H., Pastor, 208 E. Court St., Ithaca, N. Y.
Coman, A. P., District Superintendent, Syracuse, N. Y.
Woolever, H. E. (C.M.), Secretary, Executive Committee, Joint Commission on Union, Washington, D. C.
*Osborn, Mrs. H. S., Housewife, 208 S. Hill Terrace, Ithaca, N. Y.
*Odell, A. G., Physician, Clifton Springs, N. Y.
Reserves
Merring, E. E., District Superintendent, Geneva, N. Y.
Stearns, H. G., Pastor, 18 William St., Auburn, N. Y.
*Nye, Mrs. F. K., Housewife, 1600 E. Colvin St., Syracuse, N. Y.
*Jaquith, W. E. (deceased).

CENTRAL NORTHWEST—ME (2)
Sec. C; Row 14, 5 and 6
Westerberg, T. J., District Superintendent, Chicago, Ill.
*Anderson, J. E., Salesman, 87 N. Harrison St., Batavia, Ill.
Reserves
Lund, E. F., Pastor, 10 Foote Ave., Jamestown, N. Y.
*Regnell, Arthur, Contractor, 6621 N. Ashland Ave., Chicago, Ill.

CENTRAL PENNSYLVANIA—ME (4 and 1 C.M.)
Sec. D; Row 3, 1 to 6
Skillington, J. E., Pastor, 311 Market St., Bloomsburg, Pa.
Heckman, E. R., Supt., Methodist Home for Aged, Tyrone, Pa.
Swartz, M. E. (C.M.), Pastor, 909 Diamond St., Williamsport, Pa.
*Adams, C. V., Salesman, Montoursville, Pa.
*Frey, V. M., Engineer, 24 N. George St., York, Pa.
Reserves
Welliver, L. A., District Superintendent, Harrisburg, Pa.
Shue, A. C., District Superintendent, Sunbury, Pa.
*Campbell, R. W., Insurance, Altoona Trust Bldg., Altoona, Pa.
*Rich, R. F., Manufacturer, Woolrich, Pa.

CENTRAL TENNESSEE—ME (2)
Sec. B; Row 18, 11 and 12
Fesmire, W. J., District Superintendent, Baxter, Tenn.
*Holmes, Miss Leota, Teacher, 464 Jackson St., Lexington, Tenn.
Reserves
Clayburn, M. D., Pastor, Dickson, Tenn.
*Dixon, C. C., Businessman, Collinwood, Tenn.

CENTRAL TEXAS—ME,S (14)
Sec. A; Rows 18, 7 to 10; 19, 1 to 10
Hawk, E. B., Dean, School of Theology, S. M. U., Dallas, Tex.
Riley, P. E., Pastor, 304 N. 15th St., Corsicana, Tex.
Ward, W. W., Pastor, 1518 Vaughn Blvd., Fort Worth, Tex.
Goodloe, R. W., Professor, Southern Methodist University, Dallas.
Score, J. N. R., Pastor, 1111 Elizabeth Blvd., Fort Worth, Tex.
Culver, F. P., Pastor, Olney, Tex.

Chunn, M. M., Pastor, 1517 Lipscomb St., Fort Worth, Tex.
*Cherry, H. H., Conference Lay Leader, Brownwood, Tex.
*Bryan, Mrs. Gid J., Conference President, W.M.S., Hamilton, Tex.
*Sone, Law, President, Texas Woman's College, Fort Worth, Tex.
*Harris, Nat, Attorney, 1317 S. 7th St., Waco, Tex.
*Edwards, J. R., Businessman, 300 Tierney St., Fort Worth, Tex.
*Boswell, G. C., College President, Weatherford, Tex.
*Martin, Boyce, Publisher, 200 S. 18th St., Corsicana, Tex.

Reserves

Bergin, J. W., President, Southwestern University, Georgetown, Tex.
Neal, T. E., Pastor, Fort Worth, Tex.
Sory, R. O., Presiding Elder, Corsicana, Tex.
Seymour, L. W., Pastor, Georgetown, Tex.
*Wedemeyer, Mrs. B. B., Housewife, 1304 N. 15th St., Waco, Tex.
*McGlammery, B. E., State Educator, Eastland, Tex.
*Culver, F. P., Jr., Judge, Fort Worth, Tex.
*Ayers, Leake, Banker, Gatesville, Tex.

CENTRAL WEST—ME (2)
Sec. B; Row 7, 7 and 8

Abbott, B. F., Pastor, 208 N. Leffingwell Ave., St. Louis, Mo.
*Williams, Miss A. M., Teacher, St. Louis, Mo.

Reserves

Booker, B. R., District Superintendent, Sedalia, Mo.
*Lightner, L. W., Insurance, 2534 Marion St., Denver, Colo.

CHINA—ME (4 D.L.O.C.)
Sec. D; Rows 6, 8 to 10; 7, 5 to 10; 8, 5 to 10; 9, 5 to 10

Ding, Samson, S., 150 Fifth Ave., New York, N. Y.
*Miller, Miss Alpha J., 150 Fifth Ave., New York, N. Y.
*Wiant, Paul P., 150 Fifth Ave., New York, N. Y.
*Highbaugh, Miss Irma, 303 Eddy St., Ithaca, N. Y.

Reserves

James, Edward, Shanghai, China.
*Wong, Miss Pearl, University of Southern California, Los Angeles.
*Clay, E. H., 150 Fifth Ave., New York, N. Y.

CHINA—ME,S (2)
Sec. C; Row 17, 3 and 4

Kaung, Z. T., Pastor, 316 Yu Ya Ching Road, Shanghai, China.
*Yang, Y. C., University President, Shanghai, China.

Reserves

Hawk, J. C., Pastor, Huchow, Che, China.
*Tsao, Mrs. S. H., Housewife, 88 Rue Maresca, Shanghai, China.

COLORADO—ME (4 and 2 D.L. and 1 C.M.)
Sec. D; Rows 10, 7 to 10; 11, 8 to 10

Auman, O. W., Treasurer, World Service Commission, Chicago, Ill.
Schofield, C. E., President, Iliff School of Theology, Denver, Colo.
Geyer, F. L. (D.L.), Superintendent, New Mexico Mission, 4001 N.
    Fourth St., Albuquerque, N. Mex.
*Spencer, R. B., Editor, Fort Morgan, Colo.
*Harrah, E. C., Professor, 1918 13th Ave., Greeley, Colo.
*Lewis, Miss Harriet (Y.D.L.), Great Falls, Mont.
*Spurgeon, W. H. (C.M.), Attorney, Colorado Springs, Colo.

Reserves

Edwards, L. M., Pastor, Colorado Springs, Colo.
Blackstock, W. E. (R.D.L), Dist. Supt., Salt Lake City, Utah.
*Stiles, G. W., Bacteriologist, 725 Newport St., Denver, Colo.

CUBA—ME,S (2)

Sec. C; Row 21, 11 and 12

Clements, E. E., Presiding Elder, Apartdo 2252, Havana, Cuba.
*Noble, Enrique, Educator, c/o Birmingham-Southern College, Birmingham, Ala.

Reserves

Hopkins, O. K., Pastor, Virtudes 152, Havana, Cuba.
*Montes de Oca, Juan, Educator, Marianao, Havana, Cuba.

CZECHOSLOVAK—ME,S (2)

Sec. A; Row 11, 7 and 8

Bartak, J. P., Presiding Elder, Jecna 17, Prague, Czechoslovakia.
*Bartak, Mrs. M., Housewife, Jecna 17, Prague, Czechoslovakia.

Reserves

Vancura, V., Presiding Elder, Husova 14, Pilsen, Czechoslovakia.
*Vancura, Mrs. M., Housewife, Husova 14, Pilsen, Czechoslovakia.

DAKOTA—ME (2)

Sec. B; Row 13, 7 and 8

Kohlstedt, E. D., Executive Secretary, Board of Home Missions and Church Extension, Philadelphia, Pa.
*Dunbar, B. A., Professor, State College, Brookings, S. Dak.

Reserves

Lochridge, F. H., District Superintendent, Mitchell, S. Dak.
*Squire, Melvin, Real Estate, Aberdeen, S. Dak.

DELAWARE—ME (2)

Sec. A; Row 12, 7 and 8

Hargis, D. H., Pastor, 200 E. 9th St., Wilmington, Del.
*Wilson, H. S., Justice of Peace, Upper Hill, Md.

Reserves

Henry, D. W., Pastor, 514 N. 58th St., Philadelphia, Pa.
*Walker, C. D., Businessman, Atlantic City, N. J.

DETROIT—ME (6 and 3 D.L.)

Sec. C; Rows 3, 1 to 4; 4, 1 to 4

Rice, M. S., Pastor, 59 Alger Ave., Detroit, Mich.
Reed, M. R., Pastor, 5151 W. Chicago Blvd., Detroit, Mich.
Fitch, F. L., District Superintendent, Port Huron, Mich.
Crane, H. H. (D.L.), Pastor, 671 Edison Ave., Detroit, Mich.
Gray, J. M. M. (D.L.), Chancellor, American University, Washington.
Fruit, W. R. (D.L.), District Superintendent, Detroit, Mich.
*Baldwin, H. C., Attorney, 17600 Fairway Drive, Detroit, Mich.
*Pearce, Webster, College President, Marquette, Mich.
*Strong, D. F., Salesman, 7086 Senator Ave., Detroit, Mich.

Reserves

Brashares, C. W., Pastor, Ann Arbor, Mich.
Carr, H. F., Pastor, 217 W. Court St., Flint, Mich.
Eva, S. D., Area Secretary, 84 Parkhurst Ave., Detroit, Mich.

*Halmhuber, P. G., Dentist, 12715 Montevista Ave., Detroit, Mich.
*Atkinson, S. G., Retired, Millington, Mich.
*Neithercut, Charles, Attorney, Flint, Mich.

EAST GERMAN—ME (2)
Sec. B; Row 12, 7 and 8

Steinkraus, J. H., District Superintendent, Lawrence, Mass.
*Mueller, E. H., Banker, 9608 Continental Ave., Forest Hills, N.ᵞY.

Reserves

Hagner, Feodor, Pastor, 919 N. 15th St., Philadelphia, Pa.
*Windels, C. M., Secretary, Y.M.C.A., Brooklyn, N. Y.

EAST TENNESSEE—ME (2)
Sec. A; Row 1, 3 and 4

Sanders, W. L., District Superintendent, Bluefield, W. Va.
*McNorton, Mrs. D. E., Housewife, Chattanooga, Tenn.

Reserves

Haywood, J. W., President, Morristown College, Morristown, Tenn.
⁺Boyd, M. W., Teacher, Morristown College, Morristown, Tenn.

EASTERN—MP (2)
Sec. C; Row 8, 3 and 4
(No report of elections to date)

EASTERN SWEDISH—ME (2)
Sec. B; Row 12, 5 and 6

Whyman, H. C., Pastor, 422 Dean St., Brooklyn, N. Y.
*Hjerpe, O. W., Businessman, West Hartford, Conn.

Reserves

Ericson, C. G., Pastor, 57 Bay St., Springfield, Mass.
⁺Bengston, J. P., Businessman, New York, N. Y.

ERIE—ME (4)
Sec. D; Row 14, 1 to 4

Barnard, L. M., District Superintendent, Brookville, Pa.
Davison, S. T., Pastor, Girard, Pa.
*Welch, E. T., Manufacturer, Westfield, N. Y.
*McKay, L. H., Attorney, Sharon, Pa.

Reserves

Barr, H. H., District Superintendent, Jamestown, N. Y.
Davis, W. E., Pastor, Greenville, Pa.
*Gifford, B. H., Insurance, 314 E. 25th St., Erie, Pa.
*Wilkinson, J. W. F., Teacher, Clarion, Pa.

EUROPEAN CONFERENCES—ME (4 D.L.O.C.)
Sec. D; Rows 6, 8 to 10; 7, 5 to 10; 8, 5 to 10; 9, 5 to 10

Arvidson, Theodore, Box 5020, Stockholm 5, Sweden.
Haver, M. S., St. olavsgt, 28-30 Oslo, Norway.
Sigg, Ferdinand, 69 Badenerstrasse, Zurich, Switzerland.
*Stehl, Heinrich, 8 Fuerstenstr, Kassel, Germany.

Reserves

Kellar, Frederick J., 150 Fifth Ave., New York, N. Y.
Bergsten, Gote, Box 5020, Stockholm 5, Sweden.
Voellny, Eduard, Alleweg 13, Bern, Switzerland.
*Goericke, Otto, Russenstrasse 39, Radebeul bei Dresden, Germany.

FLORIDA—ME (2)

Sec. C; Row 13, 5 and 6

Bartlay, H. W., Financial Agent, Board of Home Missions and Church Extension, Jacksonville, Fla.
*Boyd, D. A., Mortician, Box 106, Palatka, Fla.

Reserves

Walker, T. H. B., Pastor, Box 837, Jacksonville, Fla.
*Hull, S. A., Railroad Postal Clerk, Jacksonville, Fla.

FLORIDA—ME,S (10)

Sec. D; Row 17, 1 to 10

Norton, M. H., Presiding Elder, 311 E. Oak St., Tampa, Fla.
Blackburn, H. W., Pastor, 508 E. Fort King Ave., Ocala, Fla.
Dunkle, W. F., Presiding Elder, Orlando, Fla.
Hardin, Smith, Presiding Elder, Bradenton, Fla.
Daniel, J. H., Pastor, 215 W. 10th St., Jacksonville, Fla.
*Wilson, Harwell (deceased).
*Godfrey, Mrs. F. B., Housewife, 700 Delaney St., Orlando, Fla.
*Griffin, DeWitt, Banker, Ocala, Fla.
*Hawkins, A. K., Real Estate, Box 960, Bradenton, Fla.
*Feaster, Mrs. J. T., Housewife, 540 N. E. 96th St., Miami, Fla.

Reserves

Myres, W. A., Presiding Elder, Gainesville, Fla.
Turner, A. F., Pastor, Orlando, Fla.
Boyd, P. M., Pastor, 2746 St. Johns Ave., Jacksonville, Fla.
*Moore, Mrs. T. V., Conference President, W.M.S., Box 1462, Buena Vista Station, Miami, Fla.
*Peeler, C. B., Attorney, Jacksonville, Fla.
*Alexander, T. F., Hospital Superintendent, Tampa, Fla.

FOOCHOW, CHINA—ME (1 D.L.)

Sec. D; Row 6, 8

Cartwright, F. T. (D.L.), 150 Fifth Avenue, New York, N. Y.

FORT SMITH-OKLAHOMA—MP (2)

Sec. C; Row 8, 1 and 2

Browers, J. W., Pastor, Prague, Okla.
*Wilson, O. L., Quinton, Okla.

Reserves

Matthews, M. L., Pastor, Fort Smith, Okla.
Mathis, W. C., Pastor, Hugo, Okla.
*Pitts, C. A., Hugo, Okla.
*Vancil, E. E., Williams, Okla.

GENESEE—ME (4)

Sec. A; Row 8, 4 to 7

Keene, S. A., District Superintendent, Buffalo, N. Y.
Searles, J. W., Pastor, 28 Landers Road, Kenmore, N. Y.
*Brown, Mrs. W. R., National Vice-President, Woman's Home Missionary Society, 65 Walnut St., East Aurora, N. Y.
*Gibbs, M. S., Attorney, Iroquois Bldg., Buffalo, N. Y.

Reserves

Olmstead, J. H., Pastor, 334 Baynes St., Buffalo, N. Y.
Henderson, J. M., Pastor, 58 Mason St., Rochester, N. Y.
*Clay, T. B., Merchant, 168 Grant St., Buffalo, N. Y.
*Simpson, L. J., Attorney, 99 Genesee St., Hornell, N. Y.
*Leighbody, G. W. (R.D.L.), Director, Goodwill Industries, Buffalo, N. Y.

GEORGIA—ME (2 and 1 C.M.)

Sec. C; Row 12, 10 to 12

Dewey, E. C., District Superintendent, Atlanta, Ga.
Hammond, E. J. (C.M.), Division of Finance, Board of Home Missions and Church Extension, Atlanta, Ga.
*McElroy, G. S., Merchant, Bowden, Ga.

Reserves

Rollins, F. J., Pastor, Tallapoosa, Ga.
*Cox, L. L., Teacher, 2131 McLendon Ave., Atlanta, Ga.

GEORGIA—MP (2)

Sec. D; Row 3, 9 and 10

Hunton, W. M., Conference President, Atlanta, Ga.
*Pace, J. W., Railroad Employee, Atlanta, Ga.

Reserves

Brantley, C. E., Pastor, Bowden, Ga.
*Simpson, W. R., Commission Merchant, Produce Row, Atlanta, Ga.

HOLSTON—ME (2 and 2 D.L. and 1 C.M.)

Sec. B; Row 1, 8 to 12

Stapleton, R. L., District Superintendent, Harriman, Tenn.
*Robb, J. L., President, Junior College, Athens, Tenn.
*Fletcher, J. S. (D.L.), Attorney, Chattanooga, Tenn.
*Black, Mrs. H. C. (D.L.), Housewife, Johnson City, Tenn.
*Trotter, F. H. (C.M.), Teacher, Chattanooga, Tenn.

Reserves

Milburn, J. E., Pastor, 839 Windsor Ave., Bristol, Tenn.
Hamilton, F. A. (R.D.L.), Pastor, Chattanooga, Tenn.
Hampton, J. M. (R.D.L.), Pastor, Chattanooga, Tenn.
*Rogers, C. E., Superintendent Public Schools, Johnson City, Tenn.

HOLSTON—ME,S (14 and 2 C.M.)

Sec. D; Rows 15, 5 to 10; 16, 1 to 10

Perry, J. W., Pastor, Abingdon, Va.
French, J. S., Pastor, 1151 Holston Ave., Bristol, Tenn.
Martin, I. P., Pastor, 123 Fountain Ave., Fountain City, Tenn.

Greer, R. E., Presiding Elder, 515 Tazewell, Wytheville, Va.
Baylor, J. A., Pastor, Tazewell, Va.
Eastwood, W. P., Pastor, 2309 Bland Road, Bluefield, W. Va.
Stevenson, M. A., Pastor, 2819 Broad, Cleveland, Tenn.
*Hillman, J. N., College President, Emory, Va.
*Sherrod, C. C., College President, Johnson City, Tenn.
*Thomas, L. M., Attorney, 610 James Bldg., Chattanooga, Tenn.
*Tynes, Mrs. L. A., Conference President, W.M.S., Tazewell, Va.
*Barnett, W. K., Government Service, Radford, Va.
*Pennington, A. S., Merchant, Appalachia, Va.
*Carter, F. A., Business Executive, Sweetwater, Tenn.
*Brock, W. E. (C.M.), Business Executive, Chattanooga, Tenn.
*Perry, Mrs. J. W. (C.M.), President, Woman's Missionary Council, Abingdon, Va.

Reserves

Worley, E. D., Pastor, Chattanooga, Tenn.
Hoppe, L. E., Presiding Elder, Sweetwater, Tenn.
Shelton, F. B., Presiding Elder, Knoxville, Tenn.
*Strader, G. S., Retired, Bluefield, W. Va.
*Harmeling, Karl, Businessman, Bristol, Va.
*Adair, H. H., Veterinarian, Bristol, Va.

IDAHO—ME (2 and 1 D.L.)

Sec. C; Row 22, 10 to 12

Hertzog, W. H., District Superintendent, Twin Falls, Idaho.
*Deal, E. H., Insurance, 210 12th Ave., Nampa, Idaho.
*Roan, H. J. (D.L.), Insurance, 1118 Pueblo St., Boise, Idaho.

Reserves

Hamilton, H. S., District Superintendent, Nampa, Idaho.
*Roan, H. J., Insurance, 1118 Pueblo St., Boise, Idaho.

ILLINOIS—ME (10 and 1 D.L.)

Sec. C; Rows 18, 1 to 6; 19, 1 to 5

Wells, A. M., Executive Secretary, Preachers' Aid Society, Decatur, Ill.
Lugg, T. B., Pastor, 365 N. Church St., Decatur, Ill.
Shaw, W. E., Corresponding Secretary, Board of Foreign Missions, 150 Fifth Ave., New York, N. Y.
Pulliam, W. G., District Superintendent, Urbana, Ill.
Sandmeyer, E. G., District Superintendent, Peoria, Ill.
McPherson, H. W. (D.L.), Executive Secretary, Board of Education, 740 Rush St., Chicago, Ill.
*Fitch, H. W., Physician, Bushnell, Ill.
*Snavely, H. R., Attorney, Marshall, Ill.
*Blackstock, Mrs. I. B., Housewife, Springfield, Ill.
*Wiley, H. S., Businessman, Buffalo, Ill.
*Martin, L. H., Attorney, Normal, Ill.

Reserves

Northcott, H. C., Pastor, 409 W. Hill St., Champaign, Ill.
Thorpe, G. H., District Superintendent, Decatur, Ill.
Grummon, A. R., Pastor, 704 S. 5th St., Springfield, Ill.
Johnson, I. M., Pastor, 825 N. Main St., Decatur, Ill.
*Weir, Benjamin, Publisher, Charleston, Ill.
*Pritchett, C. J., Insurance, Dana, Ill.
*Drysdale, W. C., Telephone Manager, Rantoul, Ill.

*Musselman, D. L., Business College, 230 S. 20th St., Quincy, Ill.
*Dillinger, Ray, Farmer, R.F.D. 6, Decatur, Ill.

ILLINOIS—ME,S (2)

Sec. C; Row 15, 11 and 12

Mathis, W. T., Pastor, 514 E. Locust St., Salem, Ill.
*Davis, J. H., Businessman, 1910 Dursius, Murphysboro, Ill.

Reserves

Humphrey, W. D., Presiding Elder, Waverly, Ill.
*Beaty, B. K., Auto Mechanic, Taylorville, Ill.

ILLINOIS—MP (2)

Sec. C; Row 17, 1 and 2

Hanna, F. B., Conference President, Cuba, Ill.
*Ruff, A. C., Banker, Ohio, Ill.

Reserves

Langdon, B. F., Pastor, 7534 Eberhart Ave., Chicago, Ill.
Reuckert, F. E., Pastor, 667 S. 2d St., Canton, Ill.
*Stevens, Miss Lucy, Teacher, Cuba, Ill.
*Collier, C. C., Teacher, West Union, Ill.

INDIA CONFERENCES—ME (4 D.L.O.C.)

Sec. D; Rows 6, 8 to 10; 7, 5 to 10; 8, 5 to 10; 9, 5 to 10

Moffatt, E. M., 150 Fifth Ave., New York, N. Y.
Rugg, E. M., 150 Fifth Ave., New York, N. Y.
*Das, Mrs. C. P., 106 Morningside Drive, New York, N. Y.
*Patel, J. S. K., Leonard Theological College, Jubbulpore, India.

Reserves

Parker, A. C., 1055 N. Kingsley Drive, Los Angeles, Calif.
McLaughlin, W. J., 85 Sherman St., Hartford, Conn.
*Stockwell, Miss G. L., Clarion, Iowa.
*Wilson, Miss Retta I., 107 Park St., Geneva, Ohio.

INDIANA—ME (6 and 1 C.M.)

Sec. D; Rows 4, 8 to 10; 5, 7 to 10

Fifer, O. W., Editor, 420 Plum St., Cincinnati, Ohio.
Hartinger, W. C., District Superintendent, Indianapolis, Ind.
Walker, J. M., Pastor, 608 W. 6th St., Bloomington, Ind.
*McDonald, T. M., Attorney, Princeton, Ind.
*Kibler, R. M., Businessman, Farmersburg, Ind.
*Asbury, Mrs. H. E., General Secretary, Woman's Foreign Missionary
    Society, 1824 Carrollton Ave., Indianapolis, Ind.
*Schwaninger, W. W. (C.M.), Retired, New Albany, Ind.

Reserves

Jones, W. T., District Superintendent, Evansville, Ind.
Woodward, A. S., District Superintendent, Bloomington, Ind.
Moore, J. G., District Superintendent, Rushville, Ind.
*Rowe, J. A., Retired, Bedford, Ind.
*Everson, R. D., Farmer, Harvey Road, Action, Ind.
*Hinkle, H. D., Attorney, Vincennes, Ind.
*Ostrom, Mrs. H. E. (R.D.L.), Housewife, Indianapolis, Ind.

INDIANA—MP (4)

Sec. C; Row 13, 1 to 4

Clarke, Fred, Conference President, Elwood, Ind.
Lineberry, F. W., Pastor, 139 Division St., Elkhart, Ind.
*DeWeese, H. O., Express Agent, 1001 S. Anderson St., Elwood, Ind.
*Arnold, W. S., Insurance, 1539 Pleasant St., Indianapolis, Ind.

Reserves

Ferris, E. L., Pastor, 1520 South D St., Elwood, Ind.
Avery, H. L., Pastor, 17 E. Main St., Logansport, Ind.
*Williams, Walter, Farmer, R.F.D. 4, Muncie, Ind.
*Harper, Leonard, Farmer, R.F.D. 4, Lawrenceburg, Ind.

IOWA-DES MOINES—ME (6)

Sec. C; Row 13, 7 to 12

Goodwin, L. P., District Superintendent, Des Moines, Iowa.
Smith, U. S., Pastor, Perry, Iowa.
Barker, A. H., Pastor, Ames, Iowa.
*Hollingsworth, Mrs. H. S., Housewife, Des Moines, Iowa.
*Taylor, Dean, Editor, *Daily Ledger*, Fairfield, Iowa.
*Peterman, J. H., Banker, Page County State Bank, Clarinda, Iowa.

Reserves

Longnecker, W. A., Pastor, New London, Iowa.
Shipman, R. M., Pastor, 1018 Des Moines St., Des Moines, Iowa.
Edwards, F. C., District Superintendent, Perry, Iowa.
*Knapp, S. A., Insurance, Masonic Bldg., Ames, Iowa.
*Beck, J. M., Publisher, *Daily Iowegian*, Centerville, Iowa.
*Gammon, B. O., Businessman, Des Moines, Iowa.

IOWA-MISSOURI—MP (2)

Sec. B; Row 15, 4 and 5

Betz, W. H., Pastor, 623 E. 8th St., Newton, Iowa.
*McComas, Warren, Stock Raiser, Osceola, Iowa.

Reserves

Williams, H. E., Conference President, Ladora, Iowa.
Green, C. R., Pastor, Maxwell, Iowa.
*Newell, C. D., Farmer, Newton, Iowa.
*Tanner, L. J., Williamsburg, Iowa.

JAPAN CONFERENCES—ME (1 D.L.O.C.)

Sec. D; Rows 6, 8 to 10; 7, 5 to 10; 8, 5 to 10; 9, 5 to 10

Berry, A. D., Mexico, N. Y.

Reserve

Smith, F. H., 2816 Hillegass Ave., Berkeley, Calif.

KANSAS—ME (6 and 2 D.L.)

Sec. C; Rows 9, 1 to 4; 10, 1 to 4

Allison, O. E., Pastor, Emporia, Kans.
Buck, E. F., District Superintendent, Manhattan, Kans.
Penick, R. O., Pastor, Independence, Kans.
Keve, W. A. (D.L.), District Superintendent, Kansas City, Kans.
*Cunningham, T. O., Businessman, Kansas City, Kans.

*French, Mrs. H. A., Housewife, Topeka, Kans.
*Gaede, J. C., Baker, Fredonia, Kans.
*Landon, A. F. (D.L.), Businessman, Topeka, Kans.

Reserves

McCormick, W. R., District Superintendent, Topeka, Kans.
Chubb, J. S., Pastor, Baldwin, Kans.
Odom, C. W., District Superintendent, Emporia, Kans.
*Case, A. S., Merchant, 115 W. Myrtle St., Independence, Kans.
*McCoy, Mrs. J. L., Housewife, Coffeyville, Kans.
*Powell, Mrs. B. M., Housewife, 1236 Mulvane St., Topeka, Kans.

KANSAS—MP (2)

Sec. C; Row 11, 11 and 12

Dixon, L. E., Conference President, Kansas City, Kans.
*Cook, A. L., 1019 Cleveland St., Kansas City, Kans.

Reserves

Pentz, D. M,. Pastor, 1019 Cleveland St., Kansas City, Kans.
*Allen, A. W., 1938 N. 28th St., Kansas City, Kans.

KENTUCKY—ME (2)

Sec. A; Row 18, 1 and 2

Rice, S. C., District Superintendent, Pineville, Ky.
*Bennett, A. S., Insurance, Hartford, Ky.

Reserves

Shepherd, W. W., District Superintendent, Wilmore, Ky.
*Zimmerman, H. M., Businessman, Covington, Ky.

KENTUCKY—ME,S (6 and 1 C.M.)

Sec. A; Row 13, 1 to 7

Clark, J. L., Presiding Elder, Lexington, Ky.
Perkins, A. R., Pastor, 303 E. Mt. Vernon St., Somerset, Ky.
Crockett, O. B., Presiding Elder, Fort Thomas, Ky.
Cram, W. G. (C.M.), Executive Secretary, General Board of Missions, Doctors' Bldg., Nashville, Tenn.
*Redwine, M. C., Attorney, 491 S. Maple St., Winchester, Ky.
*Spillman, Mrs. J. H., Housewife, Harrodsburg, Ky.
*Cannon, J. T., Banker, 315 Pike St., Cynthiana, Ky.

Reserves

Davis, W. P., Pastor, Harrodsburg, Ky.
Whitaker, H. W., Pastor, Lexington, Ky.
Clark, W. L., Pastor, Paris, Ky.
*Gibson, J. H., Banker, Somerset, Ky.
*King, L. E., Farmer, Cynthiana, Ky.
*Savage, E. W., Businessman, Lexington, Ky.

KENTUCKY—MP (2)

Sec. A; Row 14, 5 and 6

Shumway, H. L., Pastor, Catlettsburg, Ky.
*Bellomy, Edward, Merchant, Prichard, W. Va.

Reserves

Watkins, A. C., Pastor, 15 Georgia St., Winchester, Ky.
*Watkins, Mrs. A. C., Housewife, 15 Georgia St., Winchester, Ky.

The Methodist Church

KOREAN CONFERENCES—ME (1 D.L.O.C)

Sec. D; Rows 6, 8 to 10; 7, 5 to 10; 8, 5 to 10; 9, 5 to 10
*Troxel, Miss M. J., 5965 W. Huron St., Chicago, Ill.

Reserve
*Anderson, A. G., 500 N. Ashland Ave., Chicago, Ill.

LEXINGTON—ME (2 and 1 D.L.)

Sec. A; Row 10, 1 to 3
Smith, B. F., District Superintendent, 3553 S. Parkway, Chicago, Ill.
*Bethea, D. A., Physician, 1139 Field St., Hammond, Ind.
*Patton, J. A. (D.L.), Mortician, Indianapolis, Ind.

Reserves
Skelton, D. E., District Superintendent, Indianapolis, Ind.
Sweeney, S. H. (R.D.L.), Pastor, 213 E. 50th St., Chicago, Ill.
*Crolley, Richard A. (deceased).

LITTLE ROCK—ME,S (8)

Sec. B; Row 21, 1 to 8
Reves, C. M., Presiding Elder, 1301 Schiller St., Little Rock, Ark.
Baker, Clem, Executive Secretary, Conference Board of Christian
Education, 723 Center St., Little Rock, Ark.
Hammons, J. D., Vice-President, Hendrix College, Little Rock, Ark.
Rule, E. C., Pastor, 120 W. 6th St., Pine Bluff, Ark.
*Cannon, J. S. M., Mail Supervisor, 211 Arch St., Little Rock, Ark.
*Hollis, Carl, Banker, Warren, Ark.
*Moore, Fred, Public School Superintendent, Pine Bluff, Ark.
*Stinson, Mrs. J. M., Conference President, W.M.S., 509 Washington
St., Camden, Ark.

Reserves
Clegg, Leland, Presiding Elder, Camden, Ark.
Watson, W. C., Pastor, Malvern, Ark.
Mann, J. W., Presiding Elder, 508 Locust St., Texarkana, Ark.
Baker, J. D., Presiding Elder, Prescott, Ark.
*Prewitt, T. A., Merchant, Tillar, Ark.
*Fuller, T. E., Physician, National Bank Bldg., Texarkana, Ark.
*Wade, Mrs. H. K., Conference Secretary, W.M.S., Hot Springs, Ark.
*Overstreet, C. A., College President, Magnolia, Ark.

LOUISIANA—ME (2)

Sec. A; Row 2, 5 and 6
Bowen, J. W. E., District Superintendent, New Orleans, La.
*Davage, M. S., President, Clark University, S. Atlanta, Ga.

Reserves
Handy, W. T., Pastor, 2217 Jackson Ave., New Orleans, La.
*Hayes, R. B., Professor, Sam Houston College, Austin, Tex.
*Bowen, Mrs. M. D. (R.D.L.), Principal, Gilbert Academy, New
Orleans, La.

LOUISIANA—ME,S (8 and 2 C.M.)

Sec. D; Row 19, 1 to 10
Holmes, W. W., Pastor, New Orleans, La.
Duren, W. L., Editor, *New Orleans Christian Advocate*, New Orleans,
La.

Johns, H. L., Pastor, 722 Broad St., Lake Charles, La.
Dawson, Dana, Pastor, 2222 Fairfield Ave., Shreveport, La.
Parker, F. N. (C.M.), Professor, Candler School of Theology, Emory
    University, Ga.
*Holland, C. O., Vice-President, Centenary College, Shreveport, La.
*James, T. L., Investments, Ruston, La.
*Sexton, Mrs. G. S., Jr., Conference President, W.M.S., 32 Atkins
    St., Shreveport, La.
*Carter, J. H., Business Executive, New Orleans, La.
*White, H. H. (C.M.), Attorney, Alexandria, La.

Reserves

Hicks, G. M., Pastor, Ruston, La.
Harper, R. H., Presiding Elder, Alexandria, La.
Gunn, E. C., Presiding Elder, New Orleans, La.
Spann, J. R., Pastor, 138 E. Boulevard, Baton Rouge, La.
Duren, W. L. (R.C.M.), Church Editor, New Orleans, La.
*Walker, E. L., District Judge, Ruston, La.
*Brumley, R. E., Attorney, Franklin, La.
*Nichols, I. C., University Professor, Baton Rouge, La.
*Pollard, Mrs. J. B., Housewife, New Orleans, La.

LOUISIANA—MP (2)

Sec. B; Row 14, 3 and 4

Lee, J. W., Conference President, Grayson, La.
*Johnson, T. L., School Superintendent, Grayson, La.

Reserves

Yeager, I. L., Pastor, Monroe, La.
Pardue, Mrs. M. E., Pastor, Atlanta, Tex.
*Wardlow, F. W., Merchant, Montgomery, La.
*McKeithen, J. W., Contractor, Grayson, La.

LOUISVILLE—ME,S (8)

Sec. D; Row 18, 1 to 8

Short, R. H., Presiding Elder, Louisville, Ky.
Hummel, G. W., Presiding Elder, Bowling Green, Ky.
Nicholson, J. H., Pastor, 1421 23d Ave., Meridian, Miss.
Lyon, A. P.. Pastor, 1232 S. Jackson St., Louisville, Ky.
*Dickey, J. H., Insurance, Columbia Bldg., Louisville, Ky.
*Harmon, J. L., President, Bowling Green College of Commerce, Bowl-
    ing Green, Ky.
*Cash, W. L., Physician, Box 23, Princeton, Ky.
*Piggott, Mrs. J. W., Housewife, The Lindens, Irvington, Ky.

Reserves

Weldon, J. W., Presiding Elder, Hopkinsville, Ky.
Stuckey, L. N., Pastor, 1113 S. Fourth St., Louisville, Ky.
Bennett, R. V., Pastor, Campbellsville, Ky.
*Johnson, Mrs. A. C., Conference President. W.M.S., 236 Poplar St.,
    Elizabethtown, Ky.
*Hummel, Mrs. G. W., Housewife, Bowling Green, Ky.
*Butler, V. H., Insurance, Starks Bldg., Louisville, Ky.

MAINE—ME (2)

Sec. B; Row 5, 6 and 7

Callaghan, A. A., District Superintendent, Augusta, Maine.
*Baldwin, C. D., Railroad Official, Bangor, Maine.

Reserves

Robinson, E. W., District Superintendent, Portland, Maine.
*Currie, Miss Margaret, Attorney, 58 North St., Saco, Maine.

MALAYSIA AND PHILIPPINE ISLANDS CONFERENCES—ME (2 D.L.O.C.)

Sec. D; Rows 6, 8 to. 10; 7, 5 to 10; 8, 5 to 10; 9, 5 to 10

Archer, R. L., 150 Fifth Avenue, New York, N. Y.
Lyons, E. S., 1089 W. 35th St., Los Angeles, Calif.

Reserve

Amstutz, H. B., Singapore.

MARYLAND—MP (16)

Sec. C; Rows 5, 5 to 12; 6, 5 to 12

Straughn, J. H., President, General Conference, Baltimore, Md.
Sexsmith, E. A., Conference President, Baltimore, Md.
Smith, L. B., Pastor, 3612 Edmondson Ave., Baltimore, Md.
Shipley, R. L., Church Editor, 516 N. Charles St., Baltimore, Md.
Holloway, F. G., College President, Westminster, Md.
Green, J. L., Pastor, N. Division St., Salisbury, Md.
Humphreys, G. I., President, High Point College, High Point, N. C.
Makosky, E. C., Pastor, 1903 N. Monroe St., Arlington, Va.
*Benson, F. M., Attorney, 2 E. Lexington Ave., Baltimore, Md.
*Baker, J. H., Banker, 1st National Bank Bldg., Baltimore, Md.
*Gilligan, Henry, Attorney, 2304 First St., N. W., Washington, D. C.
*Adkins, F. P., Lumber Dealer, Salisbury, Md.
*Scott, W. C., Business Executive, Baltimore, Md.
*Staley, H. C., Business Executive, Baltimore, Md.
*Herrigel, Fred, Jr., Judge, Short Hills, N. J.
*MacLea, Daniel, Lumber Dealer, 4301 Greenway, Baltimore, Md.

Reserves

Nicholson, R. Y., Pastor, 2504 Garrison Ave., Baltimore, Md.
White, R. W., Pastor, 2324 1st St., N. W., Washington, D. C.
Link, J. N., Seminary Professor, Westminster, Md.
Bunce, E. L., Pastor, 2705 St. Paul St., Baltimore, Md.
Haddaway, G. W., Executive Secretary, Board of Missions, Baltimore, Md.
Stone, E. D., Pastor, 3449 Falls Road, Baltimore, Md.
Wright, W. F., Pastor, 2216 Lake Ave., Baltimore, Md.
Mulligan, J. C., Pastor, Cambridge, Md.
*Matthews, Mrs. M. B., Housewife, 4301 Greenway, Baltimore, Md.
*Jett, R. S., Tailor, 3512 Carlisle Ave., Baltimore, Md.
*Parks, N. J., Merchant, Parksley, Va.
*Dykes, L. W., Commission Merchant, Baltimore, Md.
*Ball, F. M., Attorney, 4527 17th St., Arlington, Va.
*Insley, W. H., Insurance, Salisbury, Md.
*Harrison, W. H., Retired, 3282 N St., N. W., Washington, D. C.
*Satterfield, C. N., Merchant, Chestertown, Md.

MEMPHIS—ME,S (12)

Sec. B; Row 22, 1 to 12

Jones, F. B., Presiding Elder, 1041 Jefferson St., Paducah, Ky.
Underwood, J. E., Pastor, 327 S. Royal St., Jackson, Tenn.
Estes, L. H., Pastor, 1120 Faxon Ave., Memphis, Tenn.
Hamlett, E. G., Presiding Elder, 310 Messick Bldg., Memphis, Tenn.

Peeples, F. H., Pastor, 607 E. McLemore Ave., Memphis, Tenn.
Daniel, C. C., Presiding Elder, Jackson, Tenn.
*Hedden, Henry, Superintendent, Methodist Hospital, Memphis, Tenn.
*Womack, R. E., President, Lambuth College, Jackson, Tenn.
*McMurry, W. F., Attorney, Paducah, Ky.
*Meek, Paul, President U. T. Junior College, Martin, Tenn.
*Tatum, Mrs. S. H. Conference President, W.M.S., Alamo, Tenn.
*Morelock, G. L., Executive Secretary, General Board of Lay Activities, 810 Broadway, Nashville, Tenn.

Reserves

Horton, J. L., Pastor, 154 Stonewall, Memphis, Tenn.
Selah, W. B., Pastor, 1207 Peabody Ave., Memphis, Tenn.
Mathis, E. M., Presiding Elder, Dyersburg, Tenn.
Fain, G. C., Pastor, 1762 Overton Park Ave., Memphis, Tenn.
*Peeler, J. T., Attorney, Huntingdon, Tenn.
*Elkins, R. A., District Judge, Dresden, Tenn.
*Patton, W. C., Attorney, Halls, Tenn.
*Bond, C. W., Auto Dealer, Arlington, Tenn.
*Tatum, Mrs. S. H. (R.C.M.), Conference President, W.M.S., Alamo, Tenn.

MICHIGAN—ME (6 and 1 D.L.)

Sec. A; Rows 8, 1 to 3; 9, 1 to 4

Coors, D. S., Pastor, 210 W. Ottowa St., Lansing, Mich.
Robinson, L. T., Pastor, 243 W. Webster Ave., Muskegon, Mich.
Pellowe, A. H., Pastor, 235 Calkins Ave., S. E., Grand Rapids, Mich.
Seaton, J. L. (D.L.), President Albion College, Albion, Mich.
*Dickinson, L. D., Governor, Charlotte, Mich.
*Veenboer, Mrs. W. H., Housewife, Grand Rapids, Mich.
*Burnham, Smith, Professor, Kalamazoo, Mich.

Reserves

Perdew, W. C., Pastor, 208 S. Park St., Kalamazoo, Mich.
Nixon, L. H., District Superintendent, Albion, Mich.
Seaton, J. L., President Albion College, Albion, Mich.
*Huckle, T. O., Editor, Cadillac, Mich.
*Stewart, Mrs. L. W., Housewife, 526 Union St., Ionia, Mich.
*Shumacker, W. H., Editor, Three Rivers, Mich.

MICHIGAN—MP (2)

Sec. A; Row 1, 1 and 2

Willson, E. R., Conference President, Gagetown, Mich.
*Vincent, E. R., 221 E. Corunna St., Corunna, Mich.

Reserves

Dibley, Joseph, Pastor, 811 S. Chestnut St., Lansing, Mich.
Hart, F. E., Pastor, New Lathrop, Mich.
*Hadsall, M. L., Birch Run, Mich.
*Maxwell, Gala, Clio, Mich.

MINNESOTA—ME (2)

Sec. A; Row 1, 5 and 6

Rising, L. H., Pastor, 2207 Knapp St., St. Paul, Minn.
*Reineke, G. F., Physician, New Ulm, Minn.

Reserves

Mattam, J. W., Hospital Chaplain, Rochester, Minn.
*DeVinny, Mrs. M. L., Corresponding Secretary, Woman's Home Missionary Society, St. Paul, Minn.

MISSISSIPPI—ME (2 and 1 D.L.)

Sec., A; Row 10, 4 to 6

Shaw, J. B. F., District Superintendent, W. Jackson, Miss.
Johnson, L. E. (D.L.), Pastor, Jackson, Miss.
*McAllister, R. H., Manager, *Christian Advocate*, New Orleans, La.

Reserves

Wheaton, J. D., Pastor, 209 S. Yazoo St., Yazoo City, Miss.
*Hall, E. W., Mortician, 600 Mobile St., Hattiesburg, Miss.

MISSISSIPPI—ME,S (10)

Sec. A; Row 15, 1 to 10

Sutherland, B. L., Pastor, Jackson, Miss.
Brownlee, T. M., Presiding Elder, Jackson, Miss.
Bowen, C. A., Secretary, Editorial Dept., General Board of Christian Education, 810 Broadway, Nashville, Tenn.
Hunt, B. M., Pastor, 1417 W. Capitol St., Jackson, Miss.
Alsworth, W. B., Presiding Elder, Hattiesburg, Miss.
*Sullivan, J. M., Professor, Millsaps College, Jackson, Miss.
*Stevens, B. M., Merchant, Richton, Miss.
*Arrington, Mrs. Paul, Conference President, W.M.S., Petal, Miss.
*Hawkins, W. D., Insurance, Meridian, Miss.
*Youngblood, Curtis, Merchant, Wesson, Miss.

Reserves

Campbell, J. F., Presiding Elder, Gulfport, Miss.
Leggett, J. T., Pastor, Hattiesburg, Miss.
Neill, J. L., Pastor, Brookhaven, Miss.
*Bailey, T. L., Attorney, Meridian, Miss.
*Corban, L. C., Judge, Biloxi, Miss.
*Tatum, W. O., Wholesale Lumber, Hattiesburg, Miss.

MISSISSIPPI—MP (2)

Sec. A; Row 18, 5 and 6

Sharp, F. L., Pastor, Collinsville, Miss.
*Williamson, N. S., Attorney, Meridian, Miss.

Reserves

Watson, R. H. M., Conference President, Meridian, Miss.
Hamrick, W. L., Pastor, Hattiesburg, Miss.
*Fowler, Luther, Farmer, Pickens, Miss.
*West, C. D., Avera, Miss.

MISSOURI—ME (6 and 2 D.L. and 1 C.M.)

Sec. C; Rows 5, 1 to 4; 6, 1 to 4

Kulp, E. J., Pastor, Kansas City, Mo.
King, J. F., District Superintendent, Springfield, Mo.
Wahl, F. W., Pastor, 1102 Wilmington St., St. Louis, Mo.
Hislop, Edward (C.M.), 1121 McGee St., Kansas City, Mo.
*Lyons, L. J., Attorney, 1002 Walnut St., Kansas City, Mo.
*Bragg, Grace L., Housewife, 3666a Montana Ave., St. Louis, Mo.

*Hanke, C. W., Businessman, 818 Olive St., St. Louis, Mo.
*Tucker, R. C. (D.L.), Attorney, Kansas City, Mo.
*Duhigg, Miss A. B. (D.L.), Teacher, Bingham Canyon, Utah.

Reserves

Halter, A. A., District Superintendent, Sedalia, Mo.
Garrett, E. N., District Superintendent, Kirksville, Mo.
Clark, V. C., District Superintendent, Carthage, Mo.
*Carothers, Manville, Postman, Kirksville, Mo.
*Taylor, J. A., Hotel Manager, Springfield, Mo.
*Brigham, E. T., Businessman, Kansas City, Mo.
*Mead, Mrs. C. L. (R.D.L.), Housewife, Kansas City, Mo.

MISSOURI—ME,S (8 and 1 C.M.)

Sec. A; Rows 16, 5 to 10; 17, 8 to 10

Holliday, R. C., Pastor, 211 W. Broadway, Columbia, Mo.
Tucker, F. C., Pastor, 1002 N. 25th St., St. Joseph, Mo.
Pegues, D. K., Pastor, 900 Paris St., Hannibal, Mo.
Randolph, J. D., Pastor, 215 S. Cole St., Mexico, Mo.
Alexander, W. M. (C.M.), Secretary, Department of Schools and
    Colleges, General Board of Christian Education, Nashville, Tenn.
*Stephens, F. F., University Professor, Columbia, Mo.
*Woods, J. M., Business Executive, 801 Bird St., Hannibal, Mo.
*Utz, W. H., Jr., Attorney, 903 Camby Bldg., St. Joseph, Mo.
*Marr, P. M., Merchant, Milan, Mo.

Reserves

Taylor, P. P., Pastor, Boonville, Mo.
Ruff, R. H., President, Central College, Fayette, Mo.
Smith, A. F., Publishing Agent, Nashville, Tenn.
Ruyle, C. E., Presiding Elder, Mexico, Mo.
*Pohlman, George, Postmaster, Macon, Mo.
*Cravens, W. A., Attorney, Excelsior Springs, Mo.
*Burke, Mrs. M. W., Housewife, Moberly, Mo.
*Fawks, R. W., Merchant, Forest City, Mo.

MISSOURI—MP (2)

Sec. A; Row 11, 9 and 10

Stribling, E. R., Pastor, Monett, Mo.
*Dillon, Mrs. B. E., Housewife, Rogersville, Mo.

Reserves

Henderson, C. E., Pastor, Cassville, Mo.
Saye, C. W., Pastor, Aurora, Mo.
*Hazel, Mrs. Gail, Housewife, 130 E St., St. Louis, Mo.
*Stribling, Roy, Monett, Mo.

MONTANA STATE—ME (2)

Sec. C; Row 4, 10 to 12

Morange, John, Pastor, Havre, Mont.
*Collins, E. E., Attorney, 209-211 Securities Bldg., Billings, Mont.

Reserves

Turner, Horace, District Superintendent, Billings, Mont.
*Lewis, V. E., Attorney, Fort Benton, Mont.

NEBRASKA—ME (8 and 1 D.L.)

Sec. C; Rows 7, 10 to 12; 8, 10 to 12; 9, 10 to 12

Kaub, L. H., Pastor, Beatrice, Nebr.
Hess, H. E., Superintendent, Methodist Hospital, Omaho, Nebr.
Aitken, Walter, Pastor, 12th and M Sts., Lincoln, Nebr.
Geissinger, E. L., Pastor, 401 N. 27th St., Lincoln, Nebr.
*Greenslit, H. M., Railroad Official, Lincoln, Nebr.
*Gray, G. H., Insurance, Columbus, Nebr.
*Rogers, W. S., Businessman, Ainsworth, Nebr.
*Watson, Miss E. M., Corresponding Secretary, Woman's Foreign Missionary Society, 1701 S. 17th St., Lincoln, Nebr.
*Clark, W. D. (D.L.), Banker, Omaha, Nebr.

Reserves

Hillman, P. M., District Superintendent, Kearney, Nebr.
Cutshall, E. G., Counselor of Finance, Lincoln, Nebr.
McDade, E. C., District Superintendent, Beatrice, Nebr.
Pfoutz, F. E., District Superintendent, Hastings, Nebr.
*Pennington, Mrs. F. G., Housewife, Wymore, Nebr.
*Dryden, K. H., Attorney, Kearney, Nebr.
*Seymour, Edward, Businessman, Wayne, Nebr.
*Eells, L. L., Physician, Auburn, Nebr.

NEW ENGLAND—ME (4 and 1 D.L., and 1 C.M.)

Sec. C; Row 3, 5 to 7; 4, 5 to 7

Marsh, D. L., President, Boston University, Boston, Mass.
Hartman, L. O., Editor, 581 Boylston St., Boston, Mass.
*Emery, S. T., Insurance, 35 Marshall St., Newton Center, Mass.
*MacMullen, S. O., Insurance, 25 Brackett Road, Newton, Mass.
*LeSourd, Mrs. L. L. (D.L.), Housewife, Newton, Mass.
*Clarke, V. P. (C.M.), Attorney, 93 Bacon St., Winchester, Mass.

Reserves

Ford, C. O., Pastor, 3 Franklin St., Lynn, Mass.
Jeffras, C. W., Pastor, 120 Buckingham St., Springfield, Mass.
*Bliss, E. P., Retired, 26 Bartlett St., Malden, Mass.
*Roberts, G. C., Insurance, 293 Bridge St., Springfield, Mass.

NEW ENGLAND SOUTHERN—ME (2 and 1 D.L.)

Sec. C; Row 7, 1 to 4

Claypool, J. V., District Superintendent, Providence, R. I.
Knudson, A. C. (D.L.), Professor, Boston University, Boston, Mass.
*Pritchard, W. P., Physician, 273 N. Main St., Fall River, Mass.

Reserves

Stoody, R. W., Pastor, 410 Prospect St., Fall River, Mass.
*Miner, A. T., Trustee of Estates, New London, Conn.
*McCullough, J. B. (R.D.L.), Businessman, Philadelphia, Pa.

NEW HAMPSHIRE—ME (2)

Sec. C; Row 17, 5 and 6

Stringfellow, L. W., Pastor, 66 Webster St., Haverhill, Mass.
*Davis, W. H., Manufacturer, 4 Stevens St., Nashua, N. H.

Reserves

Hawver, H. D., District Superintendent, Concord, N. H.
*Webb, C. W., Businessman, 220 Washington St., Dover, N. H.

NEW JERSEY—ME (4)

Sec. A; Row 12, 3 to 6

Brock, T. S., District Superintendent, Trenton, N. J.
Sloan, H. P., Editor, 150 Fifth Ave., New York, N. Y.
*Propert, F. C., Attorney, Haddonfield, N. J.
*Bennett, H. P., Salesman, Long Branch, N. J.

Reserves

Hann, E. F., District Superintendent, Woodbury, N. J.
Chamberlain, Leon, District Superintendent, Red Bank, N. J.
*Poffenberger, A. C., Manager, Hotel Dennis, Atlantic City, N. J.
*Matthews, E. C., Businessman, Williamstown, N. J.

NEW MEXICO—ME,S (4)

Sec. D; Row 15, 1 to 4

Barr, W. L., Presiding Elder, 2831 Lebanon St., El Paso, Tex.
Campbell, C. K., Pastor, 642 W. May St., Las Cruces, N. Mex.
*Davidson, H. O., Retired, Albuquerque, N. Mex.
*Carver, G. C., Merchant, Melrose, N. Mex.

Reserves

Bailey, W. G., Presiding Elder, Box 661, Albuquerque, N. Mex.
Shearer, G. W., Presiding Elder, Clovis, N. Mex.
*Walker, Mrs. C. S., Housewife, Albuquerque, N. Mex.
*Ables, J. H., Attorney, Denver, Colo.

NEW YORK—ME (4 and 3 D.L.)

Sec. A; Rows 9, 5 to 7; 10, 7 to 10

Sockman, R. W., Pastor, 950 Park Ave., New York, N. Y.
MacRossie, Allan, Educational Director, Commission on Courses of
    Study, 150 Fifth Ave., New York, N. Y.
*Smith, C. A., Court Stenographer, Peekskill, N. Y.
*Fowler, C. H., Attorney, 60 E. 42d St., New York, N. Y.
*Mott, J. R. (D.L.), Chairman, International Missionary Council,
    230 Park Ave., New York, N. Y.
*McConnell, Mrs. F. J. (D.L.), Housewife, New York, N. Y.
*Wagner, R. F. (D.L.), United States Senator, Washington, D. C.

Reserves

Coile, C. C., District Superintendent, New York, N. Y.
Stacey, F. W., District Superintendent, Poughkeepsie, N. Y.
*Colvin, Mrs. D. L., Housewife, New York, N. Y.
*Class, J. L., Attorney, 80 Livingston Ave., Yonkers, N. Y.

NEW YORK EAST—ME (6 and 1 D.L.)

Sec. A; Rows 2, 1 to 4; 3, 1 to 4

Langdale, J. W., Book Editor, 150 Fifth Ave., New York, N. Y.
Hough, L. H., Dean, Drew Theological Seminary, Madison, N. J.
Newell, F. B., Executive Secretary, 150 Fifth Ave., New York, N. Y.
*Carman, E. R., Attorney, 87-21 164th St., Jamaica, N. Y.
*Horne, F. A. (deceased).
*Chaffee, H. A., Banker, Norwood Road, Bridgeport, Conn.
*Hardie, Mrs. C. H. (D.L.), Secretary, Woman's Foreign Missionary
    Society, 883 E. 19th St., Brooklyn, N. Y.

Reserves

Jones, H. D., District Superintendent, Baldwin, N. Y.
Worley, L. F., District Superintendent, New Haven, Conn.
Auman, L. W. (R.D.L.), Pastor, Jackson Heights, N. Y.
*Reid, W. W., Publisher, 11-03 157th St., Beechhurst, N. Y.
*Barradell, W. H., Attorney, Rockville Center, N. Y.
*Welker, Miss Edith, Religious Education Worker, Chicago, Ill.

NEWARK—ME (4 and 1 D.L. and 1 C.M.)

Sec. B; Row 9, 8 to 12

Washabaugh, J. E., District Superintendent, East Orange, N. J.
Foster, L. E., Pastor, 351 Williams St., East Orange, N. J.
Brown, A. A. (D.L.), President, Drew University, Madison, N. J.
*Clark, S. H., Manufacturer, 7 Roosevelt Road, Maplewood, N. J.
*McNear, A. S., Insurance, 20 Gilbert Place, East Orange, N. J.
*Joy, J. R. (C.M.), 150 Fifth Ave., New York, N. Y.

Reserves

Quimby, K. K., District Superintendent, Ridgewood, N. J.
Brown, A. A., President, Drew University, Madison, N. J.
*Beattys, G. D., Attorney, 8 Stoneleigh Park, Westfield, N. J.
*Diefendorf, Mrs. Mabel, Housewife, Ridgewood, N. J.

NORTH ALABAMA—ME,S (18 and 1 C.D.)

Sec. B; Rows 18, 1 to 10; 19, 1 to 9

Davenport, G. M., Pastor, 7759 10th Ave., S., Birmingham, Ala.
Lazenby, M. E., Presiding Elder, 819 Line St., Decatur, Ala.
Henry, W. G., Presiding Elder, Atlanta, Ga.
Kimbrough, S. O., Pastor, 810 Greensboro Ave., Anniston, Ala.
Stevenson, H. M., Pastor, Tuscaloosa, Ala.
Morris, W. E., Presiding Elder, 824 Quintard Ave., Anniston, Ala.
Davidson, M. M., Presiding Elder, Tuscaloosa, Ala.
Freeman, A. M., Presiding Elder, Florence Ala.
Chadwick, J. S., Superannuate, Birmingham, Ala.
*Carr, R. B., Circuit Judge, 623 Highland Ave., Anniston, Ala.
*Garrison, E. J., Attorney, Ashland, Ala.
*Kirby, A. N., Merchant, 5720 5 Terrace, S., Birmingham, Ala.
*Ingram, B. L., Sheriff, 110 Avenue V, Pratt City, Ala.
*Ward, F. S., Superintendent of Education, Carrollton, Ala.
*Graves, W. D., Merchant, Alexander City, Ala.
*Morris, Mrs. Isaac, Conference President, W.M.S., Fairfield, Ala.
*Haley, P. S., Civil Engineer, Jasper, Ala.
*Self, W. D., Merchant, Trafford, Ala.
*Denman, Harry (C.M.), Secretary of Evangelism, General Board of Missions, Doctors' Bldg., Nashville, Tenn.

Reserves

Franklin, M. A., Pastor, 2133 S. 14th St., Birmingham, Ala.
Gamble, F. K., Church Editor, Birmingham, Ala.
Hunter, J. D., Pastor, Birmingham, Ala.
McNutt, D. C., Presiding Elder, Jasper, Ala.
Dill, R. L., Presiding Elder, Gadsden, Ala.
*Green, W. C., Postmaster, Birmingham, Ala.
*Sparkman, John, Attorney, Huntsville, Ala.
*Cook, F. M., College Professor, Florence, Ala.
*Napier, T. H., College Professor, Montevallo, Ala.
*Miller, Grady, Insurance, 3401 Salter Road, Birmingham, Ala.

NORTH ARKANSAS—ME,S (10 and 1 C.M.)

Sec. B; Rows 16, 9 to 12; 17, 6 to 12

Martin, A. W., Pastor, 815 S. Main St., Jonesboro, Ark.
Schisler, J. Q., Secretary, Department of the Local Church, General Board of Christian Education, Nashville, Tenn.
Johnston, Warren, Presiding Elder, Fort Smith, Ark.
Goddard, O. E., Pastor, 1922 Dodson Ave., Fort Smith, Ark.
Wayland, E. T., Presiding Elder, 1017 Clifton St., Conway, Ark.
*Pewett, Mrs. Henkel, Conference President, W.M.S., Jonesboro, Ark.
*Williams, J. M., Professor, Hendrix College, Conway, Ark.
*Stuck, C. A., Lumber, Jonesboro, Ark.
*Melton, C. G., Eye Specialist, Box 34, Fayetteville, Ark.
*Womack, J. P., College Professor, Jonesboro, Ark.
*Reynolds, J. H. (C.M.), President, Hendrix College, Conway, Ark.

Reserves

Wasson, A. W., Secretary, Department of Foreign Missions, General Board of Missions, Doctors' Building, Nashville, Tenn.
Womack, W. V., Presiding Elder, Fayetteville, Ark.
Walton, A. G., Pastor, Searcy, Ark.
Hayden, R. S., Pastor, Forrest City, Ark.
Williams, E. B., Pastor, Blytheville, Ark.
*Barnett, Nelson, Merchant, Batesville, Ark.
*Galloway, S. A., Investments, Fort Smith, Ark.
*Snetser, Mrs. B. E., Housewife, Newport, Ark.
*Stone, Mrs. Fred, Housewife, Fort Smith, Ark.
*Metcalf, C. D., Banker, Batesville, Ark.

NORTH CAROLINA—ME (2 and 1 D.L.)

Sec. C; Row 3, 10 to 12

Winchester, R. W., Pastor, High Point, N. C.
Brooks, R. N. (D.L.), Editor, 631 Baronne St., New Orleans, La.
*Jones, D. D., President, Bennett College, Greensboro, N. C.

Reserves

Brooks, R. N., Editor, 631 Baronne St., New Orleans, La.
Wright, T. S., Real Estate, 200 W. Park Ave., Winston-Salem, N. C.

NORTH CAROLINA—ME,S (14 and 1 C.M.)

Sec. B; Rows 14, 5 to 12; 15, 6 to 12

Grant, T. McM., Pastor, Box 529, Greenville, N. C.
Hillman, E. L., Presiding Elder, 31 New St., New Bern, N. C.
Ormond, J. M., Professor, Duke University, Durham, N. C.
Plyler, M. T., Editor, *North Carolina Christian Advocate*, Greensboro, N. C.
Hickman, F. S., Professor, Duke University, Durham, N. C.
Smith, H. C., Pastor, 516 W. Chapel Hill, Durham, N. C.
Love, F. S., Pastor, 221 N. 4th St., Wilmington, N. C.
*Hillman, Mrs. E. L., Conference President, W.M.S., New Bern, N. C.
*MacKinnon, Miss S. L., Secretary, Foreign Department, General Board of Missions, Doctors' Building, Nashville, Tenn.
*Greene, W. K., Dean, Duke University, Durham, N. C.
*Knight, W. L., Attorney, Weldon, N. C.
*Cooper, W. B., Broker, 608 Dock St., Wilmington, N. C.
*Chadwick, W. C., Insurance, New Bern, N. C.
*Hood, G. P., Commissioner of Banks, Raleigh, N. C.
*Few, W. P. (C.M.), President, Duke University, Durham, N. C.

Reserves

Hobbs, A. J., Presiding Elder, Durham, N. C.
Cuninggim, J. L., President, Scarritt College, Nashville, Tenn.
Bradshaw, R. W., Conference Secretary, Christian Education, Durham, N. C.
Porter, H. B., Pastor, Wilson, N. C.
*Bruton, J. F., Attorney, Wilson, N. C.
*Morris, C. G., Insurance, Washington, N. C.
*Marr, Wade, Stocks and Bonds, Elizabeth City, N. C.
*Flowers, R. L., Treasurer, Duke University, Durham, N. C.

NORTH CAROLINA—MP (14)

Sec. B; Rows 2, 6 to 12; 3, 6 to 12

Pritchard, J. E., Conference President, High Point, N. C.
Bates, C. W., Pastor, Box 51, Browns Summit, N. C.
Forlines, C. E., Seminary President, Westminster, Md.
Taylor, S. W., Pastor, Asheboro, N. C.
Andrews, R. M., Pastor-Editor, Greensboro, N. C.
Brown, G. R., Pastor, Liberty, N. C.
Paschall, F. W., Pastor, 603 E. Davis St., Burlington, N. C.
*Coble, M. A., Banker, Burlington, N. C.
*Wills, J. N., Stationer, W. Gaston St., Greensboro, N. C.
*Hammer, Mrs. W. C., Businesswoman, Asheboro, N. C.
*Wren, L. L., Manufacturer, Siler City, N. C.
*Koonce, A. J., Mortician, High Point, N. C.
*Redding, W. F., Jr., Miller, Asheboro, N. C.
*Hicks, J. B., Attorney, Henderson, N. C.

Reserves

Auman, J. C., Pastor, Thomasville, N. C.
Carroll, J. E., Pastor, 222 N. Edgeworth St., Greensboro, N. C.
Surratt, H. F., Pastor, Graham, N. C.
Whitehead, T. J., Pastor, Charles St., Henderson, N. C.
Madison, J. C., Pastor, High Point, N. C.
Lindley, P. S., College Professor, High Point, N. C.
Bethea, N. G., Pastor, 165 Hillside St., Asheville, N. C.
*Allen, J. H., Business Executive, Reidville, N. C.
*Crew, J. W., Jr., Attorney, Roanoke Rapids, N. C.
*Cutchin, J. M., Farmer, Whitakers, N. C.
*Cox, R. M., Dairyman, Rural Hall, N. C.
*Coltrane, Mrs. D. S., Housewife, Raleigh, N. C.
*Montgomery, S. P., Contractor, High Point, N. C.
*Ross, J. D., Banker, Asheboro, N. C.

NORTH DAKOTA—ME (2)

Sec. B; Row 1, 6 and 7

Burgum, L. R., District Superintendent, Fargo, N. Dak.
*Knight, G. N., Professor, Jamestown, N. Dak.

Reserves

Wallace, C. L., President, Wesley College, Grand Forks, N. Dak.
*Fawcett, W. C., Physician, Starkweather, N. Dak.

NORTH GEORGIA—ME,S (18 and 1 C.M.)

Sec. C; Rows 17, 7 to 12; 18, 7 to 12; 19, 6 to 12

King, W. P., Editor, *Christian Advocate*, Nashville, Tenn.
Jones, H. H., Pastor, 1037 Green Ave., N. W., Atlanta, Ga.

LaPrade, W. H., Pastor, 929 Waverly Place, Atlanta, Ga.
Pierce, A. M., Pastor, Milledgeville, Ga.
Jarrell, C. C., Pastor, Augusta, Ga.
Rumble, Lester, Pastor, 528 Orme Circle, Atlanta, Ga.
Shelton, W. A., Presiding Elder, Birmingham, Ala.
Rogers, Wallace, Pastor, 312 S. Hill St., Griffin, Ga.
Russell, R. L., Pastor, 205 N. Green St., Gainesville, Ga.
*Johnston, S. L., Merchant, Woodstock, Ga.
*Cox, H. W., President, Emory University, Emory University, Ga.
*Awtrey, Mrs. L. M., Conference President, W.M.S., Acworth, Ga.
*Lance, T. J., President, Young Harris College, Young Harris, Ga.
*Ingram, I. S., College President, Carrollton, Ga.
*Slaughter, N. G., Dentist, S. M. Bldg., Athens, Ga.
*Tilley, Mrs. M. E., Conference Secretary, W.M.S., Atlanta, Ga.
*Quillian, Hubert, College President, LaGrange, Ga.
*Wardlaw, J. C., Extension Department, State University, 223 Walton, N. W., Atlanta, Ga.
*Candler, J. S. (C.M.), Attorney, 199 Tuxedo Drive, Atlanta, Ga.

Reserves

Maxwell, M. M., Pastor, LaGrange, Ga.
Twiggs, L. M., Presiding Elder, Augusta, Ga.
Yarbrough, J. F., Pastor, Thomaston, Ga.
Holland, H. C., Presiding Elder, Rome, Ga.
*Wells, Jere, Superintendent, County Schools, Hapeville, Ga.
*Winter, Miss Bert, Housewife, Bowersville, Ga.
*Bell, M. S., Banker, Milledgeville, Ga.
*McElreath, Walter, Attorney, Grant Bldg., Atlanta, Ga.

NORTH INDIANA—ME (6)

Sec. A; Row 11, 1 to 6

Pugh, A. W., Pastor, 310 McCullough Blvd., Muncie, Ind.
Fribley, F. E., District Superintendent, Fort Wayne, Ind.
Sweet, W. W., Professor, 5805 Dorchester Ave., Chicago, Ill.
*Roudebush, R. R., Teacher, Charlotteville, Ind.
*Gettle, H. R., Optician, 4620 Stratford Road, Fort Wayne, Ind.
*Fenstermacher, G. E., Professor, Upland, Ind.

Reserves

Smith, C. H., Pastor, 109 Crescent Ave., Fort Wayne, Ind.
Bransford, W. H., Pastor, Anderson, Ind.
Smith, P. B., District Superintendent, Richmond, Ind.
*Elliott, L. J., Farmer, Wabash, Ind.
*Ballinger, F. E., Merchant, Daleville, Ind.
*Stump, C. R., Merchant, Marion, Ind.

NORTH MISSISSIPPI—ME,S (10)

Sec. D; Row 12, 1 to 10

Wasson, L. P., Presiding Elder, Columbus, Miss.
McIlwain, A. T., Pastor, Box 245, Greenville, Miss.
Curtis, V. C., Pastor, Church St., Louisville, Miss.
Wroten, J. D., Pastor, 612 Main St., Columbus, Miss.
Countiss, J. R., Pastor, 108 Wilson St., Starkville, Miss.
*Houston, J. G., Merchant, New Albany, Miss.
*McGowan, J. G., Supreme Court Judge, Jackson, Miss.
*Hall, D. H., Banker, New Albany, Miss.
*Talbert, Mrs. H. L., Conference President, W.M.S., Clarksdale, Miss.
*Kyle, J. W., Attorney, Sardis, Miss.

Reserves

Lott, W. R., Presiding Elder, Corinth, Miss.
Stephens, J. E., Pastor, Clarksdale, Miss.
Johnson, Mellville (deceased).
*Milden, A. W., Professor, University, Miss.
*Ratliff, Mrs. W. H., Housewife, Sherard, Miss.
*Forman, J. M., Attorney, Indianola, Miss.
*Houston, J. G. (R.C.M.), Merchant, New Albany, Miss.

NORTH MISSISSIPPI—MP (2)

Sec. D; Row 9, 1 and 2

Whitehurst, B. G., Conference President, Coldwater, Miss.
*Potts, W. O., Corinth, Miss.

Reserves

Ivy, C. L., Pastor, Dennis, Miss.
*Roy, S. A., Farmer, Corinth, Miss.

NORTH TEXAS—ME,S (12)

Sec. C; Row 20, 1 to 12

Martin, P. E., Pastor, 1312 10th St., Wichita Falls, Tex.
Barnes, S. A., Presiding Elder, 5128 Birchman St., Fort Worth, Tex.
Ryan, H. G., Pastor, 4115 Junius St., Dallas, Tex.
French, G. C., Pastor, N. Benge St., McKinney, Tex.
Spragins, C. A., Presiding Elder, 714 N. Walnut St., Sherman, Tex.
Lee, Umphrey, President, Southern Methodist University, Dallas, Tex.
*Fudge, E. S., Wholesale Merchant, 6270 Richmond St., Dallas, Tex.
*Waggoner, M. T., Cattle Buyer, 1925 9th St., Wichita Falls, Tex.
*Caldwell, Gibson, Miller, McKinney, Tex.
*Minga, Mrs. T. H., Housewife, Frisco, Tex.
*Love, M. F., Insurance, 614 Bank Bldg., Greenville, Tex.
*Jordon, Mrs. W. O., Conference President, W.M.S., Dallas, Tex.

Reserves

Mood, R. G., Presiding Elder, McKinney, Tex.
Baker, W. H., Pastor, Dallas, Tex.
Black, S. M., Presiding Elder, Paris, Tex.
*Murphree, J. C., Attorney, Iowa Park, Tex.
*Cullum, W. H., Jr., Insurance, 4805 Cedar Springs, Dallas, Tex.
*Armistead, D. F., Railway Mail Service, Denison, Tex.

NORTHEAST OHIO—ME (10 and 2 D.L., and 1 C.M.)

Sec. B; Rows 7, 1 to 6; 8, 1 to 6

Brown, E. R., District Superintendent, Cleveland, Ohio.
Olson, O. T., Pastor, 1919 E. 107th St., Cleveland, Ohio.
Wright, L. C., President, Baldwin-Wallace College, Berea, Ohio.
Ketcham, C. B., College President, Alliance, Ohio.
Courtney, H. W., District Superintendent, Cambridge, Ohio.
Davis, N. E. (D.L.), Executive Secretary, Board of Hospitals, Homes, and Deaconess Work, Columbus, Ohio.
Mueller, F. W. (C.M.), Department Superintendent, Board of Home Missions and Church Extension, Philadelphia, Pa.
*Hoover, A. L., Businessman, Lakeside, Ohio.
*Cherry, James, Businessman, Canton, Ohio.
*Archer, W. D., Manufacturer, 914 Clark St., Cambridge, Ohio.
*Robinson, M. C., Merchant, 4026 State Ave., Ashtabula, Ohio.

*Beetham, C. S., Merchant, Cadiz, Ohio.
*Oram, Miss E. J. (D.L.), National Officer, Woman's Home Missionary Society, 1831 E. 93d St., Cleveland, Ohio.

Reserves

McQueen, M. W., District Superintendent, Steubenville, Ohio.
Garth, S. E., Pastor, 283 W. Madison Ave., Youngstown, Ohio.
Green, J. D., Pastor, 242 Front St., Berea, Ohio.
Secrest, P. E., District Superintendent, Youngstown, Ohio.
Smith, W. S., Pastor, 14037 Euclid Ave., Cleveland, Ohio.
*Kendall, F. H., Retired, 143 Mentor Ave., Painesville, Ohio.
*Cartmell, B. E., Secretary, Ohio Wesleyan University, 275 N. Sandusky St., Delaware, Ohio.
*Masters, Kathryn F., Clerk, District Board of Health, 1252 Sinclair Ave., Steubenville, Ohio.
*Hoover, G. A., Attorney, Canal Fulton, Ohio.

NORTHERN MINNESOTA—ME (4 and 3 D.L.)

Sec. B; Rows 19, 10 to 12; 20, 9 to 12

Stafford, T. A., Executive Secretary, Board of Pensions and Relief, 740 Rush St., Chicago, Ill.
Mecklenburg, George, Pastor, Minneapolis, Minn.
Bugbee, L. H. (D.L.), Editor, 420 Plum St., Cincinnati, Ohio.
Raines, R. C. (D.L.), Pastor, Minneapolis, Minn.
*Douglas, H. A., Banker, Minneapolis, Minn.
*Jardine, Florence R., Accepted Supply Pastor, Minneapolis, Minn.
*Lindsay, Mrs. F. F. (D.L.), Housewife, Preston, Minn.

Reserves

Baumhofer, E. F., District Superintendent, Minneapolis, Minn.
*Ulland, J. S., Banker, Fergus Falls, Minn.
*Lindsay, Mrs. F. F., Housewife, Preston, Minn.

NORTHERN NEW YORK—ME (4)

Sec. D; Row 3, 7 and 8

Miller, F. A., Pastor, 446 Dimmick St., Watertown, N. Y.
Judd, A. G., District Superintendent, Utica, N. Y.
*Sykes, W. C., Businessman, Conifer, N. Y.
*Cheetham, A. D., Businessman, New York Mills, N. Y.

Reserves

Warren, J. W., Pastor, Fulton, N. Y.
Love, E. C., Pastor, Ilion, N. Y.
*Phelps, H. R., Businessman, North Bay, N. Y.
*Flanders, W. E., Public Officer, 40 Bay St., Potsdam, N. Y.

NORTHWEST—ME,S (2)

Sec. D; Row 8, 3 and 4

Harper, E. J., Pastor, 134 S. 5th St., Corvallis, Oreg.
*Purvance, E., Bookkeeper, Coquille, Oreg.

Reserves

Hartman, P. D., Presiding Elder, 3004 N. Lincoln St., Spokane, Wash.
*Starmer, W. B., Bookkeeper, La Grand, Oreg.

NORTHWEST INDIANA—ME (4 and 1 D.L.)

Sec. B; Row 10, 8 to 12

Davis, H. L., Secretary, Preachers' Aid Society, Indianapolis, Ind.
Beck, B. D., Pastor, 521 S. Center St., Terre Haute, Ind.
*Mann, E. M., Attorney, 21 Boston Ave., Terre Haute, Ind.
*Evans, F. C., Banker, Crawfordsville, Ind.
*McCutchan, R. G. (D.L), Retired, Claremont, Calif.

Reserves

Young, Claude, District Superintendent, LaFayette, Ind.
Williams, T. F., Pastor, 404 N. 6th St., LaFayette, Ind.
*Lee, C. O., Professor, 600 Robinson St., West LaFayette, Ind.
*Campbell, J. B., Manufacturer, 905 S. Main St., South Bend, Ind.

NORTHWEST IOWA—ME (4)

Sec. C; Row 14, 1 to 4

Walker, J. B., Pastor, 3240 Garretson Ave., Sioux City, Iowa.
Roadman, E. A., President, Morningside College, Sioux City, Iowa.
*White, Mrs. M. H., Housewife, 2109 Nebraska St., Sioux City, Iowa.
*Dolliver, J. I., Attorney, State Bank Building, Fort Dodge, Iowa.

Reserves

Davies, J. J., District Superintendent, Fort Dodge, Iowa.
Bush, M. D., Pastor, Pomeroy, Iowa.
*Morling, Mrs. W. H., Housewife, Emmetsburg, Iowa.
*Harshbarger, C. C., Retired, Onowa, Iowa.

NORTHWEST KANSAS—ME (2)

Sec. C; Row 21, 7 and 8

Smith, A. N., District Superintendent, Salina, Kans.
*Kemp, C. A., Evangelist, Winona, Kans.

Reserves

Templin, L. R., Pastor, Concordia, Kans.
*Tipton, W. H., Businessman, Goodland, Kans.

NORTHWEST TEXAS—ME,S (12)

Sec. C; Row 16, 1 to 12

Haymes, J. O., Pastor, 404 Scurry St., Big Spring, Tex.
Hooton, C. R., Presiding Elder, 501 E. 4th St., Sweetwater, Tex.
Clark, O. P., Presiding Elder, 2316 18th St., Lubbock, Tex.
Pearce, W. M., Pastor, Box 297, Pampa, Tex.
White, E. E., Presiding Elder, Box 95, Plainview, Tex.
Bickley, C. A., Presiding Elder, 1225 Sayles Blvd., Abilene, Tex.
*Nichols, R. H., Publisher, Vernon, Tex.
*Yoder, D. P., Auto Dealer, Snyder, Tex.
*Condron, S. H., College Dean, 2005 6th Ave., Canyon, Tex.
*Willson, J. M., Lumber Dealer, Floydada, Tex.
*Randal, Mrs. C. M., Conference President, W.M.S., Seymour, Tex.
*Bryant, R. B., Merchant, Stamford, Tex.

Reserves

Wright, C. C., Presiding Elder, Vernon, Tex.
Lipscomb, L. N., Pastor, Lubbock, Tex.
Young, S. H., Pastor, Sweetwater, Tex.
Grimes, C. C., Pastor, Amarillo, Tex.

*Braswell, A. M., News Editor, Clarendon, Tex.
*Boger, R. G., Dean, McMurry College, Abilene, Tex.
*Rollins, Mrs. N. G., Housewife, Abilene, Tex.
*Ellzey, T. V., Rancher, Perryton, Tex.

NORWEGIAN AND DANISH—ME (2)

Sec. A; Row 12, 1 and 2

Schevenius, C. W., District Superintendent, Minneapolis, Minn.
*Michelsen, M. E., Salesman, 7612 Creiger Ave., Chicago, Ill.

Reserves

Beckstrom, J. M., District Superintendent, Chicago, Ill.
*Hansen, A. W., 1049 Van Slyke Ave., St. Paul, Minn.

OHIO—ME (12 and 3 D.L., and 2 C.M.)

Sec. A; Rows 6, 1 to 10; 7, 3 to 10

Martin, Arba, Pastor, Portsmouth, Ohio.
Miller, I. E., Pastor, 3436 St. Johns Place, Cincinnati, Ohio.
Schatzman, A. G., District Superintendent, Columbus, Ohio.
Kestle, A. J., Pastor, 96 E. Fifth St., Chillicothe, Ohio.
Stafford, E. R., Pastor, Hartwell, Cincinnati, Ohio.
Swank, Jesse, Pastor, Limestone St., Springfield, Ohio.
Diekmann, J. A. (D.L.), Superintendent, Bethesda Hospital, Cincinnati, Ohio.
Soper, E. D. (C.M.), President, Ohio Wesleyan University, Delaware, Ohio.
*Goode, Mrs. W. H. C., President, Woman's Home Missionary Society, Sidney, Ohio.
*Jones, C. A., Executive Secretary, Community Fund, Columbus, Ohio.
*Bancroft, E. D., Field Representative, Commission on Men's Work, Urbana, Ohio.
*McKim, J. J., Secretary, Y.M.C.A., Cincinnati, Ohio.
*Appleby, T. W., Insurance, Losantiridge, Cincinnati, Ohio.
*Ivins, L. S., Dean, Defiance College, Defiance, Ohio.
*Freeman, Mrs. J. H. (D.L.), National Treasurer, Woman's Home Missionary Society, Delaware, Ohio.
*Keplinger, W. E. (D.L.), Banker, Cincinnati, Ohio.
*Cherrington, E. H. (C.M.), Executive Secretary, Board of Temperance, Prohibition, and Public Morals, Washington, D. C.

Reserves

Timerman, Donald, District Superintendent, Newark, Ohio.
Jones, J. I., District Superintendent, Columbus, Ohio.
Turley, C. E., District Superintendent, Wilmington, Ohio.
Tucker, R. L., Pastor, 242 18th Ave., Columbus, Ohio.
Wheaton, Miss R. E. (R.D.L.), Editor, Cincinnati, Ohio.
*Long, Mrs. C. C., Home Base Secretary, Woman's Foreign Missionary Society, 3434 Darwin Place, Westwood, Ohio.
*Kirk, W. F., Executive Secretary, State Grange, Port Clinton, Ohio.
*Mitchell, A. S., Attorney, Newark, Ohio.

OHIO—MP (10)

Sec. B; Rows 5, 8 to 12; 6, 8 to 12

Rosenberger, S. W., Conference President, Columbus, Ohio.
Williams, J. C., Pastor, 140 12th St., Columbus, Ohio.
Brown, F. L., Pastor, 321 E. Maynard Ave., Columbus, Ohio.
Johnson, C. S., Editor, Sunday School Literature, Pittsburgh, Pa.

Farmer, R. I., Pastor, 125 N. 9th St., Cambridge, Ohio.
*Miller, E. D., Insurance, 257 Chittenden Ave., Columbus, Ohio.
*Barss, Mrs. E. K., Housewife, 810 Walnut St., Coshocton, Ohio.
*Stottlemire, F. E., Printing Business, Cambridge, Ohio.
*Graver, E. H., Drakewood Drive, Cincinnati, Ohio.
*Ellis, P. M., Wilmington, Ohio.

Reserves

Custis, D. L., Pastor, Mount Vernon, Ohio.
Grimm, P. E., Pastor, 3799 Hyde Park Ave., Cincinnati, Ohio.
Linton, R. S., Pastor, 225 Jefferson St., Tiffin, Ohio.
Tolbert, R. C., Pastor, Sabina, Ohio.
Morton, C. J., Pastor, Attica, Ohio.
*Walker, Mrs. Mary, Businesswoman, Wheeling, W. Va.
*Rinker, C. T., Road Supervisor, Rayland, Ohio.
*Taylor, W. W., Farmer, Martins Ferry, Ohio.
*Gilhousen, Mrs. F. B., Housewife, Byesville, Ohio.
*Rosenberger, Mrs. S. W., Housewife, Columbus, Ohio.

OKLAHOMA—ME (4 and 1 C.M.)

Sec. B; Row 11, 8 to 12

Hargett, I. M., Pastor, Oklahoma City, Okla.
Deschner, Phil, District Superintendent, Tulsa, Okla.
*Wilcox, W. H., Attorney, Stillwater, Okla.
*Vickery, W. M., Real Estate, Blackwell, Okla.
*Wilcox, W. H. (C.M.), Attorney, Stillwater, Okla.

Reserves

Smith, R. J., Pastor, Enid, Okla.
Jorns, E. L., Pastor, 15th and Quaker Sts., Tulsa, Okla.
*Carter, H. V., Engineer, Tulsa, Okla.
*O'Neal, C. T., Attorney, Lawton, Okla.

OKLAHOMA—ME,S (14)

Sec. D; Rows 13, 3 to 10; 14, 5 to 10

Hutchinson, Forney, Pastor, 1307 S. Newport St., Tulsa, Okla.
Abernathy, J. R., Presiding Elder, Oklahoma City, Okla.
Morgan, R. E. L., Presiding Elder, 812 E Ave., Lawton, Okla.
Slack, W. B., Presiding Elder, Ardmore, Okla.
Evans, L. L., Presiding Elder, 1468 N. Elwood St., Tulsa, Okla.
Satterfield, R. S., Presiding Elder, 409 W. Canadian St., Vinita, Okla.
Blackburn, R. T., Presiding Elder, 1120 W. Main St., Durant, Okla.
*McFall, C. S., Insurance, Box 13, Frederick, Okla.
*Dunlap, Mrs. E. B., Housewife, 1002 B Ave., Lawton, Okla.
*Newton, H. E., Public Accountant, Muskogee, Okla.
*Clark, B. C., Jeweler, Oklahoma City, Okla.
*Orwig, S. S., Oil Business, Wewoka, Okla.
*Cole, J. R., Jr., Investments, Adams Hotel, Tulsa, Okla.
*Beeson, M. A., Educator, 309 Duck St., Stillwell, Okla.

Reserves

Curry, J. C., Pastor, Okmulgee, Okla.
Bowers, J. E., Presiding Elder, McAlester, Okla.
Chappell, C. G., Pastor, Oklahoma City, Okla.
Babcock, S. H., Executive Secretary, Conference Board of Christian Education, Oklahoma City, Okla.
Franklin, S. W., Pastor, Okemah, Okla.

Crowe, F. S., Presiding Elder, 604 E. Broadway, Muskogee, Okla.
Brooks, C. L., Pastor, Idabel, Okla.
Evans, L. L. (R.C.M.), Presiding Elder, Tulsa, Okla.
*Eakes, M. M., Attorney, Tulsa, Okla.
*Carlock, J. H., Merchant, Ardmore, Okla.
*Castle, C. E., Attorney, Waggoner, Okla.
*Wharton, J. H., Insurance, McAlester, Okla.
*Bailey, F. M., Attorney, Chickasha, Okla.
*Woodworth, W. W., Banker, Ringling, Okla.
*Summers, Mrs. L. C., Housewife, Stilwell, Okla.

ONONDAGA—MP (2)

Sec. C; Row 2, 7 and 8

Weaver, G. C., Pastor, 7 N. St. Regis Drive, Rochester, N. Y.
*Waterman, W. C., Port Byron, N. Y.

Reserves

Loomis, H. B., Pastor, Fulton, N. Y.
Spaulding, W. F., Pastor, Gerry, N. Y.
Fultz, B. J., Pastor, Arkport, N. Y.
*Coe, N. M., Mortician, Lycoming, N. Y.
*Johnson, Ramund, Gerry, N. Y.
*Haggerty, Floyd, Ilion, N. Y.

OREGON—ME (2 and 1 D.L. and 1 C.M)

Sec. C; Row 12, 10 to 12

Hall, S. W., District Superintendent, 2040 Court St., Salem, Oreg.
Harrison, J. C. (D.L.), District Superintendent, Portland, Oreg.
Mills, E. L. (C.M.), Editor, McAlister St., San Francisco, Calif.
*Peterson, E. W., Editor, 1304 S. E. 53d St., Portland, Oreg.

Reserves

Harrison, J. C., District Superintendent, Portland, Oreg.
Baxter, B. R. (R.D.L.), President, Willamette University, Salem,
    Oreg.
*Phelps, F. M., Attorney, Corbett Bldg., Portland, Oreg.

PACIFIC—ME,S (4 and 1 C.M.)

Sec. C; Rows 1, 10 to 12; 2, 11 and 12

Kenney, J. R., Pastor, 132 N. Stanislaus St., Stockton, Calif.
McPheeters, J. C., Pastor, 322 Ellis St., San Francisco, Calif.
Emmons, G. C. (C.M.), Secretary, Department of Home Missions and
    Hospitals, General Board of Missions, Nashville, Tenn.
*Newby, Nathan, Attorney, Washington Bldg., Los Angeles, Calif.
*Sweet, E. M., Jr., Insurance, Stockton, Calif.

Reserves

Fry, J. A. B., Pastor, Berkeley, Calif.
Lyons, J. L., Presiding Elder, Berkeley, Calif.
*Moore, A. H., Real Estate, 2517 Durant Ave., Berkeley, Calif.
*Haynes, N. J., Merchant, Los Angeles, Calif.

PACIFIC NORTHWEST—ME (6)

Sec. C; Row 14, 7 to 12

Magee, J. B., Pastor, 5th and Marion Sts., Seattle, Wash.
MacCaughey, Charles, District Superintendent, Seattle, Wash.

Mahoney, C. K., Pastor, 221 S. Howard St., Spokane, Wash.
*Foster, C. D., Editor, Advocate Bldg., Chehalis, Wash.
*Robbins, C. A., College Bursar, 636 N. Sprague Ave., Tacoma, Wash.
*Jeffers, D. S., Dean, University of Idaho, Moscow, Idaho.

Reserves

Adams, J. M., District Superintendent, Pullman, Wash.
Harold, E. F., District Superintendent, Spokane, Wash.
Brumblay, Robert, Pastor, 314 Fifth Ave., E., Olympia, Wash.
*Hall, J. B., Merchant, R.F.D. 1, Mount Vernon, Wash.
*Hazen, J. B., Mortician, 1306 N. Monroe St., Spokane, Wash.
*Woods, Mrs. Rufus, Housewife, 323 1st St., Wenatchee, Wash.

PHILADELPHIA—ME (6 and 1 D.L. and 1 C.M.)

Sec. C; Rows 11, 1 to 4; 12, 1 to 4

Henson, G. W., Corresponding Secretary, Methodist Hospital, 1701
  Arch St., Philadelphia, Pa.
Kitto, C. W., District Superintendent, Philadelphia, Pa.
Tyson, W. G., District Superintendent, Philadelphia, Pa.
Thomas, J. S. L. (C.M.), Pastor, 257 High St., Philadelphia, Pa.
*Eggleston, C. F., Attorney, 1701 Arch St., Philadelphia, Pa.
*Masland, J. W., Manufacturer, 1219 68th Ave., Philadelphia, Pa.
*Lynch, G. S., Salesman, 132 E. 5th St., Media, Pa.
*Elliott, W. J. (D.L.), Treasurer, Board of Home Missions and Church
  Extension, 1701 Arch St., Philadelphia, Pa.

Reserves

Hand, H. E., District Superintendent, Philadelphia, Pa.
Keiser, R. N., District Superintendent, Philadelphia, Pa.
Duncombe, Franklin, Pastor, Bala-Cydwyd, Pa.
*Dievler, Mrs. William, Housewife, Elkins Park, Pa.
*Peffer, D. R., Sr., Insurance, Fulton Bank Bldg., Lancaster, Pa.

PITTSBURGH—ME (6 and 1 D.L.)

Sec. A; Rows 13, 8 to 10; 14, 7 to 10

Corcoran, S. W., Superintendent Church Union, Pittsburgh, Pa.
Piper, J. D., District Superintendent, Pittsburgh 16, Pa.
Anderson, W. K., Pastor, 116 Tioga St., Johnstown, Pa.
*Lee, Elizabeth M., Corresponding Secretary, Woman's Foreign Mis-
  sionary Society, 400 Shady Ave., Pittsburgh, Pa.
*Howe, C. P., Editor, Tarentum, Pa.
*Jones, E. W., Banker, Lesnett Road, R. D., Bridgeville, Pa.
*McQuiston, J. C. (D.L.), Businessman, Wilkinsburg, Pa.

Reserves

Jose, J. F., District Superintendent, Pittsburgh 8, Pa.
Payton, J. S. (R.D.L.), Editor, 736 National Press Bldg., Washing-
  ton, D. C.
Spaugy, L. D., Pastor, 141 W. Second St., Greensburg, Pa.
*McQuiston, J. C., Businessman, Wilkinsburg, Pa.
*Wickline, R. L., Insurance, 4151 Jenkins Arcade, Pittsburgh, Pa.
*Humphreys, N. H., Businessman, Box 1007, Johnstown, Pa.

PITTSBURGH—MP (8)

Sec. B; Rows 7, 9 to 12; 8, 9 to 12

Hooper, T. L., Conference President, Pittsburgh, Pa.
Broomfield, J. C., Pastor, 800 4th St., Fairmont, W. Va.

Allen, A. J., Pastor, 34 Clark St., Uniontown, Pa.
Hawley, J. W., Pastor, 5415 Howe St., Pittsburgh, Pa.
*Shaw, Harry, Attorney, Fairmont, W. Va.
*Perkins, W. C., Business Executive, Ruskin Apts., Pittsburgh, Pa.
*Sproul, R. C., Auditing, 625 Fifth Ave., Pittsburgh, Pa.
*Smith, W. T., Dry Cleaning, 93 Willis Road, Connellsville, Pa.

Reserves

Daugherty, C. L., Pastor, 199 Richbarn Road, Pittsburgh, Pa.
Mansberger, A. R., Pastor, 218 E. Crawford Ave., Connellsville, Pa.
Smith, C. M. Pastor, 3603 Beechwood Blvd., Pittsburgh, Pa.
Feeman, H. L., College President, Adrian, Mich.
*Leonard, T. W., Insurance, 212 Jucunda St., Pittsburgh, Pa.
*Braun, C. A., Businessman, Heinz Terrace, Sharpsburg, Pa.
*Shell, Mrs. J. W., President, Woman's Conference, Uniontown, Pa.
*Orbin, Jess, Retired, 103 Pennsylvania Ave., Uniontown, Pa.

ROCK RIVER—ME (6 and 3 D.L. and 1 C.M.)

Sec. B; Rows 1, 1 to 5; 2, 1 to 5

Stone, F. D., Publishing Agent, 740 Rush St., Chicago, Ill.
Smith, H. G., President, Garrett Biblical Institute, Evanston, Ill.
Moore, A. S., Secretary, City Missions, Chicago, Ill.
Diffendorfer, R. E. (D.L.), Corresponding Secretary, Board of Foreign Missions, 150 Fifth Ave., New York, N. Y.
Fowler, G. A. (D.L.), Pastor, N. Oak Park Ave., Oak Park, Ill.
*Dangel, Mrs. W. H., Housewife, 175 Grove Ave., Oak Park, Ill.
*Crawford, A. C., Manufacturer, 10149 S. Hoyne Ave., Chicago, Ill.
*Cantlin, Jacob, Attorney, 1008 Leroy Ave., Rock Falls, Ill.
*Oldshue, Mrs. James (D.L.), Housewife, E. 88th St., Chicago, Ill.
*James, J. A. (C.M.), Professor, 2127 Orrington Ave., Evanston, Ill.

Reserves

Pierce, R. M., District Superintendent, Evanston, Ill.
Thompson, John, Pastor, 77 W. Washington St., Chicago, Ill.
Semans, R. L., District Superintendent, Rockford, Ill.
*Jackson, J. R., Manufacturer, Stephenson St., Freeport, Ill.
*Alderson, E. R., Businessman, 10931 Longwood Drive, Chicago, Ill.
*Timmons, Mrs. C. N., Housewife, 406 Fourth St., Sterling, Ill.
*Will, Herman, Jr. (R.Y.D.L.), Peace Educator, Chicago, Ill.
*Loucks, C. O. (R.D.L.), Attorney, 10 S. LaSalle St., Chicago, Ill.

SAINT JOHNS RIVER—ME (2 and 1 D.L.)

Sec. B; Row 4, 6 to 8

Farrar, G. E., Pastor, 109 S. Wild Olive St., Daytona Beach, Fla.
James, G. C. (D.L.), Pastor, 320 N. E. 2d Ave., Miami, Fla.
*Noble, F. B., Attorney, Jacksonville, Fla.

Reserves

Hortin, P. R. (R.D.L.), Pastor, St. Petersburg, Fla.
*Raap, Albert, Pastor's Assistant, 320 N. E. 2d Ave., Miami, Fla.

ST. LOUIS—ME,S (6)

Sec. C; Row 11, 5 to 10

Tadlock, C. W., Executive Secretary, General Board of Finance, 506 Olive St., St. Louis, Mo.
Webdell, C. W., Chaplain, Barnes Hospital, University, Mo.
Orear, E. H., Presiding Elder, 201 Beckwith St., Malden, Mo.

*Parker, W. W., College President, Cape Girardeau, Mo.
*Riggs, Mrs. Jeptha, Housewife, Westmount, Cape Girardeau, Mo.
*Williams, F. E., Attorney, 4233 Shenandoah, St. Louis, Mo.

Reserves

Brower, F. V., Assistant Secretary, General Board of Finance, 506
    Olive St., St. Louis, Mo.
Caskey, J. F., Pastor, 7163 Washington St., St. Louis, Mo.
*Brandon, Mrs. J. P., Housewife, Essex, Mo.
*Davis, H. J., St. Louis, Mo.
*Parker, W. W. (R.C.M.), College President, Cape Girardeau, Mo.

SAVANNAH—ME (2)

Sec. B; Row 6, 6 and 7

Prothro, C. W., Pastor, 1907 Burroughs St., Savannah, Ga.
*Clements, T. R., Farmer, Forsyth, Ga.

Reserves

Dougan, E. W., District Superintendent, La Grange, Ga.
*Gross, H. K., Mortician, Statesboro, Ga.

SOUTH AMERICAN CONFERENCES—ME (3 D.L.O.C.)

Sec. D; Rows 6, 8 to 10; 7, 5 to 10; 8, 5 to 10; 9, 5 to 10

Bullock, D. S., Goodrich, Mich.
Wesley, Arthur, 675 Olavarria, Buenos Aires, Argentina.
*Bell, C. S., Box 81, Puyallup, Wash.

Reserves

Stockwell, B. F., Buenos Aires, Argentina.
*Aguirre, Miss Marie, 150 Fifth Ave., New York, N. Y.

SOUTH CAROLINA—ME (2 and 1 D.L.)

Sec. A; Row 8, 8 to 10

Howard, A. R., District Superintendent, Sumter, S. C.
*Pinckney, T. H., Teacher, St. George, S. C.
*Randolph, J. B. (D.L.), President, Claflin College, Orangeburg, S. C.

Reserves

Curry, D. S., District Superintendent, Greenville, S. C.
*Caldwell, C. W., Railway Postal Clerk, Orangeburg, S. C.

SOUTH CAROLINA—ME,S (8 and 1 C.M.)

Sec. A; Rows 16, 1 to 4; 17, 3 to 7

McCoy, E. L., Presiding Elder, Florence, S. C.
Ward, Woodrow, Presiding Elder, 84 Pitt St., Charleston, S. C.
Stokes, Peter (deceased).
Garrison, E. K., Pastor, 400 E. Harrison St., Dillon, S. C.
Ford, J. E. (C.M.), Presiding Elder, Marion, S. C.
*Mobley, M. R., Physician, Cherokee Road, Florence, S. C.
*Bowman, J. S., Attorney, 254 E. Russell St., Orangeburg, S. C.
*Stockhouse, Will, Cotton Mill Executive, Marion, S. C.
*DuRant, Charlton, Attorney, Manning, S. C.

Reserves

Gleaton, W. D., Presiding Elder, 2 Church St., Sumter, S. C.
Phillips, W. R., Pastor, Marion, S. C.
*Guilds, J. C., President, Columbia College, Columbia, S. C.
*Smoak, W. W., Editor, Walterboro, S. C.

SOUTH CAROLINA—MP (2)

Sec. D; Row 5, 1 and 2

Frye, Irvin, Conference President, Effingham, S. C.
*Davis, D. H., Merchant, Bishopville, S. C.

Reserves

Frazier, F. L., Pastor, St. Stephens, S. C.
*Steele, J. T., Poultryman, West Columbia, S. C.

SOUTH FLORIDA—ME (2 and 1 D.L.)

Sec. A; Row 9, 8 to 10

Simpson, J. A., Pastor, 613 8th St., West Palm Beach, Fla.
*Smith, J. H., Physician, 2153 N. W. 3d Ave., Miami, Fla.
*Bethune, Mrs. M. M. (D.L.), President, Bethune-Cookman College,
Daytona Beach, Fla.

Reserves

Curington, N. J., Pastor, 308 E. 6th St., Sanford, Fla.
*Adams, T. A., Physician, 323 Pine St., Daytona Beach, Fla.

SOUTH GEORGIA—ME,S (14 and 1 C.M.)

Sec. B; Rows 3, 1 to 5; 4, 1 to 5; 5, 1 to 5

Freeman, H. T., Presiding Elder, 504 E. Central St., Valdosta, Ga.
Johnson, Silas, Pastor, 111 Lamar St., Macon, Ga.
Quillian, W. F., Executive Secretary, General Board of Christian
Education, 810 Broadway, Nashville, Tenn.
Meeks, C. M., Pastor, Box 183, Brunswick, Ga.
Harrell, L. A., Pastor, 402 N. Lee St., Valdosta, Ga.
Dell, J. P., Pastor, Box 336, Moultrie, Ga.
Moore, Leland, Pastor, Box 336, Cairo, Ga.
Ellis, T. D. (C.M.), Executive Secretary, General Board of Church
Extension, 1115 Fourth Ave., Louisville, Ky.
*Thrasher, T. E., Merchant, Ashburn, Ga.
*Shepard, C. L., Attorney, 203 Everett Square, Fort Valley, Ga.
*Britton, C. A., Jr., Business Manager, *Wesleyan Christian Advocate*,
Macon, Ga.
*Roberts, Warren, Attorney, 632 College St., Macon, Ga.
*Sapp, Mrs. C. C., Conference President, W.M.S., Albany, Ga.
*Anderson, W. T., Banker, Leslie, Ga.
*Wight, J. S., Nurseryman, Cairo, Ga.

Reserves

Wilson, J. H., Presiding Elder, Tifton, Ga.
Fain, J. E., Pastor, Albany, Ga.
Clary, G. E., Conference Secretary, Christian Education, Macon, Ga.
*Guerry, T. H., Lumber Dealer, Savannah, Ga.
*Wimberly, R. S., Attorney, Lumpkin, Ga.
*Anderson, D. R., President, Wesleyan College, Macon, Ga.

SOUTHERN—ME (2)

Sec. D; Row 13, 1 and 2

Leonard, H. C., Associate Secretary, Board of Home Missions and
Church Extension, 1701 Arch St., Philadelphia, Pa.
*Brandenberger, M. B., Physician, 455 E. College St., Seguin, Tex.

Reserves

Rode, L. J., District Superintendent, San Antonio, Tex.
*Carter, G. E., Businessman, Box 366, Port Arthur, Tex.

SOUTHERN CALIFORNIA—ME (8 and 2 D.L.)

Sec. C; Row 15, 1 to 10

Buckner, W. C., District Superintendent, Los Angeles, Calif.
Smith, R. L., Pastor, 8th and Hope Sts., Los Angeles, Calif.
Stevens, F. G. H., District Superintendent, Pasadena, Calif.
Warmer, G. A., Pastor, 3565 W. 6th St., Riverside, Calif.
Corley, J. L. (D.L.), Executive Secretary, Conference Board of Education, 125 Marchessault St., Los Angeles, Calif.
*Seymour, Mrs. Jerome, Secretary, Woman's Foreign Missionary Society, 952 N. Lake Ave., Pasadena, Calif.
*Hole, J. W., Treasurer, 125 Marchessault St., Los Angeles, Calif.
*Andrew, Wray, Manager, Goodwill Industries, Long Beach, Calif.
*McCulloch, S. W., Businessman, Box 73, Fullerton, Calif.
*McGiffin, J. H. S. (D.L.), Director, Young People's Work, 125 Marchessault St., Los Angeles, Calif.

Reserves

Martin, Wilsie, Pastor, 735 Plymouth Ave., Los Angeles, Calif.
Oechsli, Leonard, Pastor, 102 Alamansor St., Alhambra, Calif.
Corley, J. L., Executive Secretary, Conference Board of Education, 125 Marchessault St., Los Angeles, Calif.
Dunning, J. E., District Superintendent, Box 116, Santa Ana, Calif.
*Page, G. H., Insurance, Los Angeles, Calif.
*Leavitt, H. P., Attorney, 811 S. Catalina St., Los Angeles, Calif.
*Mather, W. W., Professor, 530 Laurel Ave., Upland, Calif.
*Whisler, A. R., Railroad Official, Oceanside, Calif.

SOUTHERN ILLINOIS—ME (4)

Sec. A; Row 14, 1 to 4

Yost, C. R., President, Lebanon, Ill.
Hall, C. C., District Superintendent, Mount Vernon, Ill.
*Johnson, W. T., Physician, Eldorado, Ill.
*Webb, Mrs. J. L., Housewife, 1405 N. 41st St., East St. Louis, Ill.

Reserves

Yates, E. U., District Superintendent, Carbondale, Ill.
Peterson, C. L., District Superintendent, Lebanon, Ill.
*Rauschkolb, F. G., Agent, McKendree College, Lebanon, Ill.
*Woodley, Mark, Banker, Marion, Ill.

SOUTHWEST—ME (2)

Sec. C; Row 12, 8 and 9

Taggart, J. H., District Superintendent, Little Rock, Ark.
*Cullins, J. S., Mail Carrier, 4103 W. 16th St., Little Rock, Ark.

Reserves

Sherrill, W. S., Pastor, 4123 W. 17th St., Little Rock, Ark.
*Fields, Mrs. Z. R., Housewife, Brickeys, Ark.

SOUTHWEST KANSAS—ME (4)

Sec. B; Row 13, 9 to 12

Harris, I. D., District Superintendent, Winfield, Kans.
Kirk, A. E., District Superintendent, N. Oliver St., Wichita, Kans.
*Mayberry, L. W., Superintendent, City Schools, Wichita, Kans.
*Gray, Mrs. C. M., Housewife, Peabody, Kans.

Reserves

Henry, A. E., Pastor, 221 Erie St., Wichita, Kans.
Gardner, N. S., District Superintendent, Hutchinson, Kans.
*McKibbin, H. B., 1500 Park Place, Wichita, Kans.
*Gibson, Miss Gladys, Medicine Lodge, Kans.

SOUTHWEST MISSOURI—ME,S (6)

Sec. A; Row 3, 5 to 10

Glenn, J. C., Pastor, 228 W. Edenton St., Raleigh, N. C.
Rand, H. J., Pastor, 1001 S. Main St., Independence, Mo.
Starkey, L. M., Presiding Elder, 806 W. 6th St., Sedalia, Mo.
*Lamb, Mrs. F. A., Housewife, Edgevale Road, Kansas City, Mo.
*Smith, R. J., Appellate Judge, 411 Normal, Springfield, Mo.
*Earp, W. L., Editor, 427 W. Walnut St., Nevada, Mo.

Reserves

Luetzow, H. H., Presiding Elder, Marshall, Mo.
Baker, E. D., Pastor, Clinton, Mo.
Prater, J. D., Presiding Elder, Webb City, Mo.
*Showalter, J. W., Merchant, Kansas City, Mo.
*Reed, I. H., Utility Manager, 111 W. 4th St., Sedalia, Mo.
*Farmer, Mrs. H. R., Conference President, W.M.S., Springfield, Mo.

TENNESSEE—ME (2)

Sec. D; Row 4, 6 and 7

Golden, J. W., District Superintendent, Memphis, Tenn.
*Freeman, S. C., Dentist, 402 8th Ave., So., Nashville, Tenn.

Reserves

Lewis, G. W., District Superintendent, Miller St., Nashville, Tenn.
*Jones, Mrs. L. L., Dressmaker, 1405 South St., Nashville, Tenn.

TENNESSEE—ME,S (12 and 1 C.M.)

Sec. C; Rows 1, 1 to 7; 2, 1 to 6

Baggett, J. F., Presiding Elder, 810 Broadway, Nashville, Tenn.
Harrell, C. J., Pastor, 2130 West End, Nashville, Tenn.
Hinkle, D. E., Presiding Elder, 118 Fifth St., Clarksville, Tenn.
Ferguson, J. L., Presiding Elder, Franklin, Tenn.
Blue, W. H., Pastor, 317 Madison St., Clarksville, Tenn.
Anderson, E. P., Pastor, 1501 Stratton Ave., Nashville, Tenn.
⁺Whitmore, B. A., Publishing Agent, Nashville, Tenn.
⁺Batts, W. O., Headmaster, Columbia Military Academy, Columbia, Tenn.
*Webb, W. R., Headmaster, Webb School, Bell Buckle, Tenn.
*O'Neal, Mrs. Robert, Conference President, W.M.S., Clarksville, Tenn.
*McGinnis, H. B., Attorney, Carthage, Tenn.
*Thompson, E. D., Merchant, Centerville, Tenn.
*Maddin, P. D. (C.M.), Attorney, Nashville, Tenn.

Reserves

Ricks, W. B., Presiding Elder, Gallatin, Tenn.
Durrett, John, Presiding Elder, Cookeville, Tenn.
Vivion, King, Pastor, McKendree Church, Nashville, Tenn.
*Wiseman, W. H., Mortician, Erin, Tenn.
*Rawls, J. F., Treasurer, General Board of Missions, Nashville, Tenn.
*Jakes, J. W., Banker, Nashville, Tenn.

TENNESSEE—MP (2)

Sec. C; Row 3, 8 and 9

Kelley, C. I., Conference President, Unionville, Tenn.
*Van Cleave, A. B., Farmer, Huntingdon, Tenn.

Reserves

Cartwright, J. L., Pastor, Horse Branch, Tenn.
*Kelley, Mrs. C. I., Housewife, Unionville, Tenn.

TEXAS—ME (2)

Sec. A; Row 12, 9 and 10

Dogan, M. W., President, Wiley College, Marshall, Tex.
*Jordan, M. W., Railroad Employee, Sydnor St., Houston, Tex.

Reserves

Scott, J. S., Pastor, 2414 Charles St., Houston, Tex.
*Johnson, Mrs. P. D., Assistant Principal, High School, Marshall, Tex.

TEXAS—ME,S (14 and 2 C.M.)

Sec. D; Rows 1, 1 to 6; 2, 1 to 10

Jones, G. F., Pastor, 1411 Eleventh St., Huntsville, Tex.
Mills, J. W., Pastor, 1205 S. Chilton St., Tyler, Tex.
McKenney, S. S., Presiding Elder, Tyler, Tex.
Wilson, G. H., Presiding Elder, 510 Rusk Ave., Marshall, Tex.
Bryan, W. F., Presiding Elder, 1328 Ave. L, Huntsville, Tex.
Tower, J. Z., Pastor, Box 3247, Beaumont, Tex.
Swain, W. R., Presiding Elder, 2434 Liberty St., Beaumont, Tex.
Quillian, Paul (C.M.), Pastor, 901 Clay St., Houston, Tex.
*Fondren, W. W. (deceased).
*Stillwell, H. W., Superintendent of Schools, Texarkana, Tex.
*Calhoun, Galloway, Attorney, Tyler, Tex.
*Banker, H. F., Insurance, 443 Austin Ave., Port Arthur, Tex.
*Lowman, H. L., Superintendent of Schools, Goose Creek, Tex.
*Mills, Mrs. J. W., Conference President, W.M.S., Tyler, Tex.
*Acker, T. E., Banker, 520 El Paso St., Jacksonville, Tex.
*Scott, J. T. (C.M.), Attorney, Houston, Tex.

Reserves

Robinson, H. I., Pastor, Galveston, Tex.
Cannon, N. D., Pastor, Jacksonville, Tex.
Whaling, H. M., Jr., Presiding Elder, 901 Clay St., Houston, Tex.
Berglund, J. V., Pastor, Houston, Tex.
Melbert, N. H., Pastor, Port Arthur, Tex.
Walker, A. T., Superannuate, Huntsville, Tex.
Stanton, E. M., Pastor, Huntsville, Tex.
*Huffor, Earl, College Professor, Huntsville, Tex.
*Windham, W. C., Physician, Center, Tex.
*Chinn, Mrs. E. C., Housewife, Houston, Tex.
*Dean, S. W., Attorney, Madisonville, Tex.
*Woodson, J. R., Merchant, Caldwell, Tex.
*Smythe, M. G., Attorney, Houston, Tex.
*Darsey, M. E., Merchant, Grapeland, Tex.

TEXAS—MP (2)

Sec. B; Row 21, 11 and 12

Richardson, J. A., Pastor, San Angelo, Tex.
*Davidson, J. D., Physician, Teague, Tex.

Reserves

Copeland, Kenneth, Pastor, Mexia, Tex.
Johnson, A. J., Pastor, 7 E. 11th St., San Angelo, Tex.
*Kuykendall, George, 1329 W. 13th St., Corsicana, Tex.
*Lewis, A. L., Coolidge, Tex.

TEXAS MEXICAN—ME,S (2)

Sec. C; Row 1, 8 and 9

Ramos, Frank, Presiding Elder, Station A, San Antonio, Tex.
*Onderdonk, Mrs. F. S., Housewife, Box 105, San Antonio, Tex.

Reserves

Nañez, Alfredo, Presiding Elder, 1317 Tyler St., Brownsville, Tex.
*Ramos, Mrs. Jovita, Housewife, Station A, San Antonio, Tex.

TROY—ME (4)

Sec. B; Row 4, 9 to 12

Douglass, G. C., Publishing Agent, 420 Plum St., Cincinnati, Ohio.
Kelley, Mark, District Superintendent, Albany, N. Y.
*Moore, V. K., Banker, Au Sable Forks, N. Y.
*Gibson, Miss Henrietta, Housewife, 415 State St., Albany, N. Y.

Reserves

Perry, J. A., Pastor, 2015 15th St., Troy, N. Y.
Tripp, E. F., District Superintendent, 97 23d St., Troy, N. Y.
*Ryder, F. H., Manufacturer, 12 Prospect St., Cobleskill, N. Y.
*Van Antwerp, Harry, Businessman, Watervliet, N. Y.

UPPER IOWA—ME (4 and 2 D.L.)

Sec. C; Row 21, 1 to 6

Baker, E. A., Pastor, Cedar Falls, Iowa.
Court, F. W., District Superintendent, Waterloo, Iowa.
Burgstahler, H. J. (D.L.), President, Cornell College, Mount Vernon, Iowa.
*Cohagen, S. A., Secretary, Y.M.C.A., Waterloo, Iowa.
*Nicholson, Mrs. E. R., Housewife, Mount Vernon, Iowa.
*Baker, R. T. (Y.D.L.), Director of Publicity, Board of Foreign Missions, 150 Fifth Ave., New York, N. Y.

Reserves

Henke, A. W., District Superintendent, Cedar Rapids, Iowa.
Burgstahler, H. J., President, Cornell College, Mount Vernon, Iowa.
*Surry, E. M., Businessman, Cedar Rapids, Iowa.
*Currie, F. R., Businessman, Mason City, Iowa.

UPPER MISSISSIPPI—ME (2 and 1 D.L.)

Sec. C; Row 12, 5 to 7

McCoy, L. M., President, Rust College, Holly Springs, Miss.
*Coleman, W. J., Baker, Aberdeen, Miss.
*Rogers, Mrs. L. P. (D.L.), Supervisor, Colored Schools, Box 133, Indianola, Miss.

Reserves

Talbert, C. A., Professor, Gammon Theological Seminary, Atlanta, Ga.
*Scarborough, Mrs. B. J., Housewife, Holly Springs, Miss.

UPPER SOUTH CAROLINA—ME,S (10 and 1 C.M.)

Sec. B; Rows 16, 1 to 6; 17, 1 to 5

Turnipseed, B. R., Pastor, Richardson Ave., Greenville, S. C.
Peele, C. E., Pastor, 1021 Elmwood Ave., Greenville, S. C.
Garrett, W. B., Presiding Elder, Box 43, Greenville, S. C.
Mullikin, W. L., Presiding Elder, Spartanburg, S. C.
Morris, R. F., Presiding Elder, E. Earle St., Greenville, S. C.
*Horton, J. B., Secretary, Y.M.C.A., Columbia, S. C.
*Holler, J. C., Superintendent of Education, Anderson, S. C.
*Babb, R. E., Attorney, Laurens, S. C.
*Hardin, J. C., Manufacturer, 320 Saluda St., Rock Hill, S. C.
*Moore, LeRoy, County Master, 720 Maple St., Spartanburg, S. C.
*Snyder, H. N. (C.M.), President, Wofford College, Spartanburg, S. C.

Reserves

Gunter, A. L., Conference Secretary, Board of Christian Education, Spartanburg, S. C.
Beach, F. C., Pastor, Spartanburg, S. C.
*Bell, O. R., Probate Judge, Lancaster, S. C.
*Gray, H. D., Merchant, Laurens, S. C.

VERMONT—ME (2)

Sec. C; Row 21, 9 and 10

Martin, E. H., District Superintendent, Saint Johnsbury, Vt.
*Clark, A. C., Customs Official, Newport, Vt.

Reserves

Lipsky, B. G., Pastor, Morrisville, Vt.
*Wright, Mrs. F. S., Housewife, Windsor, Vt.

VIRGINIA—ME,S (20 and 1 C.M.)

Sec. B; Rows 9, 1 to 7; 10, 1 to 7; 11, 1 to 7

Potts, J. M., Presiding Elder, 1705 Park Ave., Richmond, Va.
Clark, H. P., Presiding Elder, Rivermont Ave., Lynchburg, Va.
Bell, C. C., Presiding Elder, 732 Park Ave., Portsmouth, Va.
Myers, H. P., Secretary, Department of Education and Promotion, General Board of Missions, Nashville, Tenn.
Riddick, R. P., Presiding Elder, 603 Camden Ave., Salisbury, Md.
Winn, J. B., Pastor, 116 S. Main St., Danville, Va.
Wright, W. A., Presiding Elder, 841 Main St., Danville, Va.
Pearson, J. W., Pastor, 1312 Rivermont Ave., Lynchburg, Va.
Hatcher, S. C., Vice-President, Randolph-Macon College, Ashland, Va.
Robertson, J. C., Conference Secretary, Board of Christian Education, 1516 Laburnum Ave., Richmond, Va.
Moore, J. W. (C.M.), Pastor, West Ave., Newport News, Va.
*Phelps, W. R., Manufacturer, College St., Bedford, Va.
*Wells, L. W., Insurance, 1520 Porter St., Richmond, Va.
*Fisher, B. L., Businessman, Martinsville, Va.
*Brewer, R. L., Real Estate, Suffolk, Va.
*Eanes, E. E., Attorney, Box 32, Emporia, Va.
*Gregory, Lucius, Manufacturer, Chase City, Va.
*Roper, W. B., Ship Builder, 735 Yarmouth St., Norfolk, Va.
*Elliott, W. T., Banker, Painter, Va.
*Pettyjohn, O. R., Farmer, Monroe, Va.
*Newcomb, O. P., Farmer, Sassafras, Va.

Reserves

Wells, F. L,. Pastor, 1707 Park Ave., Richmond, Va.
Smart, W. A., Professor, Emory University, Ga.
Tuttle, C. O., Pastor, Rocky Mount, Va.
Chenault, F. R., Pastor, Norfolk, Va.
Hank, P. M., Presiding Elder, Petersburg, Va.
*Redd, J. H., Real Estate, Richmond, Va.
*Short, S. H., Wholesale Merchant, Petersburg, Va.
*Small, J. F., Merchant, Norfolk, Va.
*Britt, Mrs. Lee, Conference President, W.M.S., Suffolk, Va.
*Reed, G. N., Banker, Reedville, Va.

VIRGINIA—MP (2)

Sec. B; Row 21, 9 and 10

Clowers, C. D., Conference President, Greeneville, Tenn.
*Harrison, F. M., Farmer, Greeneville, Tenn.

Reserves

Robinette, W. S., Pastor, 1014 Federal St., Kingsport, Tenn.
*Poe, Cyrus, Mohawk, Tenn.

WASHINGTON—ME (4)

Sec. B; Row 12, 9 to 12

Hughes, W. A. C., Secretary, Colored Work, Board of Home Missions
and Church Extension, Philadelphia, Pa.
Williams, R. M., Pastor, 1914 11th St., N. W., Washington, D. C.
*Briscoe, A. E., Attorney, 2330 McColloh St., Baltimore, Md.
*Tyler, Fannie D., Secretary, Woman's Foreign Missionary Society,
Fairmont Heights, Md.

Reserves

Mitchell, A. J., District Superintendent, Baltimore, Md.
Love, E. A., District Superintendent, Washington, D. C.
*Jackson, Henrietta L., Secretary, Washington, D. C.
*Rawlings, G. D., Businessman, 919 Harlem Ave., Baltimore, Md.

WEST TEXAS—ME (2 and 1 C.M.)

Sec. C; Row 22, 7 to 9

Grannum, S. E., President, Sam Houston College, Austin, Tex.
King, W. J. (C.M.), President, Gammon Theological Seminary, At-
lanta, Ga.
*Cooper, E. M., Teacher, Box 823, Seguin, Tex.

Reserves

Whitiker, C. E., Pastor, 1207 Hackberry St., Austin, Tex.
*Smith, R. L., Teacher, 817 N. 4th St., Waco, Tex.

WEST TEXAS—ME,S (10)

Sec. C; Rows 7, 5 to 9; 8, 5 to 9

Spellman, L. U., Presiding Elder, S. David St., San Angelo, Tex.
Heinsohn, Edmund, Pastor, 2800 San Pedro St., Austin, Tex.
Barton, K. P., Pastor, 317 W. Concho St., San Angelo, Tex.
Curl, R. F., Pastor, 1171 W. Woodlawn St., San Antonio, Tex.
Simpson, J. F., Director, Leadership Training, General Board of
Christian Education, 810 Broadway, Nashville, Tenn.
*Jackson, W. W., President, University of San Antonio, San Antonio,
Tex.

*Jackson, H. E., Attorney, San Angelo, Tex.
*Peel, D. T., Mortician, 520 Taylor St., Corpus Christi, Tex.
*Childers, M. A., Attorney, San Antonio, Tex.
*Brooks, M. H., Jeweler, San Angelo, Tex.

Reserves

Batchelor, S. L., Pastor, 1137 W. Ashby Place, San Antonio, Tex.
Ratliff, H. M., Presiding Elder, Del Rio, Tex.
King, H. M., Conference Secretary, Board of Christian Education, San Antonio, Tex.
Mason, J. J., Presiding Elder, Uvalde, Tex.
Hartsfield, Gaston, Presiding Elder, Corpus Christi, Tex.
*Harrison, F. H., Insurance, Harlingen, Tex.
*Batchelor, Mrs. S. L., Conference President, W.M.S., San Antonio, Tex.
*Few, W. W., Superintendent of Schools, Austin, Tex.
*Montgomery, C. M., University Professor, Austin, Tex.
*Mills, O. A., Rancher, Uvalde, Tex.

WEST VIRGINIA—ME (4 and 1 D.L. and 1 C.M.)

Sec. D; Row 10, 1 to 6

Stater, C. G., District Superintendent, Wheeling, W. Va.
Miles, M. C., District Superintendent, Huntington, W. Va.
Engle, J. W. (D.L.), Missioner, Buckhannon, W. Va.
*Harmer, Mrs. H. W., Housewife, Clarksburg, W. Va.
*Evans, C. W., Insurance, Box 484, Fairmont, W. Va.
*Law, C. O. (C.M.), Insurance, Hawley Bldg., Wheeling, W. Va.

Reserves

Wark, H. E., Pastor, 170 W. Pike St., Clarksburg, W. Va.
Wolfe, J. L., Pastor, 1126 5th Ave., Huntington, W. Va.
*Hartley, C. H., Agricultural Extension Work, Morgantown, W. Va.
*Williamson, W. T., Travel Bureau, Kanawha St., Charleston, W. Va.

WEST VIRGINIA—MP (10)

Sec. B; Row 20, 1 to 8

Bee, L. E., Pastor, 257 Center St., Weston, W. Va.
Burns, J. E., Conference President, Harrisville, W. Va.
Mitchell, B. M., Pastor, Bridgeport, W. Va.
Shaffer, F. L., Pastor, Clarksburg, W. Va.
Snyder, G. H., Pastor, Flemington, W. Va.
*Locke, A. W., Banker, St. Marys, W. Va.
*Nutter, E. M., Sheriff, West Union, W. Va.
*Jenkins, U. I., Educator, Jane Lew, W. Va.
*Post, Mrs. Ancel, Housewife, Lost Creek, W. Va.
*High, J. H., Park, W. Va.

Reserves

Bright, C. R., Pastor, 215 Market St., Fairmont, W. Va.
Bennett, A. E., Pastor, 905 Lynn St., Parkersburg, W. Va.
Selby, J. A., Pastor, Rowlesburg, W. Va.
*Ash, B. G., Farmer, Watson, W. Va.
*Weekly, K. W., Merchant, Parkersburg, W. Va.
*Westgall, J. B., Retired Banker, Harrisville, W. Va.

WEST WISCONSIN—ME (2)

Sec. B; Row 8, 7 and 8

Hughes, A. F., District Superintendent, Madison, Wis.
*Whitcher, F. O. Banker, Platteville, Wis.

Reserves

Dixon, E. C., Pastor, Superior St., Wisconsin Dells, Wis.
*Watkins, W. P., Secretary, Y.M.C.A., La Crosse, Wis.

WESTERN MEXICAN—ME,S (2)

Sec. D; Row 8, 1 and 2

Gomez, A. M., Pastor, 2400 Texas St., El Paso, Tex.
*Parker, Mrs. R. J., Housewife, 3003 Montana St., El Paso, Tex.

Reserves

Hill, B. O., Conference Executive Secretary, Christian Education, Box 11, El Paso, Tex.
*Cruz-Aedo, F., College Professor, Box 11, El Paso, Tex.

WESTERN NORTH CAROLINA—ME,S (20)

Sec. A; Rows 4, 1 to 10; 5, 1 to 10

Weaver, C. C., Pastor, 1226 Dilworth Road, Charlotte, N. C.
Garber, P. N., Professor, Duke University, Durham, N. C.
Plyler, A. W., Editor, *North Carolina Christian Advocate*, 1009 W. Market St., Greensboro, N. C.
Lambuth, W. A., Presiding Elder, Winston-Salem, N. C.
Rowe, G. T., Professor, Duke University, Durham, N. C.
Craven, J. B., Pastor, 1000 Market St., Greensboro, N. C.
Stanbury, W. A., Pastor, Ravencroft Road, Asheville, N. C.
Jordan, G. R., Pastor, Virginia Road, Winston-Salem, N. C.
Smathers, M. T., Presiding Elder, Winston-Salem, N. C.
Kirkpatrick, C. S., Pastor, 447 Arlington St., Greensboro, N. C.
*Woosley, O. V., Superintendent, Children's Home, Winston-Salem, N. C.
*Ivey, J. B., Merchant, Charlotte, N. C.
*Gobbel, L. L., President, Greensboro College, Greensboro, N. C.
*Dunham, H. A., Merchant, 62 Patton Ave., Asheville, N. C.
*Jones, J. A., Building Contractor, Charlotte, N. C.
*Kirby, A. J., Manufacturer, 255 E. Main St., Gastonia, N. C.
*Evans, P. F., Superintendent of Schools, Lexington, N. C.
*Lambeth, J. E., Manufacturer, Thomasville, N. C.
*Weaver, Mrs. C. C., Conference President, W.M.S., Charlotte, N. C.
*Worth, W. H., Merchant, Jefferson, N. C.

Reserves

Moser, C. H., Presiding Elder, Gastonia, N. C.
McLarty, E. K., Pastor, Concord, N. C.
Bond, G. T., Presiding Elder, Charlotte, N. C.
Hayes, L. B., Presiding Elder, Greensboro, N. C.
*McEwen, L. B., Lumber Dealer, High Point, N. C.
*Gray, J. A., Banker, Winston-Salem, N. C.
*Cole, E. A., Manufacturer, Charlotte, N. C.
*Kesler, J. C., Real Estate, Salisbury, N. C.

WESTERN NORWEGIAN-DANISH—ME (2)

Sec. B; Row 16, 7 and 8

Engebretsen, Fredrik, Pastor, 336 N. Mesa St., San Pedro, Calif.
*Engebretsen, Glenn, Merchant, University Ave., Los Angeles, Calif.

Reserves

Bringdale, J. G., Pastor, 1010 S. 16th St., Tacoma, Wash.
*Tobson, Charles, Merchant, 1400 Polk St., San Francisco, Calif.

The Methodist Church 79

WESTERN VIRGINIA—ME,S (6 and 1 C.M.)

Sec. D; Row 11, 1 to 7

Given, W. M., Presiding Elder, Dixie St., Charleston, W. Va.
Yoak, J. B. F., Jr., Presiding Elder, Beckley, W. Va.
Foglesong, W. H., Presiding Elder, Barboursville, W. Va.
Taylor, B. P. (C.M.), Pastor, Tenth St., Huntington, W. Va.
*Downs, Mrs. W. M., Conference President, W.M.S., Fairmont, W. Va.
*Bright, G. W., Coal Executive, Woodlawn Ave., Beckley, W. Va.
*Coleman, W. H., Lumber Dealer, Charleston, W. Va.

Reserves

Clay, H. L., Presiding Elder, 2614 Lynwood Ave., Ashland, Ky.
Walton, A. J., Director of Promotion and Extension, General Board
    of Christian Education, Nashville, Tenn.
*Ferguson, C. W., Judge, Wayne, W. Va.
*Pratt, B. E., Merchant, Ashland, Ky.

WILMINGTON—ME (4 and 1 D.L.)

Sec. A; Row 2, 7 to 10

Bunting, J. J., District Superintendent, Salisbury, Md.
Jacobs, D. W., Pastor, Snow Hill, Md.
*Overdeer, W. L., 1703 West St., Wilmington, Del.
*Hooper, Granville, Cambridge, Md.
*Wright, H. B. (D.L.), Businessman, Preston, Md.

Reserves

Hallman, E. C., District Superintendent, Dover, Del.
Gunby, W. E., District Superintendent, Wilmington, Del.
*Shockley, O. M., Bishopville, Md.
*Wright, H. B., Businessman, Preston, Md.

WISCONSIN—ME (4 and 1 C.M.)

Sec. B; Row 6, 1 to 5

Schlagenhauf, I. E., District Superintendent, Appleton, Wis.
Perry, J. W., District Superintendent, Watertown, Wis.
Stansell, R. B. (C.M.), District Superintendent, Milwaukee, Wis.
*Roberts, E. H., Salesman, W. Wisconsin Ave., Wauwatosa, Wis.
*Jacobs, G. A., Insurance, Exchange Bldg., Janesville, Wis.

Reserves

Turner, F. J., Pastor, 932 Lake Ave., Racine, Wis.
Sheppard, R. B., Pastor, 1010 W. Wisconsin Ave., Milwaukee, Wis.
*Banting, G. O., Educator, 135 S. Grand Ave., Waukesha, Wis.
*Ziegler, Mrs. B. C., Housewife, West Bend, Wis.
*Friedman, O. A. (R.D.L.), Executive Secretary, Goodwill Industries,
    2103 W. Pierce St., Milwaukee, Wis.
*Hutchinson, Mrs. R. B. (R.Y.D.L.), Randolph St., Burlington, Wis.

WYOMING—ME (4)

Sec. D; Row 5, 3 to 6

Bell, G. M., District Superintendent, Kingston, Pa.
Savige, G. R., Pastor, 290 Vestal Ave., Binghamton, N. Y.
*Van Deusen, H. R., Attorney, 420 Quincy Ave., Scranton, Pa.
*Hunt, W. L., Businessman, Unadilla, N. Y.

Reserves

Vermilya, C. E., Pastor, Morris, N. Y.
Pennell, J. R. (R.D.L.), District Superintendent, Binghamton, N. Y.
*Quay, E. E., Teacher, Wyoming Seminary, Kingston, Pa.
*Lord, A. T., Merchant, 4 Summer St., Binghamton, N. Y.

WYOMING STATE—ME (2)

Sec. B; Row 14, 1 and 2

Hills, R. O., District Superintendent, Casper, Wyo.
*Hamm, A. S., Chief Biological Survey, Cheyenne, Wyo.

Reserves

Hoyt, C. C., Pastor, Laramie, Wyo.
*Mentzner, J. A., Dentist, Thermopolis, Wyo.

ALPHABETICAL LIST OF DELEGATES

(Names of Lay Delegates preceded by *. The number after each name is the number of the General Standing Committee for which that delegate was nominated by his respective Commission on Church Union, as recommended by the Joint Commission on Church Union, subject to the approval of the Uniting Conference.)

Name	Conference and Church
Abbott, Benjamin F. (1)	Central West, ME
Abernathy, John R. (1)	Oklahoma, ME,S
*Acker, T. E. (2)	Texas, ME,S
*Adams, Charles V. (4)	Central Pennsylvania, ME
*Adkins, Fred P. (1)	Maryland, MP
Aitken, Walter (2)	Nebraska, ME
Alexander, W. M. (5)	Missouri, ME,S
Allen, A. J. (8)	Pittsburgh, MP
Allison, Oscar E. (5)	Kansas, ME
Alsworth, W. B. (6)	Mississippi, ME,S
Anderson, E. P. (6)	Tennessee, ME,S
*Anderson, J. Edward (1)	Central Northwest, ME
Anderson, William K. (5)	Pittsburgh, ME
*Anderson, W. Tinley (2)	South Georgia, ME,S
*Andrew, Wray (3)	Southern California, ME
Andrews, Henry M. (2)	Alabama, ME,S
Andrews, R. M. (2)	North Carolina, MP
*Appleby, Troy W. (6)	Ohio, ME
Archer, Raymond L. (8)	Malaysia and Philippine Islands, ME
*Archer, William D. (3)	Northeast Ohio, ME
*Arnold, W. Scott (3)	Indiana, MP
*Arrington, Mrs. Paul (8)	Mississippi, ME,S
Arvidson, Theodore (1)	Europe, ME
*Asbury, Mrs. Hattie E. (4)	Indiana, ME
Auman, Orrin W. (3)	Colorado, ME
*Awtrey, Mrs. L. M. (4)	North Georgia, ME,S
*Babb, R. E. (2)	Upper South Carolina, ME,S
Baggett, John F. (2)	Tennessee, ME,S
Baker, Clem (5)	Little Rock, ME,S
Baker, Earle A. (2)	Upper Iowa, ME
*Baker, John H. (4)	Maryland, MP
*Baker, Richard T. (5)	Upper Iowa, ME
*Baldwin, Clinton D. (2)	Maine, ME
*Baldwin, Howard C. (4)	Detroit, ME
*Bancroft, E. Dow (3)	Ohio, ME
*Banker, H. F. (4)	Texas, ME,S
Barker, Alfred H. (8)	Iowa-Des Moines, ME
Barnard, Lawrence M. (1)	Erie, ME
Barnes, S. A. (4)	North Texas, ME,S
*Barnett, W. K. (5)	Holston, ME,S
Barr, Walter L. (3)	New Mexico, ME,S
*Barss, Mrs. E. K. (4)	Ohio, MP
Bartak, Joseph P. (5)	Czechoslovak, ME,S
*Bartak, Mrs. M. (6)	Czechoslovak, ME,S

81

Name	Conference and Church
Bartlay, Henry W. (4)	Florida, ME
Barton, K. P. (1)	West Texas, ME,S
Bates, C. W. (4)	North Carolina, MP
*Batts, W. O. (2)	Tennessee, ME,S
Bayley, Francis R. (2)	Baltimore, ME
Baylor, J. A. (7)	Holston, ME,S
Beck, Bert D. (2)	Northwest Indiana, ME
Bee, L. E. (7)	West Virginia, MP
Beery, Edgar C. (2)	Baltimore, ME,S
*Beeson, M. A. (2)	Oklahoma, ME,S
*Beetham, Charles S. (6)	Northeast Ohio, ME
Bell, C. C. (1)	Virginia, ME,S
*Bell, Carl S. (8)	South America, ME
Bell, George M. (2)	Wyoming, ME
*Bellomy, Edward (3)	Kentucky, MP
*Bennett, Alvis S. (5)	Kentucky, ME
*Bennett, Harry P. (3)	New Jersey, ME
*Benson, F. Murray (6)	Maryland, MP
Berry, Arthur D. (4)	Japan, ME
*Bethea, Dennis A. (3)	Lexington, ME
*Bethune, Mrs. Mary M. (2)	South Florida, ME
Betz, W. H. (3)	Iowa-Missouri, MP
*Black, Mrs. Henry C. (4)	Holston, ME
Blackburn, Henry W. (5)	Florida, ME,S
Blackburn, R. T. (1)	Oklahoma, ME,S
*Blackstock, Mrs. Ira B. (4)	Illinois, ME
Bickley, C. A. (4)	Northwest Texas, ME,S
Blue, Willard H. (4)	Tennessee, ME,S
*Boswell, G. C. (8)	Central Texas, ME,S
Bowen, C. A. (5)	Mississippi, ME,S
Bowen, John W. E. (6)	Louisiana, ME
*Bowman, John S. (3)	South Carolina, ME,S
*Boyd, David A. (1)	Florida, ME
*Bragg, Mrs. Grace L. (5)	Missouri, ME
*Brandenberger, Max B. (3)	Southern, ME
Brasher, John L. (6)	Alabama, ME
*Brawley, James P. (8)	Atlanta, ME
*Brewer, R. L., Jr. (1)	Virginia, ME,S
*Bright, George W. (2)	Western Virginia, ME,S
*Briscoe, Arthur E. (6)	Washington, ME
*Britton, Charles A., Jr. (6)	South Georgia, ME,S
Brock, Thomas S. (7)	New Jersey. ME
*Brock, W. E. (1)	Holston. ME,S
*Brooks, Morris H. (3)	West Texas, ME,S
Brooks, Robert N. (6)	North Carolina, ME
Broomfield, J. C. (7)	Pittsburgh, MP
Browers, J. W. (4)	Fort Smith-Oklahoma, MP
Brown, Arlo A. (5)	Newark, ME
Brown, Earl R. (2)	Northeast Ohio, ME
Brown, Frank L. (5)	Ohio, MP
Brown, George R. (6)	North Carolina, MP
*Brown, Mrs. W. Raymond (4)	Genesee, ME
Brownlee, T. M. (8)	Mississippi, ME,S
*Bryan, Mrs. Gid J. (4)	Central Texas, ME,S
Bryan, W. F. (3)	Texas, ME,S
*Bryant, R. B. (3)	Northwest Texas, ME,S
Buck, Ernest F. (5)	Kansas, ME

Name	Conference and Church
Buckner, Walter C. (2)	Southern California, ME
Bugbee, Lucius H. (5)	Northern Minnesota, ME
Bullock, Dillman S. (4)	South America, ME
Bunting, John J. (1)	Wilmington, ME
Burgstahler, Herbert J. (5)	Upper Iowa, ME
Burgum, Leslie R. (2)	North Dakota, ME
*Burnham, Smith (5)	Michigan, ME
Burns, J. E. (1)	West Virginia, MP
Butler, J. E. (2)	Arkansas, MP
*Caldwell, Gibson (6)	North Texas, ME,S
*Calhoun, Galloway (1)	Texas, ME,S
Callaghan, Arthur A. (5)	Maine, ME
Campbell, Clyde K. (6)	New Mexico, ME,S
*Candler, John S. (5)	North Georgia, ME,S
*Cannon, J. S. M. (3)	Little Rock, ME,S
*Cannon, James T. (4)	Kentucky, ME,S
Canter, Harry M. (1)	Baltimore, ME,S
*Canter, Noland M. (4)	Baltimore, ME,S
*Cantlin, Jacob (2)	Rock River, ME
*Carman, Edward R. (1)	New York East, ME
*Carr, R. B. (2)	North Alabama, ME,S
*Carter, Fred A. (6)	Holston, ME,S
*Carter, John H. (6)	Louisiana, ME,S
Cartwright, Frank T. (1)	China, ME
*Carver, George C. (4)	New Mexico, ME,S
Casaday, T. C. (1)	Alabama, MP
*Cash, W. L. (6)	Louisville, ME,S
Chadwick, J. S. (7)	North Alabama, ME,S
*Chadwick, W. C. (4)	North Carolina, ME,S
*Chaffee, H. Almon (3)	New York East, ME
*Cheetham, Arthur D. (8)	Northern New York, ME
*Cherrington, Ernest H. (4)	Ohio, ME
*Cherry, Hal H. (3)	Central Texas, ME,S
*Cherry, James (3)	Northeast Ohio, ME
*Childers, M. A. (2)	West Texas, ME,S
Chunn, Marcus M. (4)	Central Texas, ME,S
*Clark, Anson C. (3)	Vermont, ME
*Clark, B. C. (1)	Oklahoma, ME,S
Clark, J. L. (2)	Kentucky, ME,S
Clark, O. P. (7)	Northwest Texas, ME,S
*Clark, Samuel H. (3)	Newark, ME
*Clark, W. Dale (3)	Nebraska, ME
Clarke, Fred (1)	Indiana, MP
Clarke, Hawes P. (1)	Virginia, ME,S
*Clarke, Vincent P. (3)	New England, ME
Claypool, James V. (2)	New England Southern, ME
Clements, E. E. (4)	Cuba, ME,S
*Clements, Theodore R. (6)	Savannah, ME
Clowers, C. D. (3)	Virginia, MP
*Coble, M. A. (1)	North Carolina, MP
Cockrell, S. K. (4)	Baltimore, ME,S
*Coffman, C. S. (6)	Baltimore, ME,S
*Cohagen, Stephen A. (3)	Upper Iowa, ME
*Cole, J. R., Jr. (6)	Oklahoma, ME,S
*Coleman, Wade H. (1)	Western Virginia, ME,S
*Coleman, Walter J. (7)	Upper Mississippi, ME

Name	Conference and Church
Coleman, William H. (1)	Arizona, ME,S
*Collins, Elmer E. (1)	Montana State, ME
Coman, Alfred P. (5)	Central New York, ME
*Condron, S. H. (5)	Northwest Texas, ME,S
*Cook, A. L. (6)	Kansas, MP
*Cooper, Elridge M. (2)	West Texas, ME
*Cooper, W. B. (2)	North Carolina. ME,S
Coors, D. Stanley (3)	Michigan, ME
Corcoran, Sanford W. (4)	Pittsburgh, ME
Corley, Jesse L. (5)	Southern California, ME
Countiss, John R. (5)	North Mississippi, ME,S
Court, Frank W. (1)	Upper Iowa, ME
Courtney, Homer W. (3)	Northeast Ohio, ME
*Cox, Harvey W. (5)	North Georgia, ME,S
*Crabbe, George W. (1)	Baltimore, ME
Cram, Willard G. (4)	Kentucky, ME,S
Crane, Henry H. (2)	Detroit, ME
Cravens, J. B. (8)	Western North Carolina, ME,S
*Crawford, Alfred C. (3)	Rock River, ME
Crockett, O. B. (5)	Kentucky, ME,S
*Crummey, John D. (6)	California, ME
*Cullins, John S. (5)	Southwest, ME
Culver, Frank P. (3)	Central Texas, ME,S
*Cunningham, Thomas O. (6)	Kansas, ME
Curl, R. F. (3)	West Texas, ME,S
Curtis, V. C. (1)	North Mississippi, ME,S
Curtis, W. M. (1)	Alabama, ME,S
*Dangel, Mrs. William H. (4)	Rock River, ME
Daniel, Coleman C. (8)	Memphis, ME,S
Daniel, J. H. (6)	Florida, ME,S
*Dannelly, Clarence M. (5)	Alabama, ME,S
*Das, Mrs. C. Premnath (5)	India, ME
*Davage, Matthew S. (6)	Louisiana, ME,S
Davenport, George M. (2)	North Alabama, ME,S
*Davidson, H. O. (1)	New Mexico, ME,S
*Davidson, J. D. (6)	Texas, MP
Davidson, M. M. (8)	North Alabama, ME,S
*Davis, D. H. (2)	South Carolina, MP
Davis, Henry L. (7)	Northwest Indiana, ME
*Davis, Joseph H. (2)	Illinois, ME,S
Davis, Newton E. (4)	Northeast Ohio, ME
*Davis, Warren H. (3)	New Hampshire, ME
Davison, Samuel T. (1)	Erie, ME
Dawson, Dana (3)	Louisiana, ME,S
*Deal, Edson H. (3)	Idaho, ME
Dell, J. P. (7)	South Georgia, ME,S
*Denman, Harry (4)	North Alabama, ME,S
Deschner, Phil (2)	Oklahoma, ME
*DeWeese, H. O. (4)	Indiana, MP
Dewey, Elmer C. (2)	Georgia, ME
*Dickey, J. H. (3)	Louisville, ME,S
*Dickinson, Luren D. (1)	Michigan, ME
Diekmann, John A. (4)	Ohio, ME
Diffendorfer, Ralph E. (4)	Rock River, ME
*Dillon, Mrs. B. E. (4)	Missouri, MP
Ding, Samson S. (4)	China, ME

Name	Conference and Church
Dixon, L. E. (1)	Kansas, MP
Dogan, Matthew W. (5)	Texas, ME
*Dolliver, James I. (2)	Northwest Iowa, ME
Douglas, George C. (6)	Troy, ME
*Douglas, Hiram A. (5)	Northern Minnesota, ME
*Downs, Mrs. Ward M. (5)	Western Virginia, ME,S
*Duhigg, Miss Ada B. (4)	Missouri, ME
*Dunbar, Bertrand A. (7)	Dakota, ME
*Dunham, H. A. (1)	Western North Carolina, ME,S
Dunkle, William F. (1)	Florida, ME,S
*Dunlap, Mrs. E. B. (5)	Oklahoma, ME,S
*DuRant, Charlton (5)	South Carolina, ME,S
Duren, W. L. (6)	Louisiana, ME,S
*Eanes, E. Ennis (2)	Virginia, ME,S
*Earp, W. L. (6)	Southwest Missouri, ME,S
*Easter, John E. (1)	Baltimore, ME,S
Eastwood, W. P. (5)	Holston, ME,S
Eddins, J. S. (6)	Alabama, MP
*Edwards, J. R. (6)	Central Texas, ME,S
Edwards, John R. (1)	Baltimore, ME
*Eggleston, Charles F. (4)	Philadelphia, ME
*Elliot, William J. (4)	Philadelphia, ME
*Elliot, Wesley T. (3)	Virginia, ME,S
*Ellis, P. M. (3)	Ohio, MP
Ellis, Thomas D. (4)	South Georgia, ME,S
*Ellison, John T. (1)	Alabama, ME,S
Ellison, R. R. (5)	Alabama, ME,S
*Ellison, Mrs. R. R. (7)	Alabama, ME,S
Emmons, Grover C. (4)	Pacific, ME,S
*Emory, Sam T. (7)	New England, ME
*Engebretsen, Fredrik (1)	Western Norwegian-Danish, ME
*Engebretsen, Glenn (6)	Western Norwegian-Danish, ME
Engle, James W. (1)	West Virginia, ME
Estes, Lud H. (5)	Memphis, ME,S
*Evans, Charles W. (3)	West Virginia, ME
*Evans, Frank C. (6)	Northwest Indiana, ME
*Evans, John H. (6)	Arizona, ME,S
Evans, L. L. (5)	Oklahoma, ME,S
*Evans, Paul F. (3)	Western North Carolina, ME,S
Farmer, Roy I. (2)	Ohio, MP
Farrar, George E. (4)	Saint Johns River, ME
*Feaster, Mrs. J. T. (5)	Florida, ME,S
*Fenstermacher, George E. (6)	North Indiana, ME
Ferguson, John L. (5)	Tennessee, ME,S
Fesmire, William J. (1)	Central Tennessee, ME
*Few, W. P. (5)	North Carolina, ME,S
Fifer, Orien W. (2)	Indiana, ME
*Fisher, B. L. (6)	Virginia, ME,S
Fitch, Frank L. (6)	Detroit, ME
*Fitch, Harold W. (6)	Illinois, ME
*Fletcher, John S. (5)	Holston, ME
Fletcher, Maynard O. (2)	Blue Ridge-Atlantic, ME
Foglesong, W. H. (2)	Western Virginia, ME,S
*Fondren, W. W. (deceased) (3)	Texas, ME,S
Ford, J. Emerson (5)	South Carolina, ME,S

Name	Conference and Church
Forlines, Charles E. (5)	North Carolina, MP
*Foster, Chapin D. (6)	Pacific Northwest, ME
Foster, Lloyd E. (2)	Newark, ME
*Fowler, Carl H. (2)	New York, ME
Fowler, George A. (1)	Rock River, ME
Freeman, A. M. (5)	North Alabama, ME,S
Freeman, H. T. (2)	South Georgia, ME,S
*Freeman, Mrs. Jane H. (4)	Ohio, ME
*Freeman, Sewell C. (8)	Tennessee, ME
French, George C. (6)	North Texas, ME,S
*French, Mrs. Herbert A. (3)	Kansas, ME
French, J. Stewart (2)	Holston, ME,S
*Frey, V. Max (6)	Central Pennsylvania, ME
Fribley, Fremont E. (1)	North Indiana, ME
Fruit, Walter R. (4)	Detroit, ME
Frye, Irvin (1)	South Carolina, MP
*Fudge, Ezra S. (7)	North Texas, ME,S
*Gaede, John C. (8)	Kansas, ME
Garber, Paul N. (6)	Western North Carolina, ME,S
Garrett, W. B. (4)	Upper South Carolina, ME,S
*Garrison, E. J. (1)	North Alabama, ME,S
Garrison, Edward K. (4)	South Carolina, ME,S
Geissinger, E. Lamont (5)	Nebraska, ME
*Gettle, Homer R. (2)	North Indiana, ME
Geyer, Francis L. (7)	Colorado, ME
*Gibbs, Merton S. (2)	Genesee, ME
*Gibson, Miss Henrietta (4)	Troy, ME
*Gilligan, Henry (8)	Maryland, ME
Given, W. M. (3)	Western Virginia, ME,S
Glenn, John C. (2)	Southwest Missouri, ME,S
*Gobbel, Luther L. (5)	Western North Carolina, ME,S
*Goddard, J. J. (3)	Alabama, MP
Goddard, O. E. (4)	North Arkansas, ME,S
*Godfrey, Mrs. F. B. (4)	Florida, ME,S
Golden, James W. (2)	Tennessee, ME
Gomez, Abel M. (3)	Western Mexican, ME,S
*Goode, Mrs. W. H. C. (4)	Ohio, ME
Goodloe, Robert W. (8)	Central Texas, ME,S
Goodwin, Levi P. (2)	Iowa-Des Moines, ME
Grannum, Stanley E. (5)	West Texas, ME
Grant, Thomas McM. (2)	North Carolina, ME,S
*Graver, E. H. (1)	Ohio, MP
*Graves, W. D. (7)	North Alabama, ME,S
*Gray, Mrs. C. M. (5)	Southwest Kansas, ME
*Gray, George H. (3)	Nebraska, ME
Gray, Joseph M. M. (6)	Detroit, ME
Green, J. Leas (3)	Maryland, MP
*Greene, W. K. (3)	North Carolina, ME,S
*Greenslit, Henry M. (1)	Nebraska, ME
Greer, R. E. (1)	Holston, ME,S
*Gregory, Lucius (7)	Virginia, ME,S
*Griffin, DeWitt (2)	Florida, ME,S
*Haley, Paul S. (8)	North Alabama, ME,S
Hall, Claude C. (2)	Southern Illinois, ME
*Hall, D. H. (7)	North Mississippi, ME,S

Name	Conference and Church
Hall, Sydney W. (7)	Oregon, ME
Hamlett, Earl G. (1)	Memphis, ME,S
*Hamm, Adolph S. (8)	Wyoming State, ME
*Hammer, Mrs. W. C. (4)	North Carolina, MP
Hammond, Edmund J. (6)	Georgia, ME
Hammons, J. D. (4)	Little Rock, ME,S
*Hanke, Charles W. (3)	Missouri, ME
Hanna, Frank B. (2)	Illinois, MP
*Hardie, Mrs. Charles H. (6)	New York East, ME
*Hardin, J. C. (4)	Upper South Carolina, ME,S
Hardin, Smith (2)	Florida, ME,S
Hargett, Ira M. (1)	Oklahoma, ME
Hargis, David H. (3)	Delaware, ME
*Harman, J. L. (1)	Louisville, ME,S
*Harmer, Mrs. Harvey W. (5)	West Virginia, ME
Harmon, Nolan B., Jr. (6)	Baltimore, ME,S
Harper, E. J. (6)	Northwest, ME,S
*Harrah, Ezra C. (2)	Colorado, ME
Harrell, Costen J. (3)	Tennessee, ME,S
Harrell, L. A. (1)	South Georgia, ME,S
Harris, Innis D. (2)	Southwest Kansas, ME
*Harris, Nat (2)	Central Texas, ME,S
*Harrison, F. M. (2)	Virginia, MP
Harrison, Jabez C. (6)	Oregon, ME
Hartinger, William C. (3)	Indiana, ME
Hartman, Lewis O. (1)	New England, ME
Hatcher, Sam C. (5)	Virginia, ME,S
Haver, Mathias S. (1)	Europe, ME
Hawk, Eugene B. (5)	Central Texas, ME,S
*Hawkins, A. K. (7)	Florida, ME,S
*Hawkins, W. D. (4)	Mississippi, ME,S
Hawley, J. W. (4)	Pittsburgh, MP
Haymes, J. O. (5)	Northwest Texas, ME,S
Heckman, Edgar R. (7)	Central Pennsylvania, ME
*Hedden, Henry (4)	Memphis, ME,S
Heinsohn, Edmund (6)	West Texas, ME,S
Henry, W. G. (6)	North Alabama, ME,S
Henson, George W. (1)	Philadelphia, ME
*Herrigel, Fred, Jr. (2)	Maryland, MP
Hertzog, William H. (4)	Idaho, ME
Hess, Harry E. (4)	Nebraska, ME
Hickman, Frank S. (1)	North Carolina, ME,S
*Hicks, Jasper B. (6)	North Carolina, MP
*Highbaugh, Miss Irma (8)	China, ME
Hillman, E. L. (5)	North Carolina, ME,S
*Hillman, Mrs. E. L. (8)	North Carolina, ME,S
*Hillman, James N. (3)	Holston, ME,S
Hills, Roy O. (2)	Wyoming State, ME
Hinkle, David E. (1)	Tennessee, ME,S
Hislop, Edward (1)	Missouri, ME
*Hjerpe, Oscar W. (6)	Eastern Swedish, ME
*Hole, J. Wesley (3)	Southern California, ME
*Holland, C. O. (2)	Louisiana, ME,S
*Holler, J. C. (1)	Upper South Carolina, ME,S
Holliday, Robert C. (3)	Missouri, ME,S
*Hollingsworth, Mrs. H. S. (3)	Iowa-Des Moines, ME
*Hollis, Carl (1)	Little Rock, ME,S

88   *Journal of the Uniting Conference*

Name	Conference and Church
Holloway, Fred G. (2)	Maryland, MP
*Holmes, Miss Leota (3)	Central Tennessee, ME
Holmes, William W. (2)	Louisiana, ME,S
*Hood, Gurney P. (6)	North Carolina, ME,S
*Hooper, Granville (1)	Wilmington, ME
Hooper, T. LeRoy (5)	Pittsburgh, MP
Hooten, Caradine R. (2)	Northwest Texas, ME,S
*Hoover, Arthur L. (1)	Northeast Ohio, ME
*Horne, Frank A. (deceased) (6)	New York East, ME
*Horton, J. B. (6)	Upper South Carolina, ME,S
Hough, Lynn H. (5)	New York East, ME
*Houston, J. G. (2)	North Mississippi, ME,S
Howard, Arthur R. (4)	South Carolina, ME
*Howe, Charles P. (3)	Pittsburgh, ME
Hughes, Alfred F. (5)	West Wisconsin, ME
Hughes, William A. C. (1)	Washington, ME
Hummel, G. W. (2)	Louisville, ME,S
Humphreys, Gideon I. (5)	Maryland, MP
Hunt, B. M. (1)	Mississippi, ME,S
*Hunt, Walter L. (3)	Wyoming, ME
Hunton, W. M. (4)	Georgia, MP
Huse, Raymond H. (6)	Central New York, ME
Hutchinson, Forney (2)	Oklahoma, ME,S
*Ingram, Ben L. (6)	North Alabama, ME,S
*Ingram, I. S. (4)	North Georgia, ME,S
*Ivey, J. B. (2)	Western North Carolina, ME,S
*Ivins, Lester S. (3)	Ohio, ME
*Jackson, H. E. (5)	West Texas, ME,S
*Jackson, W. W. (6)	West Texas, ME,S
Jacobs, Disston, W. (7)	Wilmington, ME
*Jacobs, George A. (7)	Wisconsin, ME
James, Glenn C. (2)	Saint Johns River, ME
*James, James A. (3)	Rock River, ME
*James, T. L. (5)	Louisiana, ME,S
*Jardine, Mrs. Florence Resor (2)	Northern Minnesota, ME
Jarrell, Charles C. (6)	North Georgia, ME,S
*Jeffers, Dwight S. (5)	Pacific Northwest, ME
*Jenkins, U. I. (8)	West Virginia, MP
Johns, H. L. (5)	Louisiana, ME,S
Johnson, Crates S. (6)	Ohio, MP
Johnson, Levi E. (2)	Mississippi, ME
*Johnson, T. L. (5)	Louisiana, MP
Johnson, Silas (6)	South Georgia, ME,S
*Johnson, William T. (7)	Southern Illinois, ME
*Johnston, Smith L. (2)	North Georgia, ME,S
Johnston, Warren (2)	North Arkansas, ME,S
*Jones, Charles A. (4)	Ohio, ME
*Jones, David D. (1)	North Carolina, ME
Jones, Edward M. (1)	Central Alabama, ME
*Jones, Everett W. (7)	Pittsburgh, ME
Jones, Frank B. (2)	Memphis, ME,S
Jones, Guy F. (2)	Texas, ME,S
Jones, Henry H. (6)	North Georgia, ME,S
*Jones, J. A. (6)	Western North Carolina, ME,S
Jordan, G, Ray (1)	Western North Carolina, ME,S

Name	Conference and Church
*Jordan, Miles W. (1)	Texas, ME
*Jordan, Mrs. W. O. (3)	North Texas, ME,S
*Joy, James R. (6)	Newark, ME
Judd, Albert G. (1)	Northern New York, ME
*Judd, Zebulon V. (2)	Alabama, ME,S
Kaub, Louis H. (2)	Nebraska, ME
Kaung, Z. T. (4)	China, ME,S
Keene, Samuel A. (1)	Genesee, MP
Kelly, C. I. (2)	Tennessee, MP
Kelly, Mark (5)	Troy, ME
*Kemp, Cary A. (1)	Northwest Kansas, ME
*Kennedy, Mrs. Robert C. (3)	Blue Ridge-Atlantic, ME
Kenney, John R. (1)	Pacific, ME,S
*Keplinger, Warren E. (6)	Ohio, ME
Kestle, Asa J. (1)	Ohio, ME
Ketcham, Charles B. (5)	Northeast Ohio, ME
Keve, Wiley A. (1)	Kansas, ME
*Kibler, Russell M. (5)	Indiana, ME
Kimbrough, S. O. (4)	North Alabama, ME,S
King, James F. (2)	Missouri, ME
King, William P. (2)	North Georgia, ME,S
King, Willis J. (2)	West Texas, ME
*Kirby, A. J. (4)	Western North Carolina, ME,S
*Kirby, Amos N. (3)	North Alabama, ME,S
Kirk, Albert E. (4)	Southwest Kansas, ME
Kirkpatrick, Charles S. (3)	Western North Carolina, ME,S
Kitto, Charles W. (5)	Philadelphia, ME
*Knight, George N. (6)	North Dakota, ME
*Knight, W. L. (3)	North Carolina, ME,S
Knoles, Tully C. (5)	California, ME
Knudson, Albert C. (5)	New England Southern, ME
Kohlstedt, Edward D. (4)	Dakota, ME
*Koonce, A. J. (2)	North Carolina, MP
Kulp, Edmund J. (6)	Missouri, ME
*Kyle, John W. (1)	North Mississippi, ME,S
*Lamar, George H. (2)	Baltimore, ME,S
*Lamb, Mrs. Fred A. (4)	Southwest Missouri, ME,S
*Lambeth, James E. (6)	Western North Carolina, ME,S
Lambeth, W. A. (1)	Western North Carolina, ME,S
*Lance, T. Jack (6)	North Georgia, ME,S
*Landon, Alfred M. (6)	Kansas, ME
Langdale, John W. (6)	New York East, ME
LaPrade, William H. (3)	North Georgia, ME,S
*Law, Clyde O. (5)	West Virginia, ME
Lazenby, M. E. (6)	North Alabama, ME,S
*Lee, Miss Elizabeth M. (4)	Pittsburgh, ME
Lee, J. W. (3)	Louisiana, MP
Lee, Umphrey (5)	North Texas, ME,S
Leonard, Harry C. (3)	Southern, ME
*LeSourd, Mrs. Lucille L. (4)	New England, ME
*Lewis, Miss Harriet D. (5)	Colorado, ME
*Lindsay, Mrs. F. F. (4)	Northern Minnesota, ME
Lineberry, F. W. (6)	Indiana, MP
*Locke, A. W. (1)	West Virginia, MP
Love, Frank S. (4)	North Carolina, ME,S

90 Journal of the Uniting Conference

Name	Conference and Church
*Love, Marvin F. (2)	North Texas, ME,S
*Lowman, Harmon L. (5)	Texas, ME,S
Lugg, Thomas B. (5)	Illinois, ME
*Lynch, G. Stanley (3)	Philadelphia, ME
*Lynn, W. Lee (6)	Central Alabama, ME
Lyon, A. P. (6)	Louisville, ME,S
Lyons, Ernest S. (2)	Malaysia and Philippine Islands, ME
*Lyons, Leslie J. (2)	Missouri, ME
MacCaughey, Charles (2)	Pacific Northwest, ME
MacLea, Daniel (5)	Maryland, MP
*MacMullen, Stanley O. (6)	New England, ME
MacRossie, Allan (5)	New York, ME
*Maddin, Percy D. (4)	Tennessee, ME,S
Magee, John B. (3)	Pacific Northwest, ME
Mahoney, Carl K. (5)	Pacific Northwest, ME
Makosky, Eugene C. (7)	Maryland, MP
*Mann, Earl M. (6)	Northwest Indiana, ME
*Marr, P. M. (6)	Missouri, ME,S
Marsh, Daniel L. (5)	New England, ME
Martin, Arba (2)	Ohio, ME
Martin, Albert W. (3)	North Arkansas, ME,S
*Martin, Boyce (1)	Central Texas, ME,S
Martin, Eldon H. (1)	Vermont, ME
Martin, I. P. (3)	Holston, ME,S
*Martin, Lester H. (6)	Illinois, ME
Martin, Paul E. (2)	North Texas, ME,S
*Masland, J. Wesley (4)	Philadelphia, ME
Mathis, W. T. (3)	Illinois, ME,S
*Mayberry, L. W. (6)	Southwest Kansas, ME
*McAllister, Reuben H. (6)	Mississippi, ME
*McComas, Warren (1)	Iowa-Missouri, MP
*McConnell, Mrs. Francis J. (4)	New York, ME
McCoy, E. L. (1)	South Carolina, ME,S
McCoy, Lee M. (5)	Upper Mississippi, ME
*McCulloch, Stephen W. (1)	Southern California, ME
*McCutchan, Robert G. (8)	Northwest Indiana, ME
*McDonald, T. Morton (4)	Indiana, ME
*McElroy, George S. (1)	Georgia, ME
*McFall, Carl S. (3)	Oklahoma, ME,S
*McGiffin, James H. S. (5)	Southern California, ME
*McGinnis, H. B. (1)	Tennessee, ME,S
*McGowan, J. G. (5)	North Mississippi, ME,S
McIlwain, A. T. (7)	North Mississippi, ME,S
*McKay, Leo H. (2)	Erie, ME
McKenney, S. S. (8)	Texas, ME,S
*McKim, Judson J. (6)	Ohio, ME
*McKinnon, Miss Sallie L. (4)	North Carolina, ME,S
*McMurry, William F. (2)	Memphis, ME,S
*McNear, Alexander S. (7)	Newark, ME
*McNorton, Mrs. Dorothy E. (3)	East Tennessee, ME
McPheeters, J. C. (3)	Pacific, ME,S
McPherson, Harry W. (5)	Illinois, ME
*McQuiston, Jackson C. (3)	Pittsburgh, ME
Mecklenburg, George (4)	Northern Minnesota, ME
*Meek, Paul (1)	Memphis, ME,S
Meeks, Benjamin W. (6)	Baltimore, ME

Name	Conference and Church
Meeks, C. M. (3)	South Georgia, ME,S
*Melton, C. G. (4)	North Arkansas, ME,S
*Mickelsen, M. E. (6)	Norwegian and Danish, ME
Miles, Minor C. (5)	. West Virginia, ME
*Miller, Miss Alpha (1)	. . . . China, ME
*Miller, Ely D. (5)	Ohio, MP
Miller, Frederick A. (7)	Northern New York, ME
Miller, Isaac E. (2)	Ohio, ME
Mills, Edward L. (3)	Oregon, ME
Mills, J. W. (3) . . . . Texas, ME,S
*Mills, Mrs. J. W. (4) .	Texas, ME,S
*Minga, Mrs. T. H. (5)	. North Texas, ME,S
Mitchell, B. M. (6) . . . . West Virginia, MP
*Mobley, M. R. (5)	South Carolina, ME,S
Moffatt, Elbert M. (1) . . . . India, ME
Moore, Aubrey S. (4)	. Rock River, ME
*Moore, Fred (8)	. Little Rock, ME,S
Moore, J. W. (4)	Virginia, ME,S
Moore, Leland (8)	South Georgia, ME,S
*Moore, LeRoy (3) . . . . Upper South Carolina, ME,S
*Moore, Victor K. (6)	. . Troy, ME
Morange, John (4) . .	Montana State, ME
*Morelock, George L. (3)	Memphis, ME,S
Morgan, R. E. L. (6) . . . . Oklahoma, ME,S
*Morris, Mrs, Isaac (4) . . . . North Alabama, ME,S
Morris, R. F. (2) . . . . Upper South Carolina, ME,S
Morris, W. E. (3) . . . . North Alabama, ME,S
*Mott, John R. (4) . . . . New York, ME
*Mueller, Edwin H. (5)	. East German, ME
Mueller, Frederick W. (4) . . . . . . Northeast Ohio, ME
Mullikin, W. L. (5) . . . . Upper South Carolina, ME,S
Myers, H. P. (4) . . . . Virginia, ME,S
*Newby, Nathan (4)	. . . . . . Pacific, ME,S
*Newcomb, O. P. (5)	Virginia, ME,S
Newell, Fred B. (4)	New York East, ME
*Newton, H. E. (4) . . . . Oklahoma, ME,S
*Nicholas, R. H. (6)	. Northwest Texas, ME,S
*Nicholsen, Mrs. Evelyn R. (4) . . . . Upper Iowa, ME
Nicholson, J. H. (3) . . . . Louisville, ME,S
*Noble, Enrique (2) . . . . Cuba, ME,S
*Noble, Fred B. (2)	. Saint Johns River, ME
*Norman, James R. (8)	Baltimore, ME,S
Norton, M. H. (4)	. Florida, ME,S
*Nutter, E. M. (5)	West Virginia, MP
*Odell, Albert G. (2)	. Central New York, ME
*Oldshue, Mrs. James (4)	Rock River, ME
Olson, Oscar T. (8)	. Northeast Ohio, ME
*O'Neal, Mrs. Robert (6) .	. Tennessee, ME,S
*Onderdonk, Mrs. F. S. (1) .	Texas Mexican, ME,S
*Oram, Miss E. Jean (4) .	Northeast Ohio, ME
Orear, E. H. (1)	. St. Louis, ME,S
Ormond, J. M. (4)	North Carolina, ME,S
*Orwig, S. S. (5)	. . . . . Oklahoma, ME,S
*Osborn, Mrs. H. S. (7)	Central New York, ME
*Overdeer, Willis L. (4)	. . . . . . Wilmington, ME

Name	Conference and Church
*Pace, J. W. (2)	Georgia, MP
Parker, Franklin N. (1)	Louisiana, ME,S
*Parker, Mrs. R. J. (2)	Western Mexican, ME,S
*Parker, W. W. (5)	St. Louis, ME,S
*Parr, Fred D. (8)	California, ME
Paschall, Fred W. (8)	North Carolina, MP
*Patel, J. S. K. (6)	India, ME
*Patterson, D. Stewart (5)	Baltimore, ME
*Patton, John A. (1)	Lexington, ME
Pearce, W. M. (1)	Northwest Texas, ME,S
*Pearce, Webster (2)	Detroit, ME
Pearson, John W. (6)	Virginia, ME,S
*Peck, Arthur D. (3)	Alabama, ME
*Peel, David T. (4)	West Texas, ME,S
Peele, C. E. (3)	Upper South Carolina, ME,S
Peeples, Fred H. (4)	Memphis, ME,S
Pegues, David K. (4)	Missouri, ME,S
Pellowe, Albert H. (2)	Michigan, ME
Penick, Richard O. (2)	Kansas, ME
*Pennington, A. S. (8)	Holston, ME,S
Perkins, A. R. (3)	Kentucky, ME,S
*Perkins, William C. (6)	Pittsburgh, MP
Perry, Jack W. (3)	Holston, ME,S
*Perry, Mrs. Jack W. (4)	Holston, ME,S
Perry, John W. (3)	Wisconsin, ME
Peterman, James H. (6)	Iowa-Des Moines, ME
*Peterson, Ernest W. (3)	Oregon, ME
*Pettyjohn, O. R. (6)	Virginia, ME,S
*Pewett, Mrs. Henkel (2)	North Arkansas, ME,S
*Phelps, William R. (3)	Virginia, ME,S
Pierce, A. M. (1)	North Georgia, ME,S
*Piggott, Mrs. Walter J. (4)	Louisville, ME,S
*Pinckney, Thaddaeus H. (1)	South Carolina, ME
Piper, Joseph D. (2)	Pittsburgh, ME
Plyler, A. W. (2)	Western North Carolina, ME,S
Plyler, M. T. (6)	North Carolina, ME,S
*Post, Mrs. Ancel B. (4)	West Virginia, MP
Potts, J. Manning (2)	Virginia, ME,S
*Potts, W. O. (2)	North Mississippi, MP
Pritchard, J. E. (1)	North Carolina, MP
*Pritchard, William P. (4)	New England Southern, ME
*Propert, Frank C. (6)	New Jersey, ME
Prothro, Charles W. (8)	Savannah, ME
Pugh, A. Wesley (2)	North Indiana, ME
Pulliam, William G. (3)	Illinois, ME
*Purvance, Ernest (1)	Northwest, ME,S
*Quillian, Hubert (8)	North Georgia, ME,S
Quillian, Paul W. (5)	Texas, ME,S
Quillian, William F. (5)	South Georgia, ME,S
Raines, Richard C. (8)	Northern Minnesota, ME
Ramos, Frank (3)	Texas Mexican, ME,S
Rand, H. J. (8)	Southewest Missouri, ME,S
*Randal, Mrs. C. M. (2)	Northwest Texas, ME,S
Randolph, J. D. (6)	Missouri, ME,S
*Randolph, Joseph B. (5)	South Carolina, ME

The Methodist Church 93

Name	Conference and Church
*Redding, W. F., Jr. (5)	North Carolina, MP
*Redwine, Marcus C. (1)	Kentucky, ME,S
Reed, Marshall R. (5)	..... Detroit, ME
*Reineke, George F. (6)	Minnesota, ME
Reves, C. M. (2)	Little Rock, ME,S
*Reynolds, John H. (5)	North Arkansas, ME,S
Rice, Merton S. (2)	Detroit, ME
Rice, Samuel C. (1)	Kentucky, ME
Richardson, Channing A. (1)	California, ME
Richardson, J. A. (5)	Texas, MP
Riddick, Roland P. (3)	... Virginia, ME,S
*Riggs, Mrs. Jeptha (1)	St. Louis, ME,S
Riley, P. E. (7)	Central Texas, ME,S
Rising, Lloyd H. (5)	Minnesota, ME
Roadman, Earl A. (5)	Northwest Iowa, ME
*Roan, Hans J. (2)	Idaho, ME
*Robb, James L. (5)	Holston, ME
*Robbins, Charles A. (5)	Pacific Northwest, ME
*Roberts, E. Howard (1)	... Wisconsin, ME
Roberts, George A. (4)	... Africa, ME
*Roberts, Warren (1)	South Georgia, ME,S
Robertson, J. Calloway (5)	Virginia, ME,S
Robinson, LeRoy T. (4)	Michigan, ME
*Robinson, Milton C. (3)	Northeast Ohio, ME
*Rogers, A. C. (4)	Alabama, MP
*Rogers, Mrs. Lillian P. (8)	Upper Mississippi, ME
Rogers, Wallace (4)	North Georgia, ME,S
*Rogers, Walter S. (3)	Nebraska, ME
*Roper, William B. (4)	Virginia, ME,S
*Rosenberger, John H. (3)	Baltimore, ME,S
Rosenberger, S. W. (4)	.... Ohio, MP
*Roudebush, Roy R. (4)	North Indiana, ME
Rowe, Gilbert T. (6)	Western North Carolina, ME,S
*Ruff, A. C. (6)	.....................................Illinois, MP
Rugg, Earle M. (1)	.... India, ME
Rule, E. C. (6)	Little Rock, ME,S
Rumble, Lester (5)	North Georgia, ME,S
Russell, Robert L. (4)	North Georgia, ME,S
Ryan, Harry G. (1)	North Texas, ME,S
Sanders, William L. (6)	.... East Tennessee, ME
Sandmeyer, Edwin G. (1)	Illinois, ME
*Sapp, Mrs. C. C. (3)	South Georgia, ME,S
Satterfield, Robert S. (7)	.... Oklahoma, ME,S
Savige, George R. (5)	..... Wyoming, ME
Schatzman, Albert G. (4)	Ohio, ME
Schevenius, Carl W. (1)	Norwegian and Danish, ME
Schisler, John Q. (5)	North Arkansas, ME,S
Schlagenhauf, Ira E. (3)	.... Wisconsin, ME
Schofield, Charles E. (5)	...Colorado, ME
*Schwaninger, W. W. (3)	...... Indiana, ME
Score, J. N. R. (1)	Central Texas, ME,S
*Scott, John T. (6)	.Texas, ME,S
*Scott, William C. (7)	Maryland, MP
Searles, J. Wesley (2)	Genesee, ME
Seaton, John L. (5)	Michigan, ME
*Self, W. D. (1)	North Alabama, ME,S

Name	Conference and Church
Sexsmith, E. A. (5)	Maryland, MP
*Sexton, Mrs. George S., Jr. (1)	Louisiana, ME,S
*Seymour, Mrs. Jerome (6)	Southern California, ME
Shafer, A. E. (8)	Alabama, ME,S
Shaffer, F. L. (2)	West Virginia, MP
Sharp, Frank L. (3)	Mississippi, MP
Shaw, J. Beverley F. (2)	Mississippi, ME
*Shaw, Harry (3)	Pittsburgh, MP
Shaw, William E. (4)	Illinois, ME
Shelton, William A. (3)	North Georgia, ME,S
*Shepard, C. L. (4)	South Georgia, ME,S
Sherman, H. H. (5)	Baltimore, ME,S
*Sherman, L. L. (3)	Arkansas, MP
*Sherrod, Charles C. (5)	Holston, ME,S
Shipley, Richard L. (6)	Maryland, MP
Short, Roy H. (1)	Louisville, ME,S
Shumway, H. L. (4)	Kentucky, MP
Sigg, Ferdinand (1)	Europe, ME
Simpson, John A. (6)	South Florida, ME
Simpson, J. Fisher (5)	West Texas, ME,S
Skillington, J. Edgar (3)	Central Pennsylvania, ME
Slack, W. B. (4)	Oklahoma, ME,S
Slaughter, D. P. (6)	Alabama, ME,S
*Slaughter, Nat G. (1)	North Georgia, ME,S
Sloan, Harold P. (6)	New Jersey, ME
Smathers, M. T. (3)	Western North Carolina, ME,S
Smith, Albert N. (6)	Northwest Kansas, ME
Smith, Benjamin F. (4)	Lexington, ME
*Smith, Chester A. (2)	New York, ME
Smith, H. C. (3)	North Carolina, ME,S
Smith, Horace, G. (5)	Rock River, ME
*Smith, J. Harvey (8)	South Florida, ME
Smith, Leonard B. (8)	Maryland, MP
*Smith, Robert J. (3)	Southwest Missouri, ME,S
Smith, Roy L. (4)	Southern California, ME
Smith, Ulysses S. (3)	Iowa-Des Moines, ME
*Smith, Walter T. (1)	Pittsburgh, MP
*Snavely, Herschell R. (3)	Illinois, ME
*Snyder, Henry N. (5)	Upper South Carolina, ME,S
Sockman, Ralph W. (5)	New York, ME
*Sone, Law (5)	Central Texas, ME,S
Soper, Edmund D. (5)	Ohio, ME
Spellman, L. U. (2)	West Texas, ME,S
*Spencer, Robert B. (6)	Colorado, ME
*Spillman, Mrs. J. H. (7)	Kentucky, ME,S
Spragins, Charles A. (3)	North Texas, ME,S
*Sproul, R. C., Sr. (2)	Pittsburgh, MP
*Spurgeon, William H. (1)	Colorado, ME
*Stackhouse, Will (7)	South Carolina, ME,S
Stafford, Edward R. (6)	Ohio, ME
Stafford, Thomas A. (7)	Northern Minnesota, ME
*Staley, H. C. (3)	Maryland, MP
Stanbury, W. A. (5)	Western North Carolina, ME,S
Stansell, Robert B. (2)	Wisconsin, ME
Stanton, Daniel H. (1)	Atlanta, ME
Stapleton, Robert L. (1)	Holston, ME
Starkey, Lycurgus M. (3)	Southwest Missouri, ME,S

The Methodist Church 95

Name	Conference and Church
Stater, Charles G. (2)	West Virginia, ME
*Stauffacher, Charles J. (3)	Africa, ME
*Stehl, Heinrich (8)	Europe, ME
Steinkraus, John H. (1)	East German, ME
*Stephens, F. F. (3)	Missouri, ME,S
*Stevens, B. M. (1)	Mississippi, ME,S
Stevens, Frank G. H. (7)	Southern California, ME
Stevenson, Henry M. (1)	North Alabama, ME,S
Stevenson, M. A. (6)	Holston, ME,S
*Stilwell, H. W. (3)	Texas, ME,S
*Stinson, Mrs. J. M. (6)	Little Rock, ME,S
Stokes, Peter (deceased) (2)	South Carolina, ME,S
Stone, Fred D. (6)	Rock River, ME
*Stottlemire, Frank E. (6)	Ohio, MP
Straughn, James H. (4)	Maryland, MP
Stribling, E. R. (2)	Missouri, MP
Stringfellow, LeRoy W. (2)	New Hampshire, ME
*Strong, Dennis F. (3)	Detroit, ME
*Stuck, Charles A. (1)	North Arkansas, ME,S
*Sullivan, J. Magruder (3)	Mississippi, ME,S
Sutherland, Ben L. (2)	Mississippi, ME,S
Swain, W. R. (4)	Texas, ME,S
Swank, Jesse (7)	Ohio, ME
Swartz, Morris E. (2)	Central Pennsylvania, ME
*Sweet, E. M., Jr. (3)	Pacific, ME,S
Sweet, William W. (5)	North Indiana, ME
Sydenstricker, Hubert (3)	Baltimore, ME,S
*Sykes, W. Clyde (3)	Northern New York, ME
Tadlock, Charles W. (7)	St. Louis, ME,S
Taggart, James H. (3)	Southwest, ME
*Talbert, Mrs. H. L. (3)	North Mississippi, ME,S
*Tatum, Mrs. S. Homer (4)	Memphis, ME,S
Taylor, B. P. (1)	Western Virginia, ME,S
*Taylor, Dean (4)	Iowa-Des Moines, ME
Taylor, S. W. (3)	North Carolina, MP
Thomas, J. S. Ladd (8)	Philadelphia, ME
*Thomas, Lavens M. (4)	Holston, ME,S
*Thompson, E. D. (5)	Tennessee, ME,S
Thonger, William G. (4)	Belgium, ME,S
*Thrasher, T. E. (7)	South Georgia, ME,S
*Tilley, Mrs. M. E. (1)	North Georgia, ME,S
*Tompkins, O. L. (3)	Alabama, ME,S
Tower, Joe Z. (6)	Texas, ME,S
*Trotter, Frank H. (4)	Holston, ME
*Troxel, Miss Moneta J. (5)	Korea, ME
Tucker, Frank C. (2)	Missouri, ME,S
*Tucker, R. Carter (2)	Missouri, ME
*Tunnicliffe, John (2)	California, ME
Turnipseed, B. Rhett (7)	Upper South Carolina, ME,S
*Tyler, Mrs. Fannie D. (1)	Washington, ME
*Tynes, Mrs. L. A. (2)	Holston, ME,S
Tyson, W. Galloway (1)	Philadelphia, ME
Underwood, J. Edgar (6)	Memphis, ME,S
*Utz, W. H., Jr. (7)	Missouri, ME,S

Name	Conference and Church
*Van Cleave, A. B. (5)	Tennessee, MP
*Van Deusen, Henry R. (1)	Wyoming, ME
*Veenboer, Mrs. William H. (5)	Michigan, ME
*Vickery, William M. (4)	Oklahoma, ME
*Vincent, E. R. (1)	Michigan, MP
*Waggoner, Merle T. (3)	North Texas, ME,S
*Wagner, Robert F. (8)	New York, ME
Wahl, Frederick W. (1)	Missouri, ME
Walker, John B. (7)	Northwest Iowa, ME
Walker, John M. (6)	Indiana, ME
*Ward, Forrest S. (5)	North Alabama, ME,S
Ward, W. W. (2)	Central Texas, ME,S
Ward, Woodrow (8)	South Carolina, ME,S
*Wardlaw, J. C. (6)	North Georgia, ME,S
Warmer, George A. (4)	Southern California, M.E.
Washabaugh, J. Edgar (6)	Newark, ME
Wasson, L. P. (2)	North Mississippi, ME,S
Waterman, W. C. (5)	Onondaga, MP
*Watson, Miss Ella M. (4)	Nebraska, ME
Wayland, E. T. (6)	North Arkansas, ME,S
Weaver, Charles C. (4)	Western North Carolina, ME,S
*Weaver, Mrs. Charles C. (3)	Western North Carolina, ME,S
Weaver, G. Charles (4)	Onondaga, MP
*Webb, Mrs. J. L. (6)	Southern Illinois, ME
*Webb, William R. (3)	Tennessee, ME,S
Webdell, C. Wesley (7)	St. Louis, ME,S
*Welch, Edgar T. (3)	Erie, ME
Wells, Arthur M. (7)	Illinois, ME
*Wells, Luther W. (4)	Virginia, ME,S
Wesley, Arthur F. (6)	South America, ME
Westerberg, Thor J. (1)	Central Northwest, ME
*Whitcher, Frank O. (3)	West Wisconsin, ME
White, E. E. (6)	Northwest Texas, ME,S
*White, H. H. (3)	Louisiana, ME,S
*White, Mrs. M. H. (6)	Northwest Iowa, ME
Whitehurst, B. G. (3)	North Mississippi, MP
*Whitmore, Ben A. (6)	Tennessee, ME,S
Whyman, Henry C. (8)	Eastern Swedish, ME
*Wiant, Paul P. (2)	China, ME
*Wight, J. Slater (5)	South Georgia, ME,S
*Wilcox, William H. (3)	Oklahoma, ME
*Wiley, Henry, S. (6)	Illinois, ME
*Williams, Miss Arsania M. (1)	Central West, ME
*Williams, F. E. (2)	St. Louis, ME,S
*Williams, J. M. (6)	North Arkansas, ME,S
Williams, John C. (1)	Ohio, MP
Williams, Robert M. (6)	Washington, ME
*Williamson, Nate S. (5)	Mississippi, MP
*Wills, J. Norman (7)	North Carolina, ME
Willson, E. Ray (6)	Michigan, MP
*Willson, J. M. (1)	Northwest Texas, ME,S
Wilson, Guy H. (1)	Texas, ME,S
*Wilson, Harwell (8)	Florida, ME,S
*Wilson, Herbert S. (3)	Delaware, ME
*Wilson, O. L. (1)	Fort Smith-Oklahoma, MP
Winchester, Robert W. (2)	North Carolina, ME

Name	Conference and Church
Winn, J. B. (6)	Virginia, ME,S
*Womack, J. P. (5)	North Arkansas, ME,S
*Womack, Richard E. (5)	Memphis, ME,S
*Woods, J. M. (2)	Missouri, ME,S
Woolever, Harry E. (2)	Central New York, ME
Woolf, E. L. (5)	Baltimore, ME,S
*Woosley, O. V. (1)	Western North Carolina, ME,S
*Worth, W. H. (6)	Western North Carolina, ME,S
*Wren, Los L. (3)	North Carolina, MP
*Wright, Harry B. (3)	Wilmington, ME
Wright, Louis C. (4)	Northeast Ohio, ME
Wright, William A. (3)	Virginia, ME,S
Wroten, J. D. (4)	North Mississippi, ME,S
*Yang, Y. C. (5)	China, ME,S
Yoak, John B. F., Jr. (6)	Western Virginia, ME,S
*Yoder, D. P. (2)	Northwest Texas, ME,S
Yost, Clark R. (5)	Southern Illinois, ME
*Youngblood, Curtis (6)	Mississippi, ME,S

ALPHABETICAL LIST OF RESERVE DELEGATES

[Lay Delegates invariably designated by * in front of name.]
(R.C. in parentheses (R.C.) indicates that the reserve was seated the first day of the Conference on nomination of the Chairman of the delegation. The first numeral in parentheses (5-10) indicates the Report number of the Committee on Credentials; the second numeral the item in the Report showing for whom the reserve was seated. The Reports will be found in the Appendix under Reports of Special Committees.)

Name	Conference and Church
*Ables, J. H. ..	New Mexico, ME,S
*Adair, H. H.	Holston, ME,S
Adams, Joseph M..	Pacific Northwest, ME
*Adams, Texas A.	South Florida, ME
*Aguirre, Miss Marie	South America, ME
*Alderson, Edmund R. (R.C.; 2-14)	Rock River, ME
*Alexander, T. F.	Florida, ME,S
*Allen, A. W.	Kansas, MP
*Allen, J. H.	North Carolina, MP
Amstutz, Hobart B.. ...	Malaysia and Philippine Islands, ME
*Anderson, A. Garfield	Korea, ME
*Anderson, Dice R.	South Georgia, ME,S
*Armistead, D. F. (2-9; 7-1; 9-2; 10-22)	North Texas, ME,S
*Ash, B. G.	West Virginia, MP
*Atkinson, Stephen G....	Detroit, ME
Auman, J. C.	North Carolina, MP
Auman, Lester W.	New York East, ME
Avery, H. L.	Indiana, MP
*Ayers, Leake ..	Central Texas, ME,S
Babcock, Sidney H.	Oklahoma, ME,S
*Bailey, F. M. (4-2)	Oklahoma, ME,S
*Bailey, T. L..	Mississippi, ME,S
Bailey, Thomas M..	Alabama, ME
Bailey, W. G...	New Mexico, ME
Baker, E. D. (9-24)	Southwest Missouri, ME,S
Baker, J. D. (10-12)....	Little Rock, ME,S
Baker, W. Harrison (10-21)	North Texas, ME,S
*Ball, Frank M..	Maryland, MP
*Ballengee, Mrs. W. H..	Baltimore, ME,S
*Ballinger, Floyd E.	North Indiana, ME
*Banting, George O.	Wisconsin, ME
*Barnett, Nelson (R.C.; 2-7; 4-17)	North Arkansas, ME,S
Barr, Henry H. (10-23)	Erie, ME
*Barradell, William H. (R.C.)	New York East, ME
Batchelor, S. L. (7-6; 9-9; 10-40)	West Texas, ME,S
*Batchelor, Mrs. S. L. (7-3)	West Texas, ME,S
Baumhofer, Earl F.	Northern Minnesota, ME
*Baxter, Bruce R.	Oregon, ME
Beach, F. C.	Upper South Carolina, ME,S
*Beall, Bessy B.	Baltimore, ME

Name	Conference and Church
*Beattys, George D.	... Newark, ME
*Beaty, B. K.	Illinois, ME,S
*Beck, Jesse M. (R.C.; 2-12)	Iowa-Des Moines, ME
Beckstrom, John M....	Norwegian and Danish, ME
*Bell, Miller S.	North Georgia, ME,S
*Bell, O. R.	Upper South Carolina, ME,S
*Bengston, John P.	Eastern Swedish, ME
Bennett, A.E..	West Virginia, MP
Bennett, R. V.	Louisville, ME,S
Bergin, J. W.	Central Texas, ME,S
Berglund, J. V. (3-6)	Texas, ME,S
Bergsten, Gote	Europe, ME
Bethea, N. G.	North Carolina, MP
Black, S. M. (4-22)	North Texas, ME,S
Blackstock, William E.	Colorado, ME
*Bliss, Edwin P.	New England, ME
*Boger, R. G.	Northwest Texas, ME,S
*Bond, C. W.	Memphis, ME,S
Bond, G. T.	Western North Carolina, ME,S
Booker, Rosia R.	Central West, ME
*Bowen, Mrs. Margaret D.	Louisiana, ME
Bowers, Joe E..	Oklahoma, ME,S
*Boyd, Miller W.	East Tennessee, ME
Boyd, P. M.	Florida, ME,S
Bradshaw, R. W.	North Carolina, ME,S
*Brandon, Mrs. J. P. (2-2; 6-1)	St. Louis, ME,S
Brandt, C. E. (9-S-1)	Baltimore, ME,S
Bransford, Wesley H.	North Indiana, ME
Brantley, C. E.	Georgia, MP
Brashares, Charles W.	Detroit, ME
*Braswell, S..M.	Northwest Texas, ME,S
*Braun, C. A.	Pittsburgh, MP
*Brigham, Edwin T.	Missouri, ME
Bright, C. R.	West Virginia, MP
Bringdale, Joachim G.	Western Norwegian-Danish, ME
*Britt, Mrs. Lee (10-2; 12-10)	Virginia, ME,S
*Brookes, E. Luther	Atlanta, ME
Brooks,. Charles L.	Oklahoma, ME,S
Brooks, Robert N..	North Carolina, ME
Brower, F. V..	St. Louis, ME,S
Brown, Arlo A.	Newark, ME
Brumblay, Robert	Pacific Northwest, ME
*Brumby, R. E..	Louisiana, ME,S
*Bruton, J. F.	North Carolina, ME,S
Bugbee, Lucius H.	Northern Minnesota, ME
Bunce, E. L.	Maryland, MP
Burgan, Harry W.	Baltimore, ME
Burgstahler, Herbert J.	Upper Iowa, ME
*Burke, Mrs. M. W....	Missouri, ME,S
Bush, Martin D.	Northwest Iowa, ME
*Butler, V. H.	Louisville, ME,S
*Caldwell, Charles W.	South Carolina, ME
Calhoun, W. F.	Alabama, ME,S
Campbell, J. F.	Mississippi, ME,S
*Campbell, John B. (R.C.)	Northwest Indiana, ME
*Campbell, Richard W. (9-S-4)	Central Pennsylvania, ME

Name	Conference and Church
Cannon, Neal D. (6-3)	Texas, ME,S
*Carlock, John H..	Oklahoma, ME,S
*Carothers, Manville (7-2)	Missouri, ME
Carr, Harold F...	Detroit, ME
Carroll, J. E...	North Carolina, MP
*Carter, George E..	Southern, ME
*Carter, Harry V.	Oklahoma, ME
*Cartmell, Burleigh E. (10-35)	Northeast Ohio, ME
Cartwright, J. L.	Tennessee, MP
*Case, Arthur S. (9-13; 10-9)	Kansas, ME
Caskey, J. F.	St. Louis, ME,S
*Castle, C. E.	Oklahoma, ME,S
Chamberlain, Leon	New Jersey, ME
Chappell, Clovis G.	Oklahoma, ME,S
Chenault, Fred R..	Virginia, ME,S
*Chinn, Mrs. E. C. (4-8)	Texas, ME,S
*Christenberry, W. B. (1-1)	Alabama, ME,S
Chubb, James S. (11-31)	Kansas, ME
Clark, Victor C.	Missouri, ME
Clark, W. L.	Kentucky, ME,S
Clary, G. E.	South Georgia, ME,S
*Class, John L.	New York, ME
*Clay, E. H	China, ME
Clay, H. L. ...	Western Virginia, ME,S
*Clay, Thomas B.	Genesee, ME
Clayburn, Marion D.	Central Tennessee, ME
*Clayton, James W.	Blue Ridge-Atlantic, ME
Clegg, Leland (8-14)	Little Rock, ME,S
*Coe, N. M.	Onondaga, MP
Coile, Claude C.	New York, ME
*Cole, E. A...	Western North Carolina, ME,S
*Collier, C. C.	Illinois, MP
*Coltrane, Mrs. D. S.	North Carolina, MP
*Colvin, Mrs. D. Leigh	New York, ME
*Cook, F. M...	North Alabama, ME,S
Copeland, Kenneth ..	Texas, MP
Copenhaver, J. C.	Baltimore, ME,S
Corban, L. C.	Mississippi, ME,S
Corley, Jesse L.	Southern California, ME
Corn, A. R.	Arkansas, MP
*Cowart, Mrs. Bessie.	Alabama, ME,S
*Cox, Linton L.	Georgia, ME
*Cox, R. M...	North Carolina, MP
*Cravens, W. A...	Missouri, ME,S
*Crew, J. W., Jr.....;...	North Carolina, MP
*Crolley, Richard A. (deceased)	Lexington, ME
*Cross, W. R.	Baltimore, ME,S
Crowe, F. S.	Oklahoma, ME,S
*Cruz-Aedo, Francisco	Western Mexican, ME,S
Cuninggim, J. L. (1-10)	North Carolina, ME,S
*Cullum, Will H., Jr.	North Texas, ME,S
*Culver, Frank P., Jr...	Central Texas, ME,S
Curington, Norven J...	South Florida, ME
*Currie, Frank R.	Upper Iowa, ME
*Currie, Miss Margaret	Maine, ME
Curry, Daniel S.. .	South Carolina, ME
Curry, J. C. (3-2)	Oklahoma, ME,S

Name	Conference and Church
Custis, D. L.	Ohio, MP
*Cutchin, J. M.	North Carolina, MP
Cutshall, E. Guy	Nebraska, ME
*Darsey, M. E.	Texas, ME,S
Daugherty, C. L. (1-12)	Pittsburgh, MP
Davies, James J. (11-18)	Northwest-Iowa, ME
*Davis, Harry J. (12-4)	St. Louis, ME,S
Davis, W. P. (3-4; 5-3)	Kentucky, ME,S
Davis, William E. (11-24)	Erie, ME
*Dean, S. W.	Texas, ME,S
*DeVinny, Mrs. Mabel L. (12-13)	Minnesota, ME
Dibley, Joseph	Michigan, MP
*Diefendorf, Mrs. Mabel (R.C.)	Newark, ME
*Dievler, Mrs. William (12-23)	Philadelphia, ME
Dill, R. L.	North Alabama, ME,S
*Dillinger, Ray	Illinois, ME
*Dixon, Cincinnati C.	Central Tennessee, ME
Dixon, Edwin C. (10-17)	West Wisconsin, ME
Dougan, Egbert W.	Savannah, ME
*Dryden, Kenneth H.	Nebraska, ME
*Drysdale, William C.	Illinois, ME
*Dudley, Albert H.	Baltimore, ME,S
Duncombe, Franklin	Philadelphia, ME
Dunning, James E. (12-17)	Southern California, ME
Duren, W. L.	Louisiana, ME,S
Durrett, John	Tennessee, ME,S
*Dykes, L. W.	Maryland, MP
*Eakes, M. M. (6-4; 8-7)	Oklahoma, ME,S
Edwards, Frederick C.	Iowa-Des Moines, ME
Edwards, Loren M.	Colorado, ME
*Eells, Linden L.	Nebraska, ME
*Elkins, R. A. (1-9; 5-5; 9-14)	Memphis, ME,S
*Elliot, Loren J.	North Indiana, ME
*Elliott, William J.	Philadelphia, ME
*Ellzey, Tom V. (11-32)	Northwest Texas, ME,S
Ericson, Charles C.	Eastern Swedish, ME
Eva, Sidney D. (12-15)	Detroit, ME
*Evans, L. L.	Oklahoma, ME,S
*Everson, Ray D.	Indiana, ME
Fain, Galen C.	Memphis, ME,S
Fain, J. E.	South Georgia, ME,S
*Farmer, Mrs. H. R. (1-2)	Southwest Missouri, ME,S
*Fawcett, William C.	North Dakota, ME
*Fawks, R. W.	Missouri, ME,S
Feeman, H. L.	Pittsburgh, MP
*Ferguson, Arthur P.	California, ME
*Ferguson, C. W.	Western Virginia, ME,S
Ferris, E. L.	Indiana, MP
*Few, W. W.	West Texas, ME,S
*Fields, Mrs. Z. R.	Southwest, ME
*Flanders, William E.	Northern New York, ME
*Flowers, R. L.	North Carolina, ME,S
Ford, C. Oscar	New England, ME
*Forman, J. M.	North Mississippi, ME,S

Name	Conference and Church
*Fowler, Luther	Mississippi, MP
*Franke, William F. (R.C.; 2-4)	Alabama, ME
Franklin, Marvin A.	North Alabama, ME,S
Franklin, S. W.	Oklahoma, ME,S
Frazer, John W.	Alabama, ME,S
Frazier, F. L. (R.C.; 4-11)	South Carolina, MP
*Friedman, Oliver A.	Wisconsin, ME
Fry, J. A. B.	Pacific, ME,S
*Fuller, T. E.	Little Rock, ME,S
Fultz, B. J.	Onondaga, MP
*Galloway, Sam A. (R.C.; 2-8)	North Arkansas, ME,S
Gamble, Foster K. (8-1)	North Alabama, ME,S
*Gammon, Burton O.	Iowa-Des Moines, ME
Gardner, Nelson S.	Southwest Kansas, ME
Garrett, Elza N.	Missouri, ME
Garth, Schuyler E. (11-26)	Northeast Ohio, ME
*Gibson, Miss Gladys	Southwest Kansas, ME
*Gibson, J. K.	Kentucky, ME,S
*Gifford, Blaine H. (9-3)	Erie, ME
*Gilhousen, Mrs. F. B.	Ohio, MP
Gillett, Ira E.	Africa, ME
Gleaton, W. D. (R.C.; 2-10; 4-21)	South Carolina, ME,S
*Goericke, Otto	Europe, ME
*Grace, J. Harry	Baltimore, ME
*Gray, H. D.	Upper South Carolina, ME,S
*Gray, James A.	Western North Carolina, ME,S
Green, C. R.	Iowa-Missouri, MP
Green, John D.	Northeast Ohio, ME
*Green, W. Cooper	North Alabama, ME,S
Grimes, Charles C.	Northwest Texas, ME,S
Grimm, P. E.	Ohio, MP
*Gross, Hezekiah K.	Savannah, ME
Grummon, A. Ray	Illinois, ME
*Guerry, T. H. (R.C.; 2-11)	South Georgia, ME,S
*Guilds, J. C.	South Carolina, ME,S
Gunby, Walter E.	Wilmington, ME
Gunn, Elmer C.	Louisiana, ME,S
Gunter, A. L.	Upper South Carolina, ME,S
Haddaway, G. W. (10-30)	Maryland, MP
*Hadsall, M. L.	Michigan, MP
*Haggerty, Floyd	Onondaga, MP
Hagner, Feodor	East German, ME
*Hall, Elias W.	Mississippi, ME
*Hall, Joseph B.	Pacific Northwest, ME
Hallman, Ernest C.	Wilmington, ME
*Halmhuber, Paul G. (R.C.)	Detroit, ME
Halter, Arthur A.	Missouri, ME
Hamilton, Frank A.	Holston, ME
Hamilton, Hugh K.	California, ME
Hamilton, Harry S.	Idaho, ME
Hampton, Joseph M.	Holston, ME
Hamrick, W. L.	Mississippi, MP
Hand, Howard E.	Philadelphia, ME
Handy, William T. (12-9)	Louisiana, ME
Hank, P. M.	Virginia, ME,S

The Methodist Church 103

Name	Conference and Church
Hann, Edwin F.	New Jersey, ME
*Hansen, A. W.	Norwegian and Danish, ME
*Harmeling, Karl	Holston, ME,S
Harold, Ernest F. (5-11)	Pacific Northwest, ME
*Harper, Leonard	Indiana, MP
Harper, R. H.	Louisiana, ME,S
*Harrison, F. H.	West Texas, ME,S
Harrison, Jabez C.	Oregon, ME
*Harrison, W. H.	Maryland, MP
*Harshbarger, Charles C.	Northwest Iowa, ME
Hart, F. E.	Michigan, MP
*Hartley, Charles H.	West Virginia, ME
Hartman, P. D.	Northwest, ME,S
Hartsfield, Gaston (10-39; 11-30)	West Texas, ME,S
Hawk, John C.	China, ME,S
Hawver, Harley D.	New Hampshire, ME
Hayden, R. S.	North Arkansas, ME,S
Hayes, L. B.	Western North Carolina, ME,S
*Hayes, Robert B.	Louisiana, ME
*Haynes, N. J.	Pacific, ME,S
Haywood, John W. (9-5)	East Tennessee, ME
*Hazel, Mrs. Gail	Missouri, MP
*Hazen, John B.	Pacific Northwest, ME
Henderson, C. E.	Missouri, MP
Henderson, Joseph M.	Genesee, ME
Henke, Arthur W.	Upper Iowa, ME
Henry, Albert E.	Southwest Kansas, ME
Henry, David W.	Delaware, ME
*Heutess, Mrs. Arthur (R.C.; 3-9)	Alabama, MP
Hicks, Guy M. (11-21)	Louisiana, ME,S
Hill, B. O.	Western Mexican, ME,S
Hillman, Paul M. (5-10)	Nebraska, ME
*Hinkle, Hamet D. (R.C.; 2-1)	Indiana, ME
Hobbs, A. J.	North Carolina, ME,S
Holland, H. C.	North Georgia, ME,S
*Hoover, George A.	Northeast Ohio, ME
Hopkins, O. K.	Cuba, ME,S
Hoppe, J. L.	Holston, ME,S
Hortin, Paul R. (6-9; 8-11)	Saint Johns River, ME
Horton, John L. (9-15; 10-14; 11-7)	Memphis, ME,S
*Houston, J. G.	North Mississippi, ME,S
Hoyt, Clare C.	Wyoming State, ME
*Huckle, Thomas O. (10-1; 10-38)	Michigan, ME
*Huffor, Earl (2-21)	Texas, ME,S
*Hull, Samuel A.	Florida, ME
*Hummel, Mrs. G. W. (3-4; 9-1)	Louisville, ME,S
Humphrey, William D.	Illinois, ME,S
*Humphreys, Norman H.	Pittsburgh, ME
Hunter, J. D.	North Alabama, ME,S
*Hutchinson, Mrs. Ruth B.	Wisconsin, ME
*Insley, W. H.	Maryland, MP
Ivy, C. L.	North Mississippi, MP
*Jackson, Henrietta L.	Washington, ME
*Jackson, James R.	Rock River, ME
*Jakes, J. W. (1-6; 2-19)	Tennessee, ME,S

Name	Conference and Church
James, Edward	China, ME
James, Glenn C..	Saint Johns River, ME
*Jaquith, W. E. (deceased) ..	Central New York, ME
Jeffras, Charles W.	New England, ME
*Jett, Robert S. (5-7; 6-13).	Maryland, MP
*Johnson, Mrs. A. C. (10-11) . . .	Louisville, ME,S
Johnson, A. J.	Texas, MP
Johnson, Iver M. . . .	Illinois, ME
Johnson, Melville, (deceased)	North Mississippi, ME,S
*Johnson, Mrs. Pinkie D. . ..	Texas, ME
Johnson, Ramund	Onondaga, MP
Jones, Hubert D. .	New York East, ME
Jones, J. Ira	Ohio, ME
*Jones, L. L. .	Alabama, MP
*Jones, Mrs. Lillian L.	Tennessee, ME
Jones, William T. (R.C.; 2-15)	Indiana, ME
Jorns, Elza L.	Oklahoma, ME
Jose, John F. ...	Pittsburgh, ME
Keiser, Roy N.	Philadelphia, ME
Kellar, Frederick J.	Europe, ME
*Kelley, Mrs. C. I.	Tennessee, MP
*Kendall, Franklin H.	Northeast Ohio, ME
*Kesler, J. C.....	Western North Carolina, ME,S
King, H. M.	West Texas, ME,S
*King, L. E.	Kentucky, ME,S
*Kirk, Walter F.	Ohio, ME
*Knapp, Seaman A. (9-S-3)	Iowa-Des Moines, ME
*Kuykendall, George	Texas, MP
Langdon, B. F.	Illinois, MP
*Leavitt, Henry P. .	Southern California, ME
*Lee, Charles O.	Northwest Indiana, ME
Leggett, J. T.	Mississippi, ME,S
*Leighbody, Glenn W. ..	Genesee, ME
*Leonard, T. W..:	Pittsburgh, MP
*Lewis, A. L.	Texas, MP
Lewis, George W. . ..	Tennessee, ME
*Lewis, Miss Harriet . .	Colorado, ME
*Lewis, Vernon E... . . .	Montana State, ME
*Lightner, Lawrence H. .	Central West, ME
Lindley, P. E. .	North Carolina, MP
*Lindsay, Mrs. F. F..	Northern Minnesota, ME
Link, J. N. (10-32)..	Maryland, MP
Linton, R. S.	Ohio, MP
Lipscomb, L. N. (1-4)	Northwest Texas, ME,S
Lipsky, Bailey G.	Vermont, ME
Lochridge, Frank H. (10-10)	Dakota, ME
*Long, Mrs. C. C.	Ohio, ME
Longnecker, William A. (2-17) .	Iowa-Des Moines, ME
Loomis, H. B. . .	Onondaga, MP
*Lord, A. Taylor	Wyoming, ME
Lott, W. R. (4-14)	North Mississippi, ME,S
*Loucks, Charles O.	Rock River, ME
Love, Edgar A.	Washington, ME
Love, Ernest C. ...	Northern New York, ME
Luetzow, H. H. (9-12).	Southwest Missouri, ME,S

Name	Conference and Church
Lund, Elmer F.	.Central Northwest, ME
Lynch, A. H.	Alabama, MP
Lynch, W. O. (10-42)	Arkansas, MP
Lyons, J. L.	Pacific, ME,S
Madison, J. C.	North Carolina, MP
*Malone, E. R.	Alabama, ME,S
Mann, J. W.	Little Rock, ME,S
Mansberger, Arlie R. (4-1; 4-10)	Pittsburgh, MP
*Marr, Wade	North Carolina, ME,S
Martin, Wilsie	Southern California, ME
Mason, J. J.	West Texas, ME,S
*Masters, Kathryn F.	Northeast Ohio, ME
*Mather, Wiley W.	Southern California, ME
Mathis, Eugene M.	Memphis, ME,S
Mathis, W. C.	Fort Smith-Oklahoma, MP
*Matthews, Elmer C.	New Jersey, ME
Matthews, M. L.	Fort Smith-Oklahoma, MP
*Matthews, Mrs. M. B. (R.C.)	Maryland, MP
*Maxwell, Gala	Michigan, MP
Maxwell, M. M. (7-5; 8-9; 11-18)	North Georgia, ME,S
McCormack, William R.	.Kansas, ME
*McCoy, Mrs. J. L. (3-8; 4-3)	Kansas, ME
*McCullough, J. Bruce (2-20)	.New England Southern, ME
McDade, Edwin C.	Nebraska, ME
*McElreath, Walter	North Georgia, ME,S
*McEwen, W. B.	Western North Carolina, ME,S
*McGlammery, B. E.	Central Texas, ME,S
*McGough, B. F.	Arizona, ME,S
*McKeithen, J. W.	Louisiana, MP
*McKibbin, Harold B. (R.C.; 2-13)	Southwest Kansas, ME
McLarty, E. K.	Western North Carolina, ME,S
McLaughlin, Willard J.	India, ME
McLeod, J. F.	Alabama, ME,S
McNutt, D. C. (10-41)	North Alabama, ME,S
McPherson, Harry W.	Illinois, ME
McQueen, M. Wayne (9-S-5)	.Northeast Ohio, ME
*McQuiston, Jackson C.	Pittsburgh, ME
*Mead, Mrs. Charles L. (12-3)	Missouri, ME
Melbert, N. H. (5-2)	Texas, ME,S
*Mentzer, Judd A.	Wyoming State, ME
Merring, Edwin E.	Central New York, ME
*Metcalf, C. D.	North Arkansas, ME,S
Mettam, John W. (11-28)	Minnesota, ME
Milburn, James E. (9-8)	Holston, ME
*Milden, A. W.	North Mississippi, ME,S
*Miller, Miss Alpha J.	Africa, ME
*Miller, Grady	North Alabama, ME,S
*Mills, O. A.	West Texas, ME,S
*Miner, Alton T.	.New England Southern, ME
Mitchell, Albert J. (12-20)	Washington, ME
*Mitchell, Andrew S.	Ohio, ME
*Montes de Oca, Juan	Cuba, ME
*Montgomery, C. M.	West Texas, ME,S
*Montgomery, S. P.	North Carolina, MP
Mood, R. Gibbs (5-9; 7-4)	North Texas, ME,S
*Moore, A. H.	Pacific, ME,S

Name	Conference and Church
Moore, E. C.	Alabama, ME,S
Moore, Joseph G.	Indiana, ME
*Moore, Mrs. T. V.	Florida, ME,S
*Morling, Mrs. W. H.	Northwest Iowa, ME
*Morris, C. G. ..	North Carolina, ME,S
*Morris, Percy F.	California, ME
Morton, C. J.	Ohio, MP
Moser, C. H.	Western North Carolina, ME,S
Mulligan, T. C.	Maryland, MP
*Murphree, John C.	North Texas, ME,S
*Musselman, De Lafayette L.	Illinois, ME
Myres, W. A. (R.C.; 4-19; 6-15)	Florida, ME,S
Nañez, Alfredo	Texas Mexican, ME,S
*Napier, T. H.	North Alabama, ME,S
Neal, T. Edgar	Central Texas, ME,S
Neill, J. L.	Mississippi, ME,S
*Neithercut, Charles	Detroit, ME
*Newell, C. D.	Iowa-Missouri, MP
*Nichols, I. C.	Louisiana, ME,S
Nicholson, R. Y. (1-13)	Maryland, MP
*Nipper, Roy, ...	Arkansas, MP
Nixon, Lloyd H.	Michigan, ME
Northcott, H. Clifford	Illinois, ME
*Norton, E. B.	Alabama, ME,S
*Nye, Mrs. Florence K.	Central New York, ME
Odom, Clyde W. (11-25; 12-6)	Kansas, ME
Oechsli, Leonard (12-16)	Southern California, ME
Olmstead, J. Harrison (12-7)	Genesee, ME
*O'Neal, C. T.	Oklahoma, ME
*Oram, Miss Jean...	Northeast Ohio, ME
*Orbin, Jess	Pittsburgh, MP
*Ostrom, Mrs. Henry E.	Indiana, ME
*Overstreet, C. A.	Little Rock, ME,S
*Page, George H.	Southern California, ME
Pardue, Mrs. Mary E.	Louisiana, MP
Parker, Albert A.	India, ME
*Parker, W. W.	St. Louis, ME,S
*Parks, N. J.	Maryland, MP
*Patton, W. C.	Memphis, ME,S
Payton, Jacob S. (2-16; 8-5)	Pittsburgh, ME
*Peeler, C. B. (R.C.; 4-20; 6-14)	Florida, ME,S
*Peeler, J. T. (R.C.)	Memphis, ME,S
*Peffer, Daniel R., Sr.	Philadelphia, ME
Pennell, Joseph R.	Wyoming, ME
*Pennington, Mrs. Frank G.	Nebraska, ME
Pentz, D. M. (12-14)	Kansas, MP
Perdew, William C.	Michigan, ME
Perry, James A.	Troy, ME
Peterson, Charles L.	Southern Illinois, ME
Pfoutz, Frank E.	Nebraska, ME
*Phelps, Francis M...	Oregon, ME
*Phelps, Harley R...	Northern New York, ME
Phillips, W. Roy	South Carolina, ME,S
Pierce, Ralph M.	Rock River, ME

The Methodist Church 107

Name	Conference and Church
*Pitts, C. A.	Fort Smith-Oklahoma, MP
*Poe, Cyrus	Virginia, MP
*Poffenberger, Alvin C.	New Jersey, ME
*Pohlman, George (5-1; 6-5)	Missouri, ME,S
*Pollard, Mrs. J. B. (8-6)	Louisiana, ME,S
Porter, H. B.	North Carolina, ME,S
*Powell, Mrs. Benson M. (11-14)	Kansas, ME
Prater, J. D.	Southwest Missouri, ME,S
*Pratt, Ben E.	Western Virginia, ME,S
*Prewitt, T. A. (9-6)	Little Rock, ME,S
*Pritchett, Cassius J.	Illinois, ME
*Quay, Ernest E.	Wyoming, ME
Queen, Joseph W.	Atlanta, ME
Quimby, Karl K. (R.C.)	Newark, ME
*Rapp, Albert	Saint Johns River, ME
*Ramos, Mrs. Jovita	Texas Mexican, ME,S
Rankin, William P.	California, ME
Ratliff, H. M.	West Texas, ME,S
*Ratliff, Mrs. W. H. (R.C.; 4-18; 5-22; 9-22)	North Mississippi, ME,S
*Rauschkolb, Frederick G..	Southern Illinois, ME
*Rawlings, Garrett D.	Washington, ME
*Rawls, J. F. (9-4; 11-35)	Tennessee, ME,S
Ray, C. K.	Baltimore, ME,S
*Ray, John H.	Baltimore, ME,S
*Redd, J. H	Virginia, ME,S
*Reed, G. N.	Virginia, ME,S
*Reed, I. H.	Southwest Missouri, ME,S
*Regnell, Arthur	Central Northwest, ME
*Reid, William W.	New York East, ME
Reuckert, F. E.	Illinois, MP
*Rich, Robert F.	Central Pennsylvania, ME
Richardson, F. M.	Baltimore, ME,S
Ricks, William B.	Tennessee, ME,S
*Rinker, C. T.	Ohio, MP
*Roan, Hans J.	Idaho, ME
*Roberts, George C.	New England, ME
Robinette, W. S.	Virginia, MP
Robinson, Ernest W.	Maine, ME
Robinson, H. I.	Texas, ME,S
Rode, Leonard J.	Southern, ME
*Rogers, Christian E.	Holston, ME
Rollins, Frank J.	Georgia, ME
*Rollins, Mrs. Nat G. (1-3; 4-6; 12-21)	Northwest Texas, ME,S
*Rose, Mrs. H. D.	California, ME
*Rosenberger, Mrs. S. W. (9-10).	Ohio, MP
*Ross, J. D.	North Carolina, MP
*Rowe, John A.	Indiana, ME
*Roy, S. A.	North Mississippi, MP
Ruff, Robert H. (11-9)	Missouri, ME,S
Ruyle, C. E.	Missouri, ME,S
*Ryder, Frank H.	Troy, ME
*Sanks, Leroy W.	Central Alabama, ME
*Satterfield, C. N.	Maryland, MP
*Savage, E. W. (R.C.; 3-7; 4-9)	Kentucky, ME,S

Name	Conference and Church
Saye, C. W.	Missouri, MP
*Scarborough, Mrs. Bessie J.	Upper Mississippi, ME
Scott, Julius S.	Texas, ME
*Searcy, Hubert (8-4)	Alabama, ME,S
Seaton, John L.	Michigan, ME
Secrest, Paul E. (11-33)	Northeast Ohio, ME
Selah, William B. (11-6)	Memphis, ME,S
Selby, J. A.	West Virginia, MP
Semans, Ray L.	Rock River, ME
*Seymour, Edward	Nebraska, ME
Seymour, L. W. (12-11)	Central Texas, ME,S
Shearer, G. W.	New Mexico, ME,S
*Shell, Mrs. J. W. (10-6)	Pittsburgh, MP
Shelton, F. B.	Holston, ME,S
Shepherd, William W. (10-8)	Kentucky, ME
Sheppard, R. Burton	Wisconsin, ME
Sherrill, William S.	Southwest, ME
Shipman, Raymond M.	Iowa-Des Moines, ME
*Shockley, O. M.	Wilmington, ME
*Short, S. H.	Virginia, ME,S
*Showalter, J. W. (8-8; 9-23; 10-19)	Southwest Missouri, ME,S
Shue, Allen C.	Central Pennsylvania, ME
*Shumacker, William H.	Michigan, ME
*Simpson, Leverett J.	Genesee, ME
*Simpson, W. R.	Georgia, MP
Skelton, David E.	Lexington, ME
Sledd, Andrew (deceased)	Alabama, ME,S
*Small, J. F.	Virginia, ME,S
Smart, W. A.	Virginia, ME,S
Smith, Alfred F.	Missouri, ME,S
Smith, Charles H.	North Indiana, ME
Smith, Charles M.	Pittsburgh, MP
Smith, Frank H.	Japan, ME
Smith, Phillips B.	North Indiana, ME
Smith, Robert J. (R.C.; 2-6)	Oklahoma, ME
*Smith, Robert L.	West Texas, ME
Smith, W. Stanley (11-34)	Northeast Ohio, ME
*Smoak, W. W.	South Carolina, ME,S
*Smythe, M. G.	Texas, ME,S
*Snetser, Mrs. B. E.	North Arkansas, ME,S
Sory, R. O.	Central Texas, ME,S
Spann, J. Richard	Louisiana, ME,S
*Sparkman, John	North Alabama, ME,S
Spaugy, Lemon D.	Pittsburgh, ME
Spaulding, W. F.	Onondaga, MP
*Squire, Melvin	Dakota, ME
Stacey, Fred W.	New York, ME
Stanton, E. M. (3-5)	Texas, ME,S
*Starmer, W. B.	Northwest, ME,S
Stearns, Harold G.	Central New York, ME
*Steele, J. T.	South Carolina, MP
Stephens, J. E. (4-15)	North Mississippi, ME,S
*Stevens, Miss Lucy	Illinois, MP
*Stewart, Mrs. L. W. (4-7)	Michigan, ME
*Stiles, George W.	Colorado, ME
Stockwell, B. Foster	South America, ME
*Stockwell, Miss Grace L. (6-2)	India, ME

Name	Conference and Church
Stone, E. D.	Maryland, MP
*Stone, Mrs. Fred	North Arkansas, ME,S
Stoody, Ralph W.	New England Southern, ME
*Strader, G. S. (8-12)	Holston, ME,S
*Stribling, Roy	Missouri, MP
Stuckey, L. N.	Louisville, ME,S
*Stump, Charles R.	North Indiana, ME
*Summers, Mrs. L. C.	Oklahoma, ME,S
Surratt, H. F.	North Carolina, MP
*Surry, Emil M.	Upper Iowa, ME
Sweeney, Samuel H.	Lexington, ME
Talbert, Charles A.	Upper Mississippi, ME
*Tanner, L. J.	Iowa-Missouri, MP
*Tatum, Mrs. S. Homer	Memphis, ME,S
*Tatum, W. O.	Mississippi, ME,S
*Taylor, John A.	Missouri, ME
Taylor, P. P. (12-25)	Missouri, ME,S
*Taylor, W. W.	Ohio, MP
Templin, Lester R.	Northwest Kansas, ME
Thompson, John.	Rock River, ME
Thorpe, George H.	Illinois, ME
Timerman, Donald	Ohio, ME
*Timmons, Mrs. Christian N.	Rock River, ME
*Tipton, William H.	Northwest Kansas, ME
*Tobson, Charles	Western Norwegian-Danish, ME
Tolbert, R. C.	Ohio, MP
Tripp, Ernest F.	Troy, ME
*Tsao, Mrs. S. H.	China, ME,S
Tucker, Robert L.	Ohio, ME
Turley, Charles E.	Ohio, ME
Turner, A. Fred	Florida, ME,S
Turner, Frederick J.	Wisconsin, ME
Turner, Horace	Montana State, ME
Turner, Walter L.	Central Alabama, ME
Tuttle, C. O.	Virginia, ME,S
Twiggs, L. M.	North Georgia, ME,S
*Ulland, Joseph S. (8-13)	Northern Minnesota, ME
*Van Antwerp, Harry N. (3-1)	Troy, ME
*Vancil, E. E.	Fort Smith-Oklahoma, MP
*Vancura, Mrs. M.	Czechoslovak, ME,S
Vancura, V.	Czechoslovak, ME,S
Vermilya, Charles E	Wyoming, ME
Vivion, King (8-15; 9-25)	Tennessee, ME,S
Voellny, Eduard	Europe, ME
*Wade, Mrs. H. King	Little Rock, ME,S
Walker, A. T. (1-7; 2-18)	Texas, ME,S
*Walker, Mrs. C. S.	New Mexico, ME,S
*Walker, Clarice D.	Delaware, ME
*Walker, E. L.	Louisiana, ME,S
*Walker, Mrs. Mary	Ohio, MP
Walker, O. L.	Arizona, ME,S
Walker, Thomas H. B.	Florida, ME
Wallace, Charles L.	North Dakota, ME

Name	Conference and Church
Walton, A. G.	North Arkansas, ME,S
Walton, A. J.	Western Virginia, ME,S
Walton, C. W.	Alabama, MP
*Wardlow, F. W.	Louisiana, MP
Wark, Homer E. (11-11)	West Virginia, ME
Warren, John W.	Northern New York, ME
Wasson, A. W. (8-2)	North Arkansas, ME,S
Watkins, A. C.	Kentucky, MP
*Watkins, Mrs. A. C.	Kentucky, MP
*Watkins, Wilson P.	West Wisconsin, ME
Watson, R. H. M.	Mississippi, MP
Watson, W. C.	Little Rock, ME,S
*Webb, Charles W.	New Hampshire, ME
*Wedemeyer, Mrs. B. B. (9-11)	Central Texas, ME,S
*Weekly, K. W. (R.C.)	West Virginia, MP
*Weir, Benjamin	Illinois, ME
Weldon, J. W. (4-6; 5-8)	Louisville, ME,S
*Welker, Miss Edith	New York East, ME
Welliver, Lester A. (11-29)	Central Pennsylvania, ME
*Wells, F. L.	Virginia, ME,S
*Wells, Jere	North Georgia, ME,S
*West, C. D.	Mississippi, MP
*Westfall, J. B.	West Virginia, MP
Whaling, H. M., Jr.	Texas, ME,S
*Wharton, J. H.	Oklahoma, ME,S
Wheaton, James D.	Mississippi, ME
*Wheaton, Miss Ruth (10-18; 11-15; 12-8)	Ohio, ME
*Whisler, Alvin R.	Southern California, ME
Whitaker, H. W. (5-4)	Kentucky, ME,S
White, Charles M.	Blue Ridge-Atlantic, ME
White, R. W. (10-31; 11-16)	Maryland, MP
Whitehead, T. J.	North Carolina, MP
Whitiker, Charles E.	West Texas, ME
*Whitley, Henry (10-37)	Arkansas, MP
*Wickline, Robert L.	Pittsburgh, ME
*Wilkinson, J. W. F.	Erie, ME
*Will, Herman, Jr. (R.C.; 3-15; 3-17; 7-9)	Rock River, ME
Williams, E. B.	North Arkansas, ME,S
Williams, G. Ellis	Baltimore, ME
Williams, H. E.	Iowa-Missouri, MP
Williams, Thomas F.	Northwest Indiana, ME
*Williams, Walter	Indiana, MP
*Williamson, William T.	West Virginia, ME
*Wilson, Harwell	Florida, ME,S
Wilson, J. H.	South Georgia, ME,S
*Wilson, Miss Retta I.	India, ME
*Wimberly, R. S.	South Georgia, ME,S
*Windels, Charles M. (R.C.; 2-3)	East German, ME
*Windham, W. C.	Texas, ME,S
*Winter, Miss Bert	North Georgia, ME,S
*Wiseman, W. H. (6-6)	Tennessee, ME,S
Wolfe, John L.	West Virginia, ME
Womack, W. Vance (9-26; 10-23)	North Arkansas, ME,S
*Wong, Miss Pearl	China, ME
Woodard, Abram S.	Indiana, ME
*Woodley, Mark	Southern Illinois, ME
*Woods, Mrs. Rufus	Pacific Northwest, ME

The Methodist Church 111

Name	Conference and Church
*Woodson, J. R.	... Texas, ME,S
*Woodworth, W. W.	....................Oklahoma, ME,S
Worley, E. D.	. . Holston, ME,S
Worley, Lloyd F.	...............................New York East, ME
Wright, Cal C.	................Northwest Texas, ME,S
*Wright, Mrs. Frank S.	.. Vermont, ME
*Wright, Harry B.	.... Wilmington, ME
*Wright, Thomas S.	North Carolina, ME
Wright, W. F.	..Maryland, MP
Yarbrough, J. F.	.........North Georgia, ME,S
Yates, Earl U. (10-7)	Southern Illinois, ME
Yeager, I. L.	..... Louisiana, MP
Young, Claude	....Northwest Indiana, ME
Young, S. H. (1-5)	....................Northwest Texas, ME,S
*Ziegler, Mrs. Bernhard C.	.Wisconsin, ME
*Zimmerman, Henry M. (9-7)	. Kentucky, ME

GENERAL STANDING COMMITTEES

NO. 1. COMMITTEE ON CONFERENCES

"To which shall be referred all rules and regulations, memorials, petitions, etc., relating to Church, Quarterly, District, Annual, Jurisdictional, Central, General, and other Conferences."

GEORGE W. HENSON, *Chairman;* J. N. R. SCORE, *Vice-Chairman;* ROY H. SHORT, *Secretary.*

(* Denotes Lay Delegate)

Name	Annual Conference and Church
Abbott, Benjamin F.	Central West, ME
Abernathy, John R.	Oklahoma, ME,S
*Adkins, Fred P.	Maryland, MP
*Anderson, J. Edward	Central Northwest, ME
Arvidson, Theodore	Europe, ME
Barnard, Lawrence M.	Erie, ME
Barton, K. P.	West Texas, ME,S
Bell, C. C.	Virginia, ME,S
Blackburn, R. T.	Oklahoma, ME,S
*Boyd, David A.	Florida, ME
*Brewer, R. L., Jr.	Virginia, ME,S
*Brock, W. E.	Holston, ME,S
Bunting, John J.	Wilmington, ME
Burns, J. E.	West Virginia, MP
*Calhoun, Galloway	Texas, ME,S
Canter, Harry M.	Baltimore, ME,S
*Carman, Edward R.	New York East, ME
Cartwright, Frank T.	China, ME
Casaday, T. C.	Alabama, MP
*Clark, B. C.	Oklahoma, ME,S
Clarke, Fred	Indiana, MP
Clarke, H. P.	Virginia, ME,S
*Coble, M. A.	North Carolina, MP
*Coleman, Wade H.	Western Virginia, ME,S
Coleman, William H.	Arizona, ME,S
*Collins, Elmer E.	Montana State, ME
Court, Frank W.	Upper Iowa, ME
*Crabbe, George W.	Baltimore, ME
Curtis, V. C.	North Mississippi, ME,S
Curtis, W. M.	Alabama, ME,S
*Davidson, H. O.	New Mexico, ME,S
Davison, Samuel T.	Erie, ME
*Dickinson, Luren D.	Michigan, ME
*Ding, Mrs. Emily	China, ME
Dixon, L. E.	Kansas, MP
*Dunham, H. A.	Western North Carolina, ME,S
Dunkle, William F.	Florida, ME,S
*Easter, John E.	Baltimore, ME,S

The Methodist Church

113

Name	Annual Conference and Church
Edwards, John R.	Baltimore, ME
*Ellison, J. T.	Alabama, ME,S
Engebretsen, Frederik	Western Norwegian-Danish, ME
Engle, James W.	West Virginia, ME
Fesmire, William J.	Central Tennessee, ME
Fowler, George A.	Rock River, ME
Fribley, Fremont E.	North Indiana, ME
Frye, Irvin.	South Carolina, MP
*Garrison, E. J.	North Alabama, ME,S
*Graver, E. H.	Ohio, MP
*Greenslit, Henry M.	Nebraska, ME
Greer, R. E.	Holston, ME,S
Hamlett, Earl G.	Memphis, ME,S
Hargett, Ira M.	Oklahoma, ME
*Harman, J. H.	Louisville, ME,S
Harrell, L. A.	South Georgia, ME,S
Hartman, Lewis O.	New England, ME
Haver, Mathias S.	Europe, ME
Henson, George W.	Philadelphia, ME
Hickman, Frank S.	North Carolina, ME,S
Hinkle, D. E.	Tennessee, ME,S
Hislop, Edward	Missouri, ME
*Holler, J. C.	Upper South Carolina, ME,S
*Hollis, Carl	Little Rock, ME,S
*Hooper, Granville	Wilmington, ME
*Hoover, Arthur L.	Northeast Ohio, ME
Hughes, William A. C.	Washington, ME
Hunt, B. M.	Mississippi, ME,S
*Jones, David D.	North Carolina, ME
Jones, Edward M.	Central Alabama, ME
Jordan, G. Ray	Western North Carolina, ME,S
*Jordan, Miles W.	Texas, ME
Judd, Albert G.	Northern New York, ME
Keen, Samuel A.	Genesee, ME
*Kemp, Cary A.	Northwest Kansas, ME
Kenney, John R.	Pacific, ME,S
Kestle, Asa J.	Ohio, ME
Keve, Wiley A.	Kansas, ME
*Kyle, John W.	North Mississippi, ME,S
Lambeth, W. A.	Western North Carolina, ME,S
*Locke, A. W.	West Virginia, MP
*Martin, Boyce	Central Texas, ME,S
Martin, Eldon H.	Vermont, ME
*McComas, Warren	Iowa-Missouri, MP
McCoy, E. L.	South Carolina, ME,S
*McCulloch, Stephen W.	Southern California, ME
*McElroy, George S.	Georgia, ME
*McGinnis, H. B.	Tennessee, ME,S
*Meek, Paul	Memphis, ME,S
Moffatt, Elbert M.	India, ME

Name	Annual Conference and Church
*Onderdonk, Mrs. F. S.	Texas Mexican, ME,S
Orear, E. H.	St. Louis, ME,S
Parker, F. N.	Louisiana, ME,S
*Patton, John A.	Lexington, ME
Pearce, W. M.	Northwest Texas, ME,S
Pierce, A. M.	North Georgia, ME,S
*Pinckney, Thaddeus H.	South Carolina, ME
Prichard, J. E.	North Carolina, MP
*Purvance, Ernest	Northwest, ME,S
*Redwine, M. C.	Kentucky, ME,S
Rice, Samuel C.	Kentucky, ME
Richardson, Channing A.	California, ME
*Riggs, Mrs. Jeptha	St. Louis, ME,S
*Roberts, E. Howard	Wisconsin, ME
*Roberts, Warren	South Georgia, ME,S
Rugg, Earle M.	India, ME
Ryan, Harry G.	North Texas, ME,S
Sandmeyer, Edwin G.	Illinois, ME
Schevenius, Carl W.	Norwegian and Danish, ME
Score, J. N. R.	Central Texas, ME,S
*Self, W. D.	North Alabama, ME,S
*Sexton, Mrs. G. S., Jr.	Louisville, ME,S
Short, Roy H.	Louisville, ME,S
Sigg, Ferdinand	Europe, ME
*Slaughter, N. G.	North Georgia, ME,S
*Smith, W. T.	Pittsburgh, MP
*Spurgeon, William H.	Colorado, ME
Stanton, Daniel H.	Atlanta, ME
Stapleton, Robert L.	Holston, ME
Steinkraus, John H.	East German, ME
*Stevens, B. M.	Mississippi, ME,S
Stevenson, H. M.	North Alabama, ME,S
*Stuck, Charles A.	North Arkansas, ME,S
Taylor, B. P.	Western Virginia, ME,S
*Tilley, Mrs. M. E.	North Georgia, ME,S
*Tyler, Mrs. Fannie D.	Washington, ME
Tyson, W. Galloway	Philadelphia, ME
*Van Deusen, Henry R.	Wyoming, ME
*Vincent, E. R.	Michigan, MP
Wahl, Frederick W.	Missouri, ME
Westerberg, Thor J.	Central Northwest, ME
*Williams, Miss Arsania M.	Central West, ME
Williams, J. C.	Ohio, MP
*Willson, J. M.	Northwest Texas, ME,S
Wilson, Guy H.	Texas, ME,S
*Wilson, O. L.	Fort Smith-Oklahoma, MP
*Woosley, O. V.	Western North Carolina, ME,S

NO. 2. COMMITTEE ON MINISTRY AND JUDICIAL ADMINISTRATION

"To which shall be referred all rules and regulations, memorials, petitions, etc., regarding Bishops, traveling preachers, and local preachers, pastors, and presiding elders or district superintendents; trial and appeal, and the Judicial Council."

ORIEN W. FIFER, *Chairman;* HENRY M. ANDREWS, *Vice-Chairman;* FRANK L. SHAFFER, *Secretary.*

(* Denotes Lay Delegate)

Name	Annual Conference and Church
*Acker, T. E.	Texas, ME,S
Aitken, Walter	Nebraska, ME
*Anderson, W. T.	South Georgia, ME,S
Andrews, Henry M.	Alabama, ME,S
Andrews, R. M.	North Carolina, MP
Arvidson, Theodore	Europe, ME
*Babb, R. E.	Upper South Carolina, ME,S
Baggett, John F.	Tennessee, ME,S
Baker, Earle A.	Upper Iowa, ME
*Baldwin, Clinton D.	Maine, ME
*Bartak, Joseph P.	Czechoslovak, ME,S
*Bartak, Mrs. Joseph P.	Czechoslovak, ME,S
*Batts, W. O.	Tennessee, ME,S
Bayley, Francis R.	Baltimore, ME
Beck, Bert D.	Northwest Indiana, ME
Beery, Edgar C.	Baltimore, ME,S
*Beeson, M. A.	Oklahoma, ME,S
Bell, George M.	Wyoming, ME
*Bethune, Mrs. Mary M.	South Florida, ME
*Bright, George W.	Western Virginia, ME,S
Brown, Earl R.	Northeast Ohio, ME
Buckner, Walter C.	Southern California, ME
Burgum, Leslie R.	North Dakota, ME
Butler, J. E.	Arkansas, MP
*Cantlin, Jacob	Rock River, ME
*Carr, R. B.	North Alabama, ME,S
*Childers, M. A.	West Texas, ME,S
Clark, J. L.	Kentucky, ME,S
Claypool, James V.	New England Southern, ME
*Cooper, Elridge M.	West Texas, ME
*Cooper, W. B.	North Carolina, ME,S
Crane, Henry H.	Detroit, ME
Davenport, G. M.	North Alabama, ME,S
*Davis, D. H.	South Carolina, MP
*Davis, Joseph H.	Illinois, ME,S
Deschner, Phil	Oklahoma, ME
Dewey, Elmer C.	Georgia, ME
*Dolliver, James I.	Northwest Iowa, ME
*Eanes, Ennis E.	Virginia, ME,S
*Elliott, Wesley T.	Virginia, ME,S

Name	· Annual Conference and Church
Farmer, R. I....................................	Ohio, MP
Fifer, Orien W.........................	Indiana, ME
Fletcher, Maynard O..........	Blue Ridge-Atlantic, ME
Foglesong, W. H.	Western Virginia, ME,S
Foster, Lloyd E.	Newark, ME
*Fowler, Carl H.	New York, ME
Freeman, H. T.	South Georgia, ME,S
French, J. Stewart	Holston, ME,S
*Gettle, Homer R. .	North Indiana, ME
*Gibbs, Merton S.	Genesee, ME
Glenn, John C. ..	Southwest Missouri, ME,S
Golden, James W. .	Tennessee, ME
Goodwin, Levi P. ..	Iowa-Des Moines, ME
Grant, T. McM. .	North Carolina, ME,S
*Griffin, DeWitt..............................	Florida, ME,S
Hall, Claude C. ...	Southern Illinois, ME
*Hammer, Mrs. W. C. . .	North Carolina, MP
Hanna, F. B... .	Illinois, MP
Hardin, Smith	Florida, ME,S
*Harrah, Ezra C. ..	Colorado, ME
Harris, Inis D. .	Southwest Kansas, ME
*Harris, Nat .	Central Texas, ME,S
*Harrison, F. M.	Virginia, MP
*Herrigel, Fred, Jr.	Maryland, MP
Hills, Roy O..............................	Wyoming State, ME
*Holland, C. O..............................	Louisiana, ME,S
Holloway, F. G.	Maryland, MP
Holmes, W. W......	Louisiana, ME,S
Hooten, C. R. .	Northwest Texas, ME,S
*Houston, J. G. ...	North Mississippi, ME,S
Hummel, G. W...	Louisville, ME,S
Hutchinson, Forney	Oklahoma, ME,S
*Ivey, J. B.	Western North Carolina, ME,S
James, Glenn C..........................	St. Johns River, ME
*Jardine, Mrs. Florence Resor	North Minnesota, ME
Johnson, Levi E..........................	Mississippi, ME
*Johnston, Smith L. .	North Georgia, ME,S
Johnston, Warren ...	North Arkansas, ME,S
Jones, Frank B..	Memphis, ME,S
Jones, Guy F.	Texas, ME,S
*Judd, Zebulon V.	Alabama, ME,S
Kaub, Louis H..............................	Nebraska, ME
Kaung, Z. T..............................	China, ME,S
Kelley, C. I.	Tennessee, MP
King, James F.	Missouri, ME
King, William P...	North Georgia, ME,S
King, Willis J... .	West Texas, ME
*Koonce, A. J..... ..	North Carolina, MP
*Lamar, George H. . .	Baltimore, ME,S
*Love, Marvin F.. ...	North Texas, ME,S
Lyons, Ernest S. . .Malaysia and Philippine-Islands, ME

Name	Annual Conference and Church
*Lyons, Leslie J.	Missouri, ME

MacCaughey, Charles	Pacific Northwest, ME
Martin, Arba	Ohio, ME
Martin, Paul E.	North Texas, ME,S
*McKay, Leo H.	Erie, ME
*McMurry, William F.	Memphis, ME,S
Miller, Isaac E.	Ohio, ME
Morris, R. F.	Upper South Carolina, ME,S

*Noble, Enrique	Cuba, ME,S
*Noble, Fred B.	St. Johns River, ME

*Odell, Albert C.	Central New York, ME

*Pace, J. W.	Georgia, MP
*Parker, Mrs. R. J.	Western Mexican, ME,S
Pellowe, Albert H.	Michigan, ME
Penick, Richard O.	Kansas, ME
*Pewett, Mrs. Henkel	North Arkansas, ME,S
Piper, Joseph D.	Pittsburgh, ME
Plyler, A. W.	Western North Carolina, ME,S
Potts, J. Manning	Virginia, ME,S
*Potts, W. O.	North Mississippi, MP
Pugh, Abraham W.	North Indiana, ME

*Randal, Mrs. C. M.	Northwest Texas, ME,S
Reves, C. M.	Little Rock, ME,S
Rice, Merton S.	Detroit, ME
*Roan, Hans J.	Idaho, ME
Rugg, Earle M.	India, ME

Searles, J. Wesley	Genesee, ME
Shaffer, F. L.	West Virginia, MP
Shaw, J. Beverly F.	Mississippi, ME
Sigg, Ferdinand	Europe, ME
*Smith, Chester A.	New York, ME
Spellman, L. U.	West Texas, ME,S
*Sproul, R. C., Sr.	Pittsburgh, MP
Stansell, Robert B.	Wisconsin, ME
Stater, Charles G.	West Virginia, ME
Stokes, Peter (deceased)	South Carolina, ME,S
Stribling, E. R.	Missouri, MP
Stringfellow, LeRoy W.	New Hampshire, ME
Sutherland, B. L.	Mississippi, ME,S
Swartz, Morris E.	Central Pennsylvania, ME

Tucker, Frank C.	Missouri, ME,S
*Tucker, Robert C.	Missouri, ME
*Tunnicliffe, John	California, ME
*Tynes, Mrs. L. A.	Holston, ME,S

Ward, W. W.	Central Texas, ME,S
Wasson, L. P.	North Mississippi, ME,S
*Wiant, Paul P.	China, ME
*Williams, F. E.	St. Louis, ME,S
Winchester, Robert W.	North Carolina, ME
*Woods, J. M.	Missouri, ME,S

Name	Annual Conference and Church
Woolever, Harry E.	. . . . Central New York, ME

| *Yang, Y. C. | .. . . China, ME,S |
| *Yoder, D. P. | . . . . Northwest Texas, ME,S |

NO. 3. COMMITTEE ON MEMBERSHIP AND TEMPORAL ECONOMY

"To which shall be referred all rules and regulations, memorials, petitions, etc., regarding church membership, and conditions, duties, and transfer thereof; regarding Lay Activities, Stewards, Trustees, property; financial system of the general and local church; and such activities of the Church at large in and through its institutions and boards as are not made the specific responsibility of any other Standing Committee."

W. F. BRYAN, *Chairman;* W. C. HARTINGER, *Vice-Chairman;* COSTEN J. HARRELL, *Secretary.*

(* Denotes Lay Delegate)

Name	Annual Conference and Church
*Andrew, Wray	. Southern California, ME
*Archer, William D.	Northeast Ohio, ME
*Arnold, W. Scott	Indiana, MP
Auman, Orrin W.	Colorado, ME
*Bancroft, E. Dow	Ohio, ME
Barr, W. L.	New Mexico, ME,S
*Beck, Jesse M.	Iowa-Des Moines, ME
*Bellomy, Edward	Kentucky, MP
*Bennett, Harry P.	New Jersey, ME
*Bethea, Dennis A.	Lexington, ME
Betz, W. H.	Iowa-Missouri, MP
*Bowman, John S.	South Carolina, ME,S
*Brandenberger, Max B.	Southern, ME
*Brooks, Morris H.	West Texas, ME,S
Bryan, W. F.	Texas, ME,S
*Bryant, R. B.	Northwest Texas, ME,S
*Campbell, John B.	Northwest Indiana, ME
*Cannon, J. S. M.	Little Rock, ME,S
*Chaffee, H. Almon	New York East, ME
*Cherry, Hal H.	Central Texas, ME,S
*Cherry, James	Northeast Ohio, ME
*Clark, Anson C.	Vermont, ME
*Clark, Samuel H.	Newark, ME
*Clark, W. Dale	Nebraska, ME
*Clarke, Vincent P.	New England, ME
Clowers, C. D.	Virginia, MP
*Cohagen, Stephen A.	Upper Iowa, ME
Coors, D. Stanley	Michigan, ME
Courtney, Homer W.	Northeast Ohio, ME
*Crawford, Alfred C.	Rock River, ME
Culver, Frank P.	Central Texas, ME,S
Curl, R. F.	West Texas, ME,S
*Davis, Warren H.	New Hampshire, ME
Dawson, Dana	Louisiana, ME,S

Name	Annual Conference and Church
*Deal, Edson H......	Idaho, ME
*Dickey, J. H...	...Louisville, ME,S
*Ellis, P. M.	Ohio, MP
*Evans, Charles W.	West Virginia, ME
*Evans, Paul F.	Western North Carolina, ME,S
*Fondren, W. W. (deceased)......................	Texas, ME,S
*French, Mrs. H. A.	Kansas, ME
Given, W. M.	Western Virginia, ME,S
*Goddard, J. J...........................	Alabama, MP
Gomez, Abel M.	Western Mexican, ME,S
*Gray, George H.	Nebraska, ME
Green, J. L.	Maryland, MP
*Greene, W. K.	North Carolina, ME,S
*Hanke, Charles W.	Missouri, ME
Hargis, David H.	Delaware, ME
Harrell, Costen J. .	Tennessee, ME,S
Hartinger, William C.	Indiana, ME
*Hillman, J. N.	Holston, ME,S
*Hole, John W.	Southern California, ME
Holliday, Robert C. . . . .·-·· ...	Missouri, ME,S
*Hollingsworth, Mrs. H. S..	Iowa-Des Moines, ME
*Holmes, Miss Leota	Central Tennessee, ME
*Howe, Charles P...	Pittsburgh, ME
*Hunt, Walter L.	Wyoming, ME
*Ivins, Lester S...	.... Ohio, ME
*James, James A.	Rock River, ME
*Jordan, Mrs. W. O.	North Texas, ME,S
*Kennedy, Mrs. Robert C. . . .	Blue Ridge-Atlantic, ME
*Kirby, A. N.	North Alabama, ME,S
Kirkpatrick, Charles S. . ..	Western North Carolina, ME,S
*Knight, W. L.	North Carolina, ME,S
LaPrade, W. H.	North Georgia, ME,S
Lee, J. W.	Louisiana, MP
Leonard, Harry C.	Southern, ME
*Lynch, G. Stanley	Philadelphia, ME
Magee, John B...	Pacific Northwest, ME
Martin, Albert W. . . .	.North Arkansas, ME,S
Martin, I. P.	Holston, ME,S
Mathis, W. T.	Illinois, ME,S
*McFall, Carl S.	Oklahoma, ME,S
*McNorton, Mrs. Dorothy E.. . .	East Tennessee, ME
McPheeters, J. C.....................	Pacific, ME,S
*McQuiston, Jackson C. . . .	Pittsburgh, ME
Meeks, C. M. .	South Georgia, ME,S
Mills, Edward L.	Oregon, ME
Mills, J. W..	Texas, ME
*Moore, LeRoy.	Upper South Carolina, ME,S
*Morelock, George L.	Memphis, ME,S

Name	Annual Conference and Church
Morris, W. E.	North Alabama, ME,S
Nicholson, J. H.	Louisville, ME,S
*Peck, Arthur D.	Alabama, ME
Peele, C. E.	Upper South Carolina, ME,S
Perkins, A. R.	Kentucky, ME,S
Perry, John W.	Wisconsin, ME
*Phelps, W. R.	Virginia, ME,S
Pulliam, William G.	Illinois, ME
Ramos, Frank	Texas Mexican, ME,S
Riddick, R. .P.	Virginia, ME,S
*Robinson, Milton C.	Northeast Ohio, ME
*Rogers, Walter S.	Nebraska, ME
*Rosenberger, J. H.	Baltimore, ME,S
*Sapp, Mrs. C. C.	South Georgia, ME,S
Schlagenhauf, Ira E.	Wisconsin, ME
*Schwaninger, W. W.	Indiana, ME
Sharp, F. L.	Mississippi, MP
*Shaw, Harry	Pittsburgh, MP
Shelton, William A.	North Georgia, ME,S
*Sherman, L. L.	Arkansas, MP
Skillington, J. Edgar	Central Pennsylvania, ME
Smathers, M. T.	Western North Carolina, ME,S
Smith, H. C.	North Carolina, ME,S
*Smith, R. J.	Southwest Missouri, ME,S
Smith, Ulysses S.	Iowa-Des Moines, ME
*Snavely, Herschell R.	Illinois, ME
Spragins, C. A.	North Texas, ME,S
*Staley, H. C.	Maryland, MP
Starkey, L. M.	Southwest Missouri, ME,S
*Stauffacher, Charles J.	Africa, ME
*Stephens, F. F.	Missouri, ME,S
*Stilwell, H. W.	Texas, ME,S
*Strong, Dennis F.	Detroit, ME
*Sullivan, J. M.	Mississippi, ME,S
*Sweet, E. M., Jr.	Pacific, ME,S
Sydenstricker, Hubert	Baltimore, ME,S
*Sykes, W. Clyde	Northern New York, ME
Taggart, J. H.	Southwest, ME
*Talbert, Mrs. H. L.	North Mississippi, ME,S
Taylor, S. W.	North Carolina, MP
*Tompkins, O. L.	Alabama, ME,S
*Waggoner, Merle T.	North Texas, ME,S
*Weaver, Mrs. C. C.	Western North Carolina, ME,S
*Webb, W. R.	Tennessee, ME,S
*Welch, Edgar T.	Erie, ME
*Whitcher, Frank O.	West Wisconsin, ME
*White, H. H.	Louisiana, ME,S
Whitehurst, B. G.	North Mississippi, MP
*Wilcox, William H.	Oklahoma, ME
*Wilson, Herbert S.	Delaware, ME
*Wren, Los L.	North Carolina, MP

Name	Annual Conference and Church
*Wright, Harry B.	Wilmington, ME
Wright, William A.	Virginia, ME,S

NO. 4. COMMITTEE ON MISSIONS, CHURCH EXTENSION, ETC.

"To which shall be referred all rules and regulations, memorials, petitions, etc., relating to all Missions and Missionary Organizations, Church Extension, Hospitals, Homes, Deaconesses, Temperance and Public Morals, Evangelism, and the American Bible Society."

JOHN R. MOTT, *Chairman;* NATHAN NEWBY, *1st Vice-Chairman;* MRS. W. C. HAMMER, *2d Vice-Chairman;* H. P. MYERS, *Secretary.*

(* Denotes Lay Delegate)

Name	Annual. Conference and Church
*Adams, Charles V.	Central Pennsylvania, ME
*Asbury, Mrs. Hattie E.	Indiana, ME
*Awtrey, Mrs. L. M.	North Georgia, ME,S
*Baker, John H.	Maryland, MP
*Baldwin, Howard C.	Detroit, ME
*Banker, H. F.	Texas, ME,S
Barnes, S. A.	North Texas, ME
*Barss, Mrs. E. K.	Ohio, MP
Bartlay, Henry W.	Florida, ME
Bates, C. W.	North Carolina, MP
Berry, Arthur D.	Japan, ME
Bickley, C. A.	Northwest Texas, ME,S
*Black, Mrs. Henry C.	Holston, ME
*Blackstock, Mrs. Ira B.	Illinois, ME
Blue, Willard H.	Tennessee, ME,S
Browers, J. W.	Fort Smith-Oklahoma, MP
*Brown, Mrs. W. Raymond	Genesee, ME
*Bryan, Mrs. Gid J.	Central Texas, ME,S
Bullock, Dillman S.	South America, ME
*Cannon, James T.	Kentucky, ME,S
*Canter, Noland M.	Baltimore, ME,S
*Carver, G. C.	New Mexico, ME,S
*Chadwick, W. C.	North Carolina, ME,S
*Cherrington, Ernest H.	Ohio, ME
Chunn, Marcus M.	Central Texas, ME,S
Clements, E. E.	Cuba, ME,S
Cockrell, S. K.	Baltimore, ME,S
Corcoran, Sanford W.	Pittsburgh, ME
Cram, Willard G.	Kentucky, ME,S
*Dangel, Mrs. William H.	Rock River, ME
Davis, Newton E.	Northeast Ohio, ME
*Denman, Harry	North Alabama, ME,S
*DeWeese, H. O.	Indiana, MP
Diekmann, John A.	Ohio, ME
Diffendorfer, Ralph E.	Rock River, ME
*Dillon, Mrs. B. E.	Missouri, MP
Ding, Samson S.	China, ME
*Duhigg, Miss Ada B.	Missouri, ME
*DuRant, Charlton	South Carolina, ME,S

Name	Annual Conference and Church
*Eggleston, Charles F.	Philadelphia, ME
*Elliott, William J.	Philadelphia, ME
Ellis, Thomas D.	South Georgia, ME,S
Emmons, Grover C.	Pacific, ME,S
Farrar, George E.	St. Johns River, ME
*Freeman, Mrs. Jane H.	Ohio, ME
Fruit, Walter R.	Detroit, ME
Garrett, W. B.	Upper South Carolina, ME,S
Garrison, E. K.	South Carolina, ME,S
*Gibson, Miss Henrietta	Troy, ME
Goddard, O. E.	North Arkansas, ME,S
*Godfrey, Mrs. F. B.	Florida, ME,S
*Goode, Mrs. W. H. C.	Ohio, ME
*Hammer, Mrs. W. C.	North Carolina, MP
Hammons, J. D.	Little Rock, ME,S
*Hardin, J. C.	Upper South Carolina, ME,S
*Hawkins, W. D.	Mississippi, ME,S
Hawley, J. W.	Pittsburgh, MP
*Hedden, Henry	Memphis, ME,S
Hertzog, William H.	Idaho, ME
Hess, Harry E.	Nebraska, ME
Howard, Arthur R.	South Carolina, ME
Hunton, W. M.	Georgia, MP
*Ingram, I. S.	North Georgia, ME,S
*Jones, Charles A.	Ohio, ME
Kaung, Z. T.	China, ME,S
Kimbrough, S. O.	North Alabama, ME,S
*Kirby, A. J.	Western North Carolina, ME,S
Kirk, Albert E.	Southwest Kansas, ME
Kohlstedt, Edward D.	Dakota, ME
*Lamb, Mrs. Fred A.	Southwest Missouri, ME,S
*Lee, Elizabeth M.	Pittsburgh, ME
*LeSourd, Mrs. Lucile L.	New England, ME
*Lindsay, Mrs. F. F.	Northern Minnesota, ME
Love, F. S.	North Carolina, ME,S
*MacKinnon, Miss Sallie Lou	North Carolina, ME,S
*Maddin, P. D.	Tennessee, ME,S
*Masland, J. Wesley	Philadelphia, ME
*McConnell, Mrs. Francis J.	New York, ME
*McDonald, T. Morton	Indiana, ME
Mecklenberg, George	Northern Minnesota, ME
*Melton, C. G.	North Arkansas, ME,S
*Mills, Mrs. J. W.	Texas, ME,S
Moore, Aubrey S.	Rock River, ME
Moore, J. W.	Virginia, ME,S
Morange, John	Montana State, ME
*Morris, Mrs. Isaac	North Alabama, ME,S
*Mott, John R.	New York, ME
Mueller, Frederick W.	Northeast Ohio, ME
Myers, H. P.	Virginia, ME,S

Name	Annual Conference and Church
*Newby, Nathan	Pacific, ME,S
Newell, Fred B.	New York East, ME
*Newton, H. E.	Oklahoma, ME,S
*Nicholson, Mrs. Evelyn R.	Upper Iowa, ME
Norton, M. H.	Florida, ME,S
*Oldshue, Mrs. James.	Rock River, ME
*Oram, Miss E. Jean	Northeast Ohio, ME
Ormond, J. M.	North Carolina, ME,S
*Overdeer, Willis L.	Wilmington, ME
*Peel, David T.	West Texas, ME,S
Peeples, Fred H.	Memphis, ME,S
Pegues, D. K.	Missouri, ME,S
Perry, Jack W.	Holston, ME,S
*Perry, Mrs. Jack W.	Holston, ME,S
*Piggott, Mrs. W. J.	Louisville, ME,S
*Post, Mrs. Ancel B.	West Virginia, MP
*Pritchard, William P.	New England Southern, ME
Roberts, George A.	Africa, ME
Robinson, LeRoy T.	Michigan, ME
*Rogers, A. C.	Alabama, MP
Rogers, Wallace	North Georgia, ME,S
Rosenberger, S. W.	Ohio, MP
*Roudebush, Roy R.	North Indiana, ME
Russell, Robert L.	North Georgia, ME,S
Schatzman, Albert G.	Ohio, ME
Shaw, William E.	Illinois, ME
*Shepard, C. L.	South Georgia, ME,S
Shumway, H. L.	Kentucky, MP
Slack, W. B.	Oklahoma, ME,S
Smith, Benjamin F.	Lexington, ME
Smith, Roy L.	Southern California, ME
Straughn, James H.	Maryland, MP
Swain, W. R.	Texas, ME,S
*Tatum, Mrs. S. Homer	Memphis, ME,S
*Taylor, Dean	Iowa-Des Moines, ME
*Thomas, Lavens M.	Holston, ME,S
Thonger, William G.	Belgian, ME,S
*Trotter, Frank H.	Holston, ME
*Vickery, William M.	Oklahoma, ME
Warmer, George A.	Southern California, ME
*Watson, Miss Ella M.	Nebraska, ME
Weaver, C. C.	Western North Carolina, ME,S
Weaver, G. Charles	Onondaga, MP
*Wells, Luther W.	Virginia, ME,S
Wright, Louis C.	Northeast Ohio, ME
Wroten, J. D.	North Mississippi, ME,S

NO. 5. COMMITTEE ON EDUCATION

"To which shall be referred all rules and regulations, memorials, petitions, etc., relating to all Universities, Colleges, Wesley Foundations, Schools, Seminaries, Ministerial Training, World Peace, Religious Education in the local church, including Young People's Activities and literature for church schools."

PAUL W. QUILLIAN, *Chairman;* DANIEL L. MARSH, *Vice-Chairman;* DWIGHT S. JEFFERS, *Secretary.*

(* Denotes Lay Delegate)

Name	Annual Conference and Church
Alexander, W. M.	Missouri, ME,S
Allison, Oscar E.	Kansas, ME
Anderson, William K.	Pittsburgh, ME
Baker, Clem.	Little Rock, ME,S
*Baker, Richard T.	Upper Iowa, ME
*Barnett, W. K.	Holston, ME,S
Bartak, J. P.	Czechoslovak, ME,S
*Bennett, Alvis S.	Kentucky, ME
Blackburn, Henry W.	Florida, ME,S
Bowen, C. A.	Mississippi, ME,S
*Bragg, Mrs. Grace L.	Missouri, ME
Brown, Arlo A.	Newark, ME
Brown, F. L.	Ohio, MP
Buck, Ernest F.	Kansas, ME
Bugbee, Lucius H.	Northern Minnesota, ME
Burgstahler, Herbert J.	Upper Iowa, ME
*Burnham, Smith	Michigan, ME
Callaghan, Arthur A.	Maine, ME
*Candler, John S.	North Georgia, ME,S
*Carter, Harry V.	Oklahoma, ME
Coman, Alfred P.	Central New York, ME
*Condron, S. H.	Northwest Texas, ME,S
Corley, Jesse L.	Southern California, ME
Countiss, John R.	North Mississippi, ME,S
*Cox, Harvey W.	North Georgia, ME,S
Crockett, O. B.	Kentucky, ME,S
*Cullins, John S.	Southwest, ME
*Dannelly, C. M.	Alabama, ME,S
*Das, Mrs. C. Premnath	India, ME
Dogan, Matthew W.	Texas, ME
*Douglas, Hiram A.	Northern Minnesota, ME
*Downs, Mrs. Ward M.	Western Virginia, ME,S
*Dunlap, Mrs. E. B.	Oklahoma, ME,S
Eastwood, W. P.	Holston, ME,S
Ellison, R. R.	Alabama, ME,S
Estes, Lud H.	Memphis, ME,S
Evans, L. L.	Oklahoma, ME,S
*Feaster, Mrs. J. T.	Florida, ME,S
Ferguson, John L.	Tennessee, ME,S
*Few, W. P.	North Carolina, ME,S
*Fletcher, John S.	Holston, ME
Ford, J. Emerson	South Carolina, ME,S
Forlines, C. E.	North Carolina, MP
Freeman, A. M.	North Alabama, ME,S

Name	Annual Conference and Church
Geissinger, E. Lamont	Nebraska, ME
*Gobbel, L. L.	Western North Carolina, ME,S
Grannum, Stanley E.	West Texas, ME
*Gray, Mrs. C. M.	Southwest Kansas, ME
*Halmhuber, Paul G.	Detroit, ME
*Harmer, Mrs. Harvey W. . . .	West Virginia, ME
Hatcher, Sam C.	Virginia, ME,S
Hawk, E. B.	Central Texas, ME,S
Haymes, J. O.	Northwest Texas, ME,S
Hillman, E. L.	North Carolina, ME,S
Hooper, T. LeRoy	Pittsburgh, MP
Hough, Lynn Harold	New York East, ME
Hughes, Alfred F.	West Wisconsin, ME
Humphreys, G. I.	Maryland, MP
*Jackson, H. E.	West Texas, ME,S
*James, T. L.	Louisiana, ME,S
*Jeffers, Dwight S.	Pacific Northwest, ME
Johns, H. L.	Louisiana, ME,S
*Johnson, T. L.	Louisiana, MP
Kelley, Mark	Troy, ME
Ketcham, Charles B.	Northeast Ohio, ME
*Kibler, Russell M.	Indiana, ME
Kitto, Charles W.	Philadelphia, ME
Knoles, Tully C.	California, ME
Knudson, Albert C.	New England Southern, ME
*Law, Clyde O.	West Virginia, ME
Lee, Umphrey	North Texas, ME,S
*Lewis, Miss Harriet	Colorado, ME
*Lowman, H. L.	Texas, ME,S
Lugg, Thomas B.	Illinois, ME
MacLea, Daniel	Maryland, MP
MacRossie, Allan	New York, ME
Mahoney, Carl K.	Pacific Northwest, ME
Marsh, Daniel L.	New England, ME
McCoy, Lee M.	Upper Mississippi, ME
McGiffin, James H. S.	Southern California, ME
*McGowan, J. G.	North Mississippi, ME,S
McPherson, Harry W.	Illinois, ME
Miles, Minor C.	West Virginia, ME
*Miller, Ely D.	Ohio, MP
*Minga, Mrs. T. H.	North Texas, ME,S
*Mobley, M. R.	South Carolina, ME,S
Mullikin, W. L.	Upper South Carolina, ME,S
*Newcomb, O. P.	Virginia, ME,S
*Nutter, E. M.	West Virginia, MP
*Orwig, S. S.	Oklahoma, ME,S
*Parker, W. W.	St. Louis, ME,S
*Patterson, D. Stewart	Baltimore, ME

Name	Annual Conference and Church
Quillian, Paul	Texas, ME,S
Quillian, William F.	South Georgia, ME,S
*Randolph, Joseph B.	South Carolina, ME
*Redding, W. F., Jr.	North Carolina, MP
Reed, Marshall R.	Detroit, ME
*Reynolds, John H.	North Arkansas, ME,S
Richardson, J. A.	Texas, MP
Rising, Lloyd H.	Minnesota, ME
Roadman, Earl A.	Northwest Iowa, ME
*Robb, James L.	Holston, ME
*Robbins, Charles A.	Pacific Northwest, ME
Robertson, J. Calloway	Virginia, ME,S
*Roper, W. B.	Virginia, ME,S
Rumble, Lester	North Georgia, ME,S
Savige, George R.	Wyoming, ME
Schisler, J. Q.	North Arkansas, ME,S
Schofield, Charles E.	Colorado, ME
Seaton, John L.	Michigan, ME
Sexsmith, E. A.	Maryland, MP
Sherman, H. H.	Baltimore, ME,S
*Sherrod, C. C.	Holston, ME,S
Simpson, J. Fisher	West Texas, ME,S
Smith, Horace G.	Rock River, ME
Snyder, G. H.	West Virginia, MP
*Snyder, Henry N.	Upper South Carolina, ME,S
Sockman, Ralph W.	New York, ME
*Sone, Law	Central Texas, ME,S
Soper, Edmund D.	Ohio, ME
Stanbury, W. A.	Western North Carolina, ME,S
Sweet, William W.	North Indiana, ME
*Thompson, E. D.	Tennessee, ME,S
*Troxel, Miss Moneta J.	Korea, ME
*Van Cleave, A. B.	Tennessee, MP
*Veenboer, Mrs. William H.	Michigan, ME
*Ward, F. S.	North Alabama, ME,S
*Waterman, W. C.	Onondaga, MP
*Wight, J. Slater	South Georgia, ME,S
*Williamson, Nate S.	Mississippi, MP
*Womack, J. P.	North Arkansas, ME,S
*Womack, Richard E.	Memphis, ME,S
Woolf, E. L.	Baltimore, ME,S
*Yang, Y. C.	China, ME,S
Yost, Clark R.	Southern Illinois, ME

NO. 6. COMMITTEE ON PUBLISHING INTERESTS

"To which shall be referred all rules and regulations, memorials, petitions, etc., relating to Publishing Houses, Book Committees, and the publication of periodicals and books."

ALFRED M. LANDON, *Chairman;* PAUL N. GARBER, *1st Vice-Chairman;* GEORGE R. BROWN, *2d Vice-Chairman;* JOHN B. F. YOAK, JR., *Secretary.*

Name	Annual Conference and Church
Alsworth, W. B.	Mississippi, ME,S

(* Denotes Lay Delegate)

Name	Annual Conference and Church
Anderson, E. P. ...	Tennessee, ME,S
*Appleby, Troy W. .	Ohio, ME
*Barradell, William H. . .	New York East, ME
*Bartak, Mrs. M.	Czechoslovak, ME,S
*Beetham, Charles S. . .	Northeast Ohio, ME
*Benson, F. Murray	Maryland, MP
Bowen, John W. E.	Louisiana, ME
Brasher, John L.	Alabama, ME
*Briscoe, Arthur E...	Washington, ME
*Britton, Charles A., Jr. .	South Georgia, ME,S
Brooks, Robert N.	North Carolina, ME
Brown, George R. ...	North Carolina, MP
*Caldwell, Gibson ...	North Texas, ME,S
Campbell, C. K.	New Mexico, ME,S
*Carter, Fred A.	Holston, ME,S
*Carter, J. H.	Louisiana, ME,S
*Cash, W. L.	Louisville, ME,S
*Clements, Theodore R.	Savannah, ME
*Coffman, C. S.	Baltimore, ME,S
*Cole, J. R., Jr.	Oklahoma, ME,S
*Cook, A. L.	Kansas, MP
*Crummey, John D...	California, ME
*Cunningham, Thomas O. .	Kansas, ME
Daniel, J. H.	Florida, ME,S
*Davage, Matthew S. .	Louisiana, ME
*Davidson, J. D....	Texas, MP
Douglass, George C.	Troy, ME
Duren, W. L.	Louisiana, ME,S
*Earp, W. L...	Southwest Missouri, ME,S
Eddins, J. S.	Alabama, MP
*Edwards, J. R.	Central Texas, ME,S
*Engebretsen, Glenn	Western Norwegian-Danish, ME
*Evans, John H.	Arizona, ME,S
*Fenstermacher, George E.	North Indiana, ME
*Fisher, B. L.	Virginia, ME,S
Fitch, Frank L.	Detroit, ME
*Fitch, Harold W.	Illinois, ME
*Foster, Chapin D.	Pacific Northwest, ME
French, George C.	North Texas, ME,S
*Frey, V. Max	Central Pennsylvania, ME
Garber, Paul N.	Western North Carolina, ME,S
Gray, Joseph M. M.	Detroit, ME
Hammond, Edmund J.	Georgia, ME
*Hardie, Mrs. Charles H.	New York East, ME
Harmon, Nolan B., Jr.	Baltimore, ME,S
Harper, E. J...	Northwest, ME,S
Harrison, Jabez C.	Oregon, ME
Heinsohn, Edmund .	West Texas, ME,S
Henry, W. G.	North Alabama, ME,S
*Hicks, J. B.	North Carolina, MP

Name	Annual Conference and Church
*High, J. H..	West Virginia, MP
*Hjerpe, Oscar W.	Eastern Swedish, ME
*Hood, Gurney P.	North Carolina, ME,S
*Horton, J. B.	Upper South Carolina, ME,S
Huse, Raymond H.	Central New York, ME
*Ingram, Ben L.	North Alabama, ME,S
*Jackson, W. W.	West Texas, ME,S
Jarrell, Charles C.	North Georgia, ME,S
Johnson, C. S.	Ohio, MP
Johnson, Silas	South Georgia, ME,S
Jones, Henry H.	North Georgia, ME,S
*Jones, J. A.	Western North Carolina, ME,S
*Joy, James R.	Newark, ME
*Keplinger, Warren H.	Ohio, ME
*Knight, George N.	North Dakota, ME
Kulp, Edmund J.	Missouri, ME
*Lambeth, James E.	Western North Carolina, ME,S
*Lance, T. Jack	North Georgia, ME,S
*Landon, Alfred M.	Kansas, ME
Langdale, John W.	New York East, ME
Lazenby, M. E.	North Alabama, ME,S
Lineberry, F. W.	Indiana, MP
*Lynn, Lee W.	Central Alabama, ME
Lyon, A. P.	Louisville, ME,S
*Mann, Earl M.	Northwest Indiana, ME
*Marr, P. M.	Missouri, ME,S
*Martin, Lester H.	Illinois, ME
*McAllister, Reuben H.	Mississippi, ME
*McKibben, Harold B.	Southwest Kansas, ME
*McKim, Judson J.	Ohio, ME
*McMullen, Stanley O.	New England, ME
Meeks, Benjamin W.	Baltimore, ME
*Mickelsen, M. E..	Norwegian and Danish, ME
Mitchell, B. M.	West Virginia, MP
*Moore, Victor K.	Troy, ME
Morgan, R. E. L.	Oklahoma, ME,S
*Nichols, R. H..	Northwest Texas, ME,S
*O'Neal, Mrs. Robert	Tennessee, ME,S
*Patel, J. S. K.	India, ME
Pearson, J. W.	Virginia, ME,S
*Perkins, W. C.	Pittsburgh, MP
*Peterson, Ernest W.	Oregon, ME
*Pettyjohn, O. R.	Virginia, ME,S
Plyler, M. T.	North Carolina, ME,S
*Propert, Frank C.	New Jersey, ME
Randolph, J. D..	Missouri, ME,S
*Reineke, George F.	Minnesota, ME
Rowe, Gilbert T.	Western North Carolina, ME,S

Name	Annual Conference and Church
*Ruff, A. C.	Illinois, MP
Rule, C. E.	Little Rock, ME,S

Sanders, William L.	East Tennessee, ME
*Scott, John T............................. ...	Texas, ME,S
*Seymour, Mrs. Jerome	Southern California, ME
Shipley, R. L.............................	Maryland, MP
Simpson, John A...........................	South Florida, ME
Slaughter, D. P.	Alabama, ME,S
Sloan, Harold P......................... .	New Jersey, ME
Smith, Albert N.......................	Northwest Kansas, ME
*Spencer, Robert B.	Colorado, ME
Stafford, Edward R..	Ohio, ME
Stevenson, M. A.....	Holston, ME,S
*Stinson, Mrs. J. M.	Little Rock, ME,S
Stone, Fred D.	Rock River, ME
*Stottlemire, F. E.	Ohio, MP

Tower, Joe Z.	Texas, ME,S

Underwood, J. Edgar	Memphis, ME,S

Walker, John M.............................	Indiana, ME
*Wardlaw, J. C.......................	North Georgia, ME,S
Washabaugh, J. Edgar	Newark, ME
Wayland, E. T.	North Arkansas, ME,S
*Webb, Mrs. Edna	Southern Illinois, ME
Wesley, Arthur.........................	South America, ME
White, E. E..	Northwest Texas, ME,S
*White, Mrs. M. H.	Northwest Iowa, ME
*Whitmore, Ben A.	Tennessee, ME,S
*Wiley, Henry S.	Illinois, ME
*Williams, J. M.	North Arkansas, ME,S
Williams, Robert M.	Washington, ME
Wilson, E. R.............................	Michigan, MP
*Windels, Charles M....	East German, ME
Winn, J. B..	Virginia, ME,S
*Worth, W. H.	Western North Carolina, ME,S

Yoak, J. B. F., Jr.....................	Western Virginia, ME,S
*Youngblood, Curtis	Mississippi, ME,S

NO. 7. COMMITTEE ON SUPERANNUATE SUPPORT

"To which shall be referred all rules and regulations, memorials, petitions, etc., relating to the support of superannuated or retired ministers, supernumerary ministers, and widows and dependent children of deceased ministers."

THOMAS S. BROCK, *Chairman;* A. M. WELLS, *Vice-Chairman;* A. T. MCILWAIN, *Secretary;* L. E. BEE, *Assistant Secretary.*

(* Denotes Lay Delegate)

Name	Annual Conference and Church
Baylor, J. A.............................	Holston, ME,S
Bee, L. E.............................	West Virginia, MP
Brock, Thomas S......	New Jersey, ME
Broomfield, J. C.	Pittsburgh, MP

Name	Annual Conference and Church
Chadwick, J. S.	North Alabama, ME,S
Clark, O. P.	Northwest Texas, ME,S
*Coleman, Walter J.	Upper Mississippi, ME
Davis, Henry L.	Northwest Indiana, ME
Dell, J. P.	South Georgia, ME,S
*Dunbar, Bertrand A.	Dakota, ME
*Ellison, Mrs. R. R.	Alabama, ME,S
*Emery, Sam T.	New England, ME
*Fudge, Ezra S.	North Texas, ME,S
Geyer, Francis L.	Colorado, ME
*Graves, W. D.	North Alabama, ME,S
*Gregory, Lucius	Virginia, ME,S
*Hall, D. H.	North Mississippi, ME,S
Hall, Sydney W.	Oregon, ME
*Hawkins, A. K.	Florida, ME,S
Heckman, Edgar R.	Central Pennsylvania, ME
Jacobs, Disston W.	Wilmington, ME
*Jacobs, George A.	Wisconsin ME
*Johnson, William T.	Southern Illinois, ME
*Jones, Everett W.	Pittsburgh, ME
Makosky, E. C.	Maryland, MP
McIlwain, A. T.	North Mississippi, ME,S
*McNear, Alexander S.	Newark, ME
Miller, Frederick A.	Northern New York, ME
*Osborn, Mrs. H. S.	Central New York, ME
Riley, P. E.	Central Texas, ME,S
Satterfield, Robert S.	Oklahoma, ME,S
*Scott, W. C.	Maryland, MP
*Spilman, Mrs. J. H.	Kentucky, ME,S
*Stackhouse, Will	South Carolina, ME,S
Stafford, Thomas A.	Northern Minnesota, ME
Stevens, Frank G. H.	Southern California, ME
Swank, Jesse	Ohio, ME
Tadlock, C. W.	St. Louis, ME,S
*Thrasher, T. E.	South Georgia, ME,S
Turnipseed, B. Rhett.	Upper South Carolina, ME,S
*Utz, W. H., Jr.	Missouri, ME,S
Walker, John B.	Northwest Iowa, ME
Webdell, C. Wesley	St. Louis, ME,S
Wells, Arthur M.	Illinois, ME
*Wills, J. Norman.	North Carolina, MP

NO. 8. COMMITTEE ON RITUALS AND ORDERS OF WORSHIP

"To which shall be referred all rules and regulations, memorials, petitions, etc., relating to these subjects."

OSCAR T. OLSON, *Chairman;* LEONARD B. SMITH, *Vice-Chairman;* ROBERT W. GOODLOE, *Secretary.*

(* Denotes Lay Delegate)

Name	Annual Conference and Church
Allen, A. J.	Pittsburgh, MP
Archer, R. L.	Malaysia and Philippine Islands, ME
*Arrington, Mrs. Paul	Mississippi, ME,S
Barker, Alfred H.	Iowa-Des Moines, ME
*Bell, Carl S.	South America, ME
*Boswell, G. C.	Central Texas, ME,S
*Brawley, James P.	Atlanta, ME
Brownlee, T. M.	Mississippi, ME,S
*Cheetham, Arthur D.	Northern New York, ME
Craven, J. B.	Western North Carolina, ME,S
Daniel, Coleman C.	Memphis, ME,S
Davidson, M. M.	North Alabama, ME,S
*Freeman, Sewell C.	Tennessee, ME
*Gaede, John C.	Kansas, ME
*Gilligan, Henry	Maryland, MP
Goodloe, R. W.	Central Texas, ME,S
*Haley, Paul S.	North Alabama, ME,S
*Hamm, Adolph S.	Wyoming State, ME
*Highbaugh, Miss Irma	China, ME
*Hillman, Mrs. E. L.	North Carolina, ME,S
*Jenkins, U. I.	West Virginia, MP
*McCutchan, Robert G.	Northwest Indiana, ME
McKenney, S. S.	Texas, ME,S
*Moore, Fred	Little Rock, ME,S
Moore, Leland	South Georgia, ME,S
*Norman, J. R.	Baltimore, ME,S
Olson, Oscar T.	Northeast Ohio, ME
*Parr, Fred D.	California, ME
Paschall, F. W.	North Carolina, MP
*Pennington, A. S.	Holston, ME,S
Prothro, Charles W.	Savannah, ME
*Quillian, Hubert	North Georgia, ME,S
Raines, Richard C.	Northern Minnesota, ME
Rand, H. J.	Southwest Missouri, ME,S
*Rogers, Mrs. Lillian P.	Upper Mississippi, ME

Name	Annual Conference and Church
Shafer, A. E.	Alabama, ME,S
*Smith, J. Harvey	South Florida, ME
Smith, L. B.	Maryland, MP
*Stehl, Heinrich	Europe, ME
Thomas, J. S. Ladd	Philadelphia, ME
*Wagner, Robert F.	New York, ME
Ward, Woodrow	South Carolina, ME,S
Whyman, Henry C.	Eastern Swedish, ME
*Wilson, Harwell (deceased)	Florida, ME,S

SPECIAL COMMITTEES

BUSINESS COMMITTEE

Bishop Edwin H. Hughes, Chairman; Bishop John M. Moore, Vice-Chairman; Bishop James H. Straughn, Secretary; Hiram A. Douglas, Thomas D. Ellis, Fremont E. Fribley, Eugene B. Hawk, Gideon I. Humphreys, H. E. Jackson, Dwight S. Jeffers, Zebulon V. Judd, Albert C. Knudsen.

COMMITTEE ON COURTESIES, PRIVILEGES, AND INTRODUCTIONS

Joseph M. M. Gray, Chairman; W. W. Jackson, Secretary; T. LeRoy Hooper, Assistant Secretary; Harvey W. Cox, G. Ray Jordan, Clyde O. Law, Umphrey Lee, Stanley O. MacMullen, John B. Magee.

COMMITTEE ON CREDENTIALS

Earl R. Brown, Chairman; W. W. Jackson, Vice-Chairman; Charles A. Robbins, Secretary; Henry M. Andrews, Alfred C. Crawford, Frank B. Hanna, Carl S. McFall, Roy H. Short, Frank G. H. Stevens.

COMMITTEE ON EDITORIAL REVISION

John L. Ferguson, Chairman; William K. Anderson, Vice-Chairman; Earle M. Rugg, Secretary; Henry L. Davis, James R. Joy, W. T. Mathis, Hubert Quillian, Frank L. Shaffer, Richard E. Womack.

COMMITTEE ON ENABLING ACTS AND LEGAL FORMS

Arthur A. Callaghan, Chairman; C. L. Daugherty, Vice-Chairman; William M. Alexander, Secretary; Howard C. Baldwin, John C. Broomfield, George R. Brown, J. S. M. Cannon, Frank T. Cartwright, Ernest H. Cherrington, Sanford C. Corcoran, Willard G. Cram, Matthew S. Davage, George M. Davenport, Mrs. W. H. C. Goode, W. K. Greene, Jabez C. Harrison, Jasper B. Hicks, James N. Hillman, David D. Jones, Wiley A. Keve, George H. Lamar, Mrs. F. F. Lindsey, Ernest S. Lyons, Albert W. Martin, Arba Martin, Mrs. T. H. Minga, George L. Morelock, Frederick W. Mueller, W. L. Mullikin, Nathan Newby, J. Manning Potts, Paul W. Quillian, Mrs. George S. Sexton, Jr., Herschell R. Snavely, William H. Spurgeon, Ben L. Sutherland, Nate S. Williamson.

COMMITTEE ON JOURNAL

Joseph D. Piper, Chairman; John R. Kenney, Secretary; Robert B. Spencer, E. T. Wayland, G. Charles Weaver.

JUDICIARY COMMITTEE

Francis R. Bayley, Chairman; M. A. Childers, Vice-Chairman; Fred Herrigal, Jr., Secretary; Walter C. Buckner, Leslie R. Burgum, J. E. Butler, Charles F. Eggleston, John T. Ellison, John S. Fletcher, Nolan B. Harmon, Jr., W. G. Henry, Leslie J. Lyons, William F. McMurry, J. W. Mills, Robert J. Smith, Frank C. Tucker, Henry R. VanDusen, William H. Wilcox.

COMMITTEE ON PRESIDING OFFICERS

Levi P. Goodwin, Chairman; William A. Shelton, Secretary; George W. Crabbe, John D. Crummey, Orion W. Fifer, Nat Harris, Forney Hutchinson, Henry N. Snyder, John C. Williams.

COMMITTEE OF REFERENCE

Lud H. Estes, Chairman; Edgar R. Heckman, Vice-Chairman; Cuthbert W. Bates, Secretary; J. L. Clark, Robert B. Spencer.

COMMITTEE ON RULES

J. Edgar Skillington, Chairman; Costen J. Harrell, Secretary; Lud H. Estes, Ex Officio; George W. Henson, Lavens M. Thomas, Fred W. Paschall.

133

RULES OF ORDER

I. DAILY SCHEDULE

Rule 1. The following shall be the daily order for the Uniting Conference, Sundays excepted:

a. 8:30 A.M. to 9 A.M.—Devotional Service under the direction of the Council of Bishops.

b. 9 A.M. to 12:30 P.M.—Conference business with recess for ten minutes at 10:30.

c. 2:30 P.M. to 5 P.M.—Committee meetings.

Rule 2. After devotional services the regular meetings shall be conducted as follows:

(1) (For the first day only) Calling of the roll of delegates and alternates, or reserves, by the respective Secretaries of the three uniting Churches.

(2) Approval of the Journal of the previous meeting or meetings.

(3) Report of the Committee on Courtesies, Privileges, and Introductions.

(4) Reports of Committees.

(5) Calendar.

(6) Miscellaneous business.

II. PRESIDING OFFICERS

Rule 3. The Bishop presiding shall be the legal president of the Uniting Conference. He shall decide points of order raised by the members and shall rule on points of order not raised by the members, as he deems necessary to conform to these Rules of Order, subject, in both cases, to an appeal to the Conference by any member without a second; which appeal shall be decided by vote without debate, except that the appellant and the Chairman shall each have five minutes for a statement in support of their respective positions. A tie vote in the case of an appeal shall sustain the Chair. When any member raises a point of order he shall cite by number the rule he adjudges to have been violated.

Rule 4. When the Chairman stands in his place and calls the Conference to order, no member shall speak, address the chair, or stand while the Chairman stands.

III. DUTIES AND PRIVILEGES OF MEMBERS

Rule 5. No member (delegate), unless hindered by sickness, or otherwise, from being present, shall absent himself from the sessions of the Conference without permission of the Conference, and all absentees shall be reported by the Chairman of the several Annual Conference delegations to the Committee on Credentials. No alternate, or reserve, delegate shall have the privilege of membership until the substitution has been approved by the Conference.

Rule 6. When a delegate desires to speak to the Conference, he shall arise at his assigned seat, respectfully address the Presiding Officer, and, after recognition, proceed to the speaker's platform, where, before speaking, he shall give the Chairman, in writing, his name and that of the Annual Conference from which he comes; which, in turn, the Chairman shall then announce to the Body.

Rule 7. No member who has the floor may be interrupted except for a breach of order, or a misrepresentation, or to direct the attention of the Conference to the fact that the time has arrived for a special order, or to raise a very urgent question of high privilege.

Rule 8. No member shall speak a second time on the same question if any member who has not spoken desires the floor, nor more than twice on the same subject under the same motion, nor longer than ten minutes unless his time shall be extended by the Conference.

Rule 9. A member claiming the floor at any time for what he believes is a very urgent question of high privilege, shall be allowed to indicate briefly the nature of the question, and if it be adjudged by the Chair to be such, he may proceed at his pleasure or until the Chairman judges that he has exhausted his privilege.

Rule 10. Only delegates within the bar of the Conference when the vote is taken shall be entitled to vote. Every delegate within the bar at the time a question is put, shall vote, unless for special reasons he is excused by the Conference.

Rule 11. Voting shall be by a show of hands unless otherwise ordered by the Conference. An "aye" or "no" vote, if taken, shall be by signed ballot. A count vote may be ordered, in which case the delegates shall rise from their seats and stand until counted.

Rule 12. When a vote is about to be taken any delegate shall have the right to call for a division of any question if it is subject to such division as he indicates.

Rule 13. The ministerial and lay delegates shall deliberate in one body; but upon a call, by motion, of any delegate, seconded by another delegate of the same order and supported by one third of the members of that order voting, the ministerial and lay delegates shall vote separately. But no measure shall be passed without the concurrence of a majority of both classes of delegates. In case of such a vote the order calling for it shall vote first.

Rule 14. Nothing else shall be in order when a vote is being taken or when the pending or previous question has been called until the process is completed.

IV. BUSINESS PROCEDURE

Rule 15. Reports and resolutions shall be presented in triplicate, and when requested by the Secretary motions shall be presented in writing.

Rule 16. All resolutions, reports, and communications to the Conference shall be read by the Secretary except as otherwise provided for in Rule 29. When a motion is made and seconded, or a resolution is introduced and seconded, or a report is read by the Secretary, it shall be deemed in the possession of the Conference.

Rule 17. The following motions shall be taken without debate:

(1) To adjourn.
(2) To suspend the rules.
(3) To lay on the table.
(4) To take from the table.
(5) To call for the pending or previous question.
(6) To reconsider a nondebatable motion.

Rule 18. The main proposition may be opened to debate under the following motions: to adopt; to commit; to substitute; to postpone, and to reconsider. No new motion, resolution, or subject shall be entertained until the one under consideration shall have been disposed of; but one or more of the following motions may be made, and they shall have precedence in their order; namely:

(1) To fix the time to which the Conference shall adjourn. (This motion is subject to amendment, substitution, or it may be laid on the table.)
(2) To adjourn.
(3) To take a recess.
(4) To order the pending or previous question. (This motion cannot be laid on the table.)
(5) To lay on the table.
(6) To postpone to a given time.
(7) To refer.
(8) To substitute. (See Rule 19.)
(9) To amend. (One amendment to an amendment being allowed.)
(10) To postpone indefinitely.

Rule 19. A substitute shall consist of a minority report, or a resolution, and the motion to adopt it shall be a rival principal question, and shall be in order while an amendment to the principal proposition is pending. To substitute shall require a motion and shall be subject to amendment the same as a principal question, after which the principal proposition shall be subject to amendment, an amendment to an amendment being allowed. After amendments have been made, or if no amendments are made, the vote shall be taken first on the substitution, and if ordered, the substitute becomes the main question.

Rule 20. A motion calling for the putting of the pending question shall be decided without debate, and if adopted, the pending question shall be put to a vote without further debate.

Rule 21. A motion calling for the putting of the previous question shall be decided without debate, and if adopted, all motions before the Conference shall be put to a vote in their order without further debate, except as provided for in Rule 32.

Rule 22. It shall not be in order for a delegate after discussing the pending question to make a motion that closes debate.

Rule 23. A majority of those voting, a quorum being present, shall decide all questions except the call for the "ayes" and "noes," which shall be ordered by one fifth of those voting; and it shall require a two-thirds majority, a quorum being present, to suspend or amend the Rules of Order; to set aside a special order; to consider a special order before the set time; or to sustain any motion that would stop debate.

Rule 24. A motion to reconsider an action of the Conference shall be in order at any time if offered by a member who voted with the prevailing side. If the motion being reconsidered is nondebatable, the motion to reconsider may not be debated.

Rule 25. The Secretary shall keep a chronological record of Orders of the Day, of reports of Committees (see Rule 28), and all reports placed on record by vote. This record shall be called the Calendar, and the matters of business placed on it shall be considered in order, unless by a vote of the Conference an item is taken up out of its order.

Rule 26. The motion to adjourn shall be taken without debate, and shall always be in order except

(1) When a delegate has the floor.

(2) When a question is actually put, or a vote is being taken, and before it is finally decided.

(3) When the pending or previous question has been ordered and action thereunder is pending.

(4) When a motion to adjourn has been lost, and no business or debate has intervened.

(5) When the motion to fix the time to which the Conference shall adjourn is pending.

V. COMMITTEES: DUTIES AND PREROGATIVES

Rule 27. When a memorial or resolution, or any such thing, is referred to one of the several General Standing Committees, it shall be understood that the whole question with which the paper has to do is referred to that Committee for such action as it may deem wise. Committee reports recommending no concurrence, with no minority report, shall be kept upon a separate Calendar, which Calendar shall be taken up when the regular Calendar is completed.

Rule 28. At the close of each day's meeting, the Chairmen and Secretaries of the General Standing Committees shall hand to the Secretary of the Uniting Conference, or to someone designated by him, reports of their action in triplicate. The Secretary shall enter the several reports on the Calendar in order in which they reach him; and shall hand to the editor of the *Daily Advocate* one copy of the Calendar to be published in the *Advocate* the following day.

Rule 29. A report of any Committee signed by the Chairman and Secretary thereof; and a minority report of any General Standing Committee signed by at least ten members thereof; and a minority report of any other Committee, except the Judiciary Committee, signed by at least one fourth of the members thereof; and a minority report of the Judiciary Committee signed by one or more members thereof; having been printed in the *Daily Advocate* for at least one day, shall be considered to be in possession of the Conference. Minority reports shall bear the same serial numbers, with proper alphabetical notations, as the Committee reports for which they are offered as substitutes. If there be two or more of such reports, they may be considered in their alphabetical order. All Committee reports shall be presented to the Conference upon paper bearing at the top the number of the report, the name of the Committee, the total membership of the Committee, the number present at the time the report was adopted, the number voting for the report, and the number voting against the report. Reports of the eight General Standing Committees shall be printed in the *Daily Advocate* for at least one day before being presented to the Conference, and they shall not be read unless by its order.

Rule 30. When the Chairman of a Committee is not in harmony with a report adopted by the Committee, it shall be his duty to state the fact to the Committee, which shall elect one of its members to represent it in the presentation and discussion of the report in the Conference; but if, in such a case, the Committee shall fail to select a representative, the Chairman shall designate a member to represent the Committee, and said representative shall have all the rights and privileges of the Chairman in relation to such report.

Rule 31. A member selected by the signers of a minority report of a Committee to present the same shall have the same rights and privileges in relation thereto which belong to the Chairman in the presentation of the regular (majority) report of the Committee, except that he may not present said minority report until the majority report has been presented, and shall then offer it as a substitute thereof, and except, further, that in closing the debate on the question of making the substitution the member presenting the minority report shall speak first and the Chairman last.

Rule 32. When the report of a Committee is under consideration, it shall be the duty of the Presiding Officer to ascertain, when he recognizes a member of the Conference, on which side he proposes to speak, and he shall not assign the floor to any member proposing to speak on the same side of the pending question as the speaker immediately preceding if any member desires to speak on the other side thereof.

No report shall be adopted or question relating to the same decided without opportunity having been given for at least one speech for and one against the said proposal, providing this right is claimed before the Chairman or duly authorized member presenting the Committee's report or the minority report, if there be one, is presented to close the debate.

When all have spoken who desire to do so, or when (and after) the pending or previous question has been ordered, the Chairman or/and duly authorized member or members presenting the Committee's report (and the minority report if ere be one) shall be entitled to speak before the vote is takhn.

VI. SUSPENDING OR AMENDING RULES

Rule 33. The operation of these Rules may be suspended at any time by a two-thirds vote of the Conference.

Rule 34. These Rules of Order may be amended or

changed by a two-thirds vote of the Conference; provided the proposed change or amendment has been presented to the Conference in writing and referred to the Committee on Rules, which Committee shall report thereon not later than the day following.

Rule 35. In all matters not specified, proceedings of the Uniting Conference shall be governed by Robert's "Rules of Order."

PLAN OF ORGANIZATION
TEMPORARY ORGANIZATION

1. The Presiding Officer for the temporary organization of the Uniting Conference shall be one of the Chairmen of the Joint Commission on Union as provided below in the *Plan of Organization,* who shall serve in this capacity until a Plan of Organization and Rules of Order have been adopted and a permanent organization effected.

2. The Secretarial Staff for temporary organization shall be the respective Secretaries of the General Conferences of the three uniting Churches, with such assistants as they may choose, who shall serve until a permanent secretarial staff shall have been chosen.

3. Immediately after the devotional service appropriately opening the Uniting Conference, the calling of the roll, and the transaction of such privileged business as may require immediate attention, the Conference shall proceed to effect a permanent organization by (1) Receiving nominations and taking a ballot for permanent Secretary; (2) by consideration of the Plan of Organization and Rules of Order hereinafter recommended; (3) by completing the permanent organization so far as practical at this stage of the Conference in accordance with such plans and rules as shall be adopted.

PLAN OF ORGANIZATION
I. Presiding Officers

A Committee of Nine, composed of four delegates from the Methodist Episcopal Church, four from the Methodist Episcopal Church, South, and one from the Methodist Protestant Church, of whom five shall be ministers and four laymen, shall be nominated by the Joint Commission on Union and elected and empowered by the Uniting Conference to designate from among the Bishops of the three uniting Churches those who shall preside over the Conference in its various sessions; except that during the first three days the three Chairmen of the Joint Commission shall preside in an order agreed upon among themselves.

II. Secretarial Staff

The Uniting Conference shall have a Secretary and two Associate Secretaries, and as many Assistant Secretaries as

141

need may require. They shall be chosen from the membership of the Conference in the following manner:

1. A Secretary shall be elected by ballot after nominations from the floor.

2. The Secretary so elected shall nominate for Associate
Secretaries two members of the Conference, one representing each of the uniting Churches other than the one to
which he himself belongs.

3. Nominations for Associate Secretaries shall also be
permitted from the floor, which nominations shall be limited
to members of the Conference representing the two uniting
Churches other than that to which the Secretary elected
belongs.

4. From these so nominated the Conference shall elect by
ballot one Associate Secretary representing each of the two
uniting Churches other than that which the Secretary
elected represents.

5. The Secretary and the two Associate Secretaries so
elected shall nominate for election by the Conference as
many Assistant Secretaries as in their judgment the work of
the Conference may require.

6. The Secretary and the Associate Secretaries shall continue in office until the meeting of the first General Conference of The Methodist Church, performing such duties
as may be assigned them.

III. COMMITTEES

The Uniting Conference shall have General Standing
Committees as hereinafter indicated, and such Special Committees as need may require.

1. GENERAL STANDING COMMITTEES

(1) *Conferences*—to which shall be referred all rules and
regulations, memorials, petitions, etc., relating to Church,
Quarterly, District, Annual, Jurisdictional, Central, General, and other Conferences.

(2) *Ministry and Judicial Administration*—to which shall
be referred all rules and regulations, memorials, petitions,
etc., regarding bishops, traveling preachers, and local
preachers, pastors and district elders or district superintendents; trial and appeal; and the Judicial Council.

(3) *Membership and Temporal Economy*—to which
shall be referred all rules and regulations, memorials, petitions, etc., regarding church membership and conditions,
duties and transfer thereof; regarding Lay Activities, Stewards, Trustees, properties; financial system of the general

and local church; and such activities of the church at large in and through its institutions and boards as are not made the specific responsibility of any other Standing Committee.

(4) *Missions*—to which shall be referred all rules and regulations, memorials, petitions, etc., relating to all missions and missionary organizations, church extension, hospitals, homes, deaconesses, and temperance and public morals, evangelism, and the American Bible Society.

(5) *Education*—to which shall be referred all rules and regulations, memorials, petitions, etc., relating to all Universities, Colleges, Wesley Foundations, Schools, Seminaries, Ministerial Training, Religious Education in the local church, including young people's activities, literature for church schools, and World Peace.

(6) *Publishing Interests*—to which shall be referred all rules and regulations, memorials, petitions, etc., relating to Publishing Houses, Book Committees, and the publication of periodicals and books.

(7) *Superannuate Support*—to which shall be referred all rules and regulations, memorials, petitions, etc., relating to the support of superannuated or retired ministers, and widows and dependent children of deceased ministers.

(8) *Rituals and Orders of Worship*—to which shall be referred all rules and regulations, memorials, petitions, etc., relating to these subjects.

2. MEMBERSHIP OF GENERAL STANDING COMMITTEES

(1) The membership of the foregoing General Standing Committees shall be made up on the basis of representation in the Uniting Conferences; namely, 4-4-1.

(2) The following General Standing Committees, (1) Conferences, (2) Ministry and Judicial Administration, (3) Membership and Temporal Economy, (4) Missions, (5) Education, (6) Publishing Interests, shall each be constituted of sixty delegates of the Methodist Episcopal Church, sixty delegates of the Methodist Episcopal Church, South, and fifteen delegates of the Methodist Protestant Church.

(3) The Committees, (7) Superannuate Support and (8) Ritual and Orders of Worship, shall be constituted of twenty delegates of the Methodist Episcopal Church, twenty delegates of the Methodist Episcopal Church, South, and five delegates of the Methodist Protestant Church.

(4) No delegate shall be a member of more than one of the foregoing General Standing Committees.

(5) Delegates shall be nominated for membership in the foregoing General Standing Committees by their respective

Commissions on Church Union and approved by the Uniting Conference.

3. ORGANIZATION OF GENERAL STANDING COMMITTEES

The eight General Standing Committees shall meet for organization on the first day of the Uniting Conference with a Bishop appointed by the Council of Bishops presiding, and with one of the Secretarial Staff keeping the record. The General Standing Committees shall meet at 2:30 P.M., organize and proceed to their respective tasks. A complete record of the organizations thus effected shall be promptly reported to the Secretary of the Uniting Conference and on the following day this record shall be printed in the *Daily Advocate;* and thus reported to the Conference and made a part of the official Journal.

4. MEETINGS OF THE EIGHT GENERAL STANDING COMMITTEES

Meetings of the eight General Standing Committees shall be held regularly each day at 2:30 P.M. unless otherwise ordered by the Conference. For the transaction of business a majority of the members of each Committee shall be regarded as a quorum in each and all these eight General Standing Committees.

5. SPECIAL STANDING COMMITTEES

There shall be the following Special Standing Committees:

(1) *Rules.* There shall be a Committee on Rules composed of five members, of which two shall be delegates from the Methodist Episcopal Church, two from the Methodist Episcopal Church, South, and one from the Methodist Protestant Church, to which shall be referred all matters and questions pertaining to the Rules of Order and parliamentary procedure in the business of the Conference and its Committees. The Secretary of the Uniting Conference shall be an additional ex-officio member of this Committee.

(2) *Journal.* There shall be a Committee of five members, two from the Methodist Episcopal Church, two from the Methodist Episcopal Church, South, and one from the Methodist Protestant Church, which shall examine the daily record of the Secretary, comparing it with the stenographic record, and shall report to the Conference in either of the following forms:

a. "We have examined the Journal and find it correct."
b. "We have examined the Journal and find it correct except in the following particulars":

The report of the Committee on Journal shall be submitted to the Uniting Conference and may be amended or adopted as submitted. Any error subsequently discovered shall be reported to the Conference, and upon its recommendation may be corrected by the Uniting Conference.

(3) *Credentials.* There shall be a Committee on Credentials composed of nine members, of whom four shall be from the Methodist Episcopal Church, four from the Methodist Episcopal Church, South, and one from the Methodist Protestant Church, which shall report the absence of delegates and the seating of alternate, or reserve, delegates and all matters relating to the attendance of delegates. The report of this Committee, when approved by the Conference, shall be the basis for settlement with delegates for their per diem allowance.

(4) *Editorial Revision.* There shall be a Committee on Editorial Revision composed of nine persons representing the three uniting Churches in the same ratio as the Committee on Credentials. To this Committee shall be referred, with a view to clarification and definiteness of statement, and for the correction of verbal errors and infelicities in expression, as needed, all Committee reports as adopted by the Conference and before they are recorded in the Journal.

(5) *Courtesies, Privileges, and Introductions.* There shall be a Committee on Courtesies, Privileges, and Introductions composed of nine persons, representing the three uniting Churches as in the two preceding Committees. Introduction of official visitors and the extending of the courtesy of the Conference to those to whom it may be due shall be a responsibility of this Committee. Questions of privileges for the Conference, or any of its members, shall first be presented to and considered by this Committee, and if it approves, they shall be presented to the Presiding Officer for consideration by the Conference immediately after the approval of the Journal at each morning session. This Committee shall also serve as a Committee on Resolutions.

(6) *Enabling Acts and Legal Forms.* There shall be a Special Committee on the Enabling Acts and Legal Forms of the Uniting Conference for inaugurating the activities of The Methodist Church. This Committee shall be composed of thirty-six persons chosen from the delegates of the three uniting Churches in the same ratio as the three Committees last preceding.

(7) *Judiciary Committee.* There shall be a Judiciary Committee composed of eighteen persons, representing proportionately the three uniting Churches, to which shall be referred all questions as to the constitutionality of any proposed action of the Uniting Conference. This Committee

shall report its recommendations to the Uniting Conference for final action.

(8) *Reference*. There shall be a Committee of Reference, composed of the Secretary and the two Associate Secretaries, and two other delegates selected by them, which shall receive all memorials, petitions, etc., and after ascertaining that they are in proper form, distribute them among the several Standing Committees according to their respective responsibilities as hereinbefore outlined. The Committee of Reference shall have power to withdraw a reference either upon request or upon its own motion. The Committee shall also have power to withhold from reference or publication any document which it shall deem improper. Any document not referable to any existing Committee shall be submitted by the Committee to the Conference.

(9) *Business Committee*. There shall be a Business Committee consisting of twelve members composed of the three Chairmen of the Commission on Church Union, four members from the Methodist Episcopal Church, four members from the Methodist Episcopal Church, South, and one member from the Methodist Protestant Church. This Committee shall be chosen by the Uniting Conference upon nomination of the Executive Committee of the Commission on Church Union. All questions, proposals, resolutions, communications, or other matter not included in the regular business of the Uniting Conference as fixed by the Plan of Union shall be referred without debate or motion to the Business Committee, which shall decide whether or not the matter presented shall be considered by the Conference. It shall also be the duty of the Business Committee to see that all provisions and requirements of the Plan of Union shall be considered by the Uniting Conference.

6. ORGANIZATION AND MEETINGS OF SPECIAL STANDING COMMITTEES AND SPECIAL COMMITTEES

The first person named on any Committee, except the eight General Standing Committees, shall convene the same for organization, unless otherwise ordered by the Uniting Conference, and all such Committees shall determine their respective times and places of meeting, unless otherwise ordered by the Conference. For these Committees a majority of all members shall constitute a quorum for the transaction of business.

7. MEMBERSHIP ON ALL SPECIAL COMMITTEES

Unless otherwise ordered by the Conference, membership on all Special Committees shall be constituted through nomination by the Council of Bishops and election by the Conference; and if not previously published in the *Daily Advocate* a two-thirds vote shall be required for election.

IV. MISCELLANEOUS

1. *Seating of Delegates.* The seating of delegates, elected or appointed, to the Uniting Conference shall be by Annual Conferences.

2. *Payment of Delegates' Expenses.* Each Church represented in the Uniting Conference shall be responsible for the payment of its delegates' expenses according to its usages until such time as the Uniting Conference shall order otherwise.

3. *Jurisdictional Conference Boundaries.* The delegates shall meet in their respective Jurisdictional groups on Monday, May 1, at 8 P.M., for arranging to carry out the provisions of Article VIII of the Plan of Union under procedure. For the organization of each group a Bishop appointed by the Council of Bishops and an Assistant Secretary shall be assigned as for the organization of Standing Committees.

THE EPISCOPAL ADDRESS TO THE UNITING CONFERENCE

Members of the Uniting Conference, Representatives of the Methodist Episcopal Church, the Methodist Episcopal Church, South, and the Methodist Protestant Church:

Grace be unto you, and peace, from God our Father, and from the Lord Jesus Christ.

We salute you in the Lord and in the fellowship of the hosts of God's people.

Eight million Methodist communicants and a constituency of 20,000,000 adherents stand at attention today as this Uniting Conference throws wide the gates to a new era in American Church life. The entire Protestantism of the nation turns eager eyes toward this city. No more notable and responsible Christian body has ever assembled on this continent than this Uniting Conference. The authority of the Churches that you represent has bestowed upon you by legal and constitutional procedure and action the great and grave responsibility of building the governmental structure of the new Methodist Church out of the elements of polity and practice that inhere in the three uniting Churches. You are to set the course for a powerful ecclesiastical organization upon its high and holy mission. God only in His wisdom, might, and love, can make you equal to this task and this obligation.

Methodism in America proclaims to the world today, with great joy, the culmination of one of the most outstanding and far-reaching union movements which the Church of Christ has ever witnessed. Christendom for a quarter of a century has deplored its divisions and bewailed its rivalries, and has cried aloud for peace and a new Christian and ecclesiastical unity. Great Ecumenical Councils have sounded loudly the call to Christian forces to close their ranks and present a solid front to a wretched and wayward world. Our three Churches have heard that cry, and have answered by consolidating their forces, unifying their divisions, and moving majestically to a more responsible place in Christian adventure. The process and spirit that have wrought this achievement are prophetic of other Methodist unions and of speedy correlations that will give this country a Methodism of co-ordinated oneness and of mobilized evangelical power.

148

THE AIM OF THIS ADDRESS

The Bishops have agreed that this address shall be confined to the meaning of this Uniting Conference, which has no distinct precedent, and will have no distinct successor. Within recent months the three merging Churches in their General Conferences received quadrennial messages such as have featured our larger gatherings for more than a century. We do not deem it appropriate or desirable to repeat or even closely imitate those state papers that were prepared to inspire and guide the lawmaking bodies. This address is framed with the dominant purpose of exalting the mission of a Conference unique in Methodist history.

APPROACHING THE TASK

One hundred fifty-five years deliver to us today rare rewards of experience, understanding, and triumphant effort. The Christmas Conference of 1784 created an independent organized Methodist Church in America. It established the Methodist Episcopacy upon foundations genuine and historic and without sacramentarian implication. The General Conference of 1808 created an essential and elemental constitution in Church government. These have been our great constructive, stabilizing, and directive forces. The quadrenniums have brought interpretations, amplifications, and applications, but the principles have held permanently in power. The General Superintendency of bishops has long been supplemented by the superintendency of departmental boards. With the growth of the Church there has come an increase of administrative and promotional agencies and a multiplying of rules and regulations for the systematic procedure of a vast complex organization.

The Uniting Conference will be gratified to find that these Methodist Churches have wrought so admirably in the development of a sufficient and commendable church polity, that their existing processes of government along with those supplied by the Plan of Union are ample and adequate for the governmental structure of the United Church.

In accordance with the provision of the Plan of Union, "in order to facilitate the work of the Uniting Conference," able committees appointed by the Joint Commission on Church Union have prepared harmonizations of the provisions, rules, and regulations of the three Churches. After review by the Joint Commission these are respectfully delivered to the delegates here for such use and action as their judgment may approve. We may be allowed to express our high appreciation of the remarkable and efficient labors of the splendid committees, working in limited time and under difficult conditions.

The Uniting Conference has full power to put together compactly and substantially the governmental structure of The Methodist Church. Union was accomplished by the constitutional action of the three Churches. But it could not become operative without a governmental structure which this Uniting Conference was created to provide. After the governmental structure has been agreed upon Union can go fully into effect, at such time and in such manner as the Uniting Conference by enabling acts may determine. These enabling acts may provide a point at which certain features of the government become effective, and a period in which certain other features may be made effective. In these matters the sound judgment of the Uniting Conference will make reasonable decision.

A GLANCE AT HISTORY

These three Churches, remembering today their origins and the conditions that gave them existence, have only pride in the capabilities and the achievements of their ecclesiastical ancestors. Stalwart men of noble purpose and eminent ability differed in principles and convictions and took divergent ways to build a Methodism that accorded with their consciences and their judgment. Their voices rang clear for what to them was right. By their molds, their ecclesiastical posterity have wrought faithfully and well for a century and have produced Methodism of distinction and power. We give reverent praise to the men who established the ways of our going and made possible the Churches through which we have lived, moved, and had our being. But from the high level of their characters and attainments we are able today to press across and above the lines of cleavage for the building of a greater and finer Methodism to the glory of God and the establishment of Christ's Kingdom on Earth.

The separations in Methodisms brought neither disaster nor decadence. That of 1828 which resulted in the organization of the Methodist Protestant Church dramatized the importance of lay representation in the councils of the Church; and lay representation has long been a fundamental principle in our several branches, and is such in the Plan of Union. Without the separation of 1844 Methodism would have been a house of contention and condemnation from two sides; but with separation it won honorable standing, steadfast sympathy, and unfailing support from both sections of a divided people. The tragic era of the nation seriously affected the mind and spirit of the great ecclesiastical bodies; but the people continued increasingly loyal to their respective Methodist Churches, which never receded from each other in doctrinal beliefs nor in essential elements of governmental polity. While Methodists have been distressingly divided, Methodism has continued inherently one. Its faith, its polity, its thought, its life, whatever the realm, never failed its founders. Methodism has had a basal unity, central, elemental, and enduring. No divisions of men could destroy that deeper harmony which is ever the primary basis for governmental oneness.

Faith and order are fundamental for real union in Church life and structure. The Church itself as an instrument for stabilizing the Kingdom of God has become more and more central in all Ecumenical thinking. Before its parts can be co-ordinated those parts must show integrity, and the valid and intrinsic elements of the whole. Any proposal for any Church union must take cognizance of the order involved. Without unity of thought and polity only federation may be possible. Councils may effect co-operation in life and labor, but only kinship can furnish the true and enduring basis of a united Church. Religious faiths go in families, and the normal procedure for union is along family lines. This procedure Methodism has adopted. When families have healed their own separations they will be in position to consider and accept the larger unities.

The problem of Methodist Union has not been solely ecclesiastical, but largely social and human. It has not been really a Methodist problem, but an American problem, the problem of restoring to two great peoples on opposite sides of a chasmic line the mutual good will, the respect, the esteem, and the confidence which had been disrupted by a great political upheaval. For fifty years the suggestion of union received little sympathetic response. Fraternal messages, however felicitous and forceful, were largely formal. The prevailing attitudes, sentiments, and even normal prejudices on both sides had first to be recognized, appraised, and appeased. There was the need for the show of consideration, of understanding, of Christian virtues as prerequisites to any merger. Following the first fifty years of unyielding separateness were two decades, from 1894 to 1914, during which joint Commissions on Federation tempered the winds, softened the atmosphere, and brought in a new climate of springtime and hope. In that period the old family love began to come back; the grandchildren sought fellowship with their unknown but worthy kin; and family gatherings and homecomings gradually increased. Where contacts were most numerous and associations most frequent, respect and confidence most rapidly returned. Union is here today because good will, genuine respect, mutual confidence, and Christian love widely and substantially prevail among the Methodists of the country. Union in American Methodism has been and is a matter of American life. Its consummation is linked with national understanding and national solidarity. This union of ours performs a triple service: It restores unity, harmony, and love to its own religious family; it creates a mighty bond among the great sections of this country; it sets before the religious forces of Christendom an example which is both appealing and challenging. With the consciousness of this duty performed, Methodism again faces the world in faith, hope, and love.

THE SPIRIT OF THIS CONFERENCE

The length of our separations has covered a century; the differences due to geographical divisions are not insignificant; the involved corporate life is immense, the ancient memories have vividly lingered; yet we can boldly declare that no similar movement in history has proceeded in a more kindly and fraternal mood. Those who have been in the inner circles of the Joint Commission know no chapters that they would wish to have canceled. The Commissioners will bear grateful testimony that the discussions have been so uniting in spirit that they must be classed not merely among the polite rules prevailing among gentlemen, but as among the Christlike codes prevailing among believers.

This fraternal spirit may be expected to have full sway in this Uniting Conference. On the larger matters we are already in agreement. Since we have never been separated in faith, we will have no theological debates. Inasmuch as in the broader outlines of government we are as one, these can occasion no arguments. The tasks of harmonization lie within the minor, though important, realms—realms made important because the whole scheme of union is meaningful. The call therefore will be for the kindly adept in constructive legislation rather than for the genius in parliamentary obstruction. This is a well-informed body. Condensed wisdom will be more acceptable than exhibits of extended knowledge! This Conference has difficult duties. It has been constitutionally invested with adequate power to discharge them. The ratio basis of its structure is of such significance that it calls for the consummation of its designated task without needless postponement of important matters to later gatherings of the Church. Postponement of the completion of the governmental structure might bring injury to the spirit and purpose that gave the Uniting Conference its form and character. Our work here will not be the utter finality, but it will be of utter importance. The proper union of Methodism, far more than the superficial mind can see, now becomes a program of the spirit. A preference is not necessarily a conviction, nor a custom an everlasting law. The spirit that controls our deliberations will measure the value of the cause advocated and the worth of the conclusion reached. For that reason prayers should invariably be the prelude of our discussions. The ways of debate should lead from altar to altar. This whole city should feel the devout pressure of this gathering. These days and labors should be kept holy unto God. The faithfulness and spirit with which the trust committed to us is loyally fulfilled will determine the future ways of Methodism in its extensive service to God and man.

LOCAL MERGERS

This Methodism is no fabrication of ambitious, selfish ecclesiastics. It is rather the flowing together of great streams going out to the same seas. When separations lose their motives, meaning, and value, union becomes a normal movement and act. This is just as true in local communities as with the denominational bodies. Union of the three denominations puts all local churches under the same family, but it does not require any local mergers. These are left entirely to the will, judgment, and action of the memberships of the local churches involved. When the Plan of Union was first submitted to the three Churches the Joint Commission warned against the quick amalgamation of churches and societies that are geographical neighbors. That warning this Uniting Conference may well repeat and re-enforce. Some local unions will become desirable and even necessary, but they should not be made in haste nor urged from merely economic considerations. Great loyalties and holy sentiments cluster about many altars and they should be respected. Sacred memories attach to the very aisles. These should not be sacrificed without due consideration. The economic argument, the saving of money, standing alone, may be regarded with suspicion. The sale of a place of worship to a body of irregular religionists only increases the problem of division in any community. Two wholesome Methodist Churches are apt to do more for Christ than one if the other is sacrificed upon a strange altar. When local unions are made, the congregations should keep in mind the ministers who are serving them. What will become of them? Their interests should be regarded and protected and their families should have care when mergers are being planned. This Conference should lift all mergers above the plane of financial selfishness to high places of Christian motive and service.

AN INTELLIGENT CHURCH

Methodism in this great day finds itself with large numbers of communicants and adherents who have little knowledge of its activities, plans, purposes, happenings, and movements. They are not, except in the most meager way, Methodistically informed. The Church must keep them in touch with its thought, life, and activity. It has great Publishing Houses and all necessary facilities for spreading vital intelligence. The greatest modern agencies for taking the message of this Church to its own people and all people must be called into full action. No feature of possible work offers a larger field for service than this of Church and Christian intelligence through varied papers, pamphlets, and leaflets that exhibit and interpret the life, thought, and action of Methodism. A department of Methodist intelligence in the proper boards, adequate in equipment, capable in management, and vigorous in action will have extraordinary possibilities for the United Church.

OUR CENTERS OF LEARNING

A great body such as Methodism in America now imposes upon itself an obligation to be more than a body. It must be a soul. It must be a spirit. It must be a mind. These come not save by purpose, resolution, and effort. Great souls and great spirits come by many processes, but they do not prevail long without great minds. From them and through them come light and power. Every church must either create or borrow its thinking. What it thinks, and whether it thinks, depends upon its ability or lack of ability to think. Its intellectual life determines in no small measure its standing, its stability, its course, its momentum. Borrowed thinking, or reflected thinking, eventually wears down intellectual self-respect and invites intellectual deterioration. The production of thinkers is not optional with a great Church. If it fails here it passes its leadership to other hands. The vigor of a Church's intelligence will deeply affect its spiritual understanding, its spiritual energy, its spiritual power, and fix its place among the churches.

Great thinking and high intellectual life and genuine intellectual freedom find their source, their support, and their inspiration in centers of learning. John Harvard left his modest estate for "the pious work of building a college." The theme of Harvard College's Tercentenary celebration was not the glory of Harvard but the advancement of learning. That is the note which Methodism must sound in every one of its college halls. The advancement of learning in an atmosphere of religion is the true aim of every Christian college and the indispensable objective of every great Christian Church. Its colleges and universities and seminaries should be given new significance and new accentuation in the new Methodism. Methodist colleges are largely of local origin and exist to too large a degree by local interests and local support. They are separate and distinct from each other, often in competition, and without co-ordinate consideration and encouragement. The mortality among them in recent years has been high. The time has come when something to insure permanence must be done or church colleges may pass out of existence. The Church has an educational responsibility which it dare not ignore, and which it can meet only by an adequate educational system. Our Methodism should know what colleges and universities and seminaries it should have and could properly sustain, and where it should have them. It should then put upon them its educational stamp, behind them the forces that will maintain them in educational excellence and in intellectual power, and within them the spiritual zeal that will dominate their life. In addition, it should continue and increase its plans for the spiritual care of many thousands of Methodist students in our privately endowed and tax-supported institutions as carried on by the Wesley Foundations. What this Church should do it can do. This Uniting Conference can open the way for a greater era in educational service by the provision it makes for all student life and for the administration, promotion, and permanence of its colleges and universities.

The theological seminaries of the new Church will come into a greatly enlarged responsibility. Producing master builders of Methodism, ministerial workmen with genius, ecclesiastical statesmen with foresight and power, genuine prophets with vision and authority is their great mission and task. They will require suitable student material, adequate facilities, competent faculties, and supporting resources equal to their mission and worthy of their Church. Their products can be made more serviceable to the Church. They can be given that knowledge, understanding, wisdom, conviction, and spirit which the genuine Methodist minister must have. Methodism has fundamentals of doctrine, life, and thought upon which our coming ministers must stand if they are to be its exponents. A ministry made up of functionaries can never advance the Church of God. The urgent and increasing need of Methodism is ministers of ability, broad sweep, deep thought, fine loyalty, and vital piety. Methodism is girding for a new day. An adequate ministry can come only by great seminaries kept close to the heart of the Church and sustained by its generous love.

THE HOME TASK

The Methodist Church finds itself at the open door of great, inviting, challenging, appealing service of all kinds and to many classes of people. With its consolidated forces and vast resources it is morally and religiously compelled to think and plan in terms of an encompassing, constructive, and vigorous movement in three extensive home fields: comprehensive home missions activity, local church education and Sunday school extension, and general Methodist intelligence and promotion through well-planned and well-executed publicity. Methodism must seek new powers and enter upon new processes for taking the Christian gospel to the people of all sections of our country. The rural areas, the tenant populations, the foreign settlements, the industrial districts, the race divisions, the peripheral parts of our villages, towns, and cities in all jurisdictions of the new Church present alarming moral and religious destitution. In many places only the small sects that magnify marginal doctrinal emphasis have any hearing and give any religious service. That condition cannot continue and America be sanely Christian. This Church must attempt more and do more to make our land Christian than has ever entered its dreams, much less its planning, and it should begin here. This Uniting Conference can provide for Boards, general, regional and local, and fix responsibilities which will put our Church at its great work of reforming the continent and spreading scriptural holiness over the land.

THE WORK ABROAD

This union of Methodism finds the foreign missionary work of the uniting churches in great need of special inspiration and encouragement. The missionary passion in the home churches must be renewed and strengthened. For a decade the work of foreign missions has gone on with too slow a pace. The old epoch has closed. Each field has developed its own problems, and all are difficult. The entire structure and movement of our overseas work service calls for new strategy, new statesmanship, new forces. An adequate program and system must be set up by which these may be attained. This Uniting Conference has no greater responsibility, no finer task. The new Methodist Church must not fail the nations that this day need the light, the truth, and the salvation that are in Jesus Christ. The world is still our parish. The last commission of our Lord is the first claim upon our Church.

The query has come in from our mission fields as to the place in the United Church of our heroic people on the distant frontiers. Our three Churches have worked in the lands where our people needed unity. In Japan and Korea they proceeded to form independent churches. In Mexico civil laws, and in Brazil national consciousness, made autonomous churches desirable. There are decided indications that some of our Methodist Churches would like a more definite and official relation to the Mother Churches now exchanging multiplicity for unity. Many of our leaders have hoped that the federal ties of Methodism might be lengthened and strengthened so that it might be said that the continents, though separated, had one ecumenical church. Our Plan of Union, and its scheme of Jurisdictional and Central Conferences, provides splendid possibilities for a federal or dominional government that will still allow room for a proper national or wider geographical autonomy. We are confident that this Uniting Conference will give assurance to our widely scattered children that the hearthstone still belongs to them. Our paternal feeling will meet their filial feeling in love. As far as may be wise and possible governmental provisions will be set up for making Methodism a united body in all parts of the world, thus fulfilling Wesley's goal of the "World is my parish."

Here we may be allowed to express our great joy at the marvelous growth and development of the Christian Church, and especially the Methodist Church, in the fields abroad. Many have been the prayers, the tears, the sacrifices, and gifts of love and service which have gone into them from our Methodist people for over a century. The vigor and vitality of the younger churches are being increasingly shown even today in the midst of gravest economic and political difficulties. We have here a convincing evidence of the soundness of our missionary enterprise and a tremendous challenge to enlarge our co-operation to the utmost. Our service for them should be continued and can be continued with enlarged possibilities if the bond between our people and the young churches is kept intimate and strong, but there is grave danger that they will weaken if that bond becomes greatly attenuated. Autonomous Churches and Central Conferences have come about normally in the gratifying growth of the Church in those various lands. However, we may be allowed to point out that liberty in their

Church government could go so far as to destroy elemental
and fundamental relationships with the sustaining life of
the Mother Church, and that would be deeply regretted by
all.

The Mother Church must be to the younger churches more
than an appropriating Board, however large or small the
funds bestowed, or it may sooner or later cease to be even
that.. Funds will be supplied only when and where the life
of the Church is interested. That connectionalism which
gives unity and strength to Methodism at home should embrace as far as practicable the younger Methodisms abroad.
This Uniting Conference may well make such provisions as
will keep open and render effective large possibilities of interest, watch care, and service from the Church at home to
the Churches abroad.

REFORMING CONTINENTS

The Christian Church cannot exclude itself from social
and moral reforms and be true and loyal to its own life and
responsibility. Human rights and human justice cannot be
violated without disaster to man and civilization. The des-
potism of the State is utterly destructive of human liberty
and exhaustive of human personality. The thirst for governmental power, human greed and political, economic and
social injustice, give rise to rebellion and conflict. The
Church must aid in finding a solution to these difficulties
based upon honor, humanity, and reason. War with its inevitable barbarism, murder, theft, and indescribable atroc-
ity, cannot be tolerated as a system of settling international
disputes and establishing international relationships. The
Church cannot be silent while blatant forces of evil, gross
wickedness and vile destruction stride the earth. It shall
ever endeavor to create those attitudes, powers, and processes that will produce a new earth wherein dwelleth righteousness.

THE SPREAD OF HOLINESS

When a group of eighty pioneer preachers organized the
Methodist Episcopal Church in 1784, they solemnly asked,
"What may we reasonably believe to be God's design in raising up the Methodist preachers?" They devoutly replied,
"To reform the continent and spread scriptural holiness over
these lands." They were plain, God-conscious, sin-conscious,
Christ-conscious, salvation-conscious men. They believed
in· the distinctive religious life of Methodism, its indispensable gospel, and its undeniable, irrevocable mission. They were apostolic in faith, speech, and action. It

is marvelous what they accomplished in sixty years. They: lifted the wild frontier of a vast continent out of social chaos; they redeemed the people from moral and religious destitution; they created character and civilization every-: where. These religious progenitors, these fathers in a forceful faith, were the master builders of the resplendent Kingdom which has become our rich and glorious inheri-: tance. Their power was not in their reforms but in their spiritual dynamic. Their unabated emphasis was upon the healing and the health of the heart. Redemption was their theme and reconcilation to God their goal. Not strategies, not technique, but fervent, forceful, full religious life was their power and their salvation.

Methodism came to strength through its spiritual dy-namic. That has been its distinctive contribution to American Christianity, and that must continue to be its driving power. When it is neglected, atrophy and decay come upon the Church. When nurtured it has produced strength, growth, and advance. For it no substitute has been found. It has accounted for many and far-reaching reforms, but none has ever wholly accounted for Methodism. Where the religious life is strongest there the reforms are most effective and constructive enterprises most numerous. The early Wesleyans in their spread of scriptural holiness shook a nation and awoke a great people. There resulted the greatest reforms which that country ever witnessed. Re-ligion, as religious experience and religious life, has in it power for the remaking of the world. These facts point out the trunk line for the Methodism of tomorrow, as they mark the highway of yesterday. Spiritual dynamic is the essential equipment for any triumphant Church. Its attain-ment should continually possess the leadership of the Church.

THE EVANGELISTIC CALL

This address cannot ignore the duty of emphasizing the evangelistic spirit that gave the Wesleyan movement its power and our three Churches their foundations. Evan-gelism today is in grave danger of being weakened into a generality; or narrowed into an advocacy of some frag-ment of Christian conduct; or of being defined as a sort of climatic influence. It is our solemn judgment that Method-ism can have no powerful and expanding life unless it re-covers the seeking spirit of Christ, of St. Paul, and of John Wesley. It is our judgment also that this supreme phase of our Church's life merits and requires the most distinct and powerful leadership. We are warranted, therefore, in expressing the earnest hope that the program here adopted for the Methodist Church shall include as its most vital factor a plan that shall seek to promote in all our borders an intelligent, intense, ardent, throbbing evangelism to the end that there may be added unto the Church constantly multitudes that are being saved.

It is a matter of great gratification that Methodism today in many sections of this country is in a state of decided revival. A great awakening is in progress. The Aldersgate Commemorations of these Churches, the Church-wide Evangelistic movements, and the Youth Crusades are having marvelous effect. Similar activities are on in the North and East, and in the South and West. Names for it may change, but this movement should not halt. It may take ten years to awaken this country, but Methodism has ten years to give to that sacred task. What better service could it render? All leaders in this country, educational, economic, political, and social, are saying that this nation's greatest need is a revival of religion. They know. Why not give America a revival that it will not lose from its life for a hundred years? The stage is set. It can be done. United Methodism has come to the Kingdom for such a time as this.

THE VALUATION OF THE CHURCH

Methodism in America is a great religious force. Beginning as a society in the Church of England, Methodism has become a Church in its own name, right, polity and faith. As such it is obligated to set forth, promote, and preserve its tenets, the integrity of its orders, the sanctity of its sacraments, the validity of its ministry, the redemptiveness of its religious life, and its distinctive characteristics as a legitimate and co-ordinate part of the Ecumenical Church. The founder of Methodism is universally recognized as the world's great evangelist. For fifty years he carried the torch of sacred fire to the darkened spots of England's life. But John Wesley was great as a Churchman as he was great as an evangelist. The ministry, the sacraments, and the ritual were all sacred to him. He taught his ministers and his people loyalty to the Church, its faith and its order. He made innovations under religious necessity, but he violated no Churchman's code. Before acting he established for himself and his followers a historic foundation for ordaining bishops for America and Scotland, and provided for the setting up of separate churches of apostolic content and historic lineage.

Methodism passed rapidly from the state of a society to the standing of a responsible Church of Christ. Its denominationalism was strong and assertive yet commendable, but its position as a substantial division of the Ecumenical Church became more and more established. Today the Methodist Church is a Christian Church of historic faith, order, and structure with a religious life, zeal, thought, and movement that are distinctive and dynamic. Herein lie its significance, its obligation, and its power. Such a Church, with such position and possibilities in fulfillment of its divine mission, can build itself into the life of America and the life of the world. Men await its coming as those that watch for the morning. "Awake, awake, put on strength, O arm of the Lord, as in the ancient days!"

CONCLUSION

The Methodist Church sets forth anew upon a great adventure. Whither, and to what end? The master of the ship at sea each day at noon finds his bearings from the heavenly bodies, sets his course, and steams ahead. This is a parable —Methodism, mid-ocean, a mighty vessel, a precious cargo! Whither and to what end? The setting of the course, the safety of the voyage, the splendor of the adventure are with the men who man the bridge!

No ruler takes a throne nor chief magistrate a scepter of government without a solemn oath to protect, preserve, and defend the constitution of the country. At this glorious inauguration in Methodism with uplifted hand we and you take such an oath of allegiance to our great Church. To its preservation, promotion, and advance we pledge our loyalty, our lives, and our sacred honor. The torch set aflame by our ancestors by their faith, sacrifice, and apostolic heroism shall never go out. By it men shall have the light of the world to the glory of God the Father, and Jesus Christ the Son, unto the uttermost salvation of all mankind.

In the background of all our counsels stand two towering figures, heroes, saints: the immortal founder and the sacrificial prophet of the long road. In all the changing decades we have never lost sight of their faces, the might of their faith, the example of their ardor, or the inheritance of their toil. They speak to us today from the hilltops of eternal glory. Hear them! "The best of all is, God is with us." It is the voice of the founder. God is with us! God is with us! The Father, the Son, the Holy Spirit are with us!

Hear the other voice. The prophet of the long road is speaking, echoing the words read to him by his companion at the end of his last journey as he stepped into the chariot that took him away to his Father's house. "I am Alpha and Omega, the beginning and the end. He that overcometh shall inherit all things, and I shall be his God and he shall be my Son." Down from the sky comes the assurance that victory is the ultimate portion for God's people. "God buries his workmen but carries on his work." Our illustrious human founders still speak to us in living words. Let us in the name of God of our fathers unfurl the banners and sound the trumpets and speak unto the children of Methodism that they go forward—

"God of our fathers, known of old,
Be with us yet, be with us yet."

Bishops of the Methodist Episcopal Church: William F. Anderson, John L. Nuelsen, Edwin H. Hughes, Francis J. McConnell, Frederick D. Leete, Herbert Welch, Thomas Nicholson, Adna W. Leonard, Charles B. Mitchell, John W. Robinson, Eben S. Johnson, Ernest L. Waldorf, Charles Edward Locke, Ernest G. Richardson, Edgar Blake, Frederick T. Keeney, H. Lester Smith, Charles L. Mead, Robert E. Jones, Matthew W. Clair, George A. Miller, Titus Lowe, Brenton T. Badley, Wallace E. Brown, Raymond J. Wade, James C. Baker, J. Ralph Magee, Ralph S. Cushman, Wilbur E. Hammaker, Charles W. Flint, Alexander P. Shaw, G. Bromley Oxnam, Edwin F. Lee, John M. Springer, Ralph A. Ward, John Gowdy, Jashwant R. Chitambar, J. Waskom Pickett, Juan E. Gattinoni, Roberto Elphick, F. H. Otto Melle.

Bishops of the Methodist Episcopal Church, South: Warren A. Candler, John M. Moore, Urban V. W. Darlington, H. M. Du Bose, William N. Ainsworth, Samuel R. Hay, James Cannon, Jr., Hoyt M. Dobbs, Hiram A. Boaz, Arthur J. Moore, Paul B. Kern, A. Frank Smith, Ivan Lee Holt, William W. Peele, Clare Purcell, Charles C. Selecman, J. Lloyd Decell, William C. Martin, William T. Watkins.*

President of the General Conference, Methodist Protestant Church: James H. Straughn.

---

*Bishop Collins Denny, of the Methodist Episcopal Church, South, who has declined to become a Bishop of The Methodist Church, refused to sign the foregoing address.

MESSAGE FROM THE COUNCIL OF BISHOPS

The Methodists of America have entered into a new sense of brotherhood. They have consummated the largest union of Protestant Christians ever achieved. The full significance of what has occurred is beyond our present understanding; only eternity can properly evaluate the deeper meaning of what we have here done.

Of greater significance than the act of union is the result of union. The spiritual oneness so conspicuous at the Uniting Conference must be made to permeate the whole body of Methodism. Out of this union must spring a new and more intense loyalty to our Wesleyan heritage. Above all, this Methodist Church must immediately project a program of service commensurate with its latent powers and its unparalleled opportunity.

In the providence of God our Churches have come together at a moment of world crisis. In every land there is perplexity and fear. The priceless values of life are everywhere threatened. Never in modern times was there such an imperative demand for the proclamation and application of the Gospel. At the very instant of its new birth, The Methodist Church is faced with a challenge to summon all men to behold the redemptive power which has always been resident in the eternal Christ.

The burden of our duty in this hour has been upon our hearts. In response to inner promptings, no less than to the request of the Conference, your Bishops express the need for a mighty resurgence of spiritual life and its inevitable moral overflow, and their willingness to help lead the Church in a movement to bring about its consummation.

Such a forward movement should be all-inclusive, and should be dynamic, inspirational, and educational in nature and method. It should involve a dissemination among our people of information concerning the history, genius, theology, policy, and program of Methodism.

It should inculcate a new loyalty to all our institutions. It should interpret unification to our people and weld them together in understanding, sympathy and a sense of fellowship. It should emphasize our world-wide missionary enterprise and stimulate the passion to evangelize all peoples.

It should promote Christian stewardship and bring about a greater liberality for the larger benevolent work of our

Church. It should lay bare the social and personal sins of our time and call men to repentance and reformation. It should place emphasis upon personal religious experience and seek to revive in the hearts of our people the seeking spirit of the compassionate Christ.

Such a movement must be more than a temporary enterprise of an inspirational nature. Its foundations must be wide and deep; its cultivation fundamental and constant. The best of our thought and the most competent advice we can secure shall be devoted to projecting the details of a plan, which in due time will be announced to the Church. With the hearty and unselfish co-operation of all our preachers, people, and organizations, the movement contemplated should bring the Church to its first General Conference having witnessed a revival of deep religious experience, with all its forces mobilized for the inauguration of the third century of vital Methodism.

No cause is forlorn with Christ at its head. We look up and behold the morning. Christ is out on the highways of the world's needs. No ingenuity of wickedness, no indifference or scorn of men can stop His unceasing march of redemption. We resolve anew to evade no peril and to seek no discharge from the tasks, but take our appointed way with Him until the gospel has been given in its uniqueness and redeeming power to all men.

"We will rejoice in Thy salvation, and in the name of our God will we set up our banner."

JOURNAL

of the

Uniting Conference, 1939

WEDNESDAY MORNING, APRIL 26, 1939

THE UNITING CONFERENCE OF THE METHODIST EPISCOPAL CHURCH, THE METHODIST EPISCOPAL CHURCH, SOUTH, AND THE METHODIST PROTESTANT CHURCH opened its proceedings with the observance of the Sacrament of the Lord's Supper, at 8:30 A.M., Wednesday, April 26, 1939, in the Protestant Episcopal Cathedral of Grace and Holy Trinity, Kansas City, Mo.

APRIL 26
FIRST DAY

Morning

Opening

The Sacrament of the Lord's Supper was administered by Bishops Herbert Welch, Wallace E. Brown, and Wilbur E. Hammaker, of the Methodist Episcopal Church; Bishops Samuel R. Hay, William W. Peele, and Charles C. Selecman, of the Methodist Episcopal Church, South; and Doctors E. A. Sexsmith and S. W. Rosenberger of the Methodist Protestant Church.

Sacrament
of the
Lord's
Supper

At the conclusion of this solemn and impressive service, the delegates-elect, led by the Bishops of the Methodist Episcopal Church and the Methodist Episcopal Church, South, and the President of the General Conference of the Methodist Protestant Church, marched in a body to the Municipal Auditorium, where the business sessions of the Conference were held.

Procession

At 10 o'clock Judge Leslie J. Lyons, Chairman of the Local Committee on Entertainment, requested the members of the Conference to stand, as the Bishops were approaching.

The Bishops of the Methodist Episcopal Church and the Methodist Episcopal Church, South, came to the platform, led by Bishop Edwin H. Hughes, of the Methodist Episcopal Church, Bishop John M. Moore, of the Methodist Episcopal Church, South, and Dr. James H. Straughn, President of

APRIL 26
FIRST DAY
Morning

the General Conference of the Methodist Protestant Church, the three Co-Chairmen of the Joint Commission on Church Union.

Fanfare

As the Bishops came to the platform, sixteen trumpeters from the Central Junior High School of Kansas City sounded a fanfare under the direction of Dr. James R. Houghton, director of Music of Boston University. Led by Dr. Houghton and the Seminary Singers of Boston University, the audience joined in singing "All Hail the Power of Jesus' Name."

After the Bishops had reached the platform the trumpeters rendered another selection.

Call to Order

Bishop Edwin Holt Hughes called this momentous Conference to order, as follows:

This is the day which the Lord hath made; we will rejoice and be glad in it.

The hour cometh, and now is, when the true worshipers shall worship the Father in spirit and in truth.

The sacrifices of God are a broken spirit; a broken and a contrite heart, O God, thou wilt not despise.

Let the words of my mouth, and the meditation of my heart, be acceptable in thy sight, O Lord, my strength and my redeemer.

Devotions

Bishop John M. Moore announced, and the Conference joined in singing Hymn 381, "The Church's One Foundation Is Jesus Christ Her Lord."

President James H. Straughn then led the audience in the recital of the Apostles' Creed.

Prayer

Dr. J. C. Broomfield, former President of the General Conference of the Methodist Protestant Church, led in prayer, as follows:

For bringing us to this high moment we render Thee thanks, our Father in Heaven, and now that we are here we are happy in the thought that we can depend upon Thee. We can draw upon Thy strength, and upon Thy wisdom, and upon Thy forebearance, and upon Thy patience. We would place our feet afresh upon the great promise that "my God shall supply all your needs according to his riches and glory." We pray Thee, our Father, that in like manner all of us shall be at Thy disposal, and from this opening service until the close may we be under the control of Thy Spirit; that we can follow in the path which He indicates and be brave enough to do what He wants done, rather than what we may choose to do ourselves. And may there be such a high note struck in this service as shall resound throughout this entire Uniting Conference. We acknowledge Thee as our Father; we acknowledge Jesus Christ as the Great Head of the

Church; we acknowledge the Holy Spirit as our Sanctifier, Comforter, and Guide. Through Jesus Christ our Lord. Amen.

Bishop Urban V. W. Darlington, Senior effective Bishop of the Methodist Episcopal Church, South, then led the Conference in the responsive reading "God's Unsearchable Greatness," found on page 604 of the *Methodist Hymnal.*

The Conference then joined heartily in the singing of the Gloria Patri.

Bishop Frederick T. Keeney, of the Methodist Episcopal Church, read the New Testament lesson from John 17: 1-23.

Bishop Francis J. McConnell, of the Methodist Episcopal Church, led in prayer, as follows:

Almighty God, our Father in Heaven, we praise Thee as we come before Thee upon this occasion. We can feel that Thou art very near unto us. We know that Thou art near in the sense that Thy power is round about us, and that Thy wisdom is manifest in all the works which Thou hast made, and in all the revelations which Thou dost make of Thyself to us. But we thank Thee that there come particular times when it is in a peculiar sense that Thou art near. We are indeed near unto Thee in the sense that in Thee we live and move and have our being. But Thou art near unto us also in a peculiarly intimate sense when we feel that we stand close to Thee to carry out in some special way a manifestation of Thy purpose. We come together at this time feeling the commission of a great purpose which we believe is inspired by Thee. We thank Thee for the revelations that Thou hast made through these different branches of Thy Church, for the distinctiveness of point of view, for the uniqueness of approach of each of the groups to Thee, and for the degree of success which Jesus had in carrying out Thy plans for men. And now we come together thanking Thee for the way in which Thou hast manifested Thyself, praising Thee for all the victories which the various branches have won with Thy help, and asking Thee for a larger portion even of Thy Spirit as we look to the days ahead. We praise Thee for that power by which human effort can be multiplied as men come together to do Thy will. We thank Thee for the individual experience, for the way in which we can feel that Thou dost understand each one of us. Thou knowest our downsitting and art acquainted with all our ways. Thou knowest also our uprising as we go forth to the work of the day. And we praise Thee for the revelations which have come to each of these groups of Thy servants as they have been brought together. And we thank Thee that we can feel that as the days come and go in the years that are ahead there can be a peculiar multiplication of divine force in the united body; that we have not merely the addition of one group to another, but we have also the peculiar intensification and spread of power, as these separate bodies maintain every distinctivity in their spiritual approach, nevertheless go forth in a new union of purpose and of will to accomplish that to which they have been sent on earth. Be with us then, we beseech Thee. And now deliver us from any pride in organization or any exaltation of organization for its purpose. Help us to see the peculiarities of each organization which has given to each organization its might, but deliver us, we beseech Thee, from worshiping anything that is merely instrumental. Help us to keep in mind the great end toward which we all aim. Deliver us from idolatry. May the blessed Spirit give us a sense of perspective that shall kept all things in their proper place and shall order all things aright so that nothing shall stand out at the end except the revelation of Thy Son our Lord Jesus Christ, and the means by which we attain the birth of understanding. May we think that in a sense we have come to a new kingdom for such a time as this. We see the world distraught, if not by war, at least disturbed by rumors of war. We see class arrayed against class, and race against race. We feel somehow that we have the forces that can heal these divisions and bring them into something that approaches to a body of Christ. May the spiritual aim, then, be uppermost in our minds, an aim that shall include all men. Deliver us from any false limitation of our thoughts to any one group. Above all the thought of one particular nation, may we see the nations of the earth coming together to worship Thee. Above all the thoughts of all particular races and all particular organizations may we see the common purpose for which Thou hast sent us into the world. We praise Thee for the honor Thou hast bestowed upon us. In humility we confess our sins. At times we are affrighted with the thought that Thine eyes are in every place beholding the evil, and we forget that Thou dost also behold the good. Without any trace of spiritual conceit or arrogance, may we be looking upon ourselves as possessed of an inherent dignity because we are Thy sons. What are we that Thou art mindful of us, and yet Thou hast bestowed upon us dominion over some things. May we have dominion over ourselves and in powers of persuasion and of life may we have dominion over those round about us. So may all our sessions be in a deep sense of waiting upon Thee. And may we attain here to that lofty experience of communion with Thee which comes from laboring together with Thee. We thank Thee for the enlightenment of our minds which comes out of contemplation of that truth. We thank Thee for the quickening of our wills and for the responsiveness of our hearts. But help us to understand that the true, the deepest revelation, comes, after all, as we look in the direction in which Thou art looking, as we look out to the men that know Thee not, as we see the sorrow and distress of the world. May we feel then that Thine eyes and the eyes of Thy people are centered upon the same needs and upon the same task, and grant that out of this common working together we may attain to a new sense of communion with Thyself. May we look back always, and may the Church look back always upon these days as a time when Thy people came to understand Thee better; be more nearly instantaneous in response to the promptings of Thy Spirit; be more thoroughly devoted to carrying Thy plans *Morning* out in the world. And we ask it all in the name of our Prayer Christ. Amen.

Bishop James Cannon, Jr., of the Methodist Episcopal Church, South, announced and the Conference joined in singing one of Charles Wesley's greatest hymns, No. 162 in *The Methodist Hymnal*, "O for a Thousand Tongues to Sing."

Bishop Hughes called the Uniting Conference Business to order for the transaction of business, as follows: Session

> For the formal call for the Uniting Conference, the delegates will stand.

The Conference arose and Bishop Hughes proceeded:

> Dear Brothers and Sisters: The Methodist Episcopal Church, South, the Methodist Episcopal Church, and the Methodist Protestant Church have by their regular constitutional processes voted to unite, and to become The Methodist Church. According to the Plan of Union adopted by them, a Uniting Conference was provided for, that it might consummate union and combine the laws of the three Disciplines. Delegates have been duly elected according to the provisions adopted by the three Churches to represent them.
> The time having arrived for the meeting of this Uniting Conference, I now call its first session to order and declare it duly convened.

Bishop John M. Moore, of the Methodist Episcopal Church, South, and Dr. James H. Straughn, President of the General Conference of the Methodist Protestant Church, together with Bishop Edwin H. Hughes, of the Methodist Episcopal Church, Co-Chairmen of the Joint Commission on Church Union, jointly made the following declaration:

> This we do reverently, in the name of the Father, and of the Son, and of the Holy Spirit. Amen.

Bishop Hughes announced that the first order Organization of business was the calling of the roll. Roll Call

Bishop H. Lester Smith, Secretary of the Board Bishops of Bishops of the Methodist Episcopal Church, Present stated that the following active Bishops of that Church were present: John L. Nuelsen, Edwin

APRIL 26
FIRST DAY

Morning

Bishops
Present
H. Hughes, Francis J. McConnell, Adna W. Leonard, Ernest L. Waldorf, Ernest G. Richardson, Edgar Blake, H. Lester Smith, Charles L. Mead, Robert E. Jones, Titus Lowe, Brenton T. Badley, Wallace E. Brown, Raymond J. Wade, James C. Baker, J. Ralph Magee, Ralph S. Cushman, Wilbur E. Hammaker, Charles W. Flint, Alexander P. Shaw, G. Bromley Oxnam, Edwin F. Lee, John M. Springer, Ralph A. Ward, John Gowdy, Jashwant R. Chitambar, J. Waskom Pickett, Roberto Elphick, F. H. Otto Melle. Absent: Juan E. Gattinoni.

Retired Bishops present: William F. Anderson, Frederick D. Leete, Herbert Welch, John W. Robinson, Charles E. Locke, Frederick T. Keeney, Matthew W. Clair, George A. Miller. Absent: Thomas Nicholson, Charles B. Mitchell, Eben S. Johnson.

Bishop Paul B. Kern, Secretary of the College of Bishops of the Methodist Episcopal Church, South, announced that the following active Bishops of that Church were present: Urban V. W. Darlington, Arthur J. Moore, Paul B. Kern, A. Frank Smith, Ivan Lee Holt, William W. Peele, Clare Purcell, Charles C. Selecman, J. Lloyd Decell, William C. Martin, William T. Watkins. Absent: Hoyt M. Dobbs.

Retired Bishops present: John M. Moore, James Cannon, Jr., Samuel R. Hay, Hiram A. Boaz. Absent: Warren A. Candler, Collins Denny, Horace M. Du Bose, William N. Ainsworth.

Bishop Hughes then announced that the respective Secretaries of the last General Conferences of the three uniting Churches would call the roll of delegates of their respective Churches after the manner agreed upon—namely, by Conferences, with the Chairman of each Conference delegation reporting the number present in this delegation; sending to the Secretary's table the names of all absent members of the delegation, and at the same time making any necessary substitutions.

John M. Arters, Secretary of the last General Conference of the Methodist Episcopal Church, was present; but being physically incapacitated, under his direction the roll of Conferences of that Church was called by Edgar R. Heckman, his first

Assistant Secretary, and the following were certified as being present:

APRIL 26
FIRST DAY
Morning
Delegates
Present

ALABAMA.—Ministerial: J. L. Brasher. Lay: W. F. Franke substituted for A. D. Peck.
ATLANTA.—Ministerial: D. H. Stanton. Lay: J. P. Brawley.
BALTIMORE.—Ministerial: F. R. Bayley, B. W. Meeks, J. R. Edwards. Lay: D. S. Patterson, G. W. Crabbe.
BLUE RIDGE-ATLANTIC.—Ministerial: M. O. Fletcher. Lay: Mrs. R. C. Kennedy.
CALIFORNIA.—Ministerial: T. C. Knowles, C. A. Richardson, F. D. Parr. Lay: J. D. Crummey, John Tunnicliffe.
CENTRAL ALABAMA.—Ministerial: E. M. Jones. Lay: L. W. Lynn.
CENTRAL NEW YORK.—Ministerial: R. H. Huse, A. P. Coman, H. E. Woolever. Lay: Mrs. H. S. Osborn, A. G Odell.
CENTRAL NORTHWEST.—Ministerial: T. J. Westerberg. Lay: J. E. Anderson.
CENTRAL PENNSYLVANIA.—Ministerial: J. E. Skillington, E. R. Heckman, M. E. Schwartz. Lay: O. V. Adams, V. M. Frey.
CENTRAL TENNESSEE.—Ministerial: W. J. Fesmire. Lay: Miss Leota Holmes.
CENTRAL WEST.—Ministerial: B. F. Abbott. Lay: Miss A. M. Williams.
COLORADO.—Ministerial: O. W. Auman, C. E. Schofield, F. L. Geyer. Lay: R. B. Spencer, E. C. Harrah, Herman Wills, Jr., substituted for Miss Harriett Lewis, W. H. Spurgeon.
DAKOTA.—Ministerial: E. D. Kohlstedt. Lay: B. A. Dunbar.
DELAWARE.—Ministerial: D. H. Hargis. Lay: H. S. Wilson.
DETROIT.—Ministerial: M. S. Rice, M. R. Reed, F. L. Fitch, H. H. Crane, J. M. M. Gray, W. R. Fruit. Lay: H. C. Baldwin, P. G. Halmhuber substituted for Webster Pearce, D. T. Strong.
EAST GERMAN.—Ministerial: J. H. Steinkraus. Lay: C. M. Windels substituted for E. H. Mueller.
EAST TENNESSEE.—Ministerial: W. L. Sanders. Lay: Mrs. D. E. McNorton.
EASTERN SWEDISH.—Ministerial: H. C. Whyman. Lay: O. W. Hjerpe.
ERIE.—Ministerial: L. M. Barnard, S. T. Davison. Lay: E. T. Welch, L. H. McKay.
FLORIDA.—Ministerial: H. W. Bartlay. Lay: D. A. Boyd.
GENESEE.—Ministerial: S. A. Keen, J. W. Searles. Lay: Mrs. W. R. Brown, M. S. Gibbs.
GEORGIA.—Ministerial: E. C. Dewey, E. J. Hammond. Lay: G. S. McElroy.
HOLSTON.—Ministerial: R. L. Stapleton. Lay: J. L. Robb, J. S. Fletcher, Mrs. H. C. Black, F. H. Trotter.
IDAHO.—Ministerial: W. H. Hertzog. Lay: E. H. Deal, H. J. Roan.

ILLINOIS.—Ministerial: A. M. Wells, T. B. Lugg, W. E. Shaw, W. G. Pulliam, E. G. Sandmeyer, H. W. McPherson. Lay: H. W. Fitch, H. R. Snavely, Mrs. I. B. Blackstock, H. S. Wiley, L. H. Martin.

INDIANA.—Ministerial: O. W. Fifer, W. C. Hartinger, W. T. Jones substituted for J. M. Walker. Lay: R. M. Kibler, Mrs. H. E. Asbury, W. W. Schwaninger, H. D. Hinkle substituted for T. M. McDonald.

IOWA-DES MOINES.—Ministerial: L. P. Goodwin, U. S. Smith, W. A. Longnecker substituted for A. H. Barker. Lay: Mrs. H. S. Hollingsworth, Dean Taylor, J. M. Beck substituted for J. H. Peterman.

KANSAS.—Ministerial: O. E. Allison, E. F. Buck, R. O. Penick, W. A. Keve. Lay: Mrs. H. A. French, J. C. Gaede, A. F. Landon.

KENTUCKY.—Ministerial: S. C. Rice. Lay: A. S. Bennett.

LEXINGTON.—Ministerial: B. F. Smith. Lay: D. A. Bethea, J. A. X. Patton.

LOUISIANA.—Ministerial: J. W. E. Bowen. Lay: M. S. Davage.

MAINE.—Ministerial: A. A. Callaghan. Lay: C. D. Baldwin.

MICHIGAN.—Ministerial: D. S. Coors, L. T. Robinson, A. H. Pellowe, J. L. Seaton. Lay: L. D. Dickinson, Mrs. W. H. Veenboer, Smith Burnham.

MINNESOTA.—Ministerial: L. H. Rising. Lay: G. F. Reineke.

MISSISSIPPI.—Ministerial: J. B. F. Shaw, L. E. Johnson. Lay: R. H. McAllister.

MISSOURI.—Ministerial: E. J. Kulp, J. F. King, F. W. Wahl, Edward Hislop. Lay: L. J. Lyons, Grace L. Bragg. C. W. Hanke, R. C. Tucker, Miss A. B. Duhigg.

MONTANA STATE.—Ministerial: John Morange. Lay: E. E. Collins.

NEBRASKA.—Ministerial: L. H. Kaub, H. E. Hess, Walter Aitken, E. L. Geissinger. Lay: H. M. Greenslit, G. H. Gray, W. S. Rogers, Miss E. M. Rogers, W. D. Clark.

NEW ENGLAND.—Ministerial: D. L. Marsh, L. O. Hartman. Lay: S. T. Emery, S. O. MacMullen, Mrs. L. L. LeSourd, V. P. Clarke.

NEW ENGLAND SOUTHERN.—Ministerial: J. V. Claypool, A. C. Knudson. Lay: W. P. Pritchard.

NEW HAMPSHIRE.—Ministerial: L. W. Stringfellow. Lay: W. H. Davis.

NEW JERSEY.—Ministerial: T. S. Brock, H. P. Sloan. Lay: F. C. Propert, H. P. Bennett.

NEW YORK.—Ministerial: Allan MacRossie. Lay: C. A. Smith, C. H. Fowler, J. R. Mott, Mrs. F. J. McConnell.

NEW YORK EAST.—Ministerial: J. W. Langdale, L. H. Hough, F. B. Newell. Lay: E. R. Carman, H. A. Chaffee, Mrs. C. H. Hardie, W. H. Barradell substituted for F. A. Horne.

NEWARK.—Ministerial: J. E. Washabaugh, A. A. Brown, K. K. Quimby substituted for L. E. Foster. Lay: A. S. McNear, J. R. Joy, Mrs. Mabel Diefendorf substituted for S. H. Clark.

NORTH CAROLINA.—Ministerial: R. W. Winchester, R. N. Brooks. Lay: D. D. Jones.

NORTH DAKOTA.—Ministerial: L. R. Burgum. Lay:
G. N. Knight.
NORTH INDIANA.—Ministerial: A. W. Pugh, F. E. Fribley, W. W. Sweet. Lay: R. R. Roudebush, H. R. Gettle,
G. E. Fernstermacher.
NORTHEAST OHIO.—Ministerial: E. R. Brown, O. T.
Olson, L. C. Wright, C. B. Ketcham, H. W. Courtney, N.
E. Davis, F. W. Nueller. Lay: A. L. Hoover, James
Cherry, W. D. Archer, M. C. Robinson, Miss E. J. Oram.
NORTHERN MINNESOTA.—Ministerial: T. A. Stafford,
George Mecklenburg, L. H. Bugbee, R. C. Raines. Lay:
H. A. Douglas, Florence R. Jardine, Mrs. F. F. Lindsay.
NORTHERN NEW YORK.—Ministerial: F. A. Miller, A.
G. Judd. Lay: W. C. Sykes, A. D. Cheetham.
NORTHWEST INDIANA.—Ministerial: H. L. Davis, B. D.
Beck. Lay: E. M. Mann, J. B. Campbell substituted for
F. C. Evans, R. G. McCutchan.
NORTHWEST IOWA.—Ministerial: J. B. Walker, E. A.
Roadman. Lay: Mrs. M. H. White, J. I. Dolliver.
NORTHWEST KANSAS.—Ministerial: A. N. Smith. Lay:
C. A. Kemp.
NORWEGIAN AND DANISH.—Ministerial: C. W. Schevenius. Lay: M. E. Michelsen.
OHIO.—Ministerial: Arba Martin, I. E. Miller, A. G.
Schatzman, A. J. Kestle, E. R. Stafford, Jesse Swank,
J. A. Diekmann, E. D. Soper. Lay: Mrs. W. H. C. Goode,
C. A. Jones, E. D. Bancroft, J. J. McKim, T. W. Appleby,
L. S. Ivins, Mrs. J. H. Freeman, W. E. Keplinger, E. H.
Cherrington.
OKLAHOMA.—Ministerial: I. M. Hargett, R. J. Smith
substituted for Phil Deschner. Lay: H. V. Carter substituted for W. H. Wilcox, W. M. Vickery.
OREGON.—Ministerial: S. W. Hall, J. C. Harrison, E.
L. Mills. Lay: E. W. Peterson.
PACIFIC NORTHWEST.—Ministerial: J. B. Magee, Charles
MacCaughey, C. K. Mahoney. Lay: C. D. Foster, C. A
Robbins, D. S. Jeffers.
PHILADELPHIA.—Ministerial: G. W. Henson, C. W. Kitto,
W. G. Tyson, J. S. L. Thomas. Lay: C. F. Eggleston,
J. W. Masland, G. S. Lynch, W. J. Elliott.
PITTSBURGH.—Ministerial: S. W. Corcoran, J. D. Piper,
W. K. Anderson. Lay: Elizabeth M. Lee, C. P. Howse, E.
W. Jones.
ROCK RIVER.—Ministerial: F. D. Stone, H. G. Smith,
A. S. Moore, R. E. Diffendorfer, G. A. Fowler. Lay: Mrs.
W. H. Dangel, A. C. Crawford, E. R. Alderson substituted
for Jacob Cantlin, Mrs. James Oldshue, J. A. James.
SAINT JOHNS RIVER.—Ministerial: G. E. Farrar, G. C.
James. Lay: F. B. Noble.
SAVANNAH.—Ministerial: C. W. Prothro. Lay: T. R.
Clements.
SOUTH CAROLINA.—Ministerial: A. R. Howard. Lay:
T. H. Pinckney, J. B. Randolph.
SOUTH FLORIDA.—Ministerial: J. A. Simpson. Lay:
J. H. Smith,
SOUTHERN.—Ministerial: H. C. Leonard. Lay: M. B.
Brandenberger.
SOUTHERN CALIFORNIA.—Ministerial: W. C. Buckner,
R. L. Smith, F. G. H. Stevens, G. A. Warmer, J. L. Cor-

ley. Lay: Mrs. Jerome Seymour, J. W. Hole, Wray Andrew, S. W. McCulloch, J. H. S. McGiffin.

SOUTHERN ILLINOIS.—Ministerial: C. R. Yost, C. C. Hall. Lay: W. T. Johnson, Mrs. Edna Webb.

SOUTHWEST.—Ministerial: J. H. Taggart. Lay: J. S. Cullins.

SOUTHWEST KANSAS.—Ministerial: I. D. Harris, A. E. Kirk. Lay: Mrs. C. M. Gray, H. B. McKibben substituted for L. W. Mayberry.

TENNESSEE.—Ministerial: J. W. Golden. Lay: S. C. Freeman.

TEXAS.—Ministerial: W. M. Dogan. Lay: W. M. Jordan.

TROY.—Ministerial: G. C. Douglass, Mark Kelley. Lay: V. K. Moore, Miss Henrietta Gibson.

UPPER IOWA.—Ministerial: E. A. Baker, F. W. Court, H. J. Burgstahler. Lay: S. A. Cohagen, Mrs. E. R. Nicholson, R. T. Baker.

UPPER MISSISSIPPI.—Ministerial: L. M. McCoy. Lay: W. J. Coleman.

VERMONT.—Ministerial: E. H. Martin. Lay: A. C. Clark.

WASHINGTON.—Ministerial: W. A. Hughes, R. M. Williams. Lay: A. E. Briscoe, Fannie D. Tyler.

WEST TEXAS.—Ministerial: S. E. Grannum, W. J. King. Lay: E. M. Cooper.

WEST VIRGINIA.—Ministerial: C. G. Stater, M. C. Miles, J. W. Engle. Lay: Mrs. H. W. Harmer, C. W. Evans, C. O. Law.

WEST WISCONSIN.—Ministerial: A. F. Hughes. Lay: F. O. Whitcher.

WESTERN NORWEGIAN-DANISH.—Ministerial: Fredrik Engebretsen. Lay: Glenn Engebretsen.

WILMINGTON.—Ministerial: J. J. Bunting, D. W. Jacobs. Lay: W. L. Overdeer, Granville Hooper, H. B. Wright.

WISCONSIN.—Ministerial: I. E. Schlagenhauf, J. W. Perry, R. B. Stansell. Lay: E. H. Roberts, G. A. Jacobs.

WYOMING.—Ministerial: G. M. Bell, G. R. Savige. Lay: H. R. Van Deusen, W. L. Hunt.

WYOMING STATE.—Ministerial: R. O. Hills. Lay: A. S. Hamm.

Bishop H. Lester Smith, Secretary of the Board of Bishops of the Methodist Episcopal Church, called the roll of foreign delegates by name, as they had not been elected by Conferences but had been appointed by the Board of Bishops. The following answered to their names:

AFRICAN CONFERENCES.—Ministerial: George A. Roberts. Lay: C. J. Stauffacher.

CHINA CONFERENCES.—Ministerial: Samson S. Ding. Lay: Miss Alpha J. Miller, P. P. Wiant, Miss Irma Highbaugh.

FOOCHOW CONFERENCE, CHINA.—Ministerial: F. T. Cartwright.

EUROPEAN CONFERENCES.—Ministerial: Theodore Arvidson, Mathias S. Haver, Ferdinand Sigg. Lay: Heinrich Stehl.
INDIAN CONFERENCES.—Ministerial: E. M. Moffatt, E. M. Rugg. Lay: Mrs. C. Premnath Das, J. S. K. Patel.
JAPANESE CONFERENCES.—Ministerial: A. D. Berry.
KOREAN CONFERENCES.—Lay: Miss M. J. Troxel.
MALAYSIAN AND PHILIPPINE ISLAND CONFERENCES.—Ministerial: R. L. Archer, E. S. Lyons.
SOUTH AFRICAN CONFERENCES.—Ministerial: D. S. Bullock, Arthur Wesley. Lay: C. S. Bell.

Lud H. Estes, Secretary of the last General Conference of the Methodist Episcopal Church, South, called the roll of that Church, and the following were certified as being present:

ALABAMA.—Ministerial: H. M. Andrews, R. R. Ellison, W. M. Curtis, A. E. Shafer, D. P. Slaughter. Lay: Zebulon Judd, C. M. Dannelly, Mrs. R. R. Ellison, J. T. Ellison, W. B. Christenberry substituted for O. L. Tompkins.
ARIZONA.—Ministerial: W. H. Coleman. Lay: J. H. Evans.
BALTIMORE.—Ministerial: N. B. Harmon, Jr., E. L. Woolf, H. M. Canter, E. C. Berry, Hubert Sydenstricker, S. K. Cockrell, H. H. Sherman. Lay: J. H. Rosenberger, J. E. Easter, N. M. Canter, C. S. Coleman, G. H. Lamar, J. R. Norman.
BELGIAN.—Ministerial: W. G. Thonger.
CENTRAL TEXAS.—Ministerial: E. B. Hawk, P. E. Riley, W. W. Ward, R. W. Goodloe, J. N. R. Score, F. P. Culver, M. M. Chunn. Lay: H. H. Cherry, Mrs. Gid J. Bryan, Law Sone, Nat Harris, J. E. Edwards, G. C. Boswell, Boyce Martin.
CHINA.—Ministerial: Z. T. Kaung. Lay: Y. C. Yang.
CUBA.—Ministerial: E. E. Clements. Lay: Enrique Noble.
CZECHOSLOVAK.—Ministerial: J. P. Bartak. Lay: Mrs. M. Bartak.
FLORIDA.—Ministerial: W. A. Myres substituted for M. H. Norton, H. W. Blackburn, W. F. Dunkle, Smith Hardin, J. H. Daniel. Lay: C. B. Peeler substituted for Harwell Wilson, Mrs. F. B. Godfrey, DeWitt Griffin, A. K. Hawkins, Mrs. J. T. Feaster.
HOLSTON.—Ministerial: J. W. Perry, J. S. French, I. P. Martin, R. E. Greer, J. A. Baylor, W. P. Eastwood, M. A. Stevenson. Lay: J. N. Hillman, C. C. Sherrod, L. M. Thomas, Mrs. L. A. Tynes, W. K. Barnett. A. S. Pennington, F. A. Carter, W. E. Brock, Mrs. J. W. Perry.
ILLINOIS.—Ministerial: W. T. Mathis. Lay: J. H. Davis.
KENTUCKY.—Ministerial: J. L. Clark, A. R. Perkins, O. B. Crockett, W. G. Cram. Lay: M. C. Redwine, E. W. Savage substituted for Mrs. J. H. Spillman, J. T. Cannon.
LITTLE ROCK.—Ministerial: C. M. Reves, Clem Baker, J. D. Hammons, E. C. Rule. Lay: J. S. M. Cannon, Carl Hollis, Fred Moore, Mrs. J. M. Stinson.

LOUISIANA.—Ministerial: W. W. Holmes, W. L. Duren, H. L. Johns, Dana Dawson, F. N. Parker. Lay: C. O. Holland, T. L. James, Mrs. G. S. Sexton, Jr., J. H. Carter, H. H. White.
LOUISVILLE.—Ministerial: R. H. Short, G. W. Hummel, J. H. Nicholson, A. P. Lyon. Lay: J. H. Dickey, J. L. Harman, W. L. Cash, Mrs. J. W. Piggott.
MEMPHIS.—Ministerial: F. B. Jones, J. E. Underwood, Lud H. Estes, E. G. Hamlett, F. H. Peeples, C. C. Daniel. Lay: Henry Hedden, R. E. Womack, W. F. McMurry, J. T. Peeler substituted for Paul Meek, Mrs. S. H. Tatum, G. L. Morelock.
MISSISSIPPI.—Ministerial: B. L. Sutherland, T. M. Brownlee, C. A. Bowen, B. M. Hunt, W. B. Alsworth. Lay: J. M. Sullivan, B. M. Stevens, Mrs. Paul Arrington, W. D. Hawkins, Curtis Youngblood.
MISSOURI.—Ministerial: R. C. Holliday, F. C. Tucker, D. K. Pegues, J. D. Randolph, W. M. Alexander. Lay: F. F. Stephens, J. M. Woods, W. H. Utz, Jr., P. M. Marr.
NEW MEXICO.—Ministerial: W. L. Barr, C. K. Campbell. Lay: H. O. Davidson, G. C. Carver.
NORTH ALABAMA.—Ministerial: G. M. Davenport, M. E. Lazenby, W. G. Henry, S. O. Kimbrough, H. M. Stevenson, W. E. Morris, M. M. Davidson, A. M. Freeman, J. S. Chadwick. Lay: R. B. Carr, E. J. Garrison, A. N. Kirby, B. L. Ingram, F. S. Ward, W. D. Graves, Mrs. Isaac Morris, Paul S. Haley, W. D. Self, Harry Denman.
NORTH ARKANSAS.—Ministerial: A. W. Martin, J. Q. Schisler, Warren Johnston, O. E. Goddard, E. T. Wayland. Lay: Mrs. Henkel Pewett, J. M. Williams, Nelson Barnett substituted for C. A. Stuck, S. A. Galloway substituted for C. G. Melton, J. P. Womack, J. H. Reynolds.
NORTH CAROLINA.—Ministerial: T. McM. Grant, E. L. Hillman. J. M. Ormond, M. T. Plyler, F. S. Hickman, H. C. Smith, F. S. Love. Lay: Mrs. E. L. Hillman, Miss Sallie Lou MacKinnon. W. K. Greene. W. L. Knight, W. B. Cooper, W. C. Chadwick, G. P. Hood, W. P. Few.
NORTH GEORGIA.—Ministerial: W. P. King, H. H. Jones, W. H. LaPrade. A. M. Pierce. C. C. Jarrell. Lester Rumble, W. A. Shelton, Wallace Rogers, R. L. Russell. Lay: S. L. Johnston, H. W. Cox, Mrs. L. M. Awtrey, T. J. Lance, I. S. Ingram. N. G. Slaughter, Mrs. M. E. Tilley, Hubert Quillian, J. C. Wardlaw, J. S. Candler.
NORTH MISSISSIPPI.—Ministerial: L. P. Wasson, A. T. McIlwain, V. C. Curtis. J. D. Wroten, J. R. Countiss. Lay: J. G. McGowan, D. H. Hall, Mrs. H. L. Talbert, Mrs. H. W. Ratliff substituted for J. W. Kyle.
NORTH TEXAS.—Ministerial: P. E. Martin, S. A. Barnes, H. G. Ryan, G. C. French. C. A. Spragins, Umphrey Lee. Lay: E. S. Fudge. M. T. Waggoner, Gibson Caldwell, Mrs. T. H. Minga. M. F. Love. Mrs. W. O. Jordan.
NORTHWEST.—Ministerial: E. J. Harper. Lay: E. Purvance.
NORTHWEST TEXAS.—Ministerial: J. O. Haymes, C. R. Hooton, O. P. Clark, W. M. Pearce, E. E. White, C. A. Bickley. Lay: Mrs. N. G. Rollins substituted for R. H. Nichols. D. P. Yoder, S. H. Condron, J. M. Willson, Mrs. C. M. Randal, R. B. Bryant.
OKLAHOMA.—Ministerial: Forney Hutchinson, J. R.

Abernathy, R. E. L. Morgan, W. B. Slack, L. L. Evans,
R. S. Satterfield, R. T. Blackburn. Lay: C. S. McFall,
Mrs. E. B. Dunlap, H. E. Newton, B. C. Clark, S. S.
Orwig, J. R. Cole, Jr., M. A. Beeson.
PACIFIC.—Ministerial: J. R. Kenney, J. C. McPheeters,
Gro er C. Emmons. Lay: Nathan Newby, E. M. Sweet,
Jr. v
ST. LOUIS.—Ministerial: C. W. Tadlock, C. W. Webdell,
E. H. Orear. Lay: W. W. Parker, Mrs. Jeptha Riggs,
F. E. Williams.
SOUTH CAROLINA.—Ministerial: E. L. McCoy, Woodrow
Ward, W. D. Gleaton substituted for Peter Stokes (deceased), E. K. Garrison, J. E. Ford. Lay: M. R. Mobley,
Will Stackhouse, Charlton DuRant.
SOUTH GEORGIA.—Ministerial: H. T. Freeman, Silas
Johnson, W. F. Quillian, C. M. Meeks, L. A. Harrell, J. P.
Dell, Leland Moore, T. D. Ellis. Lay: T. E. Thrasher,
C. L. Shepard, C. A. Britton, Jr., Warren Roberts, Mrs.
C. C. Sapp, T. H. Guerry substituted for W. T. Anderson,
J. S. Wright.
SOUTHWEST MISSOURI.—Ministerial: J. C. Glenn, H. J.
Rand, L. M. Starkey. Lay: Mrs. F. A. Lamb, R. J. Smith,
W. L. Earp.
TENNESSEE.—Ministerial: J. F. Baggett, C. J. Harrell,
D. E. Hinkle, J. L. Ferguson, W. H. Blue, E. P. Anderson.
Lay: B. A. Whitmore, W. O. Batts, W. A. Webb, Mrs.
Robert O'Neal, H. B. McGinnis, E. D. Thompson, P. D.
Maddin.
TEXAS.—Ministerial: G. F. Jones, J. W. Mills, A. T.
Walker substituted for S. S. McKenney, G. H. Wilson,
W. F. Bryan, J. Z. Tower, W. R. Swain, Paul Quillian.
Lay: H. F. Banker, H. L. Lowman, Mrs. J. W. Mills,
T. E. Acker, J. T. Scott.
TEXAS MEXICAN.—Ministerial: Frank Ramos. Lay:
Mrs. F. S. Onderdonk.
UPPER SOUTH CAROLINA.—Ministerial: B. R. Turnipseed, C. E. Peele, W. B. Garrett, W. L. Mullikin, R. F.
Morris. Lay: J. B. Horton, J. C. Holler, R. E. Babb, J. C.
Hardin, LeRoy Moore, H. N. Snyder.
VIRGINIA.—Ministerial: J. M. Potts, H. P. Clark, C. C.
Bell, H. P. Myers, R. P. Riddick, J. B. Winn, W. A.
Wright, S. C. Hatcher, S. C. Robertson, J. W. Moore.
Lay: W. R. Phelps, L. W. Wells, B. L. Fisher, R. L. Brewer, E. E. Eanes, Lucius Gregory, W. B. Roper, W. T. Elliott, O. R. Pettyjohn, O. P. Newcomb.
WEST TEXAS.—Ministerial: L. U. Spellman, Edmund
Heinsohn, K. P. Barton, R. F. Curl, J. Fisher Simpson.
Lay: W. W. Jackson, H. E. Jackson, D. T. Peel, M. A.
Childers, M. H. Brooks.
WESTERN MEXICAN.—Ministerial: A. M. Gomez. Lay:
Mrs. R. J. Parker.
WESTERN NORTH CAROLINA.—Ministerial: C. C. Weaver,
P. N. Garber, A. W. Plyler, W. A. Lambeth, G. T. Rowe,
J. B. Craven, W. A. Stanbury, G. R. Jordan, M. T.
Smathers, C. S. Kirkpatrick. Lay: O. V. Woosley, J. B.
Ivey, L. L. Gobbell, H. A. Dunham, J. A. Jones, A. J.
Kirby, P. F. Evans, J. E. Lambeth, Mrs. C. C. Weaver,
W. H. Worth.

APRIL 26
FIRST DAY
Morning

Delegates
Present

WESTERN VIRGINIA.—Ministerial: W. M. Given, J. B. F. Yoak, Jr., W. H. Foglesong, B. P. Taylor. Lay: Mrs. W. M. Downs, G. W. Bright, W. H. Coleman.

C. W. Bates, Secretary of the last General Conference of the Methodist Protestant Church, called the roll of that Church and the following were certified as being present:

ALABAMA.—Ministerial: J. S. Eddins, T. C. Casaday. Lay: A. C. Rogers, Mrs. Arthur Heustess substituted for J. J. Goddard.

ARKANSAS.—Ministerial: J. E. Butler. Lay: L. L. Sherman.

EASTERN.—No delegates elected.

FORT SMITH-OKLAHOMA.—Ministerial: J. W. Bowers. Lay: O. L. Wilson.

GEORGIA.—Ministerial: W. M. Hunton. Lay: J. W. Pace.

ILLINOIS.—Ministerial: F. B. Hanna. Lay: A. C. Ruff.

INDIANA.—Ministerial: Fred Clarke, F. W. Lineberry. Lay: H. O. DeWeese, W. S. Arnold.

IOWA-MISSOURI.—Ministerial: W. H. Betz. Lay: Warren McComas.

KANSAS.—Ministerial: L. E. Dixon. Lay: A. L. Cook.

KENTUCKY.—Ministerial: H. L. Shumway.

LOUISIANA.—Ministerial: J. W. Lee. Lay: T. L. Johnson.

MARYLAND.—Ministerial: J. H. Straughn, E. A. Sexsmith, L. B. Smith, R. L. Shipley, F. G. Holloway, J. L. Green, G. I. Humphreys, E. C. Makosky. Lay: Mrs. M. B. Matthews substituted for F. M. Benson, J. H. Baker, Henry Gilligan, F. P. Adkins, W. C. Scott, H. C. Staley, Fred Herrigel, Jr., Daniel MacLea.

MICHIGAN.—Ministerial: E. R. Willson. Lay: E. R. Vincent.

MISSISSIPPI.—Ministerial: F. L. Sharp. Lay: N. S. Williamson.

MISSOURI.—Ministerial: E. R. Stribling. Lay: Mrs. B. E. Dillon.

NORTH CAROLINA.—Ministerial: J. E. Pritchard, C. W. Bates, C. E. Forlines, S. W. Taylor, R. M. Andrews, G. R. Brown, F. W. Paschall. Lay: M. A. Coble, J. N. Wills, Mrs. W. C. Hammer, A. J. Koonce, W. F. Redding, Jr., J. B. Hicks.

NORTH MISSISSIPPI.—Ministerial: B. G. Whitehurst.

OHIO.—Ministerial: S. W. Rosenberger, J. C. Williams, F. L. Brown, C. S. Johnson, R. I. Farmer. Lay: E. D. Miller, Mrs. E. K. Barss, F. E. Stottlemire, E. H. Graver, P. M. Ellis.

ONONDAGA.—Ministerial: G. C. Weaver. Lay: W. C. Waterman.

PITTSBURGH.—Ministerial: T. L. Hooper, J. C. Broomfield. A. J. Allen, J. W. Hawley. Lay: Harry Shaw, W. C. Perkins, R. C. Sproul, W. T. Smith.

SOUTH CAROLINA.—Ministerial: F. L. Frazier substituted for Irvin Frye. Lay: D. H. Davis.

TENNESSEE.—Ministerial: C. O. Kelley.

The Methodist Church 179

TEXAS.—Ministerial: J. A. Richardson. Lay: J. D.
Davidson.
VIRGINIA.—Ministerial: C. D. Clowers.
WEST VIRGINIA.—Ministerial: L. E. Bee, J. E. Burns,
B. M. Mitchell, F. L. Shaffer, G. H. Snyder. Lay: K. W.
Weekly substituted for A. W. Locke, E. M. Nutter, U. I.
Jenkins, J. H. High.

APRIL 26
FIRST DAY
Morning
Delegates
Present

Bishop Hughes then stated that the next business would be the receiving of nominations and the election of a Secretary of the Uniting Conference.

Motion of J. Edgar Skillington, Central Pennsylvania, seconded by Lud H. Estes, Memphis, prevailed that we do now adopt that part of the Plan of Organization which applies to temporary organization. The following was adopted:

Temporary Organization

TEMPORARY ORGANIZATION

1. The Presiding Officer for the temporary organization of the Uniting Conference shall be one of the Chairmen of the Joint Commission on Union as provided below in the *Plan of Organization,* who shall serve in this capacity until a Plan of Organization and Rules of Order have been adopted and a permanent organization effected.
2. The Secretarial Staff for temporary organization shall be the respective Secretaries of the General Conferences of the three uniting Churches, with such assistants as they may choose, who shall serve until a permanent secretarial staff shall have been chosen.
3. Immediately after the devotional service appropriately opening the Uniting Conference, the calling of the roll, and the transaction of such privileged business as may require immediate attention, the Conference shall proceed to effect a permanent organization by: (1) Receiving nominations and taking a ballot for permanent Secretary; (2) by consideration of the Plan of Organization and Rules of Order hereinafter recommended; (3) by completing the permanent organization so far as practical at this stage of the Conference in accordance with such plans and rules as shall be adopted.

Motion of J. Edgar Skillington, Central Pennsylvania, seconded by C. W. Bates, North Carolina, prevailed, that we adopt tentatively the Rules of Order in the *Prospectus of the Discipline* for our guidance until we have adopted permanent Rules of Order.

J. Edgar Skillington nominated Edgar R. Heckman, of the Central Pennsylvania Conference, for the position of Secretary-in-Chief of the Uniting Conference, and the nomination was duly seconded.

Fred H. Peeples, Memphis, nominated Lud H. Estes, of the Memphis Conference, for Secretary-in-Chief of the Uniting Conference, and the nomination was duly seconded.

Leslie R. Burgum, North Dakota, moved that nominations be closed, and that the Conference proceed to ballot. The motion was duly seconded and prevailed.

The following were designated to act as tellers: By Bishop H. Lester Smith for the Methodist Episcopal Church:

Ministers: Glenn Engebretsen, Western Norwegian-Danish; Frank H. Trotter, Holston; Reuben H. McAlister, Mississippi; Walter S. Rogers, Nebraska; Homer R. Gettle, North Indiana; Paul P. Wiant, China; Miss Irma Highbaugh, China; H. Almon Chafee, New York East.
Ministerial Reserves: Charles A. Jones, Ohio; Mrs. W. H. Dangel, Rock River; John A. Patton, Lexington.
Laymen: Lawrence M. Barhard, Erie; Edson H. Deal, Idaho; Claude C. Hall, Southern Illinois; Harry C. Leonard, Southern; Charles W. Kitto, Philadelphia; Glenn C. James, Saint Johns River; Elbert M. Moffatt, India; Alfred F. Hughes, West Wisconsin.
Lay Reserves: R. L. Archer, Malaysia; Theodore Arvidson, Europe.

By Bishop Paul B. Kern for the Methodist Episcopal Church, South:

Ministers: Dana Dawson, Louisiana; Ernest L. Woolf, Baltimore; H. W. Blackburn, Oklahoma; James D. Wroten, North Mississippi; Clem Baker, Little Rock; Clyde K. Campbell, New Mexico; Edward E. White, Northwest Texas; J. Fisher Simpson, West Texas.
Ministerial Reserves: John C. Glenn, Southwest Missouri; R. E. Greer, Holston; Earl G. Hamlett, Memphis.
Laymen: Clarence M. Dannelly, Alabama; C. C. Sherrod, Holston; Paul S. Haley, North Alabama; W. O. Batts, Tennessee; W. H. Utz, Jr., Missouri; Merle T. Waggoner, North Texas; E. M. Sweet, Jr., Pacific; G. W. Bright, Western Virginia.
Lay Reserves: Boyce Martin, Central Texas; J. S. M. Cannon, Little Rock; Carl S. McFall, Oklahoma; W. H. Wiseman, Tennessee.

By Dr. James H. Straughn for the Methodist Protestant Church:

Ministers: J. S. Eddins, Alabama; F. L. Brown, Ohio.
Laymen: F. P. Adkins, Maryland; A. J. Koonce, North Carolina.

C. W. Bates was designated as the Secretary to accompany the Tellers, and J. S. Eddins, F. L.

Brown, F. P. Adkins, and A. J. Koonce were designated as Recording Tellers.

APRIL 26
FIRST DAY

Morning

The Tellers were assigned to their stations in the Conference room. The ballot was spread, the votes were collected, and the tellers retired to determine the result.

Lud H. Estes, Memphis, for the Committee on Rules of Order and Plan of Organization, presented the Plan of Organization, and moved its adoption. The motion was duly seconded. Arba Martin, Ohio, moved to amend Section 3, "Organization of General Standing Committees," under general head "III. Committees," by inserting the following after the word "record," in the fifth line:

Plan of
Organizatioı

There shall be elected three Co-Chairmen for each General Standing Committee, one from each of the three Uniting Churches. Each Co-Chairman shall be elected by those members of the General Standing Committee who represent the Church whence he comes. The three Co-Chairmen of any General Standing Committee shall preside in turn over the deliberations of that Committee and share equally the responsibility of Committee Chairmanship.

The motion being duly seconded, Dr. Martin spoke to the proposed amendment.

J. Edgar Skillington, Central Pennsylvania, offered the following amendment to the Martin amendment, by substituting for all of Section 3, general head III, except the last sentence of said Section 3, the following:

General
Standing
Committees

The eight General Standing Committees shall meet for organization at 2:30 P.M. on the first day of the Uniting Conference, with a Bishop appointed by the Council of Bishops presiding and with one of the Secretarial Staff keeping the record. Each of these Committees shall elect a Chairman, a Vice-Chairman, and a Secretary, and such other officers as need may require. The Chairman of one of these Committees shall be a representative of the Methodist Protestant Church, the Chairmen of not fewer than three, representatives of the Methodist Episcopal Church, South, and of the Methodist Episcopal Church each.

The Chairmen of the Joint Commission, or others whom they shall appoint, shall be constituted a committee to determine by lot and/or otherwise from which of the Uniting Churches the Chairman of the Eighth Committee shall come and likewise which Committee shall be headed by a representative of the Methodist Protestant Church, which Committees by representatives of the Methodist Episcopal Church, South, and which by representatives

APRIL 26
FIRST DAY
Morning

of the Methodist Episcopal Church. In no case shall the Chairman and Vice-Chairman of one of these Committees both be representatives of the same Church.

The motion being duly seconded, Dr. Skillington spoke to the question.

General
Standing
Committees

Motion of W. G. Cram, Kentucky, duly seconded, prevailed laying the Skillington substitute on the table.

Harold P. Sloan, New Jersey, spoke against the Martin amendment.

Motion of T. D. Ellis, South Georgia, duly seconded, prevailed laying the Martin amendment on the table.

The report of the Committee was adopted as presented. For report, see page 141.

Report of
Committee
on Rules

Lud H. Estes, for the Committee on Rules, presented the report of the Committee relative to Rules of Order and moved its adoption. The motion was duly seconded. Francis R. Bayley, Baltimore, ME, moved the following amendment:

That any suggested amendments go automatically to the Committee on Rules for their study and report.

The amendment, duly seconded, was adopted. The report of the Committee, as amended, was adopted. For report, see page 134.

Committees
Elected

J. Emerson Ford, South Carolina, one of the Co-Secretaries of the Joint Commission on Church Union, presented the following:

On behalf of the Joint Commission on Interdenominational Relations and Church Union we present the nominations of the Commission of each of the three Churches for the assignment of delegates to the eight General Standing Committees, as follows: [These nominations are printed in the *Hand Book*, pages 126-153 inclusive, and are correct except as follows. The necessary corrections will be indicated by the Secretary of each separate Commission. See below for corrections.]
We move the election of these General Standing Committees, with the proviso that Reserve delegates, who may be seated for principal delegates, shall take the places of the absent delegates on the Committees.
J. EMERSON FORD, *Secretary Commission ME,S;*
HARRY E. WOOLEVER, *Secretary Commission ME;*
LEONARD B. SMITH, *Secretary Commission MP.*

The above report was adopted, with the following corrections:
Methodist Episcopal Church: Corrections pre-

The Methodist Church 183

sented by Harry E. Woolever, Central New York, as follows:

Ministry and Judicial Administration: Delete name of Webster Pearce, Detroit.
Membership and Temporal Economy: Delete name of Ernest W. Peterson, Oregon. Add names of Jesse M. Beck, Iowa-Des Moines, and John B. Campbell, Northwest Indiana.
Education: Delete name of Edwin H. Mueller, East German. Add names of H. V. Carter, Oklahoma, and Paul G. Halmhuber, Detroit.
Publishing Interests: Delete names of Frank C. Evans, Northwest Indiana, Frank A. Horne, New York East, L. W. Mayberry, Southwest Kansas, and James H. Peterman, Iowa-Des Moines. Add names of William H. Barradell, New York East, Harold B. McKibben, Southwest Kansas, Ernest W. Peterson, Oregon, and Charles M. Windels, East German.

Methodist Protestant Church: Leonard B. Smith, Maryland, Secretary of the Commission of that Church, made the following statement:

There will be added two delegates from the West Virginia delegation. Their assignment to Committees is in the hands of the Secretary of the delegation, of the entire Methodist Protestant delegation, and he is engaged at present. They will be notified, and, if acceptable, they will be assigned to the Committees to which they are already assigned.

Methodist Episcopal Church, South: J. Emerson Ford, South Carolina, Secretary of the Commission of that Church, made the following correction:

Missions: Delete the name of W. B. Roper, Virginia. Add the name of Charlton DuRant, South Carolina.
Education: Delete the name of Charlton DuRant, South Carolina. Add the name of W. B. Roper, Virginia.

For list of Committees, see pages 112-132.
J. Emerson Ford, South Carolina, presented the nominations of the Joint Commission on Church Union for the Committee to Nominate the Presiding Officers, as called for in Section I of the Plan of Organization, and the same were confirmed as follows:

Methodist Episcopal Church: Orien W. Fifer, Indiana; Levi P. Goodwin, Iowa-Des Moines; George W. Crabbe, Baltimore; John D. Crummey, California.
Methodist Episcopal Church, South: William A. Shelton, North Georgia; Forney Hutchinson, Oklahoma;

APRIL 26 FIRST DAY — Morning — Corrections — Committee to Nominate Presiding Officers

APRIL 26
FIRST DAY
Morning

Henry N. Snyder, Upper South Carolina; Nat Harris, Central Texas.
Methodist Protestant Church: J. C. Williams, Ohio.

C. W. Bates, North Carolina, reported the result of the ballot for Secretary-in-Chief as follows: Total number of votes cast, 862. Necessary for a choice, 432. Lud H. Estes, 553; Edgar R. Heckman, 304; scattering, 5.

Secretary
Elected

Bishop Hughes announced that Lud H. Estes had been elected Secretary of the Uniting Conference.

Associate
Secretaries
Elected

The Secretary nominated for Associate Secretaries, Edgar R. Heckman, Central Pennsylvania, and Cuthbert W. Bates, North Carolina, and they were confirmed.

John M. Arters

Bishop Hughes introduced to the Conference Dr. John M. Arters, Secretary of the last General Conference of the Methodist Episcopal Church. The delegates rose and applauded.

Special
Standing
Committees

On nomination of the Bishops of the respective Churches and Dr. James H. Straughn of the Methodist Protestant Church, the following were elected to constitute the Special Standing Committees:

RULES: J. Edgar Skillington, Central Pennsylvania, ME; George W. Henson, Philadelphia, ME; Costen J. Harrell, Tennessee, ME,S; Lavens M. Thomas, Holston, ME,S; Fred W. Paschall, North Carolina, MP.

JOURNAL: John R. Kenney, Pacific, ME,S; E. T. Wayland, North Arkansas, ME,S; G. Charles Weaver, Onondaga, MP; Joseph D. Piper, Pittsburgh, ME; Robert B. Spencer, Colorado, ME.

CREDENTIALS: F. B. Hanna, Illinois, MP; Earl R. Brown, Northeast Ohio, ME; Frank G. H. Stevens, Southern California, ME; Charles A. Robbins, Pacific Northwest, ME; Alfred C. Crawford, Rock River, ME; Roy H. Short, Louisville, ME,S; Henry M. Andrews, Alabama, ME,S; Carl S. McFall, Oklahoma, ME,S; W. W. Jackson, West Texas, ME,S.

EDITORIAL REVISION: John L. Ferguson, Tennessee, ME,S; W. T. Mathis, Illinois, ME,S; Richard E. Womack, Memphis, ME,S; Hubert Quillian, North Georgia, ME,S; William K. Anderson, Pittsburgh, ME; Henry L. Davis, Northwest Indiana, ME; Earle M. Rugg, India, ME; James R. Joy, Newark, ME; F. L. Shaffer, West Virginia, MP.

COURTESIES, PRIVILEGES, AND INTRODUCTIONS: Joseph M. M. Gray, Detroit, ME; John B. Magee, Pacific Northwest, ME; Clyde O. Law, West Virginia, ME; Stanley O. MacMullen, New England, ME; Umphrey Lee, North Texas, ME,S; G. Ray Jordan, Western North Carolina, ME,S; Harvey W. Cox, North Georgia, ME,S; W. W.

Parker, St. Louis, ME,S; T. LeRoy Hooper, Pittsburgh, MP.

ENABLING ACTS AND LEGAL FORMS: Arthur A. Callaghan, Maine, ME; Frank T. Cartwright, Foochow, ME; Sanford W. Corcoran, Pittsburgh, ME; Jabez C. Harrison, Oregon, ME; Ernest S. Lyons, Philippine Islands; Wiley A. Keve, Kansas, ME; Arba Martin, Ohio, ME; Frederick W. Mueller, Northeast Ohio, ME; Howard C. Baldwin, Detroit, ME; David D. Jones, North Carolina, ME; Ernest H. Cherrington, Ohio, ME; Mrs. W. H. C. Goode, Ohio, ME; Matthew S. Davage, Louisiana, ME; Mrs. F. F. Lindsey, Northern Minnesota, ME; Herschell R. Snavely, Illinois, ME; William H. Spurgeon, Colorado, ME; G. M. Davenport, North Alabama, ME,S; William M. Alexander, Missouri, ME,S; J. Manning Potts, Virginia, ME,S; Paul W. Quillian, Texas, ME,S; Willard G. Cram, Kentucky, ME,S; Ben L. Sutherland, Mississippi, ME,S; A. W. Martin, North Arkansas, ME,S; W. L. Mullikin, Upper South Carolina, ME,S; W. K. Greene, North Carolina, ME,S; George L. Morelock, Memphis, ME,S; J. S. M. Cannon, Little Rock, ME,S; George H. Lamar, Baltimore, ME,S; Mrs. George Sexton, Jr., Louisiana, ME,S; J. N. Hillman, Holston, ME,S; Mrs. T. H. Minga, North Texas, ME,S; Nathan Newby, Pacific, ME,S; John C. Broomfield, Pittsburgh, MP; George R. Brown, North Carolina, MP; J. B. Hicks, North Carolina, MP; Nate S. Williamson, Mississippi, MP.

JUDICIARY: Nolan B. Harmon, Jr., Baltimore, ME,S; W. G. Henry, North Alabama, ME,S; Frank C. Tucker, Missouri, ME,S; J. W. Mills, Texas, ME,S; William C McMurry, Memphis, ME,S; Mark A. Childers, West Texas, ME,S; R. J. Smith, Southwest Missouri, ME,S; J. T. Ellison, Alabama, ME,S; Francis R. Bayley, Baltimore, ME; Walter C. Buckner, Southern California, ME; Leslie R. Burgum, North Dakota, ME; Leslie J. Lyons, Missouri, ME; Henry R. VanDusen, Wyoming, ME; John S. Fletcher, Holston, ME; Charles F. Eggleston, Philadelphia, ME; William H. Wilcox, Oklahoma, ME; Fred Herrigal, Jr., Maryland, MP; J. E. Butler, Arkansas, MP.

BUSINESS: Bishop Edwin H. Hughes, ME; Bishop John M. Moore, ME,S; Dr. James H. Straughn, MP; Thomas D. Ellis, South Georgia, ME,S; Eugene B. Hawk, Central Texas, ME,S; Zebulon Judd, Alabama, ME,S; H. E. Jackson, West Texas, ME,S; G. I. Humphreys, Maryland, MP; Albert C. Knudson, New England Southern, ME; Fremont E. Fribley, North Indiana, ME; Hiram A. Douglas, Northern Minnesota, ME; Dwight S. Jeffers, Idaho, ME.

REFERENCE: Lud H. Estes, Memphis, ME,S; J. L. Clark, Kentucky, ME,S; Edgar R. Heckman, Central Pennsylvania, ME; Robert G. Spencer, Colorado, ME; Cuthbert W. Bates, North Carolina, MP.

Bishop Hughes stated that the next item of business would be the hearing of the Declarations of the Adoption of the Plan of Union, as adopted by the three Uniting Churches, and that

APRIL 26
FIRST DAY

Morning
Declarations of
Adoption of
Plan of
Union
these Declarations would be given in the order of
the final action of the three Churches, the Declaration of the Methodist Protestant Church coming first.

Dr. James H. Straughn, Chairman of the Commission on Church Union of the Methodist Protestant Church, then presented the Declaration of
that Church, as follows:

The General Conference of The Methodist Protestant
Church, at its quadrennial session in the First Church,
High Point, North Carolina, May 23, 1936, approved
the Plan of Union and submitted the same to the Annual
Conferences of the Church as an overture amending the
constitution of the Church as follows:
On Methodist Union known as the Plan of Union:
Moved that the Report of the Commission on Union be
received and that the Plan of Union therein reported be
approved and that the said Plan of Union forthwith,
upon the adjournment of this General Conference, be sent
and transmitted to the several Annual Conferences of
this Church for action thereon, as provided in Article 17
of the constitution of The Methodist Protestant Church.
This motion was adopted on roll call by a vote of 142
to 39.
The Secretary of the General Conference transmitted
the approved action, with a copy of the Plan of Union,
to each of the Annual Conferences of the Church, twenty-
five in all. Twenty of the Annual Conferences have certified their ratification of the said overture, the Plan of
Union.
Inasmuch as two-thirds and more of the Annual Conferences have certified their ratification of the overture, I,
therefore, by the authority vested in me as President of
the General Conference, do hereby declare the said overture, known as the Plan of Union, approved and ratified
by the Methodist Protestant Church.
                              J. F. STRAUGHN, *President;*
                              C. W. BATES, *Secretary.*
Baltimore, Maryland, November 12, 1936.

Bishop Edwin H. Hughes, Chairman of the
Commission on Church Union of the Methodist
Episcopal Church, next presented the Declaration
of that Church, as follows:

The Bishops of the Methodist Episcopal Church, in
fulfilment of their responsibility as prescribed in the Discipline, Paragraph 91, now make official announcement to
the Church and to all interested persons as follows:
"The General Conference of the Methodist Episcopal
Church did, on May 24, 1936, at Columbus, Ohio, act favorably on the Plan of Union for the Methodist Episcopal
Church, the Methodist Episcopal Church, South, and the
Methodist Protestant Church, casting a vote of 553, of
which 470 were in the affirmative and 83 in the negative,

thus by more than the two-thirds majority required for constitutional changes. The Plan of Union was sent down to the Annual Conferences for their consideration in the sessions of the ensuing year.

APRIL 26
FIRST DAY

Morning

Declarations of
Adoption of
Plan of
Union

"The Annual Conferences of the Methodist Episcopal Church, in their sessions, voted as follows: for the Plan, laymen, 6,747; against the Plan, laymen, 585. For the Plan, ministers, 10,195; against the Plan, 1,284. The vote thus given was more than the two-thirds favorable vote required for constitutional changes.

"Inasmuch, therefore, as the General Conference and the Annual Conferences of the Methodist Episcopal Church have voted as above in favor of the Plan of Union, with all the constitutional changes therein involved, and this by more than the required majority of two-thirds of those present and voting, we, the Bishops of the Methodist Episcopal Church, do now officially declare that the said Plan of Union of the Methodist Episcopal Church, the Methodist Episcopal Church, South, and the Methodist Protestant Church, has been legally and constitutionally adopted by the Methodist Episcopal Church."

Upon this action of our Church and upon all measures to be taken in consummating the Union of the three branches of Methodism, we now reverently invoke the blessing of Almighty God.

WILLIAM F. ANDERSON,	H. LESTER SMITH,
JOHN L. NUELSEN,	CHAS. L. MEAD,
EDWIN H. HUGHES,	ROBERT E. JONES,
FRANCIS J. MCCONNELL,	MATTHEW W. CLAIR,
FREDERICK DELAND LEETE,	GEORGE A. MILLER,
HERBERT WELCH,	TITUS LOWE,
THOMAS NICHOLSON,	BRENTON T. BADLEY,
ADNA WRIGHT LEONARD,	WALLACE E. BROWN,
CHARLES BAYARD MITCHELL,	RAYMOND J. WADE,
JOHN W. ROBINSON,	JAMES C. BAKER,
EBEN S. JOHNSON,	J. RALPH MAGEE,
ERNEST LYNN WALDORF,	RALPH S. CUSHMAN,
CHARLES EDWARD LOCKE,	WILBUR E. HAMMAKER,
E. G. RICHARDSON,	CHARLES W. FLINT,
EDGAR BLAKE,	ALEXANDER P. SHAW,
F. T. KEENEY,	G. BROMLEY OXNAM.

MISSIONARY BISHOPS

EDWIN F. LEE,	JOHN M. SPRINGER.

BISHOPS ELECTED BY CENTRAL CONFERENCES

RALPH A. WARD,	JUAN E. GATTINONI,
JOHN GOWDY,	R. ELPHICK,
JASHWANT R. CHITAMBAR,	F. H. OTTO MELLE.
J. WASKOM PICKETT,	

Bishop John M. Moore, Chairman of the Commission on Church Union of the Methodist Episcopal Church, South, next presented the Declaration of that Church, as follows:

APRIL 26   The College of Bishops of the Methodist Episcopal
FIRST DAY   Church, South, in fulfillment of their responsibility under
Morning   the law of the Church as recorded in the *Discipline*, par-
Declarations of   agraph 43, made the following declaration to the General
Adoption of   Conference and the Church on May 4, 1938:
Plan of   "The several Annual Conferences of the Methodist
Union   Episcopal Church, South, in their sessions in the Con-
ference year, beginning May 1, 1937, voted on the fol-
lowing constitutional question:

"Shall the Annual Conferences of the Methodist
Episcopal Church, South, approve and authorize
the adoption of the Plan of Union of the Methodist
Episcopal Church, the Methodist Episcopal Church,
South, and the Methodist Protestant Church, as proposed and recommended by the Commissions on Interdenominational Relations and Church Union, duly
appointed by the General Conferences of these three
Churches, and attached hereto?"

"The total vote of the members of the several Annual
Conferences was 8,897, of which 7,650 voted in the affirmative and 1,247 in the negative.

"The General Conference of the Methodist Episcopal
Church, South, voted on the Plan of Union of the three
said churches on April 29, 1938, casting a vote of 460,
of which 434 were in the affirmative and 26 were in the
negative.

"Inasmuch as the several Annual Conferences, by a
vote of more than three-fourths of all their members present and voting, did make concurrent recommendation that
the Plan of Union be adopted by the General Conference,
and inasmuch as the General Conference on April 29,
1938, did vote affirmatively upon this joint recommendation of the Annual Conferences by a majority of more than
two-thirds, we the College of Bishops do hereby announce
and declare that the said Plan of Union of the Methodist
Episcopal Church, the Methodist Episcopal Church, South,
and the Methodist Protestant Church has been legally
and constitutionally adopted by the Methodist Episcopal
Church, South."

JOHN M. MOORE,	HOYT M. DOBBS,
U. V. W. DARLINGTON,	HIRAM A. BOAZ,
H. M. DUBOSE,	ARTHUR J. MOORE,
JAMES CANNON, JR.,	PAUL B. KERN,
SAM R. HAY,	A. FRANK SMITH.

Attest:

JOHN M. MOORE, *President of College of Bishops during the General Conference of 1938.*

LUD H. ESTES, *Secretary of General Conference,
Methodist Episcopal Church, South.*

The report of the Joint Commission on Methodist Union was then presented by Dr. Harry E.
Woolever, as follows:

PRESENTATION OF ADOPTED PLAN OF UNION
AND PROSPECTUS OF THE DISCIPLINE OF
THE METHODIST CHURCH

APRIL 26
FIRST DAY
Morning

Presentation
of Plan of
Union and
Prospectus
of Discipline

Fathers and Brethren of The Methodist Church: The members of the Joint Commission on Methodist Union composed of the proper Commissions of the three Uniting Churches as legally constituted, appointed, and authorized by the respective General Conferences of the Methodist Protestant Church, the Methodist Episcopal Church, South, and the Methodist Episcopal Church, now come to report and transfer to this delegated Uniting Conference, au-thorized and composed by the respective Churches concerned, the results of the labors as indicated and contained in the Plan of Union and the *Prospectus of the Discipline* of The Methodist Church.

The authorized bodies creating the Joint Commission on Methodist Union, as in order raised and empowered by the respective General Conferences, are:

THE COMMISSION ON INTERDENOMINATIONAL RELATIONS
OF THE METHODIST EPISCOPAL CHURCH

Bishops: Edwin Holt Hughes (Chairman), Frederick D. Leete, Edgar Blake, Robert E. Jones, Ernest G. Richardson.
Ministers: J. S. Ladd Thomas, Edmund D. Soper, Edward Hislop, F. W. Mueller, Edward Laird Mills, Harry E. Woolever (Secretary), E. J. Hammond, Willis J. King, Morris E. Swartz, Robert B. Stansell.
Lay Members: Ernest H. Cherrington, James R. Joy, James A. James, Fred D. Parr, Vincent P. Clarke, William H. Spurgeon, W. H. Wilcox, W. W. Schwaninger, Clyde O. Law, F. H. Trotter.

THE COMMISSION ON METHODIST UNION OF THE
METHODIST PROTESTANT CHURCH

Ministers: James H. Straughn (Chairman), John C. Broomfield, Leonard B. Smith (Secretary), J. C. Williams, E. A. Sexsmith, Roby F. Day, L. E. Bee, F. W. Lineberry, S. W. Taylor, Charles S. Bragg, J. S. Eddins, G. C. Weaver, F. B. Hanna, C. R. Green.
Lay Members: Harry Shaw, J. H. Baker, Nate S. Williamson, P. M. Ellis, W. C. Perkins, J. N. Wills.

THE COMMISSION ON INTERDENOMINATIONAL RELATIONS
AND CHURCH UNION OF THE METHODIST EPISCOPAL
CHURCH, SOUTH

Bishops: John M. Moore (Chairman), Paul B. Kern, Arthur J. Moore, A. Frank Smith, Ivan Lee Holt.
Ministers: T. D. Ellis, F. N. Parker, Grover C. Emmons, J. W. Moore, Paul W. Quillian, B. P. Taylor, J. Emerson Ford (Secretary), H. H. Sherman, Willard G. Cram, W. M. Alexander.
Laymen: John S. Candler, Percy D. Maddin, H. H. White, H. N. Snyder, J. H. Reynolds, W. E. Brock, John T. Scott, Harry Denman, W. P. Few, Mrs. J. W. Perry.

The Joint Commission of these three Churches held its first authorized meeting on August 28, 1934, at the Union

APRIL 26
FIRST DAY
Morning
Presentation
of Plan of
Union and
Prospectus
of Discipline
League Club in Chicago. After a series of extended meetings the Plan of Union of The Methodist Church was completed and submitted to the Editorial Committee at a session in Evanston, Ill., on the morning of August 16, 1935. It received the approval of the entire Joint Commission without a dissenting vote. The authorized Committee of Fifteen having final review approved the final draft in the Cincinnati Club, Cincinnati, Ohio, at 2 P.M., December 3, 1935, and the Secretary was instructed to present it to the Churches.

The Plan of Union received the affirmative vote of the succeeding General Conferences and the Annual and Lay Conferences by decisive constitutional majorities.

Carrying out the requirements of the Plan of Union, the Commissions with the aid of authorized and carefully selected Committees, with a personnel of over two hundred, prepared the Prospectus of the Discipline of the Methodist Church. This document was placed in the hands of all delegates for preliminary study and is now, with the Plan of Union, turned over to this Uniting Conference for such use as the authorized delegates deem wise. It is not a perfect document. It is submitted as the work of earnest, consecrated, and experienced committee men and women and the Commissioners of the three Churches. It is subject to any change, substitution, and amendment which further counsel may indicate as wise. There are also supplemental memorials and materials which will be submitted at the proper time to the Uniting Conference and the various General Standing Committees.

There is in possession of the Joint Commission a petition from the Methodist Church of Mexico to be included in The Methodist Church. This will come to your attention at a later session.

The Secretaries in behalf of the Joint Commissioners desire to express the deep appreciation which they hold for the fine and helpful co-operation and the prayers which have upheld the labors of these years of earnest effort. We labored to build upon firm foundations laid by other hands. These workmen of God whose labors do abide, although they watch us from higher ground today, are too numerous to list here. We feel that justice and love compel the naming of two of our noble Chairmen of the Commissions who have gone to their crowning since their names were attached to the Plan of Union, William Fraser McDowell and Edwin DuBose Mouzon.

Our closing work is an expression of the hope that the spirit born of prayer and fasting, which characterized the signers of "The Plan of Separation" in an effort to save American Methodism, may characterize this body of delegates as they build around the Plan of Union the Church of the future, The Methodist Church.

Respectfully and humbly submitted by authority of the Joint Commission on Methodist Union.

HARRY EARL WOOLEVER,
For the Methodist Episcopal Church;
J. EMERSON FORD,
For the Methodist Episcopal Church, South;
LEONARD B. SMITH,
For the Methodist Protestant Church.

Motion of John W. Langdale, New York East, seconded by Lud H. Estes, Memphis, prevailed that the three Declarations, together with the Report of the Joint Commission, be received and placed on record in the Journal of the Uniting Conference.

Motion of F. W. Lineberry, Indiana, duly seconded, prevailed that the time be extended for the reading of the Episcopal Address.

Bishop John M. Moore, Chairman of the Commission on Union of the Methodist Episcopal Church, South, then presented the Episcopal Address. At the conclusion of the presentation the delegates arose and applauded. For the Episcopal Address, see page 148.

The Secretary and Associate Secretaries presented nominations for the Secretarial Staff. The Conference confirmed the same as follows:

Journal: Edgar R. Heckman, Central Pennsylvania, ME; Cuthbert W. Bates, North Carolina, MP.

Standing Votes: Cuthbert W. Bates, North Carolina, MP; J. Leas Green, Maryland, MP; C. S. Kirkpatrick, Western North Carolina, ME,S; R. F. Curl, West Texas, ME,S; John C. Glenn, Southwest Missouri, ME,S; Arthur A. Callaghan, Maine, ME; Asa J. Kestle, Ohio, ME; Albert G. Judd, Northern New York, ME; Charles A. Robbins, Pacific Northwest, ME.

Calendar: John B. F. Yoak, Jr., Western Virginia, ME; D. Stewart Patterson, Baltimore, ME.

Non-Concurrent Calendar: Robert N. Brooks, North Carolina, ME.

Daily Advocate: Robert S. Satterfield, Oklahoma, ME,S.

Ballots and Tellers: John J. Bunting, Wilmington, ME.

Discipline: Fred B. Newell, New York East, ME; T. LeRoy Hooper, Pittsburgh, MP; Grover C. Emmons, Pacific, ME,S.

T. McM. Grant, North Carolina, ME,S, stated that it would be impossible for him to serve on the Committee on Journal, due to other duties, and offered his resignation. It was accepted by the Conference. On nomination of the College of Bishops of the Methodist Episcopal Church, South, John R. Kenney, Pacific, ME,S, was elected a member of the Committee on Journal.

The following Bishops and Secretaries were appointed for the purpose of organizing the eight General Standing Committees:

APRIL 26
FIRST DAY
Morning

Organization
of General
Standing
Committees

No 1, Conferences: Bishops E. G. Richardson, W. W. Peele; Secretary, J. J. Bunting.

No. 2, Ministry and Judicial Administration: Bishops Edgar Blake, Clare Purcell; Secretary, J. C. Glenn.

No. 3, Membership and Temporal Economy: Bishops Frederick D. Leete, A. Frank Smith; Secretary, J. Leas Green.

No. 4, Missions, Church Extension, Hospitals, etc.: Bishops Edwin H. Hughes, Arthur J. Moore; Secretary, C. W. Bates.

No. 5, Education: Bishops G. Bromley Oxnam, Paul B. Kern; Secretary, Lud H. Estes.

No. 6, Superannuate Support, Pensions, and Relief: Bishops E. L. Waldorf, U. V. W. Darlington; Secretary, J. B. F. Yoak, Jr.

No. 7, Publishing Interests: Bishops H. Lester Smith, J. Lloyd Decell; Secretary, Edgar R. Heckman.

No. 8, Ritual: Bishops James C. Baker, Ivan Lee Holt; Secretary, R. N. Brooks.

Motion of Harry E. Woolever, Central New York, duly seconded, prevailed that, owing to the lateness of the hour of adjournment this morning, the eight General Standing Committees meet at 3 P.M. instead of 2:30 P.M., this change of time being for today only.

Adjournment   Motion of Thomas D. Ellis, South Georgia, duly seconded, prevailed that we do now adjourn. After various announcements the opening session of the Uniting Conference adjourned at 1:15 P.M. with the benediction pronounced by Bishop William F. Anderson of the Methodist Episcopal Church.

THURSDAY MORNING, APRIL 27, 1939

The Conference met in second day's session, April 27, 1939, at 8:30 A.M., with Bishop John M. Moore presiding.

Bishop Ivan Lee Holt conducted the opening devotions, at the request of the Council of Bishops.

Bishop Ernest L. Waldorf brought the morning address, using as the basis for his remarks Matthew 13: 13.

Journal   The report of the Committee on Journal was adopted, as follows:

We have examined the Journal and found it correct.
JOSEPH D. PIPER, *Chairman;*
JOHN R. KENNEY, *Secretary.*

Isaac E. Miller, Ohio, Chairman of the Commission on Entertainment, presented Report No. 1 of that Committee, calling attention to the fact that Kansas City had turned over the auditorium, with its splendid facilities, without any expense whatsoever to the Uniting Conference for its use. The report being in two Sections, Section I was adopted.

Section II was then presented. Fred B. Stone, Rock River, moved to amend the report by adding after "$4 per day" the words, "or such portion as the funds available will permit." This amendment was accepted by Dr. Miller. Ben A. Whitmore, Tennessee, moved as a substitute for the whole that the per diem be fixed at $3 per day, and the motion was duly seconded. By common consent the request of Frank W. Lineberry, Indiana, that the Methodist Protestant delegates be excused from voting on this motion, because their expenses were all provided, was granted.

Francis R. Bayley, Baltimore, moved that the matter be referred back to the Book Committee of the Methodist Episcopal Church, and the proper authorities of the Methodist Episcopal Church, South, with power to act in the matter of fixing the per diem, and the motion was duly seconded.

Nathan Newby, Pacific, raised the point of order that the Uniting Conference had the power to settle the question, and the Chair ruled the point well taken.

Lud H. Estes, Memphis, spoke in favor of the report.

The motion of F. R. Bayley, being put, did not prevail. The motion of B. A. Whitmore, being put, did not prevail.

Section II as amended was adopted. The report was then adopted as a whole, as follows:

COMMISSION ON ENTERTAINMENT, REPORT NO. 1

SECTION I

To the Members of the Uniting Conference:

The Commission on Entertainment for the Uniting Conference of The Methodist Church presents for your approval the following:

I. That your Commission did, pursuant to authority given it by the three uniting Churches, proceed in due time and form to select the city in which the Uniting Conference would be held and has selected the city of

APRIL 27
SECOND DAY
Morning
Commission on
Entertain-
ment,
Report No. 1

Kansas City, Missouri; that it has designated the seat of the Conference to be the New Municipal Auditorium in said city and recommends that its action in this respect be approved.

II. That it has allocated the seats in the arena of said Auditorium by lot among the several Conferences of the three Churches involved and that the allocation of seats as published in the seating plan as given on pages 14 and 15 of *The Daily Christian Advocate* of this date, April 26, 1939, be approved as the official seating plan of this Conference, this plan subject to such minor changes as may be found necessary; and your Commission requests that it be authorized to make such adjustments and changes.

Committee
Meeting
Plans

III. That the meeting places for the proposed General Standing Committees shall be:

(1) Committee on Conferences, Room 500.

(2) Committee on Ministry and Judicial Administration, Room 400.

(3) Committee on Membership and Temporal Economy, west concourse, arena floor.

(4) Committee on Missions, Room 600.

(5) Committee on Education, Room 501.

(6) Committee on Publishing Interests, Room 401.

(7) Committee on Superannuate Support, Central Street mezzanine lobby, west side of Auditorium.

(8) Committee on Ritual and Orders of Worship, second floor, room under stage. (Take elevator from main foyer.)

IV. We have provided offices for the general officers of the Conference as follows:

(1) The secretaries of the Uniting Conference and editors of *The Daily Christian Advocate* in Room 100 at the south end of the mezzanine floor.

(2) The treasurers of the three Churches involved, in Room 203, first balcony floor on the west side of the Auditorium.

(3) The publishing agencies in Room 201, first balcony floor, west side of the Auditorium.

(4) We have provided offices for the Committee on Ushers and Pages in Room 205, balcony floor, east side of the Auditorium.

(5) For the representatives of the Church papers and secular press and news agents, south half of the east concourse, Wyandotte Street entrance to the Auditorium.

(6) For the use of stenographers for the bishops and chairmen of the general committees, north end of the east concourse, Wyandotte Street entrance.

V. Your Commission further reports that the general Program Committee of the Uniting Conference has arranged for a Youth Rally in the Auditorium for Saturday night, April 29, 1939, and that the general local committees of the Methodist Youth Rally have, in connection with said program and entertainment, arranged for twenty-three seminars to be held during the afternoon of Saturday, April 29, and have requested us to suggest to the Conference that it grant the use of the bar of the Conference to the Youth for the purpose of holding said seminars, there being an insufficient number of committee rooms to accommodate said meetings. Your Commissioners have considered this application on the part of the Youth and believe it is meritorious and therefore recommend to the Uniting Conference that it grant to the Youth the use of the bar of the Uniting Conference.

VI. We recommend that the bar of the Conference be fixed to include the arena floor of the main assembly room of the Municipal Auditorium.

VII. We have provided press tables in front of the platform and we recommend that the representatives as designated by this Commission be given seats there.

VIII. We recommend that fraternal delegates and distinguished guests be seated on the platform.

IX. The Commission is glad to report that there was in due time organized locally a General Committee on the entertainment of this Conference and that it and its subcommittees have co-operated in a fine way and have given every assistance that the Commission could ask in perfecting the set-up of the Conference, and we heartily commend said Committtee and its members for its action in respect thereto.

X. In making this report, we wish to express to the Conference that it has been a joy to serve in this capacity and we are herewith handing over to the Conference physical equipment which we believe to be unsurpassed; and in particular we want the Conference to know that Kansas City has furnished this magnificent Auditorium without a penny of cost to the uniting Churches; and we pray God's richest blessing upon the sessions of this Conference during its stay in Kansas City.

SECTION II

We recommend that the Uniting Conference vote a per diem of $4 per day or such portion as the funds available will permit for the delegates representing the Methodist Episcopal Church and the Methodist Episcopal Church, South.

> ISAAC E. MILLER, *Chairman,*
> *Methodist Episcopal Church.*
> F. W. LINEBERRY, *Vice-Chairman,*
> *Methodist Protestant Church.*
> H. P. MYERS, *Secretary,*
> *Methodist Episcopal Church, South.*

Dr. Miller presented Judge Leslie J. Lyons, Missouri, a member of the Commission on Entertainment, and requested him to present Report No. 2 of the Commission. Before presenting the report Judge Lyons stated that the family of Bishop Eugene R. Hendrix had presented for the use of the Conference the desk at which the Secretary sits, the desk having been used by the Bishop during his lifetime in the preparation of many of his articles advocating Unification, and that the flow-

Marginal notes:
APRIL 27
SECOND DAY
Morning
Committee
Meeting
Plans

Per Diem

Commission on
Entertain-
ment,
Report No. 2

APRIL 27
SECOND DAY
Morning
Commission on Entertainment, Report No. 2

ers in front of the desk were a gift of the family in his memory.

Judge Lyons then presented Report No. 2. Because the report changed the time of the meeting of the Committees involved, Judge Lyons moved that the Rules be amended in that respect and that the Committee meetings be held at the hours specified. The motion, duly seconded, prevailed and the report was adopted, as follows:

COMMISSION ON ENTERTAINMENT, REPORT NO. 2

Your Commission on Entertainment suggests for your action certain changes in the meetings of General Standing Committees, as follows:

Committee No. 1—Conferences. Meeting in Room 500. Meet at 2:45 instead of 2:30 P.M. Begin to take elevator in foyer at 2:35.

Committee No. 2—Ministry and Judicial Administration. Meet at Grace and Holy Trinity Cathedral at 2:30 P.M. The Cathedral is located at 415 West 13th Street.

Committee No. 4—Missions. Room 500. Meeting at 2:15 P.M. instead of 2:30. Members of this committee begin to take elevator in foyer at 2:00.

Committee No. 5—Education. Room 501. Meeting at 3 P.M. instead of 2:30. Begin to take elevator in Main foyer at 2:45.

Committee No. 6—Publishing Interests. Room 401. Meet at regular hour, 2:30 P.M. Begin to take elevator in foyer at 2:20 P.M.

ISAAC E. MILLER, *Chairman;*
F. W. LINEBERRY, *Vice-Chairman;*
H. P. MYERS, *Secretary.*

Fraternal Delegates Introduced

Joseph M. M. Gray, Detroit, Chairman of the Committee on Courtesies, Privileges, and Introductions, was recognized and introduced the following Fraternal Delegates to the Presiding Officer, who in turn presented them to the Conference: The Right Reverend John W. Woodside, D.D., President and Moderator of the United Church of Canada; The Reverend Doctor Gordon A. Sisco, General Secretary of the General Council of the United Church of Canada; The Right Reverend Doctor Robert Bond, former President of the British Methodist Conference; The Hon. Isaac Foot, M.P., lay representative of the British Methodist Church; The Rev. Yotara Koizumi, President of the Methodist Protestant Church of Japan; The Rev. Kyugoro Obata, of the East Annual Conference of the Methodist Church of Japan; Eleazer Guerra, General Superintendent of the Methodist Church of Mexico.

As each was separately introduced the Con- APRIL 27 SECOND DAY
ference rose in welcome to these Fraternal Delegates and Bishop John M. Moore appropriately *Morning*
replied to each address. (For addresses see Section in Appendix, "Fraternal Addresses.")
Announcements were made and the Bishop de- Recess
clared the Conference to be in recess.
After a recess of ten minutes Bishop Moore Reconvene
called the Conference to order, and Dr. James R.
Houghton presented the Seminary Singers of
Boston University, who rendered De Profundis,
the 130th Psalm which John Wesley heard in St.
Paul's Cathedral on the particular day on which
he had his strange heart-warming experience.
The Conference stood during the rendition of the
anthem.
Bishop Moore made the following special an- Methodist Protestants
nouncement:

> The Methodist Protestant delegates and alternates will
> meet tonight (Thursday) at 7:45 o'clock at the Grand
> Avenue Methodist Church. This will be an Executive
> session and will not be open to the public.

Bishop Moore stated that this meeting was
called in accordance with the provision in the Plan
of Union, at which meeting the brethren from the
Methodist Protestant Church would elect two of
their number to be Bishops in The Methodist
Church, and requested that all be much in prayer
for God's guidance.
The following announcement of the organiza- Organization of Standing Committees
tion of the General Standing Committees was
made, to become a part of the record of the Uniting Conference:

COMMITTEE ON CONFERENCES: George W. Henson, Chair-
man; John N. R. Score, Vice-Chairman; J. E. Burns,
Secretary. (Later J. E. Burns resigned and Roy H. Short
was elected Secretary.)
COMMITTEE ON MINISTRY AND JUDICIAL ADMINISTRA-
TION: Orien W. Fifer, Chairman; Henry M. Andrews,
Vice-Chairman; Frank L. Shaffer, Secretary.
COMMITTEE ON MEMBERSHIP AND TEMPORAL ECONOMY:
W. F. Bryan, Chairman; William C. Hartinger, Vice-
Chairman; Costen J. Harrell, Secretary.
COMMITTEE ON MISSIONS, CHURCH EXTENSION, HOS-
PITALS, HOMES, ORPHANAGES, EVANGELISM, DEACONESS
WORK, TEMPERANCE AND SOCIAL SERVICE: John R. Mott,
Chairman; Nathan Newby, Vice-Chairman; Mrs. W. C.
Hammer, Vice-Chairman; H. P. Myers, Secretary.

APRIL 27
SECOND DAY
Morning
Organization
of Standing
Committees

COMMITTEE ON EDUCATION: Paul W. Quillian, Chairman; Daniel L. Marsh, Vice-Chairman; Dwight S. Jeffers, Secretary.
COMMITTEE ON PUBLISHING INTERESTS: Alfred M. Landon, Chairman; Paul N. Garber, Vice-Chairman; George R. Brown, Vice-Chairman; John B. F. Yoak, Jr., Secretary.
COMMITTEE ON SUPERANNUATE SUPPORT, PENSIONS, AND RELIEF: Thomas S. Brock, Chairman; Arthur M. Wells, Vice-Chairman; A. T. McIlwain, Secretary; L. E. Bee, Assistant Secretary.
COMMITTEE ON RITUALS AND ORDERS OF WORSHIP: Oscar T. Olson, Chairman; Leonard B. Smith, Vice-Chairman; Robert W. Goodloe, Secretary.

Special
Committees

The following, on motion of C. W. Bates, North Carolina, duly seconded, were confirmed as representatives of the Methodist Protestant Church on the Special Committees:

RULES: Fred W. Paschall, North Carolina.
JOURNAL: G. Charles Weaver, Onondaga.
CREDENTIALS: Frank B. Hanna, Illinois.
EDITORIAL REVISION: Frank L. Shaffer, West Virginia.
COURTESIES, PRIVILEGES, AND INTRODUCTIONS: T. LeRoy Hooper, Pittsburgh.
ENABLING ACTS: John C. Broomfield, Pittsburgh; George R. Brown, North Carolina; Jasper B. Hicks, North Carolina; Nate S. Williamson, Mississippi.
JUDICIARY: J. E. Butler, Arkansas; Fred Herrigal, Jr. Maryland.
BUSINESS: Gideon I. Humphreys, Maryland.

The Secretary presented the list of nominations from the Methodist Episcopal Church for membership on the Business Committee, and they were duly confirmed, as follows:

BUSINESS COMMITTEE: Albert C. Knudsen, New England Southern; Fremont E. Fribley, North Indiana; Hiram A. Douglas, Northern Minnesota; Dwight S. Jeffers, Pacific Northwest.

Fraternal
Delegate
Speaks

Dr. Joseph M. M. Gray, Detroit, Chairman of the Committee on Courtesies, presented Dr. E. P. Blamires, Ex-President of the New Zealand Conference of the Methodist Church of New Zealand, and Honorary Secretary of the New Zealand Council of Religious Education, to Bishop Moore, who in turn presented him to the Conference. The Conference rose in recognition. At the conclusion of his address, Bishop Moore made appropriate reply. (For address, see Appendix, "Fraternal Addresses.")

Bishop Moore read the following cable and telegrams:

Tokyo, April 27, 1939.
Methodist Conference, Kansas City.
Greetings. Prayers for divine guidance.
AOYAMA GAKUIN.

Keijo, April 27, 1939.
Uniting Conference, Methodist Church, Kansas City.
Korean Methodists pray God's richest blessing on this historic occasion.

Keijo, April 26, 1939.
Uniting Conference, Kansas City.
Greetings and love. Ephesians four three.
MANCHURIA MISSION,
BY RYANG.

Montevideo, April 26, 1939.
General Conference, Methodist Church, Kansas City.
God bless Methodist Unification.
URUGUAYAN METHODIST ASSOCIATION,
BY DANIEL HALL.

Washington, April 25, 1939.
Uniting Methodist Assembly, Kansas City, Mo.
Sino-Korean People's League extends heartiest and warmest congratulations to the leaders and the members of all the Methodist Denominations who made this union of Methodism possible. Christianity is surely marching on. We sincerely pray God may bestow upon this union his richest blessings, wisdom, and positive action for the advancement of Christ's spirit.
KILSOO HAAN, *Washington Representative.*

Lake Grove, N. Y., April 26, 1939.
Reuniting Methodist Conference, care Rev. Thomas B. Mather, D.D., Kansas City.
The Suffolk Association of Congregational Churches and ministers in annual meeting today at Lake Grove, N. Y., sends greetings and heartiest congratulations on convening of this historic Conference for reuniting branches of American Methodists and its significance for the Church of Christ Universal. The world is our common parish.
REV. WELLS H. FITCH, *Registrar.*

Amarillo, Tex., April 27, 1939.
Bishop Ivan Lee Holt, Methodist Church Conference.
The hearts of all American Christians who pray the Saviour's prayer for the unity of God's people are with you and all Methodists assembled in your great Conference where we believe the Holy Spirit will preside filling your hearts with peace and power.
E. CECIL SEAMAN,
Protestant Episcopal Bishop of North Texas.

APRIL 27
SECOND DAY
Morning
Messages Read
Claremore, Okla., April 26, 1939.
The Secretary of Uniting Conference.
At one minute after ten ground was broken for the new
Methodist Church at Claremore, Okla. First new church
with the name "The Methodist Church."
                                W. C. HEATON, *Pastor.*

On motion of Edward D. Kohlstedt, Dakota,
duly seconded, the Secretary was requested to
make appropriate reply to the telegrams. On
motion of the Secretarial Staff, John N. R. Score,
Central Texas, was confirmed as Secretary of
Telegrams.

Greetings from
the President
Bishop Moore called attention to the message
of greetings sent this body by President Roosevelt and read last evening. Motion of Chester A.
Smith, New York, duly seconded, prevailed that
we make the letter a part of our records, and that
we send the President a message expressive of our
gratitude. Bishop Hughes delivered the following
letter from the President:

MESSAGE FROM THE PRESIDENT
WARM SPRINGS, GA., Easter Day, 1939.
My dear Friends: News that three long-separated Methodisms are to hold a Uniting Conference in Kansas City
will bring hope and happiness to earnest souls within these
three communions who for decades have worked and
prayed and petitioned for reunion. I deeply regret that
circumstances make it impossible for me to accept your
kind invitation to attend this significant gathering. To
a world distracted by malice, envy, and ill will, the Kansas
City assembly is a harbinger of better things.

It will, I venture to say, be hailed with satisfaction by
communions outside the Methodist fold as an indication
that the spiritual forces of this nation are determined to
minimize differences which hitherto have tended to arti-
ficial and unnecessary divisions.

This does not mean that honest differences in religious
belief are not to be recognized. It must remain a part of
our American heritage of complete freedom of conscience
to respect those differences in the spirit of toleration which
is of the very essence of our American tradition. I like,
therefore, to think that the cause of religious tolerance is
being advanced by the action of the Uniting Conference,
that as a result of this union of the forces of Methodism
we shall all advance a little nearer to the goal of the
philosopher whose ideal was: Unity in essentials, liberty
in nonessentials—in all things, charity.

A solution of the problems that ever more darkly over-
shadow the world today is impossible without recourse to
the forces of religion. By this, I mean recognition by
men and nations of the spiritual power beyond ourselves
which makes for righteousness, which transcends the order

of mundane culture, and enters the penumbra of divine mystery.

APRIL 27
SECOND DAY
Morning
Greetings from
the President

The American conscience has been shocked in these anxious times to witness a trampling underfoot of the sacred right of freedom of conscience—the right of every man to worship God according to the dictates of his own heart. In the bitter conflict of principles and policies which we witness today the American nation will continue to sustain before all the world the torch of complete liberty of conscience. Beyond the turmoil of the passing day we seek for peace, the peace that passeth understanding. With us freedom and order are moral requisites. Without freedom all is chaos.

These are some of the thoughts which come to me on this Easter Day, the day of hope and happiness and re-awakening to newness of life. In sending my felicitations to the new Methodist Church which is to emerge from the Uniting Conference may I express the hope that the spirit of unity will increase among all our people. The need for union is great, particularly so, since to the democracies of the world has fallen the task of defending and perpetuating freedom of conscience.

The Methodists have pointed the way to union. May God prosper the work and hasten the day when Christians of all confessions shall present a united front to combat the forces of strife that threaten our heritage of religion.

Very sincerely yours,

FRANKLIN D. ROOSEVELT.

Bishop Edwin Holt Hughes,
Bishop John M. Moore,
The Reverend Dr. James H. Straughn, Chairmen,
Commission of the Uniting Churches, Kansas City, Mo.

Mr. Smith presented a resolution which was referred to the Business Committee.

Dr. Isaac E. Miller, Ohio, Chairman of the Entertainment Committee, announced that the Hymnal found on the desk of each delegate was presented by the Publishing Houses of The Methodist Church.

Bishop John M. Moore presented Bishop Paul B. Kern, who in turn presented Bishop Cesar Dacorso Filho of the Methodist Church of Brazil. The Conference arose to greet Bishop Dacorso. At the close of his address Bishop John M. Moore appropriately replied. (For address see Appendix, "Fraternal Addresses.")

Bishop U. V. W. Darlington presented a communication from Bishop Collins Denny; Bishop Arthur J. Moore presented a communication from Bishop W. N. Ainsworth; Bishop John M. Moore presented a communication from Bishop H. M. Du Bose. Motion of Thomas D. Ellis, South

Resolution
Hymnals
Presented
Bishop Dacorso
Presented
Communications

APRIL 27
SECOND DAY
Morning
Absent Bishops
Georgia, prevailed, referring these communications, without reading, to the Committee of Reference for their consideration and report.
Motion of Orien W. Fifer, Indiana, duly sec-
oned, prevailed, requesting the three Co-Chairman
of the Joint Commission on Union, and the Secretary of the Uniting Conference, to send a message
of affectionate greeting to all the absent Bishops.

Memorials
Harry E. Woolever, Central New York, Secretary of the Joint Commission on Church Union,
presented the following resolution and moved its
adoption. Being duly seconded, this was done.

> WHEREAS, there are in the hands of the Secretary of
> the Executive Committee of the Joint Commission on
> Methodist Union a number of memorials from Church
> organizations whose opinion should be before the proper
> committees, and other material which will be of value in
> the deliberation of these committees;
> *Be It Resolved,* That the Uniting Conference, in order
> to facilitate the placing of said memorials and other
> documents into the possession of the committees concerned,
> authorize the Secretary of the Joint Executive Committee
> or the Secretaries of the General Conferences who have
> received such memorials and documents to place the same
> in the hands of the secretaries of the respective General
> Standing Committees for which they are clearly intended:
> That such material and memorials hereinafter received
> shall go to the Business Committee for proper examination
> and disposition.

Dr. Woolever began reading the list, when Fred
D. Stone, Rock River, raised the point of order
that this was equivalent to the presenting of an
argument to this body and therefore was out of
order. The Chair sustained the point of order.
Motion of Arlo A. Brown, Newark, duly seconded, prevailed that we reconsider the action just
taken. Motion of Arlo A. Brown, duly seconded,
then prevailed that the resolution of Dr. Woolever
be laid on the table.

Adjournment
Motion of Thomas D. Ellis, South Georgia, duly
seconded, prevailed that we do now adjourn. The
Conference adjourned with the benediction pronounced by Bishop Hiram A. Boaz.

FRIDAY MORNING, APRIL 28, 1939

Bishop John M. Moore called the Conference to order at 8:30 A.M. and announced that Bishop Ernest G. Richardson would conduct the devotions of the morning.

The devotional address was made by Bishop Urban V. W. Darlington, who spoke from the theme "I Will Build My Church."

Bishop John M. Moore read the following Certificate of Election:

To the Uniting Conference in session at Kansas City, Missouri: This is to certify that the delegates from the Annual Conferences of the Methodist Protestant Church in the Uniting Conference met in the Grand Avenue Temple Methodist Episcopal Church, Kansas City, Missouri, on Thursday, April 27, 1939, for the purpose of electing two Bishops in accordance with the provisions of the Plan of Union. The lot was cast and the choice fell upon James Henry Straughn and John Calvin Broomfield, and they are hereby certified to the Uniting Conference as having been duly elected to the office of Bishop.

Signed by order and in behalf of the Methodist Protestant delegation of the Uniting Conference, this the 28th day of April, 1939.

C. W. BATES, *Secretary.*

Bishop John M. Moore requested Dr. E. A. Sexsmith, President of the Maryland Conference, Methodist Protestant Church, and John H. Baker, senior ranking lay delegate of that Conference, to escort Bishop-elect Straughn from his seat to the head of his aisle, where Bishops Edwin H. Hughes and Arthur J. Moore met him and escorted him to the platform and presented him to the presiding Bishop. Bishop John M. Moore had designated Bishop Urban V. W. Darlington to act with Bishop Hughes, but Bishop Darlington had left the platform after his morning address. Bishop John M. Moore presented Bishop-elect Straughn with the following statement:

Bishop-elect Straughn, once a totalitarian leader and now a colleague in the ranks of benevolent democracy, I present to the Bishops and to the Uniting Conference, Bishop-elect James Henry Straughn.

The Conference rose and applauded.

Bishop John M. Moore then resigned the Chair to Dr. James H. Straughn, a Co-Chairman of the Joint Commission on Church Union.

Bishop-elect Straughn briefly addressed the Conference.

The report of the Committee on Journal was adopted, as follows:

> We have examined the Journal and found it correct.
> JOSEPH D. PIPER, *Chairman;*
> JOHN R. KENNEY, *Secretary.*

Chester A. Smith, New York, was recognized on a question of personal privilege and stated that on yesterday he had presented a resolution in connection with the action of the Conference relative to the letter received from President Roosevelt, but that the resolution failed to appear in today's *Daily Christian Advocate.* Bishop John M. Moore, who presided yesterday, read the paragraph on the duties of the Business Committee found on page 15 of the *Prospectus of the Discipline.* Bishop Moore stated that in as much as Mr. Smith's resolution was on "other matter not included in the regular business of the Uniting Conference, as fixed by the Plan of Union" he had erred in allowing it to come before the Uniting Conference without knowing its content, and that the official record should simply show that it had been received and had been referred.

Joseph M. M. Gray, Chairman of the Committee on Courtesies, Privileges, and Introductions, presented Luren D. Dickinson, senior ranking lay delegate from the Michigan Conference and Governor of Michigan, to Dr. Straughn, who in turn presented him to the Conference. Governor Dickinson addressed the Conference. Dr. Straughn replied appropriately.

The following telegrams were read by the Presiding Officer, and the Secretary, by common consent, was instructed to make appropriate reply:

> New York, N. Y., April 26, 1939.
> Methodist Conference, Grace and Holy Trinity Cathedral, Kansas City.
> The National Council of the Protestant Episcopal Church sends cordial greetings to you and prayers for the success of your endeavor.
> H. ST. GEORGE TUCKER, *Presiding Bishop.*

> Wichita Falls, Texas, April 28, 1939.
> Methodist Commission on Unity, Kansas City.
> Disciples of Christ in Texas State Convention assembled

felicitate their Methodist brethren met to perfect union
and pray God's richest blessings upon them.
   O. L. SHELTON, Wichita Falls;
   GRAHAM FRANK, Dallas;
   EDGAR DEWITT JONES, Detroit.

     Sedalia, Mo., April 27, 1939.
Methodist Uniting Conference, Municipal Auditorium.
 Missouri Convention Disciples of Christ unanimously
vote greetings and felicitations to your great Conference
of United Methodism. Sincere prayers for your success.
   JOHN STUART MILL, *General Secretary*.

     Fresno, Calif., April 26, 1939.
Unifying Conference, Care Grover C. Emmons, Kansas
City.
 Greetings from Pacific Woman's Missionary Confer-
ence assembled Fresno. Prayers attend in your great task.
   FLORENCE GOODYEAR, *Recording Secretary*.

Report No. 1 of the Committee on Credentials
was presented by the Chairman, Earl R. Brown,
Northeast Ohio, and on his motion was adopted.
(For report see Appendix, "Special Committee
Reports," page 828.) Committee on
Credentials,
Report No. 1

 Charles C. Jarrell, North Georgia, presented Episcopal
Assignments
the following resolution:

 WHEREAS, the Plan of Union (Division Three, Article
VI) imposes on the Uniting Conference the duty of assigning the effective Bishops for service to the various
Jurisdictional Conferences; therefore be it
 Resolved, That the presiding Bishop be requested to
appoint a Nominating Committee to consist of six members—one from each Jurisdiction—whose duty it shall be
to nominate for election by this body a Committee on
Episcopal Assignments, to consist of thirty-six members
—six from each Jurisdiction. That Committee shall recommend to this body for adoption a Plan of Episcopal
Assignments to the various Jurisdictions, together with a
Plan of Episcopal Residences throughout the Church.
     T. D. ELLIS,
     J. C. WARDLAW,
     CHARLES C. JARRELL.

 Edward Hislop, Missouri, was recognized and
moved a suspension of the Rules that he might
present a substitute for the resolution before the
Conference. The Chair ruled that no suspension
of the Rules was necessary. Dr. Hislop then presented the following substitute:

 Since it is stated in the Plan of Union, Article VI,
Division Three, that "The effective Bishops shall be assigned for service to the various Jurisdictional Confer-

L 28
DAY
ing
1
ments

ences by the Uniting Conference," and since there is no Standing Committee to which this responsibility has been committed, it is therefore moved, that a committee be raised by this Conference for this specific purpose, this committee to be created as follows: Five ministers and five laymen from each Jurisdiction, making sixty in all. The members of the committee are to be elected by the delegates of each Jurisdiction at the Jurisdictional Meetings to be held on Monday evening, May 1. This committee, after making survey of the field and verifying the number of Bishops legally allotted to each jurisdiction and verifying the number of effective Bishops available for service, shall report the assignments of Bishops to this Conference not later than Monday, May 8.

Dr. Hislop moved its adoption, and the motion was duly seconded.

Merton S. Rice, Detroit, moved that the whole matter be referred to General Standing Committee No 2, Ministry and Judicial Administration. The motion was duly seconded.

Lewis O. Hartman, New England, moved that the motion to refer be laid on the table. The motion was duly seconded.

J. Edgar Skillington, Central Pennsylvania, raised the point of order that the motion to lay on the table was out of order. The Chair ruled that the motion to lay on the table was in order. The motion to lay on the table was put and was lost.

Orien W. Fifer, Indiana, spoke in favor of referring the matter to the Committee on Ministry and Judicial Administration.

Fred D. Stone, Rock River, spoke in favor of the substitute of Dr. Hislop.

Merton S. Rice, Detroit, spoke in favor of the motion to refer.

Edward Hislop, Missouri, spoke in favor of the substitute.

The motion to refer the matter to the Committee on Ministry and Judicial Administration was put, and the motion to refer was lost.

The Conference then adjourned for recess.

ing

At 10:40 A.M. Dr. Straughn called the Conference to order.

The Seminary Singers from Boston University rendered a selection, after which Dr. James R. Houghton sang as a solo "The Holy City" by special request. The Conference stood and applauded.

As a matter of high privilege Bishop John M. Moore assumed the Chair. Bishop Moore appointed Dr. T. LeRoy Hooper, President of the Pittsburgh Conference of the Methodist Protestant Church, and Judge Harry Shaw, senior ranking lay delegate from the same Conference, to escort Bishop-elect Broomfield from his seat to the head of the aisle, where Bishops Adna W. Leonard and William W. Peele met him and escorted him to the platform, presenting him to the presiding Bishop, who in turn presented him to the Conference with the following statement:

APRIL 28
THIRD DAY

Morning
Bishop-elect
Broomfield
Escorted to
Platform

> Bishops of the Church, members of the Uniting Conference, I present to you with great joy Bishop-elect John Calvin Broomfield, born a Scotsman on the Fourth of July, a Methodist Protestant elected a Bishop in The Methodist Church.

The Conference rose and applauded.

Dr. Straughn resumed the Chair.

Lynn Harold Hough, New York East, spoke in favor of the Hislop substitute.

Episcopal
Assignments

Lewis O. Hartman, New England, proposed the following amendment to the Hislop substitute:

> I move that five lay delegates and five ministerial delegates from the foreign field be added to the sixty representatives from the Jurisdictions in the United States, and that the foreign representatives shall be chosen at a meeting of all the delegates from the foreign field, to be held on May 1.

Dr. Hislop accepted this amendment.

Nolan B. Harmon, Jr., Baltimore, raised the question as to whether the report of this Special Committee called for in the Hislop substitute would be final. That portion of the substitute was read indicating that it would be final.

Merton S. Rice, Detroit, spoke against the substitute.

Daniel L. Marsh, New England, offered the following:

> At the point where the committee shall report its action to this Conference, amend as follows: "Report to the Uniting Conference its recommendations for the assignment of Bishops, for such action as the Conference deems meet and proper."

This amendment was accepted by Dr. Hislop.

Orien W. Fifer, Indiana, spoke in opposition to the substitute.

Harold Paul Sloan, New Jersey, spoke in favor of the substitute.

Frank W. Court, Upper Iowa, moved the previous question and the motion, being duly seconded, was ordered.

The motion to substitute the Hislop paper for the Jarrell paper was adopted. The Hislop substitute was then adopted.

Daniel L. Marsh, New England, as a matter of high privilege for the entire house, asked for and was granted the privilege of changing the wording of the Hislop substitute as follows: Instead of the words, "the delegates of each Jurisdiction," make it read, "the delegates from the Annual Conferences composing the Jurisdictions respectively."

The amended resolution is as follows:

> Since it is stated in the plan of Union, Article VI, Division Three, that "the effective Bishops shall be assigned for service to the various Jurisdictional Conferences by the Uniting Conference," and since there is no Standing Committee to which this responsibility has been committed, it is therefore moved, that a committee be raised by this Conference for this specific purpose, this Committee to be created as follows: Five ministers and five laymen from each Jurisdiction, making sixty in all. The members of the committee are to be elected by the delegates from the Annual Conferences composing the Jurisdictions respectively, at the Jurisdictional meetings to be held on Monday evening, May 1.
>
> That five lay delegates and five ministerial delegates from the foreign field be added to the sixty representatives from the Jurisdictions in the United States, and that the foreign representatives shall be chosen at a meeting of all the delegates from the foreign field, to be held on May 1.
>
> This Committee, after making survey of the field and verifying the number of Bishops legally allotted to each Jurisdiction, shall report to the Uniting Conference its recommendations for the assignment of Bishops, for such action as the Conference deems meet and proper.

A. Wesley Pugh, North Indiana, moved that Paragraph (9), page 161, of the *Handbook* be referred to the Committee on Rules for clarification and interpretation, with special reference to the sentence beginning, "All questions, proposals, resolutions, communications, or other matters not included in the regular business of the Uniting

Conference." The motion, duly seconded, prevailed.

Benjamin W. Meeks, Baltimore, presented the following resolution:

Resolved, That when a resolution is presented to the Uniting Conference and is referred to the Business Committee, it be not printed in the *Daily Advocate* until after the Business Committee has reported it to this body.

Motion of Lewis O. Hartman, New England, duly seconded, prevailed referring the Meeks resolution to the Committee on Rules.

Levi P. Goodwin, Iowa-Des Moines, Chairman of the Committee on Presiding Officers, reported for the Committee that Bishop Charles L. Mead would preside tomorrow, Saturday, April, 29. The report was adopted.

H. T. Freeman, South Georgia, presented the following paper:

The statement was made and the resolution calling for a Special Committee on Assignment of Bishops to the Jurisdictions implied that the Uniting Conference has no Committee on the Episcopacy. According to Chapter VIII, page 59, of the Prospectus, there are other matters concerning the Episcopacy which need to be dealt with by this Conference. Is the Standing Committee on the Ministry and Jurisdictional Administration competent to deal with these matters?

The Chair replied that the Committee on Ministry and Judicial Administration had full authority in all matters, except those things otherwise designated by this body.

It was called to the attention of the Conference that Dr. J. Emerson Ford, Secretary of the Commission on Union of the Methodist Episcopal Church, South, and a member of this body, was in deep sorrow over the sudden death of his father. Motion of Harry E. Woolever, Central New York, duly seconded, prevailed instructing the Secretary to convey to Dr. Ford the deepest sympathy of the Conference.

Bishop Roberto Elphick, of Chile, was presented to the Conference by Dr. Straughn. Bishop Elphick addressed the Conference relative to the great earthquake which had recently visited Chile and thanked all those who in any way had contributed to the relief of his stricken countrymen.

APRIL 28
THIRD DAY
Morning
Adjournment

Motion of John F. Baggett, Tennessee, duly seconded, prevailed that, after the necessary announcements, we do adjourn. Various announcements were made and the Conference adjourned with the benediction pronounced by Dr. Merton S. Rice.

SATURDAY MORNING, APRIL 29, 1939

APRIL 29
FOURTH DAY
Morning
Opening

Bishop Charles L. Mead called the Uniting Conference to order at 8:30 A.M., for the session of the fourth day. The Seminary Singers of Boston University approached the platform as a processional.

Bishop Mead announced that the devotions of the morning would be conducted by Bishop William W. Peele.

The devotional message of the morning was delivered by Bishop G. Bromley Oxnam from the theme "He Came Too Soon, This Christ."

The report of the Committee on Journal was adopted as follows:

Journal

We have examined the Journal and found it correct.
JOSEPH D. PIPER, *Chairman;*
JOHN R. KENNEY, *Secretary.*

Committee on
Credentials,
Report No. 2

Report No. 2 of the Committee on Credentials was presented by Earl R. Brown, Chairman, who moved its adoption. The motion, duly seconded, prevailed. (For report see Appendix, "Special Committee Reports," page 829.)

Mrs. J. W.
Hawley

Bishop Mead announced the death of Mrs. J. W. Hawley, wife of Dr. J. W. Hawley, a member of the Pittsburgh Conference delegation of the Methodist Protestant Church, and called on Bishop Paul B. Kern to lead in prayer. The Conference stood while Bishop Kern offered prayer. The Secretary was instructed to express the sympathy of the Conference to the family.

W. F. Bryan, Texas, gave notice that at the proper time he would move a reconsideration of the action of yesterday, whereby the Conference ordered a Special Committee to be created for the assignment of Bishops to Jurisdictions.

Reconsider

Fred D. Stone, Rock River, having voted with the majority on yesterday, moved that we do now reconsider the action of yesterday relative to the assignment of Bishops, not for the purpose of changing the method of procedure, but for the purpose of changing the ratio of representation on the Committee ordered. The motion to reconsider, being duly seconded, was adopted.

Fred D. Stone, Rock River, then offered the following amendment:

Amend the report so that the basis of representation shall be ten each—five lay and five clerical—in the Northeastern, North Central, Western, and Central Jurisdictions; that it shall be twenty each—ten lay and ten clerical—in the Southeastern and South Central Jurisdictions; and that in the ten representatives from the foreign fields, the four-four-one ratio provided for this Conference shall prevail as nearly as possible.

Isaac E. Miller, Ohio, spoke against the adoption of the resolution.

Edward Hislop, Missouri, spoke in favor of the resolution.

Merton S. Rice, Detroit, spoke against the adoption of the pending matter.

Hans J. Roan, Idaho, moved that the matter be referred to the Committee on Judiciary for an opinion regarding the legality of said action under the Rules of the Uniting Conference. The motion was duly seconded.

Chester A. Smith, New York, offered the following as a substitute for all that was before the Conference:

Resolved, That this Uniting Conference refer the matter of assigning the Bishops for service to the Committee on Ministry and Judicial Administration, which is hereby d rec ed to present to this body its report not later than May t6.

The motion to substitute was declared out of order, since, under the Rules of Order, a motion to refer (said motion of Hans J. Roan being before the Conference) takes precedence over a motion to substitute.

W. F. Bryan, Texas, moved that the motion to refer to the Committee on Judiciary be tabled. The motion, being duly seconded, prevailed.

Francis R. Bayley, Baltimore, moved that the whole matter before the Conference be laid on the table. The motion was duly seconded, but did not prevail.

Harold Paul Sloan, New Jersey, spoke in favor of the amendment.

Harry E. Hess, Nebraska, offered as a substitute a motion to refer this matter to the Committee on Ministry and Judicial Administration. The motion was declared out of order on the ground that it was a new motion and not germane to the pending matter.

William F. Quillian, South Georgia, moved the previous question. The motion, duly seconded, prevailed and the previous question was ordered.

By a count vote of 470 for and 360 against, the Stone amendment prevailed.

By a count vote of 463 against to 361 for, the Hislop resolution, adopted on yesterday, reconsidered and amended this morning, was not adopted.

Fred D. Stone then offered the following motion:

> That the assignment of Bishops to the residences and the Jurisdictions, according to the Plan of Union, according to the privilege given to this Uniting Conference, be referred, with authority and with instructions to report their action to this Conference, to the Committee on Ministry and Judicial Administration.

The motion was seconded by Orien W. Fifer, Indiana, who also offered the following amendment:

> That the same groups, which assigned the delegates to the different committees, shall assign nine additional delegates from the foreign field in the ratio of four-four-one to the General Committee on Ministry and Judicial Administration, they to serve upon the subcommittee or Episcopacy."

Dr. Stone accepted the Fifer amendment. The motion of Fred D. Stone was adopted.

Time Extended   Motion of the Secretary, duly seconded, prevailed extending the time in order that Judge Lyons might make an important announcement for the Local Committee on Entertainment.

Judiciary
Committee
Excused   Francis R. Bayley, Baltimore, Chairman of the Committee on Judiciary, requested that the Committee be excused to consider matters of immediate concern. The Committee was excused.

Recess   The Conference then adjourned for recess.

At 10:55 A.M. the Conference reconvened, with Bishop Charles L. Mead in the chair.

Madame Yoshika Saito, of Tokyo, Japan, sang as a solo "Alleluia," by Mozart. She then sang in her native tongue "I Need Thee Every Hour." Rendering the same song in English, at the suggestion of the presiding Bishop, the Conference joined in singing the chorus.

Dr. Joseph M. M. Gray, Detroit, Chairman of the Committee on Courtesies, Privileges, and Introductions, presented to the presiding Bishop Dr. Eric M. North, Secretary of the American Bible Society. Bishop Mead presented him to the Conference. Dr. North briefly addressed the Conference and presented it with a copy of the Bible for its use. Bishop Mead replied appropriately in behalf of the Conference.

J. Edgar Skillington, Central Pennsylvania, Chairman of the Committee on Rules, was recognized. He presented Report No. 1 of the Committee and moved that it be printed in the *Daily Christian Advocate* for consideration on Monday. The motion, being duly seconded, prevailed.

Dr. Skillington presented Report 2, which was read by the Secretary, under the Rules of Order, as it had not been published.

Thomas D. Ellis, South Georgia, moved the adoption of the report.

Dr. Skillington spoke to the report.

Chester A. Smith, New York, offered as an amendment the following resolution:

Resolved, That any paper or resolution presented to and read to the Conference by a member thereof, and upon which the question of consideration has not been raised and sustained, shall be printed in the *Daily Advocate.*

George W. Henson, Philadelphia, a member of the Committee on Rules, spoke in favor of the report.

Motion of Charles A. Robbins, Pacific Northwest, duly seconded, prevailed, laying the Smith amendment on the table.

The report was then adopted. (For report see Appendix, "Special Committee Reports," page 825.)

George C. Douglass, Troy, presented and moved the reference of the following resolution:

Marginal notes:
APRIL 29
FOURTH DAY
Morning
Reconvene
Madame Yoshika Saito Sings
Dr. Eric M. North Introduced
Committee on Rules of Order, Report No. 1
Report No. 2
Bishops' Salaries, etc.

Resolved, That the proper committee consider methods of paying salaries and allowances to the two newly elected Bishops, and that the Secretary place this Resolution in the hands of the proper committee, accompanied by information which this committee will need.

The resolution was ordered referred.

Levi P. Goodwin, Iowa-Des Moines, Chairman of the Committee on Presiding Officers, presented Report No. 2, which was adopted, as follows:

COMMITTEE TO SELECT PRESIDING OFFICERS, REPORT NO. 2

Your committee presents the following selections for Presiding Officers:

Monday, May 1—Bishop Paul B. Kern.
Tuesday, May 2—Bishop Adna W. Leonard.
Wednesday, May 3—Bishop U. V. W. Darlington.
The committee will meet in Room 310 on Monday at 1:45 P.M.   LEVI P. GOODWIN, *Chairman;*
W. A. SHELTON, *Secretary.*

The following communication from the Central Conference of American Rabbis, addressed to Bishop Mead, was read by the Secretary:

GREETINGS FROM AMERICAN RABBIS

May I through you extend to the Uniting Conference of the Methodist Episcopal Church the hearty fraternal greetings of the Central Conference of American Rabbis? I send you also our warm congratulations on the success of the effort to unite the branches of the Methodist Episcopal Church. It is all the more significant a spiritual victory because it is a conspicuous example of the success of a sincere effort to achieve the religious ideal of unity in a day when division and dissension rule in a large part of the world.

We pray with you that God will bless your broader fellowship and make the greater Methodist Episcopal Church an effective instrument to do his will.

With further greetings of peace and brotherhood, I am,
Fraternally yours,   MAX C. CURRICK.

Motion of Thomas D. Ellis, South Georgia, duly seconded, prevailed instructing the Secretary to make proper reply.

Bishop Adna W. Leonard was granted the privilege of the floor to announce the arrangements for the consecration of Bishops-elect James H. Straughn and John C. Broomfield. Bishop Mead stated that Bishop Leonard had been requested by the Council of Bishops to preach the consecration sermon.

Motion of Thomas D. Ellis, South Georgia, duly

seconded, prevailed, that when we adjourn it be to meet in regular session Sunday afternoon for the p u r p o s e of consecrating Bishops-elect Straughn and Broomfield.

Alfred F. Hughes, West Wisconsin, moved that the paragraph of the Episcopal Address appearing on page 30 of the *Daily Christian Advocate* under the sub-title "An Intelligent Church," be referred to the General Standing Committee on Education. The motion, duly seconded, prevailed.

Fred D. Stone, Rock River, announced that the Book Concerns of the three Churches were to celebrate one hundred years of service next Tuesday night, May 2, with a pageant and program in the Music Hall of the auditorium. Motion of Daniel L. Marsh, New England, seconded by Nathan Newby, Pacific, prevailed that we make this meeting an official session of the Conference.

Motion of Edgar R. Heckman, Central Pennsylvania, duly seconded, prevailed that after necessary announcements we adjourn.

George A. Fowler, Rock River, called the attention of the Conference to the fact that Sunday, April 30, 1939, is the 150th anniversary of the inauguration of George Washington as the first President of the United States, and that our Church was the first religious organization to recognize the Constitution and the Chief Magistrate just inaugurated in 1789.

Francis R. Bayley, as a matter of privilege, stated that the Committee on Judiciary had no report to make to the Conference at this time.

After various announcements the Conference adjourned with the benediction pronounced by Bishop Charles L. Mead.

SUNDAY AFTERNOON, APRIL 30, 1939

Pursuant to the order of adjournment the Uniting Conference convened at 3:30 o'clock for the purpose of consecrating Bishops-elect James H. Straughn and John C. Broomfield.

The session opened with the singing of the Processional (Hymn 315, "How Firm a Foundation"), led by Dr. James R. Houghton and the Seminary Singers of Boston University.

The following order of service was observed: Dr. Houghton announced and the Conference joined in singing Hymn 379, "I Love Thy Kingdom, Lord."

Bishop John M. Moore led in prayer.

The Boston Seminary Singers, led by Dr. Houghton, sang the Apostles' Creed, set to music by the eminent Russian composer, Gretchaninoff, the audience standing.

The Collect was read by Bishop Edwin H. Hughes.

The first Scripture lesson, Acts 20: 17-35, was read by Bishop Paul B. Kern.

The second Scripture lesson, John 21: 15-17 and Matthew 28: 18-20, was read by Bishop H. Lester Smith.

Consecration Sermon

The Consecration Sermon was delivered by Bishop Adna Wright Leonard, from the text Matthew 20: 22 and from the theme "Are Ye Able?" as follows:

ARE YE ABLE?

I shall read a few verses from the Gospel according to St. Matthew, the twentieth chapter, and will then read again the words that I take as the text of the afternoon sermon.

The Gospel according to St. Matthew, twentieth chapter, beginning at the twentieth verse: "Then came to him the mother of Zebedee's children with her sons, worshiping him, and desiring a certain thing of him. And he said unto her, What wilt thou? She saith unto him, Grant that these my two sons may sit, the one on thy right hand, and the other on the left, in thy kingdom. But Jesus answered and said, Ye know not what ye ask. Are ye able to drink of the cup that I shall drink of, and to be baptized with the baptism that I am baptized with? They say unto him, We are able."

Listen then to the words of the text taken from the twenty-second verse of the twentieth chapter of the Gospel according to St. Matthew: "Are ye able to drink of the cup that I shall drink of? They say unto him, We are able."

This question grew out of a conversation between Jesus and the two sons of Zebedee after their mother had requested that places of preferment be given to them in His kingdom. The Master must have experienced a keen sense of disappointment as He listened to their request. It was the case of an ambitious mother and her two sons who shared her ambitions for them. It is clear there was indignation among the disciples, for the Word says, "And when the ten heard it, they were moved with indignation against the two brethren." The feeling of indignation was not against the mother, but against the two sons who were thinking of the Kingdom in terms of reward and emolument. The element of jealousy was not wanting and a generous attitude on the part of the disciples was hard to discover.

The question which Jesus put to those two young men was in the nature of a challenge and an appeal. By this question, He challenged their conception of the Kingdom. They had not grasped what the Kingdom really meant. They conceived it to be an opportunity to possess power and position. They had not realized that all true greatness is in service and that His only power was the might of His love. Let us be careful how we judge, for possibly many of us have not yet faced all that is involved in the truth that the really big man, in God's sight, the truly great man is he who serves the most.

Jesus was straightforward and frank in dealing with people. He could not tolerate duplicity or deception. He told them they were to go into the world as sheep among wolves and again and again made it plain that the spirit of the Kingdom of God and the spirit of the world were in eternal conflict. All worthy enterprises and all great undertakings are fraught with difficulties, discouragements, and dangers. Everyone who engages in a great task or enterprise must expect to lay his course with trial. The disciples discovered this to be the case. They were ignorant of what awaited them. They wanted thrones, but he gave them a cross. One would be put to the sword, while another best loved and most tried of all would know the meaning of utter loneliness.

He did not place a glittering crown above the gate and hide the cross behind the wall. He told them plainly that the road over which they were to go, if they followed Him, would be rough and rugged. In all of this He was not disappointed with their imperfections and was patient with them in their shortcomings. He knew they did not know what was ahead of them.

When on the Damascus Road the crisis came in Paul's life, how much did he know what experiences awaited him? The other disciples had been three years under the personal leadership and teaching of Jesus. After all that they were contentious, reaching out for rewards and benefits. With Paul it was different. He came directly to the question as to who Jesus was and the claim made by Him and His disciples regarding His relation to God. When he surrendered to Jesus Christ, when he accepted the Messiahship of Jesus, when he proclaimed the Lordship of Jesus, he staked his all on that act of faith. He never raised the question about what he would get out of it. But Paul did not know what awaited him on the new and untrod way. His was the act of faith.

So it was with Luther, so it was with Wesley, and so it has been with a company which no man can number. The same principle obtains in the adventure upon which we as Methodists have embarked. That there are problems ahead goes without saying. But who is wise enough to say just what those problems will be? Again it is the act of faith.

In winning men for the Kingdom they were not to be unmindful of the fact that it was to be a Kingdom of right relationships. He did not want His followers to win men to Him by obscuring the nature of the cause or by blunting the edge of moral demands. The disciples had to learn that only when we think aright of Christ and are rightly disposed toward Him, can we have fellowship one with another and experience the great fact that the blood of Jesus Christ cleanses us from sin.

He not only challenged their conception of the Kingdom, but He accepted their appraisal of their ability to drink His cup. He took them as they were that He might make them what they ought to be. Jesus knew that if He was to accomplish anything with his disciples, He must in the first instance accept them as He found them.

In other words Jesus was willing to accept those two young men, notwithstanding their ignorance of what awaited them, provided He could have their love, their allegiance, and their devotion. He was wise enough to see that these are the creative and uplifting elements in all true discipleship. A man may say, "I am able to share The Cup," not knowing all that is involved in thus committing himself. The Master's reply is "You shall share it," provided your love for me is supreme and your loyalty is without taint. He was willing to accept their love mixed with their ignorance, but first of all He wanted their love. He was getting back to the essentials—He was testing the sincerity of their love for Him.

I am persuaded that the greatest need of the Church is to get back to the essentials of the gospel and offer to men, without mental reservation, a God who is able to meet their every need "through riches in glory by Christ Jesus." Every one is in quest of the mastery of the art of living. The church has the secret. If we obviously have the secret, the world will come in quest of it. We do not need more machinery, but we do need to go back to the essentials and get power to drive the machinery we now have built up. We do not need more whirring of the wheels, but the roar of power.

If only in the spirit of utter dedication we could answer, "Lord, by thy grace we are able," we could carry the battle to the very gates and win this world for Christ. The Church must be brought once again to the place of a mighty fellowship, offering the privilege of service for Christ in heroic and adventurous endeavor, to bring this world "back to God."

The day in which we live in many respects resembles the world that confronted the early church. Waking philosophers have rendered themselves important. Skepticism, infidelity, and practical materialism abound. Man has become the slave of the very machinery he has created. In blindness and confusion, the world is groping after a new social order. Europe is witnessing today the return to Caesar worship. The difference between the more ancient Caesar worship and that of today is that the former is a bit more picturesque.

It is the duty of the Church to tell the world there is in Christ the sure Word of God, for lack of which the world

is perishing. The Church must be careful not to become
panic-stricken. She must be careful not to declare her
message in terms of defeat. Paul said, "We are perplexed,
but not in despair."
Man reaches out for something mightier than himself.
Time is on the side of Christian faith. Someday men will
discover that the price demanded by the totalitarian states
is too much and that the boasted benefits of totalitarianism
are not what they are claimed to be.

The Christian Church has always appealed to the higher elements in man. It has assumed a larger capacity for
thought than its rivals have allowed. It has taught man
to think and has lifted up the dignity and worth of the individual. It has stood for the Saviourhood of Jesus and
His ultimate supremacy. It has stood for the love of God
the forgiveness of God, for human redemption, for social
justice, economic righteousness, and the brotherhood of
man, in the fatherhood of God through Jesus Christ our
Lord. This testimony has not at all times been clear and
her courage in the face of certain wrongs has not been
all that could be desired. Nevertheless, the Church has
stood for these things and she stands for them today.

The age of dictators will pass and possibly sooner than
some are disposed to think. Men are beginning to see
that "man cannot live by bread alone."

The disciples learned by bitter experience the meaning
of absolute trust in God. They discovered that by the
grace of God, they were able. Ignorance gave way to
knowledge and faith in Christ made them triumphant.
God can do anything with a man who depends utterly upon
Him.

These men who are to be consecrated this afternoon to
the office of Bishop in The Methodist Church have known
the meaning of great responsibilities. Today they enter
upon a field of service peculiar to Methodism. They are
to be set apart for a great and holy task—a task so great,
and at times so delicate, as to require the utmost of body,
mind, and spirit. What awaits them, God alone knows.

In the fascinating story of the life of Whymper, the famous mountain climber, there is an interesting account of
achievement through co-operation.

At one of the stations on the trail up the mountain,
there lived a dwarf. He was a hunchback and was a poor,
misshapen thing. It was his duty to attend to the needs
of the climbers as they tarried for rest at the station before making the final dash to the summit. The heights
were not for him, because he simply was not equal to it.
Everyone else had long since come to the same conclusion.
The heights were not for the likes of him.

But one day Whymper, the world renowned mountain
climber, was guiding a small company of men up the mountain. They rested at the station before attempting to
reach the summit. Whymper learned that it had been the
desire of the poor hunchback some day to climb to the top
of the mountain. His eyes shone and hope leaped into his
soul. So Whymper bade him come and follow him and he
would see him through. There were many tight and difficult places where it seemed his strength would utterly

APRIL 30
FIFTH DAY

Afternoon
Consecration
Sermon

fail and he must give up. But when his strength was weakest, Whymper was at his side. When he staggered and seemed about to fall, the great mountain climber put out his strong right hand. He struggled along and kept at it until they reached the summit. When the old mountain was beneath their feet the grateful hunchback fell at the feet of Whymper in a burst of gratitude and amazement. The little fellow achieved because he did his best in co-operation with the great, strong man.

The Methodist Church is now launched upon one of the most significant adventures in the history of the Christian centuries. In a very real sense our faces are toward the heights. Difficulties of which now we are ignorant undoubtedly are in the offing and also our greatest achievements for the Kingdom of God.

Constitutional rights and privileges, Christian education, the redemption of this world from sin, sacred sentiments and glorious loyalties, missionary enterprises, brotherhood, fellowship, youth looking hopefully and determinedly into the future, these and all other matters relating to the Kingdom are before us.

Hear the Master say, "Are ye able to drink the cup?" O Methodist Church, "put on thy strength" and answer, "Lord—'We are able' by thy grace, if only Thou wilt be with us on the upward way."

At the conclusion of the sermon, the Boston Seminary Singers sang Hymn 268, "Are Ye Able?" the Conference standing and joining in the singing of the last stanza.

Bishop-elect
Straughn
Presented
for
Consecration

Bishop-elect James Henry Straughn was presented for consecration by Dr. E. A. Sexsmith, President of the Maryland Conference, Methodist Protestant Church, and Dr. George R. Brown, of the North Carolina Conference, Methodist Protestant Church.

Bishop-elect
Broomfield
Presented
for
Consecration

Bishop-elect John Calvin Broomfield was presented for consecration by Dr. T. LeRoy Hooper, President of the Pittsburgh Conference, Methodist Protestant Church, and Dr. C. L. Daugherty, of the Pittsburgh Conference, Methodist Protestant Church.

The exhortation to the Bishops-elect was given by Bishop John M. Moore, who then led in prayer.

Bishop Edwin H. Hughes then examined the Bishops-elect, using the questions in the Ritual Service of Consecration of a Bishop.

The audience was requested to bow their heads in silent prayer, praying God's richest blessings upon those about to be consecrated Bishops.

At the conclusion of the season of silent prayer

Bishop Paul B. Kern led in the recital of *Veni,*
Creator Spiritus.
Bishop H. Lester Smith then led in prayer.
At the conclusion of the prayer Bishop-elect
James Henry Straughn was consecrated to the office of Bishop in The Methodist Church by Bishops Edwin Holt Hughes, Adna Wright Leonard, and Paul Bentley Kern.
Bishop-elect John Calvin Broomfield was then consecrated to the office of Bishop in The Methodist Church by Bishops John Monroe Moore, H. Lester Smith, and Adna Wright Leonard.
The Ritual prayers were offered by Bishop Kern.
Bishop H. Lester Smith announced and the congregation joined in singing Hymn 164, "All Hail the Power of Jesus' Name."
The Conference adjourned with the benediction
pronounced by Bishop John M. Moore.

MONDAY MORNING, MAY 1, 1939

The Conference was called to order at 8:30 A.M.
by Bishop John M. Moore, who introduced Bishop
H. Lester Smith to lead the devotions of the morning. The Devotional Address of the morning was
given by Bishop William C. Martin, who based his remarks on the prayer of St. Paul found in Ephesians 3: 14-19.
At 9 A.M. Bishop Moore resigned the chair to Bishop Paul B. Kern for the business session.
The Report of the Committee on Journal was
adopted, as follows:

We have examined separately the Journal of Saturday morning's and Sunday afternoon's sessions and find them correct.
JOSEPH D. PIPER, *Chairman;*
JOHN R. KENNEY, *Secretary.*

Report No. 3 of the Committee on Credentials
was presented by the Chairman, Earl R. Brown, Northeast Ohio, who moved that it be adopted without reading and published in the *Daily Christian Advocate.* The motion, duly seconded, prevailed. For report, see Appendix, "Special Committee Reports," page 830.
Clarence M. Dannelly, Alabama, addressed the Conference on a question of high privilege, and

suggested the Conference quicken its pace of working.

Leslie J. Lyons, Missouri, made important announcements relative to speeding up the work of the Conference.

Motion of Orien W. Fifer, Indiana, duly seconded, prevailed, that each General Standing Committee be given the privilege of deciding the hour of its meeting from day to day.

Social Creed   William P. King, North Georgia, presented the following resolution:

WHEREAS, we have no section in the Prospectus that has any reference to a Social Creed and to social and economic questions, and whereas a harmonization is necessary of the Disciplines of the three uniting Churches; therefore be it

Resolved, That the Council of Bishops appoint a committee of 18 in the 4-4-1 ratio of the three Uniting Churches, whose function it shall be to prepare and submit to this Conference a Social Creed for the United Church. This Committee shall consist of an equal number of preachers and laymen. The Committee is to make a report to the Conference by May 8.

Ernest W. Peterson, Oregon, spoke in opposition to the resolution, stating that the matters involved should go to the General Standing Committee on Membership and Temporal Economy.

Lynn Harold Hough, New York East, on a question of privilege, requested a ruling from the Chair as to whether or not the resolution should go automatically to the above-mentioned Committee. The Bishop ruled that it does not, unless a special motion is made placing it there.

Nathan Newby, Pacific, moved, as an amendment, that the resolution be referred to the General Standing Committee on Membership and Temporal Economy. The motion was duly seconded.

Chester A. Smith, New York, moved as a further amendment that the report should include our position on some of the questions of the day, especially the resolution which he had offered at the beginning of the session. The Chair ruled this amendment out of order.

The amendment of Nathan Newby was adopted. The resolution as amended was then adopted, and the matter referred to the General Standing Committee on Membership and Temporal Economy.

The Methodist Church 223

Report No. 1 of the Committee of Reference was presented and adopted, as follows: MAY 1
SIXTH DAY

COMMITTEE OF REFERENCE, REPORT NO. 1 *Morning*

The communications of Bishops W. N. Ainsworth, Collins Denny, and H. M. DuBose, referred to the Committee by the Uniting Conference, have been duly considered and all properly answered. Committee of Reference, Report No. 1

LUD H. ESTES, *Chairman;*
C. W. BATES, *Secretary.*

Calendar No. 1, Report No. 1 of the Committee on Superannuate Support, printed on page 86 of the *Daily Christian Advocate*, was presented by Thomas S. Brock, New Jersey, Chairman of the Committee. Dr. Brock explained the provisions of the report and moved its adoption. The motion was duly seconded. Committee on Superannuate Support, Report No. 1

Francis R. Bayley, Baltimore, inquired if the words "unless dissolved as hereinafter provided," found at the end of Section 2, Paragraph 1304, of the printed report should not be omitted. The Chairman replied as follows in explanation: "This particular phrase is put in here in order to protect the Methodist Protestant Church so that if they wish to dissolve that corporation they have the right to do it without waiting until General Conference legislation."

George C. French, North Texas, moved that we consider the report section by section. The motion was duly seconded, but did not prevail.

Edward D. Kohlstedt, Dakota, moved to amend Paragraph 1303, Section 1, line 7 of the printed report by changing the expression "two Executive Secretaries" to read "one or more Executive Secretaries."

Charles V. Adams, Central Pennsylvania, suggested that it should read "one or two Executive Secretaries," and Dr. Kohlstedt accepted the suggestion.

Fred B. Newell, New York East, spoke against the amendment.

Willard G. Cram, Kentucky, moved to lay the amendment on the table. The Chair ruled that an amendment cannot be laid on the table.

J. Edgar Skillington, Central Pennsylvania, moved the pending question. The motion, being duly seconded, prevailed.

Dr. Brock spoke in favor of the report as print-

MAY 1
SIXTH DAY

Morning

Committee on
Super-
annuate
Support,
Report No. 1

ed. The vote was taken on the Kohlstedt amendment. The amendment did not prevail.

Frank W. Court, Upper Iowa, moved to insert
in line 4, Paragraph 1307, of the printed report,
the word "necessary" just before the word "expenses." The motion was duly seconded.

J. Edgar Skillington, Central Pennsylvania,
moved as an amendment that all after the word
"denomination" should be stricken out, and there
should be added after that word, "As provided for
in ——," the blank to be filled by inserting the
number of the paragraph which shall contain this
provision when known. Dr. Court accepted this
amendment.

Arthur M. Wells, Illinois, spoke in favor of the
report as presented by the Chairman.

On a count vote of 450 for to 336 against, the
Skillington amendment, accepted by Dr. Court,
prevailed.

Thomas S. Brock, Chairman, closed the debate
for the Committee.

The report as amended was then adopted. For
report, see Appendix, "General Standing Committees," page 642.

Committee on
Conferences,
Reports Nos.
1 and 2

John B. F. Yoak, Jr., Western Virginia, moved
that the Rules be suspended in order that Reports
1 and 2 of the Committee on Conferences, appearing in this morning's *Daily Christian Advocate*,
might be taken up and acted on at this time. The
motion, duly seconded, prevailed.

Mrs. J.
Premnath
Das
Introduced

Joseph M. M. Gray, Detroit, Chairman of the
Committee on Courtesies, Privileges, and Introductions, presented Mrs. J. Premnath Das, a distinguished member of the Uniting Conference.
Mrs. Das graduated from Goucher College, Baltimore, and then taught in Isabella Thoburn College, India. At the recent annual meeting of the
Board of Governors she was elected President of
the College, the first Indian woman to be thus
honored.

Order of the
Day

Motion of George W. Henson, Philadelphia,
duly seconded, prevailed, making as the Order of
the Day, after recess, the consideration of Reports
1 and 2 of the Committee on Conferences.

Bishop H. Lester Smith, Secretary of the
Council of Bishops, and Lud H. Estes, Memphis,
Secretary of the Uniting Conference, separately

presented the names of those who had been nomi- MAY 1
nated to organize the Jurisdictional Conference SIXTH DAY
meetings, to be held tonight, and Leslie J. Lyons, *Morning*
Missouri, announced the place of meetings. The Jurisdictional
nominations were approved, as follows: Meetings

Northeastern Jurisdiction: Bishop Edwin H. Hughes;
Secretary, Edgar R. Heckman; meeting place, Room 400.
Southeastern Jurisdiction: Bishop U. V. W. Darling-
ton; Secretary, C. W. Bates; meeting place, Grace and
Holy Trinity Cathedral.
Central Jurisdiction: Bishop Robert E. Jones; Secre-
tary, R. N. Brooks; meeting place, Room 314.
North Central Jurisdiction: Bishop E. L. Waldorf;
Secretary, T. LeRoy Hooper; meeting place, Room 401.
South Central Jurisdiction: Bishop A. Frank Smith;
Secretary, J. N. R. Score; meeting place, Room 600.
Western Jurisdiction: Bishop Titus Lowe; Secretary,
Grover C. Emmons; meeting place, Room 311.

J. L. Harman, Louisville, requested the Chair Parliamentary
to make a ruling on the following matter: "Can Inquiry
an amendment to a motion or resolution be put on
the table without carrying with it the whole matter?" The Chair ruled that the Uniting Conference was governed by the Rules of Order in the
Handbook, and in all matters not specifically provided for we are governed by Robert's Rules of
Order. Robert's Rules of Order, pages 10 and 55,
show that an amendment cannot be laid on the
table, because the process of laying an amendment
on the table is virtually to close a debate.

Various announcements were made and the Recess
Conference recessed for ten minutes.

At 10:40 A.M. the Conference resumed its ses- Reconvene
sion, with Bishop Paul B. Kern in the chair.

The Boston Seminary Singers presented "Let
Thy Holy Spirit Come Unto Me," by Peter Tsche-
snokoff, under the direction of Dr. James R.
Houghton. Bishop Kern then led in prayer.

The Conference had previously ordered that Ministry and
additional members from the Foreign Field be Judicial
added to the General Standing Committee on tion
Ministry and Judicial Administration, the nominations to be made by those who had made the
previous nominations for the General Standing
Committees. The Conference confirmed the following:

Methodist Episcopal Church, South: Clerical, J. P.
Bartak, Czechoslovakia, and Z. T. Kaung, China. Lay,

MAY 1
SIXTH DAY
Morning

Y. C. Yang, China, and Mrs. J. P. Bartak, Czechoslovakia. Methodist Protestant Church: Lay, Mrs. W. E. Hammer, North Carolina. Methodist Episcopal Church: Clerical, Theodor Arvidson and Ferdinand Sigg, Europe. Lay, Paul P. Wiant, China, and Earle M. Rugg, India.

Committee on Conferences, Report No. 1

Calendar No. 2, Report No. 1 of the Committee on Conferences, page 104 of the *Daily Christian Advocate,* was presented by George W. Henson, Philadelphia, Chairman, who explained its provisions and moved its adoption. The motion was duly seconded.

W. F. Bryan, Texas, moved as a substitute that the General Conference meet in 1941, and the motion was duly seconded. John T. Ellison, Alabama, spoke for the substitute; Elmer E. Collins, Montana State, against the substitute; Harold Paul Sloan, New Jersey, for the substitute; A. P. Lyon, Louisville, against the substitute; Thomas S. Brock, New Jersey, for the substitute; Roy L. Smith, Southern California, against the substitute; George Mecklenburg, Northern Minnesota, for the substitute; Nathan Newby, Pacific, against the substitute.

Frank P. Culver, Central Texas, moved the previous question, and the motion was duly seconded. The previous question was ordered.

At the request of Dr. Henson, J. N. R. Score, Central Texas, Chairman of the sub-committee handling the matter under consideration, closed the debate. The substitute of W. F. Bryan did not prevail. The report, printed on page 104 of the *Daily Christian Advocate,* was adopted. For report, see Appendix, "General Standing Committees," page 420.

Committee on Conferences, Report No. 2

Calendar No. 3, Report No. 2 of the Committee on Conferences, page 104 of the *Daily Christian Advocate,* was presented by the Chairman, George W. Henson, Philadelphia, who moved its adoption. The motion was duly seconded. Dr. Henson requested common consent to insert after the words "place of," in the sixth line, the following: "and make the arrangements with the Local Committee for." Common consent was granted, and the report was adopted as amended. For report, see Appendix, "General Standing Committees," page 420. Before the vote was taken Bishop Kern called attention to Article II of Section I of the Plan of Union and asked if the Conference desired the Committee proposed to report back to the Uniting Conference in order that it may proceed in line with your Plan of Union? Dr. Henson replied: "I think this body is actually carrying out that purpose by voting upon this resolution." This explanation was accepted by the Conference, by common consent

On motion of George C. Douglass, Troy, duly seconded, the following resolution was adopted:

Resolved, That each Committee, in making its proposals for the future Methodist Church, state whether or not the proposals increase overhead; and if so, estimate the amount."

The following resolution was presented by W. G. Cram, Kentucky, who moved its adoption. The motion was duly seconded.

That the Editorial Committee, which is to prepare and edit the New Discipline of The Methodist Church, be instructed to place in the New Discipline, in proper order, the matter that occurs in the Prospectus as follows:
1. All the matter that occurs on pages 5, 6, 7, 8, 9, and 10, inclusive, which is the Plan of Union.
2. The matter that occurs on pages 21, 22, and 23, inclusive, which is the Articles of Religion.*
3. The matter that occurs on pages 24 and 25, inclusive, which is the General Rules.
4. The matter that occurs on pages 19 and 20, inclusive, which is the Historical Statement.†

Henry M. Andrews, Alabama, called attention to the fact that in the Historical Statement, page 19, middle of the second column, appeared this statement, "Dr. Coke then, with the assistance of several Presbyters, was consecrated a Bishop." This he stated was evidently an error. Bishop Edwin H. Hughes replied that this was true and that it had been corrected in the regular documents of the Joint Commission.

Henry M. Greenslit, Nebraska, asked a question about a certain date. The Editors of the *Disci-*

* Note the Cherrington substitute for the Taylor Amendment, which was adopted, concerning matters in this section. See page 229.—EDITORS.

† For all matters referred to in Sections 2, 3, and 4 see Appendix.

pline, by common consent, were instructed to make all necessary historical corrections.

Harry Van Antwerp, Troy, moved that the words "The following article is found in the Methodist Protestant Articles of Religion," found on page 23 of the *Prospectus of the Discipline*, second column, be stricken out. The motion was duly seconded.

Thomas D. Ellis, South Georgia, raised the point of order that it was a part of the Plan of Union, and therefore could not be stricken out, as the Plan of Union had been constitutionally adopted. Bishop Edwin H. Hughes stated that the Article mentioned had been placed where it was at the request of the Methodist Protestant brethren for information and as a witness of their stand and of the stand of Methodism down over the time of its history, and that it was not a part of the Plan of Union.

Herbert J. Burgstahler, Upper Iowa, moved that the motion just made be made the first Order of the Day tomorrow morning after the report of the Committee on the Journal. The motion was duly seconded.

M. A. Childers, West Texas, made the following point of order: "The whole question of whether or not that should be in the *Discipline* is out of order because Article III of the Plan of Union says that the Articles of Religion shall be those historically held in common by the three Uniting Churches. Therefore if this last paragraph is not held in common by all three it cannot be put into our Articles of Religion by this Uniting Conference."

The Chair ruled the point well taken and that the motion to postpone debate on the matter and the motion to strike out certain wording are automatically therefore out of order.

Dean Taylor, Iowa-Des Moines, moved that the paragraph on page 23, now under discussion, be transferred to the Historical Section. The motion was duly seconded. The amendment was accepted by Dr. Cram.

J. C. McPheeters, Pacific, spoke against the transposition of the paragraph.

Grover C. Emmons, Pacific, made the point of order that we cannot transfer the paragraph to another place in the *Discipline,* because it had been placed where it was in the Plan of Union. The Chair ruled the point not well taken if "the verbiage as is here printed and as was an original part of the original Plan of Union is simply transferred without alteration."

Ernest H. Cherrington, Ohio, moved the following substitute for the Taylor motion: "That the footnote which appears at the end of the Articles of Religion in the *Prospectus* be placed at the end of the Articles of Religion in the *Discipline* of The Methodist Church with the statement that it was placed there by action of the Uniting Conference and not by the constitutional process by which the Articles of Religion for The Methodist Church were adopted."

The substitute, duly seconded, prevailed.

The motion of Dr. Cram, thus amended, was then adopted.

G. C. Boswell, Central Texas, moved that the date of final adjournment be set for Sunday evening, May 7. The motion did not prevail.

Report No. 3 of the Committee on Rules, on motion of the Secretary, was ordered printed in the *Daily Christian Advocate* for action tomorrow.

Motion of John F. Baggett, Tennessee, duly seconded, prevailed that we adjourn after the announcements. Various announcements were made and the Conference adjourned with the benediction pronounced by Bishop Cesar Dacorso Filho.

TUESDAY MORNING, MAY 2, 1939

The Conference convened at 8:30 A.M. with Bishop Adna W. Leonard in the chair. Bishop Leonard announced that Bishop Clare Purcell would be in charge of the morning worship service and that Bishop Charles W. Flint would bring the devotional address.

Bishop Flint brought a timely message descriptive of "A Good Man," found in the first Psalm, centering his remarks about the key clause "In His law doth he meditate day and night."

Bishop Leonard called the business session of the Conference to order at 9 A.M.

The report of the Committee on Journal was adopted, as follows:

We have examined the Journal and find it correct.
JOSEPH D. PIPER, *Chairman;*
JOHN R. KENNEY, *Secretary.*

J. T. Ellison, Alabama, was recognized on a question of high personal privilege and moved that the words in lines 14 and 15, page 119, of the *Daily Christian Advocate*, column 3, in his speech of yesterday, be deleted. The motion, duly seconded, prevailed.

Early
Adjourn-
ment

Herbert J. Burgstahler, Upper Iowa, moved that we do now adjourn until tomorrow morning and go at once to the work of the General Standing Committees. The motion was duly seconded.

J. Edgar Skillington, Central Pennsylvania, raised the point of order that there were in the *Daily Christian Advocate* two reports that, under the order of business, should be considered at this time. The Bishop ruled the point of order well taken.

Committee on
Rules,
Report No. 1

Report No. 1 of the Committee on Rules, page 126 of the *Daily Christian Advocate*, was read by the Secretary. Dr. Skillington explained the report and moved its adoption. The motion, duly seconded, prevailed. For report, see Appendix, "Special Standing Committees," page 824.

Report No. 3

Report No. 3 of the same Committee was read by the Secretary. Dr. Skillington explained its provisions and moved its adoption. The motion, duly seconded, prevailed. For report, see Appendix, "Special Standing Committees," page 825.

Committee on
Credentials,
Report No. 4

Earl R. Brown, Northeast Ohio, Chairman of the Committee on Credentials, presented Report No. 4 of the Committee, and moved that it be adopted without reading and published in the *Daily Christian Advocate* of tomorrow. The motion, duly seconded, prevailed. For report see Appendix, "Special Standing Committees," page 832.

The following recommendation of the Committee on Credentials, on motion of Earl R. Brown, Northeast Ohio, duly seconded, prevailed:

The Committee on Credentials submits the following recommendation:

When an alternate, or reserve delegate, is seated in the Conference for from one to three days only, he shall occupy both the principal's seat in the Uniting Conference and be seated in the Committees to which the principal is assigned, and the alternate, or reserve delegate, shall receive the per diem allowance for the day or days approved. EARL R. BROWN, *Chairman;* CHARLES A. ROBBINS, *Secretary.*

Herbert J. Burgstahler, Upper Iowa, renewed his motion that we do now adjourn and proceed to the work of the General Standing Committees. The motion was duly seconded. Dr. Burgstahler spoke to the motion. The Chair held the motion to adjourn in abeyance until James A. James, Rock River, could present a privileged resolution, and also that some other miscellaneous matters requiring action under our Rules of Order could be attended to. Dr. Burgstahler changed the wording of his motion so that the matters announced by the Chair might be attended to before adjournment.

On motion of James A. James, Rock River, duly seconded, the following was adopted:

RECOGNITION BY WORLD METHODISM OF THE CENTENARY OF THE BIRTH OF FRANCES E. WILLARD

In view of the fact that Frances E. Willard was an honored and faithful member of the Methodist Episcopal Church during her entire adult life, in view of the fact that she was one of the first five women to be elected as delegates to a General Conference; in view of the fact, further, that she is now recognized as one of the world's greatest leaders, it is thought fitting that The Methodist Church should be among the first to honor her memory. The resolution here presented implies the calling upon all of our schools, colleges, and universities to recognize this significant event, upon all Methodist churches to carry out appropriate programs on the Sunday nearest September 28, which shall include exercises in the Church school and in the preaching services; and the issuing of special editions of all church *Advocates;* that this Uniting Conference go on record in support of the movement for the issuing, upon the order of the Post Master General, of special memorial Frances E. Willard centenary stamps.

Arthur M. Wells, Illinois, moved, as an amendment to the Burgstahler motion, that we adjourn at ten o'clock, instead of immediately. The amendment was accepted by Dr. Burgstahler.

Willard G. Cram, Kentucky, and J. Edgar Skillington, Central Pennsylvania, spoke against the motion to adjourn.

Arthur A. Callaghan, Maine, moved the previous question on all that was before the Confer-

MAY 2
SEVENTH DAY
Morning

Frances E.
Willard

Rules
Suspended

Committee on
Super-
annuate
Support,
Report No. 2

Committee on
Missions,
Report No. 1

ence. The motion, duly seconded, prevailed, and the previous question was ordered. The motion to adjourn at ten o'clock did not prevail on being put to a vote.

James A. James, Rock River, obtained common consent of the Conference to insert in his resolution, previously adopted, relative to Frances E. Willard, a paragraph concerning the issuance of special memorial stamps by the Post Office Department.

Motion of Nathan Newby, Pacific, duly seconded, prevailed, that the rules be suspended that we might take up the Calendar and consider the reports appearing in today's issue of the *Daily Christian Advocate.*

Calendar No. 4, Report No. 2 of the Committee on Superannuate Support, entitled "Permanent and Pension Fund," and appearing on page 127 of the *Daily Christian Advocate,* was presented by the Chairman, Thomas S. Brock, New Jersey. Dr. Brock explained the provisions of the report and moved its adoption. The motion, duly seconded, prevailed. For report, see Appendix, "General Standing Committees," page 645.

Calendar No. 5, Report No. 1 of the Committee on Missions, entitled "The Board of Temperance" and appearing on page 127 of the *Daily Christian Advocate,* was presented by the Chairman, John R. Mott, New York. Dr. Mott explained in detail the provisions of each Article and moved the adoption of the report. The motion was duly seconded.

Daniel L. Marsh, New England, moved to amend Section III, Conference Boards, Article 1, on page 128 of the *Daily Christian Advocate,* by inserting after the word "Cabinet," in the second line, the words, "or otherwise, as the Conference may direct." This amendment was accepted by the Chairman.

George C. French, North Texas, raised the point of order that the Conference was ignoring the action of yesterday which called for a careful estimate of overhead expenses to accompany each report where such was involved, and moved that we observe the rule. Bishop Leonard ruled that, in view of the action of yesterday, the report could not be received at this time. Dr. Mott stated that the proposed legislation would not call for an increase in overhead.

Francis R. Bayley, Baltimore, moved that we suspend this particular rule at this time and adopt the report under consideration. The motion, duly seconded, prevailed.

Report No. 1 of the Committee on Missions was then adopted. For report, see Appendix, "General Standing Committees," page 547.

On motion of Orien W. Fifer, Indiana, duly seconded, the following resolution was adopted:

Resolved, That if and when Reports Nos. 6 and 7 on the Calendar, or Report No. 3 of the Committee on Conferences and Report No. 1 of the Committee on Membership and Temporal Economy, be adopted, the Secretary be authorized to change the term "District Elder" to whatever term this Conference may adopt when the report of the Committee on Ministry and Judicial Administration is presented concerning this title; this resolution, if adopted, to apply to all other reports which may carry the term "District Elder."

Calendar No. 6, Report No. 3 of the Committee on Conferences, entitled "District Conferences" and found on page 128 of the *Daily Christian Advocate,* was presented by George W. Henson, Philadelphia, Chairman. Dr. Henson explained the provisions of the report and moved that it be adopted. The motion was duly seconded.

Leslie R. Burgum, North Dakota, raised the question that there seemed to be no provision for a presiding officer in case the District Superintendent should be absent. Dr. Henson asked that the Committee be granted common consent to add, at the close of paragraph 169 of the printed report, "If the District Superintendent be absent, the District Conference is authorized to elect a Chairman." Common consent was given for this amendment.

A. Wesley Pugh, North Indiana, moved to amend Paragraph 175 of the printed report by adding in line 3, after the words "suitable candidates," the words "for acceptance as Accepted Supply Pastors." This amendment was accepted by Dr. Henson for the Committee.

Thomas D. Ellis, South Georgia, inquired if there would be any provision made for licensing local preachers if no District Conference were

MAY 2
SEVENTH DAY

Morning
Committee on
Missions,
Report No. 1

Committee on
Conferences,
Report No. 3
—"District
Conferences"

MAY 2
SEVENTH DAY
Morning
Committee on
Conferences,
Report No. 3
—"District
Conferences" held. Chairman Henson stated that this would be taken care of in a later report under "Quarterly Conferences."

Charles MacCaughey, Pacific Northwest, raised the question as to whether or not this was new legislation, because it considered the question of Accepted Supply Pastors. Dr. Henson stated that the term "Accepted Supplies" appeared many times in the Discipline of the Methodist Episcopal Church and there would be no reason why it should not be placed here. The Chair asked if there were any objections to this being received as suggested by Dr. Henson. There were none, and by common consent the explanation of Dr. Henson was accepted.

Samuel C. Rice, Kentucky, offered the following as a substitute for Paragraph 177 of the printed report:

> Before the ballot for the license of an applicant is taken, he must present written answers to the following questions, namely:
> 1. Will you abstain from the use of tobacco and other indulgences which may injure your influence?
> 2. Are you in debt so as to interfere with your work in the ministry?

The motion, duly seconded, did not prevail.

Edward R. Stafford, Ohio, moved to amend Paragraph 172 of the printed report by adding, "Such called sessions of the District Conference may be held at the time and place of the Annual Conference session." The motion was duly seconded. Chairman Henson stated that the District Elder shall fix the date of the District Conference, "and that means also the special sessions doubtless that he is to call, and he could call one if he sees fit at the Annual Conference." The proposed amendment, duly seconded, being put, was not adopted.

Edgar T. Welch, Erie, stated that the matter of elections provided for in Paragraph 171 was also being considered by a subcommittee of the General Standing Committee on Membership and Temporal Economy, and moved that the matter be referred to a conference of the two committees involved for action. The motion, seconded by George W. Henson, prevailed.

Francis R. Bayley, Baltimore, moved the previous question. The motion, duly seconded, prevailed and the previous question was ordered. Chairman Henson closed the debate for the committee and asked common consent, which was granted, to make the following minor changes for clarification: In Paragraph 170, after the word "superannuated," add the words "or retired." In the same paragraph let the wording relating to "Church School Superintendents" be "Church School Superintendent from each church in the charge." The report was then adopted, with the understanding that Paragraph 171 was referred for conference, as previously acted upon. For report, see Appendix, "General Standing Committees," page 420.

MAY 2
SEVENTH DAY

Morning
Committee on
Conferences,
Report No. 3
—"District
Conferences"

Calendar No. 7, Report No. 1 of the Committee on Membership and Temporal Economy, printed on pages 128 and 129 of the *Daily Christian Advocate*, and entitled "The Local Church," was presented by the Chairman, W. F. Bryan, Texas. Dr. Bryan stated that there would be no overhead expense with reference to this report. He explained its provisions and moved its adoption. The motion was duly seconded.

Committee on
Membership
and
Temporal
Economy,
Report No. 1
—"The Local
Church"

John Q. Schisler, North Arkansas, moved to amend Paragraph 426, third line, by deleting the words "eighteen years old and over." The motion was duly seconded and Dr. Schisler spoke to the motion.

J. C. McPheeters, Pacific, spoke against the amendment.

Joseph M. M. Gray, Detroit, spoke in favor of the amendment. The Schisler amendment to delete was adopted.

Robert S. Satterfield, Oklahoma, requested an interpretation of Paragraph 431, beginning of line 7, asking, "Does this take away or interfere in any way with the duties of the stewards?" Chairman Bryan replied, "It does not."

Oscar T. Olson, Northeast Ohio, moved to amend Paragraph 430 by adding after the words "the stewards," in line 5, the words "the leaders" and add the words "and where desired, the director of music" after the words "the director of religious education" in lines 6 and 7. The motion was duly seconded, but the amendment was accepted by Chairman Bryan.

MAY 2
SEVENTH DAY
Morning
Committee on
Membership
and
Temporal
Economy,
Report No. 1
—"The Local
Church"

By common consent the time was extended to complete this item of business and the hearing of announcements before recess.

W. C. Perkins, Pittsburgh, raised a question in regard to Paragraph 429. Dr. Perkins stated that the Prospectus contained four items while the printed report contained only three, and asked if the item omitted, relative to the election of Annual Conference delegates and Church officers, had been provided for elsewhere. Chairman Bryan assured him that it had.

George W. Henson, Philadelphia, moved to amend Paragraph 437 of the printed report by adding at the close of the paragraph the words "except where otherwise authorized by the Quarterly Conference." The amendment was accepted by Chairman Bryan.

Sanford W. Corcoran, Pittsburgh, moved to amend Paragraph 430, last sentence, by changing the language to read as follows: "The Chairman shall be the pastor or, if the Board desires, it may elect the Chairman. The Board shall also elect a Secretary and a Treasurer." The motion was duly seconded.

Costen J. Harrell, Tennessee, spoke in favor of the report as presented.

William F. Quillian, South Georgia, moved that the amendment lie on the table, and the motion, duly seconded, prevailed.

James W. Engle, West Virginia, moved to amend Paragraphs 434 and 436 by changing the word "twenty-one" to "eighteen" in each separate paragraph.

Costen J. Harrell, Tennessee, spoke against the proposed amendment, explaining the paragraph as printed.

The amendment was not adopted.

J. C. McPheeters, Pacific, moved to amend Paragraph 426 by adding after the words "Annual Meeting" at the close of the fifth line the words "The Quarterly Conference may establish an age limit for membership in this meeting when desired." The motion, duly seconded, did not prevail.

Benjamin W. Meeks, Baltimore, moved to amend Paragraph 431, line three, by changing the word "or" to "and." The motion, duly seconded, did not prevail.

Edward D. Kohlstedt, Dakota, moved the previous question on all that was before the Conference. The motion, duly seconded, prevailed, and the previous question was ordered.

The report was adopted as amended. For report, see Appendix, "General Standing Committees," page 509.

Various announcements were made and the Conference stood at recess at 10:40 A.M.

At 10:50 A.M. Bishop Leonard called the Conference to order.

The Seminary Singers of Boston University, under the direction of Dr. James R. Houghton, presented a negro spiritual, "Climbing Up the Mountain, Children."

Calendar No. 8, Report No. 1 of the Committee on Ministry and Judicial Administration, printed on page 129 of the *Daily Christian Advocate* and entitled "Number of Bishops in Jurisdictional Conferences," was presented by Orien W. Fifer, Indiana, Chairman. Dr. Fifer explained the provisions of the report and moved its adoption. The motion, duly seconded, prevailed. For report, see Appendix, "General Standing Committees," page 457.

Calendar No. 9, Report No. 2 of the Committee on Ministry and Judicial Administration, printed on pages 129 and 130 of the *Daily Christian Advocate* and entitled "The Judicial Council," was presented by the Chairman, Orien W. Fifer, Indiana. Dr. Fifer requested Francis R. Bayley, Baltimore, Chairman of the subcommittee, to represent the Committee in presenting the report.

Dr. Bayley called attention to a typographical error in Paragraph 301. In line 10, immediately following the word "nominees," should be inserted the words "or from such other nominees." Dr. Bayley explained, in detail, the provisions of the report and moved its adoption.

George C. French, North Texas, raised the point of order that, according to Article VII of the Plan of Union, page 10 of the *Prospectus*, there is a provision that no new legislation may be enacted at this Uniting Conference, and that

Marginal notes: MAY 2 SEVENTH DAY — Morning — Committee on Membership and Temporal Economy, Report No. 1—"The Local Church" — Recess — Reconvene — Seminary Singers — Committee on Ministry and Judicial Administration, Report No. 1—"Bishops in Jurisdictional Conferences" — Committee on Ministry and Judicial Administration, Report No. 2—"The Judicial Council"

MAY 2
SEVENTH DAY
Morning
Committee on
Ministry and
Judicial Ad-
ministration,
Report No. 2
—"The Judi-
cial Council"
Dr. Bayley had stated that Paragraph 309 was a new provision in the report of the Committee, growing out of the fact that we would soon be operating under Jurisdictional Conferences.

Dr. Bayley replied that the basis of this legislation was already in the *Discipline* of the Methodist Episcopal Church, South, and that it was clearly within the power of this body to adapt it to the use of The Methodist Church.

After this explanation by Dr. Bayley, the Chair ruled the point of order, raised by Dr. French, to be out of order.

Chester A. Smith, New York, disagreeing with the ruling of the Chair, appealed to the Conference. On a standing vote the ruling of the Chair was overwhelmingly sustained.

Lynn Harold Hough, New York East, and Thomas D. Ellis, South Georgia, both spoke in favor of the report.

Chester A. Smith, New York, spoke against the report and moved to amend it at three different places, as follows:

I move to amend the report as follows:

1. By striking· out of Paragraph 301, the second subdivision thereof, the words, "The Council of Bishops shall nominate by a majority vote of the effective Bishops twenty traveling elders and sixteen lay members of the church and from such nominees or from such other nominees as may be named from the floor of the conference, without discussion," and inserting in their place the following: "Nominees for the Judicial Council shall be made, without discussion, from the floor of the Conference, and from such nominees," and by striking out in the eleventh line of that subdivision the word "five" and inserting in place thereof the word "four," and by striking out in the twelfth line of said second subdivision the word "four" and inserting the word "five," so that the first sentence of said second subdivision shall read: "Nominees for the Judicial Council shall be made, without discussion, from the floor of the Conference, and from such nominees the General Conference shall elect, by ballot, and without discussion, five traveling elders and four lay members, and from the remaining nominees the General Conference shall elect by separate ballot four traveling elders and five lay members as alternate members of the Judicial Council."

2. From Paragraph 312, the third subdivision, strike out the words "The Council of Bishops" in the first line, and insert in place thereof the words "The Secretary of the Conference."

Leslie R. Burgum, North Dakota, raised the point of order, after the first amendment had been offered, that its provisions are not contained in any of the *Disciplines* of the three Churches, and therefore is out of order because it lacks harmonization.

The Chair ruled the point not well taken, on the ground that the report of the Committee itself is before the body and any member may offer the amendment which is proposed, the Conference itself being the judge of the final disposition of the offered amendment.

The motion to amend was duly seconded and Mr. Smith spoke to the question before the Conference.

George A. Fowler, Rock River, moved that the proposed amendments lie on the table.

Daniel L. Marsh, New England, raised the point of order that our Rules of Order give to anybody who wishes to speak on the opposite side the right to do so before debate is shut off. The Chair ruled the point well taken.

George H. Lamar, Baltimore, spoke against the amendments.

Arthur A. Callaghan, Maine, moved the previous question. The motion, duly seconded, prevailed, and the previous question was ordered.

Francis R. Bayley, as Chairman in charge of the report, closed the debate. The Smith amendments were not adopted. The report was then adopted. For report, see Appendix, "General Standing Committees," page 457.

Bishop Leonard requested the privilege of the house for Bishop James Cannon, Jr., who made the following statement:

MAY 2
SEVENTH DAY
Morning
Committee on Ministry and Judicial Administration, Report No. 2 —"The Judicial Council"

Statement of Bishop James Cannon, Jr.

STATEMENT BY BISHOP CANNON

Mr. Chairman and brethren of the Uniting Conference of The Methodist Church: I have received word from my son, Dr. James Cannon of Duke University, that another son, David P. Cannon of Arlington, Va., was being brought to Duke University Hospital for treatment for gastric ulcer of the stomach, from which a severe hemorrhage had already resulted.

As my son Dr. Wallace B. Cannon died very suddenly a few years ago from a similar gastric ulcer, I am compelled to decide that my duty constrains me to leave the Conference and go to Durham.

I am constrained to make another statement before leaving the Conference: On May 16, 1938, there appeared in the widely circulated, illustrated paper *Life*, this statement: "In Birmingham, over the protest of its bigoted

MAY 2
SEVENTH DAY
Morning
Statement of
Bishop
James
Cannon, Jr. Bishop James Cannon, Jr., and many other irreconcilables the Quadrennial General Conference of the M. E. Church, South, voted to end the slavery-born split of American Methodism."

I received numerous letters and personal denunciations of this libelous statement, but up to this time I have made no reply. My brethren who have been associated with me in the General Conferences of the Church for over thirty years know my record.

In 1914, at the Oklahoma City General Conference, I offered the amendment which smoothed the way for the appointment of the first Commission on Unification. In 1918, as chairman of the Commission on Church Relations, I advocated the continuation of that Commission. As a member of that Commission I, with Bishop Edgar Blake as co-chairman of a subcommittee which met in Richmond, worked out a Plan of Union which was adopted by the Joint Commission and became the basis of the Plan which was voted upon in 1924 and 1925.

When it became evident that, while the Chattanooga General Conference of our Church had given the constitutional majority, it was possible that the Annual Conference might not ratify, I was requested to be the chairman of a committee to advocate ratification and by most strenuous efforts, while the constitutional majority was not given, an actual majority of 420 was secured.

Concerning the present plan of Unification, the fact is that I have stated most unequivocally that I favored the Plan, but in order that there might be no opportunity for successful obstruction in the Civil Courts, I urged that any possible legal complication be thoroughly considered by the Judicial Council.

I have most earnestly advocated Unification since the General Conference of my Church in 1910. It was one of the great moments of my life when I faced this great Conference and announced Charles Wesley's great hymn, "O for a Thousand Tongues to Sing," and recognized that there were more than one thousand tongues of delegates, Bishops, and alternates of United Methodism to sing that hymn.

It is with great regret that I must leave before the Conference adjourns.

May I say to you, my brethren, I fully realize that there will be difficulties in making some adjustments, but not more difficulties than we have had in each of our three denominations.

My brethren, patience and brotherly love will be effective oil!

And now, I commend you to God and to the word of His grace, which is able to build you up and give you an inheritance among all them that are sanctified.

God bless you, one and all!

The Conference and visitors rose and applauded. Bishop Leonard replied appropriately and called upon Bishop Herbert Welch to offer prayer. Bishop Welch prayed God's richest blessings upon Bishop Cannon and his loved ones.   -

Clarence M. Dannelly, Alabama, was recognized on a question of high personal privilege and stated that the article appearing in the local morning paper under the caption ·"Delegates from Dixie Win Skirmishes at Conference" was misleading in its implications and not in harmony with the facts, as the members of the Uniting Conference were all working wholeheartedly for the welfare of The Methodist Church.

Bishop James H. Straughn, in behalf of the delegates from the Methodist Protestant Church, also protested that there was no intent or purpose on the part of the Methodist Protestant group to form a bloc with any other group in the Uniting Conference.

Bishop Leonard announced and the members of the Conference stood and all joined heartily in singing the first stanza of "Blest Be the Tie That Binds."

Roy L. Smith, Southern California, having previously voted for, moved a reconsideration of Calendar No. 7, Report No. 1 of the Committee on Membership and Temporal Economy, for the purpose of offering a simple amendment. The motion, duly seconded, prevailed. Dr. Smith then offered the following amendment: Paragraph 431, beginning of line 3 to end of first sentence should read "Board, on joint call of the pastor and the Chairman, or on written petition of fifteen per cent of the membership of said Board." The motion being duly seconded, Dr. Smith spoke to his proposed amendment.

Committee on
Membership
and
Temporal
Economy,
Report No. 1
Reconsidered

Fred D. Stone, Rock River, spoke in opposition to the amendment.

On being put to a vote, the Smith amendment was not adopted. The original report was then adopted. For report, see Appendix, "General Standing Committees," page 509.

Willard G. Cram, Kentucky, raised a question concerning the legality of a portion of an action taken by the Uniting Conference on April 29, recorded on page 98, column 3 of the *Daily Christian Advocate*, whereby the matter of assigning Bishops to residences was referred to the Committee on Ministry and Judicial Administration. Dr. Cram now moved that the matter be referred to the Committee on Judiciary for a decision. The

MAY 2
SEVENTH DAY

Morning

motion being duly seconded, Dr. Cram spoke to his motion.

Fred D. Stone, Rock River, seconding the motion, spoke in favor of the reference. The Cram motion to refer the matter prevailed.

Report of Committee on Presiding Officers

The Committee on Presiding Officers presented their report and it was adopted, as follows:

COMMITTEE OF NINE TO SELECT PRESIDING OFFICERS, REPORT No. 3

Your committee presents the following selections for Presiding Officers: Thursday, May 4, Bishop E. G. Richardson; Friday, May 5, Bishop Arthur J. Moore; Saturday, May 6, Bishop E. L. Waldorf; Monday, May 8, Bishop A. Frank Smith.   LEVI P. GOODWIN, *Chairman;*
                                      W. A. SHELTON, *Secretary.*

Night Session

Motion of the Secretary, duly seconded, prevailed that when we adjourn it be to meet in the Music Hall at 8 P.M. in harmony with previous action making the presentation of the pageant "The Spreading Word," and presented by the Publishing Houses of the three uniting Churches, an official session of the Conference.

Telegram from Bishop Dobbs

The Secretary read the following telegram from Bishop Hoyt M. Dobbs:

Sanatorium, Miss., May 1, 1939.
Dr. Lud H. Estes, Auditorium.
Please express to my colleagues and to the Conference my grateful thanks and appreciations. I am with you in thought, purpose, and affections. My prayer is for the highest and happiest consummation of union.
                                      HOYT M. DOBBS.

Deceased Members

The Secretary of the Conference was instructed to send messages of sympathy to the families of those delegates who had died before the convening of the Conference, provided he was given correct names and addresses. The name of Mrs. Dan Brummitt was included in the list, by common consent.

Announcements

Various announcements were made. Bishop Leonard requested that we have a moment of reverent quiet, after which he pronounced the benediction and the Conference adjourned.

Adjournment

TUESDAY EVENING, MAY 2, 1939

Pursuant to adjournment, the Conference convened at 8 P.M. in the Music Hall for the purpose of witnessing the presentation of the pageant "The Spreading Word" sponsored by the Publishing Houses of the three uniting Churches. Briefly, this was "A Pageant of the People Called Methodist—They of a Thousand Books and Two," celebrating the Sesquicentennial of the Publishing House of the Church. More than 250 men and women, old and young, took part in presenting the pageant in four Episodes, as follows:

Episode I. The Organization of American Methodism. The Christmas Conference—Lovely Lane Chapel, Baltimore, Maryland, December 24, 1784-January 3, 1785.

Episode II. A Methodist Publishing House Is Authorized by the Conference of 1789 at Wesley Chapel (John Street Church) in New York.

Episode III. Presentation of the Conference Address to President Washington, June 1, 1789. The scene takes place at the President's House on Franklin Square, New York.

Episode IV. The First Book Room. 43 Fourth Street, between Race and Arch Streets, Philadelphia, 1789.

Following the Episodes moving pictures were introduced showing the circuit rider on his rounds, printing processes of a century ago and those now in general use in our several printing plants. As a grand finale the roll of active Publishing Agents and Editors of the Uniting Churches was called and those present responded and took their places on the platform.

The Conference then adjourned with the benediction pronounced by Bishop William F. Anderson.

WEDNESDAY MORNING, MAY 3, 1939

The Conference was called to order at 8:30 A.M. by Bishop Urban V. W. Darlington. The Bishop announced that Bishop Charles L. Mead would be in charge of the worship service and that Bishop A. Frank Smith would bring the devotional address of the morning.

Bishop Smith addressed the Conference on "The Christian Grace of Gratitude," basing his remarks on Colossians 3: 15 and 17.

MAY 3
EIGHTH DAY
Morning
Journal

Bishop Darlington called the Conference to order for the business session at 9 A.M.

The report of the Committee on Journal was presented and adopted, as follows:

We have separately examined the journal of yesterday morning and last evening and found both correct.
JOSEPH D. PIPER, *Chairman;*
JOHN R. KENNEY, *Secretary.*

Committee on Credentials, Report No. 5

Earl R. Brown, Northeast Ohio, Chairman of the Committee on Credentials, presented Report No. 5 and moved its adoption without reading, the report to be published in the *Daily Christian Advocate* of tomorrow. The motion, duly seconded, prevailed. For report, see Appendix, "Special Standing Committees," page 833.

Flowers in Memory of Bishop Mouzon

It was announced that the large bouquet of beautiful white flowers on the left of the platform had been placed there in memory of Bishop Edwin DuBose Mouzon, by his former students in Southwestern University.

Bishop Darlington led in an appropriate prayer in memory of the work and influence of Bishop Mouzon.

Committee on Conferences, Report No. 3 Referred

A. Wesley Pugh, North Indiana, moved that Paragraph 177, Report No. 3 of the Committee on Conferences, Calendar No. 6, adopted May 2, 1939, be made to conform to whatever report is adopted from the Committee on Ministry and Judicial Administration relating to the same subject.

George W. Henson, Philadelphia, stated that the matter was being considered by the several committees.

Nathan Newby, Pacific, moved that the matter be referred to the newly created Special Standing Committee of Chairmen of General Standing Committees. The motion, duly seconded, prevailed.

The Press

Costen J. Harrell, Tennessee, presented the following resolution, which was adopted:

Resolved, That we hereby express our appreciation for the courteous reporting by the daily papers of Kansas City of the proceedings of this Uniting Conference. While we regret an article appearing in yester-

day's paper, we wish to record our sincere appreciation
of the just and considerate publicity as a whole.

EARL G. HAMLETT,
C. M. DANNELLY,
COSTEN J. HARRELL.

J. Edgar Washabaugh, Newark, under a question of privilege, told of the great sorrow which
had come to Samuel H. Clark, lay delegate of the
Newark Conference, in the sudden death of his
brother and mother-in-law since the convening
of the Uniting Conference; of his making air-
plane trips to both funerals; and that he was
present at his post of duty in his delegation this
morning. Dr. Washabaugh moved that the Uniting Conference express to Brother Clark our
deepest sympathy and commend him for his loyalty and love for The Methodist Church. The motion, duly seconded, prevailed unanimously. Bishop Edwin H. Hughes, at the request of Bishop
Darlington, prayed God's richest blessings upon
Brother Clark and his loved ones.

Charles MacCaughey, Pacific Northwest, moved
that we recognize the faithful services of some
thirty subcommittee members present, for their
arduous work in helping to prepare the *Prospectus of the Discipline*, and that they be granted
seats on the main floor of the Auditorium, without
the power to vote or debate. The motion, duly
seconded, prevailed.

Arthur A. Callaghan, Maine, Chairman of the
Committee on Enabling Acts and Legal Forms,
presented the following recommendation:

Your Committee on Enabling Acts and Legal Forms
recommends that each of the regular Standing Committees of this Uniting Conference be requested to prepare
proper Enabling Acts to take care adequately of its interests between the date of the adjournment of this Conference and the completing of the cycle of organization
of General Boards and interests following the initial
meetings of the several Jurisdictional Conferences.

A. A. CALLAGHAN, *Chairman;*
W. M. ALEXANDER, *Secretary.*

On motion of Thomas D. Ellis, South Georgia,
duly seconded, the recommendation was adopted.

William F. Quillian, South Georgia, presented
the following resolution:

Resolved, That the Uniting Conference requests the
Committee on Rules to make a recommendation as to a

correct and uniform term to be used in addressing the Chair; and that this recommendation be made as early as possible.

The resolution, being duly seconded, was adopted and referred to the Committee on Rules.

Lud H. Estes, Memphis, presented the following amendment to Rule 27 and moved its reference to the Committee on Rules:

> When an amendment is offered to a report of any of the eight General Standing Committees, the Chair shall ascertain if the proposed amendment had previously been offered in any of the meetings of the Standing Committee, or its subcommittee. If the proposed amendment had previously been presented in committee meetings and voted down, the Chair shall declare the proposed amendment out of order.

On motion of Daniel L. Marsh, New England, duly seconded, the amendment was laid on the table.

M. A. Childers, West Texas, moved that the Rules be suspended in order that we might take up the Calendar. The motion, duly seconded, prevailed.

J. Edgar Skillington, Central Pennsylvania, spoke with reference to the danger of adopting reports taken from the Calendar under the suspension of the Rules and moved that we adjourn and go into committee work.

Paul M. Hillman, Nebraska, made the point of order that Dr. Skillington's motion was out of order, as he had made the motion after he had made his speech. The Chair ruled the point of order well taken.

E. M. Sweet, Jr., Pacific, moved that we do now adjourn and go into committee work. The motion, duly seconded, did not prevail.

Nathan Newby, Pacific, presented the following:

> *Resolved,* That the resolution requiring each committee to furnish with each report a statement as to whether or not the report, if adopted, will increase the overhead expense, be and the same is hereby rescinded.

The motion was seconded and Judge Newby spoke to the motion to rescind.

George C. Douglass, Troy, spoke against the motion to rescind.

J. W. Moore, Virginia, moved to lay Judge Newby's motion on the table. The motion, duly seconded, prevailed.

Orien W. Fifer, Indiana, moved that we reconsider the action taken on Monday, May 1, whereby "each committee" in making its proposals for the future Methodist Church state whether or not the proposals increase overhead, etc. The motion, duly seconded, prevailed.

Dr. Fifer then moved that the matter be referred to the Committee on Rules, and the motion, duly seconded, prevailed.

Calendar No. 10, Report No. 4 of the Committee on Conferences, printed on pages 160 and 161 of the *Daily Christian Advocate* and entitled "The General Conference," was presented by George W. Henson, Philadelphia, Chairman, who explained its provisions and moved its adoption. The motion was duly seconded.

Charles V. Adams, Central Pennsylvania, proposed the following addition to Section II, Paragraph 102: "except that in an Annual Conference, meeting within sixty days prior to the opening of a General Conference, said Annual Conference may elect its delegates at any session, special or otherwise, within fourteen months immediately preceding the General Conference." The motion was duly seconded and Dr. Adams spoke to the question.

Francis R. Bayley, Baltimore, moved that the Adams amendment be referred back to the Committee for their consideration. The motion, duly seconded, did not prevail.

The Adams amendment, on being put to a vote, did not prevail.

L. A. Harrell, South Georgia, moved to amend Paragraph 101, line 5, by substituting the word "majority" for "major." Chairman Henson accepted the proposed amendment.

George C. French, North Texas, moved to amend Section I, Paragraph 101, by inserting in line 7, after the word "members," the words "all of whom shall be elected by ballot and by majority vote." Chairman Henson accepted this proposed amendment.

Robert N. Brooks, North Carolina, proposed an

MAY 3
EIGHTH DAY

Morning

Committee on
Conferences,
Report No. 4
—"The Gen-
eral Confer-
ence"

Committee on
Education,
Report No. 1
—"General
Orzani-
zation"

amendment to Section IV, Paragraph 108, Article 2, by substituting "1940" for "beginning with such year." It was explained that this Article is a part of the Plan of Union, and cannot be changed, and that the "1940" would find its proper place in the *Discipline* of 1939.

The report, amended by agreement, was then adopted. For report, see Appendix, "General Standing Committees," page 422.

Calendar No. 11, Report No. 1 of the Committee on Education, printed on page 161 of the *Daily Christian Advocate* and entitled "General Organization," was presented by the Chairman, Paul Quillian, Texas, who explained its provisions and made the following editorial changes in the printed report because of stenographic errors: Paragraph 1005, last sentence, the words "A majority" at the beginning of the sentence should read "Three-fifths." In the first paragraph of Paragraph 1008 insert just before the last sentence, beginning "A majority of the members," the following sentence: "The Vice-President and Recording Secretary shall be included in the representation of their respective Advisory Committees."

Henry Gilligan, Maryland, a member of the Legal Committee on Permanent Funds, proposed an amendment to this particular report relative to the continuance of all existing corporations of the former Churches in connection with education in order that trust funds may be safeguarded. Chairman Quillian stated that the matter referred to would be taken up in the proper section on Enabling Acts. This was satisfactory to Brother Gilligan.

J. W. Moore, Virginia, asked "What is the cost?" Chairman Quillian stated that the new Board would have a membership of seventy as against eighty-six in the three Boards now in existence, and that there would be nine administrative officers in the new Board as against fourteen in the Boards now in operation, and that the overhead would not be increased.

Ralph E. Diffendorfer, Rock River, requested more information in regard to the Enabling Acts, and asked two questions: (1) Should not Paragraph 1001 denote the legal succession of the new

Board of Education? (2) Are all our interests properly safeguarded in Paragraph 1013? Chairman Quillian assured him that this would all be taken care of in the Enabling Acts, which are yet to come before the Conference for action.

George W. Henson, Philadelphia, moved as an amendment to Paragraph 1003 that the Executive Secretaries be elected by the General Conference, instead of by the Board of Education. The motion was seconded by Edward D. Kohlstedt, Dakota.

Arlo A. Brown, Newark, spoke against the amendment.

Joseph M. M. Gray, Detroit, spoke in favor of the Henson amendment.

The Chair called attention to the fact that we were within two minutes of the time for recess.

J. T. Ellison, Alabama, moved that the time be extended. There was no second to the motion.

Daniel L. Marsh, New England, moved that we do now go into recess. The motion, duly seconded, prevailed, and the Conference adjourned for recess.

At 10:40 A.M. Bishop Darlington called the Conference to order. The Conference stood and joined in singing "Blest Be the Tie That Binds."

The Seminary Singers of Boston University, under the direction of Dr. James R. Houghton, rendered the composition by Palestrina, "Adoramus Te, Christe," "Christ, We Do All Adore Thee."

Leslie J. Lyons, Missouri, was recognized to make some announcements on behalf of the Committee on Entertainment. Judge Lyons moved that when we adjourn it be to meet in official session at 7 P.M. to hear the address of Governor Alfred M. Landon. The motion, duly seconded, prevailed.

Joseph M. M. Gray, Detroit, Chairman of the Committee on Courtesies, Privileges, and Introductions, presented Dr. Robert Bond and the Hon. Isaac Foot, Fraternal Delegates from Great Britain, to the presiding Bishop, who in turn presented them to the Uniting Conference to bid the Conference farewell. The Conference rose and applauded the appearance of the distinguished visitors. Each addressed the Conference. Bish-

MAY 3
EIGHTH DAY
Morning
Report No. 1
on Education
Continued
op Darlington replied, appropriately, and the Conference stood and joined heartily in singing "All Hail the Power of Jesus' Name."

The pending question was resumed. ·

Nathan Newby, Pacific, spoke against the Henson amendment.

Harold P. Sloan, New Jersey, spoke in favor of the amendment.

Daniel L. Marsh, New England, spoke against the amendment.

Edmund J. Kulp, Missouri, spoke in favor of the amendment.

M. C. Redwine, Kentucky, spoke against the amendment.

Jesse L. Corley, Southern California, moved the pending question. The motion, duly seconded, prevailed and the pending question was ordered.

Chairman Quillian closed the debate for the Committee.

W. C. Perkins, Pittsburgh, raised the point of order that the recommendation of the Committee violates the provision of the Plan of Union which states that no new legislation shall be enacted. ·

Willard G. Cram, Kentucky, asked if it is·in order to raise a point of order under the previous question. The Chair ruled that it was.

Clem Baker, Little Rock, called attention to the fact that we were not electing an Executive Secretary for the Board of Education, but were dealing with the election of Executive Secretaries for the three Divisions of the Board of Education.

Fred D. Stone, Rock River, spoke against the point of order raised by W. C. Perkins.

Bishop Darlington ruled the point of order not well taken on the ground that it was the election of Executive Secretaries for the three Divisions of the Board of Education and not the election·of an Executive Secretary for the General Board·of Education that was involved.

The amendment of George ·W. Henson, being put to a vote, did not prevail.

Nathan Newby, Pacific, moved the previous question. The motion, being duly seconded, prevailed and the previous question was ordered. ·

The report of the Committee was adopted. For report, see Appendix, "General Standing Committees," page 592.

Paul M. Hillman, Nebraska, on a question of privilege for the entire Conference, requested the delegates to sign the cards that had been distributed, in order that a correct and complete list of the Delegates and Bishops might be obtained for printing in the *Daily Christian Advocate* of tomorrow.

MAY 3
EIGHTH DAY
Morning
Privilege

Frank B. Jones, Memphis, moved that, after announcements, we do now adjourn. The motion, duly seconded, prevailed.

Motion to Adjourn

The following letter was read to the Conference:

Letter from J. Emerson Ford

Dr. Lud H. Estes, Secretary Uniting Conference, Kansas City, Mo.

My Dear Doctor Estes: Permit me to express to you, and through you to the Uniting Conference, my deep gratitude for the gracious and friendly expression of sympathy which you have conveyed on behalf of the Conference.

While there are no words to describe my deep sense of loss in the passing of my father, there is genuine satisfaction in the memory of his consistent devotion to Christ and His Church and in the assurance that he has entered into a still more glorious fellowship in the Kingdom of God.

Likewise there is great joy in the knowledge that my comrades are remembering me in the presence of Him whose grace is sufficient for every need.

Sincerely, J. EMERSON FORD.

Various announcements were made and the Conference adjourned with the benediction pronounced by Dr. Robert Bond of England.

Announcements
Adjournment

WEDNESDAY EVENING, MAY 3, 1939

Pursuant to the adjournment order, the Conference convened at 7 P.M., with Bishop G. Bromley Oxnam presiding, at the request of Bishop Urban V. W. Darlington.

MAY 3
EIGHTH DAY
Evening
Opening

The Boston University Seminary Singers, under the direction of Dr. James R. Houghton, sang "The Lord Have Mercy," by Lvosky.

Bishop Oxnam introduced Dr. Ralph W. Sockman, Chairman, and Charles F. Boss, Executive Secretary, of the World Peace Commission of the Methodist Episcopal Church.

Bishop Oxnam introduced Hon. Alfred M. Landon, Delegate-at-Large of the Methodist Episcopal Church, from the Kansas Conference. Governor Landon addressed the Conference on the

Address by Governor Landon

MAY 3
EIGHTH DAY
Evening
Adjournment

world outlook for peace and its relationship to
the foreign policy of the United States, his subject being "Is a World Peace Conference Practical?" For address, see Appendix, "Addresses,"
page 894.

The Conference adjourned with the singing of
the National Anthem, "My Country, 'Tis of Thee."

THURSDAY MORNING, MAY 4, 1939

MAY 4
NINTH DAY
Morning
Opening

Bishop Ernest G. Richardson called the Conference to order for the worship service at 8:30
A.M., this being the ninth day of the Conference.
He announced that the worship service would be
in charge of Bishop J. Lloyd Decell and that
Bishop Francis J. McConnell would bring the devotional address of the morning. Bishop Mc-
Connell read Ephesians 3: 14-21, and brought a
timely message on "The Rich Man's Heaven and
the Poor Man's Hell."

The business session was called to order at
9 o'clock by Bishop Richardson.

Journal

The report of the Committee on Journal was
presented and adopted, as follows:

We have examined separately the Journal of the morning and evening sessions of Wednesday, May 3, 1939, and
find both correct.   JOSEPH D. PIPER, *Chairman;*
JOHN R. KENNEY, *Secretary.*

Committee on
Credentials,
Report No. 6

Earl R. Brown, Northeast Ohio, Chairman of
the Committee on Credentials, presented Report
No. 6, and moved its adoption without reading
and its publication in the *Daily Christian Advocate* of tomorrow. The motion, duly seconded,
prevailed. (See report, page 834.)

Committee on
Rules,
Report No. 4

J. Edgar Skillington, Central Pennsylvania,
Chairman of the Committee on Rules, presented
Report No. 4, printed on page 193 of the *Daily
Christian Advocate*. The Secretary read the report to the Conference. Dr. Skillington explained
its provisions and moved its adoption. The motion, duly seconded, prevailed. For report, see
Appendix, "Special Standing Committees," page
826.

Entertainment
Commission

Bishop H. Lester Smith, Secretary of the Council of Bishops, presented the following nominations for membership on the Commission on Entertainment of the first General Conference of

The Methodist Church: Northeastern Jurisdiction, Rev. J. Edgar Washabaugh, J. H. Baker; Southeastern Jurisdiction, Rev. T. D. Ellis, E. C. Watson; Central Jurisdiction, Rev. Stanley E. Grannum, John A. Patton; North Central Jurisdiction, Rev. Aubrey S. Moore, Troy W. Appleby; South Central Jurisdiction, Rev. C. M. Reves, Leslie J. Lyons; Western Jurisdiction, Rev. Roy O. Hill, Nathan Newby.

MAY 4
NINTH DAY
Morning
Entertainment
Commission

Motion of Elmer E. Collins, Montana State, duly seconded, prevailed, confirming the nominations.

J. H. Dickey, Louisville, moved that when we adjourn at noon today, the Bishops and Delegates retire to the north front of the Auditorium to have a Conference picture made. The motion, duly seconded, prevailed.

Conference
Picture

Fred D. Stone, Rock River, presented the following resolution and moved its adoption:

Conference
Expense

I move that the Committee on Conferences be requested to report to this Uniting Conference, as soon as possible, legislation to provide for the expenses of the first General Conference, and that they be requested to report to the Uniting Conference suggestions as to the manner in which the Jurisdictional Conferences should meet their expenses.

The motion, seconded by George W. Henson, Philadelphia, was adopted.

Francis R. Bayley, Baltimore, Chairman of the Committee on Judiciary, was recognized for a privileged matter. Dr. Bayley stated that several reports from the Committee on Judiciary were being published in the *Daily Christian Advocate,* and when so published should be considered as privileged matters. By common consent this was agreed to by the Uniting Conference.

Judiciary

Mark Kelley, Troy, under Rule 24, moved a reconsideration of Calendar No. 7, Report No. 1 of the Committee on Membership and Temporal Economy found on pages 128 and 129 of the *Daily Christian Advocate,* which was adopted on Tuesday, May 2, 1939. The motion, duly seconded, prevailed by a slight majority.

Reconsider Report No. 1,
Committee on Membership and Temporal Economy

Mark Kelley then offered the following amendment: Strike out all that follows "to" in line 2 of Paragraph 435 and substitute therefor the following: "not less than two nor more than

MAY 4
NINTH DAY
Morning
Reconsider Report No. 1, Committee on Membership and Temporal Economy

thirty-five stewards, except that in charges of more than five hundred members there may be added two stewards for each additional one hundred members." The motion was duly seconded.

J. N. R. Score, Central Texas, moved to amend the Kelley amendment by striking out all after the words "thirty-five stewards," and inserting, "provided that in churches of more than five hundred members, one additional steward shall be elected for each additional thirty members."

The Score motion, duly seconded, prevailed. The Kelley amendment, as thus amended, was adopted.

Chester A. Smith, New York, moved to amend Paragraph 434 by striking out in the fifth line thereof the words "of which the pastor shall be Chairman." The motion was duly seconded.

W. F. Bryan, Texas, Chairman of the Committee, explained the provisions of this paragraph and spoke against the Smith amendment.

Francis R. Bayley, Baltimore, moved that the amendment be laid on the table.

Lynn Harold Hough, New York East, raised the point of order that an amendment cannot be laid on the table. The Chair stated that the point of order was well taken.

The Smith amendment was not adopted.

The original report, as amended at this session, was then adopted. For report, see Appendix, "General Standing Committees," page 509.

Assistant
Secretaries

On motion of the Secretarial Staff, Dr. Curtis B. Haley and Dr. Thomas P. Potter were confirmed as Assistant Secretaries for work on the *Discipline*.

Calendar

The Calendar was then taken up. Secretary Estes called attention to a typographical error in the headings of Calendar Nos. 12 and 13. The number voting for both reports was 98 instead of 49 as stated in the printed reports in the *Daily Christian Advocate*.

Committee on
Ministry and
Judicial Administration,
Report No. 3
—"Ministry"

Calendar No. 12, Report No. 3 of the Committee on Ministry and Judicial Administration, printed on pages 161 and 162 of the *Daily Christian Advocate*, and entitled "Chapter IX, Ministry," was presented by Orien W. Fifer, Indiana, Chairman, who explained its provisions and moved its adoption. The motion, duly seconded, prevailed. For report, see Appendix, "General Standing Committees," page 460.

Calendar No. 13, Report No. 4 of the Committee on Ministry and Judicial Administration, printed on page 162 of the *Daily Christian Advocate*, entitled "District Superintendents," was presented by Orien W. Fifer, Indiana, Chairman, who explained its provisions and moved its adoption. The motion was duly seconded.

Leslie R. Burgum, North Dakota, called attention to the fact that in Paragraph 215, Article 2, the term "District Elder" appeared. Chairman Fifer replied that this was an error and the term "District Superintendent" should be inserted. This was done by common consent.

J. S. Ladd Thomas, Philadelphia, moved to amend Paragraph 215, Article 2, Item 15 as follows: In (b) change the word "unreached" to "unevangelized"; in (d) add after the word "hospitals" the words "homes and orphanages"; in (e) add after the word "colleges" the words "Wesley Foundations."

These changes were accepted by the Chairman and approved by the Conference by common consent.

Bertrand A. Dunbar, Dakota, inquired if any provision had been made as to the term of office of the District Superintendent. Chairman Fifer answered that this would be taken care of in a later report.

The report was then adopted. For report, see Appendix, "General Standing Committees," page 461.

Calendar No. 14, Report No. 2 of the Committee on Membership and Temporal Economy, entitled "Church Property," and printed on pages 162 and 163 of the *Daily Christian Advocate*, was presented by W. F. Bryan, Texas, Chairman. Dr. Bryan requested that Vincent P. Clarke, New England, Chairman of the Subcommittee on Church Property of the Committee on Membership and Temporal Economy, represent the Committee in the presentation of the report. Mr. Clarke presented the report, explaining its provisions, and moved its adoption. The motion was duly seconded.

Marshall R. Reed, Detroit, moved to amend

MAY 4 NINTH DAY *Morning* Committee on Ministry and Judicial Administration, Report No. 4 —"District Superintendents"

Committee on Membership and Temporal Economy, Report No. 2 —"Church Property"

MAY 4
NINTH DAY

Morning

Committee on
Membership
and
Temporal
Economy,
Report No. 2
—"Church
Property"

Paragraph 452 by striking out the words at the end of the paragraph reading "discharge all indebtedness against it" and substituting the following: "have secured and paid in cash two-thirds of the total cost of the project, and that the remaining one-third of the total cost may be secured by responsible subscriptions and satisfactory loans." The motion being duly seconded, Dr. Reed spoke to his amendment.

Harry C. Leonard, Southern, spoke against the amendment.

Harry G. Ryan, North Texas, moved to lay the Reed amendment on the table.

Daniel L. Marsh, New England, raised the point of order that an amendment cannot be laid on the table. The Chair sustained the point of order.

William H. Barradell, New York East, offered the following substitute for Paragraph 452: "Before any church building may be formally dedicated, it shall have secured in cash or its equivalent sixty-five per cent of the cost of land, building, furnishings, and fixtures, and the remainder shall have been covered by good subscriptions." Mr. Barradell spoke to the substitute, as it had been duly seconded.

G. M. Davenport, North Alabama, moved the previous question on all that was before the Conference. The motion, duly seconded, did not prevail.

J. H. Nicholson, Louisville, called for a division on the motion of G. M. Davenport. The Chair put the question again and the call for the previous question was voted down.

Arlo A. Brown, Newark, moved the pending question. The motion, duly seconded, prevailed, and the pending question was ordered.

Louis C. Wright, Northeast Ohio, inquired if this involved new legislation. The Bishop replied that the principle involved is in at least one of the *Disciplines* of the Uniting Churches.

Vincent P. Clarke, for the Committee, closed the debate under the pending question.

The vote was taken upon the Barradell substitute and it did not prevail.

The vote was then taken upon the Reed amendment and it did not prevail.

Concerning Paragraph 438 Francis R. Bayley, Baltimore, suggested that the word "church" be substituted for "charge" in the first line. Mr. Clarke replied that the Committee could not accept this. Dr. Bayley then asked that, after the word "chairman" in the next to the last line, there be inserted the words "except where the charter otherwise provides." With the consent of the Conference, Mr. Clarke accepted this suggestion. MAY 4
NINTH DAY
Morning
Committee on Membership and Temporal Economy, Report No. 2 —"Church Property"

Thomas D. Ellis, South Georgia, moved to amend Paragraph 449 by inserting after the words "District Superintendents," at the end of line 8, the words "and the preacher in charge." The motion was duly seconded, and Dr. Ellis spoke to the motion. This was accepted by the Chairman, there being no objection from the Conference.

Lewis O. Hartman, New England, moved the following amendment to this section of the report: "That the legislation of this whole section shall not apply in the territory of Central Conferences or Provisional Central Conferences." The motion was seconded and Dr. Hartman spoke to the question. This amendment was accepted by the Chairman, with the consent of the Conference.

Benjamin W. Meeks, Baltimore, moved that Paragraph 446, with a slight change of wording, be added to Paragraph 438, the wording to be as follows: "When a charge consists of two or more churches located in different places, the foregoing provisions shall apply to each church with the same force and effect as though it were a separate charge."

Dr. Meeks asked the Chairman if he would accept this amendment. The Chairman said "No." The motion of Dr. Meeks was duly seconded, and he spoke to the same.

J. Edgar Skillington, Central Pennsylvania, called attention to the words "the foregoing provisions" and their proposed place at the heading of this Chapter. Dr. Meeks then changed, with the consent of his second, the words to read "these provisions."

A. Wesley Pugh, North Indiana, moved to amend Paragraph 446 by adding these words:

MAY 4.
NINTH DAY

Morning

Committee on
Membership
and
Temporal
Economy,
Report No. 2
—Continued

Edward E. White, Northwest Texas, moved the pending question. The motion, duly seconded, prevailed, and the pending question was ordered. The amendment, being put to vote, did not prevail.

Alvis S. Bennett, Kentucky, moved to amend Paragraphs 451 and 454 by changing "ten per cent" to "twenty per cent" in each paragraph. The motion was duly seconded and Dr. Bennett spoke to the question. The motion did not prevail.

D. E. Hinkle, Tennessee, moved to amend Paragraph 442, line 5, by striking out the word "control," so that the wording would be "Trustees of the charge shall hold and manage," etc. This was accepted by the Chairman, there being no objection from the Conference.

Walter C. Buckner, Southern California, moved to amend Paragraph 442 by adding the following: "The Trustees shall not prevent or interfere with the pastor or other duly authorized ministers of The Methodist Church in the use of said property for religious services or other proper meetings recognized by the law and usage of The Methodist Church."

The motion, duly seconded, prevailed.

Earl G. Hamlett, Memphis, moved to amend Paragraph 451 by adding after the words "estimated cost," in line 31, the following: "except in church buildings costing less than $15,000 where only thirty per cent shall be required." The motion being duly seconded, Dr. Hamlett spoke to the question.

Edmund J. Hammond, Georgia, spoke against the motion.

M. A. Childers, West Texas, moved the previous question. The motion, duly seconded, prevailed and the previous question was ordered.

Chairman Clarke not desiring to speak, Bishop Richardson put the motion on the Hamlett amendment. The motion did not prevail.

The report was adopted as amended. For report, see Appendix, "General Standing Committees," page 512.

Resolution
Referred to
Committee
on Rules

Nolan B. Harmon, Jr., Baltimore, presented and moved that the following resolution be referred to the Committee on Rules: -

Resolved, That no amendment to the report of the Standing Committees shall be considered by this Conference unless and until such amendments are seconded by at least ten members of the Conference.

NOLAN B. HARMON, JR.,
H. H. SHERMAN,
ALF M. LANDON.

The motion being duly seconded, Dr. Harmon spoke to the matter in hand. The motion to refer, being put, prevailed.

Orien W. Fifer, Indiana, under a question of privilege, moved that the Committee on Publishing Interests prepare a suitable memoir and tribute for Dr. Dan B. Brummitt and Dr. Claudius B. Spencer, both of whom had worked ardently for the cause of Church Union, and that the memoirs be presented to this Conference for adoption and have a place in its Journal. The motion, duly seconded, prevailed.

Memoirs for Drs. Brummitt and Spencer

Frank P. Culver, Central Texas, moved that we suspend the Rules and take up the Calendar appearing in the *Daily Christian Advocate* of today. The motion, duly seconded, prevailed.

Rules Suspended

Clarence M. Dannelly, Alabama, moved that the Conference fix Tuesday, May 9, 1939, as the closing date of its deliberations. The motion being duly seconded, Mr. Dannelly spoke to the question.

Final Closing

Isaac E. Miller, Ohio, moved that the matter be referred to the Committee of Elected Chairmen, and that they be requested to report to the body as soon as possible. The motion to refer, duly seconded, prevailed.

George E. Farrar, Saint Johns River, moved to defer action on Calendar 15, Report No. 3 of the Committee on Superannuate Support, until tomorrow, and the motion was duly seconded.

Calendar

Thomas S. Brock, New Jersey, Chairman of the Committee, spoke against postponement.

John R. Edwards, Baltimore, moved, as an amendment, that we pass over all printed reports from the Committee on Publishing Interests and the Committee on Superannuate Support, and take up the other reports on the printed Calendar. Dr. Farrar accepted this amendment. The motion, being put, did not prevail.

Calendar 15, Report No. 3 of the Committee on

MAY 4
NINTH DAY

Morning

Committee on
Super-
annuate
Support,
Report No. 3
—"Ministers'
Reserve
Pension
Fund"

Committee on
Conferences,
Report No. 5

Superannuate Support, entitled "Ministers' Reserve Pension Fund" and printed on pages 186-188 of the *Daily Christian Advocate,* was presented by Thomas S. Brock, New Jersey, Chairman, who explained its provisions and moved its adoption. The motion, duly seconded, prevailed. For report, see Appendix, "General Standing Committees," page 648.

George W. Henson, Philadelphia, Chairman of the Committee on Conferences, moved that we do now take up Calendar 25, Report No. 5 of the Committee on Conferences, out of its order. The motion, being duly seconded, prevailed by more than the required two-thirds vote.

At the request of Dr. Henson, Frank W. Court, Upper Iowa, Chairman of the subcommittee which prepared this particular report, came to the platform to assist in presenting the report. Dr. Henson explained the provisions of the report and moved its adoption. The motion was duly seconded.

Robert G. McCutchan, Northwest Indiana, moved to amend Paragraph 178, Article 2, by making the Director of Music a member of the Quarterly Conference, at the discretion of the local church, provided the Director of Music was a member of The Methodist Church. The motion was seconded. Dr. Court explained the provisions of the paragraph. The motion, being put, did not prevail.

Henry Gilligan, Maryland, moved to amend Paragraph 181, Article 1, by omitting from lines 6 to 8 the words, "or to confirm the stewards who have been elected by the members of the charge (Paragraph 434)." The motion was duly seconded.

L. B. Smith, Maryland, raised the point of order that in Section X, Article II, page 8, Plan of Union, it says that the membership of the Church should have the right to elect their Church officers. The Bishop ruled that these officers elected by the congregation did not need to be confirmed, but that they might be.

Dr. Court accepted the amendment with the consent of the Conference.

Henry Gilligan, Maryland, moved to amend Paragraph 181, Article 6, by striking out the last

line, which reads "where the Quarterly·Confer- ᴹᴬʸ 4
ence so directs," and inserting "as· provided in ᴺᴵᴺᵀᴴ ᴰᴬʸ
Article 2 of this paragraph." The motion being *Morning*
duly seconded, Dr. Gilligan spoke to the question.· Committee on
Dr. Court spoke against its adoption. The mo- Report No. ᶠ
tion to amend, being put, did not prevail.

Charles MacCaughey, Pacific Northwest, moved
to·amend Paragraph 181, Article 6, by striking
out the word "annually" in the first·line. The
motion·being duly seconded,··Dr. MacCaughey·
spoke to it.

Dr. Court stated that the Committee could not
accept the proposed amendment.

Paul. M. Hillman, Nebraska, spoke against the
amendment.

Warren Roberts, South Georgia, moved the
previous question on all matters before the Con-·
ference. The motion, duly seconded, prevailed
and the previous question was ordered.

Chairman Brock not desiring to speak, the motion was put on the amendment of Charles·Mac-
Caughey, but it did not prevail. The report was
adopted. For report, see Appendix,·"General
Standing Committees," page 427.

Daniel L. Marsh, New·England, moved that Announce-
after the hearing of announcements we adjourn. ments
The motion, duly·seconded, prevailed. Various Adjournment
announcements were made and the Conference
adjourned with the benediction pronounced by
Bishop Jashwant R. Chitambar.

· FRIDAY MORNING, MAY 5, 1939

·Bishop Arthur J. Moore called the Conference ᴹᴬʸ 5
to order at 8:30 A.M., and announced that Bishop ᵀᴱᴺᵀᴴ ᴰᴬʸ
Robert E. Jones would conduct the worship serv- *Morning*
ice, and Bishop John C. Broomfield would·bring Opening
the devotional address of· the morning. Bishop
Broomfield brought a timely message on "Re-
leasing God."·

At 9 A.M. Bishop Arthur J. Moore called the·
business·session to order.

The Committee on·Journal· reported. The re- Journal
port·was adopted, as follows: ·

We have examined the Journal and found it correct.
JOSEPH D. PIPER, *Chairman;*·
JOHN R. KENNEY, *Secretary.*

MAY 5
TENTH DAY
Morning
Committee on
Publishing
Interests,
Report No. 3
—"Church
School
Publica-
tions"
Calendar No. 18, Report No. 3 of the Commit-
tee on Publishing Interests, printed on pages 189
and 190 of the *Daily Christian Advocate*, and en-
titled "Church School Publications," was pre-
sented by Dr. Garber, who requested Dr. Lang-
dale to be in charge of the report. Dr. Langdale
explained its provisions.

William F. Quillian, South Georgia, moved the
following addition to the report, the amendment
to be numbered Section 9: "The provisions of
Paragraph 1208 shall not apply to the promotional materials of the Division of Educational
Institutions or of the Division of the Local
Church." The motion being duly seconded, Dr.
Quillian explained its import. The Chairman,
with the consent of the Conference, accepted the
amendment.

Frank C. Propert, New Jersey, raised a question of the constitutionality of the method of the
election of the Editor of Church School Publications, and moved that the matter be referred to
the Committee on Judiciary for consideration and
report. The motion was duly seconded.

Bishop Arthur J. Moore called attention to the
parliamentary situation—namely, the adoption of
the report of the Committee on the motion, duly
seconded, already before the Conference—and requested Brother Propert to withhold his motion
for the time being. Brother Propert agreed to
this.

Daniel L. Marsh, New England, inquired how
the new Section 9 could be reconciled with Section
3 of the report. Dr. Langdale replied that the
new Section 9 had to do with "promotional" material alone and not "curriculum" material mentioned in Section 3. This explanation was satis-.
factory.

Dr. Marsh raised a further question as to how
the rest of the Committee on Curriculum was to
be constituted. J. Calloway Robertson, Virginia,
being recognized, stated that the matter would be
taken care of in a report of the Committee on
Education.

J. Calloway Robertson, Virginia, moved to
amend Paragraph 1208, Section 8, by inserting
the words "without vote" after the words "the
privilege of the floor," in lines 7 and 14. Dr.

Langdale, with the consent of the Conference, accepted this amendment.

Warren Roberts, South Georgia, moved the previous question. The motion, duly seconded, prevailed and the previous question was ordered. The report was adopted. For report, see Appendix, "General Standing Committees," page 635.

Frank C. Propert, New Jersey, moved that the question of the method of the election of the Editor of Church School Publications, found in Paragraph 1208, Section 1, of the report just adopted be referred to the Committee on Judiciary for consideration and report as to the constitutionality of the method. The motion, duly seconded, prevailed.

Calendar No. 19, Report No. 4 of the Committee on Publishing Interests, printed on page 190 of the *Daily Christian Advocate* and entitled "Church Press," was presented to the Conference by Paul N. Garber, who moved its adoption, and requested Nolan B. Harmon, Jr., Baltimore, Chairman of the subcommittee on the Church Press, to present the report. The motion was duly seconded. Dr. Harmon explained the provisions of the report.

The time of recess nearing, motion of Elmer E. Collins, Montana State, duly seconded, prevailed extending the time for Dr. Harmon to complete his remarks.

Daniel L. Marsh, New England, suggested that the word "next," found at the beginning of the fourth line in the fourth paragraph, be stricken out. This suggestion was accepted by the Chairman, with the consent of the Conference.

The report was then adopted. For report, see Appendix, "General Standing Committees," page 636.

The Conference recessed at 10:31 A.M.

At 10:41 Bishop Arthur J. Moore called the Conference to order.

The Conference stood and, under the leadership of Dr. James R. Houghton, joined in singing the first verse of "Thus far the Lord hath led us on."

The Council of Bishops, with Bishop Adna W. Leonard as Precentor, sang, to the delight of the Conference, the Bishops' song, "Beloved, we

Marginal notes:

MAY 5
TENTH DAY

Morning

Committee on Publishing Interests, Report No. 3 —"Church School Publications"

Referred

Committee on Publishing Interests, Report No. 4 —"Church Press"

Recess

Reconvene

Bishops' Song

⁵
ᴬʸ

ᵍ

ₐnt

are now the sons of God." The Conference rose and applauded.

Dr. James R. Houghton sang, by special request, "Open the Gates of the Temple."

George W. Henson, for the Committee of Elected Chairman, presented the following report:

1. There will be no change in the plan of morning worship.
2. Monday, May 8. Morning session at 8:30 o'clock; afternoon session at 2:15 o'clock; a Special Order of the Day at 4:30 P.M.; Evening session at 7:45 o'clock with an address by Dr. Albert W. Palmer, President of the Chicago Theological Seminary.
3. Tuesday, May 9. Three sessions on Monday. Order of the Day at 4:30 P.M. to have the scheduled program "The Negro in Methodism." Evening session to open with a twenty-minute address by Dr. Charles W. Welch, Moderator of the Presbyterian Church. At 5:30 P.M. celebration of the two hundredth anniversary of the building of the First Methodist Church of the world, in Exhibition Hall.
4. Wednesday, May 10. Three sessions as on Monday and Tuesday, closing with the Declaration of Union Service, Wednesday night, with suitable devotions.

Dr. Henson, for the Committee, presented the following and moved its adoption:

The Committee of Chairmen recommend that we adopt the program as announced and fix adjournment on Wednesday night after the Declaration of Union Service and closing devotions.

The motion was seconded.

At the request of Dr. Henson, Horace G. Smith, Rock River, William A. C. Hughes, Washington, and Frederick W. Mueller, Northeast Ohio, spoke to the report of the Committee.

The report of the Committee was adopted.

Dr. Henson, on behalf of the Committee of Elected Chairmen, expressed regret that in the readjusted program no suitable place could be found for the program the women of the Church had arranged, and that they had graciously withdrawn their program.

Thomas S. Brock, New Jersey, Chairman, requested common consent to take up Calendar No. 21 now instead of Calendar No. 20, both being reports from the Committee on Superannuate Support.

Calendar No. 21, Report No. 5 of the Committee

on Superannuate Support, printed on page 191 of the *Daily Christian Advocate* and entitled "Section III, Board of Conference Claimants; Organization and Duties," was presented by Dr. Brock, who explained its provisions and moved its adoption. The motion was duly seconded.

Fred B. Newell, New York East, moved to amend Paragraph 1314, Section 2, by striking out the words "effective ministers and laymen in equal number," found in lines 3 and 4. No objection being raised, the amendment was accepted by the Chairman.

George C. French, North Texas, raised the question about the method of the creation of the Board. The Chairman replied that the District Superintendents would nominate to the Annual Conference the members, and that the Annual Conference would act on the nominations.

George C. Douglass, Troy, asked a question regarding Section 5: "Can the local Conference Stewards borrow money on a vote of the united session?" The Chairman replied: "The Board itself cannot borrow money for the payment of the annuities. If an Annual Conference takes action borrowing the money itself, it assumes the responsibility."

Stanley O. MacMullen, New England, moved to amend the report by inserting the words "effective ministers and laymen in equal numbers," stricken out a little while ago. The motion was duly seconded.

Arthur M. Wells, Illinois, moved to lay this amendment on the table. The Chair ruled the motion out of order.

J. Edgar Skillington, Central Pennsylvania, moved the previous question. The motion, duly seconded, prevailed and the previous question was ordered.

The amendment of S. O. MacMullen was adopted. The report was adopted as amended. For report, see Appendix, General Standing Committees," page 660.

Calendar No. 20, Report No. 4 of the Committee on Superannuate Support, printed on pages 190 and 191 of the *Daily Christian Advocate* and entitled "Section V, Regulations for the Territory of the Missouri Corporation, Rules and Regula-

MAY 5
TENTH DAY

Morning

Committee on Superannuate Support, Report No. 5 —"Organization and Duties"

Committee on Superannuate Support, Report No. 4 —"Missouri Corporation"

MAY 5
TENTH DAY

Morning

Committee on
Superannu-
ate Support,
Report No. 4
—"Missouri
Corpora-
tion"
tions," was presented by Thomas S. Brock, Chairman, who explained its provisions and moved its adoption. The motion was duly seconded. Dr. Brock requested Charles W. Tadlock, St. Louis, to answer any questions raised.

George E. Farrar, Saint Johns River, moved to amend Paragraph 1340 by adding Section 2, as follows:—

> The Missouri Corporation is authorized and directed to make a comprehensive study of the Clearing House System of the distribution of divided annuities responsibilities and shall report its findings to the General Conference of 1940.

The motion was duly seconded. The amendment was accepted by the Chairman, no objection being raised.

The report was adopted. For report, see Appendix, "General Standing Committees;," page 657.

Committee on
Superannu-
ate Support,
Report No. 6
—"Divided
Annuity Re-
sponsibility"
Calendar No. 22, Report No. 6 of the Committee on Superannuate Support, printed on page 191 of the *Daily Christian Advocate* and entitled "Divided Annuity Responsibility," was presented by Thomas S. Brock, Chairman, who explained its provisions and moved its adoption. The motion was duly seconded.

Benjamin W. Meeks, Baltimore, asked for a clarification of Paragraph 1330, Section 1, after the word "provided," the question being about the support of ministers who came from the Missouri Corporation into the territory of the Illinois Corporation. Chairman Brock replied as follows:

> The Missouri Corporation, at the present time, is paying $2.13 per service year to all the annuitants for which that Board is responsible. That money was raised for the benefit of these members of the Methodist Episcopal Church, South. The responsibility of the Annual Conferences under the jurisdiction of the Missouri Board will be for the moneys that come from the churches and from the Chartered Fund and the dividends or produce of the Book Concern, and such other moneys that may come into these particular Annual Conferences. Then, all those members who were originally members of the Methodist Episcopal Church, South, for which this $6,000,000 fund was raised, will, in addition, receive the $2.13 for service years as long as they continue to be annuitants in The Methodist Church.

Thomas A. Stafford, Northern Minnesota, made further explanations concerning this paragraph and section. The report was adopted. For report, see Appendix, "General Standing Committees," page 661.

MAY 5
TENTH DAY
Morning

Calendar No. 23, Report No. 2 of the Committee on Missions, printed on page 191 of the *Daily Christian Advocate*, concerning the American Bible Society, was presented by John R. Mott, New York, Chairman, who explained its provisions and moved its adoption. The motion, duly seconded, prevailed. For report, see Appendix, "General Standing Committees," page 549.

Committee on Missions, Report No. 2

Costen J. Harrell, Tennessee, raised a point of order that Rule 27-A, adopted yesterday, was not being observed in the reports of the last two committees. The Chair inquired of Dr. Brock if the reports adopted from the Committee on Superannuate Support would increase the overhead. Dr. Brock replied that there would be no increase. Dr. Jarrell, speaking for the Committee on Publishing Interests, said the legislation adopted would diminish the overhead.

Estimated Cost

Calendar No. 24, Report No. 3 of the Committee on Membership and Temporal Economy, printed on pages 191 and 192 of the *Daily Christian Advocate* and entitled "District Parsonages," was presented by W. F. Bryan, Texas, Chairman, who stated that there would be no expense incurred whatsoever. Dr. Bryan requested Vincent P. Clarke, New England, to be in charge of the report. Brother Clarke explained its provisions, and stated that the word "and" should be inserted after the words "state of Maryland" in the fourteenth line of Paragraph 461. Brother Clarke moved the adoption of the report, and the motion was duly seconded.

Committee on Membership and Temporal Economy, Report No. 3 —"District Parsonages"

Thomas S. Brock moved to amend Paragraph 457 by inserting the words "the District Stewards or by" after the words "elected by" in the thirteenth line. No objection being raised, Chairman Clarke accepted the amendment.

Arthur M. Wells, Illinois, moved to amend Section VI, Paragraph 459, by adding the words "No such residence shall be sold until authorized by two-thirds of the Annual Conferences compris-

MAY 5
TENTH DAY

Morning

Committee on Membership and Temporal Economy,

Report No. 3 —"District Parsonages"

ing the Episcopal Area." The motion, duly seconded, did not prevail.

A. Wesley Pugh, North Indiana, moved to amend the report by adding a new paragraph to be headed "Parsonage Trustees," which paragraph shall immediately precede Section IV of the report under consideration, and shall read as follows:

Whenever there are two or more churches on a pastoral charge, a separate Board of Trustees, consisting of not less than three nor more than nine persons, shall be elected by the churches of such charge, to be the custodians of the parsonage property on such charge. Such Trustees shall have the same qualifications as required for Trustees of church property.

George C. French, North Texas, moved to amend the amendment by changing the number "nine" to "five." This was accepted by A. Wesley Pugh.

W. F. Bryan, Texas, suggested that the trustees be elected by the "Quarterly Conference" instead of by the "churches." Dr. Pugh accepted this suggestion.

Vincent P. Clarke spoke against the Pugh amendment.

Alfred F. Hughes, West Wisconsin, spoke in favor of the Pugh amendment.

Arthur A. Callaghan, Maine, spoke to the amendment.

G. M. Davenport, North Alabama, moved the previous question. The motion, duly seconded, prevailed and the previous question was ordered.

Guy F. Jones, Texas, raised the point of order that the matter had been cared for in Paragraph 441, which required the Charge Board of Trustees to make a written report to the last Quarterly Conference concerning all property in their hands. The Chair ruled the point not well taken on the ground that the section referred to seems to deal with local church property and not with a parsonage in which several churches have ownership.

The amendment of A. Wesley Pugh was adopted. The report was then adopted as amended. For report, see Appendix, "General Standing Committees," page 517.

Bishop Edwin H. Hughes, under a matter of

high privilege, called the attention of the Conference to the presence, in the balcony, of Dr. George H. Clarke of the New England Conference. Dr. Clarke is 88 years of age and the father of Vincent P. Clarke, a member of the Uniting Conference. Bishop Hughes requested Dr. Clarke to stand. He arose and the Conference applauded.

Elridge M. Cooper, West Texas, moved a reconsideration of Calendar No. 7, Report No. 1 of the Committee on Membership and Temporal Economy, that he might offer an amendment to Paragraph 430 which would include "class leaders" in the membership of the Quarterly Conference.

Oscar T. Olson, Northeast Ohio, raised the point of order that this was done yesterday, when, on his motion, the words "the leaders," were inserted after the words "the stewards." The Chair ruled the point well taken.

George W. Henson, Philadelphia, Chairman of the Committee of Elected Chairmen, presented the following Readjusted Program, and it was adopted by common consent, as follows:

READJUSTED PROGRAM

Monday, May 8. Morning session of the Uniting Conference at 8:30 A.M., with no change in plan of morning worship; 2:15 P.M., Afternoon session; 7:45 P.M., Evening session, opening with an address by Dr. Albert W. Palmer, President of the Chicago Theological Seminary.

Tuesday, May 9. Three sessions as on Monday. An Order of the Day at 4:30 P.M., to have the scheduled program on "The Negro in Methodism." The evening session will open with a twenty-minute address by Dr. Charles W. Welch, Moderator of the Presbyterian Church. At 5:30 P.M. the program arranged for celebrating the two hundredth anniversary of the building of the first Methodist Church of the world, the New Room in Bristol, England. This will be held in Exhibition Hall.

Wednesday, May 10. Three sessions as on Monday and Tuesday. At 4:30 P.M. a special Order of the Day for our institutions of higher learning with brief addresses by Dean Lynn Harold Hough and Dr. Umphrey Lee. As the grand finale of the evening session, the Declaration of Union followed by closing devotions and final adjournment.

The following letter, received from Bishop Collins Denny, was read by the Secretary:

Marginal notes:

MAY 5
TENTH DAY
Morning
George H. Clarke

Reconsider

Readjusted Program

Letter from Bishop Denny

MAY 5
TENTH DAY
·*Morning*
Letter from
Bishop
Denny

To the Uniting Conference of The Methodist Church.

Dear Brethren: Very heartily I accept and reciprocate your assurance of your affectionate greetings. I appreciate greatly the fact that you should have me in mind at this time so full of great business for all of you; and I pray that the Father of us all may ever have you in His gracious care and grant you success in all your undertakings.

Fraternally,   COLLINS DENNY,
Bishop of the Methodist Episcopal Church, South.

Letter from
Bishop
Ainsworth

The following letter from Bishop W. N. Ainsworth was read by the Secretary:

To the Methodist Uniting Conference, Kansas City, Mo.

Dear Fathers and Brethren: It is a matter of keen regret that the condition of my health makes it imprudent for me to attend the sessions of the Uniting Conference. The fellowship, which I enjoyed through many sessions of the Joint Commission, heightened the expectation of this perfect day, when the ardent hope of years would be fulfilled in sight.

Though absent in the body, I will be with you in spirit every hour of your deliberations. And, as our expectant eyes look up, may the heart of United Methodism burn again with the warmth that comes alone from the Living Spirit and feel a fresh outbreak of the redeeming passion of our founder and forefathers, proclaiming in all our world parish the great and acceptable year of the Lord and the salvation of our God!

Please record my name on some inconspicuous page as a humble member of the United Church.

Affectionately your Brother in Christ,
WILLIAM N. AINSWORTH.

Letter from
Bishop
Du Bose

The following letter from Bishop H. M. Du Bose was read by the Secretary.

To the Uniting Conference of The Methodist Church,

Dear Brethren: The fact that I find my physical strength so depleted that I must forego attendance upon the Uniting Conference is a source of almost agonizing disappointment to me.

But God is good. I shall pray for His favor upon you and all the brethren.

Fraternally and faithfully,

H. M. DU BOSE.

Motion of Elmer E. Collins, Montana State, duly seconded, prevailed that we adjourn after necessary announcements were made.

Announcements

Various announcements were made and the Conference adjourned with the benediction pronounced by Bishop F. H. Otto Melle.

Adjournment

SATURDAY MORNING, MAY 6, 1939

Bishop Ernest L. Waldorf called the Conference to order at 8:30 A.M., and announced that Bishop Wallace E. Brown would be in charge of the morning worship service and will introduce the speaker who is to bring the devotional message. Bishop Brown conducted the service and announced that Bishop Charles C. Selecman would deliver the devotional message. Bishop Selecman spoke on "The Evangelistic Mission of Methodism," using as the basis of his remarks Luke 19: 10, "For the Son of man is come to seek and to save that which was lost," and John 20: 21, "As my Father hath sent me, even so send I you."

At 9 A.M. Bishop Waldorf called the Conference to order for the business session.

The report of the Committee on Journal was adopted, as follows:

Morning

Opening

Journal

> We have examined the Journal and find it correct.
> JOSEPH D. PIPER, *Chairman;*
> JOHN R. KENNEY, *Secretary.*

On motion of Earl R. Brown, Northeast Ohio, Chairman, duly seconded, the following recommendation was adopted:

Credentials

> The Committee on Credentials recommends that reserve or alternate delegates seated after May 6, 1939, shall be seated at no expense to the Conference.
> EARL R. BROWN, *Chairman;*
> CHARLES A. ROBBINS, *Secretary.*

Dr. Brown presented Report No. 8 of the Committee on Credentials and moved that it be adopted without reading and printed in the *Daily Christian Advocate* of Monday, May 8. The motion, duly seconded, prevailed. For report, see Appendix, "Special Standing Committees," page 836.

Committee on Credentials, Report No. 8

Bishop H. Lester Smith, Secretary of the Council of Bishops, requested the Chairmen of Conference delegations with which Delegates-at-large are seated to include in their reports the attendance or nonattendance of all such delegates.

Bishop H. Lester Smith, Secretary of the Council of Bishops, presented the following nominations for membership on the Judicial Council, in

Nominations—Judicial Council

MAY 6
ELEVENTH DAY
ı *Morning*
Nominations—
Judicial
Council

accordance with the action of the Uniting Conference on Tuesday, May 2, 1939, in adopting
Calendar No. 9, Report No. 2 of the Committee
on Ministry and Judicial Administration:

METHODIST PROTESTANT CHURCH

Ministers: A. J. Allen, Pittsburgh Conference; George
R. Brown, North Carolina Conference; G. I. Humphreys,
Maryland Conference; S. W. Rosenberger, Ohio Confer-
ence.

METHODIST EPISCOPAL CHURCH, SOUTH

Ministers: J. B. Craven, Western North Carolina Con-
ference; W. L. Duren, Louisiana Conference; J. Stewart
French, Holston Conference; W. G. Henry, North Georgia
Conference; J. W. Johnson, North Georgia Conference;
A. C. Millar, Little Rock Conference; J. Richard Spann,
Louisiana Conference; A. J. Weeks, North Texas Con-
ference.
Laymen: John H. Carlock, Oklahoma Conference; M. A.
Childers, West Texas Conference; R. L. Flowers, North
Carolina Conference; G. H. Lamar, Baltimore Conference;
Martin E. Lawson, Southwest Missouri Conference; W. F.
McMurry, Memphis Conference; C. E. Mead, New Mexico
Conference; O. A. Park, South Georgia Conference.

METHODIST EPISCOPAL CHURCH

Ministers: Francis R. Bayley, Baltimore Conference;
Walter C. Buckner, Southern California Conference; Les-
lie R. Burgum, North Dakota Conference; Sanford W.
Corcoran, Pittsburgh Conference; Mark Kelley, Troy Con-
ference; Charles B. Ketcham, Northeast Ohio Conference;
Ernest F. Lyons, Los Angeles, Calif.; Carl K. Mahoney,
Pacific Northwest Conference.
Laymen: Jacob Cantlin, Rock River Conference; Vin-
cent P. Clarke, New England Conference; James I. Dol-
liver, Northwest Iowa Conference; Fred C. Huebner, Iowa-
Des Moines Conference; Benjamin A. Matthews, New
York Conference; Sidney R. Redmond, Central West
Conference; William H. Spurgeon, Colorado Conference;
Henry R. Van Deusen, Wyoming Conference.

Bishop H. Lester Smith announced that the
Council of Bishops had appointed a committee of
their number to arrange the ballot for the Judicial
Council according to the legislation and had
named Bishops G. Bromley Oxnam, Clare Purcell, and James H. Straughn.

George C. French, North Texas, moved that the
Order of the Day for 10 A.M. on Monday, May 8,
be the election of the Members of the Judicial
Council. The motion, duly seconded, prevailed.

Lynn Harold Hough, New York East, on a question of privilege for the Conference, called the

attention of the body to the fact that previous action had set apart May 8, for the consideration of the report of the Committee on Membership and Temporal Economy concerning "A Social Creed for United Methodism," but that in as much as the report had not been printed, by common consent we request the Committee to have it printed in the *Daily Advocate* of Monday, May 8, for consideration on May 9. This action was taken by common consent.

G. M. Davenport, North Alabama, moved that the Conference proceed to receive nominations from the floor for membership on the Judicial Council. The motion was duly seconded. Leslie J. Lyons, Missouri, moved to amend by making the matter the Order of the Day immediately following recess this morning. Dr. Davenport accepted the amendment, and the motion prevailed.

Francis R. Bayley, Baltimore, Chairman, requested that Report No. 3 of the Committee on Judiciary, printed on page 258 of the *Daily Christian Advocate*, be taken up. By common consent this was done and the Secretary read the report. Dr. Bayley moved its adoption. The motion being seconded, Dr. Bayley spoke to the report, stating that the word "areas" in line 5 of the last paragraph should read "residences."

Motion of J. Edgar Skillington, Central Pennsylvania, duly seconded, prevailed extending the time of Dr. Bayley one minute in order to complete his remarks.

M. A. Childers, West Texas, spoke to the report, stating that if "areas" and "residences" mean the same thing he was in favor of joining the Chairman of the Committee in making the change, but if they were different he suggested voting for the report as printed. Dr. Bayley made a brief statement and M. A. Childers withdrew his suggestion.

L. P. Wasson, North Mississippi, spoke to the report suggesting a different method for the assignment of the Bishops.

Orien W. Fifer, Indiana, spoke in favor of the report, with the word "residences" inserted.

Bishop Waldorf stated that he understood the word "residences" was accepted, and therefore is in the report. No objection was raised.

MAY 6
ELEVENTH DAY

Morning

Social Creed

Judicial Council

Committee on Judiciary, Report No. 3

MAY 6
ELEVENTH DAY
Morning
Committee on Judiciary, Report No. 3

J. W. Mills, Texas, moved the previous question. The motion, duly seconded, prevailed and the previous question was ordered.

The report, with the word "residences" inserted for the word "areas," was adopted. For report, see Appendix, "Special Standing Committees," page 819.

Reconsider

Frank W. Court, Upper Iowa, moved a reconsideration of Calendar No. 14, Report No. 2 of the Committee on Membership and Temporal Economy, adopted May 4, in order to make the following amendment to Paragraph 439 by adding the words "on nomination of the Nominating Committee, of which the pastor shall be Chairman," in the sixth line. The motion, duly seconded, did not prevail.

Time Limit

George W. Henson, Philadelphia, speaking for the Committee of Elected Chairmen, moved that, beginning at this time, speeches be limited for delegates to three minutes and for the Chairmen of Committees to five minutes. The motion was duly seconded.

J. Edgar Skillington, Central Pennsylvania, moved that the Rules be suspended that the matter might be considered. The motion, duly seconded, prevailed. The Rules were suspended and the motion of George W. Henson prevailed.

South Central Jurisdiction

J. N. R. Score, Central Texas, as a matter of privilege, presented the report of the delegates of the South Central Jurisdiction relative to Annual Conference boundaries. By common consent the report was order to record. For report, see Appendix, "Jurisdictions," page 863.

Support of Bishops

L. O. Hartman, New England, presented the following resolution and moved its reference to the Committee on Enabling Acts and Legal Forms:

Resolved, That, pending appropriate action by the General Conference, the Book Committee of the former Methodist Episcopal Church and the Publishing Agents of the former Methodist Episcopal Church, South, shall be given joint responsibility in securing funds for Episcopal support and for fixing and paying the salaries and allowances of the effective Bishops and the allowances for the retired Bishops and the widows and minor children of deceased Bishops.

The motion was duly seconded. W. F. Bryan, Texas, Chairman of the Committee on Membership and Temporal Economy, stated that his Committee had this matter under consideration and would bring in a report later.

Dr. Hartman spoke in favor of his motion to refer. The motion to refer was adopted.

A. Wesley Pugh, North Indiana, raised a question as to whether or not this resolution had reference to all the Bishops, including those who have been elected Missionary Bishops? The Chair replied that the report refers to "Episcopal support" and includes all Bishops.

Arba Martin, Ohio, moved to reconsider Calendar No. 24, Report No. 3 of the Committee on Membership and Temporal Economy, adopted May 5, for the purpose of considering the number of Trustees in an Annual Conference and moving an amendment thereto. The motion, duly seconded, did not prevail.

Thomas D. Ellis, South Georgia, presented the following resolutions and moved their reference to the Committee on Enabling Acts and Legal Forms:

WHEREAS, it is necessary at all times to safeguard the titles to and interest in the property of The Methodist Church, local and general, and to protect the interest of the various organizations of said Church in trust and other forms of holding property; therefore be it

Resolved, That we authorize the Bishops of the Jurisdictional Conference within which a suit or suits may be brought, if in their judgment it is proper to do so, to employ competent attorneys to defend and protect the interests of The Methodist Church, local and general, in such property and to cause such suit or suits to be brought as may in their judgment be necessary to protect the interests of The Methodist Church.

If an emergency arises and it appears to one of the Bishops that action should be taken quickly, he may do so until the opinion of the Bishops of the Jurisdictional Conference may be obtained. In such case or cases, the expense of such litigation and such employment of attorneys, properly payable by the Church, shall be paid out of such general fund as may be provided to pay the expenses of the General Conference, or from such fund or funds as may be designated by the General Conference for the purpose.

The motion, duly seconded, prevailed.

Edgar R. Heckman, Central Pennsylvania, one of the Associate Secretaries, under a question of privilege, in behalf of the Secretarial Staff, presented the following:

When Calendar No. 7, Report No. 1 of the Committee on Membership and Temporal Economy, was being considered on May 2, it was stated that "class or unit leaders" were not to be included in the membership of the Official Board, according to Paragraph 430, so that the Board might not be too large.

Later, Robert G. McCutchan, Northwest Indiana, attempted to secure adoption of a resolution to include the Director of Music as a member of the Official Board.

Oscar T. Olson, Northeast Ohio, offered an amendment to amend Paragraph 430 as follows: "and where desired, the Director of Music."

None of the Secretarial Staff understood the motion to include the words "the leaders" to be inserted after the word "Stewards" in the fifth line of Paragraph 430 as appears in the *Daily Christian Advocate.*

The Chairman of the Committee in charge of this Report accepted the suggestion relative to "director of music," but had no knowledge of having accepted the words "the leaders."

The Committee on the Journal also, from their notes, did not have this item.

It is therefore asked by common consent that this be inserted by the Committee on the Journal.

Daniel L. Marsh, New England, moved that we reconsider Calendar No. 7, Report No. 1 of the Committee on Membership and Temporal Economy, that these words might be included.

W. F. Bryan, Texas, Chairman of the Committee on Membership and Temporal Economy, approved the statement just made so far as the Committee was concerned.

The motion, duly seconded, prevailed.

Daniel L. Marsh, New England, then moved that the words be inserted.

Oscar T. Olson, Northeast Ohio, explained that he had submitted his amendment in writing, and that the record of the *Daily Christian Advocate* was correct.

Arthur A. Callaghan, Maine, inquired whether the term "the leaders" was meant to include "Class Leaders or Unit Leaders." Dr. Olson stated that his amendment included both.

The motion of Dr. Marsh, duly seconded, prevailed. The report was then adopted, as amended. For report, see Appendix, "General Standing Committees," page 509.

Rules   Frank C. Propert, New Jersey, presented the following resolution and moved its adoption:

Resolved, That the Committee on Rules of this Conference be continued and instructed to prepare and to submit to the General Conference rules for the conduct of the business of that Conference.

The motion, duly seconded, prevailed,

Frank C. Propert, New Jersey, presented the following and moved its reference to the Committee on Enabling Acts and Legal Forms:

Resolved, That the Committee on Enabling Acts and Legal Forms be requested to prepare and submit to this Conference a report expressly fixing the effective date of the new *Discipline* of The Methodist Church, except as to those provisions for which effective dates may be expressly stated elsewhere in that *Discipline.*

The motion, duly seconded, prevailed.

Ernest W. Peterson, Oregon, presented the following and moved its reference to the Committee on Missions:

A few months ago American Methodism lost from her midst Dr. Clarence True Wilson, militant foe of alcohol and all forms of unrighteousness.

I move that the General Standing Committee on Missions, to which has been referred all matters pertaining to the temperance work of the Church, be requested to prepare a suitable memoir and tribute concerning the late Dr. Clarence True Wilson, for over a quarter of a century the militant leader of the temperance forces of the Methodist Episcopal Church, for adoption by this Uniting Conference and publication in the Journal.

The motion duly seconded prevailed.

J. Edgar Skillington, Central Pennsylvania, presented an amendment to Standing Rule 31 and also a resolution as to a uniform term to be used in addressing the Chair. Motion, duly seconded, prevailed that these be referred, without reading, to the Committee on Rules for their consideration and report.

W. F. Dunkle, Florida, presented the following and moved its reference to the Committee on Enabling Acts and Legal Forms:

WHEREAS the Plan of Union under the caption of Procedure in Article VI says, "All Annual Conferences of the three Churches shall retain their existing status until by the action of the Uniting Conference it shall be determined otherwise," and whereas the boundaries of some Annual Conferences have been changed by the creating of Jurisdictions and others may be changed here by the delegates from the several Jurisdictions as provided in Article VIII of the Plan of Union; and whereas these changes may produce some confusion as to the status of the Conferences thus affected; therefore be it

Resolved and Enacted by the Uniting Conference:
1. That Annual Conferences of The Methodist Church from and after the adjournment of the Uniting Conference shall be those named in the *Discipline* with such powers and duties and bounds as described in the *Discipline;*
2. That any Annual Conference which existed at the time of the meeting of the Uniting Conference may have one or more sessions to finish its business and arrange for the corporate and institutional areas.

The motion, duly seconded, prevailed.

Committee on
Publishing
Interests,
Report No. 5
—"Publish-
ing Agents"

Calendar No. 26, Report No. 5 of the Committee on Publishing Interests, printed on page 221 of the *Daily Christian Advocate* and entitled "Publishing Agents," was presented by Paul N. Garber, Western North Carolina, Chairman, who stated that there would be no increase in overhead in the adoption of the report. Dr. Garber requested Charles C. Jarrell, North Georgia, Chairman of the Subcommittee on Administration of the General Committee, to explain the report. Dr. Jarrell explained the report and moved its adoption. The motion, duly seconded, prevailed. For report, see Appendix, "General Standing Committees," page 637.

Committee on
Education,
Report No. 2
—"Sugges-
tions in
Episcopal
Address"

Calendar No. 27, Report No. 2 of the Committee on Education, printed on page 221 of the *Daily Christian Advocate* and entitled "Suggestions in Episcopal Address," was presented by Paul Quillian, Texas, Chairman, who explained its provisions and moved its adoption. The motion, duly seconded, prevailed. For report, see Appendix, "General Standing Committees," page 595.

Committee on
Membership
and Tem-
poral Econ-
omy,
Report No. 4
—"Board of
Lay Activi-
ties"

Calendar No. 28, Report No. 4 of the Committee on Membership and Temporal Economy, printed on pages 221 and 222 of the *Daily Christian Advocate,* and entitled "Board of Lay Activities," was presented by W. F. Bryan, Texas, Chairman, who stated that the overhead would be increased because provision is made in the report for Jurisdictional Conferences to have Secretaries of Lay Activities. Dr. Bryan requested Edgar T. Welch, Erie, to present the report. Brother Welch explained the report and moved its adoption.

The Conference recessed at 10:30 A.M.

Bishop Waldorf called the Conference to order at 10:40 A.M. The Conference joined in singing the Doxology. Dr. Houghton announced and the Conference joined in singing a new hymn on

Unification, "Clear the Way for the Eternal," composed by Dr. William L. Stidger. The musical arrangement was by Dr. Houghton.

MAY 6
ELEVENTH DAY
Morning

Leonard B. Smith, Maryland, was recognized on a matter of courtesy and stated that the flowers in front of the Secretary's desk had been placed there by a visiting member of the Maryland Conference, Methodist Protestant Church, in memory of Thomas Hamilton Lewis, a prominent member of the Methodist Protestant Church, and a great leader in the cause of Unification.

Thomas
Hamilton
Lewis

Harry E. Woolever, Central New York, as a matter of courtesy, stated that the Fraternal Delegates from the Methodist Church of Great Britain had reached Washington, and read a telegram from the District Superintendent, stating:

Courtesy to
British
Delegates

The President graciously received Dr. and Mrs. Bond, Mr. Foot, and myself today and requested me to express to Bishop Hughes his deep regret over inability to go to Kansas City. We entertained in their honor and took them to Mount Vernon.

Bishop Waldorf inquired of the Conference whether it wished to take up the Order of the Day—namely, the nominations for membership on the Judicial Council—or to continue consideration of the pending report.

Committee on
Membership
and Tem-
poral Econ-
omy,
Report No. 4
(Continued)

Motion of Nathan Newby, Pacific, duly seconded, prevailed that we complete consideration of the pending report.

Fred D. Stone, Rock River, moved to amend Paragraph 604 by substituting the word "Board" for the word "General" at the end of the first line. The motion was duly seconded.

Herbert J. Burgstahler, Upper Iowa, spoke in favor of the amendment.

Alfred C. Crawford, Rock River, raised the point of order that the General Conference of the former Methodist Episcopal Church, South, elected the Executive Secretary of the General Board of Lay Activities.

Francis R. Bayley, Baltimore, Chairman of the Committee on Judiciary, reminded the Conference that a similar question had been referred to the Committee on Judiciary, and that they were going forward in their consideration of the matter as rapidly as possible. Dr. Bayley stated that he

MAY 6
ELEVENTH DAY
Morning
Committee on
Membership
and Tem-
poral Econ-
omy,
Report No. 4
thought the matter of the point of order could be held in abeyance until the Committee on Judiciary had reported on the matter. This statement was accepted by the Conference, by common consent, and the amendment of Fred D. Stone was adopted.

Thomas D. Ellis, South Georgia, moved to amend Paragraph 608, line 1, by substituting the word "may" for the word "shall," and that the same change be made in the report wherever the word "shall" appears with reference to the Jurisdictional Conference. The motion was duly seconded, but was accepted by Chairman Welch.

William K. Anderson moved to amend Paragraph 625 by substituting the words "Chairman of Lay Activities" for the words "Charge Lay Leader" found in the second line. The motion was duly seconded and Dr. Anderson spoke to the amendment.

Arba Martin, Ohio, asked if the term "Chairman of Lay Activities" refers to men only. Bishop Waldorf replied that in his judgment it did not, as a woman is a layman.

Lynn Harold Hough, New York East, raised a point of order relative to the amendment of T. D. Ellis, asking if it referred to all reports or to this particular report. The Chair stated that it referred to this report alone.

The amendment of W. K. Anderson was not adopted.

D. Stewart Patterson, Baltimore, moved to amend Paragraph 615 as follows: After the word "the," end of line 2, insert the words "lay members of the"; after the word "Conference" in line 3 place a period; strike out the remainder of the paragraph and insert in place thereof the following: "Nominations shall be made by the Conference Board of Lay Activities, and other nominations may be made from the floor." The motion being duly seconded, Brother Patterson spoke to the question. The amendment was adopted.

D. Stewart Patterson, Baltimore, moved to amend Paragraph 620 by adding in line 5, after the words "District Superintendent," the following: "or by a Committee of the District Board of Lay Activities, of which Committee the District Superintendent may be a member." The motion was duly seconded.

George W. Henson, Philadelphia, spoke in favor of the amendment. The amendment was adopted.

D. Stewart Patterson, Baltimore, moved to amend Paragraph 622 by striking out the words "The District Superintendent" and inserting therefor the words "The District Board of Lay Activities." The motion, duly seconded, prevailed.

Charles V. Adams, Central Pennsylvania, moved as a substitute for Paragraph 625 the following: "The Charge Lay Leader shall be elected by the Official Board." The motion being duly seconded, Brother Adams spoke to the substitution.

W. K. Greene, North Carolina, spoke against the substitute.

J. Edgar Skillington, Central Pennsylvania, spoke in favor of the substitution.

G. M. Davenport, North Alabama, moved the previous question. The motion, duly seconded, prevailed and the previous question was ordered. The substitute was adopted.

Lester S. Ivins, Ohio, called attention to a typographical error in the third line from the bottom of Paragraph 603, stating that the word "and" had been omitted between the words "District" and "Conference" in said line. The chairman accepted this correction. Lester S. Ivins then spoke in favor of the report.

Thomas D. Ellis, South Georgia, moved the previous question on all before the Conference. The motion, duly seconded, prevailed and the previous question was ordered.

The Chairman closed the debate and the report was adopted, as amended. For report, see Appendix, "General Standing Committees," page 521.

The Order of the Day, nominations from the floor for membership on the Judicial Council, was then taken up.

The following ministers were nominated from the Methodist Episcopal Church: Henry W. Bartlay, Florida Conference, by David A. Boyd, Florida Conference; Thomas A. Stafford, Northern Minnesota, by Henry L. Davis, Northwest Indiana. When informed that if elected Dr. Stafford would have to resign his present position as

MAY 6
ELEVENTH DAY

Morning
Committee on Membership and Temporal Economy, Report No. 4

Nominations Judicial Council

MAY 6
ELEVENTH DAY
Morning
Nominations—
Judicial
Council
Executive Secretary of the Board of Pensions and Relief, H. L. Davis withdrew the nomination.

The following laymen were nominated from the Methodist Episcopal Church: Howard C. Baldwin, Detroit Conference, by Paul G. Halmhuber, Detroit Conference; Fred B. Noble, Saint Johns River Conference, by George E. Farrar, Saint Johns River Conference; Joseph B. Randolph, South Carolina Conference, by J. Harvey Smith, South Florida Conference; William H. Wilcox, Oklahoma Conference, by Ira M. Hargett, Oklahoma Conference.

The following ministers were nominated from the Methodist Episcopal Church, South: J. W. Bergin, Central Texas Conference, by Frank P. Culver, Central Texas Conference; B. R. Turnipseed, Upper South Carolina Conference, by Henry M. Stevenson, North Alabama Conference; Paul N. Garber, Western North Carolina Conference, by Mrs. T. H. Minga, North Texas Conference.

The following laymen were nominated from the Methodist Episcopal Church, South: Sam G. Bratton, New Mexico Conference, by H. O. Davidson, New Mexico Conference; R. B. Carr, North Alabama Conference, by G. M. Davenport, North Alabama Conference; H. B. McGinnis, Tennessee Conference, by John F. Baggett, Tennessee Conference; J. G. McGowen, North Mississippi Conference, by L. P. Wasson, North Mississippi Conference; Nathan Newby, Pacific Conference, by J. C. McPheeters, Pacific Conference; M. C. Redwine, Kentucky Conference, by W. L. Cash, Louisville Conference; T. D. Samford, Alabama Conference, by Zebulon Judd, Alabama Conference; H. H. White, Louisiana Conference, by W. W. Holmes, Louisiana Conference; J. T. Ellison, Alabama Conference, by L. O. Hartman, New England Conference; Mrs. J. W. Perry, Holston Conference, by W. G. Cram, Kentucky Conference.

On motion of Albert N. Smith, Northwest Kansas, duly seconded, the nominations were closed.

Clyde O. Law, West Virginia, moved that the nominees of the Council of Bishops and those made from the floor of the Conference be separated on the printed ballot. The motion, duly seconded, did not prevail.

Frank C. Propert, New Jersey, moved that Paragraph 604 of Calendar No. 28, Report No. 4 of the Committee on Membership and Temporal Economy, as amended and adopted this morning, be referred to the Committee on Judiciary that they may report to us their opinion as to whether or not that paragraph as amended is unconstitutional. The motion, duly seconded, prevailed.

Calendar No. 29, Report No. 5 of the Committee on Ministry and Judicial Administration, printed on pages 222 to 228 inclusive of the *Daily Christian Advocate* and entitled "Offenses for Which a Bishop or a Traveling Preacher May Be Tried," was taken up for consideration. Orien W. Fifer, Indiana, Chairman of the Committee, requested Francis R. Bayley, Baltimore, Chairman of the subcommittee having in charge the preparation of this Report, to present it to the Conference. Dr. Bayley requested M. A. Childers, West Texas, Vice-Chairman of the subcommittee, to assist him. Dr. Bayley explained the revisions of the report and called attention to the fact that no provision was included for the trial of a Missionary Bishop, but that this would be covered by locating men in Jurisdictions who are in service in the foreign field, and therefore they would be amenable to the Jurisdictional Conferences. Dr. Bayley moved the adoption of the report.

George A. Fowler, Rock River, moved to amend Paragraph 342, Article 2, by substituting the word "may" for the word "shall" in the third line from the end of the paragraph. The motion was duly seconded and Dr. Fowler spoke to the amendment. Dr. Bayley spoke against the proposed amendment. The amendment was not adopted.

J. Edgar Skillington, Central Pennsylvania, moved to amend Paragraph 348-A by adding the following words: "and except also that in case of a charge involving dishonestly securing possession or being in possession of money or property, this limitation shall not apply if restitution has not been made." The motion was duly seconded. Dr. Skillington raised the question as to whether or not there was provision in this legislation for the trial of a person who may be *alleged* to have committed offense, being a member of one of these

MAY 6
ELEVENTH DAY

Morning

Committee on Ministry and Judicial Administration,

Report No. 5 —"Offenses"

Judicial Council

three Uniting Churches before this Conference sat and this legislation was passed.

Nathan Newby, Pacific, being recognized, replied that a person can be tried only under the laws that obtained when the offense was committed.

Fred B. Noble, Saint Johns River, called attention to the fact that there was a five-year limitation in the 1936 *Discipline* of the Methodist Episcopal Church, Paragraph 751 (f).

Elmer E. Collins, Montana State, spoke in favor of the printed report.

W. C. Perkins, Pittsburgh, raised the question as to the trial of a retired Bishop and the provision made therefor. Dr. Bayley stated that the matter was taken care of in Paragraph 316.

Leslie R. Burgum, North Dakota, moved the pending question. The motion, duly seconded, prevailed and the pending question was ordered.

The Skillington amendment was not adopted.

George C. French, North Texas, moved that Paragraph 348-A be deleted. The motion, duly seconded, did not prevail.

Gurney P. Hood, North Carolina, moved the previous question on all before the Conference. The motion, duly seconded, prevailed and the previous question was ordered.

M. A. Childers closed the debate for the Committee. He called attention to Section XV, Paragraphs 366 to 370 inclusive, and stated that the matter of Annual Conference Deaconess Boards was being considered by another committee, but had not been acted upon by the Uniting Conference up to this time, and asked that, in the adoption of the Report, Section XV be adopted with the provision that whatever Board is provided by the Uniting Conference for the trial of a Deaconess, said Section XV be amended to conform thereto.

The report was adopted. For report, see Appendix, "General Standing Committees," page 463.

Paul N. Garber, J. T. Ellison, and Mrs. J. W. Perry severally appeared before the Uniting Conference and requested that they be allowed to withdraw their names from the list of nominees for membership on the Judicial Council. Their request was granted by common consent.

Levi P. Goodwin, Iowa-Des Moines, Chairman of the Committee on Presiding Officers, presented the following report and moved its adoption. The report was adopted, as follows:

MAY 6
ELEVENTH DAY
Morning
Presiding
Officers

REPORT NO. 4

In accordance with the action of yesterday morning fixing the sessions of the Conference for next week, your Committee presents the following selections for Presiding Officers:

Monday, May 8—8:30 A.M., Bishop ̀A. Frank Smith; 2:15 P.M., Bishop H. Lester Smith; 7:45 P.M., Bishop Ivan Lee Holt.

Tuesday, May 9—8:30 A.M., Bishop Francis J. McConnell; 2:15 P.M., Bishop J. C. Broomfield; 7:45 P.M., Bishóp Edgar Blake.

Wednesday, May 10—8:30 A.M., Bishop C. C. Selecman; 2:15 P.M., Bishop Titus Lowe; 7:45 P.M., The Three Co-Chairmen of the Joint Commission on Union.

LEVI P. GOODWIN, *Chairman.*

Bishop Edwin H. Hughes, for the Council of Bishops, presented a letter from the Federal Council of Churches of Christ in America. On motion of Costen J. Harrell, Tennessee, seconded by John W. Langdale, New York East, the letter was received and ordered to record, as follows:

Letter from
Federal
Council of
Churches

Bishop Edwin Holt Hughes, Bishop John M. Moore, Rev. James H. Straughn, D.D., Kansas City, Mo.

Dear Friends: In behalf of the Federal Council of the Churches of Christ in America we desire to express our heartfelt interest in the great Conference which is effecting the unification of the Methodist Episcopal Church, the Methodist Episcopal Church, South, and the Methodist Protestant Church. We rejoice that under the leadings of the Holy Spirit this unprecedented achievement in Christian unity has been brought about. We extend fraternal greetings in behalf of the other Christian bodies associated in the Federal Council and pray God's richest blessings upon your gathering.

We gratefully recognize the fact that the reunion of your three denominations is the greatest ever achieved in Christian history in the number of people affected. It is our earnest hope and belief that the influence of your reunion may have a profound and far-reaching effect upon American Christianity as a whole and that the example which you have set may soon be followed by other denominational families.

It is a matter of deep satisfaction to us that the Methodist Episcopal Church, the Methodist Episcopal Church, South, and the Methodist Protestant Church have all been associated with the Federal Council of the Churches of Christ in America from the very beginning. It would be impossible to exaggerate the contribution which your

MAY 6
ELEVENTH DAY
Morning
Letter from
Federal
Council of
Churches
three churches have made to church federation and unity through the leadership given by your outstanding personalities and also through the devoted interest of the rank and file of your membership.

We rejoice that The Methodist Church will now take the place of your three former denominations in the membership of the Federal Council and we earnestly covet your continuing and ever-increasing participation in the fellowship and service of the Council. We are sure that it is not necessary to request you to continue to make provision for undiminished financial support of the Council under the new arrangements which will be made in connection with your reunion, but in order that this item may not run the risk of being overlooked in the pressure of the weighty matters which you will be considering at Kansas City we would respectfully suggest that in some proper way you make certain that the present contributions from your three bodies be continued and, if possible, increased.

With hearty congratulations and boundless good wishes, we remain,

Fraternally yours,

GEORGE A. BUTTRICK, *President;*
JOHN R. MOTT, *Vice-President;*
SAMUEL McCREA CAVERT, *General Secretary.*

Bishop Waldorf read to the Conference the following telegram:

Lud H. Estes, Secretary, Kansas City, Mo.

Sincere congratulations to your Uniting Conference over its ideal accomplishment in so happily combining three of America's great denominations for service to America.

F. H. LAGUARDIA, *Mayor, City of New York.*

Motion of John F. Baggett, Tennessee, duly seconded, prevailed referring to the Commission on Entertainment of the General Conference of 1940 Mayor LaGuardia's invitation to hold the first General Conference of The Methodist Church in New York City.

Motion of Joseph M. M. Gray, Detroit, duly seconded, prevailed that after the necessary announcements we adjourn.

Various announcements were made and the

Conference adjourned with the benediction pronounced by Bishop William F. Anderson.

MONDAY MORNING, MAY 8, 1939

Bishop A. Frank Smith called the Conference to order at 8:30 A.M., for the session of the twelfth day and announced that Bishop James C. Baker would be in charge of the worship service and that Bishop Edgar Blake would bring the devotional message. Bishop Blake brought a timely message from the Parable of the Fig Tree as found in the thirteenth chapter of the Gospel by St. Luke. *Morning
Opening*

The report of the Committee on Journal was adopted, as folows: *Journal*

We have examined the Journal and found it correct.
JOSEPH D. PIPER, *Chairman;*
JOHN R. KENNEY, *Secretary.*

Earl B. Brown, Northeast Ohio, Chairman, presented Report No. 9 of the Committee on Credentials, and moved its adoption without reading, the report to be printed in tomorrow's *Daily Christian Advocate.* The motion, duly seconded, prevailed. For report, see Appendix, "Special Standing Committees," page 837. *Committee on Credentials, Report No. 9*

W. F. Bryan, Texas, Chairman of the Committee on Membership and Temporal Economy, moved that consideration of Calendar Reports Nos. 42 and 43, being Reports Nos. 5 and 6 of the committee dealing with the financial plan for the Church, be made the Order of the Day for Tuesday, May 9, at 10 A.M. The motion, duly seconded, prevailed. *Committee on Membership and Temporal Economy, Reports Nos. 5 and 6*

J. Edgar Skillington, Central Pennsylvania, Chairman of the Committee on Rules, presented Report No. 7 of the Committee, printed on page 293 of the *Daily Christian Advocate,* and requested that it be read. The Secretary read the report to the Conference. Dr. Skillington asked common consent to make the following change for the clarification of the report: Strike out, beginning in line 11, the words "consideration of the majority report, together with amendments proposed thereto, shall have been completed," and substituting therefor the following: "the report of the committee has had such consideration as the Conference may wish to give it." Common consent was granted. On motion of Dr. Skillington, duly seconded, the report was adopted. For report, *Committee on Rules, Report No. 7*

MAY 8
TWELFTH DAY
Morning
Committee on
Rules,
Report No. 8
see Appendix, "Special Standing Committees," page 827.

Report No. 8 of the same committee, printed on page 293 of the *Daily Christian Advocate*, was presented by the Chairman and read to the Conference by the Secretary. On motion of Dr. Skillington, duly seconded, the report was adopted. For report, see Appendix, "Special Standing Committees," page 828.

World Council of Churches
The Chair recognized Bishop Edwin H. Hughes on a matter of personal privilege. Bishop Hughes stated he had received an invitation from the officers of the Provisional Committee of the World Council of Churches, asking the Methodist Episcopal Church to become a member of that great body, and that Dr. John R. Mott, a member of the Uniting Conference, was one of the Provisional Officers of that organization. He requested Dr. Mott to come to the platform. Dr. Mott, being recognized, offered the following resolution:

A letter has been received by Bishop Hughes from the officers of the Provisional Committee of the World Council of Churches, inviting the Methodist Episcopal Church to join this World Council. Presumably such an invitation has been sent, as well, to other branches of Methodism.

While it evidently does not lie within the province of this Uniting Conference to accept this invitation in an official way, we do vote to send it to the General Conference of 1940 with a recommendation for favorable action.

On motion of Dr. Mott, duly seconded, the resolution was adopted.

Leave of Absence
The Chairman of the Sub-subcommittee on Assignment of Bishops asked that the members of this committee be excused from the afternoon and evening sessions of today in order that the committee might meet at 2 P.M. and 7 P.M. to complete their work. Permission was granted, by common consent.

Referred
Fred D. Stone, Rock River, offered the following resolution:

Resolved, That the Committee on Enabling Acts, in considering the motion of L. O. Hartman presented to this Conference on Saturday, May 6, and referred to them, be requested to consider the matter as including the Book Committees or Publishing Boards of the three former Churches that are participating parties to this Union.

The resolution, on motion of Dr. Stone, duly seconded, was referred to the Committee on Enabling Acts and Legal Forms.

On motion of Thomas D. Ellis, South Georgia, duly seconded, the following resolution was adopted:

Resolved, That we request the Council of Bishops to formulate and present to the Uniting Conference for its adoption a program for The Methodist Church in the following areas:
1. The advancement of the spiritual life of the Church.
2. Increased support of the Benevolences.
3. The deepening of the educational and missionary conviction of the Church.
4. A comprehensive and forward-looking program in every Local Church.
Signed: T. D. Ellis, John W. Langdale, James A. James, L. O. Hartman, Harold Paul Sloan, Fred D. Stone, Harry E. Woolever, Robert B. Stansell, J. W. Hawley, W. F. McMurry, Orien W. Fifer, W. G. Henry, W. F. Bryan, Charles M. Meeks, Harry Denman, Ralph W. Sockman, M. S. Rice, W. C. Perkins, Wm. H. LaPrade, O. W. Auman, W. P. King.

Bishop Hughes stated that the Council of Bishops unanimously approved this resolution and would greatly rejoice in its adoption.

At the request of Francis R. Bayley, Baltimore, Chairman of the Committee, the Secretary read Report No. 4 of the Committee on Judiciary, printed on page 292 of the *Daily Christian Advocate.*

Dr. Bayley explained its provisions and moved its adoption. The motion, duly seconded, prevailed. For report, see Appendix, "Special Standing Committees," page 820.

Report No. 5 of the same Committee, printed on page 293 of the *Daily Advocate,* was read by the Secretary at the request of Dr. Bayley, who moved its adoption. The motion, duly seconded, prevailed. For report, see Appendix, "Special Standing Committees," page 820.

Dr. Bayley, on a matter of privilege, moved that the Secretary of the Uniting Conference write a letter of thanks to Rev. W. G. McKenney, Baltimore Conference of the former Methodist Episcopal Church, for the gift of a gavel being used today and brought to the Uniting Conference by S. S. McKenney, Texas Conference of the form-

Greetings to
European
Methodists

er Methodist Episcopal Church, South, and a brother of W. G. McKenney. The motion, duly seconded, prevailed.

The following resolution, presented by Ralph E. Diffendorfer, Rock River, was, on his motion, duly seconded, adopted:

GREETINGS TO EUROPEAN METHODISTS

The Uniting Conference of The Methodist Church convened in Kansas City, Missouri, U. S. A., on April 26, 1939, sends fraternal greetings to our brethren in Europe. Through your representatives who are to assemble in Copenhagen, Denmark, for fellowship and the discussion of matters of mutual concern, we assure you of our continued love and co-operation as a part of our world-wide Methodism.

We commend to you the spirit of unity—the Christ which dominates our present assembly. We pray that the blessing of God and the guidance of the Holy Spirit be yours to the end and that your respective lands and the entire Continent of Europe may be led to accept the Gospel of Christ as the only sure hope of peace and salvation for all men and nations.

Thanksgiving
Resolution

Leslie R. Burgum, North Dakota, presented the following resolution:

I move that the last Thursday of November in this present year be made a day of Thanksgiving to God throughout The Methodist Church for the perfecting of the union we now enjoy, and that the various agencies of our Church co-operate in such observance; and that, since this year marks the one hundred and fiftieth anniversary of the issuance of the first Thanksgiving Day Proclamation by George Washington in the month of November, 1789, then to a new nation and to a new Church, particular attention be paid to the content of that message and to its value for a people who seek to make vital religion effective in our national life.

The motion being duly seconded, Dr. Burgum spoke to the question. The motion prevailed.

Referred to
Business
Committee

George C. French, North Texas, moved the following:

I move that we do now refer the question of studying the written Constitutions now found in the *Disciplines* of the Methodist Episcopal Church and the Methodist Protestant Church to a special committee, with instructions to report to this Conference, for its consideration not later than 11 A.M., Tuesday, May 9, 1939; and that said Special Committee be composed as follows:

One clerical and one lay representative to be elected by and from the delegates from the various Annual Conferences now composing our Jurisdictional and Central Conferences.

The motion was duly seconded. Thomas D. Ellis, South Georgia, moved its reference to the
Business Committee. The motion, duly seconded,
prevailed.

Motion of Daniel L. Marsh, New England, duly
seconded, prevailed that we do now take up the
Calendar.

John B. F. Yoak, Jr., Western Virginia, Calendar Secretary, moved that Calendar No. 43, Report No. 6 of the Committee on 'Membership and
Temporal Economy, and Calendar No. 52, Report
No. 11 of the Committee on Conferences, be referred back to their respective Committees, as
both reports had been inadvertently passed without a quorum being present, and that the Reports
retain their place on the Calendar. The motion,
duly seconded, prevailed.

Orien W. Fifer, Indiana, Chairman of the Committee on Ministry and Judicial Administration,
moved that Calendar No. 61, Report No. 12 of the
Committee, printed on page 311 of the *Daily
Christian Advocate,* exchange places on the Calendar with Calendar No. 30, Report No. 6 of the
same Committee, printed on page 228 of the *Daily
Christian Advocate,* as this exchange of reports
would expedite the business of the Conference.
The motion, duly seconded, prevailed by more
than the two-thirds majority.

Dr. Fifer then presented Calendar No. 61, Report No. 12 of the Committee on Ministry and
Judicial Administration, and requested that the
Conference give common consent for the following changes before the report was read by the
Secretary. The Conference, by common consent,
separately approved the following changes: Omit
the third paragraph, which is in parentheses, and
starts with the word "Suggestion'; at the close of
Section 3 strike out the last sentence, which reads
as follows: "Said Bishops shall have their relation to the Jurisdictional Conferences in the
United States." In Section 4 let the last line read,
"already fixed by the Uniting Conference." Re-
arrange the paragraphs, letting Section 5 follow
Section 1, becoming Section 2; Section 4 should
be Section 3; Section 3 should be Section 4; and
Section 2 should be Section 5.

Dr. Fifer then explained the provisions of the

MAY 8
TWELFTH DAY

Morning

Committee on
Ministry
and Judicial
Administra-
tion, Re-
port No. 12
report and moved its adoption. The motion was duly seconded.

Ralph E. Diffendorfer, Rock River, asked a question relative to Sections 6 and 7 as to whether their adoption would mean that we are permanently adopting the policy of Missionary Bishops. Dr. Fifer answered in the negative.

Francis R. Bayley, Baltimore, being recognized, stated: "I do not so understand that this commits us to a permanent policy of the Missionary Bishops: but these two sections, it seems to me, are absolutely necessary for this ad interim period."

Motion of John F. Baggett, Tennessee, duly seconded, prevailed that the time be extended to complete the pending matters, as the Order of the Day was near at hand.

A. Wesley Pugh, North Indiana, stated, as the author of Sections 6 and 7, that they were adopted in the committee meeting with the understanding that they would become a special section in the chapter on Episcopacy. Dr. Fifer concurred in the statement and asked common consent of the Conference for the Editors of the *Discipline* to allocate Sections 6 and 7 properly. Common consent was granted.

Arlo A. Brown, Newark, moved the pending question. The motion, duly seconded, prevailed and the pending question was ordered.

Dr. Fifer requested that the words "not included in Central Conferences," in lines 5 and 6 of Section 3, be stricken out. This was done by common consent.

The Report was then adopted. For report, see Appendix, "General Standing Committees," page 497.

Leslie J. Lyons, Missouri, moved that the temperance address of Bishop Edwin H. Hughes, delivered yesterday afternoon, be printed in the *Daily Christian Advocate.* The motion, duly seconded, prevailed.

The Order of the Day having arrived, the Conference proceeded to the election of members of the Judicial Council. The Secretary explained the method of taking the vote and assigned the tellers to their stations at the request of John J. Bunting, Wilmington, Secretary of Ballots and Tellers.

Daniel L. Marsh, New England, moved that a majority vote be required for election. The motion, duly seconded, prevailed.

George C. French, North Texas, moved that no ballot be counted as legal that has fewer or more than the number called for upon that particular ballot. The motion, duly seconded, prevailed.

Gideon I. Humphreys, Maryland, being recognized, requested permission to withdraw his name from the list of nominees. This was granted by common consent.

Frank W. Court, Upper Iowa, moved that the delegates who are prevented from being present on account of illness be allowed the right to vote. There was no second to this motion.

Carl K. Mahoney, Pacific Northwest, being recognized, asked permission to withdraw his name from the list of nominees. This was granted by common consent.

Arthur A. Callaghan, Maine, raised the question if any mark appearing against the name of a nominee would be valid.

Ralph E. Diffendorfer, Rock River, moved that the mark be an X. The motion was duly seconded.

Fred D. Stone, Rock River, moved as an amendment that any mark clearly indicating the voter's choice would be valid. Dr. Diffendorfer and his second accepted the amendment, and the motion prevailed.

The ballot was spread, the vote taken and declared officially closed, and the Tellers retired to determine the results, under the supervision of John J. Bunting, Wilmington, Secretary of Ballots and Tellers.

George W. Henson, Philadelphia, Chairman, presented Calendar No. 31, Report No. 6 of the Committee on Conferences, printed on page 228 of the *Daily Christian Advocate*, and moved its adoption with the substitution for Item (4) of the resolution of Frank C. Propert, New Jersey, which had been adopted Saturday, May 6, but with this additional sentence: "and to publish the same in the Church Press at least thirty days before the convening of the said Conference." The report as amended was then adopted on motion of Dr. Henson, duly seconded. For report,

MAY 8
TWELFTH DAY
Morning
Recess

Reconvene

Kansas Wesleyan University
Harmonic Choir

Introductions

see Appendix, "General Standing Committees," page 429.

The Bishop declared the Conference to be in recess.

Bishop A. Frank Smith called the Conference to order at 10:40 A.M.

Dr. James R. Houghton presented Bishop Charles L. Mead to the Conference. Bishop Mead in turn presented the Kansas Wesleyan University Harmonic Choir of Salina, Kansas. Under the leadership of Dr. Leon A. Wilgus the Choir rendered three beautiful selections. Bishop Smith, for the Conference, thanked Dr. Wilgus and the Choir for their contribution to the work of the Uniting Conference.

Joseph M. M. Gray, Detroit, Chairman of the Committee on Courtesies, Privileges, and Introductions, presented Bishop Charles L. Mead, Chairman of the Local Committee on Entertainment of the Uniting Conference, in order that Bishop Mead might present his co-workers who had so efficiently provided for the welfare of the delegates and visitors attending the Uniting Conference. Bishop Mead introduced the following: Bishop W. T. Watkins, Co-Chairman; Dr. Thomas B. Mather, Executive Vice-President; Dr. C. E. Street, Secretary; Mr. Kenneth Robertson, Treasurer; Dr. E. L. Dixon, Dr. Edward Hislop, Dr. W. A. Keve, Ex-officio members of the Executive Committee. The following Committee Chairmen were introduced: Mr. R. Carter Tucker, Finance; Mr. T. O. Cunningham, Budget; Dr. E. J. Kulp, Hotels; Dr. E. L. Hobbs, Ushers; Mr. J. W. Miller, Transportation; Dr. W. C. Hanson, Hospitality; Mrs. Fred A. Lamb, Women's Activities; Dr. G. F. Tipton, Negro Activities; Dr. S. B. Edmondson, Pulpit Supply; Mr. Powell Weaver, Music; Dr. King D. Beach, Broadcasting; Mr. C. M. Hayman, Restaurants; Mr. Frank Tucker, Press; Mr. Ed J. Barnes, Decorations; Rev. George Ryder, Information; Dr. Mills Anderson, Housing; Mrs. J. W. Showalter, Telephone; Mr. A. A. McCullum, Post Office; Mr. W. J. Campbell, Physical Arrangements; Mr. George L. Goldman, Director of the Auditorium; Mr. C. A. Mook, Superintendent of the Auditorium; Mr. Abe W. Conners, Assistant Superintendent of the Auditorium; Mr. Ed

Roach, Loud Speaking Equipment Engineer; Mr. Lawrence Riley, Electrician.

Dr. Gray spoke of the work of the women and then presented and introduced the Presidents of the Woman's Missionary Societies of the three former Churches: Mrs. J. W. Shell, Reserve, Pittsburgh, President of the Woman's Missionary Convention of the Methodist Protestant Church; Mrs. J. W. Perry, Holston, President of the Woman's Missionary Council of the Methodist Episcopal Church, South; Mrs. W. H. C. Goode, Ohio, President of the Woman's Home Missionary Society of the Methodist Episcopal Church; Mrs. Thomas Nicholson, Upper Iowa, President of the Woman's Foreign Missionary Society of the Methodist Episcopal Church.

Morning

Introductions

Dr. Gray next introduced the Right Reverend Robert Nelson Spencer, Bishop of the Diocese of West Missouri, and the Very Reverend Claude W. Sprouse, Dean of Grace and Holy Trinity Cathedral. Each, in turn, briefly addressed the Conference.

Bishop Spencer and Dean Sprouse Address the Conference

Bishop Smith replied appropriately for the Conference, and also in behalf of the Conference thanked all those who in any way had contributed to the comfort and inspiration of the Uniting Conference.

Bishop Smith called attention to the report of the Southeastern Jurisdiction Boundaries printed on page 292 of the *Daily Christian Advocate*. Motion of the Secretary, duly seconded, prevailed that it be received and go to record.

Southeastern Jurisdiction Boundaries

Frank C. Propert, New Jersey, called the attention of the Conference to the fact that in the adoption of Reports Nos. 4 and 5 of the Committee on Judiciary, printed on pages 292 and 293 *Daily Christian Advocate*, certain sections of other reports, previously adopted by the Uniting Conference, had been declared unconstitutional. He now moved that the subject matter of Paragraph 1208, Section 1, Calendar No. 18, Report No. 3 of the Committee on Publishing Interests, printed on page 189 of the *Daily Christian Advocate*, be referred to the Committee on Publishing Interests, in order that they might present another section within the limits of the Plan of Union. The motion, duly seconded, prevailed.

Referred

MAY 8
TWELFTH DAY
Morning
Referred

Frank C. Propert, New Jersey, moved that amended Paragraph 604, Calendar No. 28, Report No. 4 of the Committee on Membership and Temporal Economy, printed on page 221 of the *Daily Christian Advocate*, be referred to the Committee on Membership and Temporal Economy for restatement in the light of Report No. 5 of the Committee on Judiciary. The motion, duly seconded, prevailed.

Certain papers on the Secretary's desk were referred, by common consent, to the Committee of Reference.

A Resolution
Precautionary

W. F. Dunkle, Florida, presented the following, which, on his motion, duly seconded, was referred to the Committee on Enabling Acts and Legal Forms:

A RESOLUTION PRECAUTIONARY

In order to provide for any work or rule of the Church which may be inadvertently overlooked by the Uniting Conference; therefore be it

Resolved, That any work or rule of any one of the three Uniting Churches which inadvertently has not been provided for by the Uniting Conference, may and shall be provided for and administered as provided for in the *Disciplines* of the affected Churches until the General Conference shall provide otherwise.

Report of
Special
Committee
on Memoirs

M. T. Plyler, North Carolina, presented the report of the Special Committee on Memoirs, appointed by the Committee on Publishing Interests, and moved that it be placed on the Calendar. The motion, duly seconded, prevailed.

Excused

Arthur A. Callaghan, Maine, Chairman of the Committee on Enabling Acts and Legal Forms, moved that the members of the Committee be excused from attendance upon the afternoon session, in order that they might meet and complete their work. This was granted by common consent.

Southeastern
Jurisdiction
Boundaries

J. W. Perry, Holston, asked common consent to correct the report of the Southeastern Jurisdiction, printed on page 292 of the *Daily Christian Advocate*, and which was ordered to record this morning, by deleting the word "west" in the third line from the end of Paragraph (3), Holston Conference. This was granted by common consent.

George W. Henson, Philadelphia, Chairman, presented Calendar No. 32, Report No. 7 of the

Committee on Conferences, printed on pages 228 and 229 of the *Daily Christian Advocate* and entitled "Church Conference." He requested Roy H. Short, Louisville, Chairman of the Subcommittee preparing this report, to come to the platform. Dr. Henson explained the provision of the report and moved its adoption. The motion, duly seconded, prevailed. For report, see Appendix, "General Standing Committees," page 430. MAY 8
TWELFTH DAY
Morning
Committee on
Conferences,
Report No. 7
—"Church
Conference"

Paul Quillian, Texas, Chairman, presented Calendar No. 33, Report No. 3 of the Committee on Education, printed on pages 229 and 230 of the *Daily Christian Advocate* and entitled "Division of Educational Institutions," and moved its adoption. The motion was duly seconded. Dr. Quillian requested Herbert J. Burgstahler, Upper Iowa, Chairman of the subcommittee, to be in charge of the Report and answer any questions that should arise. The report was adopted. For report, see Appendix, "General Standing Committees," page 596. Committee on
Education,
Report No. 3
—"Division
of Educa-
tional Insti-
tutions"

Thomas S. Brock, New Jersey, Chairman, presented Calendar No. 34, Report No. 7 of the Committee on Superannuate Support, printed on pages 252 and 256 inclusive in the *Daily Christian Advocate* and entitled "Regulations for the Territory of the Illinois Corporation." Dr. Brock requested Thomas A. Stafford, Northern Minnesota, Executive Secretary of the Illinois Corporation, to come to the platform and assist in the presentation of the report. Dr. Brock called attention to typographical errors as follows: The word "appointment" should read "apportionment"; the word "cash" before the word "salary" should be deleted; in the twentieth line of Paragraph 1319 (1) the word "before" should read "after." Dr. Brock explained the provisions of the report and requested common consent to make the following corrections: Article V, Paragraph 1319 (1), after the word "Elder" in the ninth line, add the words "or President of a Methodist Protestant Conference." Article IX, Paragraph 1323, Section 5: Add after the word "Conference" in the first line the following words: "Claimants may apportion annually to." Article XIII, Paragraph 1327: Add Section 2, which was passed unani- Committee on
Superannu-
ate Support,
Report No. 7
—"Regula-
tions for the
Territory of
the Illinois
Corpora-
tion"

MAY 8
TWELFTH DAY
Morning

mously by the Committee but does not appear in the printed report, and is as follows:

Committee on
Superannu-
ate Support,
Report No. 7
—"Regula-
tions for the
Territory of
the Illinois
Corpora-
tion"

Paragraph 1327, Section 2. Annual Conferences may file with other Conferences claims against members, whose membership has been changed by transfer, who have such unpaid assessments and pledges for Conference Claimants' causes and funds. Boards of Conference Claimants for which claims are filed shall collect the same on retirement of members.

Common consent was granted for these corrections. Dr. Brock then moved the adoption of the report.

William F. Quillian, South Georgia, asked an explanation of the fourth paragraph of Article XXIII. Dr. Brock replied that Article XXIII was simply added as a matter of reference, because it represented judicial decisions, and stated that the committee had nothing to do with Article XXIII.

George C. French, North Texas, asked if there would be any objection to substituting the words "Board of Conference Claimants" for the words "Conference Stewards." Dr. Brock replied that that was purely an editorial matter and that the commitee had nothing to do with the judicial decisions.

The report was adopted. For report, see Appendix, "General Standing Committees," page 662.

Constitution-
ality

W. C. Perkins, Pittsburgh, presented the following resolution and moved its adoption:

Resolved, That the reports that have been adopted by this Conference in which the method of election of any Secretary or other officers may be in question on the basis of the constitutionality of the procedure provided, be now referred to the Committee on Judiciary for their consideration and report as to the constitutionality of the election provisions set up in these reports."

Paul Quillian, Texas, Chairman of the Committee on Education, raised the point of order that before this resolution could be considered, the proper procedure would be to move a reconsideration of Report No. 1 of the Committee of Education, which was adopted May 3, 1939, as in the adoption of this Report the matter of the constitutionality of elections was called into question, and that the Chair had ruled upon it and the decision was so recorded in the Journal of the Unit- ing Conference. The point of order was sus- tained by the Chair and the resolution was not adopted.

Paul Quillian, Texas, Chairman, presented Cal- endar No. 35, Report No. 5 of the Committee on Education, printed on page 256 of the *Daily Chris-* *tian Advocate* and entitled "Enabling Act," and requested common consent to strike out the last sentence beginning "The Commission is given, etc." This was granted by common consent. Motion of Dr. Quillian, duly seconded, prevailed adopting the report. For report, see Appendix, "General Standing Committees," page 602.

Orien W. Fifer, Indiana, Chairman, presented Calendar No. 36, Report No. 7 of the Committee on Ministry and Judicial Administration, printed on page 256 of the *Daily Christian Advocate* and entitled "The Episcopacy—Duties, Powers, and Limitations." Dr. Fifer asked common consent to make the following corrections: In Paragraph 204, Section 1, the word "delegation" at the beginning of the fifth line should be "declaration." In Section 3, Paragraph 204, strike out the words "not included in Central Conferences" found in lines nine and ten. Paragraph 205, Section 4, the word "permit" at the end of the first line should be "appoint." By common consent this was done. Dr. Fifer then explained the provisions of the report and moved its adoption.

Leslie R. Burgum, North Dakota, moved to amend Paragraph 204, Section 3, by substituting, at the end of line four, the word "four" for the word "six"; at the beginning of line six substitute the word "four" for the word "six" and in the same line substitute the word "eight" for the word "nine." The motion was duly seconded and Dr. Burgum spoke to the question.

Harold Paul Sloan, New Jersey, spoke against the amendment.

J. Edgar Skillington, Central Pennsylvania, moved the pending question. The motion was duly seconded.

A division of the vote being called for, a count vote was had and resulted as follows: Total vote cast, 778; necessary to order the pending ques-

MAY 8
TWELFTH DAY
Morning

tion, 518; for the pending question, 547; against the pending question 231.

The pending question being ordered, Dr. Fifer, Chairman, closed the debate for the committee. The amendment was not adopted.

Committee on Ministry and Judicial Administration, Report No. 7 —"Duties and Powers of Episcopacy"

Disston W. Jacobs, Wilmington, moved to amend Section 5 of Paragraph 204 by substituting the word "three-fourths" for the word "two-thirds" in the third line. The motion was duly seconded and Dr. Jacobs spoke to the question. The amendment did not prevail.

The report was then adopted. For report, see Appendix, "General Standing Committees," page 487.

Elmer E. Collins, Montana State, moved that after the necessary announcements the Conference adjourn. The motion, duly seconded, prevailed.

After various announcements the Conference adjourned with the benediction pronounced by Bishop Edwin H. Hughes.

MAY 8
TWELFTH DAY
Afternoon
Opening

MONDAY AFTERNOON, MAY 8, 1939

Bishop H. Lester Smith called the Conference to order at 2:15 P.M. The Conference stood and joined in singing Hymn 147, "Ask Ye What Great Thing I Know."

At the request of Bishop H. Lester Smith, Jesse Swank, of the Ohio Conference, led the Conference in prayer.

Dr. Kyugoro Obata Introduced

Bishop Arthur J. Moore was recognized for a question of privilege. Representing the Council of Bishops, Bishop Moore introduced Rev. Dr. Kyugoro Obata, Fraternal Delegate of the Japan Methodist Church.

The Secretary read the credentials of Dr. Obata, as follows:

To the Uniting Conference of The Methodist Episcopal Church, The Methodist Episcopal Church, South, The Methodist Protestant Church.

Dear Fathers and Brethren: We, your daughter Church across the Western Sea, the Japan Methodist Church, send you our affectionate and prayerful greetings.

This message will be conveyed to you by our brother, Rev. Kyugoro Obata, M.A., D.D., L.L.D., who was educated in your schools and served in your pulpits before he returned to work among us here. We desire him to express to you our gratitude for the devoted service you have rendered our land in helping to lay the foundations of the Kingdom of God. With the Methodist Episcopal Church it is a story of sixty-six years of devoted service; with the Methodist Protestant Church fifty-nine years; with the Methodist Episcopal Church, South, fifty-three years. We feel that eternity alone will tell the true story of that service. And we have faith to believe that you are to render us in the days to come, as a great United Church, a service which will be even more abundant than in the past.

You may be sure that we, members of the Japan Methodist Church, your children in the faith, are praying that God's richest blessing may be granted you in this Uniting Conference, and that His benediction may rest upon your great United Church as it goes forth to do even a more glorious work for Him.

Your brother in Christ,
TOKIO KUGIMIYA,
Bishop of the Japan Methodist Church.

Dr. Obata then spoke to the Conference. For his address, see Appendix, "Fraternal Addresses," page 876.

At the close of Dr. Obata's address the Conference stood and applauded.

Dr. Obata brought to the Conference greetings from the National Christian Council of Japan, the East Annual Conference and the West Annual Conference of the Methodist Church of Japan.

Arthur A. Callaghan, Maine, Chairman of the Committee on Enabling Acts and Legal Forms, stated that it was necessary for the Committee to meet immediately in their room and requested that ballots for the election of members of the Judicial Council be sent to their room that they might vote. This request was granted by the Conference, by common consent.

Motion of Daniel L. Marsh, New England, duly seconded, prevailed that the Rules be suspended to receive the results of the first ballot for members of the Judicial Council, and take another ballot, if necessary, before proceeding with the regular order of business.

By common consent blank ballots were distributed to the delegates that they might check the results of the first ballot. The Chair announced that W. O. Wiseman, Tennessee, was now serving as Teller in place of W. O. Batts, Tennessee. Blank ballots were also sent to the members of the Committee on Enabling Acts and Legal Forms,

MAY 8
TWELFTH DAY
Afternoon
Dr. Kyugoro Obata Introduced

Privilege

First Ballot for Members of Judicial Council

MAY 8
TWELFTH DAY

Afternoon

First Ballot
for Members
of Judicial
Council

and the Sub-subcommittee on Episcopal assignments, as previously ordered by the Conference. The results of the first ballot were announced by the Chair, as follows:

Votes cast, 779; defective, 2; ballots counted, 777; necessary to elect 389. Francis R. Bayley, Baltimore, 735; J. Stewart French, Holston, 443; Martin E. Lawson, Southwest Missouri, 438. Francis R. Bayley, J. Stewart French, and Martin E. Lawson, each having received the required majority, were declared elected members of the Judicial Council of The Methodist Church. The complete ballot is as follows:

Ministers from the Methodist Episcopal Church: Francis R. Bayley, Baltimore, 735; Walter C. Buckner, Southern California, 169; Ernest S. Lyons, Los Angeles, Calif., 169; Sanford W. Corcoran, Pittsburgh, 163; Charles B. Ketcham, Northeast Ohio, 160; Mark Kelley, Troy, 89; Leslie B. Burgum, North Dakota, 86; Henry W. Bartlay, Florida, 61; Carl K. Mahoney, Pacific Northwest, 12.

Laymen from the Methodist Episcopal Church: Henry R. VanDeusen, Wyoming, 312; Vincent P. Clarke, New England, 308; Benjamin A. Matthews, New York, 224; James I. Dolliver, Northwest Iowa, 214; Howard C. Baldwin, Detroit, 169; Joseph B. Randolph, South Carolina, 87; William H. Spurgeon, Colorado, 69; William H. Wilcox, Oklahoma, 65; Fred B. Noble, Saint Johns River, 60; Sidney R. Redmond, Central West, 50; Jacob Cantlin, Rock River, 47; Fred C. Heubner, Iowa-Des Moines, 43.

Ministers from the Methodist Protestant Church: George R. Brown, North Carolina, 352; A. J. Allen, Pittsburgh, 253; S. W. Rosenberger, Ohio, 193; G. I. Humphreys, Maryland, 12.

Ministers from the Methodist Episcopal Church, South: J. Stewart French, 443; W. G. Henry, North Georgia, 203; A. C. Millar, Little Rock, 196; B. R. Turnipseed, Upper; South Carolina, 164; A. J. Weeks, North Texas, 164; J. B. Craven, Western North Carolina, 121; J. W. Johnson, North Georgia, 112; J. W. Bergin, Central Texas, 106; W. L. Duren, Louisiana, 96; J. Richard Spann, Louisiana, 43.

Laymen from the Methodist Episcopal Church, South: Martin E. Lawson, Southwest Missouri, 438; M. A. Childers, West Texas, 325; Nathan Newby, Pacific, 265; R. L. Flowers, North Carolina, 108; O. A. Park, South Georgia, 98; W. F. McMurry, Memphis, 89; G. H. Lamar, Baltimore, 59; M. C. Redwine, Kentucky, 50; R. B. Carr, North Alabama, 44; S. G. Bratton, New Mexico, 42; J. H. Carlock, Oklahoma, 38; J. G. McGowen, North Mississippi, 34; H. B. McGinnis, Tennessee, 25; H. H. White, Louisiana, 22; C. E. Mead, New Mexico, 14; T. D. Samford, Alabama, 10.

Henry W. Bartlay, Florida, and H. B. McGinnis, Tennessee, asked permission to withdraw their names from the list of nominees for membership on the Judicial Council. By common consent their request was granted.

A second ballot for members of the Judicial Council was spread and the votes collected. The Chair declared the ballot officially closed and the Tellers retired to determine the results.

Earl R. Brown, Northeast Ohio, Chairman of the Committee on Credentials, was recognized and stated that the Committee had many requests for courtesy seatings for only one session of the three sessions now being held daily, but the Committee felt that, in view of the previous action of the Conference, they had no authority to take such action unless the Conference authorized the same, and that the Committee was willing to do the extra work entailed. By common consent the courtesy seatings for one session only were ordered by the Uniting Conference.

The Committee of Reference presented the following messages to the Conference:

May 3, 1939

To the Bishops, Elders, Deacons and Laity Members, United Methodist Church of America.

Greetings:

We, the National Officers, National Councilors, and Members of the Indian Association of America, Inc., send our hearty greetings in behalf of your wonderful Christian spirit and efforts of true Americanism of uniting the three great Methodist bodies as one—Christ Jesus had prayed that all Christians may be one.

We pray that your Christian work will continue to be blessed, and we ask you all—The Methodist Church—to remember the Red Race, the native sons and daughters of America, and pray for them, and pray for our work, and we in return gladly co-operate with your Indian Mission work, if you only give us that Christian privilege to do so.

The blessing of the Lord be upon you.

Fraternally,   BARNABAS S'HIUHUSHU, PH.D.,
                                        Chief Executive.

Dr. Lud Estes, Secretary, Uniting Conference, Kansas City, Mo.

Because the step is so definitely in the right direction and has such possibilities for good, I am constrained, as I pass through Kansas City en route west, to send my congratulations on your being able to bring the Methodist Episcopal Church, the Methodist Episcopal Church, South, and the Methodist Protestant Church together into The Methodist Church.

This is a challenge to all other denominations. It has long been my reasoned judgment that a more consolidated front of the organized forces of religion would be an immeasurable aid toward reaching the objectives, and to reach the objectives of religion is the most important purpose in the world.

As a deeply interested Presbyterian layman whose grandfather was a Methodist minister, I do want to commend the action, and I am sure that not the least good which may come from the general application of your accomplishment will be the more efficient organization insuring our capacity to take better care of our ministers, which in itself is of the very utmost significance.

I sincerely hope your example may be followed by other denominations and I most sincerely wish you the greatest success.   WILL H. HAYS.

May 6, 1939
Unification Conference of American Methodism, Kansas City Mo.

Dear Brethren: The Executive Committee and Board of Managers of the Lord's Day Alliance of the United States extend their heartiest congratulations to the three bodies of Methodism now in the Unifying Conference for the merging into the greater body.

May the benediction of the God and Father of our Lord and Saviour Jesus Christ rest upon the conclusions of judgment reached in the Unification Conference, and may His grace and favor through the guidance of the Holy Spirit attend the future way of what is now the largest body of Protestantism in the United States of America; and may the voice and action of this United Methodism be heard and felt the nation through and all the world around.

Fraternally and faithfully yours, for the Executive Committee and the Board of Managers.

JOHN H. WILLEY, *Chairman;*
HARRY L. BOWLBY, *Secretary.*

Uniting Conference: Grace be unto you and peace from God our Father and from the Lord Jesus Christ.

Mt. Vernon Church, Houston, Tex., salutes you in the work that you have done and will do. After prayer of thankfulness and an entreaty for continued divine direction in these last strenuous hours of your work, Sunday we assumed official session at 11:45 A.M. for a vote of thanks to you and a covenant of fellowship in the task which is yet ahead.

Yours for Kingdom building,
W. H. HIGHTOWER, *Pastor.*

The Methodist Unifying Conference, Kansas City, Mo.

Dear Brethren: At the State Conference of the Congregational-Christian Churches of Oklahoma, held at Kingfisher, Okla., May 4 and 5, the following resolution was adopted and ordered sent to you:

"WHEREAS the Northern M. E. Church, the Southern M. E. Church, and the Protestant Methodist Church are now in session in Kansas City, Mo., with the purpose of forming a Unity of the three denominations; therefore be it

"*Resolved*, That the following message be sent that organization:

"The 50th Annual Conference of the Congregational-Christian Churches of Oklahoma, now in session at the Methodist-Congregational Church of Kingfisher on the 4th and 5th of May, 1939, do hereby send greetings to the Unification Conference of the branches of the Methodist Church and do hereby extend hearty congratulations to the said body as the evidence of progressive unity in Christ and do hereby express our hopeful prayers for your ultimate success."

Fraternally yours,   MRS. E. P. REIKOW, *Scribe*.

Edmund D. Soper, Ohio, presented the following resolution, which, on his motion, duly seconded, was adopted:

ECUMENICAL METHODIST COUNCIL

The Plan of Unification recommends that the worldwide character of Methodism shall be recognized by the participation of The Methodist Church in the Ecumenical Methodist Conference and its constituent organization; therefore be it

Resolved, That the membership of this Church in the Ecumenical Methodist Council, Western Section, be continued. The editors of the new *Discipline* are directed, in accordance with this action and with the former practice of the three bodies now combined into the united Church, to print under the appropriate title the names of the Ecumenical Council members as the same appear in the present *Disciplines* of the Churches.

W. P. KING,
HARVEY W. COX,
F. N. PARKER,
EDMUND D. SOPER.

Under a privileged matter John R. Mott, New York, was recognized and moved the following:

In view of the necessarily prolonged time required to complete the main report of the Committee on Missions and the importance of the issues involved, I move that the consideration of this report be made the order immediately following the recess on Tuesday morning, May 9, and I also move that the rule requiring the printing of the Report at least one day before its consideration be suspended. The report will appear in the *Daily Advocate* tomorrow morning.

The Chair called attention to an Order of the Day previously set for 10 A.M., Tuesday, May 9, and suggested that this might not be completed by recess time. Dr. Mott agreed to have consideration of the Report of the Committee on Missions to follow immediately after the completion of the previously set Order of the Day on Tues-

Margin notes:
MAY 8
TWELFTH DAY
Afternoon
Communications

Ecumenical Methodist Council

Order of the Day

day, May 9. The motion, with this understanding, duly seconded, prevailed.

John B. F. Yoak, Jr., Western Virginia, Calendar Secretary, stated that the Committee on Publishing Interests was ready to report on Paragraph 1208, Section 1, Calendar No. 18, Report No. 3, which had been referred for restatement to the Committee by the adoption of Report No. 4 of the Committee on Judiciary. By common consent it was agreed to receive the report. On motion of Dr. Yoak, duly seconded, the following was adopted:

> Paragraph 1208, Section 1. There shall be an Editor of Church School Publications, elected quadrennially by the General Conference. In the event of a vacancy in the office, the Board of Publication shall have the authority to elect an editor to serve until the ensuing General Conference.

Judicial
Council

The question was raised as to whether or not a delegate now seated, but elected a member of the Judicial Council, should vacate his seat at this time. Motion of Lewis O. Hartman, New England, duly seconded, prevailed, that all members-elect of the Judicial Council retain their seats and privileges as delegates in the Uniting Conference until its final adjournment.

Committee on
Conferences,
Report No. 8
—"Jurisdic-
tional Con-
ference"

George W. Henson, Philadelphia, Chairman, presented Calendar No. 37, Report No. 8 of the Committee on Conferences, printed on page 257 of the *Daily Christian Advocate* and entitled "Jurisdictional Conference." Dr. Henson requested Frank S. Hickman, North Carolina, Chairman of the Subcommittee on Jurisdictional Conferences, to assist in the presentation of the report. Dr. Henson explained the provisions of the report and moved its adoption.

Orien W. Fifer, Indiana, moved to amend Paragraph 128 in Section I, by striking out the last sentence and substituting the following:

> The said Committee shall recommend to the Jurisdictional Conference, the assignments of the said Bishops to their respective residences; and may make recommendations to the Bishops of its Jurisdiction concerning the formation of the Episcopal Areas within its Jurisdiction.

Elmer E. Collins, Montana State, spoke against the amendment.

Lynn Harold Hough, New York East, spoke in favor of the amendment.

Leslie J. Lyons, Missouri, inquired whether or not the action of the Committee would be final or will it report back for the approval of the Jurisdictional Conference?

MAY 8
TWELFTH DAY
Afternoon
Committee on
Conferences,
Report No. 8
—"Jurisdic-
tional Con-
ference"

Dr. Henson replied that it was the thought to have the Committee report back to the body, but was not so specified in the paragraph, and could be easily written in.

Frank S. Hickman, North Carolina, spoke to the pending matter opposing the amendment.

Daniel L. Marsh, New England, stated that in the light of Dr. Henson's reply to Judge Lyons the printed Paragraph 128 should state that the Committee should report its recommendation to the Jurisdictional Conference for such action as it desired to take. Dr. Hickman accepted this suggestion for the Committee, and Dr. Henson said it would appear in the following words: "The Committee shall report their recommendations to the Jurisdictional Conference for final action."

Thomas S. Brock, New Jersey, asked how this report could be harmonized with Calendar No. 61, Report No. 12 of the Committee on Ministry and Judicial Administration, adopted this morning.

The Chair replied that they do not harmonize.

Dr. Fifer spoke to his amendment saying it would harmonize both reports.

John R. Kenney, Pacific, raised the point of order that Dr. Fifer was arguing the question and the Chair ruled the point well taken.

The Fifer amendment, duly seconded, was adopted.

Harry Van Antwerp, Troy, moved to amend Paragraph 134 by adding the following words: "but this shall not be done without the consent of the Conferences affected." The motion being duly seconded, Brother Van Antwerp spoke to the question.

J. R. Edwards, Central Texas, spoke against the amendment.

J. Edgar Skillington, Central Pennsylvania, called attention to Article V under Section IV of the Plan of Union and raised the question of the constitutionality of the amendment.

MAY 8
TWELFTH DAY
Afternoon
Committee on
Conferences,
Report No. 8
—"Jurisdic-
tional Con-
ference"

George A. Fowler, Rock River, referred to Article III, Section VIII of the Plan of Union for the same purpose.

J. W. Moore, Virginia, moved to lay the amendment on the table. The Chair ruled that this could not be done.

M. C. Redwine, Kentucky, spoke against the amendment.

Charles V. Adams, Central Pennsylvania, moved the pending question. The motion, duly seconded, prevailed and the pending question was ordered.

Dr. Hickman closed the debate for the Committee. The amendment was not adopted.

Charles A. Robbins, Pacific Northwest, inquired if the Committee intended to omit all reference to reserve delegates. Dr. Henson replied that was not the intention and asked permission for the Committee to bring in a supplemental report covering this point. Permission was granted the Committee by common consent.

Fred D. Stone, Rock River, moved to amend Paragraph 137 by inserting after the word "concerned" in the tenth line these words: "and civil court approval where necessary." The Chairman accepted the amendment.

M. C. Redwine, Kentucky, called attention to the legal language of Paragraph 135, first five lines. Dr. Hickman called attention to the fact that they were quoted from the Prospectus, page 33, Paragraph 139.

Benjamin W. Meeks, Baltimore, moved that Paragraphs 135, 136, and 137 be referred to the Committee on Enabling Acts and Legal Forms. The suggestion was accepted by Dr. Hickman for the Committee, and approved by the Conference by common consent.

Dr. Hickman further explained the report, and moved its adoption. The motion was duly seconded. The report was adopted as amended with the understanding that if the Committee on Enabling Acts and Legal Forms found it necessary to amend or change the paragraphs referred to them, Paragraphs 135, 136, and 137, they would bring in their recommendation later, otherwise the report will stand as adopted. For report, see

Appendix, "General Standing Committees," page 431.

William R. Phelps, Virginia, moved a reconsideration of Calendar No. 28, Report No. 4 of the Committee on Membership and Temporal Economy, adopted May 6, 1939, for the purpose of restating Paragraph 604, to comply with Report No. 5 of the Judiciary Committee. The motion, duly seconded, prevailed and reconsideration was ordered. Brother Phelps then moved that the wording of Paragraph 604, printed on page 221 of the *Daily Christian Advocate*, be substituted for the action of the Conference when the report was adopted May 6, 1939. The motion, duly seconded, prevailed. The report was then adopted as restated. For report, see Appendix, "General Standing Committees," page 521.

Motion of Daniel L. Marsh, New England, duly seconded, prevailed that we suspend the rules which require the printing of reports in the *Daily Advocate* a day in advance of their consideration, in order that the reports appearing in today's issue of the *Daily Advocate* might be taken up.

George C. French, North Texas, moved that Calendar No. 27, Report No. 8 of the Committee on Conferences, adopted this morning, be referred to the Committee on Judiciary to find out whether or not we have adopted legislation which conflicts with our power. The motion was seconded by Frederick W. Wahl, Missouri.

Francis R. Bayley, Chairman of the Committee on Judiciary, stated that the Committee ought not to be expected to consider anything but definite questions regarding constitutionality.

Frank S. Hickman, North Carolina, raised the point of order that Paragraph 129, especially mentioned by Dr. French, had been taken verbatim from the Plan of Union and therefore it is out of order to refer it to anybody. The Chair ruled that, in view of this fact, the point of order was well taken and therefore the motion was out of order.

Calendar No. 38, Report No. 1 of the Committee on Rituals and Orders of Worship, printed on page 294 of the *Daily Christian Advocate*, was presented by Oscar T. Olson, Northeast Ohio, Chair-

MAY 8
TWELFTH DAY

Afternoon

Committee on
Rituals and
Orders of
Worship,
Report No. 1
man. Dr. Olson explained the report and asked for the privilege of the floor for Robert G. Mc-Cutchan, Northwest Indiana. Dean McCutchan was recognized and made the following motion:

I move that the Methodist Hymnal and the Responsive Readings as adopted officially by the former Methodist Episcopal, the former Methodist Church, South, and the former Methodist Protestant Church, be the official Hymnal and Responsive Readings for The Methodist Church.

The motion was duly seconded.

Elmer E. Collins, Montana State, moved to amend by adding these words: "and that orchestration thereof be prepared and published by the Methodist Publishing House." The motion was duly seconded.

Daniel L. Marsh, New England, requested that the motion of Brother Collins be made as a separate motion and Brother Collins yielded to the request.

The motion of Dean McCutchan prevailed and the report was adopted. For report, see Appendix, "General Standing Committees," page 679.

Elmer E. Collins, Montana State, moved that the Methodist Publishing House be authorized to prepare and publish an orchestration of the new Methodist Hymnal. The motion being duly seconded, Brother Collins spoke to the question.

John W. Langdale, New York East, moved that the matter of the orchestration of The Methodist Hymnal be referred to the Publishing Houses. The substitute motion, duly seconded, prevailed.

Bishop John M. Moore was recognized for a privileged matter and presented the following letter from Josephus Daniels, Ambassador of the United States to Mexico:

Dear Bishop: It is an achievement for thanksgiving that in the domain of Methodism the middle wall or partition has broken down and Mason and Dixon's line is wiped out.

I had hoped to be present, at least at the final sessions of the Uniting Conference, as all branches of our Communion adopted plans for the perfect union in one effective and militant organization.

This unification has long been my heart's desire. Speaking at the General Conference of the Southern division of the Church in 1918, I plead for an end of separation and the mobilization of all Methodists into one mighty army under one banner, "The world is my parish," marching to the uplifting music of Wesleyism.

With the end of division and duplication of agencies, the way is now open for a greater revival of Evangelism for which mankind in travail waits. For, what anxious and disturbed men yearn for today is to have their hearts warmed by the fire of religious experience and their lives freed from love of material things and lifted out of dependence upon force. There is no hope for a jittery world except in faith in the teaching of the Prince of Peace. Wars and rumors of war will vanish when men everywhere seek spiritual guidance, and not until then.

I join with all who believe that religion alone can raise people out of their present harm and into prayer that a united Methodism co-operating with all other Christians may be a chosen instrument in hastening the day when brotherhood and that peace which passeth all understanding will supplant greed and hate of war. That must be the goal of Christendom today. May its coming be hastened by the spirit that has guided the action of the first great Conference of the United Methodists in the new world.

With faith strengthened by the spirit of the deliberation and the declaration of this Uniting Conference, I am,.
Faithfully yours, JOSEPHUS DANIELS.

(margin: MAY 8 TWELFTH DAY Afternoon Letter from Josephus Daniels)

By common consent the letter was received for record and the Secretary was requested to make suitable reply.

The result of the second ballot for members of the Judicial Council was announced as follows by Bishop Lester H. Smith:

(margin: Result of Second Ballot for Members of Judicial Council)

Total number of votes cast, 820; votes counted, 820; necessary for a choice, 411. George R. Brown, North Carolina, 568; Henry R. Van Deusen, Wyoming, 497; Vincent P. Clarke, New England, 493; M. A. Childers, West Texas, 480.

George R. Brown, Henry R. VanDeuseń, Vincent P. Clarke, and M. A. Childers, each having received the required majority, were declared elected members of the Judicial Council of The Methodist Church.

The Secretary then read the complete returns of the second ballot, as follows:

Ministers from the Methodist Episcopal Church: Walter C. Buckner, Southern California, 225; Ernest S. Lyons, Los Angeles, Calif., 194; Sanford W. Corcoran, Pittsburgh, 150; Charles B. Ketcham, Northeast Ohio, 141; Mark Kelley, Troy, 49; Leslie R. Burgum, North Dakota, 45; Carl K. Mahoney, Pacific Northwest, 4; Henry W. Bartlay, Florida, 2.

Laymen from the Methodist Episcopal Church: Henry R. Van Deusen, Wyoming, 497; Vincent P. Clarke, New England, 493; James I. Dolliver, Northwest Iowa, 189; Benjamin A. Matthews, New York, 176; Howard C. Bald-

MAY 8
TWELFTH DAY

Afternoon

Result of Second Ballot
for Members
of Judicial
Council
win, Detroit, 110; Joseph B. Randolph, South Carolina, 38; Sidney R. Redmond, Central West, 35; Fred C. Huebner, Iowa-Des Moines, 23; Fred B. Noble, Saint Johns River, 23; William H. Spurgeon, Colorado, 22; William H. Wilcox, Oklahoma, 16; Jacob Cantlin, Rock River, 10.

Ministers from the Methodist Protestant Church: George R. Brown, North Carolina, 568; A. J. Allen, Pittsburgh, 171; S. W. Rosenberger, Ohio, 76; G. I. Humphreys, Maryand, 1.

Ministers from the Methodist Episcopal Church, South: W. G. Henry, North Georgia, 360; A. C. Millar, Little Rock, 128; B. R. Turnipseed, Upper South Carolina, 92; A. J. Weeks, North Texas, 65; J. B. Craven, Western North Carolina, 58; J. W. Johnson, North Georgia, 52; W. L. Duren, Louisiana, 32; J. W. Bergin, Central Texas, 27; J. Richard Spann, Louisiana, 8.

Laymen from the Methodist Episcopal Church, South: M. A. Childers, West Texas, 480; Nathan Newby, Pacific, 185; R. L. Flowers, North Carolina, 46; O. A. Park, South George, 23; W. F. McMurry, Memphis, 18; R. B. Carr, North Alabama, 14; M. C. Redwine, Kentucky, 10; S. G. Bratton, New Mexico, 7; J. G. McGowen, North Mississippi, 7; G. H. Lamar, Baltimore, 2; H. B. McGinnis, Tennessee, 2; J. H. Carlock, Oklahoma, 1; C. E. Mead, New Mexico, 1.

The third ballot for members of the Judicial Council was spread. The votes were collected, the ballot declared officially closed, and the Tellers retired to determine the result.

Calendar No. 39, Report No. 2 of the Committee on Rituals and Orders of Worship, printed on page 294 of the *Daily Christian Advocate*, was presented by Oscar T. Olson, Chairman, who explained the report and moved its adoption. The motion, duly seconded, prevailed. For report, see Appendix, "General Standing Committees," page 679.

Calendar No. 40, Report No. 3 of the Committee on Rituals and Orders of Worship, printed on pages 294, 295, and 296 of the *Daily Christian Advocate*, was presented by Oscar T. Olson, Chairman, who explained its provisions and moved its adoption. The motion was duly seconded.

Nolan B. Harmon, Jr., Baltimore, moved to amend the report by striking out in "Section V, The Burial of the Dead," the passage of Scripture taken from 2 Samuel 12: 16-23 and found printed on page 296, column 2 of the *Daily Christian Advocate*, the motion duly seconded, prevailed.

Chester A. Smith, New York, moved to amend

the report by substituting the word "cup" for the word "wine" at the end of the third line from the bottom, in the first column of page 305 of the Prospectus, and then in the fourteenth line of the paragraph following the Prayer of Consecration, page 295 of the *Daily Christian Advocate*, first column, change the words "these thy creatures of bread and wine" to read "this bread and this cup." The motion being duly seconded, Brother Smith spoke to the question.

MAY 8
TWELFTH DAY
Afternoon
Committee on
Rituals and
Orders of
Worship.
Report No. 3

Daniel L. Marsh, New England, spoke against the amendment.

The amendment was not adopted.

The report, as amended, was adopted. For report, see Appendix, "General Standing Committees," page 699.

Calendar No. 41, Report No. 4 of the Committee on Rituals and Orders of Worship, printed on pages 296 and 297 of the *Daily Christian Advocate*, was presented by Oscar T. Olson, Chairman, who moved its adoption. The motion, duly seconded, prevailed. For report, see Appendix, "General Standing Committee," page 797.

Bishop H. Lester Smith announced that the Seminary Singers of Boston University were to return to Boston early tomorrow morning and requested that they sing for the Conference.

Under the leadership of Dr. James R. Houghton they rendered "The Nicene Creed," the Conference standing during its rendition. The final number of the Boston Seminary Singers was "The Pilgrim's Chorus" from the opera of Tannhauser by Wagner.

The Conference rose and applauded.

Bishop Smith, in well chosen words, in behalf of the Uniting Conference thanked Dr. Houghton and the Seminary Singers for the contribution they had made to the inspiration and success of the Conference. Dr. Houghton replied appropriately.

Horace G. Smith, Rock River, moved "That the records of the Uniting Conference show our high appreciation of the great contribution the chorus singers have made to the life and work of this Conference, and that we pray God to grant them mercies as they return to 72 Mt. Vernon, and make

⁸ them fruitful in all good works as they move out
DAY into the ministry of our great Church."
oon   , Arlo A. Brown, New Jersey, seconded the motion, which was unanimously adopted by the
Uniting Conference.

Oscar E. Allison, Kansas, was recognized for a
matter of privilege. He called attention to the
last paragraph of Report No. 1 of the Committee
on Judiciary, appearing on page 231 of the *Daily
Christian Advocate,* and moved that in the light
of this paragraph the following be referred to the
Committee on Judiciary for an opinion:

> Does the Committee on Judiciary now find the delegates
> of the South Central Jurisdiction were within their rights
> in changing Conference boundary lines in Kansas so as
> to make two Conferences instead of three, thus merging
> the Northwest Kansas Conference and Southwest Kansas
> Conference and somewhat altering the lines of the Kansas
> Conference, as reported in Report No. 1, Committee on
> South Central Jurisdiction, page 256, the *Daily Christian
> Advocate?*

The motion, duly seconded, prevailed.

Third   The results of the third ballot for members of
for   the Judicial Council were announced by Bishop
rs of   Smith, as follows:
1
1

> Ballots cast, 798; ballots counted, 798; necessary for
> a choice, 400. W. G. Henry, North Georgia, 672; Walter
> C. Buckner, Southern California, 532.

W. G. Henry and Walter C. Buckner, each having received the required majority, were declared
elected members of the Judicial Council of The
Methodist Church. This ballot completed the election of the Judicial Council.

The Secretary read the complete result of the
third ballot, as follows:

> Ministers from the Methodist Episcopal Church: Walter
> C. Buckner, Southern California, 532; Ernest S. Lyons,
> Los Angeles, Calif., 109; Sanford W. Corcoran, Pittsburgh,
> 68; Charles B. Ketcham, Northeast Ohio, 59; Leslie R.
> Burgum, North Dakota, 14; Mark Kelley, Troy, 8; Carl
> K. Mahoney, Pacific Northwest, 1.
>
> Ministers from the Methodist Episcopal Church, South:
> W. G. Henry, North Georgia, 672; A. C. Millar, Little
> Rock, 36; B. R. Turnipseed, Upper South Carolina, 20;
> A. J. Weeks, North Texas, 20; J. B. Craven, Western
> North Carolina, 19; W. L. Duren, Louisiana, 6; J. W.
> Johnson, North Georgia, 6; J. W. Bergin, Central Texas,
> 1; J. Richard Spann, Louisiana, 1.

The Methodist Church

The Judicial Council is composed of the following:
Ministers—Francis R. Bayley (1), Walter C. Buckner
(3), George R. Brown (2), J. Stewart French (1), W. G.
Henry (3). Laymen—Vincent P. Clarke (2), Henry R.
Van Deusen (2), M. A. Childers (2), Martin E. Lawson
(1). (Note: the figures in parentheses ( ) indicate the
ballot on which the member was elected.)

Motion of Óscar T. Olson, duly seconded, prevailed that we take the first ballot for alternate
members of the Judicial Council.

The Chair announced that William D. Archer,
Northeast Ohio, would serve as Teller in Section A.

The first ballot was spread for alternate members of the Judicial Council. The votes were collected, the ballot declared officially closed, and the
Tellers retired to determine the result.

Motion of William C. Hartinger, Indiana, duly
seconded, prevailed that after the necessary announcements we adjourn, to meet at 7: 45 P.M.

Various announcements were made and the
Conference adjourned with the benediction pronounced by Bishop H. Lester Smith.

MONDAY EVENING, MAY 8, 1939

Pursuant to adjournment, the Conference convened in evening session, Monday, May 8, at 7:45
o'clock, with Bishop Ivan Lee Holt in the chair.

Bishop Holt announced and the Conference
joined in singing Hymn 73, "Be Still, My Soul:
The Lord Is on Thy Side."

At the request of Bishop Holt, Dr. Ralph W.
Sockman, New York, Chairman of the World
Peace Commission of the former Methodist Episcopal Church, conducted the devotions. Dr. Sockman read a Scripture lesson from Luke 4: 16-21
and led in prayer.

Bishop Holt introduced the speaker of the evening, Dr. Albert W. Palmer, President of Chicago
Theological Seminary. Dr. Palmer addressed the
Conference on the social message of the Church,
discussing the question, "Can We Build a Christian Social Order?" For address, see Appendix,
"Addresses," page 906.

At the close of the address the following telegram was read by the Secretary:

Chicago, Ill., May 5, 1939.
Bishop Ivan Lee Holt, Kansas City, Mo.
Because of our conviction that religion is the source of

MAY 8
TWELFTH DAY
Afternoon

First Ballot for Alternate Members of Judicial Council

Announcements

Adjournment

MAY 8
TWELFTH DAY
Evening Opening

Albert W. Palmer Addresses Conference

Telegram

MAY 8
TWELFTH DAY
Evening

a nation's strength and that the welfare and happiness of our citizens are intimately associated with the place that religion is accorded in our national life, the Co-Chairmen of the National Conference of Christians and Jews send greetings to the Uniting Conference of Methodism in Kansas City now engaged in a task of great moment to those of every religious faith and extend good wishes for the successful conclusion of its labors.

ARTHUR H. COMPTON,
CARLTON J. H. HAYES,
ROGER WILLIAMS STRAUS.

Concerning Woman's Night

On a matter of privilege, the Chair recognized Mrs. Thomas Nicholson, Upper Iowa, who read the following:

The early closing of the Uniting Conference has eliminated the program for Woman's Night. As members of the Program Committee we wish to extend here our gratitude to Mrs. Fred A. Lamb, Chairman of the Local Committee of Woman's Activities, and to Mrs. William C. Hanson, Chairman of the Local Program Committee, and to many who co-operated in the preparation of a colorful, impressive, and informational program to which the women throughout this whole section were planning to come.

We thank the Missouri Pacific Railroad for their promise to run a special train from other parts of the State.

We express our appreciation to Dr. Georgia Harkness, who was to fly from Mount Holyoke to speak on the topic, "What Price Unity?"

May we also express to the Local Committee our sincere thanks on behalf of the women of the Conference, and on our own behalf for many courtesies extended by the Local Committee to the women in attendance on the Uniting Conference.

MRS. J. W. SHELL,
President Woman's Convention of the Methodist Protestant Church;
MRS. J. W. PERRY,
President of the Woman's Missionary Council, Methodist Episcopal Church, South;
MRS. THOMAS NICHOLSON,
President of the Woman's Foreign Missionary Society of the Methodist Episcopal Church;
MRS. W. H. C. GOODE,
President of the Woman's Home Mission Society of the Methodist Episcopal Church.

By common consent, the message was received and ordered to record.

Temperance, Prohibition, Public Morals

Ernest H. Cherrington, Ohio, was recognized for a privileged motion. Dr. Cherrington moved the following:

I move that the Editors of the *Discipline* be instructed to include in the forthcoming *Discipline* of The Methodist

Church, the legislation, advices, and pronouncements in Paragraph 655 of the 1938 *Discipline* of the Methodist Episcopal Church, South, and Paragraphs 166 and 1465 of the 1936 *Discipline* of the Methodist Episcopal Church, with authority to make such editorial revision as may seem necessary or desirable, but preserving the substance of those paragraphs which set forth the attitude of Methodism on Temperance, Prohibition, and Public Morals. MAY 8 TWELFTH DAY *Evening*

The motion, duly seconded, prevailed.

Motion of the Secretary, duly seconded, prevailed suspending the Rules in order that reports appearing in the *Daily Christian Advocate* of May 8, 1939, might be taken up and acted upon. Calendar

Calendar No. 44, Report No. 9 of the Committee on Conferences, printed on pages 299 to 302 inclusive of the *Daily Christian Advocate* and entitled "Central Conferences," was presented by George W. Henson, Philadelphia, Chairman. Dr. Henson requested Lewis O. Hartman, New England, Chairman of the Subcommittee which prepared the report, to present and explain the repor . Committee on Conferences, Report No. 9 —"Central Conferences"

Dr. Hartman stated that the net cost of administration under The Methodist Church would be less than administering through the three constituent former Churches. He requested common consent to make the following corrections, which was granted by the Conference:

Designate the subheads in the "paragraphs" by figures in parentheses ( ) instead of using the term "Section."

Paragraph 143, fifth line, the word "General" should read "Central."

Section III, Paragraph 148 (3), "Section 3, Paragraph 2," should read "Paragraph 148 (2)."

The time of the speaker having expired, motion of J. T. Elliston, Alabama, duly seconded, prevailed extending Dr. Hartman's time until he could finish explaining and presenting the report.

Section IV, Paragraph 149 (4), sixth line, after the words "shall be fixed by the," insert the words "Committee administering the"; line 8, after the word "with" at the beginning of the line insert the words "representatives of." Begin the next sentence with a capital "A" and change the word "Conferences" to "Conference."

Section IV, Paragraph 149 (12), the word "elective," fourth line from the bottom, should read "election of."

Section V (2), add after the word "India," in the fourth line, the words "and Burma."

MAY 8
TWELFTH DAY
Evening
Committee on
Conferences,
Report No. 9
—"Central
Confer-
ences"

Section VI, Paragraph 152, strike out the words "Dhulia Mission (M.P.)" at beginning of the paragraph.

Section VI, Paragraph 156, insert after "Finland Annual Conference (M.E.)" the words "Finland-Swedish Annual Conference (M.E.)"

Enabling Acts, Paragraph 160, line 5, insert after the words "Central Conference" the words "or otherwise."

Enabling Acts, Paragraph 160, strike out the word "now" at the beginning of the second line of the second paragraph.

Enabling Acts, Paragraph 162, second line, insert after the word "Provisional" the word "Central."

Enabling Acts, Paragraph 163, last line, strike out the word "Foreign."

Dr. Hartman then moved the adoption of the report and the motion was duly seconded.

Ralph E. Diffendorfer, Rock River, asked what was meant by the phrase "co-ordinate authority" in line 5 of Paragraph 145. Dr. Hartman answered the question and Dr. Diffendorfer moved to amend by changing the wording from "co-ordinate authority with" to "authority similar to that exercised by." This was accepted by the Chairman.

Dr. Diffendorfer raised a question relating to Section VII, Paragraph 157 (4), asking why Japan and Korea were listed among the Provisional Central Conferences and stated that he thought the entire Section 4 should be omitted from the list because they are not in any sense Provisonal Central Conferences. Dr. Hartman replied that the question is answered in Paragraph 157 and that the grouping in Section 4 is purely for the time being for administrative purposes. This was satisfactory to Dr. Diffendorfer.

Dr. Diffendorfer moved to amend Section IV, Paragraph 149 (3), second paragraph, by striking out all that follows the words "Central Conference," in line 3. The motion being duly seconded, Dr. Diffendorfer spoke to the question.

Dr. Hartman spoke against the amendment. The amendment was not adopted.

Willard G. Cram, Kentucky, moved to amend Enabling Acts, Paragraph 159, by striking out the word "and" in line 4 immediately preceding the words "Central Mission Conferences" and inserting a comma in its place; in the same line, after the word "Conferences," place a comma and add the words "Annual Conferences, Mission Confer-

ences, and Missions." The motion was duly sec- MAY 8
onded. Dr. Hartman stated that he would accept TWELFTH DAY
the amendment for the Committee if there was no Evening
objection. No objections was raised and the Committee on
amendment was accepted by common consent. Report No. 9
George C. Douglass, Troy, raised the question Confer-
as to where this report shows the method of sup- ences"
port for the Central Conference Bishops. Dr.
Hartman replied that it would be found in Section
IV (4). Dr. Douglass, after this explanation,
moved to amend Section IV (4) by adding "That
the General Conference shall fix the amount of
grant-in-aid necessary until such time as the said
Central Conferences shall be able to provide complete support for such Bishops or General Superintendents." The motion was duly seconded.
Dr. Hartman spoke for the report as printed.
The amendment was not adopted.

J. P. Bartak, Czechoslovak, moved to amend
Section IV (17) by substituting the word "fifteen"
for the word "twenty" found in the last line. The
motion, duly seconded, prevailed.

William K. Anderson, Pittsburgh, asked if the
wording of Section II, Paragraph 144, was correct. Dr. Hartman replied that the point was
well taken and that the English was not good.
Dr. Anderson then moved that the Chairman of
the Committee be authorized to edit Paragraph
144 correctly. The motion, duly seconded, prevailed.

The report was adopted as amended. For report, see Appendix, "General Standing Committees," page 434.

Orien W. Fifer, Indiana, moved that the Rules
be suspended in order to present the Report of
the Committee on Ministry and Judicial Administration concerning the assignment of the Bishops
to their Jurisdictional Conferences and their residences. The motion, duly seconded, prevailed.

Dr. Fifer then presented the report as follows:

REPORT OF COMMITTEE ON MINISTRY AND
JUDICIAL ADMINISTRATION

The Assignment of Bishops to Jurisdictions and to Assignments
Residences follows (first the Jurisdictions, then the names of Bishops
of the Bishops within the Jurisdiction, then their assignments):

326   *Journal of the Uniting Conference*

MAY 8
TWELFTH DAY
Evening,
Assignments
of Bishops

Northeastern Jurisdiction: Bishop G. Bromley Oxnam, Boston; Bishop F. J. McConnell, New York; Bishop Ernest G. Richardson, Philadelphia; Bishop Adna W. Leonard, Pittsburgh; Bishop Charles W. Flint, Syracuse; Bishop Edwin H. Hughes, Washington.

Southeastern Jurisdiction: Bishop J. Lloyd Decell, Birmingham; Bishop William T. Watkins, Atlanta; Bishop Clare Purcell, Charlotte; Bishop Hoyt M. Dobbs, Jackson; Bishop U. V. W. Darlington, Louisville; Bishop Paul B. Kern, Nashville; Bishop William W. Peele, Richmond.

North Central Jurisdiction: Bishop Ernest L. Waldorf, Chicago; Bishop H. Lester Smith, Cincinnati; Bishop Edgar Blake, Detroit; Bishop J. Ralph Magee, Des Moines; Bishop Titue Lowe, Indianapolis; Bishop Ralph S. Cushman, St. Paul.

South Central Jurisdiction: Bishop Ivan Lee Holt, Dallas; Bishop A. Frank Smith, Houston; Bishop Charles L. Mead, Kansas City; Bishop Charles C. Selecman, Oklahoma City; Bishop William C. Martin, Omaha; Bishop John C. Broomfield, St. Louis.

Western Juristiction: Bishop Wilbur E. Hammaker, Denver; Bishop Wallace E. Brown, Portland; Bishop James C. Baker, Los Angeles.

Central Jurisdiction: Bishop Robert E. Jones, Columbus; Bishop Alexander P. Shaw, New Orleans.

Assignments to Foreign Fields: Bishop John L. Nuelsen, Geneva—North Central Jurisdiction. Bishop Raymond J. Wade, Stockholm—North Central Jurisdiction. Bishop Brenton C. Badley, Dehli—Northeastern Jurisdiction.

Missionary Bishops: Bishop Edwin F. Lee, Singapore-Manila—North Central Jurisdiction. Bishop John M. Springer, Elisabethville, Belgian Congo—Northeastern Jurisdiction.

Special Assignments: In accordance with the action of this Uniting Conference we recommend that the Council of Bishops assign Bishop Arthur J. Moore, attached to the Southeastern Jurisdiction, for special service outside the United States, and Bishop James H. Straughn, attached to the Northeastern Jurisdiction, to special service within the United States.

In view of the recommendation with reference to Bishop Arthur J. Moore and Bishop James H. Straughn, we recommend that they be permitted to select their own places of residence within their respective Jurisdictions until the next General Conference.

ORIEN W. FIFER, *Chairman;*
FRANK L. SHAFFER, *Secretary.*

Dr. Fifer moved the adoption of the report. The motion, duly seconded, prevailed.

Offering   By common consent an offering was taken for the Entertainment Fund in behalf of the Local Committee.

J. W. Mills, Texas, moved that after announcements we adjourn. The motion, duly seconded, did not prevail.

Calendar No. 45, Report No. 4 of the Committee on Education, printed on page 320 of the *Daily Christian Advocate* and entitled "Commission on World Peace," was presented by Paul Quillian, Texas, Chairman, who explained its provisions. Dr. Quillian asked common consent to insert the words "method of" in line 5 after the words "the same." Common consent was granted. Dr. Quillian moved the adoption of the report. The motion, duly seconded, prevailed. ' For report, see Appendix, "General Standing Committees," page 602.

MAY 8
TWELFTH DAY
Evening
Committee on
Education,
Report No. 4
—"Commis-
sion on
World
Peace"

Calendar No. 46, Report No. 6 of the Committee on Education, printed on pages 302 and 303 of the *Daily Christian Advocate* and entitled "Ministerial Education; Standards," was presented by Paul Quillian, Texas, Chairman. Dr. Quillian called attention to a stenographic error in leaving out some words and asked common consent to insert them, as follows: In line 19 insert after the words "budget askings for their" the words "adequate support. After an adequate presentation of the claims of these."

Committee on
Education,
Report No. 6
—"Ministe-
rial Educa-
tion;
Standards"

Common consent was granted for the correction.

Dr. Quillian requested Charles E. Schofield, Colorado, Chairman of the Subcommittee on this matter, to present the report.

Dr. Schofield explained the report and moved its adoption.

J. C. McPheeters, Pacific, moved to amend Paragraph 1048 by inserting in lines 8 and 10, after the word "Senate," the following words: "or the State University, or the educational accrediting agency of the State in which the institution is located." The motion being duly seconded, Dr. McPheeters spoke to the question.

John L. Seaton, Michigan, spoke in opposition to the amendment.

A. Wesley Pugh, North Indiana, spoke in favor of the amendment.

Dr. Schofield spoke in favor of the report. The motion was put and the amendment was not adopted.

A. Wesley Pugh, North Indiana, moved to amend Paragraph 1063 by adding at the end of the paragraph these words: "The requirements of

MAY 8
TWELFTH DAY
Evening
Committee on
Education,
Report No. 6
—"Ministe-
rial Educa-
tion;
Standards"

this paragraph shall not apply to Accepted Supply Pastors who have previously completed the Course of Study as prescribed for Local Preachers." This was accepted by the Chairman for the Committee.

The report was adopted. For report, see Appendix, "General Standing Committees," page 603.

W. F. Bryan, Texas, moved that we do now adjourn. The motion, duly seconded, prevailed.

Announce-
ments

After various announcements the Conference

Adjournment

adjourned with the benediction pronounced by Bishop Edgar Blake.

TUESDAY MORNING, MAY 9' 1939

MAY 9
THIRTEENTH
DAY
Morning
Opening

The Uniting Conference convened in the session of the thirteenth day on Tuesday, May 9, at 8:30 A.M., with Bishop Francis J. McConnell in the chair. Bishop McConnell announced that the devotional service would be conducted by Bishop Jashwant R. Chitambar of India and the address of the morning would be given by Bishop William T. Watkins. Bishop Watkins, citing the experiences of the early Christians found in the Book of Acts, challenged The Methodist Church to face and meet three great tasks as the early disciples met them, namely: the task of evangelism, the demands of human brotherhood, and the missionary demand.

Bishop McConnell called the Conference to be in business session at 9 A.M.

Journal

The Report of the Committee on Journal was adopted, as follows:

> Your Committee has separately examined the Journal of the sessions of yesterday morning and yesterday afternoon, and find both correct.
>
> JOSEPH D. PIPER, *Chairman;*
> JOHN R. KENNEY, *Secretary.*

Assistant
Secretaries

On nomination of the Secretary, Dr. Harry L. Upperman and Mrs. Alice Hardy were confirmed as Assistants to the Journal Secretary.

Committee on
Credentials,
Report No.
10

Earl R. Brown, Northeast Ohio, Chairman of the Committee on Credentials, presented Report No. 10 and moved that it be adopted and made a part of the Journal of the Uniting Conference.

The motion, duly seconded, prevailed. For report, see Appendix, "Special Standing Committees," page 839.

Motion of Earl R. Brown, Chairman, duly seconded, prevailed that the Committee on Credentials be authorized to complete the work of approving future changes in seating and to file with the Secretary of the Uniting Conference the final list without formal action, and that this list shall become a part of the official Journal.

On behalf of the Committee, Dr. Brown presented the following:

MAY 9
THIRTEENTH
DAY

Morning

Committee on
Credentials,
Report No.
10

The members of the Committee on Credentials wish to express to our Secretary, Mr. Charles A. Robbins, our deep appreciation for his painstaking and efficient work in checking all changes in seating and preparing the daily reports for publication.

Motion of Dr. Brown, duly seconded, unanimously prevailed adopting the resolution.

The result of the first ballot for alternate members of the Judicial Council was announced by Bishop McConnell, as follows:

Result of First
Ballot for
Alternate
Members of
Judicial
Council

Ballots cast, 693; ballots counted, 693; necessary for a choice, 347.. A. J. Allen, Pittsburgh, 555; Nathan Newby, Pacific, 513; Ernest S. Lyons, Los Angeles, Calif., 484; James I. Dolliver, Northwest Iowa, 408; Sanford W. Corcoran, Pittsburgh, 394; Benjamin A. Matthews, New York, 392.

A. J. Allen, Nathan Newby, Ernest S. Lyons, James I. Dolliver, Sanford W. Corcoran, and Benjamin A. Matthews, each having received the required majority, were declared elected alternate members of the Judicial Council of The Methodist Church.

The complete result of the ballot was read by the Secretary, as follows:

Ministers from the Methodist Episcopal Church: Ernest S. Lyons, Los Angeles, Calif., 484; Sanford W. Corcoran, Pittsburgh, 394; Charles B. Ketcham, Northeast Ohio, 251; Leslie R. Burgum, North Dakota, 113; Mark Kelley, Troy, 90; Carl K. Mahoney, Pacific Northwest, 9; Henry W. Bartlay, Florida, 5.

Laymen from the Methodist Episcopal Church: James I. Dolliver, Northwest Iowa, 408; Benjamin A. Matthews, New York, 392; Howard C. Baldwin, Detroit, 225; Joseph B. Randolph, South Carolina, 57; Fred B. Noble, Saint Johns River, 54; William H. Spurgeon, Colorado, 52;

MAY 9
THIRTEENTH
DAY

Morning

Result of First
Ballot for
Alternate
Members of
Judicial
Council

Sidney R. Redmond, Central West, 41; William H. Wilcox, Oklahoma, 40; Fred C. Heubner, Iowa-Des Moines, 31; Jacob Cantlin, Rock River, 21.

Ministers from the Methodist Protestant Church: A. J. Allen, Pittsburgh, 555; S. W. Rosenberger, Ohio, 112; G. I. Humphreys, Maryland, 7.

Ministers from the Methodist Episcopal Church, South: A. C. Millar, Little Rock, 340; B. R. Turnipseed, Upper South Carolina, 287; A. J. Weeks, North Texas, 217; J. B. Cravan, Western North Carolina, 142; J. W. Johnson, North Georgia, 135; W. L. Duren, Louisiana, 100; J. W. Bergin, Central Texas, 95; J. Richard Spann, Louisiana, 45.

Laymen from the Methodist Episcopal Church, South: Nathan Newby, Pacific, 513; R. L. Flowers, North Carolina, 321; W. F. McMurry, Memphis, 126; O. A. Park, South Georgia, 98; R. B. Carr, North Alabama, 66; M. C. Redwine, Kentucky, 51; G. H. Lamar, Baltimore, 43; J. G. McGowen, North Mississippi, 33; H. B. McGinnis, Tennessee, 32; S. G. Bratton, New Mexico, 25; J. H. Carlock, Oklahoma, 23; H. H. White, Louisiana, 20; C. E. Mead, New Mexico, 9; T. D. Samford, Alabama, 3.

Second Ballot
for Alternate Members of Judicial Council

The second ballot was spread for alternate members of the Judicial Council. Boyce Martin, Central Texas, was announced to serve as Teller in the place of Clarence M. Dannelly, Alabama. The ballot was taken, the votes collected, the ballot was officially declared closed, and the Tellers retired to determine the result.

T. D. Ellis

Thomas D. Ellis, South Georgia, was recognized on a matter of personal privilege and made the following statement:

It is not my purpose to criticize those who have given us the fine record of this Conference, but I cannot permit one statement to go without correction. It states in the *Daily Christian Advocate*, page 318, "I have never found any Bishop to have the backing of the Church." I did not say that. What I tried to say is, "It will help the great program to be brought forward by the Bishops to have the backing of this Conference and of the Church."

Committee on
Judiciary,
Report No. 6

Francis R. Bayley, Baltimore, Chairman, presented Report No. 6 of the Committee on Judiciary. Dr. Bayley explained its provisions and moved its adoption. The motion, duly seconded, prevailed. For report, see Appendix, "Special Standing Committees," page 821.

As a matter of privilege Dr. Bayley requested that the duly elected Judicial Council be excused for a special matter. The request was granted by common consent.

Lewis O. Hartman, New England, presented the following motion:

MAY 9
THIRTEENTH
DAY
Morning
Central Con-
ferences

I move that to the Central Conferences, to the Provisional Central Conferences, and to the Annual Conferences, Mission Conferences, and Missions within their territory, permission be given to embody in parentheses the word "Episcopal" between the words "Methodist" and "Church" in the official title "The Methodist Church."

The motion being duly seconded, Dr. Hartman spoke to the question. The motion prevailed.

Innis D. Harris, Southwest Kansas, under a question of privilege, moved the reference of the following matter to the Committee on Judiciary:

Referred

In view of the fact that in the recent formation of the boundaries of the West Oklahoma Conference, by the South Central Jurisdiction, as it appears on page 258 of the *Daily Christian Advocate*, Report No. 1, Section 3, that in the formation of these boundary lines, long established by the Methodist Episcopal Church and the Methodist Episcopal Church, South, involving the territory known as the Panhandle, it is respectfully asked by the three Conferences involved—namely, the Southwest Kansas Conference, the Northwest Texas Conference, and the West Oklahoma Conference—that this matter be referred to the Committee on Judiciary for a decision as to its legality.

IRA M. HARGITT, *Chairman, West Oklahoma Conference;*
J. O. HAYES, *Chairman, Northwest Texas Conference;*
INNIS D. HARRIS, *Chairman, Southwest Kansas Conference.*

The motion, duly seconded, prevailed.

George H. Lamar, Baltimore, raised a point of order in connection with the motion of L. O. Hartman relative to the Central Conferences, stating that the action taken was not within the power of this body according to the Plan of Union, and suggested that the matter be referred to the Committee on Judiciary. Point of
Order

The Chair stated that the action would have to be reconsidered to refer. L. O. Hartman moved that we reconsider the action. The motion, duly seconded, prevailed, and reconsideration was ordered.

On motion of L. O. Hartman, duly seconded, the matter was referred to the Committee on Judiciary. Referred

Stanley O. MacMullen, New England, moved that we do now take up the Calendar. The motion, duly seconded, prevailed. Calendar

9
NTH
g

Arthur M. Wells, Illinois, stated that the Committee on Enabling Acts and Legal Forms was ready to report, and that Committee Reports come before the Calendar. The Chair ruled the point well taken.

Edward R. Carman, New York East, under the question of privilege, presented the following:

A TRIBUTE TO FRANK A. HORNE

"Men are of two kinds, and he
Was of the kind I'd like to be."

He was born in Brooklyn, N. Y., February 25, 1869, and at an early age entered the business world and became a man of note, influence, and prominence.

From his youth to the day of his death he was very active in the work of the Lord Jesus and His Church. Elected superintendent of Simpson Sunday School while still in his teens, he made such an impression that he was appointed to the Board of Foreign Missions of the Methodist Episcopal Church and served many years, finally becoming Vice-President thereof.

In his local church he was Chairman of its governing body.

For more than twenty-five years a member of the Book Committee of the Methodist Episcopal Church, for years Chairman of its Executive Committee and in May, 1932, Chairman of the Book Committee; President of the Lay Conference of the New York East Conference; President of the Methodist Hospital in Brooklyn, N. Y,; Vice-President of the Brooklyn and Long Island Church Society; member of the Advisory Board of the Methodist Home; Trustee of Drew and Goucher Colleges; and a member of six General Conferences, 1916 to 1936.

Elected a delegate to this Uniting Conference and appointed by the Joint Commission to the Committee on Publishing Interests, he aided in the preparation of that part of the Prospectus relating to this interest.

He was truly a servant of God, "a workman that needeth not to be ashamed."

Dr. Horne departed this life March 22, 1939.

"And when he passed, I think there went
A soul to yonder firmament
So white, so splendid, and so fine
It came almost to God's design."

JOHN W. LANGDALE,	H. ALMON CHAFFEE,
LYNN HAROLD HOUGH,	MAUDE W. HARDIE,
FRED B. NEWELL,	WILLIAM H. BARRADELL.
EDWARD R. CARMAN,	

Brother Carman moved that the paper be received and go to record in the Journal of the Uniting Conference. The motion, seconded by Chester A. Smith, New York, prevailed.

Frank B. Jones, Memphis, on a question of privilege, announced that Dr. G. L. Morelock, a member of the Memphis Conference delegation and General Secretary of the General Board of Lay Activities of the Methodist Episcopal Church, South, had been ill throughout the sessions of the Uniting Conference and was now a patient in Trinity Hospital, Kansas City, Mo.

By common consent the Rules were suspended to take up and act upon reports printed in the *Daily Christian Advocate* of today, May 9.

Arthur A. Callaghan, Maine, Chairman, presented Report No. 1 of the Committee on Enabling Acts and Legal Forms, printed on pages 367 and 368 of the *Daily Christian Advocate*. Dr. Callaghan requested W. M. Alexander, Missouri, to help in the presentation of the report.

Dr. Callaghan stated that there were some typographical errors in Section 1. The word "between" in the third line should read "before." Dr. Callaghan stated that there was some editorial work needed on the whole paragraph. Dr. Callaghan explained the report Section by Section and moved its adoption. His time expiring before the complete presentation of the report, motion of Aubrey S. Moore, Rock River, duly seconded, prevailed extending Dr. Callaghan's time until he could complete its presentation.

Henry M. Greenslit, Nebraska, raised the question as to whether or not this body is satisfied to have nothing as our Constitution other than the Plan of Union, which is found in the first seven lines of Section 13. The Chairman replied: "It seemed to the Committee on Enabling Acts and Legal Forms that, inasmuch as the Constitution had been set up, we could not go much further than that."

John R. Edwards, Baltimore, moved to amend Section 7 by adding, "The Publishing Agents of the Book Concern, in correspondence with the Benevolence Boards, are authorized to furnish statistical blanks for use in Annual Conferences." This was accepted by the Chairman.

The report was adopted. For report, see Appendix, "Special Standing Committees," page 798.

Report No. 2 of the Committee on Enabling Acts and Legal Forms was presented by Arthur

MAY 9
THIRTEENTH DAY

Morning
G. L. Morelock

Committee on Enabling Acts and Legal Forms, Report No. 1

Committee on Enabling Acts and Legal Forms, Report No. 2

Committee on
Enabling
Acts and
Legal
Forms, Re-
port No. 2

A. Callaghan, Maine, Chairman, who explained the provisions of the report and moved its adoption. The motion was duly seconded.

W. C. Perkins, Pittsburgh, raised the question as to whether or not the word "Boards," in the fourth line of Section 2, should not read "Committees."

Nathan Newby, Pacific, was recognized and stated that the wording of the Section was in the exact language proposed by the brethren of the Methodist Protestant Church.

C. W. Bates, North Carolina, Secretary of the last General Conference of the Methodist Protestant Church, was recognized and stated, "I am sure the language here is what was intended."

The report was adopted. For report, see Appendix, "Special Standing Committees," page 802.

Death of Mrs.
E. A.
Sexsmith

Leonard B. Smith, Maryland, under a question of high personal privilege, announced the sudden death of Mrs. E. A. Sexsmith, the wife of the President of the Maryland Conference, Methodist Protestant Church, and moved that the Uniting Conference appropriately express itself in offering sympathy to our bereaved brother, Dr. E. A. Sexsmith, a member of this Uniting Conference. The motion, duly seconded, was unanimously adopted.

Committee on
Membership
and Tem-
poral Econ-
omy, Report
No. 5—"Fi-
nancial
Plan"

The Order of the Day having arrived, Calendar No. 42, Report No. 5 of the Committee on Membership and Temporal Economy, printed on page 297 of the *Daily Christian Advocate* and entitled "Financial Plan," was presented by W. F. Bryan, Texas, Chairman. Dr. Bryan requested Orrin W. Auman, Colorado, James A. James, Rock River, J. L. Green, Maryland, and Costen J. Harrell, Tennessee, to come to the platform to assist in presenting the report.

Dr. Bryan stated that the proposed legislation would materially decrease the overhead. He also called attention to the following typographical errors: Paragraph 500, line 6, change the word "their" to the word "the"; line 7, change the word "and" to the word "of." Dr. Bryan then began an explanation of the provisions of the report. His time expiring, motion of John F. Baggett, Ten-

nessee, duly seconded, prevailed extending the
time to finish the explanation of the report. Completing the explanation, Dr. Bryan moved the
adoption of the report. The motion, duly seconded, prevailed. For report, see Appendix,
"General Standing Committees," page 526.

Calendar No. 43, Report No. 5-A of the Committee on Membership and Temporal Economy,
printed on pages 297, 298, and 299 of the *Daily
Christian Advocate* and entitled "Section II, Annual Conference Commission on Finance," was
presented by W. F. Bryan, Texas, Chairman, who
explained the provisions of the report and moved
its adoption.

Thomas S. Brock, New Jersey, moved to amend
Paragraph 516 by inserting after the word
"Treasurer," at the beginning of the twelfth line,
the following: "or District Treasurers elected by
the Annual Conference." The Chairman accepted
the proposed amendment.

Edward D. Kohlstedt, Dakota, asked if the
word "Benevolent" in the last line of Paragraph
524 should not be "Benevolence." The Chairman
replied that "Benevolence" was the right term.

James J. James, Rock River, moved to amend
Paragraph 523 by inserting in line 12 immediately
preceding the word "General" at the end of the
line, the words "General Conference or the." This
was accepted by the Chairman.

Robert S. Satterfield, Oklahoma, inquired if
Paragraph 517 meant a flat salary for all District
Superintendents — no exceptions made. Dr.
Bryan replied: "No, that can be left to the Annual
Conference when the Annual Conference so de-
sires to fix the salary of the District Superintend-
ent."

Benjamin W. Meeks, Baltimore, raised a question relative to designated gifts as set forth in
Paragraph 528 and asked if there was any provision for making the special offering on World's
Temperance Sunday for the Board of Temperance
an exception to the principle set forth in said
paragraph.

Orrin W. Auman, Colorado, replied that such
exceptions should not be pressed and suggested
that a committee of three be appointed to consider the matter and report later.

MAY 9
THIRTEENTH
DAY

Morning

Committee on
Membership
and Tem-
poral Econ-
omy, Report
No. 5-A—
"Annual
Conference
Commission
on Finance"

MAY 9

THIRTEENTH
DAY

Morning

Committee on
Membership
and Tem-
poral Econ-
omy, Report
No. 5-A—
"Annual
Conference
Commission
on Finance"

Motion of Daniel L. Marsh, New England, duly
seconded, prevailed authorizing O. W. Auman,
W. F. Bryan, and B. W. Meeks to prepare the suggested amendment, with the clear understanding
that the name of no Board or Agency will be
mentioned.

M. C. Redwine, Kentucky, asked if the committee would substitute the word "and" for the
word "or" in the ninth line following the words
"District Steward" in Paragraph 525. The Committee accepted the change and no objection was
raised.

The time of recess nearing, motion of Daniel
L. Marsh, New England, duly seconded, prevailed
that the time be extended only for the completion
of this report.

Lewis O. Hartman, New England, called attention to the fact that the matter of the support of
Central Conference Bishops, mentioned in the last
sentence of Paragraph 519, was provided for last
night in the adoption of Calendar No. 44, Report
No. 9 of the Committee on Conferences and entitled "Central Conferences." The Chair replied
that he thought the pending matter went beyond
that provision last night.

The report was adopted. For report, see Appendix, "General Standing Committees," page
529.

Charles W.
Welch
Introduced

Joseph M. M. Gray, Detroit, Chairman of the
Committee on Courtesies, Privileges, and Introductions, introduced the Reverend Dr. Charles W.
Welch, Moderator of the Presbyterian Church of
the United States of America, to the Conference.

Recess

The Conference was then in recess for ten
minutes.

Reconvene

Bishop McConnell called the Conference to
order at 10:45 A.M. The Conference stood and
joined in singing "Onward Christian Soldiers,"
under the leadership of Dr. James R. Houghton.

Committee
Reports

Joseph M. M. Gray, Detroit, moved that the
Committee of Elected Chairmen be instructed to
select the order in which the remaining reports
shall be presented to the Conference. George W.
Henson, Philadelphia, moved to amend by suggesting that this order begin with the afternoon
session of today. The amendment was accepted

by Dr. Gray, and the motion, duly seconded, prevailed.

Under the question of privilege for the entire Conference, Isaac E. Miller, Ohio, Chairman of the Joint Commission on Entertainment of the Uniting Conference, made announcements concerning the service of Wednesday night incident to the proclamation of the Declaration of Union.

Dr. Miller presented Dr. John A. Rinkel, of Minneapolis, a member of the Joint Commission, stating that he had made a very large contribution to the comfort of the delegates of the Uniting Conference, by the tireless and efficient service he had rendered in so many ways.

Dr. Miller requested, in behalf of the Conference, that Dr. Houghton sing "The Glory Road" tomorrow immediately after recess.

Bishop McConnell announced the result of the second ballot for alternate members of the Judicial Council as follows:

Ballots cast, 741; ballots counted, 741; necessary to a choice, 371. R. L. Flowers, North Carolina, 584; A. C. Millar, Little Rock, 570; R. B. Turnipseed, Upper South Carolina, 410.

R. L. Flowers, A. C. Millar, and B. R. Turnipseed, each having received the required majority, were declared elected alternate members of the Judicial Council of The Methodist Church.

The Secretary read the complete result, as follows:

Ministers from the Methodist Episcopal Church, South: A. C. Millar, Little Rock, 570; B. R. Turnipseed, Upper South Carolina, 410; A. J. Weeks, North Texas, 212; J. B. Craven, Western North Carolina, 104; J. W. Johnson, North Georgia, 89; W. L. Duren, Louisiana, 50; J. W. Bergin, Central Texas, 28; J. Richard Spann, Louisiana, 12.

Laymen from the Methodist Episcopal Church, South: R. L. Flowers, North Carolina, 584; W. F. McMurry, Memphis, 54; O. A. Park, South Georgia, 24; M. C. Redwine, Kentucky, 14; R. B. Carr, North Alabama, 10; G. H. Lamar, Baltimore, 10; S. G. Bratton, New Mexico, 8; J. G. McGowen, North Mississippi, 6; H. H. White, Louisiana, 5; J. H. Carlock, Oklahoma, 4; H. B. McGinnis, Tennessee, 4; C. E. Mead, New Mexico, 2; T. D. Samford, Alabama, 1.

The alternate members of the Judicial Council are as follows: Ministers: Sanford W. Corcoran (1), Ernest S. Lyons (1), A. J. Allen (1), A. C. Millar (2), B. R. Turnip-

---

Marginal notes:

MAY 9
THIRTEENTH DAY

Morning

Announcements Concerning the Declaration of Union Service

John A. Rinkel Presented

Result of Second Ballot for Alternate Members of Judicial Council

MAY 9
THIRTEENTH
DAY
Morning

seed (2). Laymen: James I. Dolliver (1), Benjamin A. Matthews (1), R. L. Flowers (2), Nathan Newby (1). The figure in parentheses ( ) indicates the ballot on which election occurred.

Organization
of Judicial
Council

The organization of the Judicial Council of The Methodist Church was reported, as follows:

President, Fracis R. Bayley; Vice-President, Martin E. Lawson; Secretary, Henry R. Van Deusen.

Rules of Prac-
tice and
Procedure
for Judicial
Council

Henry R. Van Deusen, Wyoming, stated that the Judicial Council had adopted certain Rules of Practice and Procedure, and moved that they be printed in the *Daily Advocate* and also in the Appendix to the *Discipline*. The motion, duly seconded, prevailed. For Rules of Practice and Procedure, see Appendix, "Miscellaneous," page 928.

Time Limit

Cary A. Kemp, Northwest Kansas, moved to amend the Rule of Order which limits the Chairman of a Committee to five minutes in presenting the report of the Committee, by removing the five-minute limit. The motion, duly seconded, did not prevail.

Committee on
Missions,
Report No. 5
—"Board of
Missions
and Church
Extension"

The Order of the Day having arrived, Calendar No. 71, Report No. 5 of the Committee on Missions, printed on pages 351 to 360, inclusive, of the *Daily Christian Advocate* and entitled "Board of Missions and Church Extension," was presented by John R. Mott, New York, Chairman, who started explaining its provisions. In the midst of the explanation, Dr. Mott's time expiring, motion of Daniel L. Marsh, New England, duly seconded, prevailed, extending the time for the consideration of the report. Dr. Mott completed his explanation and moved the adoption of the report. The motion was duly seconded.

Roy L. Smith, Southern California, spoke for the adoption of the report.

Frank W. Court, Upper Iowa, stated that Mrs. Evelyn R. Nicholson, Upper Iowa, a member of the Committee on Missions, had called his attention to a typographical error in Paragraph 859, and requested permission to correct the same by inserting after the words "young people" in the seventh line of the paragraph, the words "and children in behalf of native and foreign groups, needy childhood." This was accepted by the Chairman.

MAY 9
THIRTEENTH
DAY

Morning
Committee on
Missions,
Report No. 5
—"Board of
Missions
and Church
Extension"

Paul P. Wiant, Foochow (China), moved to amend Paragraph 842 by striking out the word "or" in the fourth line and placing a comma in its place, and then adding after the words "Mission Conference," in the same line, the words "or Annual Conference." This was accepted by the Chairman.

Charles F. Eggleston, Philadelphia, moved to amend Paragraph 838, Article 2, Section 1, by inserting in line 14, after the words "Charter and Constitution," the words "and with the Constitution of the Board, and to recommend Constitutions." The Chairman accepted the proposed amendment.

Charles F. Eggleston, Philadelphia, moved to amend Paragraph 893 by adding the following at the end: "The Committee may meet as a whole as it determines, and members of the Committee carrying on the same class of work may also meet separately for consultation and co-operation." The Chairman accepted this proposed amendment.

Charles A. Jones, Ohio, moved to amend Paragraph 833, Article 6, by substituting the words "Two, one man and one woman" for the word "one" at the end of line 4 and the words "or more" at the beginning of line 5. This was accepted by the Chairman. Brother Jones then spoke in favor of the report.

Edward D. Kohlstedt, Dakota, spoke in favor of the report.

G. M. Davenport, North Alabama, moved the previous question.

Fred D. Stone, Rock River, raised the question of the apparent omission of legislation covering the licensing and consecration of Deaconesses and asked if this would be cared for. The Chairman assured him that it would be.

The motion for the previous question, duly seconded, prevailed, and the previous question was ordered.

George C. French, North Texas, raised the question concerning the overhead. The Chairman replied that, taking into view all the Boards involved, there would be no increase in the overhead.

MAY 9
THIRTEENTH
DAY
Morning

Dr. Mott then closed the debate for the Committee.

The report was adopted. For report, see Appendix, "General Standing Committees," page 555.

Committee to
Study
Property
Interests

John R. Mott, New York, presented the following resolution and moved its adoption:

That the Council of Bishops in due time appoint a Study Committee of four persons (two men and two women) from each Jurisdiction, and one representative from each of the Central Conferences, not officers or paid executives of any Board or Society, to study the property interests of the Boards involved in the Report of the Committee on Missions and Church Extension, together with other financial implications, also to take account of any inaccuracies and contradictions in the report; it being understood, however, that the Study Committee shall not be authorized to change the substance of said report in any particular, but may recommend to the General Conference any legislation which it may conclude would perfect the processes of the Board of Missions and Church Extension.

JOHN R. MOTT, *Chairman;*
NATHAN NEWBY, *Vice-Chairman.*

Lewis O. Hartman, New England, asked if Dr. Mott would be willing to accept some representatives from the foreign field on the proposed committee. Dr. Mott accepted the amendment, "and one representative from each of the Central Conferences," to be inserted after the words "from each Jurisdiction."

The resolution was unanimously adopted.

Committee on
Missions
Report No. 6
—"Methodist
Participa-
tion in
China Civil-
ian Relief"

Calendar No. 72, Report No. 6 of the Committee on Missions, printed on page 360 of the *Daily Christian Advocate* and entitled "Methodist Participation in China Civilian Relief," was presented by John R. Mott, New York, Chairman. Dr. Mott spoke to the report and moved its adoption.

Chester A. Smith, New York, moved to amend the report by adding either to Section 1 or Section 2 the following:

It is unfair to ask the charitable-minded members of our Christian Churches to send their money to China and then permit the munition makers of this country to sell to Japan fifty-four per cent of all her war materials with which she is devastating China; therefore I move that we call upon the Congress of the United States of America to pass such legislation as will prevent the sale and shipment to Japan of all war materials of every kind and description.

The ·motion being duly seconded, Brother Smith spoke to the question.

Nathan Newby, Pacific, spoke in opposition to the amendment.

Arlo A. Brown, Newark, moved that the amendment be referred to the Business Committee. The motión was seconded by Ralph E. Diffendorfer, Rock River.

W. F. Bryan, Texas, Chairman of the Committee on Membership and Temporal Economy, stated that his Committee was dealing with the question, and moved as a substitute that the matter be referred to the Committee on Membership and Temporal Economy instead of to the Business Committee. This was accepted by Dr. Brown and his second, and the motion was adopted to refer.

The Report of the Committee on Missions was then adopted. For report, see Appendix, "General Standing Committees," page 591.

Bishop McConnell, on a matter of privilege for the Chair, stated that this morning he had replied to Dr. Hartman that the Chair thought the matter of the support of the Bishops of Central Conferences had been provided for. He said further: "It now appears that there is a contradiction between the methods proposed as have been set up by the adoption of Calendar No. 44, Report No. 9 of the Committee on Conferences, adopted Monday night, May 8, and Calendar No. 43, Report No. 6 of the Committee on Membership and Temporal Economy, adopted this morning. It is only fair to Dr. Hartman that I make this statement. If he wishes to make any further statement, he is privileged to do so."

Lewis O. Hartman, New England, moved that the matter be referred to the Chairman of the Committee on Temporal Economy and the Chairman of the Subcommittee on Central Conferences. The motion, duly seconded, prevailed.

Bishop McConnell recognized Bishop Edwin H. Hughes on the matter of a privileged communication from the Council of Bishops.

Bishop Hughes made the following statement:

"This relates to your instruction, brethren, to one of your Committees; likewise to the Council of Bishops. The feeling ran contemporaneously in this body, and likewise in the Council of Bishops, that one of the most

Margin notes:

MAY 9
THIRTEENTH
DAY

Morning

Committee on
Missions
Report No. 6
—"Methodist
Participation in
China Civilian Relief"

Privilege for
the Chair

Forward Program of The
Methodist
Church

MAY 9
THIRTEENTH
DAY

Morning

Forward Pro-
gram of The
Methodist
Church

important things in following up the spirit of this Uniting Conference should be an attempt to increase the spiritual and evangelistic life of our beloved Church.

"It is not, of course, possible for us thus quickly to
bring in anything like a detailed program. Bishop Kern,
on behalf of the Council of Bishops, will give a brief
statement as to some of the things that are proposed,
after which I will be glad to read a paper that is a sum-
mons to all our hearts."

Bishop Paul B. Kern outlined some of the preliminary plans contemplated by the Council of
Bishops concerning this great forward movement
of The Methodist Church.

Bishop Hughes made the following statement
with reference to the paper he later read:

"I may say, in frankness, it was written with the pen
and heart of Bishop Arthur J. Moore. On reading it to
the Council of Bishops, it was the feeling that the document was so sacred that we scarcely dared to change a
word of any of its paragraphs. You will allow me to add
that many times more interest was shown in the subject
matter of this paper and in the program which is here
generally proposed than has been shown in our Council
of Bishops in connection with any other matter that has
been referred to them.

"I feel like asking you to pray while this is being read,
and to ask God to send it down to our Church as a call
to our people."

Bishop Hughes then read the following paper:

The Methodists of America have entered into a new
sense of brotherhood. They have consummated the largest
union of Protestant Christians ever achieved. The full
significance of what has occurred is beyond our present
understanding; only eternity can properly evaluate the
deeper meaning of what we have here done.

Of greater significance than the act of union is the
result of union. The spiritual oneness so conspicuous at
the Uniting Conference must be made to permeate the
whole body of Methodism. Out of this union must spring
a new and more intense loyalty to our Wesleyan heritage.
Above all, this Methodist Church must immediately project
a program of service commensurate with its latent powers
and its unparalleled opportunity.

In the providence of God our Churches have come together at a moment of world crisis. In every land there is
perplexity and fear. The priceless values of life are everywhere threatened. Never in modern times was there such
an imperative demand for the proclamation and application of the gospel. At the very instant of its new birth,
The Methodist Church is faced with a challenge to summon all men to behold the redemptive power which has
always been resident in the eternal Christ.

The burden of our duty in this hour has been upon our

MAY 9

THIRTEENTH
DAY

Morning

Forward Pro-
gram of The
Methodist
Church

hearts. In response to inner promptings, no less than to the request of the Conference, your Bishops express the need for a mighty resurgence of spiritual life and its inevitable moral overflow, and their willingness to help lead the Church in a movement to bring about its consummation.

Such a forward movement should be all-inclusive, and should be dynamic, inspirational, and educational in nature and method. It should involve a dissemination among our people of information concerning the history, genius, theology, policy, and program of Methodism. It should inculcate a new loyalty to all our institutions. It should interpret unification to our people and weld them together in understanding, sympathy, and a sense of fellowship. It should emphasize our world-wide missionary enterprise and stimulate the passion to evangelize all peoples.

It should promote Christian stewardship and bring about a greater liberality for the larger benevolent work of our Church. It should lay bare the social and personal sins of our time and call men to repentance and reformation. It should place emphasis upon personal religious experience and seek to revive in the hearts of our people the seeking spirit of the compassionate Christ.

Such a movement must be more than a temporary enterprise of an inspirational nature. Its foundations must be wide and deep; its cultivation fundamental and constant. The best of our thought and the most competent advice we can secure shall be devoted to projecting the details of a plan, which in due time will be announced to the Church. With the hearty and unselfish co-operation of all our preachers, people, and organizations, the movement contemplated should bring the Church to its first General Conference having witnessed a revival of deep religious experience, with all its forces mobilized for the inauguration of the third century of vital Methodism. No cause is forlorn with Christ at its head. We look up and behold the morning. Christ is out on the highways of the world's needs. No ingenuity of wickedness, no indifference or scorn of men can stop His unceasing march of redemption. We resolve anew to evade no peril and to seek no discharge from the tasks, but take our appointed way with Him until the gospel has been given in its uniqueness and redeeming power to all men.

"We will rejoice in Thy salvation, and in the name of our God will we set up our banner."

Thomas D. Ellis, South Georgia, moved that the Conference stand in approval of this great paper and challenge to The Methodist Church. The motion was seconded by Paul M. Hillman, Nebraska, and the members of the Uniting Conference rose to express unanimous approval.

Nathan Newby, Pacific, moved that the paper be received and printed in the *Daily Christian Advocate*. The motion, duly seconded, prevailed.

MAY 9

THIRTEENTH
DAY

Morning

Committee on
Enabling
Acts and
Legal
Forms,
Report No. 3
Report No. 3 of the Committee on Enabling Acts
and Legal Forms printed on pages 368 and 369
of the *Daily Christian Advocate*, was presented by
Arthur A. Callaghan, Maine, Chairman, who ex-
plained its provisions. Dr. Hartman requested
Nathan Newby, Pacific, and W. M. Alexander,
Missouri, to come to the platform and help in the
presentation of the reports of the Committee.
The report, on motion of the Chairman, duly sec-
onded, was adopted. For report, see Appendix,
"Special Standing Committees," page 803.

Committee on
Enabling
Acts and
Legal
Forms,
Report No. 4
Report No. 4 of the same Committee, printed on
page 369 of the *Daily Christian Advocate*, was
presented and explained by the Chairman. Motion of Arthur A. Callaghan, duly seconded, prevailed adopting the report. For report, see Appendix, "Special Standing Committees," page
805.

Committee on
Enabling
Acts and
Legal
Forms,
Report No. 5
Report No. 5 of the same Committee, printed on
page 369 of the *Daily Christian Advocate*, was
presented by the Chairman, who explained its pro-
visions and moved its adoption. The motion, duly
seconded, prevailed. For report, see Appendix,
"Special Standing Committees," page 805.

Committee on
Enabling
Acts and
Legal
Forms,
Report No. 6
Report No. 6 of the same Committee, printed
on page 369 of the *Daily Christian Advocate*, was
presented by the Chairman, who explained its
provisions. On his motion, duly seconded, the
report was adopted. For report, see Appendix,
"Special Standing Committees," page 806.

Committee on
Enabling
Acts and
Legal
Forms,
Report No. 7
Report No. 7 of the same Committee, printed
on page 369 of the *Daily Christian Advocate*, was
presented by Dr. Callaghan, who moved its adop-
tion, after explaining its provisions. The motion,
duly seconded, prevailed. For report, see Appen-
dix, "Special Standing Committees," page 806.

Committee on
Enabling
Acts and
Legal
Forms,
Report No. 8
Report No. 8 of the same Committee, printed on
pages 369 and 370 of the *Daily Christian Advocate*, was presented by the Chairman, who explained its provisions and stated that the word
"Prospectus" in the last line of Paragraph 1130
should read "Discipline." Motion of Dr. Callaghan, duly seconded, prevailed, adopting the
report. For report, see Appendix, "Special Standing Committees," page 807.

Report No. 9 of the same Committee, printed on

page 370 of the *Daily Christian Advocate*, was presented and explained by the Chairman. On his motion, duly seconded, the Report was adopted. For report, see Appendix, "Special Standing Committees," page 809.

Report No. 10 of the same Committee, printed on page 370 of the *Daily Christian Advocate*, was presented and explained by Dr. Callaghan, on whose motion, duly seconded, the report was adopted. For report, see Appendix, "Special Standing Committees," page 811.

Report No. 11 of the same Committee, printed on page 370 of the *Daily Christian Advocate*, was presented and explained by the Chairman, who moved its adoption. The motion, duly seconded, prevailed. For report, see Appendix, "Special Standing Committees," page 811.

Report No. 12 of the same Committee, printed on page 370 of the *Daily Christian Advocate*, was presented by Dr. Callaghan, who explained its provisions and moved its adoption with the deletion of the word "hereinafter" in line 3. The motion, duly seconded, prevailed. For report, see Appendix, "Special Standing Committees," page 812.

George C. French, North Texas, asked if there would be any increase in overhead occasioned by any of these reports.

Dr. Callaghan replied that, as far as they were able to determine, there would be none.

Dr. Callaghan requested that the members of the Committee on Enabling Acts and Legal Forms be excused from attending the afternoon session that they might complete their work. The request was granted, by common consent.

Lewis O. Hartman, New England, Chairman of the Subcommittee on Central Conferences, reported that he had conferred with W. F. Bryan, Texas, Chairman of the Committee on Membership and Temporal Economy, in regard to the matter referred to them by the action of the Uniting Conference this morning; that at the suggestion of Dr. Bryan he had also conferred with Orrin W. Auman, Colorado, a member of the Subcommittee on Financial Plan of the Committee on Membership and Temporal Economy, and that the three would like to have common consent of

MAY 9
THIRTEENTH
DAY

Morning

Committee on
Enabling
Acts and
Legal
Forms,
Report No. 9

Committee on
Enabling
Acts and
Legal
Forms, Report No. 10

Committee on
Enabling
Acts and
Legal
Forms, Report No. 11

Committee on
Enabling
Acts and
Legal
Forms, Report No. 12

Support of
Bishops

MAY 9
THIRTEENTH
DAY
Morning

Mrs. Francis
J. McConnell

Jurisdictions

Bishop
Asbury's
Birthplace

the Uniting Conference to delete the last sentence of Paragraph 519 of Calendar No. 43, Report No. 6 (5-A) of the Committee on Membership and Temporal Economy, said sentence starting in line 11 and beginning with the words "He is, furthermore." No objection being raised, common consent was given for the deletion.

Mrs. Francis J. McConnell, New York, was recognized on a matter of personal privilege and addressed the Conference in behalf of the women concerned with the adoption of the Report of the Committee on Missions, which report had projected the great program for Missions for The Methodist Church, and assured the Uniting Conference of the loyal support of the women of Methodism in bringing the projected program to pass. The time of Mrs. McConnell expiring before she had finished her remarks, on motion of Daniel L. Marsh, New England, duly seconded, her time was extended.

The Report on Annual Conference Boundaries of the Northeastern Jurisdiction, printed on pages 363, 364, and 365 of the *Daily Christian Advocate,* was ordered to record.

The Report of the Central Jurisdiction on Boundaries, printed on page 365 of the *Daily Christian Advocate,* was ordered to record.

The Report of the North Central Jurisdiction concerning Boundaries, printed on pages 365, 366, and 367 of the *Daily Christian Advocate,* was ordered to record.

The following resolution was presented, and upon motion, duly seconded, it was adopted:

FROM SOUTHEASTERN JURISDICTION

The following resolution was adopted at a meeting of the delegates from the Annual Conferences comprising the Southeastern Jurisdiction held May 6, 1939.

T. D. ELLIS, *Chairman;*
HARRY DENMAN, *Secretary.*

RESOLUTION No. 7

WHEREAS Dr. Bond, our fraternal messenger from British Methodism, has called to our attention the possibility of purchasing the house in which Bishop Francis Asbury was born; and

WHEREAS, Bishop Asbury spent most of his life of service within those states which are now a part of the Southeastern Jurisdiction; therefore be it

Resolved, That the delegates of the Southeastern Juris-

diction herewith request that common consent be given for
this Jurisdiction to inaugurate plans for the possible purchase of this historic shrine to be rebuilt on the Campus of
Scarritt College in Nashville, Tennessee.

MAY 9
THIRTEENTH
DAY
Morning

J. P. MARTIN,	D. E. HINKLE,
J. S. FRENCH,	E. P. ANDERSON,
J. W. PERRY,	E. D. THOMPSON,
A. W. PLYLER,	COSTEN J. HARRELL,
CHAS. C. WEAVER,	W. E. BROCK,
W. G. HENRY,	F. H. TROTTER,
JAS. N. HILLMAN,	R. L. STAPLETON,
JOHN L. FERGUSON,	MRS. H. C. BLACK,
MRS. ROBERT O'NEAL,	WM. F. QUILLIAN,
BEN A. WHITMORE,	HARRY DENMAN.
WM. R. WEBB,	

Motion of Daniel L. Marsh, New England, duly
seconded, prevailed that after the necessary announcements we adjourn.

The Secretary read the following cablegram:

Cablegram
from
Methodist
Seoul

Uniting Conference, Kansas City, Mo.·
Philippians four twenty-three. Uniting session three
Annual Conferences. METHODIST SEOUL.

The following telegram was read:

Telegram from
Bishop
Johnson

Portland, Oregon, May 9, 1939.
Uniting Conference Methodist Church, Kansas City, Mo.
Many thanks for sympathetic greetings from Conference. I rejoice greatly in the effectual working among
you of the cementing power and love of Christ and pray
that He will lead us in helping to bring this world under
His sway. BISHOP E. S. JOHNSON.

The following was received and ordered to record, by common consent:

Stenographers

We, the stenographers of this Uniting Conference,
do hereby wish to express our appreciation for the fine
co-operation given us by the delegates of this Conference.
We consider it a privilege to have been able to help in
some way with the forwarding of Methodism and Christianity in the world.

HARRIET PAGE, · ' ·	MARY EVA GIBBS,
DOROTHY OTTMAN,	THELMA TRIPLETT.
EMILY LOUISE TIEMANN,	

Bishop Charles Flint was recognized and read
the following telegram:

Telegram from
Robert F.
Wagner

Having already wired presiding Bishop of Uniting Conference expressing my inability to attend the sessions due

MAY 9
THIRTEENTH
DAY
Morning

to pendency of important legislative matters in the Senate. I am extremely honored to have been appointed as delegate. I rejoice with you over the happy outcome of the long negotiations which result in making one Methodist body in this country. I am greatly indebted to the Methodist Church for my early training and the formation of my social convictions which I have tried to work out in legislation.   ROBERT F. WAGNER.

Adjournment

The Conference adjourned with the benediction pronounced by Bishop J. Lloyd Decell.

TUESDAY AFTERNOON, MAY 9, 1939

MAY 9
THIRTEENTH
DAY
Afternoon

Opening

Pursuant to adjournment, the Conference was called to order at 2:15 P.M. by Bishop John C. Broomfield.

The Conference stood and joined in singing Hymn No. 4, "O Worship the King, All-Glorious Above," after which Dr. A. J. Allen, Pittsburgh, led in prayer.

Solo by Dr. Houghton

At the request of the Conference, Dr. James R. Houghton sang as a solo "God Is Our Refuge," based on the forty-sixth Psalm.

On a question of privilege Horace G. Smith, Rock River, moved the following:

Gavels

Because of the widespread interest shown in the historic gavels used by the presiding officers of this Uniting Conference, I move that Dr. Thomas P. Potter, who has provided most of these gavels, be asked to prepare a brief written statement concerning these gavels to be sent to the Church Press, and, if space permits, to be printed in the last issue of the *Daily Christian Advocate*.

The motion, duly seconded, prevailed. For this article, see Appendix, "Miscellaneous," page 930.

Committee of
Elected
Chairmen

George W. Henson, Philadelphia, made the following statement for the Committee of Elected Chairmen:

Three of the General Standing Committees have completed their work and their reports have been adopted. There are twenty-three Calendar Reports and six Resolutions yet to be acted on. These can be taken care of in their regular order in the sessions yet to be held.

By common consent the program as outlined was adopted.

Referred

Arthur A. Callaghan, Maine, moved to refer to the Committee on Judiciary the question, "Who are the legal delegates to the Annual Conference?" The motion, duly seconded, prevailed.

Calendar No. 47, Report No. 8 of the Committee on Ministry and Judicial Administration, printed on pages 303 and 304 of the *Daily Christian Advocate* and entitled "Retired Bishops," was presented by Orien W. Fifer, Indiana, Chairman, who explained its provisions and moved its adoption, with the understanding that Sections ·V and VI be omitted from this report, as the matters contained therein had been taken care of by previous action of the Uniting Conference. The motion, duly seconded, prevailed and the report. was adopted. For report, see Appendix, "General Standing Committees," page 489.

MAY 9

THIRTEENTH
DAY

Afternoon

Committee on
Ministry and
Judicial Ad-
ministration,
Report No. 8
—"Retired
Bishops"

Calendar No. 48, Report No. 9 of the Committee on Ministry and Judicial Administration, printed on page 304 of the *Daily Christian Advocate* and entitled "Pastors," was presented by Orien W. Fifer, Indiana, Chairman. Dr. Fifer requested J. Manning Potts, Virginia, Chairman of the Subcommittee, to be in charge of. the report. Dr. Potts explained its provisions and moved the adoption of the report. The motion was duly seconded.

Committee on
Ministry and
Judicial Ad-
ministration,
Report No. 9
—"Pastors"

Thomas S. Brock, New Jersey, spoke against the third item of Paragraph 217, Article 2, stating that the term "Accepted Supply" needed to be clarified for the Conference.

J. W. Moore, Virginia, spoke for the report.

Disston W. Jacobs, Wilmington, moved to amend Paragraph 217, Article 2, by striking out the word "an" in line 2, and inserting therefor the words "a full time." The motion being duly seconded, Mr. Jacobs spoke to the question.

Thomas D. Ellis, South Georgia, was recognized, but yielded the floor to William P. King, North Georgia, who spoke for the report.

Daniel L. Marsh, New England, called for the reading of the amendment and then spoke in its favor.

Joseph M. M. Gray, Detroit, moved as a substitute for the Jacobs amendment that Item 3 of Paragraph 217, Article 2, be stricken from the report. The motion being duly seconded, . Dr. Gray spoke to the question.

· Roy·O. Hills, Wyoming State, spoke against the substitute.

MAY 9
THIRTEENTH
DAY
Afternoon
Committee on
Ministry and
Judicial Ad-
ministration,
Report No. 9
—"Pastors"

Nolan B. Harmon, Jr., Baltimore, spoke in favor of the substitute.

Earl R. Brown, Northeast Ohio, raised the point of order that if the substitute was adopted it would take away the right to administer the Sacrament of Baptism. The Chair ruled the point of order not well taken.

Harry G. Ryan, North Texas, moved the previous question.

The Chair stated that he had recognized Fred B. Noble, Saint Johns River, before the motion for the previous question was made.

F. B. Noble spoke against the substitute.

The Chair stated that the previous question had been called for. Lewis O. Hartman, New England, called attention to the fact that the vote had not been taken.

Daniel L. Marsh, New England, raised the point of order that "because somebody wanted to move the previous question before the last speaker spoke, it does not mean that the motion for the previous question is now pending. The Chairman did not recognize anybody who made the motion for the previous question since the other man spoke." The Chair ruled the point well taken.

Harold Paul Sloan, New Jersey, spoke for the substitute.

Charles A. Robbins, Pacific Northwest, moved the pending question. The motion, duly seconded, prevailed and the pending question was ordered.

Dr. Potts closed the debate for the Committee. The vote was taken on the Gray substitute and it did not prevail.

A. Wesley Pugh, North Indiana, offered the following amendment to the Jacobs amendment: "An unordained pastor or an Accepted Supply Pastor, giving full-time pastoral service, shall have authority, etc." This was accepted by Dr. Jacobs.

Elmer C. Dewey, Georgia, moved as a substitute for the Jacobs amendment the following: In line 9, after the word "Superintendent," insert the words "and with his permission."

Alvis S. Bennett, Kentucky, spoke against the substitute.

Elmer E. Collins, Montana State, moved the previous question on all that was before the Conference. The motion, duly seconded, prevailed and the previous question was ordered.

The vote on the Dewey substitute was taken and it did not prevail.

The vote on the Jacobs amendment was taken and it did not prevail.

Dr. Potts called attention to a typographical error in Paragraph 219, Article 4, line 4, stating that the words "without the consent of the Quarterly Conference" had been inadvertently omitted before the words "and the."

The report was adopted. For report, see Appendix, "General Standing Committees," page 491.

Calendar No. 49, Report No. 10 of the Committee on Ministry and Judicial Administration, printed on page 305 of the *Daily Christian Advocate* and entitled "Pastors," was presented by Orien W. Fifer, Indiana, Chairman, who moved its adoption. The motion was duly seconded.

Leonard B. Smith, Maryland, moved to substitute Paragraph 220, Article 5, page 69 of the *Prospectus of the Discipline*, which reads as follows:

No minister shall perform the marriage of a divorced person whose divorced wife or husband is living; but this rule shall not apply to the innocent person when it is clearly established by competent testimony that the true cause for the divorce was such as to justify remarriage in the light of the teachings of Scripture concerning marriage and divorce, nor to divorced persons seeking to be reunited in marriage.

The motion being duly seconded, Dr. Smith spoke to the question.

George Mecklenberg, Northern Minnesota, spoke against the substitute.

W. L. Duren, Louisiana, spoke in favor of the substitute.

J. Edgar Skillington, Central Pennsylvania, moved the pending question. The motion, duly seconded, prevailed and the pending question was ordered.

Dr. Fifer closed the debate for the Committee.

The substitute was voted on and did not prevail. A division was called for, but was not sustained by the vote of the Conference. The Chair again

---

Marginal notes:

MAY 9
THIRTEENTH
DAY
Afternoon

Committee on Ministry and Judicial Administration, Report No. 9 —"Pastors"

Committee on Ministry and Judicial Administration, Report No. 10—"Pastors" put the question of voting on the substitute, and the substitute did not prevail.

The report was adopted. For report, see Appendix, "General Standing Committees," page 494.

Bishop Ernest L. Waldorf was recognized for a special privilege and presented to the Conference forty students of Garrett Biblical Institute, Evanston, Ill., who were attending the Conference and were seated in the gallery. Bishop Waldorf requested Horace G. Smith, Rock River, President of Garrett and a member of this Conference, to stand, and also the students. The Conference applauded.

Committee on
Ministry and
Judicial Ad-
ministration,
Report No.
11—"Recep-
tion of
Preachers
on Trial"

Calendar No. 50, Report No. 11 of the Committee on Ministry and Judicial Administration, printed on page 305 of the *Daily Christian Advocate* and entitled "Reception of Preachers on Trial," was presented by Orien W. Fifer, Indiana, Chairman. Dr. Fifer requested J. Manning Potts, Virginia, to be in charge of the report. Dr. Potts explained the provisions of the report, stating that the word "satisfactory" should appear before the words "written answers" in line 6 of Paragraph 222, Article 2. He moved the adoption of the report and the motion was duly seconded.

Raymond H. Huse, Central New York, moved to amend Paragraph 228, Article 3, Item (19) (a), by striking out, at the end of the item, the words "neither spend any more time at any one place than is strictly necessary." The motion, duly seconded, did not prevail.

Albert N. Smith, Northwest Kansas, moved to amend Paragraph 229 by striking out the word "not" in line 3 following the words "They need." The motion, duly seconded, prevailed.

Hawes P. Clarke, Virginia, moved the previous question. The motion, duly seconded, prevailed and the previous question was ordered.

The report, as amended, was adopted. For report, see Appendix, "General Standing Committees," page 494.

J. Fisher Simpson, West Texas, moved a reconsideration of Calendar No. 48, Report No. 9 of the Committee on Ministry and Judicial Administration, in order that he might offer an amendment to Paragraph 217 concerning the instruction

of parents and young people in Christian homemaking. The motion, duly seconded, did not prevail.

Harold Paul Sloan, New Jersey, presented the
following resolution and moved its adoption:

> *Resolved,* That Report No. 11 of the Committee on
> Ministry and Judicial Administration, found on page 305
> of the *Daily Christian Advocate,* be referred to the Com-
> mission on Ritual with instruction to prepare a form of
> service or services and to report the same to the General
> Conference of 1940.

The motion, duly seconded, prevailed.

Calendar No. 51, Report No. 10 of the Committee on Conferences, printed on pages 305 and 306
of the *Daily Christian Advocate* and entitled
"Mission Conferences," was presented by George
W. Henson, Philadelphia, Chairman, who moved
its adoption. The motion, duly seconded, prevailed. For report, see Appendix, "General
Standing Committees," page 446.

Calendar No. 52, Report No. 11 of the Committee on Conferences, printed on page 306 of the
Daily Christian Advocate and entitled "Administration of Missions (In the Home Field)," was
presented by George W. Henson, Philadelphia,
Chairman. Dr. Henson explained the provisions
of the report and asked common consent to strike
out the words "using a language other than the
English," found in lines 1 and 2 of Section 4.
Common consent was given by the Conference.
Dr. Henson then moved the adoption of the report. The motion, duly seconded, prevailed. For
report, see Appendix, "General Standing Committees," page 448.

Calendar No. 53, Report No. 12 of the Committee on Conferences, printed on page 306 of the
Daily Christian Advocate and entitled "Missions
(On Foreign Fields)," was presented by George
W. Henson, Philadelphia, Chairman, who explained the report and moved its adoption. The
motion, duly seconded, prevailed. For report, see
Appendix, "General Standing Committees," page
449.

Calendar No. 54, Report No. 13 of the Committee on Conferences, printed on page 306 of the
Daily Christian Advocate, was presented by

Side notes: MAY 9 THIRTEENTH DAY Afternoon; Referred; Committee on Conferences, Report No. 10—"Mission Conferences"; Committee on Conferences, Report No. 11—"Administration of Missions (In the Home Field)"; Committee on Conferences, Report No. 12—"Missions (On Foreign Fields)"; Committee on Conferences, Report No. 13

MAY 9
THIRTEENTH
DAY
Afternoon

George W. Henson, Philadelphia, Chairman. Dr. Henson requested J. N. R. Score, Central Texas, to come to the platform and answer any questions that might be raised. Dr. Henson moved the adoption of the report. The motion, duly seconded, prevailed. For report, see Appendix, "General Standing Committees," page 450.

Committee on
Missions,
Report No. 3
—"Board of
Hospitals
and Homes
of The
Methodist
Church"

Calendar No. 55, Report No. 3 of the Committee on Missions, printed on page 307 of the *Daily Christian Advocate* and entitled "Board of Hospitals and Homes of The Methodist Church," was presented by John R. Mott, New York, Chairman, who explained its provisions and moved its adoption. Dr. Mott requested Albert G. Schatzman, Ohio, Chairman of the Subcommittee which prepared this report, to assist in its presentation.

Charles C. Jarrell, North Georgia, moved to amend Paragraph 822, Section 2, by adding the following sentence:

In those Conferences where civil law requires the election of Boards of Trustees or Managers by the Annual Conference, it shall be the duty of the Conference Board of Hospitals and Homes to nominate persons for such election.

This amendment was accepted by the Chairman, and no objection was raised. The report was adopted. For report see Appendix, "General Standing Committees," page 550.

Committee on
Missions,
Report No. 4
—"General
Commission
on Evangel-
ism"

Calendar No. 56, Report No. 4 of the Committee on Missions, printed on pages 307 and 308 of the *Daily Christian Advocate* and entitled "General Commission on Evangelism," was presented by John R. Mott, New York, Chairman. Dr. Mott requested that S. O. Kimbrough, North Alabama, Chairman of the Subcommittee preparing this report, assist in its presentation.

Dr. Mott moved the following amendments: In the fourth unnumbered paragraph, insert in line 5 after the words "Annual Conference may" the words "by a two-thirds vote of the Conference"; and in line 4 of the ninth unnumbered paragraph insert the word "of" after the words "in the field." The motion, duly seconded, prevailed.

Dr. Mott then moved the adoption of the report as amended. The motion, duly seconded, pre-

vailed. For report, see Appendix, "General Standing Committees," page 553. *MAY 9*
THIRTEENTH DAY
Afternoon

George W. Henson, Philadelphia, Chairman of the Committee of Elected Chairmen, called attention to the Special Order of the Day set for 4:30 P.M. for consideration of the prepared program of "The Negro in Methodism." Bishop Broomfield urged the visitors in the galleries to remain for the Order of the Day. *Program on "The Negro in Methodism"*

Francis R. Bayley, Baltimore, Chairman of the Committee on Judiciary, under a question of privilege, announced a very important meeting of the Committee at 7:45 P.M. *Judiciary*

Jesse L. Corley, Southern California, offered the following resolution: *Resolution Referred*

A city as gracious and generous as is Kansas City deserves the best government that can be secured. As guests of this beautiful city and recipients of her extraordinary hospitality, we have been made aware—by expressions of her citizens and from the Press—of the humiliation and chagrin suffered by the good citizens of the community because of the amazingly traitorous graft, greed, and exploitation . . . .

Fred D. Stone, Rock River, raised the point of order that this resolution is clearly one that should be referred to the Business Committee. The Chair ruled the point well taken.

Dr. Corley then moved that the resolution be referred to the Business Committee.

Costen J. Harrell, Tennessee, raised the point of order that it would go automatically to the Business Committee under our Rules of Order. The Chair ruled the point well taken and the resolution was referred to the Business Committee.

The Secretary announced that the Norwegian and Danish Conference and the Central Northwest Conference should be recorded in the North·Central Jurisdiction and not the Northeastern Jurisdiction, as printed in the *Daily Christian Advocate*, page 363.

Following various announcements by the Secretary, the Order of the Day was taken up. . *Order of the Day*

Bishop Broomfield presented Bishop Alexander P. Shaw to be in charge of the Order of the Day, "The Negro in Methodism." *Bishop Shaw Presented*

The following program was presented:

The audience stood and joined in singing "My Country, 'Tis of Thee."

A combined Chorus from the local Churches and Lincoln High School, under the direction of Prof. J. O. Morrison of Kansas City, rendered an anthem, "Lift Every Voice and Sing."

Lewis O. Hartman, New England, led the Conference in prayer.

Dr. W. Aiken Smart, of Candler School of Theology, Emory University, Atlanta, Ga., addressed the Conference on "Barriers Burned Away." The Conference stood in applause at the conclusion of the address. [The Editors deeply regret that they were unable to secure the address of Dr. Smart, through circumstances over which the Editors had no control.]

The Chorus rendered a spiritual, "Listen to the Lamb."

Dr. Matthew S. Davage, President of Clark University, Atlanta, Ga., addressed the Conference on "Methodism: Our Heritage and Hope." For address, see Appendix, "Regular Addresses," page 884. The Conference stood in appreciation and applauded the address.

Three selections were rendered by the Chorus at the conclusion of the address by Dr. Davage.

The Conference adjourned with the benediction pronounced by Benjamin F. Abbott, Central West.

TUESDAY EVENING, MAY 9, 1939

The Conference convened at 7:45 P.M., Tuesday, May 9, for the evening session with Bishop Edgar Blake in the chair. The Bishop announced and the Conference joined in singing Hymn 73, "Be Still, My Soul: The Lord Is on Thy Side."

Bishop John W. Gowdy of China led in prayer, after which the Conference joined in singing Hymn 268, "Are Ye Able? Said the Master."

Merton S. Rice, Detroit, at the request of Bishop Blake, introduced the speaker of the evening, Dr. Charles W. Welch, Moderator of the Presbyterian Church in the United States of America.

Dr. Welch addressed the Conference on the subject of "Evangelism." Bishop Blake replied appropriately in behalf of the Conference.

-ɔDr. James R. Houghton sang as a solo "The
Ninety and Nine."
Bishop Edwin H. Hughes, at the request of
Joseph M. M. Gray, Detroit, Chairman of the
Committee of Courtesies, Privileges, and Introduc-
tions, presented Judge Richard J. Hopkins, the
only United States District Judge in the State of
Kansas.
Dr. Gray presented Dr. Walter Van Kirk, who
spoke to the Conference and told of his work in
broadcasting the news of the Uniting Conference.
Henry H. Crane, Detroit, moved to refer to the
Committee on Judiciary, for their decision, the
question of the legality of deleting from the new
Discipline the footnote to the twenty-third Article
of Religion, found on page 23 of the *Prospectus
of the Discipline.* The motion being duly seconded, Dr. Crane spoke to the question.
His time expiring before he had finished his
remarks, motion of Daniel L. Marsh, New England, duly seconded, prevailed extending the time
not to exceed five minutes.
The motion to refer was adopted.
Ernest H. Cherrington, Ohio, presented a
memoir of Dr. Clarence True Wilson, and moved
that it be received and adopted, without reading,
and made a part of the Journal of the Uniting
Conference. The motion, duly seconded, prevailed. Dr. Cherrington spoke briefly to the
motion. For memoir, see Appendix, "Miscellaneous," page 925.
The following resolution, offered by William F.
Quillian, South Georgia, was adopted:

WHEREAS, a resolution offered by E. D. Soper, page
333, *Daily Christian Advocate,* May 9, 1939, provides that
"The editors of the new *Discipline* are directed . . . .
to print under the appropriate title the names of the
members of the Methodist Ecumenical Council as they
appear in the present *Disciplines* of the Churches"; and
WHEREAS, the list of names thus recorded is incomplete;
therefore be it
Resolved, That the names of these members be printed
in the new *Discipline* as they may be furnished by the
Secretary of the Methodist Ecumenical Council, Western
Section, Dr. A. J. Weeks.

WM. F. QUILLIAN,	EDMUND D. SOPER,
PAUL N. GARBER,	H. W. COX.

MAY 9
THIRTEENTH
DAY
Evening
Referred

Motion of the Secretary, duly seconded, prevailed that the request of the Central Northwest Conference and of the Norwegian-Danish Conference for an Enabling Act in relation to their boundaries, be referred to the Committee on Enabling Acts and Legal Forms, to be reported on tomorrow.

Calendar

On motion of Daniel L. Marsh, New England, duly seconded, the Calendar was taken up.

W. F. Bryan, Texas, stated that a motion of Chester A. Smith, New York, concerning war had been referred to his Committee for consideration; that he had consulted with Brother Smith and the Committee thought it better to consider the Smith resolution as a separate matter, rather than in connection with the report of the Committee touching a Social Creed. Dr. Bryan moved a suspension of the Rules for the purpose of hearing the Smith resolution. The motion did not prevail.

Committee on
Membership
and
Temporal
Economy,
Report No. 6
—"A Social
Creed"

Calendar No. 57, Report No. 6 of the Committee on Membership and Temporal Economy, printed on pages 308 and 309 of the *Daily Christian Advocate* and entitled "A Social Creed," was presented by W. F. Bryan, Texas, Chairman. Dr. Bryan requested John B. Magee, Pacific Northwest, to present the report. Dr. Magee presented the report and moved its adoption. The motion was duly seconded.

John B. Campbell, Northwest Indiana, moved to amend the report by deleting Section 7. The motion being duly seconded, Brother Campbell spoke to the question.

Dr. Magee spoke for the Committee.

The motion being put, Section 7 was deleted.

Alfred M. Landon, Kansas, moved that Section 16 be referred back to the Committee on Membership and Temporal Economy for harmonization with the resolution already referred to that Committee calling for national action against the sale of munitions to Japan. The motion being duly seconded, Governor Landon spoke to the question.

Edmund Heinsohn, West Texas, spoke against the motion to refer.

Nathan Newby, Pacific, spoke in favor of the motion.

Herman Will, Jr., Rock River, spoke against the motion to refer.

Edmund J. Kulp, Missouri, spoke in favor of referring.

William P. King, North Georgia, spoke against the motion to refer.

J. L. Harman, Louisville, spoke in favor of the motion.

Paul M. Hillman, Nebraska, spoke against the motion to refer.

Joseph M. M. Gray, Detroit, spoke in favor of the motion.

Lloyd E. Foster, Newark, spoke against the motion to refer.

Alfred M. Landon, Kansas, on a matter of high personal privilege, suggested that some of the comments were not entirely proper.

Richard T. Baker, Upper Iowa, spoke against the motion to refer.

John B. F. Yoak, Western Virginia, moved the pending question. The motion, duly seconded, prevailed and the pending question was ordered.

Dr. Magee closed the debate for the Committee. The motion to refer Section 16 was put and did not prevail.

Lynn Harold Hough, New York East, spoke in favor of the report.

George E. Farrar, Saint Johns River, moved the previous question. The motion, duly seconded, prevailed, and the previous question was ordered.

The report was adopted as amended. For report, see Appendix, "General Standing Committees," page 535.

George W. Henson, Philadelphia, Chairman of the Committee of Elected Chairmen, reported on the status of the Calendar, and moved to suspend the Rules that we might consider Calendar Reports Nos. 61, 64, 63, and 62 in that order.

The Secretary called attention to the fact that Report No. 61 had been considered in the place of Report No. 30, and now Calendar Report No. 30 takes the place of No. 61. With this explanation the motion of George W. Henson, duly seconded, prevailed.

Calendar No. 30, Report No. 6 of the Committee on Ministry and Judicial Administration, printed

MAY 9
THIRTEENTH
DAY
Evening
Committee on
Membership
and
Temporal
Economy,
Report No. 6
—"A Social
Creed"

MAY 9
THIRTEENTH DAY

Evening

Committee on Ministry and Judicial Administration, Report No. 6—"The Episcopacy—Duties, Powers, and Limitations"

Committee on Education, Report No. 9 —"The Christian Sabbath"

Committee on Education, Report No. 8 —"The Editorial Division"

Committee on Education, Report No. 7 —"The Division of the Local Church"

on page 228 of the *Daily Christian Advocate,* and entitled "The Episcopacy—Duties, Powers, and Limitations," was presented by Orien W. Fifer, Indiana, Chairman, who explained its provisions and moved its adoption. The motion, duly seconded, prevailed. For report, see Appendix, "General Standing Committees," page 486.

Calendar No. 64, Report No. 9 of the Committee on Education, printed on page 346 of the *Daily Christian Advocate* and entitled "The Christian Sabbath," was presented by Paul Quillian, Texas, Chairman. Dr. Quillian requested Lester Rumble, North Georgia, Clem Baker, Little Rock, and J. Calloway Robertson, Virginia, who had helped in the preparation of reports, to come to the platform. Dr. Quillian explained the provisions of the report before the Conference and moved its adoption. The motion, duly seconded, prevailed. For report, see Appendix, "General Standing Committees," page 617.

Calendar No. 63, Report No. 8 of the Committee on Education, printed on pages 345 and 346 of the *Daily Christian Advocate* and entitled "D. The Editorial Division," was presented by Paul Quillian, Texas, Chairman, who requested Dr. Robertson to be in charge of the presentation of the report.

Dr. Robertson explained the provisions of the report and asked common consent to substitute for Paragraph 1084 in the printed report the following:

> There shall be elected quadrennially by the General Conference an Editor of Church School Publications who shall be the Executive Secretary in charge of the Editorial Division of the Board of Education.

Common consent was granted. Dr. Robertson moved the adoption of the report, and the motion, duly seconded, prevailed. For report, see Appendix, "General Standing Committees," page 615.

Calendar No. 62, Report No. 7 of the Committee on Education, printed on pages 344 and 345 of the *Daily Christian Advocate* and entitled "C. The Division of the Local Church," was presented by Paul Quillian, Texas, Chairman. Dr. Quillian asked common consent to make the following change in Paragraph 1071-A: Strike out in lines 25 and 26 the words "and determine" and insert in their place the words "and shall co-operate with the Curriculum Committee in determining." Common consent was granted and the change was made. Dr. Quillian then explained the provisions of the report and moved its adoption. The motion was duly seconded. Dr. Quillian in explaining Paragraph 1080-B gave the nominations for the nine additional persons proposed, not nominated by the Committee on Education, but by the Joint Committee of the Committee on Missions and the Committee on Education, as follows: Jesse L. Corley, Alfred F. Hughes, Wade Crawford Barclay, Roy R. Roudebush, J. Emerson Ford, Clem Baker, J. M. Ormond, Mrs. J. W. Perry, J. Leas Green.

MAY 9
THIRTEENTH DAY
Evening
Committee on Education, Report No. 7 —"The Division of the Local Church"

George C. French, North Texas, raised the question of the overhead and Dr. Quillian replied that the cost will be decreased and not increased.

Chester A. Smith, New York, asked if there was anything in the report or any other report that would prevent Churches now having Epworth Leagues continuing them. The Chairman replied that there was not.

The motion to adopt the report prevailed. For report, see Appendix, "General Standing Committees," page 609.

Motion of George W. Henson, duly seconded, prevailed that we adjourn after Dr. John W. Langdale has presented the memoirs of Dr. Spencer and Dr. Brummitt for publication in the Journal of the Uniting Conference.

Memoirs of Drs. Spencer and Brummitt

Calendar No. 69, Report No. 6 of the Committee on Publishing Interests, printed on pages 350 and 351 of the *Daily Christian Advocate*, being the memoir of Dr. Claudius B. Spencer, was presented by John W. Langdale, New York East, who moved that the report be received and go to record, without reading. The motion, duly seconded, prevailed. For memoir, see Appendix, "General Standing Committees," page 639.

Committee on Publishing Interests, Report No. 6

Calendar No. 70, Report No. 7 of the Committee on Publishing Interests, printed on page 351 of the *Daily Christian Advocate*, being the memoir

Committee on Publishing Interests, Report No. 7

MAY 9
THIRTEENTH
DAY
Evening

of Dr. Dan B. Brummitt, was presented by John W. Langdale, New York East, who moved that the report be received and go to record without reading. The motion, duly seconded, prevailed. For memoir, ˌsee Appendix, "General Standing Committees," page 640.

Adjournment

The Conference adjourned with the benediction pronounced by Bishop Edwin F. Lee of Singapore.

MAY 10
FOURTEENTH
DAY
Morning

Opening

WEDNESDAY MORNING, MAY 10, 1939

Bishop Charles C. Selecman called the Conference to order at 8:30 A.M., Wednesday, May 10, and announced that the worship service would be in charge of Bishop Wilbur E. Hammaker, and that Bishop J. Ralph Magee would deliver the devotional address.

Bishop Magee brought his message from Matthew 4: 1 on the greatest problem ever faced by any man, "How to Make the Kingdom of God Come upon Earth As It Is in Heaven."

Bishop Selecman called the business session of the Conference to order at 9 A.M.

Journal

The Committee on Journal reported as follows:

ſ We have examined the Journal of Monday night; the Journal of Tuesday morning and of Tuesday afternoon, and find them correct.

JOSEPH D. PIPER, *Chairman;*
JOHN R. KENNEY, *Secretary.*

The report was approved.

At the request of the Committee on Journal, the Secretary moved that the approval of the Journal of the session of last night, Tuesday, May 9, and of the three sessions of today, be left to the Secretarial Staff, backed up by the stenotype record. The motion, duly seconded, prevailed.

Patriotic
Devotion

Harold Paul Sloan, New Jersey, presented the following and moved its adoption:

The Methodist Episcopal Church, which before it was divided was foremost among American Churches to declare its devotion to the Federal Government, and to present its duty to President Washington, has to no degree departed from its historic position. As a reunited body we therefore now renew our former expressions of loyalty.

We cherish the freedom secured to mankind by this republic as among our own and the human race's most precious possessions. Political liberty is indeed nothing less than a necessary fruition of the gospel of Jesus Christ: so that devotion to it must of course command the Christian's utmost resource, being conditioned only by that loyalty to the Living God, Himself, by which alone free government can either be, or be made strong.

Being thus exalted and blessed in this liberty of Christian men and Americans, reunited Methodism publishes anew its thanksgiving for the great republic of the West; and pledges its devotion, its sacrifice, and its unceasing prayers that this high heritage received from our fathers may be preserved for our children, and our children's children; and not only as undiminished, but as increased as in each advancing decade made more nobly fair.

[Signed by L. O. Hartman, Harold Paul Sloan, Daniel L. Marsh, Frank S. Hickman, T. D. Ellis, T. S. Ladd Thomas, Orien W. Fifer, H. J. Burgstahler, Fred D. Stone, Leslie J. Lyons, Arlo A. Brown, Thomas S. Brock, John R. Mott, Frank C. Propert, Harry P. Bennett.]

The motion, duly seconded, prevailed.

Report No. 7 of the Committee on Judiciary, printed on page 418 of the *Daily Christian Advocate*, was presented by Francis R. Bayley, Baltimore, Chairman, who moved its adoption. The motion, duly seconded, prevailed. For report, see Appendix, "Special Standing Committees," page 822.

Report No. 8 of the Committee on Judiciary, printed on page 419 of the *Daily Christian Advocate*, was presented by Francis R. Bayley, Baltimore, Chairman, who moved its adoption. The motion, duly seconded, prevailed. For report, see Appendix, "Special Standing Committees," page 822.

Report No. 9 of the Committee on Judiciary, printed on page 419 of the *Daily Christian Advocate*, was presented by Francis R. Bayley, Chairman, who moved its adoption. The motion, duly seconded, prevailed. For report, see Appendix, "Special Standing Committees," page 823.

Francis R. Bayley, Baltimore, moved a reconsideration of the action of last night in referring the footnote to the twenty-third Article of Religion to the Committee on Judiciary for a decision. The motion, duly seconded, prevailed and reconsideration was ordered.

Dr. Bayley then moved to amend Dr. Crane's motion by referring the matter to the Council of Bishops for their study and for them to report their findings to the General Conference of 1940.

MAY 10
FOURTEENTH
DAY

Morning

War and Peace

The motion being seconded, Dr. Bayley spoke to the question. The motion to refer the matter to the Council of Bishops was adopted.

Frank S. Hickman, North Carolina, presented and moved the adoption of the following resolution:

WHEREAS, in the present extremely dangerous state of affairs existing among the nations of the world, it is imperative that every possible influence looking toward the establishment of universal peace be exerted by the followers of the Prince of Peace; and

WHEREAS, a reunited and powerful Church is just now coming into existence whose voice in this grave situation ought to be unequivocal; and

WHEREAS, there exists an honest difference of opinion in regard to the particular form which the conviction of tha Church in this crucial issue ought to take; therefore be tit

Resolved, that the Methodist Church:

1. Takes its stand undivided in its opposition to the spirit of war now raging through the world;

2. Pledges itself to exert every possible influence at its command to persuade belligerent peoples to find such ground of settlement of their difficulties as shall result in lasting peace between them;

3. Urges the President and the Congress of the United States to take every possible step to avoid the entanglement of our country in a world-wide conflagration of war which we are convinced would bring our civilization into ruins; and

4. Commits to our Board of Education the responsibility of laying the foundation of a system of Christian education which shall seek to eradicate the causes of war and train our children for Christian participation in the arts of peace.

<table>
<tr><td>T. D. ELLIS, •</td><td>E. D. KOHLSTEDT,</td></tr>
<tr><td>WM. F. QUILLIAN,</td><td>HAROLD PAUL SLOAN,·</td></tr>
<tr><td>NOLAN B. HARMON, JR.,</td><td>GEORGE W. CRABBE,</td></tr>
<tr><td>M. S. RICE,</td><td>J. EMERSON FORD,</td></tr>
<tr><td>FRANK S. HICKMAN, •</td><td>A. W. PUGH,</td></tr>
<tr><td>HARRY E. WOOLEVER,</td><td>B. D. BECK,</td></tr>
<tr><td>J. M. ORMOND, · -</td><td>F. W. WAHL.</td></tr>
<tr><td>J. L. BRASHER, · ..</td><td></td></tr>
</table>

Bishop and
Mrs. Flint

The motion, duly seconded, prevailed.

Mrs. Mary McCloud Bethune, South Florida, under the question of personal privilege, presented the greetings of the women of her race to the United Conference. Asking Bishop and Mrs. Charles W. Flint and the delegation of the Atlanta Area to stand, she then presented to Bishop and Mrs. Flint, on behalf of the Atlanta Area, a bouquet of beautiful flowers as a token of their appreciation of the faithful service rendered the Area by Bishop and Mrs. Flint. Bishop Flint replied appropriately and Mrs. Flint received the bouquet amid the applause of the delegates.

Report No. 11 of the Committee on Credentials was presented by Earl R. Brown, Northeast Ohio. By common consent, according to previous action, the report was received and ordered printed in the *Daily Advocate*. (See report, page 842.)

Willard G. Cram, Kentucky, .presented the following resolution:

Resolved, That the Council of Bishops be requested to appoint a Committee of two representatives from each Jurisdiction to consider the matter of the location of Boards and Commissions authorized by the Uniting Conference and make report to the General Conference of 1940, the expenses of the Committee to be paid from the Administrative Fund.

JOHN R. MOTT,	JOHN W. LANGDALE,
W. M. ALEXANDER,	THOMAS S. BROCK,
FRED D. STONE,	HAROLD PAUL SLOAN,
JOSEPH M. M. GRAY,	A. W. WASSON,
T. D. ELLIS,	WM. K. ANDERSON,
WM. F. QUILLIAN,	W. G. CRAM.

On the motion of Dr. Cram, duly seconded, the resolution was adopted.

George W. Henson, Philadelphia, moved that the Rules be suspended and that the Calendar be taken up in its regular order, to be followed by the Reports of the Committee on Enabling Acts and Legal Forms. The motion, duly seconded, prevailed.

Calendar No. 58, Report No. 7 of the Committee on Membership and Temporal Economy, printed on page 309 of the *Daily Christian Advocate*, was presented by W. F. Bryan, Texas, Chairman, who requested Costen J. Harrell, Tennessee, to be in charge of the report. Dr. Bryan stated that this report was simply the clarification of a matter already passed.

Committee on
Membership
and
Temporal
Economy,
Report No. 7

Dr. Harrell moved a reconsideration of Calendar No. 7, Report No. 1 of the Committee on Membership and Temporal Economy, printed on pages 128 and 129 of the *Daily Christian Advocate*, in order to harmonize both reports. The motion, duly seconded, prevailed and reconsideration was ordered.

Committee on
Membership
and
Temporal
Economy,
Report No. 1
—Reconsidered

MAY 10
FOURTEENTH
DAY

Morning

Dr. Harrell requested common consent to amend Paragraph 430 by adding to the fourth line the words "as may be authorized by the Quarterly Conference," and in the last line of the report to change the figure "450" to "430·" This was granted by the Conference.

Dr. Harrell moved to amend Paragraph 430, Calendar No. 7, Report No. 1 of the Committee on Membership and Temporal Economy, by substituting Paragraph 430 as presented in Calendar No. 58, Report No. 7 of the same Committee, now before the Conference. The motion, duly seconded, prevailed. Calendar No. 7, Report No. 1 of the Committee on Membership and Temporal Economy, as amended, was then adopted. For report, see Appendix, "General Standing Committees," page 509.

Committee on
Membership
and
Temporal
Economy,
Report No. 7

Calendar No. 58, Report No. 7 of the Committee on Membership and Temporal Economy, on motion of Dr. Harrell, duly seconded, was adopted. For report, see Appendix, "General Standing Committees," page 538.

Committee on
Membership
and
Temporal
Economy,
Report No. 8
—"Ministe-
rial Sup-
port"

Calendar No. 59, Report No. 8 of the Committee on Membership and Temporal Economy, printed on pages 309 and 310 of the *Daily Christian Advocate* and entitled "Ministerial Support," was presented by W. F. Bryan, Texas, Chairman, who requested R. F. Curl, West Texas, to represent the Committee. Dr. Curl explained the provisions of the report and moved its adoption. The motion was duly seconded.

Arthur A. Callaghan, Maine, moved to amend Paragraph 536 by substituting the word "accepted" for the word "adopted" in line 9. This was accepted by the Chairman for the Committee, no objection being raised.

Mrs. J. W. Perry, Holston, moved to amend the report by striking out Paragraph 546.

John R. Edwards, Baltimore, spoke against the motion to delete Paragraph 546 and recommended that the word "pastor" be included in the report. The Chairman of the Committee accepted the recommendation.

Lovick P. Wasson, North Mississippi, moved, as a substitute for the Perry motion to delete, that the paragraph be amended by substituting for the words "be responsible," in line 3, the words "have special responsibility" and by striking out line 6. This was accepted by the Chairman, no objection being raised.

A. W. Martin, North Arkansas, moved to amend Paragraph 546 by striking out the words "Board of Lay Activities and the Woman's Missionary organizations," in lines 1, 2, and 3, and substituting therefor the words "Official Board." The motion was duly seconded.

J. C. McPheeters, Pacific, spoke against the Martin amendment.

William E. Shaw, Illinois, moved to amend by adding to the personnel of Paragraph 546 the "Local Council of Missions and Church Extension" provided for in the Report of the Committee on Missions adopted yesterday. The motion was duly seconded.

Elmer E. Collins, Montana State, moved the previous question on all before the Conference. The motion, duly seconded, prevailed, and the previous question was ordered.

R. F. Curl closed the debate for the Committee.

The vote was taken on the Shaw amendment, and it did not prevail.

The vote was taken on the Martin amendment, and it did not prevail.

The vote was then taken on the Perry substitute to strike out Paragraph 546 and it did not prevail.

Henry M. Andrews raised a point of order that the adoption of the report would be contradictory to one already adopted. The Chair ruled the point of order not well taken.

The report was then adopted. For report, see Appendix, "General Standing Committees," page 538.

Calendar No. 60, Report 9 of the Committee on Membership and Temporal Economy, printed on pages 310 and 311 of the *Daily Christian Advocate* and entitled "Admission into the Church," was presented by W. F. Bryan, Texas, Chairman, who requested William C. Hartinger, Indiana, to be in charge of the report.

Dr. Hartinger explained the provisions of the

MAY 10
FOURTEENTH
DAY
Morning

Committee on
Membership
and
Temporal
Economy,
Report No. 8
—"Ministe-
rial Sup-
port"

Committee on
Membership
and
Temporal
Economy,
Report No. 9
—"Admis-
sion into the
Church"

MAY 10
FOURTEENTH
DAY

Morning

Committee on
Membership
and
Temporal
Economy,
Report No. 9
—"Admis-
sion into the
Church"

report and moved its adoption. The motion was duly seconded.

Thomas S. Brock, New Jersey, asked an interpretation of Paragraph 419. Dr. Hartinger asked common consent to insert after the words "Request give" the words "a certificate of membership and," stating that they had been left out. Common consent was given, there being no objection.

William K. Anderson, Pittsburgh, moved to amend Paragraph 415 by adding Section A as follows: "The continual cleansing of nonresident lists is enjoined upon churches, and all nonresidents whose addresses have been lost shall be stricken from the roll as "withdrawn without Certificate."

The motion was duly seconded and Dr. Anderson spoke to the question. Dr. Hartinger stated that the matter was taken care of in Paragraphs 423 and 424.

Daniel L. Marsh, New England, moved the pending question. The motion, duly seconded, prevailed and the pending question was ordered.

The Anderson amendment, being put to a vote, did not prevail.

The hour of recess having arrived, motion of Daniel L. Marsh, New England, duly seconded, prevailed that the time be extended to complete consideration of this report.

R. F. Curl, West Texas, moved to amend Paragraph 405 by inserting before the words "upon giving," in line 4, the words "upon the presentation of a Certificate of membership from their Church or." The motion being duly seconded, Dr. Curl spoke to the question.

Lynn Harold Hough, New York East, moved the previous question. The motion, duly seconded, prevailed and the previous question was ordered.

Dr. Hartinger closed the debate for the Committee.

The vote was taken on the Curl amendment and it did not prevail.

The report was adopted. For report, see Appendix, "General Standing Committees," page 542.

The Conference recessed at 10:40 A.M.

Bishop Selecman called the Conference to order

at 10:50 A.M. The Conference stood and sang Hymn 209, "Amazing Grace! How Sweet the Sound," led by Dean Robert G. McCutchan, Northwest Indiana.

Dr. James R. Houghton presented the choir of the National Training School for Christian Workers, Kansas City, Mo., and stated that the school was under the sponsorship of the Woman's Home Missionary Society. Dr. Houghton requested Bishop Charles L. Mead to present the Choir to the Conference. Bishop Mead introduced Dr. Anna Neidherheiser, President of the School, and Miss A. Louise Sumwalt, Director of Music. The Choir sang the "Hallelujah Chorus," by Beethoven.

Joseph M. M. Gray, Detroit, Chairman of the Committee on Courtesies, Privileges, and Introductions, presented Mr. J. Max Kruwel, Minister of Music, Boulevard Methodist Church of Kansas City, the official organist of the Uniting Conference.

Mr. Kruwel
Presented

The following resolution was presented by Leslie J. Lyons, Missouri:

Conference
Sessions

WHEREAS, it will be necessary in a substantial number of States, in the formation of new Conferences authorized by the Uniting Conference and in adjusting boundary lines changed by the action of the Uniting Conference, to arrange sessions of the Conferences involved at the same time or approximately at the same time; and

WHEREAS, it would be a great waste of time and expense if said Conferences could be authorized to hold their final sessions outside of their boundaries; therefore be it

Resolved, That we request the Committee on Enabling Acts and Legal Forms to prepare and submit to this Conference for its action an appropriate Enabling Act authorizing Conferences to hold their final sessions outside their boundaries, and that the first sessions of the new Conferences may be held outside their boundaries but within their Jurisdictions.

The resolution, duly seconded, was adopted.

Under a question of privilege, Bishop A. Frank Smith presented the booklet prepared by Dr. Harry E. Woolever, Central New York, concerning Methodist Union, and urged all to secure copies.

History of
Union

George W. Henson, Philadelphia, raised the point of order that recess did not cancel the order of the Calendar. The Chair ruled the point well taken.

MAY 10
FOURTEENTH
DAY
Morning

Under a matter of high privilege for the Conference, George C. Douglass, Troy, presented the following:

Jurisdictional
Conference
Expense

The Council of Bishops requests the Committee on Membership and Temporal Economy to bring in a resolution to the following effect: That the Bishops of each Jurisdiction shall appoint a Committee composed of three laymen and three ministers, who with the Bishops of the Jurisdiction shall determine a method of raising the fund necessary for the expenses of the first Jurisdictional Conference.

George C. French, North Texas, moved to amend by adding the words "subject to the approval of the Jurisdictional Conference." On being informed that this resolution was to cover a temporary situation only, he withdrew his amendment.

On motion of Dr. Douglass, duly seconded, the request was approved.

Special
Collections

W. F. Bryan, Texas, Chairman of the Committee on Membership and Temporal Economy, under a question of privilege for the Conference, requested that Orrin W. Auman, Colorado, be permitted to present a brief paper relative to Special Collections, the preparation of said paper having been ordered by the Uniting Conference at its session on Tuesday morning, May 9. Dr. Auman presented the following as an addition to Paragraph 405, Calendar No. 42, Report No. 5 of the Committee on Membership and Temporal Economy, and to go to record:

Any General Board or Agency requesting the privilege of a Church-wide collection in the interests of its work shall present such request to the Commission on World Service and Finance when the askings of the Board or Agency for the ensuing quadrennium are presented to the Commission.

The Commission shall make recommendations to the General Conference as to the special collection and special days to be authorized. The Commission shall bring to the General Conference a recommendation in the case of each collection as to whether the income from such special collection shall constitute a part of the support from the Benevolence Funds by the Board receiving such collection, or whether the income from such special collection shall be over and above the support of the Board or Agency from the General Benevolence Funds.

By common consent the paper was ordered to record at the proper place.

Calendar No. 65, Report No. 10 of the Committee on Education, printed on pages 346 and 347 of the *Daily Christian Advocate* and entitled "Jurisdictional Board of Education," was presented by Paul Quillian, Texas. Dr. Quillian requested Clem Baker, Little Rock, and Lester Rumble, North Georgia, to come to the platform. Dr. Quillian explained the provisions of the report, stating that Paragraph 1103 needed a correction and asked common consent to change the words "Annual Conference," in line 6, to read "Division of the Local Church." Common consent was granted, no objection being raised. Dr. Quillian moved the adoption of the report and the motion was duly seconded.

Francis R. Bayley, Baltimore, moved to amend Paragraph 1091 by substituting the word "may" for the word "shall" in line 2. This was accepted by the Chairman, no objection being raised.

The report was adopted. For report, see Appendix, "General Standing Committees," page 618.

Dr. Quillian asked common consent to refer to the Committee on Location of Boards and Commissions, authorized this morning by the Uniting Conference, Report No. 13 of the Committee on Education relative to the same matter, Report No. 13 not being a Calendar Report. By common consent, this request was granted.

Calendar No. 66, Report No. 11 of the Committee on Education, printed on page 347 of the *Daily Christian Advocate* and entitled "Annual Conference Board of Education," was presented by Paul Quillian, Texas, Chairman, who explained its provisions and moved its adoption. The motion was duly seconded.

Cary A. Kemp, Northwest Kansas, raised the question if the word "shall" in line 2 should not be "may" in the light of the motion made by Dr. Bayley in the adoption of the previous report. Dr. Quillian replied that the pending report dealt with the *Annual Conference* and there should be authorized an Annual Conference Board of Education.

Charles V. Adams, Central Pennsylvania, moved to amend Paragraph 1112 by inserting the

MAY 10
FOURTEENTH
DAY

Morning

Committee on
Education,
Report No.
10—"Jurisdictional
Board of
Education"

Referred

Committee on
Education,
Report No.
11—"Annual Conference Board
of Education"

words "portion of a" before the word "session" in
line 4. This was accepted by Dr. Quillian, no objection being raised.

John R. Edwards, Baltimore, moved to amend
Paragraph 1107 by inserting after the words "Executive Secretary," in line 4, the words "who may
serve for two or more contiguous Conferences."
This was accepted by the Chairman, no objection
being raised.

J. Edgar Skillington, Central Pennsylvania,
asked for an explanation of Paragraph 1114 concerning "receipts from Missionary offerings in
Church schools."

The Chairman stated that the *Disciplines* of the
former Methodist Episcopal Church and of the
former Methodist Episcopal Church, South, provided for a certain portion of the Missionary offering from Church schools to be returned to Annual
Conferences for the support of extension and
rural work and neglected areas.

Dr. Skillington asked further if the Conference
Board of Education can determine the fraction or
portion of these offerings that are to be available.

Dr. Quillian stated that the General Conference
only had this authority.

Frank C. Propert, New Jersey, moved to amend
Paragraph 1107 by omitting the words "Executive Secretary" and add the following sentence:
"At the option of the Annual Conference, an Executive Secretary may be employed." The motion
was duly seconded, but did not prevail.

The report was adopted. For report, see Appendix, "General Standing Committees," page
621.

Calendar No. 67, Report No. 12 of the Committee on Education, printed on pages 347, 348, and
349 of the *Daily Christian Advocate* and entitled
"The Local Church," was presented by Paul Quillian, Texas, Chairman, who explained its provisions and moved its adoption. The motion was
duly seconded.

Dr. Quillian asked common consent to make the
following corrections in Paragraph 1120: Insert
the words "pastor and the" before the word "general" in line 10, and insert the word "assistant"
after the words "elect the" in line 11. Common
consent was granted, no objection being raised.

The time of Dr. Quillian expiring before the end of the explanation of the provisions of the report, motion of Daniel L. Marsh, New England, duly seconded, prevailed extending the time to complete the explanation.

Ralph E. Diffendorfer, Rock River, called attention to the last sentence of Paragraph 1124, and Section 4 of Paragraph 1126, stating that a very important question was raised and that these paragraphs he thought did not harmonize the *Discipline*. Dr. Diffendorfer suggested that these paragraphs be referred to the Commission authorized by the Uniting Conference to study all phases of the Missionary work, and which Commission is to report to the 1940 General Conference. Dr. Quillian stated that he would be glad to refer the paragraphs to the Commission.

J. Fisher Simpson, West Texas, moved to amend Paragraph 1122 by adding an item to come after present Item 4 to read as follows:

> To provide opportunities for parents and young people to have studies in marriage and Christian homemaking.

This was accepted by the Chairman, no objection being raised.

The report was adopted. For report, see Appendix, "General Standing Committees," page 624.

Calendar No. 68, Report No. 14 of the Committee on Conferences, printed on pages 349 and 350 of the *Daily Christian Advocate* and entitled "Annual Conferences," was presented by George W. Henson, Philadelphia, Chairman, who explained its provisions. Dr. Henson called attention to a typographical error in Article 3 of Paragraph 162. In line 9, after the words "in the" at the end of the line, add the words "General Conference shall be representatives in that body. Additional delegates shall be elected to complete the number determined by the ratio for representation in the." Then add to Article 4, Paragraph 164, the following: "The Annual Conference shall have power to locate a ministerial member for unacceptability and inefficiency." By common consent these additions were made, no objection being raised.

MAY 10
FOURTEENTH
DAY
Morning
Committee on
Education,
Report No.
12—"The
Local
Church"

Committee on
Conferences,
Report No.
14—"An-
nual Confer-
ences"

The time of Dr. Henson expiring before he had finished his explanation of the provisions of the report, motion of Nathan Newby, Pacific, duly seconded, prevailed extending the time to complete the presentation of the report.

Dr. Henson moved the adoption of the report. The motion, duly seconded, prevailed. For report, see Appendix, "General Standing Committees," page 451.

Business
Committee

Bishop Edwin H. Hughes reported for the Business Committee as follows:

We recommend that the following action be taken on the matters referred to your Business Committee:

1. Local condition in this city. No action recommended.

2. That the Bishops study the written Constitutions now found in the *Disciplines* of the several churches with instructions to report to this Conference. No action recommended.

3. The international matter relating to munitions. No action recommended.

4. A resolution of Chapin D. Foster, relative to a day of national prayer. We recommend that Mr. Foster be heard, if the paper will provoke no debate.

Day of Prayer

By common consent the report was adopted.

Chapin D. Foster, Pacific Northwest, offered the following resolution and moved its adoption:

Resolved, That The Methodist Church earnestly requests the President of the United States to give serious consideration to the setting aside by Proclamation of a National Day of Prayer, urging all denominations and all civic and service organizations to unite both in the fact and in the spirit of such an occasion, to the end that this Nation may humbly ask Divine guidance in these critical days, and courage to follow that guidance.

The Methodist Church firmly believes that a Day of Prayer, honestly and conscientiously observed, would make a contribution of inestimable value to the cause of World Peace and understanding.

In the event that the President of the United States finds that such a Day of Prayer might be set aside, The Methodist Church pledges him the sincere co-operation of eight million members of a United Church.

The motion, duly seconded, prevailed.

Motion of Daniel L. Marsh, duly seconded, prevailed that after announcements we adjourn.

Announce-
ments

Adjournment

Various announcements were made and the Conference adjourned with the benediction pronounced by Bishop Raymond J. Wade.

WEDNESDAY AFTERNOON, MAY 10, 1939

Pursuant to adjournment, the Uniting Conference convened at 2:15 P.M. with Bishop Titus
Lowe in the chair. The Bishop announced and
the Conference stood and joined in singing Hymn
487, "The Morning Light Is Breaking."
The Conference was led in prayer by Bishop
Edwin F. Lee of Singapore.

Opening

Bishop Lowe requested the privilege of having
four of the Bishops who had served on the wide-
flung line of missions to address the Conference
briefly. This was ordered by common consent.
Bishop Lowe then separately presented Bishop
John Gowdy of China, Bishop J. Waskom Pickett
of India, Bishop John M. Springer of Africa, and
Bishop Ralph J. Ward of China. Each spoke op-
timistically of the several fields represented. The
Conference rose and applauded at the close of
the addresses. At the request of Bishop Lowe,
Merton S. Rice, Detroit, led in prayer.

Bishops Gowdy, Pickett, Springer, and Ward Address the Conference

Motion of Leslie J. Lyons, Missouri, duly seconded, prevailed that the photographers be permitted to take a picture of the Conference at this
time. The picture was taken.

Conference Picture

Joseph M. M. Gray, Detroit, Chairman of the
Committee on Courtesies, Privileges, and Intro-
ductions, requested that Umphrey Lee, North
Texas, of the Committee, present Resolutions of
Appreciation at this time.

Resolutions of Appreciation

Dr. Lee presented the report of the Committee
and moved its adoption. The motion, duly seconded, prevailed and the following resolutions
were adopted:

REPORT ON RESOLUTIONS

Upon the success of this Uniting Conference, upon its
spirit as well as its enactments, depends in a large way
the future of American Methodism. We are, therefore,
especially grateful to all who have made it possible for
the Conference to work in comfort in spite of its size and
the magnitude of its task.

We acknowledge our obligations to the Committee on
Entertainment of the Uniting Conference, the Local Committee on Entertainment, to the Co-Chairmen, Bishop
Charles L. Mead and Bishop William T. Watkins, and to
the Executive Committee, Dr. L. E. Dixon, Dr. Edward
Hislop, Dr. Thomas B. Mather, and Dr. W. A. Keve, and
to the individual members of the various committees
working with them, whose chairmen were introduced to

MAY 10
FOURTEENTH
DAY
Afternoon

Resolutions of
Appreciation the Conference on Tuesday, May 9. Their very difficult task has been performed so that the Conference has been free of minor irritations and has been comfortable during an arduous session. Our thanks are due to the Very Reverend Claude Sprouse, Dean of Grace and Holy Trinity Cathedral, who made possible the use of the Cathedral for our opening Communion services.

We would remember especially the ushers, who have given their time and have worked hard for the convenience of the delegates and guests, and the pages, who have been alert and gracious.

The thanks of the Conference are due to the City and to the Convention Bureau of the Chamber of Commerce through whom we have the use of this great Auditorium and to the superintendent and technicians who have prepared the Auditorium for our use. Other courtesies of the City, especially the services of the Traffic Squad of the Kansas City Police, are acknowledged with our sincere thanks.

The Uniting Conference wishes to express its deep appreciation of the efficient work of E. B. Chappell, Jr., Paul M. Hillman, and Charles M. Smith, Editors, and Harry L. White and his associates on the stenotype force in providing *The Daily Christian Advocate.*

The Uniting Conference wishes to express its gratitude to the dailies of the country which have maintained representatives at the Conference for accurate and adequate reporting of the proceedings of the Conference. The Conference wishes also to express its appreciation to the national press associations and news-distribution agencies, to the National Broadcasting Company, the Columbia Broadcasting System, the Mutual Broadcasting System, the radio stations of Kansas City, Trans-Radio Press, the Fox Movietone Corporation, and to the Rev. Dr. Walter Van Kirk, commentator on religious news for the Federal Council of Churches of Christ in America, for valued assistance in telling the story of Methodism Unification to America.

We thank the National Committee on Publicity, Dr. Miron A. Morrell, Dr. Elmer T. Clark, Crates S. Johnson, and their assistants for their excellent work in making it possible for the press to obtain accurate and complete news reports of the proceedings of this Conference.

The officials responsible for the exhibits of the various Boards and causes of the Church displayed in this building are offered this expression of our gratitude.

In the work of the Conference, many have contributed to expedite business and to handle the endless detail of this unique gathering. Committee members and especially the officers of the various committees, who worked long hours to prepare the voluminous reports submitted to this body should know that this Conference and all Methodism in America are grateful to them for their unselfish service.

The Bishops, who have presided with such fairness and courtesy, are assured of our very real gratitude.

We thank the Secretary, Dr. Lud Estes, and his assistants for their efficient work.

All who participated in the worship services deserve the gratitude of the Conference, as this has been helpful in every way in promoting our main objective, the creation of spiritual unity. This Committee desires to express to Dr. James R. Houghton, the Precentor of the Conference, the unqualified thanks of the body for the work that he has done in preparing and directing the music of the Conference.

The organist, the Boston University School of Theology's chorus, the Kansas Wesleyan University's Harmonic Choir, and all other organizations and individuals who have helped in the music of this Conference, will be gratefully remembered.

In such a large Conference, with so elaborate a program, it is impossible to mention all who have helped in entertainment and inspiration. We are grateful for the evangelistic services, the pageants, and the special services, although they cannot here be reviewed. And we appreciate the spirit of those who have cut short their programs to enable this Conference to complete its work tonight.

In carrying out the work set for this Uniting Conference, the delegates have always been conscious of their great debt to the Joint Commission on Interdenominational Relations and Church Union of the former Methodist Churches now united in The Methodist Church, and to the Preparatory Committees appointed by this Joint Commission. Their long and careful labor has made it possible for a Conference to meet and complete the legal steps necessary to the formation of a great United Church. The Chairmen of the Joint Commission, Bishop Edwin Holt Hughes, Bishop John M. Moore, and Bishop James H. Straughn, have been not only co-laborers but symbols of the movement for unity in American Methodism.

Most of all we are thankful for the spirit of this Uniting Conference, for the tolerance, the courtesy, the brotherly love which have here prevailed. With great care the Conference was so constituted that the rights of each of the three Churches participating might be protected; it is the justification of this Conference that the safeguards have grown to be unnecessary. We have done much toward perfecting the organization of The Methodist Church; we have done more in demonstrating our spiritual unity.

For all of this we offer humble thanks to Almighty God, who has brought us to this good hour; and we pray that He may increase our faith, confirm our hope, and perfect us in love.   STANLEY O. MCMULLEN,
                              T. LEROY HOOPER,
                              UMPHREY LEE.

Bishop Lowe introduced Francis R. Bayley, Baltimore, President of the Judicial Council of The Methodist Church. Dr. Bayley introduced his colleagues with the statement, "This is the Supreme Court of The Methodist Church." The Conference rose in applause as the members were introduced as follows: Martin E. Lawson, Southwest Missouri, Vice-President; Henry R. Van

Margin notes:
MAY 10
FOURTEENTH
DAY

Afternoon

Resolutions of
Appreciation

Judicial
Council
Members
Introduced

10

ENTH
Y

noon

Deusen, Wyoming, Secretary; Dr. Walter C. Buckner, Southern California; Dr. George R. Brown,
North Carolina; Dr. W. G. Henry, North Alabama; Dr. J. Stewart French, Holston; Vincent
P. Clarke, New England; M. A. Childers, West
Texas, had to leave the Conference before the Judicial Council was presented.

ee on
ns.
: No.
ser-

John R. Mott, New York, Chairman of the
Committee on Missions, presented three recommendations for record and for insertion at the
proper place in Calendar No. 71, Report No. 5 of
the Committee on Missions. These recommendations were relative to the Bureau of Deaconess
Work, and had been inadvertently omitted in the
drafting of the Report of the Committee. Report
No. 5 of the Committee on Missions was adopted
Tuesday morning, May 9, 1939, with the understanding that this matter would be looked into and
properly taken care of by the Chairman. Motion of John R. Mott, duly seconded, prevailed
adopting the recommendations and ordering them
to record at their proper place.

Motion of George W. Henson, Philadelphia,
Chairman of the Committee of Elected Chairmen,
duly seconded, prevailed that we proceed with the
Calendar.

ee ' on
y and
l Ad-
ation,
No.

ns"

Calendar No. 73, Report No. 13 of the Committee on Ministry and Judicial Administration,
printed on pages 360 to 363 inclusive of the *Daily
Christian Advocate* and entitled "Deacons," was
presented by Orien W. Fifer, Indiana, Chairman,
who requested J. Manning Potts, Virginia, to
be in charge of the report. Dr. Potts stated that
the report would be presented in three divisions.
Dr. Potts explained the provisions of Section VI,
Deacons. Dr. Potts stated that, due to a secretarial error, Paragraph 252 was worded as in the
Prospectus of the Discipline, page 76, but that
the Committee recommended a change and that by
common consent he was offering the following as
a substitute for Paragraph 252:

252. (1) Whenever it is determined by the Committee
on Conference Relations or the Ministerial Qualifications
Group that, in their judgment, a member of the Annual
Conference is unacceptable, inefficient, or indifferent in
the work of the ministry, or that his conduct is such as
to impair seriously his usefulness as a minister, or that

his engagement in secular business, except as required by the ill health of himself or of his family, disqualifies him for pastoral work, they shall notify him in writing, and ask him to request location at the next session of the Annual Conference. If he refuses or neglects to locate as requested, the Conference may, by count vote, upon recommendation of the Committee on Conference Relations, locate him without his consent, and deprive him of the right to exercise the ministerial office.

(2) Whenever it is unanimously determined by the District Superintendents that a member of the Annual Conference should be located for any of the reasons cited in Section 1, they shall notify him in writing of their judgment at least six months before the next session of the Annual Conference, and ask him to request location at such session under the provisions of Paragraph 251. If he refuses or neglects to locate as requested, the District Superintendents shall certify the facts to the Committee on Conference Relations or Ministerial Qualifications Group, which Committee shall proceed to recommend his immediate location without his consent, and the discontinuance of his right to exercise the ministerial office.

(3) However, if any located person remains a member in good standing of The Methodist Church until the age of sixty-five years, he shall thereby retain the right to make an annuity claim, based upon the years of his effective ministry and subject to the action of the Annual Conference. FRANK L. SHAFFER, *Secretary.*

MAY 10
FOURTEENTH DAY
Afternoon
Committee on Ministry and Judicial Administration, Report No. 13—
"Deacons"

(Note the Brock amendment in the next paragraph, which was accepted.)

Thomas S. Brock, New Jersey, at the request of Dr. Potts, explained the provisions of the paragraph and suggested the following rewording for clarification: Change the last clause of Section 1, which reads "and deprive him of the right to exercise the ministerial office," and change the last clause in Section 2, which reads "and the discontinuance of his right to exercise the ministerial office," so that the clauses shall read in both Sections 1 and 2 as follows: "which discontinues his right to exercise the ministerial office." This was accepted by Dr. Potts. The Conference then gave common consent to make the substitution as requested. Dr. Potts then moved the adoption of Section VI and the motion was duly seconded.

William F. McMurry, Memphis, raised the following question:

Does Paragraph 252, Article 3, providing that a located minister retains certain annuity rights under certain circumstances, apply to ministers under voluntary as well as involuntary location?

MAY 10
FOURTEENTH
DAY

Afternoon

Committee on
Ministry and
Judicial Ad-
ministration,
Report No.
13—
"Deacons"

Dr. Potts replied that 'it is the intention to apply it to any located minister.

W. F. McMurry called attention to an apparent conflict between Paragraph 252, Article 3, now pending, and Paragraph 1341 of Calendar No. 20, Report No. 4 of the Committee on Superannuate Support, printed on pages 190 and 191 of the *Daily Christian Advocate.*

Thomas S. Brock, New Jersey, Chairman of the Committee on Superannuate Support, replied that Paragraph 1341, referred to, related to Judicial decisions in the old *Disciplines,* and not to the forthcoming *Discipline,* and were simply placed in the report as a matter of reference.

Thomas A. Stafford, Northern Minnesota, asked an interpretation of the following words in Paragraph 252, Section 3: "the right to make an annuity claim, based upon the years of his effective ministry and subject to the action of the Annual Conference." Dr. Stafford's question is as follows:

What is that action? That is what I want answered. Is that an action restoring his membership in the Conference so he can be in a position to make a claim, or is it an action restoring the claim without restoring membership in the Conference?

Dr. Potts replied as follows:

The action only restores the claimant's membership in the Conference. The point has been made that a man may serve up until the age of sixty-five and that though he may have served for part of that time, or all of it, ineffectively, that should not destroy his claim to an annuity. If the Conference allowed him to remain in it, and he probably did the best he could with what he had to work with, they feel that he should have a claimant annuity.

Arthur M. Wells, Illinois, raised the question, "When a man takes a location on his own request to avoid charges or expulsion, then what effect does it have on his claim to be made later?"

The Chairman replied: "We do not think that he would have that claim, then."

Section VI, on motion of Dr. Potts, duly seconded, was adopted.

Dr. Potts proceeded to explain Section VII, Local Preachers, and moved its adoption. The motion was duly seconded.

A. Wesley Pugh, North Indiana, moved to amend Paragraph 261, Article 7, by inserting after the words "of Baptism," in line 5, the words "and of the Lord's Supper." This was accepted by the Chairman for the Committee, no objection being raised.

Dr. Pugh moved to further amend Paragraph 261, Article 7, by striking out all after the word "fields" at the beginning of line eight, and inserting the following: "the conferring of such authority shall rest with the Central Conferences in which they are pastors." This was accepted by Dr. Potts for the Committee, no objection being raised.

Mrs. Florence R. Jardine, Northern Minnesota, presented a minority report, printed on page 363 of the *Daily Christian Advocate*, for Paragraph 266, Article 12 of Section VII, now pending, and moved its adoption as a substitute for Paragraph 266 of the majority report. The motion being duly seconded, Mrs. Jardine spoke to the question.

Her time expiring before she had finished her remarks, motion of J. Manning Potts, Virginia, duly seconded, prevailed extending her time.

Mrs. Jardine moved the adoption of the substitute and the motion was duly seconded.

Isaac E. Miller, Ohio, spoke against the substitute.

George W. Henson, Philadelphia, Chairman of the Committee of Elected Chairmen, being recognized, called attention to the Order of the Day for four-thirty, the amount of business yet to be presented to the Conference, and moved that the speeches be limited to three on each side and then to the closing speech by the minority and the majority. The motion was duly seconded.

Daniel L. Marsh, New England, moved to amend the motion by making it one speech instead of three speeches before the closing arguments by the respective Chairmen. Dr. Henson and his second accepted the amendment, and the motion prevailed.

Miss Irma Highbaugh, China, spoke for the substitute. Her time expiring before she had finished her remarks, motion of Herbert J. Burg-

MAY 10
FOURTEENTH
DAY

Afternoon

Committee on
Ministry and
Judicial Administration,
Report No.
13—
"Deacons"

MAY 10
FOURTEENTH
DAY

Afternoon

Committee on
Ministry and
Judicial Ad-
ministration,
Report No.
13—
"Deacons"

stahler, Upper Iowa, duly seconded, prevailed extending her time.

Mrs. T. H. Minga, North Texas, spoke against the substitute.

John R. Edwards, Baltimore, raised the question as to what would be the status of women already ordained and in Annual Conference membership if the majority report were adopted.

The Chairman replied: "This does not take away from any women who are ordained the rights that they now have."

Mrs. Jardine closed the debate for the minority report.

J. Manning Potts closed the debate for the majority report.

By a count vote of 384 against and 371 for, the minority report was not adopted.

Dr. Potts moved the adoption of Section VII, and the motion, duly seconded, prevailed.

J. Manning Potts moved that Paragraph 177 of Calendar No. 6, Report No. 3 of the Committee on Conferences, printed on page 128 of the *Daily Christian Advocate*, as regards the use of tobacco, be made to conform to Paragraph 258, Section 1, item "Third" in Section VII, just adopted. The motion, duly seconded, prevailed.

Dr. Potts explained Sections VIII and IX and moved their adoption. The motion, duly seconded, prevailed.

Dr. Potts then moved the adoption of the report. The motion, duly seconded, prevailed. For report, see Appendix, "General Standing Committees," page 498.

George W. Henson, Philadelphia, Chairman of the Committee on Conferences, offered the following resolution:

Resolved, That General or Executive Secretaries of the General Boards of the Church who are not elected members of the General Conference shall have the privilege of the floor on matters affecting the interests of their Boards, but without vote and at the expense of their respective Boards.

The resolution was adopted on motion of Dr. Henson, duly seconded.

Dr. Henson presented the following resolution:

Where an Annual Conference meets in the regular session on the eve of the 1940 General Conference, if it is desired, it may hold a called session of the Annual Conference at which may be considered the matter of electing delegates to the General and Jurisdictional Conferences; *provided* such called session shall not be held earlier than nine months preceding the General Conference. An adjourned session may be held for the same purpose.

The motion of Dr. Henson, duly seconded, prevailed.

Lewis O. Hartman, under a question of high privilege, presented the following resolution:

Mr. Chairman, I desire to present a resolution having to do with the only Bishop in the history of Methodism who has been retired twice. At Atlantic City in 1932 a piece of legislation was embodied in the *Discipline* of the Methodist Episcopal Church which made it possible in an emergency situation to appoint a Bishop in the retired relation to active service in an area or part of an area for a period not extending beyond the session of the ensuing General Conference.

Early in the year 1938, by the sudden death of the much-beloved Bishop Charles Wesley Burns of Boston, it became necessary for the first time in the history of the Church to invoke the provisions of this new law, and the Board of Bishops appointed Bishop Herbert Welch to fill the vacancy. He immediately came to Boston with his gracious wife, and addressed himself once more to the episcopal task. For more than a year now he has carried forward the full-time work of a Bishop with all the vigor of youth and has endeared himself everywhere to the preachers and laymen of New England.

He has traveled many times in each of the six states, preaching in the churches, holding Annual and District Conferences, and engaging in committee work. He has also attacked with keen discernment and courageous directness not a few of the knotty institutional problems of the area, and has greatly helped in their solution.

Always friendly and accessible, Bishop Welch during these few months by his sympathetic attitude and sound judgment in critical situations has gained not only the deep respect but also the abiding affection of New England Methodists.

We desire, therefore, in this public way to acknowledge with gratitude his high service to the Church and the kingdom, and we pray God's richest blessing upon him and his good wife.

Before the adoption of the resolution, at the request of Dr. Hartman, Mrs. Lucile L. LeSourd, New England, in behalf of the Boston Area, presented Mrs. Welch with a bouquet of flowers.

The resolution was adopted on the motion of Dr. Hartman, duly seconded. Bishop Welch replied appropriately.

MAY 10
FOURTEENTH
DAY
Afternoon

Merton S. Rice, Detroit, under a question of privilege for the Conference, presented the following resolution:

Retired
Bishops

The Council of Bishops shall have authority to assign a retired Bishop to a Jurisdiction for Episcopal service, up to the General Conference in 1940, where such service is needed for the adequate supervision of the work of the Church in that Jurisdiction.

The resolution, on the motion of Dr. Rice, duly seconded, was adopted.

The reports of the Committee on Enabling Acts being called for, Arthur A. Callaghan, Maine, the Chairman, requested that Nathan Newby, Pacific, and W. M. Alexander, Missouri, come to the platform and assist in the presentation of the reports.

Committee on
Enabling
Acts and
Legal
Forms,
Report No.
13

Report No. 13 of the Committee on Enabling Acts and Legal Forms, printed on page 418 of the *Daily Christian Advocate*, was presented by Arthur A. Callaghan, Maine, Chairman, who explained its provisions and moved its adoption. The motion, duly seconded, prevailed. For report, see Appendix, "Special Standing Committees," page 812.

Committee on
Enabling
Acts and
Legal
Forms,
Report No.
14

Report No. 14 of the same Committee, printed on page 418 of the *Daily Christian Advocate*, was presented by the Chairman, who explained its provisions and moved its adoption. The motion, being duly seconded, the report was adopted. For report, see Appendix, "Special Standing Committees," page 812.

Committee on
Enabing
Acts and
Legal
Forms,
Report No.
15

Report No. 15 of the same Committee, printed on page 418 of the *Daily Christian Advocate*, was presented by Dr. Callaghan, who explained its provisions and moved its adoption. The motion, duly seconded, prevailed and the report was adopted. For report, see Appendix, "Special Standing Committees," page 813.

Committee on
Enabling
Acts and
Legal
Forms,
Report No.
16

Report No. 16 of the same Committee, printed on pages 418 and 419 of the *Daily Christian Advocate*, was presented by the Chairman, who explained its provisions and moved its adoption. The motion, duly seconded, prevailed and the report was adopted. For report, see Appendix, "Special Standing Committees," page 813.

All the printed reports of the Committee on Enabling Acts and Legal Forms having been presented, motion of Arlo A. Brown, Newark, duly seconded, prevailed that the rules be suspended, and the remaining reports be considered.

The following reports were separately explained by the Chairman, and each, separately, on motion duly made and seconded, was adopted:

Committee on
Enabling
Acts and
Legal
Forms, Re-
ports Nos.
17, 18, 19,
20, 21

No. 17. Boundaries of the Central Northwest Conference.

No. 18. Boundaries of the Norwegian-Danish Conference.

No. 19. Election of Lay Delegates to Annual Conferences.

No. 20. Concerning Paragraphs 135, 136, 137, Calendar No. 37, Report No. 8 of the Committee on Conferences, printed on page 257 of the *Daily Christian Advocate*.

No. 21. Where sessions of Annual Conferences may be held.

For these reports, see Appendix, "Special Standing Committees," pages 814-816.

Arthur A. Callaghan, Maine, presented the following resolution:

Resolved, That authorization be given the Editors of the new *Discipline* of The Methodist Church, to lift all Enabling Acts out of the main body of the *Discipline* and place them together in one group in the Appendix. The Chairman and Secretary of the Committee on Enabling Acts and Legal Forms volunteer their assistance in the accomplishment of this task.

A. A. CALLAGHAN, *Chairman;*
W. M. ALEXANDER, *Secretary.*

The resolution, on motion of Dr. Callaghan, duly seconded, was adopted.

Nathan Newby, Pacific, moved to add the following statement to Paragraph 893 of Report No. 9 of the Committee on Enabling Acts and Legal Forms, printed on page 370 of the *Daily Christian Advocate.*

Paragraph 983. This Committee shall be called together by the President of the first-named organization at such time and in such place as shall be decided upon by a majority of the Presidents of the organizations named.

The motion, duly seconded, prevailed.

Francis R. Bayley requested that the matter of the election of Lay Delegates to Annual Con-

MAY 10
FOURTEENTH
DAY
Afternoon

ferences be also printed in the Appendix to the new *Discipline*. The Chairman of the Committee on Enabling Acts and Legal Forms accepted the suggestion.

Bishop Keeney
Presented

Bishop Lowe presented to the Uniting Conference Bishop Frederick T. Keeney, who so effectively led in the Million Unit Fellowship Movement of the former Methodist Episcopal Church.

Appreciation
of Bishop
Burns

Daniel L. Marsh, New England, presented the following resolution:

WHEREAS, since the last meeting of the General Conference of his branch of the Uniting Church (The Methodist Episcopal), Bishop Charles Wesley Burns, of the Boston Area, has been divinely promoted by death; therefore be it

Resolved: 1. That we record our appreciation of Bishop Charles Wesley Burns, a good shepherd of the flock, a kind brother beloved, an eloquent and scholarly preacher, a wise and faithful Bishop of the Church of God.

2. That we pray God's blessing upon his widow and children and upon this new Church which he foresaw and loved with pure devotion.

On motion of Dr. Marsh, duly seconded, the resolution was adopted. The Conference bowed for prayer, led by Bishop Titus Lowe.

estern
Jurisdiction

Motion of the Secretary, duly seconded, prevailed that the report of the Western Jurisdiction, printed on pages 417 and 418 of the *Daily Christian Advocate,* be received and placed on the records of the Uniting Conference.

piscopal
Supervision

Lewis O. Hartman, New England, presented the following resolution:

I move that the Uniting Conference, under the authority in Paragraph 160, page 301 of the *Daily Christian Advocate,* refer the question of adequate Episcopal supervision in the Central Conference of Southern Asia, for such action as may meet their judgment, to the Council of Bishops.

utonomous
Methodist
Churches

The resolution, on motion of L. O. Hartman, duly seconded, was adopted.

Lewis O. Hartman, New England, moved that the Uniting Conference go on record as expressing our abiding love for and, unwaning interest in the future development of the autonomously independent Methodist Churches which have been affiliated with The Methodist Church—namely, the Japan Methodist Church, The ⸱Methodist

Church of Brazil, the Methodist Church of Mexico, and the Korean Methodist Church, and that we assured them of our prayers for their prosperity in establishing the Kingdom of God in their lands. The motion, duly seconded, prevailed.

James A. James, Rock River, presented the following resolution and moved its adoption:

MAY 10
FOURTEENTH
DAY

Afternoon

Joint Commission on
Union

WHEREAS, the Uniting Conference has undertaken a great work which has been characterized with a spirit of devotion, unity, and brotherhood, and which cannot be completed in important details within the time it is possible for us to remain, in so large a delegated body, thereby leaving many important and existing projects to be completed; and

WHEREAS, the union which has been established by the Uniting Conference has now to be carried to the Annual Conferences and local churches throughout the United States and the world, and many local unions of institutional life, properties, and congregations will naturally follow, but which should be afforded uniform and constructive guidance when requested; therefore be it

Resolved, in order to further carry forward the spirit of unifying and harmonizing the *Disciplines* and the work of these three former Churches, that we hereby authorize, until the meeting of the General Conference, the Commission on Interdenominational Relations and Union of the three Churches to serve as a Joint Commission on Union and to be known as The Methodist Church Commission on Interdenominational Relations and Union; and that such Commission be authorized to take such steps as seem best to further the purpose of our union.

This Commission is to be composed of twenty-five members, five effective Bishops, ten ministers, and ten lay members, appointed by the Council of Bishops, the expenses of such Commission to be met from the administrative funds.

Motion of A. P. Lyon, Louisville, duly seconded, prevailed that the paper be laid on the table.

Guy F. Jones, Texas, presented the following and moved its adoption:

Abbreviated
Digest

Resolved, That the Editors of the *Discipline* of The Methodist Church be requested and authorized to prepare and make available for early use by District Superintendents, Pastors, and others engaged in administering the new legislation, an abbreviated digest of all that legislation having to do with administration in the Annual and District Conferences, pastoral charges, and local churches.

John W. Langdale, New York East, said the Editors of the *Discipline* expected to get it out promptly. On motion, duly made and seconded, the resolution was laid on the table.

MAY 10
FOURTEENTH
DAY
Afternoon

Appreciation
of Bishop
Mouzon

J. W. Moore, Virginia, for the Uniting Conference, requested Bishop A. Frank Smith, a former pupil of Bishop Edwin D. Mouzon, to write an appreciation of Bishop Mouzon and that the same be published in the *Daily Advocate* of tomorrow. The motion, duly seconded, prevailed.

Dr. Morelock
Presented

Leslie J. Lyons, Missouri, presented to the Conference Dr. George L. Morelock, Memphis, General Secretary of the General Board of Lay Activities of the former Methodist Episcopal Church, South, who had been ill in a local hospital during the Uniting Conference.

No Pages at
Evening
Session

By common consent the Uniting Conference requested that no pages be used to carry messages among the delegates during the evening session of The Declaration of Union.

"Our Higher
Institutions
of
Learning"

"Our Higher Institutions of Learning," the Order of the Day, having arrived, Bishop Lowe resigned the chair to Bishop James H. Straughn.

The Conference stood and joined in singing No. 279, "God of Grace and God of Glory."

Bishop Paul B. Kern led in prayer.

Dr. Lee Addresses the
Conference

Dr. William F. Quillian, General Secretary of the General Board of Christian Education, former Methodist Episcopal Church, South, presented Dr. Umphrey Lee, President of Southern Methodist University, Dallas, Tex., who addressed the Conference on "The Church-Related College and University." For address, see Appendix, "Regular Addresses," page 901.

Dean Hough
Addresses
the
Conference

Dr. H. W. McPherson, Executive Secretary of the General Board of Education, former Methodist Episcopal Church, presented Dean Lynn Harold Hough, Drew Theological Seminary, Madison, N. J., who addressed the Conference on "The Theological Seminary in The Methodist Church." For address, see Appendix, "Regular Addresses," page 890.

The Conference stood in appreciation and applause at the conclusion of the addresses.

Addresses
Ordered
Printed

Daniel L. Marsh, New England, presented the following resolution:

I move that Dr. Umphrey Lee and Dean Lynn Harold Hough be requested to submit the manuscripts of these addresses to the *Daily Christian Advocate*, and that the *Advocate* be requested to print them.

Harry W. McPherson, Illinois, moved to amend by including the addresses of Dr. W. Aiken Smart and Dr. Matthew S. Davage. Dr. Marsh accepted the amendment. The motion, duly seconded, prevailed.

Motion of Daniel L. Marsh, New England, duly seconded, prevailed that we do now adjourn.

The Conference adjourned with prayer by Dr. Merle N. Smith, formerly of First Methodist Church, Pasadena, Calif.

MAY 10
FOURTEENTH DAY
Afternoon

Adjournment

WEDNESDAY EVENING, MAY 10, 1939

THE DECLARATION OF UNION

MAY 10
FOURTEENTH DAY

Pursuant to adjournment, the Uniting Conference convened on Wednesday evening, May 10, for the closing session of this historic Conference, for the Declaration of Union of The Methodist Church, the three Co-chairmen of the Joint Commission on Interdenominational Relations and Church Union presiding.

Evening

Opening

Bishop John M. Moore called the Conference to order at 7:45 P.M.

Bishop Ivan Lee Holt announced and the Conference joined in singing Hymn No. 381, "The Church's One Foundation."

Dr. James R. Houghton led in this and the other Hymns sung by the Conference at this session.

After the singing of the Hymn, the Conference joined in the Call to Worship, led by Bishop Ernest G. Richardson, as follows:

Call to Worship

The Bishop: It shall come to pass, saith God, I will pour out my spirit upon all flesh.
The People: God hath not given unto us the spirit of fear, but of power and love and a sober mind.
The Bishop: The promise is unto you to your children and to as many as the Lord our God shall call.
The People: As many as are led by the Spirit of God, they are the children of God. Amen.

Bishop Richardson then led in prayer and the people joined in the Collect, as follows:

Prayer

The Bishop: Almighty God, our Father, who by Thy Holy Spirit dost enlighten, bless, and sanctify the hearts that seek Thee: pour forth upon us and Thy whole Church this day the blessing and power of Thy life. Look upon us who are assembled here with our mind and heart to worship Thee, and renew to us the baptism of inspiration and grace that Thou hast always given to Thy devoted servants. So fill us with Thy Spirit, that the words of our mouth, and the fervor of our service, and the courage of our devotion to witness for Thee, may be made manifest among men, that Thy name, O Father, our God, may be widely glorified: through Jesus Christ our Lord. Amen.

The Collect: O God, our Father, we have come unto Mount Zion. We have built the altar; send thou the fire from heaven. We have spread the table; break thou the bread. We have opened the Book; shine Thou upon its pages. We have gathered about the Cross of our Lord; be Thou in our midst. Here, in this high hour, we would gain strength for our labors and consecration for Thy kingdom. Fulfill now the desires and hopes of Thy servants, granting us in this world knowledge of Thy truth and in the world to come life everlasting: through Jesus Christ our Lord. Amen.

Bishop Robert E. Jones announced and the Conference joined in singing Hymn No. 162, "O for a Thousand Tongues to Sing."

The people being seated and bowing their heads, Bishop Arthur J. Moore led in the Prayer of Thanksgiving, the people joining in the Collect, as follows:

The Bishop: O God, the Father of all mankind, we lift up our hearts in gratitude for the devoted and good through whom we have received our evangelical heritage of fellowship in Thy Church and Kingdom; those who having experienced the Christian purpose have wrought well and built nobly, into the fruit of whose labor we have entered. We give Thee hearty thanks for our fathers and brethren who beheld the vision of a community of faith within Thy Church Universal spreading Scriptural Holiness throughout the world, into whose goodly inheritance we have come. We pray that a double portion of the spirit that lived in their souls may possess our lives, that with steadfast courage and unwavering hope we may fulfill in our time the tasks put into our hands to do; through Jesus Christ our Lord. Amen.

The Collect: O God our Father, Thou Spirit of holiness and truth, bring us into a unity of love and consecration which may bear some likeness to the blessed nature of our Lord; grant us the spirit of peace and grace, that Thy universal family may be devoted to Thee with their whole heart, and kept in the unity of Thy Spirit in the bond of peace: through Jesus Christ our Lord. Amen.

The Conference stood and joined in singing the Doxology, and remaining standing were led in the recitation of The Canticle of the Church by Bishop Frederick DeLand Leete, as follows:

The Bishop: Arise, shine; for thy light is come: and the glory of the Lord is risen upon thee.

The People: For behold, the darkness shall cover the earth: and gross darkness the people;

The Bishop: But the Lord shall arise upon thee: and his glory shall be seen upon thee.

The People: And the Gentiles shall come to thy light: and the kings to the brightness of thy rising.

The Bishop: Lift up thine eyes round about, and see: all that gather themselves together, they come to thee;

The People: Thy sons shall come from far: and thy daughters shall be nursed at thy side.

The Bishop: Then thou shalt see, and flow together: and thine heart shall fear, and be enlarged;

The People: Because the abundance of the sea shall be converted unto thee: the wealth of the Gentiles shall come unto thee.

The Bishop: I will make thee an eternal excellency: a joy of many generations.

The People: Violence shall no more be heard in thy land: wasting nor destruction within thy borders;

The Bishop: But thou shalt call thy walls Salvation; and thy gates Praise.

The People: And the Lord shall be unto thee an everlasting light; and thy God thy glory.

The Bishop: Now unto the God of grace, for the might of his Spirit and the love of Christ;

The People: Be glory in the Church throughout all ages; world without end. Amen.

Dr. James R. Houghton led in the singing of the Gloria Patri.

Bishop Paul B. Kern read the New Testament Scripture lesson from the seventeenth chapter of the Gospel by St. John, verses 1, 2, 6, 17 to 23 inclusive.

Bishop Ivan Lee Holt announced the taking of a Thank offering, and the ushers waited upon the audience for this act of worship.

Bishop John C. Broomfield announced and the Conference joined in the singing of The Litany Hymn, No. 380, "Jesus, with Thy Church Abide."

Bishop Edgar Blake then called the names of six heroes of Methodist Union who rest from their labors in the Divine Land:

William Norman Ward, of the former Methodist Protestant Church.

Thomas Hamilton Lewis, of the former Methodist Protestant Church.

Marginal notes:
MAY 10
FOURTEENTH DAY
Evening
Doxology
The Canticle
Names of Heroes of Methodist Union Called

MAY 10
FOURTEENTH
DAY

Evening

Bishop Eugene Russell Hendrix, of the former Methodist Episcopal Church, South.
Bishop Edwin DuBose Mouzon, of the former Methodist Episcopal Church, South.
Bishop Earl Cranston, of the former Methodist Episcopal Church.
Bishop William Fraser McDowell, of the former Methodist Episcopal Church.

As their names were separately called a photo-
graph of each was presented on a specially prepared screen.

Bishop Hughes
Addresses
the
Conference

Bishop John M. Moore then presented Bishop
Edwin Holt Hughes who delivered the following
address:

ADDRESS BY BISHOP HUGHES

My comrades have deputed me to prepare and speak
the final word for this Uniting Conference. I am pre-
suming that the aim is to secure an interpretation and
a prospectus. Neither part of the task is easy. How
shall one interpret a vast river, cleaving a continent and
emptying into a gulf whose waters finally will touch the
shores of the planet? Or how shall one interpret a lofty
mountain that pierces the sky with its whiteness and lifts
its testimony beyond all clouds? As for a prospectus, who
can describe the future errands of the Mississippi's cur-
rents or tell of the soil that Shasta sheds for the enrich-
ing of a great coast? For all of us these figures of speech
do not overstate the significance of this Conference. The
greatest of rivers and the tallest peaks would alone be
worthy metaphors in the making of a review or a preview.
So let me say, quite frankly and humbly, that I have
prayed much in my preparation and that in these three
near days the toils of the light and the watches of the night
have moved my pen across the pages to the accompani-
ment of music, both solemn and glad.

I. THE PAST

Even as it is not good for man to be alone, so is it not
good for a fact to stand alone. A river is not a speedy
miracle, nor is a mountain a quick creation. This gathering is no extemporized event. If all who have wrought
and prayed to make it possible should come here, lifting
their "white shields of expectation," we should have an
audience many times larger than this. The building itself
would plead for more room while all the approaching
streets would be made dense with visitors from the shad-
owy lands of God's other countries.

We reached this altar by reverent kneeling at thousands of other altars. The worship of millions of Christ's
people has been consecrated here in this city, now made
more truly historic. Not only have the great leaders
whose faces have been just flashed upon our grateful
memories brought service to this shrine; but their minor
comrades in the long crusade have by countless supplica-

tions made this place the depository of their hopes and the goal of their endeavors. Some, still living, have seen the day afar off and have been glad with a joy that was but the prelude of this ecstasy. We have watched and prayed full many a year, and to all that we have added our labor of expectant love.

On this night our century plant comes to the glory of its bloom. We stand entranced as we behold the color and know the fragrance of the garden of the Lord where the Lord of the garden meets with us in the holy companionship of his grace. We have waited patiently for him, and he hath brought this thing to pass. Praise be to his holy Name!

Perhaps I may be permitted to say, with no personal tribute whatever for myself, that I have never known finer and more thorough preparation for a great event than has been made for this Council of God's people. We may have sometimes faced unexpected difficulties or noted troublesome omissions in our Plan of Union. But the real surprise is that we have not found more of these!

In the multitude of our counselors we have secured much wisdom. We need not even hint at individual credits. This would be too much like debating as to how we should distribute the shares of the ocean. Continuing a sea metaphor, we may repeat the shrewd remark of a New England statesman: "That the man on top of the wave was frequently mistaken for the wave itself." Only one Person has lived of whom we could say that he was "all in all." Yet this one has, in the longer and more immediate preparation for this day, had so many faithful comrades that we must leave it to him in the final judgment to assess the credits to his beloved helpers.

Those of us who have been most intimate with the lengthy toil that preceded this Uniting Conference approached April 26, 1939, with proper tremblings, bearing with us such assurance as came from our study of the finest *Prospectus* that mine eyes have ever beheld. Yet one by one the obstacles disappeared or were surmounted.

What explains all this? In the spiritual background were millions of prayers. In the recent months heaven has become custodian of the countless petitions that were offered in our cathedrals and in tiny rural meeting houses. Old people spoke to God, and he had so long been in the habit of listening to them that he could not close his heart against their loving demands. In our council rooms, little and big, the Lord of wisdom heard our plea for light and often touched us with the radiance of his own purpose.

No Conference was ever preceded by more faithful work of appointed committees. So far as the past is concerned, it has poured its plentiful measure into these days until we have had the right to feel that the providence of God has been expressed in the providence of God's people, and until we felt, as well, that our prepared delegates came through these doors shouting to the great Companion who walked with us—"Hosanna! Blessed is He that cometh in the name of the Lord."

MAY 10
FOURTEENTH
DAY

Evening

Bishop Hughes
Addresses
the
Conference

II. THE PRESENT

So came we to the date and the place of our hopes. Ere we reached the point of legislation, the Saviour put upon us the certificate of his grace. We can never forget that Communion Service in the Cathedral. There the doctrine of "the real Presence" came to larger meaning for us. The fact that we did not go to the formal altar, according to our dear custom, did not prevent our hearts from reaching the inner shrine, or from beholding the shekinah that shone over the invisible holy of holies.

Some strange and lovely thing happened in that intense and glorious service. We found the place where we left our sorrows. Both worlds came into our fellowship. It was as if the Lord himself were instituting for us anew the Holy Supper of his remembrance and his companionship. But the influence went farther, though not higher, than that: We placed our *problems* at the foot of the cross. We were conscious of a Saviour, great enough to ease our griefs, to carry our burdens, and also to make us more nearly equal to our sacred responsibilities.

We came from that hour in the mood of triumph. The procession that moved toward these doors stepped to the music of victory. We had a fresh experience of conversion, of transformation, of love, of peace. Our fears had been left in the Cathedral, in the care of God; our hopes came with us to the Auditorium, in the same care. We bore in our spirits an unforgettable glory: and while we did no shouting, we could have whispered to these entrances, "Lift up your heads, O ye gates; and the King of Glory shall come in!" and when we came He made one with us all.

The prophecy of that Communion has not failed us. Some of us have had to confess to God the folly of our anxieties. As we have gone along these legislative roads, the valleys have been lifted and the mountains have been laid low.

One illustration has occurred to me many, many times —a parable gained from earth's roadways. Often as we look ahead we see the rising hill that our automobile must conquer. We wonder whether it has the power to climb those steeps. Yet as we move onward some miracle-worker seems to bring the ascent to the level of our powers and we are soon capturing the heights.

It has been so here, dear brothers and sisters. An old lady, being asked what things in her lifetime had troubled her most, made reply: "The things that never happened." How true that homely suggestion has been of our Conference! We came with trembling to task after task, only to find that the weight of the burden had been decreased by a Helper. Our morning prayers, prompted often by solicitude, ended in evening prayers, prompted by gratitude. If tears brimmed our eyes when the dawn had come, more plentiful tears surprised our pillows in the evening time. In the quiet of our rooms we were tempted to revive the tradition of the "shouting Methodist" and to cry aloud, "Glory be to God on high," even as on this part of the earth we have "peace among men of good will."

III. THE FUTURE

MAY 10
FOURTEENTH
DAY

Evening

Bishop Hughes
Addresses
the
Conference

If it be true that the effective past that made this Conference and the effective present that crowned it with success have been compounded of a certain spirit, then we have discovered the secret of our effective future. Hundreds of you have said to me, "If we can carry to our pastors and people the atmosphere of this gathering, unification will succeed beyond all compare."

We who have been here must be the ambassadors of this spirit. Having seen what right attitudes can accomplish, we must scatter those attitudes over all our borders. The future may be spoiled by the mood of fear, or it may be glorified by the mood of love. To the cultivation of that love we now dedicate ourselves, and to the increase of that love we now challenge our companions in the faith. In all our problems the Lover has been the Solver, even as the Mightiest of all Lovers is alone to be the Solver of the world's perplexities.

Many years ago I heard my dear and splendid father preach a sermon that entered my boyish heart to abide there through the decades. You will allow me to pay him tribute in this supreme hour. He was a hero of the saddlebags; an itinerant of the mountain roads; a gentleman of the log-house; a cultured evangelist of the Gospel of his Lord; a preacher who after sixty years of work left his children no legacy save that of character, no treasure save that which lies beyond the reach of moth or rust. His text was, "Keep yourselves in the love of God." His emphasis was on the imperative. By deliberate will we were to work at love; to put upon ourselves the compulsion that would make us stay within its blessed territory; to avoid the dispositions and deeds that would destroy the climate of affection; to insist that the definite purpose of love should be the commanding force of life.

Down over nearly sixty years of time I still see that stalwart form in the pulpit; and I still hear that wonderful voice instructing men in the gracious imperative mood: "Keep yourselves in the love of God." Carry your free will into the realms of your immortal soul. Dispose your disposition.

It is true word forever, if only we may keep it and ourselves close to Christ. As we leave this Auditorium, it is the will of God for us. St. Paul seized the heart of his Lord's teaching and, showing us "the higher talents," showed us, too, the path that is "still higher," even the more excellent way. He said that it was better than eloquence, surpassing the tongues of men and of angels.

He esteemed it higher than knowledge, more important than the power to fathom mysteries and secret lore. He made it loftier than faith that could move hills from their bases. He declared it more worthy than a stubborn and devoted sacrifice that surrendered goods to benevolences and the living body to the flames.

He said that it is "very patient, very kind"; "knows no jealousy; makes no parade"; "gives itself no airs"; "is never rude, never selfish, never irritated, never resentful"; "is gladdened by goodness"; "always eager to believe the best"; ever "hopeful."

MAY 10
FOURTEENTH
DAY

Evening

Bishop Hughes
Addresses
the
Conference

Above the wreck of all worlds he saw its banner flying. He epitomized its conquests in the unwavering claim, "Love never faileth."

If that spirit has made our Conference successful, it can empower all our coming programs, whether of inner spirit or of outer service. So we may repeat each to the other, and each to himself, the apostolic command, "Make love your aim."

Let us, therefore, set ourselves to a rivalry of affection. Once I said jocularly, and yet seriously, to my Comrade-Chairmen of the Commissions that I would seek to surpass them in the contest of love, so that when God gave his recognitions he would say: "First Prize, Edwin H. Hughes: Honorable Mention, John M. Moore and James H. Straughn."

I pass that challenge on to all of you. The recent months have shown that an early and blessed result of union is an enlarged census of loving hearts. We love more people and they love us in return. If some of us were to go to heaven tonight, we should take with us a far greater freight of affection than we had two years ago. We should bear its glory and honor into the city where naught but love dwells and where the center of all life is One who loved us and gave himself for us.

I am myself weary of the initialed abortions—M. E., M. P., and M. E. C., S. They have become my favorite aversions; and I am willing to leave to Washington all the residue of alphabetical lists. I say now to the ex-M. E.'s and to the ex-M. P.'s and to the ex-M. E. C., S.'s, the words of Longfellow addressed by him to the children of his household, but now addressed by me to the children of God:

> "I have you fast in my fortress
> And I will not let you depart,
> But put you down in the dungeon
> Of the round-tower of my heart.
> And there I will keep you forever,
> Yes, forever and a day,
> Till the walls shall crumble to ruin,
> And moulder to dust away."

We have not lost our old Churches. They are the portable treasures that we bear into the larger associations —our baptisms, our conversions, the patient instructions of our wayward youth, our educations, our ordinations, our accretions of heart garnered for the service of Christ, our thousands of good and tender memories, our filial gratitude toward the ministers who claimed us for the Redeemer—all these are kept in the vaults secure.

We have more people to love, and more kinds of people to love, and larger areas for our harvests of love. We find our lips uttering in affection the new name "The Methodist Church," glad that the scorn that once made it an epithet has been supplanted by the tribute that recognizes two centuries of a wide and holy service. Not only in the formal documents where we must mingle love and legality, but also in all the inner declarations of our hearts, we yield it anew to Him who said, "I will build my Church; and the gates of hell shall not prevail against it.".

Certainly the larger present, held in the days of this Conference, has seen the flow of our hearts toward union. This feeling has made its own slogans. Many have sought to put the spirit into some condensed phrase, to make for it a fitting frame of words.

Some of our delegates have found themselves repeating the title of Professor Garber's book, "The Methodists Are One People." Any unconscious attempts here made to discount, or check, or cancel that feeling have met resistless torrents of conviction.

Looking upon the mingling of many nations, upon the meeting of the cross-currents of a wide internationalism, we have uttered the words, "The Methodists are one people." Gazing with curious interest upon the racial composite, black, brown, yellow, and upon other colors not known among the primary rays, we have felt that God wrote in the rainbow across the skies, "The Methodists are one people." Knowing that here were gathered men holding all political opinions and advocating the several theories of government, we have all come to believe so sincerely and strongly in the merging program as to win from our lips the cry, "The Methodists are one people."

Beholding the changes in law according to which our Woman's Societies come into a new alignment and under which loyal women have given us the best missionary organizations known on earth today, now yield to other plans, we have politely said across the gentle barriers of sex, "The Methodists are one people."

Made aware occasionally of a line once drawn by two surveyors named Mason and Dixon, and kindly regarding the differing emphases that have been fashioned by the years lived in the memories of Lincoln and of Lee, we have waved the banner, "The Methodists are one people."

Amid all the slashing of temperaments, the cool statements of deliberation and the fervencies of more eager debate, wherein Peter and James and John funded their varying dispositions, we have still declared, "The Methodists are one people."

Listening to three episcopal groups and bringing into the circle of the Northern adn Southern Bishops the Protestant twins, we have in differing accents known how to pronounce the motto, "The Methodists are one people."

Carrying hither the loyal remembrances of our spiritual forefathers, touchingly recalling the sacrificial lives and loves of our nearer religious ancestry, we have done away with the Jericho walls between our camps by trumpeting the challenge, "The Methodists are one people."

Gazing upward toward another world whose portals have opened to Snethen and Lewis, Capers and Andrew and Haygood and Hendrix, Ward and Mouzon, and Cranston and McDowell, we have sent over wireless waves the message to the unified hosts of heaven, "The Methodists are one people."

Moving reverently into the sacred precincts of the seventeenth chapter of John's Gospel and listening to the

MAY 10
FOURTEENTH
DAY
Evening

Bishop Hughe
Addresses
the
Conference

MAY 10
FOURTEENTH
DAY

Evening

Bishop Hughes
Addresses
the
Conference

praying voice of the Redeemer Himself as he speaks to
the Father concerning the disciples of his earthly ministry
and his disciples in this room, "Nor do I pray for these
alone, but for all who believe in me by their spoken word,
may they all be one," we have answered the petition of the
beseeching Christ by saying, "The Methodists are one
people."

Is it any wonder then that we have been lifted toward
a seventh heaven, and that we have known something
more of the mystical glory wherein one declares:
"I looked, and behold there was a great host whom
no one could count, from every nation and people and
tribe, standing before the throne and before the Lamb,
clad in white robes, with palm branches in their hands;
and they cried with a loud voice, 'Saved by our God who
is seated on the throne and by the Lamb!' And all of the
angels surrounded the throne and the presbyters and the
four living creatures, and fell on their faces before the
throne, worshiping God, and crying, 'Even so. Blessing
and glory and wisdom and thanksgiving and honor and
power and might be to our God forever and ever! Amen.' "

This matter is too sacred for any literary climax. We
must now transfer it to the rhetoric of action. We have
been on the mountain of transfiguration where we have
met the lawgiver, and the prophet, and the Master Himself. As John Wesley said, "We must not build taber-
nacles." Our hosannas must not yield to misgivings. We
should go forward into the mightiest and most constructive movements that Methodism has ever promoted in the
name of Christ. We must say to sinners of whatever
kind that we know a saving name. We must pray, and
pray, and pray. We must evangelize, and evangelize, and
evangelize. We must carry a throbbing Gospel beyond
all rivers and plains and deserts and mountains and
oceans. In the ceaseless program of redemption, inspired
by our Lord, we must go on with the proclamation of
grace until the last rebel against the infinite mercy of the
Most High lays down his arms of mutiny and cries out,
"Nay, but I yield, I yield, I yield. I can hold out no more."
All this we do for the dear Redeemer's sake. Amen.

Preamble to
the Declara-
tion of
Union

The entire audience of twelve thousand people
arose as Bishop James H. Straughn read the following Preamble to the Declaration of Union:

WHEREAS, The Methodist Episcopal Church, the Methodist Episcopal Church, South, and the Methodist Protestant Church did through their respective General Conferences appoint Commissions on Interdenominational Relations and Church Union; and whereas these Commissions acting jointly did produce, propose, and present to
the three Churches a Plan of Union; and whereas these
three Churches, each acting separately for and in its
own behalf, did by more than the constitutional majorities endorse and adopt this Plan of Union, in accord
with their respective Constitutions and *Disciplines*, and
did effect the full consummation of union in accordance
with the Plan of Union; and whereas these three Churches

in adopting this Plan of Union did authorize and provide for a Uniting Conference with certain powers and duties as therein set forth; and whereas the Uniting Conference, duly authorized and legally chosen in accordance with the Plan of Union, is now in session in the city of Kansas City, Mo.: MAY 10 FOURTEENTH DAY *Evening*

Bishop Edwin Holt Hughes read the Affirmation, as follows: Affirmation

NOW, THEREFORE, we, the members of the Uniting Conference, the legal and authorized representatives of the Methodist Episcopal Church, the Methodist Episcopal Church, South, and the Methodist Protestant Church, in session here assembled on this the tenth day of May, 1939, do solemnly, in the presence of God and before all the world, make and publish the following Declarations of fact and principle.

Bishop John M. Moore then read the Declarations of Union, the responses being made by the Bishops and members of the Uniting Conference standing, and with uplifted right hand, as follows: Declarations of Union

I

The Bishop: The Methodist Episcopal Church, the Methodist Episcopal Church, South, and the Methodist Protestant Church are and shall be one United Church.

The Delegates: We do so declare.

II

The Bishop: The Plan of Union as adopted is and shall be the Constitution of this United Church, and of its three constituent bodies.

The Delegates: We do so declare.

III

The Bishop: The Methodist Episcopal Church, the Methodist Episcopal Church, South, and the Methodist Protestant Church had their common origin in the organization of the Methodist Episcopal Church in America in 1784, A.D., and have ever held, adhered to, and preserved a common belief, spirit, and purpose, as expressed in their common Articles of Religion.

The Delegates: We do so declare.

IV

The Bishop: The Methodist Episcopal Church, the Methodist Episcopal Church, South, and the Methodist Protestant Church, in adopting the name "The Meth-

odist Church" for the United Church, do not and will
not surrender any right, interest, or title in and to
these respective names which, by long and honored
use and association, have become dear to the ministry
and membership of the three uniting Churches and
have become enshrined in their history and records.

The Delegates: We do so declare.

V

The Bishop: The Methodist Church is the ecclesiastical
and lawful successor of the three uniting Churches,
and through which the three Churches as one United
Church shall continue to live and have their existence,
continue their institutions, and hold and enjoy their
property, exercise and perform their several trusts
under and in accord with the Plan of Union and Discipline of the United Church; and such trusts or corporate bodies as exist in the constituent Churches
shall be continued as long as legally necessary.

The Delegates: We do so declare.

VI

The Bishop and the Delegates: To The Methodist Church
thus established we do solemnly declare our allegiance,
and upon all its life and service we do reverently invoke the blessing of Almighty God. Amen.

The people were seated and bowing their heads
were led in and responded to the Hallowing
Prayer of Union, by Bishop A. Frank Smith, as
follows:

The Bishop: In the name of the Father, our God by whose
favor we live in this heritage of faith;
To the honor of Jesus Christ, the Son of the living
God, our Lord and Saviour;
To the praise of the Holy Spirit, source of light and
power;
We consecrate this communion of faith that is The
Methodist Church.

The People: Holy, holy, holy, Lord God of Hosts: heaven
and earth are full of thy glory. Glory be to thee, O
Lord most high.

The Bishop: We consecrate this Church
For the worship of God in praise and prayer;
For the ministry of the Word;
For the celebration of the Holy Sacraments.

The People: God is a Spirit, and they that worship him
must worship him in spirit and in truth.

The Bishop: We consecrate this Church
For the guidance of childhood;
For the sanctification of the family;
For the training of youth in faith and knowledge.

The People: Remember now thy Creator in the days of
thy youth.

The Bishop: We consecrate this Church
For the edifying of the body of Christ;
For the cure of souls that doubt;
For the persuasion of those who have not yet believed;
For the evangelization of the world;
For the promotion of righteousness, Christian unity, and good-will.

The People: All souls are mine, saith the Lord. Inasmuch as ye did it unto the least of these my brethren, ye did it unto me.

The Bishop: We consecrate this Church
For the redemption of characters;
For brotherhood with all men; ·
For the ennobling of this life and the deepening of the assurance of the life eternal.

The People: The ransomed of the Lord shall come to Zion with songs and everlasting joy.

The Bishop: We consecrate this Church
In grateful remembrance of all who have loved and served the cause that is here consummated;
In loving memory of those who have fared forth from this earthly habitation;
In high hope for those who shall share in this heritage of faith in days to come.

The People: Holy, holy, holy, Lord God of hosts! Heaven and earth are full of thee. Heaven and earth are praising Thee, O Lord most high!

The Bishop and People: Having part among the people of God and the Church Universal in the inheritance of apostles and prophets, fathers and teachers, martyrs and evangelists; we give thanks unto the Father who hath made us meet to be partakers of the inheritance of the saints in light. Compassed about by so great a cloud of witnesses, we do here and now consecrate The Methodist Church to the worship of God and the establishment of His Kingdom among men everywhere, through Jesus Christ our Lord. Amen.

MAY 10
FOURTEENTH
DAY

Evening

Hallowing
Prayer of
Union

Bishop John M. Moore: "We have now before us the Declaration of Union. Will you adopt this Declaration, including the Preamble and the Affirmation and the Declarations? I recognize Judge H. H. White, who has been a member of the Commission on Unification since 1916; a citizen of the State of Louisiana."

Judge H. H. White, Louisiana: "I consider it a high privilege and honor to move that the Declaration of Union which has been adopted, Section by Section, be now adopted as a whole."

Bishop John M. Moore: "I ask for a second, and will recognize Dr. James R. Joy, of Newark, long years the Editor of *The Christian Advocate*,

MAY 10
FOURTEENTH
DAY

Evening

who has been a member of the Commission since 1916."

Dr. James R. Joy, Newark: "Mr. Chairman, I have the honor to second the motion of Judge White."

Bishop Moore: "I will recognize Judge Harry Shaw of Fairmont, W. Va., a distinguished jurist of his own state, who has been a member of the Methodist Protestant Church in great activity and efficiency."

Hallowing
Prayer of
Union

Judge Harry Shaw, Pittsburgh: "Mr. Chairman, members of the Uniting Conference: I take great pleasure in seconding the motion of Judge White, that we do now adopt this Declaration of Union."

Vote on
Declaration
of Union

Bishop Moore: "I shall take the vote first of those standing in favor of adoption, and after you are seated I will take the vote for those who oppose the adoption. If you will adopt this Declaration of Union as a whole, you will stand and lift your right hand. The Bishops will do likewise."

The entire assemblage of Bishops and delegates arose, right hands uplifted. There was prolonged applause and the Bishops and delegates were seated.

Bishop Moore: "If you oppose the adoption of this Declaration, will you stand and lift your right hand."

After a few moments of impressive silence, Bishop John M. Moore said: "No one stands."

The entire Conference arose and there was prolonged applause.

Declaration of
Union
Adopted

Bishop John M. Moore: "The Declaration of Union has been adopted! The Methodist Church is! Long live The Methodist Church!"

The Greater Kansas City Messiah Chorus, conducted by Mr. Powell Weaver, then rendered the Hallelujah Chorus by George Friedrich Handel.

Exhortation
and
Ascription

Bishop Urban V. W. Darlington read the Exhortation and Ascription, the people joining in the close, as follows:

The Bishop: Now, therefore, in the sight of ,all the con-

gregation of the Lord, and in the audience of our
God, keep and search for the commandments of the
Lord our God, that ye may possess this good land
and leave it for an inheritance for your children after
you forever.

The Bishop and the People: Now unto Him that is able
to do exceeding abundantly above all that we ask or
think, according to the power that worketh in us,
unto Him be glory in the Church by Christ Jesus
throughout all ages, world without end. Amen.

Bishop Darlington announced and the Conference joined in the closing Hymn No. 533, "O God,
Our Help in Ages Past."

Bishop Edwin Holt Hughes: "This being a regular session of the Uniting Conference, we will adjourn in due order. The Chair recognizes Dr.
T. D. Ellis, of the South Georgia Conference, for
the motion to adjourn."

Dr. Thomas D. Ellis, South Georgia: "I move
that the Uniting Conference now adjourn *sine
die.*"

Bishop Hughes: "The Chair recognizes Dr.
Ernest H. Cherrington, of the Ohio Conference,
for the seconding of this motion."

Dr. Ernest H. Cherrington, Ohio: "I second
the motion that we do now adjourn."

Bishop Hughes: "Those who will vote to adjourn after receiving the benediction from the
Senior Bishop of the Methodist Episcopal Church,
now the Senior Bishop of The Methodist Church,
Bishop John L. Nuelsen, will lift your hands; contrary. We will be adjourned."

The Uniting Conference of the Methodist Episcopal Church, the Methodist Episcopal Church,
South, and the Methodist Protestant Church,
which convened in Kansas City, Mo., Wednesday,
April 26, 1939, for the purpose of officially uniting and merging the three major branches of
American Methodism, having accomplished its
purpose in more ways than one, adjourned *sine
die* at 9:12 P.M., on Wednesday, May 10, 1939,
with the benediction pronounced by the Senior
Bishop of The Methodist Church, Bishop John L.
Nuelsen, as follows: "Now the God of peace, that
brought again from the dead our Lord Jesus
Christ, that great Shepherd of the sheep, through
the blood of the everlasting covenant, make you
perfect in every good work to do His will, work-

MAY 10

FOURTEENTH
DAY

Evening

Benediction
and Ad-
journment

ing in you that which is well pleasing in His sight, through Jesus Christ; to whom be glory for ever and ever. Amen."

EDWIN H. HUGHES,
JOHN M. MOORE,
JAMES H. STRAUGHN,
CHARLES L. MEAD,
PAUL B. KERN,
A. W. LEONARD,
U. V. W. DARLINGTON,
E. G. RICHARDSON,
ARTHUR JAMES MOORE,
ERNEST LYNN WALDORF,
A. FRANK SMITH,
H. LESTER SMITH,
IVAN LEE HOLT,
FRANCIS J. McCONNELL,
JOHN C. BROOMFIELD,
EDGAR BLAKE,
CHARLES C. SELECMAN,
TITUS LOWE,
Presiding Officers of The Uniting Conference;
LUD H. ESTES,
Secretary, The Uniting Conference;
R. EDGAR HECKMAN,
J. C. BATES,
Associate Secretaries, The Uniting Conference.

APPENDIX

HISTORICAL STATEMENT

The doctrine and spirit of Primitive Christianity have existed at different times and in different degrees in all branches of the Kingdom of Christ. They were embodied in a new form on this wise:

"In 1729 two young men in England, reading the Bible, saw that they could not be saved without holiness, followed after it, and incited others so to do. In 1737 they saw, likewise, that men are justified before they are sanctified; but still holiness was their object. God then thrust them out to raise a holy people."

This was the rise of Methodism, as given in the words of its founders, John and Charles Wesley, of Oxford University, Presbyters of the Church of England.

On the evening of May 24, 1738, John Wesley had undergone his "heart-warming" experience at a meeting of a Religious Society in Aldersgate Street, in London, an experience which his brother Charles had previously found.

In the latter part of 1739, eight or ten persons came to John Wesley in London. They appeared to be deeply convinced of sin, and earnestly groaning for redemption. They desired (as did two or three more the next day) that he would spend some time with them in prayer. That they might have more time for this great work, he appointed a day when they might all come together, which from thenceforward they did every week, namely, on Thursday, in the evening. Their number increased daily. To all these he gave those advices which he judged most needful for them; and they always concluded their meeting with prayer suited to their several necessities.

After this rise of the United Societies in Europe, the spiritual movement fostered by them spread to America. In the year 1766 Philip Embury, a local preacher from Ireland, began to preach in New York City and formed a Society, now the John Street Church. Another local preacher, Thomas Webb, Captain in the British Army, soon joined him and began preaching. About the same time Robert Strawbridge, from Ireland, settled in Frederick County, Maryland, preaching there and forming Societies. In 1769 Mr. Wesley sent Richard Boardman and Joseph Pilmoor to America, and in 1771 Francis Asbury and Richard Wright.

Their work was signally owned of God, so that, at the close of the War of the Revolution, the number of traveling preachers was about eighty and the members in the Societies about fifteen thousand.

When the Independence of the United States was acknowledged by the Treaty of 1783, the American Methodists, most of whom had been members of the Church of England, were, according to the declaration of Mr. Wesley, "totally disentangled both from the State and the English hierarchy." He added: "They are now at full liberty to follow the Scriptures and the Primitive Church, and we judge it best that they should stand fast in that liberty wherewith God has so strangely made them free."

But, as the parish clergy had mostly returned to England, the Methodist Societies were without ordained pastors. "For hundred of miles together" they were destitute of the Christian sacraments. They appealed to Mr. Wesley. He finally responded by ordaining Richard Whatcoat and Thomas Vasey as Presbyters (or Elders) for America; and also, since he preferred the Episcopal form of Church government, by setting apart, by prayer and the imposition of hands, the Reverend Thomas Coke, Doctor of Civil Law, a Presbyter of the Church of England, to be a Superintendent, "to preside over the flock of Christ' in America. In these services he was assisted by other ordained ministers. He also commissioned Dr. Coke to ordain, as joint Superintendent with himself, the Reverend Francis Asbury, then General Assistant for the American Societies. Mr. Wesley also abbreviated the "Articles of Religion" and a "Sunday Service" from the Book of Common Prayer of the Church of England; providing forms, likewise, for the administration of the Sacraments and the ordination of ministers. With this was sent also "A Collection of Psalms and Hymns."

At the Christmas Conference, begun in Baltimore, Maryland, December 24, 1784, sixty preachers met Dr. Coke and his companions. The plan of Mr. Wesley was unanimously and heartily approved. They organized the *Methodist Episcopal Church*, and adopted the Articles of Religion and the Sunday Service prepared by Mr. Wesley, adding to the articles one containing a recognition of Civil Government, and inserting in the Ritual a prayer for the rulers of the United States. Mr. Asbury accepted the Episcopal office only after he and Dr. Coke were elected by the Conference. Mr. Asbury then, with the assistance of Dr. Coke and several Presbyters, who had been ordained by

Mr. Wesley in England, was consecrated as a Bishop. Others were ordained Deacons, and thirteen were elected Elders. This conference also enacted laws for the government of the new church.

Such was the origin of the Methodist Episcopal Church, the first with an Episcopal form of government to attain an independent existence in the United States. It continued its work with holy zeal and grew to large numbers and commanding influence. But in 1828 a group of earnest and godly persons, largely moved by an insistence on lay representation, separated and became the Methodist Protestant Church. The history of this movement may be read in the last *Discipline* of the Methodist Protestant Church, published in 1936, a history penned by the late President of that body, the Reverend Thomas Hamilton Lewis, an earnest advocate of Methodist Union.

In 1844 there occurred another division, the cause being construed by some as the question of slavery; by others as a constitutional issue over the powers of Episcopacy. After years of discussion, negotiation, and even litigation, the Cape May Commission, 1876, representing in its joint membership and action both bodies—the Methodist Episcopal Church and the Methodist Episcopal Church, South—reached terms of amity, according to which each body recognized the other as a legitimate branch of Methodism and laid the basis for a peace which moved steadily and slowly toward union.

The Methodist Protestant Church had a most honorable and useful life for more than a century. Its voting constituency then, feeling that the issue that caused its independent organization had been met in the gradual legislation of its sister Methodisms, voted overwhelmingly in favor of the Plan of Union as submitted by the authorized Joint Commission.

The Methodist Episcopal Church achieved many victories and builded many institutions, especially in the Northern States, and in Missionary work throughout the world. By far more than constitutional majorities in the General Conference and in the Annual and Lay Conferences it adopted the Plan of Union.

The Methodist Episcopal Church, South, began its work in 1845. Its service was largely rendered in the Southern Section of the United States, but its frontiers were extended widely and hopefully into many foreign lands. Its General Conference acting on April 29, 1938, completed its constitutional voting process and by a great majority put its seal in favor of the Plan of Union.

Thus The Methodist Church, with a membership of approximately 8,000,000, enters upon its career as a merged and consolidated ecclesiastical body. In its Declaration of Union, proclaimed at the Uniting Conference May 10, 1939, at Kansas City, Missouri, it keeps legal title to the names— The Methodist Episcopal Church; The Methodist Episcopal Church, South; and the Methodist Protestant Church, affirming that because of long and honored use and association these titles are enshrined in history and record and are to be carried perpetually in the *Discipline* as the names of the constituent Churches of The Methodist Church.

This is for our people a brief summary of the history of Methodism through approximately two centuries, a history whose wide reading and careful study we earnestly recommend to our ministers and members. The three branches that have united to form The Methodist Church have always believed that the only infallible proof of any genuine Church of Christ is its ability to seek and save the lost; to disseminate the Pentecostal Spirit and life; to spread Scriptural holiness over all lands and to reform all continents by the Gospel of Christ. And the sole object of the rules, regulations, and usages of The Methodist Church is that it may fulfil in all places and years its original divine commission as a leader in evangelism, in reforms, and in fraternal relations with all branches of the one Church of Christ, with which it gladly confesses its partnership in the spiritual conquest of the whole world for the Son of God.

ARTICLES OF RELIGION

I. *Of Faith in the Holy Trinity*

¶ 1. There is but one living and true God, everlasting, without body or parts; of infinite power, wisdom, and goodness; the Maker and Preserver of all things, both visible and invisible. And in unity of this Godhead, there are three persons of one substance, power, and eternity; the Father, the Son, and the Holy Ghost.

II. *Of the Word, or Son of God, who was made very Man*

¶ 2. The Son, who is the Word of the Father, the very and eternal God, of one substance with the Father, took man's nature in the womb of the blessed Virgin; so that two whole and perfect natures, that is to say, the Godhead and manhood, were joined together in one person, never to be divided, whereof is one Christ, very God and very man, who truly suffered, was crucified, dead, and buried, to reconcile his Father to us, and to be a sacrifice, not only for original guilt, but also for actual sins of man.

III. *Of the Resurrection of Christ*

¶ 3. Christ did truly rise again from the dead, and took again his body, with all things appertaining to the perfection of man's nature, wherewith he ascended into heaven, and there sitteth until he return to judge all men at the last day.

IV. *Of the Holy Ghost*

¶ 4. The Holy Ghost, proceeding from the Father and the Son, is of one substance, majesty, and glory, with the Father and the Son, very and eternal God.

V. *Of the Sufficiency of the Holy Scriptures for Salvation*

¶ 5. Holy Scripture containeth all things necessary to salvation; so that whatsoever is not read therein, nor may be proved thereby, is not to be required of any man, that it should be believed as an article of the faith, or be thought requisite or necessary to salvation. In the name of the Holy Scripture, we do understand those canonical books of the Old and New Testament, of whose authority was never any doubt in the Church.

Of the Names of the Canonical Books—Genesis, Exodus, Leviticus, Numbers, Deuteronomy, Joshua, Judges, Ruth,

The First Book of Samuel, The Second Book of Samuel, The First Book of Kings, The Second Book of Kings, The First Book of Chronicles, The Second Book of Chronicles, The Book of Ezra, The Book of Nehemiah, The Book of Esther, The Book of Job, The Psalms, The Proverbs, Ecclesiastes, or the Preacher, Cantica, or Songs of Solomon, Four Prophets the Greater, Twelve Prophets the Less.

All the Books of the New Testament, as they are commonly received, we do receive and account canonical.

VI. *Of the Old Testament*

¶ 6. The Old Testament is not contrary to the New; for both in the Old and New Testament everlasting life is offered to mankind by Christ, who is the only Mediator between God and man, being both God and man. Wherefore they are not to be heard, who feign that the old fathers did look only for transitory promises. Although the law given from God by Moses, as touching ceremonies and rites, doth not bind Christians, nor ought the civil precepts thereof of necessity to be received in any commonwealth; yet, notwithstanding, no Christian whatsoever is free from the obedience of the commandments which are called moral.

VII. *Of Original or Birth Sin*

¶ 7. Original sin standeth not in the following of Adam (as the Pelagians do vainly talk), but it is the corruption of the nature of every man, that naturally is engendered of the offspring of Adam, whereby man is very far gone from original righteousness, and of his own nature inclined to evil, and that continually.

VIII. *Of Free-Will*

¶ 8. The condition of man after the fall of Adam is such, that he cannot turn and prepare himself by his own natural strength and works to faith, and calling upon God; wherefore we have no power to do good works, pleasant and acceptable to God, without the grace of God by Christ preventing us, that we may have a good will, and working with us, when we have that good will.

IX. *Of the Justification of Man*

¶ 9. We are accounted righteous before God, only for the merit of our Lord and Saviour Jesus Christ, by faith, and not for our own works or deservings; wherefore, that we are justified by faith only, is a most wholesome doctrine, and very full of comfort.

X. *Of Good Works*

¶ 10. Although good works, which are the fruits of faith, and follow after justification, cannot put away our sins and endure the severity of God's judgment; yet are they pleasing and acceptable to God in Christ, and spring out of a true and lively faith, insomuch that by them a lively faith may be as evidently known, as a tree discerned by its fruit.

XI. *Of Works of Supererogation*

¶ 11. Voluntary works, besides, over and above God's commandments, which they call works of supererogation, cannot be taught without arrogancy and impiety. For by them men do declare, That they do not only render unto God as much as they are bound to do, but that they do more for his sake than of bounden duty is required: whereas Christ saith plainly, When ye have done all that is commanded you, say, We are unprofitable servants.

XII. *Of Sin after Justification*

¶ 12. Not every sin, willingly committed after justification, is the sin against the Holy Ghost, and unpardonable. Wherefore the grant of repentance is not to be denied to such as fall into sin after justification; after we have received the Holy Ghost, we may depart from grace given, and fall into sin, and by the grace of God rise again, and amend our lives. And therefore they are to be condemned who say they can no more sin as long as they live here, or deny the place of forgiveness to such as truly repent.

XIII. *Of the Church*

¶ 13. The visible Church of Christ is a congregation of faithful men, in the which the pure word of God is preached, and the sacraments duly administered according to Christ's ordinance, in all those things that of necessity are requisite to the same.

XIV. *Of Purgatory*

¶ 14. The Romish doctrine concerning purgatory, pardons, worshiping, and adoration, as well of images as of relics, and also invocation of saints, is a fond thing vainly invented, and grounded upon no warrant of Scripture, but repugnant to the word of God.

XV. *Of Speaking in the Congregation in such a Tongue as the People understand*

¶ 15. It is a thing plainly repugnant to the word of God, and the custom of the Primitive Church, to have public prayer in the Church, or to minister the sacraments in a tongue not understood by the people.

XVI. *Of the Sacraments*

¶ 16. Sacraments ordained of Christ, are not only badges or tokens of Christian men's profession; but rather they are certain signs of grace, and God's good will toward us, by the which he doth work invisibly in us, and doth not only quicken, but also strengthen and confirm our faith in him.

There are two sacraments ordained of Christ our Lord in the Gospel; that is to say, Baptism and the Supper of the Lord.

Those five commonly called sacraments; that is to say, Confirmation, Penance, Orders, Matrimony, and Extreme Unction, are not to be counted for Sacraments of the Gospel, being such as have partly grown out of the corrupt following of the apostles, and partly are states of life allowed in the Scriptures, but yet have not the like nature of Baptism and the Lord's Supper, because they have not any visible sign or ceremony ordained of God.

The sacraments were not ordained of Christ to be gazed upon, or to be carried about; but that we should duly use them. And in such only as worthily receive the same, they have a wholesome effect or operation; but they that receive them unworthily, purchase to themselves condemnation, as St. Paul saith. I Cor. 11: 29.

XVII. *Of Baptism*

¶ 17. Baptism is not only a sign of profession and mark of difference, whereby Christians are distinguished from others that are not baptized; but it is also a sign a regeneration, or the new birth. The baptism of young children is to be retained in the Church.

XVIII. *Of the Lord's Supper*

¶ 18. The Supper of the Lord is not only a sign of the love that Christians ought to have among themselves one to another, but rather is a sacrament of our redemption by Christ's death: insomuch, that to such as rightly, worthily, and with faith receive the same, the bread which we break is a partaking of the body of Christ; and likewise the cup of blessing is a partaking of the blood of Christ.

Transubstantiation, or the change of the substance of bread and wine in the Supper of the Lord, cannot be proved by Holy Writ; but is repugnant to the plain words of Scripture, overthroweth the nature of a sacrament, and hath given occasion to many superstitions.

The body of Christ is given, taken, and eaten in the Supper, only after an heavenly and spiritual manner. And the mean whereby the body of Christ is received and eaten in the Supper, is faith.

The sacrament of the Lord's Supper was not by Christ's ordinance reserved, carried about, lifted up, or worshiped.

XIX. *Of Both Kinds*

¶ 19. The cup of the Lord is not to be denied to the lay-people; for both the parts of the Lord's Supper, by Christ's ordinance and commandment, ought to be administered to all Christians alike.

XX. *Of the One Oblation of Christ, finished upon the Cross*

¶ 20. The offering of Christ once made, is that perfect redemption, propitiation, and satisfaction for all the sins of the whole world, both original and actual; and there is none other satisfaction for sin but that alone. Wherefore, the sacrifice of masses, in which it is commonly said that the priest doth offer Christ for the quick and the dead, to have remission of pain or guilt, is a blasphemous fable, and dangerous deceit.

XXI. *Of the Marriage of Ministers*

¶ 21. The ministers of Christ are not commanded by God's law either to vow the estate of single life, or to abstain from marriage; therefore it is lawful for them, as for all other Christians, to marry at their own discretion, as they shall judge the same to serve best to godliness.

XXII. *Of the Rites and Ceremonies of Churches*

¶ 22. It is not necessary that rites and ceremonies should in all places be the same, or exactly alike; for they have been always different, and may be changed according to the diversity of countries, times, and men's manners, so that nothing be ordained against God's word. Whosoever, through his private judgment, willingly and purposely doth openly break the rites and ceremonies of the Church to which he belongs, which are not repugnant to the words of God, and are ordained and approved by common authority, ought to be rebuked openly, that others may fear to do the like, as one that offendeth against the common order of the Church, and woundeth the consciences of weak brethren.

Every particular Church may ordain, change, or abolish rites and ceremonies, so that all things may be done to edification.

XXIII. *Of the Rulers of the United States of America*

¶ 23. The president, the congress, the general assemblies, the governor, and the councils of state, as the delegates of the people, are the rulers of the United States of America, according to the division of power made to them by the constitution of the United States, and by the constitutions of their respective states. And the said states are a sovereign and independent nation, and ought not to be subject to any foreign jurisdiction.*

XXIV. *Of Christian Men's Goods*

¶ 24. The riches and goods of Christians are not common as touching the right, title, and possession of the same, as some do falsely boast. Notwithstanding, every man ought, of such things as he possesseth, liberally to give alms to the poor according to his ability.

XXV. *Of a Christian Man's Oath*

¶ 25. As we confess that vain and rash swearing is forbidden Christian men by our Lord Jesus Christ and James his apostle; so we judge that the Christian religion doth not prohibit, but that a man may swear when the magistrate requireth, in a cause of faith and charity, so it be done according to the prophet's teaching, in justice, judgment, and truth.

The following article is found in the Methodist Protestant Articles of Religion:

Of Sanctification

Sanctification is that renewal of our fallen nature by the Holy Ghost, received through faith in Jesus Christ, whose blood of atonement cleanseth from all sin; whereby we are not only delivered from the guilt of sin, but are washed from its pollution, saved from its power, and are enabled, through grace, to love God with all our hearts and to walk in his holy commandments blameless.

---

* The Twenty-Third Article of Religion in the *Disciplines* of all our Churches in foreign lands shall read:

XXIII. Of the Duty of Christians to the Civil Authority.

"It is the duty of all Christians, and especially of all Christian ministers, to observe and obey the laws and commands of the governing or supreme authority of the country of which they are citizens or subjects, or in which they reside, and to use all laudable means to encourage and enjoin obedience to the powers that be."

THE GENERAL RULES

¶ 31. In the latter end of the year 1739 eight or ten persons who appeared to be deeply convicted of sin, and earnestly groaning for redemption, came to Mr. Wesley in London. They desired, as did two or three more the next day, that he would spend some time with them in prayer, and advise them how to flee from the wrath to come, which they saw continually hanging over their heads. That he might have more time for this great work, he appointed a day when they might all come together; which from thenceforward they did every week, namely, on Thursday, in the evening. To these, and as many more as desired to join with them (for their number increased daily), he gave those advices from time to time which he judged most needful for them; and they always concluded their meeting with prayer suited to their several necessities.

¶ 32. This was the rise of the United Society, first in Europe, and then in America. Such a society is no other than "a company of men having the form and seeking the power of godliness, united in order to pray together, to receive the word of exhortation, and to watch over one another in love, that they may help each other to work out their salvation."

¶ 33. That it may the more easily be discerned whether they are indeed working out their own salvation, each Society is divided into smaller companies, called Classes, according to their respective places of abode. There are about twelve persons in a Class, one of whom is styled The Leader. It is his duty,

1. To see each person in his Class once a week at least; in order, (1) To inquire how his soul prospers. (2) To advise, reprove, comfort, or exhort, as occasion may require. (3) To receive what he is willing to give toward the relief of the Preachers, Church, and poor.

2. To meet the Ministers and the Stewards of the Society once a week; in order, (1) To inform the Minister of any that are sick, or of any that walk disorderly and will not be reproved. (2) To pay the Stewards what he has received of his Class in the week preceding.

¶ 34. There is only one condition previously required of those who desire admission into these Societies—"a desire to flee from the wrath to come, and to be saved from their sins." But wherever this is really fixed in the soul it will be shown by its fruits.

¶ 35. It is therefore expected of all who continue therein that they shall continue to evidence their desire of salvation.

First: By doing no harm, by avoiding evil of every kind, especially that which is most generally practiced; such as,

The taking of the name of God in vain.

The profaning the day of the Lord, either by doing ordinary work therein or by buying or selling.

Drunkenness, buying or selling spirituous liquors, or drinking them, unless in cases of extreme necessity.

Slaveholding; buying or selling slaves.

Fighting, quarreling, brawling, brother going to law with brother; returning evil for evil, or railing for railing; the using of many words in buying or selling.

The buying or selling goods that have not paid the duty.

The giving or taking of things on usury—that is, unlawful interest.

Uncharitable or unprofitable conversation; particularly speaking evil of Magistrates or of Ministers.

Doing to others as we would not they should do unto us.

Doing what we know is not for the glory of God, as:

The putting on of gold and costly apparel.

The taking such diversions as cannot be used in the name of the Lord Jesus.

The singing those songs, or reading those books, which do not tend to the knowledge or love of God.

Softness and needless self-indulgence.

Laying up treasure upon earth.

Borrowing without a probability of paying; or taking up goods without a probability of paying for them.

¶ 36. It is expected of all who continue in these Societies that they shall continue to evidence their desire of salvation,

Second: By doing good; by being in every kind merciful after their power; as they have opportunity, doing good of every possible sort, and, as far as possible, to all men:

To their bodies, of the ability which God giveth, by giving food to the hungry, by clothing the naked, by visiting or helping them that are sick or in prison;

To their souls, by instructing, reproving, or exhorting all we have any intercourse with; trampling under foot that enthusiastic doctrine, that "we are not to do good unless our hearts be free to it."

By doing good, especially to them that are of the household of faith or groaning so to be; employing them preferably to others; buying one of another; helping each other in business; and so much the more because the world will love its own and them only.

By all possible diligence and frugality, that the Gospel be not blamed.

By running with patience the race which is set before them, denying themselves, and taking up their cross daily; submitting to bear the reproach of Christ, to be as the filth and offscouring of the world; and looking that men should say all manner of evil of them falsely, for the Lord's sake.

¶ 37. It is expected of all who desire to continue in these Societies that they shall continue to evidence their desire of salvation.

Third: by attending upon all the ordinances of God; such are,

The Public Worship of God.

The Ministry of the Word, either read or expounded.

The Supper of the Lord.

Family and private Prayer.

Searching the Scriptures.

Fasting or Abstinence.

¶ 38. These are the General Rules of our Societies; all of which we are taught of God to observe, even in his written Word, which is the only rule, and the sufficient rule, both of our faith and practice. And all these we know his Spirit writes on truly awakened hearts. If there be any among us who observes them not, who habitually breaks any of them, let it be known unto them who watch over that soul as they who must give an account. We will admonish him of the error of his ways. We will bear with him for a season. But, if then he repent not, he hath no more place among us. We have delivered our own souls.

REPORTS ADOPTED

REPORTS OF GENERAL STANDING COMMITTEES *

I. COMMITTEE ON CONFERENCES

REPORT No. 1. CONCERNING FIRST GENERAL CONFERENCE

Calendar No. 2. Adopted May 1. See Journal, page 226.

Membership of Committee, 135; present when report was adopted, 115; voting for adoption, 93; voting against adoption, 22.

Your Committee on Conferences recommends that the first General Conference be convened on the last Wednesday in April, 1940.

REPORT No. 2. CONCERNING FIRST GENERAL CONFERENCE

Calendar No. 3. Adopted May 1. See Journal, Page 226.

Membership of Committee, 135; present when report was adopted, 114; voting for adoption, 114.

Your Committee on Conferences recommends that the Council of Bishops be requested to nominate to the Uniting Conference a commission composed of one preacher and one layman from each Jurisdiction to determine the place of and make arrangements with the Local Committee for holding the first General Conference.

REPORT No. 3. DISTRICT CONFERENCES

Calendar No. 6. Adopted May 2. See Journal, Page 235.

Membership of Committee, 135; present when report was adopted, 117; voting for adoption, 117.

¶ 169. A District Conference shall be held annually in each District if authorized by the Annual Conference. The District Superintendent shall preside. If the District Superintendent be absent, the District Conference is authorized to elect a Chairman.

¶ 170. A District Conference shall be composed of all the preachers, traveling, superannuated or retired, supernumerary and local, the exhorters, Church School Superin-

*The original reports of all General Standing Committees were signed by their respective Chairmen and Secretaries.—EDITORS.

tendent from each Church in the charge, the District Stewards, District Trustees, the District Lay Leader and Associate Lay Leaders, the Charge Lay Leaders, the District Secretary or President of the Women's Organizations, the District Directors of Young People's Work, of Adult Work, of Children's Work, and such other persons as the Annual Conference may determine.

¶ 171. Upon nomination of the District Board of Lay Activities in consultation with the District Superintendent, the District Conference shall .elect a District Lay Leader and two Associate District Lay Leaders. The District Superintendent and the two remaining Lay Leaders shall have authority to fill vacancies occurring *ad interim* in the office of District and Associate District Lay Leaders.

¶ 172. The District Superintendent shall fix the date of the District Conference but the District Conference shall fix the place. Should it become necessary to change the place, the District Superintendent shall have authority to change it. The District Superintendent may call special sessions when necessity requires.

¶ 173. The District Conference shall inquire particularly into the condition of the several charges concerning: (1) Their spiritual state; (2) the missionary work of and in the' Districts; (3) the Christian education work through the Church Schools, vacation schools, young people's organizations; (4) the women's work; (5) the support of the Church colleges and the attendance upon them; (6) the work done in and for the American Bible Society; (7) the lay activities and especially in behalf of benevolences and in promoting worship in unserved sections and communities; (8) the work of and for our hospitals and homes; (9) the patronage of the Church papers and our Publishing Houses; (10) the candidates for the Ministry from the District and aid in their preparation; (11) concerning the support of the Church, its ministry and its benevolences and the financial systems that are being used.

¶ 174. The District Conference shall license proper persons to preach, when, in its judgment, their gifts, grace, and usefulness warrant. All votes to license shall be by ballot. It shall renew the licenses of Local Preachers when satisfied with their fitness, their usefulness, and their labors. Local preachers shall present to the Conference written reports of their work. Preachers on trial in all Annual Conferences are not subject to the District Conferences for the passage of character and the renewal of license. The District Conference may license a preacher in his absence, provided his examination is satisfactory to the Conference.

¶ 175. The District Conference shall recommend to the Annual Conference suitable candidates for acceptance as Accepted Supply Pastors, for admission on trial, for Local Deacon's orders, for Local Elder's orders, for readmission into the traveling connection, for the restoration of Local Preacher's credentials. No person shall be recommended to the Annual Conference for admission on trial or for ordination until he passes before a committee of three, to be appointed by the District Superintendent, an approved examination in the prescribed course of study. All votes to recommend Preachers for admission on trial, for readmission, for Deacon's or Elder's Orders, or for restoration of credentials shall be by ballot. No recommendation from a District Conference shall be valid after the session of the Annual Conference next following the grant of the recommendation.

¶ 176. The District Conference upon the nomination of the District Superintendent, shall elect a Licensing Committee of six or four. The District Superintendent shall fill any vacancy in the Committee. The Committee shall serve until the ensuing Annual Conference. It shall have the power, by unanimous vote, after thorough and satisfactory examination in the prescribed Course of Study, to license proper and duly recommended persons to preach, and to recommend proper persons for admission on trial or for readmission. The District Superintendent and the Secretary of the Licensing Committee shall furnish a certified record of the proceedings to the Secretary of the District Conference for record in the Journal. The District Superintendent shall be a member and Chairman of this Committee.

¶ 177. Before the ballot for the license of an applicant is taken, either in the District Conference or Licensing Committee, he shall have agreed wholly to abstain from the use of tobacco.

¶ 178. The District Conference may choose its own order of business provided that all the business committed to it is transacted. The Secretary duly elected shall keep an accurate record of the proceedings, and submit it to the Annual Conference for examination.

REPORT No. 4.   THE GENERAL CONFERENCE

Calendar No. 10.   Adopted May 3.   See Journal, Page 248.

•Membership of Committee, 135; present when report was adopted, 94; voting for adoption, 94.

SECTION I. HOW COMPOSED

¶ 101. The General Conference shall be composed of one Ministerial Member for every seventy Ministerial Members of each Annual Conference and one additional Member for a majority fraction thereof, and an equal number of lay members, all of whom shall be elected by ballot and by a majority vote. Every Annual Conference shall be entitled to at least one Ministerial and one Lay Member. The Secretaries of the several Annual Conferences shall furnish certificates of election to the Delegates severally, and shall send a certificate of such election to the Secretary of the preceding General Conference immediately after the adjournment of said Annual Conference.

SECTION II. ELECTION OF DELEGATES

¶ 102. The Ministerial Delegates and Alternates to the General Conference shall be elected by ballot by the ministerial members of the Annual Conference; *provided* that such Delegates shall have been traveling preachers in the constituent Churches forming this union, or in The Methodist Church, for at least four years next preceding their election and are in full connection with the Annual Conference electing them when elected and at the time of holding the General Conference. The lay Delegates and Alternates to the General Conference shall be elected by ballot by the Lay Members of the Annual Conference, *provided* that such delegates be at least twenty-five years of age and shall have been members of the constituent Churches forming this union, or of The Methodist Church, for at least four years next preceding their election, and are members thereof within the Annual Conference electing them at the time of holding the General Conference. The election of Delegates by ballot shall be held at the session of the Annual Conference immediately preceding the General Conference.

SECTION III. RULES

¶ 103. When the General Conference is in session it shall require the presence of a majority of the whole number of Delegates to the General Conference to constitute a quorum for the transaction of business; but a less number may take a recess or adjourn from day to day in order to secure a quorum, and at the final session may approve the Journal, order the record of the roll call, and adjourn *sine die*.

¶ 104. The Ministerial and Lay Members shall deliberate as one body. They shall vote as one body; but a separate vote shall be taken on any question when requested by one third of either order of Delegates present and voting. In all cases of separate voting it shall require the concurrence of a majority of each order to adopt the proposed measure. However, in the case of changes in the Constitution a vote of two thirds of the General Conference as provided in the Plan of Union shall be required.

¶ 105. The General Conference shall determine the manner by which the Jurisdictional Conferences shall elect their representatives on the General Boards.

¶ 106. The General Conference shall establish the basis for the election of Delegates to the Central Conference. It may change the number and boundaries of the Ceneral Conferences.

¶ 107. The Council of Bishops by two-thirds majority vote or two-thirds of all the Annual Conferences by a majority vote of each Conference shall have the power to call at any time an extra session of the General Conference to be held at such time as the Council of Bishops may choose and at such place as a committee chosen by the Council of Bishops may fix. The General Conference thus called shall be composed of the Delegates elected to the preceding General Conference, except when an Annual Conference shall prefer to have a new election.

SECTION IV.   GENERAL CONFERENCE POWERS

¶ 108. The following are the rules and regulations as to the composition and the powers of the General Conference as given in the Plan of Union:

Article 1.   The General Conference shall be composed of not less than 600 nor more than 800 Delegates, one half of whom shall be Ministers and one half Lay Members, to be elected by the Annual Conferences.

Art. 2.   The General Conference shall meet in the month of April or May once in four years, beginning with such year, and at such place as shall be fixed by the Uniting Conference, and thereafter at such time and in such place as shall be determined by the General Conference or by its duly authorized committees.

Art. 3.   The General Conference shall fix the ratio of representation in the General, Jurisdictional and Central Conferences from the Annual Conferences, with the total ministerial membership in the Annual Conference as a basis; *provided* that each Annual Conference shall be entitled to at least one Ministerial and one Lay Delegate in the General Conference and also in the Jurisdictional or Central Conference.

Art. 4. The General Conference shall have full legislative power over all matters distinctively connectional, and in the exercise of said power shall have authority as follows:

1. To define and fix the conditions, privileges, and duties of Church membership.

2. To define and fix the qualifications and duties of Elders, Deacons, Supply Preachers, Local Preachers, Exhorters, and Deaconesses.

3. To define and fix the powers and duties of Annual Conferences, Mission Conferences, and Missions, and of District, Quarterly, and Church Conferences.

4. To provide for the organization, promotion, and administration of the work of the Church outside of the United States of America.

5. To define and fix the powers, duties, and privileges of the Episcopacy; to adopt a plan for the support of the Bishops, to provide a uniform rule for their superannuation, and to provide for the discontinuance of a Bishop because of inefficiency or unacceptability.

6. To provide and revise the *Hymnal* and Ritual of the Church and to regulate all matters relating to the form and mode of worship, subject to the limitations of the First Restrictive Rule.

7. To provide a Judicial system and a method of Judicial procedure for the Church, except as herein otherwise prescribed.

8. To initiate and to direct all connectional enterprises of the Church, such as publishing, evangelistic, education, missionary, and benevolent, and to provide boards for their promotion and administration.

9. To determine and provide for raising the funds necessary to carry on the connectional work of the Church.

10. To fix a uniform basis upon which Bishops shall be elected by the Jurisdictional Conferences and to determine the number of Bishops that may be elected by Central Conferences.

11. To select its presiding officers from the Bishops, through a committee, *provided* that the Bishops shall select from their own number the president for the opening session.

12. To change the number and the boundaries of Jurisdictional Conferences upon the consent of a majority of the Annual Conferences in each Jurisdictional Conference involved.

13. To establish such commissions for the general work of the Church as may be deemed advisable.

14. To enact such other legislation as may be necessary,

subject to the limitations and restrictions of the Constitution of the Church.

SECTION V. RESTRICTIVE RULES

¶ 109. The General Conference shall not revoke, alter, or change our Articles of Religion, or establish any new standards or rules of doctrine contrary to our present existing and established standards of doctrine.

¶ 110. The General Conference shall not change or alter any part or rules of our government so as to do away with Episcopacy, or destroy the plan of our itinerant General Superintendency.

¶ 111. The General Conference shall not do away the privileges of our Ministers or Preachers of trial by a committee and of an appeal; neither shall it do away the privileges of our members of trial before the Church, or by a committee, and of an appeal.

¶ 112. The General Conference shall not revoke or change the General Rules of the United Societies.

¶ 113. The General Conference shall not appropriate the produce of the Publishing House, the Book Concern, or the Chartered Fund to any purpose other than for the benefit of the traveling, supernumerary, superannuated and worn-out preachers, their wives, widows, and children.

SECTION VI. AMENDMENTS

¶ 114. Amendments to the Constitution may originate in either the General Conference or an Annual Conference.

¶ 115. Amendments to the Constitution shall be made upon a two-thirds majority of the General Conference present and voting and a two-thirds majority of all the members of the several Annual Conferences present and voting, except in the case of the First Restrictive Rule, which shall require a three-fourths majority of all the members of the Annual Conferences present and voting. The vote, after being completed, shall be canvassed by the Council of Bishops and the amendment voted upon shall become effective upon their announcement of its having received the required majority.

¶ 116. A Jurisdictional Conference may by a majority vote propose changes in the Constitution of the Church, and such proposed changes shall be submitted to the next General Conference. If the General Conference adopts the measure by a two-thirds vote, it shall be submitted to the Annual Conferences according to the provision for amendments.

REPORT NO. 5. QUARTERLY CONFERENCES

Calendar No. 25. Adopted May 4. See Journal, Page 263.

Membership of Committee, 135; present when report was adopted, 92; voting for adoption, 89.

¶ 178, *Article 1.* A Quarterly Conference shall be organized in each Pastoral Charge.

Art. 2. The Quarterly Conference shall be composed of all traveling, supernumerary, and superannuated or Retired Preachers, residing within the Circuit or Charge; all Local Preachers, exhorters, Deaconesses, class leaders and secretaries of the Annual Meetings, stewards, trustees, financial Secretaries, and Treasurers of the local churches; superintendents of Church Schools; Presidents of Young People's Divisions, Epworth Leagues, Christian Endeavors, and kindred organizations; Woman's Missionary Societies, Ladies' Aid Societies, Deaconess Circles, and Brotherhoods; Directors of Christian Education, Social and Recreational Life, and Golden Cross; Chairmen of Missionary Committees, and of the Local Church Boards of Education; Secretaries of Good Literature; and presidents or superintendents of other organizations which are approved by the Quarterly Conference for membership therein; *provided* that all members of the Quarterly Conference shall be members of The Methodist Church.

¶ 179. The District Superintendent or an Elder designated by him shall preside. In the absence of the District Superintendent or the designated Elder, the Pastor shall preside. The District Superintendent shall fix the time for the meeting of the Quarterly Conference, but the Conference may appoint the place. The District Superintendent and the Pastor shall have authority to change the place, and also to call special sessions of the Quarterly Conference. Quarterly Conferences for two or more Pastoral Charges may be held at the same time and place.

¶ 180. There shall be held on each charge a First and Fourth Quarterly Conference. The Second and Third Quarterly Conferences shall be held at the discretion of the District Superintendent. A Recording Steward shall be elected, who shall keep an accurate and permanent record of the proceedings and shall be the custodian of all records and reports. A Secretary shall be elected for each meeting who, with the President, shall sign the proceedings and transmit them to the Recording Steward.

¶ 181. The Quarterly Conference shall have the following powers, duties, and responsibilities:

Article 1.   To elect the stewards for the Circuit, Station, or Mission, on nomination of the Pastor, or on nomination of a committee of which the Pastor shall be the chairman, as the Quarterly Conference may direct, and to provide for the election of trustees in accordance with provisions hereinafter set forth; and to elect a District Steward on nomination of a committee of which the District Superintendent shall be a member.

Art. 2.   To arrange for the election of church officers by vote of the Church membership, whenever the sentiment of the Church or Charge is evidently in favor of this process, by calling a Church Conference for this purpose, giving notice of not less than ten days.

Art. 3.   To elect, or confirm the election of, a superintendent or superintendents of Church Schools, as provided in ¶ 1135 of this *Discipline*.

Art. 4.   To elect such Standing Committees for the Charge as may be ordered by the General, Jurisdictional, or Central Conference, or by its own action in harmony with the *Discipline*.

Art. 5.   To elect or provide for the election of other officers as provided in Section 10, Article 2, of the Plan of Union.   "Unless the General Conference shall order otherwise the officers of the Church or Churches constituting a Pastoral Charge shall be elected by the Quarterly Conference or by the members of said Church or Churches at a meeting called for that purpose, as may be arranged by the Quarterly Conference, unless the election is otherwise required by local Church charters or state laws."

Art. 6.   To elect annually or quadrennially, as the Annual Conference may determine, one Lay Delegate and one reserve Lay Delegate, to the Annual Conference; *provided,* that the Lay Delegate and the reserve Lay Delegate to the Annual Conference may be elected by the Annual Meeting of the church or charge where the Quarterly Conference so directs.

Art. 7.   To recommend by ballot proper persons to the District Conference for license to preach, when in its judgment their gifts, graces, and usefulness will warrant; and in case no District Conference is authorized by the Annual Conference, to license such person to preach.

Art. 8.   To recommend the restoration of credentials by the Annual Conference to a Preacher who has surrendered his credentials, should he give satisfactory evidence to the Conference of his amendment or innocense, and procure a certificate of the Quarterly Conference of the Charge in which he resides, or of the Annual Conference that admitted him on trial, recommending their restoration by the Annual Conference to which he surrendered his credentials.

Art. 9. To license proper persons to exhort and to inquire annually into the gifts, labors, and usefulness of each exhorter on the Circuit, Station, or Mission.

Art. 10. To supervise and promote the financial interests of the Pastoral Charge, particularly for the support of the ministry, the payment of benevolences, the prompt discharge of financial obligations for the building, repair, and general physical conditions of the Church houses and parsonages of the Pastoral Charge.

Art. 11. To accept or reject any conveyance, gift, donation, legacy, bequest, or devise, for the benefit of any Church under its jurisdiction, or for the whole Charge.

Art. 12. To appoint at the Fourth Quarterly Conference a committee to examine and audit the books of the Church treasurers, and make a written report to the first Quarterly Conference following, as to whether they have been accurately kept.

Art. 13: To promote all the spiritual as well as temporal interests of the Church—evangelistic, educational, missionary and benevolent.

¶ 182. The Order of Business in the Quarterly Conference shall be such as is necessary to take care of the business committed to its charge. A printed Order of Business covering the items referred by this Uniting Conference or any subsequent General Conference to the Quarterly Conference shall be printed by the Publishing House.

If the observation of this complete Order of Business is likely to protract a session beyond a reasonable limit, the Chairman may select the more important matters and bring them forward.

REPORT NO. 6. CONCERNING FIRST GENERAL CONFERENCE *Calendar No. 31.* *Adopted May 8.* *See Journal, Page 299.*

Membership of Committee, 135; present when report was adopted, 86; voting for adoption, 86.

In accord with Section 11, ¶ 6 of the Plan of Organization which reads, "The Secretary and the Associate Secretaries shall continue in office until the meeting of the first General Conference of The Methodist Church, performing such duties as may be assigned them." *Be It Resolved:* (1) That the Secretary of the Uniting Conference is appointed, authorized and instructed to prepare and call the roll of members of the first General Conference of The Methodist Church to be held in 1940.

(2) That all memorials, petitions, resolutions, and miscellaneous papers relating to or addressed to the first General Conference of The Methodist Church shall be mailed to the Secretary of the Uniting Conference not later than ten days preceding the convening of the first General Conference, and thereafter all such memorials, petitions, resolutions, and miscellaneous papers shall be mailed to the Secretary of the Uniting Conference at the seat of the General Conference for purposes of classification and reference to the Standing Committees of the General Conference.

(3) That the Treasurer of the General Conference is authorized to pay the necessary expense of the Secretary of the Uniting Conference in carrying out the provisions of this paper and in making necessary preparation for the secretarial work of the first General Conference.

(4) That the Committee on Rules of Order of this Uniting Conference be continued and instructed to prepare and submit to the 1940 General Conference rules for the conduct of the business of that Conference, and to publish the same in the Church Press at least thirty days before the convening of the said Conference.

REPORT NO. 7.   CHURCH CONFERENCES

Calendar No. 32.   Adopted May 8.   See Journal, Page 303.

Membership of Committee, 135; present when report was adopted, 74; voting for adoption, 72; voting against adoption, 2.

A Church Conference may be held in every Local Church, composed of the members of the Church who are eighteen years of age or over, as frequently as the work of the Church may require. The Conference shall be called by the Pastor. The Pastor or, in his absence, a chairman elected by the body shall preside. The Conference may act on such matters as are referred to it by the Quarterly Conference, may review the work of the Church and adopt plans for its promotion, subject to the *Discipline* of The Methodist Church, to such limitations and provisions as are committed to the Quarterly Conference, and the Official Board or the Board of Stewards. The Secretary of the Church Conference shall present for inspection to the last Quarterly Conference of the year the records of the Church Conference. The Secretary of the Church Conference shall be a member of the Quarterly Conference.

REPORT NO. 8. JURISDICTIONAL CONFERENCES

Calendar No. 37. Adopted May 8. See Journal, Page 312.

Membership of Committee, 135; present when report was adopted, 112; voting for adoption, 111.

SECTION I. AUTHORIZATION

¶ 117. All Jurisdictional Conferences shall have the same status and the same privileges of action within the limits fixed by the Plan of Union.

¶ 118. The Jurisdictional Conference shall be composed of one Ministerial Delegate for every thirty Ministerial Members of each Annual Conference, or major fraction thereof, and an equal number of Lay Delegates, *provided* that no Annual Conference shall be denied the privilege of two Delegates, one Lay and one Ministerial.

¶ 119. The Ministerial Delegates shall be elected by ballot by the Ministerial Members of the Annual Conference, *provided* that such delegates shall have been Traveling Preachers in the constituent Churches forming this union, or of The Methodist Church, for at least four years next preceding their election, and are in full connection with the Annual Conference electing them when elected and at the time of holding the General and Jurisdictional Conferences.

¶ 120. The Lay Delegates shall be elected by ballot by the Lay Members of the Annual Conference; *provided* that such delegates be at least twenty-five years of age, and shall have been members of the constituent Churches forming this union, or of The Methodist Church, for at least four years next preceding their election, and are members thereof within the Annual Conference electing them.

¶ 121. The Ministers and Lay Delegates shall deliberate in one body.

¶ 122. Each Jurisdictional Conference shall meet within the twelve months succeeding the meeting of the General Conference at such time and place as shall have been determined by the preceding Jurisdictional Conference, or by its properly constituted committee.

[Note: The first meeting of each Jurisdictional Conference after the General Conference shall be called by the Council of Bishops at a date fixed by them and at a place selected by a Committee on Entertainment appointed by them.]

¶ 123. The Jurisdictional Conference shall adopt its own procedure, rules, and plan of organization, except at all times when the Conference is met, it shall take a majority of the whole number of delegates elected to make a quorum for the transaction of business. But a less number may take a recess or adjourn from day to day, and at the final session may approve the Journal and order the record of the roll call and adjourn *sine die.*

¶ 124. The Jurisdictional Conference shall provide for the expenses of its sessions.

¶ 125. The Bishops of a Jurisdictional Conference, by a two-thirds vote, shall have authority to call a special session of the Conference when necessary. A called session cannot transact any other business than that indicated in the call.

¶ 126. The Jurisdictional Conference shall be presided over by the Bishops of the Jurisdiction, except as provided for in Division Three, Article V, of the Plan of Union governing episcopal administration. In case no Bishop of the Jurisdiction is present, the Conference may elect a President from the Ministerial Delegates.

¶ 127. A Bishop elected by or administering in a Jurisdictional Conference shall be amenable for his conduct to his Jurisdictional Conference. Any Bishop shall have the right of appeal to the Judicial Council.

¶ 128. The Jurisdictional Conference shall elect a Standing Committee on Episcopacy, to consist of one Ministerial and one Lay Delegate from each Annual Conference. The said Committee shall review the work of the Bishops, pass on their character and official administration, and report to the Jurisdictional Conference its findings for such action as the Conference may deem appropriate within its constitutional warrant of power. The said Committee shall recommend to the Jurisdictional Conference the assignments of the said Bishops to their respective residences, and may make recommendations to the Bishops of its Jurisdiction concerning the formation of the Episcopal Areas within its Jurisdiction.

¶ 129. The Jurisdictional Conferences shall have the following powers and duties and such others as may be conferred by the General Conference:

1. To promote the evangelistic, educational, missionary, and benevolent interests of the Church, and to provide for interests and institutions within their boundaries.

2. To elect Bishops and to co-operate in carrying out such plans for their support as may be determined by the General Conference.

3. To establish and constitute Jurisdictional Conference Boards as auxiliary to the General Boards of the Church as the need may appear, and to choose their representatives on

the General Boards in such manner as the General Conference may determine.

4. To determine the boundaries of their Annual Conferences, provided that there shall be no Annual Conference with a membership of fewer than fifty Ministers in full connection, except by the consent of the General Conference.

5. To make rules and regulations for the administration of the work of the Church within the Jurisdiction, subject to such powers as have been or shall be vested in the General Conference.

6. To appoint a Committee on Appeals to hear and determine the appeal of a Traveling Preacher of that Jurisdiction from the decision of a trial committee.

¶ 130. The Jurisdictional Conference shall have authority to examine and acknowledge the Journals of the Annual Conferences within their bounds, and shall make such rules for the drawing up of the Journals as may seem necessary.

¶ 131. The Jurisdictional Conference. shall keep an official Journal of their proceedings, duly signed by the Secretary and President, the same to be sent for examination to the ensuing General Conference.

SECTION II. JURISDICTIONAL BOUNDARIES

¶ 132. The Methodist Church in the United States of America shall have Jurisdictional Conferences constituted as follows:

Northeastern: Maine, New Hampshire, Vermont, Massachusetts, Connecticut, Rhode Island, New York, Pennsylvania, New Jersey, Maryland, West Virginia, Delaware, District of Columbia, Puerto Rico.

Southeastern: Virginia, North Carolina, South Carolina, Georgia, Florida, Alabama, Tennessee, Kentucky, Mississippi, Cuba.

Central: The Negro Annual Conferences, the Negro Mission Conferences and Missions in the United States of America.

North Central: Ohio, Indiana, Illinois, Michigan, Wisconsin, Minnesota, Iowa, North Dakota, South Dakota.

South Central: Missouri, Arkansas, Louisiana, Nebraska, Kansas, Oklahoma, Texas, New Mexico.

Western: Washington, Idaho, Oregon, California, Nevada, Utah, Arizona, Montana, Wyoming, Colorado, Alaska, Hawaiian Islands.

¶ 133. Changes in the number, names, and boundaries of the Jurisdictional Conferences may be effected by the General Conference upon the consent of a majority of the

Annual Conferences of each of the Jurisdictional Conferences involved.

¶ 134. Changes in the number, names, and boundaries of the Annual Conferences may be effected by the Jurisdictional Conferences in the United States according to the powers vested in the Jurisdictional Conference.

¶ 135. The Jurisdictional Conference shall not alienate any property or institution, or the proceeds derived from the sale or transfer of any property or institution from The Methodist Church, nor shall the Jurisdictional Conferences of any of its Boards involve the General Conference Boards or any other organization of the Church in any financial obligation without the official approval of said Board or organization.

¶ 136. When property rights are involved by the change of boundary lines of Annual Conferences within the Jurisdiction, the Jurisdictional Conference shall constitute a Committee of Arbitration to adjust all claims and make final settlement of the same. In case of inter-Jurisdictional conflicts, the said committee shall act with a like committee from each of the other Jurisdictions involved, to reach a proper settlement.

¶ 137. No invested funds, fiduciary trusts, or property acquired by bequest, donation, or otherwise, for specific objects within the boundaries of an Annual Conference or Conferences may be diverted to other purposes except by the consent of the Annual Conference or Conferences involved and with the consent of the Jurisdictional Conference or Conferences concerned, and civil-court approval where necessary; *provided* that local churches possessing such funds or property shall not be required to obtain the consent of the Jurisdictional Conferences. The same rule shall apply to similar funds or properties acquired by the Jurisdictional Conferences for work specifically Jurisdictional in its scope. In such cases the Jurisdictional Conference shall determine the disposition of the interests involved, subject to an appeal to the Judicial Council.

(Note: See Report No. 20 of the Committee on Enabling Acts and Legal Forms concerning ¶¶ 135, 136, and 137 of the above Report.)

REPORT NO. 9.   CENTRAL CONFERENCES

Cálendar No. 44.   Adopted May 8.   See Journal, Page 323.

Membership of Committee, 135; present when report was adopted, 88; voting for adoption, 88.

SECTION I. AUTHORIZATION

¶ 142. In territory outside the United States of America, Annual Conferences, Mission Conferences, and Missions in such numbers as the General Conference by a two-thirds vote shall determine may be organized by the General Conference into Central Conferences or Provisional Central Conferences with such duties, privileges, and powers as the General Conference by a two-thirds vote shall prescribe.

SECTION II. CENTRAL CONFERENCE BISHOPS

¶ 143. The Central Conferences shall elect Bishops, in the number determined by the General Conference, whose Episcopal supervision shall be within the territory included in the Central Conference by which they have been elected, subject to such other conditions as the General Conference shall prescribe; *provided*, however, that a Bishop elected by one Central Conference may exercise Episcopal supervision in another Central Conference when so requested by such other Central Conference.

¶ 144. A Bishop elected by a Central Conference shall be constituted by the election of the Central Conference, and then consecrated by the laying on of hands of three Bishops, or at least of one Bishop and two Elders.

¶ 145. A Bishop elected by a Central Conference shall have, within the bounds of the Central Conference by which he is elected or within which he is administering, authority similar to that exercised by Bishops elected by or administering in a Jurisdictional Conference. He shall also be subject to the same rules and regulations for retirement, trial, and appeal as apply in the case of Bishops elected by or administering in a Jurisdictional Conference.

¶ 146. A Bishop elected by a Central Conference shall have the status, rights, and duties within his territory of a Bishop elected by or functioning in a Jurisdictional Conference. A Bishop elected by a Central Conference shall have membership in the General Council of Bishops and shall have the privilege of full participation with vote in the meetings of the Council, whenever the interest of his Central Conference or the interests common to all Central Conferences are involved. Attendance upon the annual meetings of the General Council of Bishops by Bishops elected by Central Conferences shall be left to the option of the Bishops in each Central Conference.

¶ 147. A Bishop elected by a Central Conference shall be amenable to the Central Conference, with right of appeal to the Judicial Council.

SECTION III.   ORGANIZATION OF CENTRAL CONFERENCES

¶ 148, (1) There shall be such Central Conferences as are hereinafter authorized; or shall be hereafter authorized by the General Conference, or as may develop from authorized Provisional Central Conferences as set forth in Section III (9). They shall have the privileges and powers as hereinafter set forth, *provided* that a Central Conference shall have at least a total of twenty Ministerial and twenty Lay Delegates on the basis of representation as set forth in Item (2) hereof: except that in cases wherein reasons may be deemed sufficient by the General Conference, said General Conference may fix a different number.

(2) The Central Conferences shall be composed of Ministerial Members elected by Ministers and Lay Members elected by Laymen, in equal numbers, chosen in such manner and with such qualifications as the Central Conference shall itself determine. Each Annual Conference and Mission Conference shall be entitled to at least two Ministerial and two Lay Delegates and no other selection of Delegates shall be authorized which would provide for more than one Ministerial Delegate for every six Ministerial Members of an Annual Conference or Mission Conference, except that a majority of the number fixed by a Central Conference as the ratio of representation shall entitle an Annual Conference or Mission Conference to an additional Ministerial Delegate, and to an additional Lay Delegate. A Mission is authorized to elect and send one of its members to the Central Conference concerned as the representative of the Mission, said representative to be accorded the privilege of sitting with the Committees of the Central Conference, with the right to speak in the Committees, or in the regular sessions of the Central Conference, but without the right to vote. The representatives of the Mission shall have the same claim for payment of expenses as is allowed to members of the Central Conference.

(3) The first meeting of a Central Conference shall be called by the Bishop or Bishops in charge, at such time and place as he or they may select, to which members of the Annual Conferences, Mission Conferences, and Missions concerned shall be elected on the basis of representation in accordance with ¶ 148 (2). The time and place of future meetings shall be determined by the Central Conference.

(4) Each Central Conference shall meet within the year succeeding the session of the General Conference of The Methodist Church at such time and place as the Central

Conference itself or its Bishops may determine. The sessions of said Conference shall be presided over by the Bishops. In case no Bishop be present, the Conference shall elect a temporary president from among its own members. The Bishops resident in a Central Conference, or a majority of them, with the concurrence of the Executive Committee or other authorized Committee shall have the authority to call an extra session of the Central Conference to be held at the time and place designated by them.

(5) The Council of Bishops may assign one of their number to visit any Central Conference. When so assigned, the Bishop shall be an accredited representative of the general Church; and when requested by the Bishops resident in that Central Conference may exercise therein the functions of the Episcopacy.

(6) The presiding officer of the Central Conference shall decide questions of order, subject to an appeal to the Central Conference, and he shall decide questions of law subject to an appeal to the Judicial Council; but questions relating to the interpretation of the rules and regulations made by the Central Conference for the governing of its own sessions shall be decided by the Central Conference.

(7) Central Conferences shall maintain a co-operative and consulative relationship through duly continued Executive Committees, Executive Boards, or Councils of Co-operation with the Board of Missions and Church Extension authorized by the General Conference which have work within the bounds of said Central Conferences, but the legal distinction between the Board of Missions and Church Extension and the organized Church on the field shall always be kept clear.

(8) The Journal of the proceedings of a Central Conference, duly signed by the President and Secretary, shall be sent for examination to the General Conference.

(9) Provisional Central Conference may become a Central Conference upon the fulfillment of the necessary requirements, Section III (1), and upon the authorization of the General Conference.

SECTION IV. CENTRAL CONFERENCE POWERS

¶ 149, (1) To a Central Conference shall be committed for supervision and promotion, in harmony with the *Discipline* and interdenominational contractual agreements, the missionary, educational, evangelistic, industrial, publishing, medical, and other connectional interests of the Annual Conferences, Mission Conferences, and Missions within its territory, and such other matters as may be referred to it by said bodies, or by order of the General Conference; and it shall provide suitable organizations for such work and elect the necessary officers for the same. A Central Conference, however, may not enter upon such work outside its borders without first consulting the Board of Missions and Church Extension and securing their approval.

(2) A Central Conference, when authorized by a specific enabling act of the General Conference, may elect one or more Bishops from among the traveling elders of The Methodist Church. The number of Bishops to be elected by each Central Conference shall be determined from time to time by the General Conference.

(3) When a Central Conference shall have been authorized to elect Bishops, such elections shall be conducted under the same general procedure as prevails in the Jurisdictional Conferences for the election of Bishops.

A Central Conference shall have power to fix the tenure of Bishops elected by the said Central Conference, provided that such tenure shall not be for a term longer than that in force at the time of Bishops elected by the Jurisdictional Conferences.

(4) The amount of support and all other allowances (including office, house rent, travel, retirement allowances, and provisions for health and education of children) for Bishops elected by the Central Conferences shall be fixed by the Committee administering the General Episcopal Fund, after consultation with representatives of the Episcopal Fund Committees of the various Central Conferences and with the Bishops whose cases are under consideration. These amounts shall be paid from the General Episcopal Fund, according to the regulations adopted by the General Conference. A Central Conference shall co-operate in building up the General Episcopal Fund by seeing that the amounts for this purpose apportioned to the Annual Conferences within its bounds (on the same ratio basis as prevails for the Annual Conferences in the Jurisdictional Conferences) are raised.

(5) A Central Conference, in consultation with the Bishops of that Central Conference, shall fix the Episcopal areas and residences and make assignments to them of the Bishops who are to reside in that Central Conference. The Bishops of a Central Conference shall arrange the plan of Episcopal visitation within its bounds.

The Secretary of a Central Conference, where one or more Bishops have been chosen, shall report to the Secretary of the General Conference the names of the Bishop or

Bishops and the residences to which they have been assigned by the Central Conference.

(6) Subject to the approval of the Bishops resident in a Central Conference, a Central Conference shall have the power to prescribe Courses of Study, including those in the vernaculars, for its Ministry both foreign and indigenous, including Local Preachers, Exhorters, Bible Women, Deaconesses, Teachers, both male and female, and all other workers whatsoever, ordained or lay. It shall also make rules and regulations for examinations in these courses.

(7) A Central Conference shall have power to make such changes and adaptions as the peculiar conditions on the fields concerned require, regarding Church membership, special advices, worship, and the Ministry within its territory, and shall have power to decide the official status and ordination of women; *provided* that no action shall be taken which is contrary to the general book of *Discipline* of The Methodist Church.

(8) A Central Conference shall have the authority to change the provisions for the ordination of Ministers in such way that the ordination of an Elder may follow his ordination as Deacon after one year.

(9) A Central Conference shall have the power to conform the detailed rules, rites, and ceremonies for the solemnization of marriage, to the statute laws of the country or countries within its Jurisdiction.

(10) A Central Conference is authorized to prepare and translate simplified or adapted forms of such parts of the Ritual as it may deem necessary; such changes to receive the approval of the Resident Bishop or Bishops of the Central Conference.

(11) A Central Conference shall have authority to edit and publish a Central Conference *Discipline* which shall contain, in addition to the Constitution of the Church, such sections from the general book of *Discipline* of The Methodist Church as may be pertinent to the entire Church; and also such revised, adapted, or new sections as shall have been enacted by the Central Conferences concerned under the powers given by the General Conference, with the understanding that legislation passed by the General Conference becomes effective immediately throughout the entire Church.

(12) In a Central Conference, or Provisional Central Conference, using a language other than English, however, legislation passed by a General Conference shall not take effect until six months after the close of that General Conference, in order to afford the necessary time to make adap-

tations and to publish a translation of the legislation which has been enacted, which translation shall be approved by the Resident Bishop or Bishops of the Central Conference. This provision, however, shall not exclude the election of delegates to the General Conferences by Annual Conferences within the territory of Central Conferences or Provisional Central Conferences.

(13) A Central Conference, where the laws of the country permit, shall have the power to incorporate one or more Executive Committees, Executive Boards or Councils of Co-operation, with such membership and such powers as may have been granted by the Central Conference, for the purpose of transacting any necessary business that may arise in the interval between the sessions of the Central Conference, or that may be committed to said Boards or Committees by the Central Conference.

(14) A Central Conference is authorized to interpret Article XXIII of the Articles of Religion so as to recognize the government or governments of the country or countries within its territory.

(15) The Central Conference, with the concurrence of the Resident Bishop or Bishops concerned, shall have authority to supervise such institutions, interests, and properties of The Methodist Church in the territory of that Central Conference as may have been provided by funds raised within said Central Conference, or as may be entrusted to it. It shall have the power to make rules and regulations for the purchase, holding, and transfer of any such property or institution secured or established from resources raised within the Central Conference, and of any other properties as may be transferred to it by the Annual Conferences or any other organizations, local or general, holding same; provided, however, (a) that all procedure shall be subject to the laws of the country or countries concerned; (b) that no transfer of property shall be made from one Annual Conference to another without the consent of the Conference holding title to such property; (c) that the existing status of properties held by local Trustees or other holding bodies that be recognized. The Central Conference shall not alienate any property or institution, or the proceeds derived from the sale or transfer thereof, from The Methodist Church, nor shall the Central Conference involve the Board of Missions and Church Extension, or any other organization of the Church, in any financial obligation without the official approval of said Boards or organizations.

The provisions of Chapter XIII in the Prospectus governing Church property shall not apply in the territory of Central Conferences and Provisional Central Conferences except in cases where such Conferences have not been fully organized with their own rules and regulations.

(16) A Central Conference shall have power to authorize the congregations in a certain state or country to form special organizations in order to receive the acknowledgment of the state or country according to the laws of that state or country. These organizations shall be empowered to represent the interests of the Church to the authorities of the state or country according to the rules and principles of The Methodist Church, and they shall be required to give regular reports of their activities to their respective Annual Conferences.

(17) A Central Conference shall fix the boundaries of the Annual Conferences, Mission Conferences, and Missions within its bounds, proposals for changes first having been submitted to the Annual Conferences concerned as prescribed in the general book of *Discipline* of The Methodist Church; *provided,* however, that the number of Annual Conferences which may be organized within the bounds of a Central Conference shall first have been determined by the General Conference. No Annual Conference shall be organized with fewer than twenty-five ministerial members, nor shall an Annual Conference be continued with fewer than fifteen members.

(18) A Central Conference may, with the consent of the Bishops resident in that Conference, enter into agreements with Churches or Missions of other denominations for the division of territory or of responsibility for Christian work within the territory of the Central Conference.

(19) A Central Conference shall have power to add to the business of the Annual Conference supplementary questions considered desirable or necessary for meeting its own needs; to make such changes and adaptations in procedure as the peculiar conditions of the fields require; and to adapt the temporal economy of the Church within its own territory, including orders of business suitable for District and Quarterly Conferences.

(20) The Central Conference shall have a Standing Committee on Women's Work. This Committee should preferably be composed of the women delegates and such other persons as the Central Conference may elect. The duty of this Committee shall be to study the relation of women to the Church and to devise ways and means of developing this portion of the Church membership to the end that it may assume its rightful responsibilities in the extension of

the Kingdom. The Committee shall make recommendations to the Central Conference regarding women's organizations within its areas.

(21) A Central Conference shall be authorized to adopt rules of procedure for the trial and appeal of its ministers as the necessities of the field may require; to appoint a Committee on Appeals to hear and determine the appeal of a Traveling Preacher of that Central Conference from the decision of a Committee of Trial; *Provided*, however, that these rules shall in all respects conform to the restrictions and limitations prescribed in the chapter on Judicial Administration.

(22) A Central Conference shall have authority to elect and support general officers in all departments of the work of the Church within the boundaries of the Central Conferences, but may not determine the number of Bishops.

(23) A Central Conference shall have authority to examine and acknowledge the Journals of the Annual Conferences, Mission Conferences and Missions located within its bounds, and to make rules for the drawing up of the Journals as may seem necessary.

SECTION V. SPECIFIC AUTHORIZATIONS

¶ 150. (1) *The China Central Conference.* The China Central Conference is hereby authorized to elect —— Bishop (s) for China, *provided* that by such election there shall not be more than —— Bishop(s) resident in this field during the quadrennium ending in ——.

(2) *The Central Conference of Southern Asia.* The Central Conference of Southern Asia is hereby authorized to elect —— Bishop(s) for India and Burma; *provided* that by such election there shall not be more than —— Bishop(s) resident in that field during the quadrennium ending in ——.

(3) *The Latin America Central Conference.* The Latin America Central Conference is hereby authorized to elect —— Bishop(s) for South America provided that by such election there shall not be more than —— Bishop(s) resident in that field during the quadrennium ending in ——. The Central Conference, however, of Latin America is authorized (Chapter III, Section III (1)) by the General Conference to conduct a Central Conference with the privileges and power as provided under Central Conference legislation, *provided* that it shall have at least a total of fifteen ministerial and fifteen lay delegates on the regular basis of representation.

(4) *The Germany Central Conference.* The Germany

Central Conference is hereby authorized to elect ——— Bishop (s) for Germany, *provided* that by such election there shall not be more than ——— Bishop (s) resident in that field during the quadrennium ending in ———.

(5) *The Northern Europe Central Conference.* The Northern Europe Central Conference is hereby authorized to elect ——— Bishop (s) for Northern Europe, *provided* that by such election there shall not be more than ——— Bishop (s) resident in that field during the quadrennium ending in ———.

(6) *The Philippine Islands Central Conference.* The Philippine Islands Central Conference is hereby authorized to elect ——— Bishop (s) for the Philippine Islands, *provided* that by such election there shall not be more than ——— Bishop (s) resident in that field during the quadrennium ending in ———. The Central Conference of the Philippine Islands, however, is authorized (Chapter III, Section III (1)) by the General Conference to conduct a Central Conference with the privileges and powers as provided under Central Conference legislation, *provided* that it shall have at least a total of fifteen ministerial and fifteen lay delegates on the regular basis of representation.

SECTION VI. BOUNDARIES OF CENTRAL CONFERENCES

¶ 151. *China Central Conference.*
China Annual Conference (M. E. S.)
China Mission Conference (M. P.)
Central China Annual Conference (M. E.)
Foochow Annual Conference (M. E.)
Hinghwa Annual Conference (M. E.)
Kiangsi Annual Conference (M. E.)
North China Annual Conference (M. E.)
Shantung Annual Conference (M. E.)
West China Annual Conference (M. E.)
Yenping Annual Conference (M. E.)

¶ 152. *Central Conference of Southern Asia.*
Bengal Annual Conference (M. E.)
Bhabua Mission (M. E.)
Bombay Annual Conference (M. E.)
Burma Annual Conference (M. E.)
Central Provinces Annual Conference (M. E.)
Gujarat Annual Conference (M. E.)
Hyderabad Annual Conference (M. E.)
Indus River Annual Conference (M. E.)
Lucknow Annual Conference (M. E.)
North India Annual Conference (M. E.)

Northwest India Annual Conference (M. E.)
South India Annual Conference (M. E.)
¶ 153. *Philippine Islands Central Conference.*
Philippine Annual Conference (M. E.)
Philippine North Annual Conference (M. E.)
¶ 154. *Latin America Central Conference.*
Bolivia Mission Conference (M. E.)
Central America Mission Conference (M. E.)
Chile Annual Conference (M. E.)
Eastern South America Annual Conference (M. E.)
Peru Mission Conference (M. E.)
¶ 155. *Germany Central Conference.*
Central Germany Annual Conference (M. E.)
Northeast Germany Annual Conference (M. E.)
Northwest Germany Annual Conference (M. E.)
South Germany Annual Conference (M. E.)
Southwest Germany Annual Conference (M. E.)
¶ 156. *Northern Europe Central Conference.*
Baltic and Slavic Annual Conference (M. E.)
Denmark Annual Conference (M. E.)
Finland Annual Conference (M. E.)
Finland-Swedish Annual Conference (M. E.)
Norway Annual Conference (M. E.)
Sweden Annual Conference (M. E.)
Russia Mission Conference (M. E.)

SECTION VII. PROVISIONAL CENTRAL CONFERENCES

¶ 157. The work of The Methodist Church outside the United States and its possessions, not organized into Central Conferences, shall be administered as follows:

(1) *Central and Southern Europe.*
Switzerland Annual Conference (M. E.)
Belgium Annual Conference (M. E. S.)
Czechoslovak Annual Conference (M. E. S.)
Poland Mission Conference (M. E. S.)
Italy Annual Conference (M. E.)
Hungary Mission Conference (M. E.)
Bulgaria Mission Conference (M. E.)
Jugoslavia Mission Conference (M. E.)
North Africa Annual Conference (M. E.)
France Mission Conference (M. E.)
Madeira Mission (M. E.)
Spain Mission (M. E.)
(2) *Africa Provisional Central Conference.*
Angola Mission Conference (M. E.)

Congo Mission Conference (M. E.)
Congo Mission (M. E. S.)
Liberia Annual Conference (M. E.)
Rhodesia Annual Conference (M. E.)
Southeast Africa Mission (M. E.)
(3) *Southeastern Asia Provisional Central Conference.*
Malaya Annual Conference (M. E.)
Malaysia Chinese Mission Conference (M. E.)
Sumatra Mission Conference (M. E.)
Sarawak (Borneo) Mission Conference (M. E.)
(4) *Japan and Korea.*
Japan Mission (M. E. S.)
Japan Mission Council (M. E.)
Japan Mission Conference (M. P.)
Japan Mission (M. P.)
Korea Mission (M. E.)
Korea Mission (M. E. S.)

ENABLING ACTS

¶ 158. Until legislation enacted by the General Conference of 1940 becomes effective the several Central Conferences, Central Mission Conferences, Annual Conferences, Mission Conferences, and Missions now in existence in the constituent Churches are authorized to perform their functions within the legislation provided in the *Discipline* of the constituent churches.

¶ 159. The Uniting Conference shall set up an Ad Interim Committee on Central Conferences composed of two representatives from each Central Conference, one representative from each Provisional Central Conference and two representatives from each Jurisdictional Conference to be nominated by the Council of Bishops. This Committee is instructed to study all questions relating to Central Conferences and to report their findings to the General Conference of 1940.

¶ 160. In the territory of Central Conferences and Provisional Central Conferences where no provision has been made for adequate Episcopal supervision by a Central Conference, or otherwise, the Uniting Conference shall make such provision either by direct assignment of a Bishop from one of the Jurisdictions or by referring the matter to the Council of Bishops for action; *provided* that the Missionary Bishops administering the territories of Africa, Southeastern Asia, and the Philippine Islands shall be responsible for the Episcopal supervision and administration of the Annual Conference, Mission Conferences, and Missions within their respective areas. In case of the death, disability, or resignation of a Missionary Bishop, the Council of Bishops shall provide for the supervision of the work under his care until the meeting of, the General Conference of 1940.

¶ 161. If an Episcopal vacancy should occur, by death, resignation, or otherwise, within the bounds of the Central Conferences of Latin America, China, Southern Asia, Germany, Northern Europe, and the Philippine Islands, during the interim between this Uniting Conference and the first General Conference, the Central Conference concerned is authorized to fill the vacancy by an election of a Bishop. If the Central Conference does not meet before the first General Conference, then the vavancy may be filled by the Council of Bishops. If an Episcopal vacancy should occur within the bounds of a provisional Central Conference during the interim between this Uniting Conference and the first General Conference, the vacancy shall be filled by the Council of Bishops.

¶ 162. The Bishops assigned to Provisional Central Conference Areas shall be responsible for the Episcopal supervision and administration of the Annual Conferences, Mission Conferences, and Missions within their respective areas. When requested by one of these Bishops, the Council of Bishops may assign one of their number for presidential administration within the area of the Provisional Central Conference concerned.

¶ 163. When there are missionaries of the Board of Missions working within any of the Provisional Central Conferences, the Bishop in charge may hold an Annual Meeting of the Missionaries for the consideration of all matters relating to the policy and work of the Board of Missions.

¶ 164. In countries where there is an autonomous Methodist Church and in which the Board or Boards of Missions have worked, the Council of Bishops, whenever it may be deemed desirable, shall authorize one of its members to visit such autonomous areas as the accredited representative of The Methodist Church. He shall advise and co-operate with the missionaries of the Board of Missions, and shall counsel with the Bishop of the autonomous Church when invited to do so.

REPORT NO. 10.   MISSION CONFERENCES

Calendar No. 51. Adopted May 9. See Journal, Page 353.

Membership of Committee, 135; present when report was adopted, 84; voting for adoption, 84.

Section 1. Any Mission established under the provisions of the *Discipline* may be constituted a Mission Conference by the General Conference; *provided* that no Mission Conference shall have less than 20 Ministerial Members; and *provided* that within the territory of a Central Conference or a Provisional Central Conference four Ministerial Members may constitute a Mission Conference.

Section 2. A Mission Conference is authorized to exercise the powers of an Annual Conference subject to the approval of the presiding Bishop; and its members shall share *pro rata* in the produce of The Methodist Publishing House with members of the Annual Conferences, and they may elect one Ministerial and one Lay Delegate to the Jurisdictional Conference. A Mission Conference, within the territory of a Central Conference or a Provisional Central Conference, may elect Delegates to a Central Conference or Provisional Central Conference on the same basis as an Annual Conference, but may not elect Delegates to a General Conference.

Section 3. The Bishop having Episcopal Supervision of a Mission Conference in a foreign or a home mission field may appoint a representative as Superintendent, to whom may be committed specific responsibility for the representation of the Board of Missions and Church Extension and of the Woman's Division of Christian Service in their relation to the indigenous Church and also in co-operation with other recognized evangelical missions. Such duties shall be exercised so as not to interfere with the work of the District Superintendent. This Superintendent may also be a District Superintendent, where there are two or more Districts. He shall be responsible directly to the Bishop appointed to administer the work in the Area, and he shall make adequate reports of the work and needs of his field, to the Bishop, to the Secretaries of the Board of Missions and Church Extension immediately concerned, and to the Secretary for the field representing the Woman's Division of Christian Service.

Section 4. If there is no Bishop present at an annual session of a Mission Conference, the Superintendent shall preside; but if there is no Superintendent present the presidency shall be determined as in an Annual Conference.

Section 5. Each Mission Conference or Mission at its Annual Session shall appoint a Standing Committee, whose duty it shall be, with the concurrence of the President of the Conference, to make an estimate of the amount necessary for the support of each Pastoral Charge, either in full or supplementary to the amount raised by the Charge.

Such estimates shall be subject to modification by the Division of the Board of Missions and Church Extension immediately concerned.

Section 6. A charge within a Mission Conference or Mission may receive aid from the Board of Missions and Church Extension without having been designated by the Conference at its meeting.

Section 7. In Mission Conferences in the home field there shall be a Board of Home Missions and Church Extension constituted as in an Annual Conference, and having the same duties and powers.

Section 8. Under special conditions, Mission Conferences, within the territory of a Central Conference or a Provisional Central Conference, may designate a member to sit with the Standing Committees of the General Conference, without expense to the General Conference.

REPORT NO. 11. MISSIONS IN THE HOME FIELD

Calendar No. 52. Adopted May 9. See Journal, Page 353.

Membership of Committee, 135; present when report was adopted, 68; voting for adoption, 68.

Section 1. A Mission shall meet annually at the time and place appointed by the Bishop in charge, who shall preside. In the absence of the Bishop the Superintendent of the Mission shall preside. The presiding officer shall bring forward the regular business of the meeting, and arrange the work. This Annual Session shall possess the functions and powers of a District Conference, although the authority to license Local Preachers, and to renew the licenses of Local Preachers and Exhorters, shall remain with the Quarterly or District Conference.

Section 2. The Bishop in charge of a Mission may appoint a Superintendent of the Mission, or as many Superintendents as, in the judgment of the Bishop, may appear necessary or wise and for whom support has been provided. The Bishop shall determine the Groups or Charges over which the respective Superintendents shall have supervision.

Section 3. In the case of a Mission using more than one foreign language, and extending over a wide geographical territory, the Bishop may assemble in Annual Sessions the members of the Mission on a racial or geographical basis. The Mission may delegate to such sub-groups the work of examining and recommending to an Annual Conference candidates for Admission on Trial, under such limitations as the *Discipline* provides.

Section 4. In Annual Sessions examinations of Local and Traveling Preachers shall be held by the Mission, and certified to the Annual Conference concerned. The Mission shall also make the recommendation for Reception on Trial in an Annual Conference.

REPORT NO. 12. MISSIONS IN FOREIGN FIELDS

Calendar No. 53. Adopted May 9. See Journal, Page 353.

Membership of Committee, 135; present when report was adopted, 80; voting for adoption, 80.

Section 1. Foreign fields outside of an Annual Conference working under the care of the Board of Missions and Church Extension, not having met the requirements for the organization of a Mission Conference, may be organized into a Mission.

Section 2. The Mission shall meet annually, and shall be composed of all regularly appointed missionaries and mission Traveling Preachers, with lay members, the number of whom and the mode of their appointment each Mission shall determine for itself.

Section 3. A Bishop, or, in his absence, one of the Superintendents chosen by ballot by the Mission, shall preside in the annual meeting. This meeting shall exercise in a general way the functions of a District Conference. It shall have power to license suitable persons to preach and to pass upon the character of Preachers not members of an Annual Conference, to receive on trial mission Traveling Preachers, and to recommend proper persons for Deacons' and Elders' orders. At the Annual Meeting the Bishop or President shall assign the missionaries and Traveling Preachers to the several Charges for the ensuing year; *provided*, that no missionary shall be transferred to or from a Mission without previous consultation with the Board of Missions and Church Extension.

Section 4. The work of a Mission shall be divided, when necessary, into Districts, over each of which a missionary shall be placed as Superintendent. It shall be the duty of the Superintendent, in the absence of a Bishop, to take general supervision of the work in his District with all its interests, and to report the state of that work and its needs to the Bishop in charge and to the Board of Missions and Church Extension.

Section 5. For the consideration of financial and other matters relative to the policies of the Board of Missions and Church Extension, and the work of the missionaries, the missionaries of each Mission field shall hold an annual Missionaries' Meeting and report their proceedings to the Board of Missions and Church Extension. In the absence of a Bishop one of the missionaries shall be elected by ballot to preside.

REPORT No. 13. CONCERNING EXPENSE OF FIRST
GENERAL CONFERENCE

Calendar No. 54. Adopted May 9. See Journal, Page 353.

Membership of Committee, 135; present when report was adopted, 112; voting for adoption, 112.

Section 1. We estimate the expense of the first General Conference to be $150,000. This amount should be asked of The Methodist Church as a net and preferred claim.

Section 2. We recommend that the spreading of this apportionment and the method for collecting the same be referred to the Co-ordinating Committee established in the Enabling Act in Report No. 1 of the Committee on Publishing Interests, Page 189, Column 2, Section 1, of *The Daily Christian Advocate,* together with the Treasurers of the Uniting Conference Expense Fund. A threefold basis of distribution shall be used—namely, the ministerial membership, total lay membership, and cash pastoral support of the several Annual Conferences of each of the several Jurisdictions. The several Annual Conferences are instructed to raise this money as the Annual Conference itself may direct, or by following as nearly as possible the methods previously used for collecting the Uniting Conference Expense Fund.

Section 3. The special apportionment shall be announced not later than sixty days after the adjournment of the Uniting Conference.

Section 4. In Annual Conferences meeting before the announcement of the special apportionment provision shall be made for assuming the same and apportioning it to Districts or Charges within the Annual Conferences for the collection of the same.

Section 5. This Committee shall also make an estimate of the probable cost of the first sessions of the several Jurisdictional Conferences and report its findings, together with any suggestions for raising the moneys necessary, to the first General Conference.

REPORT No. 14. ANNUAL CONFERENCES

Calendar No. 68. Adopted May 10. See Journal, Page 373.

Membership of Committee, 135; present when report was adopted, 71; voting for adoption, 71.

SECTION I.   COMPOSITION AND CHARACTER

¶ 162. *Article* 1. The Annual Conference shall be composed of all the Traveling Preachers in full connection with it, together with a lay member elected by each Pastoral Charge. The lay members shall be at least twenty-one years of age and shall have been for the four years preceding their election, members of one of the constituent Churches forming this union, or of The Methodist Church.

Art. 2. The Annual Conference is the basic body in the Church, and as such shall have reserved to it the right to vote on all constitutional amendments, on the election of Ministerial and Lay Delegates to the General and Jurisdictional or Central Conferences, on all matters relating to the character and Conference relations of its Ministerial Members, and on the ordination of ministers, and such other rights as have not been delegated to the General Conference under the Constitution, with the exception that the Lay Members may not vote on matters of ordination, character, and Conference relations of Ministers. It shall discharge such duties and exercise such powers as the General Conference under the Constitution may determine.

Art. 3. The Annual Conference shall elect by ballot Ministerial and Lay Delegates to the General Conference and to its Jurisdictional or Central Conference in the manner provided in this section Articles IV and V, at the session preceding the General Conference. The persons first elected up to the number determined by the ratio for representation in the General Conference shall be representatives in that body. Additional Delegates shall be elected to complete the number determined by the ratio for representation in the Jurisdictional or Central Conference, who, together with those first elected as above, shall be Delegates in the Jurisdictional or Central Conference. The additional Delegates to the Jurisdictional or Central Conference shall in the order of their election be the reserve Delegates to the General Conference. The Annual Conference shall also elect reserve Ministerial and Lay Delegates to the Jurisdictional or Central Conference as it may deem desirable.

Art. 4. The Ministerial Delegates to the General Conference and to the Jurisdictional or Central Conference shall be elected by the Ministerial Members of the Annual Conference, *provided* that such Delegates shall have been Traveling Preachers in the constituent Churches forming this union, or in The Methodist Church, for at least four years next preceding their election and are in full connection with the Annual Conference electing them when elected and at the time of holding the General and Jurisdictional or Central Conferences.

Art. 5. The Lay Delegates to the General Conference and to the Jurisdictional or Central Conference shall be elected by the lay members of the Annual Conference, *provided* that such Delegates be at least twenty-five years of age and shall have been members of the constituent Churches forming this union, or of The Methodist Church, for at least four years next preceding their election, and are members thereof within the Annual Conference electing them at the time of holding the General and Jurisdictional or Central Conferences.

SECTION II.   ORGANIZATION

¶ 163. *Article* 1. Annual Conferences may become severally bodies corporate, wherever practicable, under the law of the Countries, States, and Territories within whose bounds they are located.

Art. 2. The Bishops shall appoint the times for holding the Annual Conferences.

Art. 3. The Annual Conference or a Committee thereof shall select the places for holding the Conference, but should it become necessary for any reason to change the place of meeting, a majority of the District Superintendents, with the consent of the Bishop in charge, may change the place. The Annual Conference has the right and power to provide for an adjourned session. The Bishop, with the concurrence of three-fourths of the District Superintendents, may call a Special Session of the Annual Conference. This special session shall be composed of the Ministerial Members of the Annual Conference and of the Lay Members elected for the previous session of the Annual Conference.

Art. 4. A Bishop shall preside over the Annual Conference. In the absence of a Bishop, the Conference shall by ballot, without nomination or debate, elect a President from among the Traveling Elders. The President thus elected shall discharge all the duties of a Bishop except Ordination.

SECTION III.   POWERS AND DUTIES

¶ 164. *Article* 1. ' The Annual Conference at the first session following the General Conference or Jurisdictional or Central Conference shall appoint or elect such Quadrennial Boards, Commissions or Committees as shall be ordered by the General Conference or the Jurisdictional or the Central Conference, of which the said Annual Conference is a part, or by the Annual Conference itself, for the purpose of promoting the work of The Methodist Church within the bounds of the said Annual Conference. The powers and duties of said Boards, Commissions and Committees shall be prescribed by. the Conference authorizing them or as may be defined in certain paragraphs of this *Discipline*. Members of the above Boards, Commissions and Committees shall hold office until their successors are elected.

Art. 2. The Annual Conference may make rules to govern its own procedure, provided that no Annual Conference shall make any rule contrary to the Constitution or to the powers granted it by the General Conference.

Art. 3. An Annual Conference may admit into membership only those who have met all the disciplinary requirements for membership and only in the manner prescribed in the *Discipline*.

Art. 4. The Annual Conference shall have power to hear complaints against its Ministerial Members and may try, reprove, suspend, deprive of ministerial office and credentials, expel, or acquit any against whom charges may have been preferred. The Annual Conference shall have power to locate a ministerial member for unacceptability or inefficiency.

Art. 5. The relation of a Ministerial Member of the Annual Conference shall not be changed until he has had an opportunity to appear either in person or through a representative before the Committee on Conference Relations and Ministerial Qualifications except as provided in ¶ 252.

Art. 6. The Annual Conference shall keep an exact record of its proceedings, according to the forms provided by the General and Jurisdictional Conferences. It shall send to its Jurisdictional Conference or Central Conference, as may be required, a copy signed by the President and Secretary. It shall also send to the Book Committee and the Editor of the General Minutes a printed or written copy of the Journal.

Art. 7. All members of the Annual Conference, including probationers and accepted supplies, shall attend the sessions of the Annual Conference, and they shall furnish to the Annual Conference such reports and in such form as the laws of the Church may require.

Art. 8. Every transfer of a Traveling Preacher is conditioned on the passage of his character, by the Conference from which he is amenable up to the time of his transfer. The official announcement that a Preacher is transferred changes his membership so that his rights and responsibilities in the Conference to which he goes, begin from the date of his transfer.

Art. 9. The status of a member of the Annual Conference or probationer is further determined by those sections of the *Discipline* governing the Ministry.

Art. 10. The Annual Conference shall provide adequate surety bonds for all officers handling funds of the Conference and shall have the books of said officers audited annually.

Art. 11. All records of Secretaries, Treasurers, and Statisticians shall be kept according to the forms prescribed by the laws of the Church.

Art. 12. (1) The Annual Conference shall elect a Committee of Traveling Elders on Conference Relations and Ministerial Qualifications. This Committee shall consist of not fewer than six members, arranged as far as practicable in classes to serve three years each. This Committee may be divided into two groups: (1) on Conference Relations, (2) on Ministerial Qualifications.

(2) The Conference Relations Group shall give consideration to matters pertaining to the relations of ministers of the Annual Conference belonging to the following: Superannuates, or Retired Ministers, Supernumeraries, Ministers asking Sabbatical leave, Accepted Supply Pastors, students appointed to attend schools, local Deacons and Elders.

(3) The Ministerial Qualifications Group shall make full inquiry as to the fitness of candidates for admission on trial and into full connection. This must be an examination as to character, habits of life, conversion, call to the Ministry, Christian experience, age, domestic situations, co-operation with others, ability to lead a service of worship, and understanding of the Church's mission. The answers to these questions may be submitted in writing. In the case of those coming from other Churches, inquiry must also be made as to the educational qualifications. The Committee shall report recommendations concerning each candidate to the Annual Conference as the Bishop or the Conference shall call for such report.

SECTION IV. THE BUSINESS OF THE CONFERENCE

¶ 165. After religious services the Secretary of the previous Annual Conference shall call the roll. The Conference shall complete its organization and proceed with its business.

Article 1. Inquiries shall be made in the open Conference as to whether all the Ministerial Members of the Conference are blameless in their life and official administration. The District Superintendent may answer for all the preachers in his District in one answer, if it be desired to call the name of each and every Preacher in open session, or the Committee on Conference and Ministerial Relations may make inquiry of each District Superintendent about each man in his District and make one report to the Bishop and the Conference in open session; *provided,* that the Conference may order an executive session of the Ministerial Members, to consider questions relating to matters of ordination, character, and Conference relations.

Art. 2. The Committee on Conference Relations and Ministerial Qualifications shall be prepared to report at the call of the Bishop the questions regarding the standing of all ministers in the Conference: (a) All members of the Annual Conference whether effective, supernumerary, superannuated, on Sabbatical leave, or students; (b) on trial and pursuing Courses of Study, and whether for admission into full connection or for orders; (c) those to be admitted on trial or into full connection; (d) those to be elected to orders; (e) all accepted supplies; (f) those to be received from other Churches; (g) those transferred to other Conferences during the year; (h) those transferred into the Conference during the year.

Art. 3. At the conclusion of the examination of the standing of the ministers in the Conference the presiding Bishop may call to the bar of the Conference the class to be admitted into full connection, and receive them into Conference membership after asking the questions to be found in the *Discipline.* This examination of the ministers, and the passing of their characters, should be the business of one session.

Art. 4. Since the Annual Conference is to include laymen and Preachers it is suggested that one single sitting of the Conference should consider reports of the year's work. After the statistical questions have been answered let the Boards and Committees of the Conference make their reports for discussion and adoption. The special interests of the Conference may also present reports of their work, due regard being given by the Bishop to a proper allotment of time.

Art. 5. It is suggested, for one or more sittings, that the Conference give due consideration to the work of the coming year. The representatives of connectional interests and Church-wide movements, as well as those charged with the responsibility for Conference work and programs, should present their challenge and their objectives.

Art. 6. The business of the Annual Conference shall be to inquire

1. What are the reports of the District Superintendents as to the status of the work within their Districts?

2. Are all the Preachers blameless in their life and official administration?

. What Preachers have died during the year?

. Who are discontinued?

. Who are located?

. Who have withdrawn or been expelled?

&. Who are transferred to other Conferences?

. Who are supernumerary?

&. Who are retired?

10. Who are granted Sabbatical leave?

11. Who are admitted on trial?

12. Who are readmitted?

13. Who are received from other Churches as Traveling Preachers?

14. Who are received by transfer from other Conferences?

15. Who have completed their studies
   (a) Of the first year?
   (b) Of the second year?
   (c) Of the third year?
   (d) Of the fourth year?

16. Who have been continued
   (a) In their studies of the first year?
   (b) In their studies of the second year?
   (c) In their studies of the third year?
   (d) In their studies of the fourth year?

17. Who are admitted into full connection?

18. What Traveling Preachers and what Local Preachers have been elected Deacons?

19. Who have been ordained Deacons?

20. What Traveling Preachers and what Local Preachers have been elected Elders?

21. Who have been ordained Elders?

22. Who are Accepted Supply Pastors?

23. What Accepted Supply Pastors now in charge are taking
   (a) The Conference Course of Study?
   (b) The Local Preachers' Course of Study?

24. Are the Accepted Supply Pastors blameless in their life and official administration?

25. What Preachers coming from other Churches with recommendations from the District Conference or Quarterly Conference have had their orders recognized as Local Deacons or Local Elders?

26. Who constitute the Conference Committee of Investigation?

27. Who is elected Conference Lay leader?

28. What is the report of the Conference Treasurer?

29. What is the report of the Statistician?

30. What are the reports, recommendations, and plans of the Boards of the Conference?

31. What are the objectives of this Conference for the coming year as stated by the Bishop in charge or a committee appointed by him?

32. Where shall the next session of the Conference be held?

33. Where are the Preachers stationed this year?

II. COMMITTEE ON MINISTRY AND JUDICIAL ADMINISTRATION

REPORT NO. 1. NUMBER OF BISHOPS IN JURISDICTIONAL CONFERENCES

Calendar No. 8. Adopted May 2. See Journal, Page 237.

Membership of Committee, 135; present when report was adopted, 118; voting for adoption, 117; voting against adoption, 1.

Each Jurisdictional Conference having 500,000 church members or less shall be entitled to four Bishops, and for each additional 500,000 Church members or two-thirds thereof shall be entitled to one additional Bishop.

REPORT NO. 2. JUDICIAL ADMINISTRATION

Calendar No. 9. Adopted May 2. See Journal, Page 237.

Membership of Committee, 135; present when report was adopted, 108; voting for adoption, 105; voting against adoption, 1; not voting, 2.

SECTION I. THE JUDICIAL COUNCIL

¶ 301. The Judicial Council shall be composed of nine members, of whom five shall be Ministers and four shall be Laymen—to be nominated and elected in the following manner;

The Council of Bishops shall nominate by a majority vote of the effective Bishops twenty traveling Elders and sixteen Lay Members of the Church and from such nominees or from such other nominees as may be named from the floor of the Conference, without discussion, the General Conference shall elect, by ballot, and without discussion, five traveling Elders and four Lay Members, and from the remaining nominees the General Conference shall elect by separate ballot five traveling Elders and four Lay Members as alternate members of the Judicial Council. These alternates shall be eligible to fill vacancies occuring from any cause in the membership of the Council for the remainder of the term of the member whose place the alternate may have been called to fill, and in the event of a vacancy it shall be the duty of the President and Secretary to notify the alternate of each class in order of his election. In the event of vacancies occurring after the exhaustion of the list of alternate members, the Council shall be authorized to fill such vacancies for the remainder of the quadrennium. Members of the Council shall be at least forty years of age. The term of office shall be for eight years, and until their successors are elected and qualified; provided that at the first General Conference the three traveling Elders and the two Lay Members receiving the highest majority of votes shall be elected for eight years, and the two from each class receiving the next highest majority vote shall be elected for four years. Thereafter all elections shall be for a term of eight years, and all elections shall be by a majority vote.

¶ 302. Members of the Council shall be ineligible for membership in the General Conference or Jurisdictional Conference or in any General or Jurisdictional Board or for administrative service in any connectional office.

¶ 303. The Judicial Council shall provide its own method of organization and procedure. It shall meet at the time and place of the meeting of the General Conference and shall continue in session until the adjournment of that body. It shall meet at such other times and places as it may deem necessary. Seven members shall constitute a quorum. An affirmative vote of at least six members of the Council shall be necessary to declare any act of the General Conference unconstitutional. On other matters a majority vote of the entire Council shall be sufficient.

¶ 304. The Judicial Council shall determine the constitutionality of any act of the General Conference upon an appeal of a majority of the Council of Bishops, or" one-fifth of the members of the General Conference.

¶ 305. The Judicial Council shall determine the constitutionality of any act of a Jurisdictional or a Central Conference upon an appeal of a majority of the Bishops of that
Jurisdictional or Central Conference, or upon the appeal
of ·one-fifth of the members of that Jurisdictional or Central
Conference.

¶ 306. The Judicial Council shall hear and determine the
legality of any action taken therein by any General Conference Board or Jurisdictional or Central Conference
Board or Body, upon appeal by one-third of the members
thereof, or upon request of the Council of Bishops, or a
majority of the Bishops of the Jurisdictional or Central
Conference.

¶ 307. The Judicial Council shall hear and determine any
appeal from a Bishop's decision on a question of law made
in the Annual or District Conference when said appeal has
been made by one-fifth of that Conference present and
voting.

¶ 308. The Judicial Council shall meet at least once a
year and pass upon the decisions of law made by the Bishops
in Annual and District Conferences upon questions submitted to them in writing, and reported in writing to
the Council with a syllabus of each case, and affirm, modify or reverse them. Before affirmation no Episcopal decision shall be authoritative except in the case pending.
When the decisions are affirmed, they shall become the law
of the Church.

¶ 309. The Judicial Council shall hear and determine an
appeal of a Bishop when taken from the decision of the
Trial Court in his case.

¶ 310. The Judicial Council shall have such other duties
and powers as may be conferred upon it by the General
Conference.

¶ 311. All decisions of the Judicial Council shall be final.
However, when the Judicial Council shall declare any act
of the General Conference unconstitutional, that decision
shall be reported back to that General Conference immediately.

ENABLING ACTS

¶ 312. The Uniting Conference shall elect a Judicial
Council whose members shall serve until their successors
are elected by the General Conference. Such Judicial Council shall consist of five Ministers and four Laymen holding
membership in The Methodist Church and having the qualifications hereinabove provided for membership in the Judicial Council. The method of electing such Judicial Coun-

cil shall be that hereinabove provided for election by the General Conferences of a Judicial Council; *provided* that in order to preserve the spirit of unity, and give fair representation upon such Judicial Council to each of the Churches united, membership thereon shall be distributed as follows:

Two Ministers and two Laymen who, prior to union, held membership in the Methodist Episcopal Church; two Ministers and two Laymen who, prior to union, held membership in the Methodist Episcopal Church, South; one Minister who, prior to union, held membership in the Methodist Protestant Church.

The Council of Bishops is directed to arrange the official ballot of nominees for the election in such a manner as to carry out in said election this provision as to distribution of membership among the constituency of the respective Churches united in The Methodist Church. Such Judicial Council shall have all the powers provided herein in the Plan of Union for the Judicial Council.

¶ 313. This Judicial Council shall determine all appeals from any one of the uniting Churches which remain undetermined at the time of the Uniting Conference.

REPORT No. 3. THE MINISTRY

Calendar No. 12. Adopted May 4. See Journal, Page 254.

Membership of Committee, 135; present when report was adopted, 98; voting for adoption, 98.

SECTION I. THE CALL TO PREACH

¶ 213. In order that we may try those persons who profess to be moved by the Holy Spirit to preach, let the following questions be asked, namely:

1. Do they know God as a pardoning God? Have they the love of God abiding in them? Do they desire nothing but God? Are they holy in all manner of conversation?

2. Have they gifts, as well as grace, for the work? Have they a clear, sound understanding; a right judgment in the things of God; a just conception of salvation by faith? Do they speak justly, readily, clearly?

3. Have they fruit? Have any been truly convinced of sin and converted to God, and are believers edified by their preaching?

4. As long as these marks concur in anyone, we believe he is called of God to preach. These we receive as. sufficient proof that he is moved by the Holy Spirit.

REPORT NO. 4. DISTRICT SUPERINTENDENTS

Calendar No. 13. Adopted May 4. See Journal, Page 255.

Membership of Committee, 135; present when report was adopted, 98; voting for adoption, 98.

SECTION II

¶ 214. *Article* 1. District Superintendents are to be chosen and appointed by the Bishop.

¶ 215. *Art.* 2. The duties of a District Superintendent are:

1. To travel through his District, in order to preach and to oversee the spiritual and temporal affairs of the Church.

2. In the absence of the Bishop, to have charge of all the traveling ministers and local preachers in his District.

3. To change, receive, or appoint Preachers during the intervals between Conferences and in the absence of the Bishop, as the *Discipline* directs; *provided,* that he shall not appoint any Preacher who has been rejected as an applicant, or who has been discontinued or located, unless the Conference at the time of such rejection, discontinuance, or location, shall grant such authority; and he shall not appoint any Preacher who has previously been expelled from the ministry, or has surrendered his credentials to an Annual Conference, unless the Conference to which he surrendered his credentials, or from which he was expelled, restores his credentials or recommends him; and he shall not appoint any Local Preacher who is not listed as an Accepted Supply Pastor, except between sessions of the Annual Conference, and then only until its next session.

4. To issue Licenses for Local Preachers and to renew them in accordance with the action of the District or Quarterly Conference.

5. To preside in the Quarterly Conferences of each Pastoral Charge, and at the District Conference.

6. To take care that every part of the *Discipline* is observed in his District.

7. To see that all charters, deeds, and other conveyances of Church property in his District conform to the *Discipline* and to the laws, usages, and forms of the county, state, territory, or country within which such property is situated.

8. To counsel with the Pastors in his District in regard to their pastoral responsibilities and other matters affecting their ministry.

9. To advise and encourage Local Preachers, candidates

for the ministry and Conference undergraduates in their studies.

10. To report the names and addresses of all Local Preachers in his District to the Secretary of the Annual Conference for insertion in the Conference Journal; and to report the names and addresses of all who have been licensed to preach during the year and all candidates for the ministry to the Department of Ministerial Supply and Training.

11. To prepare and deliver to his successor an official list of all abandoned church buildings, parsonages, cemeteries, and other such property within the bounds of his District, and also a list of all endowments, annuities, trust funds, investments, and unpaid legacies belonging to any Pastoral Charge or organization thereof in his District.

12. To report annually an accurate record of all financial transactions pertaining to abandoned properties to the Annual Conference.

13. To procure statistics from every Charge and report them to the Annual Conference, in case the pastor should fail to make report; and to have the records of his District Conference at the Annual Conference for examination.

14. To decide all questions of law which may arise in the business of the Quarterly or District Conference, when submitted to him in writing, subject to an appeal to the President of the next Annual Conference.

15. To promote all the interests of the Church within the bounds of his District, in co-operation with the Pastors and the Quarterly Conferences, giving particular attention to the following:

(a) The cultivation of personal religion and the sharing of spiritual experience;

(b) Evangelistic interest and activity among the churches and in behalf of the unevangelized.

(c) Establishment of new preaching places and organization of new congregations wherever needed;

(d) Missionary and social service interests and activities, including the Women's Missionary Societies, hospitals, homes and orphanages;

(e) Christian Education, including the Church Schools, and youth organizations and the Church-related Colleges, Wesley Foundations, and all other educational institutions and work;

(f) Christian Literature, especially the circulation of our Church papers and the distribution of literature and books issued by our own Publishing Houses;

(g) Lay Activities, including Personal Evangelism, Christian Stewardship, proper Financial Systems, Temperance, Social and Economic Justice, World Peace, Benevolences, and Christian Life Service.

(h) Administration of the Ordinances and Sacraments.

16. To perform such other duties as the *Discipline* may direct.

REPORT NO. 5. JUDICIAL ADMINISTRATION

Calendar No. 29. Adopted May 6. See Journal, Page 289.

Membership of Committee, 135; present when report was adopted, 83; voting for adoption, 81; not voting, 2.

SECTION II. OFFENSES FOR WHICH A BISHOP OR A TRAVELING PREACHER MAY BE TRIED

¶ 314. A Bishop or Traveling Preacher shall be liable to accusation and trial upon any of the following charges:

(a) Immorality or crime.

(b) Disseminating, publicly or privately, doctrines which are contrary to the Articles of Religion, or the established standards of doctrine.

(c) Habitual neglect of his Episcopal or ministerial duties.

(d) Imprudent or unministerial conduct.

(e) Disobedience to the Order and Discipline of the Church.

(f) Improper tempers, words, or actions.

(g) Maladministration.

SECTION III. INVESTIGATION AND TRIAL OF A BISHOP

¶ 315. A Bishop is amenable for his conduct to the Jurisdictional Conference.

¶ 316, *Article 1.* If a Bishop shall be accused in writing of any of the offenses hereinbefore mentioned (¶ 314) in the interval between sessions of the Jurisdictional Conference, the District Superintendent within whose District the offense is said to have been committed shall call the Committee of Investigation of that Annual Conference who shall carefully inquire into the case; and if, in the judgment of a majority of them, there is reasonable ground for such accusation, they shall prepare and sign the proper charges, and send a copy of the same to the accused, and to the President of the Bishops of his Jurisdiction. The President shall call together at some convenient place within thirty days of the time he receives the charges not less than nine traveling Elders and also the witnesses by whom the accusation is expected to be established; and if two-thirds of these nine traveling Elders believe a trial' necessary, they shall suspend the Bishop until he can be tried as hereinafter provided.

Art. 2. The President of the Bishops shall, within thirty days of the suspension, convene the Bishops within the Jurisdiction and they shall appoint one of their number who shall fix the place and time for the trial and convene the Committees of Investigation of not fewer than four Conferences within the Jurisdiction, of whom thirteen shall be chosen as the Trial Court, provided that the Committee of Investigation which prepared and signed the charges shall not be included therein. The Church and the accused each shall have, in addition to the right of unlimited challenge for cause, the right of peremptory challenge to the number of four. The Bishop so appointed shall preside at the trial and appoint a Secretary who shall keep a record of the proceedings and the testimony.

Should the accused be the President then a copy of the charges shall be sent to some other Bishop of the Jurisdiction, who shall perform the duties hereinabove prescribed for the President.

Art. 3. The Court as thus constituted shall have full power to try the accused and by a majority vote suspend him from the functions of his office; to depose him from his office or the ministry or both; or expel him from the Church; or in case of minor offenses to fix a lesser penalty. Its findings shall be final, subject to appeal to the Judicial Council as hereinafter provided, and shall be reported to the Jurisdictional Conference for entry on its Journal. The records of the trial, including the testimony, shall be signed by the President and Secretary of the trial Court and shall be placed in the custody of the Secretary of the Jurisdictional Conference, together with all the documents in the case, for preservation with the papers of the Jurisdictional Conference, and shall be the basis of any appeal which may be taken.

Art. 4. In case challenge for cause, sustained by the Bishop presiding at the trial, shall reduce the number of Investigating Committee members below thirteen, additional eligible Committees of Investigation from other Conferences within the Jurisdiction may be summoned by him to take the place of the member challenged, so that the membership of the Trial Court shall consist of thirteen members.

Art. 5. An accusation preferred during the session of a Jurisdictional Conference shall be made directly to the

Committee on Episcopacy, which shall investigate the charges, and, if it consider a trial necessary, shall report to the Jurisdictional Conference. If the Committee on Episcopacy should decide a trial necessary, it shall formulate charges and specifications, conforming them to the grade of offense involved in the accusation, and it shall appoint one or more of its members to prosecute the case. The bill of charges and specifications shall be a part of the report of the Committee to the Jurisdictional Conference. Every case to be tried under this process, upon the finding of a bill of charges, shall be referred to a Committee of Elders, who shall be appointed by the President in the chair or in such manner as the Conference may determine. Said Committee to consist of not more than twenty-five nor less than thirteen. The Church and the accused each shall have, in addition to the right of unlimited challenge for cause, the right of peremptory challenge to the number of four. The court as thus constituted shall have full power to try the accused and by a majority vote suspend him from the functions of his office; to depose him from his office or the ministry or both; or expel him from the Church; or in case of minor offenses to fix a lesser penalty. Its finding shall be final, subject to appeal to the Judicial Council as hereinafter provided.

¶ 317. A Bishop suspended or deposed shall have no claim upon the Episcopal Fund for salary, house rent, or any other expenses from the date of such suspension or deposition; but in case he is thereafter found not guilty of the charge or charges for which he was suspended or deposed, his claim upon the Episcopal Fund for the period during which he was deprived of the function of his office shall be paid to him.

¶ 318. If an alleged offense has been committed beyond the bounds of any District the District Superintendent within the bounds of whose District the Bishop resides shall proceed as hereinbefore provided.

¶ 319. The several Central Conferences shall make suitable rules for the investigation and trial of charges against Bishops elected by them. In the absence of such rules the same procedure shall be followed as is provided for the investigation and trial of Bishops in Jurisdictional Conferences; provided, however, that an appeal may be taken to the Judicial Council.

SECTION IV.   APPEAL OF A BISHOP

¶ 320, *Article* 1. A Bishop shall have the right of appeal to the Judicial Council in case of an adverse decision by the Trial Court; *provided*, that within thirty days after his

conviction he notify the Secretary of the Jurisdictional Conference in writing of his intention to appeal, unless such decision shall be rendered within thirty days prior to the meeting of such Conference in which case notice shall be given
within ten days after his conviction.

Art. 2. A Bishop elected by a Central Conference shall
have the right of appeal to the Judicial Council in case of an
adverse decision by the Central Conference; *provided,* that
within thirty days after the decision of the Central Conference he shall notify the Secretary of the Central Conference in writing of his intention to appeal, unless such decision shall be rendered within thirty days prior to the meeting of such Conference, in which case notice shall be given
within ten days after his conviction.

Art. 3. It shall be the duty of the Secretary of the Jurisdictional or the Central Conference, on receiving notice of
such appeal, to notify the Secretary of the Judicial Council,
and the Council shall fix the time and place for the hearing
of the appeal, and shall give due notice of the same to the
appellant and to the Secretary of the Jurisdictional or Central Conference who in turn shall notify the counsel for the
Church.

SECTION V.   TRIAL OF A TRAVELING PREACHER

¶ 321, *Article 1.* Each Annual Conference at each session, upon nomination of the Presiding Bishop, shall elect
five Elders, men of experience and sound judgment in the
affairs of the Church, who shall be known as the Committee of Investigation, and two reserves. The reserves shall
serve in the absence or disqualification of the principals.

Art. 2. If a Traveling Preacher, in the interval between
sessions of his Conference, shall be accused of any of the
offenses enumerated in ¶ 314, his District Superintendent,
or the District Superintendent of the District within the
bounds of which such acts are alleged to have taken place,
shall call the Committee of Investigation to investigate the
same, and, if possible, bring the accused and accuser face
to face; the accused shall have the right to make a statement
in his own behalf, but shall not present any witnesses. The
District Superintendent shall preside throughout the proceedings, and shall certify and declare the judgment of the
Committee.

Art. 3. If the accused is a District Superintendent, the
Bishop in charge shall call in the District Superintendent of
any other District of the Annual Conference, who shall
summon the Committee of Investigation of the Annual Conference of which the accused is a member to investigate the

case; and he shall preside at the investigation; but in case there is only one District Superintendent in the Conference, or if the other District Superintendents are so related to the case as to make it improper for any one of them to serve, then the Bishop shall appoint an Elder to act in the case.

Art. 4. If in either case, in the judgment of a majority of the Committee of Investigation, there is reasonable ground for such accusation, they shall prepare and sign the proper charges, send a copy of the same to the accused, to the Bishop in charge, and to the Secretary of the Annual Conference. The accused shall be suspended from all ministerial services until the trial of the charges.

Art. 5. The Bishop in charge, within not less than thirty days nor more than sixty days after the receipt of a copy of such charges, shall appoint counsel for the Church and notify the accused in writing to appear at a fixed time and place no less than ten days after service of such notice to select the effective Elders who shall try the charges presented. At the appointed time the Bishop, upon nomination of a majority of the District Superintendents, and in the presence of the accused and his counsel, if requested, and counsel for the Church, shall select effective Elders of the Annual Conference of which the accused is a member. The counsel for the Church and the accused each shall have peremptory challenges to the number of four, and challenges for cause without limit. If by reason of challenges which are sustained the number is reduced below thirteen, additional Elders shall be named to take the place of the members challenged so that the membership of the Trial Court shall consist of thirteen members. The Bishop in charge shall also fix the time and place for the trial, notice of which shall be given in writing to the accused by the counsel for the Church fifteen days in advance of the time fixed. The Bishop in charge or another Bishop appointed by him shall preside at the trial. The Presiding Bishop shall appoint a Secretary, who shall keep a record of the proceedings and of the testimony. The Court thus constituted shall have full power to try the accused and upon conviction to suspend him from the functions of his office; or to depose him from his office or the ministry or both; or to expel him from the Church; or in case of minor offenses to fix a lesser penalty. Its finding shall be final, subject to appeal to the Committee on Appeals of the Jurisdictional Conference. It shall make a faithful report in writing of all its proceedings, signed by the President and Secretary of the Committee, to the Secretary of the Annual Conference for entry in its Journal, and deliver up to him there-with the bill ·of charges, and evidence taken, and the decision rendered, with all documents brought into the trial:

¶ 322, *Article* 1. When accusation against a Traveling Preacher is preferred during the session ·of an Annual Conference, it shall first be referred for investigation to a committee of three traveling Elders, appointed by the President, which committee shall report to the Conference whether or not a trial is deemed necessary. If it report a trial unnecessary, and the Conference differ in judgment from the Committee, a second committee shall be appointed to inquire into the facts, and its report shall be final. The Committee of Investigation when reporting a case for trial, shall formulate a bill of charges, and shall appoint some member of the Conference to prosecute the case. The Annual Conference, at its ·discretion, shall then try an accused Traveling Preacher by one of the following methods:

Art. 2. The Conference may appoint a committee of thirteen effective Elders to try the accused, who shall have the right of unlimited challenge for cause and peremptory challenge of three. The Committee in the presence of a Bishop ·or of a Chairman whom the President of the Conference shall have appointed, and one of the Secretaries of the Conference shall try the case. The Committee thus constituted shall have full power upon his conviction to suspend him; to depose him; to expel him; or to fix a lesser penalty. Its finding shall be final, subject to appeal to the Committee on Appeals of the Jurisdictional Conference. It shall make a faithful report in writing of all its proceedings, duly signed by the President and Secretary of the Committee, to the Secretary of the Annual Conference for entry in its Journal before its final adjournment, and deliver up to him therewith the bill of charges, the evidence taken, and the decision rendered, with all documents brought into the trial.

Art. 3. The trial, including the examination of witnesses, may be by the Conference in executive session.

Art. 4. The Bishop may appoint an Elder as a Commissioner to take evidence in the case, in whole or in part. The Commissioner shall cause a correct record of the proceedings and the evidence, taken by a stenographer where possible, and signed by the witnesses respectively, to be laid before the Annual Conference; upon which evidence and such other evidence as may be admitted the case shall be determined.

Art. 5. When an accused is tried and the specific charge is not sustained by·the evidence, but the accused has been found guilty of imprudent or of unministerial conduct, this fact may be so declared and a suitable penalty imposed by the committee.

¶ 323. In cases of improper temper, words, or actions, the Traveling Preacher so offending shall be admonished by his senior in office. If he offends again one or more Ministers are to be taken as witnesses. If he continues to offend, the District Superintendent shall proceed as directed in ¶ 321.

¶ 324. Any Traveling Preacher who shall hold a religious service within the bounds of a Pastoral Charge, when requested by the Preacher in Charge or the District Superintendent not to hold such service, shall be deemed guilty of disobedience of the Order of Discipline of the Church; and if he shall not refrain from such conduct, he shall be liable to investigation, and trial.

¶ 325. If a Traveling Preacher is charged with disseminating publicly or privately doctrines which are contrary to our Articles of Religion, or to our other existing and established standards of doctrine, and the Minister so offending shall solemnly promise the Committee of Investigation not to disseminate such erroneous doctrines in public or private, it may waive suspension in order that the case may be laid before the next Annual Conference, which shall determine the matter.

¶ 326. Whenever specific complaint is made in writing and signed by five responsible persons who are members or Ministers of The Methodist Church, charging a teacher in one of our theological schools, who is a minister, with violating his pledge of loyalty to our doctrine and polity, said complaint shall be lodged with the District Superintendent within whose District the accused holds his Quarterly Conference membership, who with two Elders chosen by him shall carefully consider the same; and if in their opinion the complaint is of sufficient gravity to require an investigation, he shall immediately proceed according to the provisions of the *Discipline* in ¶ 321.

¶ 327. If the teacher referred to in ¶ 326 is a Lay Member or Local Preacher, the complaint shall be lodged with the Preacher in Charge of the Church to which the said teacher belongs, who shall proceed in accordance with the provisions of the *Discipline* for the investigation or trial of members or local preachers.

¶ 328. Any Traveling Preacher residing beyond the bounds of his own Conference shall be subject to the investigation and trial prescribed in ¶ 321, under the authority of the District Superintendent of the District within which he resides or within which he is employed. And the Committee of Investigation shall consist of the Committee of Investigation of that Conference. If he resides or is employed within the bounds of a Mission, he shall be subjected to investigation under the authority of the District Superintendent of the District within which he holds his Quarterly Conference membership or of the Superintendent of the Mission and the Committee of Investigation of the same. If he is the Superintendent of the Mission, the Bishop in charge shall appoint an Elder to act in the case.

¶ 329. An Annual Conference may entertain and try charges against its Ministerial members though no investigation of them has been held, or though the investigation has not resulted in suspension.

Maladministration

¶ 330, *Article* 1. Complaint against the administration of a Bishop may be forwarded to the Jurisdictional or Central Conference and entertained there; *provided* at least thirty days' notice in writing shall have been given to the accused and to the Secretary of the Conference.

Art. 2. A Traveling Preacher shall be answerable to his Conference on a charge of maladministration, but not for error in judgment. The violation of the advice concerning divorce shall be considered an act of maladministration.

Art. 3. Errors or defects in judicial proceedings shall be duly considered when presented on appeal.

(a) In regard to cases where there is an investigation under ¶ 321, but no trial is held as a result thereof, errors of law or administration committed by a District Superintendent are to be corrected by the President of the next Annual Conference on request in open session and in such event the Conference may also order just and suitable remedies if injury resulted from such error.

(b) Errors of law or defects in judicial proceeding, which are discovered on appeal, are to be corrected by the President of the next Annual Conference upon request in open session and in such event the Conference may also order just and suitable remedies, if injury has resulted from such errors.

Art. 4. Errors of administration not connected with judicial proceedings may be presented in writing to the Bishop presiding for his decision thereon; and the Annual Conference may order just and suitable remedies when the rights of ministers or members of the Church have been injuriously affected by such errors.

Status of a Bishop or Traveling Preacher Deposed or Expelled

¶ 331, *Article* 1. In case a Bishop or a Traveling Preacher shall have been deposed from the Ministry without being expelled from the Church, he shall be given a certification of membership in the Church signed by the President and Secretary of the Conference.

Art. 2. In case a Bishop or a Traveling Preacher shall have been deposed from the Ministry or expelled from the Church for teaching publicly or privately doctrines contrary to our Articles of Religion, or our other established standards of doctrine, he shall not again be licensed to preach until, if a Traveling Preacher, he shall have satisfied the Conference from which he was deposed or expelled; or, if a Bishop, he shall have satisfied the Annual Conference from which he was elected Bishop, and shall have promised in writing to desist wholly from disseminating such doctrine.

Withdrawal Under Complaints or Charges

¶ 332, *Article* 1. When a Bishop is accused of any of the offenses named in ¶ 314 and desires to withdraw from the Church, the Jurisdictional or Central Conference may permit him to withdraw; in which case the record shall be "Withdrawn under Complaints." If formal charges have been presented, he may be permitted to withdraw; in which case the record shall be "Withdrawn under Charges." In either case his status shall be the same as if he had been expelled.

Art. 2. When a Traveling Preacher is accused of any of the offenses enumerated in ¶ 314 and desires to withdraw from the Church, the Annual Conference may permit him to withdraw under the same conditions as are set forth in Article 1, ¶ 332.

SECTION VI. TRIAL OF A PREACHER ON TRIAL OR AN ACCEPTED SUPPLY PASTOR

¶ 333. A Preacher on Trial in an Annual Conference or an Accepted Supply Pastor, in reference to amenability and appeal, is considered as a Local Preacher; but in his case the District Superintendent shall perform the duties which are assigned to the Preacher in Charge in the case of an accused Local Preacher.

SECTION VII. TRIAL OF A LOCAL PREACHER

¶ 334. When a Local Preacher, ordained or unordained, is accused of any of the offenses enumerated in ¶ 314 the

Preacher in Charge shall call a Committee of Investigation, consisting of three or more Local Preachers, or if Local Preachers cannot be obtained, three or more members of the Church, before which it shall be the duty of the accused to appear, and by which, if the charge is sustained, he shall be suspended from all Ministerial functions until the next District or Quarterly Conference; which Conference shall try the case, and if the accused is found guilty the Conference shall suspend, deprive of Ministerial office and credentials, or expel the accused. But a Local Preacher may be tried by a District or Quarterly Conference without preliminary investigation, provided at least fifteen days' notice in writing shall have been given him by the Preacher in Charge. Such notice shall contain a statement of the charges.

¶ 335. Should the District Conference having jurisdiction in the case of an accused Local Preacher judge it expedient to try him by a Committee, it may appoint nine of its members for that purpose, the accused having the right of challenge for cause and three peremptory challenges, which Committee in the presence of the President of the District Conference, or of an Elder appointed by him, and a Secretary appointed by the said Conference, shall have full power to consider and determine the case; and the Secretary shall make a correct report in writing of all the proceedings and evidence to the Secretary of the District Conference, and shall deliver to him all the papers in the case.

¶ 336, *Article 1.* In case of improper temper, words, or actions, the Local Preacher so offending shall be admonished by the Preacher in Charge. Should a second transgression take place, one or two members of the Church are to be taken as witnesses. If he continues to offend, the case shall be investigated as provided in ¶ 334 or he shall be tried at the next District or Quarterly Conference, and, if he is found guilty, the Court shall fix the penalty.

Art. 2. If, on due trial by the District or Quarterly Conference, a Local Preacher is found neglectful of his duties as a Local Preacher or unacceptable in his Ministry, he may be deprived of his Ministerial office; in which case, if he is ordained, the District Superintendent shall require him to surrender his credentials, that they may be returned to the Annual Conference.

¶ 337, *Article 1.* If a Local Preacher disseminates, publicly or privately, doctrines which are contrary to our Articles of Religion, or to our other present existing and established standards of doctrine, the same procedure shall be observed as prescribed in ¶ 336.

Art. 2. A Local Preacher who shall hold religious services within the bounds of a Pastoral Charge when requested not to do so by the Preacher in Charge or District Superintendent, shall be deemed guilty of disobedience to the Order and Discipline of the Church, and shall be brought to investigation or trial.

¶ 338. When a Local Preacher or Deacon is complained of as being so unacceptable or inefficient as to be no longer useful in his work, and the District or Quarterly Conference for that reason refuses to pass his character, the District or Quarterly Conference shall investigate the case; and if it appears that the complaint is well founded, and if he fails to give the Conference satisfactory assurance that he will amend, or voluntarily surrender his credentials, the Conference may depose him from the Ministry. He may defend himself before the Conference, in person or by representative. The President of the District or Quarterly Conference shall in this case comply with the requirements of ¶ 316.

¶ 339. If, in the judgment of the District Superintendent, a fair and impartial trial cannot be had in the Quarterly Conference where the accused holds his membership, the District Superintendent shall refer the case for trial to some other Quarterly Conference within the bounds of his District.

¶ 340. If the trial is by the Quarterly Conference, the accused shall have the right of challenge for cause. If by reason of said challenge or other cause the number of the members of the Quarterly Conference present shall fall below seven, which number shall be required for a quorum in any such trial, the Quarterly Conference, if the District Superintendent so request, shall adjourn to a subsequent date, to be named by him to try the case; or, the District Superintendent may refer it to some other Quarterly Conference in his District.

¶ 341. In Mission Conferences or Missions in the United States, its Territories, and Insular Possessions the power to try Local Preachers shall remain with the respective District or Quarterly Conference; but Local Preachers so tried and convicted shall have the right of appeal to the Annual Session of the Mission Conference or the Mission.

SECTION VIII. TRIAL OF A CHURCH MEMBER

Offenses for Which a Lay Member May Be Tried

¶ 342, *Article* 1. A member shall be liable to accusation and trial upon any of the following charges:

(a) Immorality or crime.

(b) Disseminating, publicly or privately, doctrines which are contrary to the Articles of Religion or the established standard of doctrine.

(c) Disobedience to the Order and Discipline of the Church.

Art. 2. A member of the Church, who after private reproof and admonition by the Pastor or Class Leader, persists in using, buying, or selling intoxicating liquors as a beverage, or who signs a petition in favor of granting a license for the sale of such liquors, or who signs a petition of consent for the sale of such liquors, or who applies for a license for the sale of such liquors, or who as attorney or otherwise procures a license for himself or another for the sale of such liquors, or who becomes bondsman of any person or persons engaged in such traffic, or who rents his property as a place in which or on which to manufacture or sell intoxicating liquors, shall be brought to trial, and if when found guilty he evinces no purpose to amend, he shall be expelled.

¶ 343. In cases of neglect of duties of any kind; imprudent conduct; indulging in sinful tempers or words; "taking such diversions as cannot be used in the name of the Lord Jesus"; or disobedience to the Order and Discipline of the Church; on the first offense, let private reproof be given by the Pastor or Class Leader, and if there is an acknowledgment of the fault and proper humiliation, the person may be borne with. On further offense the Pastor or Class Leader may take with him one or two discreet members of the Church. On continued offense let him be brought to trial, and if when found guilty he evinces no purpose to amend, he shall be expelled.

¶ 344. If a member of the Church shall be accused of endeavoring to sow dissention in the Church by inveighing against its Doctrines or Discipline, its ministers or members, or in any other manner, the person so offending shall first be reproved by the Preacher in Charge; and if he persists in such practice, he shall be brought to trial, and if found guilty, shall be expelled.

¶ 345. In all the foregoing cases of trial enumerated in this section the accused member shall be brought to trial before a Committee of not less than seven members of the Church. They shall be chosen by the Quarterly Conference or Official Board by ballot. The accused may challenge for cause and shall have three peremptory challenges and in case of such challenge if the Preacher in Charge judge it advisable for the obtaining of a fair trial he shall call in a committee of seven from any part of the District. The Preacher in Charge shall preside at the trial.

Penalties

¶ 346. If the accused person shall be found guilty by the decision of a majority of the Committee, the Preacher in Charge then and there shall pronounce the sentence of expulsion.

¶ 347. If, in view of mitigating circumstances or other sufficient reason, the Committee shall find that a lower penalty would be proper, it may impose such penalty.

¶ 348. An expelled person shall have no privileges of the society or of the Sacraments of the Church without confession, contrition, and satisfactory reformation.

SECTION IX. GENERAL DIRECTIONS

Limitations

¶ 348-A. No charge shall be entertained for any alleged offense which shall not have been committed within five years immediately preceding the filing of the complaint except in cases where there is a conviction in a Civil or Criminal Court and in such cases the charges must be filed within one year after the entry of the final judgment.

Notice

¶ 348-B. All notices required or provided for in this Chapter shall be in writing signed by or on behalf of the person or body giving or required to give such notice and shall be addressed to the person to whom it is required to be given. Such notices shall be served by delivering a copy thereof to the party or chief officer of the body to whom it is addressed in person (or by registered mail addressed to the last known residence, or address of such party). The fact of the giving of the notice shall affirmatively appear over the signature of the party required to give such notice and become a part of the record of the case.

Testimony

¶ 349, *Article* 1. The testimony shall be taken by a stenographer, if convenient, and reduced to writing, and certified by the presiding officer and secretary. The record, which shall include all documents, papers, and evidence in the case, shall be the basis of any appeal which may be taken.

Art. 2. The testimony of a witness who is not a member of The Methodist Church shall not be rejected on that account.

Art. 3. It shall be the duty of a Minister and a member of the Church to appear and testify when summoned.

Art. 4. The presiding officer of any Court before which a case may be pending or the Bishop in charge of an Annual Conference shall have power, whenever the necessity of the parties or of witnesses shall require, to appoint, on the application of either party, a commissioner or commissioners, either a minister or layman or both, to examine witnesses; provided due notice (thirty days) of the time and place of taking of such testimony shall have been given to the adverse party; counsel for both parties shall be permitted to examine and cross-examine the witness or witnesses whose testimony is thus taken. The commissioners so appointed shall take such testimony in writing as may be offered by either party.

Art. 5. The testimony properly certified by the signature of the commissioner or commissioners shall be transmitted to the presiding officer of the Court before which the case is pending. All questions as to relevancy or competency of the testimony so taken shall be determined by the presiding officer of the Court when the evidence is considered.

Art. 6. If in any case the accused person, after due notice (thirty days) has been given him, shall refuse or neglect to appear at the time and place set forth for the hearing, the investigation or trial may proceed in his absence.

Art. 7. In all cases wherein it is provided that notice shall be given to a Bishop or District Superintendent and the charges or complaints are against that particular person, then such notice, if a Bishop, shall be given to another Bishop within the same Jurisdiction; if a District Superintendent, to the Bishop in charge.

Records

¶ 350, *Article* 1. In all investigations or trials the records shall be accurate and full; they shall include the proceedings in detail and all the evidence taken stenographically, if possible, including the documents admitted, together with the charges, specifications, and findings, and shall be approved and attested by the presiding officer and Secretary. In all investigations the presiding officer shall appoint a Secretary to keep a record of the proceedings and documents, of which records, when properly attested, the said presiding officer shall be the custodian. The custodian shall deliver the entire record to the President or Secretary of the Conference or Court to which the case shall go for final disposition.

Art. 2. In the trial of a member of the Church the

Preacher in Charge shall appoint the Secretary, and said Preacher in Charge shall be the custodian of the records, when properly attested. If no appeal be taken, he shall deliver the records to the Recording Steward for preservation. If an appeal be taken, he shall deliver the records to the President of the proper Appellate Court, and after they have been used in the Court they shall be returned by the Secretary to the Recording Steward of the Charge from which they came.

Art. 3. The Secretaries of Quarterly, District, and Annual Conferences and of the Jurisdictional Conference shall be the custodians of the records, which in all cases shall be made by them or their assistants, of all trials occurring in their bodies respectively; and in case of appeal they shall deliver said records to the President or Secretary of the proper Appellate Court. After the said appeal has been heard, the records shall be returned to the Conference from which they came.

Counsel

¶ 351. In all cases of investigation or trial the accused shall be entitled to appear and to be represented by counsel of his own selection and to be heard in oral or written argument. Such counsel shall be a Traveling Preacher if the accused is a Bishop or a Traveling Preacher, or a member in good standing in The Methodist Church if the accused be a Lay Member.

¶ 352. In all cases where counsel has not been provided for either the Church or the accused such counsel shall be appointed as follows:

Article 1. In the investigation of a Bishop, counsel shall be appointed by the officer presiding; and in case of a trial by the Jurisdictional Conference, counsel shall be appointed by it. Such counsel shall be an effective Elder or Elders.

Art. 2. In the investigation of a Traveling Preacher, counsel shall be appointed by the District Superintendent; and in case of trial the appointment shall be by the Bishop in charge or President of the Annual Conference. In either case such counsel shall be a Traveling Preacher.

Art. 3. In all other cases, counsel shall be appointed by the presiding officer and shall be a Traveling Preacher or a member in good standing in The Methodist Church.

Charges

¶ 353, *Article* 1. Amendments may be made to a bill of charges up to the time of the opening of the trial, at the discretion of the presiding officer; *provided* they relate to the form of statement only and do not change the nature of the alleged offense and do not introduce new matter of which the accused has not had due notice (thirty days).

Art. 2. Amendments to charges against Traveling Preachers shall be presented and ruled upon by the presiding officer before the case is committed to the Committee for trial.

' *Art.* 3. In case of improper words, tempers, and actions, a charge of slander shall not be entertained unless signed by a person alleged to have been slandered.

Art. 4. Charges and specifications for the trial of a Bishop, Minister, Local Preacher, Deaconess, or Member shall define the offense by its generic term.

Trials

¶ 354, *Article* 1. In all cases of investigation or trial at least thirty days' notice in writing shall be given to the persons accused. Notice shall be given also to such witnesses as either party may name, and shall be issued in the name of the Church and be signed by the President of the tribunal which is to investigate or try the case.

Art. 2. In all cases, sufficient time shall be allowed for the person to appear at the given place and time, and for the accused to prepare for the investigation or trial. The President of the tribunal to investigate or try the case shall decide what constitutes "sufficient time."

Art. 3. In all cases of investigation or trial both parties shall have the right of challenge for cause and such peremptory challenges as herein provided. It shall be the duty of the presiding officer to see, if possible, that there be present a sufficient number of properly qualified persons as substitutes to prevent the number from being reduced below that required for the investigation or trial.

Art. 4. As soon as the Court has convened, the accused shall be called upon by the Chairman to plead to the charge and his pleas shall be duly recorded; and on his neglect or refusal to plead, the plea of not guilty shall be entered for him, and the trial shall proceed; *provided,* that for sufficient cause the Court may adjourn from time to time as convenience or necessity may require; and *provided,* also, that the accused shall, at all times during the trial, have liberty to be present except as hereinafter mentioned and in due time and order to produce his testimony and to make his defense.

Art. 5. The Court shall be a continuing body until the final disposition of the charge. In case any member of the Court shall be unable to attend all of the sessions, he shall not vote upon the final determination of the case, but in such case the remainder of the Committee may proceed to judgment and it shall require a majority of the original membership of the Court to sustain the charges.

Art. 6. All objections to the regularity of the proceedings and the form and substance of charges and specifications shall· be made at the first session of the trial. The presiding officer upon the filing of such objection shall, or on his own motion, may determine all such preliminary objection and may dismiss the case or in the furtherance of the truth and justice permit amendments to the specifications or charges not changing the general nature ·of the same.·

Art. 7. Objections of any party to the proceedings shall be entered on the record.

Art. 8. A charge shall not allege more than one offense; several charges against the same person, however, with the specifications under each of them, may be presented at one and the same time and may be tried together. When several charges are tried at the same time a vote on each specification and charge must be separately taken.

Art. 9. No witness afterward to be examined, shall be present during the examination of another witness, if the opposing party objects. Witnesses shall be examined first by the party producing them; then cross-examined by the opposite party, after which any member of the Court or either party may put additional questions. Irrelevant or frivolous questions shall not be permitted, nor leading questions by the parties producing the witnesses except ·under permission of the Court as necessary to elicit the truth. The general rule against admission of hearsay testimony shall be applied and enforced.

Art. 10. In case of investigation, trial, or appeal the presiding officer shall not deliver a charge, reviewing or explaining the evidence or setting forth the merits of the case. He shall remain and preside until the judgment is expressed, the findings completed, and the record signed; but without expressing any opinion on the law or facts unless the parties in interest be called in. Counsel and witnesses shall withdraw and not return unless recalled for the above mentioned purpose.

Appeals

¶ 355, *Article* 1. An appeal shall not be allowed in any case in which the accused has failed or refused to be present in person or by counsel at his trial. Appeals, regularly taken, shall be heard by the proper Appellate Court unless it shall appear to the said Court that the Appellant has forfeited his right to appeal by misconduct, such as refusal to abide by the findings of the Committee of Investigation or of the Trial Court or withdrawal from the Church, or failure to appear in person or by counsel to prosecute the appeal, or prior to the final decision on appeal from his conviction resorting to suit in the Civil Courts against the complainant or any of the parties connected with the Ecclesiastical Court in which he was tried.

Art. 2. The right of appeal when once forfeited by neglect or otherwise cannot be revived by any subsequent Appellate Court.

Art. 3. The right to take and to prosecute an appeal shall not be affected by the death of the person entitled to such right. His heirs or legal representatives may prosecute such appeal as he would be entitled to do if he were living.

Art. 4. In no case shall an appeal operate as suspension of sentence. The finding of the Trial Court must stand until it is modified or reversed by the proper Appellate Court.

Art. 5. The records and documents of the trial, including the evidence, and these only, shall be used in the hearing of any appeal, except as set forth in ¶ 330.

Art. 6. In all cases where an appeal is made, and admitted, by the Appellate Court, after the charges, findings, and evidence have been read and the arguments concluded, the parties shall withdraw, and the Appellate Court shall consider and decide the case. It may reverse, in whole or in part, the findings of the Trial Court, or it may remand the case for a new trial. It may determine what penalty, not higher than that affixed at the trial, shall be imposed. If it neither reverses, in whole or in part, the judgment of the Trial Court, nor remands the case for a new trial, nor modifies the penalty, that judgment shall stand. The Appellate Court shall not reverse the judgment nor remand the case for a new trial on account of errors plainly not affecting the result.

Art. 7. In all cases the right to present evidence shall be exhausted when the case has been heard once on its merits in the proper Court; but Questions of Law may be carried on appeal, step by step, to the Judicial Council.

Art. 8. If in any case of appeal of a Traveling Preacher, or of a Bishop, the Appellate Court is convinced that new evidence has been discovered material to the issue, it may remand the case for a new trial.

Art. 9. If, within sixty days after the conviction of a member of the Church, he shall make application in writing

·to the Preacher in Charge for ·a new trial on the ground of newly discovered ·evidence, and submit therewith a written statement of the same, and if it shall appear to the Preacher in Charge that such evidence is material to the issue involved, he shall grant a new trial.

Art. 10. In no case shall a new trial be ·granted upon newly discovered evidence which could have been obtained for the trial in the exercise of due diligence, or which is merely cumulative in its effect.

Art. 11. In all cases of appeal the appellant, at the time he gives notice of appeal, shall furnish to the officer receiving such notice, and to the counsel for the Church, a written statement of the grounds of his appeal and the hearing in the Appellate Court shall be limited to the grounds set forth in such statement.

Art. 12. When any Appellate Court shall reverse, in whole or in part, the findings of a Trial Court, or remand the case for a new trial, or change the penalty imposed by that court, it shall return to the Annual Conference or to the Secretary of the Trial Court a statement of the grounds of its action.

Art. 13. The order of appeals on Questions of Law shall be as follows: From the decision of the Preacher in Charge to the District Superintendent presiding in the Quarterly or District Conference; from the decision of the District Superintendent to the Bishop presiding in the Annual Conference; and from the decision of a Bishop presiding in an Annual Conference to the Jurisdictional Conference; otherwise to the Judicial Council; and from a Central Conference to the Judicial Council.

Art. 14. When an appeal ·is taken on a Question of Law, written notice of the same shall be served on the Secretary of the body in which the decision has been rendered, whose duty it shall be to see that an exact statement of the question submitted and the ruling of the Chair thereon shall be entered on the Journal. He shall then make and certify a copy of the question and ruling and transmit the same to the Secretary of the body to which the appeal is taken. The Secretary who thus receives said certified copy shall present the same in open Conference and as soon as practicable lay it before the presiding officer for his ruling thereon; which ruling must be rendered before the final adjournment of that body, that said ruling together with the original question and ruling may be entered on the Journal of that Conference. The same course shall be followed in all subsequent appeals.

Art. 15. The various Boards, Committees, or Commissions, elected, authorized, or provided for by the General Conference, shall have full power and authority to remove and dismiss at their discretion any member, officer, or employee thereof who shall be guilty of any immoral conduct, breach of trust, or who for any reason is unable to, or fails to perform the duties of his or her office, or other misconduct which any of said Boards, Committees, or Commissions may deem sufficient to warrant such dismissal and removal. In the event any member, officer, or employee of such Board, Committee or Commission, including the Board of Publication, elected, authorized, or provided for by the General Conference, is indicted for or found guilty of any felony or misdemeanor by a verdict of any Trial Jury in any Court of any state or county where such offense shall have been committed, or who shall plead quilty to or confess his or her guilt thereto, then and in that event, the Board, Committee, or Commission of which he or she is a member, officer, or employee shall be and is hereby authorized to remove such officer, member, or employee so charged or convicted, and the place so vacated shall be filled as provided in the *Discipline*. The action of such Board, Committee, or Commission in removing such member, officer, or employee in the circumstances above set forth shall be final, and such member, officer, or employee so removed shall have no further authority to participate in any way in the affairs of such Board, Committee, or Commission.

SECTION X. APPEAL OF A TRAVELING PREACHER

¶ 356, *Article* 1. Each Jurisdictional Conference, upon nomination of the Bishops, shall elect a Committee of Appeals composed of nine Traveling Elders who have been at least six years successively members of The Methodist Church or one of the Uniting Churches, and an equal number of alternates. This Committee shall serve until its successors have been confirmed. This Committee shall have full power to hear and determine appeals of Traveling Preachers taken from any Annual Conference within the Jurisdiction. The Committee shall adopt its own rules of procedure and its decisions shall be final.

Art. 2. When notice of an appeal has been given to the President of an Annual Conference, he shall give notice of the same to the Secretary of the Committee on Appeals of the Jurisdictional Conference and submit the documents in the case. The Jurisdictional Conference Committee on Appeals shall give notice to the President of the Conference from which the appeal is taken and to the Appellant of the time and place where the appeal will be heard. Both the Annual

Conference and the Appellant may be represented by counsel. The President of the Conference shall appoint counsel for the Church.

, *Art.* 3. The Committee on Appeals of the Jurisdictional Conference when acting as a court of appeals shall determine two questions only:

(a) Does the evidence sustain the charge or charges?

(b) Were there such errors of law as to vitiate the verdict?

These questions shall be determined by the records of the trial and the argument of counsel for the Church and for the accused. The Committee shall in no case hear witnesses.

SECTION XI. APPEAL OF A LOCAL PREACHER

¶ 357, *Article* 1. In cases of conviction, a Local Preacher shall be allowed to appeal to the Annual Conference; provided that within thirty days after his conviction he shall signify in writing to the District Superintendent of the District his determination to appeal.

Art. 2. An appeal by a Local Preacher from a Quarterly Conference within the jurisdiction of a Mission shall be to the Annual Meeting of the said Mission.

'SECTION XII. APPEAL OF A CHURCH MEMBER

¶ 358, *Article* 1. Any suspended or expelled member may appeal to the next Quarterly Conference. If appeal be made, the Preacher in Charge shall present to the Conference the record of the trial, from which record the case shall finally be determined.

· *Art.* 2. No member of the Committee of Trial shall vote on the appeal.

Art. 3. The appellant, in person or by his representative (who shall be a member of the Chuch), shall state the grounds of his appeal, and shall be permitted to make his argument without interruption, so long as his defense is within the record of the case. The representative of the Committee of Trial shall then be permitted to respond, and the appellant may reply. The appellant and the representative of the Committee shall then withdraw, and the majority of the members of the Quarterly Conference present shall finally determine the case.

Art. 4. No member, after trial and explusion, shall be restored until he give satisfactory evidence of repentance of the offense for which he was expelled, unless the Quarterly Conference become convinced of his innocence, in which case he may be restored.

SECTION XIII. THE DEPRIVATION AND RESTORATION OF
CREDENTIALS

Article 1. Of the Credentials of Traveling Deacons or Elders

¶ 359. When a Traveling Deacon or Elder is deprived of his credentials of ordination, by expulsion or otherwise, they shall be filed with the papers of his Annual Conference.

¶ 360. When a traveling Deacon or Elder desires to surrender his credentials and retain his membership in our Church, he shall be permitted to do so, and to designate the Church to which he will hold membership; and the Secretary of the Conference to which he surrenders his credentials shall issue to him a certificate of membership in the Church; *provided,* that no Minister shall be permitted to take such action when charges involving his character have been made and sustained or are pending. However, when his character is involved in cases where the law permits final adjustment by the surrender of credentials, this shall be also the surrender of membership in the Church.

¶ 361. Should he later give satisfactory evidence to the Conference of his amendment or innocence, and procure a certificate of the Quarterly Conference of the charge in which he resides, or of the Annual Conference that admitted him on trial recommending their restoration by the Annual Conference to which he surrendered his credentials, the Conference may restore them.

Article 2. Of the Credentials of Local Deacons or Elders

¶ 362. When a Local Deacon or Elder is deprived of his credentials of ordination, by expulsion or otherwise, the District Superintendent shall require them of him, and file them with the Annual Conference in the bounds of which the Local Preacher resides.

¶ 363. Should he later produce to the Annual Conference a recommendation from the District Conference for the restoration of his credentials, signed by its President and Secretary, they may be restored to him.

Article 3. Of the Restoration of Lost Credentials

¶ 364. Should the credentials of any Deacon or Elder be destroyed or lost, the Bishop who ordained him, or the Bishop in whose territory he resides, upon ascertaining the necessary facts, may issue duplicate credentials.

SECTION XIV. MISSION CONFERENCES

¶ 365. In all matters of Judicial Administration the rights, duties, and responsibilities of Ministerial members of Missions and Mission Conferences are the same as those in Annual Conferences and the procedure is the same.

SECTION XV. DEACONESSES

¶ 366. When a Deaconess is accused of any violation of a moral law, the District Superintendent under whose supervision she works, shall call a Committee of three or more for investigation. This Committee shall consist of one representative of the Deaconess administration under which the accused serves, and two or more members of the Annual Conference Deaconess Board of which the accused is a member. She shall appear before this Committee and, if charges are sustained, she shall be suspended from all Deaconess services until the next regular meeting of the Annual Conference Deaconess Board, or until a special meeting of said Board shall be held. If the accused is found guilty, the Annual Conference Deaconess Board shall suspend, or deprive her of office and credentials. A Deaconess may be tried by an Annual Conference Deaconess Board without preliminary investigation, provided fifteen days' written notice shall have been given her.

¶ 367. In case of improper temper, words, actions, or disloyalty to the rules and regulations of the administration or other organization with which she serves, the Deaconess so offending shall be admonished by the President of the Annual Conference Deaconess Board. If she continues to offend, the case shall be investigated as provided in ¶ 366, or she shall be tried at the next meeting of the Annual Conference Deaconess Board or at a special meeting of the Annual Conference Deaconess Board; and if found guilty and impenitent, shall be expelled from her Deaconess relationship.

¶ 368. If a Deaconess shall contract debts which she is not able to pay, the President of the Annual Conference Deaconess Board shall appoint three judicious members of the Annual Conference Deaconess Board to consider her accounts, contracts, and circumstances. If, in their opinion, she has behaved dishonestly, or contracted debts without the probability of paying, the same procedure shall be followed as defined in ¶ 366 or ¶ 367 of this Chapter.

¶ 369. In case of conviction, a Deaconess shall be allowed to appeal to the Board of Hospitals and Homes; *provided* that within thirty days after her conviction, she shall signify in writing to the District Superintendent or President of the Annual Conference Deaconess Board by which she was tried, her determination to appeal to the Board of Hospitals and Homes, which in full session, or by a special

Committee of not less than seven nor more than nine, shall hear the appeal, and its decision shall be the final determination of the case, subject only to an appeal to the Jurisdictional Conference by either party on questions of law.

¶ 370. An appeal by a Deaconess from an Annual Conference Deaconess Board within the jurisdiction of a Mission Conference, shall be to the Board of Hospitals and Homes.

REPORT NO. 6. THE EPISCOPACY—DUTIES, POWERS, AND LIMITATIONS

Calendar No. 30. Adopted May 9. See Journal, Page 360.

Membership of Committee, 135; present when report was adopted, 83; voting for adoption, 81; not voting, 2.

¶ 203. The duties of a Bishop are:

1. To preside in the General, Jurisdictional, Central, and Annual Conferences.

2. To form the Districts according to his judgment, after consultation with the District Superintendents, and after the number of the same has been determined by vote of the Annual Conference.

3. To fix the appointments of the preachers in the Annual Conferences, Mission Conferences, and Missions, as the *Discipline* may direct. He may appoint an Associate Pastor for a Charge when in his judgment such an appointment is necessary.

4. To appoint the deaconesses.

5. To fix, either within their own Conference or within the Conference where they attend school, the Quarterly Conference membership of all ministers who are left without appointment to attend school.

6. To travel through the Connection at large.

7. To oversee the spiritual and temporal affairs of the Church.

8. To send immediately to the Secretaries of both Conferences involved, written notices of the transfer of a member, and his standing in the Course of Study if an undergraduate.

9. To organize such Missions as shall have been authorized by the General Conference.

10. To consecrate Bishops, to ordain Elders and Deacons, to consecrate Deaconesses, and to see that the names of the persons ordained and consecrated by him be entered on the journals of the Conference.

The Methodist Church   487

REPORT No. 7. THE EPISCOPACY—DUTIES, POWERS, ETC.
Calendar No. 36. Adopted May 8. See Journal, Page 305.

Membership of Committee, 135; present when report
was adopted, 88; voting for adoption, 87; voting no, 1.

¶ 204. The following provisions and limitations shall be
observed by the Bishop when fixing the appointments:

1. He shall appoint Preachers to Pastoral Charges annually after consultation with the District Superintendents;
provided that, before the official declaration of the assignments of the Preachers, he shall announce openly to the
cabinet his appointments.

2. He may make or change the appointments of Preachers
in the interval between sessions of the Annual Conference
as necessity may require, after consultation with the District Superintendents.

3. He shall choose and appoint the District Superintendents annually, but he shall not appoint any Minister a District Superintendent for more than six consecutive years,
nor for more than six years in any consecutive nine years,
except in Annual Conferences, Missions and Mission Conferences outside the United States and its possessions, and
Foreign Language work in the United States; provided that
the years of service in such relationship in one of the Uniting Churches shall be counted.

(In view of administrative problems and emergencies
that may arise in the merging of the Uniting Churches, a
Bishop if he deem it necessary for the completion of union
may continue a District Superintendent beyond his tenure
of six years, but such extension of tenure shall not continue
beyond the first session of his Annual Conference following
the first General Conference of The Methodist Church.)

4. He may make the following appointments annually:
The Publishing Agents; Corresponding Secretaries, Assistant Corresponding Secretaries, Treasurers, and Recording
Secretaries of the connectional benevolence Boards and Societies; Editors and Assistant Editors; Chaplains in the
army and navy and to prisons, reformatories, hospitals,
sanatoriums, and charitable institutions; Preachers for sea-
men; Ministers for community and federated churches;
Ministers in the service of the American Bible Society or
of any state Bible Society auxiliary thereto, or of the Sunday League of America; the President, Principals, and
Teachers in institutions of learning under our auspices;
Secretaries and Superintendents of City Missions, Executive
and Extension Secretaries of Annual Conference Boards of
Christian Education, Conference Missionary Secretaries.

5. On the recommendation of the District Superintendents confirmed by a two-thirds vote of the Annual Conference, he may appoint:

An agent to travel throughout such Conference for the purpose of distributing tracts; an Agent or Agents, to promote the cause of temperance; Instructors in institutions of learning not under our auspices; an Agent or Agents for the benefit of our institutions of learning; Superintendents, Secretaries, and Agents of hospitals and homes under our auspices; agents for other benevolence institutions; editors of unofficial papers or magazines published in the interest of The Methodist Church; *provided* that in no such case shall the Church incur any financial responsibility; one or more members of an Annual Conference to do evangelistic work in the Conference.

¶ 205. 1. When a Bishop judges it necessary he may divide a Circuit, Station, or Mission into two or more and appoint the Pastors thereto; and he may unite two or more Circuits or Stations and appoint one Pastor for the united congregations.

2. A Bishop may appoint a Preacher on Trial or a Member of an Annual Conference who desires to attend school to any college or theological seminary approved by the standardizing agency of The Methodist Church.

3. Whenever a Conference or Mission Conference shall become a part of an autonomous Methodist Church, as, for example, in Korea or Mexico, the Council of Bishops may at their discretion, transfer members of said Conference or Mission Conference, who desire transfer, to the Conference from which they went to the mission field. In case any members of said Conference or Mission Conference have not previously had membership in another Conference of The Methodist Church, the Council of Bishops may, at its discretion, transfer said members to Conferences as determined by the Council of Bishops.

4. A Bishop shall not appoint any Preacher who has been rejected as an applicant, or who has been discontinued or located except at his own request, unless the Conference, at the time of such rejection, discontinuance, or location, shall give such liberty; and he shall not appoint as a supply any Preacher who has previously been expelled from the ministry or has surrendered his credentials to an Annual Conference unless the Conference to which he surrendered his credentials, or from which he was expelled, restores his credentials or recommends it.

5. The Council of Bishops shall promote the evangelistic activities of the Church and shall appoint annually one of

their number, who shall preside over the Commission on Evangelism and furnish such inspirational leadership as the need and opportunity may demand.

6. The Bishops shall discharge such other duties as the *Discipline* may direct.

¶ 206. Any minister who has been in effective relation in any Annual Conference or Conferences for ten consecutive years from the time of his Admission on Trial may be granted a Sabbatical Leave by a Bishop for one year without losing his relationship as an effective Minister. This Sabbatical Leave is to be allowed for travel, study, rest, or for other justifiable reasons. Sabbatical Leave granted by the Bishop holding the Conference must be upon the vote of the Annual Conference to which the Minister belongs, after said Minister has given notice to his District Superintendent, and after the District Superintendent has given to the Bishop of his intention to request such Sabbatical Leave. A Sabbatical Leave shall not be granted to one man more frequently than one year in seven.

REPORT NO. 8. RETIRED BISHOPS

Calendar No. 47. Adopted May 9. See Journal, Page 349.

Membership of Committee, 135; present when report was adopted, 89; voting for adoption, 88; voting against adoption, 1.

¶ 207. 1. If a Bishop cease from traveling at large among the people without the consent of the Jurisdictional Conference, he shall not thereafter exercise in any degree the Episcopal office in The Methodist Church.

2. A Bishop may voluntarily resign from the Episcopacy at any session of his Jurisdictional Conference. A Bishop so resigning shall surrender to the Secretary of his Jurisdictional Conference his consecration papers and he shall be furnished with a certificate of his resignation which shall entitle him to membership as a Traveling Elder in the Annual Conference of which he was last a member or its successor.

3. A Bishop who by reason of impaired health is temporarily unable to perform full work may be released by the Jurisdictional Conference from the obligation to travel through the Connection at large. He may choose the place of his residence and the Council of Bishops shall be at liberty to assign him to such work as he may be able to perform. He shall receive his support as provided by the *Discipline*. This release shall not be granted for more than one quadrennium.

¶ 208.   1.   A Bishop whose seventieth birthday precedes the first day of the regular session of his Jurisdictional Conference shall be released at the close of that Conference from the obligation to travel through the Connection at large, and from residential supervision.

2.   A Bishop, at any age and for any reason deemed sufficient by his Jurisdictional Conference, may be released by that body from the obligation to travel through the Connection at large, and from residential supervision.

3.   A Bishop who has reached the age of sixty-seven years, or who within the quadrennium preceding his required retirement, makes such a request, may be released from both the obligation to travel through the Connection at large and from residential supervision by giving written notice that he so elects to the Bishops of his Jurisdictional Conference; and when a Bishop has been released in this manner the Bishops shall report the fact to the next Jurisdictional Conference.   His support as a retired Bishop, dating from his written notice concerning release, shall be provided according to the *Discipline*.

4.   A Bishop who has been retired under provisions 1, 2, or 3 may, on vote of the Council of Bishops, be appointed to take charge of an Episcopal Area, or parts of an Area, in case of the death, resignation, or disability of the Resident Bishop or because of judicial procedure (provided the request is made by a majority of the Bishops in the Jurisdiction of the proposed change).   This appointment shall not continue beyond the next session of his Jurisdictional Conference.

5.   The Council of Bishops shall have authority to assign a retired Bishop to a Jurisdiction for episcopal service up to the General Conference of 1940, where such service is needed for the adequate supervision of the work of the Church in that Jurisdiction.

¶ 209.   1.   A Bishop who has been released from the obligation to travel through the Connection at large in accordance with any of the foregoing provisions shall not preside thereafter over any Annual Conference, Mission Conference, or Mission, nor make appointments, nor preside at the Jurisdictional or Central Conference, but may take the chair temporarily in any Conference if requested to do so by the Bishop presiding.   He may participate in the Council of Bishops but without vote.   In case, however, a retired Bishop shall be appointed by the Council of Bishops to take charge of a vacant Area, or parts of an Area, under the provisions of ¶ 208, Section 4, he may preside over sessions of an Annual Conference, Mission Conference, or

Mission, make appointments, and participate in the vote of the meetings of the Bishops.

2. A Bishop who has been released under any of the foregoing provisions may continue to exercise all the rights and privileges which pertain to the Episcopal office, except as herein otherwise provided.

REPORT NO. 9. PASTORS

Calendar No. 48. Adopted May 9. See Journal, Page 349.

Membership of Committee, 135; present when report was adopted, 80; voting for adoption, 80.

¶ 216, *Article* 1. A Pastor is a preacher who, by appointment of the Bishop or the District Superintendent, is in charge of a Station or Circuit.

¶ 217, *Art.* 2. The duties of a pastor are:

1. To preach the gospel; to perform the marriage ceremony, and to administer the Sacraments of Baptism and the Lord's Supper, according to the *Discipline.*

2. To visit from house to house in order to give pastoral guidance and oversight to the members of the Church and others in need of a pastor's help.

3. An unordained Pastor or a Local Preacher serving as an "Accepted Supply" shall have authority to perform the marriage ceremony, provided it is not in conflict with the civil laws; and to administer the Sacrament of Baptism and the Lord's Supper in the bounds of his own Charge, in the absence of the District Superintendent, with the understanding that no permanent powers of ordination are conferred until granted by the laying on of hands after he has met the Disciplinary requirements.

4. To have the oversight of the other preachers in his Pastoral Charge; and to arrange the appointments, wherever practicable, so as to give the Local Preachers regular employment on the Sabbath.

5. To see that Class Leaders are chosen and to change them when necessary and to examine each of them concerning his method of leading a class.

6. In the absence of the District Superintendent and the Bishop, to control the appointment of all services to be held in the Churches in his Charge.

7. To hold Quarterly Conferences, at the request of the District Superintendent and to serve as Chairman of the Official Board, unless a Chairman has been elected by the Official Board.

8. To instruct candidates for membership in the Church,

in the doctrines, rules, and regulations of the Church; to receive persons into membership; to receive and dismiss members by Certificate.

9. To administer all the provisions of the *Discipline* in his Pastoral Charge.

10. To see that the ordinances and regulations of the Church are duly observed and that the General Rules are read and explained once a year in each congregation.

11. To hold or appoint Prayer Meetings, Love Feasts, and Watch Night Meetings, wherever advisable.

12. To see that the people in the bounds of his Charge are supplied with our Church literature, including books, periodicals, and Church School literature.

13. To form Classes of the children, youth, and adults for instruction in the Word of God and to perform the duties prescribed for the training of children.

14. To organize and maintain Church Schools, Woman's Missionary Societies, Young People's Organizations, and Brotherhoods.

15. To preach on the subject of Missions, and to nominate at the fourth Quarterly Conference a Missionary Committee for each congregation, and to report the name and address of the Chairman of the Missionary Committee to the District Superintendent.

16. To preach on the subject of Christian Education, and to urge upon parents the importance of educating their children, advising them to patronize the institutions of learning of our Church.

17. To teach and preach on Christian Stewardship, Temperance, the Claims of the Ministry, and World Peace, and to promote those causes within the bounds of his Charge.

18. To preach on the subject of the Bible and its circulation.

19. To explain the meaning and importance of the Benevolences and to urge their support by all the people in his Charge.

20. To make a written report to each Quarterly Conference on the following items:

(a) The general state of the Church in his Charge.

(b) The names of all who have been received into the Church, with the method of reception indicated, and of all who have died, removed, withdrawn, or been expelled during the preceding quarter.

(c) Number and condition of Church Schools, including Sunday School meetings, weekday meetings of children, meetings of young people, fellowship meetings of adults, and Vacation Schools.

(d) Number of sermons preached to children.

(e) Other religious instruction conducted, with children and adults, including Training Classes.

(f) Number of pastoral visits, and the use of the Church-School roll in pastoral visitation.

(g) Subscribers to our Church Periodicals.

(h) Collections for Benevolences.

(i) Missions, including Woman's Missionary Societies, Church Extension, and missionary education in the Church School.

(j) Lay Activities, including the financial system, lay speaking, training of the Official Boards, 'Christian Stewardship, and the Wesley Brotherhood.

(k) Other items worthy of record.

(l) Plans for future work.

21. To keep a membership record for his Charge in which shall be noted the name, with the time and manner of reception and disposal, of every member of the Church. In Charges containing more than one organized congregation, the names of the members shall be arranged under the name of the Church to which they belong.

22. To keep a permanent record of all baptisms and marriages in the bounds of his Charge.

23. To keep and transmit to his successor two directories, one in which the residences of all the members shall be recorded, and a constituency roll.

24. To furnish to every person uniting with the Church on profession of faith, or from preparatory membership, a certificate of membership.

25. To leave to his successor an account of his Charge, including a list of subscribers to the benevolences and to our periodicals.

26. To make report to the Annual Conference of all items required for the statistics of the Conference, and to deliver to the Conference Treasurer all moneys raised for benevolent causes, or satisfactory vouchers for the same, using the forms prescribed by the *Discipline.* '

¶ 218, *Art. 3.* No Pastor shall engage other than an Accredited Methodist Evangelist without first obtaining the written consent of his District Superintendent.

¶ 219, *Art. 4.* No preaching place shall be discontinued in the interval between the sessions of the Annual Conference without the consent of the Quarterly Conference and the District Superintendent. If thus discontinued, the names of the members shall be transferred to such Churches as the members may select.

REPORT NO. 10. PASTORS

Calendar No. 49. Adopted May 9. See Journal, Page 351.

Membership of Committee, 135; present when report was adopted, 83; voting for adoption, 70; voting against adoption, 9..

¶ 220, *Article 5.* No Minister shall solemnize the marriage of a divorced person whose wife or husband is living and unmarried; but this rule shall not apply (1) to the innocent person when it is clearly established by competent testimony that the true cause for divorce was adultery or other vicious conditions which through mental or physical cruelty or physical peril invalidated the marriage vow, nor (2) to the divorced persons seeking to be reunited in marriage.

REPORT NO. 11. CONCERNING PREACHERS ON TRIAL

Calendar No. 50. Adopted May 9. See Journal, Page 352.

Membership of Committee, 135; present when report was adopted, 81; voting for adoption, 79; voting against adoption, 2.

SECTION IV. RECEPTION OF PREACHERS ON TRIAL

¶ 221, *Article 1.* A preacher is to be received on Trial by an Annual or Mission Conference.

¶ 222, *Art. 2.* He must present a recommendation duly signed by the President and Secretary of the District Conference, or by the Chairman and Secretary of the Licensing Committee of the District, or by the Quarterly Conference where no District Conference exists; give to the Annual or Mission Conference satisfactory evidence of his knowledge of the studies prescribed for candidates for Reception on Trial; and have previously deposited with the Committee on Conference Relations in duplicate (on a form prepared by the Commission on Courses of Study, to whom one completed copy shall be sent—¶ 1068) satisfactory written answers to certain questions concerning his age, health, religious and church experience, call to the ministry, educational record and plans, including the following questions, namely:

(1) Are you convinced that you should enter the ministry of the Church?

(2) Are you willing to face any sacrifices that may be involved?

(3) Are you in debt so as to interfere with your work

or have you obligations to others which will make it difficult for you to live on the salary you are to receive?

(4) Will you abstain from the use of tobacco and other indulgences which may injure your influence?

·(5) Will you keep before you as the one great objective of your life the advancement of God's Kingdom? ·

·¶ 223, Art. 3. Observe!—This relation of being on Trial embraces the requisites of a competent pastorate, and must apply as well to proper administrative qualifications as to acceptable preaching ability. - One on Trial may be discontinued without doing him any wrong; otherwise it would be no trial at all.

·¶ 224, Art. 4. While he is on Trial the Annual Conference alone has jurisdiction over the question of his authority to preach; and his continuance on Trial shall be equivalent to the renewal of his License to preach. If he shall be discontinued, he shall be a member of the Quarterly Conference of the Charge where he resides at the time; and if he is not a Deacon or Elder, his License shall expire within one year unless it be renewed.

¶ 225, Art. 5. When an unordained preacher is on trial in an Annual Conference, and, without an ordained colleague, is regularly appointed to a Pastoral Charge, he shall be authorized to administer the Sacraments of Baptism and the Lord's Supper and to perform the marriage ceremony, if the laws of the state permit.

SECTION V. ADMISSION INTO FULL CONNECTION

¶ 226, Article 1. A preacher on Trial who has been appointed in the regular itinerant work on Circuits or Stations, or as instructor in one of our institutions of learning for two successive years from the time he was received on Trial, may be admitted into Full Connection in the Annual Conference after he has given satisfactory evidence of his knowledge of the first two years of the Conference Course of Study, and after the examination before the Conference prescribed in Article 3 of this section; provided, this shall not be so construed as to prevent the admission into Full Connection of one who, while a student in any College or Theological Seminary of The Methodist Church approved by the Authorized Standardizing Agency, or other College or Evangelical Theological Seminary of equal rank, has been for the proper length of time regularly appointed as Pastor in a Circuit or Station under the appointment of the District Superintendent.

·¶ 227, Art. 2. An Annual Conference may require a,

physical examination of a candidate before his admission either on trial or into Full Connection from membership on Trial, or on credentials from other churches.

¶ 228, *Art.* 3. In admitting a preacher at the Conference into Full Connection, after solemn fasting and prayer, he shall be asked, before the Conference, the following questions, with any others which may be thought necessary, namely:

(1) Have you faith in Christ?

(2) Are you going on to perfection?

(3) Do you expect to be made perfect in love in this life?

(4) Are you earnestly striving after it?

(5) Are you resolved to devote yourself wholly to God and his work?

(6) Do you know the General Rules of our Church?

(7) Will you keep them?

(8) Have you studied the Doctrines of The Methodist Church?

(9) After full examination do you believe that our Doctrines are in harmony with the Holy Scriptures?

(10) Will you preach and maintain them?

(11) Have you studied our form of Church Discipline and Polity?

(12) Do you approve our Church Government and Polity?

(13) Will you support and maintain them?

(14) Will you diligently instruct the children in every place?

(15) Will you visit from house to house?

(16) Will you recommend fasting or abstinence, both by precept and example?

(17) Are you determined to employ all your time in the work of God?

(18) Are you in debt so as to embarrass you in your work?

(19) Will you observe the following directions?

(a) Be diligent. Never be unemployed. Never be triflingly employed. Never trifle away time; neither spend any more time at any one place than is strictly necessary.

(b) Be punctual. Do everything exactly at the time. And do not mend our rules, but keep them; not for wrath, but for conscience' sake.

¶ 229. These questions are asked for individual examination and heart-searching, and are to be answered orally. The Bishop shall then say: *The questions you have heard relate to faith and conduct and you have answered them in your own heart. In the presence of God and your Confer-*

ence *I must now ask you these questions which you are to answer in an audible voice:*

Question: Have you faith in Christ and His gospel as revealed in the New Testament?

ᵢ *Answer:* That is my faith.

Question: Will you be diligent in observing all the admonitions as to conduct and official administration?

Answer: That is my purpose, God being my helper.

¶ 230,- *Art.* 4. A Missionary employed in a Mission may be admitted into Full Connection, if recommended by the Superintendent of the Mission where he labors, without being present at his Annual Conference for examination; but, whenever practicable, he shall be asked the questions in ¶¶ 228 and 229 in the presence of the members of the Mission at the Annual Meeting, otherwise in the presence of the Superintendent.

¶ 231, *Art.* 5. A Minister who has been located at his own request may be readmitted by an Annual Conference, at its discretion, upon presentation of his certificate of location and the recommendation of his Quarterly or District Conference and of the Annual Conference from which he located.

REPORT NO. 12. ASSIGNMENT OF BISHOPS

Calendar No. 61. Adopted May 8. See Journal, Page 297.

Membership of Committee, 135; present when report was adopted, 92; voting for adoption, 92.

¶ 212, *Section* 1. Effective Bishops in residence in the United States shall be assigned to the Jurisdictional Conferences in the United States by the Uniting Conference.

2. Effective Bishops in residence in foreign lands or under assignment to foreign service shall have their relation to such Jurisdictional Conferences in the United States as the Uniting Conference may determine.

3. The Bishops assigned to such service shall be in addition to the quota already fixed by the Uniting Conference.

4. The Council of Bishops may appoint one or more of their number to administer Annual Conferences, Mission Conferences, and Missions outside the United States and its possessions not included in Central Conferences or for special service within the United States in the interim between the Uniting and the first General Conference.

5. Each Jurisdictional Conference may fix the Episcopal Residences within its Jurisdiction and assign the Bishops to the same. The Bishops of the Jurisdiction shall fix the boundaries of the Episcopal Areas.

SECTION —. MISSIONARY BISHOPS

¶ —.

1. A Missionary Bishop is a Bishop who has been elected for a specified Foreign Mission Field with full Episcopal Powers, but with Episcopal Jurisdiction limited to the Foreign Mission Field for which he was elected.

2. Missionary Bishops shall be included in all other provisions for the Episcopacy including relation to Jurisdictional Conferences, amenability, and provisions for support and retirement.

(NOTE. The Uniting Conference instructed the Editors of the *Discipline* to make a separate section of these two items, Sections 6 and 7, and place it at the proper place in the *Discipline*.)

REPORT NO. 13. MINISTERIAL RELATIONS

Calendar No. 73. Adopted May 10. See Journal, Page 378.

Membership of Committee, 135; present when report was adopted, 104; voting for adoption, 104.

SECTION VI. DEACONS

¶ 232. A Deacon is constituted by the election of the Annual Conference and the laying on of the hands of a Bishop.

¶ 233. A Deacon has authority to preach; to conduct Divine Worship; to perform the Marriage Ceremony; to administer Baptism; and to assist an Elder in administering the Lord's Supper (¶ 217, Article 2, Section 3, shall apply).

Preachers of the following Classes are eligible to the Order of Deacon:

A. *As Local Preachers*

¶ 234. Those who have been Local Preachers for four consecutive years; shall present a recommendation for Deacon's Orders from the District Conference or from the Quarterly Conference where no District Conference exists, duly attested by the President and Secretary thereof; and shall have completed, satisfactorily to the Annual Conference, the studies prescribed for Local Preachers who are candidates for Deacon's Orders.

B. *As Accepted Supply Pastors*

¶ 235. Those who have been Accepted Supply Pastors in regular service for two full years; and shall have completed the first two years of the Conference Course of

Study, together with the Studies indicated under the Examination for Reception on Trial, under the Conference Board of Ministerial Training.

C. *As Having Been Received on Trial*

¶ 236. Those who have been ordained as Local Deacons under Class A or B and in addition have been received on Trial will continue to Elder's Orders in Class C.

D. *As Members On Trial in the Course of Study*

¶ 237. Those who have been on Trial in an Annual Conference for two years, and shall have completed, satisfactorily to the Annual Conference, the first two years of the Conference Course of Study.

E. *Under the Seminary Rule*

¶ 238. Those who have been Local Preachers for two full years; and during the same time have been regular students in one of our Theological Seminaries or in other Theological Seminaries whose standing is approved by The Standardizing Agencies; shall have been received on Trial or shall have been on Trial for at least one year; and shall have completed, satisfactorily to the Annual Conference, the first two years of the Conference Course of Study.

F. *Under the Missionary Rule*

¶ 239. Those Preachers on Trial who shall be appointed by a Bishop to a Foreign Mission, or to a remote field in any Conference, or to a Church in a Foreign Country outside of the Boundary of a Mission or Annual Conference, or to a Chaplaincy in the Army or Navy, in a Prison, Reformatory, Sanatorium, or a Charitable Institution; *provided,* that the presiding Bishop and a majority of the District Superintendents recommend such an election.

ELDERS

¶ 240. An Elder is constituted by the election of the Annual Conference, and by the laying on of hands of a Bishop and of Elders.

¶ 241. An Elder has authority to preach; to conduct Divine Worship; to administer the Sacraments of Baptism and the Lord's Supper, and to perform the Marriage Ceremony.

Preachers of the following classes are eligible to the Order of Elder:

A. *As Local Preachers*

¶ 242. Those who have been for four consecutive years Local Deacons, or shall have served as regularly appointed Supply Pastors for two full years after having been ordained Deacons; and shall present a recommendation for Elder's Orders from the District Conference, or from the Quarterly Conference where no District Conference exists, duly signed by the President and Secretary thereof; and shall have completed, satisfactorily to the Annual Conference, the Studies prescribed for Local Deacons who are candidates for Elder's Orders.

B. *As Accepted Supply Pastors*

¶ 243. Those who shall have been ordained Deacons under the provisions of ¶ 235, who shall have been serving as regular Accepted Supply Pastors for two full years since their ordination; and shall have satisfactorily completed the full Conference Course prescribed.

C. *As Local Deacons Who Have Been Received on Trial*

¶ 244. Those who have been in Full Connection in the Annual Conference; have been Local Deacons for two consecutive years immediately preceding such election; and have completed, satisfactorily to the Annual Conference, the first two years of the Conference Course of Study.

D. *As Conference Members in the Conference Courses*

¶ 245. Those who have been in Full Connection in the Annual Conference for two successive years, and also Deacons during the same time; and shall have completed, satisfactorily to the Conference, the Conference Course of Study.

E. *Under the Seminary Rule*

¶ 246. Those who have been received on Trial, and elected to the office of Deacon under the provisions of ¶ 238, and have completed, satisfactorily to the Conference, the Conference Course of Study, have been Deacons at least one year, and have been admitted into Full Connection.

F. *Under the Missionary Rule*

¶ 247. Those who are members of, or have been received on Trial in an Annual Conference; and have been appointed to a Chaplaincy in the Army or Navy, or to a Foreign Mission, or to the pastorate of a Church in a foreign country outside of a Mission or Conference, or to a Mission among foreign people within an English-speaking Conference.

When a Preacher shall have passed his examination, and shall have been admitted into Full Connection, and elected to the Order of Deacon, but fails of his Ordination through the absence of the Bishop, his eligibility to the Order of Elder shall count from the time of his election to the Order of Deacon.

No person shall be elected to Elder's Orders except such as are of unquestionable moral character, genuine piety, and sound in the fundamental Doctrines of Christianity and faithful in the discharge of gospel duties.

MISSION TRAVELING PREACHER

¶ 248. A Mission Traveling Preacher, Deacon or Elder, is one who is a member of a Mission without being a member of an Annual Conference. In the election of Mission Traveling Deacons and Elders the Mission shall require of all applicants the conditions and qualifications demanded of Traveling Deacons and Elders by an Annual Conference. The duties, responsibilities, rights, and privileges of Mission Traveling Deacons and Elders shall be the same as those of Traveling Deacons and Elders who are members of an Annual Conference and may be transferred to an Annual Conference with the status attained in the Mission.

SUPERNUMERARY MINISTERS

¶ 249. A Supernumerary Minister is one who, because of impaired health, or other equally sufficient reason, is temporarily unable to perform full work. This relation shall not be granted for more than five years in succession except by a two-thirds vote of the Conference, upon recommendation of the Committee on Conference Relations, and a statement of the reason for such recommendation. He may receive an appointment, or be left without one, according to the judgment of the Annual Conference of which he is a member; and he shall be subject to all limitations of the *Discipline* in respect to reappointment and continuance in the same charge that apply to Effective Ministers. In case he has no Pastoral Charge he shall have a seat in the Quarterly Conference, and all the privileges of membership, in the place where he resides. He shall report to the Fourth Quarterly Conference, and to the Pastor, all Marriages performed and all Baptisms administered. Should he reside beyond the bounds of his Annual Conference, he shall forward to it annually a certificate similar to that required of a Retired Minister, and in case of failure to do so the Annual Conference may locate him without his consent. He shall have no claim on the Conference funds except by vote of the Conference.

RETIRED MINISTERS

¶ 250, *Article 1.* A Retired Minister is one who, at his own request, or by action of the Annual Conference, upon recommendation of the Committee on Conference Relations, has been placed in the retired relation.

Art. 2. Every Retired Minister who is not appointed as Pastor of a Charge shall have a seat in the Quarterly Conference, and all the privileges of membership in the Church where he resides, except as set forth in Article 3. He shall report to the Fourth Quarterly Conference and to the Pastor all Marriages performed and Baptisms administered. If he resides without the bounds of the Conference, he shall forward annually to his Conference a certificate of his Christian and his Ministerial conduct, together with an account of the number and circumstances of his family, signed by the District Superintendent or the Pastor of the Charge within the bounds of which he resides. Without this certificate the Conference may, after due notice (thirty days), locate him without his consent.

Art. 3. In the case of a Quarterly Conference in a Mission among non-English-speaking people, Retired Ministers of different race shall have a vote in the Quarterly Conference only when they shall have been duly elected to the same.

TERMINATION OF ANNUAL CONFERENCE MEMBERSHIP

By Voluntary Location

¶ 251, *Article 1.* An Annual Conference, first having examined a Member's character at the session of the Conference when a request for Location is made, and finding him in good standing, may at his request grant him a Certificate of Location, providing such relation be granted only to persons who avowedly intend to discontinue regular ministerial or evangelistic work, which relation shall be certified by the President of the Conference. Such Minister shall thereupon hold his membership, as Local Elder or Deacon, in the Quarterly Conference where he resides, and shall be held amenable for his conduct and the continuance of his ordination rights to the Annual Conference within which the Quarterly Conference membership is held.

Art. 2. Whenever a Member of the Annual Conference applies for a Location it shall be asked: Is he indebted to the Publishing House? If it be ascertained that he is so indebted, the Conference shall require him to secure said debt, if judged necessary or proper, before a Location is granted.

By Involuntary Action

¶ 252. (1) Whenever it is determined by the Committee on Conference Relations or Ministerial Qualifications that in their judgment a Member of the Annual Conference is unacceptable, inefficient, or indifferent in the work of the Ministry, or that his conduct is such as to impair seriously his usefulness as a Minister, or that his engagement in secular business, except as required by the ill health of himself or of his family, disqualifies him for Pastoral work, they shall notify him in writing, and ask him to request location at the next session of the Annual Conference. If he refuses or neglects to locate as requested, the Conference may, by count vote, upon recommendation of the Committee on Conference Relations, locate him without his consent, which discontinues his right to exercise the Ministerial Office.

(2) Whenever it is unanimously determined by the District Superintendents that a Member of the Annual Conference should be located for any of the reasons cited in Section 1, they shall notify him in writing of their judgment at least six months before the next session of the Annual Conference, and ask him to request location at such session under the provisions of ¶ 251. If he refuses, or neglects to locate as requested, the District Superintendents shall certify the facts to the Committee on Conference Relations, or Ministerial Qualifications Group, which Committee shall proceed to recommend his immediate location without his consent, which discontinues his right to exercise the Ministerial office.

(3) However, if any located person remains a Member in good standing of The Methodist Church until the age of sixty-five years, he shall thereby retain the right to make an annuity claim, based upon the years of his Effective Ministry and subject to the action of the Annual Conference.

By Surrender of the Ministerial Office

¶ 253. Any member of an Annual Conference in good standing, who may desire to surrender his Ministerial Office and withdraw from the Conference, may be allowed to do so by the Conference at its session; in which case his Credentials shall be filed with the papers of the Annual Conference of which he was a Member, and his membership in the Church shall be recorded in the Society where he resides at the time of such surrender.

By Withdrawal

¶ 254. When a Minister in good standing withdraws to unite with another Church, his Credentials should be surrendered to the Conference, and, if he shall desire it, they may be returned to him with the following inscription written plainly across their face, namely:

"A .... B.....................
has this day been honorably dismissed by the . ...
Annual Conference from the ministry of The Methodist Church.

"Dated . ...
" ...., President,
" ...., Secretary."

¶ 255. When in the interval between sessions of Annual Conferences a Member thereof shall deposit with a Bishop or with his District Superintendent a letter of withdrawal from our Ministry or his Credentials, or both, the same shall be presented to the Annual Conference at its next session for its action thereon.

SECTION VII. LOCAL PREACHERS

¶ 256, *Article* 1. No member of the Church shall be at liberty to preach without a license.

¶ 257, *Art.* 2. Wherever a District Conference exists, the powers hereinafter conferred on Quarterly Conferences in relation to Local Preachers shall be exercised only by the District Conference; but it shall not license any persons to preach, without the previous recommendation of the Quarterly Conference.

¶ 258, *Art.* 3. The Quarterly Conference, where no District Conference exists, shall have authority:

Section 1. To license proper persons to preach, provided the following steps have been taken, and in order:

(1) They shall have been recommended by the Church of which they are members.

(2) They shall have been before the District Committee, and shall have been recommended by it.

(3) They shall have passed a satisfactory examination in the studies prescribed for candidates for License to preach, and shall have been examined by the District Committee on the subjects of Doctrine and Discipline, and shall have agreed wholly to abstain from the use of tobacco.

Section 2. To examine Local Preachers other than Accepted Supply Pastors in the Course of Study prescribed for them; to inquire into the gifts, labors, and usefulness of each by name, and to renew their licenses annually when in the judgment of the Conference their gifts, grace, and usefulness, and their faithfulness and proficiency in study, warrant such renewal. In the case of Local Preachers who are candidates for the Traveling Ministry, examinations may be suspended while they are pursuing regular courses of study in our Theological Seminaries or in Universities or Colleges approved by the Authorized Standardizing Agency.

Section 3. To recommend to the Annual Conference Local Preachers who are suitable candidates for Deacons' or Elders' Orders, for Recognition of Orders, for Readmission, for Reception on Trial; or for acceptance as Accepted Supply Pastors; such candidates having been previously examined by the District Committee on the subjects of Doctrine and Discipline.

Section 4. To try, suspend, deprive of Ministerial Office and Credentials, expel, or acquit any Local Preacher of the Circuit or Station against whom charges may have been preferred.

¶ 259, *Art.* 4. The District Committee on Qualifications of Local Preachers shall be annually nominated by the District Superintendent and approved by the Annual Conference.

¶ 260, *Art.* 5. Local Preachers, ordained or unordained, not having a Pastoral Charge, shall be members of, and amenable to, the Quarterly Conference where they reside, except as hereinafter stated. When they shall change their residence they shall procure from the Pastor of the Charge from which they remove, or from the District Superintendent, a Certificate of their Official Standing and of Dismissal and shall present it to the Pastor of the Charge to which they remove. If they neglect to do this they shall not be recognized nor use their office as Local Preachers in the Charge to which they have removed; and they shall continue to be amenable to the Quarterly Conference of the Charge from which they have removed, which, if the neglect be long continued, after due notice (thirty days), may try them for persistent disobedience to the order of the Church, and upon conviction thereof deprive them of Ministerial Office and Credentials.

Art. 6. Local Preachers appointed to a Pastoral Charge shall procure from the Pastor of the Charge from which they remove, or from the District Superintendent, a Certificate of their Official Standing and of Dismissal, and at its next session shall present it to the Quarterly Conference of the Pastoral Charge to which they have been appointed and their Church and Quarterly Conference Membership shall be in that Charge.

. But so long as they are regular Supply Pastors giving full-time service they shall be responsible to the Annual Conference in which they receive an appointment as well as to the District and Quarterly Conference of the Pastoral Charge in which they are serving.

¶ 261, *Art.* 7. Unordained Local Preachers, only while serving as regularly appointed Pastors of Charges, shall be authorized to administer the Sacraments of Baptism and of the Lord's Supper, and, when the laws of the state permit, to perform the marriage ceremony, but in all foreign mission fields, the conferring of such authority shall rest with the Central Conferences in which they are Pastors.

¶ 262, *Art.* 8. Whenever a Preacher is located or discontinued by an Annual Conference, he shall thereupon hold his Quarterly Conference membership as Local Elder or Deacon where he resides at the time of location or discontinuance.

¶ 263, *Art.* 9. Whenever Local Preachers, ordained or unordained, shall sever their relation with The Methodist Church in any way whatsoever, they shall deposit their Credentials with the proper authorities.

¶ 264, *Art.* 10. District Superintendents and the Pastors are required to arrange appointments, wherever it is practicable, so as to give the Local Preachers regular and systematic employment.

¶ 265, *Art.* 11. Local Preachers shall make to the District or Quarterly Conference a report of their labors, as follows: 1. Number of sermons preached. 2. Number of funerals conducted. 3. Number of marriages performed, with the names of persons married. 4. Number of baptisms administered, with the names and ages of the persons baptized. 5. Miscellaneous Items. 6. Items 2, 3, and 4 shall be reported to the Pastor for entry in the church records.

¶ 266, *Art.* 12. Women are included in the foregoing provisions, except in so far as they apply to candidates for the Traveling Connection.

SECTION VIII.   ACCEPTED SUPPLY PASTORS

¶ 267, *Article* 1. The Bishops and District Superintendents shall appoint at each Annual Conference Session a Committee on Accepted Supply Pastors, to be composed of not more than ten members, taken equally from the Committee on Conference Relations and the Board of Ministerial Training, which Committee shall recommend to the Annual

Conference each year the list of Accepted Supply Pastors. Any Local Preacher who is employed as a Pastor in Charge must have his character, fitness, training, and effectiveness passed, and be accepted as Supply Pastor, by a majority vote of the District Conference and Annual Conference after reference to and recommendation by the Committee on Accepted Supply Pastors. Between sessions of the Annual Conference, a District Superintendent may employ, but only until the next session of the Annual Conference, as a Supply Pastor, a Local Preacher who is not listed as an Accepted Supply Pastor.

¶ 268, *Art.* 2. The acceptance of a Local Preacher as a Supply Pastor does not guarantee him an appointment. The list of Accepted Supply Pastors is merely an eligibility list from which Supplies can be accepted, and not a roll of those entitled to appointment. Such listing shall not be for more than one year at a time, and an Accepted Supply Pastor may be relieved of his Charge at any time during the Conference year by a majority vote of the District Superintendents.

¶ 269, *Art.* 3. An Accepted Supply Pastor who is in charge of a pastoral appointment shall attend the sessions of the Annual Conference and shall have the privilege of speaking on any question, but without vote.

¶ 270, *Art.* 4. The roll of Accepted Supply Pastors shall be called at Annual Conference immediately following the regular Roll Call.

¶ 271, *Art.* 5. When a Local Preacher is accepted as a Supply Pastor the Annual Conference alone has jurisdiction over his authority to preach. Continuance in this relation shall be equivalent to renewal of his license to preach. Upon the discontinuance of this relation his status becomes again in all regards that of a Local Preacher without pastoral appointment.

SECTION IX. MINISTERS FROM OTHER CHURCHES

¶ 272, *Article* 1. Ministers coming from other Evangelical Churches provided they present suitable testimonials of good standing, and give assurance of their faith, Christian experience and other qualifications, and give evidence of their agreement with us in doctrine and discipline, may be received into our Ministry in the following manner:

1. The Quarterly Conference may receive them as Local Preachers, not entitled to administer the Sacraments, pending the recognition of their Orders by the Annual Conference. The Annual Conference may recognize their Orders as Local Deacons or Elders, provided they stand an

approved examination in the Course of Study prescribed for Local Preachers.

2. Upon recommendation by the District Conference, or the Quarterly Conference where no District Conference exists, the Annual Conference may recognize their Orders and admit them into the membership of the Conference either on Trial or in Full Connection, and may, at its discretion, require them to pursue, in whole or in part, the Conference Course of Study.

3. Ministers from other Churches may apply directly to the Annual Conference, which may recognize their Credentials, and receive them into the Full Membership of the Conference; *provided,* that in all such cases the Candidates for Admission into Full Membership must answer satisfactorily the questions set forth in ¶ 228; and, further, that those from other than Methodist Churches must take upon themselves our ordination vows, without the reimposition of hands.

4. The Annual Conference may also receive on equal standing preachers who are on Trial in the Ministry of another Methodist Church, using, however, special care that before they are admitted to Full Membership their examination be entirely satisfactory.

¶ 273, *Art. 2.* Wherever the Orders of a Minister are recognized according to the foregoing provision, he shall be furnished with a Certificate signed by the Bishop according to the form.

"This is to certify that the . . . .
Annual Conference of The Methodist Church, having examined the Credentials of the Rev. . . . . as
. . . . (an Elder or a Deacon) of the . . . .
Church, and having received other testimonials of his Grace, Gifts, and Usefulness, and being satisfied therewith, has this day . . . . accepted and recognized him in due form as . . . . (an Elder or a Deacon) in The Methodist Church, entitled to exercise under its authority all the functions pertaining to that ordination, so long as his life and doctrine become the Gospel of Christ.

"Given under my hand and seal at . . . .
this   day of . . . . in the year of our Lord . . . .
              "... . . . . President."

¶ 274, *Art. 3.* When the Orders of a Minister of another Church shall have been duly recognized, his Certificate of Ordination by said Church shall be returned to him with the following inscription written plainly across its face:

"Accredited by the .... Annual
Conference of The Methodist Church, this .... day of
.... 19 , as the basis of new Credentials.
"........................., President,
"........................., Secretary."

MINORITY REPORT

We move to substitute for Article 12, ¶ 266, the following:
. "Women are included in all provisions, both for the
local and for the traveling Ministry."

MRS. FLORENCE RESOR JARDINE,	A. J. KOONCE,
JOHN TUNNICLIFFE,	MRS. MARY M. BETHUNE,
E. R. STRIBLING,	W. P. KING,
Y. C. YANG,	E. M. RUGG,
JOS. H. DAVIS,	FORNEY HUTCHINSON,
C. I. KELLEY,	CLINTON D. BALDWIN,
MRS. M. BARTAK,	MRS. L. A. TYNES,
A. W. PUGH,	A. W. PLYLER,
CHESTER A. SMITH,	F. G. HOLLOWAY.

Failed of adoption, May 10.

III. COMMITTEE ON MEMBERSHIP AND TEMPORAL ECONOMY

REPORT NO. 1. THE LOCAL CHURCH

*Calendar No. 7. Adopted May 2. See Journal, Pages 235,
241, 253, 282, 365.*

Membership of Committee, 134; present when report was adopted, 117; voting for adoption, 117.

SECTION I. DUTIES OF DISTRICT SUPERINTENDENT AND PASTOR

¶ 425. In order that each local Church or Congregation
may be an effective unit it shall be the duty of all District
Superintendents and Pastors to organize and administer
the Charges and Churches committed to their care in accordance with the plan set forth in this chapter.

SECTION II. ANNUAL MEETING

¶ 426. There shall be held in every charge an annual
Church meeting. All persons holding their membership in
the Charge shall be members of the Annual Meeting. The
District Superintendent or, in his absence, the Pastor shall
preside. In the absence of both, the meeting shall elect a
Chairman from its own number. The meeting shall elect
a secretary, who may be the Recording Steward of the

Charge, and the minutes shall be recorded in the Quarterly Conference Record Book.

¶ 427. The Annual Meeting may be held at the call of the Pastor, in conjunction with or preceding the Fourth Quarterly Conference; *provided*, that if the Quarterly Conference and the Annual Meeting are held jointly, matters reserved to the jurisdiction of the Quarterly Conference shall be voted on by the members of the Quarterly Conference only.

¶ 428. The Annual Meeting shall be a rallying point for the membership of the Charge to review the work of the year, to consider the local opportunities and needs, to acquaint the members with the general program of The Methodist Church, and to lay plans for the ensuing year. It shall be the duty of the Pastor, District Superintendent, and Lay Leader to arrange a program of addresses and discussions on such phases of the general and local work of the Church as may, in their judgment, be most needed at that time and place, to distribute literature prepared by our Church boards and agencies, and diligently to urge the membership of the Charge to attend.

¶ 429. The following shall be the order of business for the Annual Meeting:

1. To hear the written report of the Pastor, presenting a review of the outstanding achievements of the year, including a statement of gains and losses in membership and of attendance on public worship and the Church School, together with recommendations for the future. He may include in this report the work of the organizations in the Charge, or he may appoint representatives from those organizations to report separately.

2. To hear a written report from the Chairman of the Official Board of each church on the charge relating to the work of the Board during the year.

3. To hear the report of a Committee on Policy, previously appointed by the Pastor, who shall be its chairman. On Charges of more than one church, he shall appoint to this committee at least one member from each Church. This committee, after a careful survey of the work of the Charge, shall make recommendations to the Annual Meeting concerning improvement of the financial system employed, new territory to be occupied, Church Schools, temperance, missionary education, circulation of Christian literature, religion in the home, and any other matters relating to the work of the Church. After discussion of these recommendations and such revisions as the meeting may deem wise, a general policy of the Charge for the following year

shall be adopted, subject to the approval of the Quarterly Conference.

SECTION III. THE OFFICIAL BOARD

¶ 430. In every Church there shall be an executive body called the Official Board, organized by either of the following ways, as may be authorized by the Quarterly Conference: The Board may be composed as follows: The Pastor, Assistant Pastor, Deaconess serving the Charge, the stewards, the unit or class leaders, the trustees, the church treasurer, the director of religious education, where desired the director of music, the superintendent of the Church School, the chairman of the local Board of Christian Education, president or presidents of the women's auxiliaries authorized by the General Conference, a representative elected by the Young People's Division, and the chairman of the local Missionary Council. It shall be organized with a Chairman, a Secretary, and a Treasurer. If the Official Board is not composed and organized as above, the Board of Stewards shall assume all powers and duties prescribed in this section of the *Discipline* and shall be the Official Board.

¶ 431. The Official Board may meet monthly at a time designated by the Board, or on the call of the Chairman or the Pastor. This Board shall promote and have oversight of the work of the local Church under the general direction of the Pastor. It shall provide for the financial needs of the Church by means of an every-member canvass or some other method, and it shall see that its current financial obligations, including the benevolences, are promptly met. It shall promote, through proper committees or otherwise, evangelism, missions, Christian education, lay activities, social service, and other enterprises as directed by the General, Jurisdictional, Central, and Annual Conferences, and shall administer such other affairs as shall arise in the work of the Church, subject to such limitations and provisions as are committed to the Quarterly Conference.

¶ 432. At each meeting of the Official Board let the following items, with any others that may be necessary, be considered: (1) Are there any strangers in the community, or any sick or distressed, or others who should be visited? (2) What is the report from the treasurer or treasurers of the church, and are the current obligations paid? (3) Does the work of the Church School and other Church organizations prosper, and what may be done to improve them? (4) Are there any committees to report? Any unfinished business? Any new business?

SECTION IV. OTHER ORGANIZATIONS

¶ 433. Other organizations and enterprises authorized by the General Conference shall be instituted in the local Church in accordance with the *Discipline*.

SECTION V. STEWARDS

¶ 434. The Stewards of the Charge shall be elected annually by the Quarterly Conference on nomination of the Pastor or on nomination of a committee of which the Pastor shall be chairman; or they shall be elected by the members of the Charge, twenty-one years of age and over, at a meeting called for that purpose as may be arranged by the Quarterly Conference. Where desired, a Church treasurer may be elected in a similar manner. In case of Circuits, each Church may elect its respective officials.

¶ 435. Each Charge shall be entitled to not less than two nor more than thirty-five Stewards; *provided,* that in Churches of more than five hundred members one Steward shall be elected for each additional thirty members.

¶ 436. Stewards shall be not less than twenty-one years of age, members of The Methodist Church, persons of genuine Christian character, who love the Church and are competent to administer its affairs.

¶ 437. Stewards shall be members of the Quarterly Conference and of the Official Board, and their duties and responsibilities shall be as defined in those sections of the *Discipline* which declare the functions of these organizations.

REPORT NO. 2. CHURCH PROPERTY

Calendar No. 14. Adopted May 4. See Journal, Page 260.

Membership of Committee, 134; present when report was adopted, 116; voting for adoption, 115; not voting, 1.

CHAPTER XII

SECTION I. TRUSTEES OF CHARGES

¶ 438. For each Charge there shall be a Board of Trustees of Church property consisting of not less than three or more than nine persons, each of whom shall be not less than twenty-one years of age and at least two-thirds of whom shall be members of The Methodist Church. They shall be elected for a term of three years or until their successors shall have been duly elected; *provided,* that one-third shall be elected each year. Such Board shall elect its own chairman except where the charter otherwise provides, and such other officers as it may desire. When a Charge consists of two or more Churches located in different places, these provisions shall apply to each Church with the same force and effect as though it were a separate Charge.

¶ 439. Except as the laws of the state, territory, or country, or the existing charter of any incorporated charge or Church prescribe otherwise, such Board of Trustees shall be elected by the Quarterly Conference on nomination of the Pastor, or in his absence, of the District Superintendent; or they may be elected by the membership of the Charge not less than twenty-one years of age at a meeting called for that purpose, as may be arranged by the Quarterly Conference. At least ten days' notice of such meeting and the purpose of thereof shall be given from the pulpit of the Charge.

¶ 440. Any vacancy in the Board of Trustees may be filled until the next annual election by the Quarterly Conference of the Charge, or pending action by the Quarterly Conference by the majority vote of the remaining Trustees, except as the civil laws shall prescribe otherwise.

¶ 441. The Board of Trustees of the Charge shall be responsible to the Quarterly Conference and annually shall make a written report to the Fourth or last Quarterly Conference of the Charge, which report shall include the following items: (1) Number of Churches and Parsonages; (2) Their probable values; (3) Other real estate and personal property held; (4) Title by which each piece of real estate is held; (5) Income therefrom and how expended; (6) Amount received during the year for building, rebuilding, and improving Churches and Parsonages and how expended; (7) Debts and how contracted; (8) Amount of insurance on each property and whether restricted by coinsurance or other limiting conditions; (9) Who is custodian of and where the legal papers are kept; (10) Detailed lists of trusts: funds, where invested; incomes, how applied.

¶ 442. Except as in this chapter otherwise provided and subject to the direction of the Quarterly Conference, the Board of Trustees of the Charge shall hold and manage all real property of the Charge and such other property as may be committed to them, receive and administer all bequests made to the Charge, receive and administer all trusts and invest all trust funds of the Charge in conformity with the laws of the state, territory, or country in which the Charge is located. The Trustees shall not prevent or interfere with the Pastor or other duly authorized Ministers of The Methodist Church in the use of said property for religious services or other proper meetings recognized by the law and usage of The Methodist Church.

¶ 443. Charges may be incorporated when permitted so to do under the laws of the state, territory, or country in which they are located. In the Articles of Incorporation or Charter it shall be provided: (1) That the corporation shall support the doctrine and shall be subject to the laws, usages, and ministerial appointments of The Methodist Church as from time to time established, made, and declared by the lawful authority of said Church; (2) That the directors of the corporation shall be the Board of Trustees of Church property elected and organized as prescribed in the *Discipline* of The Methodist Church unless the laws of the state, territory, or country in which the Charge is located prescribe otherwise; (3) That the corporation shall have the power to secure, hold, improve, encumber, sell, convey, and dispose of property, both real and personal, in fee simple and otherwise.

¶ 444. If and when incorporated, all real estate owned or thereafter acquired by the Charge shall be deeded directly to it in its corporate name. If not incorporated, all real estate owned or acquired by the Charge shall be deeded to the trustees of the Charge, their successors and assigns in trust for the use and benefit of the Charge and of The Methodist Church. All deeds by which premises are hereafter acquired for use as a place of divine worship shall contain the following trust clause: "In trust, that said premises shall be used, kept, maintained, and disposed of, as a place of divine worship of the Methodist ministry and members of The Methodist Church; subject to the discipline, usage, and ministerial appointments of said Church as from time to time authorized and declared by the General Conference and by the Annual Conference within whose bounds the said premises are situated."

All deeds by which premises are hereafter acquired for use as a parsonage shall contain the following trust clause: "In trust, that such premises shall be held, kept, maintained, and disposed of, as a place of residence for the use and occupancy of the Preachers of The Methodist Church, who may from time to time be appointed in said place; subject to the usage and Discipline of said Church, as from time to time authorized and declared by the General Conference of said Church, and by the Annual Conference within whose bounds the said premises are situated."

If the law of the state, territory, or country in which the property is located requires a different method or means for conveying or acquiring fee simple title to such property, the same shall apply and be substituted for the means and method prescribed in this paragraph.

¶ 445. When two or more churches are united, merged, or consolidated, the Boards of Trustees or other proper officials of the constituent Churches shall take such steps to affect the transfer of the property, both real and personal, as the laws of the state shall require.

¶ 446. When two or more Churches comprise a single Charge and one or more thereof is separated from such Charge and established as a Charge or united with another Charge which does not own a parsonage, each such Church shall be entitled to receive its just share of the then reasonable value of the parsonage in which it had invested funds, and the amount of such value and just share shall be determined by a committee of three persons appointed by the District Superintendent who shall not be members of any of the interested churches. From any such determination there is reserved unto each of the interested Churches the right of appeal to the next succeeding Annual Conference. Any sum received as or from such share shall be used for no purpose other than the purchase or building of a parsonage.

¶ 447. In no event shall the Trustees mortgage or encumber real estate on which a church or parsonage is located for the current expense of a Charge, nor shall the principal of the proceeds of the sale of such property be so used.

¶ 448. Except as in this chapter otherwise provided and except as the laws of the state, territory, or country in which the property is located prescribe otherwise, property belonging to a charge may be mortgaged or sold and conveyed by the Board of Trustees but only with the written consents of the District Superintendent and the Preacher in charge, and with the authorization of the Quarterly Conference by a majority of those present and voting at a meeting of the Quarterly Conference; *provided,* that not less than ten days' notice of such meeting and proposed action shall have been given from the pulpit of the Charge.

¶ 449. With the consent of the presiding Bishop and of a majority of the District Superintendents the Annual Conference may declare any Charge or Church within its bounds discontinued or abandoned. Upon a Charge or Church being thus discontinued or abandoned it shall be the duty of its Board of Trustees to make such disposition of the property thereof as the Annual Conference shall direct, and if no such lawful trustees remain or if for any reason said Trustees fail to make such disposition, then it shall be the duty of the Trustees of the Annual Conference to sell or dispose of said property in accordance with the direction of the Annual Conference.

The legislation of this whole section shall not apply in the territory of Central or Provisional Central Conferences.

SECTION II. BUILDING AND REMODELING CHURCH AND
PARSONAGE PROPERTY

¶ 450. Any Church desiring to purchase, build, or remodel a church shall first secure the District Superintendent's written consent thereto and the Quarterly Conference's authorization thereof after not less than ten days' notice of such proposed action shall have been given from the pulpit of the Charge. Thereupon the Quarterly Conference shall appoint a committee of not less than three members of such Church who shall make an estimate of the amount required to complete such undertaking or enterprise, and such estimate, amount, and proposed undertaking shall be submitted for approval to the members of the Church not less than twenty-one years of age at a meeting called for that purpose. If such undertaking is that of building a church the purchase price of the lot or lots on which such church is to be erected shall be paid in full, and before any such building is begun or contract is entered into for the construction thereof or for the purchase or remodeling of an already erected church, it shall be the duty of the Quarterly Conference to acquire a fee simple title to such premises by deed of conveyance executed in the form and manner as in this chapter provided, and to secure in cash and tangible assets one-half of said estimated cost. When such undertaking is that of building a church the purchase price paid for the lot or lots on which the church is to be erected may be credited as a tangible asset secured. The provisions of this paragraph shall not apply to any repairs or remodeling, the cost of which will not exceed ten per cent of the value of the building affected.

¶ 451. Before any church building may be formally dedicated it shall be necessary to discharge all indebtedness against it.

SECTION III. BOARD OF CHURCH LOCATION AND BUILDING

¶ 452. There shall be in each District of an Annual Conference a Board of Church Location and Building consisting of the District Superintendent, three Ministers and three Laymen nominated by the District Superintendent and elected annually by the Annual Conference:

¶ 453. Before beginning or contracting for the building,

purchase, or remodeling of church or parsonage property, the price of such purchase, the plans, specifications, and location of such building or remodeling and the probable cost thereof shall be submitted to the Board of Church Location and Building of the District in which the property is located. The provisions of this paragraph shall not apply to remodeling, the cost of which does not exceed ten per cent of the value of the building affected.

¶ 454. It shall be the duty of this Board to study carefully the feasibility and financial soundness of said undertaking and to report its conclusions to the Charge making such proposal.

¶ 455. A decision of this Board disapproving such purchase, building, or remodeling shall be final unless overruled by the Annual Conference to which there is reserved unto such Charge the right of appeal.

REPORT NO. 3. CONCERNING CHURCH PROPERTY

Calendar No. 24. Adopted May 5. See Journal, Page 274.

Membership of Committee, 134; present when report was adopted, 111; voting for adoption, 111.

SECTION III. PARSONAGE TRUSTEES

¶ 456. Wherever there are two or more Churches on a pastoral Charge, a separate Board of Trustees, consisting of not less than three nor more than five persons, shall be elected by the Quarterly Conference of such Charge, to be the Custodians of the Parsonage Property. Such Trustees shall have the same qualifications as are required for Trustees of Church Property.

SECTION IV. DISTRICT PARSONAGES

¶ 457. When authorized by the Quarterly Conferences of two-thirds of the Charges in the District a residence for the District Superintendent may be acquired, the title to which may be held in trust by a District Board of Trustees of not less than three nor more than nine persons of the same qualifications as in this chapter provided for Trustees of Charges, who shall be nominated by the District Superintendent and elected by the District Conference. Where there is no District Conference the Trustees may be elected by the District Stewards or by the Annual Conference on nomination of the District Superintendent. They shall be elected for a term of one year and until their successors shall have been elected, and shall report annually to the District Conference or Annual Conference. If the title to the District parsonage is not held by a District Board of Trustees, the same shall be held in trust by Trustees of the Annual Conference of which such District is a part, and such Trustees shall report annually to the Annual Conference. Except as the laws of the state, territory, or country prescribe otherwise, district property held in trust by a District Board of Trustees may be mortgaged or sold and conveyed by them only by authority of the District Conference or Annual Conference; or if such property is held in trust by the Trustees of the Annual Conference, it may be mortgaged or sold and conveyed by such Trustees only by authority of the Annual Conference. The purchase price and maintenance cost of District parsonages shall be equitably distributed among the charges of the District by the District Stewards.

SECTION V.   TRUSTEES OF ANNUAL CONFERENCE

¶ 458. There shall be an incorporated Board of Trustees of each Annual Conference. This Board shall consist of nine persons of the same qualifications as in this chapter provided for Trustees of Charges, and such persons shall be the directors of the corporation. They shall be elected by the Annual Conference for a term of three years, except as to the first Board so elected, one-third of whom shall be elected for a term of one year, one-third for a term of two years, and one-third for a term of three years and until their successors shall have been elected; *provided,* however, that existing incorporated Trustees of any Annual Conference may continue unaffected by this section unless and until such Charter is amended.

SECTION VI.   BISHOP'S RESIDENCE

¶ 459. When authorized by two-thirds of the Annual Conferences comprising an Episcopal Area a residence for the resident Bishop may be acquired which shall be under the management and control of and the title to which shall be held in trust by the Trustees of the Annual Conference within which the residence is located, and the purchase price and maintenance cost thereof shall be equitably distributed by the Trustees among the several Conferences in the Area. Should an Annual Conference contribute to the purchase of an Episcopal residence and later be transferred to an area not owning one, if it shall ask payment for its equity, such claim shall not be denied.

The Methodist Church 519

SECTION VII. INCORPORATED TRUSTEES OF THE
METHODIST CHURCH

¶ 460. There shall be a Board of Trustees incorporated under the name of "The Board of Trustees of The Methodist Church." This Board shall be composed of six Ministers and six Lay Members. At least one of its members shall be chosen from the bounds of each Jurisdictional Conference in the United States. They shall be elected for a term of eight years by the General Conference on nominations of the Council of Bishops, except as to the first such Board, of which three Clerical and three Lay Members thereof shall be elected for a term of four years and three Clerical and three Lay Members thereof shall be elected for a term of eight years and until their successors shall have been elected and qualified.

¶ 461. This corporation shall receive and administer new trusts and funds and so far as may be legal be the successors in trust of "The Trustees of The Methodist Episcopal Church," a corporation incorporated under the laws of the state of Ohio, and of "The Board of Trustees of the Methodist Episcopal Church, South," a corporation incorporated under the laws of the state of Tennessee, and of the "Board of Trustees of the Methodist Protestant Church," a corporation incorporated under the laws of the state of Maryland and, so far as is legal and as such successors in trust it shall be and is authorized and empowered to receive from its said predecessor corporations all trust funds and assets of every kind and character, real, personal or mixed, held by them or either of them, and it shall be and is authorized to administer such trusts and funds in accordance with the conditions under which they have been previously received and administered by said predecessor corporations. But nothing herein contained shall be construed to require the dissolution of the three corporations above mentioned and they shall continue to administer such funds as may not be legally transferred to the new corporation. There shall be a correlating Committee of nine members of which three shall be appointed by each of the existing corporations. This committee shall have authority to secure a charter for the new corporation and to arrange the details for handling the trusts in accordance with their terms.

¶ 463. The object and duty of this Board shall be to receive, collect, and hold in trust for the benefit of The Methodist Church any and all donations, bequests and devises of any kind or character, real or personal, that may be given, devised, bequeathed, or conveyed unto said Board or to The

Methodist Church as such for any benevolent, charitable or religious purpose and to administer the same and the income therefrom in accordance with the directions of the donor, trustor, or testator and in the interests of the Church, society, institution or agency contemplated by such donors, trustors, or testators under the direction of the General Conference. The Board shall have power to invest, reinvest, buy, sell, transfer, and convey any and all funds and properties which it may hold in trust subject always to the terms of the legacy, devise, or donation. When the use to be made of any such donation, bequest, or devise is not otherwise designated, the same shall be added to and become a part of "The Permanent Fund" of the Methodist Church.

¶ 464. The Board may intervene and take all necessary legal steps to safeguard and protect the interests and rights of The Methodist Church anywhere, in all matters relating to property and rights to property whether arising by gift, devise, or otherwise, or where held in trust or established for the benefit of The Methodist Church or its membership; or abandoned Church property where Annual Conference Trustees neglect to take necessary steps to protect the interests of the members of The Methodist Church in such property.

¶ 465. It shall be the duty of the Pastor within the bounds of whose Charge any such gift, bequest, or devise is made to give prompt notice thereof to said Board which shall proceed to take such steps as are necessary and proper to conserve, protect, and administer the same. But the Board may decline to receive or administer any such gift, devise, or bequest for any reason satisfactory to the Board.

¶ 466. The Board shall make to each General Conference a full, true and faithful report of its doings, of all funds, moneys, securities and property held in trust by it and of its receipts and disbursements during the quadrennium.

¶ 467. There shall be a fund known as "The Permanent Fund" to be held and administered by the Board, the principal of which shall be kept intact forever and the interest accumulating from said Fund shall be used by the Board as the General Conference shall direct.

SECTION VIII. TRUSTEES OF SCHOOLS AND OTHER INSTITUTIONS

¶ 468. Trustees of schools, colleges, universities, hospitals, homes, orphanages, institutes and other institutions owned or controlled by The Methodist Church shall be at least twenty-one years of age. At all times not less than three-fourths of them shall be members of The Methodist Church and all must be nominated, confirmed or elected by some governing body of the Church or by some body or officer thereof to which or to whom this power has been delegated by the governing body of the Church; *provided* that when an institution is owned and operated jointly with some other denomination or organization, said requirement that three-fourths of the Trustees shall be members of The Methodist Church shall apply only to the portions of the Trustees representing The Methodist Church.

SECTION IX. AUDITING AND BONDING

¶ 469. All persons holding trust funds, securities or moneys of any kind belonging to the General Conference or to Annual or Mission Conferences or to those organizations under the control of the General, Annual or Mission Conferences shall be bonded in a reliable company in such good and sufficient sum as the Conference may direct. The accounts of such persons shall be audited at least annually, preferably by a certified public accountant or a competent auditing committee carefully chosen by the Commission on Finance and the findings of such audit shall be published in the Conference Minutes.

SECTION X. PROVISION FOR LOCAL LAWS

¶ 470. Whenever the law of the state, territory, or country in which is located any property of The Methodist Church, its agencies or subdivisions, or the provisions of an existing charter of a corporation organized and holding property for such purposes, requires otherwise than in this chapter prescribed, such law or charter shall apply and be substituted for such of the provisions of this chapter as are in conflict with such law or charter.

REPORT NO. 4. BOARD OF LAY ACTIVITIES

Calendar No. 28. Adopted May 6. See Journal, Page 287.

Membership of Committee, 134; present when report was adopted, 89; voting for adoption, 89.

SECTION I. GENERAL BOARD OF LAY ACTIVITIES

¶ 601. The purpose of the Board of Lay Activities shall be to deepen the spiritual life of the laymen of the Church and to secure among laymen an increasing loyalty and interest with the ultimate end in view of an active working force in each local Church.

¶ 602. The General Board of Lay Activities shall be com-

posed of six active Bishops, one from each Jurisdiction;
six active Ministers, one from each Jurisdiction; twenty-
four Lay Members, elected by the several Jurisdictional
Conferences on the basis of Church membership; *provided*
that these Lay Members shall be elected from the Conference Lay Leaders of the several Annual Conferences in
the Jurisdiction. The headquarters of the General Board
shall be fixed by the General Conference.

¶ 603. The Board shall promote a program of Lay Activities which shall include Christian stewardship, Christian
fellowship, personal evangelism, lay speaking or preaching,
the circulation of Church papers and other Christian literature, the Benevolences, adequate support of the Ministry,
sound Church finance in the Local Church, attendance upon
worship services, men's work (including Brotherhoods),
the training of official boards, work for boys and youth,
the Christianizing of personal and community life, co-
operation with other General Boards and Agencies, and
District and Conference organizations to make more effective the entire program of Lay Activities.

¶ 604. The General Conference shall elect an Executive
Secretary, who shall have general supervision of the work
under the direction of the Board and who shall be subject
to the authority and control of the Board. On nomination
of the General Secretary such Associate Secretaries as the
Board deems necessary shall be elected by the Board. The
Board shall have authority to fill vacancies occurring *ad
interim,* including that of the Executive Secretary.

¶ 605. The work of this Board shall be considered a
benevolent interest of the Church, and the General Commission on World Service and Finance shall include in the appropriations recommended for adoption by the General
Conference such sum as may be necessary for the proper
support of the Board. This Board shall report to the Commission its estimate of the amount needed annually for its
work.

¶ 606. This Board shall report quadrennially to the General Conference and to the several Jurisdictional Conferences.

¶ 607. This Board shall be organized by the election of a
President, a Vice-President, a Recording Secretary, and a
Treasurer. It shall have authority to regulate its own pro-
ceedings.

SECTION II. JURISDICTIONAL BOARDS

¶ 608. There may be in every Jurisdiction a Jurisdictional
Board of Lay Activities composed of the Conference Lay

Leaders of the several Annual Conferences in the Jurisdiction; two active Bishops, one of whom shall be a member of the General Board of Lay Activities, three active Ministers, one of whom shall be a member of the General Board of Lay Activities, elected by the Jurisdictional Conference on the nomination of the Committee on Lay Activities.

¶ 609. Within the Jurisdiction this Board shall promote the program of Lay Activities as outlined by the General Board of Lay Activities under the authority of the General Conference.

¶ 610. The Jurisdictional Conference may elect a Secretary of Lay Activities, who shall have general supervision of the work in the Jurisdiction under the direction of the Board, and who shall be subject to the authority and control of the Board. The Board shall have authority to fill vacancies occurring *ad interim*, including that of Secretary.

¶ 611. The work of this Board shall be considered a benevolent interest of the Church within the Jurisdiction, and the Jurisdictional Conference Commission on Budget shall include in the appropriations recommended for adoption by the Jurisdictional Conference such sum as may be necessary for the support of the Board. This Board shall report to the Jurisdictional Conference Commission on Budget its estimate of the amount needed annually for its work.

¶ 612. This Board shall report quadrennially to the Jurisdictional Conference.

¶ 613. This Board shall be organized by the election of a President, a Vice-President, a Recording Secretary, and a Treasurer. It shall have authority to regulate its own proceedings.

SECTION III. ANNUAL CONFERENCE BOARDS

¶ 614. There shall be in every Annual Conference a Conference Board of Lay Activities, composed of the Conference Lay Leader, who shall be Chairman of the Board, the District Lay Leader and the two Associate District Lay Leaders from each district, and the District Superintendents of the Conference.

¶ 615. The Conference Lay Leader shall be elected annually by the Lay Members of the Annual Conference. Nominations shall be made by the Conference Board of Lay Activities, and other nominations may be made from the floor.

¶ 616. This Board shall report to the Annual Conference at its annual session and shall hold an anniversary, or otherwise provide for an adequate representation of the work of Lay Activities, during the session of the Conference. This Board shall carry out the program of Lay Activities as outlined under the direction of the General and Jurisdictional Boards of Lay Activities, and also co-operate with the other Conference Boards in executing their plans for larger service in the work of the Church.

¶ 617. This Board shall hold one annual meeting each year in connection with the Annual Conference session and such other meetings as may be deemed advisable by the Board and upon the call of the Chairman. The Conference Board shall have authority to fill a vacancy in the office of Conference Lay Leader.

¶ 618. The Annual Conference Board shall estimate annually the amount necessary for the support of its work and report this amount to the Annual Conference Commission on Budget for its consideration and recommendation to the Annual Conference.

SECTION IV. DISTRICT BOARDS

¶ 619. There shall be in every District a District Board of Lay Activities composed of the District Lay Leader, who shall be Chairman of the Board, two Associate District Lay Leaders, the District Superintendent, and the Lay Leader of each Charge in the District.

¶ 620. The District and Associate District Lay Leaders shall be elected annually by the District Conference upon nomination of a Committee to be named by the District Superintendent or by a Committee of the District Board of Lay Activities, of which Committee the District Superintendent may be a member. In Annual Conferences where District Conferences are not held, the Annual Conference shall elect the District and Associate District Lay Leaders upon nomination of a Committee named by the District Superintendents.

¶ 621. This Board shall co-operate with the Annual Conference Board of Lay Activities in promoting the program of Lay Activities outlined under the direction of the General, Jurisdictional, and Conference Boards of Lay Activities.

¶ 622. The District Board of Lay Activities shall have authority to fill vacancies occurring *ad interim* in the office of District and Associate District Lay Leaders.

SECTION V. CHARGE BOARDS

¶ 623. The Official Board, in co-operation with the Pastor, shall be responsible for the program of Lay Activities in the Station Church as outlined under the direction of the General, Jurisdictional, Conference, and District Boards of Lay Activities.

¶ 624. The Pastor shall call this Board to meet as soon as practicable after the session of the Annual Conference for organization and for perfecting plans for the work of the year.

¶ 625. The Charge Lay Leader shall be elected by the Official Board.

SECTION VI. THE CIRCUIT BOARD

¶ 626. The Official Boards of the several Churches of the , Circuit, in co-operation with the Pastor, shall be responsible for the program of Lay Activities as outlined under the direction of the General, Jurisdictional, Conference, and District Boards of Lay Activities.

¶ 627. These Boards shall also promote harmony and Christian fellowship among the Churches of the Circuit to the end that a larger service may be rendered by the Circuit.

¶ 628. The Pastor shall call these Boards to meet as soon as practicable after the session of the Annual Conference for organization and for perfecting plans for the work of the year.

¶ 629. The Charge Lay Leader of the Circuit shall be elected annually by the Quarterly Conference at the session next preceding the session of the Annual Conference.

¶ 630. The Chairmen of the Official Boards of the several Churches of the Charge shall be the Church Lay Leaders, except that where the Pastor is Chairman, the Official Boards shall elect the Church Lay Leaders.

SECTION VII. DUTIES OF LAY LEADERS

¶ 631. The Conference Lay Leaders shall give direction to the work of the Conference Board of Lay Activities, make a written report to the Board at its regular annual session, and make a written report to the Jurisdictional Secretary at the close of the Conference year, which shall include the names and correct addresses of the District, Associate District, and Charge Lay Leaders of the several Districts and Charges.

¶ 632. The District and Associate District Lay Leaders shall co-operate with the District Superintendent in giving direc on to the work of the District Board of Lay Activities. ti

¶ 633. The District Lay Leader shall make a written report to the District Board of Lay Activities at its regular annual session and also a written report to the Conference Lay Leader at the close of the Conference year, which shall include the names and correct addresses of the two Associate District Lay Leaders and the Charge Lay Leaders of the several Charges in the District.

¶ 634. The Charge Lay Leader of the station church shall co-operate with the Pastor in giving full direction to the work of the Official Board, co-operate with the District Lay Leader in the program of Lay Activities for the District, and make a written report to the Quarterly Conference and annually to the District Lay Leader.

¶ 635. The Charge Lay Leader of the Circuit Charge ι shall co-operate with the Pastor in giving full direction to the work of Lay Activities within the Circuit, co-operate with the District Lay Leader in the program of Lay Activities for the District, and make a written report to the Quarterly Conference and annually to the District Lay Leader which shall include the correct names and addresses of the several Church Lay Leaders of the Circuit.

¶ 636. The Church Lay Leader shall co-operate with the Pastor in directing the work of the Official Board of the Church, co-operate with the Charge Lay Leader in the program of Lay Activities for the Circuit and make a written quarterly report to the Charge Lay Leader.

REPORT NO. 5.   FINANCIAL PLAN

Calendar No. 42.   Adopted May 9.   See Journal, Pages 293, 334

Membership of Committee, 134; present when report was adopted, 103; voting for adoption, 98; voting against adoption, 5.

¶ 500. Provision for receiving and distributing the incomes from askings of the various Church Boards and Commissions, both General and Annual Conference; for the support of the ministry, including Bishops, the widows and minor children of deceased Bishops, District Superintendents, Pastors, and Conference Claimants; the support of the local Church and for meeting the needs of the General Conference and of all other interests or institutions asking for financial support, shall be made according to the following plan:

SECTION I.   GENERAL COMMISSION ON WORLD SERVICE AND FINANCE

¶ 501. There shall be a General Commission on World Service and Finance constituted as follows: Two Ministers and two Lay Members elected by the General Conference from each Jurisdiction nominated by the Bishops thereof; six Members at large, two of whom shall be Bishops, nominated by the Council of Bishops and elected by the General Conference. No member, including said Bishops, or employee of any connectional board or agency shall be eligible to membership. The Bishops shall not be present in the sessions of the Commission when the salaries of the Bishops or matters pertaining to the Episcopal Fund are being considered. Vacancies during the quadrennium shall be filled by the Commission.

The Commission shall meet annually or on call of the Chairman. Sixteen members shall constitute a quorum. The expenses of the Commission shall be paid by the Treasurer of the General Administration Fund. It shall serve four years and until the adjournment of the next succeeding General Conference.

¶ 502. *Officers.* The officers of the Commission shall be a President, a Vice-President, a Recording Secretary and a Treasurer elected by the Commission who shall serve four years and until their successors are duly elected and qualify. The President, Vice-President and Secretary shall be elected from the membership of the Commission. The officers shall perform the duties usually attached to their respective offices.

The Treasurer shall receive from the Annual Conference Treasurers and all other sources all funds intended (1) for the support of the General Benevolences, (2) for the General Administration Fund, and (3) for the Episcopal Fund, and shall disburse the same as may be ordered by the General Conference or by the General Commission on World Service and Finance. No one of these funds shall be drawn on for the benefit of another.

The Treasurer shall report annually to the Commission on World Service and Finance and to the Annual Conference Commissions as to all amounts received and disbursed during the year. He shall also give to the General Conference a full and detailed report of the financial transactions of the Commission for each succeeding quadrennium. The Treasurer shall be bonded in such amount as may be determined by the Commission.

¶ 503. The Executive Secretary, or duly authorized representative, of each of the Boards and other agencies for which askings are authorized by the General Conference shall appear before the Commission to represent interests for which each is responsible.

¶ 504. The General Commission on World Service and Finance, after making diligent effort to secure full information regarding the general interests of the Church, in order that none may be neglected, jeopardized, or excluded, shall recommend to the General Conference for its action and determination in a single budget the total amount to be apportioned for all connectional interests. The apportionments for connectional causes in the interval between General Conferences may be changed when such adjustment is required by an emergency, but such change must receive a three-fourths vote of the members of the Commission present and voting, together with the concurrence of the Council of Bishops.

Any General Board or agency requesting the privilege of a Church-wide collection in the interests of its work shall present such request to the Commission on World Service and Finance when the askings of the Board or agency for the ensuing quadrennium are presented to the Commission.

The Commission shall make recommendations to the General Conference as to the special collections and special days to be authorized. The Commission shall bring to the General Conference a recommendation in the case of each collection as to whether the income from such special collection shall constitute a part of the support from the Benevolence funds by the Board receiving such collection, or whether the income from such special collection shall be over and above the support of the Board or agency from the General Benevolence funds.

¶ 505. The General Commission on World Service and Finance shall determine the ratio of total apportionments and receipts to be allotted to each of the interests included in the budget, and submit the same to the General Conference for approval. Thereafter, no benevolent interest shall be allowed to have a prior or preferred claim except by a three-fourths vote of those present and voting at a regular or called meeting of the Commission, with the concurrence of the Council of Bishops. The Commission shall act as arbiter in all cases of interboard disagreement on financial matters and shall consider complaints from contributors, both individual and organization. It shall preserve the principle of voluntary acceptance of apportionments by the local Church.

¶ 506. The General Commission on World Service and Finance shall recommend to the General Conference the salaries of the effective Bishops, the allowance for their expense of house, office, and travel, the support of retired Bishops and the widows and. minor children ōf deceased Bishops; and the total amount adopted by the General

Conference shall be included in the apportionment for the Episcopal Fund.

¶ 507. The apportionments approved by the General Conference for the General Benevolences and the General Administration Fund shall be transmitted by the Commission on World Service and Finance to the several Annual Conferences and apportioned on an equitable basis, having regard to the number of members in each Annual Conference, as the first factor, and to the amounts contributed by it for ministerial support (not counting missionary aid), current expenses (exclusive of money raised for debt, interest, building and improvements and all special campaigns), and for Annual Conference and General Benevolences, as the second factor. The median of the two fractions thus attained for any Annual Conference shall constitute the fractional part of each of the several askings upon the Church at large to be apportioned to it. Proper adjustment shall be made for any changes in Conference boundaries. The percentage fixed by the Commission for transmittal to the several Annual Conferences shall be reported to the General Conference before adjournment and recorded in the Journal.

¶ 508. The Commission shall aid in standardizing annuity rates and formulating policies for the writing of annuities by institutions and agencies operating under the auspices of The Methodist Church.

¶ 509. The Commission may receive, take title to, sell, dispose of, or hold absolutely or in trust, property, real and personal, for the benefit of the General Benevolences of the Church and for distribution thereto.

¶ 510. The fiscal year for the Commission on World Service and Finance and for the Boards and agencies related to it shall be from June 1 to May 31.

REPORT NO. 5-A. CONCERNING WORLD SERVICE AND FINANCE

Calendar No. 43. Adopted May 9. See Journal, Page 335.

Membership of Committee, 134; present when report was adopted, 62; voting for adoption, 62.

SECTION II. ANNUAL CONFERENCE COMMISSION ON FINANCE

¶ 511. There shall be in each Annual Conference a Commission on World Service and Finance composed of five Ministers and six Lay Members, nominated by the District Superintendents and elected by the Annual Conference next succeeding the General Conference. They shall serve for four years, beginning with the adjournment of that Annual Conference. No member or employee of any Conference or Connectional Board shall be eligible. The Chairman of each Conference Board or Commission, or some person appointed by it, shall have opportunity to represent the claims of his Board or Commission before the Annual Conference Commission on World Service and Finance.

¶ 512. The Commission shall make diligent effort to secure full information regarding all Conference interests that none may be neglected, jeopardized, or excluded and shall recommend to the Annual Conference for its action andh determination the total amount to be appointed for eac .

¶ 513. The Commission shall recommend to the Annual Conference for its action the percentage of the total sum for Annual Conference interests which shall be allotted to each such interest.

¶ 514. The Commission shall determine the amounts to be apportioned to each District of the Annual Conference for both General and Annual Conference budgets, when these have been determined as previously set forth, and shall report them to the Annual Conference for approval.

¶ 515. The Commission shall organize by electing a President and Secretary. The Treasurer of the Annual Conference shall be the Treasurer of the Commission. The Treasurer shall be bonded in a surety company approved by the auditing committee of the Annual Conference.

¶ 516. It shall be the duty of the Commission, unless otherwise provided for, to estimate the amount necessary to furnish a sufficient and equitable support for the District Superintendent of each District in the Conference, including salary, suitable provision for rent, travel and office expense. It shall report this estimate to the Annual Conference for approval. The Conference Treasurer, or District Treasurers, elected by the Annual Conference, shall remit monthly to the several District Superintendents the amounts due them, and with the approval of the Annual Conference may borrow the funds necessary to make this possible.

¶ 517. Annual Conferences which elect to do so may provide for the support of District Superintendents through a District Stewards' Meeting instead of the Annual Conference Commission on World Service and Finance. In that case, there shall be held annually in such Districts a meeting composed of the District Stewards. Under- the Chairmanship of the District Superintendent the meeting shall estimate and apportion the salary and expenses of the

District Superintendent among the several Charges, according to their ability. They shall distribute to the Charges the total apportionments ordered by the General and Annual Conferences, and transmitted to the District by the Annual Conference Commission on World Service and Finance. The amount apportioned for the support of the District Superintendent shall be added by the Official Board of each Charge to the salary estimated for the Pastor and its collection shall be provided for in the same way. Distribution shall be made on a pro rata basis. The District Stewards may elect a Treasurer, or payment may be made direct by the Treasurer or disbursing Steward of each Pastoral Charge. There shall be a settlement day at least once a quarter when proportional payments for the various items of ministerial support shall be made.

SECTION III. GENERAL ADMINISTRATION

¶ 518. The General Administration Fund shall provide for the expenses of the Judicial Council, the sessions of the General Conference, such General Conference Commissions and Committees as may be appointed, and for authorized interchurch activities. The Episcopal Fund, raised separately from the benevolences, shall provide for the salary and expenses of effective Bishops, for the support of Retired Bishops and of the widows and minor children of deceased Bishops. The Treasurer shall pay these claims upon proper voucher. Subject to the approval of the General Commission on World Service and Finance, they shall have authority to borrow such amounts as may be necessary for the proper execution of the orders of the General Conference.

¶ 519. The Treasurer of the General Commission on World Service and Finance is directed to send monthly to each Bishop and Missionary Bishop a check covering one-twelfth of the annual salary, the house rent, or maintenance, and office expenses, as estimated by the Commission. He shall also pay the claim for official travel of a Bishop, or a Missionary Bishop, upon presentation of an itemized voucher.

¶ 520. "Official travel" of an effective Bishop shall be interpreted to include all visitations within his Area to Church institutions or enterprises of The Methodist Church, where the call of need or opportunity warrants his presence and service. "Official travel" shall include also such journeys outside his Area as are within the meaning of "travel through the Connection at large." For all such official travel within and outside his Area, an effective Bishop, upon presentation of an itemized voucher, shall have the right of claim on the Episcopal Fund, within such limits as may be set by the General Commission on World Service and Finance. No part of the expense of such visitations shall be accepted from local Methodist Churches or enterprises within the Bishop's Area or for visitations made while in official "travel through the Connection at large."

Nothing in this interpretation is intended to preclude the acceptance of an honorarium for special or nonofficial engagements of a Bishop outside his Area or for services rendered upon invitations from other than Methodist Church enterprises within his Area, provided that such engagements do not interfere with his official duties.

¶ 521. The General Commission on World Service and Finance shall apportion among the several Annual Conferences the sum required to be raised for all connectional purposes. The Annual Conference Commission on World Service and Finance shall apportion the same to the several Districts. The District Superintendent, or the District Stewards' Meeting, shall apportion the same to the several Charges of each District as the Annual Conference may order.

¶ 522. Each Annual Conference shall elect a Conference Treasurer at the first session of the Annual Conference after the adjournment of the General Conference on nomination of the Annual Conference Commission on World Service and Finance. He shall serve for a quadrennium or until his successor shall be elected and qualify. The Conference Commission on World Service and Finance shall have full authority and supervision over the Treasurer, and after consultation with the Bishop in charge shall have the power to remove him from office for cause and to fill vacancies *ad interim*. The Commission on World Service and Finance shall have the books of the Conference Treasurer audited within forty days after the close of the Annual Conference.

¶ 523. All amounts collected in the local Churches on General and Conference askings shall be sent monthly by the local church Treasurer to the Treasurer of the Annual Conference. Annual Conference Treasurers shall make monthly distribution of the funds received to the Treasurers of the several boards or institutions for Conference work and to the Treasurer of the General Commission on World Service and Finance for connectional work according to the precentages fixed by the General Conference or the General Commission on World Service and Finance. The Annual Conference Commission on World Service and

Finance shall provide suitable bonds for the Annual Conference Treasurer and the Treasurers of the several Annual Conference Boards and causes and shall designate a depository or depositories for Annual Conference funds. It shall require the Treasurers of all boards, societies, and institutions to be bonded in companies approved by the Annual Conference Committee on Audit.

SECTION IV. THE COMMISSION ON THE PROMOTION OF THE BENEVOLENCES

¶ 524. There shall be a Commission for the Promotion of the General Conference Benevolences. This Commission shall be composed of one effective Bishop from each Jurisdiction appointed by the Council of Bishops, one Minister and one Lay Member elected by each Jurisdictional Conference, and the Executive Secretaries of the General Conference Benevolence Boards. It shall be the duty of this Commission to promote a Church-wide interest in home and foreign missions, in Christian education and in all of the benevolent causes authorized by the General Conference. The expenses of this Commission and of its promotional work shall be paid by the General Conference Benevolence Boards and agencies.

SECTION V. CULTIVATION AND COLLECTION

¶ 525. As soon as practicable after the session of the Annual Conference the District Superintendent shall present to every Charge in the District the amount apportioned to it by the General Commission on World Service and Finance for Connectional and Conference benevolences. It shall be the joint responsibility of the Pastor, the District Steward, and the Church Lay Leader to present to a meeting of each congregation in a Charge the program of benevolonces and administration, an explanation of the various causes supported, and a statement of the amount of askings from that congregation and the manner in which it was determined. Such presentation to each local congregation shall be made before the Quarterly Conference of that Charge shall set the amount of its acceptance. The First or Second Quarterly Conference may accept, increase, or decrease the amount apportioned. The amount voted by the Quarterly Conference shall be the amount apportioned for the charge.

¶ 526. The District Superintendent shall report to the Chairman of the Annual Conference Commission the amounts that have been accepted by the District, charge by charge, and the Chairman shall inform the Commission and the various Conference interests regarding the total amounts which have been accepted by that Conference for the current year. The Bishops, District Superintendents, Pastors, and official Laymen shall make diligent effort to raise the full amount of the askings accepted by the Charges. In the case of Charges which have not been using this plan heretofore it is advised that they arrange their affairs so as to inaugurate it immediately following the first General Conference of The Methodist Church.

SECTION VI. MISCELLANEOUS

¶ 527. Special gifts, bequests, and annuities for endowment purposes made to colleges, universities, hospitals, orphanages, and other authorized institutions and boards shall not be charged against the askings for any institution or Board from the benevolent collections.

¶ 528. Pastoral Charges, individuals or groups may designate their gifts to the work of any Board or agency or to one or more projects or types of work under their direction; *provided* that these have been included in the program of the Boards as approved by the General Commission on World Service and Finance. Such gifts shall be applied to the work to which they have been designated and when credited on the apportionment of a local Church shall be charged as a part of the ratio share of the Board or Boards receiving them in the distributable General Benevolence Funds.

¶ 529. When the total amount to be apportioned to the several claims has been determined by the General Conference and in the case of Conference causes by the Annual Conference, the following principle shall apply:

No General Board or interest, such as a school, college, university, or hospital, shall make a special Church-wide appeal for funds without the approval of the General Conference, or in the interim between General Conferences, without the approval of the Council of Bishops and the General Commission on World Service and Finance; no Annual Conference Board or interest as above defined shall make a special Conference-wide appeal for funds to the Churches without the approval of the Annual Conference.

¶ 530. The salaries and any expense items paid to all connectional officers and their chief assistants shall be published in the report of the General Commission on World Service and Finance to the General Conference. The various Annual Conference Boards and agencies shall report to the Annual Conferences the salaries and traveling expenses allowed to all Secretaries in their employ.

REPORT NO. 6. REPORT OF SOCIAL CREED COMMITTEE

Calendar No. 57. Adopted May 9. See Journal, Page 358.

Membership of Committee, 134; present when report was adopted, 91; voting for adoption, 84; voting against adoption, 6; not voting, 1.

A SOCIAL CREED

The interest of The Methodist Church in Social Welfare springs from the labors of John Wesley, who ministered to the physical, intellectual, and social needs of the people to whom he preached the gospel of personal redemption.

In our historic position we have followed Christ in laboring to bring the whole of life with its activities, possessions, and relationships into conformity with the will of God.

The followers of Christ and a depressed world look to a United Methodism for a statement of its position on social and economic questions.

RELIGIOUS POSITION

1. The Methodist Church aims to view the perplexing times and problems which we face today in the light of the teachings of Jesus. We believe that to be silent in the face of need, injustice and exploitation would be to deny Him.

2. We believe that God is Father of all peoples and races, Jesus Christ is His Son, that we and all men are brothers, and that man is of infinite worth as a child of God.

3. We believe that personality possesses the highest value. We test all institutions and practices by their effect upon personality. Since personality is being oppressed in so many parts of the world, we seek for its emancipation and for those things which will enrich and redeem it. Since Jesus died for the redemption of human life we believe we should live to fulfill our obligation to help save man from sin and from every influence which would harm or destroy him.

OUR SOCIAL CREED

1. The Methodist Church stands for equal rights and complete justice for all men in all stations of life; for the protection of both the individual and the family by the single standard of purity; education for marriage, parenthood, and home-building, proper housing, proper regulation of marriage, and uniform divorce laws.

2. We stand for a proper regulation of working conditions for women, especially mothers, and the safeguarding

of their physical and moral environment; for the abolition of child labor; adequate provision for the protection, education, spiritual nurture and wholesome recreation of every child; and for the provision of educational programs which will attain these ends.

3. We stand for the abatement and prevention of poverty by protection against all forms of social, economic and moral waste, and by the conservation of human values by the protection of the worker from dangerous machinery, from unsafe and unsanitary working conditions, and from occupational diseases.

4. We stand for the rights of all men to live and to have adequate means of livelihood, and for the safeguarding of workers from the devastating results of enforced unemployment.

5. We stand for reasonable hours of labor, for just wages, for a fair day's work for a fair day's wage, for fair working conditions, for periods of leisure for those who work, and for an equitable division of the product of industry.

6. We stand for some form of security for old age, for insurance against injury to the worker, and for increased protection against those preventable conditions which produce want.

7. We stand for the right of employees and employers alike to organize for collective bargaining and social action; protection of both in the exercise of their right; the obligation of both to work for the public good.

8. We stand for the principle of the acquisition of property by Christian processes, and believe in stressing the principle of stewardship in its use; in the practical application of the Christian principle of social well-being to the acquisition and use of wealth and the subordination of the profit motive to the creative and co-operative spirit.

9. We stand for the safeguarding of the farmer and his family and for the preservation of all the values of rural life.

10. We stand for all workers having at least one day of rest in seven.

11. We stand for the protection of the individual, the home, and the society from the social, economic, and moral waste of any traffic in intoxicants and habit-forming drugs.

12. We stand for the application of the redemptive principle to the treatment of offenders against the law, to reform of penal and correctional methods, and to criminal court procedure.

13. We stand for the rights of racial groups, and insist

that the above social, economic, and spiritual principles apply to all races alike.

14. We recognize the need of an army and navy for police purposes. We stand for the repudiation of war and for the discovery and development of all reasonable methods to attain peace, for the reduction of armaments by all nations, participation in international agencies for the peaceable settlement of controversies, and for the building of a co-operative spirit among the nations. We insist that the agencies of the Church shall not be used in the preparation for war, but in the promulgation of peace. We believe that war is utterly destructive and is our greatest collective social sin and a denial of the ideals of Christ. We stand upon this ground, that The Methodist Church as an institution cannot endorse war nor support or participate in it.

15. The Methodist Church, true to the principles of the New Testament, teaches respect for properly constituted civil authority. It holds that government rests upon the support of its conscientious citizenship, and that conscientious objectors to war in any or all of its manifestations are a natural outgrowth of the principle of good will and the Christian desire for universal peace; and holds that such objectors should not be oppressed by compulsory military service anywhere or at any time. We ask and claim exemption from all forms of military preparation or service for all conscientious objectors who may be members of The Methodist Church. In this they have the authority and support of their Church. However, we recognize the right of the individual to answer the call of his government in an emergency according to the dictates of his Christian conscience.

16. We stand for the recognition and maintenance of the rights and responsibilities of free speech, free assembly, and a free press; and for the encouragement of free communication of mind with mind, as essential to the discovery of truth.

17. We stand upon the right of various groups to believe in various peaceful methods for solving the problems that confront us; some, who believe that we need a drastic readjustment of the social order to correct the acquisitiveness which characterizes us; others, who believe in the correctional method for an economic order which they believe possesses the inherent good which has produced prosperity and is able to do so again; and still others, who believe in producers' and consumers' co-operatives. We stand by the

single measure of testing every proposal in the light of the teachings of Jesus.

18. We believe that society has a right to expect that every person not physically nor mentally incapacitated, shall be constantly engaged, so far as possible, in some vocation productive of common good.

19. We recommend that this Social Creed be read to our congregations at least once a year or placed in their hands in printed form.

REPORT NO. 7. CONCERNING OFFICIAL BOARDS

Calendar No. 58. Adopted May 10. See Journal, Page 366.

Membership of Committee, 134; present when report was adopted, 87; voting for adoption, 87.

In order to clarify provisions already adopted by the Uniting Conference (Pages 128 and 129 of the *Advocate,* with certain amendments) we recommend reconsideration of Report No. 1, and we recommend that ¶ 430 be amended to read as follows:

¶ 430. In every Church there shall be an executive body called the Official Board, organized by either of the following ways as may be authorized by the Quarterly Conference: "The Board may be composed as follows: The Pastor, Assistant Pastor, Deaconess serving the Charge, the stewards, the unit or class leaders, the trustees, the church treasurer, the director of religious education, where desired the director of music, the superintendent of the Church School, the chairman of the local Board of Christian Education, president or presidents of the women's auxiliaries authorized by the General Conference, a representative elected by the Young People's Division, and the chairman of the local Missionary Council. It shall be organized with a chairman, a secretary, and a treasurer. If the Official Board is not composed and organized as above, the Board of Stewards shall assume all powers and duties prescribed in this section of the *Discipline* and shall be the Official Board."

We recommend that the last sentence in ¶ 437 be deleted, its provisions being written in ¶ 430.

REPORT NO. 8. CONCERNING SUPPORT OF MINISTRY

Calendar No. 59. Adopted May 10. See Journal, Page 366.

Membership of Committee, 134; present when report was adopted, 95; voting for adoption, 95.

SECTION VII. MINISTERIAL SUPPORT

¶ 531. Assumption of the obligations of the itinerancy required to be made at the time of admission into the traveling connection puts upon the Church the counter-obligation of providing support for the entire Ministry of the Church. In view of this the claim for ministerial support in each Pastoral Charge shall include provision for the support of Pastors, District Superintendents, Bishops, and Conference Claimants.

. ¶ 532. The specific amount of the payment for the support of the Pastor having been determined, the other three items of ministerial support shall be related to the Pastor's salary on a percentage basis, so that the respective payments required for the support of Bishops, District Superintendents, and Conference Claimants in each Pastoral Charge shall be exactly proportional to the amount paid to the Pastor.

¶ 533. The Treasurer or Treasurers of each Pastoral Charge shall make proportional distribution of the funds raised in that Pastoral Charge for the support of the ministry and remit monthly the items for Bishops, District Superintendents, and Conference Claimants to the proper treasurer.

. ¶ 534. It shall be the duty of the Quarterly Conference of each Pastoral Charge or of the Stewards of the Charge as the Quarterly Conference may elect, at the session immediately preceding the Annual Conference and after consultation with the Pastor, to agree upon the minimum salary of the Pastor of the Charge for the ensuing year. In Charges of more than one organized congregation, the amount allotted to each Church shall be recorded in the minutes of the Quarterly Conference. The Pastor's salary, thus agreed upon, shall not include the traveling and moving expenses of a new appointee to the Charge. Where traveling and moving expenses of a new appointee to a Charge are paid by the Charge, this amount shall be a separate and additional item.

¶ 535. No Pastor shall be entitled to any claim for unpaid salary against any Church or Charge he has served after his pastoral connection with the Church or Charge has ceased.

. ¶ 536. Each Annual Conference, after careful study of its needs and its sources of income for ministerial support, may adopt a Schedule of Minimum Support for its pastors. This schedule shall specify the minimum financial support necessary for effective service for Clerical Members of the Conference and for Supply Pastors who are accepted by the Annual Conference and who are giving full time to pastoral work. his schedule may allow for differences in living conditions, number of dependents in the family, or any other variants, as desired by the Annual Conference.

¶ 537. When adopted by vote of the Annual Conference, this Schedule of Minimum Support shall be observed by the Bishops and District Superintendents in arranging the appointments.

¶ 538. If it is necessary in order to maintain a satisfactory Schedule of Minimum Support or to assist its Pastors in special need, a Sustentation Fund may be apportioned to the Pastoral Charges, collected and disbursed as the Annual Conferences may direct.

¶ 539. In order to supplement such a Fund an equitable apportionment may be made on that part of the salaries of all effective Ministerial Members of an Annual Conference above the minimum salary fixed by said Annual Conference.

¶ 540. Every Ministerial Member of an Annual Conference appointed to any other field than the Pastorate or District Superintendency shall furnish annually to the Secretary of his Conference, at the time of the Conference Session, a statement of his financial support, and the salaries or remuneration of all men in special service shall be published in the *Journal* of the Annual Conference.

SECTION VIII.   FINANCIAL SYSTEM IN THE LOCAL CHURCH

¶ 544, Section 1. The financial plan of the local Church should be founded upon the principles of Christian Stewardship, so that when followed it will provide sufficient support for the local and World Service of The Methodist Church. The following essential features apply to every Pastoral Charge; the details may be adapted to local conditions.

Section 2. Every member should be fully informed regarding the extent and needs of the local and World Service of his Church.

Section 3. Systematic contributions should be sought and envelopes provided that contributions may be received weekly and credited to the individual contributors.

Section 4. Quarterly or semi-annual statements should be issued and arrears collected as far as possible.

Section 5. The ideal of "Every Member a Recorded Contributor" can be more nearly achieved when the Budget includes every item, both local and connectional, to which the local congregation is asked to contribute.   -

Section 6. Budget envelopes should be assigned to each

new member taken into the Church; the envelopes should be assigned before the following Sunday, with an introductory letter explaining briefly the plan for the financial support of the Church.

Section 7. The control of the expenditures of moneys should be with the Official Board, the Board of Stewards, the Finance Committee, as the Quarterly Conference may direct, and no appropriations should be made for items not included in the Budget without also providing additional funds for these items, and not until the Official Board, Board of Stewards, or Finance Committee, shall have approved such appropriation.

Section 6. Payments to Local Expenses, Ministerial Support, and Benevolences shall be prorated, as nearly as possible, in the relative proportions these items represent in the approved budget.

¶ 545. The Finance Committee shall consist of not less than three members. It shall be the duty of the Finance Committee before the close of the fiscal year:

1. In collaboration with the Financial Secretary, or Treasurer, and Pastor to prepare a local budget in the following form:

Ministerial Support—namely, Pastor's Salary, House Rent (if paid in cash to owners or trustees), apportionment for District Superintendent, apportionment for Bishops, and apportionment for Conference Claimants.

Benevolences (or World Service), which shall include the World Service Acceptance of the Charge, the Acceptance for Conference Causes, and the amounts sought by the authority of the Official Board for Special Benevolences other than those for which special collections may be ordered by the Official Board.

Local Expenses, which shall include salaries for music, janitor, religious education directors, Church School budget, repairs, supplies, and all other purely local expenses.

2. To present, previous to the end of the fiscal year, the Budget to a specially called meeting of the Official Board for approval or revision.

3. To proceed immediately, by personal canvass of the entire membership of the Church, congregation, Church School, Epworth League, Young People's organization, and other supporters of the Church, to secure pledges and to determine the probable income for the coming year.

4. If the probable income is insufficient to meet budgets as made, to report to the first Quarterly Conference recommendations as to how the balance needed can be raised, or

to recommend that the budget be reduced to correspond to the probable income.

¶ 546. The Pastor, the Board of Lay Activities, and the Women's Missionary organizations shall have special responsibility for the promotion of Benevolences and World Service in the Local Church—

1. To inculcate the principles of Christian Stewardship.

2. To arrange continual, periodic, and special presentation to the members and various organizations of the charge, of the interests and work included in tthe World Service of The Methodist Church.

3. To ascertain apportionments for the World Service, Annual and Quarterly Conference Benevolences, and with the Finance Committee of the Official Board make up the Benevolence Budget.

4. Wherever pledges and receipts seem to indicate failure to raise the complete Benevolence Budget, to report recommendations to the Official Board.

¶ 547. The duties of the Church Treasurer or Financial Secretary are:

1. To receive and record in approved classified form all moneys coming to the Church, not subject to immediate control of the Trustees.

2. To keep an account with each individual contributor.

3. To deposit promptly all funds in a Bank or Trust Company approved by the Official Board.

4. To report to each monthly meeting of the Official Board and to the Quarterly Conference as may be required.

5. To assist the Finance Committee in forming the Budget of the Pastoral Charge.

6. To co-operate with the Committee on Benevolences in promoting the Benevolent Interests of the Church.

¶ 548. Pastoral charges that so desire may elect a local treasurer, who shall handle all moneys for Ministerial Support and purely local expense and a connectional Treasurer, who shall handle all Benevolence moneys.

REPORT NO. 9.   CONCERNING CHURCH MEMBERSHIP

Calendar No. 60.   Adopted May 10.   See Journal, Page 367.

Membership of Committee, 134; present when report was adopted, 70; voting for adoption, 68; voting against adoption, 2.

SECTION I.   ADMISSION INTO THE CHURCH

¶ 401. All persons seeking to be saved from their sins and desiring to live the Christian life are eligible for membership in The Methodist Church.

¶ 402. It shall be the duty of the Pastor to instruct, or to appoint suitable leaders to instruct, all persons offering themselves for Church membership in the principles of the Christian life, in the baptismal and membership vows, and in the rules and regulations of The Methodist Church.

¶ 403. When the Pastor is satisfied as to the genuineness of their faith, their acceptance of the baptismal and membership vows, and their knowledge of and willingness to keep the rules and regulations of The Methodist Church, he shall present the candidates to the congregation; and after the candidates who have been baptized and the members of the church have entered into solemn covenant with one another as provided in the Ritual, he shall receive them into Church membership according to the prescribed form.

¶ 404. If any candidates for Church membership are unable to appear before the congregation for reasons satisfactory to the Pastor, he may receive them elsewhere according to the prescribed form, subject to the approval of the Official Board. This approval shall be secured in advance except in cases of emergency.

¶ 405. Members in good standing in any evangelical Church who desire to unite with us may be received into membership upon giving satisfactory evidence of their willingness to support The Methodist Church and to keep its rules and regulations, and after they and the members of the Church have entered into solemn covenant with one another as provided in the Ritual.

¶ 406. A permanent record of membership shall be kept, both resident and non-resident, including all changes of relation in the same. Each entry shall bear its proper date, and the Pastor shall report all such changes in membership at the next Quarterly Conference.

¶ 406A. Each Pastor shall also keep and transmit to his successor a constituency roll, containing the names and addresses of all persons related to the membership of the Church and Church School, either by kinship or preference.

¶ 406B. It is recommended that each Church shall provide, in addition to such records of membership, a Membership Register having space for home address and date and manner of admission into membership. Each person, at the time of admission into membership, shall be requested to sign this register. This register shall be bound and not a loose-leaf volume.

SECTION II. BAPTIZED CHILDREN AND THE CHURCH

¶ 407. We hold that all children, by virtue of the unconditional benefits of the atonement, are members of the

Kingdom of God, and therefore graciously entitled to baptism. The minister shall earnestly exhort all parents to dedicate their children to the Lord in baptism as early as convenient and, before baptism is administered, shall diligently instruct the parents regarding the vows which they assume in this Sacrament. It is expected of parents or guardians who present their children for Baptism, that they use all diligence in bringing them up in conformity to the Word of God; and they shall be admonished of this obligation and earnestly exhorted to faithfulness therein.

¶ 408. We regard all children who have been baptized as being in visible covenant relation to God and as preparatory members under the special care and supervision of the Church, and they shall be so reported.

¶ 409. The Pastor shall keep and transmit to his successor an accurate register of the names of baptized children within his Pastoral Charge, giving the dates of their birth and baptism, the names of their parents, and the places of their residence. He shall also enroll their names as preparatory members. Should they remove, he shall issue to them Certificates of Registration.

¶ 410. The Pastor shall organize into classes the baptized children of the Church when they shall have reached the age of ten years, or at an earlier age when it is deemed advisable, and shall meet them at least once a week for a reasonable period to instruct them in the nature, design, and obligations of baptism, and in the truths of the Scriptures; to urge them to give regular attendance upon the public worship of the Church; to advise, exhort, and encourage them to an immediate personal acceptance of Jesus Christ as Lord and Saviour, and to instruct them in the use of the means of grace in living the Christian life; provided, that unbaptized children may likewise be included in such classes. Such unbaptized children may with the consent of their parents or guardians, be recognized and recorded as preparatory members. If need be, the Pastor may appoint one or more suitable persons to assist him in such class instruction.

¶ 411. Whenever baptized children shall give evidence of understanding their Christian privileges and obligations and of their Christian faith and purpose they may be admitted into full membership in the Church according to the provisions of the Discipline for admission into the Church (¶ 403).

SECTION III.   AFFILIATED MEMBERSHIP

¶ 412. Members of our Church residing elsewhere for an extended period may upon application be enrolled as

Affiliated Members of The Methodist Church located in the vicinity of their temporary residence. Such membership shall entitle them to the privileges of that Church, to its pastoral oversight, to engage in its active service, and to hold office therein; but they shall be counted and reported only in the membership of their home churches.

SECTION IV. RESIDENT AND NONRESIDENT MEMBERS

¶ 413. All members living in the community, and those living elsewhere who continue to manifest interest in the Church from which they have moved, either by visitation, correspondence, or contributions, shall be reported as Resident Members of that Church.

¶ 414. When a member has resided in another community for at least one year, and has manifested no interest in continuing his membership in the Church from which he has moved, either by visitation, correspondence, or contributions, after attempts by correspondence or visitation to relate said member to a church in the community where he resides have proved ineffectual, he shall be reported as a Nonresident Member.

¶ 415. The Resident and Nonresident Members shall be counted in making the Annual Conference reports of total membership, but they shall be reported in separate columns, and only the number of Resident Members shall be considered in making the apportionments.

¶ 416. When a member is about to move to a new community, it shall be the duty of the Pastor to call upon him and ascertain his wishes as to his future church relations. In case a member moves without making such arrangements, the Pastor shall address an inquiry to such member together with a blank form for reply. Notice of such removal shall be sent to a Pastor near the place of residence of the member, together with return blank.

SECTION V. TRANSFER OF MEMBERSHIP

¶ 417. When a member desires a transfer of membership from one pastoral charge to another the Pastor, or if there is no pastor the District Superintendent, shall send a Certificate of Transfer to the pastor of the charge to which the member is to be transferred. Such certificate when requested shall not be refused except for reasons that justify judicial proceedings against such member. Notice of the issuing of a Certificate of Transfer shall be given to the member who is thus transferred. The person being thus transferred until received elsewhere shall be amenable to and shall support the Church issuing the Certificate of Transfer.

¶ 418. The Pastor of the Church to whom a Certificate of Transfer has been sent upon receiving the member thus transferred shall so notify the Pastor or District Superintendent issuing such Certificate. Upon receipt of such notice, the Pastor shall record in the Permanent Record of Membership, after the name of the person, the date of transfer and the name of the charge to which he has been transferred.

¶ 419. A Pastor shall upon request give a Certificate of Membership and of Recommendation to any member in good standing who wishes to unite with any other evangelical denomination.

SECTION VI.   TERMINATION OF MEMBERSHIP

¶ 420. Membership in the Church can be terminated only by withdrawal, expulsion, or death.

¶ 421. When any member in good standing proposes to withdraw from The Methodist Church, he shall communicate his purpose in writing to the Pastor of the Church in which his membership is held. On receiving such notice of withdrawal, the Pastor shall enter the fact of withdrawal upon the record of Church Membership. If requested, the Pastor shall give a "Letter of Withdrawal" to such member. Such withdrawal, however, may be retracted after obtaining the consent of the Pastor and the Quarterly Conference.

¶ 422. A member of the Church who has united without notice with another demonination shall be recorded as "Withdrawn."

¶ 423. A person who has been a Nonresident Member for three consecutive years, upon recommendation of the Membership Committee and by vote of the Quarterly Conference, shall no longer be counted in the statistical returns, and there shall be written after his name, "Removed without Certificate." But no name shall be so designated until the Pastor and the Membership Committee shall have made faithful effort to find and relate said member to a church in the community where he resides. Such member, upon application to the Pastor, may be restored to Resident Membership.

¶ 424. A member who has become neglectful of his vows and without good and sufficient reason has continuously absented himself from the services of the Church or has persistently refused to support the Church, shall be visited by the Pastor or Membership Committee and entreated to renew his vows, his loyalty to and his support of the Church.

If the member refuses to give heed to such entreaty, upon recommendation of the Pastor and Membership Committee, the Quarterly Conference may order written after his name "Removed without Certificate." Such person shall no longer be counted in the statistical returns. He may, upon application to the Pastor, be restored to the roll of membership.

IV. COMMITTEE ON MISSIONS

REPORT NO. 1. THE BOARD OF TEMPERANCE

Calendar No. 5. Adopted May 2. See Journal, Page 233.

Membership of committee, 135; present when report was adopted, 102; voting for adoption, 102.

I. CONSTITUTION

Article 1. In order to make more effectual the efforts of The Methodist Church in creating a Christian public sentiment, and in crystallizing opposition to all public violations of the moral law, there shall be a Board of Temperance, with headquarters in Washington, D. C. The Board of Temperance (hereinafter known as the Board) shall be incorporated in the District of Columbia under this title, and work under the following constitution. ·

Art. 2. The object and duty of this Board shall be to promote by an intensive educational program, including publication and distribution of literature, voluntary total abstinence from all intoxicants and narcotics; to promote observance and enforcement of constitutional provisions and statutory enactments which suppress the traffic in alcoholic liquors and in narcotic drugs; and to promote the speedy enactment of such legislation throughout the world.

It shall be the object and duty of this Board also actively to seek the suppression of salacious and corrupting literature and degrading amusements, lotteries and other forms of gambling, and in every wise way to promote the public morals.

Art. 3. The Board shall consist of one Bishop from each Jurisdictional Conference, elected by the Bishops of the Jurisdiction, one Minister and one Lay Member elected by each Jurisdiction, and ten members-at-large, of whom five shall be women, to be elected by the Board.

Art. 4. In the event of vacancies occurring in the Board by death or resignation, the Board may fill such vacancies by election, having regard for Jurisdictions, such elected members to serve until the meeting of the next Jurisdictional Conference of which they are members.

Art. 5.. The officers of the Board shall be a President, who shall be a Bishop, a Vice-President, a Second Vice-President, a Recording Secretary, a Treasurer, and an Executive Secretary.

The Board shall appoint an Executive Committee which shall consist of the officers of the Board, the Executive Secretary *ex officio*, and seven additional members selected by the Board. This Committee shall have the power *ad interim* to fill any vacancies in the field and office representatives and to transact such business as is necessary in the interim of the annual meetings and report the work annually for confirmation by the Board.

Art. 6. The Executive Secretary shall be elected quadrennially by the General Conference, and shall be *ex-officio* a member of the Board and its executive officer. In the event of his death or resignation, the Board shall have authority to fill the vacancy until the ensuing General Conference.

Art. 7. The Board shall hold an annual meeting, on a date and at a place to be determined by the Executive Committee of the Board, and other meetings as the work of the Board may require, and shall enact suitable bylaws governing the activities of the Board and its employees.

II. JURISDICTIONAL CONFERENCE BOARD OF TEMPERANCE

Art. 1. There may be in each Jurisdiction a Board of Temperance auxiliary to the General Board of Temperance hereinafter called the Board. The Board shall have headquarters to be located by the Jurisdictional Conference.

Art. 2. If and when established, the Board shall be composed of the active Bishops of the Jurisdiction and eighteen other members, six of whom shall be Ministers, and twelve Laymen, two of whom shall be young people under the age of twenty-five, five of whom shall be men, and five of whom shall be women, elected by the Jurisdictional Conference on nomination of the Committee on Temperance. This Committee shall have as a basis of choice one Minister and two Lay Members from each Annual Conference of the Jurisdiction, who shall be nominated by the Annual Conference on the recommendation of the Board of Temperance. Members of the General Board of Temperance resident in the Jurisdiction shall be *ex officio* members of the Jurisdictional Board.

Art. 3. The Board shall elect a President, Vice-President, and Recording Secretary at its first meeting following the meeting of the Jurisdictional Conference. It shall have an Executive Committee of seven members whose duties shall be determined by the Board. The Board shall meet annually at a time and place to be designated by its Executive Committee. Nine members shall constitute a quorum.

Art. 4. In case there should develop special conditions which, in the judgment of a Jurisdictional Board, would justify employment of a Jurisdictional Secretary for a particular time and purpose, such employment may be made subject to the approval of the General Board of Temperance.

III. CONFERENCE BOARDS

Art. 1. Each Annual Conference shall elect, on the nomination of the Cabinet, or otherwise as the Conference may direct, a Conference Board of Temperance consisting of not less than ten members and not more than eighteen members, with equal representation of Ministers and Lay members, two of whom shall be young people under twenty-five years of age, and the remainder of the Lay membership shall consist of an equal number of men and women, whose duty shall be to promote the work of the Board within the bounds of the Annual Conference, and with power to elect its own officers and raise its own funds; *provided* that no General Funds collected for the General Board shall be allocated to the Conference Board, except by action of the General Board.

IV. THE LOCAL CHURCH

Art. 1. Each Pastor should actively promote a vigorous program of temperance education in all departments of his Church or Churches, and members of both the Church and the Church School should be pledged to total abstinence.

Art. 2. Each Pastor should present the cause of Temperance on or near World Temperance Sunday and take a freewill offering for the General Board of Temperance.

REPORT NO. 2. AMERICAN BIBLE SOCIETY

Calendar No. 23. Adopted May 5. See Journal, Page 273.

Membership of Committee, 135; present when report was adopted, 97; voting for adoption, 97.

Your Committee on Missions recommends that the following paragraph be adopted as part of the *Discipline* of The Methodist Church to be placed as the Committee editing the *Discipline* may decide:

"To encourage the wider circulation of the Holy Scriptures and their translation, publication, and distribution in the United States and abroad, the American Bible Society shall be recognized as one of the Connectional missionary agencies of The Methodist Church and the General Commission on World Service and Finance shall make appropriate provision for sharing in its support."

REPORT NO. 3. BOARD OF HOSPITALS AND HOMES OF THE METHODIST CHURCH

Calendar No. 55. Adopted May 9. See Journal, Page 354.

Membership of Committee, 135; present when report was adopted, 111; voting for adoption, 111.

SECTION I. CONSTITUTION

¶ 812. *Name and Purpose.* There shall be a Board of Hospitals and Homes of The Methodist Church for the promotion and general advisory supervision of all hospitals or other organizations and institutions not affiliated with any other Board of the Church, for the care of the sick, homes for the aged and children, to preserve and promote the Christian character of these institutions and conserve their spiritual value as institutions of the Church.

¶ 813. *Incorporation.* The Board of Hospitals and Homes of The Methodist Church shall be duly incorporated according to the laws of any state selected by said Board.

¶ 814. *Management.* The management of the Board shall be vested in a Board of twenty-four managers, consisting of one Bishop from each Jurisdiction elected by the Bishops of the Jurisdiction, and one Minister, and two Lay Members, one of whom shall be a woman, to be elected by the Jurisdictional Conference.

¶ 815. *Officers.* (1) The Officers of the Board of Managers shall be a President elected by said Board from among the Bishops who are members of the Board of Managers, a Vice-President, a Recording Secretary, a Treasurer, elected by the Board of Managers for the quadrennium, and such other officers and agents as the Board of Managers may from time to time determine.

(2) The Board of Managers may elect an Executive Secretary and provide for his salary and necessary help. This Secretary shall be subject to the authority and control of the Board of Managers.

¶ 816. *Meetings.* (1) An Annual Meeting of the Board shall be held at such time and place as the Board may determine.

(2) An Executive Committee of eleven members shall be elected by the Board of Managers, such Committee to include the officers of the Board, and seven additional members to be elected by the Board, the Executive Secretary being a member of the Executive Committee *ex officio*. Seven members of the Executive Committee shall constitute a quorum.

¶ 817. *Affiliation and Membership.* Hospitals or homes, using the name Methodist and maintaining Christian standards, or looking to a Methodist constitutency for support, and not under the direct supervision of any other Methodist Board, may affiliate with the Board of Hospitals and Homes when the Trustees have been confirmed according to the *Discipline* of the Church.

¶ 818. *Financial Support.* The support of the Board of Hospitals and Homes shall be derived from the following sources:

1. From affiliated institutions.

2. A percentage of the American White Cross and Golden Cross Collections of not more than ten per cent.

3. From gifts, devises, wills, etc.

4. Such share in the General Benevolences of the Church as the General Conference may order.

¶ 819. *Powers.* (1) The Board may make surveys, disseminate information, suggest plans for securing funds, maintain a bureau for the purpose of securing experts in all lines of work, provide architectural data, and render assistance in the promotion and establishment of new institutions.

(2) The Board shall encourage and assist all institutions within its jurisdiction in attaining the highest possible professional, spiritual, and financial standards and shall set such required attainments as may be necessary to protect the aims and ideals of The Methodist Church.

(3) The Board of Managers is authorized to organize committees, set up financial accounts, assist institutions in efforts to secure funds, and perform such other functions as the normal work of the Board may require.

¶ 820. *The American White Cross and Golden Cross.* There shall be an American White Cross and Golden Cross Society of The Methodist Church which shall include in its responsibility the interests and activities formerly promoted by the White Cross Society of the Methodist Episcopal Church, and the Golden Cross Society of the Methodist Episcopal Church, South, which shall promote the hospital work under the direction of the Board of Hospitals and Homes, and shall collect moneys and other material assistance in providing hospitalization for the worthy and deserving poor, and the care of the aged and children. The enrollment shall be held annually on a date to be determined by the patronizing Annual Conference or Annual Conferences, funds raised in such enrollment to be used as directed by action of the Annual Conference in keeping with the policies of said society.

¶ 821. *Jurisdictional Conference Board of Hospitals and Homes.*

(1) There may be in each Jurisdiction a Board of Hospitals and Homes auxiliary to the General Board of Hospitals and Homes hereinafter called the Board. The Board shall have headquarters to be located by the Jurisdictional Conference.

(2) The Board shall be composed of the active Bishops of the Jurisdiction, eighteen managers, six of whom shall be Ministers, twelve Lay Members, six of whom shall be women, elected by the Jurisdictional Conference on nomination of the Committee on Hospitals and Homes, which shall have as a basis of choice one Minister and two Laymen, one of whom shall be a woman, from each Annual Conference of the Jurisdiction nominated by the Annual Conference Board of Hospitals and Homes. The Jurisdictional members and advisory members, if any, of the General Board of Hospitals and Homes shall be *ex officio* members of the Board.

(3) The Board shall elect a President, Vice-President, and Recording Secretary at its first meeting following the meeting of the Jurisdictional Conference. It shall have a General Committee of nine members. Its duties shall be determined by the Board. The Board shall meet annually at such time and place as may be fixed by its General Committee. Nine members shall constitute a quorum.

(4) The Jurisdictional Board shall be advisory to the Hospitals and Homes of the Jurisdiction in harmony with the general plans of the Church as outlined by the General Board.

(5) The Jurisdictional Board may elect a Secretary, who shall carry out the plans of the Church for the Board of Hospitals and Homes in co-operation with the Executive Secretaries of the General Board.

¶ 822. *Annual Conference Board of Hospitals and Homes.*

(1) Each Annual Conference may provide from within its bounds a Conference Board of Hospitals and Homes provided as follows:

(a) Seven members shall be elected, three from the ministerial and four from the Lay Members (two of whom shall be women) of the Conference.

(b) All Jurisdictional Members of each Conference shall be *ex officio* members of such Conference Board.

(2) Such Conference Board shall meet at least once during the regular session of each Annual Conference and shall seek, in co-operation with the Jurisdictional Board, to promote the interests of the Hospitals and Homes within the bounds of said Annual Conference. In those Conferences where civil law requires the election of Boards of Trustees and Managers by the Annual Conference, it shall be the duty of the Conference Board of Hospitals and Homes to nominate persons for such election.

(3) Each District Conference and Pastoral Charge shall appoint a Committee on Hospitals and Homes whose duty it shall be to promote the general interests of hospitals and homes of The Methodist Church and the particular hospitals and homes, to whose support they are respectively allocated.

(4) The American White Cross Society and the Golden Cross Society are authorized to make an enrollment of members and adherents, in order to secure their interest in and support of Hospitals and Home. The enrollment shall be held annually in every congregation, on a date to be determined by the patronizing Annual Conference or Annual Conferences. The week following Enrollment Sunday shall be known as Hospitals and Homes Week. Funds raised through said enrollment shall be used as directed by the Annual Conference in keeping with the policies of said societies.

REPORT NO. 4. GENERAL COMMISSION ON EVANGELISM

Calendar No. 56. Adopted May 9. See Journal, Page 354.

Membership of Committee, 135; present when report was adopted, 78; voting for adoption, 72; not voting, 6.

In response to the clamant call to evangelism contained in the Episcopal Address to the Uniting Conference, and, therefore, in order that this all-important subject may be lifted up and held in the place of central prominence throughout the Methodist communion, the Conference authorizes the creation of a Commission on Evangelism which shall devote itself to the promotion of evangelism in all its types and phases.

¶ . There shall be a General Commission on Evangelism composed of six Bishops, one from each Jurisdiction, elected by the Council of Bishops, one of whom shall be designated as Chairman of the Commission; the Executive Secretaries of the Board of Missions, the Executive Secretaries of the Board of Education, the Editor of the Church School Publications, the General Secretary of the Board of Lay Activities (who shall be members *ex officio*) ; and one Minister, one Layman, one Laywoman, and one Youth member from each Jurisdiction to be elected by each Jurisdictional Conference, and ten others, three of whom shall be evangelists to be elected by the Commission.

¶   . The Chairman of the General Commission on Evangelism shall make a report of the work of the Commission to the Council of Bishops and shall submit a program of work for the General Commission on Evangelism to the Council of Bishops for their consideration and approval.

¶   . The financial support of the General Commission on Evangelism shall be derived from the General Benevolence funds of the Church.

¶   . The General Commission on Evangelism shall have authority to set up standards for General and Conference Evangelists. The Bishop in charge of an Annual Conference may, by a two-thirds vote of the Conference, appoint members of an Annual Conference as general or approved evangelists, provided the Conference Commission on Evangelism recommends and the General Commission on Evangelism approves.

¶   . The headquarters of the General Commission on Evangelism shall be determined by the Commission.

¶   . The General Commission on Evangelism shall elect an Executive Secretary, and provide such other help as may be needed.

¶   . The annual meeting of the General Commission on Evangelism shall be held at such time and place as the Commission may determine.

¶   . The General Commission on Evangelism is charged with the responsibility of creating an intelligent interest and passion for evangelism and promoting all types and phases of evangelism among the ministers and laity throughout the entire Church.

¶   . The General Commission on Evangelism shall cooperate as far as possible in the training of our Ministry for leadership in the field of Evangelism and in co-operation with the various agencies of the Church in creating a literature to serve the cause of Evangelism.

¶   . The General Commission on Evangelism shall promote the practice of intercession and family worship and stimulate the enlistment of inactive members in worship and Christian service.

¶   . Each Jurisdictional Conference may have a Commission on Evangelism which shall promote the program of the General Commission on Evangelism.

¶ . Each Annual Conference shall provide for a Conference Commission on Evangelism which shall promote the program as outlined by the General Commission on Evangelism.

¶ . The Annual Conference Commission on Evangelism shall be authorized to recommend to the presiding Bishop for appointment as Conference Evangelists such members of the Conference as meet the requirements of that work. Such evangelists shall make report of their work and labors and their financial receipts to their respective Commissions as soon as may be required.

REPORT NO. 5. BOARD OF MISSIONS AND CHURCH EXTENSION

Calendar No. 71. Adopted May 9. See Journal, Pages 338 and 378

Membership of Committee, 135; present when report was adopted, 105; voting for adoption, 81; voting against adoption, 19; not voting, 5.

SECTION I. THE AIM OF MISSIONS

¶ 826. The supreme aim of Missions is to make the Lord Jesus Christ known to all peoples in all lands as their divine Saviour, to persuade them to become His disciples, and to gather these disciples into Christian Churches; to enlist them in the building of the Kingdom of God; to co-operate with these Churches; to promote world Christian Fellowship, and to bring to bear on all human life the spirit and principles of Christ.

SECTION II. INCORPORATION

¶ 827. *Article* 1. (1) There shall be an incorporated Board of Missions and Church Extension of The Methodist Church, hereinafter called the Board. It shall conduct its operations through three administrative divisions, each of which shall be incorporated. The Board and its Divisions shall be domiciled and incorporated in such state or states as the Board may select. Subject to the limitations hereinafter specified each of the incorporated divisions shall be subject to the supervision and control of the Board, and all shall be under the direction and control of the General Conference of The Methodist Church in all things not inconsistent with the constitution and laws of the United States and of the states of incorporation.

(2) The Board shall have control of all the work former-

ly controlled and administered by the following: The Missionary Society, the Board of Foreign Missions, the Board of Home Missions and Church Extension, the Woman's Foreign Missionary Society, the Woman's Home Missionary Society, the Wesleyan Service Guild, and the Ladies' Aid Societies of the Methodist Episcopal Church; the Board of Missions, including the Woman's Missionary Society, the Woman's Board of Foreign Missions, the Woman's Board of Home Missions, and the Woman's Missionary Council, and the Board of Church Extension of the Methodist Episcopal Church, South, and the Board of Missions of the Methodist Protestant Church, and such other corporations or agencies of the General Conference which do similar work, but this recital shall not be construed as exclusive.

SECTION III.   CONSTITUTION

¶ 828, *Article 1. Name and Object.* The name of this organization shall be the Board of Missions and Church Extension of The Methodist Church. Its objects are religious, philanthropic and educational, designed to diffuse more generally the blessings of Christianity in every part of the world, by the promotion and support of all phases of missionary and Church extension activity in the United States and other countries; to promote missionary intelligence, interest and zeal throughout The Methodist Church, and to aid in Christianizing personal life and the social order in all lands and among all peoples. Other agencies of The Methodist Church shall conduct work in foreign fields only in co-operation with the Board of Missions and Church Extension.

¶ 829, *Art. 2. Authority.* The Board shall have authority to regulate its own proceedings in accordance with its Constitution and Charter; to buy, acquire, receive by gift, devise, bequests of property, real, personal, and mixed, and to hold, sell and dispose of property; to secure, appropriate and administer funds for its work; to sue and be sued; to elect the necessary officers and members of its staff, remove them for cause and fill vacancies; to make bylaws in harmony with the *Discipline* of The Methodist Church and the Charter of the Board, and to administer its affairs through its respective Divisions, and shall be clothed with the power and shall have the right to do any and all things which shall be authorized by its Charter.

¶ 830, *Art 3. Board of Managers.* (1) The management and disposition of the affairs of the Board, the making and administration of appropriations, and all other activities, shall be vested in a Board of Managers.

(2) The Board of Managers shall be elected quadrennially and shall be composed of all active Bishops of The Methodist Church resident in the United States; one Minister, and three Laymen, two of whom shall be women, from each Jurisdiction for each 450,000 members, or major fraction thereof, in the Jurisdiction, elected by the Jurisdictional Conference on nomination of its Committee on Missions and Church Extension; *provided*, that no Jurisdiction, in addition to its active Bishops, shall have fewer than two Ministers and six Laymen, four of whom shall be women, and two Youth members, one young man and one young woman, under twenty-five years of age, from each Jurisdiction, elected by the Jurisdictional Conference. In nominating and electing such Jurisdictional members the Jurisdictional Conference, through its Committee on Missions and Church Extension, shall have as a basis of choice one Minister and one Layman designated by each Annual Conference of the Jurisdiction, on nomination of its Committee on Missions and Church Extension; three Laywomen nominated by each Conference Woman's Society of Christian Service within the Jurisdiction from which number the Woman's Jurisdictional Society shall nominate to the Jurisdictional Conference the number to be elected to the Board; and one young man and one young woman from those nominated by the Youth Organization of each Annual Conference in the Jurisdiction. Vacancies in the Board of Managers shall be filled by the Bishops of the Jurisdiction in which the vacancies occur *ad interim*, having regard to the various classifications of members.

(3) The Board of Managers shall meet annually, at such time and place as it may determine. Forty members shall constitute a quorum. Special meetings may be called by the President on order of the Executive Committee or may be ordered by the Board of Managers.

(4) The Board of Managers shall elect quadrennially a President, who shall be the presiding officer, three Vice-Presidents, one upon nomination of each of the three administrative divisions and other Vice-Presidents if the Board shall so determine, a Recording Secretary, and such other officers as it may need. Their duties shall be those usually performed by such officers. The Board may also elect annually such committees as may be necessary to the carrying on of its business.

(5) The Board shall elect annually upon nomination of the respective Divisions an Executive Committee of thirty-seven members: nine members from the Division of Foreign Missions; nine members from the Division of Home Mis-

sions and Church. Extension; eighteen women from the
Woman's Division of Christian Service—a majority of
whom shall constitute a quorum. The President of the
Board shall be the Chairman of the Executive Committee.
This Executive Committee shall exercise the powers of the
Board *ad interim.* For the more efficient performance of
its duties the Executive Committee shall constitute from its
own body three subcommittees on (1) Foreign Missions,
(2) Home Missions and Church Extension, (3) Woman's
Division of Christian Service—composed of the members
elected from these Divisions, and such other subcommittees
as may be found necessary for the carrying on of the work,
having regard to equal representation of the Divisions.
These subcommittees shall have such powers as the Executive Committee shall delegate to them.

¶ 831, *Art.* 4. The duties of the Board shall be:

A. To have the general oversight of the missionary and
church extension program of The Methodist Church, with
special reference to its development and expansion.

B. .To determine the broad lines of policy and program,
and through the respective Divisions, to carry out the program.

C. To determine fields to be occupied and the nature of
the work to be undertaken; to build and maintain churches,
hospitals, homes, schools, parsonages, and other institutions
of Christian service; and to enlist, train and support the
workers.

D. To safeguard for each Division the fullest measure of
autonomy consistent with presenting a united front and a
mutually-supporting program.

E. To foster, as between the respective Divisions, united
fellowship, planning and action.

F. To elect and commission the executive officers of the
respective Divisions, on nominations of the Divisions.

G. To appropriate and expend money for the support of
all work under its care, to receive and properly administer
all properties and trust funds coming in any manner into
its possession for missionary or other purposes, except as
hereinafter provided.

H. To assist in the organization of and in the maintenance of co-operative relations with the Boards, committees
and other agencies of the General Conference; also with the
Jurisdictional, Central and Annual Conference missionary
boards, committees and agencies; likewise with interdenominational and other missionary agencies in the home and
foreign fields.

Section 2. The Board shall provide for the correlation

and harmonization of the work of its various Divisions, Departments, and Bureaus. It shall do any and all things consistent with its Constitution and Charter to accomplish the purpose of The Methodist Church in establishing missionary and Church extension work at home and abroad.

¶ 832, *Art. 5. Divisions.* The Board shall conduct its activities through three Administrative Divisions and a Joint Division of Education and Cultivation, namely:

(1) Division of Foreign Missions,
(2) Division of Home Missions and Church Extension,
(3) Woman's Division of Christian Service,
(4) Joint Division of Education and Cultivation.

¶ 833, *Art. 6. Executive Secretaries.* The Board shall elect one or more Executive Secretaries for each of the three Administrative Divisions, and two (one man and one woman) for the Joint Division of Education and Cultivation. Said Secretaries shall be nominated by their respective Divisions, and shall be elected by the Board.

These Secretaries shall have co-ordinate power. They shall be subject to the direction of the Board and of their respective Divisions. Their salaries shall be fixed and paid as the Board may determine. They shall be employed exclusively in the work of the Board, promoting the missionary cause by such activities as the Board may approve. The Executive Secretaries shall be members *ex officio* of the Board.

¶ 834, *Art. 7. Treasurers and Trust Officers.* (1) The Board shall elect a Treasurer for the Division of Foreign Missions, a Treasurer for the Division of Home Missions and Church Extension, and a Treasurer for the Woman's Division of Christian Service, upon nomination by the respective Divisions. The Board may also provide the Treasurers with such assistants as it may deem necessary.

(2) The Treasurers shall be responsible for receiving the funds of the Board and of the respective Divisions, holding the same in a safe depository and disbursing them according to the regulations of the Board or the respective Divisions upon proper order. The Board or the respective Divisions shall designate depositories for their funds.

(3) The Board shall elect one or more Trust Officers who shall be charged with the responsibility of receiving, holding and properly disbursing the returns from all trust funds, endowments and securities of the Board according to the regulations of the Board.

(4) All properties, trust funds, permanent funds and other special funds and endowments now held and administered by the several organizations merging into the Board

of Missions and Church Extension shall be carefully safeguarded and administered in the interest of those persons and causes for which said funds were established; *provided,* that the properties, trust funds, permanent and endowment funds shall be transferred to the Board of Missions and Church Extension from other Boards and Departments of Boards only when such transfers may be made according to the laws of the states where the several Boards are chartered and upon the recommendation of the respective Divisions. Funds of the three administrative Divisions and their preceding corporations and societies, which are subject to appropriation, shall be appropriated only upon recommendation of the respective Divisions and for the work for which the respective Divisions are responsible.

(5) The Treasurers and Trust Officers of the Board shall be bonded by the Board in such sums and upon such conditions as the Board may determine. Their books shall be audited annually by certified public accountants chosen by the Board, and their reports shall be presented to the Board at each annual meeting.

¶ 835, *Art. 8. Joint Committee on Personnel.* There shall be a Joint Committee on Personnel of the several Divisions of the Board, which shall be responsible for the enlistment, cultivation, training and recommendation of candidates for missionary service at home and abroad.

¶ 836, *Art. 9. Missionaries.* (1) Standards and qualifications of Missionary candidates for home and foreign service, including Deaconesses, shall be determined by the Board on the recommendation of the Joint Committee on Personnel.

(2) A person shall be constituted and acknowledged as a Missionary or Deaconess and receive support as such from the funds of the Board only when such person has been approved by the Board and has been assigned to some definite field.

SECTION IV. DIVISION OF FOREIGN MISSIONS

¶ 837, *Article 1.—Organization.* (1) Within the Board there shall be a Division of Foreign Missions, hereinafter called the Division, which shall be one of the co-ordinate administrative Divisions of the Board.

(2) The Division shall be incorporated as hereinbefore provided.

(3) The Division shall be composed as nearly as possible of one-third of the active Bishops, and the remaining members shall be as follows: one-half of the Ministers, one-half of the Laymen, one-third of the Laywomen, and one-third

of the Youth members of the Board. The Division shall meet annually at the time of the meeting of the Board, and at such other times as it may deem necessary. ! .. ,.

¶ 838, *Art. 2.—Authority.* (1) The Division shall have authority to regulate its own proceedings; to select fields of labor; to accept, train, commission, and maintain workers; to sue and be sued; to buy and sell property; to secure and administer funds for the support of all work under its charge; to solicit and accept contributions subject to annuity; to make appropriations for its work; to select the necessary officers; to remove any officer for cause and fill vacancies; to make Bylaws in harmony with its Charter and Constitution and with the Constitution of the Board; and to recommend Constitutions and Bylaws for Jurisdictional and Annual Conference Boards related to the Division.

(2) The Division shall administer and promote the work of Missions outside the United States and its dependencies formerly administered by the Board of Foreign Missions of the Methodist Episcopal Church, and the work outside of the United States of the Board of Missions, General Section, of the Methodist Episcopal Church, South, and the Board of Missions of the Methodist Protestant Church, except such activities of the Woman's Convention of the Methodist Protestant Church, and shall have committed to it all the general foreign missionary activities of The Methodist Church in foreign fields.

(3) This Division shall estimate the needs of the work under its care and shall present the same to the Board for consideration and approval. It shall present to the Board for appointment Missionaries for its various fields of service, who have been approved by the Personnel Committee. '

(4) The Division, in co-operation with the Departments of Work in Foreign Fields of the Woman's Division, shall formulate plans and policies for the administration of Foreign Missions, shall consider lines of work, fields to be occupied, and various enterprises, and make recommendations to the Board for approval. There shall be an Inter-Division Committee in Foreign Work with equal representation from the Division of Foreign Missions and the Department of Foreign Work of the Woman's Division of Christian Service, which shall co-ordinate and correlate the programs and policies for foreign fields subject to the approval of the Board.

(5) This Division shall recommend to the Board for appropriation an emergency or contingent fund not to exceed five per cent of the total amount appropriated for the Divi-

sion. This Division shall not recommend to the Board for appropriations including the emergency fund for a fiscal year more than the total amount received for this Division from all sources during the preceding fiscal year.

¶ 839, *Article 3.—Foreign Field Committees, Budgets, and Estimates.* (1) In a Foreign Mission field of the Board each Annual Conference, Mission Conference, or Mission shall have a Field Committee. This Committee shall consist of the following members: The Resident Bishop, the Mission Treasurers, and the Mission Superintendents. It shall also include such other persons as the Annual Conference, Mission Conference, or Mission may elect, provided there be an equal number of missionaries of the Division of Foreign Missions and of the Woman's Division of Christian Service and where possible an equal number of national men and women.

This Field Committee shall be the unifying and co-ordinating agency for both the Division of Foreign Missions and the Foreign Department of the Division of Woman's Christian Service.

The personnel of this Committee shall be subject to the approval of and shall be responsible to the Board for the administration of funds provided by the Board. The Committee shall elect its own Chairman.

(2) In a mission field, where there is a Central Conference in which there is an Executive Board or Council of Co-operation duly constituted, the budget estimates for the development of the work, prepared by the various Field Committees, shall be presented to the Division of Foreign Missions and to the Division of Woman's Christian Service after approval by said Executive Board or Council of Co-operation. The budgets shall be presented, Conference by Conference, and by projects within the Conference. These estimates shall be prepared and submitted separately for the General and Woman's Work in such form as may be required, and shall be the basis for appropriation of mission funds.

(3) In Provisional Central Conferences, where there is no Executive Board or Council of Co-operation, the estimates shall be sent direct to the Division of Foreign Missions and to the Division of Woman's Christian Service from the Field Committee of each Annual Conference; Mission Conference or Mission.

¶ 840, *Art. 4.—Administration of Missions.* (1) Foreign fields outside of an Annual Conference working under the care of the Board of Missions not having met the requirements for the organization of a Mission Conference may be organized into a Mission.

(2) The Mission shall meet annually, and shall be composed of all regularly appointed Missionaries and Mission Traveling Preachers, with Lay Members, the number of whom and the mode of their appointment each Mission shall determine for itself.

(3) The Bishop, or in his absence one of the Superintendents chosen by ballot by the Mission, shall preside in the annual meeting. This meeting shall exercise in a general way the functions of a District Conference. It shall have power to license suitable persons to preach and to pass upon the characters of preachers not members of an Annual Conference, to receive on Trial Mission Traveling Preachers, and to recommend proper persons for Deacons' and Elders' Orders. The Bishop or President shall at the Annual Meeting assign the Missionaries and Mission Traveling Preachers to the several Charges for the ensuing year; *provided,* that no Missionary shall be transferred to or from a Mission without previous consultation with the Board.

(4) The work of a Mission shall be divided, when necessary, into districts, over each of which a Missionary shall be placed as Superintendent. It shall be the duty of the Superintendents, in the absence of the Bishop, to take general supervision of the work in his District with all its interests, and to report the state of that work and its needs to the Bishop in charge and to the Board.

(5) For the consideration of financial and other matters relative to the policies of the Board, and the work of the Missionaries, the Missionaries of each Mission shall hold an annual Missionaries' Meeting and report their proceedings to the Board. In the absence of a Bishop one of the Missionaries shall be elected by ballot to preside.

¶ 841, *Art. 5.—Mission Fields in Which There are Autonomous or Independent Methodist Churches.* (1) The missionaries of The Methodist Church appointed to work in Mission fields where there are autonomous or independent Methodist Churches, while retaining their membership in their home Local Churches and Annual Conferences and without impairing their relationship to the Board of Missions and Church Extension and the appointing authority of The Methodist Church, shall, while in service in such fields, be free to accept the rights and privileges of membership in the Local Churches and the Annual Conferences of the national Methodist Churches as offered to them by such Churches.

(2) The Missionaries in such mission fields may be organized into Mission Councils under constitutions approved by the Board of Missions and Church Extension.

(3) A Mission Council shall be authorized to elect and send one of its members to the General Conference of The Methodist Church as its representative. Such representative shall have his expenses paid from the General Conference funds and shall be accorded the privilege of sitting with the Committee of the General Conference with the right to speak when questions relating to our work in foreign fields are being considered.

(4) Wherever desired by an autonomous Methodist Church and the missionaries working in relation to such Church, there shall be a Central Council composed of members of the autonomous Church and the missionaries of the Board working in that field, under a constitution approved by the Board of Missions and Church Extension. This Central Council shall be the agency through which the Board shall co-operate with such autonomous Church.

. (5) Mission Councils and Central Councils shall not be constituent parts of Central Conferences, but many maintain fraternal relations with neighboring Central Conferences.

¶ 842, *Art. 6.—Lay Missionaries.* Lay Missionaries of the Board, men and women, shall be associate members of their Mission, Mission Conference, or Annual Conference, and be permitted all privileges of the floor and the right to vote on all questions not Ministerial or constitutional and shall be eligible for election to Mission or Conference Committees.

SECTION V. DIVISION OF HOME MISSIONS AND CHURCH EXTENSION

¶ 843, *Article 1.—Organization.* (1) Within the Board there shall be a Division of Home Missions and Church Extension, hereinafter called the Division, which shall be one of the co-ordinate administrative Divisions of the Board.

(2) The Division shall be incorporated as hereinbefore provided.

(3) The Division shall be composed as nearly as possible of one-third of the active Bishops, and the remaining members shall be as follows: one-half of the Ministers, one-half of the Laymen, one-third of the Laywomen, and one-third of the Youth members of the Board. The Division shall meet annually at the time of the meeting of the Board.

¶ 844, *Art. 2.—Authority.* (1) The Division shall have authority to regulate its own proceedings; to select fields of labor; to accept, train, commission, and maintain workers; to sue and be sued; to buy and sell property; to secure and administer funds for the support of all work under its charge; to solicit and accept contributions subject to annuity; to make appropriations for its work; to select the necessary officers; to remove any officer for cause and fill vacancies; to make Bylaws in harmony with its Charter and Constitution, and with the Constitution of the Board; and to recommend Constitutions and Bylaws for Jurisdictional and Annual Conference Boards related to the Division.

(2) The Division shall elect its own Chairman, Vice-Chairman, and Recording Secretary, and such committees as it may deem necessary.

(3) The Division shall meet at the time of the annual meeting of the Board and may meet at other times at the call of the Chairman.

(4) The Division shall have two Sections: The Section of Home Missions, and the Section of Church Extension, with one or more Executive Secretaries for each section, having co-ordinate authority in their respective fields of administrative responsibility.

(5) The Board, upon nomination and with the joint concurrence of the Executive Secretaries of the Division, may elect Superintendents of Departments and Directors of other organizational units as needs may require.

¶ 845, *Art. 3.—Functions.* The Division shall have general supervision and administration of the work of Home Missions and Church Extension in the United States of America and its territories, not including the Philippine Islands; the deepening of the spiritual life of the Church; the promotion and direction of movements relative to the spiritual meaning and work of Methodism; and administration of all Donation Aid, Loan Funds, and Endowments contributed and established for the work of Church Extension, except such as may be administered by the Jurisdictional and Annual Conferences. The plans and policies of the Division shall be submitted to the Board for approval.

¶ 846, *Art. 4.—Revenue.* The revenues for the work of the Division shall be derived from the amounts apportioned to the several Annual Conferences by the General Conference or its authorized agency, and gifts, donations, devises, bequests, annuities and special gifts for the work of this Division.

· ¶ 847, *Art. 5.—Section of Home Missions.* (1) The Section of Home Missions shall have the following departments, plus such organizational units as the Board, upon the recommendation of the section, may determine:

(a) Department of City Work,
(b) Department of Town and Country Work,
(c) Department of Goodwill Industries,
(d) Department of Negro Work.

(2) The Secretary or Secretaries of this Section shall supervise, administer, and promote the work of Home Missions. They shall communicate to any Bishop assigned to the presidency of an Annual Conference, Mission Conference, or Mission in the time of his presidency, such information as the Section of Home Missions may possess touching said Annual Conference, Mission Conference, or Mission for the guidance of the Bishop in administration.

A. Department of City Work

¶ 848. The Department of City Work shall promote missionary work in cities with a population of ten thousand or more. It shall aid in making surveys in cities with special reference to the religious conditions of foreign-speaking, Negro, or other groups; the necessary location and adaptation of church buildings, and the programs required for needy and congested communities. It shall also aid in the organization and development of adequate religious centers in city territory. It shall administer such appropriations as may be committed to it by the Division. All askings for missionary work in cities of ten thousand population or more shall require the review and recommendation of the Department or its Superintendent.

¶ 849, *Article 1.* The Department of City Work shall promote the organization of City Missionary Societies wherever possible and practicable.

Art. 2. A City Missionary Society may be organized under such name and control as it may determine, wherever, in cities of at least ten thousand population, there are two or more Pastoral Charges, and where, in the judgment of the Bishop or Bishops and District Superintendent or Superintendents concerned, it is deemed advisable. The purpose of such a society is to promote evangelization and to co-ordinate the work of the church in such cities and contiguous communities. All Bishops, District Superintendents, and Superintendents of Missions or Mission Conferences having jurisdiction within the geographical territory covered by the Society, and all Pastors therein, shall be *ex officio* members of said Society or its Board of Managers. Each Quarterly Conference shall be entitled tô at least one Lay representative in the Society or Board.

Art. 3. The City Society may include in its work the organization of Church Schools, and the organization (but not the constituting) of Churches, the aid of weak Churches, the acquisition of real estate, and the erection of buildings, the adaptation of downtown Churches to their altered environment, the securing and holding of endowments for the City Society and dependent Churches, the conducting of missions among foreign-speaking and other needy peoples, the development of well-organized open-air evangelism, the maintenance of kindergartens and industrial schools, the promotion of social and settlement work, including services rendered in connection with juvenile court cases, the support of rescue missions and of institutions for the relief of the sick and the destitute. A City Society may also devise plans for promoting the connectional life of Methodism, and for co-operation and federation with other Evangelical Churches.

Art. 4. A City Society may elect, either from within or from without its membership, not more than three persons, members of The Methodist Church, as members of the Quarterly Conference of any Church under its supervision or the object of its benefactions. The persons so chosen shall enjoy all the rights and privileges of Quarterly Conference membership, when so approved by the Quarterly Conference.

Art. 5. In Annual Conferences where there exists a City Society having an executive officer giving his entire time to the work, it is recommended that said executive officer shall be invited into consultation with the Bishop and District Superintendents in the consideration of the appointments that affect missions or Churches administered or aided by said Society.

Art. 6. A City Society shall have authority in the territory covered by its Constitution or Charter, to make appropriations to the Pastoral Charges, and to collect and disburse moneys for all the objects contemplated in its organization.

Art. 7. It is recommended that any church within its territory expecting to receive aid for building or improvement from the City Society, be required to secure, as a condition to receiving such aid, the approval of the City Society with respect to location, plans and methods of financing.

Art. 8. A City Society, in order to receive appropriations from the Board through the Divisions, shall meet the following conditions: (a) It shall be organized according to the *Discipline;* (b) it shall have an Executive Committee meeting at least once every quarter; (c) it shall be actively at work; (d) it shall have made a report as required by the Department of City Work; (e) it shall raise annually by collections or otherwise an amount at least equal to that appropriated to it by the Board, exclusive of appropriations made for work among foreign-speaking peoples.

Art. 9. It shall be the duty of the District Superintendent whose district covers in whole or in part a city, or contains communities contiguous to each other in which there are two or more Charges, to co-operate with the Department of City Work in securing wherever practicable, the organization of a City Society as herein provided. Charges in communities adjacent to a city, and not attached to any other Society, may be included in the Society of the adjacent city.

Art. 10. It shall be the duty of each pastor whose Charge lies within the territory of a City Society, once each year to present the interests of the Society to his congregation, take a collection for the same, or provide for the amount apportioned in the Benevolent Budget, and report the amount received to the Annual Conference.

Art. 11. The Annual Conferences are directed to take such friendly interest in the City Societies within their bounds as shall promote their efficiency and facilitate their work; to arrange for the publication of their reports in the Conference *Journal,* and to provide a separate column in connection with the statement of the Benevolence collections for the itemized report of the offerings for this work.

Art. 12. All City Societies shall be auxiliary to the Division, and shall make each year to the Department of City Work a detailed statement which shall include: (1) Number of Ministers or Missionaries supported in whole or in part, the amount paid to each, and the kind of work in which each is engaged; (2) expenses of administration; (3) the total amount raised by the Society and how expended. The report shall also include such other items as the Department shall require.

¶ 850, *Article* 1. The Department of City Work shall promote the Council of Cities of the Board of Missions and Church Extension. The Council shall be composed of the Secretary, the Superintendent and members of the Department, and two delegates from each organized City Society. The Council may be convened annually, or at such other times as the Department may determine.

Art. 2. The purpose of the Council shall be to promote the study of City Church work, with all that relates to a better understanding of the religious needs of urban communities. It shall present methods for city surveys, practical methods of Church development and administration, having in view the city-wide responsibility of the Church. It shall seek by papers and discussions to present the social, economic, industrial, and spiritual needs of the cities.

B. *Department of Town and Country Work*

¶ 851. The Department of Town and Country Work shall promote all phases of the work of the Church in rural territory and in places of less than ten thousand population; conduct surveys and research studies of rural conditions and use the findings for more effective rural Church work; develop a co-operative procedure among all Church and other agencies that serve rural people; promote among our Ministers and in colleges and theological schools the study of town and country life; co-operate with the allies of the Church in improving the economic, social, educational, and religious life of the people in town and rural areas.

(1) The Department shall promote a constructive policy for supplying rural Churches with weekly public worship either by the service of regular Ministers, or competent religious Lay workers; develop a system for training the officeholders in the Local Church, and devise a plan for providing adequate financial support for rural Ministers.

(2) The Department shall give instruction, encouragement and support to Annual Conference Boards of Missions and Church Extension in the prosecution of Conference plans for carrying forward the work of Christianity in village and rural communities, and to the Jurisdictional Boards in their regional movements and methods for establishing the Church and preaching the gospel of Christ to all the people in their territory.

(3) The Department shall review and administer maintenance askings from the field for town and country work, and recommend to responsible organizations, after a careful survey of the field, essential denominational exchanges, mergers, or other co-operative plans to prevent overlapping by religious organizations.

(4) There shall be set up in each Annual Conference a Town and Country Life Commission composed of the District Superintendents, a representative from each of the participating Boards, including the Woman's Division of Christian Service. This Commission shall meet annually at least four weeks before the session of the Annual Conference. At this meeting the Commission shall outline a program of work to be presented to the participating Conference Boards and seek to co-ordinate all the work of the various Boards.

(5) The Town and Country Life Commission may promote the organization of Town and Country Societies where such societies seem to be needed, these societies to select their own name, determine their own organization and prosecute such work as they deem best in co-operation with the Department of Town and Country Work.

C. Department of Goodwill Industries

¶ 852. The Section of Home Missions shall maintain a Department of Goodwill Industries, the purpose of which shall be to provide for the religious, educational, social, and industrial welfare of the handicapped and unfortunate. This Department shall consist of the Executive Secretary or Secretaries of the Section of Home Missions, and sixteen other persons, three-fourths of whom shall be actively associated with Goodwill Industries, and one-half of whom shall be executives of autonomous auxiliary Goodwill Industries. Members of the Department shall be elected by the Division, on joint nomination of the Executive Secretary or Secretaries of the Section of Home Missions; *provided*, however, that the Executives of local Goodwill Industries to be nominated for election to the Department shall be selected from among nominations submitted by auxiliary Goodwill Industries.

The Department shall promote and establish Goodwill Industries in various centers; shall review missionary askings and administer appropriations for Goodwill Industries; shall endorse and assist only those local Goodwill Industries which are organized and conducted according to its established standards, rules, and regulations, and shall urge them to co-operate in programs of service promoted by other boards, divisions, sections, departments, or agencies of The Methodist Church.

The Department may conduct national and regional institutes, and such other special training activities as will help to develop the specialized leadership required for the direction of Goodwill Industries.

D. Department of Negro Work

¶ 853. The Division shall organize a Department for work among Negroes which shall co-operate with the Boards and agencies of the Central Jurisdictional Conference; and with the several agencies and Boards of the Colored Methodist Episcopal Church as authorized in the Plan of Union.

E. Bilingual Work

¶ 854. (1) Bilingual Work in the United States, except in organized Bilingual Conferences and Missions, shall be administered through the English-speaking Conferences under the supervision of the Section of Home Missions.

(2) To insure a nation-wide sense of responsibility, it shall be the duty of the District Superintendent and Pastor to remind the Quarterly Conference of each English-speaking Methodist Church in America of its missionary obligation to any Bilingual peoples resident in the charge.

F. *Section of Church Extension*

¶ 855. The work of Church Extension shall be conducted under the following provisions and regulations:

(1) The Section of Church Extension shall encourage the erection of churches in communities not already adequately supplied; shall assist in the building of churches, parsonages and other mission buildings where assistance is most needed; and shall give special attention to church architecture.

(2) The Board shall appropriate money for the various types of work in the field and the conduct of the office; it shall determine what amount should be donated or loaned to each applicant; and do such other business as may be legitimate and proper for it to do.

(3) Aid in the form of donations in the erection, remodeling, and repairing of churches and parsonages shall be made available primarily to clearly missionary projects. Assistance in the development of other types of Church property, if and when granted, shall be provided as loans.

(4) All applications for Church Extension aid shall be made through the Annual Conference Board of Missions and Church Extension, or a similar Board in the Jurisdiction. Grants shall be made by the Board or the Executive Committee upon recommendation of the Section and the Secretary or Secretaries.

(5) In granting donations to churches and parsonages the Board shall require from the trustees of each aided Church an obligation, which shall be a lien upon the property involved, for the return of the amount donated, with lawful interest thereon in the event that the work shall cease or the property shall be alienated from The Methodist Church. In case of relocation, the Board's investment and lien may be transferred to the new property.

(6) When a donation is granted by the Board where the property involved is held in trust by the Board of Trustees of the Annual Conference no lien shall be required by the Board; *provided* the Trustees of the Annual Conference agree with the approval of the Annual Conference that the property shall not be conveyed without protecting the

Church Extension claim, and that appropriations to the Conference may be withheld if need be to insure such protection.

(7) The Board shall raise and administer a loan fund which shall be held separate from funds secured for general distribution. It shall consist of all money or other properties specially donated or bequeathed to the Board as a Permanent Fund, subject to annuity or otherwise, where the gift is intended to assist in the building and financing of Churches and parsonages. It shall be used only as loans on adequate security to be determined by the Board.

(8) It shall be lawful for the Board to accept contributions to its funds from any person or persons capable of making the same subject to annuity, payable to the persons making such donations, or other contractual beneficiaries; *provided*, however, that all amounts so received shall be loaned by the Board on adequate security; and *provided*, further, that the aggregate amounts of annuities that the said Board shall assume to pay shall never be allowed to exceed the annual interest receivable on the loans made. Expenses incurred in the administration of such funds shall be charged to and defrayed out of the income received therefrom. The requirement of the Charter of the Board of Church Extension of the Methodist Episcopal Church, South, which states that, "the aggregate of annuities that the Board shall assume to pay shall never be allowed to exceed one-half of the annual interest receivable on the loans made by said Board," shall be binding and in effect on all annuities made by it.

(9) There shall be a fund known as the "Revolving Fund" which shall consist of such sums as may be released from the General Fund or appropriated by the Board or the Executive Committee, all returned donations, and such other funds as may be made available. Loans from the Revolving Fund shall be made to churches and parsonages upon such terms and conditions as the Board or the Executive Committee shall from time to time determine.

(a) The Section shall organize and conduct a service to the field known as the Department of Finance and Debt-Raising for the purpose of securing funds for new church building enterprises or debt-burdened Churches and of assisting and guiding Churches in developing effective budget and other financial plans. Churches receiving this service shall make such payment therefor as the Section shall determine.

(b) A fund may be set up by the Section to be secured from gifts and legacies and the income therefrom to be used in supporting the work of the Department of Finance and Debt-Raising.

(c) The Board of Church Extension of the Methodist Episcopal Church, South, the Department of Church Extension of the Board of Home Missions and Church Extension of the Methodist Episcopal Church and the Board of Missions of the Methodist Protestant Church shall continue to operate under the present charters of these Boards until all endowments, trust funds and annuity contracts can be transferred by legal processes to the Board, so that these funds, endowments and annuities may be administered "in the interest of those persons and causes for which these funds were established." The General Conference can make the necessary changes in the Constitution of the several Boards in order to make practical this regulation.

Inter-Division Committee on Home Work

¶ 856. There shall be an Inter-Division Committee on Home Work which, in co-operation with a similar committee from the Woman's Division of Christian Service, shall co-ordinate and correlate plans and policies for Home Missions, and arrange for such co-operative activities and joint projects as may be mutually acceptable.

SECTION VI. THE WOMAN'S DIVISION OF CHRISTIAN SERVICE

¶ 857, *Article 1.—Organization.* (1) Within the Board there shall be a Woman's Division of Christian Service, hereinafter called the Division, which shall be one of the co-ordinate administrative Divisions of the Board.

(2) The Division shall be incorporated as hereinbefore provided.

(3) The Division shall be composed of all the women members of the Board, one Bishop from each Jurisdiction and one-third of the Youth representatives. This Division may increase its working force by electing quadrennially advisory members not to exceed twenty. These advisory members shall not be members of the Board nor serve on the Board Committees.

(4) The Woman's Division shall include in its scope the interests and activities formerly promoted and administered by the Woman's Foreign Missionary Society, the Woman's Home Missionary Society, the Wesleyan Service Guild, the Ladies' Aid Societies of the Methodist Episcopal Church; the types of work and interests included in the Board of Missions, Section of Woman's Work, the Woman's Missionary Council and former Boards and Societies (the Woman's Missionary Society, the Woman's Board of For-

eign Missions, and the Woman's Board of Home Missions) of the Methodist Episcopal Church, South; such activities of the Woman's Convention of the Methodist Protestant Church as logically fall within the organization and all Deaconess work carried on by the Uniting Churches within the United States.

¶ 858, *Art. 2.—Authority.* The Woman's Division shall have authority to regulate its own proceedings; to select fields of labor; to accept, train, commission and maintain workers; to sue and be sued; to buy and sell property; to secure and administer funds for the support of all work under its charge; to solicit and accept contributions subject to annuity; to make appropriations for its work; to select the necessary officers; to remove any officer for cause and fill vacancies; to make bylaws in harmony with its Charter and Constitution and with the Constitution of the Board; and to recommend Constitutions and Bylaws for Jurisdictional, Conference, District and local organizations related to the Woman's Division.*

¶ 859, *Art. 3. Purpose.*—The purpose of the Woman's Division shall be to develop and maintain Christian work among women and children at home and abroad; to cultivate Christian family life; to enlist and organize the efforts of Christian women, young people, and children in behalf of native and foreign groups, needy childhood, and community welfare; to assist in the promotion of a missionary spirit throughout the Church; to select, train, and maintain Christian workers; to co-operate with the Local Church in its responsibilities, and to seek fellowship with Christian women of this and other lands in establishing a Christian social order around the world.

¶ 860, *Art. 4.—Officers.* (1) The Division shall nominate

---

* Pending further action by the General Conference and in Churches where there is not a united program under the Woman's Division provision is hereby made for Ladies' Aid Societies to organize and operate in harmony with provisions formerly made in the *Discipline* of the Methodist Church within the Charge, she shall then become a promotion of the financial, social, and spiritual interests of the Church, Ladies' Aid Societies, or Societies of similar designation and purpose, may be organized in the Pastoral Charge, which Societies shall be under the control of the Quarterly Conference.

2. The President of a Ladies' Aid Society shall be elected by the Society and confirmed by the Quarterly Conference. If a member of The Methodist Church within the Charge, she shall then become a member of the Quarterly Conference if approved by it for membership therein. It shall be her duty to present to the Quarterly Conference a report of her Society, together with such other information as the Quarterly Conference may require and she may be able to give.

a Vice-President of the Board, who shall be Chairman of the Division. It shall also nominate for election by the Board, its Administrative Secretaries, its Treasurer or Treasurers, its trust officer or officers. Vacancies shall be filled on nomination of the Division. Such other officers as the Division may need it shall provide. The Division shall determine the powers and duties of its officiary and the remuneration of any employed officers and workers.

(2) The Treasurers and trust officers of the Division shall be bonded in such sums and upon such conditions as the Division may determine. The accounts of these officers shall be audited annually by a certified accountant.

Departments

¶ 861, *Art. 5.—Organization.* (1) The Division shall be organized into two administrative Departments:

(a) Department of Work in Foreign Fields.

(b) Department of Work in the United States and its dependencies, excepting the Philippine Islands.

There shall be a Department of Christian Social Relations and Local Church Activities.

(2) There shall be such bureaus, committees, and other organizational units in each Department as shall best promote its interest. The functions of these, other than hereinafter determined, shall be defined by the Division.

(3) There shall be a Secretary or Secretaries in each Department. The number and duties of the Secretaries shall be determined and defined by the Division.

(4) The cultivation and promotion of the work of the Women's Division shall be under its direction. Plans and policies for the same shall be carried out by the Woman's Secretary of the Joint Division of Education and Cultivation.

¶ 862, *Art. 6.—The Department of Work in Foreign Fields* shall promote the work of Missions outside the United States and its dependencies.

(1) There shall be a Standing Committee composed of the Administrative Secretary or Secretaries of the Department of Work in Foreign Fields and the Jurisdictional representatives of the Department of Work in Foreign Fields.

(2) There shall be a Committee which, in conjunction with a Committee of equal representation from the Division of Foreign Missions, shall consider policies, programs, and estimates which come from Field Committees to the Divisions. See ¶ 839. They shall report their recommendations regarding correlation and co-ordination to the Board of Missions and Church Extension for final action.

. There shall also be a Standing Committee of similar composition which in co-operation with the Secretaries of Education and Cultivation shall correlate the missionary program at the home base.

(3) ·There shall be a Standing Committee on the World Federation of Methodist Women. The Department shall create such other Committees as the needs of the work may demand.

· *The Department. of Work in the United States. and Its Dependencies* shall supervise and promote the Home Missionary work of ·the Division. This Department shall have a Standing Committee on Work in Home Fields. This Committee, in conjunction with a Standing Committee in the Division of Home Missions and Church Extension, shall constitute an Inter-Division Committee on Home Work which shall. co-ordinate and correlate the programs and policies in the Home Fields. In the Department of Work in Home Fields there shall be a Bureau of Deaconess Work. The Department shall create such other Bureaus and Committees for the administration of the various types of work as the needs may demand.

The Bureau of Deaconess Work

.1. The office of Deaconess is hereby authorized in The Methodist Church.

. .(a) All Deaconess Work in Foreign fields shall be under the supervision of the Central Conference or Provisional Central Conferences concerned. All deaconess work in Europe shall be under the supervision of the Central Conferences or Provisional Central Conferences in Europe.

' (b). All Deaconess work in the United States and its dependencies shall be under the supervision of the Bureau of Deaconess Work of the Woman's Division of Christian Service.

.2. All properties, trust funds, permanent funds, other special funds and endowments now held and administered by or for the several forms of administration of Deaconess Work under the three Uniting Churches shall be carefully safeguarded and administered by the several forms of administration in the interest of those persons and causes for which said funds were established.

3. The Bureau of Deaconess Work shall be composed of a Bishop, chosen by the Council of Bishops, the Secretaries of the Department of Home Missions of the Woman's Division, the Secretaries of the Deaconess Bureau, and two persons chosen by each Jurisdictional Deaconess Association, one of whom shall be a Deaconess member of that Association, and

the other an officer of the Jurisdictional Woman's Society of Christian Service.

4. *Candidates.* A candidate shall meet the following requirements: She shall be a woman having the necessary qualifications who has been led by the Holy Spirit to devote herself to full-time service of the Church. She shall be a member of The Methodist Church in good standing between the ages of twenty-three and thirty-five and shall have shown fitness for such service by some form of active Christian work. She shall be recommended by the Quarterly Conference of the Charge of which she is a member. She shall have completed the required course in a standard high school, and at least two years of accredited college work or its scholastic equivalent, and shall have had two years of specialized preparation in an accredited training school, college, or other educational institution approved by the Bureau.

5. A Sabbatical year, a part of which shall be spent in special study, may be granted with full or part salary upon recommendation of the Secretary of the Bureau of Deaconess Work and the Jurisdictional Deaconess Association.

6. A Deaconess shall be retired at the age of sixty-five unless by a two-thirds vote of the Association her term of service is lengthened, and shall receive a pension proportioned to her years of service.

7. A Deaconess uniform shall be prescribed, but the wearing of it shall be optional.

8. *Jurisdictional Deaconess Association:*

(a) All Deaconesses working in Annual Conferences, Mission Conferences or Missions of the Jurisdiction shall be members of the Association. The Association shall elect its own officers.

(b) One Bishop, elected by the Bishops of the Jurisdiction, one minister from each Conference, elected by the Conference, and the President of each Conference Woman's Society of Christian Service of the Jurisdiction shall be members of the Association.

(c) The Jurisdictional Deaconess Association shall recommend to the Bureau of Deaconess Work the transfer of Deaconesses to and from its Jurisdiction. It shall also recommend Deaconesses who are eligible for retirement or relief. It shall recommend the renewal of certificates or licenses of Deaconesses annually to the Bureau of Deaconess Work and shall make a report to this Bureau. It shall recommend to the Committee on Candidate Work and Training of the Woman's Division all applicants for Deaconess work.

(d) Annual Conference Deaconess Boards may be set up in all Conferences where five or more Deaconesses are working. All licensed Deaconesses of the Conference shall be members of the Conference Deaconess Board. Two District Superintendents of districts in which there is Deaconess work, and two representatives of the Conference Society of the Woman's Board of Christian Service shall be members of the Conference Deaconess Board. It shall approve annually the standing of all Deaconesses within the Conference and report the same to the Jurisdictional Deaconess Association.

(e) The Conference Deaconess Board shall have the oversight of all Deaconess work within the bounds of the Conference. It shall have authority to license Deaconesses who have been recommended by the Bureau of Deaconess Work, approve annually their standing as Deaconesses, arrange for their consecration at the Annual Conference by the presiding Bishop, and transfer Deaconesses from one Annual Conference to another within the Jurisdiction. This provision shall not apply where the Deaconess is otherwise appointed. Officers and Committees shall be elected as the needs of the work require. The Conference Deaconess Board shall meet annually, preferably at the seat of the Annual Conference.

(f) The appointment of Deaconesses to their respective fields of labor shall be made by the Bishop presiding at the Annual Conference upon recommendation of the Conference Deaconess Board of the Jurisdictional Deaconess Association.

(g) The minutes of the Conference Deaconess Board shall be reported to the Annual Conference for publication in the Conference Journal, to the Jurisdictional Deaconess Association, and to the Bureau of Deaconess Work.

(h) All Deaconesses shall receive financial compensation on either an allowance or a salary basis, the minimum of which shall be fixed by the Bureau of Deaconess Work.

(9) *Department of Christian Social Relations and Local Church Activities.*

The Department of Christian Social Relations and Local Church Activities shall supervise and promote the work of the Division along the lines of community service and social relations.

It shall seek to make real and effective the teachings of Jesus as applied to individual, class, racial, and national relationships. It shall endeavor to enlist the participation of Church women in such questions as have a moral or religious significance or an important bearing on public welfare. It shall seek to inspire in the women of the local Church a greater devotion to its spiritual interests; to cooperate with its educational agencies, and to develop Christian fellowship and concern for the financial responsibilities of the Church.

¶ 863, *Art. 7.—Committees.* (1) The Division shall be empowered to create such Bureaus and Committees as the work may demand. There shall be an Executive Committee, a Committee on Candidates, a Committee on Trust Funds and Investments, a Committee on Finance and Estimates.

(2) The cultivation and promotion of the Woman's Christian Service organization shall be under the direction of the Division, and plans and policies for the same shall be carried out by the Woman Secretary or Secretaries of the Joint Division of Education and Cultivation.

¶ 864, *Art. 8.—Funds.* (1) The Funds of the Division shall be derived from annual pledges or dues, special memberships, devises, bequests, annuities, special offerings, gifts and collections taken in meetings held in the interest of the organization. All undesignated funds shall be allocated by the Finance Committee of the Division on a definite percentage basis to the work of the Department of Foreign Missions and the Department of Home Missions of the Division, and shall be forwarded through Conference Treasurers to the Treasurers of the Division.

(2) All properties, trust funds, permanent funds, and other special funds and endowments now held and administered by the several organizations merging into the Woman's Division of Christian Service shall be carefully safeguarded and administered in the interests of those persons and causes for which said funds were established.

(3) The annual appropriations for any year shall not exceed the income of the preceding year.

¶ 865. *The Jurisdictional Woman's Society of Christian Service.* If and when the Jurisdictional Conference establishes a Jurisdictional Board of Missions and Church Extension, there shall be a Jurisdictional Woman's Society of Christian Service auxiliary to the Woman's Division of Christian Service of the Board.

The Jurisdictional Society shall be composed of thirty-six members elected by the Jurisdictional Conference, on nomination of its Woman's Jurisdictional Society, which shall have, as a basis of choice, three officers from each Conference Society of the Jurisdiction nominated by the Conference Society at its meeting preceding the session of the Jurisdictional Conference; also any members of the Woman's Division of Christian Service living within the Jurisdiction, two Bishops chosen by the Bishops from the Jurisdiction. One Secretary of the Jurisdictional Division of Foreign Missions, and one from the Jurisdictional Division of Home Missions and Church Extension, and one from the Jurisdictional Board of Education shall be members of the Jurisdictional Society.

The Society shall elect a President, a Vice-President, Recording Secretary and Treasurer or Treasurers at its first meeting following the meeting of the Jurisdictional Conference. The Society shall meet annually at such time and place as it may determine. Nineteen members shall constitute a quorum.

The Society shall have authority to promote its work in accordance with the program and policy of the Woman's Division of Christian Service; it shall have supervision of all institutions within the Jurisdiction which are the responsibility of the Woman's Conference Societies of the Jurisdiction.

The Jurisdictional Society shall elect Secretaries, Superintendents and Treasurers as the work may demand in accordance with the plans of the Woman's Division of Christian Service.

Auxiliary to the Jurisdictional Society there shall be Conference Woman's Societies of Christian Service; in the district and local Churches there shall be adult, young people's, and children's societies auxiliary to the Woman's Conference Society of Christian Service.

¶ 866. *The Assembly.* There shall be a delegated body termed the Assembly which shall meet at such time and place as the Division may determine. The purpose of the Assembly shall be to promote and deepen interest in the work of the Woman's Division. The Division shall determine the composition, functions and power of the Assembly.

SECTION VII.   JOINT DIVISION OF EDUCATION AND CULTIVATION

¶ 867, *Article* 1. The Joint Division of Education and Cultivation shall be composed of six Bishops, one from each Jurisdiction; six men and two women from the Division of Foreign Missions, elected by that Division; six men and two women from the Division of Home Missions and Church Extension, elected by that Division; eight women from the Woman's Division of Christian Service, elected by that Division. In all these selections there must be due regard to equitable representation from the Jurisdictions. This Division shall undergird with Education and Cultivation the total program of the Board.

¶ 868, *Art.* 2. The Division shall publish, sell, and circulate books, literature and periodicals for all the work of the Board and shall be responsible for editing and preparing the same. It shall co-operate with the Board of Education and all agencies of The Methodist Church and with interdenominational agencies in the preparation and distribution of missionary literature.

¶ 869, *Art.* 3. The Division shall edit, publish, and distribute throughout the Church such periodicals for missionary education as the needs may require.

¶ 870, *Art.* 4. The Division shall promote Missionary Councils, Conventions, Institutes and other meetings throughout the Church for the purpose of developing a missionary spirit, spreading missionary information, and acquainting the Church with the plans and policies of the Board. The Department shall seek the co-operation of Jurisdictional and Annual Conferences, District Superintendents, Pastors, Missionary Societies, and other agencies of the Church.

¶ 871, *Art.* 5. The Division shall have charge of all plans for cultivating missionary giving, placing missionary specials, and for promoting the missionary program of the Church; *provided,* however, that all such plans shall be subject to and in harmony with the general financial system of The Methodist Church as adopted by the General Conference.

¶ 872, *Art.* 6. The Division shall co-operate with the Inter-Board Committee on Missionary Education of the Board of Missions and Church Extension and the Board of Education.

¶ 873, *Art.* 7. The Division shall also co-operate with Theological Seminaries and Departments of Missions in the conduct of Missionary Institutes in such institutions, and shall develop other plans for affording missionary information and inspiration to students.

¶ 874, *Art.* 8. The Woman Secretary and Woman Editor of this Division shall carry out the plans and policies of the Woman's Division of Christian Service in promoting organizations for the various age groups in local Churches, Districts, Conferences, and Jurisdictions; in providing missionary education for Woman's, Young Woman's, and Children's Societies; in creating, editing and publishing such periodicals, books, and leaflets as the work of the societies may necessitate. This Division shall co-operate in all plans necessary for the efficiency of the Christian Service Societies in the Jurisdictions, Conferences, Districts, and Churches.

SECTION VIII

¶ 875, *Art. 1.—Secretarial Council.* There shall be a Secretarial Council composed of all the Executive Secretaries of the four Divisions of the Board. The Council shall elect its own Chairman annually from the Divisions in rotation, and shall have regular meetings at such times and places as the Council or the Board may determine. It shall be the duty of this Council to recommend plans for the correlation and harmonization of the work of the various Divisions. Each Division shall keep the Council fully informed concerning its activities and plans. The Council shall prepare items of business for presentation to its four Divisions and to its committees.

¶ 876, *Art. 5.—Revenues.* (1) The income of the Divisions of the Board, exclusive of the Woman's Division of Christian Service, shall be derived from apportionments, assessments, or askings distributed to Jurisdictions, Annual Conferences, and Pastoral Charges by the budget-making agency of the General Conference in such manner as the General Conference may prescribe, from Church Schools, gifts, donations, freewill offerings, annuities, bequests, specials, and other sources from which Missionary and Benevolence funds are usually derived, in harmony with the *Discipline* of The Methodist Church and actions of the General Conference.

(2) Askings shall be received from the fields and budgets prepared by the Division of Foreign Missions and the Division of Home Missions and Church Extension in such manner as the Board may prescribe, consistent with its Constitution and its Charter; and this combined budget shall be presented to the budget-making agency of the General Conference on the basis of an equal division between Home and Foreign Missions; *provided* that in case the budget-making agency shall consider the needs of one Division as imperative it may allow a ten-per-cent increase for that Division for a year.

(3) The Board shall not appropriate for the regular maintenance of its work in any one year more money than was received by it for appropriation the previous fiscal year.

(4) The funds for the maintenance of the work of the Woman's Division of Christian Service shall be derived

from annual pledges or dues, special memberships, devises, bequests, annuities, special offerings, gifts, and collections taken in meetings in the interest of the work of the Division; *provided* that the funds thus raised shall be appropriated to the work established by the several uniting organizations comprising the Woman's Division, or work hereafter to be entered upon by the Woman's Division. All undirected funds shall be divided on a percentage basis to the work of the several departments. All funds, except those designated for local purposes, shall be forwarded through Conference Treasurers to the Treasurer of the Board for the Woman's Division of the Board.

(5) The funds for the Joint Division of Education and Cultivation shall be appropriated by the Board and charged proportionately to each Division.

¶ 877, *Art. 3.—General Missionary Council.* There shall be a General Missionary Council composed of the members of the Board and the Secretaries, Assistant Secretaries, Superintendents, Directors, and other members of the full-time employed staff of the Board of Missions and Church Extension, Jurisdictional Boards of Missions and Church Extension, and Annual Conference Boards of Missions and Church Extension. This Council shall meet biennially at such time and place as the Board or the Council itself shall determine. The Council shall study and discuss all matters relating to the work of Missions and Church Extension as promoted by the General, Jurisdictional, and Conference Boards; it shall disseminate missionary information and inspiration throughout the Church.

¶ 878, *Art. 4.—Co-operation with Other Boards and Agencies.*

A. *Joint Committee on Religious Education in Foreign Fields.*

For the purpose of more effectively promoting religious education outside the United States there shall be a Joint Committee on Religious Education in Foreign Fields composed of the Executive Secretary of the Division of the Local Church of the Board of Education and seven other persons appointed by the Division; a Secretary of the Division of Foreign Missions of the Board of Missions and Church Extension and three other persons appointed by the Division; and a Secretary of the Woman's Division of Christian Service of the Board of Missions and Church Extension and three other persons appointed by the Division.

There shall be an Executive Secretary of the Joint Committee who shall be Secretary of the Board of Missions and Church Extension for Religious Education in countries outside the United States. The Secretary shall be elected by the Board of Missions and Church Extension upon nomination of the Joint Committee.

The Joint Committee shall meet annually, and at such other times as the committee shall itself determine, and shall make report of its actions to the Boards of Education and Missions and Church Extension at their annual meetings.

The budget of the Joint Committee shall be prepared by the Committee subject to the approval of the co-operating Boards.

B. *Interboard Committee on Missionary Education.*

For the purpose of promoting effective co-operation between the Board of Missions and Church Extension and the Board of Education in missionary education there shall be an Inter-Board Committee between the two Boards, composed of the Executive Secretary of the Division of the Local Church, the Executive Secretary of the Division of Church School Publications, the Executive Secretary of the Division of Educational Institutions of the Board of Education, and five other persons to be appointed by that Board, and an equal number from the Board of Missions and Church Extension which shall include the following—the Secretaries of the Division of Education and Cultivation; two Secretaries from the Division of Foreign Missions, two from the Division of Home Missions and Church Extension, and two from the Woman's Division of Christian Service, to be nominated by the several Divisions.

The duties of this Committee shall be: (a) To develop a unified program of missionary education for all age-groups in the Local Church and in the colleges, universities, and theological seminaries; (b) to represent the two Boards in disseminating missionary information through Church School literature and in the preparation of curricular material on Missions; and (c) to co-operate in the publication of books for missionary education in the Church School.

There shall be an Executive Secretary of the Committee who shall be elected by the Division of the Local Church of the Board of Education, on nomination of the Inter-Board Committee, and who shall be the Secretary of the Division of the Local Church of the Board of Education for Missionary Education in the Church School. The Committee shall have a budget for its work provided by the two Boards as they may decide.

The Division of the Local Church may, in co-operation with other missionary agencies, through the Inter-Board Committee on Missionary Education, develop co-operative plans for the Missionary Education of children, young people, and adults.

C. The Board may co-operate with other Agencies and Boards of The Methodist Church in such manner as the Board may determine. It shall co-operate with such National and International Missionary and such other Agencies as the Board may determine.

SECTION IX. JURISDICTIONAL BOARDS

¶ 879, *Article* 1. The Plan of Union gives the Jurisdictional Conference authority "to establish and constitute Jurisdictional Boards of the Church as the needs may appear." However, in the interest of uniformity in the several Jurisdictions, it is suggested that the Jurisdictional Conferences give serious consideration to the following:

¶ 880, *Art.* 2. The Board shall be composed of the active Bishops of the Jurisdiction, and eighteen managers, half of whom shall be women, elected by the Jurisdictional Conference, on nomination of the Committee on Missions and Church Extension, which shall have as a basis of choice one Minister, one Layman and one Laywoman from each Annual Conference of the Jurisdiction, the men upon the nomination of the Annual Conference Board of Missions and Church Extension, and the women upon the nomination of the Woman's Conference Society of Christian Service. The members of the General Board residing within the Jurisdiction shall be *ex-officio* members of the Jurisdictional Board.

¶ 881, *Art.* 3. The Jurisdictional Board shall elect a President, Vice-President, and Recording Secretary at its first meeting following the meeting of the Jurisdictional Conference. The Board shall meet annually at such time and place as it may determine. The Bishops of the Jurisdiction shall fill all *ad interim* vacancies, having regard for the various classifications.

¶ 882, *Art.* 4. The Jurisdictional Board shall have authority to promote the entire program of Missions and Church Extension in harmony with the general plans of the Church as outlined by the Board in all its Divisions, and such other duties as the Jurisdictional Conference shall provide.

¶ 883, *Art.* 5. The Jurisdictional Board may elect two Secretary-Treasurers, a man and a woman, with such assistants as may be needed, who shall carry out the total program of the Board in all its Divisions.

¶ 884, *Art.* 6. The Jurisdictional Board shall have such revenue as the Jurisdictional Conference may apportion to the Annual Conferences over and above the apportionments approved by the General Conference and such other revenues for the Woman's Division as the Woman's Annual Conference Societies of Christian Service may pledge.

SECTION X.   ANNUAL CONFERENCE BOARDS

¶ 885, *Art.* 1. (1) The Annual Conference Boards of Missions and Church Extension shall be auxiliary to the General Board and to the Jurisdictional Conference Board and shall be composed of one Lay member from each District and an equal number of Ministers, elected quadrennially, and an additional five members, should the Conference desire them.

(2) The Board shall elect its own officers, hold its Annual Meeting at the call of the President, and other meetings may be called by the President, or any three members, on due notice. The transactions of the year shall be reported by the President to the Annual Conference and a detailed statement of all disbursements of missionary aid within the Conference shall be printed in the Annual Conference Minutes. The President shall have charge of the Annual Conference Anniversary of the Board.

(3) The Board, in making payments to meet appropriations, may send drafts to the Secretary of the Conference Board, payable to the Treasurer; but duly authorized City Societies or Town and Country Societies may receive their remittances direct.

(4) The Board, in its activities, may pursue either of the following systems:

(1) The Conference Board shall review, approve, or adjust the askings of the District Superintendents for the maintenance program within the bounds of the Annual Conference before they are presented to the Board. In making final decisions on all askings from the several Annual Conferences, the Board shall take into account the comparative missionary needs of each project and its permanent value of service to the entire Church.

(2) The Conference Board shall estimate annually the amount that may be necessary for the support of Conference Missionary Work and also the amount necessary for Conference Church Extension, and shall report both estimates to the Conference Commissions on Budget (or Benevolences). The amount raised on these appor-

tionments shall be administered by the Board and applied respectively to Home Missions and to Church Extension. The work of the Board shall be subject to the approval of the Annual Conference. The Board shall seek to cover all unoccupied territory in the Conference by the establishment and support of Missions, but Missions shall be established only with the consent of the Bishop in charge. The Board shall co-operate with the General Board, and the Jurisdictional Conference Board of Missions and Church Extension, in carrying out the policies and promoting the movements which they propose and adopt for any and all phases of the work of Missions and Church Extension.

¶ 886, *Art. 2.—Administration of Missions.* (1) Work outside the boundaries of an Annual Conference or work among racial groups within the bounds of Annual Conferences now cared for by the Board of Missions and Church Extension not having met the requirements for the organization of a Mission Conference may be organized into a Mission. A Mission shall be composed of all regularly appointed Missionaries and Mission Traveling Preachers, with Lay members, the number of whom, and the mode of their appointment, each Mission shall determine for itself.

(2) A Mission shall meet annually at the time and place appointed by the Bishop in charge, who shall preside, if present. In the absence of the Bishop the Superintendent of the Mission shall preside. The Presiding Officer shall bring forward the regular business of the meeting, and arrange the work. This Annual Meeting shall possess in a general way the functions and powers of a District Conference.

(3) The Bishop in charge of a Mission may appoint a Superintendent of the Mission, or as many Superintendents as, in the judgment of the Bishop, may appear necessary or wise and for whom support has been provided. The Bishop shall determine the Groups or Charges over which the respective Superintendents shall have supervision.

(4) In case of a Mission using more than one foreign language, and extending over a wide geographical territory, the Bishop may assemble in Annual Meetings the members of the Mission on a racial or geographical basis. The Mission may delegate to such subgroups the work of examining and recommending to an Annual Conference candidates for Admission on Trial, under such limitations as the *Discipline* provides.

(5) In Missions using a language other than English examinations of Local and Traveling Preachers shall be held by the Mission, and certified to an Annual Conference.

The Missions also shall make recommendations for Reception on Trial in an Annual Conference.

¶ 887, *Art. 3.—Missionary Secretaries.* The Conference Board of Missions and Church Extension shall elect annually a Conference Missionary Secretary, who shall carry out all plans for Missionary Education except those committed to the Conference Woman's Society of Christian Service. He may be a part-time or a full-time salaried officer at the discretion of the Board, and his salary and expenses, if any, shall be paid by the Conference Board. The Conference Board shall also provide for the selection of a District Missionary Secretary in each District of the Conference, who shall labor under the direction of and in co-operation with the Conference Missionary Secretary. The Conference Missionary Secretaries and the District Missionary Secretaries, after proper election or nomination, shall be appointed by the Bishop in charge of the Conference.

¶ 888, *Art. 4.—District Missionary Institutes.* There shall be held annually in each District a District Missionary Institute for purposes of missionary education and the spreading of missionary information among the people. These Institutes shall be promoted by the Conference Missionary Secretary in co-operation with the District Missionary Secretaries and the District Superintendents. These Institutes shall be exclusively missionary in character and separated from all other causes and interests and the program shall deal exclusively with missionary matters. The plans of the Board of Missions and Church Extension and the Jurisdictional Board concerning mission study, the circulation of the missionary periodical and other literature, and all other plans and policies of missionary education and information of the Church shall be presented at these Institutes. Speakers provided by the General and Jurisdictional Boards shall be used for the programs of these Institutes in so far as possible.

SECTION XI. LOCAL CHURCH COUNCILS

¶ 889, *Article 1.* There shall be in each local Church a Council of Missions and Church Extension whose membership shall be as follows:

1. Pastor or Pastors.
2. General and Missionary Superintendents of the Church School.
3. Two Youth representatives to be nominated by the Youth organizations of the Church and elected by the Quarterly Conference.
4. At least two Laymen, elected by the Quarterly Con-

ference, and at least two Laywomen, elected by the Local Church Woman's Society of Christian Service.

It shall be the duty of the Pastor to convene the members of this Council who shall elect such officers and Committees as may be determined.

¶ 890, *Art. 2.* It shall be the duty of the Local Church Council of Missions and Church Extension, aided by the Pastor, to co-ordinate all phases of missionary promotion in the local Church; to provide for the diffusion of missionary information among the members of the Church and congregation, the Church School and Youth organizations, through sermons, missionary addresses, special programs; to appoint representatives from the local Church to District or Annual Conference missionary meetings for the regular presentation of the cause of Missions and Church Extension; to institute mission study classes, to see that each Church School observes the offerings on the fourth Sunday for the Home and Foreign Missionary Enterprise; to support the Pastor in his plans for raising funds for missions; to co-operate with the work of the Woman's Society of Christian Service, and in every possible way to develop a missionary-minded Church which will co-operate loyally with the Board.

SECTION XII. ENABLING ACT FOR AD INTERIM ADMINISTRA-
TION OF THE BOARD OF MISSIONS AND CHURCH EXTENSION ·

¶ 891. The work of the Board of Missions and Church Extension shall be administered through eleven corporate bodies: The Board of Home Missions and Church Extension of the Methodist Episcopal Church operating under a Charter of the state of Pennsylvania; The Board of Foreign Missions of the Methodist Episcopal Church operating under a Charter of the state of New York; The Board of Church Extension of the Methodist Episcopal Church, South, operating under a Charter of the state of Kentucky; the Woman's Foreign Missionary Society of the Methodist Episcopal Church, operating under a Charter of the state of New York; the Woman's Home Missionary Society of the Methodist Episcopal Church, operating under a Charter of the state of Ohio; the Board of Missions of the Methodist Episcopal Church, South, operating under a Charter of the state of Tennessee; The Woman's Missionary Society of the Methodist Episcopal Church, South, operating under a charter of the state of Tennessee; the Woman's Board of Foreign Missions of the Methodist Episcopal Church, South, operating under a Charter of the state of Tennessee; the Woman's Board of Home Missions of the Methodist Episcopal Church, South, operating under a Charter of the state of Mississippi; the Board of Missions of the Methodist Protestant Church, operating under a Charter of the state of Pennsylvania; and the Board of Hospitals, Homes and Deaconess Work of the Methodist Episcopal Church, operating under a Charter of the state of Illinois. The Trust, Permanent, Endowment and Annuity Funds and Properties now held and administered for specific purposes under the Charters of these Corporations shall be safeguarded, controlled and administered by them in the "interest of those persons and causes for which these funds were established."

¶ 892. During the period between the time of the Uniting Conference and the time when the Board shall be constituted according to the Plan of Union and begin to assume its functions, the work of the Board of Missions and Church Extension of The Methodist Church shall be administered as follows:

The Missionary and Church Extension Work now being administered by the Boards enumerated in ¶ 891 shall be administered by the respective organizations now in existence. The terms of office of the present officers and members of these Boards shall continue until their successors shall have been elected by the Jurisdictional Conferences and until the new Board of Missions and Church Extension shall be assembled and duly organized.

¶ 893. In order to secure co-operation between the Boards, and in order to assist in administering the total program under their care, and in order to suggest any further steps for the merger and administration of the Board in The Methodist Church, there shall be a Joint Committee composed of five representatives of the Woman's Foreign Missionary Society of the Methodist Episcopal Church; five representatives of the Home Missionary Society of the Methodist Episcopal Church; five representatives of the Board of Foreign Missions of the Methodist Episcopal Church; six representatives of the Board of Home Missions and Church Extension of the Methodist Episcopal Church; and three representatives of the Board of Hospitals, Homes and Deaconess Work of the Methodist Episcopal Church; six representatives of the Board of Missions of the Methodist Protestant Church; six representatives of the Board of Church Extension of the Methodist Episcopal Church, South; eighteen representatives of the Board of Missions of the Methodist Episcopal Church, South.

This Committee shall be called together by the President

of the first-named organization at such time and in such place as shall be decided upon by a majority of the Presidents of the organizations named.

The Committee may meet as a whole as it determines, and members of the Committee carrying on the same class of work may meet separately for consultation and co-operation.

¶ 894. The constitutions of the Boards mentioned in ¶ 891, adopted by the respective General Conferences of the three Churches, shall remain as the Constitution of the eleven corporations until the General Conference shall order otherwise.

REPORT NO. 6. METHODIST PARTICIPATION IN CHINA CIVILIAN RELIEF

Calendar No. 72. Adopted May 9. See Journal, Page 340.

Membership of Committee, 135; present when report was adopted, 107; voting for adoption, 107.

In China, one of the greatest mission fields of Methodism, a terrible war has been raging. Invading armies have passed over hundreds of thousands of square miles, leaving behind them destroyed cities, destitute millions, and human suffering perhaps unparalleled in history. Millions of our brothers and sisters in China are in sore distress.

In this terrible crisis in the life of a nation among whose people we have so long labored, The Methodist Church must extend the hand of helpfulness. Our Missionaries and Churches in China are serving to the best of their ability, but the need is so overwhelming that their efforts must be supplemented by unusual liberality on the part of the Methodists of America. The urgency of the situation calls for immediate response. Therefore,

Resolved, That this Uniting Conference: 1. Calls upon the members and constituents of all Methodist Churches in the name of Christ to share in self-denial with those who are so desperately in need of food, clothing, shelter, medical attention, help to become self-supporting, and the other ministries of the Church;

2. Upon our Bishops, District Superintendents, Presiding Elders, and Pastors to interpret the appalling situation, and to lead all our congregations to include relief for China in their current plans and programs and to co-operate in community efforts for China Relief.

3. We recognize the Church Committee, as constituted by the Federal Council of Churches of Christ in America, the Foreign Missions Conference of North America, and China

Famine Relief, U. S. A. Inc., as the agency through which The Methodist Church co-operates with other denominations in a united endeavor for China Relief.

4. Contributions may be sent direct to the Church Committee for China Relief, or to the Foreign Missionary agencies of the Church, which will transmit all money received for the purpose to the Church Committee for China Relief. We request the Board of Missions, the World Service Commission, and other missionary agencies of the Church to recognize contributions for China Relief by the issuance of World Service Honor Vouchers, or through any method by which such recognition is given for special contributions.

5. We name the following as a Committee which, in consultation with the Church Committee for China Relief, will plan to make the above recommendations effective: Herbert Welch, Ivan Lee Holt, James H. Straughn, Paul B. Kern, Ernest L. Waldorf, Miss Bettie Brittingham, A. W. Wasson, Ralph E. Diffendorfer, J. Q. Schisler, N. F. Forsyth, Mrs. J. W. Perry, R. N. Brooks, F. L. Gibbs, Mrs. J. W. Masland, Miss S. L. MacKinnon, Merle N. English.

V. COMMITTEE ON EDUCATION

REPORT NO 1. GENERAL ORGANIZATION

Calendar No. 11. Adopted May 3. See Journal, Page 250.

Membership of Committee, 135; present when report was adopted, 100; voting for adoption, 100.

¶ 1001. There shall be a Board of Education of The Methodist Church for the promotion of Christian Education. The Board shall have general oversight of the educational interests of the Church in the United States. It may co-operate with the Board of Missions for the advancement of Christian Education in other lands.

¶ 1002. The Board shall be constituted as follows: Each Jurisdictional Conference shall elect to membership in the Board, as the General Conference may provide, one Bishop, one Minister, one Layman, and one Youth representative twenty-five years of age or under at the time of his election and chosen from nominations made by the youth organizations within the Jurisdiction. Then, in addition thereto, each Jurisdiction shall elect one Minister and one Layman for each 300,000 members or major fraction thereof. At least three of the members thus elected shall be members of the Jurisdictional Board of Education, and not more than two of them shall come from one Annual Conference. Care shall be taken to elect men and women who are qualified by experience in educational institutions or in the local Church, and by training and interest, for the work of the Board in its three Divisions. *Ad interim* vacancies on the Board shall be filled by the Board from the Jurisdictions in which the vacancies occur.

The Board, on nomination of its Committee on Nominations, shall elect the members to three Divisions—Educational Institutions, Local Church, and Editorial—in the ratio of five, five, and two.

¶ 1003. As soon as possible after their election the members shall be assembled by a convener designated by the Council of Bishops to organize in the following manner: A Committee of seven elected upon nomination from the floor shall nominate a President, one or more Vice-Presidents, a Recording Secretary, and a Treasurer for each of the two Divisions, Educational Institutions and the Local Church. These officers shall be elected quadrennially from the membership of the Board except the Treasurers, who may be elected from outside the membership of the Board. The Executive Secretary of the Division of Educational Institutions and the Executive Secretary of the Division of the Local Church shall be elected by the Board from nominations made by their respective divisions. The Executive Secretary of the Editorial Division (Editor of Publications of the Board) shall be elected as hereinafter provided. Other employees may be elected as the Board may direct. The salaries and duties of all officers and employees except in the Editorial Division shall be fixed by the Board.

¶ 1004. The Board of Education shall be incorporated under the laws of whatever state the Board may determine. The Division of Educational Institutions shall be located in Chicago, Illinois; the Division of the Local Church and the Editorial Division in Nashville, Tennessee.

¶ 1005. The Board shall meet annually at such time and place as it may determine, subject to the provisions of the Act of Incorporation, and may hold such special meetings as may be necessary. Three-fifths of the members of the Board shall constitute a quorum.

¶ 1006. The Board shall appoint such Committees as may be necessary for the proper discharge of its business. It may adopt such bylaws for the regulations of the affairs of the Board and its Divisions and Committees as are not inconsistent with the Act of Incorporation or with General Conference legislation.

¶ 1007. The President who shall be a presiding, not an administrative officer, shall preside over the meetings of the Board and of the Executive Committee.

¶ 1008. The Executive Committee of the Board shall be composed of the President, Vice-President, and Recording Secretary of the Board and the members of the Advisory Committees of the three Divisions as hereinafter provided: Educational Institutions, seven; Local Church, seven; and Editorial, four. The Vice-President and Recording Secretary shall be included in the representation of their respective Advisory Committees. A majority of the members shall constitute a quorum.

The Executive Committee shall manage the funds of the Board under such regulations as the Board may adopt; fix the official bond of the Treasurers and of any other officers entrusted with the handling of funds; consider and approve the administrative budgets of the Board and its Divisions, except the Editorial Division.

The Board may commit to the Executive Committee such other powers and duties as it may determine. Minutes of the Executive Committee shall be sent to the members of the Board and submitted to the annual meeting of the Board for approval. Meetings of the Committee shall be held at least quarterly.

¶ 1009. Each of the Divisions as provided in ¶¶ 1002-1003, shall elect from its members an Advisory Committee as follows: Educational Institutions, seven; Local Church, seven; Editorial, four. These Committees shall assist in the conduct of the work and serve as members of the Executive Committee of the Board.

¶ 1010. Each of the Divisions shall provide for a review of the work of the Division, pass upon recommendations of the Executive Secretary and staff of the Division, and make recommendations to the Board concerning the needs and programs of the Division.

¶ 1011. The Executive Secretaries of the Division shall be the administrative officers of their respective Divisions under such regulations as the Board may make. They shall present annually to the Board reports of their work and recommendations as approved by the Divisions, including organization and budget. Assistants to the Executive Secretaries of the Division of the Educational Institutions and the Division of the Local Church shall be elected annually by the Board upon nomination of the respective Executive Secretaries. Assistants to the Executive Secretary of the Editorial Division shall be elected as hereinafter provided. In determining the number of Assistants due consideration shall be given to the varieties of work to˙be undertaken and the funds prospectively available.

The Executive Secretaries of the Divisions shall have the

privilege of membership, without vote, in the Board, in the Executive Committee, and in their respective Divisions.

¶ 1012. The Board shall be authorized to solicit and create special funds; to receive gifts and bequests; to hold properties and securities in trust; and to administer all these financial affairs in accordance with its own rules and the provisions of the *Discipline.*

The Board shall present quadrennially to the General Commission on World Service and Finance a statement of the amount required for its general expenses and for the support of each Division of its work, except the Editorial Division, which shall be financed as elsewhere provided. An apportionment to meet the approved needs shall be transmitted to the Church by the Commission.

From the funds derived from these and other sources, the Board shall appropriate annually such amounts as it may deem necessary for the support of the Division of Educational Institutions and the Division of the Local Church.

In all cases, the purposes for which funds are committed to the Board shall be strictly observed.

¶ 1013. All assets and liabilities existing at the time of union in the funds of the Board of Education of the three uniting Churches shall be the assets and liabilities of the corresponding Divisions in the new Board of Education.

¶ 1014. The Board shall have authority to make provision at its discretion for co-operation with any of the General Boards or agencies of the Church in any matters which, in the judgment of the Boards concerned, may be provided for jointly.

¶ 1015. The Board shall have authority to arrange for co-operation in its field of work with other denominations and with interdenominational agencies. Each Annual Conference shall determine for itself to what extent it will undertake to co-operate with other denominations or agencies in its own territory.

⁚ REPORT No. 2. SUGGESTIONS IN EPISCOPAL ADDRESS

Calendar No. 27. Adopted May 6. See Journal, Page 284.

Membership of Committee, 135; present when report was adopted, 87; voting for adoption, 85; not voting, 2.

Pursuant to the request of the Council of Bishops in the Episcopal Address, as printed in the *Daily Advocate* on the subject, "An Intelligent Church," the Committee on Education desires to co-operate in the plan proposed. This plan contemplates the setting up of a Department of Promotion and Publicity which is to be supported by the Boards and other agencies.

It is our understanding that perhaps the agents already at work, in the field of publicity and promotion in the several Boards, may be co-ordinated to discharge this responsibility. We are, therefore, recommending that a Commission be appointed by the Council of Bishops to study this entire question and make a report to the General Conference in 1940. This Commission would co-operate with the Boards in securing data and information as to what is now being done, as to the possible additional expense involved, and also as to what additional service might be rendered by such a Commission.

REPORT No. 3. DIVISION OF EDUCATIONAL INSTITUTIONS

Calendar No. 33.   Adopted May 8.   See Journal, Page 303.

Membership of Committee, 135; present when report was adopted, 115; voting for adoption, 115.

¶ 1016. There shall be a Division of Educational Institutions which shall perform such functions of the Board of Education as hereinafter set forth.

¶ 1017. The Division of Educational Institutions shall have an advisory relation to the business and educational management of all universities, colleges, schools, theological schools, Wesley Foundations, and other educational institutions related to The Methodist Church in the United States except those institutions owned by other Boards. It shall devise ways and means for the aid of such educational institutions; shall receive and disburse funds which may be committed to the Board for the purposes of the Division; may serve as a Board of Reference or Arbitration; and when necessary it may take measures to protect the property and other interests in such educational institutions. It may establish and conduct schools in the United States in communities in which facilities for education are not adequately provided. It shall promote the cause of education throughout the Church by collecting and distributing statistics and other information, by giving counsel concerning the planning of educational buildings and the location and organization of educational institutions. Through the properly constituted agencies it shall provide courses designed to meet the needs of every classification in our ministry. It shall seek to promote the religious training and activities of students at institutions of The Methodist Church and of Methodist students at tax supported and other institutions not related to The Methodist Church. It may also serve as a general medium of communication between teachers desiring employment and institutions needing their services.

¶ 1018. The Executive Secretary of the Division of Educational Institutions shall have general supervision of the affairs of the Division and shall be the administrative and legal executive thereof. In all his official relations he shall be subject to the authority and control of the Board. He shall report annually to the Board on the work of the Division. In case the office of the Executive Secretary shall become vacant, the Board shall elect his successor.

¶ 1019. The Division shall organize such departments and appoint such committees as may be necessary for the proper discharge of its business. It may adopt bylaws for the regulation of the affairs of the Division and of its several departments and committees not inconsistent with the Act of Incorporation of the Board of Education or with General Conference legislation.

¶ 1020. The Division shall receive such funds as are contributed for its work through the General Benevolences of the Church and shall appropriate the same for the maintenance of the work committed to it under such rules as the Board may adopt; *provided* that they are in accord with General Conference legislation.

¶ 1021. The Division shall have power to administer under the rules and regulations of the Board any and all funds, gifts, and bequests which have been or may be committed to the Board for the purpose of the Division; and to solicit or create any special funds for its projects. The purposes for which the funds are given and accepted shall be sacredly observed.

Appropriations

¶ 1022. The Division, through such officers, Committees, and Commissions as it may deem necessary, shall provide for the co-operative study of the special problems of the educational institutions and effective operation of plans for further integrating the work of our educational institutions with the Church's program of Christian education.

¶ 1023. The Division shall promote Annual Conference co-operation in order that cultivation periods may be developed in every congregation under the leadership of the Pastor for the purpose of deepening the interest of the Church in the educational institutions of the Church.

¶ 1024. Appropriations to institutions from funds at the disposition of the Division shall not debar those institutions from soliciting aid from their supporting Conferences or from other sources. In making appropriations for the support of educational institutions, the Division shall give due consideration to the actual current needs of such institutions as shown in carefully prepared reports presented by them on budget forms provided by the Division.

¶ 1025. No institutions hereafter established or acquired shall be aided by the Division unless the Division shall have been consulted and shall have approved the expenditures involved in the establishment or acquisition of such institutions, and the University Senate shall have approved its proposed classification before the project was undertaken. No institution, receiving an annual appropriation from the Division, shall incur debt obligations—bonded or otherwise —for building and for expansion programs not justified by property assets and sound pledges without first submitting its proposed plans to the Division for consideration and counsel. Any such institution failing to observe this regulation relinquishes its right to appropriations until the debt so incurred is liquidated. In no case shall the Division aid an institution which changes its classification until the University Senate shall have approved the classification.

¶ 1026. The Division shall recommend to the several Jurisdictional Conference Boards of Education and to the Annual Conference Boards of Education that the appropriation of Annual Conference funds shall be made only to those approved institutions whose educational and religious aims and programs are in active accord with the policies of the Church as expressed in the *Discipline,* and through special General Conference enactments.

¶ 1027. In fulfillment of its responsibility for the religious training and activities of Methodist students, the Division shall make such appropriations as the funds at its disposition shall warrant for the maintenance of Wesley Foundations and other organizations with similar purposes in the United States, which have been established or which may hereafter be established, under conditions approved by the Division. A Wesley Foundation in a non-Methodist institution or a student religious program in a Methodist institution making request for financial aid shall submit for consideration carefully prepared reports on budget forms provided by the Division. Appropriations by the Division toward the maintenance of student religious work at a given institution shall not debar it from soliciting additional support from its patronizing Conferences.

The University Senate

¶ 1028. The University Senate of The Methodist Church shall be composed of twenty-one persons, not members of the Board of Education, who are actively engaged in the work of education and are fitted by training and experience for the technical work of establishing standards and evaluating educational institutions in accordance with such standards. Eleven of these members shall be elected quadrennially by the Board of Education: and ten shall be appointed by the Council of Bishops. Due regard shall be given to representation from the various types of institutions included in the University Senate's classification of educational institutions. If, in consequence of the retirement of a member from educational work or for any other cause, a vacancy occurs in the Senate during the quadrennium, it shall be filled by the agency by which the retiring member was elected, at its next meeting.

¶ 1029. The Senate shall establish and assist in maintaining standards for the educational institutions related to The Methodist Church in the United States, and shall sustain an advisory relation to the Board of Education in matters of educational policy. It shall report to the Board, at least quadrennially, a proper classification for each educational institution or foundation in the United States which is related to The Methodist Church, and on the basis of this report the Division shall prepare its official lists of institutions and shall be governed in its administration.

¶ 1030. At the request of the Executive Secretary of the Division of Educational Institutions, the Senate shall investigate the resources, scholastic requirements, and procedure of any designated educational institution claiming or adjudged to be under the patronage or supervision of the Division, and shall report to the Division its decisions as to whether or not the requirements and educational and religious services of that institution are such as to justify its official recognition by the Church.

¶ 1032. At the request of the President or the Executive Secretary of any of the Boards of the Church, or at the written request of its own members, the Senate shall examine the quality and standards of the educational work done under the auspices of such Board and shall report to the Board concerned its estimate of the merit of such educational work and its recommendations as to what particular changes or improvements, if any, should be accepted.

· ¶ 1033. The Senate shall elect its own Presiding Officer and may appoint such Committees and may delegate to them such powers as are incident to its work. The Executive Secretary of the Division of Educational Institutions shall be the Executive Secretary of the Senate.

¶ 1034. The Senate shall meet annually at such time and

place as it may determine. Special meetings may be called on the written request of five members or at the discretion of the Presiding Officer and the Executive Secretary of the Division of Educational Institutions.

¶ 1035. After consultation with the officers of the Senate, the Division of Educational Institutions shall provide in its annual budget, as it may deem sufficient, for the expense of the Senate, except that expenses incurred by the Senate on behalf of any other Board of the Church shall be borne by that Board.

Classification of Schools

¶ 1036. The educational institutions in the United States related to The Methodist Church are classified as follows:
1. Universities.
2. Colleges of Liberal Arts.
3. Schools of Theology.
4. Schools of Religion for Lay Workers.
5. Other Professional Schools.
6. Junior Colleges.
7. Secondary Schools.
8. Wesley Foundations and Similar Organizations.
9. Training Schools for Religious Workers.

It shall be the duty of the President or other administrative officer of each educational institution to furnish statistics and other information to the Division of Educational Institutions and to the University Senate, also to report to the Division on forms which it shall supply, such information as may be needed for an understanding of the status, the work, and the progress of his institution. No institution having been classified by the University Senate shall announce a different classification without first securing the approval of the Senate and of the Division.

¶ 1037. No educational institution or foundation of The Methodist Church shall hereafter be established until its plans and organization shall have been approved by the University Senate and the Division of Educational Institutions; and no Annual or Mission Conference in the United States shall acquire, through any Board or Society, a school, college, university, or other educational institution, unless the approval of the Division shall have been previously obtained and unless, in the judgment of the Division, there is reasonable assurance of financial support sufficient to equip and maintain the institution in the classification approved for it by the University Senate.

¶ 1038. The Board of Education shall publish at least quadrennially a list of all the educational institutions related to The Methodist Church, classified by the University Senate in accordance with the provisions of ¶ 1036.

Education for Negroes

¶ 1039. The Division shall be the agency of the Board in administering institutions for Christian education among Negroes except those institutions owned by other agencies. The Division shall have authority to recommend to the Board plans by which schools sponsored by it may cooperate with or may unite with schools of other denominations or under independent control; *provided* the interests of The Methodist Church are adequately protected. Special effort shall be made to secure permanent endowments for schools under the direction of the Division, and whenever the Board is assured that their support will be adequate and that their property will be conserved and perpetuated, the schools may, on the recommendation of the Division, be transferred to local Boards of Trustees.

¶ 1040. As a means of educating the Church on the needs of Negro Schools, Race Relations Sunday (the second Sunday in February) shall be observed as the time when the interests of Christian Education for Negro Youth shall be presented. The Board shall receive all moneys derived from the observance of this day for the sole use of the Division for the advancement of this cause.

Educational Foundations

¶ 1041. Educational societies or foundations created by Annual Conferences may be recognized as auxiliaries of the Board of Education when their objects and purposes, their articles of incorporation, and their methods of administration shall have been approved by the Annual Conference within whose bounds they are incorporated and by the Division. All auxiliaries thus formed shall be required to send annually a report of their fiscal and administrative affairs to the Division.

Loan Funds

¶ 1042. The Division shall promote and administer the student loan fund and other funds established for the aid of students in accordance with Disciplinary provisions governing said funds in the former Methodist Episcopal Church, the former Methodist Episcopal Church, South, and the former Methodist Protestant Church. These funds shall be administered as heretofore until legislation governing the relation and administration of these funds shall be enacted by the General Conference.

Work for Methodist Students

¶ 1043. The Division may employ one or more persons whose duty it shall be to organize and carry on Wesley Foundations at state and independent institutions where practicable, and may co-operate with the colleges of the Church in promoting student religious activities. It shall also be its duty to study the religious needs of the campus, to offer advice in planning programs, to enlist suitable candidates for full-time religious vocations, and to assist in evangelistic work.

¶ 1044. It is recommended that there be a Campus-Church Relations Committee in the Board of Education composed of the Executive Secretaries of the three Divisions and two staff members of the Division of Educational Institutions and two staff members of the Division of the Local Church. It shall be the duty of this Committee to study and make recommendations to the Board concerning the relationship of the Campus and the Local Church in student religious activities. There shall be a Campus-Church Relations Committee in every college situation where The Methodist Church is at work. The Boards of Education of the Annual Conferences of a given state may create an Inter-Conference Commission on Student Religious Work to give general oversight to all such projects in the institutions of higher learning within the state.

REPORT NO. 4. COMMISSION ON WORLD PEACE

Calendar No. 45. Adopted May 8. See Journal, Page 327.

Membership of Committee, 135; present when report was adopted, 105; voting for adoption, 105.

We recommend continuation of the Commission on World Peace, authorized by the General Conference of 1936 of the Methodist Episcopal Church, as at present constituted and with the same method of financial support as now provided, until the meeting of the General Conference of The Methodist Church.

REPORT NO. 5. ENABLING ACT

Calendar No. 35. Adopted May 8. See Journal, Page 305.

Membership of Committee, 135; present when report was adopted, 105; voting for adoption, 105.

Provision for the Continuation of the General Conference Commission on the Youth Crusade

Pending action by the General Conference of The Methodist Church, the Youth Crusade Commission shall be authorized to continue the functions and activities stipulated by the General Conference of the Methodist Episcopal Church, South, at Birmingham in 1938, with continuation of financial support as at present.

REPORT NO. 6. MINISTERIAL EDUCATION; STANDARDS

Calendar No. 46. Adopted May 8. See Journal, Page 327.

Membership of Committee, 135; present when report was adopted, 87; voting for adoption, 87.

¶ 1046. The Division of Educational Institutions shall assist other properly constituted agencies of the Church in the training of our ministers while they are in residence in our educational institutions. Through the Commission on Courses of Study it is directly responsible for the training of all classifications of our ministry while they are pursuing their regular Conference Courses of Study and the courses provided for them in our Pastors' Schools and other agencies of ministerial training.

¶ 1047. It is expected of all candidates for the ministry that they shall complete a four-year college course of study leading to a Bachelor of Arts degree or its equivalent, and complete a course leading to the Bachelor of Divinity, or an equivalent degree in one of our Schools of Theology.

¶ 1048. No candidate shall be received on trial in an Annual Conference until he has given clear evidence that he possesses the preaching gift, and until he shall have completed at least four full years of college work in an institution approved for that purpose by the University Senate, or has earned a higher degree from an institution approved by the University Senate; *provided,* that, under special conditions clearly recognized as unusual, the Annual Conference may by a three-fourths vote admit a candidate who has satisfactorily completed two years of work in a four-year college, approved by the University Senate, or is a graduate of a junior college approved by the University Senate, in which case the District Superintendent and the Board of Ministerial Training shall furnish to the Conference written statements of particulars showing definitely in what respect the case is special and unusual before the vote is taken. After the admission of such candidate into full connection, and after his completion of the four-year Conference Course of Study, he shall be required to pursue two years of such graduate study as may be prescribed by the Commission on Courses of Study, this work to be taken under the direction of the Conference Board of Ministerial Training.

In the admission of young men to Annual Conferences,

the General Conference recognizes that our Theological Schools necessarily exercise a considerable influence. It, therefore, recommends to these schools that, before admitting any candidate for the pastoral ministry into their student body, they inquire fully into his preaching gift and make this also a condition of admission.

¶ 1049. Central Conferences shall fix the educational standards and all other requirements for admission to the Annual Conferences within their borders; all other Annual Conferences and Mission Conferences outside of the United States of America shall fix their own standards and requirements for admission. Mission Conferences in the United States shall require of all applicants the conditions and qualifications demanded of Traveling Deacons and Elders by an Annual Conference.

¶ 1050. When a Minister in full connection fails to be advanced in his work in the Conference Course of Study for a given year, said year shall not be counted as a year of effective service unless he is in attendance upon a school approved by the University Senate or is excused by a two-thirds vote of his Conference upon the recommendation of the Board of Ministerial Training.

¶ 1051. Any member on trial who does not complete the first two years of the Course of Study within four years shall be discontinued, and any full member who fails to complete the entire four years of the Course of Study within six years shall be located, unless, in either case, extension of time shall be recommended by a two-thirds vote of the Board of Ministerial Training and authorized by a two-thirds vote of the Annual Conference. In no case shall a person have a larger total than eight years in the Course of Study, and any person failing to complete the Course within this eight-year period shall not be permitted to join a Conference again on trial. This section, however, shall not apply for the period of time in which the candidates are carrying regular work in residence in a school of theology approved by the University Senate.

Theological Schools

¶ 1052. The Theological Schools of the Church are established and maintained for the training of Ministers. They exist for the benefit of the whole Church, and their support shall be provided by the whole Church as a part of its general benevolence giving. Furthermore, in case the support from this source is inadequate, each school shall have the right to appeal to the Jurisdictional Conference in which it is located and to the Annual Conference comprising that

Jurisdiction for additional support. For the purpose of carrying out the provision for the better support of the Theological Schools of the Church, the Division of Educational Institutions, in consultation with the administrative officers of these Schools, shall establish budget askings for their adequate support, after an adequate presentation of the needs of these institutions by a representative of the Schools of Theology. The amount necessary for such support shall be added as a separate item in the annual askings of the Board of Education from the Benevolence funds as determined by the authoritative body. No Theological School or Department of Theology in a College or University shall be established without first submitting its proposed organization and classification to the University Senate for approval and consent of both the Senate and the Division.

It is expected that our schools of theology will acquaint their students with the current programs of The Methodist Church, such as its educational, missionary, social and other service programs, and with the organizations and terminology of the Church.

Examinations and Credits

¶ 1053. Graduates of Colleges who are also graduates of a School of Theology approved by the University Senate shall be exempt from examination in the Conference Course of Study except on the *Discipline*. However, the Board of Ministerial Training shall discuss with each candidate his preparation for admission on trial. This section shall apply only to Schools of Theology of recognized standing which admit only graduates of colleges as degree students and are approved by the University Senate in respect to their requirements.

¶ 1054. Credits from Graduate Schools of Theology and other educational agencies approved by the University Senate, submitted by students who have not completed the theological course, shall be accepted by the Conferences on the basis of studies pursued in the same text or courses in the same subject judged to be equivalent by the Conference Board of Ministerial Training. However, all candidates shall be examined in the *Discipline*.

¶ 1055. Credits from other Theological Schools of The Methodist Church, not of graduate rank, may be accepted on the basis of studies pursued in the same text or of courses in the same subject judged to be equivalent by the Conference Board of Ministerial Training.

¶ 1056. Credits from colleges other than those of The Methodist Church may be accepted in studies not Biblical or theological, if the University Senate recognizes the colleges as of equal grade with those approved by the Senate.

¶ 1057. Credits, as provided in ¶¶ 1053 to 1056, shall be accepted only on the basis of certificates issued by the schools in question, stating the time when the courses were taken and the standing attained. Credits shall not be determined by individual members of the Board but by the Board of Ministerial Training in each Conference.

Conference Board of Ministerial Training

¶ 1058. In each Annual Conference the Presiding Bishop, after consultation with the Chairman of the Board of Ministerial Training of the previous quadrennium, or a committee of the Board, or in the case of a new Conference, after consultation with the cabinet, shall appoint a Board of Ministerial Training, consisting of not fewer than six nor more than sixteen members, care being taken to select men with special qualifications for this work. This Board shall be appointed at the first session following the General Conference for a term of four years. The Board of Ministerial Training shall urge all Conference and undergraduates to attend a School of Theology approved by the University Senate, and shall encourage and assist them in every practicable way to complete the course leading to a Bachelor of Divinity or its equivalent degree in the School of Theology. The Board shall require all Conference undergraduates who are not attending a School of Theology approved by the University Senate to pursue their work promptly in a standard Pastors' School or Summer School for Ministerial Training, or by correspondence. It shall co-operate with our Schools of Theology by recommending from the Annual Conference students with definite ministerial promise. Vacancies in the Board of Ministerial Training shall be filled by the Bishop after consultation with the Chairman of the Board.

¶ 1059. This Board shall organize by electing one of its members Chairman and another Registrar, the latter to keep a permanent record of the standing of the students, and report to the Conference when required. This record shall include the credits allowed students for work done in Schools of Theology, Colleges, standard Pastors' Schools, Summer Schools for Ministerial Training and by correspondence, and shall be filed with the Commission on Courses of Study.

¶ 1060. The Board of Ministerial Training in each Annual Conference shall seek, through co-operation with the District Superintendents and Pastors of the Conference, to enlist suitable candidates for the Christian Ministry, and shall keep a list of all persons enlisted within the bounds of the Conference, and shall seek in every way practicable to provide guidance and counsel to them in their training and preparation for the ministry.

¶ 1061. The course for Reception on Trial and the courses for undergraduates shall be taken by correspondence, or part by correspondence and part in a standard Pastors' School or Summer School for Ministerial Training, except that credits for the Courses of Study may be accepted from the Schools of Theology and Colleges as described in ¶¶ 1054 to 1056.

¶ 1062. The Board of Ministerial Training shall convene at the seat and time of the Annual Conference, preferably the day before the session opens, to review and complete the work of the year and to arrange for the work of the year to come.

¶ 1063. Accepted Supply Pastors who are giving their full time to pastoral work under the District Superintendents shall be required to take the Conference Course of Study, including the course for admission on trial. The Courses shall be taken by correspondence, or part by correspondence and part in a standard Pastors' School or Summer School for Ministerial Training, except that credits for the Courses of Study may be accepted from the Schools of Theology and Colleges, as described in ¶¶ 1054 to 1056. Any Accepted Supply Pastor who fails to observe the requirements of this section, or who shall fail to complete two years of the Course of Study within four years and the entire course within eight years, shall not be employed by a District Superintendent. The requirements of this paragraph shall not apply to Accepted Supply Pastors who have previously completed the Course of Study as prescribed for Local Preachers.

Commission on Courses of Study

¶ 1064. Within the Division there shall be a Commission on Courses of Study for ministers which shall be composed of three Bishops and three other ministers to be appointed by the Council of Bishops, three members from the faculties of the educational institutions of the Church elected by the Division of Educational Institutions, the Executive Secretary of the Division, and the Book Editor, *ex officio*. The members of this Commission shall hold office until their successors are duly appointed. There shall be a Director of this work elected by the Commission who by virtue of his office shall be an Assistant Secretary of the Division. The work of the Commission shall be reported to the annual meeting of the Board and the Division shall serve as the repository of the records of the Commission.

¶ 1065. The Commission shall study the needs of our ministry in the field of training and shall prescribe the Courses of Study upon which those applying for license to preach, for orders as Local Preachers and for reception on trial, respectively, shall be examined; also a Course of Study extending through four years to be pursued by those who have been received on trial in the Annual Conference and by Accepted Supply Pastors. It shall recommend courses of reading for all Preachers who have finished their undergraduate studies, and it shall also provide postgraduate Courses of Study for use in the Annual Conferences.

¶ 1066. The Commission shall meet at such times during the quadrennium as it may deem advisable to give consideration to the program of ministerial training, as it is related to Schools of Theology, College Departments of Religion, and correspondence courses, and shall give advice and counsel concerning postgraduate Courses of Study to be offered in our standard Pastors' Schools or Summer Schools for Ministerial Training.

¶ 1067. The work of the Commission on Courses of Study shall be supported from the General Benevolences of the Church, the amount to be determined by the authoritative body.

¶ 1068. The Division, in co-operation with Graduate Schools of Theology approved by the University Senate, may arrange for correspondence work as may be needed to provide for the study of all the courses prescribed by the Commission on Courses of Study. The Postgraduate Courses of Study, which may be developed by the Commission on Courses of Study, may be taken also by correspondence. All correspondence work shall be related to one or more of the Graduate Schools of Theology approved by the University Senate.

¶ 1069. The Division, in co-operation with the Boards of Ministerial Training and the Boards of Education of any group of Conferences, may establish standard Pastors' Schools or Summer Schools for Ministerial Training to provide for the study of the courses prescribed by the Commission on Courses of Study. Courses may be provided for both undergraduates and those Ministers who have completed the Conference Course of Study.

¶ 1070. During the period between the Uniting Conference and the appointment of the new Commission on Courses of Study for The Methodist Church, the Commission on Courses of Study as at present constituted in the three uniting Churches shall continue to function as at present and shall co-operate in every practicable way.

REPORT NO. 7. DIVISION OF THE LOCAL CHURCH

Calendar No. 62. Adopted May 9. See Journal, Page 360.

Membership of Committee, 135; present when report was adopted, 87; voting for adoption, 87.

¶ 1071-A. The Division of the Local Church shall develop a comprehensive and unified program of Christian education which shall lead to a knowledge of the Holy Scriptures, the Christian religion, and the Christian Church. It shall provide for worship, fellowship, study and service, including social, recreational, evangelistic and missionary activities, and education in the Christian way of life. It shall be responsible for forming standards and preparing programs for the organization and work of Christian education in the Local Church in accordance with provisions as set forth in Section IV.

The term "Church School," used in the *Discipline,* is understood to include Sunday Church Schools, week-day Church Schools, vacation Church Schools, leadership educational agencies; and other educational work of the Local Church with children, young people, and adults. The Division, in co-operation with the Editorial Division, shall seek to inform the Church on all phases of Church School work, shall establish and maintain standards, and shall co-operate with the Curriculum Committee in determining the curricula of the Church School, including the courses of leadership education; and give direction to a comprehensive and unified program of Christian education in the Local Church. It shall provide for instruction concerning the significance and work of the Church and the functions of its various officers and Boards.

The Division shall have supervision of all the training processes of the Church for both Lay and Ministerial workers, except where these have been specifically delegated to other agencies.

The Division shall co-operate with other agencies in the promotion of Brotherhoods, Men's Councils, and kindred organizations to the end that the different organizations of the Church may be correlated under a unified program for aggressive Christian service.

¶ 1071-B. The Executive Secretary of the Division of the Local Church shall have general supervision of the affairs of the Division and shall be the administrative and legal executive thereof. In all his official acts he shall be subject to the authority of the Board. He shall report annually to the Board. In case the office of Executive Secretary should become vacant, the Board shall elect his successor.

¶ 1071-C. The Division shall organize such departments as may be necessary for the proper promotion of Christian education of children, young people, and adults in local churches; and for leadership education, evangelism, and missionary education in the Church Schools.

¶ 1072. The Division shall provide programs for the training of Pastors, teachers, officials, and others in the work of the Local Church, and promote these programs through various types of training schools, correspondence work, and such other agencies as it may see fit to establish. It shall have authority also to promote and conduct educational conferences, councils, assemblies, and other meetings in the interest of Church Schools and the Christian education of children, young people, and adults, and in the interest of an improved leadership. The Division in co-operation with the Division of Educational Institutions, shall have authority to develop within the Church, democratic organizations of youth nationally and in Jurisdictions, Annual Conferences, Districts and subdivisions of districts; *provided*, however, that such organizations shall include all groups within a given age range within the Local Church.

¶ 1073. In order that Church Schools may be made available for those for whom The Methodist Church is responsible, the Division of the Local Church shall be authorized to project and promote plans for Church School extension throughout the Church, and to contribute to the support of Church Schools requiring assistance in mission territory.

¶ 1074. The Division shall have authority to enter into agreements with Jurisdictional Conference Boards of Education by which Jurisdictional Boards may promote a program of Church School extension in accordance with the policies of the Board and employ Extension Secretaries for work in rural and neglected areas. As a part of this agreement, the Jurisdictional Board shall make an annual budget for the extension program which shall be submitted, together with quarterly reports on the distribution of the funds herein provided for, to the Executive Secretary of the Division of the Local Church, who shall transmit the same to the Joint Committee, as provided for in ¶ 1080-A.

¶ 1075. The Division of the Local Church shall have the responsibility for working out, in co-operation with Jurisdictional Boards of Education, a general program and plan of organization for the furtherance within the Annual Conference of all the interests of Christian education with the supervision of which the Division is charged. This shall include the holding within the Conference territory of training schools, conferences, educational councils, federations, assemblies, and such other meetings in the interest of Christian education as the Division may deem wise. It shall call together the officers and representatives of the Jurisdictional Boards for counsel regarding Annual Conference organization and program of work in the field of Christian education in the local church.

Joint Committee on Religious Education in Foreign Fields

¶ 1076. For the purpose of more effectively promoting religious education outside the United States there shall be a Joint Committee on Religious Education in Foreign Fields composed of the Executive Secretary of the Division of the Local Church of the Board of Education and seven other persons appointed by the Division; a Secretary of the Division of Foreign Missions of the Board of Missions and three other persons appointed by the Division; and a Secretary of the Woman's Division of Christian Service of the Board of Missions and three other persons appointed by the Division.

There shall be an Executive Secretary of the Joint Committee who shall be the Secretary of the Board of Missions for Religious Education in countries outside the United States. The Secretary shall be elected by the Board of Missions upon nomination of the Joint Committee.

The Joint Committee shall meet annually, and at such other times as the Committee shall itself determine, and shall make report of its actions to the Boards of Education and of Missions at their annual meetings.

The budget of the Joint Committee shall be prepared by the committee subject to the approval of the co-operating boards.

Ad Interim Plan for Administration of Religious Education in Foreign Fields

¶ 1077. 1. During the period between the time of the Uniting Conference and the time when the General Conference shall otherwise order, the work of Religious Education in Foreign Fields shall be administered as follows:

(1) The work of Religious Education in Foreign Fields now being administered by the Joint Committee on Reli-

gious Education in Foreign Fields of the Methodist Episcopal Church shall continue to be so administered.

(2) The promotion of Religious Education in Foreign Fields under the Joint Committee of Co-operation and Counsel of the Methodist Episcopal Church, South, shall continue as heretofore.

(3) The work of Religious Education in Foreign Fields now being administered by the Foreign Department of the Board of Missions of the Methodist Protestant Church shall be administered by the Board of Missions of that Church.

2. In order to assure the co-ordination of existing programs of Religious Education in Foreign Fields of the three previously existing churches, and co-operation in the administration of these programs, and to develop plans in detail for the merging and unified administration of the work of Religious Education in Foreign Fields, there shall be a Joint Committee on Co-operation and Co-ordination of ten members, composed as follows: The secretary of the Joint Committee on Religious Education in Foreign Fields, and one member each from the Board of Education, the Board of Foreign Missions, and the Woman's Foreign Missionary Society of the Methodist Episcopal Church, these members to be designated by the respective agencies; four members from the Methodist Episcopal Church, South, two each from the Board of Missions and the General Board of Christian Education, these members to be designated by the respective Boards; and two members from the Methodist Protestant Church, one each from the Board of Missions and the Board of Christian Education, these members to be designated by their respective Boards.

Inter-Board Committee on Missionary Education

¶ 1078-A. For the purpose of promoting effective co-operation between the Board of Missions and the Board of Education in missionary education there shall be an Inter-Board Committee between the two Boards composed of the Executive Secretary of the Division of the Local Church, the Executive Secretary of the Division of Church School Publications, the Executive Secretary of the Division of Educational Institutions of the Board of Education, and five other persons to be appointed by that Board, and an equal number from the Board of Missions which shall include the following: The Secretaries of the Division of Education and Cultivation; two Secretaries from the Division of Foreign Missions, two from the Division of Home Missions and Church Extension, and two from the Woman's Division of Christian Service to be nominated by the several Divisions.

The duties of this Committee shall be: (a) to develop a unified program of Missionary Education for all age-groups in the Local Church and in the colleges, universities, and theological seminaries; (b) to represent the two Boards in disseminating missionary information through Church School literature and in the preparation of curricular material on Missions; and (c) to co-operate in the publication of books for Missionary Education in the Church School.

The Inter-Board Committee shall meet annually, and at such other times as the Committee itself may determine, and shall make report of its actions to the Boards of Education and of Missions at their annual meetings.

There shall be an Executive Secretary of the Committee, who shall be elected by the Board of Education, on nomination of the Inter-Board Committee, and who shall be the Secretary of the Division of the Local Church of the Board of Education for Missionary Education in the Church School. The Committee shall have a budget for its work provided by the two Boards as they may decide.

Ad Interim Plan for Administration of Missionary Education

¶ 1078-B. 1. During the period between the time of the Uniting Conference and the time when the General Conference shall otherwise order, the work of Missionary Education in the Methodist Churches of the United States shall be administered as follows: (1) The work of Missionary Education now being administered by the Board of Foreign Missions, the Board of Home Missions and Church Extension, the Woman's Foreign Missionary Society, the Woman's Home Missionary Society, the Board of Education, and the Secretarial Council of the Methodist Episcopal Church shall continue to be so administered; (2) the work of Missionary Education now being administered by the Department of Missionary Education of the General Board of Education, and the Department of Education and Promotion in the Board of Missions, of the Methodist Episcopal Church, South, shall continue as heretofore; (3) the Missionary Educational work now being done by the Board of Missions and the Board of Education of the Methodist Protestant Church shall continue to be so administered.

2. To assure the co-ordination of the existing programs of Missionary Education in the three previously existing Churches, co-operation in the administration of these programs and the development of plans in detail for the merging and unified prosecution of Missionary Education in the Methodist Churches of the United States, there shall be an

Inter-Board Committee on Missionary Education and Co-ordination which shall be composed of sixteen members, as follows: One member each from the Board of Foreign Missions, the Board of Home Missions and Church Extension, the Board of Education, the Secretarial Council, the Woman's Foreign Missionary Society and the Woman's Home Missionary Society, of the Methodist Episcopal Church; six members from the Methodist Episcopal Church, South—three each from the Board of Missions and the General Board of Christian Education; and four members from the Methodist Protestant Church, two each from the Board of Missions and the Board of Education; all the foregoing members to be elected by their respective Boards and Societies. The Secretaries of Missionary Education from each denomination shall be ex-officio members without vote.

¶ 1079. There shall be a Joint Committee on Architecture composed of the Executive Secretary of the Division of the Local Church of the Board of Education, three others to be elected by said Board of Education, and four other persons, elected by the Board responsible for Church Extension. This Committee shall have authority to prepare standards for the architecture of churches and educational buildings and to recommend them to the co-operating Boards; and shall be authorized, under such provisions as the Boards may agree upon, to offer counsel in the erection of such buildings. The Joint Committee shall meet annually and at such other times as its work may require.

¶ 1080-A. In the discharge of its responsibility for supervising Missionary Education in the Church Schools, the Division of the Local Church shall provide for the participation by Church Schools in Missionary Enterprises at home and abroad, such as the "Home and Foreign Missionary Enterprise," the "World Comradeship Plan," and "World Service."

(Until the General Conference shall provide otherwise the contributions for these various plans shall be handled, distributed, and used in harmony with the provisions heretofore obtaining in the three uniting Churches.)

¶ 1080-B. For the purpose of study of the problems involved in the various plans for missionary and Benevolence giving in Church Schools and in other children's and youth organizations of the Church, the distribution of the funds, and for report to the General Conference of 1940, there shall be a Committee of nineteen members composed as follows: ten members from the Inter-Board Committee on Missionary Education and Co-ordination (¶ 1078-B, Section

2) and nine additional persons elected by the Uniting Conference on nomination of the Joint Committee of the General Standing Committee on Missions and the General Standing Committee on Education, as follows: Jesse L. Corley, Alfred F. Hughes, Wade Crawford Barclay, Roy R. Roudebush, J. Emerson Ford, Clem Baker, J. M. Ormond, Mrs. J. W. Perry, J. Leas Green.

¶ 1080-C. The Division of the Local Church may, in co-operation with other missionary agencies, through the Inter-Board Committee on Missionary Education, develop co-operative plans for the Missionary Education of children, young people, and adults.

¶ 1081. The Division shall have authority to receive and administer funds, gifts, or bequests that may be committed to it for any Division of its work; and to solicit, establish, and administer any special funds that may be found necessary for the carrying out of its plans and policies.

¶ 1082. The Division shall, in co-operation with the Division of Educational Institutions, discover and give guidance to volunteers for all forms of vocational religious work, including training courses and all other procedures designed to provide vocational guidance for all young people of the Church.

¶ 1083. The Division may place specials in the Church Schools in its own area of work. Only such specials as are approved by the Divisional Committee on the Local Church may be placed in the Church Schools.

REPORT NO. 8. D. THE EDITORIAL DIVISION

Calendar No. 63. Adopted May 9. See Journal, Page 360.

Membership of Committee, 135; present when report was adopted, 74; voting for adoption, 74.

¶ 1085. There shall be elected quadrennially by the General Conference an Editor of Church School Publications who shall be the Executive Secretary in charge of the Editorial Division of the Board of Education.

¶ 1086. The assistants in the Editorial Division shall be elected annually by the Board of Publication upon nomination of the Editor of Church School Publications. The Board of Publication shall fix and pay the salaries of the Editor of Church School Publications and his assistants and shall have full financial responsibility for all other expenses connected with the work of the Editorial Division of the Board of Education.

¶ 1087. The publications of the Board of Education shall be manufactured, promoted, and distributed through The Methodist Publishing House. In matters involving financial responsibility the final determination in every case shall lie with the Board of Publication. After consultation with the Publishing Agents, the Editor of Church School Publications shall prepare a complete budget for his work, including salaries of assistants and office secretaries, and travel, to be effective when approved by the Board of Publication, and shall direct its operation from year to year.

¶ 1088. Through the Editorial Division, working in cooperation with the Curriculum Committee, the Board of Education shall provide all curriculum materials necessary for carrying on its work. The Editor of Church School Publications shall be responsible for the preparation of all curriculum materials, including periodicals, undated materials, and books authorized for use in the program of Christian education. The circulation of the literature prepared by this Division shall be a joint responsibility of the Board of Education and the Board of Publication.

¶ 1089. (1) There shall be a Curriculum Committee which shall determine the curricula of the Church School and recommend to the Editor of Church School Publications for final approval by the Board of Education the materials to be produced for use in Church Schools, young people's societies, training schools, and all other agencies related in any way to the work of the Board of Education. The Committee shall also make plans for the improvement and circulation of the Church School literature.

(2) The Curriculum Committee shall consist of not fewer than eleven nor more than seventeen members of which the Executive Secretaries of the three Divisions, the Book Editor, and two Publishing Agents shall be members. Other members shall be appointed by the Executive Committee of the Board of Education, who shall give due consideration to the necessity of having members on the Committee representing agencies of the Church which use teaching material. The Executive Committee of the Board shall have power to invite other individuals to act as consulting members of the Curriculum Committee without power to vote.

¶ 1090. The Chairman of the Committee on the Editorial Division and the Editor of Church School Publications may sit with the Board of Publication for the consideration of matters pertaining to the joint interests of the Board of Publication and the Board of Education and shall have the privilege of the floor. The Publishing Agents may sit with the Board of Education for the consideration of matters pertaining to the joint interests of the Board of Education and the Board of Publication and shall have the privilege of the floor.

¶ 1015-B. There shall be an advisory relation between the Board of Education and the General Conference Commission on World Peace. The Board in co-operation with the Commission on World Peace shall develop plans and curricula for the education of children, young people, and adults in the principles of peace and international co-operation.

(NOTE.—¶ 1015-B has been placed with this Report according to the instructions of the Committee on Education See Calendar No. 67, Report No. 12 of the General Standing Committee on Education.)

REPORT NO. 9. THE CHRISTIAN SABBATH

Calendar No. 64. Adopted May 9. See Journal, Page 360.

Membership of Committee, 135; present when report was adopted, 73; voting for adoption, 73.

Complying with the request contained in numerous memorials referred to this Committee, we recommend the retention in the *Discipline* of the following statement on "The Christian Sabbath," found in Paragraph 167 of the *Discipline* of the Methodist Episcopal Church, 1936 Edition:

"¶ 167. We recognize the claims of the Christian Sabbath as an institution made to meet man's deepest need for worship and rest. These claims are re-enforced by both State and Church and the moral mandate of the law and the gospel. John Wesley made the observance of the Lord's Day by cessation of 'ordinary work therein or by buying or selling,' a requirement among the General Rules of the people called Methodists.

"This particular rule needs frequent emphasis in our time, when the progress of the kingdom of God is retarded by the encroachments of unnecessary labor and commercialized amusements upon the sanctity of the Lord's Day. While it is true that works of necessity have been enlarged to meet modern conditions, and some latitude must be granted in the matter of real recreation, the right use of the Lord's Day is not optional but imperative for the Christian conscience. The Church cannot compromise with an invasion of the Lord's Day that violates its fundamental principles of worship and rest. Such rest as does not interfere with true worship is allowable; such worship as is consistent with true rest is a high obligation. We remember to the emphasis of our Lord upon doing good on the Sabbath day, and urge our people to follow his example in ministering to the sick and needy on that day.

"We therefore recommend that all our Pastors give the Lord's Day the place it deserves in the educational and preaching program of the Church; and that our District Superintendents be requested to bring this vital concern to the attention of the Quarterly Conferences for inclusion in the reports rendered by the Pastor, the Presidents of the Epworth Leagues or other young people's societies, and the Church School Superintendent. Only thus can we promote a revival of Sabbath observance as a necessity of our human nature for worship and rest and make effective a united protest against all efforts to make the Lord's Day a holiday instead of a holy day and thus destroy this primary institution."

REPORT No. 10

SECTION II.   JURISDICTIONAL BOARD OF EDUCATION

Calendar No. 65.   Adopted May 10.   See Journal, Page 371.

Membership of Committee, 135; present when report was adopted, 73; voting for adoption, 73.

¶ 1091. In each Jurisdiction there may be a Board of Education to promote the program of Christian Education and Church School Extension within the Jurisdiction.

¶ 1092. The Jurisdictional Board shall be auxiliary to the General Board and shall co-operate with it in advancing the interest of educational institutions, Wesley Foundations and similar work in Methodist Colleges, and of the entire program of Christian Education in the Local Church. It also shall conduct Training Schools, Assemblies, and other gatherings for religious purposes, promote intelligent use of the literature of the General Board, and hold at least one meeting annually at which a representative of the General Board shall be present.

¶ 1093. The Board shall be composed of the effective Bishops within the Jurisdiction, and one Minister and one Layman from each Annual Conference, at least one of whom shall be a member of the Annual Conference Board of Education. The Annual Conference representatives on the Jurisdictional Board shall be elected by the Conference from nominations made by the Annual Conference Board of Education, at its session next preceding the Jurisdictional

Conference. In addition there shall be youth members at large, one from each Episcopal Area within the Jurisdiction. These youth members shall be twenty-five years of age or under at the time of election, and shall be chosen as the Annual Conference youth organizations within the area may determine. Care shall be taken to elect persons who are qualified for the work of the Board by experience in educational institutions, and in the Local Church, and by training and interest. No salaried officer of the Board shall be a member of the Board. The Executive Secretary of the Board shall be an *ex officio member*.

¶ 1094. The officers of the Board shall be a President, a Vice-President, a Recording Secretary, a Treasurer, and an Executive Secretary. These officers shall be elected quadrennially by the Board by ballot. A majority of the members of the Board shall constitute a quorum.

¶ 1095. There shall be an Executive Committee of the Board, of which the President shall be a member, which shall be chosen by the Board on nomination of the Nominating Committee. The Executive Committee shall meet on call of the President or of one third of its members and shall transact all necessary business of the Board *ad interim* under such regulations as the Board may adopt.

Its acts shall be reported in writing to the members of the Board. The Executive Committee shall act as the Finance Committee of the Board and shall prepare and recommend to the Jurisdictional Conference a quadrennial budget which shall include all the financial needs of the Board.

¶ 1096. The organization of the new Board shall be effected at the beginning of the quadrennium in the following way: A convener, appointed by the Bishops of the Jurisdiction, shall assemble the members of the new Board for organization at the earliest possible date after their election; *provided* that ample notice shall be given to all members to enable them to be present at the organizational meeting. The convener shall effect a permanent organization as prescribed in ¶ 1094.

¶ 1097. The President shall be a presiding, not an administrative, officer. The Treasurer, who shall be adequately bonded, shall deposit the funds of the Board in a designated depository.

¶ 1098. The Board shall elect quadrennially from its membership, upon nomination of the Nominating Committee, two Standing Committees of such number as the Board may determine. These Committees shall be known as:

(1) The Committee on Educational Institutions.

(2) The Committee on the Local Church.

The Committee on Educational Institutions shall study the needs of the institutions within the territory of the Jurisdictions, shall hear the recommendations of the Executive Secretary of the Jurisdictional Board, and shall make recommendations to the Board.

The Committee on the Local Church shall study the educational needs of local Churches and of Annual Conference Boards of Education, shall consider the recommendations of the Executive Secretary of the Jurisdictional Board, and shall make recommendations to the Board.

¶ 1099. The Executive Secretary shall have responsibility for the general oversight and promotion of all the work of the Board and in the direction and supervision of its salaried workers. On nomination of the Executive Secretary such other salaried workers as the Board may deem necessary shall be elected. Due consideration shall be given to the need for specialized leadership in college institutional promotion and in the field of work with children, with young people including student religious activities, with adults, and in the areas of missions and social problems, extension work in rural areas, and in leadership education and training. All salaried officers shall attend the meetings of the Jurisdictional Board and shall have all the privileges of members except the privilege of voting. The Executive Secretary shall make a full report to the Board annually, and to the General Board of Education. Other salaried workers shall report as may be required to the Executive Secretary.

¶ 1100. The Board shall meet annually. A majority of the members shall constitute a quorum. The President and the Executive Secretary shall prepare the order of business.

¶ 1101. The Executive Secretary of the Board shall prepare a report of its proceedings and submit it to the Jurisdictional Conference. Each Jurisdictional Conference shall set apart a session at which time the interests of Christian education shall be emphasized. Immediately following the session of the Jurisdictional Conference, the Board, through its Executive Secretary, shall report to the Executive Secretaries of the three Divisions of the Board of Education a summary of its acts and the names of its officers and salaried workers and such other information as may be needed by the Board of Education.

¶ 1102. The Board shall have authority to co-operate with other Jurisdictional Boards in matters of common interest. It shall also have authority to co-operate with interchurch organizations and agencies. Each Annual Conference shall determine for itself to what extent it will co-operate with these agencies within its own territory.

¶ 1103. The sources of income of the Board shall be as follows: First, from gifts of donors who are particularly interested in the work represented by the Division of Educational Institutions and by the Division of the Local Church; second, from apportionments allotted to the Churches within the Jurisdiction for the work of the Jurisdictional Board of Education; third, from such per cent of the total amount raised for missions by the Church Schools within the Jurisdiction as the General Conference may direct.

REPORT No. 11. ANNUAL CONFERENCE BOARDS

Calendar No. 66. Adopted May 10. See Journal, Page 371.

Membership of Committee, 135; present when report was adopted, 70; voting for adoption, 70.

¶ 1104. In each Annual Conference there shall be a Board of Education elected by the Conference to promote Church School Extension and the program of Christian Education.

¶ 1105. The Conference Board shall be auxiliary to the Jurisdictional Board and shall co-operate with it and the General Board in advancing the interests of Christian Education. It shall help to secure statistics and other information concerning the colleges and local Churches within its borders; to develop support of educational institutions, Wesley Foundations, and similar work in Methodist Colleges, and for the entire program of Christian Education in the Local Churches, and to promote intelligent use of the literature of the General Board. It shall hold at least one meeting annually in which the Jurisdictional Board may have representation.

¶ 1106. The Board shall be composed of an equal number of Laymen and Ministers, the number and manner of election to be determined by the Annual Conference; and in addition, the President of the Conference Youth Organization and two other young people, twenty-five years of age or under at time of election, chosen by the Conference Youth Organization, shall be members of the Board. Care shall be taken to elect persons who are qualified for the work of the Board by experience in educational institutions and in the Local Church, and by training and interest. No salaried officer of the Board shall be a member. A majority of the members shall constitute a quorum. The members shall continue in office until their successors are elected.

¶ 1107. The officers of the Board shall be a President, a Vice-President, a Recording Secretary, a Treasurer, and an Executive Secretary (who may serve two or more contiguous Conferences), elected by the Board in such manner as it may determine. The retiring Board shall complete the business and make its annual report to the Conference. The retiring Board shall make such recommendations as it may desire to the new Board, which Board shall take charge immediately upon its organization and shall make recommendations to the Annual Conference.

¶ 1108. There shall be an Executive Committee of the Board, of which the President shall be a member. The Executive Committee shall meet on the call of the President or of one-third of the members and shall transact all necessary business of the Board *ad interim*, under such regulations as the Board may adopt. Its acts shall be reported to the annual meetings of the Board. The Executive Committee shall act as the Finance Committee of the Board, and shall prepare a statement of its financial needs for the next year. The President, or someone designated by him, shall present to the Commission on World Service and Finance of the Conference the financial needs of the Board.

¶ 1109. Organization of the new Board shall be effected at the beginning of the quadrennium in the following way: The Bishop shall appoint a convener of the Board who shall assemble the Board to effect a permanent organization as prescribed in ¶ 1107.

¶ 1110. The President shall be a presiding, not an administrative, officer. The Treasurer, who shall be adequately bonded, shall receive, and receipt for, all funds of the Board and disburse them by check as ordered by the Board. All checks must be countersigned by the Executive Secretary or some other person duly authorized by the Board.

¶ 1111. The Executive Secretary shall have responsibility for the general oversight and promotion of all the work of the Board and in the direction and supervision of its salaried and voluntary workers. On nomination of the Executive Secretary, such other salaried and volunteer workers as the Board may deem necessary shall be elected. In the case of Annual Conference Directors of Young People's Work the nomination shall be made after consultation with the responsible officers of the Annual Conference Young People's Organization. The Executive Secretary, after conference with the District Superintendent, and with the responsible officers of the age-group organizations within the Annual Conference, may report to the Board for confirmation by the Annual Conference the following workers for each District who, with the District Superintendent, shall constitute the District Staff of Christian Education: District Director of Adult Work, District Director of Young People's Work, District Director of Children's Work. The Executive Secretary shall make a full report annually. The other salaried workers shall report as may be required to the Executive Secretary.

¶ 1112. The Board shall hold at least one annual meeting and such other meetings as it may determine. Each Annual Conference shall set apart a portion of a session in which the interests of Christian Education shall be adequately considered.

¶ 1113. The Board shall make a report of its proceedings and policies to the Annual Conference. This report shall carry the Treasurer's report showing all resources and liabilities of the Board, its income from all sources, and its expenditures for every purpose. Immediately following the session of the Annual Conference, the Board, through its Executive Secretary, shall report to the Jurisdictional Board of Education a summary of its acts and the names of its officers and salaried workers. It shall transmit to the Jurisdictional Board the names and addresses of Church School Superintendents and the officers of the District and Annual Conference organizations operating under the Conference Board and of Young People's Assemblies and other organizations.

¶ 1114. In accordance with the financial plan of the Church, an apportionment shall be allotted to the Churches within the Conference for the work of the Conference Board of Education. Other sources of income shall be gifts, returns from special days, and receipts from Missionary offerings in the Church School. The Board shall determine the distribution of the funds thus received to each of the general interests under the care of the Board.

¶ 1115. The Executive Secretary of the Conference Board of Education, and two other persons to be elected by this Board, together with the Conference Missionary Secretary and two other persons to be elected by the Conference Board of Missions, shall constitute a Joint Committee for the purpose of considering, reaching agreements, and making recommendations to the two Boards regarding Church School and rural Church work.

REPORT NO. 12. THE LOCAL CHURCH

Calendar No. 67. Adopted May 10. See Journal, Page 372.

Membership of Committee, 135; present when report was adopted, 70; voting for adoption, 70.

¶ 1116. Each Church shall be organized so as to discharge its responsibility for the religious development of its entire constituency in accordance with the policies of the Board of Education and the requirements of the *Discipline* as indicated in ¶ 1071.

¶ 1117. In the program of work herein outlined it is understood that the Pastor is, as elsewhere in all the work of the Pastoral Charge, the Preacher in charge, and is responsible for the total educational program of the Church. Nothing in this plan is to be construed as interfering with his authority and responsibility.

¶ 1118. Each Local Church shall organize a Church Board of Education which shall be composed of the Pastor, the Church School Superintendent, the Director of Christian Education, the three Assistant Superintendents, one representative elected by each of the Women's Societies, the Board of Stewards, and other agencies in the Church, and not less than two, nor more than four young people, elected by the young people. In addition there may be not more than five members at large, elected by the Quarterly Conference, chosen for their fitness for leadership in Christian education.

In small Churches the Board may be composed of the Pastor, the Church School Superintendent, one teacher of children, one teacher of youth, one young person chosen by the youth of the Church, one person representing the adult organization, and a member of the Board of Stewards, elected by that body. Three persons at large, chosen for special fitness for leadership, may be added by the Quarterly Conference or the members of the Church.

The Church Board of Education shall have supervision of the total program of Christian education in each Local Church. The Board shall be auxiliary to the Annual Conference Board of Education, the Jurisdictional Board of Education and the General Board of Education and shall seek to maintain the standards of an effective Church program of Christian education as they shall be worked out democratically from time to time in harmony with the standards of the Boards of Education.

¶ 1119. There may be in each Church a Council of Children's Workers and a Council of Adult Workers. Each

Council shall be composed of the Superintendents of the respective age-group divisions and departments in the Church School and heads of all other groups and agencies in the Church working with children and adults.

There may be a Council of Youth Workers consisting of representatives selected by the department councils in the Youth Division outlined in ¶ 1125.

Each Council shall meet monthly or as often as necessary and exercise such supervision over the various programs being promoted within the Church for its respective age groups as shall avoid duplications and omissions and contribute to the total religious needs of the age group concerned.

¶ 1120. Prior to the beginning of the Church School year, the Quarterly Conference or the members of said Church shall, on nomination of the Pastor (or by a nominating committee, selected by the Board of Education, of which the Pastor shall be Chairman) elect a General Superintendent, and not more than five persons at large for membership on the Board; and on nomination of the Pastor and General Superintendent, shall elect three Assistant Superintendents—viz., a Superintendent of the Children's Division, a Superintendent of the Youth Division, and a Superintendent of the Adult Division, who shall supervise the work of their respective Divisions. The General Superintendent shall be the administrative officer of the Church Board of Education. He shall make regular reports to this Board and to the Quarterly Conference concerning the Church School, giving the information called for by the Division of the Local Church of the General Board.

¶ 1121. As early in the autumn as practicable the Pastor shall call the members of the new Board of Education together for the purpose of organizing the work of the new Church School year, at which time they shall elect a Chairman, who shall be a member of The Methodist Church, a Vice-Chairman, and a Secretary from among their members; and the officers and teachers of the Church School as provided for in ¶ 1118. The Secretary of the Church School may serve as Secretary of the Church Board of Education.

¶ 1122. It shall be the further duty of the Church Board of Education:

(1) To make provision for the organization, guidance, and supervision of the three Divisions of the Church, as follows: The Children's Division (one to eleven years inclusive); the Young People's Division (twelve to twenty-three

years inclusive), and the Adult Division (twenty-four years and over) ; *provided* that the General Board of Education may modify these age provisions as needed.

(2) To develop a program of Christian education which shall include: worship, fellowship, study and service; use of literature approved by the General Board; missionary education in the Church School; and other activities as provided for in ¶ 1071.

(3) To provide for budgeting and expending funds raised throughout the Church School.

(4) To plan a program of leadership education for the improvement of the workers in service, and for the discovery, selection and training of prospective workers and leaders.

(5) To provide opportunities for parents and young people to have studies in marriage and Christian homemaking.

(6) To continue the observance of the special days, such as Rally Day, Children's Day, Church School Day, College Day, Young People's Day, with offerings as are now authorized by the three Uniting Churches until these special days may be changed by the General or Jurisdictional Conferences.

(7) To observe one Sunday in each month, preferably the fourth, as Missionary Sunday and to take an offering on that day. Until the General Conference shall order otherwise this offering shall be handled in harmony with the provisions in the *Disciplines* of the three Churches which are being united.

(8) To insure that records are accurately kept by the officials in the Church School in form approved by the Division of the Local Church, and to make regular reports to the Quarterly Conference.

(9) To see that information concerning the work of our schools, colleges, universities and specified student work, such as the Wesley Foundation program, is given regularly in the Church through appropriate programs and promotion.

(10) To hold regular meetings (preferably monthly) for the purpose of receiving and passing on reports and recommendations and for the study of the educational work of the Church; and in advance of the opening of the Church School year, on nomination of the General Superintendent in concurrence with the Pastor, to elect all officers and teachers of the Church School not herein otherwise provided for.

(11) To fill vacancies occurring during the year in any of the elective positions provided in subsection 10 above,

and to remove officers and teachers of the Church School for habitual neglect, inefficiency, or improper conduct, upon recommendation of the Superintendent or Pastor.

¶ 1123. There shall be a Workers' Conference in each Church composed of the Pastor, the General Superintendent, the Assistant Superintendents, other general officers of the Church School, and all adult officers and teachers and student officers in the departments of the Young People's Division. The General Superintendent shall be the presiding officer of the Workers' Conference, which shall meet at least quarterly. The Workers' Conference shall provide for study and discussion of the educational task of the Church, and for making such recommendations to the Church Board of Education as it may deem advisable; *provided,* that in small Churches, at the discretion of the Pastor and the General Superintendent, the Workers' Conference may meet with the Church Board of Education and the combined body may perform all the duties of both bodies except the election and confirmation of officers and teachers specified in ¶ 1126, in which case the Board of Education itself, as provided for in ¶ 1122 (10) shall act. Provision shall be made for such age-group divisional and departmental conferences as may be needed.

¶ 1124. The Children's Division shall be organized into classes and departments appropriate to the age group involved. It shall conduct its work with children in harmony with the standards established by the General, Jurisdictional, and Conference Boards of Education, and shall include in its work such Sunday and weekday activities as are necessary for a complete and unified program of Christian education for children, in harmony with ¶ 1071. The Woman's Missionary Society and the Church Board of Education are authorized to co-operate in the missionary education of children in accordance with plans to be determined by the General, Jurisdictional, and Annual Conferences.

¶ 1125. (1) The Youth Division shall be subdivided by ages into departments; *provided,* however, that in small Churches where it is not possible to subdivide the Youth Division, the entire Youth Division may be organized as one department.

(2) Each department shall seek to develop its work in harmony with the Disciplinary provisions and with the standards established by the Conference, the Jurisdictional, and the General Boards of Education. Each department may include in its work Sunday morning, Sunday evening, and such other meetings and activities as are appropriate

to a complete program of Christian education for young people; *provided*, that the result shall be a unified, or correlated, program of work in each department.

(3) Each department shall organize in accordance with one or the other of the two following plans (to be outlined fully by the General Board of Education) as may be determined by the membership concerned and the Church Board of Education.

(a) Plan I. Where a unified organization is desired, one organization, with one set of officers and one program planning Department Council, shall be responsible for carrying on all the activities of the department as outlined in subsection 2, above.

(b) Plan II. Where two or more correlated organizations are desired they may be provided within the department to carry on activities outlined in subsection 2, above. Each may have its own officers, program committees and separate memberships. Suitable representatives from each organization within the Department shall meet together as a Department Council monthly or as often as necessary to give such supervision over the programs of the organizations concerned as shall avoid duplications and omissions and meet the total needs of the age group concerned. The Department Council shall represent the entire Department in matters which concern that age group of the Local Church.

(4) The Church Board of Education and all other agencies concerned shall encourage and maintain in the organization and program of the Youth Division opportunity for initiative and expression on the part of Youth, as well as opportunity for adult counsel.

(5) The use of Methodist literature and programs shall be promoted in connection with the youth organizations.

¶ 1126. (1) For the Adult Division there shall be a Superintendent who shall be an Assistant to the General Superintendent, and who shall be Chairman of the Adult Council.

(2) The Adult Council, in accordance with the plans and policies of the Division of the Local Church and the Church Board of Education, may elect such other administrative officers for the Adult Division of the Church School as may be needed.

(3) The Adult Council, in accordance with the plans and policies of the Conference, Jurisdictional and General Boards of Education and the Church Board of Education, may organize Wesley Classes, organizations for young adults, a Church Fellowship for men, Methodist Brother-

hoods, Men's Clubs, and such other groups as shall promote the purpose of the Church. Each class or group may select its own officers and teachers, *provided* that the teachers in the Church school shall be confirmed by the Church Board of Education with concurrence of the Pastor and the General Superintendent.

(4) The Woman's Missionary Society is a group in the Adult Division on a co-operative basis. It shall maintain its relationship to the overhead agencies of the General Conference to which it is an auxiliary so as to preserve the interests and fulfill the responsibilities to its organization.

¶ 1127. On nomination of the Pastor, with the concurrence of the Church Board of Education, the Quarterly Conference may employ annually a Director of Christian Education, whose duties shall be defined and whose work shall be supervised by the Church Board of Education in accordance with the standards of the General, Jurisdictional and Conference Boards of Education. The Director shall be a member of the Quarterly Conference, of the Church Board of Education in an advisory capacity, and of all committees and Councils under the Church Board of Education.

¶ 1128. We hold that all children, by virtue of the unconditional benefits of the atonement, are members of the Kingdom of God, and are therefore graciously entitled to baptism; but, as infant Baptism contemplates a course of religious instruction and discipline, it is expected of all parents or guardians who present their children for Baptism that they will use all diligence in bringing them up in conformity to the Word of God.

¶ 1129. It shall be the duty of the officers and teachers of the Church School in co-operation with the pastor to lead all members of the Church School to make a profession of faith in Christ, to have a comprehension of the responsibilities involved in such profession, and to give evidence of a sincere and earnest determination to discharge them. The Minister shall prepare the teachers of the Church School in connection with their regular duties to instruct all members in the Junior Department and above in the meaning and practice of Church membership, and shall supplement such instruction as he may deem necessary. He shall plan carefully for the reception of members of the Church according to the provisions of the *Discipline*.

¶ 1130. It shall be the duty of the District Superintendent to bring the subject of Christian education before the Quarterly Conference of each Pastoral Charge within his district.

At least once each year he shall inquire into the character and effectiveness of the program of Christian education of every Charge within his District. He shall co-operate with the Conference Secretary of Education, where there is one, and with the Annual Conference Board of Education in promoting in all the Churches of his district the plan of organization, the standards, and the literature provided or recommended by the General and Jurisdictional Boards of Education. He shall use the record and report forms provided by the Board of Education for the use of District Superintendents.

¶ 1015-B. There shall be an advisory relation between the Board of Education and the General Conference Commission on World Peace. The Board in co-operation with Commission on World Peace shall develop plans and curricula for the education of children, young people, and adults in the principles of peace and international co-operation.

(NOTE.—This paragraph has been placed at the close of Calendar No. 63, Report No. 8 of the General Standing Committee on Education.)

VI.   COMMITTEE ON PUBLISHING INTERESTS

REPORT NO. 1.   THE METHODIST PUBLISHING HOUSE

Calendar No. 16.   Adopted May 5.   See Journal, Page 267.

Membership of Committee, 135; present when report was adopted, 121; voting for adoption, 121.

¶ 1201, (1).   The Methodist Publishing House comprises the publishing interests of The Methodist Church.

(2) The objects of The Methodist Publishing House shall be: The advancement of the cause of Christianity by disseminating religious knowledge and useful literary and scientific information in the form of books, tracts, and periodicals; the promotion of Christian education; the transaction of any and all business properly connected with the publishing, manufacturing, and distribution of books, tracts, periodicals, materials and supplies for Churches and Church Schools; and such other business as the General Conference may authorize and direct.

(3) The Methodist Publishing House shall be under the direction and control of a Board of Publication, acting through Publishing Agents elected by the Board and through such other officers as the Board may find it necessary or expedient to establish.

(4) The several corporations through and by means of which the publishing interests shall be conducted by the Board of Publication shall be collectively known as The

Methodist Publishing House; each corporation having power to transact its business under its own corporate name, as the Board may direct.

(5) The four corporations, known by the following names, to-wit: The Methodist Book Concern, a corporation existing under the laws of the state of New York; The Methodist Book Concern, a corporation existing under the laws of the state of Ohio; The Board of Publication of the Methodist Protestant Church, a corporation existing under the laws of the state of Pennsylvania; and the Book Agents of the Methodist Episcopal Church, South, a corporation existing under the laws of the state of Tennessee; shall be presently continued, the members of the Board of Publication serving and acting as trustees and directors of each such corporation. The Board is empowered and authorized to continue the printing and manufacturing business of the Church at New York, Cincinnati, Chicago, Nashville, Pittsburgh, and Baltimore, and later to combine the allocated activities into a smaller number of publishing units as the Board may determine to be in the best interest of the whole Church; *provided* that one of the principal plants shall be continued within the present territory served from the Publishing House located at Nashville, Tennessee. Branch houses, distributing agencies, depositories, and offices may be established or continued or discontinued, in the discretion of the Board.

(6) The members of the Board of Publication first elected under this *Discipline*, and their successors in office, are declared to be the successors of the incorporators named in the charters of The Methodist Book Concern issued by the states of New York and Ohio, and in the charter of The Board of Publication of the Methodist Protestant Church issued by the state of Pennsylvania. The Publishing Agents elected from time to time under this or any subsequent *Discipline* are declared to be the successors in office of the Book Agents of the Methodist Episcopal Church, South, named in the charter issued to the corporation of that name by the state of Tennessee.

(7) After proper reserves have been set up by the Board of Publication for the efficient operation of the business and necessary expansion, the net produce of The Methodist Publishing House shall be applied to no purpose other than to the benefit of the Traveling, Supernumerary, Superannuated, and worn-out Preachers, their wives, widows, and children.

(8) The net produce of the several corporations, after setting up proper reserves as above provided, shall be paid

into a single fund and distributed annually by the Board of Publication to the several Annual Conferences for the persons who are and shall be Conference Claimants.

(9) The property and proceeds of each corporation shall be held and managed separately, without transfer of funds or obligations of credit between them.

(10) The income of each of the several corporations of The Methodist Publishing House shall be appropriated to no other purpose than its own legitimate business, and the distribution of net produce, after setting up proper reserves as above provided.

The Board of. Publication

¶ 1202. (1) The Board of Publication shall be constituted by the respective Jurisdictional Conferences, with a representation of each in proportion to Church membership upon a basis of one member of the Board for each 150,000 Church members or major fraction thereof, within the Jurisdictional Conference, *provided* that no Jurisdictional Conference shall have fewer than three members, and *provided,* further, that the ministers and laymen shall be in equal number, as nearly as possible. In case a Jurisdictional Conference by the ratio has an odd number of representatives it shall decide whether the major number of its representatives shall be Ministers or Laymen. The term of office of the members of the Board shall be eight years, but in the first election, one-half shall be elected for only four years, the Conference determining in case of an odd number. Any vacancy occurring between sessions of the Jurisdictional Conferences for any cause, including removal from the Jurisdiction, shall be filled by the Board from that Jurisdictional Conference in whose representation the vacancy occurs. The Publishing Agents shall be *ex officio* members of the Board without vote.

(2) The Board shall meet as soon as practicable after the Jurisdictional Conferences for organization and the adoption of such regulations as it may deem necessary or desirable.

(3) The Board shall meet annually, and special meetings may be held at such times and places as the Board may appoint, or at the call of the Chairman. Special meetings shall be called by the Chairman whenever requested, in writing, by one-third of the members. At all meetings of the Board a majority of the members shall constitute a quorum.

(4) The Board shall keep a correct record of its proceedings and shall examine carefully into the condition of the affairs of The Methodist Publishing House and make report

thereof to the Annual Conferences, the Jurisdictional Conferences, and the General Conference.

(5) The Board shall fix the salaries of the following officers: The Publishing Agents, the Book Editor, the Editors of the official papers of the Church, and the Editor of the Church School Publications.

(6) The Board shall have authority to fill vacancies occurring during the intervals of Jurisdictional Conferences in any of the offices mentioned in this chapter.

(7) The members of the Board of Publication and all officers elected by it shall hold office until their successors are chosen.

Executive Committee of The Board of Publication

¶ 1203. (1) The Board of Publication shall elect from its membership an Executive Committee of sixteen members, including the Chairman of the Board, who shall serve as Chairman of the Executive Committee. Not more than four members of the Executive Committee shall be from any one of the six Jurisdictions. In addition, the Publishing Agents shall be *ex officio* members of the Executive Committee without vote. Any vacancy occurring in the membership of the Executive Committee shall be filled by it until the next meeting of the Board.

(2) The Executive Committee shall have and exercise all and only those powers which the Board of Publication may delegate to it. It shall meet quarterly to examine the affairs under its charge and shall keep and submit to the Board correct records of its proceedings. Special meetings of the Executive Committee may be called by the Chairman upon his own initiative, and shall be called upon the written request of five members of the Executive Committee. A majority of the members of the Executive Committee shall constitute a quorum.

Enabling Acts

(1) Notwithstanding the foregoing provisions, pending the meeting of the first General Conference of The Methodist Church, and the first meetings of the Jurisdictional Conferences of The Methodist Church, The Board of Publication shall consist of the members composing the Book Committees of the Methodist Episcopal Church and the Methodist Episcopal Church, South, and the Board of Publication of the Methodist Protestant Church, who shall serve and perform their customary duties regarding their respective corporate interests, until their successors are elected and qualify.

The Executive Committees or Local Committee of the respective Book Committees shall perform their customary duties regarding their respective corporate interests until such time as the Board of Publication constituted by the respective Jurisdictional Conferences shall elect an Executive Committee.

The Executive Committees of the respective Book Committees and Local Committee acting as such shall appoint a Co-ordinating Committee of nine members, four of whom being appointed by the Executive Committee of the Book Committee of the Methodist Episcopal Church, four being appointed by the Local Committee of the Book Committee of the Methodist Episcopal Church, South, and one being appointed by the Executive Committee of the Board of Publication of the Methodist Protestant Church.

(2) The Publishing Agents of the three Uniting Churches shall be continued in office and perform their customary duties under the direction and control of the respective Book Committees of the three Uniting Churches until the Jurisdictional Conferences shall have constituted a Board of Publication and until the Publishing Agents are thereafter elected.

(3) All of the present Editors who have been elected either by a General Conference or by a Book Committee of the Uniting Churches, shall be continued in office until the first Jurisdictional Conferences of The Methodist Church, and until the election of Editors by the Board of Publication. If in the interim a vacancy occurs, then the successor to such Editor shall be appointed by the entire Board of Publication, to serve until the election of Editors as above provided.

(4) Any distribution of the net produce of the several corporations to Conference Claimants prior to January 1, 1941, shall be in the customary manner, only to the Conference Claimants of that one of the Uniting Churches to which such corporation belonged.

The term "Conference Claimants" shall also include those who become such prior to January 1, 1941.

The net produce of the several corporations shall be distributed as a single fund on and after January 1, 1941.

REPORT NO. 2. BOOK EDITOR

Calendar No. 17. Adopted May 5. See Journal, Page 267.

Membership of Committee, 135; present when report was adopted, 101; voting for adoption, 101.

¶ 1207. The Board of Publication shall elect quadrennially by ballot a Book Editor, who shall edit all the books of our publication, except those edited by other agencies of the Church; and shall perform such other editorial duties as may be required of him by the Board of Publication. He shall have joint responsibility with the Publishing Agents in passing on all manuscripts considered for publication.

REPORT NO. 3. CHURCH SCHOOL PUBLICATIONS

Calendar No. 18. Adopted May 5. See Journal, Page 269.

Membership of Committee, 135; present when report was adopted, 121; voting for adoption, 121.

¶ 1208. (1) There shall be an Editor of Church School Publications, elected quadrennially by the General Conference. In the event of a vacancy in the office, the Board of Publication shall have authority to elect an Editor to serve until the ensuing General Conference.

(2) The Editor of Church School Publications shall be responsible for the preparation of all curriculum materials, including periodicals, undated materials, and books authorized for use in the program of Christian Education. The circulation of the literature prepared by the Editor of Church School Publications shall be a joint responsibility of the Board of Education and the Board of Publication.

(3) There shall be a Curriculum Committee which shall include in its membership the Editor of Church School Publications, the Book Editor, and the Publishing Agents, which shall determine the curriculum of the Church School. The Editor of Church School Publications, after final approval by the Board of Education, shall prepare the materials to be produced for use in Church Schools, young people's societies, training schools, and all other agencies related in any way to the work of the Board of Education. The Committee shall also make plans for the improvement and circulation of the Church School literature.

(4) The assistants to the Editor of Church School Publications shall be elected annually by the Board of Publication upon nomination of the Editor of Church School Publications. The Board of Publication shall fix and pay the salaries of the Editor of Church School Publications and his assistants and shall have full financial responsibility for all other expenses connected with the work of the Editor of Church School Publications.

(5) The publications of the Board of Education shall be manufactured, published, and distributed through The Methodist Publishing House. In matters involving respon-

sibility the final determination in every case shall lie with the Board of Publication. After consultation with the Publishing Agents, the Editor of Church School Publications shall prepare a complete budget for his work, including salaries of assistants and office secretaries, and travel, to be effective when approved by the Board of Publication, and shall direct its operation from year to year.

(6) There shall be one complete co-ordinated system of literature published by The Methodist Publishing House for the entire Methodist Church. This literature is to be of such type and variety as to meet the needs of all groups of our people.

(7) The Board of Publication and Publishing Agents have authority to decline to publish any item of literature when in their judgment the cost would be greater than should be borne by the publishers.

(8) The Editor of Church School Publications and the Chairman of the Committee on Editorial Division of the Board of Education shall have the right to sit with the Board of Publication for the consideration of matters pertaining to the joint interests of the Board of Publication and the Board of Education and shall have the privilege of the floor, without vote. The Publishing Agents shall have the right to sit with the Board of Education for the consideration of matters pertaining to the joint interests of the Board of Education and the Board of Publication and shall have the privilege of the floor, without vote.

(9) The provisions of ¶ 1208 shall not apply to the promotional materials of the division of Educational Institutions or of the Division of the Local Church.

REPORT No. 4. CHURCH PRESS

Calendar No. 19. Adopted May 5. See Journal, Page 269.

Membership of Committee, 135; present when report was adopted, 95; voting for adoption, 92; voting against adoption, 3.

¶ 1209. WHEREAS, the Enabling Act relating to the Publishing Interests of The Methodist Church contains the following provision: "The Executive Committees of the respective Book Committees and Local Committee acting as such shall appoint a Co-ordinating Committee of nine members, four of such Co-ordinating Committee being appointed by the Executive Committee of the Book Committee of the Methodist Episcopal Church, four being appointed by the Local Committee of the Book Committee of the Methodist Episcopal Church, South, and one being appointed by the Executive Committee of the Board of Publication of the Methodist Protestant Church." Therefore be it

Resolved, That all proposals heretofore submitted or hereafter to be submitted relating to the Church Press be referred to the Co-ordinating Committee mentioned above; and that that Committee be instructed to consider such proposals and any other plan that may develop during the course of the Committee's consideration, and to present to the next General Conference of The Methodist Church a definite plan for official organ or organs for The Methodist Church. And be it further

Resolved, That all official papers of the three Uniting Churches be published and edited until the General Conference shall order otherwise, as they were published and edited at the time of the commencement of the Uniting Conference.

REPORT NO. 5. PUBLISHING AGENTS

Calendar No. 26. Adopted May 6. See Journal, Page 284.

Membership of Committee, 135; present when report was adopted, 101; voting for adoption, 99; voting against adoption, 1; not voting, 1.

¶ 1204. (1) The Board of Publication shall elect, quadrennially, two Publishing Agents.

(2) The Board shall have power to prescribe regulations, not inconsistent with the provisions of this chapter, for the government of the Publishing Agents; and in all such regulations, as well as in their entire management, both the Board and Publishing Agents shall keep in view the object for which The Methodist Publishing House is established, and shall strive to accomplish this object in the most efficient and economical manner.

(3) The Board shall determine the functions of the Publishing Agents so that there shall be unity and efficiency in the operations of the Publishing House.

(4) The Board shall require the Publishing Agents to report to the Executive Committee at least once in each quarter the state of the current business of The Methodist Publishing House during that period.

(5) The Publishing Agents, with the approval of the

Board, shall have authority to extend the business of The Methodist Publishing House in such manner as they may judge to be for the best interests of the Church.

(6) The Publishing Agents shall be the administrative officers of The Methodist Publishing House, under the supervision and direction of the Board, subject to the adjustment of their functions by the Board as authorized in this chapter.

(7) The Board shall require the Publishing Agents to give bonds conditioned upon the faithful discharge of their duties as Publishing Agents and as Treasurers of the various funds committed to their care by action of the General Conference or other bodies of The Methodist Church. The bonds covering each account shall be determined by the Board and the several premiums paid by each account, and the Chairman of the Board shall be the custodian of the Agents' bonds above mentioned. The Publishing Agents, acting in capacity of Treasurers of these various funds, shall submit to the Board annually, and oftener if requested, an audited report of each account, the cost of said report being a charge against the account covered.

(8) The Board shall have power to suspend, after hearing, the Publishing Agents or any of the officers created by this chapter, for misconduct or failure to perform the duties of their office.

Real Estate and Buildings

¶ 1205. (1) The Methodist Publishing House shall not buy, sell, or exchange any real estate except by order of the General Conference, or, between the session of the General Conference, by a two-thirds vote of all the members of the Board of Publication; nor shall the Board authorize any new buildings, or make any improvements, alterations, or repairs to existing buildings to cost in excess of $50,000 except by order of the General Conference, or, between the sessions of the General Conference, by two-thirds vote of all members of the Board. In either case, such vote shall be taken at a regular or called meeting of the Board, and if at a called meeting the purpose of this meeting shall have been stated in the call.

(2) The erection of a new building, or the improvement, alteration, or repair of an existing building, involving an expenditure of not more than $25,000 may be authorized by the vote of a majority of the Executive Committee. These provisions shall not prevent the making of investments on

mortgage security or the protection of the same, or the collection of claims and adjustments.

Printing for Church Agencies

¶ 1206. It is recommended that the General Boards, Institutions and Commissions of The Methodist Church have all their printing done by The Methodist Publishing House.

REPORT NO. 6. TRIBUTE TO DR. CLAUDIUS BUCHANAN
SPENCER

Calendar No. 69. Adopted May 9. See Journal, Page 361.

The swift flight of years since the passing of Dr. Spencer has not dimmed the memory of his vivid personality nor dulled the sharp sense of personal loss experienced by his fellow-craftsmen of the Church Press throughout the land. He was born in Michigan in October, 1856, and died at Kansas City in July, 1934. Pious parents named him Claudius Buchanan after an eminent Baptist divine, and under their nurture and admonition he was educated for the ministry. To his first hard-scrabble appointment in a Michigan mining camp is traceable his deep and lifelong sympathy with the underprivileged. Transferred to Colorado in 1892, his journalistic gift caught the eye of the observant young Chancellor of the University of Denver, William Frazer McDowell, and upon his recommendation he was appointed editor of the *Rocky Mountain Christian Advocate*. What he did in that office for eight years made inevitable his election in 1900 to the *Central Christian Advocate*. For thirty-two years he ruled his realm—a career which is comparable, both in duration and brilliancy, to that of James Monroe Buckley of New York.

As an editor, Dr. Spencer had industry, scholarship, versatility, imagination, gentleness, wit, faith, and insatiable thirst for information. In the pursuit of essential facts he could not be drawn off the scent. Wherever he might be, he was fairly sure to be found in a library running down some blind trail to the fact he wanted to verify. Upon subjects as diverse as Mormonism, Alcohol, Egyptology, and Peace, he wrote with authority. Methodist Unification lay near his heart, and his writings contributed substantially to its consummation. A master of a mighty pen, in his facile grasp it was a lance for chivalrous combat and a trowel for building the walls of the Holy City. His style was all his own, compounded of adequate information, keen logic, and sparkling and pungent wit. Originality was Claudius' way. Finally, above all, he was everyman's friend, and the most delightful of comrades, an inimitable storyteller, and himself the theme of many stories, unselfish, even-tempered, and bubbling with quips and quiddities. His "Alhambra Hollyhocks," the seeds brought from Spain and lovingly distributed broadcast, now blooming in a thousand Western dooryards, are appropriate memorials of a rare soul which found its dearest satisfaction in giving pleasure to others.

RICHARD L. SHIPLEY,   HAROLD PAUL SLOAN,
ROBERT N. BROOKS,   W. L. DUREN,
M. T. PLYLER,   JAMES R. JOY,
CHAS. A. BRITTON, JR., JOHN W. LANGDALE.

REPORT NO. 7. TRIBUTE TO DR. DAN BREARLEY BRUMMITT

Calendar No.·70. Adopted May 9. See Journal, Page 362.

Dan Brearley Brummitt was born in Bately, England, August 13, 1867. At fifteen, Dan came with the family to America and for several years he worked as dock hand and farmer boy in New York state. He attended Kansas Agricultural College for a year, taught school for a year, and then went to Baker University, where he entered the preparatory class along with a young woman, Miss Stella Wyatt.

Before his graduation from Baker in 1894, having been ordained to the Ministry in 1893, young Dan B. Brummitt and Miss Stella Wyatt were married in September, 1894, and they together went to Altamont, Kansas, to serve the church there. Next year their one son was born. A Master of Arts degree from Baker through correspondence was won in 1898, and that year he enrolled at Drew Theological Seminary. So these first thirty years were truly years of preparation for the four marvelously busy decades to follow.

What exacting labors were his! On *The Epworth Herald*, as Circulation Manager for The Methodist Book Concern, as editor of *The Epworth Herald* and as editor of *The Christian Advocate* (Northwestern), and the vast amount of material he turned out for periodicals, these made heavy demands. Then too there were his several well-known books: *Manuel Davidson*, a novel, was published in 1925 and *Shoddy*, a novel, appeared two years later. *Words of Gold*, in which the other side of the life of his Church as portrayed in *Shoddy*, was to appear soon.

But the calendar counts for little in estimating the career of a man such as Dan Brummitt. For back of the output of those busy years given to national and international church gatherings on both sides of the Atlantic and the grind of the print shop, lives that noble soul, so genuine, so youthful, so eager. Dan B. Brummitt certainly embodied the average man of our common humanity. This enabled him to write *Justus Timberline*, which he termed the run of the mine of the members of the Methodist Church.

This man of dynamic and eager soul refused to grow old. Though the burdens pressed hard, that radiant, joyous, and buoyant spirit scattered sunshine everywhere. His was a rare capacity for fellowship, with little regard for rank or station. The average man found at all times a genuine brother in Dan Brummitt. Men came to know him in the byways and on the highways of the world as he went everywhere counting not his life dear unto himself.

His son, now a trained journalist, put a volume into these words, as he confided to his mother, "We knew that Dad was a great man, but we did not know so many other people knew it." How came this to be? Was it not due to that broad catholic spirit that dominated him? As a contender for Christian democracy, this lover of the true and beautiful and the good in mankind became a transparent soul to all of like qualities. As he enabled others to know the common touch, he disclosed the inner secrets of his own life.

Some of us feel that Dan B. Brummitt, an editor of rare qualities, was a casualty of this Uniting Conference. His unrelenting labors overtaxed his strength because of that something which drove him on unmindful of the ultimate consequences. Eighteen months ago under Wesley's oak at Savannah, Ga., stirred by the associations of the place, Dan Brummitt talked to friends with eagerness and abandon of the Methodist Union. He seemed to bear the weight of the world's misery on his heart. This constrained him to the last limit to secure Methodist union. How eagerly and devotedly labored this preacher-editor to bring in the better day! He carried the load of dozens of men in making provision for this Conference. Finally, the break came with the completion of the Uniting Conference Edition. Copy was all in, forms were made ready, the last proof OK'd, and presses were set going, as our eager and devoted brother suddenly took leave for the Conference of the Blest. *Copy all in; hearts left desolate!*

That last morning at home, with his usual tender leave-taking of her from whom he had gone away so often, he passed out of the yard with a glad wave of his hand. Across the threshold of that home no shadow had ever fallen. Since that far-off day of love's young dream at Baker and their early parsonage home-nest to this final morning hour, full and understanding love had been theirs. He who had gone away so many times fell on Wednesday of Holy Week and passed on to that appointment where, as he said so many times, "We can do all the things we haven't had time for here."

M. T. PLYLER,	HAROLD PAUL SLOAN,
W. L. DUREN,	RICHARD L. SHIPLEY,
JAMES R. JOY,	ROBERT N. BROOKS,
JOHN W. LANGDALE,	CHAS. A. BRITTON, JR.

VII. COMMITTEE ON SUPERANNUATE SUPPORT

REPORT NO. 1.   PERMANENT AND PENSION FUNDS

Calendar No. 1.   Adopted. May 1.   See Journal, Page 224.

Membership of Committee, 45; present when report was adopted, 39; voting for adoption, 39.

SECTION 1

SECTION I.   ORGANIZATION OF BOARD OF PENSIONS

¶ 1301.   (1) There shall be a Board of Pensions of The Methodist Church having the administration of the support of Conference Claimants of The Methodist Church in succession to "The Board of Pensions and Relief of The Methodist Episcopal Church," which is incorporated under the laws of the state of Illinois in that name, and in succession to "The Board of Finance of the Methodist Episcopal Church, South," which is incorporated under the laws of the state of Missouri in that name, and in succession to the Board of Managers of "The General Fund for Superannuates of The Methodist Protestant Church," which is incorporated under the laws of the state of Maryland in that name. The three Corporations aforesaid are referred to hereinafter, respectively, as the Illinois Corporation, the Missouri Corporation, and the Maryland Corporation. These three Corporations shall be continued with their headquarters in Chicago, Illinois, St. Louis, Missouri, and Baltimore, Maryland, respectively, but with their corporate names changed to, and to be known as, "The Board of Pensions of The Methodist Church, Incorporated in Illinois," and "The Board of Pensions of The Methodist Church, Incorporated in Missouri," and "The Board of Pensions of The Methodist Church, Incorporated in Maryland," respectively.

(2) The Illinois Corporation shall be responsible for the administration of funds for the support of Conference Claimants in the Northeastern, the North Central, the Western and the Central Jurisdictional Conferences, and

the Missouri Corporation shall be responsible for the administration of funds for the support of Conference Claimants in the Southeastern and the South Central Jurisdictional Conferences.

¶ 1302. (1) The Board of Pensions of The Methodist Church, hereinafter, for the sake of brevity, called the Board, shall be composed of three Bishops at large, to be chosen by the Council of Bishops, and one member of each Jurisdictional Conference for every 300,000 Church members of the Jurisdictional Conference or major fraction of that number; *provided*, that each Jurisdictional Conference shall have at least one Minister and one Layman, all to be elected by the Jurisdictional Conference. A member of the Board shall serve for a period of four years and, in any case, until his successor shall have been elected.

(2) The members of the Board shall constitute the members of the Illinois Corporation, the Missouri Corporation and the Maryland Corporation respectively, and the annual meetings of the three aforesaid Corporations and of the Board shall be held at the same place and consecutively in the order mentioned.

(3) In all matters not specifically covered by General Conference legislation, the Board shall have authority to adopt rules and policies for the administration of the support of Conference Claimants, with variations for each of the territories assigned respectively to the Illinois Corporation and to the Missouri Corporation as conditions may require. It shall meet annually for the review and consideration of the work committed to its care and shall take such measures as it may deem advisable to co-ordinate the work of the Illinois Corporation and the Missouri Corporation.

¶ 1303. (1) The Board shall elect quadrennially a President, a Vice-President, and a Recording Secretary from its own membership. At the first meeting of the Board, following the respective meetings of the Jurisdictional Conferences, it shall elect two Executive Secretaries for a term of four years. The two Executive Secretaries of the Board shall be members thereof by virtue of their office. A vacancy in the office of either of the Executive Secretaries shall be filled by the Board. One of the Executive Secretaries shall have charge of the affairs of the Illinois Corporation, the other shall have charge of the affairs of the Missouri Corporation, under the direction of the Board, in the respective Jurisdictional Conferences assigned to each, and both shall have co-ordinate powers and duties as the executive officers of the Board. The respective Treasurers of the

Illinois Corporation and the Missouri Corporation shall be elected by the Board and shall be the Treasurers of the Board.

(2) A vacancy in the membership of the Board shall be filled for the unexpired term by the Board.

(3) A majority of the members of the Board shall constitute a quorum.

SECTON II. AUTHORIZATIONS

¶ 1304. (1) The Illinois Corporation and the Missouri Corporation shall be responsible for the administration of the funds and properties already in their hands, respectively, or which shall be put into their hands hereafter for their respective groups of Jurisdictional Conference, and they shall also be responsible for the execution of the rules and policies of the Board, particularly as these rules and policies relate to their respective fields of operation.

(2) In general, the respective tasks and functions of the Illinois Corporation and the Missouri Corporation shall be those heretofore performed, respectively, by The Board of Pensions and Relief of the Methodist Episcopal Church and The Board of Finance of the Methodist Episcopal Church, South. The functions of the Maryland Corporation shall be confined to the administration of the General Fund for Superannuates, formerly of the Methodist Protestant Church, according to provisions hereinafter made, and the Maryland Corporation shall so operate until the General Conference shall order otherwise, unless dissolved as hereinafter provided.

(3) Until the total membership of the Board shall have been duly elected as herein provided, the membership thereof shall consist of the combined membership of The Board of Pensions and Relief of the Methodist Episcopal Church, The Board of Finance of the Methodist Episcopal Church, South, and The Board of Managers of the General Endowment Fund for Superannuates of the Methodist Protestant Church, as such membership stood at the beginning of the Uniting Conference, and any vacancies in such membership shall be filled for the interim period by the Board. *Ad interim*, the organization of the Board shall be the same as that provided in ¶ 1303, (1), above.

¶ 1305. (1) The Board is authorized to receive, hold in trust and administer, through its Corporations, all such funds as Connectional Permanent Funds, Reserve Pension Funds, and the Chartered Fund, and it shall have power to apportion these duties to the Illinois Corporation and the Missouri Corporation as it may deem advisable.

(2) The Board is authorized to receive, hold in trust and administer, through its Corporations, Endowment Funds belonging to Annual Conferences, or other funds for the support of Conference Claimants to be administered for the benefit of such Annual Conferences; *provided,* that at no time shall any part of the principal of the Endowment Funds be spent or appropriated for any purpose. The net income of such Endowment Funds shall be disbursed annually for the benefit of Conference Claimants of the Annual Conferences in their respective fields of operation.

(3) The Board is authorized and empowered to receive any bequest made or intended for the benefit of disabled, Superannuated and/or Retired Ministers, the widows of Ministers and the dependent minor children of Ministers, such persons being commonly called "Conference Claimants," of the Methodist Episcopal Church, the Methodist Episcopal Church, South, the Methodist Protestant Church, or The Methodist Church, and if the language of such bequest be inexact, the Board shall administer or dispose of such bequests in the manner it deems most equitable, according to the intent of the donor, after careful inquiry into the circumstances connected with the making of the bequest.

¶ 1306. The Board and each of its Corporations shall adopt ways and means of increasing the Endowment Funds to be administered either for the Board or the Annual Conferences, by obtaining gifts, annuities, and bequests and also for the purpose of increasing the current contributions of the Pastoral Charges for Conference Claimants.

¶ 1307. The Board shall share in the funds raised for the Benevolence Budget of the denomination, as provided for in ¶ 504. (NOTE. ¶ 504 is found in Calendar No. 42, Report No. 5 of the General Standing Committee on Membership and Temporal Economy.)

REPORT NO. 2.   PERMANENT AND PENSION FUND

Calendar No. 4. Adopted May 2. See Journal, Page 232.

Membership of Committee, 45; present when report was adopted, 41; voting for adoption, 41.

SECTION I.   THE CHARTERED FUND

¶ 1308. The Chartered Fund shall be administered by the Illinois Corporation for the benefit of all Annual Conferences in The Methodist Church, the boundaries of which are within the United States, unless the General Conference shall order otherwise, and once a year the net earnings of the Fund, after provision for depreciation, shall be divided equally among such Annual Conferences in accordance with the provisions of the Charter of said Fund.

¶ 1309. Until the General Conference shall order otherwise, the income from the Endowment Fund for Superannuates held by the Missouri Corporation shall be distributable as annuities on account of service of Conference Claimants formerly rendered in an Annual Conference of the Methodist Episcopal Church, South, or service rendered in an Annual Conference of The Methodist Church within the territory of the Missouri Corporation; *provided,* however, that in the case of any Annual Conference formerly of the Methodist Episcopal Church which shall remain substantially unaffected in its liability for annuities by unification, in order to participate in the distribution made by the Missouri Corporation, it shall be necessary for such Conference to deposit with the Missouri Corporation assets sufficient to produce an annual income equivalent to the amount which would be distributed to such Conference in the event it elects to participate.

¶ 1310. (1) For the rules and regulations applicable respectively to the Annuity Distribution, also to the administration of relief, in the territory of the Illinois Corporation, see ¶¶ 1315-1338.

(2) For the rules and regulations applicable respectively to the distribution, also the administration of relief, in the territory of the Missouri Corporation, see ¶¶ 1339-1341.

(3) For provisions concerning the joint operation of the Ministers' Reserve Pension Fund by the Illinois Corporation and the Missouri Corporation, and the Plan of the Fund, see ¶¶ 1342-1355.

¶ 1311. The assets of the General Funds for Superannuates of the Methodist Protestant Church shall be placed in the Chartered Fund of the Methodist Church, and the income therefrom shall be distributed by the Board to the Annual Conferences concerned according to its judgment of the relative liability for annuities to be assumed within the respective territories of the Illinois Corporation and the Missouri Corporation; *provided,* however that the annuities paid to the said claimants shall be at the annuity rate established by the Annual Conference in which membership is held.

¶ 1312. (1) There shall be set up a Distributing Committee in each Annual Conference to be merged after Unification, to be composed of three members appointed by the Conference at its session immediately succeeding the Uniting Conference, which Committee shall act jointly with simi-

lar committees of three members each from the other Annual
Conference or Conferences having an interest in the merger
of such Annual Conference; said Joint Committee to have
power to allocate the Conference Claimants and distributable assets of the Conference to be merged.

(2) The Distributing Committee shall determine the
number of service years rendered in the Annual Conferences
which will lose their identity in the merging of Conference
territory and the findings of the Committee shall be final
unless definite evidence to the contrary be discovered, and
the annuity payments by the continuing Conference shall
be made accordingly.

(3) The Distributing Committee shall keep complete minutes of its transactions, and a copy thereof shall be filed with
the Secretary of each Annual Conference of The Methodist
Church concerned in its work.

(4) Until the work of the Distributing Committee shall
have been completed, the corporate organization of the Annual Conference in process of merger shall be maintained.
After the Distributing Committee shall have completed its
work, the officers of such corporation, subject to the completion of its business, shall dissolve it, they being authorized
to do so by the Annual Conference concerned.

SECTION II. CONFERENCE ORGANIZATIONS

¶ 1313. (1) Annual Conferences are authorized to establish and maintain investment funds: Preachers' Aid
Societies and organizations and funds of similar character,
under such names, plans, rules, and regulations as they
may determine, the income from which shall be applied
to the support of Conference Claimants. It is recommended that each Annual Conference provide an incorporated
Board to administer its permanent funds, under some other
corporate name than that used by the Board of Pensions.

(2) Subject to the laws of the State in which it is incorporated, an Annual Conference shall have power to require from its members in the effective relation an annual
contribution to either its Permanent or Reserve Fund or
for current distribution or to a Preachers' Aid Society for
the benefit of its annuitants, subject to the following provisions, (1) The annual payment may be made in installments as provided by the Annual Conference; (2) the Conference may fix a financial penalty for failure of the
member to pay; (3) in case his membership in the Annual
Conference is terminated under the provisions of the *Discipline*, the Conference may refund the amount so paid, in
whole or in part, after a hearing has been given to the per-

son terminating his membership, in case such hearing is requested; (4) the making of such payment shall not be used as the ground of contractual obligations upon the part of the Conference, or as the ground of any special or additional annuity claim of a member against the Conference, neither shall it prevent disallowance of his annuity claim by Conference action.

(3) Each Annual Conference shall hold one service during its sessions, to be known as the Conference Claimants' Anniversary, for the promotion of the interests of Conference Claimants.

(4) Each congregation shall observe annually one Sunday in the interests of Conference Claimants, which shall be known as "Veterans' Day."

REPORT NO. 3. MINISTERS' RESERVE PENSION FUND

Calendar No. 15. Adopted May 4. See Journal, Page 262.

Membership of Committee, 45; present when report was adopted, 34; voting for adoption, 34.

Establishment

¶ 1342. (1) A reserve pension system, to be called the Ministers' Reserve Pension Fund of The Methodist Church, hereinafter called the Fund, is hereby established. It shall be administered by the Board of Pensions in accordance with and subject to the provisions that follow.

(2) An Annual or Mission Conference, at any time, on its own determination, by a two-thirds vote of its membership present and voting, may enter the Fund and may actively participate therein when it accepts the conditions and fulfills the requirements herein set forth.

Definitions

¶ 1343. (1) The following definitions shall apply to the interpretation of the Plan of the Fund, unless the context plainly indicates otherwise:

(2) "Employer" shall mean any connectional Board, organization, or institution that receives the services of a member of the Fund in either a pastoral or non-pastoral capacity and which shall pay therefor any form of salary, compensation, or allowance.

(3) "Support" of a member of the Fund shall mean:

(a) The sum or sums annually received from a Pastoral Charge as compensation for his services, plus an amount equivalent to fifteen per cent thereof, if the minister occupy a parsonage free of rent;

(b) The salary of a District Superintendent received from the District as compensation for his services, plus an amount equivalent to fifteen per cent thereof, if he occupy a district parsonage free of rent;

(c) The salary of a Bishop received from the Episcopal Fund as compensation for his services, plus the allowance for Episcopal residence;

(d) The salary or compensation received by a Pastor from a Federated or community Church, or from a Church of another denomination, plus an amount equivalent to fifteen per cent thereof, if he occupy a personage free of rent;

(e) The financial aid furnished by a missionary board, or other organization;

(f) The salary, compensation, or allowance received for services rendered under special Episcopal appointment.

(4) "Regular Interest" shall mean earned interest not to exceed four per cent compounded annually.

(5) "Service Annuity" shall mean an annuity payable quarterly in advance during life, beginning at the date of retirment, to be provided by the Fund on the basis of allocated credits together with the "Regular Interest" accumulated thereon.

(6) "Income Annuity" shall mean an annuity payable quarterly in advance during life, beginning at the date of retirement, to be provided by the Fund on the basis of the personal contributions of the member together with the "Regular Interest" accumulated thereon.

(7) "Pension" shall mean the total of the "Service Annuity" and the "Income Annuity."

(8) "Widow's Pension" shall mean an annuity payable quarterly in advance to the widow of a member of the Fund who dies before attaining retirement, to be provided by the Fund on the basis of the personal contributions of the deceased member, together with the "Regular Interest" accumulated thereon, plus three-fourths of his "Service Annuity" credits, together with the "Regular Interest" accumulated thereon.

(9) "Child's Annuity" shall mean an annuity payable quarterly in advance to a minor child of a deceased member of the Fund.

(10) "Minor Child" shall mean a child under twenty-one years of age.

(11) The meaning of the word "child" shall be interpreted to include "a child legally adopted."

(12) "New Entrant" shall mean a Minister in good standing in Full Membership in an Annual or Mission Conference on or after the entry of said Conference into the Fund.

(13) "Previous Entrant" shall mean a Minister in good standing in Full Membership in an Annual or Mission Conference, prior to the entry of said Conference into the Fund.

(14) "Pension Code" shall mean the rules and regulations concerning pensions and relief contained in ¶¶ 1315-1338 inclusive.

Membership

¶ 1334. (1) The membership of the Fund shall consist of the "New Entrants" in Annual or Mission Conferences in the United States of America; *provided*, however, that "New Entrants" past thirty-five years of age shall not be accepted as members of the Fund, unless an initial provision for "Service Annuity" shall be made by or for them in such manner and amount as shall be determined by the Board of Pensions.

(2) "Previous Entrants" who are Members of Annual or Mission Conferences which are participating in the Fund may become members of the Fund by a two-thirds vote of the Conference membership present and voting; *provided*, however, that accrued service obligations under the "Pension Code" shall be funded for or by such "Previous Entrants," in such manner and amount as shall be satisfactory to the Board of Pensions.

(3) A minister received by transfer into an Annual or Mission Conference on and after the date of entry of the Conference into the Fund shall be classed as a "New Entrant" while serving in such Conference. When such Minister shall transfer to an Annual or Mission Conference not participating in the Fund, he shall be subject to the provisions of the "Pension Code" for years served in such Conference, but upon subsequent entry into an Annual or Mission Conference participating in the Fund, such minister shall resume contribution and receive credits therefrom.

Contributions by the Conference

¶ 1343. (1) Each Annual or Mission Conference that enters the Fund shall contribute annually thereto, during the first decade of its participation, an amount equivalent to five and one-half per cent of the total "Support" of its Members who are also members of the Fund; the rate of contribution during the second decade of participation shall be six and one-half per cent; and thereafter the rate of contribution shall be seven and one-half per cent. With the approval of the Board of Pensions an Annual or Mission Conference may adopt the seven-and-one-half-per-cent rate initially, or at any time during the first two decades aforementioned.

(2) Each Annual or Mission Conference shall determine the plan by which it shall secure the annual contribution to the Fund required in the preceding section of this paragraph, and shall make suitable and adequate provision therefor.

(3) Each Annual or Mission Conference shall collect the contributions due the Fund, and shall have power to adjudicate all questions in connection therewith.

(4) The contributions required in subsection 1 of this paragraph shall be made to the Treasurer of the Annual or Mission Conference, or any other officer who may be designated by the Conference, who shall transmit the same to the Board of Pensions within thirty days after the session of such Conference, together with a schedule of information showing the members covered by the payment transmitted.

(5) A deficiency in the payment of the annual amount required of an Annual or Mission Conference shall reduce accordingly the "Service Annuity" credits of the members of the Fund in such Conference and also any other benefits provided by the Fund for them, unless otherwise ordered by the Conference as provided in subsection 6.

(6) In the event of the failure of a Pastoral Charge, or "Employer" to pay, in whole or in part, the amount apportioned in any year, by an Annual or Mission Conference, for the purposes of the Fund, such Conference shall reduce equitably the "Service Annuity" credit for such year of service of such member of the Fund serving said Pastoral Charge, District, or "Employer," and shall advise the Board of Pensions of its action in the case.

(7) For purposes of adjudication of matters pertaining to the contributions to the Fund in an Annual or Mission Conference for co-operation with the Board of Pensions each Conference participating in the Fund shall elect annually a Committee on Reserve Pensions to consist of not fewer than five nor more than nine persons.

¶ 1346. An annual contribution, the equivalent of two per cent of his "Support," shall be paid directly to the Fund by each member thereof in the effective relation, in quarterly installments payable in advance, on the following dates: February 15, May 15, August 15, and November 15. Such contribution shall be applicable to "Income Annuity" credit only.

¶ 1347. (1) A member of the Fund who shall have reached the age of sixty-five years and who shall have been granted the retired relation shall receive thereafter, during his lifetime, a "Service Annuity." Upon the death of a member of the Fund while receiving a "Service Annuity" the equivalent of seventy per cent of such Annuity shall be continued to his widow, if their marriage took place before the member entered into the "Service Annuity."

The "Service Annuity" and the seventy per cent thereof to be continued to the widow shall be the actuarial equivalent of his allocated "Service Annuity" credits together with the "Regular Interest" accumulated thereon, determined on the basis of the actual ages of the member and his wife at the time of entry into the "Service Annuity."

If at the time of his entry into the "Service Annuity" a member be unmarried or a widower, the calculation of the amount of such "Service Annuity" shall be made on the basis of assumed equal ages for man and wife.

The "Service Annuity" shall be determined according to the tables of annuity rates for such purpose, in current use by the Board of Pensions.

(2) At the same time that a member of the Fund, whether married or single, is granted a "Service Annuity," he shall be entitled to an "Income Annuity" of a type identical with his "Service Annuity," the amount thereof to be the actuarial equivalent of his personal contributions to the Fund together with the "Regular Interest" accumulated thereon.

The "Income Annuity" shall be determined according to the tables of annuity rates for such purpose, in current use by the Board of Pensions.

Widow's Pension

¶ 1348. (1) If a member of the Fund die while in the Effective or Supernumerary Relation, a "Pension" shall be paid to his widow, based on her age and provided by the total of her deceased husband's personal contributions, together with the "Regular Interest" accumulated thereon, plus seventy per cent of his "Service Annuity" credits together with the "Regular Interest" accumulated thereon at the time of his death.

(2) If the "Pension" of a widow whose husband died while he was in the Effective or Supernumerary Relation be less than $300, at the discretion of the Board of Pensions, she may be granted annually an additional amount; *provided*, however, that in such case the total of the "Pension"

and the Grant received by her shall not exceed $300 per annum.

Child's Pension

¶ 1349. (1) Each "Minor Child" of a deceased member of the Fund may be granted an Annuity of $75 until attainment of age sixteen, to be discontinued immediately thereafter, unless the child be enrolled and regularly attending a standard school or college.

(2) Upon presentation to it annually of a satisfactory certificate of enrollment, attendance, and work done in a standard school or college, the Board of Pensions may grant a child of a deceased member of the Fund an Annuity of $150 from age sixteen until attainment of age twenty-one.

Limitation of Annual Payments

¶ 1350. (1) If a member of the Fund die before attaining retirement, the total of the annual payments thereafter, in any year, to his widow and minor children shall not exceed seventy per cent of the average "Support" for the preceding year of the members of his Conference who were members of the Fund.

(2) If a member of the Fund die while receiving a "Pension," the total of the annual payments thereafter, in any year, to his widow and children shall not exceed the annual "Pension" which he was receiving prior to his decease.

Refund

¶ 1351. (1) Upon ceasing to be a member of an Annual or Mission Conference prior to retirement, a member of the Fund shall receive as a refund, in lieu of all other benefits, a sum equivalent to the total of his own contributions to the Fund, together with the "Regular Interest" accumulated thereon.

(2) Upon ceasing to be a Member of an Annual or Mission Conference after retirement, the "Service Annuity" shall cease automatically, and the "Income Annuity" shall be commuted in the form of a cash settlement to be actuarially determined and made by the Board of Pensions.

(3) If a member of the Fund die prior to receipt of any installment of his "Income Annuity," and without leaving a widow or minor child or children, there shall be refunded to his estate a sum equivalent to the total of his contributions to the Fund, together with the "Regular Interest" accumulated thereon.

(4) If the widow of a member of the Fund remarry, the "Service Annuity" shall cease automatically, and the "In-

come Annuity" shall be commuted in the form of a cash settlement to be actuarially determined and made by the Board of Pensions; this shall apply to a surviving widow of a member who died while in the Retired Relation, as well as to a widow of a member who died while in the Effective or Supernumerary Relation.

Disability Benefits

¶ 1352. (1) An annual Disability Allowance may be given to a disabled member of the Fund under age sixty-five, if disability shall have been evident for a period of not less than one hundred eighty days, and the member shall have submitted to such examinations as may be required by the Board of Pensions, and it shall appear from the reports that his health shall have failed as a result of disease or injury, and that presumably he is totally and permanently incapacitated for both Ministerial work and the support of his family.

The annual Disability Allowance shall not exceed one-third of the average "Support" of the members of his Conference who shall have been members of the Fund during the preceeding Annual Conference year. At the discretion of the Board of Pensions, the initial payment of the Allowance may be made to cover all or any part of the waiting period of one hundred eighty days, or only the period of disability following the termination of the waiting period.

(2) During the continuance of his disability, a member of the Fund shall receive an annual allocation to be applied on his "Service Annuity" credit, equivalent to the current "Service Annuity" credit in the Annual or Mission Conference of which he is a member, said allocation to be provided from the Disability Fund.

(3) When recommended by the Board of Pensions, the continuation of the above Disability Benefits (subsections 1, 2) shall be subject to the yearly approval of the member's Annual or Mission Conference.

(4) During the continuance of his disability, a member of the Fund shall be exempt from the requirement to contribute to the Fund, but when his disability has been terminated and he has entered into a salaried relationship with a Pastoral Charge, District, or "Employer" he shall resume contribution to the Fund.

(5) If a disabled member of the Fund recover sufficiently to resume ministerial work or to engage in a remunerative occupation, his Disability Allowance may be reduced or terminated by the Board of Pensions at its discretion.

(6). During the continuance of his disability, the member may be required, at the discretion of the Board, while still under the age of sixty-five years, to have a medical examination at any time by a physician appointed to act in behalf of the Board of Pensions.

(7) If disability continue until age sixty-five be attained, the Disability Benefits shall terminate and thereafter a disabled member of the fund shall receive his "Pension," according to the provisions of ¶ 1347.

Funds

¶ 1353. (1) The annual contributions required in ¶ 1345, sub-section 1, shall be appropriated for the purposes of the Fund according to the following percentages:

Service Annuity Fund .70%
Disability, Widow', and Children's Funds . .27%
Contingent Fund 3%

(2) The seventy per cent of the contributions of an Annual or Mission Conference for the Service Annuity Fund shall be apportioned equally among its members in the effective relation who shall be also members of the Fund, except as provided in ¶ 1345, sub-sections 5, 6, and shall be allocated to each of them annually.

The amounts so allocated together with the "Regular Interest" thereon shall be trusteed by the Board of Pensions for the Service Annuities described in ¶ 1347, sub-section 1.

(3) The twenty-seven per cent of the contributions of the Annual or Mission Conferences for the Disability, Widows', and Children's Funds shall be administered by the Board of Pensions as indicated in ¶¶ 1347-1350, 1352.

(4) The three per cent of the contributions of the Annual or Mission Conferences for the Contingent Fund shall be administered by the Board of Pensions, as hereinafter provided.

(5) A Contingent Fund shall be created and administered by the Board of Pensions to which shall be credited:

(a) The three per cent of the Annual or Mission Conference contributions provided in sub-sections 1, 4, of this paragraph;

. (b) The excess interest earnings above "Regular Interest" in any of the other Funds;

(c) The "Service Annuity" credits released when a Minister ceases to be a member of the Fund;

(d) Any resources of the Ministers' Reserve Pension Fund not otherwise designated or allocated.

(6) The Contingent Fund shall be used at the discretion

of the Board of Pensions in such ways and for such purposes as in the judgment of the said Board shall best serve the interests for which the Ministers' Reserve Pension Fund is created.

Initial Reserve Fund

¶ 1354. (1) Each Annual or Mission Conference entering the Fund shall be required to provide an Initial Reserve Fund for the liabilities assumed on account of "New Entrants." The amount of such Initial Reserve Fund, the conditions of its actuarial calculation, and the manner of financing its liabilities shall be determined by the Board of Pensions on request of the Annual or Mission Conference concerned.

(2) The Initial Reserve Fund and the earnings therefrom shall be used exclusively for the financing of the aforesaid liabilities.

Authorization

¶ 1355. (1) The Board of Pensions is authorized, instructed, and empowered to put the Ministers' Reserve Pension Fund Plan as herein set forth into operation in any Annual or Mission Conference after such Conference shall have decided to enter and shall have made provision for the requisite Initial Reserve Fund specified herein; *provided*, however, that if there be too few Conferences to secure a proper distribution of risks at the beginning of operations, the Board of Pensions may provide from its general funds a temporary subvention in amount sufficient to protect the Fund from actuarial deficit which might be caused by early claims.

(2) The Board of Pensions is hereby authorized to act as a Reserve Funding Agency for such Annual or Mission Conferences as may desire to transfer to it any or all of their obligations for "Previous Entrants" under the "Pension Code" at a fixed rate of annuity per year of service.

(3) The Board of Pensions is hereby authorized to administer the Fund and to adopt such rules and regulations as may be necessary for the efficient operation of the Fund, subject to the limitation that this power shall not be exercised so as to nullify any of the provisions of the Plan.

NOTE: The Editor of the *Discipline* is instructed to make all necessary numerical changes in the cross-references which occur in the above text which have been carried over from previous *Disciplines*.

The Methodist Church · 657

REPORT NO 4

Calendar No. 20. Adopted May 5. See Journal, Page 272.
Membership of Committee, 45; present when report
was adopted, 37; voting for adoption 37.

SECTION V. REGULATIONS FOR THE TERRITORY OF THE
MISSOURI CORPORATION

Rules and Regulations

The administration of the pensions and support of Conference Claimants within the Annual Conferences of the
Southeastern and South Central Jurisdictional Conferences
shall be with the Missouri Corporation and shall be governed
by the following rules and regulations:

¶ 1339. (1) The support of the Conference Claimants
within the Annual Conferences of the Southeastern and
South Central Jurisdictional Conferences shall be received
and administered by two bodies, The Board of Pensions—
Missouri Corporation and the Annual Conference Board of
Conference Claimants. The Missouri Corporation receives
its funds from Endowment Funds, the annual income from
which is appropriated to the total number of the Claimants
of its Area, upon the basis of service. The Annual Conference Board of Conference Claimants obtains its funds
from an apportionment upon the Conference, from the annual distribution from The Publishing House, from the
Chartered Fund and from the income from any Conference owned Endowment Funds.

(2) The Funds available for appropriation annually by
the Missouri Corporation shall be distributed to the Conference Claimants of The Methodist Church within the territory administered by said Board as follows: (a) To the
Retired Ministers, on the basis of years of service; (b) To
the widows of deceased ministers, on the basis of the number of years that they have been the wives of effective Traveling Preachers; and the amount shall be seventy per cent
of that paid to the Retired Ministers for a like number of
effective years of service.

(3) The Board of Conference Claimants shall estimate
annually the amount that will be necessary in addition to
what may be received from the Missouri Corporation, The
Publishing House, the Chartered Fund and other sources
to provide a reasonable support for the ensuing year for
Retired Ministers, and the widows and dependent orphaned
children of deceased Members of the Conference, and shall
recommend this amount for apportionment upon the Con-

ference as other funds are apportioned to the Annual Conference.

(4) The amount approved by the Annual Conference for Conference Claimants shall be apportioned to the several Districts of the Conference on the same ratio of percentage as other funds are apportioned, but shall be kept separate and distinct from the Benevolence apportionment. The District Stewards shall apportion to the Charges within their respective Districts the total amount apportioned to the Districts respectively, on a percentage basis of the salary received by the Pastor in each Charge for the preceding year.

(5) The amount apportioned to each charge for Conference Claimants shall be paid in the same proportion as the District Superintendent and the Pastor are paid, and the Claimants' *pro rata* shall be sent to the Conference Treasurer quarterly. In the Statistical Table, No. III, of the Annual Conference Minutes, there shall be provided a separate column with the caption, "Conference Claimants," which shall show the amount apportioned to each Charge and the amount paid, in the same manner as to the District Superintendent and the Pastor.

(6) The Secretary of each Annual Conference shall keep a complete service record of all Ministerial Members of the Annual Conference and, in the chronological roll of such members published annually in the Annual Minutes, he shall add a column showing the net service years of each such Member up to date of publication. The Secretary of each Annual Conference shall certify to the Secretary of the Missouri Corporation the names and years of active service of the Retired Ministers and of the widows of ministers of the Annual Conference. The years of active service of a Retired Minister shall be the years from the date of his admission on trial to the date of his retirement, less the years within this period when he may have been located, supernumerary, retired, or appointed to student work without Pastoral assignment; *provided*, however, that only two years shall be allowed for the time he was on trial. The years of service to be counted for a Minister's widow shall be the years she was his wife during his active service.

(7) The Board of Conference Claimants shall distribute the moneys received on apportionment and otherwise to the Retired Ministers, and widows and orphans of deceased Members of the Conference, as stated in subsection 1; *provided* that each Annual Conference may set apart such part of its funds as it may desire to supplement the appropriation for necessitous cases; and *provided* further, that when

a Minister breaks down in the work and is placed on the retired list, his claim shall begin from the time at which he ceased to receive any support from his last Charge.

¶ 1340. (1) Service years formerly rendered by Conference Claimants in the Methodist Episcopal Church, and the Methodist Protestant Church, respectively, except as otherwise herein provided, shall be counted for Annuity Claim without discrimination in the Annual Conferences included in the territory assigned to the Missouri Corporation.

(2) The Missouri Corporation is authorized and directed to make a comprehensive study of the clearinghouse system of distribution of Divided Annuity Responsibility and it shall report its findings to the General Conference of 1940.

Judicial Decisions

¶ 1341. The Board of Conference Claimants shall be subject to the following regulations:

The Lay Member of the Board may or may not be a Member of the Annual Conference.

The produce of The Publishing House and the Chartered Fund, set apart for Superannuate Ministers and the widows and orphans of Ministers, shall be added to the fund raised for Conference Claimants and distributed to the Claimants according to the time of active service rendered by the Claimants.

The Board may reserve, in its hands, so much of its funds as may be necessary during the year to pay on the funeral expenses of deceased Claimants, and to relieve Claimants who may be brought into unforeseen need or distress, the Conference having the right to approve, recommit, or amend its report.

An appropriation may be made by the Board to one whose claim has arisen since the preceding session of the Conference.

The claim of a superannuate is on the Conference of which he is a Member.

Conference Claimants living in the bounds of territory ceded by the Jurisdictional Conference from one Annual Conference to another should be ceded with the territory, but they have the legal right to continue to be Claimants on the Annual Conference from which the territory is ceded.

Ministers on Trial and the families of deceased Ministers on Trial are not beneficiaries of the superannuate funds.

Location for any cause instantly cancels all claims on the superannuate funds, both for the Minister and his family; but the Conference may, if it desires, levy an assessment and make an appropriation as a charity, though not so as to divert the collections taken for the Conference Claimants.

Widows of Superannuate Ministers who married them after their superannuation do not become Conference Claimants.

The widow of a Traveling Minister who withdraws from our Church and unites with another does not forfeit her legal claim on the superannuate funds; but should she in doing so, or thereafter, attack our Church, that claim shall thereby be forfeited.

Children of a deceased Minister twenty-one years of age, sound in mind and body, shall not be Claimants.

The voluntary renunciation by a Member of an Annual Conference of his claim or that of his family does not abrogate the subsequent claim of his widow and the orphaned children.

REPORT No 5

Calendar No. 21. Adopted May 5. See Journal, Page 271.

Membership of Committee, 45; present when report was adopted, 37; voting for adoption, 37.

SECTION III. BOARD OF CONFERENCE CLAIMANTS

Organization and Duties

¶ 1314. (1) There shall be organized in each Annual Conference a Conference Board, auxiliary to The Board of Pensions, to be known as the Board of Conference Claimants, which shall have charge of the interests and work of providing for the support of Conference Claimants of the Annual Conference, except as otherwise provided for by The Board of Pensions.

(2) The Board of Conference Claimants shall be composed of not less than twelve members, effective Ministers and Laymen in equal number, to be elected at the first session of the Annual Conference following the Uniting Conference and so arranged in classes that one-third may be elected annually thereafter.

(3) The Board of Conference Claimants shall report to the Annual Conference, the names, addresses, and years of service of the Conference Claimants, the names of those who have died during the year, the names of the dependent children of deceased members of the Conference and any other useful information, and show separately the amount paid to each by the Conference from the annuity and necessitious fund and by the Board of Pensions.

Retired Ministers, the widows of Ministers during their

widowhood, and dependent children of deceased Ministers are Conference Claimants.

The appropriations to the Conference Claimants shall be subject to the approval of the Annual Conference.

(4) The Board of Conference Claimants shall make a report to the Board of Pensions immediately following the session of the Annual Cnference and upon the forms provided for that purpose by the Board of Pensions.

(5) The Board of Conference Claimants shall not have power to borrow money for the purpose of making payment to the Claimants.

REPORT NO. 6

Calendar No. 22. Adopted May 5. See Journal, Page 272.

Membership of Committee, 45; present when report was adopted, 35; voting for adoption 35.

ARTICLE XVI

Divided Annuity Responsibility

¶ 1330. (1) The responsibility for annuity for the approved years of service of a Conference Claimant shall rest with the Annual Conference in which the service was performed, or its legal successor; *provided,* however, that service rendered in the territory of the Missouri Corporation prior to the Uniting Conference shall be the responsibility of the Annual Conference within the territory of the Illinois Corporation in which the retired relation has been granted.

(2) The clearinghouse system of distribution of Divided Annuity Responsibility shall be continued until the General Conference shall order otherwise, and the clearinghouse figures shall be determined by the Board of Pensions as formerly, subject to such modifications as may be necessitated by the provisions of subsection 1 above.

(3) When fixing the appropriations from the income of the Connectional Permanent Fund, the Board of Pensions through its Illinois Corporation, shall give special consideration to the exigencies arising in Annual Conferences which pay an annuity rate of $10 or less per year of service of a Retired Minister, and in which the application of the principle of Divided Annuity Responsibility has produced a notably adverse effect.

(4) The Board of Pensions is hereby authorized and directed to make a comprehensive study of the problem of devising equitable means to assign annuity responsibility, including service in Missions and Mission Conferences, and

it is instructed to recommend a plan for the samè to thè General Conferehce of 1940.

REPORT NO 7

Calendar No. 34. Adopted May 8. See Journal, Page 304.

Membership of Committee, 45; present when report was adopted, 37; voting for adoption, 37.

SECTION IV.   REGULATIONS FOR THE TERRITORY OF THE ILLINOIS CORPORATION

The administration of the pensions and support of Conference Claimants within the Annual Conferences of the Northeastern, North Central, Central, and Western Jurisdictional Conferences shall be with the Illinois Corporation and shall be governed by the rules and regulations contained in the following Code:

THE PENSION CODE

ARTICLE I

¶ 1315. *Definition of Conference Claimants*

Retired Ministers, the widows of ministers, during their widowhood, and dependent children of deceased Ministers are Conference Claimants.

ARTICLE II

¶ 1316. *Nature of Ministerial Support*

Assumption of the obligations of the Ministry required to be made at the time of his admission to membership in an Annual Conference puts upon the Church the inevitable counter-obligation of providing a comfortable support for the minister during the period of his membership in an Annual Conference and for his widow and dependent children after his death, but such counter-obligation with reference to an annuity shall not be construed as contractual unless and until provision shall have been made therefor on an actuarial reserve basis.

ARTICLE III

¶ 1317. *Approval of Claim*

The Annual Conference shall be the sole judge of the admissability and validity of annuity claims, and shall be fully competent to determine all payments, disallowances, and deductions thereunder, subject to the specific regulations relating thereto contained in the *Discipline*.

ARTICLE IV

¶ 1318. *Retirement*

(1) The Annual Conference may place any member thereof in the retired relation, with or without his consent and irrespective of his age, if such relation be recommended by the Committee on Conference Relations. If retirement takes place before attainment of age sixty-five, the right to make an annuity claim shall be unimpaired.

(2) At his own request, the Annual Conference may place any member thereof in the retired relation, with the privilege of making an annuity claim if he has attained the age of sixty-five years prior to the date of the opening session of the Annual Conference to which said request is presented.

(3) Retirement prior to attainment of age sixty-five with the privilege of making an annuity claim on the ground of a Minister's personal disability, shall be permitted only after a thorough investigation of his case by, and presentation of a medical certificate to, the Committee on Conference Relations. This certificate shall be made on a form approved by the Illinois Corporation, and shall be given by a regular medical doctor, other than the personal physician of the applicant, who has been approved by the Committee on Conference Relations. If such disability continue for more than one year, such medical certificate shall be required annually.

ARTICLE V

¶ 1319. *Definitions.*

(1) The following "Years of Approved Service" in the effective relation in an Annual Conference of The Methodist Church may be counted for the purpose of determining both the annuity claims and the annuities payable thereon: (a) as Pastor-in-Charge or Assistant Pastor; (b) as District Superintendent, Presiding Elder, or Conference President; (c) as Special Appointee to an institution or organization owned and operated by The Methodist Church and of which the entire Board of Trustees, Managers, or Directors is elected by an Annual, Jurisdictional, or General Conference of The Methodist Church; or if appointment is for service in an institution or organization other than those provided for in (c) of this section the claim for annuity shall be established annually only after approval by a three-fourths vote of the Annual Conference; (d) as a member of the Annual Conference left without appointment to attend school; (e) "leave of absence"; (f) as the wife of a Minister during his "years of Approved Service."

Two years of service on trial as Pastor-in-Charge or Assistant Pastor shall be counted also as "Years of Approved Service."

(2) The following years of service in the effective relation may not be approved as a basis of annuity claim: (a) Years for which a pension, or any other form of compensation or "deferred salary," is received from any source other than the Annual Conference; (b) years served, under a special appointment, made after May 29, 1934, with an institution or organization not formally approved by the Annual Conference. Special appointments shall be listed in the Conference Yearbook, in two divisions as follows: (1) with annuity claim, (2) without annuity claim.

(3) The "Annuity Rate" shall mean the sum determined annually by the Annual Conference, payable as an annuity for each year of "Approved Service" of a Retired Minister rendered in The Methodist Church. The "Annuity Rate" shall be determined by the Annual Conference, without restriction, but it is recommended that such rate be not less than one per cent of the "Average Salary" of the Conference, as hereinafter defined in (4).

(4) The "Average Salary" of the Conference for the purposes of this annuity plan shall mean the average salary, including house rent at a valuation equivalent to fifteen per cent of the salary, of the Ministers in the Annual Conference who are in the effective relation as Pastors or District Superintendents, based on the salaries as published in the statistical reports for the Conference Year immediately preceding the General Conference. In computing the "Average Salary" of the Conference, no account shall be taken of salaries of Ministers who shall have served less than one year on a Pastoral Charge. The "Average Salary" shall be established by the Illinois Corporation for each Annual Conference quadrenially, immediately preceding the General Conference.

(5) "Dependent Child" shall mean a child of a deceased Minister or a child legally adopted before the Minister's retirement or death, under sixteen years of age and dependent for his or her support. If the child be kept in a standard school, the age limit may be extended not to exceed two additional years by action of the Board of Conference Claimants.

(6) "The Methodist Church" shall mean The Methodist Church after the Uniting Conference of 1939, also any of the Churches, united in 1939, as they were constituted prior to 1939.

(7) "Methodist Minister" shall mean a Minister of The Methodist Church as defined above.

(8) "Illinois Corporation" shall mean the corporation of the Board of Pensions having the administration of pension work in the Northeastern, the North Central, the Western and the Central Jurisdictions.

(9) "Missouri Corporation" shall mean the corporation of the Board of Pensions having the administration of pension work in the Southeastern and South Central Jurisdictions.

ARTICLE VI

¶ 1320. *Claim of a Retired Minister*

The Annuity Claim of a Retired Minister shall be for an amount equivalent to the total of his "Years of Approved Service" multiplied by the "Annuity Rate" as defined above, irrespective of breaks in the sequence of such service.

ARTICLE VII

¶ 1321. *Claim of a Widow*

(1) The Annuity Claim of a widow shall be for an amount equivalent to the total of her "Years of Approved Service" multiplied by seventy per cent of the "Annuity Rate" (See Article V, subsections 1-2). The fact that a widow served as the wife of a Minister of The Methodist Church until his death and, after an intervening period of widowhood, served again as the wife of another Minister of The Methodist Church, shall not prevent the approval of all such years of service for the purpose of computing her "Annuity Claim."

(2) The Annuity Claim of a widow shall become effective immediately upon the death of her husband. (See Article XI, subsections 6, 7, for amplification of this section.)

(3) The Annuity Claim of the widow shall be valid, whether or not a located preacher had been restored to membership in the Annual Conference at the time of his death.

(4) A certificate of the fact that a widow remains unmarried and continues as a member of The Methodist Church shall be obtained annually by the Board of Conference Claimants on a form to be provided by the Illinois Corporation.

(5) If a widow reside in a foreign land, or in a community where there is no Methodist Church accessible, she may

receive permission from the Annual Conference, by a two-thirds vote, to join or affiliate with any other Evangelical Church in such place of residence. In such case, her marital status and Christian character shall be certified by her Pastor annually on a form to be provided by the Illinois Corporation.

ARTICLE VIII

¶ 1322. *Claim of a Dependent Child*

(1) The Annuity Claim of a "Dependent Child" shall be determined by multiplying the father's "Years of Approved Service" by one-fourth of the "Annuity Rate" (see Article V, subsection 3), *provided*, however, that in no case shall the total of the annuity claims of the dependent children exceed the Annuity Claim of the father.

(2) The Annuity Claim of a "Dependent Child" shall become effective immediately upon the death of the father, and shall cease upon attainment of age sixteen. If the child be kept in a standard school, the age-limit may be extended, not to exceed two additional years, by action of the Board of Conference Claimants.

(3) A certificate of attendance of a "Dependent Child," at a standard school, shall be obtained annually between the ages of sixteen and eighteen by the Board of Conference Claimants, on a form to be provided by the Illinois Corporation.

(4) A child born of a marriage consummated after the father has been placed in the retired relation shall not be entitled to benefits from the Conference Claimants Funds.

ARTICLE IX

¶ 1323. *Apportionment*

(1) The apportionment to the Pastoral Charges for the purpose of providing for annuity claims shall be determined by the Board of Conference Claimants by multiplying the total "Years of Approved Service" (see Article V, subsections 1, 2) of the Conference Claimants (for this purpose the total of widows' years of service shall be reduced thirty per cent, and the total years of the deceased fathers of "Dependent Children" shall be reduced seventy-five per cent) by the "Annuity Rate" determined by the Annual Conference, and subtracting therefrom the total of all moneys received for annuity distribution from sources other than the Pastoral Charges. In figuring the "Years of Approved Service," for purposes of computing the apportionment, the Board of Conference Claimants shall take

account of the probable net increase of such years which may be caused by deaths during the year or by retirements likely to be effected at the next Annual Conference.

(2) The apportionment to the Pastoral Charges for both regular relief and emergency appropriations for Conference Claimants who are in distress, because of inadequacy of the annuity to meet their needs, or because of other special circumstances, shall be recommended by the Board of Conference Claimants and approved by the Annual Conference.

(3) As a general limitation, the sum total of the apportionment above mentioned shall not exceed a figure equivalent to twelve per cent of the total salaries of the Pastors and District Superintendents of the Conference; *provided,* however, that a larger apportionment may be approved by majority vote of the members of the Annual Conference present and voting. In the interest of equitable apportionment, it is recommended that the sums asked from the several Pastoral Charges for Conference Claimants be determined according to a graduated scale, devised so as to distribute the larger part of the apportionment to the Pastoral Charges paying as much or more than the average Pastoral salary of the Conference. House rent shall not be considered in making the apportionment to the Pastoral Charges, but when paid by the Pastor should be considered as a deduction from his cash salary. When requested to do so, the Board of Pensions shall assist the Board of Conference Claimants in the preparation of a graduated scale of apportionments. Under the graduated scale plan, the foregoing provisions shall not, in any case, preclude the making of a larger apportionment than twelve per cent of the Pastoral salary to an individual Pastoral Charge.

(4) The sum total of the apportionments above mentioned shall be apportioned as one amount to the several Pastoral Charges of the Conference and to self-supporting Pastoral Charges in Missions served by members of the Conference. The apportionment to the individual Charge for Conference Claimants shall be stated as a percentage of the salary to be received by the Pastor. The recommendations in this section shall not preclude the use of other methods of apportionment on a percentage basis, which may be adopted by vote of the Annual Conference.

(5) The Board of Conference Claimants may apportion annually to an organization or institution of The Methodist Church, employing a member of the Conference and which does not provide a pension for his years of service

therein, an amount not to exceed twelve times the average "Annuity Rate" established by the Conference during five years immediately preceding. Moneys collected on apportionment made under this section shall be conserved at interest by the Illinois Corporation and shall be applied in distribution only after the person involved or his widow becomes a Conference Claimant. It is recommended that such moneys be released, for distribution on account of the Conference Claimants concerned, at the regular annuity rate of the Conference. In the event of termination of membership in an Annual Conference, the Illinois Corporation shall pay the accumulated amount, as it may determine, to the Board of Conference Claimants concerned.

(6) To a Federated Church, which is under the jurisdiction of a Quarterly Conference, and served by a Minister of the Conference, the Board of Conference Claimants shall make an apportionment equivalent to the apportionment made to a Methodist Church within the Conference having membership and resources equal to the Methodist constituency of the Federated Church.

(7) A Community Church, not under the jurisdiction of a Quarterly Conference, and served by a Methodist Minister, appointed thereto on request of the Annual Conference, supported by a two-thirds vote, shall not be subject to an apportionment and the service of a Minister rendered thereto shall be without annuity claim.

ARTICLE X

¶ 1324. *Proportional Payment*

(1) The amount payable by any Pastoral Charge on the apportionment for Conference Claimants shall be directly proportional to the amount of cash received by the Pastor on his salary. The apportionment for Conference Claimants being stated as a percentage of the Pastor's salary, an amount equivalent to that percentage shall be due to the Board of Conference Claimants on the basis of the payments made to the Pastor.

(2) The Treasurer of the Pastoral Charge shall be primarily responsible for the application of the provisions of the first section of this Article, but in the event of his failure to apply such provisions the Pastor shall adjust his cash salary and the payment to the Conference Claimants according to the proper ratio, as provided above, before he enters the respective amounts in his statistical report to the Annual Conference. And on retirement, the amount of such defaults shall be deducted from his annuity subject to the limitations of deduction provided hereinafter.

(3) It shall not be permissible for a Pastor-in-Charge to receive a bonus or other supplementary compensation intended to defeat the object of the regulation in subsection 2 of this Article by the stipulation that such bonus, or other supplementary compensation, be not counted on his salary. For so doing, on the complaint of the Board of Conference Claimants, his annuity claim may be disallowed by Conference order for the particular year of service during which such bonus or supplementary compensation was so received.

ARTICLE XI

¶ 1325. *Distribution*

(1) Moneys for Annuity and Relief distribution shall be derived from public collections, private gifts, bequests, and other sources; and in order that the Church may effectually meet the obligation to provide a comfortable support for Conference Claimants, the rules and regulations for obtaining and administering the funds established for such purposes shall be observed by all Pastors, District Superintendents, and Bishops, and by all Pastoral Charges, Quarterly, and Annual Conferences.

(2) The amount received each year from the Pastoral Charges shall be divided at the end of the Conference Year between Annuity Distribution and the Relief Fund in proportion to the amount asked from the Pastoral Charges for each fund respectively at the previous session of the Annual Conference. Any part of such amount received in advance of the annual session of the Conference shall be reserved for appropriation and expenditure during the ensuing Conference year.

(3) Moneys designated for Annuities shall be distributed on the basis of service, and shall consist of:

(a) The dividend of The Methodist Publishing House.

(b) The income from any investments of the Annual Conference for Annuity Distribution held for this purpose.

(c) Gifts and bequests for Annuity Distribution.

(d) Such proportion of the money received from the Pastoral Charges for Conference Claimants as is for Annuity Distribution.

(4) Moneys designated for Relief on the basis of special need shall consist of:

(a) The appropriation for Connectional Relief paid to the Annual Conference by the Illinois Corporation.

(b) Such proportion of the money received from the Pastoral Charges as is for Relief on the basis of special need.

(c) The income from such gifts and bequests as are made for Relief on the basis of special need.

(d) Income arising from investments made by Relief and Aid Societies of the Annual Conferences, if so designated by them.

(5) Money designated for Emergency Relief shall consist of:

(a) The dividend of the Chartered Fund.

(b) Special collections at the Annual Conference for Emergency Relief.

(c) Gifts and bequests for immediate distribution as Emergency Relief.

(6) The Annual Conference may authorize the Board of Conference Claimants to pay annuities and relief benefits quarterly or semi-annually in advance. In such case, upon the death of a Retired Minister, the first subsequent payment to his widow and children, if there be any surviving, shall be the next periodical payment due to all Claimants of the Conference, and upon the death of a widow no further payment shall be made on her account beyond the last payment regularly due and payable while she was living; the same rule, regarding after-death payment, shall apply to a "Dependent Child" deceased prior to attainment of age sixteen. In the case of a widow whose husband died while in the effective relation, the first payment of annuity to be made immediately shall cover *pro rata* the unelapsed portion of the installment period during which his death occurred.

(7) In case the Annual Conference authorizes the Board of Conference Claimants to pay annuities and relief benefits either quarterly or semi-annually at the end of whichever installment period it may select, rather than in advance, as indicated in subsection 6 of this Article, then the first periodical payment due after retirement of a Minister shall not be payable until one such installment period has elapsed following the session of the Conference at which he was placed in the retired relation. In such case, upon the death of a Retired Minister, the first subsequent payment to his widow and "Dependent Children," if there be any surviving, shall be the balance due to him for the elapsed portion of the installment period which he failed to outlive plus the payment due to them for the unelapsed portion of such period. Furthermore, upon the death of the widow, any balance due to her may be paid to the surviving "Dependent Children," if there be any, but her estate shall have no claim thereto. In the event of the death of a Retired

Minister who received his annuity payments under the provisions of this section, and who died leaving neither widow nor "Dependent Children," no payment shall be made to his estate. In the event of the death of a Minister in the effective relation the first payment to the widow and "Dependent Children," if there be any surviving, shall be made *pro rata* for the period elapsed between the time of his death and the date of the next regular payment.

(8) The Board of Conference Claimants shall investigate carefully all claims made on the basis of special need and the Secretary of the Board shall obtain annually in advance as much information regarding their condition as may be available, in order that the Board of Conference Claimants may have before it the facts necessary to determine equitably the amount of relief to be granted in each case.

A Minister in the supernumerary relation cannot make an annuity claim and may be granted Relief by the Board of Conference Claimants only when it is so ordered by the Annual Conference.

(9) The Board of Conference Claimants may establish a fund for the purpose of granting Emergency Relief to Conference Claimants in cases of special need. Normally, such fund should not exceed the equivalent of ten per cent of the total amount appropriated for regular Relief grants.

(10) The Annual Conference, upon recommendation of the Board of Conference Claimants, shall designate a bank or other depository, for deposit of the funds held by the Board of Conference Claimants.

(11) When it is deemed expedient, the Board of Conference Claimants may build up a reserve fund from the income for Conference Claimants in order to stabilize the annuity rate payable in the Conference. Such reserve fund should be, at least, twenty-five per cent of the average annual income of the Board of Conference Claimants for all purposes for the five years immediately preceding. Such reserve fund shall be held as the Annual Conference shall direct and shall be subject to the requirements described in subsection 10 of this Article.

(12) Whenever it is deemed advisable because of the problems arising from a merger of Conferences, two or more Conferences may pool or combine all or a part of their incomes for Conference Claimants and administer the same jointly under their combined Conference Boards of Conference Claimants.

¶ 1326. *Operation Through Illinois Corporation*

(1) When authorized by the Annual Conference, the Board of Conference Claimants may deposit all or any part of the funds under its control with the Illinois Corporation.

(2) The Annual Conference may authorize the Illinois Corporation to make the periodical payments to the Conference Claimants and, in such case, the Board of Conference Claimants shall prepare annually a complete schedule of the plan of distribution for the guidance of the Illinois Corporation in making such payments, and shall co-operate fully with it, in order to insure efficient and prompt service. Checks issued by the Illinois Corporation under the provisions of this section shall show plainly the name of the Conference for which the disbursements are made.

(3) The Illinois Corporation shall be entitled to collect an annual service fee, figured on a cost basis, for the work specified in the preceding section.

(4) The Illinois Corporation shall furnish annually to the Board of Conference Claimants a report showing full details of the transactions under subsection 2 of this Article.

¶ 1327. *Liens on Annuities*

(1) Whenever a Conference Claimant shall be in debt to The Methodist Publishing House, or to the Conference or to any of its organizations, on account of unpaid assessments, and pledges for the benefit of Conference Claimants, such debt shall constitute a lien on the annuity of the person involved, and the Conference shall have power to appropriate and apply his or her annuity, or any part thereof, to the payment of such debt; *provided,* however, that not more than one-quarter of the annuity shall be appropriated in any year for such purpose and, furthermore, *provided* that such power shall not be interpreted as applying to the settlement of other debts of a Conference Claimant.

(2) An Annual Conference may file with another Annual Conference a claim against a member transferred thereto while he was owing all or part of any assessment or pledge for the benefit of funds for Conference Claimants and, upon retirement of such member, the Board of Conference Claimants shall collect, on behalf of the Conference making the claim, the amount owed, subject to the provisions in subsection 1 of this Article.

ARTICLE XIV

¶ 1328. *Relinquishment*

For a year at a time, a Conference Claimant may voluntarily relinquish in writing his or her Annuity Claim and any amount payable thereunder; *provided* that the disposal of the relinquished amount shall be entirely under the control of the Board of Conference Claimants.

ARTICLE XV

¶ 1329. *Disallowance of Annuities*

(1) Upon recommendation of the Board of Conference Claimants, after opportunity has been given for either a written or oral statement by the Claimant, any "Annuity Claim" may be disallowed, in whole or in part, for any cause cited by the Board of Conference Claimants; *provided,* that in case of disallowance for such cause, approval shall be given of two-thirds of the members of the Annual Conferences present and voting.

(2) When an "Annuity Claim" shall have been disallowed, under subsection 1 of this Article, it may be reconsidered at any subsequent annual session of the Conference, upon recommendation of the Board of Conference Claimants, or two-thirds vote of the Conference.

(3) For disallowance on account of accepting a bonus or other supplementary compensation with intention to defeat the plan of proportional payment of Ministerial Support, see Article X, subsection 3.

ARTICLE XVII

¶ 1331. *Fund for Accepted Supply Pastors*

(1) Each Annual Conference which utilizes the services of Accepted Supply Pastors shall create and maintain a relief fund for Accepted Supply Pastors to be administered by the Board of Conference Claimants for the purpose of granting relief to aged and disabled Accepted Supply Pastors who shall have given not less than twenty years of full-time pastoral service under the direction and control of a District Superintendent. Claimants on this fund shall be known as "Special Conference Claimants" and all accounting on their behalf shall be kept separate from the accounts for "Regular Conference Claimants." (¶ 1315.) ·

(2) On and after attainment of the age specified in the *Discipline* for the retirement of Ministers who are Members of an Annual Conference, Accepted Supply Pastors may be-

come "Special Conference Claimants" upon recommendation of the Committee on Conference Relations and the approval of the Annual Conference.

(3) As soon as practicable after the death of an Accepted Supply Pastor, the Board of Conference Claimants shall consider the case of his widow, if any, and grant such relief as may be available, subject to the service requirements in subsection 1 of this Article, and provided that she retain membership in The Methodist Church.

(4) The Board of Conference Claimants shall require an annual statement from each "Special Conference Claimant," and a report with certificate of character which may be furnished by either the Quarterly Conference, Pastor, or District Superintendent where the Claimant resides.

(5) Application for disability relief by an Accepted Supply Pastor, prior to attainment of the age specified in the *Discipline* for the retirement of Ministers who are Members of an Annual Conference, and before completion of the minimum number of required years of service, must be accompanied by the recommendation of the District Superintendent with a full statement of need and a physician's certificate.

(6) The Annual Conference, acting through the Board of Conference Claimants, shall determine the method to be used in raising moneys for this fund.

(7) The Annual Conferences may create and maintain a reserve fund for the aid of its aged and disabled Accepted Supply Pastors. Such fund shall be invested and administered in such manner as the Annual Conference shall determine, but the accounting shall be kept separate.

ARTICLE XVIII

¶ 1332. *Committee on Proportional Payments*

The Annual Conference may constitute its Board of Conference Claimants a Committee on Proportional Payment of Ministerial Support for the purpose of comparing the records of amounts paid on the support of Pastors and Conference Claimants by each Pastoral Charge, computing the proportional distribution thereof, and keeping a permanent record of defaults, or the Conference may organize a special Committee on Proportional Payment of Ministerial Support, which shall keep permanent records and furnish necessary information to the Board of Conference Claimants regarding adjustment of annuities.

ARTICLE XIX

¶ 1333. *Adherence to Plan*

The Annual Conference shall not subvert, contravene, or modify the provisions of the *Discipline* for the support of Conference Claimants by entering into special contracts with organizations not under the control of The Methodist Church for the payment of annuities; *provided*, however, that the Annual Conference shall be free to make such arrangements for Group Life Insurance as it may deem necessary.

ARTICLE XX

¶ 1334. *Reserve Funding*

The Illinois Corporation is authorized to enter into an agreement with any Annual Conference whereby arrangements can be made to fund in advance, on an actuarial reserve basis, any part or all of the annuities for which the Conference is responsible, subject to the following general provisions:

(1) An annual contribution not to exceed the equivalent of two per cent of the current average salary of the Conference shall be required from all members entering the fund under the provisions of this Article.

(2) The yearly contribution to be made by the Annual Conference shall be determined by it after consultation with the Illinois Corporation.

(3) Annuities funded on an actuarial reserve basis shall conform as closely as practicable to the types indicated in the Annuity Plan for Conference Claimants as amended from time to time.

(4) The plan in this paragraph may be used in conjunction wi   and supplementary to the Ministers' Reserve Pension Plan.

ARTICLE XXI

¶ 1335. *Financial Policy*

The following rules shall apply to financial administration of Annual Conference Boards:

(1) Persons connected in any way with the securities, real estate, or other forms of investment sold to or purchased from the Annual Conference, shall be ineligible to serve on the investment committees of Annual Conference Boards, societies, or institutions.

(2) No officer or member of an Annual Conference Board, society, or institution shall receive a personal commission,

bonus, or remuneration in connection with the purchase or sale of securities for such board, society or institution.

(3) The principle of diversification of investments shall be observed, in order to obtain proper geographical and class distribution of investment commitments.

(4) Real property shall be accepted as consideration for life annuity agreements only with the stipulation that the annuity shall not exceed the net income on the property until such property shall have been liquidated. Upon liquidation, the annuity shall be paid upon the net proceeds at the established annuity rate.

(5) Annual Conference Boards, societies, and institutions shall not offer higher rates of annuity than those listed in the annuity schedules approved by the General Boards of The Methodist Church.

(6) Upon the order of the Annual Conference, there shall be printed in its Yearbook a list of the investments held by each of the organizations directly or indirectly under the control of the Conference, or such list may be distributed directly to the members of the Conference at their request. A copy of all lists concerning Conference Claimants shall be filed annually with the Illinois Corporation.

(7) Borrowing money in any Conference year, to enable the Board of Conference Claimants to complete payment of annuities at a designated annuity rate, shall be done only on authority of the Annual Conference granted by a three-fourths count vote.

. (8) No officer or member of any Annual Conference Board, society, institution, or Board of Trustees of any Church or Church organization, shall be eligible to obtain a loan in any amount from funds committed to the care of such Board, society, or institution.

ARTICLE XXII

¶ 1336. *Transfers from Foreign Language Conferences*

When a Local Church supporting a pastor in the effective relation, or a group of Local Churches comprising a Pastoral Charge and supporting a Pastor, is transferred to the jurisdiction of an English-speaking conference, a Conference Member in the effective relation from said Foreign Language Conference shall also be transferred to the same English-speaking Conference, and all liability for annuities on account of service in the effective relation rendered in the Foreign Language Conference prior to such transfer shall rest with the Annual Conference to which the Member is being transferred.

ARTICLE XXIII

¶ 1337. *Judicial Decisions*

The following Judicial Decisions shall apply to this Code:
A divorced wife of a Minister cannot be a Conference Claimant.

A retired Minister's Annuity Claim is not invalidated by service as a Supply Pastor. A Retired Minister should have the privilege of serving as a Supply Pastor, especially when the annuity is insufficient to afford him "comfortable support."

Power to revise, correct, or adjust a Minister's record, as it concerns his annuity, lies with the Annual Conference and not with the General Conference.

A Minister who refuses to prorate Ministerial support may be brought to trial for violation of a law of the Church.

Annuities are granted by the Annual Conference annually, including those granted on the ground of disability; the determination of what constitutes disability lies with the Annual Conference.

Retirement can only be effected at the Annual Conference; the Annuity Claim of a Minister over age sixty-five cannot be recognized by the Conference Stewards without Conference action.

The Annuity Claim of an Effective Minister cannot be recognized by the Conference Stewards between annual sessions of the Conference; he must be retired first.

Proceeds of sales of church property may not be used for endowment for Retired Ministers.

Not more than two years on Trial can be counted for Annuity Claim in any case.

A minor child of a living Minister cannot be a Conference Claimant.

An Annuitant who entered the ministry in a Spring Conference and retired in a Fall Conference, having a fractional period of seven months at the close of his service in the Effective Relation was held to have the right to claim an extra year of annuity credit on account of the fractional period.

Although the Annual Conference has power to require a contribution to its funds and to fix a financial penalty for defaults, a Minister cannot be brought to trial for failure to make such required contribution.

An Annual Conference may withhold money from a Conference Claimant in order to discharge his obligation for assessments voted by the Annual Conference for Conference Claimants.

A Minister cannot be retired automatically by operation of a rule of an Annual Conference fixing an age of retirement.

A Minister cannot present his credentials to and be accepted into the Ministry of another denomination and at the same time retain his standing in an Annual Conference of our Church. Such action constitutes withdrawal from our Ministry and automatically terminates his right to make a claim for an annuity.

A member of an Annual Conference cannot relinquish his Annuity Claim at Conference time and then ask for it, or a portion of it, during the Conference year.

It was held that if an Annual Conference entered into a group contract with a life insurance company to provide annuities for its Ministers it would nullify the annuity plan established by the General Conference and such action would have a demoralizing effect on our pension system as a whole.

ARTICLE XXIV

¶ 1338 *Operation in Foreign Countries*

The provisions in this Pension Code need not be binding in Conferences of The Methodist Church in foreign countries. However, the general principles involved in the Code shall be duly regarded and employed in such Conferences, until the General Conference shall order otherwise.

VIII. COMMITTEE ON RITUALS AND ORDERS OF WORSHIP

EDITORIAL NOTE

Chapter XXV of the *Prospectus of the Discipline of The Methodist Church*, pages 293 to 301 inclusive, which was presented to the Uniting Conference at Kansas City, Mo., by the General Standing Committee on Rituals and Orders of Worship in their Report No. 2, Calendar No. 39, together "with additions as hereinafter noted," and which was adopted by the Uniting Conference on May 8, 1939, follows Report No. 2.

Chapter XXVI of the *Prospectus of the Discipline of The Methodist Church*, pages 302 to 335 inclusive, which was presented to the Uniting Conference at Kansas City, Missouri, by the General Standing Committee on Rituals and Orders of Worship in their Report No. 3, Calender No. 40, together "with amendments and additions as hereinafter noted," and which was amended and adopted by the Uniting Conference on May 8, 1939, follows Report No. 3.

LUD H. ESTES,
Secretary of Uniting Conference.

REPORT No. 1. METHODIST HYMNAL AND
RESPONSIVE READINGS

Calendar No. 38. Adopted May 8. See Journal, Page 315.

Membership of Committee, 45; present when report
was adopted, 37; voting for adoption, 37.

The Committee on Rituals and Orders of Worship recommends that *The Methodist Hymnal* and "The Responsive Readings" as adopted officially by the Methodist Episcopal Church, the Methodist Episcopal Church, South, and the Methodist Protestant Church be the official *Hymnal* and Responsive Readings for The Methodist Church.

REPORT No. 2. CONCERNING CHAPTER XXV OF PROSPECTUS

Calendar No. 39. Adopted May 8. See Journal, Page 318.

Membership of Committee, 45; present when report
was adopted, 37; voting for adoption, 37.

The Committee on Rituals and Orders of Worship recommends for adoption Chapter XXV of the *Prospectus* (pp. 293 to 301 inclusive), "The Orders of Worship of The Methodist Church"—with additions as hereinafter noted.

1. After the first sentence of ¶ 1401, be added "But while liberty is given in the use of these orders of worship, it is urged that all ministers and congregations make use of some one of these orders."

2. To the third sentence of ¶ 1401 be added, *The Methodist Hymnal.*

WORSHIP AND RITUAL

CHAPTER XXV

THE ORDERS OF WORSHIP OF THE METHODIST CHURCH

THE USE OF THE ORDERS OF WORSHIP

¶ 1401. In recognition of the various needs of our several congregations four orders of worship have been provided which may be used according to desire. But while liberty is given in the use of these Orders of Worship, it is urged that all ministers and congregations make use of some one of these Orders.

Let each service proceed without announcement, as far as possible.

Choral responses may be used as desired. See Numbers 589-624, *The Methodist Hymnal.*

For Calls to Worship, Invocations and Confessions, Words of Assurance, Affirmations of Faith, Prayers, see ¶ 1407.

Where there is a Junior Service or Sermon, it should immediately precede or follow the Offertory.

(The Prayer for the Church is by Walter Rauschenbusch, and is used by permission of The Pilgrim Press.)

THE SUNDAY SERVICE OF JOHN WESLEY

¶ 1402. In commending the Sunday Service to "Our Societies in America" Mr. Wesley wrote: "I believe there is no Liturgy in the World, either in ancient or modern language, which breathes more of a solid, scriptural, rational piety than the Common Prayer of the Church of England. And though the main of it was compiled considerably more than two hundred years ago, yet is the language of it not only pure, but strong and elegant in the highest degree."

When this Service is to be used for Evening Prayer, the following changes shall be made:

The *Magnificat* shall be used in place of the *Te Deum.*

The *Nunc Dimittis* shall be used in place of the *Jubilate Deo.*

In place of the Collect for Grace shall be said the following Collects:

Lighten our darkness, we beseech Thee, O Lord; and by Thy great mercy defend us from all perils and dangers of this night; for the love of Thine only Son, our Saviour, Jesus Christ. *Amen.*

Direct us, O Lord, in all our doings, with Thy most gracious favor, and further us with Thy continual help; that in all our works, begun, continued, and ended in Thee, we may glorify Thy holy Name, and finally, by Thy mercy, obtain everlasting life; through Jesus Christ our Lord. *Amen.*

¶ 1403.   ORDER OF WORSHIP I

Let the services of worship begin at the time appointed, and let the people kneel or bow in silent prayer upon entering the sanctuary.

THE PRELUDE: The people in devout meditation.

THE CALL TO WORSHIP. Which may be said or sung.

A HYMN. If a Processional, the hymn shall precede the Call to Worship, and the people shall then rise at the second stanza and join in singing.

THE PRAYER OF CONFESSION. To be said by all, the people
seated and bowed, or kneeling. The following or other
Prayer of Confession may be said:

Our Heavenly Father, who by Thy love hast made us,
and through Thy love hast kept us, and in Thy love
wouldst make us perfect, we humbly confess that we have
not loved Thee with all our heart and soul and mind and
strength, and that we have not loved one another as Christ
hath loved us. Thy life is within our souls, but our selfishness hath hindered Thee. We have resisted Thy Spirit. We have neglected Thine inspirations.

Forgive what we have been; help us to amend what we
are; and in Thy Spirit direct what we shall be; that Thou
mayest come into the full glory of Thy creation, in us and
in all men, through Jesus Christ our Lord. *Amen.*

THE SILENT MEDITATION. The people seated and bowed, or
kneeling.

THE WORDS OF ASSURANCE. By the minister.

THE LORD'S PRAYER. Which may be said or sung.

THE ANTHEM OR CHANT. Which may be the *Venite* or the
Te Deum.

THE RESPONSIVE READING. The people to stand and remain standing until after the Affirmation of Faith.

THE GLORIA PATRI.

THE AFFIRMATION OF FAITH. To be said by the Minister
and people.

THE LESSON FROM THE HOLY SCRIPTURES. The Old and
New Testament.

THE PASTORAL PRAYER. The people seated and bowed, or
kneeling.

THE OFFERTORY. The Dedication of Offerings. With
Prayer or Offertory Sentences.

A HYMN. The people standing.

THE SERMON.

THE PRAYER. The people seated and bowed, or kneeling.

THE INVITATION TO CHRISTIAN DISCIPLESHIP.

A HYMN OR DOXOLOGY. The people standing. The closing
hymn may be a Recessional hymn.

THE BENEDICTION. The people seated and bowed, or kneeling.

THE SILENT PRAYER.

THE POSTLUDE.

¶ 1404.   ORDER OF WORSHIP II

Let the services of worship begin at the time appointed, and let the people kneel or bow in silent prayer upon entering the sanctuary.

THE PRELUDE.
THE CALL TO WORSHIP.
THE INVOCATION.
A HYMN.
THE AFFIRMATION OF FAITH.

I believe in God, the Father Almighty, Maker of heaven and earth; and in Jesus Christ, His only Son our Lord; who was conceived by the Holy Spirit, born of the Virgin Mary, suffered under Pontius Pilate, was crucified, dead, and buried; the third day He rose from the dead; He ascended into heaven, and sitteth at the right hand of God the Father Almighty; from thence He shall come to judge the quick and the dead. I believe in the Holy Spirit; the holy catholic Church; the communion of saints; the forgiveness of sins; the resurrection of the body, and the life everlasting. *Amen.*

THE ANTHEM.
THE RESPONSIVE READING.
THE GLORIA PATRI.
THE LESSON FROM THE HOLY SCRIPTURES.
THE SILENT MEDITATION.
THE PASTORAL PRAYER.
THE LORD'S PRAYER.
THE OFFERTORY. The Dedication of Offerings with Prayer
        or Offertory Sentences.
A HYMN.
THE SERMON.
A PRAYER.
THE INVITATION TO CHRISTIAN DISCIPLESHIP.
A HYMN.
THE BENEDICTION.
THE POSTLUDE.

¶ 1405.   ORDER OF WORSHIP III

Let the services of worship begin at the time appointed, and let the people kneel or bow in silent prayer upon entering the sanctuary.

THE PRELUDE. The people in devout meditation.

THE CALL TO WORSHIP. Which may be said or sung.

A HYMN. If a Processional, the Hymn shall precede the Call to Worship, and the people shall then rise at the second stanza and join in the singing.

THE PRAYER OF CONFESSION. To be said by all, the people seated and bowed, or kneeling. The following or other Prayer of Confession, may be said:

Almighty God, from whom every good prayer cometh, and who pourest out, on all who desire it, the spirit of grace and supplication: deliver us, when we draw nigh to Thee, from coldness of heart and wanderings of mind; that with steadfast thoughts, and kindled affections, we may worship Thee in spirit and in truth; through Jesus Christ our Lord. *Amen.*

THE SILENT MEDITATION. The people seated and bowed, or kneeling.

THE LORD'S PRAYER. Which may be said or sung.

THE ANTHEM.

THE LESSONS FROM THE HOLY SCRIPTURE. If a Responsive Reading is used, it should be followed by the *Gloria Patri*, the people standing.

THE PASTORAL PRAYER. The people seated and bowed, or kneeling.

THE PRESENTATION OF OFFERINGS.

A HYMN. The people standing.

THE SERMON.

THE INVITATION TO CHRISTIAN DISCIPLESHIP.

A HYMN OR DOXOLOGY. The people standing.

THE SILENT PRAYER.

THE BENEDICTION. The people seated and bowed, or kneeling.

THE POSTLUDE.

¶ 1406.   ORDER OF WORSHIP IV

AN ORDER FOR MORNING OR EVENING PRAYER. ADAPTED FROM THE SUNDAY SERVICE OF JOHN WESLEY

(For Evening Prayer, see suggested changes in ¶ 1402.)

Suggested for Occasional Use

Let the services of worship begin at the time appointed, and let the people kneel or bow in silent prayer upon entering the sanctuary.

THE PRELUDE. The people in devout meditation.

SCRIPTURE SENTENCES. One or more of them to be read by the Minister, the people standing.

The Lord is in His holy temple: let all the earth keep silence before Him.

Let the words of my mouth, and the meditation of my heart, be acceptable in Thy sight, O Lord, my strength, and my redeemer.

This is the day which the Lord hath made; we will rejoice and be glad in it.

The hour cometh, and now is, when the true worshipers shall worship the Father in spirit and in truth.

The sacrifices of God are a broken spirit: a broken and a contrite heart, O God, Thou wilt not despise.

HYMN. If a Processional, the Hymn shall precede the Scripture Sentences, and the people shall then rise at the second stanza and join in singing.

CALL TO CONFESSION. By the Minister, the people standing.

Dearly Beloved, the Scripture moveth us to acknowledge and confess our sins before Almighty God, our Heavenly Father, with an humble, lowly, penitent, and obedient heart; to the end that we may obtain forgiveness, by His infinite goodness and mercy. Wherefore I pray and beseech you, as many as are here present, to accompany me with a pure heart and a humble voice unto the throne of Heavenly Grace. Let us pray.

GENERAL CONFESSION. To be said by all, the people seated and bowed, or kneeling.

Almighty and most merciful Father: We have erred and strayed from Thy ways like lost sheep. We have followed too much the devices and desires of our own hearts. We have offended against Thy holy laws. We have left undone those things which we ought to have done, and we have done those things which we ought not to have done. But Thou, O Lord, have mercy upon us. Spare Thou those, O God, who confess their faults. Restore Thou those who are penitent; according to Thy promises declared unto mankind in Christ Jesus our Lord. And grant, O most merciful Father, for His sake, that we may hereafter live a godly, righteous, and sober life; to the glory of Thy holy Name. *Amen.*

PRAYER OF PARDON. By the Minister.

O Lord, we beseech Thee, absolve Thy people from their offenses; that, through Thy bountiful goodness, we may be delivered from the bonds of those sins which by our frailty we have committed. Grant this, O Heavenly

Father, for Jesus Christ's sake, our blessed Lord and Saviour. *Amen.*

The people shall answer here, and at the end of all other prayers, *Amen.*

THE LORD'S PRAYER. To be said by all.

The Minister: O Lord, open Thou our lips.

The People: And our mouth shall show forth Thy praise.

The Minister: Praise ye the Lord.

The People: The Lord's Name be praised.

VENITE. To be said or sung by all, the people standing.

PSALTER. To be said by all, the people standing.

GLORIA PATRI. To be said by all, the people standing.

THE LESSON. From the Old Testament.

TE DEUM. To be said or sung by all, the people standing.

THE LESSON. From the New Testament.

JUBILATE DEO. To be said or sung by all, the people standing.

THE DECLARATION OF FAITH. Here shall be said the Apostles' Creed.

The Minister: The Lord be with you.

The People: And with thy spirit.

The Minister: Let us pray.

COLLECT FOR GRACE. To be said by all, the people seated and bowed, or kneeling.

O Lord, our Heavenly Father, Almighty and everlasting God, who hast safely brought us to the beginning of this day: defend us in the same with Thy mighty power; and grant that this day we fall into no sin; neither run into any kind of danger; but that all our doings may be ordered by Thy governance, to do always that which is righteous in Thy sight, through Jesus Christ our Lord. *Amen.*

PRAYER. Then may the Minister offer a Prayer, ending with:

The grace of our Lord Jesus Christ, the love of God, and the fellowship of the Holy Spirit, be with us all evermore. *Amen.*

THE OFFERTORY. Then may be sung an Anthem, and an Offering may be received.

THE SERMON. When the service is followed by a Sermon or the Holy Communion, the Minister shall make use of appropriate Hymns and Prayers. Otherwise, the

service may close with a Hymn and the following Benediction:

THE BENEDICTION.

The peace of God, which passeth all understanding,
keep our hearts and minds in the knowledge and love of
God, and of His Son, Jesus Christ our Lord: and the
blessing of God Almighty, the Father, the Son, and the
Holy Spirit, be among you, and remain with you always.
Amen.

¶ 1407.

AIDS TO INDIVIDUAL AND CONGREGATIONAL DEVOTION

A CALL TO HOLY SILENCE

The Lord is in His holy temple:
Let all the earth keep silence before Him.

CALLS TO WORSHIP AND PRAISE

O come, let us sing unto the Lord:
Let us make a joyful noise unto the Rock of our salvation,
Let us come before His presence with thanksgiving,
And make a joyful noise unto Him with psalms.

O praise the Lord, all ye nations:
Praise Him, all ye people.
For His merciful kindness is great toward us:
And the truth of the Lord endureth for ever.
Praise ye the Lord.

O be joyful in the Lord, all ye lands:
Serve the Lord with gladness: come before His presence
    with singing.
Know ye that the Lord, He is God:
It is He that hath made us, and not we ourselves;
We are His people,
And the sheep of His pasture.

The Lord is good: His mercy endureth for ever;
And His truth endureth to all generations.
This is the day which the Lord hath made,
We will rejoice and be glad in it.
Enter into His gates with thanksgiving,
And into His courts with praise.
O magnify the Lord with me, and let us exalt His Name to-
    gether,
For with Him is the fountain of life, and in-Him shall we
    see light.

The Minister: O Lord, open Thou our lips.
The People: And our mouth shall show forth Thy praise.
The Minister: Praise ye the Lord.
The People: The Lord's Name be praised

CALLS TO PRAYER

O come, let us worship and bow down:
Let us kneel before the Lord, our Maker.
For He is the Lord, our God:
And we are the people of His pasture, and the sheep of His hand.

Bless the Lord, O my soul, and all that is within me bless His holy Name.
Bless the Lord, O my soul, and forget not all His benefits:
Who forgiveth all thine iniquities;
Who healeth all thy diseases;
Who redeemeth thy life from destruction;
Who crowneth thee with loving kindness and tender mercies.
What shall I render unto the Lord for all His benefits toward me?
I will pay my vows unto the Lord, in the presence of all His people.
O come, let us worship and bow down,
Let us kneel before the Lord, our Maker.

Hear, O Israel, The Lord our God is one Lord: And thou shalt love the Lord thy God with all thy heart, and with all thy soul, and with all thy mind, and with all thy strength.

Give unto the Lord. O ye mighty, give unto the Lord glory and strength. Give unto the Lord the glory due unto His Name; worship the Lord in the beauty of holiness.

The hour cometh, and now is, when the true worshipers shall worship the Father in spirit and in truth. For the Father seeketh such to worship Him.

God is a Spirit. Let us worship Him in spirit and in truth.

Seek ye the Lord while He may be found; call ye upon Him while He is near.

Let the wicked forsake his way and the unrighteous man his thoughts.

And let him return unto the Lord, and He will have mercy upon him:

And to our God, for He will abundantly pardon.

INVOCATIONS

For a Devout Mind

Almighty God, from whom every good prayer cometh, and who pourest out on all who desire it the spirit of grace and supplication, deliver us, when we draw nigh to Thee, from coldness of heart and wanderings of mind: that with steadfast thoughts, and kindled affections, we may worship Thee in spirit and in truth; through Jesus Christ our Lord. *Amen.*

For the Vision of God

Gracious God, in Thee we live and move and have our being. In Thy presence is fullness of joy. Break the spell of that which binds our minds. Purify our hearts that we may see Thee. Renew our inward life through the unseen and eternal. Visit our spirits and witness with them that we are Thy children. *Amen.*

Our Heavenly Father, we adore Thee, whose name is love, whose nature is compassion, whose presence is joy, whose word is truth, whose spirit is goodness, whose holiness is beauty, whose will is peace, whose service is perfect freedom, and in knowledge of whom standeth our eternal life. *Amen.*

For Purity of Heart

Almighty God, unto whom all hearts are open, all desires known, and from whom no secrets are hid, cleanse the thoughts of our hearts by the inspiration of Thy Holy Spirit, that we may perfectly love Thee, and worthily magnify Thy holy Name, through Jesus Christ our Lord. *Amen.*

For the Spirit of Worship

O our God, we humbly beseech Thee to purify our hearts from all vain and worldly and sinful thoughts, and thus prepare our souls to worship Thee this day acceptably, with reverence and godly fear. O Lord, set our affection on things above, all the day long, and give us grace to receive Thy word which we shall hear this day, into honest and good hearts, and bring forth fruit with patience. Hear us, O God, for the sake of Jesus Christ, our Saviour. *Amen.*

PRAYERS OF CONFESSION

Have mercy upon us, O God, according to Thy loving kindness; according to the multitude of Thy tender mercies blot out our transgressions. Wash us thoroughly from our iniquities, and cleanse us from our sins. For we acknowledge our transgressions, and our sin is ever before us.

Create in us clean hearts, O God, and renew a right spirit within us, through Jesus Christ our Lord. *Amen.*

Almighty and most merciful Father, we have erred and strayed from Thy ways like lost sheep. We have followed too much the devices and desires of our own hearts. We have offended against Thy holy laws. We have left undone those things which we ought to have done, and we have done those things which we ought not to have done. But Thou, O Lord, have mercy upon us. Spare Thou those, O God, who confess their faults. Restore Thou those who are penitent; according to Thy promises declared unto mankind in Christ Jesus our Lord. And grant, O most merciful Father, for His sake, that we may hereafter live a godly, righteous, and sober life; to the glory of Thy holy Name. *Amen.*

Our Heavenly Father, who by Thy love hast made us, and through Thy love hast kept us, and in Thy love wouldst make us perfect, we humbly confess that we have not loved Thee with all our heart and soul and mind and strength, and that we have not loved one another as Christ hath loved us. Thy life is within our souls, but our selfishness has hindered Thee. We have not lived by faith. We have resisted Thy Spirit. We have neglected Thine inspirations. Forgive what we have been; help us to amend what we are; and in Thy Spirit direct what we shall be; that Thou mayest come into the full glory of Thy creation, in us and in all men, through Jesus Christ our Lord. *Amen.*

Almighty God, Father of our Lord Jesus Christ, Maker of all things, Judge of all men, we acknowledge and bewail our manifold sins and wickedness, which we from time to time most grievously have committed, by thought, word, and deed, against Thy Divine majesty. We do earnestly repent, and are heartily sorry for these, our misdoings; the remembrance of them is grievous unto us. Have mercy upon us, have mercy upon us, most merciful Father; for Thy Son, our Lord Jesus Christ's sake, forgive us all that is past; and grant that we may ever hereafter serve and please Thee in newness of life, to the honor and glory of Thy Name, through Jesus Christ our Lord. *Amen.*

WORDS OF ASSURANCE AND PROMISES OF PARDON

Hear what comfortable words our Saviour Christ saith unto all that truly turn to Him: Come unto Me, all ye that labor and are heavy laden, and I will give you rest.

Hear also the words from Saint John's Gospel: God so loved the world, that He gave His only begotten Son, that whosoever believeth in Him should not perish, but have everlasting life.

Here also these words of Scripture:
The Lord is gracious, and full of compassion;
Slow to anger, and of great mercy.
The sacrifices of God are a broken spirit:
A broken and a contrite heart, O God, Thou wilt not despise.

If we confess our sins, God is faithful and just to forgive us our sins, and to cleanse us from all unrighteousness.

As the heaven is high above the earth, so great is His mercy toward them that fear Him. As far as the east is from the west, so far hath He removed our transgressions from us.

Like as a father pitieth his children, so the Lord pitieth them that fear Him.

Jesus said: Be of good cheer; thy sins are forgiven.

He that spared not His own Son, but delivered Him up for us all, how shall He not with Him also freely give us all things?

There is therefore now no condemnation to them who are in Christ Jesus, who walk not after the flesh, but after the Spirit.

This is the message which we have heard of Him and declare unto you, that God is light, and in Him is no darkness at all. If we walk in the light, as He is in the light, we have fellowship one with another, and the blood of Jesus Christ His Son cleanseth us from all sin.

AFFIRMATIONS OF FAITH

The Apostles' Creed

I

I believe in God the Father Almighty, Maker of heaven and earth; and in Jesus Christ, His only Son our Lord; who was conceived by the Holy Spirit, born of the Virgin Mary, suffered under Pontius Pilate, was crucified, dead, and buried; the third day He rose from the dead; He ascended into heaven, and sitteth at the right hand of God the Father Almighty; from thence He shall come to judge the quick and the dead. I believe in the Holy Spirit; the holy catholic Church; the communion of saints; the forgiveness of sins; the resurrection of the body, and the life everlasting. *Amen.*

II

The Minister: Where the Spirit of the Lord is, there is

the one true Church, Apostolic and Universal, whose Holy Faith let us now reverently and sincerely declare:

The Minister and People: We believe in God the Father, infinite in wisdom, power and love, whose mercy is over all His works, and whose will is ever directed to His children's good.

We believe in Jesus Christ, Son of God and Son of man, the gift of the Father's unfailing grace, the ground of our hope and the promise of our deliverance from sin and death.

We believe in the Holy Spirit as the Divine Presence in our lives, whereby we are kept in perpetual remembrance of the truth of Christ, and find strength and help in time of need.

We believe that this faith should manifest itself in the service of love as set forth in the example of our blessed Lord, to the end that the kingdom of God may come upon the earth. *Amen.*

III

We believe in the one God, Maker and Ruler of all things, Father of all men; the source of all goodness and beauty, all truth and love.

We believe in Jesus Christ, God manifest in the flesh, our Teacher, Example, and Redeemer, the Saviour of the world.

We believe in the Holy Spirit, God present with us for guidance, for comfort and for strength.

We believe in the forgiveness of sins, in the life of love and prayer, and in grace equal to every need.

. We believe in the Word of God contained in the Old and New Testaments as the sufficient rule both of faith and of practice.

We believe in the Church as the fellowship for worship and for service of all who are united to the living Lord.

We believe in the kingdom of God as the divine rule in human society; and in the brotherhood of man under the Fatherhood of God.

We believe in the final triumph of righteousness, and in the life everlasting. *Amen.*

PRAYERS AND COLLECTS

For Grace and Guidance

O Lord, our Heavenly Father, Almighty and Everlasting God, who hast safely brought us to the beginning of this day, defend us in the same with Thy mighty power; and grant that this day we fall into no sin, neither run into any kind of danger; but that all our doings may be ordered by Thy governance, to do always that which is righteous in Thy sight; through Jesus Christ our Lord. *Amen.*

For Grace to Profit by Scriptures

Blessed Lord who hast caused all Holy Scriptures to be written for our learning; grant that we may in such wise hear them, read, mark, learn, and inwardly digest them, that by patience, and comfort of Thy Holy Word, we may embrace and ever hold fast the blessed hope of everlasting life, which Thou hast given us in our Saviour, Jesus Christ. *Amen.*

For the Spirit of Wisdom

O God, by whom the meek are guided in judgment, and light riseth up in darkness for the godly, grant us, in all doubts and uncertainties, the grace to ask what Thou wouldst have us to do, that the spirit of wisdom may save us from all false choices, and that in Thy light we may see light and in Thy straight path may not stumble; through Jesus Christ our Lord. *Amen.*

For Pardon

Almighty God, our Heavenly Father, who of Thy great mercy hast promised forgiveness of sins to all them that with hearty repentance and true faith turn unto Thee, have mercy upon us; pardon and deliver us from all our sins; confirm and strengthen us in all goodness; and bring us to everlasting life, through Jesus Christ our Lord. *Amen.*

O Lord, we beseech Thee, absolve Thy people from their offenses; that, through Thy bountiful goodness, we may be delivered from the bonds of those sins which by our frailty we have committed. Grant this, O Heavenly Father, for Jesus Christ's sake, our blessed Lord and Saviour. *Amen.*

For Love to God and Man

O Lord, grant us to love Thee with all our heart, with all our mind, and all our strength; and to love our neighbors for Thy sake, that the grace of charity and brotherly love may dwell in us, and that all envy, harshness, and ill will may die. Fill our hearts with kindness and compassion. May we constantly rejoice in the happiness and good success of others and sympathize with them in their sorrows. May we put away all harsh judgments and envious thoughts. So shall we follow Thee, who are Thyself the true and perfect Love; through Jesus Christ our Lord. *Amen.*

For God's Continual Help

Direct us, O Lord, in all our doings, with Thy most gracious favor, and further us with Thy continual help, that in all our works, begun, continued, and ended in Thee, we may glorify Thy holy Name, and, finally, by Thy mercy, obtain everlasting life, through Jesus Christ our Lord. *Amen.*

For Divine Wisdom and Strength

O Lord, we beseech Thee mercifully to receive the prayers of Thy people who do call upon Thee; and grant that they may both perceive and know what things they ought to do, and that they also may have grace and power faithfully to fulfill the same; through Jesus Christ our Lord. *Amen.*

For All Conditions of Men

O God, the Creator and Preserver of all mankind, we humbly beseech Thee for all sorts and conditions of men; that Thou wouldst be pleased to make Thy ways known unto them, Thy saving health unto all nations. More especially we pray for Thy holy Church universal; that it may be so guided and governed by Thy good Spirit, that all who profess and call themselves Christians may be led into the way of truth, and hold the faith in unity of spirit, in the bond of peace, and in righteousness of life. Finally, we commend to Thy Fatherly goodness all those who are in any way afflicted or distressed in mind, body, or estate, that it may please Thee to comfort and relieve them according to their several necessities; giving them patience under their suffering, and a happy issue out of all their afflictions. And this we ask for Jesus Christ's sake. *Amen.*

General Intercession

O God, at whose word man goeth forth unto his work and to his labor until the evening, be merciful to all whose duties are difficult or burdensome, and comfort them concerning their toil. Shield from bodily accident and harm the workmen at their work. Protect the efforts of sober and honest industry, and suffer not the hire of the laborers to be kept back. Incline the hearts of employers and of those whom they employ to mutual forbearance, fairness, and good will. Give the spirit of grace and of a sound mind to all in places of authority. Bless all those who labor in works of mercy and schools of good learning. Care for all aged persons, and all little children, the sick and the afflicted, and those who travel by land or by sea. Remember all who by reason of weakness are overtasked, or because of poverty are forgotten. Let the sorrowful sighing of the prisoners come before Thee, and according to the greatness of Thy power preserve Thou those that draw nigh unto death. Give ear unto our prayer, O merciful and gracious Father, for the love of Thy dear Son our Saviour Jesus Christ. *Amen.*

General Thanksgiving

Almighty God, Father of all mercies, we, Thine unworthy servants, do give Thee most humble and hearty thanks for all Thy goodness and loving kindness to us, and to all men. We bless Thee for our creation, preservation, and all the blessings of this life; but above all, for Thine inestimable love in the redemption of the world by our Lord Jesus Christ; for the means of grace, and for the hope of glory. And we beseech Thee, give us that due sense of all Thy mercies, that our hearts may be unfeignedly thankful, and that we may show forth Thy praise, not only with our lips, but in our lives; by giving up ourselves to Thy service, and by walking before Thee in holiness and righteousness all our days, through Jesus Christ our Lord, to whom, with Thee and the Holy Spirit, be all honor and glory, world without end. *Amen.*

Prayer of Saint Chrysostom

Almighty God, who hast given us grace, at this time, with one accord to make our common supplications unto Thee; and dost promise that, when two or three are gathered in Thy Name, Thou wilt grant their requests; fulfill now, O Lord, the desires and petitions of Thy servants, as may be most expedient for them; granting us in this world knowledge of Thy truth, and in the world to come life everlasting. *Amen.*

For a Blessing on Families

Almighty God, our Heavenly Father, who settest the solitary in families, we commend to Thy continual care the homes in which Thy people dwell. Put far from them, we beseech Thee, every root of bitterness, the desire of vainglory, and the pride of life. Fill them with faith, virtue, knowledge, temperance, patience, godliness. Knit together in constant affection those who, in holy wedlock, have been made one. Turn the hearts of the fathers to the children, and the hearts of the children to the fathers; and so kindle charity among us all, that we may ever have for each other kindly affection and brotherly love; through Jesus Christ our.Lord. *Amen.*

For the Church

O God, we pray for Thy Church, which is set today amid the perplexities of a changing order, face to face with a great new task. We remember with love the nurture she gave to our spiritual life in its infancy, the tasks she set for our growing strength, the influence of the devoted hearts she gathers, the steadfast power for good she has exerted. When we compare her with all human institutions, we rejoice, for there is none like her. But when we judge her by the mind of her Master, we bow in contrition. Oh, baptize her afresh in the life-giving spirit of Jesus! Put upon her lips the ancient gospel of her Lord. Fill her with the prophet's scorn of tyranny, and with a Christlike tenderness for the heavy-laden and downtrodden. Bid her cease from seeking her own life, lest she lose it. Make her valiant to give up her life to humanity, that like her crucified Lord she may mount by the path of the cross to a higher glory. *Amen.*

For Missions

O Thou who art the Light and the Life of the world, have compassion, we pray Thee, upon those who are sitting in darkness and in the shadow of death; and as Thou didst at the first, by the preaching of Thine apostles, cause the Light of Thy gospel to shine throughout the world, be pleased to make Thy ways known upon earth, Thy saving health unto all nations. Bless Thy servants who have gone into hard fields and unto distant lands to proclaim the message of salvation. Endue them with Thy Holy Spirit, enrich them with Thy heavenly grace, prosper them in all their labors, and give them souls as their reward. And, O Thou Lord of the harvest! we pray Thee to send forth more laborers into Thy harvest. May they both sow the seed and reap the fruit of their labors! And give us grace to do our part in the great field of this world in sowing and in reaping, through the grace of Jesus Christ. *Amen.*

For Evangelism

Increase, O God, the faith and the zeal of all Thy people, that they may more earnestly desire, and more diligently seek, the salvation of their fellow men, through the message of Thy love in Jesus Christ our Lord. Send forth a mighty call unto Thy servants who labor in the gospel, granting unto them a heart of love, sincerity of speech, and the power of the Holy Spirit, that they may be able to persuade men to forsake sin and return unto Thee. And so bless and favor the work of Thine evangelists, that multitudes may be brought from the kingdom of evil into the kingdom of Thy dear Son, our Saviour, Jesus Christ. *Amen.*

For Social Service

O Lord, our Heavenly Father, who by Thy blessed Son hast taught us that Thou art Love, we beseech Thee graciously to bless all those who, following His steps, give themselves to the service of their fellow men. Grant unto them clear vision to perceive those things which in our social order are amiss; give them true judgment, courage, and perseverance to help those to right that suffer wrong, and endue them with unfailing love to minister to the poor, the suffering, and the friendless. Make us sensible of our union one with another as Thy children, that we may strive wisely to order all things among us according to Thy will; for the sake of Him who laid down His life for us, Thy Son, our Saviour, Jesus Christ. *Amen.*

For the President and Others in Authority

O God, who art the Hope of all the ends of the earth, remember us in love, and guide us by Thine infinite wisdom. Most heartily we beseech Thee to grant Thy· blessing upon Thy servants, the President of the United States, the Governor of this state, and all others in authority. Imbue them with the spirit of wisdom, goodness, and truth; and so rule their hearts, and bless their endeavors, that law and order, justice and peace, may everywhere prevail, to the honor of Thy holy Name, through Jesus Christ our Lord. *Amen.*

For the Country

Almighty God, who in the former time didst lead our fathers forth into a wealthy place; give Thy grace, we humbly beseech Thee, to us, their children, that we may always approve ourselves a people mindful of Thy favor, and glad to do Thy will. Bless our land with honorable industry, sound learning, and pure religion. Defend our liberties, preserve our unity. Save us from violence, discord, and confusion, from pride and arrogancy, and from every evil way. Fashion into one happy people the multitudes brought hither out of many kindreds and tongues. Endue with the spirit of wisdom those whom we intrust in Thy Name with the authority of governance, to the end that there be peace at home, and that we keep a place among the nations of the

earth. In the time of prosperity fill our hearts with thank-
fulness; and in the day of trouble suffer not our trust in
Thee to fail; all of which we ask for Jesus Christ's sake.
Amen.

Grant us peace, Thy most precious gift, O Thou eternal
Source of peace. Bless our country, that it may ever be
a stronghold of peace, and the advocate of peace in the
councils of nations. May contentment reign within its
borders, health and happiness within its homes. Strengthen
the bonds of friendship and fellowship between all the in-
habitants of our land. Plant virtue in every soul; and may
the love of Thy Name hallow every home and every heart.
Praised be Thou, O Lord, Giver of Peace. *Amen.*

For the Advancement of the Kingdom

Almighty God, from whom all thoughts of truth and
peace proceed; kindle, we pray Thee, in the hearts of all
men the true love of peace, and guide with Thy pure and
peaceable wisdom those who take counsel for the nations
of the earth; that in tranquillity Thy kingdom may go forward till the earth is filled with the knowledge of Thy love;
through Jesus Christ our Lord. *Amen.*

For Quietness of Spirit

O God, from whom all holy desires, all good counsels, and
all just works do proceed; give unto Thy servants that
peace which the world cannot give, that our hearts may be
set to obey Thy commandments and that, by Thee, we may
pass our time in rest and quietness; through the merits of
Jesus Christ, our Saviour. *Amen.*

For Use after the Sermon

Grant, we beseech Thee, Almighty God, that the words
which we have heard this day with our outward ears may,
through Thy grace, be so grafted inwardly in our hearts
that they may bring forth in us the fruit of good living, to
the honor and praise of Thy Name; through Jesus Christ
our Lord. *Amen.*

For the Communion of Saints

We thank Thee for the dear and faithful dead, for those
who have made the distant heavens a home for us, and
whose truth and beauty are even now in our hearts. One
by one Thou dost gather the scattered families out of the
earthly light into the heavenly glory, from the distractions
and strife and weariness of time to the peace of eternity.

We thank Thee for the labors and the joys of these mortal
years. We thank Thee for our deep sense of the mysteries
that lie beyond our dust, and for the eye of faith which
Thou hast opened for all who believe in Thy Son. May we
live altogether in Thy faith and love, and in that hope
which is full of immortality. *Amen.*

> O Lord, support us all the day long
> Of this troublous life,
> Until the shadows lengthen,
> And the evening comes,
> And the busy world is hushed,
> And the fever of life is over,
> And our work is done.
> Then, of Thy great mercy,
> Grant us a safe lodging
> And a holy rest,
> And peace at the last;
> Through Jesus Christ, our Lord. *Amen.*

OFFERTORY SENTENCES

I

All things come of Thee, O Lord,
And of Thine own have we given Thee. *Amen.*

II

> We give Thee but Thine own,
> Whate'er the gift may be;
> All that we have is Thine alone,
> A trust, O Lord, from Thee. *Amen.*

III

The Minister: To the preaching of the good tidings of
salvation
The People: We consecrate our gifts.
The Minister: To the teaching of Jesus' way of life
The People: We consecrate our gifts.
The Minister: To the healing of broken bodies and the
soothing of fevered brows
The People: We consecrate our gifts.
The Minister: To the leading of every little child to the
knowledge and love of Jesus.
The People: We consecrate our gifts.
The Minister: To the caring for helpless age and the re-
lief of all who look to us for help.
The People: We consecrate our gifts.

The Minister: To the evangelization of the world and the building of the kingdom of God

The People: We consecrate our wealth, our efforts, and our lives.

BENEDICTIONS

The grace of the Lord Jesus Christ, and the love of God, and the communion of the Holy Spirit, be with you all. *Amen.*

The peace of God which passeth all understanding, keep your hearts and minds in the knowledge and love of God, and of His Son, Jesus Christ our Lord; and the blessing of God Almighty, the Father, the Son, and the Holy Spirit, be amongst you and remain with you always. *Amen.*

And now may the blessing of God Almighty, Father, Son, and Holy Spirit, be amongst you and abide with you, now and evermore. *Amen.*

The Lord bless you and keep you; the Lord make His face to shine upon you and be gracious unto you; the Lord lift up His countenance upon you and give you peace; both now and evermore. *Amen.*

Now unto Him that is able to keep you from falling, and to present you faultless before the presence of His glory with exceeding joy, to the only wise God our Saviour, be glory and majesty, dominion and power, both now and evermore. *Amen.*

Now the God of peace, that brought again from the dead our Lord Jesus, that great Shepherd of the sheep, through the blood of the everlasting covenant, make you perfect in every good work to do His will, working in you that which is well pleasing in His sight, through Jesus Christ; to whom be glory for ever and ever. *Amen.*

Now unto Him who is eternal, immortal, invisible, the only just and all-wise God, be glory and honor, dominion and power, now and for ever. *Amen.*

REPORT NO 3. CONCERNING CHAPTER XXVI OF PROSPECTUS

Calendar No. 40. Adopted May 8. See Journal, Page 318.

Membership of Committee, 45; present when report was adopted, 38; voting for adoption, 38.

The Committee on Rituals and Orders of Worship recommends for adoption Chapter XXVI of the *Prospectus* (pp. 302 to 335, inclusive), with amendments and additions as hereinafter noted.

The last sentence of the first rubric to read: "The portions to be used as responses are especially indicated by bold-faced type."

I. The Lord's Supper or Holy Communion

¶ 1408. *The Order for the Administration of the Sacrament of the Lord's Supper.*

1. In the rubric, first sentence, omit the word "white."
2. In the rubric, fifth sentence, add the words, "in the *Methodist Hymnal.*"
3. The closing response after the Beatitudes, page 303, to be properly placed.
4. After the Beatitudes the rubric to read: (Here the minister may use an alternative responsive reading Isaiah 53: 1-10.) The verses to be read by the people to be indicated in bold-faced type.

Vote on this section: Present, 38; for, 34; against, 2; not voting, 2.

¶ 1409. *An Alternative Order for the Administration of the Sacrament of the Lord's Supper.*

The Minister shall read one or more of these sentences, during the reading of which the stewards shall take up the collection for the poor.

Let your light so shine before men, that they may see your good works, and glorify your Father which is in heaven. Matt. v. 16.

Lay not up for yourself treasures upon earth, where moth and rust doth corrupt, and where thieves break through and steal: but lay up for yourselves treasures in heaven, where neither moth nor rust doth corrupt, and where thieves do not break through nor steal. Matt. vi. 19, 20.

Whatsoever ye would that men should do to you, do ye even so to them: for this is the law and the prophets. Matt. vii. 12.

Not every one that saith unto me, Lord, Lord, shall enter into the kingdom of heaven; but he that doeth the will of my Father which is in heaven. Matt. vii. 21.

Zacchaeus stood, and said unto the Lord; Behold, Lord, the half of my goods I give to the poor; and if I have taken anything from any man by false accusation, I restore him fourfold. Luke xix. 8.

He which soweth sparingly shall reap also sparingly; and he which soweth bountifully shall reap also bountifully. Every man according as he purposeth in his heart, so let him give; not grudgingly, or of necessity: for God loveth a cheerful giver. 2 Cor. ix. 6, 7.

As we have therefore opportunity, let us do good unto all men, especially unto them who are of the household of faith. Gal. vi. 10.

Godliness with contentment is great gain. For we brought nothing into this world, and it is certain we can carry nothing out. 1 Tim. vi. 6, 7.

Charge them that are rich in this world, that they be ready to distribute, willing to communicate; laying up in store for themselves a good foundation against the time to come, that they may lay hold on eternal life. 1 Tim. vi. 17-19.

God is not unrighteous to forget your work and labor of love, which ye have showed toward his name, in that ye have ministered to the saints, and do minister. Heb. vi. 10.

To do good and to communicate forget not: for with such sacrifices God is well pleased. Heb. xiii. 16.

Whoso hath this world's good, and seeth his brother have need, and shutteth up his bowels of compassion from him, how dwelleth the love of God in him? 1 John iii. 17.

He that hath pity upon the poor lendeth unto the Lord; and that which he hath given will he pay him again. Prov. xix. 17.

Blessed is he that considereth the poor: the Lord will deliver him in time of trouble. Ps. xli. 1.

Then shall the Minister read this invitation:

Ye that do truly and earnestly repent of your sins, and are in love and charity with your neighbors, and intend to lead a new life, following the commandments of God, and walking from henceforth in his holy ways; draw near with faith, and take his Holy Sacrament to your comfort: and make your humble confession to Almighty God, meekly kneeling upon your knees.

Then shall this general confession be made by the Minister and all those who are minded to receive the Holy Communion, both he and they humbly kneeling, and saying:

Almighty God, Father of our Lord Jesus Christ, Maker of all things, Judge of all men: we acknowledge and bewail our manifold sins and wickedness, which we from time to time most grievously have committed, by thought, word, and deed, against Thy Divine Majesty, provoking most justly Thy wrath and indignation against us. We do earnestly repent, and are heartily sorry for these our misdoings; the remembrance of them is grievous unto us. Have mercy upon us, have mercy upon us, most merciful Father;

for Thy Son our Lord Jesus Christ's sake, forgive us all that is past; and grant that we may ever hereafter serve and please Thee in newness of life, to the honor and glory of Thy name, through Jesus Christ our Lord. *Amen.*

Then shall the Minister say:

O Almighty God, our Heavenly Father, who of thy great mercy hast promised forgiveness of sins to all them that with hearty repentance and true faith turn to thee: have mercy upon us; pardon and deliver us from all our sins, confirm and strengthen us in all goodness, and bring us to everlasting life, through Jesus Christ our Lord. *Amen.*

The Collect

Almighty God, unto whom all hearts be open, all desires known, and from whom no secrets are hid: cleanse the thoughts of our hearts by the inspiration of Thy Holy Spirit, that we may perfectly love Thee, and worthily magnify Thy holy Name, through Christ our Lord. *Amen.*

Then shall the Minister say:

It is very meet, right, and our bounden duty, that we should at all times, and in all places, give thanks unto Thee, O Lord, holy Father, almighty, everlasting God.

Therefore with angels and archangels, and with all the company of heaven, we laud and magnify Thy glorious Name, evermore praising Thee, and saying, Holy, holy, holy, Lord God of hosts, heaven and earth are full of Thy glory. Glory be to Thee, O Lord most high. *Amen.*

Then shall the Minister say:

We do not presume to come to this Thy table, O merciful Lord, trusting in our own righteousness, but in Thy manifold and great mercies. We are not worthy so much as to gather up the crumbs under Thy table. But Thou art the same Lord whose property is always to have mercy: Grant us, therefore, gracious Lord, so to eat the flesh of Thy Son Jesus Christ, and to drink His blood, that our sinful souls and bodies may be made clean by His death, and washed through His most precious blood, and that we may evermore dwell in Him, and He in us. *Amen.*

Then the Minister shall say the prayer of consecration as followeth:

Almighty God, our Heavenly Father, who of Thy tender mercy didst give Thine only Son Jesus Christ to suffer death upon the cross for our redemption; who made there (by His oblation of Himself once offered) a full, perfect, and sufficient sacrifice, oblation, and satisfaction for the sins of the whole world; and did institute, and in His holy gospel command us to continue, a perpetual memory of that His precious death until His coming again: hear us, O merciful Father, we most humbly beseech Thee, and grant that we, receiving these Thy creatures of bread and wine, according to Thy Son our Saviour Jesus Christ's holy institution, in remembrance of His death and passion, may be partakers of His most blessed body and blood; who in the same night that He was betrayed took bread; and when He had given thanks, He brake it, and gave it to His disciples, saying, Take, eat; this is My body which is given for you; do this in remembrance of me. Likewise after supper He took the cup; and when He had given thanks, He gave it to them, saying, Drink ye all of this; for this is My blood of the New Testament, which is shed for you and for many, for the remission of sins; do this, as oft as ye shall drink it, in remembrance of me. *Amen.*

Then shall the Minister first receive the communion in both kinds himself, and then proceed to deliver the same to the other Ministers in like manner, if any be present. Then shall he say the Lord's Prayer, the people still kneeling and repeating after him every petition:

Our Father, who art in heaven, hallowed be Thy Name: Thy kingdom come: Thy will be done on earth as it is in heaven: give us this day our daily bread; and forgive us our trespasses, as we forgive those who trespass against us; and lead us not into temptation, but deliver us from evil; for Thine is the kingdom, and the power, and the glory, forever and ever. *Amen.*

Then a hymn may be sung, and the communicants shall be invited to the table. The Minister shall deliver both kinds to the people into their hands. When he delivereth the bread, he shall say:

The body of our Lord Jesus Christ, which was given for *thee*, preserve *thy soul* and *body* unto everlasting life. Take and eat this in remembrance that Christ died for *thee*, and feed on Him in *thy heart* by faith with thanksgiving.

And the Minister that delivereth the cup shall say:

The blood of our Lord Jesus Christ, which was shed for *thee*, preserve *thy soul* and *body* unto everlasting life. Drink this in remembrance that Christ's blood was shed for *thee*, and be thankful.

[When all have communicated, the Minister shall return to the Lord's Table, and place upon it what remaineth of the consecrated Elements, covering the same with a fair linen cloth.]

The Minister may then say as followeth:

O Lord and Heavenly Father, we Thy humble servants desire Thy Fatherly goodness mercifully to accept this our sacrifice of praise and thanksgiving; most humbly beseeching Thee to grant that, by the merits and death of Thy Son Jesus Christ, and through faith in His blood, we and Thy whole Church may obtain remission of our sins, and all other benefits of His Passion. And here we offer and present unto Thee, O Lord, ourselves, our souls and bodies, to be a reasonable, holy, and lively sacrifice unto Thee; humbly beseeching Thee that all we who are partakers of this holy communion may be filled with Thy grace and heavenly benediction. And although we be unworthy, through our manifold sins, to offer unto Thee any sacrifice, yet we beseech Thee to accept this our bounden duty and service; not weighing our merits, but pardoning our offenses, through Jesus Christ our Lord: by whom, and with whom, in the unity of the Holy Spirit, all honor and glory be unto Thee, O Father Almighty, world without end. *Amen.*

Then may be said or sung:

Glory be to God on high, and on earth peace, good will toward men. We praise Thee, we bless Thee, we worship Thee, we glorify Thee, we give thanks to Thee for Thy great glory, O Lord God, Heavenly King, God the Father Almighty.

O Lord, the only-begotten Son, Jesus Christ; O Lord God, Lamb of God, Son of the Father, that takest away the sins of the world, have mercy upon us. Thou that takest away the sins of the world, have mercy upon us. Thou that takest away the sins of the world, receive our prayer. Thou that sittest at the right hand of God the Father, have mercy upon us.

For Thou only art holy; Thou only art the Lord; Thou only, O Christ, with the Holy Spirit, art most high in the glory of God the Father. *Amen.*

Then the Minister, if he see it expedient, may offer an extemporaneous prayer; and afterward shall let the people depart with this blessing:

May the peace of God, which passeth all understanding, keep your hearts and minds in the knowledge and love of God, and of his Son Jesus Christ our Lord; and the blessing of God Almighty, the Father, the Son, and the Holy Ghost, be among you, and remain with you always. *Amen.*

If the Minister be straitened for time, he may omit any part of the service except the prayer of consecration.

(The Editors of the Discipline are authorized to harmonize the rubrics in this Order with the rest of the rituals.)

Vote on this section: Present, 38; for, 34; against, 2; not voting, 1.

II. BAPTISM

THE ORDER FOR THE ADMINISTRATION OF THE SACRAMENT OF BAPTISM

¶ 1410. *The Baptism of Infants.*

(Editor: "extempore" instead of "extemporary," in rubric.)

Vote on this section: Present, 38; for, 37; not voting, 1.

¶ 1411. *A Briefer Order for the Baptism of Infants.*

Vote on this section: Present, 38; for, 37; not voting, 1.

¶ 1412. *The Order for the Baptism of Children and Youth.*

The Minister, coming to the Font, shall say:

Hear the words of the Gospel, written by St. Matthew, in the twenty-eighth chapter, beginning at the sixteenth verse.

Then the eleven disciples went away into Galilee, into a mountain where Jesus had appointed them. And when they saw Him, they worshiped Him; but some doubted. And Jesus came and spake unto them, saying, All power is given unto Me in heaven and in earth. Go ye therefore, and make disciples of all nations, baptizing them in the name of the Father, and of the Son, and of the Holy Ghost: teaching them to observe all things whatsoever I have commanded you: and lo, I am with you alway, even unto the end of the world. *Amen.*

Then shall the Minister say:

Let us pray.

Almighty and everliving God, whose most dearly beloved Son Jesus Christ gave Himself for our salvation, and did command His disciples that they should go teach all nations, and baptize them in the name of the Father, and of the Son, and of the Holy Spirit: regard, we beseech Thee, the supplications of Thy congregation; and grant that *these persons* now to be baptized may so open *their* hearts to Thee as that *they* may receive the fulness of Thy grace, and may ever remain in the number of Thy faithful children, through Jesus Christ our Lord. *Amen.*

Then the Minister shall say to the *persons* to be baptized:

Well beloved, who are come hither, desiring to receive holy baptism, you have heard how the congregation hath prayed that God would assist you to open your hearts to His love and direction, that you may be faithful disciples of our Lord.

Wherefore, for your part, it is needful that in the presence of Almighty God and the hearing of this congregation, you should now make known your purpose to accept the obligations of this holy Sacrament, by answering the following questions:

Will you faithfully put away from you every known sin, of thought, word, or deed, and accept and confess Jesus Christ as your Saviour and Lord?

God helping me, I will.

Will you diligently study the Bible as God's Holy Word, and in all things strive to make it the rule of your life?

God helping me, I will.

Having been taught how the Spirit of our Lord separates right from wrong, will you faithfully endeavor to live so as to be pleasing unto Him?

God helping me, I will.

Will you be baptized in this faith?

This is my desire.

Then shall the Minister ask each person his name, and shall baptize him, saying:

N. I baptize thee in the name of the Father, and of the Son, and of the Holy Spirit. *Amen.*

Here the Minister shall offer a suitable prayer.

Vote on this section: Present, 34; for, 32; against, 1; not voting, 1.

¶ 1413. *The Order for the Baptism of Adults.* ¶ 1412 in the *Prospectus.*

(Editorial note: The. phrase "These persons" and the pronouns "them" referring to "these persons" to be in italics.)

Vote on this section: Present, 38; for, 38.

III. RECEPTION OF MEMBERS

¶ 1414. *The Order for Receiving Persons into the Church.* ¶ 1413 in the *Prospectus.*

'(Editorial note: The final paragraph following "Then shall the people say:" to be in bold-faced type.)

Vote on this section: Present, 38; for, 38.

¶ 1415. *The Order for Receiving Children and Youth into the Church.*

After the Minister previously shall have formed the children into a class (baptizing any whose baptism may have been delayed or neglected), and shall have instructed them in the things necessary for them to know as to the Doctrines and Rules of the Church, he shall cause them to be conveniently placed before the Congregation, and after inviting their Parents and Teachers to stand with them on either hand, he shall say:

Brethren of the household of faith, let our hearts be lifted up in thanksgiving to Almighty God, who by the Holy Spirit hath inclined *these children* to desire and ask for membership in the Church. Having arrived at years of discretion, and now of *their* own accord appearing before this congregation to take upon *themselves* the vows and enter upon the privileges and duties of the Church, let us with one mind and heart most earnestly invoke in *their* behalf the blessings of Father, Son, and Holy Spirit.

Then shall the Minister say:

Let us pray.

Almighty and everliving God, giver of every good and perfect gift, accept our hearty thanks for the children whom Thou hast committed to our love and care. As Thou didst bring them into the world, now renew in Thy servants, their parents, pastors, and teachers, wisdom to train them in the way they should go. Grant unto these Thy children that from this day forth they may grow in grace, and wisdom, and in favor with God and man, through Jesus Christ our Lord. *Amen.*

Then shall the Minister address the Parents or Sponsor:

Dear fathers and mothers, let this be to you a day of peculiar joy and thanksgiving in that *these who are* of your flesh and blood have also entered into a holier spiritual kinship with you in Jesus Christ. While the Church will continue to share with you the duty and privilege of bringing up *these children* in the nurture and admonition of the Lord, it renews its solemn injunction to you as parents, by God's help, faithfully to continue both to teach and train *them*, by example and precept, in the way of the Lord. Will you accept this duty, in the fear and by the favor of God, and here and now, in the presence of Almighty God and this congregation, renew the vows made by you as fathers and mothers in the baptism of *these children?*

With God's help, I will.

Then shall the Minister address the *children* who are candidates and say:

Beloved *Children,* our Lord Jesus, by His Holy Word hath expressly given to everyone who believe in Him a place in His Kingdom and Church. Before you are admitted into the Church, it becomes my duty to inquire of you as to your purpose of mind and heart:

Do you, *each of you,* believe in God as your heavenly Father?

I do.

Do you accept Jesus Christ as your personal Saviour?

I do.

Do you believe in the Bible as God's Holy Word?

I do.

Will you be loyal to The Methodist Church and uphold it by your prayers, your presence, your gifts, and your service?

I will.

Here the Minister may offer an extemporary prayer.

Then those to be received shall kneel and the Minister laying his hands upon every one of them severally shall say:

I receive you into the Church of Christ and pray God's blessing upon you.

Then shall the Minister, the People, and the Children say:

Our Father Who art in heaven, hallowed be Thy name: Thy kingdom come: Thy will be done on earth as it is in heaven: give us this day our daily bread; and forgive us our trespasses, as we forgive those who trespass against us;

and lead us not into temptation, but deliver us from evil; for Thine is the kingdom, and the power, and the glory, forever and ever. *Amen.*

Vote on this section: Present, 38; for, 38.

IV. MATRIMONY.

¶ 1416. *The Order for the Solemnization of Matrimony.* ¶ 1414 in the *Prospectus.*

Vote on this section: Present: 38; for, 38.

V. THE BURIAL OF THE DEAD

¶ 1417. *The Order for the Burial of the Dead.* ¶ 1415 in the *Prospectus.*

¶ 1418. *The Order for the Burial of a Child.* ¶ 1416 in the *Prospectus.*

Vote on this section: Present, 38; for, 38.

VI. CONSECRATION AND ORDINATION

¶ 1419. *The Order for the Consecration of Deaconesses.* ¶ 1417 in the *Prospectus.*

¶ 1420. *The Order for the Ordination of Deacons.* ¶ 1418 in the *Prospectus.*

¶ 1421. *The Order for the Ordination of Elders.* ¶ 1419 in the *Prospectus.*

¶ 1422. *The Order for the Consecration of Bishops.* ¶1420 in the *Prospectus.*

Vote on this section: Present, 38; for, 38.

VII. THE LAYING OF A CORNER STONE

¶ 1423. *The Order for the Laying of the Corner Stone of a Church.* ¶ 1421 in the *Prospectus.*

¶1424. *A Briefer Form for the Laying of a Corner Stone.* ¶ 1422 in the *Prospectus.*

Vote on this section: Present, 38; for, 38.

·· VIII. THE DEDICATION OF A CHURCH

¶ 1425. *The Order for the Dedication of a Church.* ¶ 1423 in the *Prospectus.*

Vote on this section: Present, 38; for, 38.

IX. THE DEDICATION OF AN ORGAN

¶ 1426. *The Order for the Dedication of an Organ.* ¶ 1424 in the *Prospectus.*

Vote on this section: Present, 38; for, 38.

X. THE DEDICATION OF A PARISH HOUSE

¶ 1427. *The Order for the Dedication of a Parish House.* ¶ 1425 in the *Prospectus.*

Vote on this section: Present, 38; for, 38.

XI. THE DEDICATION OF A HOSPITAL

¶ 1428. *The Order for the Dedication of a Hospital.* ¶ 1426 in the *Prospectus.*

Vote on this section: Present, 38; for, 38.

XII. THE DEDICATION OF A COLLEGE OR UNIVERSITY BUILDING

¶ 1429. *The Order for the Dedication of an Educational Building.* ¶ 1427 in the *Prospectus.*

Vote on this section: Present, 38; for, 38.

XIII. THE DEDICATION OF A HOME

¶ 1430. *The Order for the Dedication of a Home.* ¶ 1428 in the *Prospectus.*

Vote on this section: Present, 38; for, 38.

CHAPTER XXVI

THE RITUAL OF THE METHODIST CHURCH

We call upon all our Ministers to make faithful use of the forms and orders here provided, without other deviation than is here indicated.

We urge all Ministers to encourage and train the people to participate audibly in those portions of the service provided for this purpose, particularly in the celebration of the Lord's Supper. The portions to be used as responses are especially indicated by *bold-faced type.*

THE LORD'S SUPPER OR HOLY COMMUNION

¶ 1408. THE ORDER FOR THE ADMINISTRATION OF THE SACRAMENT OF THE LORD'S SUPPER

[The Lord's Table should have upon it a fair linen cloth.
Let the pure unfermented juice of the grape be used.
It is our custom to receive the Sacrament of the Lord's Supper kneeling, but if persons so desire, they may receive the Elements while seated or standing.
Upon entering the church let the communicants bow in prayer and in the spirit of prayer and meditation approach the blessed Sacrament.

The Responses throughout may be sung if desired. See Hymns 565-624 in *The Methodist Hymnal.*

The following Order has been prepared to take the place of the regular order of the morning worship. Everything preceding the Invitation may be omitted if the occasion demands such brevity. If further straitened for time, as in the sickroom, the Minister may omit any part of the service except the Invitation, the Confession, the Prayer of Consecration, the usual sentences for the distribution of the Elements, and the Benediction. But it is highly to be desired that the longer form be followed for Public Worship.]

The People shall stand and join in singing the hymn, "Holy, Holy, Holy, Lord God Almighty," or other suitable Hymn and remain standing until after the singing of the *Gloria Patri.*

God is a Spirit. They that worship Him must worship Him in spirit and in truth.

Glory be to God on high.

God is Light. If we walk in the light as He is in the light, we have fellowship one with another; and truly our fellowship is with the Father and with His Son, Jesus Christ,

Glory be to God on high.

God is Power. They that wait upon the Lord shall renew their strength: they shall mount up with wings as eagles: they shall run and not be weary: and they shall walk and not faint.

Glory be to God on high.

God is Love. Behold what manner of love the Father hath bestowed upon us that we should be called the sons of God. Hereby perceive we the love of God, because He laid down His life for us.

Glory be to God on high.

Then shall be said or sung:

Glory be to the Father, and to the Son, and to the Holy Ghost; as it was in the beginning, is now and ever shall be, world without end. *Amen.*

Then shall the Minister say:

Let us pray.

Almighty God, unto whom all hearts are open, all desires known, and from whom no secrets are hid, cleanse the thoughts of our hearts by the inspiration of Thy Holy Spirit, that we may perfectly love Thee, and worthily magnify Thy Holy Name, through Jesus Christ our Lord. *Amen.*

Our Father, who art in heaven:
Hallowed be Thy name, Thy kingdom come, Thy will be done on earth as it is in heaven.
Give us this day our daily bread. And forgive us our trespasses, as we forgive those who trespass against us. And lead us not into temptation, but deliver us from evil.
For thine is the kingdom, and the power, and the glory, for ever. *Amen.*

[Then may the Minister read the Ten Commandments, and the People, still in the attitude of prayer, shall in response ask God's mercy for their transgressions in times past and grace to keep the law in time to come.]

God spake these words, and said: I am the Lord thy God: Thou shalt have no other gods before Me.
Thou shalt not make unto thee any graven image, or any likeness of anything that is in heaven above, or that is in the earth beneath, or that is in the water under the earth: thou shalt not bow down thyself to them, nor serve them: for I the Lord thy God am a jealous God, visiting the iniquity of the fathers upon the children unto the third and fourth generations of them that hate Me; and showing mercy unto thousands of them that love Me, and keep My commandments.
Lord, have mercy upon us, and write all these Thy laws in our hearts, we beseech Thee.
Thou shalt not take the Name of the Lord thy God in vain; for the Lord will not hold him guiltless that taketh His Name in vain.
Remember the Sabbath day, to keep it holy. Six days shalt thou labor, and do all thy work: but the seventh day is the Sabbath of the Lord thy God: in it thou shalt not do any work, thou, nor thy son, nor thy daughter, thy manservant, nor thy maidservant, nor thy cattle, nor thy stranger that is within thy gates: for in six days the Lord made heaven and earth, the sea, and all that in them is, and rested the Sabbath day: wherefore the Lord blessed the Sabbath day, and hallowed it.
Lord, have mercy upon us, and write all these Thy laws in our hearts, we beseech Thee.
Honor thy father and thy mother: that thy days may be long upon the land which the Lord thy God giveth thee.
Thou shalt not kill.
Thou shalt not commit adultery.
Thou shalt not steal.
Thou shalt not bear false witness against thy neighbor.

Thou shalt not covet thy neighbor's house, thou shalt not covet thy neighbor's wife, nor his manservant, nor his maidservant, nor his ox, nor his ass, nor anything that is thy neighbor's.

Lord, have mercy upon us, and write all these Thy laws in our hearts, we beseech Thee.

[In place of or in addition to the Ten Commandments the Minister may read the summary of the Divine Law in the words of Jesus, and the People, in the attitude of prayer, shall ask God's mercy and gracious aid.]

Hear what our Lord Jesus Christ saith:

Thou shalt love the Lord thy God with all thy heart, and with all thy soul, and with all thy mind. This is the first and great commandment. And the second is like unto it, Thou shalt love thy neighbor as thyself.

Lord, have mercy upon us, and write all these Thy laws in our hearts, we beseech Thee.

Then may the Minister read the Beatitudes of the Lord Jesus, and the People, still in the attitude of prayer, shall humbly ask God that they may be fulfilled in their hearts.

Hear the Beatitudes of our Lord Jesus Christ.

Blessed are the poor in spirit: for theirs is the kingdom of heaven.

Lord, be gracious unto us, and help us to obtain this blessing.

Blessed are they that mourn: for they shall be comforted.

Lord, be gracious unto us, and help us to obtain this blessing.

Blessed are the meek: for they shall inherit the earth.

Lord, be gracious unto us, and help us to obtain this blessing.

Blessed are they which do hunger and thirst after righteousness: for they shall be filled.

Lord, be gracious unto us, and help us to obtain this blessing.

Blessed are the merciful: for they shall obtain mercy.

Lord, be gracious unto us, and help us to obtain this blessing.

Blessed are the pure in heart: for they shall see God.

Lord, be gracious unto us, and help us to obtain this blessing.

Blessed are the peacemakers: for they shall be called the children of God.

Lord, be gracious unto us, and help us to obtain this blessing.

Blessed are they which are persecuted for righteousness' sake: for theirs is the kingdom of heaven.

Blessed are ye, when men shall revile you, and persecute you, and shall say all manner of evil against you falsely, for My sake.

Rejoice and be exceeding glad: for great is your reward in heaven: for so persecuted they the prophets which were before you.

Grant unto us Thy Holy Spirit, O God, and enable us to obtain all these blessings, through Jesus Christ our Lord. *Amen.*

[If desired, the following form may be used:]

Hear the Beatitudes of our Lord Jesus Christ:

Blessed are the poor in spirit: for theirs is the kingdom of heaven.

Blessed are they that mourn: for they shall be comforted.

Blessed are the meek: for they shall inherit the earth.

Lord, be gracious unto us, and help us to obtain these blessings.

Blessed are they which do hunger and thirst after righteousness: for they shall be filled.

Blessed are the merciful: for they shall obtain mercy.

Blessed are the pure in heart: for they shall see God.

Blessed are the peacemakers: for they shall be called the children of God.

Lord, be gracious unto us, and help us to obtain these blessings.

Blessed are they which are persecuted for righteousness' sake: for theirs is the kingdom of heaven.

Blessed are ye, when men shall revile you, and persecute you, and shall say all manner of evil against you falsely, for My sake.

Rejoice, and be exceeding glad: for great is your reward in heaven: for so persecuted they the prophets who were before you.

Grant unto us Thy Holy Spirit, O God, and enable us to obtain all these blessings, through Jesus Christ our Lord. *Amen.*

[Here the Minister may use as an alternate responsive reading Isaiah 53: 1-10:]

Who hath believed our report? and to whom is the arm of the Lord revealed?

For he shall grow up before him as a tender plant, and as a root out of a dry ground; he hath no form nor comeliness, and when we shall see him, there is no beauty that we should desire him.

He is despised and rejected of men; a man of sorrows, and acquainted with grief; and we hid as it were our faces from him; he was despised, and we esteemed him not.

Surely he hath borne our griefs and carried our sorrows: yet we did esteem him stricken, smitten of God and afflicted.

But he was wounded for our transgressions, he was bruised for our iniquities; the chastisement of our peace was upon him, and with his stripes we are healed.

All we like sheep have gone astray; we have turned every one to his own way: and the Lord hath laid on him the iniquity of us all.

He was oppressed, and he was afflicted, yet he opened not his mouth: he is brought as a lamb to the slaughter, and as a sheep before his shearers is dumb, so he openeth not his mouth.

He was taken from prison and from judgment and who shall declare his generation? for he was cut off out of the land of the living; for the transgression of my people was he stricken.

And he made his grave with the wicked, and with the rich in his death; because he had done no violence, neither was any deceit in his mouth.

Yet it pleased the Lord to bruise him; he hath put him to grief; when thou shalt make his soul an offering for sin, he shall see his seed, he shall prolong his days, and the pleasure of the Lord shall prosper in his hands.

[Then may the Minister read the Epistle, to be followed by the Gospel.

Here may the Minister and People repeat the Apostles' Creed or some other of the authorized Affirmations of Faith, the People standing.

Then may follow the Sermon or Communion meditation and suitable Hymn (see Hymns 408-415, inclusive). During the singing of this Hymn the Minister shall remove the linen cloth that covers the Elements.]

After the Hymn has been sung, the Minister, standing by the Lord's Table, shall announce the Offering for the needy, using one or more of the following groups of sentences.

I

Remember the words of the Lord Jesus, how He said: It is more blessed to give than to receive.

Let your light so shine before men, that they may see your good works, and glorify your Father which is in heaven.

Not every one that saith unto Me, Lord, Lord, shall enter into the kingdom of heaven; but he that doeth the will of My Father which is in heaven.

And the King shall answer and say unto them, Verily I say unto you, Inasmuch as ye have done it unto one of the least of these My brethren, ye have done it unto Me.

Therefore all things whatsoever ye would that men should do to you do ye even so to them: for this is the law and the prophets.

II

They shall not appear before the Lord empty. Every man shall give as he is able, according to the blessing of the Lord thy God which He hath given thee.

Blessed is he that considereth the poor: the Lord will deliver him in time of trouble.

Thou shalt open thine hand wide unto thy brother, to thy poor, and to thy needy, in thy land.

Be merciful after thy power. If thou hast much, give plenteously: if thou hast little, do thy diligence gladly to give of that little: for so gatherest thou thyself a good reward in the day of necessity.

He that hath pity upon the poor lendeth unto the Lord; and that which he hath given will He pay him again.

III

To do good and to communicate forget not: for with such sacrifices God is well pleased.

As we have therefore opportunity, let us do good unto all men, especially unto them who are of the household of faith.

He which soweth sparingly shall reap also sparingly; and he which soweth bountifully shall reap also bountifully. Every man according as he purposeth in his heart, so let him give; not grudgingly, or of necessity: for God loveth a cheerful giver.

Whoso hath this world's good, and seeth his brother have need, and shutteth up his compassion from him, how dwelleth the love of God in him?

God is not unrighteous to forget your work and labor of love, which ye have showed toward His Name, in that ye have ministered to the saints, and do minister.

IV

Offer unto God thanksgiving; and pay thy vows unto the Most High.

Lay not up for yourselves treasures upon earth, where moth and rust doth corrupt, and where thieves break through and steal: but lay up for yourselves treasures in heaven, where neither moth nor rust doth corrupt, and where thieves do not break through nor steal: for where your treasure is, there will your heart be also.

Zacchaeus stood, and said unto Jesus, Behold, Lord, the half of my goods I give to the poor; and if I have taken anything from any man by false accusation, I restore him fourfold.

Charge them that are rich in this world, that they be rich in good works, ready to distribute, willing to communicate; laying up in store for themselves a good foundation against the time to come, that they may lay hold on eternal life.

Godliness with contentment is great gain. For we brought nothing into this world, and it is certain we can carry nothing out.

As the Minister receives the Offering, the people shall stand, and the following may be said or sung:

All things come of Thee, O Lord, and of Thine own have we given Thee.

Then may the Minister say:

Thine, O Lord, is the greatness, and the power, and the glory, and the victory, and the majesty: for all that is in the heaven and in the earth is Thine; Thine is the kingdom, O Lord, and Thou art exalted as Head above all.

The People shall remain standing while the Minister reads the Invitation.

Ye that do truly and earnestly repent of your sins, and are in love and charity with your neighbors, and intend to lead a new life, following the commandments of God, and walking from henceforth in His holy ways, draw near with faith, and take this holy Sacrament to your comfort; and devoutly kneeling make your humble confession to Almighty God.

Then shall this general Confession be made by the Minister and those who are minded to receive the Holy Communion, the Minister kneeling, facing the Lord's Table, and all the People in the attitude of prayer.

Almighty God, Father of our Lord Jesus Christ, Maker of all things, Judge of all men, we acknowledge and bewail our manifold sins and wickedness, which we from time to time most grievously have committed, by thought, word, and deed, against Thy Divine Majesty. We do earnestly repent, and are heartily sorry for these our misdoings; the remembrance of them is grievous unto us. Have mercy upon us, have mercy upon us, most merciful Father, forgive us all that is past; and grant that we may ever hereafter serve and please Thee in newness of life, to the honor and glory of Thy Name, through Jesus Christ our Lord. *Amen.*

Then shall the Minister offer this Prayer:

Almighty God, our Heavenly Father, who of Thy great mercy hast promised forgiveness of sins to all them that with hearty repentance and true faith turn unto Thee, have mercy upon us; pardon and deliver us from all our sins; confirm and strengthen us in all goodness; and bring us to everlasting life, through Jesus Christ our Lord. *Amen.*

Then shall the Minister say:

Hear what the Scripture saith to those of a humble and contrite heart:

If any man sin, we have an Advocate with the Father, Jesus Christ the righteous: and He is the propitiation for our sins: and not for ours only, but also for the sins of the whole world.

This is a faithful saying, and worthy of all acceptation, that Christ Jesus came into the world to save sinners.

God so loved the world, that He gave His only begotten Son, that whosoever believeth in Him should not perish, but have everlasting life.

Come unto Me, all ye that labor and are heavy laden, and I will give you rest.

After which the Minister and People may say:

Lift up your hearts.

We lift them up unto the Lord.

Let us give thanks unto the Lord.

It is meet and right so to do.

Then the Minister, still kneeling and facing the Lord's Table, shall say:

It is very meet, right, and our bounden duty that we should at all times and in all places give thanks unto Thee, O Lord, Holy Father, Almighty, Everlasting God.

Then shall be said or sung:

Therefore with angels and archangels, and with all the company of heaven, we laud and magnify Thy glorious Name, evermore praising Thee, and saying:

Holy, holy, holy, Lord God of Hosts, heaven and earth are full of Thy glory. Glory be to Thee; O Lord most high! *Amen.*

Then shall the Minister offer the Prayer of Consecration:

Almighty God, our Heavenly Father, who of Thy tender mercy didst give Thine only Son Jesus Christ to suffer death upon the cross for our redemption: who made there by the one offering of Himself, a full, perfect, and sufficient sacrifice for the sins of the whole world; and did institute, and in His holy gospel command us to continue this memorial of His precious death: hear us, O merciful Father, we most humbly beseech Thee, and grant that we, receiving this bread and wine, according to Thy Son, our Saviour Jesus Christ's holy institution, in remembrance of His death and Passion, may also be partakers of the divine nature through Him, who in the same night that He was betrayed took bread [1] and when he had given thanks, He brake it, and gave it to His disciples, saying, Take, eat; this is My body which is given for you; do this in remembrance of Me. Likewise after supper He took the cup [2] and when He had given thanks, He gave it to them, saying, Drink ye all of this, for this is My blood of the new covenant which is shed for you, and for many, for the remission of sins; do th s, as oft as ye shall drink it, in remembrance of Me. *Amen.*

[1. Here may the Minister take the plate in his hands.]
[2. Here may the Minister take the cup in his hands.]

Then shall the Minister, kneeling before the Lord's Table, unite with the People in this Prayer:

We do not presume to come to this, Thy table, O merciful Lord, trusting in our own righteousness, but in Thy manifold and great mercies. We are not worthy so much as to gather up the crumbs under Thy table, but Thou art the same Lord, whose mercy is unfailing. Grant us, therefore, gracious Lord, so to partake of these memorials of Thy Son Jesus Christ, that we may be filled with the fullness of His life, may grow into His likeness and may evermore dwell in Him, and He in us. *Amen.*

Then shall the Minister first receive the Holy Communion in both kinds himself, after which he shall proceed to deliver the same to other Ministers in like manner, if any be present. After this, the Minister shall administer the Holy Communion to the People, while they are devoutly kneeling.

[Before giving the bread, the Minister shall say:]

Jesus said, "This is My body which is given for you." Take and eat this in remembrance that Christ died for you, and feed on Him in your heart by faith, with thanksgiving.

[Likewise, before giving the cup he shall say:]

Jesus said, "This cup is the new covenant in My blood, which is shed for you." Drink this in remembrance that Christ died for you, and be thankful.

[When all have communed, the Minister shall place upon the Lord's Table what remains of the consecrated Elements, covering the same with the linen cloth.]

Then shall the Minister and People say:

O Lord, our Heavenly Father, we, Thy humble servants, desire Thy Fatherly goodness mercifully to accept this our sacrifice of praise and thanksgiving; most humbly beseeching Thee to grant, that, by the merits and death of Thy Son Jesus Christ, and through faith in His blood, we and Thy whole Church may obtain forgiveness of our sins, and all other benefits of His Passion. And here we offer and present unto Thee, O Lord, ourselves, our souls and bodies, to be a reasonable, holy, and living sacrifice unto Thee; humbly beseeching Thee that all we who are partakers of this Holy Communion may be filled with Thy grace and heavenly benediction. And although we be unworthy, through our manifold sins, to offer unto Thee any sacrifice, yet we beseech Thee to accept this our bounden duty and service; not weighing our merits, but pardoning our offenses, through Jesus Christ our Lord; by whom, and with whom, in the unity of the Holy Spirit, all honor and glory be unto Thee, O Father Almighty, world without end. *Amen.*

Then shall be said or sung the *Gloria in Excelsis*, the People standing:

Glory be to God on high, and on earth peace, good will toward men. We praise Thee, we bless Thee, we worship Thee, we glorify Thee, we give thanks to Thee for Thy great glory, O Lord God, Heavenly King, God the Father Almighty!

O Lord, the only begotten Son Jesus Christ: O Lord God,

Lamb of God, Son of the Father, that takest away the sins of the world, have mercy upon us. Thou that takest away the sins of the world, have mercy upon us. Thou that takest away the sins of the world, receive our prayer. Thou that sittest at the right hand of God the Father, have mercy upon us. For Thou only art holy; Thou only art the Lord, Thou only, O Christ, with the Holy Spirit, art most high in the glory of God the Father. *Amen.*

Then shall the Minister let the People depart with this blessing:

. ' The peace of God, which passeth all understanding, keep your hearts and minds in the knowledge and love of God, and of His Son Jesus Christ our Lord: and the blessing of God Almighty, the Father, the Son, and the Holy Spirit, be among you and remain with you always. *Amen.*

¶ 1409. *An Alternative Order for the Administration of the Sacrament of the Lord's Supper.*

The Minister shall read one or more of these sentences, during the reading of which the stewards shall take up the collection for the poor.

,. Let your light so shine before men, that they may see your good works, and glorify your Father which is in heaven. Matt. v. 16.

Lay not up for yourself treasures upon earth, where moth and rust doth corrupt, and where thieves break through and steal: but lay up for yourselves treasures in heaven, where neither moth nor rust doth corrupt, and where thieves do not break through nor steal. Matt. vi. 19, 20.

Whatsoever ye would that men should do to you, do ye even so to them: for this is the law and the prophets. Matt. vii. 12.

Not every one that saith unto me, Lord, Lord, shall enter into the kingdom of heaven; but he that doeth the will of my Father which is in heaven. Matt. vii. 21.

Zacchaeus stood, and said unto the Lord; Behold, Lord, the half of my goods I give to the poor; and if I have taken anything from any man by false accusation, I restore him fourfold. Luke xix. 8.

He which soweth sparingly shall reap also sparingly; and he which soweth bountifully shall reap also bountifully. Every man according as he purposeth in his heart, so let him give; not grudgingly, or of necessity: for God loveth a cheerful giver. 2 Cor. ix. 6, 7.

As we have therefore opportunity, let us do good unto all men, especially unto them who are of the household of faith. Gal. vi. 10.

Godliness with contentment is great gain. For we brought nothing into this world, and it is certain we can carry nothing out. 1 Tim. vi. 6, 7.

Charge them that are rich in this world, that they be ready to distribute, willing to communicate; laying up in store for themselves a good foundation against the time to come, that they may lay hold on eternal life. 1 Tim. vi. 17-19.

God is not unrighteous to forget your work and labor of love, which ye have showed toward his name, in that ye have ministered to the saints, and do minister. Heb. vi. 10.

To do good and to communicate forget not: for with such sacrifices God is well pleased. Heb. xiii. 16.

Whoso hath this world's good, and seeth his brother have need, and shutteth up his bowels of compassion from him, how dwelleth the love of God in him? 1 John iii. 17.

He that hath pity upon the poor lendeth unto the Lord; and that which he hath given will he pay him again. Prov. xix. 17.

Blessed is he that considereth the poor: the Lord will deliver him in time of trouble. Ps. xli. 1.

Then shall the Minister read this invitation:

Ye that do truly and earnestly repent of your sins, and are in love and charity with your neighbors, and intend to lead a new life, following the commandments of God, and walking from henceforth in his holy ways; draw near with faith, and take this holy Sacrament to your comfort: and make your humble confession to Almighty God, meekly kneeling upon your knees.

Then shall this general confession be made by the Minister and all those who are minded to receive the Holy Communion, both he and they humbly kneeling, and saying:

Almighty God, Father of our Lord Jesus Christ, Maker of all things, Judge of all men: we acknowledge and bewail our manifold sins and wickedness, which we from time to time most grievously have committed, by thought, word, and deed, against Thy Divine Majesty, provoking most justly Thy wrath and indignation against us. We do earnestly repent, and are heartily sorry for these our misdoings; the remembrance of them is grievous unto us. Have mercy upon us, have mercy upon us, most merciful Father; for Thy Son our Lord Jesus Christ's sake, forgive us all that is past; and grant that we may ever hereafter serve and please Thee in newness of life, to the honor and glory of Thy name, through Jesus Christ our Lord. *Amen.*

Then shall the Minister say:

O Almighty God, our Heavenly Father, who of Thy great mercy hast promised forgiveness of sins to all them that with hearty repentence and true faith turn to Thee: have mercy upon us; pardon and deliver us from all our sins, confirm and strengthen us in all goodness, and bring us to everlasting life, through Jesus Christ our Lord. *Amen.*

The Collect

Almighty God, unto whom all hearts be open, all desires known, and from whom no secrets are hid; cleanse the thoughts of our hearts by the inspiration of Thy Holy Spirit, that we may perfectly love Thee, and worthily magnify Thy holy Name, through Christ our Lord. *Amen.*

Then shall the Minister say:

It is very meet, right, and our bounden duty, that we should at all times, and in all places, give thanks unto Thee, O Lord, holy Father, Almighty, everlasting God.

Therefore with angels and archangels, and with all the company of heaven, we laud and magnify Thy glorious Name; evermore praising thee, and saying, Holy, holy, holy, Lord God of hosts, heaven and earth are full of Thy glory. Glory be to Thee, O Lord most high. *Amen.*

Then shall the Minister say:

We do not presume to come to this Thy table, O merciful Lord, trusting in our own righteousness, but in Thy manifold and great mercies. We are not worthy so much as to gather up the crumbs under Thy Table. But Thou art the same Lord whose property is always to have mercy: Grant us, therefore, gracious Lord, so to eat the flesh of Thy Son Jesus Christ, and to drink His blood, that our sinful souls and bodies may be made clean by His death, and washed through His most precious blood, and that we may evermore dwell in Him, and He in us. *Amen.*

Then the Minister shall say the prayer of consecration as followeth:

Almighty God, our Heavenly Father, who of Thy tender mercy didst give Thine only Son Jesus Christ to suffer death upon the cross for our redemption; who made there (by His oblation of Himself once offered) a full, perfect, and sufficient sacrifice, oblation, and satisfaction for the sins of the whole world; and did institute, and in his holy gospel command us to continue, a perpetual memory of that His precious death until His coming again: hear us, O merciful Father, we most humbly beseech Thee, and grant that we, receiving these Thy creatures of bread and wine, according to Thy Son our Saviour Jesus Christ's holy institution, in remembrance of His death and passion, may be partakers of His most blessed body and blood; who in the same night that He was betrayed took bread; and when He had given thanks, He brake it, and gave it to His disciples, saying, Take, eat; this is My body which is given for you; do this in remembrance of me. Likewise after supper He took the cup; and when He had given thanks, He gave it to them, saying, Drink ye all of this; for this is My blood of the New Testament, which is shed for you, and for many, for the remission of sins; do this, as oft as ye shall drink it, in remembrance of me. *Amen.*

Then shall the Minister first receive the communion in both kinds himself, and then proceed to deliver the same to the other Ministers in like manner, if any be present. Then shall he say the Lord's Prayer, the people still kneeling and repeating after him every petition:

Our Father who art in heaven, hallowed be Thy name: Thy kingdom come: Thy will be done on earth as it is in heaven: give us this day our daily bread; and forgive us our trespasses, as we forgive those who trespass against us; and lead us not into temptation, but deliver us from evil; for Thine is the kingdom, and the power, and the glory, forever and ever. *Amen.*

Then a hymn may be sung, and the communicants shall be invited to the table. The Minister shall deliver both kinds to the people into their hands. When he delivereth the bread, he shall say:

The body of our Lord Jesus Christ, which was given for *thee*, preserve *thy soul* and *body* unto everlasting life. Take and eat this in remembrance that Christ died for *thee*, and feed on Him in *thy heart* by faith with thanksgiving.

And the Minister that delivereth the cup shall say:

The blood of our Lord Jesus Christ, which was shed for *thee*, preserve *thy soul* and *body* unto everlasting life. Drink this in remembrance that Christ's blood was shed for *thee*, and be thankful.

[When all have communicated, the Minister shall return to the Lord's Table, and place upon it what remaineth of the consecrated Elements, covering the same with a fair linen cloth.]

The Minister may then say as followeth:

O Lord and Heavenly Father, we Thy humble servants desire Thy Fatherly goodness mercifully to accept this our sacrifice of praise and thanksgiving; most humbly beseeching Thee to grant that, by the merits and death of Thy Son Jesus Christ, and through faith in His blood, we and Thy whole Church may obtain remission of our sins, and all other benefits of His Passion. And here we offer and present unto Thee, O Lord, ourselves, our souls and bodies, to be a reasonable, holy, and lively sacrifice unto Thee; humbly beseeching Thee that all we who are partakers of this holy communion may be filled with Thy grace and heavenly benediction. And although we be unworthy, through our manifold sins, to offer unto Thee any sacrifice, yet we beseech Thee to accept this our bounden duty and service; not weighing our merits, but pardoning our offenses, through Jesus Christ our Lord: by whom, and with whom, in the unity of the Holy Spirit, all honor and glory be unto Thee, O Father Almighty, world without end. *Amen.*

Then may be said or sung:

Glory be to God on high, and on earth peace, good will toward men. We praise Thee, we bless Thee, we worship Thee, we glorify Thee, we give thanks to Thee for Thy great glory, O Lord God, Heavenly King, God the Father Almighty.

O Lord, the only-begotten Son, Jesus Christ; O Lord God, Lamb of God, Son of the Father, that takest away the sins of the world, have mercy upon us. Thou that takest away the sins of the world, have mercy upon us. Thou that takest away the sins of the world, receive our prayer. Thou that sittest at the right hand of God the Father, have mercy upon us.

For Thou only art holy; Thou only art the Lord; Thou only, O Christ, with the Holy Spirit, art most high in the glory of God the Father. *Amen.*

Then the Minister, if he see it expedient, may offer an extemporaneous prayer; and afterward shall let the people depart with this blessing:

May the peace of God, which passeth all understanding, keep your hearts and minds in the knowledge and love of God, and of his Son Jesus Christ our Lord; and the blessing of God Almighty, the Father, the Son, and the Holy Ghost, be among you, and remain with you always. *Amen.*

If the Minister be straitened for time, he may omit any part of the service except the prayer of consecration.

BAPTISM

THE ORDER FOR THE ADMINISTRATION OF THE SACRAMENT OF BAPTISM

[Let every adult Person, and the Parents of every Child to be baptized, have the choice of sprinkling, pouring, or immersion.

It is proper and desirable that this Sacrament should not only be accompanied by prayer, admonition, and the reading of Scripture, as herein provided, but that it should be administered in the presence of the people, and most suitably in the house of God.]

¶ 1410. *The Baptism of Infants*

Dearly Beloved, forasmuch as all men are heirs of life eternal and subjects of the saving grace of the Holy Spirit; and that our Saviour Christ saith, Suffer the little children to come unto me, and forbid them not, for of such is the kingdom of God, I beseech you to call upon God the Father, through our Lord Jesus Christ, that of his bounteous goodness He will grant unto this child, now to be baptized, the continual replenishing of His grace that he become a worthy member of Christ's holy Church.

Then shall the Minister say:

Let us pray.

Almighty and Everlasting God, we beseech Thee, that of Thine infinite goodness Thou wilt look upon this Child and grant that by the aid of Thy Holy Spirit he may be steadfast in faith, joyful through hope, and rooted in love, and that he may so live the life which now is, that he may enter triumphantly the life which is to come; through Jesus Christ our Lord. *Amen.*

Then shall the Minister address the Parents or Sponsors, as follows:

Dearly Beloved, forasmuch as *this Child is* now presented by you for Christian baptism, and is thus consecrated to God and to His Church, it is your part and duty to see that *he* be taught, as soon as *he* shall be able to learn, the meaning and purpose of this holy Sacrament; that *he* be instructed in the principles of our holy faith and the nature of the Christian life; that *he* shall be trained to give reverent attendance upon the public and private worship of God and the teaching of the Holy Scripture, and that in every way, by precept and example, you shall seek to lead him into the love of God and the service of our Lord Jesus Christ.

Do you solemnly promise to fulfill these duties so far as in you lies, the Lord being your helper?

We do.

Then shall the·People stand and the Minister shall say:

Hear the words of the Gospel written by Saint Mark. And they brought young children to Him, that He should touch them: and His disciples rebuked those that brought them. But when Jesus saw it, He was much displeased, and said unto them, ·Let the little children come unto Me, and forbid them not: for of such is the kingdom of God. Verily I say.·unto you, Whosoever shall not receive the kingdom of God.as·a. little child, he shall not enter therein. And He took them up in His arms, put His hands upon them,·and blessed them.

Then shall the Minister, who may here take the Child in his arms, say·to the Parents or Sponsors:

What name·shall be given to this Child?

And then,·repeating the name, he shall baptize the Child, saying:

·:*N*., I.baptize thee in the Name of the Father, and, of the Son, and of the Holy Spirit. *Amen*.

Then shall the Minister say:

Let us pray.

O God, our Heavenly Father, grant that *this Child*, as *he grows* in years, may also·grow in grace and in knowledge of the Lord Jesus Christ, and that by the restraining and renewing influence of Thy Holy Spirit *he* may ever be·*a true child* of·God, serving Thee faithfully all *his* days, through Jesus Christ our Lord. *Amen*.

Almighty God, Fount of all love and wisdom, Source of all power, so guide and uphold the Parents [or Sponsors] of *this Child*, that, by loving care, wise counsel, and holy example, they may lead *him* into that life of faith whose strength is righteousness and whose fruit is everlasting joy and peace; through·Jesus Christ our Lord. ·*Amen*.

Or·the Minister may offer extemporary Prayer. Then may the Minister and People say:

·.Our,Father, who art in heaven: Hallowed be Thy Name, Thy kingdom come,.Thy will be done, on earth as it is in heaven.

Give us this day our daily bread. And forgive us our trespasses as we forgive those who trespass against us. And lead us not into temptation, but deliver us from evil. ·· For·Thine·is the kingdom, and the power, and the glory, for ever. *Amen*.

Then may be sung one or more stanzas of a Hymn, such as:

406—"Friend of the home: as when in Galilee."
407—"See Israel's gentle Shepherd stand."

Then may the Minister say:

Now unto Him that is able to keep you from falling, and to present you faultless before the presence of His glory with exceeding joy, to the only wise God our Saviour, be glory and majesty, dominion and power, now and evermore. *Amen.*

¶ 1411. *A Briefer Order for the Baptism of Infants*

The Minister, addressing the Parents or Sponsors, shall say:

Dearly Beloved, forasmuch as *this Child* is now presented by you for Christian baptism, it is your part and duty to see that *he* be brought up in the nurture and admonition of the Lord; and that in every way, by precept and example, you shall seek to lead *him* into the love of God and the service of our Lord Jesus Christ.

Do you solemnly engage to fulfill these duties so far as in you lies, the Lord being your helper?

We do.

The People stand and the Minister, who may here take the Child in his arms, shall say to the Parents or Sponsors:

What name shall be given to this Child?

Repeating the name, he shall baptize the Child, saying:

N., I baptize thee in the Name of the Father, and of the Son, and of the Holy Spirit. *Amen.*

Then shall the Minister say:

Let us pray.

Almighty God, Fount of all love and wisdom, Source of all power; so guide and uphold the Parents [or Sponsors] of this Child that, by loving care, wise counsel, and holy example, they may lead *him* into that life of faith whose strength is righteousness and whose fruit is everlasting joy and peace; through Jesus Christ our Lord. *Amen.*

Then may the Minister and People say:

Our Father, who art in heaven:
Hallowed be Thy Name, Thy kingdom come, Thy will be done, on earth as it is in heaven.

Give us this day our daily bread. And forgive us our trespasses as we forgive those who trespass against us. And lead us not into temptation, but deliver us from evil.

For Thine is the kingdom, and the power, and the glory for ever. *Amen.*

¶ 1412. *The Order for the Baptism of Children and Youth.*

The Minister, coming to the Font, shall say:

Hear the words of the Gospel, written by St. Matthew, in the twenty-eighth chapter, beginning at the sixteenth verse.

Then the eleven disciples went away into Galilee, into a mountain where Jesus had appointed them. And when they saw Him, they worshiped Him; but some doubted. And Jesus came and spake unto them, saying, All power is given unto Me in heaven and in earth. Go ye therefore, and make disciples of all nations, baptizing them in the name of the Father, and of the Son, and of the Holy Ghost: teaching them to observe all things whatsoever I have commanded you: and lo, I am with you alway, even unto the end of the world. *Amen.*

Then shall the Minister say:

Let us pray.

Almighty and everliving God, whose most dearly beloved Son Jesus Christ gave himself for our salvation, and did command His disciples that they should go teach all nations, and baptize them in the name of the Father, and of the Son, and of the Holy Spirit: regard, we beseech Thee, the supplications of Thy congregation; and grant that *these persons* now to be baptized may so open *their* hearts to Thee as that *they* may receive the fullness of Thy grace, and may ever remain in the number of Thy faithful children, through Jesus Christ our Lord. *Amen.*

Then the Minister shall say to the *persons* to be baptized:

Well beloved, who are come hither, desiring to receive holy baptism, you have heard how the congregation hath prayed that God would assist you to open your hearts to His love and direction, that you may be faithful disciples of our Lord.

Wherefore, for your part, it is needful that in the presence of Almighty God and the hearing of this congregation, you should now make known your purpose to accept the obligations of this holy Sacrament, by answering the following questions:

Will you faithfully put away from you every known sin,
of thought, word, or deed, and accept and confess Jesus
Christ as your Saviour and Lord?

God helping me, I will.

Will you diligently study the Bible as God's holy word,
and in all things strive to make it the rule of your life?

God helping me, I will.

Having been taught how the Spirit of our Lord separates
right from wrong, will you faithfully endeavor to live so as
to be pleasing unto Him?

God helping me, I will.

Will you be baptized in this faith?

This is my desire.

Then shall the Minister ask each person his name, and shall baptize him saying:

. *N.*, I baptize thee in the name of the Father, and of the
Son, and of the Holy Spirit. *Amen.*

Here the Minister shall offer a suitable prayer.

¶ 1413. *The Order for the Baptism of Adults*

The Minister, addressing the People, shall say:

Dearly Beloved, forasmuch as our Saviour Jesus Christ
sent forth His disciples to teach all nations and baptize
them in the name of the Father and of the Son, and of the
Holy Spirit; and wherefore *these persons* come now to be
baptized, I beseech you to call upon God the Father that of
His bounteous goodness He will grant unto *them* the renewing power of the Holy Spirit and enable *them* by divine
grace to attain unto the fullness of salvation in Jesus Christ
our Lord.

Let us pray.

Almighty and immortal God, the aid of all that need, the
helper of all that flee to Thee for succor, the life of them
that believe, and the resurrection of the dead: we call upon
Thee for *these persons* now to be baptized. May *they* be
filled with Thy Holy Spirit and may *they* find in Thee *their*
refuge, *their* strength, *their* wisdom and *their* joy. May
they be faithful to Thee all the days of *their* life *and* finally
come to the eternal kingdom which Thou hast promised
through Jesus Christ our Lord. *Amen.*

Then may the Minister read one or more of the following Lessons:

· Peter said unto them, Repent, and be baptized every one of you in the Name of Jesus Christ for the remission of sins, and ye shall receive the gift of the Holy Spirit. For the promise is unto you, and to your children, and to all that are afar off, even as many as the Lord our God shall call. And with many other words did he testify and exhort, saying, Save yourselves from this untoward generation. Then they that gladly received his word were baptized: and the same day there were added unto them about three thousand souls. And they continued steadfastly in the apostles' doctrine and fellowship, and in breaking of bread, and in prayers. Acts 2: 38-42.

And it came to pass, that, while Apollos was at Corinth, Paul having passed through the upper coasts came to Ephesus: and finding certain disciples, he said unto them, Have ye received the Holy Spirit since ye believed? And they said unto him, We have not so much as heard whether there be any Holy Spirit. And he said unto them, Unto what then were ye baptized? And they said, Unto John's baptism. Then said Paul, John verily baptized with the baptism of repentance, saying unto the people that they should believe on Him which should come after him, that is, on Christ Jesus. When they heard this, they were baptized in the Name of the Lord Jesus. And when Paul had laid his hands upon them, the Holy Spirit came on them. Acts 19: 1-6.

There was a man of the Pharisees, named Nicodemus, a ruler of the Jews: The same came to Jesus by night, and said unto Him, Rabbi, we know that Thou art a teacher come from God: for no man can do these miracles that Thou doest, except God be with him. Jesus answered and said unto him, Verily, verily, I say unto thee, Except a man be born again, he cannot see the kingdom of God. Nicodemus saith unto Him, How can a man be born when he is old? can he enter the second time into his mother's womb, and be born? Jesus answered, Verily, verily, I say unto thee, Except a man be born of water and of the Spirit, he cannot enter into the kingdom of God. That which is born of the flesh is flesh; and that which is born of the Spirit is spirit. Marvel not that I said unto thee, Ye must be born again. The wind bloweth where it listeth, and thou hearest the sound thereof, but canst not tell whence it cometh, and whither it goeth: so is every one that is born of the Spirit. John 3: 1-8.

For this cause I bow my knees unto the Father of our Lord Jesus Christ, of whom the whole family in heaven and earth is named, that He would grant you, according to the riches of His glory, to be strengthened with might by His Spirit in the inner man; that Christ may dwell in your hearts by faith; that ye, being rooted and grounded in love, may be able to comprehend with all saints what is the breadth, and length, and depth, and height; and to know the love of Christ, which passeth knowledge, that ye might be filled with all the fullness of God. Ephesians 3: 14-19.

Then shall the Minister say to the Persons to be baptized:

Dearly Beloved, who have come hither desiring to receive holy Baptism, the Congregation gives thanks to God for your coming, and prays that the Holy Spirit may dwell within you, and that your faith may not fail. In the hearing of this Congregation you should now make known your purpose to accept the obligations of this holy Sacrament.

Do you truly repent of your sins and accept and confess Jesus Christ as your Saviour and Lord?

I do.

Will you earnestly endeavor to keep God's Holy Will and commandments?

I will.

Do you desire to be baptized in this faith?

I do.

Then shall the Minister pray:

O merciful God, grant that all sinful affections may die in *these persons*, and that all things belonging to the Spirit may live and grow in *them*. *Amen.*

Almighty, Everliving God, regard, we beseech Thee, our supplications and grant that *these persons* may receive the fullness of Thy grace, and ever remain in the number of Thy faithful and beloved children, through Jesus Christ our Lord. *Amen.*

Then the Minister, asking the name of each Person, shall baptize him, repeating the name and saying:

N., I baptize thee in the Name of the Father, and of the Son, and of the Holy Spirit. *Amen.*

Then may the Minister offer extemporary prayer. Then may the Minister and the People say:

Our Father, who art in heaven:
Hallowed be Thy name, Thy kingdom come, Thy will be done, on earth as it is in heaven.

Give us this day our daily bread. And forgive us our trespasses as we forgive those who trespass against us. And lead us not into temptation, but deliver us from evil. For thine is the kingdom, and the power, and the glory for ever. *Amen.*

Then may be sung one or more stanzas of a Hymn, such as:

223—"Blessed Master, I have promised."
226—"O Jesus, I have promised."
257—"My gracious Lord, I own Thy right."

Then may the Minister say:

Now unto Him that is able to keep you from falling, and to present you faultless before the presence of His glory with exceeding joy, to the only wise God our Saviour, be glory and majesty, dominion and power, now and evermore. *Amen.*

RECEPTION OF MEMBERS

¶ 1414. THE ORDER FOR RECEIVING PERSONS INTO THE CHURCH

On the day appointed, all that are to be received into the Church shall be called forward, and the Minister, addressing the People, shall say:

Dearly Beloved, the Church is of God, and will be preserved to the end of time, for the promotion of His worship and the due administration of His word and ordinances, the maintenance of Christian fellowship and discipline, the edification of believers, and the conversion of the world. All, of every age and station, stand in need of the means of grace which it alone supplies.

Into this holy fellowship the Persons before you, who have received the Sacrament of Baptism, who have learned the nature of these privileges and these duties, and who have also been instructed in the teachings and the aims of the Methodist Church, come seeking admission. We now propose in the fear of God to question them as to their faith and purpose, that you may know that they are proper Persons to be admitted into this Church.

Then, addressing those seeking admission, the Minister shall say:

Beloved in the Lord, you are come hither seeking union with the Church of God. We rejoice that you are minded to undertake the privileges and the duties of membership in the Church. Before you are fully admitted thereto, you should here publicly renew your vows, confess your faith, and declare your purpose, by answering the following questions:

Do you here in the presence of God and this congregation renew the solemn promise and vow that was made at your baptism?

I do.

Do you confess Jesus Christ as your Saviour and Lord and pledge your allegiance to his kingdom?

I do.

Do you receive and profess the Christian faith as contained in the New Testament of our Lord Jesus Christ?

I do.

Will you be loyal to The Methodist Church, and uphold it by your prayers, your presence, your gifts, and your service?

I will.

Then those to be received shall kneel and the Minister, who may lay his hand upon the head of every one severally, shall say:

N., The Lord defend thee with His heavenly grace and by His Spirit confirm thee in the faith and fellowship of all true disciples of Jesus Christ. *Amen.*

Then the Minister, addressing the People, shall say:

Brethren, I commend to your love and care these persons whom we this day recognize as members of the Church of Christ. What is your mind to them?

Then shall the people say:

We rejoice to recognize you as members of the Church of Christ, and bid you welcome to all its privileges. Your peace, joy and welfare are now our own. With you we renew our pledge to God and this Church. The Lord bless thee and keep thee, the Lord make His face to shine upon thee and be gracious unto thee; the Lord lift up His countenance upon thee and give thee peace. *Amen.*

Then may be sung one or more stanzas of a Hymn, such as:

379—"I love Thy kingdom, Lord.'
380—"Jesus, with Thy Church abide."
383—"How lovely is Thy dwelling place!"

Then may the Minister say:

The blessing of God Almighty; the Father, the Son, and the Holy Spirit, be among you, and remain with you always. *Amen.*

¶ 1415 *The Order for Receiving Children and Youth into the Church*

After the Minister previously shall have formed the Children into a class (baptizing any whose baptism may have been delayed or neglected), and shall have instructed them in the things necessary for them to know as to the Doctrines and Rules of the Church, he shall cause them to be conveniently placed before the Congregation, and after inviting their Parents and teachers to stand with them on either hand, he shall say:

Brethren of the household of faith, let our hearts be lifted up in thanksgiving to Almighty God, who by the Holy Spirit hath inclined *these children* to desire and ask for membership in the Church. Having arrived at years of discretion, and now of *their* own accord appearing before this congregation to take upon *themselves* the vows and enter upon the privileges and duties of the Church, let us with one mind and heart most earnestly invoke in *their* behalf the blessings of Father, Son, and Holy Spirit.

Then shall the minister say:

Let us pray.

Almighty and everliving God, giver of every, good and perfect gift, accept our hearty thanks for the children whom Thou hast committed to our love and care. As Thou didst bring them into the world, now renew in Thy servants, their parents, pastors, and teachers, wisdom to train them in the way they should go. Grant unto these Thy children that from this day forth they may grow in grace, and wisdom, and in favor with God and man, through Jesus Christ our Lord. *Amen.*

Then shall the minister address the Parents or Sponsors:

Dear fathers and mothers, let this be to you a day of peculiar joy and thanksgiving, in that *these who are* of your flesh and blood have also entered into a holier spiritual kinship with you in Jesus Christ. While the Church will continue to share with you the duty and privilege of bringing up *these children* in the nurture and admonition of the Lord, it renews its solemn injunction to you as parents, by God's help, faithfully to continue both to teach and train *them,* by example and precept, in the way of the Lord. Will you accept this duty, in the fear and by the favor of

God, and here and now, in the presence of Almighty God and this congregation, renew the vows made by you as fathers and mothers in the baptism of *these children?*
With God's help, I will.

Then shall the minister address the *Children* who are candidates and say:

Beloved *Children,* our Lord Jesus, by His Holy word, hath expressly given to everyone who believes in Him a place in His Kingdom and Church.   Before you are admitted into the Church, it becomes my duty to inquire of you as to your purpose of mind and heart:
Do you, each of you, *believe* in God as your heavenly Father?
I do.
Do you accept Jesus Christ as your personal Savior?
I do.
Do you believe in the Bible as God's Holy Word?
I do.
Will you be loyal to The Methodist Church and uphold it by your prayers, your presence, your gifts, and your service?
I will.

Here the Minister may offer an extemporary prayer.

Then those to be received shall kneel and the Minister laying his hands upon every one of them severally shall say:

I receive you into the Church of Christ and pray God's blessing upon you.

Then shall the Minister, the People, and the Children say:

Our Father who art in heaven, hallowed be Thy name: Thy kingdom come: Thy will be done on earth as it is in heaven: give us this day our daily bread; and forgive us our trespasses, as we forgive those who trespass against us; and lead us not into temptation, but deliver us from evil; for Thine is the kingdom, and the power, and the glory, forever and ever. *Amen.*

MATRIMONY

¶ 1416. THE ORDER FOR THE SOLEMNIZATION OF MATRIMONY

At the time appointed, the persons to be married—having been qualified according to the law of the State and the standards of the

Church—standing together facing the Minister, the Man at the Minister's left hand and the Woman at the right, the Minister shall say:

Dearly Beloved, we are gathered together here in the sight of God and in the presence of these witnesses to join this man and this woman in holy matrimony, which is an honorable estate, instituted by God, and signifying unto us the mystical union which exists between Christ and His Church. It is therefore not to be entered into unadvisedly, but reverently, discreetly, and in the fear of God. Into this holy estate these two persons come now to be joined.

Speaking to the persons being married, the Minister shall say:

I charge you both, as you stand in the presence of God, to remember that love and loyalty alone will avail as the foundation of a happy home. If the solemn vows which you are about to make be kept inviolate, and if steadfastly you endeavor to do the will of your heavenly Father, your life will be full of joy, and the home which you are establishing will abide in peace. No other human ties are more tender, no other vows more sacred than those you now assume.

Then shall the Minister say to the Man, using his Christian name:

N., wilt thou have this woman to be thy wedded wife, to live together in the holy estate of matrimony? Wilt thou love her, comfort her, honor and keep her, in sickness and in health; and forsaking all other keep thee only unto her, so long as ye both shall live?

The Man shall answer:

I will.

Then shall the Minister say to the Woman, using her Christian name:

N., wilt thou have this man to be thy wedded husband, to live together in the holy estate of matrimony? Wilt thou love him, comfort him, honor and keep him, in sickness and in health; and forsaking all other keep thee only unto him, so long as ye both shall live?

The Woman shall answer:

I will.

Then may the Minister say:

Who giveth this woman to be married to this man?

The Father of the Woman, or whoever giveth her in marriage, shall answer:

I do.

Then the Minister [receiving the hand of the Woman from her Father or other Sponsor] shall cause the Man with his right hand to take the Woman by her right hand, and say after him:

I, ———, take thee, ———, to be my wedded wife, to have and to hold, from this day forward, for better, for worse, for richer, for poorer, in sickness and in health, to love and to cherish, till death us do part, and thereto I plight thee my faith.

Then shall they loose their hands; and the Woman with her right hand taking the Man by his right hand, shall likewise say after the Minister:

. I, ———, take thee, ———, to be my wedded husband, to have and to hold, from this day forward, for better, for worse, for richer, for poorer, in sickness and in health, to love and to cherish, till death us do part, and thereto I plight thee my faith.

Then shall they again loose their hands; and the Man may give unto the Woman a ring, on this wise: the Minister, taking the ring, shall say:

The wedding ring is the outward and visible sign of an inward and spiritual bond which unites two loyal hearts in endless love.

The Minister shall then deliver the ring to the Man to put upon the third finger of the Woman's left hand. The Man, holding the ring there, shall say after the Minister:

In token and pledge of the vow between us made, with this ring I thee wed: in the name of the Father, and of the Son, and of the Holy Spirit. *Amen.*

In case of a double ring ceremony, the Minister shall deliver the other ring to the Woman to put upon the third finger of the Man's left hand, and the Woman, holding the ring there, shall say after the Minister:

In token and pledge of the vow between us made, with this ring I thee wed: in the name of the Father, and of the Son, and of the Holy Spirit. *Amen.*

Then shall the Minister say:

Let us pray.

O Eternal God, Creator and Preserver of all mankind, Giver of all spiritual grace, the Author of everlasting life:

send thy blessing upon this man and this woman, whom we bless in Thy Name: that they may surely perform and keep the vow and covenant now between them made.

Look graciously upon them, that they may love, honor, and cherish each other, and so live together in faithfulness and patience, and wisdom and true godliness, that their home may be a haven of blessing and a place of peace: through Jesus Christ our Lord. *Amen.*

Then shall the Minister join their right hands together and with his hand on their united hands shall say:

Forasmuch as ———, and ———, have consented together in holy wedlock, and have witnessed the same before God and this company, and thereto have pledged their faith each to the other, and have declared the same by joining hands, and by giving and receiving a ring; I pronounce that they are husband and wife together, in the Name of the Father, and of the Son, and of the Holy-Spirit. Those whom God hath joined together, let no man put asunder. *Amen.*

Then, the Husband and Wife kneeling, the Minister may say:

Let us pray:

· Our Father, who art in heaven:
Hallowed be Thy Name, Thy kingdom come, Thy will be done, on earth as it is in heaven.

Give us this day our daily bread. ' And forgive us our trespasses as we forgive those who trespass against us. And lead us not into temptation, but deliver us from evil.

For Thine is the kingdom, and the power, and the glory, for ever. *Amen.*

Then shall the Minister add this blessing:

God the Father, the Son, and the Holy Spirit, bless, preserve, and keep you; the Lord graciously with His favor look upon you; and so fill you with all spiritual benediction and love that you may so live together in his life that in the world to come you may have life everlasting. *Amen.*

THE BURIAL OF THE DEAD

¶ 1417. THE ORDER FOR THE BURIAL OF THE DEAD

The Minister shall begin the service by reading one or more of the following sentences:

Jesus said, I am the resurrection, and the life: he that

believeth in Me, though he were dead, yet shall be live: and whosoever liveth and believeth in Me shall never die.

The eternal God is thy refuge, and underneath are the everlasting arms.

The Lord is my light and my salvation; whom shall I fear? The Lord is the strength of my life; of whom shall I be afraid?

The righteous live for ever, and the care of them is with the Most High: with His right hand He shall cover them, and with His arm shall He shield them.

For we know that if our earthly house of his tabernacle were dissolved, we have a building of God, an house not made with hands, eternal in the heaven.

Then shall the Minister say:

Let us pray:

[Here may the Minister offer one or both of the following Prayers, ending with the Lord's Prayer:]

Almighty God, Fount of all life, Thou art our refuge and strength, Thou art our help in trouble. Enable us, we pray Thee, to put our trust in Thee, that we may obtain comfort, and find grace to help in this and every time of need; through Jesus Christ our Lord. *Amen.*

Almighty God, our Father, from whom we come and unto whom our spirits return, Thou hast been our dwelling place in all generations. Thou art our refuge and strength, a very present help in trouble. Grant us Thy blessing in this hour, and enable us so to put our trust in Thee that our spirits may grow calm and our hearts be comforted. Lift our eyes beyond the shadows of earth, and help us to see the light of eternity. So may we find grace and strength for this and every time of need; through Jesus Christ our Lord. *Amen.*

Our Father, who art in heaven:

Hallowed be Thy Name, Thy kingdom come, Thy will be done, on earth as it is in heaven.

Give us this day our daily bread. And forgive us our trespasses as we forgive those who trespass against us. And lead us not into temptation, but deliver us from evil.

For Thine is the kingdom, and the power, and the glory, for ever. *Amen.*

Here may be read Lessons from the Old Testament:

The Lord is my shepherd; I shall not want.

He maketh me to lie down in green pastures:

He leadeth me beside the still waters.
He restoreth my soul:
He leadeth me in the paths of righteousness for His Name's sake.
Yea, though I walk through the valley of the shadow of death,
I will fear no evil: for Thou art with me;
Thy rod and Thy staff they comfort me.
Thou preparest a table before me in the presence of mine enemies:
Thou anointest my head with oil;
My cup runneth over.
Surely goodness and mercy shall follow me all the days of my life:
And I will dwell in the house of the Lord for ever. Psalm 23.

Lord, Thou hast been our dwelling place in all generations.
Before the mountains were brought forth,
Or ever Thou hadst formed the earth and the world,
Even from everlasting to everlasting, Thou art God.
For a thousand years in Thy sight
Are but as yesterday when it is past,
And as a watch in the night.
Thou carriest them away as with a flood; they are as a sleep:
In the morning they are like grass which groweth up.
In the morning it flourisheth, and groweth up;
In the evening it is cut down, and withereth.
So teach us to number our days,
That we may apply our hearts unto wisdom.
Let Thy work appear unto Thy servants,
And Thy glory unto their children.
And let the beauty of the Lord our God be upon us:
And establish Thou the work of our hands upon us:
Yea, the work of our hands establish Thou it. Psalm 90: 1, 2, 4-6, 12, 16, 17.

I will lift up mine eyes unto the hills: from whence shall my help come?
My help cometh from the Lord, who made heaven and earth.
He will not suffer thy foot to be moved: He that keepeth thee will not slumber.
Behold, He that keepeth Israel will neither slumber nor sleep.

The Lord is thy keeper: the Lord is thy shade upon thy right hand.

The Lord will preserve thy going out and thy coming in, from this time forth, and even for evermore. Psalm 121: 1-5, 7, 8.

The Lord is my light and my salvation; whom shall I fear?

The Lord is the strength of my life; of whom shall I be afraid?

Though an host encamp against me, my heart shall not fear; though war should rise against me, even then will I be confident.

For in the day of trouble He will keep me secretly in his pavillion: in the secret of His tabernacle will he hide me; He will lift me upon a rock.

Teach me thy way, O Lord, and lead me in a plain path.

I had fainted, unless I had believed to see the goodness of the Lord, in the land of the living.

Wait on the Lord: be of good courage, and He shall strengthen thine heart: wait, I say, on the Lord. Psalm 27: 1, 3, 5, 11, 13, 14.

Here shall be read Lessons from the New Testament:

Let not your heart be troubled: ye believe in God, believe also in Me. In My Father's house are many mansions: if it were not so, I would have told you. I go to prepare a place for you. And if I go to prepare a place for you, I will come again, and receive you unto Myself; that where I am, there ye may be also. I am the way, the truth, and the life. If ye love Me, keep my commandments. And I will pray the Father, and He shall give you another Comforter, that He may abide with you for ever; even the Spirit of truth; whom the world cannot receive, because it seeth Him not, neither knoweth Him; but ye know Him; for He dwelleth with you, and shall be in you. I will not leave you comfortless: I will come to you. Because I live, ye shall live also.

Peace I leave with you, My peace I give unto you: not as the world giveth, give I unto you. Let not your heart be troubled, neither let it be afraid. John 14: 1-3, 6, 15-18, 19, 27.

As many as are led by the Spirit of God, they are the sons of God. For ye have not received the spirit of bondage again to fear; but ye have received the spirit of adoption, whereby we cry, Abba, Father. The Spirit itself beareth witness with our spirit, that we are the children of God: and if children, then heirs; heirs of God, and joint-heirs with Christ; if so be that we suffer with Him, that we may be also glorified together.

For I reckon that the sufferings of this present time are not worthy to be compared with the glory which shall be revealed in us. :

And we know that all things work together for good to them that love God.

What shall we then say to these things? If God be for us, who can be against us? Who shall separate us from the love of Christ? shall tribulation, or distress, or persecution, or famine, or nakedness, or peril, or sword? Nay, in all these things we are more than conquerors through Him that loved us. For I am persuaded, that neither death, nor life, nor angles, nor principalities, nor powers, nor things present, nor things to come, nor height, nor depth, nor any other creature, shall be able to separate us from the love of God, which is in Christ Jesus our Lord. Romans 8: 14-18, 28, 31, 35, 37, 39.

Now is Christ risen from the dead, and become the first fruits of them that slept.

But some man will say, How are the dead raised up? and with what body do they come? Thou foolish one, that which thou sowest is not quickened, except it die: but God giveth it a body as it hath pleased Him.

So also is the resurrection of the dead. It is sown in corruption; it is raised in incorruption:

It is sown in hishonor; it is raised in glory: it is sown in weakness; it is raised in power:

It is sown in natural body; it is raised a spiritual body. There is a natural body, and there is a spiritual body.

And as we have borne the image of the earthly, we shall also bear the image of the heavenly.

For this corruptible must put on incorruption, and this mortal must put on immortality. So when this corruptible shall have put on incorruption, and this mortal shall have put on immortality, then shall be brought to pass the saying that is written, Death is swallowed up in victory. O death, where is thy sting? O grave, where is thy victory? The sting of death is sin; and the strength of sin is the law. But thanks be to God, who giveth us the victory, through our Lord Jesus Christ. Therefore, my beloved brethren, be ye steadfast, unmovable, always abounding in the work of the Lord, forasmuch as ye know that your labor is not in vain in the Lord. I Corinthians 15: 20, 35, 36, 38a, 42-44, 49, 53, 54, 56-58.

And I John saw the holy city, new Jerusalem, coming down from God out of heaven, prepared as a bride adorned for her husband. And I heard a great voice out of heaven saying, Behold, the tabernacle of God is with men, and He will dwell with them, and they shall be His people, and God Himself shall be with them, and be their God. And God shall wipe away all tears from their eyes; and there shall be no more death, neither sorrow, nor crying, neither shall there be any more pain: for the former things are passed away. Revelation 21: 2-4.

And he showed me a river of life clear as crystal, proceeding out of the throne of God and of the Lamb. In the midst of the street of it, and on either side of the river, was there the tree of life, which bare twelve manner of fruits, and yielded her fruit every month: and the leaves of the tree were for the healing of the nations. And there shall be no more curse: but the throne of God and of the Lamb shall be in it; and His servants shall serve Him: and they shall see His face; and his name shall be in their foreheads. And there shall be no night there; and they need no candle, neither light of the sun; for the Lord God giveth them light: and they shall reign for ever and ever. Revelation 22: 1-5.

For this cause I bow my knees unto the Father of our Lord Jesus Christ, of whom the whole family in heaven and earth is named, that He would grant you, according to the riches of His glory, to be strengthened with might by his Spirit in the inner man; that Christ may dwell in your hearts by faith; that ye, being rooted and grounded in love, may be able to comprehend with all saints what is the breadth, and length, and depth, and height; and to know the love of Christ, which passeth knowledge, that ye might be filled with all the fulness of God. Now unto Him that is able to do exceeding abundantly above all that we ask or think, according to the power that worketh in us, unto Him be glory in the church by Christ Jesus throughout all ages, world without end. Amen. Ephesians 3: 14-21.

Here may follow music and an Address, closing with extemporary or one of the following Prayers:

Eternal God, who committest to us the swift and solemn trust of life: since we know not what a day may bring forth, but only that the hour for serving Thee is always present, may we wake to the instant claims of Thy holy will: not waiting for tomorrow, but yielding today. Consecrate with Thy presence the way our feet may go; and the humblest work will shine, and the roughest places be made plain. Lift us above unrighteous anger and mistrust into faith and hope and love by a simple and steadfast reliance on Thy sure will. In all things draw us to the mind of Christ, that Thy lost image may be traced again, and that Thou mayest own us at one with Him and Thee. *Amen.*

O God, who art the strength of Thy saints and who redeemest the souls of Thy servants; we bless Thy Name for all those who have died in the Lord, and who now rest from their labors, having received the end of their faith, even the salvation of their souls. Especially we call to remembrance Thy loving-kindness and Thy tender mercies to this Thy servant. For all Thy goodness that withheld not his portion in the joys of this earthly life, and for Thy guiding hand along the way of his pilgrimage; we give Thee thanks and praise. Especially we bless Thee for Thy grace that kindled in his heart the love of Thy dear Name; that enabled him to fight the good fight, to endure unto the end, and to obtain the victory; yea, to become more than conqueror, through Him that loveth us. We magnify Thy holy Name that his trials and temptations being ended, sickness and death being passed, with all the dangers and difficulties of this mortal life, his spirit is at home in Thy presence, at whose right hand dwelleth eternal peace. And grant, O Lord, we beseech Thee, that we who rejoice in the triumph of Thy saints may profit by their example, that becoming followers of their faith and patience, we also may enter with them into an inheritance incorruptible and undefiled, and that fadeth not away; through Jesus Christ our Lord. *Amen.*

O God, the Lord of Life, the Conqueror of death, our help in every time of trouble, who dost not willingly grieve or afflict the children of men; comfort us who mourn, and give us grace, in the presence of death, to worship Thee, that we may have sure hope of eternal life and be enabled to put our whole trust in Thy goodness and mercy; through Jesus Christ our Lord. *Amen.*

Father of spirits, we have joy at this time in all who have faithfully lived, and in all who have peacefully died. We thank Thee for all fair memories and all living hopes; for the sacred ties that bind us to the unseen world; for the dear and holy dead who compass us as a cloud of witnesses, and make the distant heaven a home to our hearts. May we be followers of those who now inherit the promises, through Jesus Christ our Lord. *Amen.*

O Lord and Master, who Thyself didst weep beside the grave, and art touched with the feeling of our sorrows; fulfill now Thy promise that Thou wilt not leave Thy people comfortless, but wilt come to them. Reveal Thyself unto Thine sorrowing servants, and cause them to hear Thee say, "I am the resurrection and the life." Help them, O Lord, to turn to Thee with true discernment, and to abide in Thee through living faith; that, finding now the comfort of Thy presence, they may have also a sure confidence in Thee for all that is to come: until the day break, and these shadows flee away. Hear us for Thy great mercy's sake, O Jesus Christ our Lord. *Amen.*

O Thou who hast ordered this wondrous world and who knowest all things in earth and heaven; so fill our hearts with trust in Thee, that by night and by day, at all times and in all seasons, we may without fear commit those who are dear to us to Thy never-failing love for this life and the life to come. *Amen.*

O Lord, we pray Thee, give us Thy strength, that we may live more bravely and faithfully for the sake of those who are no longer with us here upon earth; and grant us so to serve Thee day by day that we may find eternal fellowship with them, through Him who died and rose again for us all, Jesus Christ our Lord. *Amen.*

Almighty God, who art leading us through the changes of time to the rest and blessedness of eternity, be Thou near to comfort and uphold. Make us to know and feel that Thy children are precious in Thy sight, that they live evermore with Thee, and that Thy mercy endureth forever. Thankful for the life which Thou hast given us for these seasons, help us now to resign it obediently unto Thee. Assist us to return to the scenes of our daily life, to obey Thy will with patience, and to bear our trials with fortitude and hope. And when the peace of death falls upon us, may we find our perfect rest in Thee: through Jesus Christ our Lord. *Amen.*

Then may the Minister say:

The grace of the Lord Jesus Christ, and the love of God, and the communion of the Holy Spirit, be with you all. *Amen.*

At the grave, when the People are assembled, the Minister shall say:

Our help is in the name of the Lord, who made heaven and earth.

. Like as a father pitieth his children, so the Lord pitieth them that fear Him.

Say to them that are of a fearful heart, Be strong, fear not: behold, your God will come and save you.

For the mercy of the Lord is from everlasting to everlasting upon them that fear Him and His righteousness unto children's children.

Then the Minister may say:

Forasmuch as Almighty God hath received unto Himself the soul of our departed *brother* we therefore tenderly commit *his* body to the ground in the blessed hope that as *he* has borne the image of the earthly so also *he* shall bear the image of the heavenly.

[Or the Minister may say:]

Forasmuch as the spirit of the departed has entered into the life immortal, we therefore commit *his* body to its resting place, but *his* spirit we commend to God, remembering how Jesus said upon the Cross, "Father, into Thy hands I commend My spirit."

[Or the Minister may say:]

Forasmuch as the spirit of the departed hath returned to the God who gave it, we therefore commit his body to the ground, earth to earth, ashes to ashes, dust to dust; looking for the general resurrection in the last day, and the life of the world to come, through our Lord Jesus Christ; at whose coming in glorious majesty to judge the world, the earth and the sea shall give up their dead; and the corruptible bodies of those who sleep in Him shall be changed and made like unto His own glorious body; according to the mighty working whereby He is able to subdue all things unto Himself.

Then may be said:

Blessed are the dead who die in the Lord from henceforth: yea, saith the Spirit, that they may rest from their labors; and their works do follow them.

Then shall the Minister say:

Let us pray:

Almighty God, with whom do live the spirits of those who depart hence in the Lord and with whom the souls of the faithful after death are in strength and gladness, we give Thee hearty thanks for the good examples of all those Thy servants who, having finished their course in faith, do now rest from their labor. And we beseech Thee that we, with all those who have finished their course in faith, may have our perfect consummation and bliss in Thy eternal and everlasting glory, through Jesus Christ our Lord. *Amen.*

O Merciful God, the Father of our Lord Jesus Christ, who is the resurrection and the life; in whom whosoever believeth shall live, though he die, and whosoever liveth and believeth in Him shall not die eternally: we meekly beseech Thee, O Father, to raise us from the death of sin unto the life of righteousness; that when we shall depart this life we may rest in Him, and may receive that blessing which Thy well-beloved Son shall pronounce to all that love and fear Thee. saying, "Come, ye blessed of My Father, receive the kingdom prepared for you from the beginning of the world." Grant this, we beseech Thee, O Merciful Father, through Jesus Christ our Mediator and Redeemer. *Amen.*

Here may the Minister and the People unite in the Lord's Prayer.

Then may the Minister say:

The grace of the Lord Jesus Christ, and the love of God, and the communion of the Holy Spirit, be with you all. *Amen.*

¶ 1418. THE ORDER FOR THE BURIAL OF A CHILD

The Minister shall begin the service by reading the following sentences:

Jesus said, I am the resurrection and the life: he that believeth in Me, though he were dead, yet shall he live: and whosoever liveth and believeth in Me shall never die.

He shall feed His flock like a shepherd: He shall gather the lambs with His arm, and carry them in His bosom.

Then shall the Minister say:

Let us pray.

Here may the Minister offer one or both of the following sentences:

Our Loving Father, comfortingly look upon us in our sorrow and abide with us in our loneliness. O Thou who makest no life in vain and who lovest all that Thou hast made, lift upon us the light of Thy countenance and give peace. *Amen.*

We pray that Thou wilt keep in tender love the life which we shall hold in blessed memory. Help us who continue here to serve Thee with constancy, trusting in Thy promise of eternal life, that hereafter we may be united with Thy blessed children in glory everlasting, through Jesus Christ our Lord. *Amen.*

Here may be read these Psalms:

The Lord is my shepherd; I shall not want.
He maketh me to lie down in green pastures:
He leadeth me beside the still waters.
He restoreth my soul:
He leadeth me in the paths of righteousness for His Name's sake.
Yea, though I walk through the valley of the shadow of death,
I will fear no evil: for Thou art with me;
Thy rod and Thy staff, they comfort me.
Thou preparest a table before me in the presence of mine enemies;
Thou anointest my head with oil;
My cup runneth over.
Surely goodness and mercy shall follow me all the days of my life:
And I will dwell in the house of the Lord for ever. Psalm 23.

I will lift up mine eyes unto the hills.
From whence shall my help come?
My help cometh from the Lord,
Who made heaven and earth.
He will not suffer thy foot to be moved:

He that keepeth thee will not slumber.
Behold, He that keepeth Israel
Shall neither slumber nor sleep.
The Lord is thy keeper:
The Lord is thy shade upon thy right hand.
The Lord shall preserve thy going out and thy coming in
From this time forth, and even for evermore. Psalm 121:
1-5, 7, 8.

Here shall be read Lessons from the Gospels:

At the same time came the disciples unto Jesus, saying, Who is the greatest in the Kingdom of heaven? And Jesus called a little child unto Him, and 'set him in the midst of them, and said, Verily I say unto you, Except ye be converted, and become as little children, ye shall not enter into the kingdom of heaven. Whosoever therefore shall humble himself as this little child, the same is greatest in the kingdom of heaven. And whoso shall receive one such little child in My Name receiveth Me.

Take heed that ye despise not one of these little ones: for I say unto you, That in heaven their angels do always behold the face of My Father which is in heaven. Matthew 18: 1-5, 10.

Let not your heart be troubled; ye believe in God, believe also in Me. In My Father's house are many mansions: if it were not so, I would have told you. I go to prepare a place for you. And if I go to prepare a place for you, I will come again, and receive you unto myself; that where I am, there ye may be also. I am the way, the truth, and the life. If ye love Me, keep My commandments. And I will pray the Father, and He shall give you another comforter, that He may abide with you for ever; even the Spirit of truth; whom the world cannot receive, because it seeth Him not, neither knoweth Him: but ye know Him; for he dwelleth with you, and shall be in you. I will not leave you comfortless: I will come to you. Because I live, ye shall live also.

Peace I leave with you, My peace I give unto you: not as the world giveth, give I unto you. Let not your heart be troubled, neither let it be afraid. John 14: 1-3, 6, 15-18, 19, 27.

Here may follow music and an Address, after which the Minister shall say:

Let us pray.

Here may the Minister offer extempore Prayer or the following Prayer:

O God, who art the Father of the families of the earth, look with compassion upon this bereaved family, and pour Thy heavenly comfort into their hearts. Help them by faith to see this child, over whom they grieve, safe in that home where sin and sorrow cannot enter. Enrich with Thy presence those who mourn; abide in their home, lift up their hearts; bless them with Thy favor, which is better than life; and so guide them through the trials and temptations of this world that their reunited family may know fullness of joy in Thy presence for evermore. Grant this through Him who loved little children and blessed them, even Thy Son Jesus Christ, our Lord. *Amen.*

Then may the Minister say:

The grace of the Lord Jesus Christ, and the love of God, and the communion of the Holy Spirit, be with you all. *Amen.*

At the grave, when the People are assembled, the Minister shall say:

Jesus saith to His disciples, Ye now therefore have sorrow: but I will see you again, and your heart shall rejoice, and your joy no man taketh from you. John 16: 22.

Forasmuch as the departed has entered into the life immortal, we therefore commit his body to its resting place, but his spirit we commend to God, remembering how Jesus said upon the cross, "Father, into Thy hands I commend My spirit."

Then shall the Minister say:

Let us pray.

Almighty God, Father of our Lord Jesus Christ, who gave His life for our redemption and who promised the Holy Spirit, the Comforter; strengthen, we beseech 'Thee, the faith of these bereaved ones, that they may contemplate with peace the blessedness of that eternal home which Thou hast prepared for all who love and serve Thee. Grant that they, and all others whose joy is turned into mourning, cleaving more closely unto Him, who is the resurrection and the life, may be led by Thy Spirit through this uncertain life, till the day break and the shadows flee away. *Amen.*

Here the Minister and the People unite in the Lord's Prayer. Then may the Minister say:

The grace of the Lord Jesus Christ, and the love of God, and the communion of the Holy Spirit, be with you all. *Amen.*

CONSECRATION AND ORDINATION

¶ 1419. THE ORDER FOR THE CONSECRATION OF DEACONESSES

[When the time appointed by the Bishop is come, with such other exercises as may be desired, a Sermon or an .Address may be given, declaring what is the office and duty of a Deaconess.]

After which, the President of the Conference Deaconess Board, or someone named, shall present to the Bishop or other Consecrator, those to be consecrated Deaconesses, saying:

I present unto you these persons to be consecrated as Deaconesses.

Then shall be sung the hymn, "Where Cross the Crowded Ways of Life," or other appropriate hymn.

Then shall the following Scripture be read by the Leader and Congregation responsively:

When the Son of man shall come in His glory, and all the holy angels with Him, then shall He sit upon the throne of His glory:

And before Him shall be gathered all nations: and He shall separate them one from another, as the shepherd divideth the sheep from the goats;

And he shall set the sheep on his right hand, but the goats on the left.

Then shall the King say unto them on His right hand, Come, ye blessed of my Father, inherit the kingdom prepared for you from the foundation of the world.

For I was an hungered, and ye gave Me meat: I was thirsty, and ye gave Me drink: I was a stranger, and ye took me in:

Naked, and ye clothed Me: I was sick, and ye visited Me: I was in prison, and ye came unto Me.

Then shall the righteous answer Him, saying, Lord, when saw we Thee an hungered and fed Thee? or thirsty, and gave Thee drink?

When saw we Thee a stranger, and took Thee in? or naked, and clothed Thee?

Or when saw we Thee sick, or in prison, and came unto Thee?

And the King shall answer and say unto them, Verily I say unto you, inasmuch as ye have done it unto one of the least of these My brethren, ye have done it unto Me. Matthew 25: 31-40.

Then shall be sung or said this or other Hymn:

Take my life, and let it be
Consecrated, Lord, to Thee.
Take my hands, and let them move
At the impulse of Thy love.
Take my feet, and let them be
Swift and beautiful for Thee.
Take my voice, and let me sing
Always, only, for my King.

Take my will, and make it Thine;
It shall be no longer mine.
Take my heart, it is Thine own;
It shall be Thy loyal throne.
Take my love; my Lord, I pour
At Thy feet its treasure store.
Take myself, and I will be
Ever, only, all for Thee.

After which the Consecrator shall say:

Let us pray.

O Eternal God, the Father of our Lord Jesus Christ, who didst call Phoebe and Dorcas into the service of Thy Church, look upon these Thy servants who are now to be set apart to the office of Deaconess.

Give to them, we pray Thee, such understanding of Thy holy Gospel, such firmness of Christian purpose, such diligence in service and such beauty of life in Christ, that they may be to all whom they teach or serve, a worthy revelation of the meaning and power of the Christian life. May they so order their time and so nourish their minds and hearts that they may constantly grow in grace and in the knowledge of our Lord Jesus Christ and steadily increase in power to lead others unto Him.

Grant that they may have strength of body, mind, and soul for the fulfillment of Thy will in the holy task to which Thou hast called them, and grant them Thy Holy Spirit, that they may worthily discharge the work committed to them, to the blessing of mankind and the praise of the Christ our adorable Saviour. *Amen.*

Then shall the Consecrator address the Candidates, saying:

Dearly Beloved, we rejoice with you that in the good providence of God a door of usefulness has been opened for you in the service of the Church of Christ. To you are accorded peculiar privileges and priceless opportunities. Released from other cares, you are to give yourselves without reservation to the service of the Lord, ready for any duty which may fall to your lot. Like our gracious Master, you will go about doing good, ministering to the wants of a suffering, sorrowing, and sin-laden world. The Church now solemnly sets you apart for this special service. You are to minister to the poor, visit the sick, pray with the dying, care for the orphan, seek the wandering, comfort the sorrowing, and lead the sinning to their Saviour. Such service confers a great honor, but also lays upon you a solemn responsibility. What you have done alone with God, in consecrating your lives to this service, you are now to do formally and publicly in the presence of the Church.

Do you believe that you have been led by the providence of God to engage in this work, and to assume the duties of this office?

I do.

Do you, in the presence of God and of this congregation, promise faithfully to perform the duties of a Deaconess in the Church of God.

I do.

Will you be diligent in prayer, in the reading of the Holy Scriptures, and in such other study as will help you to grow in your Christian life and in the knowledge of God and of His Kingdom?

I will.

Will you strive so to live that you may convey the blessed sense of God's presence, love, and power to the hearts and homes of those to whom you minister?

I will.

Will you cheerfully accept the direction of those whom the Church may place over you in the doing of your work?

I will.

Then shall the Candidates kneel for a brief season in silent Prayer, after which the Consecrator shall say:

May the Spirit of the Living God descend upon you and abide with you evermore. May He impart to you grace for every trial, and strength for every service. May His presence be to you a pillar of cloud by day, and a pillar of fire by night; and may the blessing of God the Father, the Son, and the Holy Spirit be with you now and evermore. *Amen.*

Then the Consecrator, laying his hand upon the head of every one severally, shall say:

I admit thee to the office of a Deaconess in the Church of God, in the name of the Father, and of the Son, and of the Holy Spirit. *Amen.*

Then shall be given to the Deaconess the emblem of her office, and the Consecrator shall say:

This pin is presented to you in the name of The Methodist Church. It symbolizes your call and commission as a servant of the Lord Christ. It is a visible expression of the confidence the Church has in you. May you wear it worthily.

Then may be sung the Deaconess Hymn of Service:

We thank Thee, God our Father,
For all Thy love and grace,
That service in Thy Kingdom
Finds everyone a place.
We thank Thee for the favor
That marks our work and call,
That makes our life vocation
A ministry to all.

We pray Thee give us guidance
To save lives gone astray;
And strength to share with others
The burdens of their day;
And music for the children
Their songs of life to sing;
While to the homes of sorrow
May we Thy comfort bring.

In homes and halls of mercy
Where love with knowledge shares
The joy of healing bodies,
And sickened minds, of cares;
We pray! O Great Physician,
Thy knowledge of man's needs;
That service be made perfect
And faith be crowned with deeds.

To Thee, O gracious Master,
Thou Christ of Calvary—
This life of love and service
Our off'ring glad shall be.

Be Thou our guide and pattern,
Be Thou our strength and stay,
Till earth shall end in heaven,
And time, in endless day.

Benediction

May Christ dwell in your hearts by faith; that ye, being rooted and grounded in love, may be able to comprehend with all saints what is the breadth, and length, and depth, and height; and to know the love of Christ, which passeth knowledge, that ye might be filled with all the fullness of God. Now unto Him that is able to do exceeding abundantly above all that we ask or think, according to the power that worketh in us, unto Him be glory in the Church by Christ Jesus throughout all ages, world without end. *Amen.*

¶ 1420. THE ORDER FOR THE ORDINATION OF DEACONS

[When the time appointed by the Bishop is come, a Sermon or Address may be given, declaring what is the office and duty of a Deacon.]

After which, one of the Elders shall present to the Bishop all who are to be Ordained, and say:

I present unto you these persons present, to be ordained Deacons.

Their names having been read aloud, the Bishop shall say to the people:

Dearly Beloved, these are they whom we purpose, God willing, this day to ordain Deacons. For, after due examination, we find that they are lawfully called to this Office and Ministry, and that they are persons meet for the same. But if there be any of you who knoweth any valid reason, for the which any one of them ought not to be received into this holy Ministry, let him come forth in the name of God, and disclose what the impediment is. [If any impediment be alleged, the Bishop shall desist from ordaining that person until he shall be found to be innocent.]

Then shall be read the Collect:

Almighty God, who by Thy Holy Spirit hast appointed the Ministry of Thy Church, graciously behold these Thy servants, now called to the Office of Deacon, and so replenish them with the truth of Thy doctrine, and so adorn them with innocency of life, that both by word and good example they may faithfully serve Thee in this Office to the glory of Thy name, and the advancement of Thy Church, through the merits of our Saviour Jesus Christ, who liveth and reigneth with Thee and the Holy Spirit, world without end. *Amen.*

Then shall be read the Epistle:

Likewise must the deacons be grave, not doubletongued, not given to much wine, not greedy of filthy lucre; holding the mystery of the faith in a pure conscience. They that have used the office of a deacon well purchase to themselves a good degree, and great boldness in the faith which is in Christ Jesus. Timothy 3: 8, 9, 13.

See then that ye walk circumspectly, not as fools, but as wise, wherefore be ye not unwise, but understanding what the will of the Lord is. Giving thanks always for all things unto God and the Father in the name of our Lord Jesus Christ; submitting yourselves one to another in the fear of God. Finally, my brethren, be strong in the Lord, and in the power of His might. Put on the whole armor of God, that ye may be able to stand against the wiles of the devil. For we wrestle not against flesh and blood, but aginst principalities, against powers, against the rulers of the darkness of this world, against spiritual wickedness in high places. Wherefore take unto you the whole armor of God, that ye may be able to withstand in the evil day, and having done all, to stand. Stand therefore, having your loins girt about with truth, and having on the breastplate of righteousness; and you feet shod with the preparation of the gospel of peace; above all, taking the shield of faith, wherewith ye shall be able to quench all the fiery darts of the wicked. And take the helmet of salvation, and the sword of the Spirit, which is the word of God: praying always with all prayer and supplication in the Spirit, and watching thereunto with all preseverance and supplication for all saints. Ephesians 5: 15, 17, 20-21; 6: 10-18.

Then shall the Bishop, in the presence of the People, examine every one of these to be Ordained, after this manner:

Do you trust that you are inwardly moved by the Holy Spirit to take upon you the Office of the Ministry in the Church of Christ, to serve God for the promoting of His glory and the edifying of his people?

I trust so.

Do you unfeignedly believe the Scriptures of the Old and New Testaments?

I do believe them.

Will you diligently read and expound the same unto the people whom you shall be appointed to serve?

I will.

It appertaineth to the office of a Deacon to assist the Elder of divine service, and especially when he ministereth the Holy Communion, to help him in the distribution thereof; to read and expound the Holy Scriptures; to instruct the youth; and to baptize. And, furthermore, it is his office to search for the needy, that they may be visited and relieved. Will you do this gladly and willingly?

I will do so, by the help of God.

Will you apply all your diligence to order your own lives and the lives of your families according to the teachings of Christ?

I will, the Lord being my helper.

Will you reverently heed them to whom the charge over you is committed, following with a glad mind and will their godly admonitions?

I will so do.

Then those to be ordained shall kneel and the Bishop, laying his hands severally upon the head of every one of them, shall say:

Take thou authority to execute the office of a deacon in the Church of God; in the name of the Father, and of the Son, and of the Holy Spirit. *Amen.*

Then shall the Bishop deliver to every one of them the Bible, saying:

Take thou authority to read the Holy Scriptures in the Church of God, and to preach the Word.

Then one appointed by the Bishop shall read the Gospel:

Let your loins be girded about and your lights burning: and ye yourselves like unto men that wait for their lord, when he will return from the wedding; that when he cometh and knocketh, they may open unto him immediately. Blessed are those servants, whom the lord when he cometh shall find watching: verily I say unto you, that he shall gird himself, and make them to sit down to meat, and will come forth and serve them. And if he shall come in the second watch, or come in the third watch, and find them so, blessed are those servants. Luke 12: 35-38.

Then shall be offered the following Prayers and Benediction

Almighty God, Giver of all good things, who of Thy great goodness hast vouchsafed to accept these Thy servants into the Office of Deacon in Thy Church: make them, we beseech Thee, O Lord, to be modest, humble, and constant in their ministration; and to have a ready will to observe all spiritual discipline; that they, continuing ever stable and strong in Thy Son Jesus Christ, may so well behave themselves in this Office that they may be found worthy to be called into the higher Ministry in Thy Church, through Thy Son our Saviour Jesus Christ: to whom be glory and honor, world without end. *Amen.*

Direct us, O Lord, in all our doings, with Thy most gracious favor, and further us with Thy continual help; that in all our works, begun, continued, and ended in Thee, we may glorify Thy holy Name, and finally, by Thy mercy, obtain everlasting life, through Jesus Christ our Lord. *Amen.*

The peace of God, which passeth all understanding, keep your hearts and minds in the knowledge and love of God, and of His Son Jesus Christ our Lord: and the blessing of God Almighty, the Father, the Son and the Holy Spirit, be among you, and remain with you always. *Amen.*

¶ 121. THE ORDER FOR THE ORDINATION OF ELDERS

[When the time appointed by the Bishop is come, a Sermon or Address may be given, declaring what is the office and duty of an Elder.]

After which, one of the Elders shall present unto the Bishop all who are to be Ordained, and say:

I present unto you these persons present, to be ordained Elders,

The names having been read aloud, the Bishop shall say to the People:

Brethren, these are they whom we purpose, God willing, this day to ordain Elders. For, after due inquiry, we find that they are lawfully called to this Office and Ministry, and that they are persons meet for the same. But if there be any of you who knoweth any valid reason for the which any one of them ought not to be received into this holy Ministry, let him come forth in the name of God and disclose what the impediment is. [If any impediment be alleged, the Bishop shall desist from ordaining the accused until he shall be found to be innocent.]

Then the Collect shall be read:

Almighty God, Giver of all good things, who by Thy Holy Spirit has appointed the ministry of Thy Church: graciously behold these Thy servants now called to the Office of Elders, and so replenish them with the truth of Thy doctrine, and adorn them with innocency of life, that both by word and good example they may faithfully serve Thee in this Office, to the glory of Thy Name, and the advancement of Thy Church, through the merits of our Saviour Jesus Christ, who liveth and reigneth with Thee and the Holy Spirit, world without end. *Amen.*

Then the Epistle and the Gospel shall be read:

I was made a minister, according to the gift of the grace of God given unto me by the effectual working of His power. Unto me, who am less than the least of all saints, is this grace given, that I should preach the unsearchable riches of Christ; and to make all men see what is the fellowship of the mystery, which from the beginning of the world hath been hid in God, who created all things by Jesus Christ: And He gave some, apostles; and some prophets; and some, evangelists; and some, pastors and teachers; for the perfecting of the saints, for the work of the ministry, for the edifying of the body of Christ: till we all come in the unity of the faith, and of the knowledge of the Son of God, unto a perfect man, unto the measure of the stature of the fullness of Christ: for this cause I bow my knees unto the Father of our Lord Jesus Christ, of whom the whole family in heaven and earth is named, that He would grant you, according to the riches of His glory, to be strengthened with might by His Spirit in the inner man; that Christ may dwell in your hearts by faith; that ye, being rooted and grounded in love, may be able to comprehend with all saints which is the breadth, and length, and depth, and height; and to know the love of Christ, which passeth knowledge, that ye might be filled with all the fullness of God. Now unto Him that is able to do exceeding abundantly above all that we ask or think, according to the power that worketh in us, unto Him be glory in the church by Christ Jesus throughout all ages world without end. *Amen.* Ephesians 3: 7-9; 4: 11-13; 3: 14-21.

Jesus said, I am the door: by Me if any man enter in, he shall be saved, and shall go in and out, and find pasture. The thief cometh not, but for to steal, and to kill, and to destroy: I am come that they might have life, and that they might have it more abundantly. I am the good shepherd: the good shepherd giveth his life for the sheep. But he that is an hireling, and not the shepherd, whose own the sheep are not, seeth the wolf coming, and leaveth the sheep, and fleeth; and the wolf catcheth them, and scattereth the sheep. The hireling fleeth, because he is an hireling, and careth not for the sheep. I am the good shepherd, and know My sheep, and am known of Mine. As the Father knoweth Me even so know I the Father: and I lay down My life for the sheep. And other sheep I have, which are not of this fold: them also I must bring, and they shall hear My voice; and there shall be one fold, and one shepherd. John 10: 9-16.

Then shall the Bishop say unto the Persons to be Ordained Elders:

Dearly Beloved, you have heard, in your private examination and in the Holy Scriptures, of what dignity and of how great importance is this Office whereunto you are called. And now again we exhort you, in the name of our Lord Jesus Christ, that you are to be messengers, watchmen, and stewards of the Lord; to teach and to admonish, to feed and to provide for the Lord's family; to seek for Christ's sheep that are dispersed abroad, and for His children who are in the midst of this evil world, that they may be saved through Christ forever.

Have always therefore in your remembrance how great a treasure is committed to your charge. For they unto whom you are to minister are the sheep of Christ, for whom He gave His life. The Church which you must serve is His Bride and His body. And if it shall happen, the Church or any member thereof, take any hurt or hindrance by reason of your negligence, you know the greatness of the fault. Wherefore see that you never cease your labor, your care, and diligence until you have done all that lieth in you, according to your bounden duty, to bring all such as shall be committed to your charge unto perfectness in Christ.

Forasmuch, then, as your Office is both of so great excellency and of so great difficulty, consider how you ought to forsake, as much as you can, all worldly cares, and be studious in learning the Scriptures, and in acquiring such knowledge and skill as may help you to declare the living word of God.

We have good hope that you have weighed and pondered these things with yourselves long since: and that you have clearly determined, by God's grace, to give yourselves wholly to this work, whereunto it has pleased God to call you. Also that you will continually pray that the Holy Spirit may assist you to order the lives of you and yours after the rule and doctrine of Christ, that you may grow riper and stronger in ministry and be godly and wholesome examples for the people to follow.

And now, that this congregation of Christ here assembled may also understand your purpose in these things, and that this your promise may the more move you to perform your duties, you shall answer plainly to these things which we, in the name of God and his Church, shall ask of you touching the same:

Do you believe in your heart that you are truly called, according to the will of our Lord Jesus, to the Ministry of Elders?

I do so believe.

Are you persuaded that the Holy Scriptures contain all truth required for eternal salvation through faith in Jesus Christ? And are you determined out of the same Holy Scriptures so to instruct the people committed to your charge that they may enter into eternal life?

I am so persuaded, and determined, by God's grace.

Will you give your faithful diligence duly to minister the doctrine of Christ, the Sacraments, and the discipline of the Church, and in the spirit of Christ to defend the Church against all doctrine contrary to God's Word?

I will so do, by the help of the Lord.

Will you be diligent in prayer, in the reading of the Holy Scriptures, and in such studies as help to the knowledge of God and His kingdom?

I will, the Lord being my helper.

Will you apply all your diligence to frame and fashion your own lives and the lives of your families, according to the teachings of Christ?

I will, the Lord being my helper.

Will you maintain and set forward, as much as lieth in you, quietness, peace, and love, among all Christian people, and especially among them that shall be committed to your charge?

I will so do, the Lord being my helper.

Will you reverently heed them to whom the charge over you is committed, following with a glad mind and will their godly admonitions?

I will so do.

Then shall the Bishop pray:

Almighty God, who hath given you this will to do all these things, grant also unto you power to perform the same; that He may accomplish His work which He hath begun in you, through Jesus Christ our Lord. *Amen.*

[Then the Congregation shall be requested to make their earnest supplications in silent Prayer to God for those who are to be ordained as Elders, and entire silence. shall be kept for a space.]

After which, the Persons to be ordained Elders all kneeling, shall be said the *Veni, Creator Spiritus,* the Bishop beginning, and all others answering as followeth:

Come, Holy Ghost our souls inspire,
And lighten with celestial fire.
Thou the anointing Spirit art,
Who dost Thy sevenfold gifts impart.
Thy blessed unction from above
Is comfort, life, and fire of love.
Enable with perpetual light
The dullness of our blinded sight;
Anoint and cheer our soiled face
With the abundance of thy grace;
Keep far our foes, give peace at home;
Where Thou art Guide no ill can come.
Teach us to know the Father, Son,
And Thee, of both, to be but ONE;
That through the ages all along
This may be our endless song:
Praise to Thy eternal merit,
Father, Son, and Holy Spirit.

Then shall the Bishop say

Let us pray.

Lift up your hearts.
We lift them unto the Lord.
Let us give thanks unto our Lord God.
It is meet and right so to do.

Almighty God, our Heavenly Father, we bless and magnify Thy holy Name for the gift of Thy most dearly beloved Son, Jesus Christ, our Redeemer, and for all His Apostles, Prophets, Evangelists, Teachers, and Pastors, whom He hath sent abroad into the world. For these here present whom thou hast called to the same holy Office and Ministry, we render unto Thee our most hearty thanks. And now, O Lord, we humbly beseech Thee to grant that these thy Ministers, and by those over whom they shall be appointed, Thy holy Name may be forever glorified, and Thy blessed kingdom enlarged, through Thy Son Jesus Christ our Lord, who liveth and reigneth with Thee in the unity of the Holy Spirit, world without end. *Amen.*

Then shall the Bishop and the Elders present lay their hands severally upon the head of every one that receiveth the Order of Elder: the receivers kneeling, and the Bishop saying:

The Lord pour upon thee the Holy Spirit for the Office and work of an Elder in the Church of God, now committed unto thee by the authority of the Church, through the imposition of our hands. And be thou a faithful dispenser of the Word of God, and of His Holy Sacraments; in the name of the Father, and of the Son, and of the Holy Spirit. *Amen.*

Then shall the Bishop deliver to every one of them, kneeling, the Bible into his hands, saying:

Take thou authority as an Elder in the Church, to preach the Word of God, and to administer the Holy Sacraments in the Congregation.

Then shall the Bishop pray:

Most Merciful Father, we beseech Thee to send upon these Thy servants Thy heavenly blessings, that they may be clothed with righteousness, and that Thy word spoken by them may never be spoken in vain. Grant also that we may have grace to receive what they shall deliver out of Thy Word as the means of our salvation; that in all our words and deeds we may seek Thy glory, and the increase of Thy kingdom, through Jesus Christ our Lord. *Amen.*

Direct us, O Lord, in all our doings, with Thy most gracious favor, and further us by Thy continual help: that in all our works, begun, continued, and ended in Thee, we may glorify Thy holy Name, and finally, by Thy mercy, obtain everlasting life, through Jesus Christ our Lord. *Amen.*

Then may the Bishop say:

The peace of God, which passeth all understanding, keep your hearts and minds in the knowledge and love of God, and of His Son Jesus Christ our Lord: and the blessing of God Almighty, the Father, the Son, and the Holy Spirit, be among you, and remain with you always. *Amen.*

[If on the same day the Order of Deacon be given to some, and that of Elder to others, the Deacons shall be first presented, and then the Elders. The Collect shall be said and the Epistle read, immediately after which they who are to be ordained Deacons shall be examined and ordained as is above prescribed. Then the Gospel having been read, they who are to be ordained Elders shall likewise be examined and ordained, as in this Office before appointed.]

¶ 121. THE ORDER FOR THE CONSECRATION OF BISHOPS

[This service is a consecration, not an ordination, of an Elder or Presbyter to the duties of General Superintendency in the Church.]

When the time appointed for the Consecration of Bishop is come, the service shall begin with a Hymn, such as "The Church's One Foundation Is Jesus Christ Her Lord," after which the Collect shall be read:

Almighty God, who by Thy Son Jesus Christ didst give to Thy holy Apostles, Elders, and Evangelists many excellent gifts, and didst charge them to feed Thy flock; give grace, we beseech Thee, to all Ministers and Pastors of Thy Church, that they may diligently preach Thy word and duly administer the godly discipline thereof; and grant to the people that they may faithfully follow the same, that they may receive the crown of everlasting glory, through Jesus Christ our Lord. *Amen.*

Then shall one of the Elders read:

And from Miletus he sent to Ephesus, and called the Elders of the Church. And when they were come to him, he said unto them:

Ye know, from the first day that I came into Asia, after what manner I have been with you at all seasons, serving the Lord with all humility of mind, and with many tears, and temptations, which befell me: how I kept back nothing that was profitable unto you, but have showed you,' and have taught you publicly, and from house to house, testifying both to the Jews, and also to the Greeks, repentance toward God, and faith toward our Lord Jesus Christ. And now, behold I go bound in the spirit unto Jerusalem, not knowing the things that shall befall me there: save that the Holy Spirit witnesseth in every city, saying that bonds and afflictions abide me. But none of these things move me, neither count I my life dear unto myself, so that I might finish my course with joy, and the ministry, which I have received of the Lord Jesus, to testify the gospel of the grace of God. Take heed therefore unto yourselves, and to all the flock, over the which the Holy Spirit hath made you overseers, to feed the church of God, which he hath purchased with his own blood. For I know this, that after my departing shall grievous wolves enter in among you, not sparing the flock. Also of your own selves shall men arise speaking perverse things, to draw away disciples after them. Therefore watch, and remember, that by the space of three years I ceased not to warn every. one night and day with tears. And now, brethren, I commend you to God, and to the word of his grace, which is able to build you up, and to give you an inheritance among all them which are sanctified. Acts 20: 17-24, 28-32.

Then shall another Elder read:

So when they had dined, Jesus saith to Simon Peter, Simon, son of Jonas, lovest thou Me more than these? He saith unto Him, Yea, Lord; thou knowest that I love Thee. He saith unto him, Feed my lambs. He saith to him again the second time, Simon, son of Jonas, lovest thou Me? He saith unto Him, Yea, Lord; thou knowest that I love Thee. He saith unto him, Feed my sheep. He saith unto him the third time, Simon, son of Jonas, lovest thou Me? Peter was grieved because He said unto him the third time, Lovest thou Me? And he said unto Him, Lord, Thou knowest all things; Thou knowest that I love Thee. Jesus said unto him, Feed my sheep. John 21: 15-17.

And Jesus came and spake unto them, saying, All power is given unto Me in heaven and in earth. Go ye therefore, and teach all nations, baptizing them in the Name of the Father, and of the Son, and of the Holy Spirit: teaching them to observe all things whatsoever I have commanded you: and, lo, I am with you alway, even unto the end of the world. *Amen.* Matthew 28: 18-20.

Then shall the Elected Person be presented by two Elders unto the Bishop, the Elders saying:

We present unto you this Elder chosen to be consecrated a Bishop.

Then shall the Bishop call upon the Congregation present to pray, saying:

Dearly Beloved, it is written in the Gospel of Saint Luke that our Saviour Christ continued the whole night in prayer, before He chose and sent forth His twelve apostles. It is written also in the Acts of the Apostles that the disciples who were at Antioch did fast and pray, before they laid their hands on Paul and Barnabas, and sent them forth on their first mission to the Gentiles. Let us, therefore, following the example of our Saviour Christ, and His Apostles, give ourselves to prayer, before we admit and send forth this person presented to us, to the work whereunto we trust the Holy Spirit hath called him.

Then shall the Bishop pray:

Almighty God, giver of all good things, who by Thy Holy Spirit has appointed divers offices in Thy Church; graciously behold this Thy servant now called to the Office and Ministry of a Bishop. So replenish him with the truth of Thy doctrine, and so adorn him with innocency of life, that both by word and deed he may faithfully serve Thee in this office, to the glory of Thy Name, and the edifying and well governing of Thy Church; through the merits of our Saviour Jesus Christ, who liveth and reigneth with Thee and the Holy Spirit, world without end. *Amen.*

Then shall the Bishop say to him that is to be Consecrated:

Brother, forasmuch as the Holy Scriptures command that we should not be hasty in admitting any person to government in the Church of Christ, before you are admitted to this Ministration, you will, in the fear of God, give answer to these questions:

Are you persuaded that you are truly called to this Ministration, according to the will of our Lord Jesus Christ?

I am so persuaded.

Are you persuaded that the Holy Scriptures contain sufficiently all truth required for eternal salvation through faith in Jesus Christ? And are you determined out of the same Holy Scriptures so to instruct the people committed to your charge that they may enter into eternal life?

I am so persuaded and determined, by God's grace.

Will you then faithfully exercise yourself in the Holy Scriptures, and call upon God that through study and prayer you may have true understanding of the same?

I will so do, by the help of God.

Are you ready with all faithful diligence to seek and to promote the truth of Christ and to defend the Church against all doctrine contrary to God's Word?

I am ready, the Lord being my helper.

Will you live soberly, righteously, and devoutly in this present world, that you may show yourself in all things an example of good works unto others, to the honor and glory of God?

I will so do, the Lord being my helper.

Will you show yourself gentle, and be merciful for Christ's sake to poor and needy people, and to all strangers destitute of help?

I will so do, by the help of God.

Will you maintain and set forward, as much as lieth in you, quietness, love, and peace among all men; and faithfully exercise such discipline in the Church as shall be committed unto you?

I will so do, by the help of God.

Will you be faithful in ordaining and appointing others; and will you ever seek to deal justly and kindly with your brethren of the ministry over whom you are placed as chief pastor?

I will so do, by the help of God.

Then shall the Bishop pray:

Almighty God, our Heavenly Father, who hath given you a good will to do all these things, grant also unto you strength and power to perform the same, that He may accomplish in you the good work which He hath begun, that you may be found blameless, through Jesus Christ our Lord. *Amen.*

[Then the Congregation shall be requested to make their earnest supplications in silent Prayer to God for those who are to be consecrated as Bishops, and silence shall be kept for a space.]

[After which shall be said the Veni, Creator Spiritus, the Bishop beginning and all others answering as followeth.]

Come, Holy Ghost, our souls inspire,
And lighten with celestial fire.
Thou the anointing Spirit art,
Who dost Thy sevenfold gifts impart.
Thy blessed unction from above
It comfort, life, and fire of love.
Enable with perpetual light
The dullness of our blinded sight;
Anoint and cheer our soiled face
With the abundance of Thy grace;
Keep far our foes, give peace at home;
Where thou art Guide, no ill can come.

Teach us to know the Father, Son,
And Thee, of both, to be but ONE;
That through the ages all along
This may be our endless song:
Praise to Thy eternal merit,
Father, Son, and Holy Spirit.

Then shall the Bishop say:

Let us pray.

Lift up your hearts.
We lift them up unto the Lord.
Lord, hear our prayer.
And let our cry come unto Thee.

Almighty and Most Merciful Father, who of Thine infinite goodness hast given Thine only_ and dearly beloved Son Jesus Christ to be our Redeemer; and hast made some Apostles, some Prophets, some Evangelists, some Pastors and Teachers, to the edifying and making perfect of thy Church: grant, we beseech Thee, to this Thy servant, such grace that he may evermore be ready to spread abroad Thy Gospel, the glad tidings of reconciliation with Thee, and to use the authority given him, not to destruction, but to salvation; not to hurt but to help; so that as a wise and faithful servant, giving to all their portion in due season he may at least be received into everlasting joy, through Jesus Christ our Lord, who, with Thee and the Holy Spirit, liveth and reigneth, one God, world without end. *Amen.*

Then the Bishops and Elders present shall lay their hands upon the head of the Elected Person kneeling before them, the consecrating Bishop saying:

The Lord pour upon thee the Holy Spirit for the Office and work of a Bishop in the Church of God, now committed unto thee by the authority of the Church through the imposition of our hands, in the name of the Father, and of the Son, and of the Holy Spirit. And remember that thou stir up the grace of God which is in thee; for God hath not given us the spirit of fear, but of power, and of love, and of a sound mind. *Amen.*

Then shall the Bishop deliver to him the Bible, saying:

Give heed unto reading, exhortation, and teaching. Think upon the things contained in this book. Be diligent in them, that the increase coming thereby may be manifest unto all men. Take heed unto thyself, and to thy teaching; for by so doing thou shalt save both thyself and them that hear thee. Be to the flock of Christ a shepherd. Hold up the weak, heal the sick, bind up the broken, bring again the outcast, seek the lost; faithfully minister discipline but forget not mercy; that the kingdom of God may come upon the earth and when the Chief Shepherd shall appear, that you may receive the never-fading crown of glory, through Jesus Christ our Lord. *Amen.*

Then shall the Bishop pray:

Most merciful Father, we beseech Thee to send down upon these thy servants Thy heavenly blessing, and so endue them with thy Holy Spirit that they, preaching Thy word, may not only be earnest to reprove, beseech, and rebuke with all patience and doctrine, but also may be to such as believe a wholesome example in word, in conversation, in love, in faith, in chastity, and in purity; that faithfully fulfilling their course, at the latter day they may receive the crown of righteousness laid up by the Lord, the righteous Judge, who liveth and reigneth one God with the Father and the Holy Ghost, world without end. *Amen.*

Direct us, O Lord, in all our doing with Thy most gracious favor, and further us with Thy continual help, that in all our works, begun, continued, and ended in Thee, we may glorify Thy holy Name; and finally, by Thy mercy, obtain everlasting life, through Jesus Christ our Lord. *Amen.*

Then may the Bishop say:

The peace of God, which passeth all understanding, keep your hearts and minds in the knowledge and love of God, and of His Son Jesus Christ our Lord; and the blessing of God Almighty, the Father, the Son, and the Holy Spirit be among you, and remain with you always. *Amen.*

THE LAYING OF A CORNER STONE

¶ 1423. THE ORDER FOR LAYING THE CORNER STONE OF A CHURCH

At the time appointed the Hymn, "The Church's One Foundation Is Jesus Christ Her Lord," or other Hymn may be sung, all the People standing, after which the Minister shall say:

The Lord is in His holy temple: let all the earth keep silence before Him.

I was glad when they said unto me, Let us go into the house of the Lord.

Let thy work appear unto Thy servants and thy glory unto their children; and let the beauty of the Lord, our God, be upon us, and establish thou the work of our hands upon us; yea, the work of our hands establish Thou it.

, Then shall the Minister offer a prayer. Then the following lesson from the Old Testament may be read responsively by the Minister and the People, the People standing.

The earth is the Lord's, and the fullness thereof; the world, and they that dwell therein.

For he hath founded it upon the seas, and established it upon the floods.

Who shall ascend into the hill of the Lord? or who shall stand in His holy place?

He that hath clean hands, and a pure heart; who hath not lifted up his soul unto vanity, nor sworn deceitfully.

He shall receive the blessing from the Lord, and right-. eousness from the God of his salvation.

This is the generation of them that seek him, that seek thy face, O Jacob.

Lift up your heads, O ye gates; and be ye lifted up, ye everlasting doors; and the King of Glory shall come in.

Who is this King of glory? The Lord strong and mighty, the Lord mighty in battle.

Lift up your heads, O ye gates; even lift them up, ye everlasting doors; and the King of glory shall come in.

Who is King of glory? the Lord of hosts, he is the King of Glory. Psalm 24.

Then may be said or sung:

Glory be to the Father, and to the Son, and to the Holy Ghost.

As it was in the beginning, is now, and ever shall be, world without end. *Amen.*

Then shall be read the lesson from the New Testament, the People being seated:

For we are laborers together with God: ye are God's husbandry, ye are God's building.

According to the grace of God which is given unto me, as a wise master-builder, I have laid the foundation, and another buildeth thereon. But let every man take heed how he buildeth thereon.

For other foundation can no man lay than that is laid, which is Jesus Christ.

Now if any man build upon this foundation gold, silver, precious stones, wood, hay stubble; every man's work shall be made manifest: for the day shall declare it, because it shall be revealed by fire; and the fire shall try every man's work of what sort it is.

If any man's work abide which he hath built thereon, he shall receive a reward.

If any man's work shall be burned, he shall suffer loss: but he himself shall be saved; yet so as by fire.

Know ye not that ye are the temple of God, and that the Spirit of God dwelleth in you? I Corinthians 3: 9-16.

Here may follow a Prayer, Offering, Anthem, Address and Hymn.

Standing at the side of the corner stone the following Scripture Sentences may be read:

Except the Lord build the house, they labor in vain that built it.

The Lord hath chosen thee to build a house for the sanctuary; be strong and do it. Fear not, nor be dismayed: for the Lord God, even my God, is with thee. He will not fail thee, nor forsake thee, until all the work for service of the house of the Lord is finished.

Therefore, thus saith the Lord God, Behold, I lay in Zion for a foundation a stone, a tried stone, a precious corner stone of sure foundation.

According to the grace of God which was given unto me, as a wise master builder I have laid the foundation.

Other foundation can no man lay than that is laid, which is Jesus Christ.

Then shall the Minister offer the Prayer of Consecration:

Almighty God, the Rock of Ages, on Thee we build all our hopes for this life and that which is to come. Other foundation we would not seek to lay than that is laid, which is Jesus Christ; and we are to build upon this Corner Stone a Holy Temple to the living God. Accept the act by which we lay this Corner Stone. Bless those whose offerings enable us to build this house of worship. Graciously guard and direct those who labor in erecting it, shielding them from accident and peril. May the walls of this building rise in security and in beauty; and may the hearts of these, thy people, be fitly joined together into a living temple, builded upon the foundation of the apostles and prophets, Jesus Christ being the chief Corner Stone. *Amen.*

Then shall the Minister and People recite the Litany for the Laying of a Corner Stone:

To the Glory of God our Father, to the service of our dear Master and His Church and to the abiding presence of the Holy Spirit,
We lay the corner stone of this church.
For a building of which Jesus Christ is the chief Corner Stone, the pillar and ground of the truth,
We lay this corner stone.
For a building that shall stand as a symbol of the Church Universal: the Corner Stone of which is Truth, the creed of which is Love, and its towers eternal Hope,
We lay this corner stone.
For a church that shall exalt not a religion of creed or of authority, but religion of saving grace, of personal experience and of spiritual power,
We lay this corner stone.
For a church that shall exalt the ministry of the open Bible, with its faithful record of human life, its unfolding of the redeeming Grace of God through Jesus Christ, its message of warning, inspiration, comfort and hope,
We lay this corner stone.
For a church that shall teach and incarnate the doctrine of the Fatherhood of God and the Brotherhood of Man,
We lay this corner stone.
For a church that shall fufill a ministry of social service inspired by spiritual motive,
We lay this corner stone.
For a church that shall be a renewing and cleansing power in the Community and that loves every other communion that exalts Christ in the service of man,
We lay this corner stone.
For a church with an open door for all people, rich or poor, homeless or desolate, who need the help of God through us,
We lay this corner stone.
For a church that shall gather the children in its arms and hold them close to Christ that they may grow up in the Church and never be lost from the fold,
We lay this corner stone.
For a church which stands for the sacramental truth—
It is more blessed to give than to receive,

We lay this corner stone.

For a church which takes hold on two worlds, and stands for the unseen and eternal, and which offers to men the abundant life which now is and that which is to come,

We lay this corner stone in the Name of Almighty God.

Then shall the Minister say:

In loving memory of those who have gone from us; whose hearts and hands have served in this church; with deep gratitude for all whose faith and consecrated gifts make this house possible; for all who may share this spiritual adventure; and with high hopes for all who shall worship in this house in years to come.

Then shall the People respond:

We lay this corner stone in the name of Almighty God— Father, Son and Holy Spirit—unto the ages of ages, world without end. *Amen.*

[Then shall the Minister, standing by the stone, exhibit to the people a box to be placed in the stone. It may contain such articles as a Bible, *The Methodist Hymnal,* the latest *Discipline,* Church periodicals, names of the Pastor, Official Board, the Building Committee of the Church, with such other documents as may be desired. The Minister may read the list of articles so deposited in the box. Then with the aid of the builder, the Minister shall lay the stone in its place.]

Then shall the people sing:

Praise God, from whom all blessings flow;
Praise Him, all creatures here below;
Praise Him above, ye heavenly host:
Praise Father, Son, and Holy Ghost. *Amen.*

Then shall the Minister say:

Now unto Him that is able to keep us from falling, and to present us faultless before the presence of His Glory with exceeding joy; to the only wise God our Saviour, be glory and majesty, dominion and power, both now and for evermore. *Amen.*

¶ 1423. A BRIEFER FORM FOR THE LAYING OF A CORNER STONE

At the time appointed the Hymn "The Church's One Foundation Is Jesus Christ Her Lord," or other Hymn may be sung, all the People standing, after which the Minister shall say:

Our help is in the Name of the Lord, who made heaven and earth.

Except the Lord build the house, they labor in vain that build it.

Dearly Beloved, we are assembled to lay the Corner Stone of a new house for the worship of the God of our fathers. Let us not doubt that He will favorably approve our godly purpose, and let us now, devoutly invoke His blessing on this our undertaking.

Then shall the Minister read the lesson from the New Testament.

For we are laborers together with God; ye are God's husbandry, ye are God's building.

According to the Grace of God which is given unto me, as a wise master-builder, I have laid the foundation, and another buildeth thereon. But let every man take heed how he buildeth thereon.

For other foundation can no man lay than that is laid, which is Jesus Christ.

Now if any man build upon this foundation gold, silver, precious stones, wood, hay, stubble; every man's work shall be made manifest: for the day shall declare it, because it shall be revealed by fire; and the fire shall try every man's work of what sort it is.

If any man's work abide which he hath built thereon, he shall receive a reward.

If any man's work shall be burned, he shall suffer loss: but he himself shall be saved; yet so as by fire.

Know ye not that ye are the temple of God, and that the Spirit of God dwelleth in you? I Corinthians 3: 9-16.

Then shall the Minister offer one or more of these prayers or an extemporary prayer:

Most glorious God, the heaven is Thy throne and the earth is Thy footstool; what house, then, can be builded for Thee, or where is the place of Thy rest? Yet, blessed be Thy name, O Lord God, that it hath pleased Thee to have Thy habitation among the sons of men, and to dwell in the assembly of the saints on the earth. And now, especially, we render thanks unto Thy holy Name, that Thou hast put it into the hearts of Thy servants to erect in this place a house for Thy worship. We thank Thee for Thy grace which has inclined them to contribute of their substance for the glory of Thy Name; and we pray Thee to continue Thy blessing upon this their undertaking. *Amen.*

Let Thy blessing rest upon those who labor in erecting this house; shield them from all harm, and grant unto them, and all of us here present, Thy heavenly grace, that our gifts and all our service may be sanctified, and that we may become in soul and body living temples of the Holy Spirit. *Amen.*

Grant that all who shall hereafter worship Thee in the temple here to be builded, may so serve and please Thee that in the end they may come to that temple whose builder and maker is God. This we ask through Jesus Christ our Lord. *Amen.*

[Then shall the Minister, standing by the stone, exhibit to the people a box to be placed in the stone. It may contain such articles as a Bible, *The Methodist Hymnal*, the latest *Discipline*, Church periodicals, names of the Pastor, Official Board, and Building Committee of the Church, with such other documents as may be desired. The Minister may read the list of articles so deposited in the box. Then with the aid of the builder, the Minister shall lay the stone in its place.]

Then shall the Minister say:

In the Name of the Father, and of the Son, and of the Holy Spirit, we lay this Corner Stone for the foundation of a house to be builded and consecrated to the worship and service of Almighty God according to the order and usages of The Methodist Church. *Amen.*

Here may follow an Address, and an Offering may be received.

Then may be sung a Hymn, such as:

548: "On this stone now laid with prayer."

Then may the Minister say:

The grace of the Lord Jesus Christ, and the love of God, and the communion of the Holy Spirit, be with you all. *Amen.*

THE DEDICATION OF A CHURCH

¶ 1425. THE ORDER FOR THE DEDICATION OF A CHURCH

After an Organ Prelude a Processional or Opening Hymn shall be sung; such as:

1—"Holy, holy, holy."
279—"God of grace."
382—"Glorious things of Thee are spoken."

Then shall the Minister say, the People standing and responding:

[The Responses may be said or sung:]

Dearly Beloved, as we learn from the Holy Scriptures, it is meet and right that houses erected for the worship of God should be especially set apart and dedicated to religious uses. We are, therefore, now assembled for the purpose of dedicating this house to the worship and service of Almighty God.

The Lord is in His holy temple.

Let all the earth keep silence before Him.

I saw the Lord sitting upon a throne high and lifted up; and His train filled the temple. Above it stood the seraphim; each one had six wings; with twain he covered his face, and with twain he covered his feet, and with twain he did fly. And one cried unto another:

Holy, holy, holy, Lord God of Hosts:
Heaven and earth are full of Thy glory.
Glory be to Thee, O Lord most high. *Amen.*

Here may an Anthem be sung.

Then shall be read responsively, the People standing:

The earth is the Lord's and the fullness thereof;

The world, and they that dwell therein.

For He hath founded it upon the seas,

And established it upon the floods.

Who shall ascend into the hill of the Lord?

Or who shall stand in His holy place?

He that hath clean hands, and a pure heart;

Who hath not lifted up his soul unto vanity, nor sworn deceitfully.

He shall receive the blessing from the Lord, and righteousness from the God of his salvation.

This is the generation of them that seek Him, that seek Thy face, O Lord.

Lift up your heads, O ye gates; and be ye lifted up, ye everlasting doors.

And the King of Glory shall come in.

Who is this King of Glory?

The Lord strong and mighty, the Lord mighty in battle.

Lift up your heads, O ye gates; even lift them up, ye everlasting doors.

And the King of Glory shall come in.

Who is this King of Glory?

The Lord of hosts, He is the King of Glory.

Then may be sung:

Glory be to the Father, and to the Son, and to the Holy Ghost.

As it was in the beginning, is now, and ever shall be, world without end. *Amen.*

Then shall be read a Lesson from the New Testament:

And He came to Nazareth, where He had been brought up: and, as His custom was, He went into the synagogue on the Sabbath day, and stood up for to read.

And there was delivered unto Him the book of the prophet Isaiah. And when He had opened the book, He found the place where it was written,

The Spirit of the Lord is upon Me, because He hath anointed Me to preach the gospel to the poor; He hath sent Me to heal the broken-hearted, to preach deliverance to the captives, and recovering of sight to the blind, to set at liberty them that are bruised.

To preach the acceptable year of the Lord.

And He closed the book, and He gave it again to the minister, and sat down. And the eyes of all them that were in the synagogue were fastened on Him. And He began to say unto them, This day is this scripture fulfilled in your ears.

Here may be offered extemporary Prayer, followed by the Lord's Prayer. Then may be sung a suitable Hymn or an Anthem, after which the Sermon may be delivered. An Offering may then be received.

Then shall the Trustees stand before the Altar, and one of them, or someone in their behalf, shall say unto the Minister:

We present unto you this building, to be dedicated as a Church for the worship and service of Almighty God.

Thereupon shall the Minister say these words of Dedication, all the People standing and uniting in the responses:

In the name of the Father, and of the Son, and of the Holy Spirit, we dedicate this Church to Christian Worship.

God is a Spirit, and they that worship Him must worship Him in spirit and in truth.

We dedicate this Church to the training of children in faith and knowledge and to the summoning of youth to the life of service.

Remember now thy Creator in the days of thy youth.

We dedicate this Church to the cure of souls that doubt and to the persuasion of those that have not yet believed; to the comfort of the discouraged, the relief of the distressed, the consecration of the strong, the guidance of the bewildered and the consolation of the dying; to the ennobling of this life and to confidence in the life eternal. All souls are Mine, saith the Lord. Inasmuch as ye did it unto one of the least of these, My brethren, ye did it unto Me.

We dedicate this Church to the unfinished task of the Church of Christ through Evangelism and Education; through Philanthropy and Social Justice; through National Probity and Honor; through Christian Unity and International Good Will.

Glory to God in the highest, and on earth peace, good will toward men.

We dedicate this Church in loving memory of all those who have gone before, and of all whose hearts and hands have served this Church; with deep gratitude for loyal comrades who have made with us this spiritual adventure; and with high hope for those who shall walk this way in days to come.

Holy, holy, holy, Lord God of Hosts!
Heaven and earth are full of Thee.
Heaven and earth are praising Thee,
O Lord most high!

The Minister and People: We dedicate this house to the glory of God our Father, by whose favor it has been builded; in honor of Jesus Christ, the Son of the living God our Lord and Saviour; to the praise of the Holy Spirit, the source of light and life. Except the Lord build the house, they labor in vain that build it.

We, the minister and the people of this Church and congregation, compassed about by so great a cloud of witnesses, do here and now dedicate ourselves anew to the worship of God in this sanctuary and the establishment of His kingdom among men everywhere.

Then shall be said or sung:

Therefore with angels and archangels, and with all the company of heaven,
We laud and magnify Thy glorious Name,
Evermore praising Thee and saying:
Holy, holy, holy, Lord God of Hosts,
Heaven and earth are full of Thy glory:
Glory be to Thee, O Lord most high. *Amen.*

Then shall the Minister say:

Let us pray.

O Eternal God, whom the heaven of heavens cannot contain, much less the walls of temples made with hands, graciously accept the dedication of this house to Thy honor and glory. *Amen.*

Grant, O Lord, that all who here share in the Sacraments, the ministry of the Word, and the fellowship of praise and prayer may know that God is in this place, may hear His voice within their hearts, and may go forth to extend to the uttermost bounds of life the Lord Christ's kingdom. *Amen.*

Now, therefore, O Lord, let Thine eyes be open toward this house day and night; and let Thine ears be ready toward the prayer of Thy children, which they shall make unto Thee in this place. And whensoever Thy servants shall make to Thee their petitions, do Thou hear them, and when Thou hearest, forgive. Grant, O Lord, we beseech Thee, that here and elsewhere Thy ministers may be clothed with righteousness, and Thy saints rejoice in Thy salvation. And may we all, with Thy people everywhere, grow up into a holy temple in the Lord, and be at last received into the glorious temple above; the house not made with hands, eternal in the heavens. And to the Farther, and the Son, and the Holy Spirit, be glory and praise, world without end. *Amen.*

Here may be sung a suitable Closing or Recessional Hymn, such as:

279—"God of grace and God of glory."

Then may the Minister say:

Now unto Him that is able to keep you from falling, and to present you faultless before the presence of His glory with exceeding joy, to the only wise God our Saviour, be glory and majesty, dominion and power, now and evermore. *Amen.*

THE DEDICATION OF AN ORGAN

¶ 1426. THE ORDER FOR THE DEDICATION OF AN ORGAN

After an Organ Prelude, a Processional or Opening Hymn shall be sung, such as,

15—"Angel voices, ever singing."

Then shall the Minister say, the People responding:

Dearly Beloved, we learn from the Holy Scriptures, that devout men set apart temples for the worship of God, and used musical instruments therein for His praise and adoration. We therefore assemble here for the purpose of dedicating this Organ for service in the worship of Almighty God.

The Call to Worship

Surely the Lord is in this place.

This is none other than the house of the Lord: this is the gate of heaven.

Enter into His gates with thanksgiving and into His courts with praise.

O magnify the Lord with me; let us exalt His Name together.

Then shall the *Gloria Patri* be said or sung:

Glory be to the Father, and to the Son, and to the Holy Ghost; As it was in the beginning, is now and ever shall be, world without end. *Amen.*

Then shall the Minister say:

Let us pray.

Almighty God, unto whom all hearts are open, all desires known, and from whom no secrets are hid, cleanse the thoughts of our hearts by the inspiration of Thy Holy Spirit, that we may perfectly love Thee, and worthily magnify Thy holy Name, through Jesus Christ our Lord. *Amen.*

[The Organ may then be presented for dedication by one of the Trustees, or someone designed for that purpose, in some such words, as:]

We present this Organ for dedication (if a gift or memorial so stating) the gift of ———— for the glory of God and in loving memory of ————.

Then shall the Minister say these words of Dedication, all the People standing and uniting in the responses:

In the Name of the Father, and of the Son, and of the Holy Spirit, we dedicate this Organ to the praise of Almighty God.

Praise God in His sanctuary: praise Him in the firmament of His power. Praise Him with the sound of the trumpet; Praise Him with psaltery and harp.

We dedicate this Organ to the cultivation of a high art: to the interpretation of the message of the Masters of music, to an appreciation of the great doxologies of the Church, and to the development of the language of praise which belongeth both to earth and to heaven.

Praise Him with stringed instruments and organs. Let everything that hath breath praise the Lord. Praise ye the Lord.

We dedicate this Organ to the wedding march, to thanksgiving on festal occasions, and to such inspiration in the service of song that all people may praise the Lord.

O sing unto the Lord a new song: sing unto the Lord all the earth, in psalms and hymns and spiritual songs, singing and making melody in your heart unto the Lord.

We dedicate this Organ to the healing of life's discords, and the revealing of the hidden soul of harmony; to the lifting of the depressed and the comforting of the sorrowing; to the humbling of the heart before the eternal mysteries and the lifting of the soul to abiding beauty and joy by the gospel of infinite love and good will.

That at the name of Jesus every knee should bow, of things in heaven, and things in earth, and things under the earth; and that every tongue should confess that Jesus Christ is Lord, to the glory of God the Father.

Then shall the Minister say:

Let us pray.

Our God and Father, whom the generations have worshiped with concord of sweet sound, be pleased to accept this Organ as a song of praise unto Thee. *Amen.*

Grant that its music, with accompanying song, may come as a blessed benediction upon all who worship here. *Amen.*

May this Organ become undying music in the world as its notes of cheer, comfort, communion, and courage are modulated into human lives for daily task and noble service. *Amen.*

To all organists who shall sound its notes, and to all worshipers who shall be lifted Godward by its voice, may there come at times the sweep of hallelujahs from the throne of the Redeemed until earth below shall be attuned to heaven above in singing hallelujah to Him who reigneth, Lord of Lords, the King of Kings. *Hallelujah! Amen.*

[Here may be sung a suitable Hymn or an Anthem, after which a Sermon or Address may be delivered. An Offering may then be received, followed by the singing of Hymn 552 and the Benediction.]

The Dedication of a Parish House.

¶ 1427. THE ORDER FOR THE DEDICATION OF A PARISH HOUSE.

' The People being assembled, the Minister shall say:

Dearly Beloved, by the favor of God and the labor of man, this building has been so far completed. It is to be a place where men and women, boys and girls, may find opportunities for instruction, for recreation, and for ministries of fellowship.

Let us therefore bring to the Heavenly Father our praises for His guidance and aid in this undertaking, and our prayers on behalf of those who by their gifts of their service shall unite in fulfilling the purposes of love and good will for which this building is prepared.

Let the Hymn, "For the Beauty of the Earth," or some other suitable Hymn, be sung. After which an Invocation may be offered, closing with the Lord's Prayer.

Then shall the Minister, or someone appointed by him, read:

Wherefore David blessed the Lord before all the congregation: and David said, Blessed be Thou, Lord God of Israel our father, for ever and ever. Thine, O Lord, is, the greatness, and the power, and the glory, and the victory, and the majesty: for all that is in the heaven and in the earth is thine; Thine is the kingdom, O Lord, and Thou art exalted as head above all. Both riches and honor come of Thee, and Thou reignest over all; and in Thine hand is power and might; and in Thine hand it is to make great, and to give strength unto all. Now, therefore, our God, we thank Thee, and praise Thy glorious Name. But who am I, and what is my people, that we should be able to offer so willingly after this sort? for all things come of Thee, and of Thine own have we given Thee. For we are strangers before Thee, and sojourners, as were all our fathers: our days on the earth are as a shadow, and there is none abiding. O Lord our God, all this store that we have prepared to build Thee an house for Thine holy Name cometh of Thine hand, and is all Thine own. I know also, my God, that Thou triest the heart, and hast pleasure in uprightness. As for me, in the uprightness of mine heart I have willingly offered all these things: and now have I seen with joy Thy people which are present here, to offer willingly unto Thee. I Chronicles 29: 10-17.

Though I speak with the tongues of men and of angels, and have not love, I am become as sounding brass, or a tinkling cymbal. And though I have the gift of prophecy, and understand all mysteries, and all knowledge; and though I have all faith, so that I could remove mountains, and have not love, I am nothing. And though I bestow all my goods to feed the poor, and though I give my body to be burned, and have not love, it profiteth me nothing.

Love suffereth long, and is kind: love envieth not; love vaunteth not itself, is not puffed up, doth not behave itself unseemly, seeketh not her own, is not easily provoked, thinketh no evil; rejoiceth not in iniquity, but rejoiceth in the truth; beareth all things, believeth all things, hopeth all things, endureth all things.

Love never faileth: but whether there be prophecies, they shall fail; whether there be tongues, they shall cease; whether there be knowledge, it shall vanish away. For we know in part, and we prophesy in part. But when that which is perfect is come, then that which is in part shall be done away. When I was a child, I spake as a child, I understood as a child, I thought as a child: but when I became a man, I put away childish things. For now we see through a glass, darkly; but then face to face: now I know in part; but then shall I know even as also I am known. And now abideth faith, hope, love, these three; but the greatest of these is love. I Corinthians 13.

Let the Hymn, "O Master, Let Me Walk with Thee," or some other suitable Hymn, be sung; after which may be delivered an Address. An Offering may then be received. Then shall the following Psalm be read by the Minister and People responsively; the People standing:

I will give thanks unto the Lord with my whole heart,
In the council of the upright, and in the congregation.
The works of the Lord are great,
Sought out of all them that have pleasure therein.
His work is honor and majesty;
And His righteousness endureth forever.
He hath made His wonderful works to be remembered:
The Lord is gracious and merciful.
He hath given food unto them that fear Him.
He will ever be mindful of His covenant.
He hath showed His people the power of His works,
In giving them the heritage of the nations.
The works of His hands are truth and justice;
All His precepts are sure.

They are established forever and ever;
They are done in truth and uprightness. Psalm 111: 1-8.

Then shall be said or sung:

Glory be to the Father, and to the Son, and to the Holy
Ghost; As it was in the beginning, is now, and ever shall
be, world without end. *Amen.*

Then let the Trustees or the Proper Committee stand up before
the People, and one of them say to the Minister:

We present unto you this building, to be dedicated to the
service of Almighty God and the fellowship of his people.

Then shall the People stand while the Minister pronounces the
following Declaration:

Dearly Beloved, it is right and proper that buildings
erected for such service in the Name of our Lord and
Saviour Jesus Christ should be formally and devoutly set
apart for their special uses. For such a dedication we are
now assembled. And, as the dedication of this building is
vain without the solemn consecration of those whose gifts
and labors it represents, let us now give ourselves anew to
the service of God: our souls, that they may be renewed
after the image of Christ; our bodies, that they may be
fit temples for the indwelling of the Holy Spirit; and our
labors and business, that they may be according to God's
holy will, and that their fruit may tend to the glory of
God and the advancement of His kingdom.

Then shall the Minister say these words of Dedication, the People
standing and responding:

In the Name of the Father, and of the Son, and of the
Holy Spirit, we dedicate this building as a Parish House
to the service of God and the uses of Christian fellowship.

Whether therefore ye eat or drink, or whatsoever ye do,
do all to the glory of God.

We dedicate this building to the purpose of religious education: to the work of the Church School, to the study of
the Scriptures, and to the development of Christian character.

Whatsoever things were written aforetime were written
for our learning: blessed are they that hear the word of
God and keep it.

We dedicate this building to the broadening of mental
horizons and the deepening of knowledge, that young and
old may be awakened and informed.

A man's wisdom maketh his face to shine, and the hardness of his face is changed.

We dedicate this building to those tasks and aims in which the Christian serves his place and time: to the cause of missions, of Christian citizenship, and the broad field of social relations.

The kingdoms of this world are become the kingdoms of our Lord, and of His Christ; and He shall reign for ever and ever.

We dedicate this building to Christian recreation of mind and of body.

Thou wilt show me the path of life; in Thy presence is fullness of joy; at Thy right hand there are pleasures for evermore.

Minister and People:

We dedicate ourselves anew to that service of our fellow men, wherein can best be performed our true service of God; in obedience to the spirit of the Master when He said: Thou shalt love the Lord thy God with all thy heart, and thy neighbor as thyself.

Then shall the Minister pray; the People being in the attitude of prayer:

Almighty God, our Heavenly Father, whose eyes are ever toward the righteous, and whose ears are ever open unto their cry, graciously accept, we pray Thee, this building which we now dedicate to Thee, to Thy service, and to Thy glory, that in it love and wisdom may unite to bring joy and strength to those who gather here; and we beseech Thee, receive us Thy servants who here dedicate ourselves anew to Thee and to those offices of fellowship and good will in which Thou art well pleased. Grant that those who come here may be cheered and quickened in mind and body, and that they may be stirred in spirit to serve Thee wisely and steadfastly; and the praise shall be Thine for ever, through Jesus Christ our Lord. *Amen.*

O Lord, we desire to place ourselves and what we here undertake in Thy hands. Direct us in this and all our doings with Thy most gracious favor, and further us with Thy continual help, that in all our works, begun, continued, and ended in Thee, we may glorify Thy name; through Jesus Christ our Lord. *Amen.*

O God, who by the grace of thy Holy Spirit hast poured the gifts of love into the hearts of Thy people, grant unto all Thy servants health of body and soul, that they may love Thee with all their strength, and with perfect devotion do Thy most holy will; through Jesus Christ our Lord. *Amen.*

Then may the Minister say:

The grace of the Lord Jesus Christ, and the love of God, and the communion of the Holy Spirit be with you all. *Amen.*

The Dedication of a Hospital

¶ 1428. THE ORDER FOR THE DEDICATION OF A HOSPITAL

The People being assembled, the Minister shall say:

Dearly Beloved, this building, which, by the favor of God and the labor of man, has been so far completed, is a symbol of that care for the sick and the suffering which was supremely exemplified in the Lord Jesus and which has always inspired those who follow Him. We believe that the Heavenly Father not only desires, but gladly accepts the service of comfort and healing for which this building is to provide, and that he looks with favor upon the dedication of the building to Himself and to the welfare of His children.

Let us therefore bring to Him our praises for His guidance and aid in this undertaking, and our prayers on behalf of those who by their gifts or their service shall unite in fulfilling those purposes of love and skill for which this building is prepared.

Let the Hymn, "We May Not Climb the Heavenly Steeps," or some other suitable Hymn, be sung. Afterward an invocation may be offered, closing with the Lord's Prayer.

Then shall the Minister, or someone appointed by him, read:

The Spirit of the Lord God is upon me; because the Lord hath anointed me to preach good tidings unto the meek; He hath sent Me to bind up the broken-hearted, to proclaim liberty to the captives, and the opening of the prison to them that are bound; to proclaim the acceptable year of the Lord, to comfort all that mourn; to appoint unto them that mourn in Zion, to give unto them beauty for ashes, the oil of joy for mourning, the garment of praise for the spirit of heaviness.

The wilderness and the solitary place shall be glad for them; and the desert shall rejoice, and blossom as the rose.

Strengthen ye the weak hands, and confirm the feeble knees. Say to them that are of a fearful heart, Be strong, fear not: behold, your God will come and save you. Then the eyes of the blind shall be opened, and the ears of the deaf shall be unstopped. Then shall the lame man leap as an hart, and the tongue of the dumb shall sing. Isaiah 61: 1-3; Isaiah 35: 1, 3-5.

And the disciples of John showed him of all these things. And John calling unto him two of his disciples sent them to Jesus, saying, Art thou He that should come? or look we for another? And in that same hour He cured many of their infirmities and plagues, and of evil spirits; and unto many that were blind He gave sight. Then Jesus answering said unto them, Go your way, and tell John what things ye have seen and heard; how that the blind see, the lame walk, the lepers are cleansed, the deaf hear, the dead are raised, to the poor the gospel is preached. And blessed is he, whosoever shall not be offended in Me. Luke 7: 18-22.

Let the Hymn, "O Master, Let Me Walk with Thee," or some other suitable Hymn, be sung; after which may be delivered an Address. An offering may then be received.

Then shall be read by the Minister and the People responsively, the People standing:

Bless the Lord, O my soul: and all that is within me, bless His holy Name.

Bless the Lord, O my soul, and forget not all His benefits:

Who forgiveth all thine iniquities; who healeth all thy diseases;

Who redeemeth thy life from destruction; who crowneth thee with loving-kindness and tender mercies.

Like as a father pitieth his children, so the Lord pitieth them that fear Him.

For he knoweth our frame; He remembereth that we are dust.

As for man, his days are as grass: as a flower of the field, so he flourisheth.

For the wind passeth over it, and it is gone; and the place thereof shall know it no more.

But the mercy of the Lord is from everlasting to everlasting upon them that fear Him, and His righteousness unto children's children;

To such as keep His covenant, and to those that remember His commandments to do them.

Bless the Lord, ye His angels, that excel in strength,

that do His commandments, hearkening unto the voice of His word.

Bless ye the Lord, all ye His hosts; ye ministers of His, that do His pleasure.

Bless the Lord, all His works in all places of His dominion:

Bless the Lord, O my soul. Psalm 103: 1-4, 13-22.

Then shall be said or sung:

Glory be to the Father, and to the Son, and to the Holy Ghost; As it was in the beginning, is now, and ever shall be, world without end. *Amen.*

Then let the Trustees or the proper Committee stand up before the People, and one of them say unto the Minister:

We present unto you this building, to be dedicated to the service of Almighty God in the relief of the sick and the suffering.

Then shall the People stand while the Minister pronounces the following Declaration:

Dearly Beloved, it is right and proper that buildings erected for such service, in the name of our Lord and Saviour Jesus Christ, should be formally and devoutly set apart for their special uses. For such a dedication we are now assembled. And, as the dedication of this building is vain without the solemn consecration of those whose gifts and labors it represents, let us now give ourselves anew to the service of God: our souls, that they may be renewed after the image of Christ; our bodies, that they may be fit temples for the indwelling of the Holy Spirit; our labors and business, that they may be according to God's holy will, and that their fruit may tend to the glory of God and the advancement of His kingdom.

Then shall the Minister say these words of Dedication, the People standing and responding:

In the Name of the Father, and of the Son, and of the Holy Spirit, we dedicate this building as a hospital to the holy ministry of healing.

Blessed are the merciful; for they shall obtain mercy.

We dedicate this building to Christian helpfulness.

Whosoever shall give to drink unto one of these little ones a cup of water only, shall in no wise lose his reward.

We dedicate this building to the sustaining power of the Holy Spirit in times of pain and suffering.

In all their afflictions He was afflicted, and the angel of His presence saved them.

We dedicate this building to the skill and wisdom that bring relief and cure; and to the patient research that uncovers fresh resources with which to serve the public health.

Happy is the man that findeth wisdom; length of days are in her right hand; she is a tree of life to them that lay hold upon her.

Minister and People together:

We dedicate ourselves anew to that service of our fellow men wherein can best be performed our true service of God; in obedience to the spirit of the Master when he said: Thou shalt love the Lord thy God with all thy heart, and thy neighbor as thyself.

Then shall the Minister say:

Let us pray.

Almighty God, our Heavenly Father, whose eyes are ever toward the righteous and whose ears are ever open unto their cry, graciously accept, we pray Thee, this building which we now dedicate to Thee, to Thy service, and to Thy glory, that in it skill and tenderness may unite to bring health and cure to those who come for aid; and we beseech Thee, receive us Thy servants who here dedicate ourselves anew to Thee and to those offices of love and good will in which Thou art well pleased. Grant that those who come here in weakness may be made strong, that those who come in pain may find relief, and that those who come in sorrow may find joy and gladness; and the praise shall be Thine forever, through Jesus Christ our Lord. *Amen.*

O blessed Lord, who hast power of life and death, of health and sickness, give wisdom and gentleness to all Thy ministering servants, to physicians and surgeons, nurses and watchers by the sick, that, always bearing Thy presence with them, they may not only heal but bless, and shine as lamps of hope in the darkest hours of distress and fear. Through Christ our Lord. *Amen.*

O most merciful Father, we look to Thee for Thy grace on behalf of those who, coming here in grievous illness, may not return to earthly joys and sorrows, but pass from here into that life immortal where Thou dost receive all who put their trust in Thee. Thou hast said that as the heavens are higher than the earth, so are my ways higher than your ways, but we know that all Thy children are in Thy tender and unfailing love which passes our understanding, and we pray that the blessed ministry of Thy Holy Spirit may sustain them, and that light eternal may shine upon them. *Amen.*

And now, O loving Father, we bow before Thee of whom every family in heaven and earth is named, praying that Thou wouldst grant us according to the riches of Thy glory, to be strengthened with might by Thy spirit in the inner man; that Christ may dwell in our hearts by faith; that we, being rooted and grounded in love, may be able to comprehend with all saints what is the breadth, and length, and depth, and height; and to know the love of Christ, which passeth knowledge, that we may be filled with the fullness of God. *Amen.*

Then may the Minister say:

The grace of the Lord Jesus Christ, and the love of God, and the communion of the Holy Spirit, be with you all. *Amen.*

THE DEDICATION OF A COLLEGE OR UNIVERSITY BUILDING

¶ 1429. THE ORDER FOR THE DEDICATION OF AN EDUCATIONAL BUILDING

The People being assembled, the Minister shall say:

Dearly Beloved, this building, which by the favor of God and the labor of man has been so far completed, embodies the obligation of each generation to impart its treasures of wisdom and knowledge to the generation following. For the fulfillment of this task we need not only the best that men can do but above all the blessing of Almighty God.

Let us therefore bring to Him our praises for His aid in this undertaking, and our prayers on behalf of those who by their gifts or their service shall unite in fulfilling the purpose for which this building is prepared.

Let the Hymn, "The Lord Our God Alone Is Strong," or some other suitable Hymn, be sung. Afterward an Invocation may be offered, closing with the Lord's Prayer.

Then shall the Minister, or someone appointed by him, read:

Happy is the man that findeth wisdom, and the man that getteth understanding. For the merchandise of it is better than the merchandise of silver, and the gain thereof than fine gold. She is more precious than rubies: and all the things thou canst desire are not to be compared unto her. Length of days is in her right hand; and in her left hand riches and honor. Her ways are ways of pleasantness, and all her paths are peace. She is a tree of life to them that lay hold upon her: and happy is everyone that retaineth her. The Lord by wisdom hath founded the earth; by understanding hath He established the heavens. By His knowledge the depths are broken up, and the clouds drop down the dew. My son, let not them depart from Thine eyes: keep sound wisdom and discretion: so shall they be life unto thy soul, and grace to thy neck. Then shalt thou walk in thy way safely, and thy foot shall not stumble. Proverbs 3: 13-23.

Enter ye in at the strait gate: for wide is the gate, and broad is the way, that leadeth to destruction, and many there be which go in thereat: because strait is the gate, and narrow is the way, which leadeth unto life, and few there be that find it. Therefore whosoever heareth these sayings of mine, and doeth them, I will liken him unto a wise man, which built his house upon a rock: and the rain descended, and the floods came, and the winds blew, and beat upon that house; and it fell not: for it was founded upon a rock. And everyone that heareth these sayings of mine and doeth them not, shall be likened unto a foolish man, which built his house upon the sand: and the rain descended, and the floods came, and the wind blew, and beat upon that house; and it fell: and great was the fall of it. Matthew 7: 13, 14, 24-28.

Let the Hymn, "Walk in the Light," or some other suitable Hymn, be sung; after which may be delivered an Address. An Offering may then be received.

Then shall the following Scripture be read by the Minister and the People responsively, the People standing:

Wisdom hath builded her house, she hath hewn out her seven pillars.

Doth not wisdom cry? And understanding put forth her voice?

She standeth in the top of high places, by the way in the places of the paths.

She crieth at the gates, at the entry of the city, at the coming in at the doors.

Unto you, O men, I call; and my voice is to the sons of men.

O ye simple, understand wisdom: and ye fools, be ye of an understanding heart.

Hear; for I will speak of excellent things; and the opening of my lips shall be right things.

For my mouth shall speak truth; and wickedness is an abomination to my lips.

Receive my instruction, and not silver; and knowledge rather than choice gold.

For wisdom is better than rubies; and all the things that may be desired are not to be compared to it.

But where shall wisdom be found? And where is the place of understanding?

Behold, the fear of the Lord, that is wisdom; and to depart from evil is understanding. Proverbs 8: 1, 7, 10, 11; Job 28: 12, 28.

Then shall be said or sung:

Glory be to the Father, and to the Son, and to the Holy Ghost; As it was in the beginning, is now, and ever shall be, world without end. *Amen.*

Then let the Trustees or the proper Committee stand up before the People, and one of them say unto the Minister:

We present unto you this building, to be dedicated to the service of Almighty God in the enlightenment of his children.

Then shall the People stand while the Minister pronounces the following Declaration:

Dearly Beloved, it is right and proper that buildings erected for such service in the Name of our Lord and Saviour Jesus Christ should be formally and devoutly set apart for their special uses. For such a dedication we are now assembled. And, as the dedication of this building is vain without the solemn consecration of those whose gifts and labors it represents, let us now give ourselves anew to the service of God: our souls, that they may be renewed after the image of Christ; our bodies, that they may be fit temples for the indwelling of the Holy Spirit; our labors and business, that they may be according to God's holy will, and that their fruit may tend to the glory of His Name and the advancement of His Kingdom.

Then shall the Minister say these words of Dedication, the People standing and responding:

In the Name of the Father, and of the Son, and of the Holy Spirit, we dedicate this building to the holy ministry of education.

Take fast hold of instruction; let her not go: keep her, for she is thy life.

We dedicate this building to the spiritual enrichment of all who shall come here in pursuit of knowledge.

Happy is the man that findeth wisdom, and the man that getteth understanding.

We dedicate this building to the loyal service of those whose training and devotion have prepared them to lead students toward the truth.

The Lord God hath given me the tongue of the learned that I should know how to speak a word in season to him that is weary.

We dedicate this building to that ministry of administration upon whose ability and fruitfulness depends the wise conduct of its affairs.

Who, then, is that faithful and wise steward, whom his lord shall make ruler over his household? Blessed is that servant whom his lord, when he cometh, shall find so doing.

Minister and People together:

We dedicate ourselves to that service of our fellow men, wherein can best be performed our true service of God; in obedience to the spirit of the Master when he said, Thou shalt love the Lord thy God with all thy heart, and thy neighbor as thyself.

Then shall the Minister say:

Let us pray.

Almighty God, our Heavenly Father, whose eyes are ever toward the righteous and whose ears are ever open unto their cry, graciously accept, we pray Thee, this building which we now dedicate to Thee, to Thy service and to Thy glory, that in it love and wisdom may unite to make plain the path of knowledge to those who gather here; and we beseech Thee to receive us Thy servants, who here dedicate ourselves anew to Thee and to those offices of fellowship and good will in which Thou art well pleased. Grant that those who come here, whether as administrators, teachers, or students, may come with pure minds, upright purpose, and steadfast endeavor, to learn and to do Thy holy will; through Jesus Christ our Lord. *Amen.*

God of our Fathers, we offer Thee our heartfelt thanks for all Thy servants: the parents and teachers, the benefactors and friends, by whose love and devotion we have come into our great inheritance of health, truth, and piety. Help us to guard faithfully this great boon, to profit by it, to augment it, and loyally to pass it on to the coming generation, that they through us may rise up to serve Thee; in the Name of Jesus Christ our Lord. *Amen.*

Grant, O Lord, to all teachers and students, to know that which is worth knowing, to love that which is worth loving, to praise that which pleaseth Thee most. Grant us with true judgment to distinguish truth from error, to dislike whatever is evil in Thine eyes, and above all to search out and to do those things which are right in Thy sight; through Jesus Christ our Lord. *Amen.*

Then may the Minister say:

Now unto Him that is able to keep you from falling, and to present you faultless before the presence of His glory with exceeding joy, to the only wise God our Saviour, be glory and majesty, dominion and power, now and evermore. *Amen.*

The Dedication of a Home

¶ 1430. THE ORDER FOR THE DEDICATION OF A HOME

At the time appointed, when the Minister and People have assembled in the Home, the Minister shall say:

Peace be to this house.

Dearly Beloved, members and friends of this household, it is written that, "Except the Lord build the house, they labor in vain that build it." We have therefore met here to invoke the divine blessing on this home, that its ties of love may be strong and beautiful through the blessing and the inspiration of the Heavenly Father.

Then may be sung the Hymn, "Father of All, Thy Care We Bless," or some other suitable Hymn.

This shall be followed by extemporary prayer, closing with the Lord's Prayer.

Then shall the words of Dedication be spoken by the Minister, the People standing and responding:

In the name of the Father, and of the Son, and of the Holy Spirit, we dedicate this home to the glory of God, committing to His loving care this house and all who dwell in it.

Have thou respect unto the prayer of Thy servant, O Lord, my God, which Thy servant prayeth before Thee this day; that Thine eyes may be open toward this house night and day.

We dedicate this home to the deep affections of the family circle, and to all friendly hospitalities.

Now God Himself, and our Father, and our Lord Jesus Christ make you to increase and abound in love.

We dedicate this home to the courage, patience, and self-control which make life cheerful and serene.

Let patience have her perfect work, that ye may be perfect and entire, wanting nothing.

We dedicate this home to all beautiful things of heart and mind that lead the soul to wider vision and to higher aims.

> "Whene'er a noble deed is wrought,
> Whene'er is spoken a noble thought,
> Our hearts in glad surprise
> To higher levels rise."

We dedicate this home to happiness, to hopefulness, and to health, that it may ever be, to those whose home it is, a dear haven of peace and joy.

> "Serene will be our days and bright,
> And happy will our nature be,
> When love is an unerring light,
> And joy its own security."

Then shall the Minister say:

Let us pray.

O God, our Heavenly Father, Giver of life, we pray Thee make this home an abode of light and love. May all that is pure, tender, and true, grow up under its shelter. May all that hinders godly union and concord be driven far from it. Make it the center of fresh, sweet, and holy influence. Give wisdom for life, and discretion in the guidance of affairs.

Let Thy work appear unto Thy servants, and Thy glory unto their children. Let the beauty of the Lord our God be upon us; and establish Thou the work of our hands upon us; yea, the work of our hands establish Thou it. And the praise shall be Thine forever. *Amen.*

Here may be sung the Hymn, "O Happy Home."

Then shall the Minister say:

The Lord bless us and keep us, the Lord cause His face to shine upon us and be gracious unto us, the Lord lift up the light of His countenance upon us, and give us peace, now and for evermore. *Amen.*

REPORT NO. 4. RECOMMENDATIONS

Calendar No. 41. Adopted May 8. See Journal, Page 319.

Membership of Committee, 45; present when report was adopted, 37; voting for adoption, 37.

The Committee on Rituals and Orders of Worship recommends that the Uniting Conference request the Council of Bishops to appoint a Commission on Orders of Worship, Rituals, and Aids to the Deepening of the Spiritual Life to report to the second General Conference of The Methodist Church; that the Board of Publication of The Methodist Church be authorized to provide funds for the expenses of the Commission; that the Commission seek to provide Orders of Worship and Rituals for The Methodist Church that will draw upon richer and wider resources than those that have been available up to the present time, and that the Commission seek to provide aids to the deepening of the spiritual life worthy of the new Church and designed to make Methodism a spiritually creative force in the land.

REPORTS OF SPECIAL STANDING COMMITTEES

I. COMMITTEE ON ENABLING ACTS AND LEGAL FORMS

REPORT NO. 1. CONCERNING INAUGURATING ACTIVITIES

Adopted May 9. See Journal, Page 333.

Membership of Committee, 36; present when report was adopted, 29; voting for adoption, 29.

For the purpose of inaugurating the activities of The Methodist Church the procedure for and in the Annual Conferences of the three Uniting Churches, composing The Methodist Church, under and in pursuance of the Plan of Union, shall include the following:

Section 1. All Annual Conferences of the three uniting Churches shall meet at some date before December 25, 1939, transact their usual business, including the appointment of Preachers until the successor organization of the Annual Conference of The Methodist Church, close their affairs, and adjourn finally as Conferences of these respective Churches.

Section 2. All Annual Conferences of The Methodist Church shall meet at some date prior to January 1, 1940, and following as early as practicable the final closing of the Annual Conferences to which they are the successors, organize, elect the Boards which the *Discipline* requires to act until their successors are elected following the Jurisdictional Conferences, adopt the programs and plans of service for its Boards, adopt apportionments for General and Conference work, appoint the Preachers to their Charges, and take such other action as the work of the Annual Conference requires.

Section 3. Each Annual Conference of The Methodist Church shall fix as an apportionment for General work an amount not less than that of its predecessor or predecessors nor less than the combined apportionments of any Conference, Conferences or parts of Conferences to which it is the successor, since these Benevolences are necessary to the support of the Boards that are continued until the Jurisdictional Conferences.

Section 4: Each Annual Conference in the Southeastern and South Central Jurisdictional Conferences, excepting those in Kansas and Nebraska, shall report and send its General Benevolences to the General Boards at Nashville, Louisville, and ·St. Louis, and each Annual Conference in the other four Jurisdictional· Conferences and in Kansas and Nebraska shall report and send its Benevolences for General·work to the World Service Commission at Chicago, Illinois, to be used in support of the Boards and interests to which its funds have usually been appropriated; *provided,* however, in the case of the Annual Conferences whose apportionments for General work is a combination of the· apportionments from the three uniting Churches the receipts for General Benevolences shall be divided upon the basis in the apportionments and sent respectively as above.

Any confusion or misunderstanding regarding these apportionments or the distribution of them shall be referred to the Committee on Adjustments set up by the World Service Commission of the Methodist Episcopal Church, the General Commission on Budget of the Methodist Episcopal Church, South, and the Executive Committee of the General Conference of the Methodist Protestant Church.

Section 5: All rules and regulations of the *Discipline* of The Methodist Church for Annual Conferences, District Conferences, Quarterly Conferences and· Church Conferences shall go into effect in each Annual Conference of The Methodist Church upon its organization.

Section 6. The General Boards, notwithstanding the fact that they are constituted by the Enabling Acts by the combination of previously existing bodies, having respectively a common plan and policy, as found in the *Discipline,* for the entire Church and its Annual Conferences shall be authorized to appoint Committees of co-ordination to set up and maintain a common plan and policy, until the meeting of the General Conference in April, 1940. The Boards with headquarters in Nashville, Louisville, and St. Louis, shall have the major responsibility in the area of the Southeastern and South Central Jurisdictions, and the other Boards of the three uniting· Churches wherever located shall have major responsibility in the other Jurisdictions.

Section 7. Pending the creation and organization of the General Conference Budget-making Agency as provided by the Uniting Conference, the duties committed to it by the *Discipline* shall be performed by the present existing agencies of the three Uniting Churches. All these agencies shall consult together and co-operate in a unified program and policy for the Church as a whole. They shall make provision for the promotion of the Benevolences for General and Conference work.

Said agencies of the three Uniting Churches shall insist that each Annual Conference apportion for General Benevolences not less than its predecessor, nor less than the combined apportionments of the Conferences and parts of Conferences of which it is the successor. They shall insist that the receipts from the Annual Conferences in the Southeastern and South Central Jurisdictions, excepting those in Kansas and Nebraska shall be sent to the Boards and agencies in Nashville, Louisville and St. Louis, and that the receipts from the Annual Conferences in the other four Jurisdictions shall go to the World Service Commission, and that the receipts from combined apportionments shall go respectively as the above. They shall appoint a Commission on Adjustment to serve till the Jurisdictional Conference to direct in any cases of confusion or misunderstanding.

The Methodist Publishing House, in correspondence with the Boards of Benevolence, is authorized to furnish Statistical Blanks for the use of the Annual Conferences.

Section 8. In those cases in which Annual Conferences are incorporated under the laws of the respective states in which they are located, the corporate existence of such Annual Conferences may be continued until their property may be legally transferred to and vested in their respective successors under the Plan of Union as hereinabove provided.

Section 9. Pending action by the 1940 General Conference, Jurisdictional Conference or Central Conference, in the exercise of their respective powers, an Annual Conference shall provide such Boards, Commissions and Committees as the *Discipline* of The Methodist Church provides, in order to carry forward the work of the United Church.

The Central Conferences are hereby authorized and empowered to meet in special session on call of the Council of Bishops.

Section 10. Pending the election of the Trustees of The Methodist Church by the General Conference, the existing corporations of the three uniting Churches, namely, the Trustees of the Methodist Episcopal Church, the Board of Trustees of the Methodist Episcopal Church, South, and the Board of Trustees of the Methodist Protestant Church, shall be continued and shall manage, control and administer the property of all kinds and description now vested in them, or any of them, and shall perform all the duties imposed upon them, or any of them, and discharge all the obligations resting upon them or any of them by their respective Churches until their successor, or successors, shall have been legally elected, and shall have qualified as such and all the assets of said corporations shall have been legally transferred to, and vested in the said. successor, or successors, authorized by The Methodist Church.

Section 11. All corporations, Boards of Trustees, Associations, or other agencies of the three uniting Churches holding or controlling any property of or exercising any powers vested in them by said Uniting Churches, or any of them, shall continue to operate under the existing Charters, articles of incorporation, constitutions, or other documents under which they have hitherto acted, prior to the uniting of said Churches under and in pursuance of the Plan of Union, until all property of every kind or description controlled by them, or any of them shall have been legally transferred to the successor or successors created by and representing The Methodist Church may receive all such property, including endowments, annuities, and trust funds, and be in a legal position to control and manage said property and trust funds in the interest of those persons and causes for which said funds were established.

Section 12. The paragraphs of this report shall not be construed to be exclusive, but only cumulative, and shall not have the effect of repealing or modifying any other report adopted by the Uniting Conference, dealing with any of the questions or matters herein considered.

Section 13. The Methodist Episcopal Church, the Methodist Episcopal Church, South, and the Methodist Protestant Church are and shall be one united Church. The Plan of Union as adopted is and shall be the Constitution of this united Church, and of its three constituent bodies. The Methodist Episcopal Church, the Methodist Episcopal Church, South, and the Methodist Protestant Church had their common origin in the organization of the Methodist Episcopal Church in America in 1784 A.D, and have ever held, adhered to and preserved a common belief, spirit, and purpose. The Methodist Episcopal Church, the Methodist Episcopal Church, South, and the Methodist Protestant Church, in adopting the name "The Methodist Church" for the united Church, do not and will not surrender any right, interest, or title in or to these respective names which by long and honored use and association have become dear to the Ministry and membership of the three uniting Churches and have become enshrined in their history and records. The Methodist Church is the ecclesiastical and lawful successor of the three uniting Churches, in and through which the three Churches as one United Church shall continue to live and have their existence, continue their institutions and hold and enjoy their property, exercise and perform their several trusts under and in accord with the Plan of Union and *Discipline* of the United Church; and such trusts or corporate bodies as exist in the constituent churches shall be continued as long as legally necessary.

Section 14. All acts and decisions of the Uniting Conference designed (a) to harmonize and combine the provisions in the *Disciplines* of the three Uniting Churches; (b) to provide for the unification, co-ordination and correlation of Boards, Societies, and other connectional interests of the Churches; (c) and all other acts and decisions designed to implement and make effective the Plan of Union shall take effect upon the adjournment of the Uniting Conference unless otherwise provided.

Section 15. Pending action by the 1940 General Conference, the Book Committee of the Methodist Episcopal Church, the General Commission on Budget of the Methodist Episcopal Church, South, and the Executive Committee of the General Conference of the Methodist Protestant Church, or their successor or successors, are hereby authorized, empowered, and instructed to co-operate in the maintenance of an adequate and equitable support for the Bishops of The Methodist Church. They are also authorized, empowered and instructed to make such modifications and changes in existing plans and procedure as shall accomplish said purpose.

Section 16. To The Methodist Church thus established we do now solemnly declare our allegiance, and upon all its life and service we do reverently invoke the blessing of Almighty God.

A. A. CALLAGHAN, *Chairman;*
W. M. ALEXANDER, *Secretary.*

REPORT No. 2. AD INTERIM OPERATION OF INTERESTS OF THE METHODIST PROTESTANT CHURCH

Adopted May 9. See Journal, Page 333.

Membership of Committee, 36; present when report was adopted, 25; voting for adoption, 25.

Section 1. The Executive Committee shall maintain its existence with the same authority and personnel as heretofore until the meeting of the General Conference in 1940.

Section 2. The Boards of Christian Education, of Missions, and of Publication shall continue to function as provided for in the reports of the Committees of the Uniting Conference dealing with those interests. The annual meetings of the said Boards shall be held as of the close of their fiscal years.

Section 3. Due to the fact that the Church will be merged into new Annual Conference relationships by the union of the Churches, thus cutting off these General Boards from their regular source of income, their income for a fiscal year shall be supplemented from the general income of The Methodist Church in amounts to be determined and allocated by the joint Committee on Adjustments.

Section 4. The office of Treasurer of the General Conference shall be continued with the same duties it now possesses until the next General Conference.

Section 5. The Board governing the General Fund for Superannuates is authorized to make its usual annual distribution of income, as of April 30, 1939, and to continue as a Board until its merging with the Chartered Fund, as set forth in the report of the Committee on Pensions.

Section 6. The duties and relationship to the General Boards of the President of the General Conference shall be continued by the former President, Bishop James H. Straughn.

Section 7. The Presidents of the several Annual Conferences shall be continued in office until the Annual Conferences over which they preside shall have become merged with the Annual Conferences of The Methodist Church as provided by the Uniting Conference.

A. A. CALLAGHAN, *Chairman;*
W. M. ALEXANDER, *Secretary.*

REPORT No. 3. CONTINUATION OF COLLECTION AND DISTRIBUTION OF BENEVOLENCES, ADMINISTRATION FUNDS, AND EPISCOPAL FUNDS OF UNITING CHURCHES

Adopted May 9. See Journal, Page 344.

.Membership of Committee, 36; present when report was adopted, 19; voting for adoption, 19.

Section 1. The collection and administration of the General Benevolences, the Administration funds and the Episcopal funds of the three Uniting Churches, from the ad-

journment of the Uniting Conference until the General
Conference shall otherwise provide, shall continue as provided in each denomination before unification.

Section 2. (a) As soon as practicable after the adjournment of the Uniting Conference, The World Service Commission of the Methodist Episcopal Church, the General
Commission on Budget of the Methodist Episcopal Church,
South, and the Executive Committee of the Methodist Protestant Church shall meet in joint session in order to make
necessary adjustments for the collection and administration of the general funds of the three Churches during the
interim between the adjournment of the Uniting Conference
and the meeting of the General Conference of The Methodist Church, and to arrange for a more complete merger
of these funds and to suggest to the General Conference any
additional legislation which these bodies may jointly conclude to be necessary in the financial organization of The
Methodist Church.

(b) This joint meeting shall appoint a special Committee
of nine on the ratio of four from the Methodist Episcopal
Church, four from the Methodist Episcopal Church, South,
and one from the Methodist Protestant Church to which
shall be referred all matters for adjustment arising out of
the Benevolence giving of the three Churches from the time
of the adjournment of the Uniting Conference to the meeting of the General Conference.

(c) The joint meeting of the three Budget Commissions
shall pass upon the collection and distribution of the receipts
from the monthly missionary offering in the Church School
and all other problems connected with the general funds of
the Church which may be referred to the joint meeting
for solution and any other matters that may not have been
fully provided for by the Uniting Conference. On all such
matters the joint meeting of the Commissions shall suggest
to the General Conference such additional legislation as in
the judgment of the Commissions may be wise and necessary.

(d) The joint meeting of the three Commissions, after
hearing the full presentation by the several Boards authorized by the Uniting Conference of the needs of their
fields and the estimated costs of administration shall
submit to the Budget-making Agencies of the General Conference a recommendation as to the amount to be asked
of the Church for the support of the General Benevolences.

A. A. CALLAGHAN, *Chairman;*
W. M. ALEXANDER, *Secretary.*

REPORT NO. 4. CONTINUATION OF WORLD SERVICE COMMISSION OF METHODIST EPISCOPAL CHURCH

Adopted May 9. See Journal, Page 344.

Membership of Committee, 36; present when report was adopted, 22; voting for adoption, 22.

During the period between the adjournment of the Uniting Conference and the time when the General Conference may order otherwise, the World Service Commission of the Methodist Episcopal Church shall continue to discharge its duties as now authorized in its Articles of Incorporation, its By-laws and in the provisions of the *Discipline* of 1936 of the Methodist Episcopal Church.

The funds received by the Treasurer of the World Service Commission shall be distributed to the World Service Boards, Commissions and Agencies as authorized and approved by the General Conference of 1936 of the Methodist Episcopal Church, except as provided otherwise by the Committee on Adjustments.

The terms of office of the members of the World Service Commission shall continue until their successors as members of a corresponding body shall have been elected.

A. A. CALLAGHAN, *Chairman;*
W. M. ALEXANDER, *Secretary.*

REPORT NO. 5. CONTINUATION OF GENERAL COMMISSION ON BUDGET FOR METHODIST EPISCOPAL CHURCH, SOUTH

Adopted May 9. See Journal, Page 344.

Membership of Committee, 36; present when report was adopted, 19; voting for adoption, 19.

During the period between the adjournment of the Uniting Conference, and the time when the General Conference may order otherwise, the General Commission on Budget of the Methodist Episcopal Church, South, shall continue to discharge its duties and function as now provided in the *Discipline* of 1938 of said Church.

The terms of office of the members of said Commission on Budget shall continue until the members of the Commission on World Service and Finance of The Methodist Church shall have been selected and qualified.

A. A. CALLAGHAN, *Chairman;*
W. M. ALEXANDER, *Secretary.*

REPORT NO. 6. PROVISIONS FOR CONTINUATION OF GENERAL
COMMISSION ON BENEVOLENCES

Adopted May 9. See Journal, Page 344.

Membership of Committee, 36; present when report
was adopted, 24; voting for adoption, 24.

Pending action by the General Conference of The Methodist Church, the General Commission on Benevolences shall
be authorized to continue the functions and activities stipulated by the General Conference of the Methodist Episcopal
Church, South, at Birmingham in 1938, with continuation
of financial support as at present. The provision for this
Commission or "Joint Co-operative Committee for the Promotion of General Benevolences" will be found in ¶ 571-B of
the *Discipline* of the Methodist Episcopal Church, South,
1938.   A. A. CALLAGHAN, *Chairman;*
W. M. ALEXANDER, *Secretary.*

REPORT NO. 7. TITLES TO CHURCH PROPERTY

Adopted May 9. See Journal, Page 344.

Membership of Committee, 36; present when report
was adopted, 19; voting for adoption 19.

WHEREAS, it is necessary at all times to safeguard the
titles to and interests in the property of The Methodist
Church, local and general, and to protect the interests of
the various organizations of said Church in trusts and other
forms of holding property; therefore, be it

Resolved, That we authorize the Bishops of a Jurisdictional Conference within which a suit or suits may be
brought, if in their judgment it is proper to do so, to employ competent attorneys to defend and protect the interests
of The Methodist Church, local or general, in such property,
or to cause such suit or suits to be brought as may in their
judgment be necessary to protect the interests of The Methodist Church. If an emergency arises and it appears to one
of the Bishops that action should be taken quickly he may
do so, until the opinion of the Bishops of the Jurisdictional
Conference can be obtained.

In such case or cases the expense of such litigation and of
such employment of attorneys, properly payable by the
Church, shall be paid out of such general fund as may be
provided to pay the expenses of the General Conference or

from such fund or funds as may be designated by the General Conference for the purpose.

A. A. CALLAGHAN, *Chairman;*
W. M. ALEXANDER, *Secretary.*

REPORT NO. 8. FOR CONTINUATION OF BOARD OF EDUCATION

Adopted May 9. See Journal, Page 344.

Membership of Committee, 36; present when report was adopted, 23; voting for adoption, 23.

¶ 1130. The Board of Education of The Methodist Church shall assume the functions, duties, and responsibilities of the Board of Education of the Methodist Episcopal Church incorporated under the laws of the state of New York; the Board of Sunday Schools of the Methodist Episcopal Church incorporated under the laws of the state of Illinois; the Board of Education for Negroes of the Methodist Episcopal Church incorporated under the laws of the state of Ohio; the Epworth League of the Methodist Episcopal Church incorporated under the laws of the state of Illinois; the Board of Christian Education of the Methodist Episcopal Church, South, incorporated under the laws of the state of Tennessee, and the Board of Education of the Methodist Protestant Church incorporated under the laws of the state of Pennsylvania.

The existence of the above named corporations or any other corporations through which any part of the educational work, of the former Churches, now united in The Methodist Church, is administered shall be continued in conformity with their respective charters and applicable state laws, in order adequately to safeguard annuity, permanent, and other trust funds and property, and to protect the interest of those persons and causes for which said funds exist or may have been established, until the General Conference shall direct the surrender of the respective charters of said corporations.

Said corporations shall transfer to the Board of Education of The Methodist Church their assets upon the organization of the said corporation under such provisions and terms as the General Conference of The Methodist Church shall provide in accordance with the provisions of ¶ 1013 of the Prospectus.

¶ 1131. During the period between the time of the Uniting Conference and the time when the General Conference may otherwise order, pending the organization of the Board of Education of The Methodist Church, the work of Chris-

tian Education of The Methodist Church shall be administered as follows: (1) The work of Christian Education now
being administered by the Board of Education of the Methodist Episcopal Church shall be administered by the present
Board of Education of that Church. The terms of office
of the present members of this Board and the terms of office of the officers thereof, elected by the General Conference of the Methodist Episcopal Church, shall continue until
their successors shall have been elected under the provisions adopted by the General Conference of The Methodist
Church. (2) The work of Christian Education now being
administered by the General Board of Christian Education
of the Methodist Episcopal Church, South, shall be administered by the present General Board of Christian Education
of that Church. The terms of office of the present members of this Board, and the terms of office of the officers
thereof elected by the General Conference of the Methodist
Episcopal Church, South, shall continue until their successors shall have been elected under provisions adopted
by the General Conference of The Methodist Church. (3)
The work of Christian Education now being administered by
the Board of Education of the Methodist Protestant Church
shall be administered by the present Board of Education of
that Church. The terms of office of the present members of
this Board and the terms of officers of that Board elected by
the General Conference of the Methodist Protestant Church
shall continue until their successors shall have been elected
by the General Conference of The Methodist Church.

¶ 1132. In order to secure co-operation among the three
Boards, and in order to administer the total work of Christian education under their care including affiliated editorial
work, and in order to suggest any further steps for the
merger and administration of Christian Education in The
Methodist Church, there shall be a Joint Committee on
Christian Education composed of five members representing the Board of Education of the Methodist Episcopal
Church, five representing the General Board of Christian
Education of the Methodist Episcopal Church, South, two
representing the Board of Education of the Methodist Protestant Church selected by their respective Boards, and the
Presidents of these three Boards and the Executive Sec-
retaries of the three Boards.

It is recognized that the Conferences of the Methodist
Protestant Church will be merged with other Conferences
at an early date, thus merging the sources of revenue of
the Board of the Methodist Protestant Church. It shall
be the duty of this Joint Committee to arrange for the carry-

ing on of the work of said Board by supplementing the funds of said Board or by division of its work among the other two Boards, due regard being given to the staff personnel of the present Board of Education of the Methodist Protestant Church. A. A. CALLAGHAN, *Chairman;*
W. M. ALEXANDER, *Secretary.*

REPORT NO. 9. AD INTERIM ADMINISTRATION OF BOARD OF MISSIONS AND CHURCH EXTENSION

Adopted May 9. See Journal, Page 344.

Membership of Committee, 36; present when report was adopted, 27; voting for adoption, 27.

¶ 891. The work of the Board of Missions and Church Extension shall be administered through eleven corporate bodies: The Board of Home Missions and Church Extension of the Methodist Episcopal Church operating under a Charter of the state of Pennsylvania; the Board of Foreign Missions of the Methodist Episcopal Church operating under a Charter of the state of New York; The Board of Church Extension of the Methodist Episcopal Church, South, operating under a Charter of the state of Kentucky; The Woman's Foreign Missionary Society of the Methodist Episcopal Church, operating under a Charter of the state of New York; the Woman's Home Missionary Society of the Methodist Episcopal Church, operating under a Charter of the state of Ohio; the Board of Missions of the Methodist Episcopal Church, South, operating under a Charter of the state of Tennessee; the Woman's Board of Foreign Missions of the Methodist Episcopal Church, South, operating under a Charter of the state of Tennessee; the Woman's Board of Home Missions of the Methodist Episcopal Church, South, operating under a Charter of the state of Mississippi; the Board of Missions of the Methodist Protestant Church, operating under a Charter of the state of Pennsylvania; and the Board of Hospitals, Homes, and Deaconess Work of the Methodist Episcopal Church, operating under a Charter of the state of Illinois. The Trust, Permanent, Endowment, and Annuity Funds and Properties now held and administered for specific purposes under the Charters of these Corporations shall be safeguarded, controlled, and administered by them in the "interests of those persons and causes for which these funds were established."

¶ 892. During the period between the time of the Uniting Conference and the time when the Board shall be constituted according to the Plan of Union and begin to assume its functions, the work of the Board of Missions and Church Extension of The Methodist Church shall be administered as follows:

The Missionary and Church Extension Work now being administered by the Boards enumerated in ¶ 891 shall be administered by the respective organizations now in existence. The terms of office of the present officers and members of these boards shall continue until their successors shall have been elected by the Jurisdictional Conferences and until the new Board of Missions and Church Extension shall be assembled and duly organized.

¶ 893. In order to secure co-operation between the Boards, and in order to assist in administering the total program under their care, and in order to suggest any further steps for the merger and administration of the Board of Missions and Church Extension of The Methodist Church, there shall be a Joint Committee composed of five representatives of the Woman's Foreign Missionary Society of the Methodist Episcopal Church; five representatives of the Home Missionary Society of the Methodist Episcopal Church; five representatives of the Board of Foreign Missions of the Methodist Episcopal Church; six representatives of the Board of Home Missions and Church Extension of the Methodist Episcopal Church: and three representatives of the Board of Hospitals, Homes, and Deaconess Work of the Methodist Episcopal Church; six representatives of the Board of Missions of the Methodist Protestant Church; six representatives of the Board of Church Extension of the Methodist Episcopal Church, South; eighteen representatives of the Board of Missions of the Methodist Episcopal Church, South.

This Committee shall be called together by the President of the first-named organization, at such time and in such place as shall be decided upon by the majority of the Presidents of the organizations named.

¶ 894. The Constitutions of the Boards mentioned in ¶ 891, adopted by the respective General Conferences of the three Churches shall remain as the Constitution of the eleven corporations until the General Conference shall order otherwise. A. A. CALLAGHAN, *Chairman;*
W. M. ALEXANDER, *Secretary.*

REPORT NO. 10. CONTINUATION OF MEN'S WORK COM-
MISSION OF METHODIST EPISCOPAL CHURCH

Adopted May 9. See Journal, Page 345.

Membership of Committee, 36; present when report
was adopted, 19; voting for adoption, 19.

During the period between the adjournment of the Uniting Conference and the time when the General Conference
may order otherwise, the Men's Work Commission of the
Methodist Episcopal Church shall continue to discharge its
duties under the authorization of the Board of Education,
under provisions of the *Discipline* of 1936 of the Methodist
Episcopal Church.

The Men's Work Commission shall continue to receive
financial support from the Board of Education.

The terms of office of the members of the Men's Work
Commission shall continue until their successors, as members of the General Board of Lay Activities, shall have been
elected.

The Men's Work Commission shall co-operate with the
General Board of Lay Activities of the Methodist Episcopal Church, South, in preparing the way for a unified
work under the General Board of Lay Activities that is to
be organized. To this end arrangements shall be made
for the election of Conference and District Lay Leaders
in the Conferences that meet prior to the General Conference of 1940.

A. A. CALLAGHAN, *Chairman;*
W. M. ALEXANDER, *Secretary.*

REPORT NO. 11. FOR CONTINUATION OF GENERAL CONFER-
ENCE COMMISSION ON WORLD PEACE

Adopted May 9. See Journal, Page 345.

Membership of Committee, 36; present when report
was adopted, 24; voting for adoption, 24.

Pending the meeting of the first General Conference of
The Methodist Church, the General Conference Commission
on World Peace shall be authorized to continue the functions
and activities described under ¶ 1464 of the *Discipline* of
the Methodist Episcopal Church. As at present, the financial support shall be provided by the World Service Commission or its successor in The Methodist Church.

A. A. CALLAGHAN, *Chairman;*
W. M. ALEXANDER, *Secretary.*

REPORT NO. 12.   FOR THE BOARD OF TEMPERANCE

Adopted May 9.   See Journal, Page 345.

Membership of Committee, 36; present when report was adopted, 26; voting for adoption, 26.

Pending the election and organization of the Board of Managers of the Board of Temperance as provided by the Uniting Conference, the Board of Temperance of the Methodist Episcopal Church shall be continued and discharge the duties herein committed to the Board of Temperance of The Methodist Church, and by the *Discipline* of the Methodist Episcopal Church.

A. A. CALLAGHAN, *Chairman;*
W. M. ALEXANDER, *Secretary.*

REPORT NO. 13.   FOR BOARD OF LAY ACTIVITIES OF

METHODIST EPISCOPAL CHURCH, SOUTH

Adopted May 10.   See Journal, Page 384.

Membership of Committee, 36; present when report was adopted, 22; voting for adoption, 22.

That until the convening of the General Conference of The Methodist Church to be held in 1940, and until the General and other Boards of Lay Activities of The Methodist Church are properly constituted and organized, the Boards of Lay Activities of the Methodist Episcopal Church, South, as now organized, shall continue to operate, have and perform all rights, functions, and duties as outlined and provided in the 1938 *Discipline* of the Methodist Episcopal Church, South, and shall receive from the Church the support as now set out in said *Discipline.*

That during the said period, the General Board of Lay Activities shall co-operate with the Men's Work Commission of the Methodist Episcopal Church and any lay organizations of the Methodist Protestant Church in preparing a way for the unified work of the Boards of Lay Activities of The Methodist Church to be organized and set up in The Methodist Church.

A. A. CALLAGHAN, *Chairman;*
W. M. ALEXANDER, *Secretary.*

REPORT NO. 14.   AD INTERIM ADMINISTRATION OF GENERAL
COMMISSION ON EVANGELISM

Adopted May 10.   See Journal, Page 384.

Membership of Committee, 36; present when report was adopted, 19; voting for adoption, 19.

The Methodist Church   813

The work of the General Commission on Evangelism shall be administered through the General Commission on Evangelism of the Methodist Episcopal Church and the Department of Evangelism and General Commission of Evangelism of the Board of Missions of the Methodist Episcopal Church, South, operating under a Charter of the state of Tennessee.

The terms of office of the present officers and members of these Commissions shall continue until their successors shall have been elected as directed by the Uniting Conference, and until the new Commission has been assembled and organized.

A. A. CALLAGHAN, *Chairman;*
W. M. ALEXANDER, *Secretary.*

REPORT No. 15. AD INTERIM PLANS FOR ADMINISTRATION OF HOSPITALS, HOMES, AND DEACONESS WORK

Adopted May 10. See Journal, Page 384.

Membership of Committee, 36; present when report was adopted, 20; voting for adoption, 20.

Pending the meeting of the General Conference of 1940, the Constitution of the Board of Hospitals, Homes, and Deaconess Work of the Methodist Episcopal Church, and the Board of Missions of the Methodist Episcopal Church, South, and the Woman's Home Missionary Society of the Methodist Episcopal Church, adopted by the respective General Conferences, shall remain as the Constitutions of these three Corporations administering the funds held by them under their respective Charters. All administrative responsibility shall remain as now prescribed in the *Discipline* of the respective Churches.

A. A. CALLAGHAN, *Chairman;*
W. M. ALEXANDER, *Secretary.*

REPORT No. 16. CONCERNING STATUS OF SOUTHERN METHODIST UNIVERSITY

Adopted May 10. See Journal, Page 384.

Membership of Committee, 36; present when report was adopted, 21; voting for adoption, 21.

WHEREAS, the approved Plan of Union (Section I, Article V) authorizes and requires the several Jurisdictional Conferences there set up to promote and provide for all interests and institutions within their boundaries; and

WHEREAS, such Plan of Union further directs this Uniting Conference (Section V, Article IV) "to provide a plan for the control and safeguarding of all permanent funds and other property interests of the three Churches"; and

WHEREAS, it now appears that the Southern Methodist University of Dallas, Texas, a Corporation chartered by the State of Texas, falls within the boundaries of the South Central Jurisdictional Conference of the new Methodist Church; and

WHEREAS, it further appears that in order to provide properly for the control of such institution and to safeguard its properties and interests and enable the Board of Trustees of such University, constituting as it does the directorate of aforesaid Texas Corporation to function properly and legally, it is now necessary and expedient that this Uniting Conference, acting under the authority so conferred, shall transfer to such Jurisdictional Conferences all rights, titles, and interests in and to the said Southern Methodist University, its properties, control, and management, heretofore vested in the General Conference of the Methodist Episcopal Church, South, and in certain of its Annual Conferences, agencies, and institutions; and

WHEREAS, it also appears that the Charter of Southern Methodist University authorized the General Conference of the Methodist Episcopal Church, South, to transfer the control and ownership of the University to such Jurisdictional Conference:

NOW, THEREFORE, it is ordered that all rights, titles, and interests in and to Southern Methodist University, its properties, franchises, control, management and maintenance, heretofore vested in the General Conference of the Methodist Episcopal Church, South, and in certain of its Annual Conferences, agencies and institutions shall be, and all such are here and now, transferred to and vested in the South Central Jurisdictional Conference of The Methodist Church, together with all privileges, functions, powers, discretions and authority incident or appertaining thereto as fully as this Uniting Conference has the right and power to transfer the same.   A. A. CALLAGHAN, *Chairman;*
W. M. ALEXANDER, *Secretary.*

REPORT NO. 17.   CONCERNING CONFERENCE BOUNDARIES
Adopted May 10. See Journal, Page 385.

Membership of Committee, 36; present when report was adopted, 20; voting for adoption, 20.

The Central Northwest (Swedish) Conference is permitted to retain its present boundaries until April 1, 1940.
A. A. CALLAGHAN, *Chairman;*
W. M. ALEXANDER, *Secretary.*

REPORT No. 18. CONCERNING CONFERENCE BOUNDARIES

Adopted May 10. See Journal, Page 385.

Membership of Committee, 36; present when report was adopted, 20; voting for adoption, 20.

The Norwegian-Danish Conference is granted permission to retain its present boundaries until April 1, 1940.

A. A. CALLAGHAN, *Chairman;*
W. M. ALEXANDER, *Secretary.*

REPORT No. 19. CONCERNING ELECTION OF LAY DELEGATES

Adopted May 10. See Journal, Page 385.

Membership of Committee, 36; present when report was adopted, 19; voting for adoption, 19.

The undersigned Subcommittee of the Committee on Enabling Acts and Legal Forms report as follows:

1. Article 1, Section VII of the Plan of Union requires each Lay Delegate to an Annual Conference to be elected "by each pastoral charge," and, therefore, Delegates to the successor Annual Conferences of The Methodist Church must be elected in this manner.

2. Lay Delegates to the Annual Conferences of the three Uniting Churches could be elected only in accordance with the Disciplinary requirements of the respective Churches electing such delegates, and only such delegates would be qualified to participate in closing up the business of such Annual Conferences in an orderly manner, prior to the organization of the successor Conferences, as provided by the Uniting Conference.

3. While the same persons may be elected both to the old Annual Conferences and to the new successor Annual Conferences of The Methodist Church, yet the different methods of election prescribed by the former *Disciplines* of the three Uniting Churches, respectively, and the method prescribed by the Plan of Union must be observed in order to have legally constituted Annual Conferences under the old and new regime.

Therefore, elections must be held in every Charge in accordance with the provisions of the new *Discipline* to qualify Lay Delegates to sit in the new successor Annual Conferences.

NATHAN NEWBY,
A. W. MARTIN,
HENRY GILLIGAN,
HOWARD C. BALDWIN,
GEORGE H. LAMAR,
Subcommittee.

We recommend that the foregoing conclusions be published in the *Daily Advocate,* and be widely published in the Church Press, and also in the Appendix to the new *Discipline,* for the purpose of giving advice that will aid in avoiding electing delegates to Annual Conferences in an illegal manner.

A. A. CALLAGHAN, Chairman;
W. M. ALEXANDER, Secretary.

REPORT NO. 20.   CONCERNING ADEQUACY OF ¶¶ 135, 136, 137
     ON PAGE 257 OF DAILY CHRISTIAN ADVOCATE

Adopted May 10. See Journal, Page 385.

Membership of Committee, 36; present when report was adopted, 19; voting for adoption, 19.

¶¶ 135, 136, 137, appearing on page 257 of the *Daily Christian Advocate,* are within the power of the Uniting Conference and are in proper form; *provided,* however, we desire to suggest, that trust funds may not be divided or transferred to other purposes than for the specific objects for which donated, even with the consent of Annual Conferences or Jurisdictional Conferences, unless the said Conferences are the beneficiaries of said trust funds, or control the same.   A. A. CALLAGHAN, *Chairman;*

W. M. ALEXANDER, Secretary.

REPORT NO. 21.   CONCERNING ANNUAL CONFERENCE
SESSIONS

Adopted May 10. See Journal, Page 385.

Membership of Committee, 36; present when report was adopted, 19; voting for adoption, 19.

Pending the meeting of the General Conference of 1940 and for the purpose of serving the convenience of the existing Annual and Lay Conferences as well as that of the new Annual and Lay Conferences throughout the six Jurisdictional Areas provided for in the Plan of Union and for the purpose of saving expenses incident to the holding of the final meetings of the existing Conferences and the holding of the first meetings of the new Conferences established by the action of this Uniting Conference, said existing Conferences and the new Conferences provided for by this Conference are hereby authorized, if they ˙deem it necessary for the aforementioned purposes, to hold said final and first sessions beyond the boundaries of the Conferences involved; *provided,* however, that said meetings shall be held within the Jurisdictional Area of said Conferences.

A. A. CALLAGHAN, *Chairman;*
W. M. ALEXANDER, *Secretary.*

II. COMMITTEE ON JUDICIARY

REPORT NO. 1. WYOMING CONFERENCE

Adopted May 5. See Journal, Page 265.

Membership of Committee, 18; present when report was adopted, 13; voting for adoption, 13.

The Committee on the Judiciary, to which has been referred a memorial containing two questions concerning the Wyoming State Conference which at present is composed of less than fifty members and whose boundaries require no adjustment because of the Plan of Union, reports as follows:

"The memorial cites Section IV, Article 5, Paragraph 4 of the Plan of Union concerning the powers of Jurisdictional Conferences, which reads as follows: 'To determine the boundaries of their Annual Conferences, provided that there shall be no Annual Conference with a membership of fewer than fifty ministers in full connection, except by the consent of the General Conference.'"

The first question is: "Is the Uniting Conference or the coming General Conference the consenting body to the Wyoming State Conference memorial?"

We answer: The General Conference is the body which must consent to the existence of an Annual Conference of fewer than fifty members.

The second question is: "If the General Conference is the consenting body, is an enabling act by the Uniting Conference necessary to legalize the status of the Wyoming State Conference until action by the General Conference?"

We answer: No.

The Committee on the Judiciary finds in the Plan of Union no intention or authority to destroy an Annual Conference unless the operation of Jurisdictional lines or the overlapping of Conference boundaries makes it inevitable.

F. R. BAYLEY, *Chairman;*
FRED HERRIGAL, JR., *Secretary.*

REPORT NO. 2. CONCERNING ELECTION OF MEMBERS OF GENERAL BOARDS

Adopted May 5. See Journal, Page 265.

Membership of Committee, 18; present when report was adopted, 13; voting for adoption, 13.

There has been referred to the Judiciary Committee the request of the Committee on Missions for an interpretation of Paragraph 3, Article V, Section IV of the Plan of Union, which reads as follows:

"Article V. The Jurisdictional Conferences shall have the following powers and duties. . . .

"3· To establish and constitute Jurisdictional Conference Boards as auxiliary to the General Boards of the Church as need may appear, and to choose their representatives on the General Boards in such manner as the General Conference may determine."

The Committee on Missions asks that the Judiciary Committee submit an opinion as to whether this means that "all members of the General Boards shall be elected by the Jurisdictional Conferences, or does it mean that the Boards themselves may elect additional members from the Church at large?"

This really involves two matters: (1) The right of the Jurisdictional Conferences to choose representatives on the General Boards of the Church; (2) whether the General Boards of the Church may be constituted with a membership including others than those chosen by the Jurisdictional Conferences.

First—There seems to be no doubt that the section quoted clearly grants the right to the Jurisdictional Conferences to elect representatives to be chosen in such manner and in such numbers as the General Conference may determine.

Second—It further seems clear that the foregoing section does not mean that the General Boards of the Church must be composed exclusively of members, elected by the Jurisdictions, as that section must be read in conjunction with Paragraph 8, Article IV, of Section I of the Plan of Union, which reads as follows:

"Article IV. The General Conference shall have . . . authority as follows. . . .

"8· To initiate and direct all connectional enterprises of the Church, such as publishing, evangelistic, educational, missionary, and benevolent, and to provide Boards for their promotion and administration."

The words "to provide Boards for their promotion and administration" must include the power and authority to provide for the number, the term of office, the manner of election, and all other matters that are involved in the setting up and organization of all such Boards; and therefore the General Conference may provide for the creation of General Boards of the Church which include members elected by Jurisdictions, and also include, if it so determine, additional members chosen as they may direct.

F. R. BAYLEY, *Chairman;*

FRED HERRIGAL, JR., *Secretary.*

REPORT No. 3. ASSIGNMENT OF BISHOPS

Adopted May 6. See Journal, Page 280.

Membership of Committee, 18; present when report was adopted, 15; voting for adoption, 15.

Your Committee on Judiciary, to which has been referred the question, "Has the Uniting Conference, under the Plan of Union, the authority to assign Bishops to residence within the Jurisdictions?" makes the following report thereon:

It is clear that this Uniting Conference not only has the power, but is directed by the Plan of Union to assign the effective Bishops to the respective Jurisdictions (Art. VI, Division III, Plan of Union).

It is also clear, in our opinion, that under the harmonizing provisions of the Plan of Union, the Uniting Conference does have the power to assign Bishops to definite areas and residences if such a law or regulation is contained in any one of the *Disciplines* of the Churches united.

There is no such provision in the *Discipline* of the Methodist Episcopal Church, South.

There is no such provision in the body of the *Discipline* of the Methodist Episcopal Church. There is such a provision, however, in the Appendix of the *Discipline* of the Methodist Episcopal Church, which, by custom, usage, and judicial decision at least has had all the force and power of law.

The Committee admits that the question of whether or not this provision, occurring only in such Appendix, can be used as the basis of legislation by this body is subject to debate.

In view of these facts and circumstances, we regard the pressing of the question of power to a decision by this body as unwise, especially since the determination thereof would be effective only until the Jurisdictional Conferences meet.

We, therefore, recommend that this Uniting Conference proceed to make a schedule of assignment of the effective Bishops, not only to the respective Jurisdictions, but also to Episcopal residences, and that the Bishops be requested to accept such assignments, subject only to such adjustments and modifications as to the Council of Bishops may seem wise.

F. R. BAYLEY, *Chairman;*
W. G. HENRY, *Secretary.*

REPORT NO. 4.   EDITOR OF CHURCH SCHOOL PUBLICATIONS

Adopted May 8. See Journal, Page 295.

Membership of Committee, 18; present when report was adopted, 15; voting for adoption, 15.

Your Judiciary Committee, to which was referred the question of the legality or constitutionality of Section 1, ¶ 1208 (Page 189, *The Daily Christian Advocate*, Thursday's issue), in which it is provided that the Editor of Church School Publications shall be elected by the Board of Education, submits the following report:

Under the harmonizing provisions of the Plan of Union, the Uniting Conference has the power and authority to bring forward into the new *Discipline* any rule or regulation relating to the method of electing this officer found in any one of the three *Disciplines* to be harmonized. We do not believe, however, that the authority to harmonize the *Disciplines* of the three Churches would authorize the adoption of a method of electing such officer not found in any one of the three *Disciplines*.

Each of the three *Disciplines* provides that the Editor of Church School Publications shall be elected by the General Conference. No provision authorizing that officer to be elected by a Board can be found in any one of the three *Disciplines*.

In our opinion, therefore, this particular section of ¶ 1208 is not authorized by the Plan of Union, and is, therefore, unconstitutional.

F. R. BAYLEY, *Chairman;*
W. G. HENRY, *Secretary.*

REPORT NO. 5.   GENERAL SECRETARY OF BOARD OF LAY
ACTIVITIES

Adopted May 8. See Journal, Page 295.

Membership of Committee, 18; present when report was adopted, 14; voting for adoption, 14.

Your Judiciary Committee, to which was referred the question of the legality or constitutionality of ¶ 604 (Page 221, *The Daily Christian Advocate*, Friday's issue), in which it is provided that the Executive Secretary of the

General Board of Lay Activities shall be elected by the General Board of Lay Activities, submits the following report:

In a preceding Report (No. 4) it was pointed out that under the harmonizing provisions of the Plan of Union, the Uniting Conference does not have the power and authority to provide for the election of a Connectional officer by some method not found in any one of the *Disciplines* of the Uniting Churches.

The *Discipline* of the Methodist Episcopal Church, South, provides that the General (Executive) Secretary of the General Board of Lay Activities shall be elected by the General Conference. There is nothing relating to this subject in either of the other two *Disciplines*.

In our opinion, therefore, the provision in ¶ 604 providing for the election of the Executive Secretary of the General Board of Lay Activities by the General Board of Lay Activities is not authorized by the Plan of Union, and is, therefore, unconstitutional.

REPORT NO. 6. BILINGUAL CONFERENCES

Adopted May 9. See Journal, Page 363.

Membership of Committee, 18; present when report was adopted, 14; voting for adoption, 14.

There has been referred to your Committee on Judiciary the request of the Central Northwest (Swedish) Conference and the Norwegian-Danish Conference that this Uniting Conference pass an enabling act which shall permit them to retain their present boundaries until a date not later than the convening of the first Jurisdictional Conference.

Or, that the Uniting Conference shall authorize the creation of two Bilingual Conferences, one to be called "The Central Northwest Conference" and to include all Swedish-speaking Churches within the North Central Jurisdiction, and the other to be called "The Norwegian-Danish Conference" and to include all of the Norwegian and Danish Churches located within the North Central Jurisdiction, and that the organization of these Conferences shall be effected not later than April 1, 1941.

. Your Committee is of the opinion that this Uniting Conference has the authority to fix the dates at which all existing Conferences shall be dissolved and all successor Conferences shall be established.

F. R. BAYLEY, *Chairman;*
W. G. HENRY, *Secretary.*

REPORT NO 7. USE OF CHURCH NAME IN
FOREIGN COUNTRIES

Adopted May 10. See Journal, Page 363.

Membership of Committee, 18; present when report was adopted, 11; voting for adoption, 11.

Your Judiciary Committee, to which was referred the question as to the legality of permitting the Central Conferences and the Provisional Central Conferences and the Annual Mission Conferences and Missions within their territory to use the name "The Methodist Church" with the word "Episcopal" in parentheses between the words "Methodist" and "Church," submits the following report:

It is the opinion of the Judiciary Committee that the name "The Methodist Church" is the legally adopted name of this Church and must be used as such. Therefore, the proposal made and the resolution before the Conference provides for the use of a name which is not legal. Further, in the opinion of the Committee, all legal requirements can be met by using the name "The Methodist Church" followed by the statement "successor to the Methodist Episcopal Church," or "Methodist Protestant Church," or "Methodist Episcopal Church, South," as the case might be.

F. R. BAYLEY, *Chairman;*
W. G. HENRY, *Secretary.*

REPORT NO. 8. CONCERNING BOUNDARIES IN THE
PANHANDLE

Adopted May 10. See Journal, Page 363.

Membership of Committee, 18; present when report was adopted, 11; voting for adoption, 11.

The Committee on the Judiciary, to which has been referred a question concerning the changing of boundary lines of the Methodist Episcopal Church and the Methodist Episcopal Church, South, involving the Panhandle, which consists of Beaver, Cimarron, and Texas Counties of Oklahoma, reports as follows:

We reply that clearly the delegates of the South Central Jurisdiction were within their rights in adjusting the Conference Boundaries on account of the overlapping of the boundaries of the Conferences of the two Methodisms.

(See ¶ 855 of the *Discipline* of the Methodist Episcopal Church, South.)

(See also ¶ 1377, Section 1, Article 71, M. E. Church.)

Your Committee has nothing to do with the practical wisdom of the action of the delegates of the South Central Jurisdiction in fixing these boundaries.

F. R. BAYLEY, *Chairman;*
W. G. HENRY, *Secretary.*

REPORT NO. 9. CONCERNING BOUNDARIES IN KANSAS

Adopted May 10. See Journal, Page 363.

Membership of Committee, 18; present when report was adopted, 11; voting for adoption, 11.

The Committee on the Judiciary, to which has been referred the memorial asking whether "the delegates of the South Central Jurisdiction were within their rights in changing Conference boundaries in Kansas so as to make two Conferences instead of three, thus merging the Northwest Kansas Conference and the Southwest Kansas Conference and somewhat altering the lines of the Kansas Conferences," reports as follows:

We reply that clearly the delegates of the South Central Jurisdiction were within their rights in adjusting the Conference Boundaries on account of the overlapping of the boundaries of the Conferences of the three Methodisms.

(See ¶¶ 846 and 861 of the *Discipline* of the Methodist Episcopal Church, South, 1938, which indicates that the two Missouri Conferences of that Church include the entire state of Kansas.)

(See also Chapter 6 of the *Discipline* of the Methodist Protestant Church, 1936, paragraph 9, page 132.)

(See also ¶ 1377, Section 1, Article 28, Article 54, Article 71, M. E. Church.)

Your Committee has nothing to do with the practical wisdom of the action of the delegates of the South Central Jurisdiction in fixing these boundaries.

F. R. BAYLEY, *Chairman;*
W. G. HENRY, *Secretary.*

III. COMMITTEE ON RULES

REPORT NO. 1. AMENDMENTS TO RULES ·

Adopted May 2. See Journal, Page 230.

Membership of Committee, 6; present when report was adopted, 5; voting for adoption, 5.

Your Committee on Rules recommends the following amendments to the Rules of Order:

1. That the following be added at the end of Rule 32, page 168 of the *Handbook:* "The right to close the debate shall prevail in like manner, to a limit of five minutes, when a vote is to be taken on a motion to amend, to substitute, to postpone, to refer, to lay on the table, or any other motion whose adoption is vitally related to the report in question"; and also that to Item 3 under Rule 17, page 165 of the *Handbook,* be added these words: "Except as provided in Rule 32"; and further that to Rule 8, page 164 of the *Handbook,* be added these words: "Except as provided in Rule 32."

2. That at the end of Rule 27, page 167 of the *Handbook,* the following words be added: "When a General Standing Committee ascertains that another Committee is or should, in its judgment, be considering a subject which it also is considering it shall proceed to arrange for a conference of representatives from the respective Committees in order to resolve the matter in question. If agreement cannot be reached thereby as to the location of the responsibility, the matter shall be referred to the Committee of Chairmen."

Your Committee on Rules further recommends that the Plan of Organization be amended by adding to the Special Standing Committees (pages 159 to 161 of the *Handbook*) a tenth committee, as follows:

"(10) *Committee of Chairmen.* There shall be a Committee of Chairmen composed of the Chairmen of the General Standing Committees, to which shall be referred any intercommittee disagreement or difficulty. It shall also arrange for the presentation of Committee reports to the Uniting Conference so as to expedite the business of the Conference in accordance with Rule 25."

J. EDGAR SKILLINGTON, *Chairman;*
COSTEN J. HARRELL, *Secretary.*

REPORT NO 2. INTERPRETATION OF PLAN OF ORGANIZATION

Adopted April 29. See Journal, Page 213.

Membership of Committee, 6; present when report was adopted, 6; voting for adoption, 6.

The Uniting Conference on the 28th instant referred to the Committee on Rules for interpretation the following provision in the Plan of Organization:

"All questions, proposals, resolutions, communications, or other matter not included in the regular business of the Uniting Conference as fixed by the Plan of Union shall be referred without debate or motion to the Business Committee, which shall decide whether or not the matter presented shall be considered by the Conference."

Your Committee's interpretation is as follows:

1. A member of the Conference presenting such an item or items as referred to above shall ask for its reference without motion or debate to the Business Committee.

2. If there is no such request, and if in the judgment of the Chair the item or items presented are "not included in the regular business of the Uniting Conference as fixed by the Plan of Union," he shall so rule (see Rule 3, *Handbook*, page 163) and the same shall be automatically referred without debate or motion to the Business Committee, which Committee shall decide whether or not the same shall be presented to the Conference for consideration.

3. It is the judgment of your Committee on Rules that the spirit and purpose of this provision in the Plan of Organization are to protect the Conference from the consideration and publication of irrelevant matter. It is the further judgment of your Committee that it is in keeping with the spirit and purpose of the above-named provision that any such matter shall not be published in *The Daily Advocate* unless and until the same has been approved and presented to the Conference by the Business Committee.

J. EDGAR SKILLINGTON, *Chairman;*
COSTEN J. HARRELL, *Secretary.*

REPORT NO. 3. CONCERNING MINORITY REPORTS

Adopted May 2. See Journal, Page 230.

Membership of Committee, 6; present when report was adopted, 6; voting for adoption, 6.

The Committee on Rules recommends that Rule 29 be amended by adding at the end the following words:

"*Provided*, that in the case of General Standing Committees having less than fifty duly constituted members a minority report signed by at least five members thereof, having been printed in *The Daily Advocate* for at least one day, shall be considered to be in possession of the Conference."   J. EDGAR SKILLINGTON, *Chairman;*
COSTEN J. HARRELL, *Secretary.*

REPORT NO. 4.   CONCERNING OVERHEAD COST

Adopted May 4.   See Journal, Page 252.

Membership of Committee, 6; present when report was adopted, 6; voting for adoption, 6.

Your Committee recommends the adoption of the following rule as Rule 27-A:

Rule 27-A. Each Committee in making any proposal for The Methodist Church which involves finances shall indicate whether or not, in its judgment, the adoption and operation of the same will increase or decrease overhead cost, and, if so, estimate to what amount.

J. EDGAR SKILLINGTON, *Chairman;*
COSTEN J. HARRELL, *Secretary.*

REPORT NO. 5. METHOD OF ADDRESSING THE CHAIR

Adopted May 5.   See Journal, Page 265.

Membership of Committee, 6; present when report was adopted, 4; voting for adoption, 4.

In the matter of a correct and uniform term to be used in addressing the Chair, which matter was referred by the Conference to your Committee on Rules, we recommend:

1. That Rule 6 (*Handbook*, p. 164) be amended to read as follows: "Rule 6. When a delegate desires to speak to the Conference, he shall arise at his assigned seat, respectfully address the Presiding Officer, using the term 'Mr. Chairman' "—the rule to read from this point to the end as written in the *Handbook.*

2. That Rule 3 (*Handbook*, p. 163) be amended by substituting the word "Chairman" for "President" in the second line.   J. EDGAR SKILLINGTON, *Chairman;*
COSTEN J. HARRELL, *Secretary.*

REPORT NO. 6. RECOMMENDING NONCONCURRENCE

Adopted May 5. See Journal, Page 265.

Membership of Committee, 6; present when report was adopted, 4; voting for adoption, 4.

With regard to the proposal that no amendment to a report of one of the eight General Standing Committees shall be in order unless signed by not less than ten members of the Conference, which matter was referred to your Committee on Rules, we respectfully recommend nonconcurrence.

In the judgment of your Committee this proposal, if adopted, would impose unwarranted limitations upon the liberty of the members of the Conference and doubtless prevent the presentation and consideration of important matters. In the interest of economy in time and expense your Committee takes occasion, however, to urge that only such amendments and substitutions be proposed as vitally affect the report under consideration.

J. EDGAR SKILLINGTON, *Chairman;*
COSTEN J. HARRELL, *Secretary.*

REPORT No 7. AMENDMENT TO RULE 31

Adopted May 8. See Journal, Page 293.

Membership of Committee, 6; present when report was adopted, 4; voting for adoption, 4.

Your Committee on Rules respectfully recommends that Rule 31 be amended to read as follows:

"Rule 31. A member selected by the signers of the minority report of a Committee to present the same as a substitute for the majority report, shall have the same rights and privileges in relation thereto which belong to the Chairman in the presentation of the regular (majority) report of the Committee, except the minority report, having been presented as provided in Rule 29, may not be considered until the Report of the Committee has had such consideration as the Conference may wish to give it, and except, further, that in closing debate on the question of making the substitution, the member presenting the minority report shall speak first and the Chairman last."

J. EDGAR SKILLINGTON, *Chairman;*
COSTEN J. HARRELL, *Secretary.*

REPORT NO. 8. METHOD OF ADDRESSING THE CONFERENCE

Adopted May 8. See Journal, Page 294.

Membership of Committee, 6; present when report was adopted, 4; voting for adoption, 4.

In the matter of a proper term to be used in addressing the Conference, which matter was referred to your Committee on Rules, your Committee respectfully recommends that no fixed term be established, but that each member be at liberty to address the body as his mind and heart may dictate.

J. EDGAR SKILLINGTON, *Chairman;*
COSTEN J. HARRELL, *Secretary.*

IV. COMMITTEE ON CREDENTIALS

REPORT NO. 1

Adopted April 28. See Journal, Page 205.

The Committee on Credentials has considered the following changes in seating and recommends that they be approved:

1. W. B. Christenberry, Lay Reserve from Alabama, M. E., S., seated instead of O. L. Tompkins for entire session.

2. Mrs. H. R. Farmer, Lay Reserve from Southwest Missouri, M. E., S., seated in place of Mrs. F. A. Lamb, for April 28 only.

3. Mrs. N. G. Rollins, Lay Reserve from Northwest Texas, M. E., S., seated in place of R. H. Nichols for April 26 only.

4. L. N. Lipscomb, Ministerial Reserve from Northwest Texas, M. E., S., seated in place of O. P. Clark for April 27 only.

5. S. H. Young, Ministerial Reserve from Northwest Texas, M. E., S., seated in place of W. M. Pearce for April 27 only.

6. J. W. Jakes, Lay Reserve from Tennessee, M. E., S., seated in place of W. R. Webb for the entire session.

7. A. T. Walker, Ministerial Reserve from Texas, M. E., S., seated in place of S. S. McKenney.

8. Galloway Calhoun, Lay Delegate from Texas, M. E., S., was seated, replacing no one.

9. R. A. Elkins, Lay Reserve from Memphis, M. E., S., was seated in place of George L. Morelock for entire session.

10. J. L. Cuninggim, Ministerial Reserve from North Carolina, M. E. S., seated in place of T. McM. Grant on April 27.

11. Mrs. N. G. Rollins, Lay Reserve, Northwest Texas, M. E., S., seated in place of R. B. Bryant for April 28.

12. C. L. Daugherty, Ministerial Reserve, M. P., Pittsburgh, was seated in place of Bishop-elect J. C. Broomfield for entire session.

13. R. Y. Nicholson, Ministerial Reserve, Maryland, M. P., seated in place of Bishop-elect J. H. Straughn for entire session.

EARL A. BROWN, *Chairman;*
CHAS. A. ROBBINS, *Secretary.*

REPORT NO. 2

Adopted April 29. See Journal, Page 210.

The Committee on Credentials has considered the following changes in seating and recommends that they be approved:

1. Hamet D. Hinkle, Lay Reserve from Indiana, M. E., was seated in place of T. M. McDonald for the entire session.

2. Mrs. J. P. Brandon, Lay Reserve from St. Louis, M. E., S., was seated for Mrs. Jeptha Riggs for April 29 only.

3. Charles M. Windels, Lay Reserve from East German, M. E., was seated in place of Edwin H. Mueller for the entire session.

4. Will F. Franke, Lay Reserve from Alabama, M. E., was seated in place of A. D. Peck from April 26 to May 3, inclusive.

5. C. L. Daugherty, Ministerial Reserve from Pittsburgh, M. P., was seated in place of J. C. Broomfield on April 28 for the remainder of the session.

6. Robert J. Smith, Ministerial Reserve from Oklahoma, M. E., was seated in place of Phil Deschner for the entire session.

7. Nelson Barnett, Jr., Lay Reserve from North Arkansas, M. E., S., was seated in place of C. G. Melton for the entire session.

8. Sam Galloway, Lay Reserve from North Arkansas, M. E., S., was seated in place of Charles A. Stuck for the entire session.

9. D. F. Armistead, Lay Reserve from North Texas, M. E., S., was seated in place of Marvin F. Love for April 28 only.

10. W. D. Gleaton, Ministerial Reserve from South Caro-

lina, M. E., S., was seated in place of Peter Stokes, deceased, for the entire session.

11. T. H. Guerry, Lay Reserve from South Georgia, M. E., S., was seated in place of W. T. Anderson for the entire session.

12. Jesse M. Beck, Lay Reserve from Iowa-Des Moines, M. E., was seated in place of James H. Peterman for the entire session.

13. H. B. McKibbin, Lay Reserve from Southwest Kansas, M. E., was seated in place of L. W. Mayberry for the entire session.

14. Edmund R. Alderson, Lay Reserve from Rock River, M. E., was seated in place of Jacob Cantlin on April 26.

15. William T. Jones, Ministerial Reserve from Indiana, M. E., was seated in place of John M. Walker for the entire session.

16. Jacob S. Payton, Ministerial Reserve at Large from Pittsburgh, M. E., was seated in place of Ralph Diffendorfer from Rock River, M. E., for April 28 only.

17. W. A. Longnecker, Ministerial Reserve from Iowa-Des Moines, M. E., was seated in place of A. H. Barker for April 26 and 27 only.

18. A. T. Walker, Ministerial Reserve from Texas, M. E., S., was seated in place of S. S. McKenney for April 26 only.

19. J. W. Jakes, Lay Reserve from Tennessee, M. E., S., was seated in place of W. R. Webb for April 27 only.

20. J. Bruce McCullough, Lay Reserve at Large from New England Southern M. E., will be seated in place of Robert F. Wagner, from New York, on May 1, for the remainder of the session.

21. Earl Huffor, Lay Reserve from Texas, M. E., S., was seated in place of W. W. Fondren, deceased, for the entire session.

22. Galloway Calhoun, Lay Delegate from Texas, M. E., S., resumes his seat on April 27.

23. R. B. Bryant, Lay Delegate from Northwest Texas, M. E., S., resumed his seat on April 29.

EARL R. BROWN, *Chairman;*
CHAS. A. ROBBINS, *Secretary.*

REPORT No. 3

Adopted May 1.   See Journal, Page 221.

The Committee on Credentials has considered the following changes in seating and recommends that they be approved:

1. Harry N. Van Antwerp, Lay Reserve from Troy, was

seated in place of Victor K. Moore on April 30 for the remainder of the session.

2. J. C. Curry, Ministerial Reserve from Oklahoma, M. E., S., was seated in place of Robert S. Satterfield for April 29 only.

3. Mrs. G. W. Hummel, Lay Reserve from Louisville, M. E., S., was seated in place of W. L. Cash for April 29 only.

4. W. P. Davis, Ministerial Reserve from Kentucky, M. E., S., was seated in place of A. R. Perkins on April 29.

5. E. M. Stanton, Ministerial Reserve from Texas, M. E., S., was seated in place of Joe Z. Tower on April 29.

6. John V. Berglund, Ministerial Reserve from Texas, M. E., S., was seated in place of Guy H. Wilson on April 29.

7. E. W. Savage, Lay Reserve from Kentucky, M. E., S., was seated in place of Mrs. J. H. Spilman for the entire session.

8. Mrs. J. L. McCoy, Lay Reserve from Kansas, M. E., was seated in place of T. O. Cunningham on May 1 for the remainder of the session.

9. Mrs. Arthur Heutess, Lay Reserve from Alabama, M. P., was seated in place of J. J. Goddard for the entire session.

10. W. Dale Clark, Lay Delegate at Large, Nebraska, M. E., was excused for April 27, 28, and 29.

11. L. D. Dickinson, Lay Delegate from Michigan, M. E., was excused after April 30 for the remainder of the session.

12. Mrs. F. A. Lamb, Lay Delegate from Southwest Missouri, M. E., S., resumed her seat April 29.

13. Mrs. Mary M. Bethune, Lay Delegate at Large, South Florida, M. E., was seated on April 28.

14. Phil Deschner, Ministerial Delegate from Oklahoma, M. E., S., resumed his seat on April 29.

15. Herman Will, Jr., Lay Reserve at Large, Colorado, M. E., was seated in place of Miss Harriet Lewis for April 26, 27, and 28.

16. Miss Harriet Lewis, Lay Delegate at Large, Colorado, M. E., was seated for April 29 and 30, and May 1 and 2.

17. Herman Will, Jr., Lay Reserve at Large, Colorado, M. E., was seated in place of Miss Harriet Lewis May 3 for the remainder of the session.

18. The report of the Committee for April 29 incompletely reported the name: J. M. Beck. The correct name is: Jesse M. Beck.

EARL R. BROWN, *Chairman;*
CHAS. A. ROBBINS, *Secretary.*

REPORT NO. 4
Adopted May 2.   See Journal, Page 230.

The Committee on Credentials has considered the following changes in seating and recommends that they be approved:

1. A. R. Mansberger, Ministerial Reserve, Pittsburgh, M. P., was seated in place of J. W. Hawley on May 1 until further notice.

2. Frank M. Bailey, Lay Reserve, Oklahoma, M. E., S., was seated in place of S. S. Orwig for May 1 only.

3. Mrs. J. L. McCoy, Lay Reserve, Kansas, M. E., was seated in place of J. C. Gaede for May 2.

4. W. L. Cash, Lay Delegate, Louisville, M. E., S., resumed his seat on May 1.

5. J. W. Weldon, Ministerial Reserve, Louisville, M. E., S., was seated in place of G. W. Hummel for May 1 only.

6. Mrs. N. G. Rollins, Lay Reserve, Northwest Texas, M. E., S., was seated in place of R. H. Nichols on May 2 until further notice.

7. Mrs. L. W. Stewart, Lay Reserve, Michigan, M. E., was seated in place of Lauren Dickinson on May 1 for the remainder of session.

8. Mrs. E. C. Chinn, Lay Reserve, Texas, M. E., S., was seated in place of H. W. Stilwell on May 1 until further notice.

9. E. W. Savage, Lay Reserve, Kentucky, M. E., S., was excused after May 1 for the remainder of the session.

10. A. R. Mansberger Ministerial Reserve, Pittsburgh, M. P., was seated in place of J. W. Hawley for May 1 to 9, inclusive.

11. Fred L. Frazier, Ministerial Reserve, South Carolina, M. P., was excused after May 1 for the remainder of the session.

12. D. H. Davis, Lay Delegate, South Carolina, M. P., was excused after May 1 for the remainder of the session.

13. A. R. Perkins, Ministerial Delegate, Kentucky, M. E., S., resumed his seat on May 1.

14. W. R. Lott, Ministerial Reserve, North Mississippi, M. E., S., was seated in place of L. P. Wasson for April 30 only.

15. J. E. Stephens, Ministerial Reserve, North Mississippi, M. E., S., was seated in place of J. D. Wroten for April 30 only.

16. Thomas McM. Grant, Ministerial Delegate, North Carolina, M. E., S., resumed his seat on April 28.

17. Nelson Barnett, Jr., Lay Reserve, North Arkansas, M. E., S., was seated in place of C. G. Melton on May 1.

18. Mrs. W. H. Ratliff, Lay Reserve, North Mississippi, M. E., S., was seated in place of J. W. Kyle on May 1.

19. W. A. Myres, Ministerial Reserve, Florida, M. E., S., was seated in place of M. H. Norton on May 1.

20. C. B. Peeler, Lay Reserve, Florida, M. E., S., was seated in place of Harwell Wilson, deceased, on May 1.

21. W. D. Gleaton, Ministerial Reserve, South Carolina, M. E., S., was seated in place of Peter Stokes, deceased, on May 1.

22. S. M. Black, Ministerial Reserve, North Texas, M. E., S., was seated in place of H. G. Ryan for May 1 only.

23. W. D. Graves, Lay Delegate, North Alabama, M. E., S., was excused after April 29 for the remainder of the session.

24. J. W. Pearson, Ministerial Delegate, Virginia, M. E., S., was seated on May 1, no one being in his place.

EARL R. BROWN, *Chairman;*
CHAS. A. ROBBINS, *Secretary.*

REPORT NO. 5

Adopted May 3. See Journal, Page 244.

The Committee on Credentials has considered the following changes in seating and recommends that they be approved:

1. George Pohlman, Lay Reserve, Missouri, M. E., S., was seated in place of P. M. Marr for May 2.

2. N. H. Melbert, Ministerial Reserve, Texas, M. E., S., was seated in place of W. R. Swain for May 2.

3. W. P. Davis, Ministerial Reserve, Kentucky, M. E., S., was seated in place of A. R. Perkins for May 2.

4. H. W. Whitaker, Ministerial Reserve, Kentucky, M. E., S., was seated in place of O. B. Crockett for May 2.

5. R. A. Elkins, Lay Reserve, Memphis, M. E., S., was seated in place of Henry Hedden on May 2.

6. G. L. Morelock, Lay Delegate, Memphis, M. E., S., resumed his seat on May 2.

7. R. S. Jett, Lay Reserve, Maryland, M. P., was seated on May 2 in place of H. C. Staley for the remainder of the session.

8. J. W. Weldon, Ministerial Reserve, Louisville, M. E., S., was seated in place of J. H. Nicholson for May 2.

9. R. Gibbs Mood, Ministerial Reserve, North Texas, M. E., S., was seated in place of Harry G. Ryan for May 2.

10. Paul M. Hillman, Ministerial Reserve, Nebraska, M. E., was seated in place of Harry E. Hess on May 2 for the remainder of the session.

11. Ernest F. Harold, Ministerial Reserve, Pacific Northwest, M. E., was seated in place of C. K. Mahoney for May 6 only.

12. Lloyd E. Foster, Ministerial Delegate, Newark, M. E., resumed his seat on May 1.

13. J. W. Pearson, Ministerial Delegate, Virginia, M. E., S., was seated on April 27.

14. T. O. Cunningham, Lay Delegate, Kansas, M. E., resumed his seat on May 2.

15. Ralph W. Sockman, Ministerial Delegate, New York, M. E., was seated on May 2 for the remainder of the session.

16. Lee M. McCoy, Ministerial Delegate, Upper Mississippi, M. E., was excused for May 2 and 3 only.

17. Joe Z. Tower, Ministerial Delegate, Texas, M. E., S., resumed his seat on May 1.

18. Guy H. Wilson, Ministerial Delegate, Texas, M. E., S., resumed his seat on May 1.

10. G. W. Hummel, Ministerial Delegate, Louisville, M. E., S., resumed his seat on May 2.

20. J. W. Kyle, Lay Reserve, North Mississippi, M. E., S., resumed his seat on May 2.

21. R. S. Jett, Lay Delegate, Maryland, M. P., resumed his seat on May 2.

22. Mrs. W. H. Ratliff, Lay Reserve, North Mississippi, M. E., S., was seated in place of J. W. Kyle for April 26 to May 1, inclusive.

EARL R. BROWN, *Chairman;*
CHAS. A. ROBBINS, *Secretary.*

REPORT NO. 6

Adopted May 4.   See Journal, Page 252.

The Committee on Credentials has considered the following changes in seating and recommends that they be approved:

1. Mrs. J. P. Brandon, Lay Reserve, St. Louis, M. E., S., was seated in place of W. W. Parker on May 3 for the remainder of the session.

2. Miss Grace L. Stockwell, Lay Reserve at Large, India, was seated in place of Mrs. Premnath Das on May 3 for the remainder of the session.

3. Neal D. Cannon, Ministerial Reserve, Texas, M. E., S., was seated in place of Guy H. Wilson for May 3 only.

4. M. M. Eakes, Lay Reserve, Oklahoma, M. E., S., was seated in place of M. A. Beeson on May 3 for the remainder of the session.

5. George Pohlman, Lay Reserve, Missouri, M. E., S., was seated in place of P. M. Marr for May 3 only.

6. W. H. Wiseman, Lay Reserve, Tennessee, M. E., S., was seated in place of W. O. Batts on May 3 for the remainder of the session.

7. Samuel H. Clark, Lay Delegate, Newark, M. E., resumed his seat on May 3.

8. R. W. Swain, Ministerial Delegate, Texas, M. E., S., resumed his seat on May 3.

9. Paul R. Hortin, Ministerial Reserve, Saint Johns River, M. E., was seated in place of Glenn C. James for May 6 only.

10. J. H. Nicholson, Ministerial Delegate, Louisville, M. E., S., resumed his seat on May 3.

11. A. R. Perkins, Ministerial Delegate, Kentucky, M. E., S., resumed his seat on May 3.

12. O. B. Crockett, Ministerial Delegate, Kentucky, M. E., S., resumed his seat on May 3.

13. Correcting Report No. 5, item 7, Robert S. Jett, Maryland, M. P., was seated on May 1 instead of May 2.

14. Correcting Report No. 4, item 20, C. B. Peeler, Florida, M. E., S., was seated on April 26 instead of May 1.

15. Correcting Report No. 4, item 19, W. A. Myres, Florida, M. E., S., was seated on April 26 instead of May 1.

EARL R. BROWN, *Chairman;*
CHAS. A. ROBBINS, *Secretary.*

REPORT NO. 7

Adopted May 5. See Journal, Page 264.

The Committee on Credentials has considered the following changes in seating and recommends that they be approved:

1. D. F. Armistead, Lay Reserve, North Texas, M. E., S., was seated in place of Mrs. T. H. Minga for May 3 only.

2. Manville Carothers, Lay Reserve, Missouri, M. E., was seated in place of Charles W. Hanke for May 4 to 8, inclusive.

3. Mrs. S. L. Batchelor, Lay Reserve, West Texas, M. E., S., was seated in place of Morris H. Brooks on May 4 for the remainder of the session.

4. Robert Gibbs Mood, Ministerial Reserve, North Texas, M. E., S., was seated in place of George C. French for May 4 only.

5. M. M. Maxwell, Ministerial Reserve, North Georgia, M. E., S., was seated in place of William P. King for May 5 only.

6. S. L. Batchelor, Ministerial Reserve, West Texas, M. E., S., was seated in place of J. Fisher Simpson for May 5 only.

7. John W. Hawley, Ministerial Delegate, Pittsburgh, M. P., resumed his seat on May 5.

8. Harriett D. Lewis, Lay Delegate at Large, Colorado, M. E., resumed her seat for May 3, 4, 5, and 6 only.

9. Herman Will, Jr., Lay Reserve at Large, Colorado, M. E., was seated in place of Harriet D. Lewis on May 7 for the remainder of the session, correcting Report No. 3, Item 16.

EARL R. BROWN, *Chairman;*
CHAS. A. ROBBINS, *Secretary.*

REPORT No. 8

Adopted May 6.   See Journal, Page 277.

The Committee on Credentials has considered the following changes in seating and recommends that they be approved:

1. Foster K. Gamble, Ministerial Reserve, North Alabama, M. E., S., was seated in place of M. M. Davidson for May 5 only.

2. A. W. Wasson, Ministerial Reserve, North Arkansas, M. E., S., resumed his seat on May 6.
for remainder of the session.

3. A. W. Martin, Ministerial Delegate, North Arkansas, M. E., S., was seated in place of O. E. Goddard on May 6.

4. Hubert Searcy, Lay Reserve, Alabama, M. E., S., was seated in place of W. B. Christenberry for May 8, 9, and 10.

5. Jacob S. Payton, Lay Reserve at Large, Pittsburgh, M. E., was seated in place of Henry H. Crane, Detroit, for May 6, 7, and 8.

6. Mrs. J. B. Pollard, Lay Reserve, Louisiana, M. E., S., was seated in place of T. L. James on May 5 for remainder of session.

7. M. M. Eakes, Lay Reserve, Oklahoma, M. E., S., was seated in place of M. A. Beeson on May 4 for remainder of session.

8. John W. Showalter, Lay Reserve, Southwest Missouri, M. E., S., was seated in place of Mrs. Fred A. Lamb for May 6 only.

9. M. M. Maxwell, Ministerial Reserve, North Georgia,

M. E., S., was seated in place of William P. King for May 5 only.

10. W. P. King, Ministerial Delegate, North Georgia, M. E., S., resumed his seat May 6.

11. Paul R. Hortin, Ministerial Reserve, Saint Johns River, M. E., was seated in place of Glenn C. James for May 6 only.

12. G. S. Strader, Lay Reserve, Holston, M. E., S., was seated in place of W. K. Barnett on May 6 for remainder of session.

13. Joseph S. Ulland, Lay Reserve, Northern Minnesota, M. E., was seated in place of Hiram A. Douglas on May 8 for remainder of session.

14. Leland Clegg, Ministerial Reserve, Little Rock, M. E., S:, was seated in place of E. C. Rule for May 6, 7, and 8.

15· King Vivion, Ministerial Reserve, Tennessee, M. E., S., was seated in place of J. L. Ferguson for May 5 only.

16. Willard H. Blue, Ministerial Delegate, Tennessee, M. E., S., resumed his seat on May 5.

17. Smith Burnham, Lay Delegate, Michigan, M. E., was excused after May 6 with no one in his place.

18. Miss Arsania Williams, Lay Delegate, Central West, M. E., was excused after May 8 with no one in her place.

19. N. G. Slaughter, Lay Delegate, North Georgia, M. E., S., was excused after May 6 with no one in his place.

20. Guy H. Wilson, Ministerial Delegate, Texas, M. E., S., resumed his seat on May 4.

21. A. D. Peck, Lay Delegate, Alabama, M. E., resumed his seat on May 4.

EARL R. BROWN, *Chairman;*
CHAS. A. ROBBINS, *Secretary.*

REPORT No. 9

Adopted May 8. See Journal, Page 293.

The Committee on Credentials has considered the following changes in seating and recommends that they be approved:.

1. Mrs. G. W. Hummel, Lay Reserve, Louisville, M. E., S., was seated in place of J. H. Dickey for May 6 only.

2. D. F. Armistead, Lay Reserve, North Texas, M. E., S., was seated in place of Marvin F. Love for May 6 only.

3. Blaine H. Gifford, Lay Reserve, Erie, M. E., was seated in place of L. H.' McKay on May 6 for the remainder of the session.

4. J. F. Rawls, Lay Reserve, Tennessee, M. E., S., was

seated in place of E. D. Thompson for May 9, at no expense to the Conference.

5. John W. Haywood, Ministerial Reserve, East Tennessee, M. E., was seated in place of William L. Sanders for May 6 only.

6. T. A. Prewitt, Lay Reserve, Little Rock, M. E., S., was seated in place of Fred Moore on May 6 for the remainder of session.

7. Henry Zimmerman, Lay Reserve, Kentucky, M. E., was seated in place of Alvis S. Bennett for May 6 only.

8· James Earl Milburn,ᵢ Ministerial Reserve, Holston, M. E., was seated in place of R. L. Stapleton for May 6 only without expense to the Conference.

9. S. L. Batchelor, Ministerial Reserve, West Texas, M. E., S., was seated in place of R. F. Curl for May 6 only.

10. Mrs. S. W. Rosenberger, Lay Reserve, Ohio, M. P., was seated in place of Mrs. E. K. Barss for May 8.

11. Mrs. B. B. Wedemeyer, Lay Reserve, Central Texas, M. E., S., was seated in place of G. C. Boswell on May 6 for the remainder of the session.

12. H. H. Luetzow, Ministerial Reserve, Southwest Missouri, M. E., S., was seated in place of H. J. Rand for May 8 only.

13. Arthur S. Case, Lay Reserve, Kansas, M. E., was seated in place of John C. Gaede for May 8 and 9 only.

14. R. A. Elkins, Lay Reserve, Memphis, M. E., S., was seated in place of Paul Meek on May 6 for the remainder of the session.

15. John L. Horton, Ministerial Reserve, Memphis, M. E., S., was seated in place of E. G. Hamlett for May 6 only.

16. Ben M. Stevens, Lay Delegate, Mississippi, M. E., S., was excused after May 6 for the remainder of session.

17. John C. Glenn, Ministerial Delegate, Southwest Missouri, M. E., S., resumed his seat on May 6.

18. John L. Ferguson, Ministerial Delegate, Tennessee, M. E., S., resumed his seat on May 6.

19. Nat Harris, Lay Delegate, Central Texas, M. E., S., was excused after May 6 for the remainder of session.

20. J. Fisher Simpson, Ministerial Delegate, West Texas, M. E., S., resumed his seat on May 6.

21. Galloway Calhoun, Lay Delegate, Texas, M. E., S., resumed·his seat on May 6.

22. Mrs. W. H. Ratliff, Lay Reserve, North Mississippi, M. E., S., was seated in place of J. W. Kyle on May 6 for the remainder of session.

23. Correcting Report No. 8, item 8, John W. Showalter

was seated in place of Mrs. Fred A. Lamb for May 8 instead of for May 6.

24. E. D. Baker, Ministerial Reserve, Southwest Missouri, M. E., S., was seated in place of John C. Glenn for May 5 only.

25. King Vivion, Ministerial Reserve, Tennessee, M. E., S., was seated in place of Willard H. Blue for May 4 only.

26. W. Vance Womack, Ministerial Reserve, North Arkansas, M. E., S., was seated in place of A. W. Martin for May 5 only.

EARL R. BROWN, *Chairman;*
CHAS. A. ROBBINS, *Secretary.*

SUPPLEMENT TO REPORT NO. 9

1. C. E. Brandt, Ministerial Reserve, Baltimore, M. E., S., was seated in place of Hubert Sydenstricker for May 4.

2. A. D. Peck, Lay Delegate, Alabama, M. E., resumed his seat on May 4.

3. Seaman A. Knapp, Lay Reserve, Iowa-Des Moines, M. E., was seated in place of Jesse M. Beck, Lay Reserve, on May 6 for the remainder of the session.

4. Richard W. Campbell, Lay Reserve, Central Pennsylvania, M. E., was seated in place of V. Max Frey on May 6 for the remainder of the session.

5. M. Wayne McQueen, Ministerial Reserve, North East Ohio, M. E., was seated in place of Homer W. Courtney for May 8 only.

EARL R. BROWN, *Chairman;*
CHAS. A. ROBBINS, *Secretary.*

REPORT NO. 10

Adopted May 9. See Journal, Page 328.

The Committee on Credentials has considered the following changes in seating and recommends that they be approved:

1. Thomas O. Huckle, Lay Reserve, Michigan, M. E., was seated in place of Lauren Dickinson for May 8, 9, and 10.

2. Mrs. Lee Britt, Lay Reserve, Virginia, M. E., S., was seated in place of B. L. Fisher for May 9 only.

3. J. G. McGowen, Lay Delegate, North Mississippi, M. E., S., was excused after May 6 for the remainder of the session.

4. G. M. Davenport, Ministerial Delegate, North Alabama, M. E., S., resumed his seat on May 8.

5. M. M. Davidson, Ministerial Delegate, North Alabama, M. E., S., resumed his seat on May 8.

6. A. N. Kirby, Lay Delegate, North Alabama, M. E., S., was excused after May 8.

7. Earl U. Yates, Ministerial Reserve, Southern Illinois, M. E., was seated in place of Clark R. Yost for May 9 and 10.

8. W. W. Shepherd, Ministerial Reserve, Kentucky, M. E., was seated in place of S. C. Rice for May 8 only.

9. A. S. Case, Lay Reserve, Kansas, M. E., was seated in place of J. C. Gaede for May 8 and 9.

10. Frank A. Lockridge, Ministerial Reserve, Dakota, M. E., was seated in place of Edward W. Kohlstedt for May 8 only.

11. Mrs. A. C. Johnson, Lay Reserve, Louisville, M. E., S., was seated in place of W. L. Cash for remainder of the session.

12. J. D. Baker, Ministerial Reserve, Little Rock, M. E., S., was seated in place of J. D. Hammons for afternoon of May 8.

13. Dr. Henry Hedden, Lay Delegate, Memphis, M. E., S., resumed his seat on May 8.

14. J. L. Horton, Ministerial Reserve, Memphis, M. E., S., was seated in place of F. H. Peeples for May 8, morning and afternoon.

15. E. G. Hamlett, Ministerial Delegate, Memphis, M. E., S., resumed his seat on May 8.

16. Mrs. J. W. Shell, Lay Reserve, Pittsburgh, M. P., was seated in place of Mr. Walter T. Smith on May 8 for the remainder of the session.

17. E. C. Dixon, Ministerial Reserve, West Wisconsin, M. E., was seated in place of Alfred F. Hughes for May 10, afternoon only.

18. Miss Ruth E. Wheaton, Lay Reserve at Large, Ohio, M. E., was seated in place of W. Dale Clark for May 8 only.

19. John W. Showalter, Lay Reserve, Southwest Missouri, M. E., S., was seated in place of Mrs. F. A. Lamb for May 8 only.

20. John C. Glenn, Ministerial Delegate, Southwest Missouri, M. E., S., resumed his seat May 6.

21. W. Harrison Baker, Ministerial Reserve, North Texas, M. E., S., was seated in place of Paul E. Martin for May 8, morning only.

22. D. F. Armistead, Lay Reserve, North Texas, M. E. S., was seated in place of Gibson Caldwell for May 8, 9, and 10.

23. W. V. Womack, Ministerial Reserve, North Arkansas, M. E., S., was seated in place of A. W. Martin for May 5 only.

24. Charles A. Stuck, Lay Delegate, North Arkansas, M. E., S., resumed his seat May 8.

25. J. H. Dickey, Lay Delegate, Louisville, M. E., S., resumed his seat on May 8.

26. D. S. Jeffers, Ministerial Delegate, Pacific Northwest, M. E., was excused after May 9.

27. H. W. Courtney, Ministerial Delegate, North East Ohio, M. E., resumed his seat on May 8.

28. R. F. Curl, Ministerial Delegate, West Texas, M. E., S., resumed his seat on May 8.

29. C. W. Hanke, Lay Delegate, Missouri, M. E., resumed his seat on May 8.

30. G. W. Haddaway, Ministerial Reserve, Maryland, M. P., was seated in place of E. A. Sexsmith for May 8, evening session.

31. R. W. White, Ministerial Reserve, Maryland, M. P., was seated in place of J. L. Green for May 8, evening session.

32. J. N. Link, Ministerial Reserve, Maryland, M. P., was seated in place of G. I. Humphreys for May 8, evening session.

33. Mrs. A. W. Allen, Lay Delegate, Kansas, M. P., resumed her seat on May 8.

34. A. L. Cook, Lay, Kansas, M. P., was seated May 8 and May 9.

35. B. E. Cartmell, Lay Reserve, North East Ohio, M. E., was seated for M. C. Robinson evening session only, May 8.

36. Paul E. Martin, Ministerial Delegate, North Texas, M. E., S., resumed his seat on May 8.

37. Henry Whitley, Lay Reserve, Arkansas, M. P., was seated in place of L. L. Sherman for remainder of session.

38. T. O. Huckle, Lay Reserve, Michigan, M. E., was seated in place of Smith Burnham for remainder of session.

39. Gaston Hartsfield, Ministerial Reserve, West Texas, M. E., S., was seated in place of L. U. Spellman for evening session only.

40. S. L. Batchelor, Ministerial Reserve, West Texas, M. E., S., was seated in place of K. P. Barton for evening session only.

41. D. C. McNutt, Ministerial Reserve, North Alabama, M. E., S., was seated in place of S. O. Kimbrough for May 8, night session.

42. W. O. Lynch, Lay Reserve, Arkansas, M. P., was seated in place of J. E. Butler for May 9 only.

EARL R. BROWN, *Chairman;*
CHAS. A. ROBBINS, *Secretary.*

REPORT NO. 11

Adopted May 10. See Journal, Page 365.

The Committee on Credentials has considered the following changes in seating and recommends that they be approved:

1. N. G. Slaughter, Lay Delegate, North Georgia, M. E., S., be excused after May 8 for the remainder of session.

2. I. S. Ingram, Lay Delegate, North Georgia, M. E., S., be excused after May 8 for the remainder of session.

3. Hubert Quillian, Lay Delegate, North Georgia, M. E., S., be excused after May 8 for the remainder of session.

4. Jack Lance, Lay Delegate, North Georgia, M. E., S., be excused after May 8 for the remainder of session.

5. J. S. Candler, Lay Delegate, North Georgia, M. E., S., be excused after May 8 for the remainder of session.

6. W. B. Selah, Ministerial Reserve, Memphis, M. E., S., was seated in place of E. G. Hamlett for afternoon, May 9.

7. John L. Horton, Ministerial Reserve, Memphis, M. E., S., was seated in place of J. E. Underwood for morning only, May 9.

8. W. M. Maxwell, Ministerial Reserve, North Georgia, M. E., S., was seated in place of A. M. Pierce for afternoon only, May 9.

9. R. H. Ruff, Ministerial Reserve, Missouri, M. E., S., was seated in place of J D Randolph on May 9, morning on y.

10. H. J. Rand, Ministerial Delegate, Southwest Missouri, M. E., S., resumed his seat on May 9 for remainder of session.

11. Homer E. Wark, Ministerial Reserve, West Virginia, M. E., was seated in place of Minor C. Miles on May 9 for evening session only.

12. J. D. Hammons, Ministerial Delegate, Little Rock, M. E., S., resumed his seat on May 9 for the remainder of session.

13. E. C. Rule, Ministerial Delegate, Little Rock, M. E., S., resumed his seat on May 9 for the remainder of session.

14. Mrs. B. M. Powell, Lay Reserve, Kansas, M. E., was seated in place of Mrs. H. A. French for evening session only, May 9.

15. Ruth E. Wheaton, Reserve at Large, Ohio, M. E., was seated in place of W. Dale Clark for May 9 sessions.

16. Raymond W. White, Ministerial Reserve, Maryland, M. P., was seated in place of E. A. Sexsmith on May 9 for the remainder of session.

17. R. C. Sproul, Sr., Lay Delegate, Pittsburgh, M. P., was excused on May 9 for the remainder of session.

18. J. J. Davies, Ministerial Reserve, Northwest Iowa, M. E., was seated in place of Earl A. Roadman for May 10 sessions.

19. W. L. Duren, Ministerial Delegate, Louisiana, M. E., S., resumed his seat on May 9.

20. S. T. Davidson, Ministerial Delegate, Erie, M. E., resumed his seat on May 10.

21. G. M. Hicks, Ministerial Reserve, Louisiana, M. E., S., was seated in place of W. L. Duren for night session, May 8 only.

22. L. M. Barnard, Ministerial Delegate, Erie, M. E., resumed his seat on May 10.

23. H. H. Barr, Ministerial Reserve, Erie, M. E., was seated in place of S. T. Davidson May 9, evening session only.

24. W. E. Davis, Ministerial Reserve, Erie, M. E., was \seated in place of L. M. Barnard on May 9 for evening session only.

25. C. W. Odom, Ministerial Reserve, Kansas, M. E., was seated in place of E. F. Buck.

26. Schuyler Garth, Ministerial Reserve, Northeast Ohio, M. E., was seated in place of C. B. Ketcham on May 8, evening session only.

27. M. C. Robinson, Ministerial Delegate, Northeast Ohio, M. E., resumed his seat on May 9.

28. John W. Mettam, Ministerial Reserve, Minnesota, M. E., was seated in place of Lloyd H. Rising on May 9 for afternoon only.

29. Lester A. Welliver, Ministerial Reserve, Central Pennsylvania, M. E., was seated in place of J. E. Skillington on May 9 for evening only.

30. Gaston Hartsfield, Ministerial Reserve, West Texas, M. E., S., was seated in place of Edmund Heinsohn on May 9 for evening only.

31. James C. Chubb, Ministerial Reserve, Kansas, M. E., was seated in place of R. C. Pennick on May 9 for afternoon only.

32. Tom V. Ellzey, Lay Reserve, Northwest Texas, M. E., S., was seated in place of J. M. Willson on May 9 and May 10.

33. Paul E. Secrest, Ministerial Reserve, Northeast Ohio, M. E., was seated in place of O. T. Olson on May 9 for evening session only.

34. W. Stanley Smith, Ministerial Reserve, Northeast

Ohio, M. E., was seated in place of L. C. Wright on May 9 for evening only.

35. J. F. Rawls, Lay Reserve, Tennessee, M. E., S., was seated in place of H. B. McGinnis, May 10, afternoon and evening sessions.

36. M. A. Childers, Lay Delegate, West Texas, M. E., S., was excused after May 8.

37. David T. Peel, Lay Delegate, West Texas, M. E., S., was excused after May 8.

EARL R. BROWN, *Chairman;*
CHAS. A. ROBBINS, *Secretary.*

REPORT NO. 12

Adopted May 10. See Journal, Page 365.

The Committee on Credentials has considered the following changes in seating and recommends that they be approved:

1. A. K. Hawkins, Lay Delegate, Florida, M. E., S., was excused May 7 for remainder of session.

2. C. B. Peeler, Lay Delegate, Florida, M. E., S., was excused May 7 for remainder of session.

3. Mrs. C. L. Mead, Reserve at Large, Missouri, M. E., was seated in place of Miss Ruth Wheaton on May 10, evening session only.

4. Harry J. Davis, Lay Reserve, St. Louis, M. E., S., was seated in place of F. E. Williams on May 10, afternoon session only.

5. F. E. Williams, Lay Delegate, St. Louis, M. E., S., resumed his seat on May 10 for evening session.

6. C. W. Odom, Ministerial Reserve, Kansas, M. E., was seated in place of R. O. Pennick on May 10, afternoon session only.

7. J. H. Olmstead, Ministerial Reserve, Genesee, M. E., was seated in place of S. A. Keen on May 10.

8. Ruth E. Wheaton, Lay Reserve at Large, Ohio, M. E., was seated in place of W. Dale Clark on May 10.

9. W. T. Handy, Ministerial Reserve, Louisiana, M. E., was seated in place of J. W. E. Bowen on May 9 for evening session only.

10. Mrs. Lee Britt, Lay Reserve, Virginia, M. E., S., was seated in place of W. T. Elliott on May 10.

11. L. W. Seymour, Ministerial Reserve, Central Texas, M. E., S., was seated in place of M. M. Chum on May 9 for evening session only.

12. G. L. Morelock, Lay Delegate, Memphis, M. E., S., resumed his seat on May 10.

13. Mrs. M. L. DeVinny, Lay Reserve, Minnesota, M. E., was seated in place of G. F. Reineke on May 10 for evening session only.

14. D. M. Pentz, Ministerial Reserve, Kansas, M. P., was seated in place of L. E. Dixon on May 10 for evening session only.

15. S. D. Eva, Lay Reserve, Detroit, M. E., was seated in place of Howard Baldwin on May 10.

16. Leonard Oechsli, Ministerial Reserve, Southern California, M. E., was seated in place of George A. Warmer on May 10, afternoon only.

17. James E. Dunning, Ministerial Reserve, Southern California, M. E., was seated in place of Roy L. Smith May 10, afternoon only.

18. E. D. Thompson, Lay Delegate, Tennessee, M. E., S., resumed his seat May 10 for remainder of session.

19. Lloyd H. Rising, Ministerial Delegate, Minnesota, M. E., resumed his seat May 9, evening session.

20. Albert J. Mitchell, Ministerial Reserve, Washington, M. E., was seated in place of W. A. C. Hughes May 9, evening only.

21. Mrs. N. S. Rollins, Lay Reserve, Northwest Texas, M. E., S., was seated in place of R. H. Nichols on May 1.

22. M. C. Robinson, Lay Delegate, Northeast Ohio, M. E., resumed his seat on May 9.

23. Mrs. William H. Dievler, Lay Reserve, Philadelphia, M. E., was seated in place of J. Wesley Mashland May 10, afternoon only.

24. J. Wesley Mashland, Lay Delegate, Philadelphia, M. E., resumed his seat May 10, evening session.

25. P. P. Taylor, Ministerial Reserve, Missouri, M. E., S., was seated in place of R. C. Holliday May 10, afternoon only.

EARL R. BROWN, *Chairman;*
CHAS. A. ROBBINS, *Secretary.*

REPORTS OF JURISDICTIONAL CONFERENCE MEETINGS

I. THE NORTHEASTERN JURISDICTION

REPORT ON BOUNDARIES

Ordered to Record May 9. See Journal, Page 346.

The delegates from the Annual Conferences within the Northeastern Jurisdiction, sitting apart for the purpose of adjusting boundaries and determining the composition of Annual Conferences, submit the following report:

The Methodist Church in the Northeastern Jurisdiction shall comprise the states of Maine, New Hampshire, Vermont, Massachusetts, Rhode Island, Connecticut, New York, New Jersey, Pennsylvania, Maryland, West Virginia, Delaware, District of Columbia, Puerto Rico; and shall include the following Annual Conferences bounded as follows:

(1) BALTIMORE CONFERENCE shall include the District of Columbia, the western shore of Maryland (except that part of Garrett County lying west of the dividing ridge of the Allegheny Mountains), so much of Pennsylvania as lies within Hancock, Flintstone, Union Grove, Hyndman, Warfordsburg, and Ellerslie Circuits; and including Delta, Mount Nebo, Fawn Grove, Stewartstown, Maryland Line and Bedford Circuits of the former Maryland Conference of the Methodist Protestant Church; and the counties of Jefferson, Berkeley, and Morgan in West Virginia.

(2) CENTRAL NEW YORK CONFERENCE shall be bounded on the west by the west lines of the towns of Williamson, Marion, and Palmyra, in Wayne County, and of the towns of Farmington and Canandaigua, in Ontario County, and of Yates and Schuyler Counties, and of the towns of Hornby and Caton, in Steuben County; and in Pennsylvania by the railroad running from Lawrenceville to Blossburg, including Mansfield and Blossburg charges; on the south by Central Pennsylvania Conference; on the east by Wyoming and Northern New York Conferences; on the north by Northern New York Conference and Lake Ontario.

(3) CENTRAL PENNSYLVANIA CONFERENCE shall be bounded on the south by the state line from the Susquehanna River to the west boundary of Bedford County, excepting Union Mills, Maryland, now part of the Littlestown Charge, and so much of Pennsylvania as is included in the

Baltimore Conference; on the west by the west line of the counties of Bedford, Blair, that part of Cambria County not included in the Pittsburgh Conference, namely: Patton, Hastings, Bakerton, and Barnesboro, including Cherry Tree and Glen Campbell and Smithport in Indiana County, Clearfield County, north to Saint Marys, excepting so much of Clearfield County as is embraced in the Erie Conference; on the north by a line extending from Saint Marys eastward to Emporium, including the territory formerly embraced by the Keating Summit Circuit; thence by the southern boundary of Potter and Tioga Counties, including Austin, Morris, and the territory formerly embraced by Costello, Wharton Circuit, Cross Fork, Hammersley Fort Circuit, Blackwell, and Liberty Valley Circuits; thence through Sullivan County north of Laporte to the west line of Wyoming County; thence on the east by the present limits of the Wyoming Conference, being the east line of Sullivan County, to the north line of Columbia County; thence by a line southeasterly through Luzerne County to the north line of the Philadelphia Conference, near White Haven; thence on the south by the northern line of Carbon, Schuylkill, and Dauphin Counties to the Susquehanna River, including Hickory Run, Weatherly, Beaver Meadows, and Ashland; and thence by the Susquehanna River to the place of beginning, including Harrisburg and that additional part of Dauphin County east from the city limits on the north to and including Paxonia, thence southward to Rutherford, thence west to the city of Harrisburg.

(4) EAST GERMAN CONFERENCE shall embrace all the German work east of the Allegheny Mountains, including all the German work in the state of New York.

(5) EASTERN SWEDISH CONFERENCE shall include all the Swedish work in the six New England States, the states of New Jersey and Delaware, and the territory included in the New York, New York East, and Philadelphia Conferences.

(6) ERIE CONFERENCE shall be bounded on the north by Lake Erie; on the east by a line commencing at the mouth of Cattaraugus Creek; thence up said creek to Gowanda, leaving said town in the Genesee Conference; thence to the Allegheny River at the mouth of the Tunungwant Creek; thence up said creek southward, excluding the city of Bradford on said creek, to the ridge dividing between the waters of Clarion and Sinnemahoning Creek, thence southward to Mahoning Creek, thence down said creek to the Allegheny River, excluding the Milton Society, but including Valier and the Haratio Society, and Hamilton in the Valier Charge,

the Putneyville Society in the Putneyville Circuit, Rimerton south of the Mahoning Creek, and that portion of the borough of Junxsutawney lying south and east of Mahoning Creek; thence across said river in a westerly direction to the southwest corner of Lawrence County, including Wampum; thence along the Ohio state line to the place of beginning, excluding Orangeville Church.

(7) GENESEE CONFERENCE shall include all that part of the state of New York lying west of the Central New York Conference except those parts of Chautauqua and Cattaraugus Counties which are now included in the Erie Conference. It shall also include Gowanda and Corning, in the state of New York, and so much of Tioga County, including Tioga Charge, in the state of Pennsylvania, as is not embraced in the Central New York Conference; also so much of Potter County, in the state of Pennsylvania, as is not included in the Central Pennsylvania Conference; also including so much of McKean County, in the state of Pennsylvania, as is embraced in the Olean District, including the city of Bradford; also the Negro work in the city of Buffalo.

(8) MAINE CONFERENCE shall include all Maine and that part of the state of New Hampshire east of the White Hills and north of the waters of Ossipee Lake, and the towns of Gorham and Berlin.

(9) NEWARK CONFERENCE shall include that part of the state of New Jersey not included in the New Jersey Conference, with the Borough of Richmond, City of New York, in the state of New York, and such portions of Rockland, Orange, and Sullivan Counties, in the state of New York, as lie south and west of a line extending from Tompkins Cove, on the Hudson River, intersecting the New Jersey state line at a point south of Sloatsburg; thence along said state line to the Wallkill River; thence due north, intersecting the Erie Railroad at a point west of Middletown; thence in a northwesterly direction to a point where the Port Jervis & Monticello Railroad crosses the northern line of Forestburg township in Sullivan County; thence southwest to a point on the Delaware River below Lackawaxen, in Pennsylvania; also such portions of Pike and Monroe Counties, in the state of Pennsylvania, as lie north of the Philadelphia Conference and east of the Wyoming Conference, the same being now included in the Matamoras, Milford, Dingmans, and Coolbaugh Charges.

(10) NEW ENGLAND CONFERENCE shall include all Massachusetts east of the Green Mountains not included in the

New Hampshire and the· New' England 'Southern Conferences: ·

(11) NEW ENGLAND SOUTHERN CONFERENCE shall in-
clude that part of' Connecticut lyirig east 'of the Connecticut
River, the state of Rhode Island, 'with the town of Black-
stone'in Massachusetts, and that part of the state of Massachusetts south of the towns of Wrentham, Walpole, ·Ded-
ham, Milton, and Quincy. ·:' ·

· (12) NEW HAMPSHIRE CONFERENCE shall include all New
Hampshire, except 'that part within the Maine ·Conference;
also that part of Massachusetts northeast of the Merrimac
River with the exception of that part of Lowell north of
the Merrimac.

·. ;(13) NEW JERSEY CONFERENCE ·shall include· that part
of' New' Jersey lying ·south' of the ·following line, namely:
commencing at Raritan· Bay; ·thence up said ·bay and river
to New Brunswick, at a point opposite the easterly boundary of the borough' of Highland .Park, thence along' the
easterly, northerly, and westerly ·boundaries of ·said borough,· respectively,· to the Raritan River; thence·along the
Raritan River ·to ·the· westerly limits ·of· the city of New
Brunswick; thence; southwest in; a straight line to Lambert-
ville ·on· the Delaware River, :including ·the city of New
·Brunswick, the·Borough of Highland Park,· and Lambert-
ville Station. ' ·:' ;

;·· (14) 'NEW YORK CONFERENCE; shall consist of the territory now in the New York, ·Poughkeepsie, Newburgh,· and
Kingston Districts, and 'including Five Points Mission.

·: (15) NEW YORK·EAST CONFERENCE shall include Long
·Island; those charges ·in Manhattan and Bronx east of'South
'Ferry; Whitehall Street; Broadway, Park· Row, Chatham
Square, 'Bowery, Third Avenue to Pelham Avenue; west to
the Harlem Railroad track;' north to Mount· Vernon; 'thence
including Mount Vernon, New Rochelle, Mamaroneck; Har-
rison,' and all between them and Long Island Sound to the
'Connecticut'·line; 'thence' following the state line, including
Pound' Ridge, to Sharon· Township; east to Winchester, ex-
cluding North Goshen; north to the state line, east to the
Connecticut River, and following the river. to the Sound,
and also excepting Five Points Mission.

(16) NORTHERN NEW · YORK ·CONFERENCE; shall. include
so much of·the county of.Franklin as is not .within the Troy
.Conference; and the counties of Saint· Lawrence, Jefferson,
·Lewis, Oneida;· and. Herkimer, ·and all· of ·Oswego County
except· Phoenix, and; so· much' of; the ·county of Madison· as
lies on and east· of the New York, Ontario & Western Railroad, together' with 'Cherry' Valley, 'Springfield, ·Richfield

Springs, and Salt Springville in Otsego County, Saint Johnsville in Montgomery County, and Lassellville, Oppenheim, and Stratford in Fulton County.

(17) PHILADELPHIA CONFERENCE shall be bounded on the east by the Delaware River; on the south by the Pennsylvania state line; on the west by the Susquehanna River, excluding Harrisburg and the adjoining part of Dauphin County, extending east to Paxtonia and Rutherford included in the Central Pennsylvania Conference; on the north by the north line of Dauphin, Schuylkill, Carbon, and Monroe Counties, excepting Ashland, and the Beaver Meadows Circuit.

(18) PITTSBURGH CONFERENCE shall be bounded on the north by the Erie Conference; on the east by the Central Pennsylvania Conference; on the south by the West Virginia Conference; on the west by the North-East Ohio Conference.

(19) TROY CONFERENCE shall include that portion of the state of New York embraced in the counties of Rensselaer, Washington, Clinton, Essex, Warren, Saratoga, Schenectady, Montgomery (except Saint Johnsville), Fulton (except the towns of Oppenheim and Stratford), Albany (except Coeymans Hollow and South Bethlehem), Schoharie (except Blenheim, Charlottesville, Eminence, Gilboa, Livingstonville, Summit, and West Fulton) ; in Columbia County, the town of Stuyvesant, Kinderhook, New Lebanon, and Chatham (except Chatham Village and East Chatham) ; in Franklin County, the towns of Standish, Saranac Lake, and the appointments connected with Bloomingdale Circuit; in Hamilton County, the towns of Benson, Hope, Wells, Indian Lake, Long Lake, and Blue Mountain Lake; and in Otsego County, Center Valley; also that portion of Vermont embraced in the counties of Addison (except the towns of Granville and Hancock), Bennington (except the towns of Landgrove and Peru), Rutland (except Mechanicsville and Cuttingsville, Mount Holly, East Wallingford, Summit, and Healdsville) ; and in Chittenden County, the towns of Charlotte, Minesburg, Huntington, Williston, Shelburne, Burlington, and Winooski; also in Massachusetts all that part of Berkshire County lying upon the line of the Boston & Albany Railroad, and north of said line.

(20) VERMONT CONFERENCE shall include Vermont, except that portion lying south of the Winooski River and west of the Green Mountain Divide; said boundary to leave Winooski Charge in the Troy Conference, and Mechanicsville and Cuttingsville in the Vermont Conference.

(21) WEST VIRGINIA CONFERENCE shall include West

Virginia except the counties of Jefferson, Berkley, Morgan, Brooke and Hancock; and shall also include that part of Garrett County, Maryland, lying west of the dividing ridge of the Allegheny Mountains.

(22) PENINSULA CONFERENCE shall include Delaware, and the counties of Maryland lying east of the Susquehanna River and the Chesapeake Bay.

(23) WYOMING CONFERENCE shall include that portion of the southern part of the state of New York which is not included in the New York, New York East, Newark, Central New York, and Genesee Conferences; and that part of the state of Pennsylvania which is bounded on the west by Central New York Conference, including the territory east of the Susquehanna River, and on the south by the Central Pennsylvania, Philadelphia, and Newark Conferences including Narrowsburg, and on the east by the Newark and New York Conferences.

(24) PUERTO RICO MISSION CONFERENCE shall include Puerto Rico and the adjacent islands belonging to its civil Jurisdiction, together with any work which may be established by The Methodist Church or come under its care in any of the islands known as the West Indies, except in the Republic of Cuba.

II. THE SOUTHEASTERN JURISDICTION

REPORT ON BOUNDARIES

Ordered to Record May 8. See Journal, Page 301.

After calling the roll of Conferences, one by one, and examining the situation of all Conferences, Methodist Episcopal, Methodist Episcopal, South, and Methodist Protestant in this Jurisdiction, we recommend that the following be fixed as the boundaries of the respective Conferences:

(1) ALABAMA CONFERENCE shall include West Florida (except Apalachicola), and all Alabama lying South of the following boundary line: Beginning at the southwest corner of Pickens County; then along the south of Pickens and Tuscaloosa Counties, and a direct line on the same parallel of latitude, east of the Coosa River; thence down that river to the southern boundary of Coosa County; thence east by that county line, and through Tallapoosa County to the south of Chambers County, and by that county line to Georgia. Except that part of Sumter County, north of Noxubee River, which is in the North Alabama Conference.

(2) FLORIDA CONFERENCE shall include all Florida not included in the Alabama Conference, except our Latin work.

(3) HOLSTON CONFERENCE shall include that part of Tennessee east of the eastern rim of Cumberland Mountain
and that part of Virginia west of New River to Radford
(including Big Stony Creek appointment), and all the territory in Montgomery and Floyd Counties in the Holston Conference of the former Methodist Episcopal Church, South,
and all of Dade County, Georgia, and the Lookout Mountain Circuit, and the towns of Flintstone, Rossville, and
Graysville in Georgia.

(4) KENTUCKY CONFERENCE shall embrace all Kentucky
lying north and east of the following line: Beginning at the
mouth of Harrod's Creek, on the Ohio River; thence south
on the southern line of the Middletown and Jeffersontown
Circuits, to the Bardstown turnpike; thence with the turnpike to Bardstown; thence with the direct road to Springfield; thence to the towns of Hayesville and Liberty; thence
south to Cumberland River; thence up the river to the fork;
thence up South Fork to Tennessee, including Liberty, and
the strip lying between Wolf River and Kentucky.

(5) LOUISVILLE CONFERENCE shall embrace all Kentucky
which is not included in the Memphis and Kentucky Conferences.

(6) MEMPHIS CONFERENCE shall be bounded by the
Mississippi, Ohio, and Tennessee Rivers, and by the line
between the states of Tennessee and Mississippi.

(7) MISSISSIPPI CONFERENCE shall embrace that part of
Mississippi south of the southern boundaries of Washington,
Holmes, Attala, Winston, and Noxubee Counties, and that
part of Humphreys County formerly embraced in Yazoo
County.

(8) NORTH ALABAMA CONFERENCE shall embrace all Alabama not included in the Alabama Conference.

(9) NORTH CAROLINA CONFERENCE shall be bounded on
the east by the Atlantic Ocean; thence along the southern
line of Virginia to the eastern line of Rockingham County,
North Carolina, excluding New Hope Church, in Hertford
County, North Carolina, also Knott's Island and Currituck
Inlet Churches in Currituck County, North Carolina;
thence south with the eastern boundary of Rockingham,
Guilford, and Randolph Counties to the southern boundary
of Randolph County; excluding Pelham Church in Caswell
County; thence west with the southern boundary of Randolph County to the Uwharrie River; thence with that river
to its junction with the Yadkin River; thence with the Yadkin and Pedee Rivers to South Carolina, and thence along
that state line to the Atlantic Ocean.

(10) NORTH GEORGIA CONFERENCE shall embrace all

Georgia (except a small part heretofore described as in the Holston Conference) which lies north of the following line: Beginning at Chattahoochee River, at Pine Mountain, and running along that mountain to Flint River; thence down that river to the southern line of Upson County; thence along the southern line of Monroe County to Ocmulgee River; thence along the south line of Jones, Baldwin, Hancock, Warren, and Richmond Counties to Savannah River.

(11) NORTH MISSISSIPPI CONFERENCE shall include all Mississippi not included in the Mississippi Conference.

(12) SOUTH CAROLINA CONFERENCE shall include that portion of South Carolina lying east and south of the following: Beginning at the North Carolina line, follow the line between Chesterfield and Lancaster Counties, between Kershaw and Fairfield Counties, thence across Richland County in a direct line from the junction of Kershaw and Fairfield Counties at the Richland line to the junction of the Seaboard Air Line and Southern Railways; thence in a direct line to Ridgewood, thence along the trolley line to Hyatt's Park; thence in a direct line to Simms Station on the Atlantic Coast Line Railway; thence in a direct line to the junction of Calhoun and Lexington Counties at the southern Richland line, thence along the line between Calhoun and Lexington Counties, between Orangeburg and Lexington Counties, between Orangeburg and Aiken Counties, between Barnwell and Aiken Counties to Savannah River; except that Heath Springs charge, Ebenezer and Smyrna Churches, Salley Church, Ellenton Church, and College Place charge (Columbia District) shall be in the South Carolina Conference, and Dentsville Church, Hopewell Church (Wagener Circuit), and Williston Church shall be in the Upper South Carolina Conference.

(13) SOUTH GEORGIA CONFERENCE shall include all Georgia south of the southern line of the North Georgia Conference.

(14) TENNESSEE CONFERENCE shall include Middle Tennessee, except that portion east of the western boundary of the counties of Marion, Sequatchie, Bledsoe, Rhea, Roane, Morgan, and Scott, to the top of Cumberland Mountain, and thence to Kentucky—Monteagle, in Marion County, and Bethel, in Sequatchie County, being included in the Tennessee Conference.

(15) UPPER SOUTH CAROLINA CONFERENCE shall include all South Carolina not included in the South Carolina Conference.

(16) VIRGINIA CONFERENCE shall be bounded on the east by the Atlantic Ocean and embracing that part of the state

of Virginia which is on the Eastern Shore; on the north by the Potomac River; thence west to the West Virginia state line to the line of the Holston Conference; thence south to the northern border of the Western North Carolina Conference, thence east along the northern border of the Western North Carolina and North Carolina Conferences to the Atlantic Ocean.

(17) WESTERN NORTH CAROLINA CONFERENCE shall include all North Carolina west of the North Carolina Conference, except Savannah Church, in Alleghany County, North Carolina; and also that part of North Carolina lying north of New River, and including that part of Virginia lying south of that river in the loop in Grayson County, Virginia; including all the territory in Carroll and Patrick Counties, Virginia, south of the crest of the Blue Ridge, and west of the Dan River.

(18) CUBA CONFERENCE shall include the work in the Republic of Cuba.

(19) LATIN MISSION shall include all our Latin work in the state of Florida.

The above Report was adopted at·a meeting of the delegates of the Jurisdiction held May 6, 1939.

III. CENTRAL JURISDICTION

REPORT ON BOUNDARIES

Ordered to Record May 9. See Journal, Page 346.

The delegates from Conferences of the Central Jurisdiction in meeting assembled have fixed the boundaries of the Conferences in the Central Jurisdiction as follows:

VII. UNITED STATES AND TERRITORIES

¶ 1377, *Article* 1. *Annual Conferences*

(2) ATLANTA CONFERENCE shall include the Negro work in that part of Georgia not included in the Savannah Conference.

(6)· CENTRAL ALABAMA CONFERENCE shall include the Negro work in Alabama and in that part of Florida ˙west of the Apalachicola River.

(11) CENTRAL WEST CONFERENCE shall include the Negro work in Kansas, Colorado, Nebraska, Missouri, and Iowa, and in that part of Illinois lying west of the following line: Beginning at the city of Cairo, and running north along the Illinois Central Railroad to the city of Mendota, and including all the towns on said line of railroad; thence

north to the Wisconsin state line, and thence west along said line to the Mississippi River, and all the Negro work in North and South Dakota and Montana.

(14) DELAWARE CONFERENCE shall include the Negro work in Delaware, New Jersey, and New York State, except that in the city of Buffalo and that already included in the New York Conference in the Boroughs of the Bronx and Manhattan in the city of New York; it shall also include the Negro work in the eastern Shore of Virginia, and all Maryland and Pennsylvania not included in the Washington Conference.

(17) EAST TENNESSEE CONFERENCE shall include the Negro work in that part of Tennessee which is not in the Tennessee Conference of this Jurisdiction; in that part of Virginia west of and including the counties of Carroll, Floyd, Montgomery, and Giles; and in the counties of Mercer, Wyoming, McDowell, Raleigh, Logan, and Mingo in West Virginia; and the counties of Whitley, Knox, Bell, and Harlan in Kentucky.

(20) FLORIDA CONFERENCE shall include the Negro work in Florida except that part lying west of the Apalachicola River, and that part south of twenty-nine degrees North latitude.

(30) LEXINGTON CONFERENCE shall include the Negro work in Kentucky, Ohio, Michigan, Indiana, Illinois, Wisconsin, and Minnesota, except so much of Illinois as is included in the Central West Conference, and except Whitley, Knox, Bell, and Harlan Counties in Kentucky.

(31) LOUISIANA CONFERENCE shall include the Negro work in Louisiana.

(35) MISSISSIPPI CONFERENCE shall include all the Negro work in Mississippi south of a line beginning at the northeast corner of Kemper County, and running along the northern border of said county, and of the counties of Neshoba, Leake, Madison, Yazoo, Sharkey, and Issaquena to the Mississippi River, and the part of Humphreys County formerly embraced in Yazoo County.

(46) NORTH CAROLINA CONFERENCE shall include the Negro work in North Carolina and in that part of Virginia lying south of a line beginning at Cape Henry and running to Hampton Roads; thence with Hampton Roads to the James River; thence with the southern bank of the James River to Chesterfield County; thence with the northern boundary of Prince George, Dinwiddie, Nottoway, Prince Edward, Charlotte, and Halifax Counties, to the northeast corner of Pittsylvania; thence in a southerly direction to the northeast corner of Henry; thence with the county lines of

Pittsylvania, Franklin, and Bedford to the corner of Bedford and Roanoke; thence with the Blue Ridge Mountains to the North Carolina state line.

(64) SAVANNAH CONFERENCE shall include the Negro work in that part of Georgia lying south of a line running east and west along the northern boundaries of Richmond, McGuffie, Warren, Hancock, Putnam, Jasper, and Butts Counties; that part of Spalding County embracing Liberty Hall Circuit; all of Pike County except the church known as Free Liberty; that part of Meriwether County embracing Greenville; and that part of Troup County embracing La Grange Station and La Grange Circuit.

(65) SOUTH CAROLINA CONFERENCE shall include the Negro work in South Carolina.

(69) SOUTH FLORIDA CONFERENCE shall include the Negro work in Florida lying south of twenty-nine degrees North latitude, including New Smyrna, Daytona, Armond, and DeLand.

(70) SOUTHWEST CONFERENCE shall include the Negro work in Arkansas and Oklahoma.

(72) TENNESSEE CONFERENCE shall include the Negro work in that portion of Tennessee west of and including Franklin, Coffee, Warren, White, Putnam, Overton, and Pickett Counties.

(73) TEXAS CONFERENCE shall include the Negro work in that part of Texas lying east of a line beginning at the Gulf of Mexico on the east boundary of Matagorda County, and running along said line and the east line of Wharton and Colorado Counties to the north point of Colorado County; thence north until it strikes the Southern Pacific Railroad at Calvert; thence along that railroad to the northern boundary of Texas, excluding Calvert and all the towns on the said railroad.

(76) UPPER MISSISSIPPI CONFERENCE shall include the Negro work in Mississippi not included in the Mississippi Conference.

(78) WASHINGTON CONFERENCE shall include the Negro work in western Maryland, the District of Columbia, the state of West Virginia, except Raleigh, Mercer, Wyoming, and McDowell Counties; so much of Pennsylvania as lies west of the Susquehanna River, including the towns of said river; and so much of Virginia as is not included in the East Tennessee, Delaware, and North Carolina Conferences.

(79) WEST TEXAS CONFERENCE shall embrace the Negro work in that part of Texas which is not included in the Texas Conference of this Jurisdiction, and shall include any

Negro mission work that may be established in New Mexico and Arizona.

IV. THE NORTH CENTRAL JURISDICTION

REPORT ON BOUNDARIES

Ordered to Record May 9. See Journal, Page 346.

Membership of Committee, 149; present when report was adopted, 85; voting for adoption, 85.

The delegates from the Annual Conferences within the North Central Jurisdiction, sitting apart for the purpose of adjusting boundaries and determining the composition of the Annual Conferences of The Methodist Church, submit the following report:

PART I. BOUNDARIES

The Methodist Church in the North Central Jurisdiction is comprised of the following states: Ohio, Indiana, Illinois, Michigan, Wisconsin, Iowa, Minnesota, North Dakota, South Dakota.

We recommend that there be nineteen Annual Conferences with names and boundaries as follows:

OHIO. There shall be two Conferences in the state of Ohio with boundaries as given below, provided that the Lakeside Assembly Ground at Lakeside and the Ohio Wesleyan Campus shall be common territory for Conference session purposes.

(1) OHIO CONFERENCE shall be bounded as follows: beginning at the northwest corner of Ohio; thence east on the north line of that state to a point due north of the mouth of the Sandusky River; thence south to and up said river to Upper Sandusky, excluding Port Clinton and Tiffin, and including Fremont and Upper Sandusky; thence in a southerly direction along the main road from Upper Sandusky through Marion to Delaware, Ohio, including the Wyandotte Church and Marion, Waldo, and all of Delaware west of Sandusky Street except Asbury Church; thence in an easterly direction to Dresden, Ohio, excluding the Galena, Sunbury, Homer, and Utica Circuits; thence down the Muskingum River to the Ohio River, including Dresden, Zanesville, and Marietta, Ohio; thence down the Ohio River to the west line of Ohio; thence north along said line to the place of beginning.

(2) NORTHEAST OHIO CONFERENCE shall be bounded as follows: beginning at the north point of the line separating

Ohio from Pennsylvania; thence south along said line to the Ohio River, including Orangeville Church; thence down said river to the Muskingum River; thence up the Muskingum River to Dresden, excluding Marietta, Zanesville, and Dresden; thence westerly to the main road passing through Delaware and Marion, including Utica, Homer, and Galena Circuits, and excluding Stratford; on the west by the main road passing through Delaware and Marion to Upper Sandusky, and by the Sandusky River to its mouth; thence due north to the state line, including the towns of Tiffin, Port Clinton, and Lakeside, and excluding so much of the town of Delaware as lies west of Sandusky Street, yet including Asbury Church in the city of Delaware; also excluding the towns of Marion, Fremont, and Upper Sandusky; thence east on the northern line of Ohio to the place of beginning.

INDIANA. There shall be three Conferences in the state of Indiana with boundaries as follows:

(1) INDIANA CONFERENCE shall be bounded on the north and the east by a line beginning where the National Road intersects the west line of Indiana; thence along said road to Terre Haute; thence along the Vandalia Railroad to Maywood Road, West Indianapolis; thence north on Maywood Road and Tibbs Avenue to West Tenth Street and thence east to the LaFayette and Indianapolis Railroad; thence north on said railroad to the Michigan Road; thence on said road to the north line of Marion County; thence east on said county line to the northeast corner of said county; thence south on the east line of said county to the National Road; thence east on said road to the state line; on the east by the state of Ohio including Elizabeth, Hamilton County, Ohio; on the south by the Ohio River; and on the west by Illinois.

(2) NORTH INDIANA CONFERENCE shall be bounded on the north by Michigan; on the east by Ohio, including Union City; on the south by the National Road from the state line west to Marion County; thence north to the northeast corner of said county; thence west to the Michigan Road; on the west by said Michigan Road to South Bend, excluding Lowell Heights and River Park Churches, South Bend, and thence by the Saint Joseph River to the Michigan state line, including Logansport and all the towns on the National Road east of Indianapolis.

(3) NORTHWEST INDIANA CONFERENCE shall be bounded on the north by Lake Michigan and the state line; on the east by the Saint Joseph River and the Michigan Road, including Lowell Heights and River Park Churches, South

Bend, Indiana; on the south by the Indiana Conference, and on the west by Illinois, including all the towns on the Michigan Road except Logansport; and all the towns on the southern boundary, excluding Washington Street Church in Indianapolis.

ILLINOIS. There shall be three Conferences in the state of Illinois with boundaries as follows:

(1) ILLINOIS CONFERENCE shall embrace that part of Illinois north of the Southern Illinois Conference and south of the following lines, namely; beginning on the Mississippi River at Albany, thence southeasterly to the northwest corner of Bureau County; thence south to the Chicago, Burlington & Quincy Railway crossing of the Chicago, Rock Island & Pacific Railway; thence along said railway to Bureau Junction; thence to the Illinois River; thence up the said river to the mouth of the Kankakee River; thence up the Kankakee River to a point directly west of the north line of Kankakee County; thence east to the Indiana line; leaving Albany, Leon, and Ottawa in the Rock River Conference, and Bureau Junction in the Illinois Conference.

(2) SOUTHERN ILLINOIS CONFERENCE shall include all that part of Illinois south of the following line, namely: beginning at a point on the Mississippi River at the northwest corner of Calhoun County; thence east along the north line of said County to the Illinois River; thence down the Illinois River to Columbiana; thence east to the northeast corner of Jersey County, leaving Corrallton and Rockbridge in the Illinois Conference, thence in a southeasterly direction; leaving Chesterfield in the Illinois Conference, and Litchfield in the Southern Illinois Conference; thence to Hillsboro, leaving Hillsboro in the Illinois Conference, thence to the northwest corner of Fayette County; thence along the north line of Fayette County and Effingham County to the west line of Cumberland County, leaving Herrick and Holiday in the Southern Illinois Conference; thence south to the southwest corner of Cumberland County; thence east along the south line of Cumberland and Clark Counties to the Wabash River.

(3) ROCK RIVER CONFERENCE shall include that part of Illinois north of the Illinois Conference, except East Dubuque.

MICHIGAN. There shall be two Conferences in Michigan, with boundaries as follows:

(1) DETROIT CONFERENCE shall include that part of Michigan in the Lower Peninsula east of the principal meridian as far north as the southern boundary of Roscommon County; thence west to the southwest corner of

said county; thence north to the southern boundary of Charlevoix County; thence east to the southeast corner of Charlevoix County; thence north to the Straits of Mackinac including Mackinaw City. It shall also include the Upper Peninsula.

(2) MICHIGAN CONFERENCE shall include that part of Michigan in the Lower Peninsula west of the principal meridian as far north as the southern boundary of Roscommon County; thence west to the southwest corner of said county; thence north to the southern boundary of Charlevoix County; thence east to the southeast corner of said county; thence north to the Straits of Mackinac.

SPECIAL. The Conferences in Michigan shall hold the next annual session, receive reports, transact necessary business, and make all adjustments incident to the creating of the new Conferences in the United Church. The time and place of the said Conferences of the Methodist Episcopal Church shall meet at Jackson, Michigan, on June 7, the Detroit Conference of the Methodist Episcopal Church shall meet at Adrian, Michigan, on June 21, and the Michigan Conference of the Methodist Protestant Church shall meet at Adrian, Michigan, on June 20.

WISCONSIN. There shall be two Conferences in the state of Wisconsin, with boundaries as follows:

(1) WISCONSIN CONFERENCE shall include all that part of Wisconsin lying east and north of a line beginning at the southeast corner of Green County, on the south line of the state; thence north on the range line between ranges nine and ten east, to the north line of township twenty; thence west on the said line to the east of range three; thence north on said line to the Michigan state line, excluding Avon Church, McFarland, Goodman Church, Brooklyn, and the town of Pine Grove in Portage County.

(2) WEST WISCONSIN CONFERENCE shall include that part of Wisconsin not embraced in the Wisconsin Conference.

IOWA. There shall be three Conferences in Iowa with boundaries as follows:

(1) IOWA-DES MOINES CONFERENCE shall be bounded on the east by the Mississippi River beginning at the southeast corner of Iowa and extending north to but not including the city of Davenport; thence west along the Chicago, Rock Island & Pacific Railroad to Iowa City, including all intermediate towns but not including Iowa City; thence along the Iowa River to the northeast corner of Iowa County; thence due west to the southwest corner of Marshall County; thence north to the northeast corner of Story

County; thence west to the northeast corner of Crawford County; thence south to the north line of township eighty-three; thence west to the east line of Monona County; thence south and west on the Monona County line to the Missouri River; hence along the Missouri River south to the Missouri state line; thence east along the Missouri state line to the Des Moines River; thence southeast along the Des Moines River to the Mississippi River at the extreme southeastern corner of Iowa.

(2) UPPER IOWA CONFERENCE shall be bounded as follows, namely: beginning at the northeast corner of Iowa, thence down the Mississippi River to Davenport, including East Dubuque, in Illinois, thence west on the north line of the Iowa Conference to the southeast corner of Story County; thence north to the state line so as to include Iowa Falls; thence east on said line to the place of beginning, including thirty acres known as Clear Lake Methodist Camp, located on the south shore of Clear Lake, Iowa.

(3) NORTHWEST IOWA CONFERENCE shall include that part of Iowa west of the Upper Iowa and north of the Iowa-Des Moines Conferences.

MINNESOTA. In the state of Minnesota there shall be two Conferences with boundaries as follows:

(1) MINNESOTA CONFERENCE shall include that part of Minnesota lying south of the following line: beginning at the eastern boundary of the state at the northeast corner of Washington County; thence running west in the northwest corner of said county; thence south to the northeast corner of Ramsey County; thence following the line of Ramsey County to where it strikes the east line of Hennepin County; thence following the east and south lines of Hennepin County to the point where the Hastings & Dakota Railroad crosses the line of said county, thence following the line of the Hastings & Dakota Railroad to Ortinville; all towns on the Hastings & Dakota Railroad to be in the Northern Minnesota Conference.

(2) NORTHERN MINNESOTA CONFERENCE shall include all Minnesota not included in the Minnesota Conference.

SOUTH DAKOTA. There shall be one Conference in South Dakota with boundaries as follows:

(1) DAKOTA CONFERENCE shall include South Dakota.

NORTH DAKOTA. There shall be one Conference in North Dakota with boundaries as follows:

(1) NORTH DAKOTA CONFERENCE shall include North Dakota.

CENTRAL NORTHWEST CONFERENCE shall include all the Swedish work in the state of New York west of the Genesee River, and in the state of Pennsylvania west of the Susquehanna River, and the Swedish work within the states of Ohio, Indiana, Illinois, Michigan, Wisconsin, Minnesota, Iowa, Nebraska, and Kansas; and also the Swedish work in Hamline, North Dakota; Globe, Missouri; and Denver, Colorado.

NORWEGIAN AND DANISH CONFERENCE shall include all the Norwegian and Danish work between the Atlantic Coast and the Rocky Mountains.

PART II. SPECIAL RECOMMENDATIONS

A. We recommend the approval of the tentative arrangements for holding of the Conferences in Michigan and the proposed adjustments of the problems which have arisen in Michigan. The Michigan Conference of the Methodist Episcopal Church shall meet in Jackson June 7, the Michigan Conference of the Methodist Protestant Church in Adrian June 20, and the Detroit Conference of the Methodist Episcopal Church in Adrian June 21.

B. We recommend that the Chattanooga Circuit of the Indiana Conference of the Methodist Protestant Church, lying mainly in Ohio, be continued in its present relationship temporarily for the adjustment of certain interests.

C. Pertaining to Bilingual Conferences:

(A) WHEREAS, the Bilingual Conferences by tradition and necessity cover several states, so established to reach our scattered people in different sections of our country, and our work organized into bilingual Conferences has been successful for nearly one hundred years; and

(B) WHEREAS, said Conferences have not had time to adjust many complicated conditions peculiar to our bilingual work and to get acquainted with the new Methodist Church and its setup; and

(C) WHEREAS, these churches which are located outside the North Central Jurisdiction will not be able to have any affiliation with their own national groups in the territories in which they are located;

Therefore, we recommend that the Uniting Conference grant the Central Northwest (Swedish) Conference an *Enabling Act* permitting it to retain its present boundaries until said Conference shall have opportunity to determine their future status. And this to be accomplished at the time of the First Jurisdictional Conference.

Therefore, we recommend that the Uniting Conference grant the Norwegian-Danish Conference an *Enabling Act* permitting them to retain their present boundaries until said Conferences shall have opportunity to make compliance with plans, without loss to the Conference, and this is to be accomplished not later than the convening of the First Jurisdictional Conference.

V. THE SOUTH CENTRAL JURISDICTION

REPORT ON BOUNDARIES

Ordered to Record May 6˙ See Journal, Page 280.

Membership of Committee, 184; present when report was adopted, 107; voting for adoption, 107.

The delegates from the Annual Conferences within the South Central Jurisdiction, sitting apart for the purpose of adjusting boundaries and determining the composition of Annual Conferences, submit the following report:

·The Methodist Church in the South Central Jurisdiction shall comprise the states of Missouri, Arkansas, Louisiana, Nebraska, Kansas, Oklahoma, Texas, and New Mexico, and shall include the following Annual Conferences bounded as follows:

(1) LOUISIANA CONFERENCE shall include all Louisiana.

(2) EAST OKLAHOMA CONFERENCE shall include all that part of Oklahoma lying east of the following line: Beginning with the south boundary of Oklahoma at the intersection of Red River and the eastern boundary of Love County; thence north with the eastern boundary of Love County; thence north with the eastern boundary of Love, Carter, Murray, Garvin, and McLain Counties to the South Canadian River; thence west with the north bank of said river to the intersection of said river and the eastern boundary of Cleveland County; thence north with the eastern boundary of Cleveland, Oklahoma, Logan, and Noble Counties to the Arkansas River; thence north with the west bank of said river, and the eastern boundary of Kay County to the Oklahoma line, exclusive of the Indian Mission Conference.

(3) WEST OKLAHOMA CONFERENCE shall comprise all Oklahoma not included in the East Oklahoma Conference, exclusive of Texhoma and the Indian Mission Conference.

(4) INDIAN MISSION shall include the distinctively Indian Pastoral Charges and Missions in Oklahoma.

(5) NEBRASKA CONFERENCE shall include all Nebraska.

(6) MISSOURI CONFERENCE shall comprise all Missouri north of the Missouri River except the four counties of Lincoln, Montgomery, St. Charles, and Warren, and North Kansas City and the Methodist congregation there.

(7) ST. LOUIS CONFERENCE shall comprise Lincoln, Montgomery, St. Charles, and Warren Counties in Missouri, and all that state south of the Missouri River and east of a line beginning at the north point of Moniteau County and running west of south to the southeast corner of Cooper County, thence directly south to the northwest corner of Miller County, and thence southward following the west lines of Miller, Pulaski, Texas, and Howell Counties to the Missouri-Arkansas line. On the west line of Pulaski County the boundary line shall deviate eastward to exclude the town of Richland and the Methodist congregation there.

(8) SOUTHWEST MISSOURI CONFERENCE shall comprise all Missouri south of the Missouri River not included in the St. Louis Conference. Along the boundary at Kansas City the line shall deviate northward to include North Kansas City and the Methodist congregation at that place.

(9) NORTH ARKANSAS CONFERENCE shall comprise that part of Arkansas lying north of the following line: Beginning at the mouth of White River, running up the river to the mouth of Des Arc Bayou; thence up the bayou to the mouth of Cypress Bayou; thence up Cypress Bayou to the main line of the Missouri Pacific Railroad; thence down that railroad to Arkansas River, including all towns along that railroad; thence up Arkansas River to the south line of Perry County; thence along the south lines of Perry, Yell, and Scott Counties to Oklahoma state line.

(10) LITTLE ROCK CONFERENCE shall comprise all of Arkansas not included in the North Arkansas Conference.

(11) KANSAS CONFERENCE shall comprise that part of Kansas lying east of a line traversing the west boundary of Chautauqua, Elk, and Greenwood Counties, thence along the south and west boundary of Chase County to the south and west boundary of Morris County, thence north along the east boundary of Dickinson, Clay, and Washington Counties to the Kansas state line.

(12) CENTRAL KANSAS CONFERENCE shall comprise all that part of Kansas not included in the Kansas Conference.

(13) CENTRAL TEXAS CONFERENCE shall comprise that part of Texas within the following boundaries: Beginning on Trinity River at the southwest corner of Navarro County, and running thence on the south side of the county to the northeast corner of Limestone County (including those parts of Wortham and Cotton Gin Circuits that are situated in Freestone County) to a point opposite the line between Thornton and Kosse Circuits; then west to the southeast corner of Thornton Circuit; thence in a direct line to the southeast corner of McLennan County; thence with the

south line of that county (including the Mooresville and Perry Churches in Falls County) to Bell County; thence with the east line of Bell County to Milam County; thence with the south line of Bell County to Williamson County, thence with the east line of Williamson County, exclusive of Manda, to Lee County; thence on the south line of Williamson County to the Austin & Northwestern Railroad; thence with the railroad, not including Liberty Hill and Leander charge, to Burnet County; thence with the east line of Burnet and Lampasas Counties to Hamilton County; thence west on the south side of Hamilton County to Mills County; thence north, and west with the lines of Mills County to Colorado River, including Bethany Church in Indian Creek Circuit; thence with the Colorado River to the east line of Coke County; thence with the east line of Coke County to the southeast corner of Nolan County; thence east with the county lines to the southwest corner of Eastland County and including Putnam, Cross Plains Station, and Dressy Circuit in Callahan County; thence north with the west lines of Eastland, Stephens, and Young Counties to the northwest corner of Young County; thence with the west and south boundaries of the North Texas Conference and the west boundary of the Texas Conference of this Jurisdiction to the beginning.

(14) NORTH TEXAS CONFERENCE shall comprise that part of Texas within the following boundaries: On the north by Red River, beginning at the northwest corner of Wichita County; thence east down the river to the northeast corner of Red River County; thence south along the east line of that county to its southeast corner; thence west along the south line of the county to the northeast corner of Franklin County, including the town of Talco in Titus County; thence south along the east line of Franklin County to its southeast corner, but including the town of Winnsboro; thence west along the south lines of Franklin and Hopkins Counties to the northwest corner of Rains County; thence south to the southwest corner of that county; thence west on the south of Hunt County to the northeast corner of Kaufman County; thence south with the east line of that county to its southeast corner; thence along the south and west lines of that county to the southeast corner of Dallas County; thence along the south and west lines of that county to the northeast corner of Tarrant County; thence west on the south lines of Denton, Wise, and Jack Counties to the southwest corner of Jack County; thence along the west line of that county to the northeast corner of Young County; thence west with the south line of Archer County to the

southwest corner of the county; thence north with the west lines of Archer and Wichita Counties to the beginning.

(15) NORTHWEST TEXAS CONFERENCE shall comprise that part of Texas within the following boundaries: Beginning on Red River at the northeast corner of Wilbarger County, south with the east line of Wilbarger and Baylor Counties to the northwest corner of Young County; thence south and west with the boundaries of the Central Texas Conference to Colorado River; thence west with the south lines of Mitchell and Howard Counties to the northeast corner of Glasscock County, thence south to the southeast corner of Glasscock County; thence west with the south lines of Glasscock and Midland Counties to the southwest corner of Midland County; thence north to the line of Andrews County; thence west to the corner of New Mexico; thence north along the state line to the northwest corner of the state; thence east with the state line to the northeast corner of Lipscomb County; thence south with the state line to the south fork of Red River; thence down Red River to the beginning and including the town of Texhoma, Oklahoma.

(16) TEXAS CONFERENCE shall comprise that part of Texas within the following boundaries: Beginning at the northeast corner of Red River County, thence east with Red River to the northeast corner of Texas; thence south with the state line to the Gulf of Mexico; on the south by the Gulf of Mexico to Matagorda Bay; thence to the mouth of Colorado River; thence north, up the river to the north line of Wharton County; thence east to the southeast corner of Colorado County; thence north with the west line of Austin (exclusive of Industry) County, Washington and Lee Counties to Williamson County; and on the north by the line of the Central Texas Conference, exclusive of the town of Perry, to Trinity River at the northeast corner of Freestone County; thence with Trinity River to the southwest corner of Kaufman County; thence with the boundary line of the North Texas Conference to the beginning.

(17) SOUTHWEST TEXAS CONFERENCE (formerly West Texas Conference) shall comprise that part of Texas west and south of the Texas, Central Texas, and Northwest Texas Conferences, including Industry and Manda, except the area west of Pecos River; and that embraced in the New Mexico Conference east of Pecos River.

(18) SOUTHWEST MEXICAN CONFERENCE shall include all the Spanish-language work in Texas and New Mexico.

(19) NEW MEXICO CONFERENCE shall include all New Mexico and that part of Texas beginning at the southeast corner of New Mexico, and running east along the line di-

viding Winkler and Ector Counties to the northwest corner of Midland County; thence south with the west line of Midland and Upton Counties to Pecos River; thence along the river to its mouth; thence northwest along the Rio Grande to the south line of New Mexico.

VI. THE WESTERN JURISDICTION

REPORT No. 1

Ordered to Record May 10. See Journal, Page 386.

Membership of Jurisdiction, 51; present when report was adopted, 40; voting for adoption, 40.

REPORT ON BOUNDARIES

The following report was adopted May 8, 1939, at a meeting in Kansas City, Mo., of delegates to the Uniting Conference of The Methodist Church from all the Conferences of the Methodist Episcopal Church, Methodist Episcopal Church, South, and Methodist Protestant Church placed within the bounds of the Western Jurisdiction.

In keeping with the provisions of the Plan of Union the delegates from the Western Jurisdiction recommend the following be fixed as the boundaries of the respective Conferences:

ANNUAL CONFERENCES

CALIFORNIA CONFERENCE shall include all that portion of California and all that portion of Nevada lying north of the northern boundary of the Southern California Conference, with the exception of White Pine County, Nevada.

COLORADO CONFERENCE shall include all of Colorado.

IDAHO CONFERENCE shall include all Idaho not embraced in the Pacific Northwest Conference, together with the following territory in the state of Oregon, namely: the counties of Baker, Malheur, Harney, Grant, Wallowa, and Union.

MONTANA CONFERENCE shall include all Montana.

OREGON CONFERENCE shall include all Oregon not included in the Idaho Conference.

PACIFIC NORTHWEST CONFERENCE shall include the state of Washington and that part of Idaho lying north of the southern boundary of Idaho County.

SOUTHERN CALIFORNIA CONFERENCE shall include that portion of California lying south of the line beginning at the northwest corner of San Luis Obispo County, running east along the north boundary of San Luis Obispo County to the northwest corner of Kern County; thence south along the west boundary of Kern County to the south boundary of said county; thence east along the south boundary of Kern County to the west boundary of San Bernardino County; thence north along the west boundaries of San Bernardino and Inyo Counties to the south boundary of Mono County; thence east to the California-Nevada state line; also that portion of Nevada lying south of a line beginning at a point where the thirty-seventh parallel of north latitude intersects the California-Nevada state line, thence east along said parallel to the west line of Lincoln County, Nevada; thence north and east along the line of Lincoln County to the Nevada-Utah state line; also the state of Arizona.

WYOMING STATE CONFERENCE shall include all Wyoming.

MISSION CONFERENCES AND MISSIONS

ALASKA MISSION shall include the territory of Alaska.

CALIFORNIA ORIENTAL MISSION shall include the work among Chinese, Filipino and Korean people in the Western Jurisdiction excepting that work in the Hawaii Mission.

HAWAII MISSION shall include all the work in the territory of Hawaii.

LATIN AMERICAN MISSION shall include the work among the Spanish-speaking people in the Western Jurisdiction, together with that in the states of Sonora and Lower California in the Republic of Mexico.

PACIFIC JAPANESE MISSION shall include the work among the Japanese people in the Western Jurisdiction excepting that in the Hawaii Mission.

UTAH MISSION shall include the work in Utah and in White Pine County, Nevada.

Fixing of these boundaries is intended to include the placing of all the work of the Methodist Episcopal Church, the Methodist Episcopal Church, South, and the Methodist Protestant Church within the boundaries of the Western Jurisdiction, under the jurisdiction of the above named Annual Conferences within whose geographical boundaries the individual Charges or other institutions of these three Churches lie.

FRATERNAL ADDRESSES

THE METHODIST CHURCH OF NEW ZEALAND

ADDRESS OF DR. E. P. BLAMIRES

Bishop Moore, Fellow Methodists: I come from a small country, New Zealand; but small countries have taken their place in the history of the world. New Zealand was the first country to give old-age pensions, it has adopted this month the most advanced social security legislation perhaps in the world. I am more proud of the fact that we have the lowest rate of infant mortality, taking care of life from its source. The Methodist Church effected union in 1913 and the hand of God has been upon us for good.

I bring you the greetings of my Conference and pray that God's blessing richly rests upon this great Methodist Church of America.

I want to express the gratitude of our Southern countries to the Methodist Church of America; for though we are a daughter Conference of British Methodism, you have sent visitors from time to time who have meant much to the kingdom of God in the Southern lands. Recently we have had Dr. Stanley Jones. Bishop Holt was with us at the Australian General Conference about three or four years ago.

Bishop Locke was your representative to the New Zealand Centenary Conference in 1932, and he was a very worthy and helpful representative. I would most especially mention Bishop William Taylor, for there has been a contingent of Methodist ministers with evangelistic fervor ever since his visit of more than 50 years ago.

I respect your time, and therefore put myself on the time limit, and thank you for this wonderful welcome. Looking into the eyes of those whom I have met thus far I have seen the soul of friends and brothers. I suppose it would be the same if I could come face to face with every individual in this Conference.

May God richly bless you and the world-wide Methodism fulfill her mission as part of Christ's great Universal Church.

THE METHODIST CHURCH OF GREAT BRITAIN
ADDRESS OF DR. ROBERT BOND

Mr. Chairman, I don't think that the Conference will desire to hear anything more so far as I am concerned. You listened with great patience last night, to me at any rate, when Mr. Foot and I had the opportunity of expressing the greetings of our own Church. We are looking with very great interest to this venture of yours, and with great confidence.

I don't think that you have quite the same difficulties that we had. There was scarcely a town or a city or a village in the whole of the British Isles where there were not at least two Methodist churches, and, in many cases, where only one was required. We have practiced no coercion— they have come together, where they have come together, of their own free will.

At our next Conference we hope to tie up the last remaining loose strings, and we have found it considerably easy where good will was concerned. You can do almost anything by good will, except one thing. That is what we have found difficult. You can't make one pound into two pounds, whatever the good will in the world is. Our finance has been one of our problems.

Perhaps you won't mind me just saying this, as an instance of how they have managed themselves. One of our villages has two churches where there ought only to have been one. There never should have been more than one, except that there were different denominations. When Methodist union came they set about trying to solve the problem of using one of these churches for a place of worship and the other for a Sunday school. They were on the best of terms, but neither of them desired to say to the other, "Yours is the church that is to be turned into a Sunday school."

They followed a very simple plan. One of the churches was a Wesleyan church; and the other one was a United Methodist church. They agreed on three or four men whose judgment they could all trust, and they said, "Now, then, you go into the matter and tell us what ought to be done, and we will agree to what you decide." Those men went into the matter and finally decided this: that the Wesleyan church was best suited for the purposes of a church, and therefore counseled that that should remain as the church for the two. The United Methodist church was best suited as a building to be transformed into a Sunday school.

They recommended that, and then added this: that the

furnishing of the United Methodist church was better than the furnishing of the Wesleyan church. So they made me consent that the pews and everything be taken out of the Wesleyan church, and the pews of the United Methodist church be put in. So it ended by every Wesleyan being able to worship in his own church and every United Methodist being able to sit in his own pew.

I offer that as an excellent method of solving some of the problems where there are two churches and only one is needed.

May I say how greatly we appreciate the kindly reception you have given us.

ADDRESS OF MR. ISAAC FOOT

Bishop Moore, Fathers, and Brethren: Having occupied far more time than I should have done last night, I was unaware that I was to be given the privilege of saying another word this morning. It will be very brief, but if I spoke to you for a long time I could not fully express my gratitude at your welcome and my sense of the high privilege of having been able to speak for millions of Methodist lay folk in England to the Methodists in this country over the sea.

I felt at home as a man belonging to a famous city in England. I was born in Plymouth in England, a city not as large as some, and not as wealthy as others, but for fame second to no city in the world. When I made my night journey the other night from Washington to Chicago, I arose in the morning and looked at the name of the first station through which I passed, and the name of the station was Plymouth. That shows something of the association between the two countries.

What after all, are the ties, my friends? What are the ties between the two countries? Bishop Moore has been speaking of the tie of common inheritance of John Wesley. A great Englishman who was a friend to America, Edmund Burke, spoke of those ties that, though light as air, are as strong as links of iron.

What, after all, binds together the people of these two countries? Not anything that can be expressed in statutes, nothing that can be written down, nothing that is in a certain sense material or ponderable. The things that unite us are the common inheritance, the common possession of the inheritance of liberty, and, above all, I think the possession of the Bible written in our own tongue. That is our greatest common possession. We rejoice in those, at least.

I have found my welcome as steady when I came to this

wonderful city, Kansas City. The first night I was here, two nights ago, I was aroused in the middle of the night by what you call, I think, the watchman of the hotel, who asked me to lock my door. Being a trustful Englishman, I had left my key in the door from the outside.

In the morning I asked the chambermaid if it was customary to lock doors in America. She said, "It is not usual, sir, but we have a big Conference here this week."

I therefore recognized that the Methodists here have a reputation in this part of the country and are perhaps like the Presbyterians, from whom we had a representative just now. He said they keep the Sabbath and everything else they can lay their hands on.

I conclude just with one story. I am tempted to it by the Presbyterian just now, who spoke of their high pride.

You did hear, no doubt, of the woman in my country who, after being a member for many years of the Presbyterian Church, went to Wesleyan Chapel and her minister was distressed about it. He came to her and asked her why she had done so.

"Well," she said, "it is because of the harmonium that you have brought into the Church."

"But," he said, "you have gone to the Wesleyan Chapel where they have a pipe organ."

"Yes," she said, "there is all the difference in the world between a pipe organ in the Wesleyan Chapel and a harmonium in the House of God."

It is her spirit which has prevented the unity in my country which they have been able to achieve in Canada.

If I could express in one word what I think would be the mind of millions of men and women in the country to which I am proud to belong, sent to you, their relatives over the sea, it would be this: That the God of Hope fill you with all joy and peace, that we may abound in hope through the power of the Holy Spirit.

THE METHODIST CHURCH OF BRAZIL
ADDRESS OF BISHOP CESAR DACORSO, FILHO

Dear Chairman, dear Brethren and Sisters: I convey the sincerest greetings and felicitations of the Methodist Church of Brazil to you; at the same time, the expression of profound admiration, appreciation, and gratitude for the assistance which in so many forms the Methodist Episcopal Church—I must say, you—have so graciously given us since the beginning of our history, through your missionary work, which has never failed.

The first Methodist missionary to visit our country was Rev. Fountain E. Pitts, of Nashville. He was in Brazil in 1835, one hundred four years ago. He was there only to study the country and the people.

The Methodist work in Brazil started in 1876, fifty-three years ago. The Rev. John J. Ransom, I think from Nashville, Tenn., was the first effective Methodist worker in the country.

Actually, the Church has a membership of 25,000, and about 120 ministers. I should mention also about 25,000 adherents, so in Brazil the Methodist family comes to about 50,000.

The Church is still too small, as it has to face a so large country and a so large population. We are working in about one-eighth of the national territory, and we are in contact with about 50,000 Brazilians.

Last year the increase of the membership of our Church was one-tenth of the previous year. If the base of the increase of the Brazilian population be kept for the succeeding years it will be doubled each 23 years. As you may easily see, if the increase of the membership of the Methodist Church in Brazil may be kept on the same basis, and the increase of the Brazilian population also, Methodism in Brazil will come to be in the succeeding years a great moral power and an influential force, as the Methodist Church has been in this marvelous country.

Brazil is coming very fast to the front line of the nations of this world. Even we Brazilians do not know what will be the rôle of the Brazilian people in the destiny of humanity. In this condition we Methodists in Brazil have now the best, largest, the most magnificent opportunity that we can imagine. We have only one Church, one Methodist Church, in 'Brazil.

We have no divisions in Brazil between foreign and Brazilians, whites, Indians and colored, nationals and missionaries. So in our Church at large, in our local churches, the foreigners and the nationals, the Colored people and the Whites are all mixed and joined the same. In our Church there is no difference between missionaries and nationals.

We rejoice greatly in seeing that we are a part of the long Methodist chain that goes from pole to pole in the Americas. We are willing to stretch our arms to our Methodist brethren in the West, in the East, over the seas, in order that we may fulfill what John Wesley wants to see—Methodists are one people.

Thank you very much.

THE METHODIST CHURCH OF MEXICO
ADDRESS OF BISHOP ELEAZAR GUERRA

Last year I was elected as the fraternal delegate to the last General Conference of the Methodist Episcopal Church, South. For one reason or another I did not receive my credentials on time, so I was not able to speak before that great body. So, when I arrived here, I did my very best to find my place here.

That reminds me of a little story. There was a lady, a very parsimonious lady, who had two children. This lady was in contact with high society and again and again she told her children not to interrupt when she was talking to important persons.

This lady had a visitor, and while they were in the midst of a very important conversation one of the children came in in a very desperate mood and said to the mother, "Mother, mother!"

The mother said, "Get away; don't interrupt us."

So the little child went away, and after the visit was over, the mother came out and said, "What did you want? What did you want to interrupt us for?"

The little girl said, "Mother, my little sister fell down in the water and I wanted to tell you."

I wanted to present to you the Mexican cause before it is too late, for, as this great Church goes forward, it must take into consideration the Mexican Methodist Church needs. You must not forget us.

It is my very peculiar privilege to be here at this hour to bring you the greetings of my Church, The Methodist Church of Mexico.

Eight years ago history was written in Mexico by the setting up of an autonomous Church, but that history was forced to circumstances, especially by an extreme nationalistic point of view and by legal laws of my country.

You are writing history here this hour, but a history that is the culmination of conscious process toward forming a great united Church. Whereas, in 1845 you divided and went on to minister to the world with broken hearts and tears of deep sorrow, now you are ready to go forward united to minister to the world, not with broken hearts, but with a joyous and radiant experience.

The Methodist Church of Mexico is composed of two Conferences of about equal strength. The frontier Conference works in the six northern states and the central Conference works four central states.

The actual membership of the Church is ten thousand and

the total constituency is twenty thousand. We have 248 pastoral charges and 100 ministers. The total amount raised for all purposes in the Church in 1938 was 130,000 pesos.

The Methodist Church of Mexico is marching forward in two ways especially—with great movement of spiritual value and doing all that is possible to obtain the self-support of the Church.

Our Church is in a very peculiar situation at this hour. Due to the fact that the civil laws of the country prohibit taking part in religious services to foreigners, it is going to be an impossibility to replace those that left the country in obedience to those laws. There is not a way to substitute those persons, so, with sorrow in our hearts, we are expecting the day when no more missionaries will be working in Mexico. What then?

The Mexican Methodists are urging you to work with us in order that we may have closer relations. That way may be encouraging us to develop young leaders, giving them proper training and afterward sending them to the states for further experience, so as to give them the opportunity to get in touch with your environment.

I assure you that Methodism is going to stay in Mexico because of the spirit that we got from our founder, John Wesley, in the missionaries you sent to us.

Our lives have been inspired by the work of the missionaries, but especially I want to mention two of them at this hour. One was Mrs. Streeter, a beautiful character who came into our midst and spent her whole life in behalf of the Mexican people. She went one time to a little town named Nombre de Dios. It has the name of God, but not the spirit of God. When she was there she was attacked and brutally injured. After she recovered—as a result of that experience she was permanently lame—somebody said to her, "Now, Mrs. Streeter, do you still want to go on with your missionary work in Mexico?"

She replied, "Certainly I do, and I am going back again to that same town to preach the wonderful message of Jesus Christ."

The other missionary is the Rev. Frank S. Onderdonk, one of the greatest missionaries that ever was sent to a missionary field.

Dr. Onderdonk spent the best years of his life in Mexico, but after the trouble during the revolution period, he came back to the country to work with the Mexican people in the Southwest. He was directly responsible for awakening the consciousness of young preachers. He guided them, directed them, inspired them. He kept on for years and years, dedicating his whole life in the ministry to work among the Mexican people.

During the year before he died he was afflicted with a terrible disease; and instead of taking time to restore his health, he just went on up to the last moment, holding his place of responsibility in the Church.

Certainly, when we have men and women with that spirit of sacrifice, we are bound to be inspired. That is why I am saying that Methodism in Mexico is going to stay.

How can we repay this work of sacrifice and love that you have given us? There is only one way, in my humble thinking, and it is to throw ourselves entirely into an intensive, sacrificial work for our Church.

You have proved to be a great and gracious leader in the past. Be it once more, but in a larger way; in a way that you may comfort the world.

THE METHODIST PROTESTANT CHURCH OF JAPAN

ADDRESS OF PRESIDENT YOTARO KOIZUMI ·

It is my great honor to stand here and to speak a little salutation.

I come from Japan, and I am the president of the Methodist Protestant Church of Japan. I express to you the heartfelt gratitude of our Conference.

I think that you, brothers and sisters in Christ, understand our situation in Japan.

I have many things to say, but my poor attainment in speaking English does not go so far.

I believe you always sympathize with us, encourage us, and pray for us, for the people of Japan that they may have the peace of Jesus Christ.

THE JAPAN METHODIST CHURCH

ADDRESS OF DR. KYUGORO OBATA ·

Dear Fathers and Brethren: As one of those who are deeply concerned about the world's unrest; as one of those who are constantly seeking light that may give a clue toward the solution of the grave questions of our day; and as one of those who firmly believe that the Christian force created by the union of the three Methodist Churches, and now formally declared before the Christendom of the world, will be adequate to rejuvenate the Christian faith and its activities, badly crippled by the great World War—I have come from the Far East to offer you my hearty greetings.

Ever since I heard of this Uniting Conference, there has been moving in my mind back and forth like a shuttle in the weaver's hands one significant word, with its rich contents and happy associations, and that word is "congratulation." Never before in my life have I been confronted with an object which demanded of me such an unreserved expression of congratulation as this Conference does, and there are various reasons for it. I would speak of three of them.

In the first place, I have a strong personal reason to congratulate this Conference. In the month of May, 1916, exactly twenty-three years ago, I had the privilege of attending the General Conference of the Methodist Episcopal Church held in Saratoga Springs, N. Y. as the fraternal delegate from the Japan Methodist Church. In my parting remarks, these words are found, which I ask your indulgence to quote. They read: "I have witnessed what we call psychological moments; but I doubt whether I shall see a more beautiful scene in heaven than what I have seen here, when two senior Bishops of the two Methodist Episcopal Churches, stood up on the platform and shook hands, amidst the applause from this house, and I take it as a pledge of every member of this Conference that the plan of unification can be carried and will be perfected before long."

The enthusiasm of the Committee of Sixty on Unification and of the Conference itself was so great that they thought the Uniting Conference might be called by the Board of Bishops before the General Conference of 1920 should meet. But, of course, it was quite natural for such large organizations as the two Methodist Episcopal Churches, with their respective habits, institutions, and rules of conduct, to take time in order to be welded into one organization. Moreover, the delay might be construed as providential, when we think that it furnished an opportunity for the Methodist Protestant Church to join in this Methodist trinitarianism. The entrance of the Methodist Protestant Church into this union transcends my personal congratulation, and for that reason I rejoice all the more. I hope that the brethren of the Methodist Protestant Church of Japan will not be offended when I say that the stand the Methodist Church of America has taken must needs be a prophecy or a happy augury for what they shall follow in the future. So much for my personal congratulation!

In the second place, this Conference deserves congratulation of a national scope, and let it be called a national congratulation. In speaking of the national congratulation directly touching an American question, a patriotic American may object saying that it is his own business, not that of a Japanese to attend to affairs American. But the Scriptures teach us to "rejoice with them that do rejoice." Why cannot a foreigner participate in the joy of a country which he loves? For me, as for thousands of my fellow countrymen, America is a home of Alma Mater, and I feel I have a right to claim that a matter of national congratulation for an American is also mine.

I can visualize millions of Methodist homes throughout this great Republic turning their attention to this Uniting Conference, carefully watching its deliberations. The improvement of the systems of communication and transportation has brought South and North close together. A good deal of personal contacts has been going on, thus obliterating the lines which divided them. But public and organized bodies, such as Christ Churches, have remained still divided, and as long as well-organized institutions or groups remain divided, so long will a true union be impeded. Individuals will pass away, but the groups organized will persist. Now the two well-organized institutions agree to become one. Therefore, this organization not only will permanently exist but also is bound to go far to influence national unity—a unity which is the source of strength and power for a nation.

Another wholesome influence of this union will be as an example to stimulate similar kinds of union for other divided organizations. The union of the three Methodist bodies serves as an incentive to bring about the fundamental union of the American nation. For this I offer my hearty congratulations to America.

Thirdly, I shall briefly dwell on the international congratulation. It has been a time-honored and proud slogan for Great Britain to tell the world that the sun never sets on her dominions. Just in the same way, or rather in a superior way, it can be said that the sun never sets in the countries where Methodist churches are planted. The dream of the founder of Methodism, "The world is my parish," is no longer a dream, but a fact beyond any dispute. These world-wide Methodist activities will receive a new impetus by the consummation of the union of the three Methodist Churches in America. A Methodist Church like the Japan Methodist Church will be keenly sensitive of this union and take fresh courage from the spiritual solidarity of "a truly world church" of Methodism demonstrated by this union.

In this connection, it may not be out of place to tell you

how the Japan Methodist Church has fared during the last twenty-three years. The comparative figures of 1915 and 1938 are as follows:

	1915	1938	Increase
Native Preachers	208	404	100%
Missionaries	103	105	—
Church Members	15,364	49,439	222%
Teachers, Officers and Pupils of S. S.	27,178	40,442	49%
Officers and Members of E. L.	3,103	8,590	177%
Finance (self-support)	127,091	373,162	193%

These are rough statements giving a general view of the main work. In addition, various social and charitable activities are carried on. What is true with the Japan Methodist Church must be true with other Methodist Churches throughout the world.

The Uniting Conference of The Methodist Church is now an object of congratulations from all over the world. But it should be remembered that an object of congratulation must be an object of responsibility. The greater the congraulation is, the heavier is the responsibility. Hence the new Methodism must face a responsibility in a cosmic fashion and scale, and it would not be a bad thing if some great enterprise in the fields of morality and religion should be undertaken in commemoration of this epoch-making gathering. Build a monument of divine magnitude, to which future generations of Methodism may look with pride and gratitude. As a man of Macedonia beckoned St. Paul to come over and help, so a man of the Far East may be calling to the newly awakened conscience of this great Conference. There can never be too big a problem of moral nature for United Methodism to tackle.

Let the Methodism of America transcend all the earthly confusion and strife of our day, and attune her attitude to that of Him who "maketh his sun to rise on the evil and on the good, and sendeth rain on the just and on the unjust," whenever she is called to face any grave problem.

I am not as old as Simeon of the New Testament, but feel old enough to reckon this my visit in this capacity as the last. So, borrowing his words, I conclude my message, which it has been my honor to deliver to you on behalf of the Japan Methodist Church, thus: "Lord, now lettest thou thy servant depart in peace, for mine eyes have seen . . . . a light to lighten" the world.

Thank you. I thank you especially. This is my birthday, and you could not have done greater honor to me than by giving me this opportunity to deliver a message to you.

THE UNITED CHURCH OF CANADA

ADDRESS OF DR. GORDON A. SISCO

Bishop Moore and Brethren: I have been Secretary of the General Council of the United Church for two years, but even in that short space of time I have learned that long speeches on an occasion like this are not in order. Therefore, I simply want to take this opportunity in view of the fact that I am appearing again on the program in connection with Ecumenical Night to reinforce what the Moderator has said and bring our greetings to you. You know the task that is yours. We are interested in all that pertains to your welfare, and we wish you God's blessing upon your task.

ADDRESS OF DR. J. W. WOODSIDE

Bishop Moore and Brethren: It is a very great joy to bring you the greetings and felicitations of the United Church of Canada. We rejoice with you very greatly indeed in this most happy consummation. We have followed with great interest every step of your deliberations and have given you our prayers. And we shall continue through the years to follow you with interest and pray that God's richest blessing may abide upon you.

As I look around me this morning, I am reminded of an occasion in the year 1925 in the city of Toronto, in a building similar to this, when some 8,000 people gathered together and formed the United Church of Canada, bringing together the Methodist Church of Canada and Newfoundland, the Congregational Churches of Canada, and the Presbyterian Church in Canada.

And, like you, that union was consummated as a great answer to a challenging human need. Of course, we were convinced that our action was in harmony with the teaching of the New Testament. And during these intervening years we have received confirmation, abundant confirmation, that we took the right step. Now, in your happy union, we have a further confirmation that we took the right step.

I wish I had time this morning to tell you something about our setup, because I discovered that there is a certain amount of ignorance, even in these intelligent United States, in regard to your nearest neighbor, Canada. One day last summer in the middle of July, when it was registering 90 in the shade, a man and his wife from one of the Southern states who has decided to spend a happy holiday in Canada, reached the boundary at Niagara Falls, and they had with them their fur coats, ski boots and skis, and a toboggan.

I am quite sure that such ignorance in regard to our country is not common among you, but some of it is there, and I want to tell you something about our Church.

We number among our adherents in Canada some two millions of people. That may seem like a small number in comparison to the great numbers in these Uniting Churches here, but it is a very great number in proportion to the total population of our country. It is an even larger proportion than what you represent in this Conference meeting here today.

Our missionary enterprises cover half a continent, the half of the continent which is larger in area than these United States; from the Atlantic to the Pacific, from the 49th Parallel on the south to the Artic Circle you will find the United Church of Canada everywhere. And our missions beyond the seas are in every land. It is literally true that the sun never sets on the mission fields of the United Church of Canada.

The thing that we have done in our union is a much more difficult thing than you have done, because we have united three great old denominations. Probably you know something down here of how difficult that really is, how difficult it is to unite Presbyterians and Methodists and Congregationalists. The Presbyterians with us are just like they are down here, stiff and proud in the pride of the elect. And the Methodists with us were just the same as they are here before me, always fearful lest they might fall from grace. The Congrationalists with us are just the same as they are with you, going about, doing just as they please.

However, by the grace of God we were able to mold them into one great organization, and it wasn't easy. We have set forth our beliefs in what we call twenty Articles of Faith. That was a great achievement, and something of which we are not ashamed. It would be worth your while to read those twenty Articles of Faith. We took twenty-six great boards of these different denominations and molded them into six boards. You will discover how difficult a thing that is. We have taken four great Church papers and amalgamated them into one, and three missionary papers into one. We have taken three great publishing interests and merged them into one. We have taken fifteen theological colleges and reduced them to eight. Possibly you will discover how difficult that is, too.

And I might say to you what you of course know: That we haven't yet solved all our problems by any means. But I want to say to you for your encouragement that we have arrived at that point in our life history where we know that there isn't a problem that has emerged or that will emerge that we cannot solve by the application of patience, good will, compromise, and trusting each other.

We have discovered in regard to these problems as they emerge that one of the very best means of arriving at a solution is to refuse to get tangled up with too many arbitrary measures and wait upon the expreience of living together in good will and trust it to discover the solution that is right and proper. Let me say to you again for your encouragement, we have arrived at the place where we arè sure that there is not a single problem that we cannot so ve.

I want to say this, also, that I have been a member of the great boards, some of the great boards of these United Churches in all these intervening years, and never yet on a single occasion when any matter of controversy has been before us have I seen the slightest indication of divisions along old denominational lines. I say that to you this morning as a brother and for your encouragement.

Mr. Chairman, we live under a great conviction that a greater union is still to be. I am quite sure that that is thè conviction in the hearts of all the delegates who are here this morning. It is true that the Methodist Churches of the United States have struck their tents and are on thè march, and I believe and you believe that you are on the march to an even greater and nobler youth. We in the United Church of Canada are gravely convinced that our common possessions are our greatest possessions, that those things which we hold in common are greater far than everything that keeps us apart. We live in that conviction.

Behind me here on the platform this morning I see two great flags, the flag of your country of which you are justly proud—that flag symbolizes many of those particular things in your life and history of which you have every reason to be proud; those distinctive things in this land and in your life that distinguish you from all others. But beside that flag there this morning is another, my flag, which I love, and which symbolizes for me and for all my fellow citizens those particular things that distinguish us from all others.

But, brethren, we live in a time, unhappily, when we are increasingly discovering that the great possessions we hold in common are more precious than even those great things symbolized by these glorious flags. The same is true of course of the Church. Two or three years ago I lost a great friend, a Roman Catholic Senator to Canada, Senator Charles Murphy. He was, as he described himself, a Sinn Feiner. When he was sick in the hospital in his last illness he sent for me. And this strict Roman Catholic asked me to pray with him again and again and give him the benediction, which I did.

On one occasion he said to me, "Dr.—" he called me, by the way, his Protestant Pope, if you please, his Protestant Pope—"I am a Roman Catholic. I am supposed to be a bigoted Roman Catholic, and you are a Protestant. But I want to tell you as I am nearing the end, that down beneath all the things that divide us, when you go deep enough we are one."

I said to him, "Senator, that is the God's truth," and so it is. We live in the graver conviction that we are moving toward an even larger and happier union. However, it may emerge in the providence of God. This idea of union is old. It is as old as the New Testament. It was envisaged by the Seer of Patmos. Remember how he saw before the throne of God that great multitude which no man can number, all nations and kindreds and tongues of peoples. They were all there and they were all there together. But why were they there together?

First of all, because they were there in a common attitude before the throne of God. And in the second place they were there together because they enjoyed a common redemption. They were washed in the blood of the Lamb. And, thirdly, they were there all together because they shared a common victory. They carried the palms in their hands. I do not know of any other basis of an enduring union, either in religion or among the races of the world. My brethren, church union is not enough. If we could unite all the Christians of this world into one Church, that would be no guaranty of the kind of world that we desire. That Church must be made up of the right kind of people. We need more men and women whose hearts have been strangely warmed. We have numbers enough. It sounds like heresy in these days to say that, when we are putting our trust in numbers. We have enough Christians in the world to set the world right, if they were the right kind of Christians.

I am reminded of the words of John Wesley. John Wesley said: "Give me a hundred men who hate nothing but sin and love nothing but God, and I will shake the gates of hell." And he did.

Give me a Church made up of members who love the Lord Jesus Christ, who hate nothing but sin, and love nothing by God, and I tell you, the gates of hell shall not prevail against her.

REGULAR ADDRESSES

"METHODISM—OUR HERITAGE AND HOPE"

ADDRESS OF DR. M. S. DAVAGE

In the beginning of America was the Negro. The Mayflower landed the Pilgrims at Plymouth in 1620. This was one year after a Dutch ship had landed Negroes at Jamestown. Negroes, therefore, enjoy the distinction of priority in America over the Pilgrim Fathers. It was required of these unwilling guests of the colonies that they give the strength of their bodies to the building of a new world. This they did, and more. They brought to America threefold gifts of body, mind, and soul. They gave the strength of their bodies. Their axes rang through the forests; their plows made deep furrows in the rich soil; their picks and shovels on the roadways kept time to the rhythmic music of their work songs; in field and factory and in the market places their backs bore the heavy burdens of commerce. They made deserts blossom and helped to lay the foundations of America's wealth and greatness.

They gave the strength of their minds. The gifts of our minds have to a marked degree influenced the culture of this nation. The Negro's wit, wisdom, and humorous philosophy of life have enriched the folklore of America. Negroes have inspired white men of letters, poets, novelists, and writers like Joel Chandler Harris, the beloved "Uncle Remus," to achieve fame and fortune as interpreters of Negro life and to give their best messages to the world in Negro dialect.

They likewise brought spiritual gifts. They gave love and loyalty where ordinarily they would have been least expected. Their spirituals are the songs that God gave them in the dark night of their despair, so that they did not hang their harps upon the willows but were enabled to sing the Lord's songs in a strange land.

In these spirituals, strangely devoid of bitterness and hate, we tell of our devotion to the kingdom; of our abiding faith in the goodness and merices of God; of our longing for a better day and of our unyielding belief that such a day would surely come. These songs have universal appeal and have touched the hearts of men and women of every race and nation. They are indeed America's unique contribution to the music of the world.

We are not newcomers, nor mere sojourners in this land. We are Americans with undivided loyalties. We are citizens who owe allegiance to no other flag. There is no hyphen in our patriotism.

In the beginning of Methodism was the Negro. Our fathers heard the moving messages which fell from the lips of Wesley, Asbury, and Coke. The tender hearts of Africa's sons were easily touched by the fervent appeals of the first Methodist evangelists. They were stirred by the plain but powerful exhortations of camp meeting preachers who described in vivid language the happy rewards of the righteous and the condign punishment of the wicked. Dr. Garber, in his book, *The Methodist Are One People,* quotes Richard Allen, founder and first Bishop of the African Methodist Church, as saying, "We are beholden to the Methodists under God, for the light of the gospel we enjoy; for all other denominations preach so high-flown that we are not able to comprehend their doctrine." This was, however, before the establishment of Methodist Theological Seminaries. The shoutings and other enthusiastic demonstrations generally in evidence at the early Methodist camp meetings kindled the emotions of our fathers and struck a responsive chord in their hearts. Negroes were among the 250 persons who contributed to the erection of the first permanent Methodist meetinghouse in America in 1768—eight years before the issuing of the Declaration of Independence. They have continued generous in their contributions to the total financial program of the Church, even to this day as is demonstrated in the fine records of the Columbus and New Orleans areas. From 1790 to 1810, Negroes constituted one-fifth of the entire membership of the Methodist Episcopal Church. Verily, we have a heritage in Methodism. We are the sons of Wesley. Therefore, in this Uniting Conference, we are not "strangers and foreigners, but fellow-citizens with the saints and of the household of God."

The history of our long connection with Methodism is replete with interesting incidents and stories of unique personalities. Time would fail me to tell of the contributions made by many humble black people through all the years to the growth, power, and influence of Methodism. I must, however, mention two outstanding characters. The first is Harry Hosier. Any story of the beginning of Methodism in America which does not give a prominent place to Harry Hosier, familiarly called "Black Harry," is inadequate. Though unlettered, he was evidently an unusual man. He accompained Asbury on many of his long and tiresome journeys. The *record* is that he often preached to the delight and edification of his hearers; the *tradition* is that there were many who preferred the soul stirring sermons of Black Harry to the more logical discourses of his episcopal leader and companion. When Bishop Coke undertook his long preaching tour of America on horseback, Bishop Asbury, out of his experience, recommended two prime requisites for the success of his undertaking. One was a good horse, and other was the loyal companionship of faithful Harry Hosier . . . . for "Black Harry" was wise in the ways and customs of illiterate backwoodsmen and skilled in the technique of wilderness travel. In 1784, he was at the height of his power as a preacher and was commissioned as one of the heralds sent forth to summon the widely scattered circuit-riding preachers to the first Methodist General Conference ever held. Were he alive today, how gladly would he have ridden forth to proclaim the convening of this Uniting Conference! Well, Harry Hosier, herald of the cross and the church, *we are here!* Surely he deserves a place in Methodism's Hall of Fame.

In 1815, John Stewart, who as a young man had lived a rather intemperate life, was converted in a Methodist camp meeting. He immediately experienced a call to preach. His changed heart was expanded by the warmth of the gospel. He was constrained to go forth as a missionary to the Wyandotte Indians. His authority to preach was questioned and he sought a local preacher's license. As proof and fruit of his ministry, he brought with him Indians who had been converted in his meetings. This would not be a bad test for preachers even today. So great was the success of his missionary endeavors among the Indians that he kindled the flame of missionary zeal among the people called Methodists and led to the establishment of the first Missionary Society in our Church. He was assisted in his labors by Jonathan Pointer, another Negro, who acted as interpreter. A monument to the memory of Stewart has been erected in Upper Sandusky, Ohio.

Here, let us note in passing a truly remarkable fact: two white congregations in greater Kansas City—one identified with the Methodist Episcopal Church, the other with the Methodist Episcopal Church, South—trace their origins to the missionary labors of the Negro, John Stewart, among the Indians. Whites, Negroes, and Indians, in Christian co-operation with results reaching down the years. How prophetic! How typical of the very genius of our Church. May it forever be true that all of God's children will always be welcomed to gather around the altars of Methodism and to sing together:

"Let every kindred, every tribe,
On this terrestrial ball,
To Him all majesty ascribe,
And crown Him Lord of all."

We acknowledge a debt. We are debtors to Methodism, North and South. We can never forget that in the days of our most desperate need, when we were despised and destitute, both of things for our higher wants, and of wants for higher things . . . . when our future seemed as "black as a hundred midnights in a cypress swamp" . . . . Methodism sent her sons and daughters from the North, to preach good tidings unto the meek and lowly. What a goodly company! Haven, Rust, Hartzell, Thirkield, Flora Mitchell, and others.

They established schools and homes and colleges, and said, "Arise, shine, for thy light is come."

In the South, too, was a noble band of those who sensed the deep spiritual needs of the slaves, and gladly hearkened to the call of God to minister unto them. Among these were some of the strongest and greatest men the South has produced. Chief among them was Bishop William Capers, founder of missions to the slaves, a spiritual giant among his fellows and one of America's greatest preachers. Also deserving of honorable mention as worthy successors of Bishop Capers are Bishop Atticus G. Haygood, courageous and kindly, author of *Our Brother in Black*, and Rev. George Williams Walker, great President of Paine College.

Bishop Capers was greatly helped by his experience in preaching to our people. Many of the leading preachers of the South hail with delight opportunities to preach to sympathetic colored congregations. The warm amens and hearty hallelujahs of my brethren, placed where they will do most good, never fail to call forth the best there is in a preacher. They can so inspire even an average preacher as to lift him above the levels of his accustomed mediocrity.

In a time like this, when the problem of minorities casts its ominous shadow over a frightened and bewildered world; when nations have become heathen hearts that put their trust in "reeking tube and iron shard," and having forsaken their belief in the potency of right, they are building altars to a modern Moloch of might, the music of whose ritual is attuned to the horrible rhythm of war. In the providence of God, Methodism has been granted a unique opportunity to give the world an object lesson in the treatment of minority groups. Thus far, she has made good! The Persians have a proverb, "When one wronged child cries in the dark, the throne of God rocks from side to side." In many lands and in many tongues God's children are crying in the dark, and the world is in unstable equilibrium.

While the governments of earth anxiously seek safety in military alliances and rest insecurely upon the shifting sands of fear and hatred, our United Church seeks to rest securely upon the firm foundation of Christian brotherhood. The gates of hell cannot prevail against it, for love is stronger than hate. Methodism neither requires nor permits her minorities to "cry in the dark." She gives them every opportunity for self-expression. Presiding Bishops invite delegates representing minority groups to "Come to the platform and make your wants and wishes known!" Though nothing startling may happen as the result of their coming, they thank God for the opportunity.

When the Plan of Union was proposed and adopted, two questions immediately arose. First, what will be the attitude of the United Church toward its Negro membership? and second, what course should Negro members follow in the best interest of all concerned? The answer to the first question is that *every right of the Negro has been conserved and guaranteed by the letter of the law.* It is in the Constitution. That is something! But our experience before and especially during this Conference assures us that above and in addition to the law and permeating it is a spirit of genuine Christian brotherhood which makes the law potent and vital. In this Conference, we have received every consideration and have been shown every courtesy.

Our answer to the second question is that it is our deliberate judgment that the advancement of the kingdom and the interests of all races can best be served by *co-operation,* founded on faith and goodwill, rather than by separation, motivated by fear and ill-will. We have no criticism for those of our peolpe who in an earlier day withdrew and established a Church of their own. Perhaps that was the only solution possible at that time. We have only admiration for the way in which they have maintained and carried on the work of their several denominations. We feel we should have their prayers and blessings and best wishes, as we attempt a more difficult and delicate task. But it is a task freighted with far greater potentialities for the future of our people. People who think at all must realize that without regard to denomination the success or failure of our venture in this co-operative Christian enterprise will surely affect for good or ill the destiny of every Negro in America.

This is a new day and a new Church with a new vision

and new courage. The world is shrinking and contantly growing smaller. The retreat method (running from difficulties) is outmoded because there is scarcely any place left to go. We, therefore, think it better to say, "Come and let us reason together," than to say, "Let us walk in separate and divergent paths." If civilization is to endure, nations and races must learn to live and work together in peace. If eventually and inevitably this must be done, then why not now? It is not too much to believe that God has honored us in choosing our own beloved Methodism to become a laboratory in which a great experiment in international and interracial co-operation on the highest levels is to be attempted and we hope successfully demonstrated.

No, we do not choose to establish another weak denomination whose supreme effort would of necessity be exerted in a selfish struggle to save itself. There are too many of that sort now whose only word is a wail of want and whose only message is a piteous appeal for funds. What manner of service could such an organization hope to render to a people so greatly in need of help and guidance? As Negroes, we want to be done with littleness and narrowness. We want wider horizons! We need to be identified with something large. Too often, the Negro is circumscribed and limited in his contacts and cut off from so many agencies and influences which are uplifting and ennobling. We are restricted and forced to think too much about ourselves. Our souls feel the blighting effects of frustration, and as a result, strange, weird religious cults are developing among us. We are in danger of becoming religious introverts. We want to feel the challenge and the thrill of greatness. we want to lift up our castdown eyes from the insignificant clods to the hills and even to the great stars of God. We want room in which to expand and grow and to develop to the utmost whatever talents God has given us. We are, therefore, glad to be an organic part of a great Christian fellowship—a Church whose parish is the world and whose plans and program are as broad as humanity's need. In short, we do not want to be in a Church whose *appeal is merely racial*. We want to be in a Church which embraces all mankind, and *is big enough for God*.

Negroes in the Methodist Church are more strategically situated than any other group in America or in the world. In a time of tense racial situations, when misunderstanding and suspicions are rife, we have a unique opportunity to interpret what is best and finest in one group to the other and to make a real contribution in promoting better understanding and goodwill between the races. We want to interpret the dreams and hopes and fears and needs of our people. Negroes are thinking: it is a matter of vital concern to the nation what twelve millions of her citizens think.

We go from this great Conference thrilled with a new sense of responsibility. We fell that we have been given a job to do. We have been entrusted with a great commission. We think we are able because we rely upon the continuation of your sympathetic interest and upon Him whose grace is sufficient. We do not deceive ourselves. Our yoke will not be easy nor our burden light. Mountains of wearisome heights are ahead.

We know we have chosen a hard way. We must suffer many disappointments, disillusionments, and some failures ere we reach our goal, but confidently, and with faith, we fare forward.

> "We see our way as birds their trackless way.
> We shall arrive! what time, what circuits first,
> We ask not; but unless God sends His hail
> Or blinding fireballs, sleet or stifling snow,
> In some time, in His good time, we shall arrive."

THE SCHOOL OF DIVINITY AND ITS RELATION TO THE UNITED CHURCH

ADDRESS OF DR. LYNN HAROLD HOUGH

Mr. Chairman: I am to speak of the School of Divinity and its relation to the United Church.

I believe, with Dr. Umphrey Lee, that the college and the university affiliated with the Church have a most far-reaching contribution to make to the life of the Church and to the life of the world. There are those who would debate this question, but there can be no question at all about the definitive relation of the School of Divinity to the life of the Church.

If the Church is to be a permanently powerful institution, it must possess those characteristics which it will receive from the adequate School of Divinity.

So I want to talk to you about the theological school and the work it is to do for the Church and through the Church for the world.

First of all, the Divinity School is the stronghold of theological learning. I am glad to emphasize this because it must become clear to all of us that every preacher should be a theologian. You will never hear physicians boast of their ignorance of materia medica. You never hear surgeons boast of their ignorance of human anatomy. Sometimes, curiously enough, you can hear ministers boasting of their ignorance of theology. It is as if a man should say, I know nothing about God; therefore, I am quite ready to be his representative in the world.

The truth of the matter is that a man whose life has been tinctured by the idealism which he finds in the Gospels, but has come to no profound understanding or experience of the deeper meaning of the Christian religion, is a source of infinite embarrassment to the Church. The man who gives the Christian message must have great understanding and conviction and respect of God and Christ and man and sin and the cross and the new life in this world and the infinite promise of immortality.

These theological sanctions are buttressed by profound understanding of the Old Testament and the New; of twenty centuries of Christian history and of the integration of Christian thought and a commanding theology.

It is curious to find men who think that they can bring forth the fruits of the Christian religion without the roots of the Christian religion. Patient, meticulous scholarship, thoroughgoing and disciplined thinking lie at the basis of all our work. An emotional experience cannot be a substitute for an intellectual understanding of the Christian religion.

One of the reasons why Methodism has been a happy hunting ground for intellectual obsessions is just that we have failed to understand the necessity of subjecting our deepest experience to the disciplines of the intelligence. A ministry, to whom the Christian religion has become an adequate buttressed body of convictions, burning with the fire of personal experiences, will have a great future.

In the second place, the School of Divinity is the home of creative freedom. Freedom without convictions means anarchy. Solidly held positions with no freedom reduce life to a den of slaves.

The theological school must be the home of the free scholar. He must be allowed to tell the truth as he sees it in respect of every investigation having to do with Biblical scholarship, every process of thought and every analysis of the bewildering ways of man and the life of the human spirit.

Milton was perfectly clear that even heaven could not be populated by coerced saints. It was to be the home of men who ·chose· goodness and God freely. Everything in the Church rests at last upon this freely chosen and uncoerced Christianity. It is as a home of freedom that the theological school will do its most notable work.

In the third place, the School of Divinity is the treasure house of spiritual tradition. The life of God in the soul of man became a blazing reality at Pentecost and the experience of God has been the living force which has moved through the Church's ways from the days of Paul, through the days of Origen and Clement, of Tertullian, of Augustine, of St. Thomas and St. Francis, of Luther and Calvin and of Wesley, down to the present day.

The spiritual tradition has changed the life of countries, has brought new quality into civilizations, and is, on the whole, the most notable of the forces which have influenced the life of man.

The student of the theological school must be introduced to it; not merely as the object of meticulous and microscopic investigation, but as a great and glorious reality which is to master his conscience and quicken his spirit, even as it dominates his mind.

This classic tradition of Christian religion must be made real to every minister who is sent out to declare the good tidings.

In the fourth place, the School of Divinity is a shrine of the new life in Christ. There is a sense, of course, in which these deep matters of the human spirit cannot be taught; and yet there are atmospheres and climates in which they become most potent. Whatever else a minister is, he must be a man to whom the new life in Christ is the supreme actuality of human existence. At whatever point the Divinity School fails, it must not fail here; the lights must be kept burning before this great altar.

In 1898, when I entered theological school, the typical Methodist divinity student came with a burning evangelical experience. He needed training, discipline, cultivation, and no end of guidance. Today a surprising number of men in our Divinity Schools are young men of good will who have been mastered by the idealism of Jesus, but are singularly lacking in any understanding of the vitalities of an evangelical experience.

I am perfectly willing to have a young man enter theological school without an evangelical experience. I am terribly disappointed if he leaves the theological school without crossing the great divide. The truth is, of course, that many men and many types make up the Christian ministry. The Apostle James would not have understood an evangelical experience, but it was not the Apostle James who gave passion and power to the Christianity of his period and it has always been true that it has been the men of evangelical experience who have kept the Church alive. So, the new life in Christ must have a permanent shrine in our theological schools.

In the fifth place, the School of Divinity is a mirror of the contemporary world. This, of course, is as it should be. Anyone who supposes that theological schools are spots where innocent young men of singular gentleness of spirit, unaware of what is going on in the world, and with a mysticism as unworldly as Palestrinia's music, meet together to cultivate the things of the spirit, has a singularly unrealistic picture of the theological school. Real young men of a real world who have been mastered by something beyond the borders of time, meet in our theological schools. There is no aspect of the passion and the pain of the contemporary world which is not reflected in the life of the theological school. Our young men know—and they should know— the bitter pain of the underprivileged. They know—and they should know—something of the intolerable loneliness of those to whom life has offered no real opportunity. They develop a tremendous passion to be able to be a voice for those who have no speech and a weapon for those who have no sword. The injustices of the world stir them to bitter indignation. The tyrannies of the world rouse them to magnificent wrath. They bravely resolve that there shall be no injustice upon which the light of Christ shall not be turned and no wrong which shall be safe while they can speak against it.

This passion for getting the will of Christ done in our world and for frankly facing every dark and terrible evil, until even the eyes of young ministers become dark with the strange tragedy of contemporary life, is one of the most notable characteristics of the young men who go out of our Divinity Schools. When this social passion is the by-product of a great spiritual experience, all is well. If a man's spirituality has no social expression, he is likely to harden into a Pharisee or soften into a voluptuary. And if his social passion has no basis in a life transformed by the grace of God in Christ, he is likely to be impotent and to turn at last to soured idealism. But when a man with a living Christian experience sets about the task of influencing a living world, great things begin to happen.

In the sixth place, the School of Divinity is a base of supply for a world-wide enterprise. In centuries before, our own Christianity has changed the world. In our own century it aspires to nothing less than a bringing to the life of all mankind the whole Christian message. Personal motives are to be changed all about the world. The salvation in Christ is to be realized by individuals all about the

world. Laws and customs and social modes are to be
changed all about the world. Culture and art and all the
gracious life of man is to be shot through by the splendor
which comes from the cross.

The theological school is all the while creating ambassadors of Christ for every court in the world and so it keeps
the world upon its mind and in its heart.

Leonardo da Vinci once painted a picture of Jesus holding the world in his hand. At the School of Divinity, Jesus
comes to the theological student and puts into his hands the
world which he has held in his own.

In the seventh place, the School of Divinity is a house of
God. Have you understood the final nature of our task?
It is our terrible claim that we see the world with the eyes
of God. We do not come with a worm's eye view of the universe, or a bird's eye view of the universe, or even a man's
eye view of the universe. We claim to come with a God's
eye view of the universe. Our whole commission gains its
importance from the fact that we claim to have seen life
with the eyes of God; to speak about life with the voice
which God has given us; to come to life with the will of
God drives us; to touch life with the heart of God inspiring
us.

As we look forward to the future of the Methodist Church,
the theological school stands in a place of pivotal and overwhelming importance. If it does the work I have discussed,
all will be well; if it fails to do this work, all will be ill.

It is very strange to me that there are Churches where,
every year, a collection is taken for ministers whose force
is spent, while no collection is taken for theological education. It is, of course, good and right that we should take
care of the men who have worn themselves out in the work
of God, but what about the man we are to send out to do
that work? Every Church, every year, should take a collection for which serious preparation is made in order
that the work of the theological school may be adequately
supported.

The future lies waiting for us. Can we produce men of
God for the great task? The theological school must answer the question and the Church must make it possible for
it to give the answer.

ADDRESS OF ALFRED M. LANDON

It is always a dangerous thing for a political leader to
cross party lines. Nevertheless, to support my President,
I do so. Whether he deserves it or not is not the question.

The Republic deserves it, and that is all that should count with every citizen.

A great war threatens. Millions of fathers and mothers are facing the possibility that they will soon be walking the floor as their sons go into battle. On the face of things, it seems that some nations are mad, and bent on ruin.

On closer examination, however, such is not the case. It may or may not be true of certain rulers. Certainly it is not true of the common people of any country. They live in hope of peace now, as always. In the words of the old hymn, they "longingly await the consummation of peace forevermore." But even in the case of rulers apparently bent on war, they realize they cannot lead an unwilling people into a successful war.

We must face the situation as it is, and in doing so let us face frankly the fact that the blunderings of statesmen in Britain, France, and even in America, are, to some extent at least, responsible for-what has come to pass—including Herr Hitler, also.

After all, fairness and frankness compel the observant citizen to admit that he made a rather strong case against economic injustices.

Mr. Hitler's speech, while rejecting the President's specific request, still leaves the door slightly open for further discussion of the common destiny of the common people of this world.

The United States of America is the one great power that has not yet been fully drawn into the balance-of-power game, and the ancient boundary line disputes, which have prevailed in Europe since before the Roman Republic. And, please God may we never be!

It is in the spirit of disinterestedness that I urge we explore constructively the possibility for further discussion which Herr Hitler's speech offers. Discussion is the only way known to man to settle angry disputes, whether public or private. It has the wisdom of the ages behind it. The longer a man who is spoiling for a fight talks, the less apt he is to fight.

Because we have not realized our stake in foreign affairs, we have adopted foreign policies on an emotional, spiritual, and reform basis. We have therefore acted like the proverbial "sucker" in a game with professionals. Henceforth, we must not allow friendship or animosity or emotion to influence our foreign policy. We must learn that negotiations between nations are cold and ruthless, and we must play the game the same way.

We cannot be sure what nation we can rely on in Europe.

For centuries they have been engaged in practicing the art of "double-crossing" each other.

Never has there been a more urgent call to be Americans —first, last, and all the time. There is only one people and one nation that has my immediate concern and interest, and that is the United States of America.

I do not like to see people who claim to be American citizens organizing in pro-Hitler bunds. I don't like to see people who claim to be American citizens organizing in stop-Hitler parades.

I don't like to see people who claim to be American citizens organizing as Czechoslovakians to regain the independence of that country.

I like Americans who are for our country, first, last, and all the time.

I fear for America's ability to stay out of a prolonged and general war. Already there are evidences of a weakening of our resolution not to get involved in another European war. Emotional, economic, and other pulls are already making themselves felt, and in the end would be the "pullers-in."

So it is folly to say that we can be indifferent to development of another European mess. It would be the easy thing to say, "I would let them stew in their own juice," except for its effect on us—directly if we get in, and indirectly if we don't.

It is important that we don't fool ourselves with "weasel" words. It is important that we thoroughly understand what they mean.

Now, take a look at what this "economic assistance" means. We give it. Our side is losing. Will we stay out then? I am afraid not. If the side we are helping is winning, we may be able to stay out. But the situation is different, both actually and psychologically, when our side is losing. We—a proud people—would then be in the position of starting something we won't finish. Therefore, we have an exact duplication of the situation when we entered the World War.

I am sure all of us can remember, while England and France were trying to get us to come to their assistance in the World War, they said all they wanted was money and material. But they changed their tune mighty soon after we got into the war. Then they wanted American soldiers in France as quickly as we could get them there. And it will be the same way this time.

Incidentally, until very recently, the left wing liberals who are the war party in America now were saying we went into the World War, not to save democracy but to save our investments. Now they are the loudest in arguing that we must oppose force with force to stop aggression in Europe.

And what does that mean? Well, aggression is simply the "weasel" word to fool the American people into sending their sons to Europe to fight in boundary line disputes which have been going on in Europe and Asia since before the dawn of civilization.

Let's face the fact frankly that economic assitance means, in the end, "doughboy" assistance. Let's stop fooling the American people that economic quarantines and economic assistance mean anything less than sending American boys into the cockpit of Europe to fight.

It's about time the "cannon fodder" mothers of America —and I mean the war brides of the last war—realize that fact.

There is another thing the American people should realize. The President, in so far as he speaks and is able to do so, has abandoned neutrality for the United States. Of course, the Congress is the final authority as to what our position will be. Until the American people make known their decision through the Congress, no President can speak with certainty for them.

Of course we are heading into dangerous paths. We can all remember that we were involved in the World War by another President who attempted to act as a mediator, and wrote notes in the attempt to settle the conflict or to avoid it on our part.

But notwithstanding this danger, the United States is the one great power which has the chance to offer something other than the mere choosing-up of sides before going into battle. I am in full support of a conference to prevent war, but I do not think our officials should enter any conference lined up with any group of nations.

I think we can and should support the President's appeal for a peace conference, and urge him to take such advantages of further discussion as Mr. Hitler's reply offers. The President's proposal of two weeks ago threw open the door to peaceful discussion. It specifically exempted the United States from any desire to interfere in the settlement of political questions in Europe, while he offered the co-operation of the United States, the world's most powerful single economic unit, for an adjustment of economic matters on a world-wide scale.

There might even be in the near future a general American appeal to the world for peace.

Why not state bluntly what the horrible and terrifying

prospect is, and remind everybody that war would be ruinous for all, and would achieve no real solution. It should be pointed out that continuance of the mere balance-of-power contest could have but one inevitable result. The appeal could express the truth that a fair chance must be offered to all people to prosper. It should point out that governments must stabilize on the basis of respect for compacts, and of putting bare force into the background.

Above all, it could restate America's intention to be impartial in its approach to a peaceful solution of world difficulties.

There must be but one objective in view in any effort for world peace. That objective must be justice for all nations and all peoples. No conference for peace can be successful if it is approached from a prejudicial point of view.

We should, in this appeal, reject the notion that war is inevitable between governmental theories. Also, we should reassert our creed—that we do not wish to impose our system upon any other people.

Finally, we should declare our readiness to co-operate in any move really designed to make for peace, no matter in what quarter it originates.

It is easy to ridicule the question of whether Herr Hitler left any opening for future discussion. If you say his answer is one of force, then the only thing left is war.

In that event, the American people should not be fooled as to what economic quarantine and economic assistance mean. They mean the inevitable sending of our sons to France to die, under the plea of saving democracy for a continent that has never known the true meaning of democracy as we know it.

We may think we can stay out, but even the most determined in that view will concede that it is a gamble.

It is obvious, of course, that the so-called democracies would win if there is a struggle to the death between them and the totalitarian governments. But what would such a victory mean to the democracies, or to anyone else? After all, does anyone win a war—a modern war, with its horrors and its long-lasting after effects? Would there be any real victor?

We should weigh beforehand the suffering and heartbreak, the destruction of producing power, and of the long painful period of rehabilitation for vanquished and victor alike. In other words, the winning of such a war could not mean victory for any people.

Because the issues involved mean life and death to individuals and governments, we welcome the lofty and well-meaning discussion which is now taking place.

The difference between those who believe there is danger in isolation and those who believe there is security in isolation is largely the difference between the military and the political point of view.

There is no question in my mind that the command of the sea insures security in our land, for my time and probably for my youngest child's time. But the question that is bothering me is, how long can popular government survive in a world armed to the teeth and constantly attacking or threatening to attack; with trade between nations at a low ebb; with monetary systems disorganized; and a world going bankrupt by this gigantic armament race? The fact that we would be the *last* nation to be exhausted is poor comfort for anyone.

We, all of us, are determined to defend our liberty. The best way to do it is now being debated before the American people.

Is the idea, then, of an international conference to avert the peril which confronts us merely Utopian? Have discussions between nations become obsolete? Is the idea of a world-wide conference not limited to one hemisphere and not limited to armaments or economics, ridiculous and doomed to inevitable failure? I do not think so, because I think the only way to have peace is to talk peace.

Furthermore, the word "inevitable" does not belong in the vocabulary of public affairs. To say that such a conference is doomed to failure is not an admission to make to one's self, or to put forward to someone else.

It is the clear duty of every public leader to strive to prevent war, and to postpone it as long as possible, in the spirit of the old dictum, "While there is life there is hope."

Even if such an international conference should fail, we should, nevertheless, use every effort to bring it about. At the very least, it would gain time, and time always fights on the side of peace. And who could predict, with any degree of accuracy, that events would not occur to sidetrack war? Who knows the workings of Providence?

The common people of all the countries of the world should resort to every possible means to stay in touch with each other. It is still possible to rally to this spirit by an international conference devoted to the discussion of their common interests.

Even if the attempt to hold such a conference should fail, we would know that our leaders had exerted all the moral and political influence possible to prevent the destruction of civilization. Suppose that the conference were held, and we did not find a formula on which all nations could agree. Should that prevent us from seeking to work for peace and better international understanding?

Neither must we cease to prepare ourselves to resist successfully the threat of any country, or combination of countries, who rely solely on force as a national policy.

There must be no doubt of our earnestness in either of these two matters: the willingness to seek, by discussion, a fair and just settlement of the disquietude now existing between nations, which is crippling a return to normal conditions of peace and employment; or, in plain language, a continuation of our military preparations to meet any threat which possibly could confront us.

Therefore, because of the weight of the imponderables— "the opinions, the sentiment, and the conscience of humanity," the proposal of such a conference seeking to inject moderation into the world situation, is not absurd. I say, it is practical and conceivable at this time.

Possessing manifestly superior power, confident in our strength and unity, we need not be afraid that to propose such a world conference will be construed as weakness, as some argue. It simply affords us an opportunity to show our decent feelings and sentiment when these seem to be going out of fashion.

Discussion and negotiation in conference are the only effective means available to modern men to postpone and avert war. We all know when they failed to prevent war, but it is impossible to tell how many times they have succeeded.

The love of and the instinct for liberty, the dreams that man has always had of a better international order and a reign of peace under God, are stronger than hatred, and stronger than the periodic struggle for power. The great cause of uniting the world in justice, understanding, and affection is poorly served by those who are discouraged by one failure, or by any number of failures, or by the inertia of the people.

Though the world stands today in arms, in every country—and no less than in Hitler's own country—the human heart and the human mind dream of a better, a more universal use of the creative forces of the world. Among those creative forces this dream cannot be imprisoned or killed. Exiled from one soil, it will grow upon another. Exiled from one time, it will be at home in another. Defeated in one age, it will be attempted in another. For it is part of the human soul.

There were wars and rumors of wars nineteen hundred years ago; but in the face of such, there was One who realized the folly of settling difficulties by resort to arms. "Blessed are the peacemakers" applies not only to private affairs, but also to international relations.

ADDRESS OF DR. UMPHREY LEE

I recall the exhortation of my elders that a preacher should always be willing to speak as a dying man to a dying congregation. I am not clear that one should always be willing to speak to an expiring Conference. But I am here under orders to represent the colleges and universities of united Methodism, some 140 of them, in fifteen minutes. It is certain that, if I stop to think about what I am asked to do, I shall never get it done.

Because of limitations in time I cannot clothe my statements in adroit phrases and clever innuendoes. I shall have to say what I mean—a very unfortunate position for a college president. Let me begin then by saying that united Methodism must make up its mind whether it really believes in Church-related colleges and universities. For twenty-five years—and more—there has been no inconsiderable part of the American people who seem to have taken it for granted that the day of Church-related institutions of higher learning is past. Even those who would refuse to acknowledge that such a thought ever crossed their minds have been disturbed by the lack of interest displayed by Church people in their own schools. And there has been something like a flight from Church relationships upon the part of institutions born and bred in the tradition.

All this has been reflected in the attitude of even our leaders. Occasionally I have heard churchmen speak of education in Church-related institutions in terms which reminded me of nothing so much as of the poem that was in the Fifth Reader I studied. You may remember the lines; it was something about a shipwreck:

> As we knelt below in darkness,
> Each one busy with his prayers,
> "We are lost," the captain shouted
> As he staggered down the stairs.

Leaving aside for the moment Irvin Cobb's remark, that a captain should have been doing something other than staggering all over the place bellowing that all was lost, one must ask why the gloom about Church-related institutions.

Let us consider for a moment the facts concerning education in this country during the last generation. In the first place, the last generation has seen the extension of free education to the college level. The building of great state universities and their support by taxation has placed within reach of a large part of our youth institutions without tuition and with relatively low fees. At the same time, the day of a college which consisted of a small group of professors and students without laboratories and with a library consisting mainly of a copy of Horace's Odes and a Latin grammar, has also passed. On the other hand, the State offers expensive and necessary equipment and library without tuition; on the other side, the Church school must get its equipment by the gifts of friends and then charge a relatively high tuition to help the costs of operation. There is no use charging up to naturalistic science or widespread skepticism or secularism, something which has its roots deep in economic facts.

The Church can justify its position only on the ground, either that it maintains the aristocratic tradition in education, taking care only of the few who deserve an education; or on the ground that it does its work as well in everything as the State, and in some things better than the State. We have to make up our minds.

In the second place, American education, during the last generation, has been widely permeated with a theory of education which is directly contrary to that to which Church-related colleges are by their nature committed. President Cowley of Hamilton College has pointed out recently that the German theory of higher education in many places ousted the English theory which has been traditional in this country. The English theory was that the college stands *in loco parentis*, taking the place of the home in looking after the character and general welfare of the student as well as his mental development. The German theory of higher education was that the institution has no obligations to the student save intellectual. In many places, during the last fifty years—and in some high quarters today—this has been the prevailing idea. To those who succumbed to this theory, the Church had no place in education.

Besides this, during the years when science was fighting for its place in the sun and when the new social sciences were trying to establish themselves, the predominant note of American education was freedom. Rightly or wrongly, many felt that the Church fettered them in their search for truth. It must be admitted that there have been some unhappy occurrences when authorities have mistaken their ecclesiastical powers for plenary inspiration concerning all things in the heaven above and the earth beneath—and, in a few historic cases, in the waters under the earth.

But when allowance has been made for ecclesiastical interference in the realm of science, it must be admitted that the search for freedom has been in part a search for freedom from any coherent philosophy and for freedom from commitments and devotion. The truth is that we have known a time when some part of American education has been allergic to convictions of any kind. It was thought by a few that one could not freely investigate the remains of the last ice age if he had convictions about monogamous marriage. Even those whom the Church regarded as dangerous modernists were, in turn, looked upon by their academic colleagues as having only passed from one degree of superstition to another; they were classed with that distinguished gentleman who proclaimed that he had renounced the errors of the Church of Rome and embraced those of the Church of England. This may be a bit exaggerated, but future historians will smile incredulously as they read the records of an era when men tried to divorce those which history has forever joined: relentless search for truth and great commitment of mind and heart.

But there is one more aspect of the era through which we have passed. No small section of American education succumbed to the great American salesman and subscribed to the doctrine that "the guest is always right." It has worked in the sale of safety razors and electric gadgets; why not in education? If applied to education, the conclusion is obvious. If undergraduates and alumni do not want religion, at least religion as it has been served up to them, then eliminate religion. I am not forgetting that the fault has often been in the way religion has been presented to the undergraduate; but I must insist that the time-spirit has been favorable to giving people what they think they want, forgetting that we believe in joining religion and learning; not because we think that people demand this, but because it is laid upon us so to do.

It is in such an era as this through which we have come, a time when the Church has been faced by the severe competition of tax-supported colleges, when the mental climate has been in many ways unfriendly to Church education, that the Church has found herself in difficulty in promoting her traditional program of higher education. And we shall have to confess that we have sometimes apologized for our existence and offered lame explanations as to the contributions which Church-related institutions are making. We have, so we have said, furnished atmosphere, but it has been slightly indefinite as to what we meant by atmosphere. A friend of mine, who headed a famous girls' school in the South, told me of two gentlemen from the Middle West who attended his Commencement. They saw an old lady, with a severe, high collar and a haughty air, cross the campus. One of them said: "What does she do?" The other said: "I suppose she furnishes this 'Southern culture' we're paying for."

I need not mention that often we have attempted to decorate our educational program with certain pastry-cake additions and circus entertainments to offset what we have lost in distinctiveness. Don't blame the school too much. We have been living in the era of flight from Church relationship.

I say we have been living in that era. Whether the Church has found it out or not, that era has been shattered, and we shall be picking up the pieces for a long time. What a library of books on philosophy could not have done, what no series of great leaders could have accomplished, has been brought about by grim want in the depression and by the Red rider whose shadow has been over the world for a quarter of a century. Because of these things men who can think at all are having to rethink their fundamental positions, and those who go on gaily imagining that nothing has happened to man's intellectual edifices erected so confidently during the nineteenth century are as anachronistic as the dinosaurs.

Even a child should know now that no state and no society is safe with the control of higher education in the hands of one authority. Men had to fight to free education from the absolute control of the Church, and they are in no mind now to bind education to the absolute control of the state. Recent happenings in Europe show us that for our sake we must preserve our system of multiple control. We must have state institutions; we must have our privately controlled instutions; and we must have our Church-related institutions. Somewhere in this land there must be institutions of higher learning which are tied by tradition and affection, if not by law, to the Church. Only in this way can we escape what has happened elsewhere.

And surely, in the face of this kind of world, no man will continue to contend that an educational system which is purely intellectualistic is sufficient. I am not laying a predicate for shoddy academic work, but I am pointing out to you that the Church had better take seriously this whole question of higher education. Once more the Church college is back without apology.

Moreover, the time-spirit which has made it unfashionable to associate deep convictions with intellectual freedom has itself vanished. Now we know that there can be no intellectual freedom without great convictions. Before the black shirts and the storm troopers, this fallacy of cloistered scholarship has melted like frost. Only those who believe deeply in freedom can maintain it. And once again in history the Galilean has walked down our little streets and into our fussy offices to dwarf all that seemed so fine and so final. A Church that stands for the worth of every human being regardless of creed or race or class is an institution that has a right to a place in higher education.

It is time that we cease apologizing for our place in education, and that we cease our lugubrious complaints. If we only knew it, in the educational world, we are in the position of the poor boy who is suddenly recognized as the long-lost heir. Church institutions today can give to American education a stability and a security against the domination of some one political party that no other kind of institutions can give. Eight million Methodists can be wrong, but there are some things on which they are not likely to be wrong.

If, however, we are going to continue our Church-related institutions, some things should be understood. The Church has no right to present to the world institutions which are not able to do educational work. If the Church believes in her institutions, she should put enough money into them to enable them to do decent academic work—or she should close them. The fact that the president is a pious man and the faculty believe in prayer does not make up for poor laboratory and no books. Skyscrapers do not stand up because the architect was a Methodist, and bridges do not carry their loads because the engineer's heart was pure.

The truth is, that the Church ought to put enough money into her schools that they could be opened to rich and poor alike and not reserved for those only who can afford the tuition. If the colleges are worth having, they are worth having for everybody. And if we are going to have them, whether with high tuition or low, they ought to be worth every cent that the student or his parents pay. There can be no substitution of piety for sound scholarship.

But, when that is said, this remains: there is no excuse for institutions under the auspices or related to the Church unless these institutions do make it possible for boys and girls to keep in touch with the Church and religious life. No institution can do what the home doesn't do, and Church colleges cannot inject religion as some sort of spiritual sulfanilimide. There is no place for petty restrictions and denominational narrowness. But this is no time to apologize for religion. In a world when no one seems to know what he believes save the ruthless of the earth, it is time for the Church to say a word. Out of the Middle Ages only two institutions have come into modern life: the Church and the University. These two, traditionally united, are the only institutions of our time dedicated to the principles of human worth and human hope, and they must not perish from the earth.

A Baptist preacher from Georgia told me of a church he built in a little, mountain town. He built it of cobblestones, picked off the fields. As it was being built, a mountaineer leaned against a tree, watching. Presently someone came up and asked the mountaineer what kind of rocks they were using. The mountaineer explained. "Well," asked the visitor, "will those stones last?" "Stranger," said the mountaineer, "they've lasted till now." And we have a sure word which shall not pass away.

ADDRESS OF PRESIDENT ALBERT W. PALMER

Bishop Holt, Fathers and Brethren and Sisters of the Uniting Conference: It is a very great privilege for me to be invited to come to Kansas City, because this happens to be my birthplace. I have spent ninety-five per cent of my life away from Kansas City. But, nevertheless, I am glad to come back to the place where I first lifted up my voice sixty years ago this month.

I also, however, am somewhat concerned about the topic on which I have been asked to speak. I don't quite see why you went outside the Methodist denomination to ask a Congregationalist to come to speak to you on the topic, "Can We Build a Christian Social Order?" except that in some places and on some occasions I understand that ministers are warned to soft-pedal the social gospel and not speak too frankly or too vigorously about the social problems.

I heard a story the other day, which rather troubled me, of a Methodist woman who lived next door to a Presbyterian woman, and she went over to her Presbyterian neighbor and said: "Would you mind calling up your minister and asking him to come and call on my husband who is very ill? I don't know what is the matter with him, but I wish you would ask your minister to come and call on him."

The Presbyterian sister said: "Yes, I would be glad to do that, but why don't you call your own Methodist minister?"

She said: "Well, you see, this may turn out to be a contagious disease, and I don't want to expose our pastor to any unnecessary danger."

There are many voices which are dealing with social issues today, and just as on your radio you sometimes try to tune out the discordant notes in order that you may listen to the great debate, or the symphony orchestra, so I hope tonight to try to tune out certain voices and bring to you three voices which it seems to me are significant as we face this question of whether or not we can build a Christian social order.

First of all, there is the voice of discouragement, disheartenment, and defeat. We live not only in a time of tired radicals, but, what is far more dangerous, a time of discouraged saints. There are a great many people who as they look out on the religious horizon see only the darkness and the clouds that are there. And they remember the discouragements and the disappointments which have come to them across the years.

The evangelism of the world in this generation—how our hearts once thrilled to it, but what a hollow sound it has today. A saloonless nation in 1920! Well, it came through, and yet how disappointing it has been.

Walter Rauschenbusch and Washington Gladden spoke to us in trumpet tones a generation ago on Christianity and the social crisis. But the social crisis still endures.

Jacob Riis—well, the battle of the slum still goes on, if not in Mulberry Bend, in other places quite as bad, in spite of Jacob Riis' heroic labors.

Jane Addams, and Graham Taylor, and Mary McDowell went down into the hardest and darkest places of Chicago and gave their lives for the civic betterment of Chicago. Well, go to Chicago and look at it.

General Booth hungered for hell, and he led his Salvation Army down into the depths of East London, but East London is still East London.

Thomas Mott Osborne fired our imagination with the thought of a more humane and a more effective prison system for the healing of moral diseases; but Thomas Mott Osborne is no more and our prisons are much the same.

Raymond Robbins and Sherwood Eddy. Reinhold Niebuhr and Professor Ward, Bishop McConnell and Kirby Page, and Arthur Holt have gone up and down the land, bugling for the social gospel, and yet the Church does not seem to be very deeply stirred.

People will tell you, Yes, yes, there have always been prophetic spirits like Elijah and Amos to cry out against social wrongs; but after all Naboth's Vineyard is still in jeopardy, and Ahab still sits upon the throne.

In the face of discouraging voices like these there are two answers that people make. Some of them simply take refuge in cynicism. Cynicism is simply the cyclone cellar of the defeated mind. It gives a temporary release. It is so smart to simply say, "Three sneers for everything," and pretend that you don't care what happens to the world.

Then there are other people who are not cynics by temperament, who simply turn back into a pietism as a retreat from the world. They say it always was a wicked world and it always will be a wicked world; and all that we can do is to turn our souls inward and dwell in the presence of God, let the world go by.

Or else, they may take refuge in a kind of Messianic militarism by which they wait for the coming of the Lord Jesus Christ upon the clouds of glory, with legions of angels at his back, to overturn the evil forces of the world and set up the Messianic order in some new millenius.

Neither of these reactions, however, I believe has the future with it. Because neither of them can command the support of youth. Youth will not be content merely to retreat into a pious Nirvana, merely to take his religion as an opiate. I don't think youth is going to be content to just wait till the second coming of Christ. Youth wants to do something about it. Youth wants to hear a bugle call and see the banners flying in the dawn.

It is significant that Fascism and Nazism and Communism are youth movements, that they carry on largely because they have the support of youth in Russia, Germany, and Italy. And wherever you have a religious vacuum, a Church that is not appealing to youth, that has no vital and strong and courageous note to which youth can respond, then that Church is leaving a vacuum in the religious life of the world, inviting Communism or Fascism to come in and occupy.

So I look for other voices than the voice of defeat or despair or disappointment.

The second voice is more reassuring. It is the voice of history. Can we build a Christian social order? The answer is, Yes, we already have. It is here. Not completely, not in all areas of society, not all places, not all the time; but we have built a Christian social order in certain places, samples of what a Christian civilization might be like.

One of these places is the Christian home. Out of twenty centuries of Christian idealism and faith has come the

Christian family. And in the home you do have a Christian social order in miniature. Here you have fathers and mothers and children living in a co-operative common-wealth, living in a spirit of democratic good will, of patient understanding, of sympathy, of sacrificial service, one to another. And in the spirit and loyalty and devotion, in the insight and care of the Christian home where it is to each according to his need and from each according to his ability, you do have a Christian social order already set up in miniature.

Then we have accomplished also the school, and in our great public school system where education is provided for every child, regardless of race or color, regardless of wealth or poverty, you have a great illustration of the Christian spirit at work, a high regard for human personality, albeit it be the helpless and ignorant personality of a little child.

And in the great public school system, with its splendid educational techniques, with its understanding of human personality, with its care for physical as well as mental, for psychological and personal well-being of every pupil, you have something that demonstrates the character and spirit of the Christian ideal applied on a great social frontier.

Then there are other social institutions which stretch on beyond the school. There is the hospital. (I heard it said that you have to be either very rich or very poor to obtain the best medical service in this country.) The hospital which has its beds, its free beds, and its free clinics, and where the finest medical attention is given to all sorts and kinds of people without asking any question as to race or creed or background except the physical need, the presence of disease which needs to be combated.

Then think of the great public health services in our cities, and the way in which we are providing through our public health departments protection for water and for milk and for food and for all of the other necessities of life, so that the life of everybody in the community to the very lowliest may be given equal and adequate protection. There the Christian spirit is expressing itself in social action.

The Juvenile Court is another illustration, for there you have a new adventure in the realm of judicial procedure. No longer is it the question, Has a law been broken? The question is, Has a personality been broken? What can be done to save and protect and retrieve the personality of the wrongdoer? That is the question asked in the Juvenile Court. It is the Christian approach to wrongdoing.

On our great public highways and in our great post office system you have another illustration on a large and national scale of a social service rendered with complete democracy, and without any sort or kind of discrimination.

A few years ago there was a very interesting play called "Berkeley Square" which many of you attended, and you may remember that in one act of that play a young couple are sitting in the back parlor of a London home. It is 1790. And there the young man, who is really a twentieth-century young man who has strayed back into the eighteenth century, shows the eighteenth-century girl with whom he has fallen in love what the twentieth century is like. He shows her Manhattan, the island on which New York City stands, and she is simply thrilled by it. "Why," she says, "I see great streets, and horseless carriages moving on them, and wonderful towers, and it is night now and the towers are all illuminated. Marvelous! How beautiful, how wonderful this is. Can this be heaven?"

I saw the play in New York City, and that New York City audience broke down and laughed at the idea that anybody should take New York for heaven. And yet, New York in the twentieth century is in some respects much nearer heaven than was London in the eighteenth century, London which had no pavements, no sewers, no pure water supply, no certified milk, no refrigeration, no police department, no fire department, no department of public health —I might go on almost indefinitely, and you would see the difference between the degree of socialization, between the application of Christian ideals of the worth of human life and human personality, which characterize our civilization today, as over against the civilization of even so recent a period as the eighteenth century.

Beyond this second and more encouraging voice of history I hear a third voice. It is the voice of courageous and creative Christian faith. It is saying to us that every social advance has seemed difficult if not impossible before it was actually achieved. What madness the Declaration of Independence must have seemed in 1776. Polygamy, dueling, slavery—how deeply intrenched they were. But they are gone. Equal suffrage! How Elizabeth Cady Stanton and the other pioneers of the suffrage movement must have despaired of its ever being achieved. But equal suffrage has come. I can imagine Micah saying almost with tears those sad words of his, "How shall I come before the Lord and bow myself before the high God? Shall I come with thousands of rams and ten thousands of rivers of oil? Shall I give my firstborn to my transgression, the fruit of my body, or the sin of my soul?"

Micah standing there face to face with child sacrifice

must have wondered if the day would ever come when child sacrifice would be abandoned.

But for lo these many hundred years no one has offered his child as a single sacrifice on the altars of religion. To be sure, we still offer children by the thousands in regimented battalions in time of war, but we haven't answered to the fact that that is child sacrifice.

When Moses stood before Pharaoh, people must have jeered at him and said, "Does he think that he can make Pharaoh give up these slaves of his in Goshen?" But things happened after Moses stood before Pharaoh which may well give every oppressor in all the centuries following cause to pause and question.

No, there is something creative in human life. There is an upward surge. There is a call to God to establish peace and brotherhood and good will, and it is written in the great prophecy of Isaiah. "He shall not fail nor be discouraged till he have set justice in the earth."

But someone is saying to me, These are glittering generalities. Be more specific. What can we actually do here in 1939 in order to make a Christian social order? Yesterday afternoon as I was reviewing what I was to say this evening I sat by a window on the northern side of the Abraham Lincoln Hotel in Springfield. In the immediate foreground the nearest building was the First Methodist Church. Beyond it, the city, a bank, a moving picture show, a lot of stores, an open square with a courthouse on it, a courthouse which once was the capitol of the state of Illinois where Abraham Lincoln spoke. Beyond that, homes, a public school, some factories, a grain elevator, and a railroad.

I said to myself, "What has that church down there on the corner to say to all the rest of the city that lies stretched out beyond it?" I think it has something to say. And I want to put what it has to say as definitely and concretely as I may.

First of all, the Church must lift up its voice and say in no uncertain tones, say it in Sunday school and young people's society, from the pulpit, by pageantry and by music and by drama, in its religious papers, in every vehicle of expression that is open to it: The community is the larger home. And it will not be a safe place in which we are to have our homes until the spirit and principles that govern the Christian home govern the larger home of the community as well. That means that in the community of tomorrow there must be no slums. We wouldn't want a slum in our family home. We must not tolerate the slum in our larger community home. This doesn't mean merely a clearance of old tenement houses. This doesn't mean merely the coming of federal housing projects whereby we shall have cities that may be as beautiful and as clean as Stockholm is, for example. I was thrilled when I went through Stockholm two years ago and found no slums there. But it means also that kind of industrial life, that sort of social organization, that shall not make it necessary for people to live in slums.

I am not saying that people shall not work for profits in the city, the community, that is to come. I think the word "profit" is a very dangerous word because it is so difficult to interpret. But I am saying this, and I believe, that every truly Christian soul, whether he believes that the socialist economy or the capitalist economy or possibly a communist economy is what ought to rule; I believe that every Christian soul, whatever his economic philosophy may be, will agree with me in this: That in a truly Christian civilization there is no place for exploitation.

In the home there is reward. In the home there is recompense for service rendered. Billy can have a newspaper route and still belong to the home, and Billy can employ his sister Mary to fold the papers for him before he goes out to deliver them, and he can farm out part of the route to Johnny, his younger brother, and still keep the whole thing in the family. But there is going to be a certain amount of supervision to see to it that he doesn't keep the sister working for too long hours and that he pays the younger brother a just proportion that he earns.

It is not profit that is wrong; it is profit that is purchased at the cost of exploitation; that is purchased at the cost of the deprivation of human beings, of opportunities for decent and wholesome living, and in a Christian civilization where the community is the larger home, there must be no place for such exploitation.

I saw not very long a rather interesting movie called "Human Hands." It was the picture of the automobile industry and it showed the building of an automobile from the time when the raw material comes into the factory until deftly molded by skillful hands, and it is created into an engine, created into a chassis, finally brought together on the assembly line until at last it rolls out of the factory complete and ready to go to the ends of the earth.

I thought to myself, "How Jesus would thrill to that picture." He who was the carpenter of Nazareth, he who loved craftsmanship, who was himself a master craftsman, how he would have responded to the skill of this great epic of manufacture. But I thought to myself, I think that Jesus, after he had seen all this and had thrilled to the masterly machines and the wonderful tools and the skillful organization of it all, would also have said: "I have seen the hands of men in this picture. But tell me about the rest of the men. What kind of faces have they? Are they faces of intelligence and of hope and of faith and of cheer and of courage? What kind of homes have they? Where do their children play? Under what conditions are their families living? What provision is made for their future? How do they look out upon life? Are they thrilled with this great industrial process or do they find in it something that is irksome and a slavery?

I think Jesus would ask those questions of industry.

The second great thing which the Church, it seems to me, might say to this generation is: You have in the public school a successful social pattern which deserves to be applied in other areas of our social life. Why do we have schools? Because children need to be educated and we would hate to see ignorant children in our city streets. But, more than that, we have schools because the community needs citizens; intelligent citizens; citizens who can read and think and discuss and to whom it can be safe to entrust the franchise and the ballot. Therefore, we must have schools in order that we may have the right kind of citizens."

And so we say to every child: "You are not to blame that you are born ignorant. It is for the welfare and the safeguarding of the community that we will give you the best education possible." We say to every citizen: "It is for your interest and your protection that no one should be illiterate. You will therefore pay taxes—school taxes—in order that we may have good citizens." Those taxes are paid and on the whole they are paid willingly and cheerfully. There are no taxes, I am sure, that we pay more happily than our taxes for the support of public schools—schools that serve all races, all sorts and kinds of people, without discrimination.

Why not apply this principle? Why not take this pattern which has worked so well? Why not apply it to the problem of unemployment?

In this day in which we live with ten million unemployed, the unemployed are not to blame for their unemployment any more than the children are to blame for being born ignorant. It isn't thriftlessness that makes men unemployed today; it is economic crises; it is the shifts and changes in industry.

Why should we want to do something for the unem-

914   *Journal of the Uniting Conference*

ployed? Well, for the sake of mercy. If you ever were unemployed yourself, if you had ever been hungry and out of
work, not knowing where you could find a job for a day or a
week or a month yourself, you'd know.

But more than that we have a cause for taking adequate
care of this problem of unemployment because we need
good citizens.

And what does unemployment do? It breaks down the
morale of citizenship. It destroys the fiber of manhood
and womanhood. It embitters the home, and if unemployment continues and if people have to live on doles and on
relief, they are going to become distrustful of the wisdom
of the community and embittered against the social organization in the midst of which they live. They are not going
to be good and loyal citizens. If we expect to have the kind
of citizens that we have established the public school system to train, we must meet this problem of unemployment.

The time has come for a much deeper thinking about
this and a much broader outlook upon it.

I saw a very amusing and yet a penetrating cartoon in a
Chicago paper sometime ago. It represented a couple of
WPA workers leaning on their shovels in characteristic
WPA attitude.

They were perfectly relaxed and they were leaning together on their shovels talking. Riding by on the boulevard were two rather overnourished gentlemen, leaning
back luxuriously on the cushions of their automobile. As
their chauffeur drove them down the boulevard, they were
talking. Both groups of men were each saying the same
thing. They were saying: "Lazy buggers!"

My friends, we have had too many jokes at the expense
of the WPA. I think the WPA has made mistakes. I wish
that it could speed up work so that it was real work that
would qualify men to go out and hold down a job at the
speed that industry requires today.

I think we have done some things in our relief program
that have led toward pauperism. I am not defending the
methods that have been used any more than I am defending
the kind of crude methods that we had in the earliest public
schools. I suffered from some of those methods myself. I
went to a little school where we had eight grades in one
room and an overworked teacher trying to teach forty impossible kids like me.

I am saying this: That we have got to learn a way that
does not pauperize people, a way that does not take away
their working edge. We have got to learn how to give to
the people of this country adequate and decent, properly-

paid, and properly-conditioned toil. Until we meet that problem we haven't faced one of the basic realities and necessities of a Christian civilization. We must have social security; we must have protection for the aged people; we must have unemployment insurance; we must have sickness insurance. We have built up the kind of a civilization where if we do not have these things we are embittering men's souls and opening the door to revolution and rebellion.

The Christian Church has always been the friend of the poor. I went down to try to get a minister out of jail who had been arrested because he was observing a labor riot that took place in Chicago. When I went to the police captain where I thought he might possibly be incarcerated, the captain said, in a nice Irish brogue, "What was this minister doing here? Why was not he in his church saying his prayers?"

I said, "Captain, the Church is the friend of the poor, and this young minister was in the line of duty finding out what was happening to the poor in Chicago in this labor situation."

He was a good enough Catholic to know I spoke the truth and he treated me with more consideration after that.

The Church has always been the friend of the poor. It must be equally the friend of the unemployed. The Church in St. Paul's day asked the people to lay aside on the first day of the week that they might give to the poor saints in Jerusalem. The Church in a democratic, self-governing community must say to that democratic, self-governing community, "We must so organize our social relations that we shall solve the problem of unemployment," and not to struggle with that with the utmost wisdom and power we have is to be less than Christian.

The third thing which the Church needs to say to this generation is that public morals are just as important as public health. Why do we have such great care of the public health? Well, because we are a merciful people and do not like to have people sicken and die if we can prevent it. But also because we recognize that public health affects every one of us, and that if we allow contagion to spread and great epidemics to get started in the country, epidemics know no color line, know no economic line; they go throughout the community.

And so we say that we must have pure water and pure milk and carefully inspected food. We must care for the

health of the people. Will we awaken to the fact that there
are moral delinquencies that are equally contagious?

Make a spot map of Chicago or any other great city and
what do you find? Spot the delinquency cases and then
spot the economic limitations, then spot the poor housing.
What happens? The spots are all in the same area. The
same area in Chicago was once inhabited by Irish. The
Irish moved out and the German came in. The Germans
moved out and the Poles came in. The Poles moved out
and the Negroes came in. Perhaps the Negroes moved out
and the Mexicans came in, and in that area there has been
a uniformly high incidence of juvenile delinquency. Why?
Because people are given to juvenile delinuency? Not so,
but because under those economic conditions and under
those housing conditions, and without decent recreation,
boys just inevitably succumb to the evil forces and influences of the community.

If we had an area in Chicago where typhoid fever occurred year after year and generation after generation, we
would do something about it. Why should not the Church
be concerned with the moral epidemics that afflict our communities, and say this matter of juvenile delinquency is
something that will not let us sleep nights, and say something must be done to protect us against the moral as well
as against the physical disease sof the community?

We know more about alcohol today than any generation
has ever known. We know something of its effect upon
the mental life of people. We know the effect it has in
landing people in state mental hospitals. We recognize the
way in which it paralyzes the upper levels of the brain, puts
judgment out of gear, makes people liable to get into not
only automobile accidents but into grave moral accidents as
well.

Shall we be indifferent to a brazen liquor traffic that
comes back without having learned anything and seeks once
more to put the mark of alcoholic liquor slavery upon our
country? Or shall the Church awaken anew with a deeper
understanding and a truer and more profound message
about the menace of alcohol as an individual and racial and
social posion, and do something to restrain this vast and
growing evil in the civilization of today?

We live in an age when people are tremendously concerned over the peril of Fascism and Nazism. They say
the great autocracies and dictatorships across the sea are
a menace to democratic countries, and for that reason we
are building up ourselves great armaments and spending
astonishing sums on military preparations.

We are told that we must guard against the dictatorships. I wish you would read an article in the May number of the *Survey Graphic* by Gunnar Myrdal, a Swedish economist, in which he analyzes the position of Sweden in an article entitled "With Dictators as Neighbors." He recognizes that over against the tremendous military might of Germany and of Russia the power of Sweden is very small, and yet he believes there is hope for Sweden. Why? Because he says the real Swedish frontier is within and on that frontier Sweden is impregnable.

What does he mean? He means that in Sweden, through wise economic organization, and through a consistent and long-continued and well-worked-out system of social security, there is among the rank and file of the Swedish people contentment, trust, faith in the social organization of which they are a part.

Unemployment, reduced to a minimum, protects against old age and against sickness, and because the Swedish people have developed a social order in which they are contented and in which they have confidence and trust, neither the Nazis nor the Communists can interject a decisive note. Communism and Nazism can only conquer where they can first of all divide.

It is only where they find social ills that have been neglected and social wrongs that have not been cared for that they can come in with their propaganda and arouse a party in their behalf. But in a community like Sweden, where these conditions do not exist, we find it different. Sweden is exempt from the power of Nazism or Communism. They have free speech in Sweden. They let the Communists and Nazis talk their heads off, but they know they cannot overcome the satisfaction that the Swedish people have in the efficiency of their social organization.

Some weeks ago, President Roosevelt was quoted as saying the frontier of America is on the Rhine. He vigorously denied ever having said it. I assume that denial was true; but other people are saying it. Too many people are looking to the Rhine as if that were our frontier.

My message to you tonight is that the frontier of America is not on the Rhine. The frontier of America runs down Main Street, runs through every industrial town, runs past every mortgaged farm, runs in the midst of every underprivileged and embittered racial or economic or social group anywhere in the country. That is America's most dangerous frontier. If we can change that frontier until there is contentment, until on that frontier people realize that social and industrial justice are being sought, that social security is being arrived at, that there is care for human life and human values on that frontier, then we shall have the kind of security that Sweden has, the security that will make it impossible for any Fascist or Communist attack to divide us within, and the Church can guard that frontier.

Government, in the last analysis, is by public opinion, and the Church, a great body like this reunited Methodism, par excellence, can mold the public opinion that can say to Government, "Neglect not this inner frontier."

The community is the larger home; the spirit, the ideals, the co-operation, the good will which characterize the family home must be carried out into the city streets, into the country lanes, into the community life of the nation.

The school is a successful social pattern. What we have done in the public school by way of sound and reasonable care for human life can be done and must be done in the field of unemployment. Public morals are as important as public health and what we have achieved in physical health we must now go on to achieve in moral health.

If the community can guard that inner frontier, then we shall have taken a concrete, definite, practical, immediate step toward the actual building of a Christian civilization.

ADDRESS OF MODERATOR CHARLES W. WELCH

Mr. Chairman and Fellow Christians: I bring you the greetings of the Presbyterian Church, U. S. A., and then becoming characteristically Methodist I would say there are two million of us. Of course, if the Southern Presbyterians were to join in with us like these dear friends of mine down here from the South, it would make it two million and a half. Then when the Episcopalians and we get together—

But taking it just as it is we are great spenders, we Presbyterians, U. S. A. We spend a million a week. That is fifty cents apiece, and the vast majority of that fifty cents is like the vast majority of every fifty cents you eight million people spend on the Church. It is on ourselves.

But I come to you tonight with a challenge because I know as well as Dr. Rice does that it is not this whole evening. I know better than even the presiding officer here does just how insistent you are going to be in about eighteen minutes.

I come to you with a challenge. I have been sitting in these two days feeling this Uniting Conference. I have heard your organization grind. I come now to challenge you to another unity that will not take so long getting into action. We may begin tonight—the unity of the spirit of our Lord.

However much organization you have—and how well it has been done and how splendidly executed—you and I still need that without which the Church cannot get on.

And the Church is needed today as it never was before, your Church and mine. And if you and I—my Church and your Church, and all the churches we claim to be Christian—do not become Christians pretty soon, this world is gone the way of the sinner and the transgressor who never came back until someone goes after them.

Listen to that passage of Scripture on which every Methodist preacher in the world has preached overmuch: "He came to his own, and his own received him not." That is what he has done and that is more than you and I have done. But you know that first "own" is a neuter plural and means "things," which, taken compositely, means "He came to his own task and his own [masculine plural] would not have it so."

He had a world to save. The Church has been dedicated to the task. One of the first things we did was to split all to pieces. We have twelve branches of the Presbyterian Church. Now think of that! We have not as much to brag about as you have. There have been men enough on this plaftorm every day I have been here to save America if they would go to work at it.

Instead of that here we all are.

The other day one of my friends in Detroit wrote me, "Come on up and spend the night with me and I will have one of my elders take you up to the Synod about a hundred miles away." When we had had breakfast the next morning he loaded me in on his elder and he whispered to me as he did, "Don't cross him."

I have been in the ministry long enough to know what that meant. But we drove along a while, and we made conversation, as preachers will with laymen, and laymen with ministers. Finally he said, as if by inspiration, "You see that great building over there?" I agreed that I saw it. He said, "There is where the Administration in Washington started these sit-down strikes."

Intsead of looking at the building I looked at this man. He saw I didn't agree with him and he took his hands off the steering wheel and his feet off the brakes and accelerator, and just sat there and looked at me. Remembering what my friend had said about not crossing him, I said, "You are mistaken about me." And you know, these laymen get awfully haywire sometimes in their thinking about things, I mean, going crooked. He said, "Where did they begin if they didn't begin over there, and who started them but the President?"

I said, "This sit-down strike business started in the Presbyterian Church long before you and I were ever born."

He came unto his own and his own received him not. That is the tragedy in Kentucky.

That is where I come from. Dr. Rice didn't tell you that; he didn't know. I have listened to more of his junk speeches—I mean speeches about junk. Don't tell my wife about that because she likes him. He comes and talks to us about the Goodwill Industries and when he has gone they bring the bags around and ask the Presbyterians to fill them.

Our tragedy in Kentucky is the tragedy that is in Missouri; the tragedy in Louisville is the tragedy that is in Kansas City. Our penitentiaries in Kentucky are crowded and so are our insane asylums: And you ask me what the reason for that is. I answer you: The Christian Church has been seated, O, so long, doing nothing at the task of winning men because they are not their own. It makes a difference if it is your boy or someone's else. But it is Christ's task to win them.

The Rotarians sat there that Thursday. Everyone who came in her neighborhood said to the assistant secretary something endearing and sweet and called her by her first name and as soon as the gong struck they hurried back down to Main Street without asking—without taking the trouble to ask, "What is that sign of mental unrest on your face?"

They went out and she took the elevator to the topmost floor of that building in which they meet every Thursday and then waited. What must have been her torture until the time came when the sun was setting and she threw herself out onto the pavement sixteen floors below?

There was a great crowd of great men who have it as the core of their gospel: "He profits most who serves best."

That woman, that seamstress there in a Christian home; three children. She said to the three of them, but principally to the eldest, sixteen, "Don't you ever miss going to Sunday school, because the best people of this community go to Sunday school." Then she said, "Mr. So and So, he is an elder—he is an officer in that church." It might have been an elder; I don't know. "He is responsible for the Sunday school, and you will see him there."

And so they began to look for this very representative man and never saw him. One day the boy said to his mother, who was perturbed as all mothers are who haven't a man standing by their side to help—it might be the minister in some cases, but more often than not it isn't the minister. He said to her, "I'm not going to Sunday school." Did you ever hear an expression like that?

That little woman's face went white, because she knew what happens, what happens to a boy who doesn't go to Sunday school. But he didn't feel good inside, so he went back the next Sunday. That is what happened with that man who sat there in the upper room and sent his own children on to Sunday school in order that he might read the funny papers. The first Sunday he did it he didn't feel good himself. And then the boy looked around for some more boys and he didn't see any.

Several months went by; O many months went by and this same woman, whose seamstress this boy's mother was in Kentucky, felt her employer come into the room and she felt her draw near and then she did what she had never done—she put her arms about that poor wretched woman, and then the woman and she herself went white and she cried out as only a mother like that does—whether we know it or not—"What is wrong?"

She answered, "Mary Ann has just come in and she said that they have sent your boy William to the penitentiary this afternoon." And then that poor woman's heart broke and that leading man, that official of the church, remained seated in that lovely, luxurious den of his, with luxurious bedroom slippers and his lounging robe; never knowing nor understanding that he could go down to the penitentiary where that boy was and say, "Let me see him; he is my man; he is there because I stood Christ up. I stood him up. I took everything he had to give; I took the honor; I took the place of prominence in his Church and then let one of his lambs slip through."

That is what the Church has been doing, while it has been organizing. Think! Think of what it is costing this country alone, to say nothing of the world, this matter of crime, these youngsters that grow younger every year than twenty when they become criminals. Think what it costs to keep them, when if these men had good sense and had no Christianity at all, but did put that amount in the Church's program—and I believe they will when the Church comes to unite in its spirit, for the salvation of these, for Christ's sake.

Think of those battleships they are getting ready to build. Think if we had someone who knew enough to know what a battleship would do with the backing of the spirit of

God in the hearts of his Church, around the world. It would be a different story.

And these jails, these guards, this graft! If men across America would open their eyes to these things!

I often think of H. C. Morrison, who is an evangelist down in our state. If it hadn't been for him, I likely wouldn't be here tonight. And I am always grateful to the Southern Methodist Church for H. C. Morrison. I would like to hear every sermon he preaches. A Methodist steward, whose office I swept out many a morning for a quarter, slipped up to my side and said to me, after I had slipped into the church and stood there like an adult, making out like I had been there all evening, "Don't you think it would make your mother gladder than she has been in years if, when you go home, you tell her you gave your heart and life to her Lord?" I haven't answered him yet.

There were a lot of people in the choir who couldn't sing a note. One fellow couldn't do anything but play on the piccolo; but he was there with his piccolo, and that is more than some of the members of the Church do. That was in the little old red Methodist Church in Franklin, Ky.

I have always thanked God for Dr. Morrison. But do you know, we are not doing enough of that? So this challenge tonight is in behalf of economy. If you can get these economists all together and have them advise the President that the thing for America to do is for all of us people who claim to be Christians to quit talking about it and go to practicing it—tonight! And then the penitentiaries will be lessened. Then the insane asylums will not be needed because there will not be reason for these things that cause them to exist.

Do you remember the story of the first Easter Day and those two men walking down the way, those seven miles? When they got to the end of the road and the stranger who would join them went in and sat down in the most ordinary experience, that of breaking bread, they recognized him.

You know what they did. The records say they rose up quickly and returned to Jerusalem, and they were going to tell the people gathered in the Upper Room for fear of the Jews that they had seen the Lord; but He beat them to it, for He had been there before. They had retraced the seven miles, the Sabbath journey, which was against the law and against the religion of that day. It was Rule So and So, No. 56, or whatever it is. But they arose up quickly.

When the Church does that, the newspapers across the land are going to say something about you. They are going to tell the truth. They are going to rise up and say,

"The Christians have commenced to act as if they believed the immortal word written in the greatest of books." But in that Book is one of the saddest sentences I know anywhere: "But Thomas, one of the twelve, called Didymus, was not there when Jesus came."

But Thomas—your friend, your husband, your neighbor, your golf partner—was not there!

I have spent hours trying to imagine why Thomas was not there that day. Did somebody forget? Did somebody say, "No, no, I'll not go by for him now," like you have sidestepped the old-fashioned class meeting for which many others as well as Methodists have been glad that it ever existed? No, I wouldn't do that! They left him where he was.

Can you remember tonight, and be honest about it, how many men and women are in hell because you sat where you were, claiming to be a Christian—claiming, claiming to be bound together? Think of the buildings for the punishment of crime we would not need if eight million Methodists were to be spiritually minded. You set the Presbyterians an example and may they follow it!

How much fun and happiness my intimate friend here, in The Methodist Church, must have 'way down the next block from me, and how we have gone year after year in and out each other's houses. We could do that, couldn't we? If we could do that, couldn't we go sometime to a door just outside of which He is always standing? The latch string is always on your side and my side. He is always knocking.

Down in Kentucky we have what you had here this afternoon to such great delight—the Negroes. What hearts they have, and how we white people who were reared with them love them! There came a time when the State Legislature of Kentucky said, "No more of that; no more co-educational activity with Whites and Negroes."

Then some friends of our Lord built Lincoln Institute, and then some more friends furnished it. Then they sent word to Berea, in the foothills of the Cumberland Mountains, to Dr. Thompson, "Come on!" and the message was handed him in the Chapel. He stood up and motioned to the Negroes, "Come on!" and he led that Negro migration from Berea to Lincoln Institute.

After they were all settled, my family physician and I would go there and sit on the platform with him as he talked to these young people as if they had been of his own blood. How he loved them! Christ did. Why shouldn't you and I? Then we would go away and go back again.

Then the day came when my family physician said to

me: "I examined Dr. Thompson this morning, as I do once a year, and you'd never guess what I found." I don't guess much around doctors! "Do you know, I found on each one of his knees a great upraised callous place. What does that mean?" he said.

That means what you and I tonight know it means when you and I feel it most. It meant that he was on his knees for these Negroes and for the rest of us whom he knew and for the rest of the world. That is what the world is waiting for.

Out West, when I was visiting the Presbyterian centers just a while ago, when I would mention the budget at Washington not being balanced, some of them would get a little restive, like you are; but do you know any people who are paying less attention to balanced budgets in America than are the Christian people?

When my budget was raised they telephoned me: "The budget is raised." There was $1,700 to spare and it had already been appropriated. I said to the Chairman of the Budget Committee: "What about the budget on the left-hand side?" He said: "What budget?" He thought he had left out something—as he had without knowing. The budget on the left-hand side are those people I have been talking about tonight who, if you and I do not win them to Christ, will never be won and they will go on down the way. Let's balance the budget, we Methodists.

I love The Methodist Church because I knew it when it was spiritual. That is the way it kept me from going to hell. There were five of us who came into that little Methodist Church there in the vestibule and turned to the right where there was a vacant pew. I wondered where the Presbyterian elders were that night when I found the pew vacant, or where the preachers of the town were.

One of those boys, one of the five who remained, was killed in a drunken brawl. Two others of them saw time in one of our penitentiaries. You see, the margin is getting very narrow. And Christ continues to come to his own and his own will not have it so.

If when you leave tomorrow night or the day that follows, and you pray, include the Presbyterians, Northern and Southern, and the Protestant Episcopal and all the other branches of the Presbyterian and Baptist and Christian and Disciple Churches, that all of us may hear him say to us that night, "Ye must, ye must be born again yourselves before you can bring anyone else to conversion," for no teacher, no pastor, no Bishop, no denomination can bring anyone nearer to God than he is himself.

MISCELLANEOUS

Adopted May 9, 1939

DR. CLARENCE TRUE WILSON

BY DR. ERNEST H. CHERRINGTON

The death of Dr. Clarence True Wilson on February 16, 1939, at Portland, Oregon, brought to a close the career of one of the best-known temperance leaders in America.

Dr. Wilson was born at Milton, Del., April 24, 1872. He was the son of Rev. John Alfred B. Wilson, a Methodist preacher long connected with the Wilmington Annual Conference of the Methodist Episcopal Church.

He attended a private school in Wilmington, Del., the Washington Academy at Princess Anne, Md., St. Johns College, Annapolis, Md., and the University of Southern California, from which university he was graduated in 1894 with the degree of Bachelor of Arts. As a result of his scholarship achievements in the University of Southern California, he became a member of Phi Beta Kappa. He received the degree of Bachelor of Divinity from McClay College of Theology in Los Angeles in 1895, the degree of Ph.B. from San Joaquin Valley College, California, in 1897, the degree of Doctor of Divinity from St. Johns College, Annapolis, Md., in 1900, and the degree of LL.D. from Washington College, Chestertown, Md., in 1926.

While he was a pastor in Portland, Doctor Wilson met and married Mrs. Maude Aikin Tifft, November 27, 1907, whose daughter, Virginia, is now the wife of Dr. Charles C. Petherman, of Portland. A younger daughter, Maribeth, is now a student at the University of Oregon.

On May 1, 1910, Doctor Wilson was elected General Secretary of the Temperance Society of the Methodist Episcopal Church with headquarters in Chicago.

For a year and a half after Doctor Wilson's election as secretary, the Temperance Society of the Methodist Episcopal Church continued its headquarters in Chicago. In 1912, however, the General Conference fixed Topeka, Kans., as the society headquarters. In 1916, at the General Conference of the Methodist Episcopal Church at Saratoga Springs, N. Y., the name of this society was changed to that of The Board of Temperance, Prohibition, and Public Morals of the Methodist Episcopal Church, with headquarters at Washington, D. C.   Under Doctor Wilson's leadership this Board came to be recognized as one of the most important agencies in the movement for sobriety and public morality.

The Methodist Building in Washington originated in the mind of Doctor Wilson. It is his great dream transformed into beautiful reality by his leadership, persistency, and devotion. He succeeded in demonstrating the advisability and the practicability of this building enterprise to Bishop William Fraser McDowell, who, as the President of the Board of Temperance and Resident Bishop of the Methodist Episcopal Church in Washington, gave full and most effective co-operation in bringing this great undertaking to fruition. This building of white limestone, standing between the great Senate Office Building and the magnificent building of the United States Supreme Court, and facing the east front of the National Capitol building and grounds, is a beautiful monument to the tireless efforts of Doctor Wilson.

He was the author of books which have had wide circulation, including *The Things That Are to Be,* a theological book written when the author was but 26; *Dry or Die: The Anglo-Saxon Dilemma,* published in 1912; *The Divine Right of Democracy,* in 1919; *That Flame of Living Fire,* 1930. He was one of the editors of *The Cyclopedia of Temperance, Prohibition, and Public Morals,* published in 1916, and was a co-author of *The Case for Prohibition,* 1922, said to be one of the strongest defenses of prohibition in print.

During the entire campaign for national prohibition Doctor Wilson spoke for that cause from ocean to ocean and from the Lakes to the Gulf. When at last the Eighteenth Amendment was secured, he did not cease his efforts or assume that the fight was over. He continued to fight for proper enforcement of prohibition laws, both state and national, to secure adequate action on the part of the federal and state governments against bootlegging, and to promote educational efforts teaching the value of total abstinence and respect for law. When national prohibition was finally repealed in 1933, he immediately set to work in speaking campaigns across the country to warn the Church people of the inevitable consequences of repeal and again to build sentiment for the return of the prohibition policy in the smaller communities, the counties, the states, and the nation.

Doctor Wilson was an official delegate to the General Conference of the Methodist Episcopal Church in 1916 and in 1924. He was also a delegate to the Ecumenical Conference held in London, England, in 1921. He was a member of the Simplified Spelling Board and of the National Temperance Council and was Vice-President of the International Reform Federation. He has spoken in every state of the Union, in Canada, and in England and France. He was a Mason, a member of the Odd Fellows Order, a Republican, and an ardent opponent of the beverage alcohol traffic in every form.

.For some time prior to 1936 Doctor Wilson struggled with the problem of failing health. At the General Conference of that year, which was held in Columbus, Ohio, he took the platform on a question of personal privilege and requested, on behalf of himself and Mrs. Wilson, that he be released from the position of Executive Secretary of the Board of Temperance, Prohibition, and Public Morals. He was made Secretary Emeritus of the Board, and after the General Conference he and Mrs. Wilson moved back to Oregon into a beautiful small home located at Gresham, some ten miles from the city of Portland. Suffering a stroke in 1936, from which he never fully recovered, although he had shown remarkable recuperative powers., he passed away early in the afternoon of Thursday, February 16, 1939.

Doctor Wilson was peculiarly endowed with qualities which helped to prepare him for his great task. These have been manifested in many ways in his very active life of more than sixty-six years. His educational qualifications, ability, courage, zeal, and enthusiasm, along with his courteous manner and attractive personality, gave him access to the hearts and minds of .multitudes of those with whom he came in contact. These qualities were of great value and contributed in a large way to his success. He had his share of critics and opponents, but he also had a veritable army of enthusiastic, admiring friends and devoted supporters throughout the nation. The attacks upon him by the friends of the liquor traffic gave ample proof of the effectiveness of his work. He was an eloquent and successful preacher of the gospel; he was an impressive and entertaining platform lecturer; he was a resourceful and alert debater. When it came to the temperance issue, he was an indomitable crusader of the Plumed Knight Brigade.

Doctor Wilson lived and worked in four distinct periods of the temperance movement. The earliest was that period in American life when the liquor traffic throughout the nation largely controlled business, politics, and government. He was in the midst of the activities of the period when increasingly the liquor interests were losing ground and the temperance forces were advancing to influence and power. He was very closely connected with the activities of the National Prohibition period, with its tragedy of promise without performance by public officials and willingness to sacrifice even the public safety and welfare to political expediency. He witnessed the first five years of the period of prohibition repeal and reaction with its disillusionment. Through all these periods he held strenuously to his convictions. He did not swerve from the major position he had taken. He did not lower his flag, he did not lose his faith, nor did he for a moment doubt the ultimate success of his cause.

RULES OF PRACTICE AND ORDER
Adopted by the Judicial Council of The Methodist Church

1. *Officers.* The officers of the Judicial Council shall be a President, a Vice-President, and a Secretary, to be elected quadrennially by a majority vote of the Council.

2. *Duties of President.* The President shall perform all duties incident to the office of a Presiding Officer of a judicial body, including the right to call the Judicial Council into session, as provided by the *Discipline.*

3. *Duties of the Vice-President.* In case of absence or inability of the President, or at the request of the President, the Vice-President shall preside over part or all of any session of the Judicial Council and perform all duties devolving upon the Presiding Officer while so presiding at such session.

4. *Duties of the Secretary.* The Secretary shall perform all duties incident to the position of Secretary or Clerk of a judicial body, and such other duties as shall be requested of him by the Judicial Council, among which shall be:

(1) To keep a correct and ample record of all proceedings of the Judicial Council, including discussions, opinions, and all other actions taken by the Council.

(2) To keep the docket and perform the duties incident thereto, as hereinafter provided.

(3) To furnish certified copy or copies of the record of the action of the Judicial Council, or any matter determined by it, to the party or parties interested and to such other matters as may have a right thereto.

(4) To send to the Secretary of the Council of Bishops certified copies of all decisions of the Judicial Council on questions of law, as provided by ¶ 607 of the *Discipline.*

(5) To notify the President of the Judicial Council im-

mediately upon the filing of any matter submitted to the Judicial Council for determination, giving him a full and complete statement of the matter involved, together with such additional data as he may deem necessary.

5. *Docket.* A docket shall be kept in which shall be entered on separate sheets, and consecutively numbered, all matters of whatever kind and character that may be brought before the Judicial Council for determination, on which docket the Secretary of the Council shall make notations of all actions taken during the pendency of any matter entered thereon, including the final determination thereof.

At the conclusion of any Annual or General Conference session of the Judicial Council there shall be entered upon the Record the disposition of each and every item of business pending upon the docket, whether continued or determined, and all matters finally disposed of shall be dropped from the active docket, and all papers, documents, and exhibits in all matters finally disposed of shall be returned to and preserved by the Secretary.

(6) *Proceedings Preparatory for Hearing.*

(1) When any matter is appealed to the Judicial Council for determination, the document or documents and exhibits setting forth the same shall be filed with the Secretary of the Judicial Council, and entered by him upon the docket of the Council.

(2) When a cause has been placed on the docket of the Judicial Council, the Secretary thereof shall, within thirty (30) days from said date, furnish to each member of the Council a copy of the document or documents and exhibits setting forth such appeal, or a careful and accurate digest thereof.

7. *Arguments.* Interested parties may be heard in person, or by others appearing for them, or both, but not more than two on the same side shall be heard except by consent of the Council. Arguments shall be limited to one hour for each side, but upon request before the argument is begun, the Council may allow such additional time as it may deem necessary for an adequate presentation of the issues involved.

8. *Interested Persons Not Parties May Be Heard.* Any person or persons not parties to the record, but interested in a question of law pending before the Judicial Council may, with the consent of the Council, be heard thereon before the Council in session.

9. *Decisions.* All decisions by the Council shall be in writing and shall be accompanied by an opinion in which the reasons upon which it is based shall be stated with a

citation of the pertinent authorities, and shall show whether or not all members of the Council concur in the decision, giving the names of such members as do not concur. Any member of the Council who dissents may give in writing the reasons for his dissent, which shall be entered of record.

10. *Approval and Signing of the Record.* The record of all sessions of the Judicial Council shall be approved by the Council in session and signed by the President and attested by the Secretary.

11. *Precedents.* The decisions of the Council, in which all the members concur, shall be binding as precedents, but they may be reviewed upon request and overruled, provided all members concur in overruling them. A decision in which a majority of the Council shall concur, but which is not unanimous, shall be a final decision of the matter submitted and binding on the Church, but may be overruled by a majority of the Council.

12. *Publication of Decisions.* The decisions of the Council on questions of law, with a summary of the facts and of the opinion, shall be published, as the Judicial Council may direct, in the *Christian Advocates*, and filed with the Secretary of the General Conference for publication in such form as the General Conference may determine.

13. *No Discussions Outside Council Meetings.* The members of the Judicial Council will not permit discussion with them on matters pending before them, or that may be referred to them for determination, save and except before the Judical Council in session.

14. *Rules May Be Amended.* These rules may be amended, repealed, or extended at any session of the Judicial Council by a majority vote thereof.

THE STORY OF THE GAVELS
By Thomas P. Potter

A few years ago, to preserve for myself and for the local church of which I had been pastor, a memento of the oldest known building connected with the Methodist Church in the early days in Iowa, I made some gavels from wood taken from that early log home. From this starting point I began to make gavels from historic Methodist buildings and mission fields and from this collection came the gavels that have been used in this Uniting Conference.

The head of the gavel that was used in the opening session is made of live oak taken from the tree on St. Simon's Island off the coast of Georgia under which John Wesley preached in 1737. The Wesley Oak is listed among "Famous Trees of America" in a brochure of the U. S. Department of Forestry. The handle is made of wood taken from the rotting stump of a tree on St. Simon's, the log of which was used to make the bow of the U. S. S. Constitution, Old Ironsides.

The head of the second gavel is of English oak, weathered by time, taken from the first chapel that was built in Kingswood, Bristol, England, in 1739. The handle is of wood used in the original John Street Church in New York, dedicated in 1768. Thus are joined together woods from the first Methodist buildings in England and America.

The John Street gavel shows the marks of the handmade nails by which boards were fastened to the timber from which the gavel was made.

The Strawbridge gavel is of beautifully grained oak taken from the tree under which Robert Strawbridge, an Irish local preacher, preached in Maryland at about the same time that Philip Embury began to preach in New York.

Another gavel is from St. George's Church in Philadelphia, dedicated in 1769, where Francis Asbury was pastor when the first Methodist Conference was held in 1773, and where regular services are held today—after 170 years—the oldest Methodist church building in use today.

Barratt's Chapel, in the Delaware Capes, was built in 1780, and it was here, on November 14, 1784, that Thomas Coke and Francis Asbury met to talk over Mr. Wesley's plan for the organization of the Methodists into a Church in America. The gavel is of worm-eaten chestnut.

Next in chronological order is one of oak and walnut taken from the log cabin home of Colonel Henry Hardman near Tipton, Iowa, where on July 12, 1837, the first Methodist class was organized in Cedar County, four years after Iowa was opened for settlement.

I saw a carpenter climb a ladder, take off the split siding, make an opening and climb into the attic and cut a piece from a rafter in the log cabin of John Listebarger, where, in 1841, the first sermon was preached on the banks of the Cedar at the Rapids. Today there are 4,000 Methodists in what was then an occasional preaching place on the Marion Circuit.

In 1857, a little church was built in China, built because someone dared to believe that God would win some folks, even in China. From the pine altar rail, where many found Christ, has been fashioned a gavel which symbolizes the thousands who have been won for the Kingdom.

From India comes a piece of solwood, solid and strong, taken from the first house that William Butler built in Bareilly, India, typifying the foundation upon which the church is built, and another, of Malabar teak from Baroda, India, termite proof, which withstands all persecution and flourishes when most opposed.

From Old Umtali, Southern Rhodesia, comes a gavel of ebony, beautiful in its national luster and polish, as is the life of Africa's people as they come to know our Christ.

From our mission work in North Africa, cames a flaky grained gavel of eucalyptus wood.

These are a part of the collection that has been gathered from historic Methodist spots and from our mission fields. They have been recommended for display at the World's Fair in New York this summer. If any reader has access to wood from early Methodist churches in the various states, I shall be very glad if such wood could be sent to me to build up a reminder of the early days of the Church.

MEMENTO FROM FIRST FOREIGN MISSION

Bishop John M. Springer calls the attention of the Editors to the fact that one of the gavels used in the closing session of the Uniting Conference was made of ivory from Liberia, the first foreign mission of the Methodist Episcopal Church, established in 1833, eleven years before the major separation. This gavel was also used in the opening session of the Uniting Conference.

MEMORIALS

The following memorials have been received by the Secretary of the Conference. We give the source of the memorial, the subject of which it treats, and the Committee to which it has been referred.

No. 1. Wyoming Conference by Mrs. W. Gray Jones on Missionary Society. (Missions.)

No. 2. Northeast Ohio Conference by Mrs. D. W. Mercell on Missionary Society. (Missions.)

No. 3. Oregon Conference by Mrs. Ruth L. Reed on Missionary Society. (Missions.)

No. 4. Pittsburgh Conference by Mabel Davis Crumrine on Missionary Society. (Missions.)

No. 5. New Hampshire Conference by Mrs. Phillip S. Nason on Missionary Society. (Missions.)

No. 6. Southwest Kansas Conference by Mrs. F. A. Pac on Missionary Society. (Missions.)   -

No. 7. West Virginia Conference by Mrs. Fred Helmick on Missionary Society. (Missions.)

No. 8. Southern Conference by Mrs. Hugh H. Hoff on Missionary Society. (Missions.)

No. 9. Michigan Conference by Mrs. William H. Helrigel on Missionary Society. (Missions.)

No. 10. Northern Minnesota Conference by Mrs. Leslie Keyes on Missionary Society. (Missions.)

No. 11. Oklahoma Conference by Mrs. George Kesselring on Missionary Society. (Missions.)

No. 12. New York Conference by Ruth S. Pearson on Missionary Society. (Missions.)

No. 13. Memphis Conference by Lud H. Estes on Boundaries. (Conferences.)

No. 14. Memphis Conference by Lud H. Estes on Lay Activities. (Membership—Temp. Econ.)

No. 15. Tennessee Conference by William O. Batts on Lay Activities. (Membership—Temp. Econ.)

No. 16. South Carolina Conference by George K. Hay on Minimum Salary. (Membership—Temp. Econ.)

No. 17. South Carolina Conference by George K. Hay on Literature. (Education.)

No. 18. South Carolina Conference by George K. Hay on Boundaries. (Conferences.)

No. 19. South Carolina Conference by George K. Hay on Election of Officers. (Membership—Temp. Econ.)

No. 20. Missouri Conference by Lyle L. Gaither on Boundaries. (Conferences.)

No. 21. Tennessee Conference on Pensions. (Superannuate.)

No. 22. Tennessee Conference by W. H. Blue on Lay Activities. (Membership—Temp. Econ.)

No. 23. Baltimore Conference by W. Fletcher Carey on Boundaries. (Conferences.)

No. 24. Baltimore Conference by W. Fletcher Carey on Presiding Elder. (Ministry—Jud. Adm.)

No. 25. Trustees John Street Church by Carl H. Fowler on John Street Church. (Membership—Temp. Econ.)

No. 26. New York Conference by Carl H. Fowler on Membership. (Membership—Temp. Econ.)

No. 27. Arkansas Conference by Mrs. S. W. Mooty on Women Ministers. (Ministry—Jud. Adm.)

No. 28. Arkansas Conference by Mrs. D. G. Hindman on Women Ministers. (Ministry—Jud. Adm.)

No. 29. Arkansas Conference by Mrs. Cora French on Women Ministers. (Ministry—Jud. Adm.)

No. 30. Woman's Missionary Council by Mrs. J. W. Perry on Women Ministers. (Ministry—Jud. Adm.)

No. 31. Eastern Swedish Conference by Rev. Henry C. Whyman on Boundaries. (Conferences.)

No. 32. Baltimore, South, Conference by William H. Best on Christian Sabbath. (Education.)

No. 33. Pittsburgh Conference by J. E. Morrison on Pastors' Salaries. (Membership—Temp. Econ.)

No. 34. Nashville, Tenn., by Grady L. Wall on Sabbath Observance. (Education.)

No. 35. Methodist Benevolent Association, Nashville, by E. P. Anderson on Sabbath Observance. (Education.)

No. 36. Ohio Conference by Mrs. Laden M. Layton on Missionary Society. (Missions.)

No. 37. Methodist Protestant Conference by Rev. Lula Wardlow on Women Ministers. (Ministry—Jud. Adm.)

No. 38. Methodist Protestant Conference by Mrs. K. L. Upchurch on Women Ministers. (Ministry—Jud. Adm.)

No. 39. Central Southern Asia Conference by E. M. Moffatt on Bishops Resident. (Ministry—Jud. Adm.)

No. 40. Central Southern Asia Conference by E. M. Moffatt on Finance Committee. (Membership—Temp. Econ.)

No. 41. Central Southern Asia Conference by E. M. Moffatt on Methodist Episcopal. (Conferences.)

No. 42. Central Southern Asia Conference by E. M. Moffatt on Support of Bishops. (Membership—Temp. Econ.)

No. 43. Central Southern Asia Conference by E. M. Moffatt on Central Bishops. (Ministry—Jud. Adm.)

No. 44. Methodist Protestant Conference by Rev. R. T. Griffin on Women Ministers. (Ministry—Jud. Adm.)

No. 45. Louisiana Conference by Rev. Nettie MacCook on Women Ministers. (Ministry—Jud. Adm.)

No. 46. Methodist Protestant Conference by Rev. Mary E. Bartlett on Women Ministers. (Ministry—Jud Adm.)

No. 47. Louisiana Conference by Mary Ellon Perdue on Women Ministers. (Ministry—Jud. Adm.)

No. 48. Association of Hospitals by G. N. Haimer on Hospitals. (Missions.)

No. 49. South Carolina Conference by Charlton Du Rant on Christian Teaching. (Education.)

No. 50. Northwest Iowa Conference by John B. Walker on Superannuate Funds. (Superannuate.)

No. 51. Northwest Iowa Conference by John B. Walker on Deprivation of Orders. (Ministry—Jud. Adm.)

No. 52. Northwest Iowa Conference by Board of Stewards on Pensions. (Superannuate.)

No. 53. Book Committee by Henry S. Henshen on Washington Page. (Publishing Interests.)

No. 54. Board of Education by Board of Education on Educational Institutions. (Education.)

No. 55. North Texas Conference by W. L. Tittle on District Superintendent. (Ministry—Jud. Adm.)

No. 56. Zurich Conference by Ferdinand Sigg on Boundaries. (Conferences.)

No. 57. Louisiana Conference by W. Scott Chinn on Bishop Shaw. (Ministry—Jud. Adm.)

No. 58. Genesee Conference by William H. Horner on Revision of Ritual. (Ritual.)

No. 59. New York Conference by Carl H. Fowler on Wills and Benevolences. (Membership—Temp. Econ.)

No. 60. New York Conference by Carl H. Fowler on Approval of Unification. (Conferences.)

No. 61. New York Conference by Carl H. Fowler on Insurance Plan. (Superannuate.)

No. 62. Relating to Pension Funds, referred to Superannuate.

No. 63. Philadelphia Conference by Mrs. J. S. Jacoby on Missionary Society. (Missions.)

No. 64. Rock River Conference by Nettie W. Bagg on Ladies' Activities. (Missions.)

No. 65. East German Conference by Fred C. Hansser on Inviting General Conference. (Conferences.)

No. 66. East German Conference by Fred Hansser on Continuing Conference. (Conferences.)

No. 67. Geneva Area Conference by John L. Nuelsen on Central Conference. (Conferences.)

No. 68. By Joint Commission on Youth Work. (Education.)

No. 69. Mexico Conference by Eleazar Guerra on Board of Missions. (Missions.)

No. 70. Chicago Bureau Conference by William J. Hennessey on Meeting of Conference. (Conferences.)

No. 71. By Otto Brand on Inactive Membership. (Membership.)

No. 72. Otto Brand on Inactive Membership. (Membership.)

No. 73. By Malcom C. Fowler on Refugee Commission. (Membership.)

No. 74. Florida Conference by P. M. Boyd on Boundaies. (Conferences.)

No. 75. Florida Conference by P. M. Boyd on Boundaries. (Conferences.)

No. 76. Youth National Conference on Youth Representation. (Conferences.)

No. 77. Methodist Benev. Assn. by Noah W. Cooper on Keeping Sabbath. (Education.)

No. 78. National Council of Youth on Negro Segregation. (Conferences.)

No. 79. North Mississippi Conference by W. L. Pearson on Presiding Elder. (Ministry—Jud. Adm.)

No. 80. West Texas Conference by R. F. Curl on Change Name Conference. (Conferences.)

No. 81. West Texas Conference by R. F. Curl on Fear of Superannuation. (Superannuate.)

No. 82. Kentucky Conference by S. C. Rice on Course of Study. (Education.)

No. 83. Upper Iowa Conference by Mrs. Earle A. Baker on Missionary Society. (Missions.)

No. 84. South Georgia Conference by Charles W. McKinnon on Lay Activities. (Conferences.)

No. 85. Florida Conference by Lakeland District on Boundaries. (Conferences.)

No. 86. Florida Conference by Carlock Hawk on Boundaries. (Conferences.)

No. 87. Philippine Conference by Benjamin Geransing on Bishop Edwin F. Lee. (Ministry—Jud. Adm.)

No. 88. Philippine North Conference by Felix Grospe on Uniting Conference. (Conferences.)

No. 89. Philippine Islands Conference by Marion Walker on Missions for Philippines. (Missions.)

No. 90. Philippine Conference on Missions for Philippines. (Missions.)

No. 91. Southern Asia Central Conference by E. M. Moffatt on Foreign Missions. (Missions.)

No. 92. Southern Asia Central Conference by E. F. Moffatt on Delegates to Central Conference. (Conferences.)

No. 93. Board Lay Activities by William R. Phelps on Lay Activities. (Membership—Temp. Econ.)

No. 94. Board Lay Activities by William R. Phelps on Church Press. (Education.)

No. 95. Norwegian-Danish Conference by Eastern District on Boundaries. (Conferences.)

No. 96. Newark Conference by O. C. Nelson on Boundaries. (Conferences.)

No. 97. Philippine North Conference by Felix Grospe on Bishop Edwin F. Lee. (Ministry—Jud. Adm.)

No. 98. St. Johns River Conference by James W. Marlin on Boundaries. (Conferences.)

No. 99. St. Johns River Conference by James W. Marlin on Boundaries. (Conferences.)

No. 100. By R. L. Stephenson on Women Ministers. (Ministry—Jud. Adm.)

No. 101. Goodwill Industries by Oliver A. Friedman on Goodwill Industries. (Missions.)

No. 102. Holston Conference by Mrs. J. W. Helms on Missionary Society. (Missions.)

No. 103. Delaware Conference by L. B. Jewith on Missionary Society. (Missions.)

No. 104. Southern California Conference by Mrs. L. F. Sedgwick on Missionary Society. (Missions.)

No. 105. Board Hospitals, Homes, Deaconess Work on Board of Hospitals. (Missions.)

No. 106. Methodist Home for Children by W. H. Smith on Home for Children. (Missions.)

No. 107. Korea Conference by Ruth C. Burkholder on Missions in Korea. (Missions.)

No. 108. Bible Society Conference by Eric M. North on American Bible Society. (Missions.)

No. 109. East German Conference by Fred C. Hansser on Bishop Herbert Welch. (Ministry—Jud. Adm.)

No. 110. By Committee on Missions on Judiciary. (Ministry—Jud. Adm.)

No. 111. Book Committee by Henry S. Henschen on Book Editor. (Publishing Interests.)

No. 112. Book Committee by Henry S. Henschen on Book Concern. (Publishing Interests.)

No. 113. North Georgia Conference by S. L. Johnston on Lay Activities. (Membership—Temp. Econ.)

No. 114. St. Johns River Conference by James W. Marlin on Boundaries. (Conferences.)

No. 115. Northern Minnesota Conference by Mrs. R. B. Jardine on Women Ministers. (Ministry—Jud. Adm.)

No. 116. North Indiana Conference by Samuel L. Yoder on Qualifications of Ministers. (Ministry—Jud. Adm.)

No. 117. North Indiana Conference by Samuel L. Yoder on Qualifications of Ministers. (Ministry—Jud. Adm.)

No. 118. Genesee Conference by Guy M. Ournshire on Boundaries. (Conferences.)

No. 119. Book Committee by Henry S. Henschen on National Methodist Press. (Conferences.)

No. 120. St. Johns River Conference on Bishop C. W. Flint. (Ministry—Jud. Adm.)

No. 121. North Georgia Conference by George L. King on District Elder. (Ministry—Jud. Adm.)

No. 122. Methodist Ministers Assn. by Walter M. Lockett, Jr., on National Press. (Publishing.)

No. 123. Kentucky Conference by J. Ralph Wood on Hospitals and Homes. (Missions.)

No. 124. Louisiana Conference by R. M. Davis on Southwestern Advocate. (Publishing.)

No. 125. Norway Conference by M. S. Haver on Bishop R. J. Wade. (Ministry—Jud. Adm.)

No. 126. Committee on Membership on Quality of Membership. (Membership—Temp. Econ.)

No. 127. Committee on Membership on Quality of Membership. (Membership—Temp. Econ.)

No. 128. New York Conference by Chester A. Smith on Ritual. (Ritual.)

No. 129. New York Conference by John W. Langdale on Moral and Economic Welfare. (Missions.)

No. 130. New York Conference by John W. Langdale on Bishop F. J. McConnell. (Ministry—Jud. Adm.)

No. 131. New York Conference by John W. Langdale on Peace Commission. (Education.)

No. 132. New York Conference by John W. Langdale on Courses of Study. (Education.)

No. 133. Central New York Conference by K. W. Haight on Social Action. (Missions.)

No. 134. Ohio M. P. Conference by Mrs. John F. Haas on Women Ministers. (Ministry—Jud. Adm.)

No. 135. Secretarial Council by E. M. North on Missionary Education. (Missions.)

No. 136. Penney Farms by W. A. Newing on All Questions of Law. (Superannuate.)

No. 137. Penney Farms by W. A. Newing on Retroactive Pensions. (Superannuate.)

No. 138. Rock River Conference by James O'May on Safeguarding Pensions. (Superannuate.)

No. 139. Rock River Conference by James O'May on Annuity Responsibility. (Superannuate.)

No. 140. Penney Farms by W. A. Newing on Ministerial Support. (Superannuate.)

No. 141. Rock River Conference by James O'May on Relating to Pensions. (Superannuate.)

No. 142. Rock River Conference by James O'May on Amend Pension Law. (Superannuate.)

No. 143. Rock River Conference by James O'May on Pensions. (Superannuate.)

No. 144. Penney Farms by W. A. Newing on Pension Matter. (Superannuate.)

No. 145. By Lee Ralph Phipps on Publication Matter. (Education.)

No. 146. North Mississippi Conference by C. A. Parks on Tenure Dist. Supt. (Ministry—Jud. Adm.)

No. 147. Ohio Conference by Edmund D. Soper on Epworth League. (Education.)

No. 148. Erie Conference by Dr. Charles T. Greer on Publication Matter. (Education.)

No. 149. Newark Conference by Homer Watson Henderson on Grading System (Ministry—Jud. Adm.)

No. 150. By H. O. Martin on Threefold Membership. (Ritual.)

No. 151. Omaha Chamber of Commerce by Francis P. Matthews on Conference Invitation. (Conferences.)

No. 152. Southwest Missouri Conference by L. M. Starkey on Distribution of Members. (Ministry—Jud. Adm.)

No. 153. Southwest Missouri Conference by L. M. Starkey on Property and Trustees. (Membership—Temp. Econ.)

No. 154. Detroit Conference by Mrs. Walter Conant Fruit on Missionary Society. (Missions.)

No. 155. Missouri Conference by E. L. Hobbs on Missouri Conference. (Conferences.)

No. 156. Central Northwest Conference by Thomas J. Westerberg on Boundaries of Conference. (Conferences.)

No. 157. Salaries for Bishops. (Ministry—Jud. Adm.)

No. 158. Florida Conference by W. F. Dunkle on Boundaries. (Conferences.)

No. 159. Ckengtu University by Huang Hsuing Miss on Bishop Ralph A. Ward. (Ministry—Jud. Adm.)

No. 160. Western Jurisdiction Conference by O. L. Walker on District Supt. (Ministry—Jud. Adm.)

No. 161. Baltic and Slavic Conference by Adolf Bergmann on Bishop Raymond J. Wade. (Ministry—Jud. Adm.).

No. 162. Central Northwest Conference by Carl H. Malmquist on Bishop Ernest L. Waldorf. (Ministry—Jud. Adm.)

No. 163. Pittsburgh Conference on Adequate Support. (Ministry—Jud. Adm.)

No. 164. Pittsburgh Conference on Inactive Members. (Membership—Temp. Econ.)

No. 165. Pittsburgh Conference on Petition for Pastor. (Ministry—Jud. Adm.)

No. 166. Pittsburgh Conference by J. E. Morrilton on Pension Funds. (Superannuate.)

No. 167. By John R. Kenny on Methodist Men. (Membership—Temp. Econ.)

No. 168. Wyoming State Conference on Wyoming State Conference. (Conferences.)

No. 169. Southern California Conference by Hardy A. Ingham on Deaconess Board. (Missions.)

No. 170. Southern California Conference on Deaconess Service. (Missions.)

No. 171. By American Defender Assn. on Catholic Church. (Missions.)

No. 172. By American Defender Assn. on Catholics and Governments. (Missions.)

No. 173. By American Defender Assn. on New Roman Empire. (Missions.)

No. 174. St. Johns River Conference by James W. Martin on Bishop C. W. Flint. (Ministry—Jud. Adm.)

No. 175. Northwest India Conference on Central Conference Bishops. (Ministry—Jud. Adm.)

No. 176. Northwest India Conference by William Dye on Missionary Societies. (Missions.)

No. 177. Northwest India Conference by William Dye on Central Conference Bishops. (Ministry—Jud. Adm.)

No. 178. Northwest India Conference by William Dye on Religious Education. (Missions.)

No. 179. Northwest India Conference by William Dye on Name Methodist. (Missions.)

No. 180. Northwest India Conference by William Dye on Support of Bishops. (Ministry—Jud. Adm.)

No. 181. Northwest India Conference by William Dye on Episcopal Residences. (Ministry—Jud. Adm.)

No. 182. Colorado Conference by Mrs. William Belmont on Missionary Society. (Missions.)

No. 183. Norwegian-Danish Conference by Carl W. Schevenins on Boundaries. (Conferences.)

No. 184. Minnesota Conference by Helene A. Jackson on Missionary Society. (Missions.)

No. 185. Board Missions South Conference by Arthur Moore on Union of Missions. (Missions.)

No. 186. By Esther A. Haskard on Women Ministers. (Ministry—Jud. Adm.)

No. 187. Louisiana Conference by T. R. W. Harris on Central Jurisdiction. (Conferences.)

No. 188. By R. M. Davis on Negro Jurisdiction. (Conferences.)

No. 189. Oklahoma Conference by R. S. Satterfield on Conference Claimants. (Superannuate.)   -

No. 190. Oklahoma Conference by R. S. Satterfield on Boundaries. (Conferences.)

No. 191. By J. Morris Bailey on Boundaries. (Conferences.)

No. 192. Oklahoma Conference by R. S. Satterfield on Lay Activities. (Membership—Temp. Econ.)

No. 193. By Rev. Effie Tate on Women Ministers. (Ministry—Jud. Adm.)

No. 194. East German Conference by Fred C. Hansser on Deaconesses. (Missions.)

No. 195. Northwest Kansas Conference by Herbert Jackson Roat on Boundaries. (Conferences.)

No. 196. New Mexico Conference by C. E. Mead on Lay Activities. (Membership—Temp. Econ.)

No. 197. Baltimore Conference by Carlton B. Stuckey on Boundaries. (Conferences.)

No. 198. Joint Committee Conference by Wade Crawford Barclay on Religious Education. (Education.)

No. 199. Joint Committee by Wade Crawford Barclay on Foreign Education. (Missions.)

No. 200. Indiana Conference by H. W. Baldridge on Supply Pastors. (Ministry—Jud. Adm.)

No. 201. Upper Iowa Conference by G. W. Woodall on Retroactive Pensions. (Superannuate.)

No. 202. Upper Iowa Conference by G. W. Woodall on Sixth Restrictive Rule. (Membership—Temp. Econ.)

No. 203. Northwest Iowa Conference by M. D. Bush on Retroactive Pensions. (Superannuate.)

No. 204. Northwest Iowa Conference by M. D. Bush on Ministerial Support. (Superannuate.)

No. 205. Newark Conference by Mrs. Hedley R. Woodward on Plan "A." (Missions.)

No. 206. Upper Iowa Conference on Board Hospitals. (Missions.)

No. 207. Philadelphia Conference of Laymen's Association on Organization of Missions. (Missions.)

No. 208. Upper Iowa Conference on Christian Education. (Education.)

No. 209. Northwest Iowa Conference by M. D. Bush on Board Hospitals. (Missions.)

No. 210. Nebraska Conference by Handel Collier on Board Hospitals. (Missions.)

No. 211. Southwest Kansas Conference by P. L. Maudsley on Board Hospitals. (Missions.)

No. 212. Southern Illinois Conference by Ray N. Kean on Annuitants. (Superannuate.)

No. 213. Southern Illinois Conference by Cameron Harman on Board Hospitals. (Missions.)

No. 214. North Minnesota Conference by Iva Conner on Deaconesses. (Missions.)

No. 215. Northwest Iowa Conference by M. D. Bush on Printed Forms. (Membership—Temp. Econ.)

No. 216. New York East Conference by Dr. Margaret Underhill on Missionary Society. (Missions.)

No. 217. Philadelphia Conference by George W. Henson on St. George's Church. (Membership—Temp. Econ.)

No. 218. Wisconsin Conference by Mrs. Ellis L. Haskins on Missionary Society. (Missions.)

No. 219. Detroit Conference by May Conant Fruit on Missionary Society. (Missions.)

No. 220. Kansas Conference by Mrs. E. E. Beauchamp on Missionary Society. (Missions.)

No. 221. Central New York Conference by Mrs. L. B. Chalonx on Missionary Society. (Missions.)

No. 222. New Jersey Conference by Natalie G. Heppard on Missionary Society. (Missions.)

No. 223. New Jersey Conference by Harriet B. Yard on Missionary Society. (Missions.)

No. 224. New England Southern by Sarah L. Davis on Missionary Society. (Missions.)

No. 225. Genesee Conference by Rosetta M. Bellfield on Missionary Society. (Missions.)

No. 226. Northwest Iowa Conference by M. D. Bush on Restrictive Rule. (Membership—Temp. Econ.)

No. 227. Southern California Conference by Charles A. Moore on Methodist Men. (Membership—Temp. Econ.)

No. 228. Northwest Iowa Conference by M. D. Bush on Laymen at Conference. (Membership—Temp. Econ.)

No. 229. By William R. C. Baker on Women Ministers. (Ministry—Jud. Adm.)

No. 230. Iowa-Des Moines Conference by L. P. Goodwin on Episcopacy. (Ministry—Jud. Adm.)

No. 231. Iowa-Des Moines Conference by L. P. Goodwin on Assignment of Bishop G. Bromley Oxnam. (Ministry—Jud. Adm.)

No. 232. Northwest Iowa Conference by M. D. Bush on Assignment of Bishop G. Bromley Oxnam. (Ministry—Jud. Adm.)

No. 233. Northern Minnesota Conference by Allen E. Dripps on Bishop J. Ralph Magee. (Ministry—Jud. Adm.)

No. 234. Upper Iowa Conference by Frank W. Court on Assignment of Bishop G. Bromley Oxnam. (Ministry—Jud. Adm.)

No. 235. Upper Iowa Conference by Frank W. Court on Iowa Area. (Conferences.)

No. 236. By Mrs. Hughbert A. Leitch on Women Ministers. (Ministry—Jud. Adm.)

No. 237. By Nannie B. Heath on Women Ministers. (Ministry—Jud. Adm.)

No. 238. By F. J. Wallace on Women Ministers. (Ministry—Jud. Adm.)

No. 239. By Mrs. W. R. Tonkia on Women Ministers. (Ministry—Jud. Adm.)

No. 240. By G. W. Woodall on Decision of Bishop. (Ministry—Jud. Adm.)

No. 241. Upper Iowa Conference on "All Questions of Law." (Ministry—Jud. Adm.)

No. 242. By S. E. Stroud on Course of Study. (Ministry—Jud. Adm.)

No. 243. Northern Minnesota Conference by Allen E. Dripps on Women Ministers. (Ministry—Jud. Adm.)

No. 244. Eastern Asia Central Conference by Lin Tieuho on Bishops. (Ministry—Jud. Adm.)

No. 245. Eastern Asia Central Conference by Lin Tieuho on Election of Bishops. (Ministry—Jud. Adm.)

No. 246. Eastern Asia Central Conference by Lin Tieuho on Episcopal Residences. (Ministry—Jud. Adm.)

No. 247. Nebraska Conference by J. W. Ekwall on Assignment of Bishop G. Bromley Oxnam. (Ministry—Jud. Adm.)

No. 248. Methodist Women's Assn. by Mrs. William J. Bagg on Women's Organizations. (Membership—Temp. Econ.)

No. 249. Upper Iowa Conference by G. W. Woodall on Membership in Boards. (Membership—Temp. Econ.)

No. 250. Geneva Area Conference on Bishop John L. Nuelsen. (Ministry—Jud. Adm.)

No. 251. Iowa-Des Moines Conference by L. P. Goodwin on Episcopal Residence. (Ministry—Jud. Adm.)

No. 252. Iowa-Des Moines Conference by L. P. Goodwin on Episcopal Residence. (Ministry—Jud. Adm.)

No. 253. Iowa-Des Moines Conference by L. P. Goodwin on Episcopal Residence. (Ministry—Jud. Adm.)

No. 254. Iowa-Des Moines Conference by L. P. Goodwin on Episcopal Residence. (Ministry—Jud. Adm.)

No. 255. Wyoming State Conference by George E. Hutt on Wyoming State Conference. (Conferences.)

No. 256. Iowa-Des Moines Conference by L. P. Goodwin on 'Episcopal Residence. (Ministry—Jud. Adm.)

No. 257. Nebraska Conference by J. W. Ekwall on Episcopal Residence. (Ministry—Jud. Adm.)

No. 258. By E. E. Avery on Lay Representation. (Membership—Temp. Econ.)

No. 259. Baltimore Conference on Boundaries. (Conferences.)

No. 260. Iowa Wesleyan College by H. C. Carter on Episcopal Residence. (Ministry—Jud. Adm.)

No. 261. Sumatra Mission Conference by Egon N. Osteom on Boundaries. (Conferences.)

No. 262. Malaya Conference by Willard A. Sckurr on Bishop Edwin F. Lee. (Ministry—Jud. Adm.)

No. 263. By Eleazar Guerra on Relations with Mexico. (Missions.)

No. 264. By Mrs. H. S. Hollingsworth on Episcopal Residence. (Ministry—Jud. Adm.)

No. 265. Northwest Iowa Conference by W. G. Muhleman on Episcopal Residence. (Ministry—Jud. Adm.)

No. 266. Eastern Asia Central Conference by Lin Tieuho on Eastern Asia Conference. (Conferences.)

No. 267. By Deaconess Association on Board of Hospitals. (Missions.)

No. 268. By Frank T. Cartwright on Names on Ministry. (Committee on Relations.)

No. 269. New York Area on Bishop Francis J. McConnell. (Ministry—Jud. Adm.)

No. 270. Oklahoma Conference by W. E. Garrison on Bishop Charles C. Selecman. (Ministry—Jud. Adm.)

No. 271. Oklahoma Conference by R. E. L. Morgan on Bishop Charles C. Selecman. (Ministry—Jud. Adm.)

No. 272. Oklahoma Conference by Virgil Alexander on Bishop Charles C. Selecman. (Ministry—Jud. Adm.)

No. 273. U. S. Commission by J. E. Skillington on Enabling Act. (Membership—Temp. Econ.)

No. 274. Norway Conference by M. S. Haver on Authority's Deaconesses. (Ministry—Jud. Adm.)

No. 275. New York East Conference by Mrs. Margaret Underhill on Missionary Society. (Missions.)

No. 276. Southern California Conference by F. G. H. Stevens on Pension Code. (Superannuate.)

No. 277. By W. R. King on Social Creed. (Membership—Temp. Econ.)

No. 278. Oklahoma Conference by Joe E. Bowers on Bishop Charles C. Selecman. (Ministry—Jud. Adm.)

No. 279. Oklahoma Conference by R. S. Satterfield on Bishop Charles C. Selecman. (Ministry—Jud. Adm.)

No. 280. Oklahoma Conference by John R. Abernathy on Bishop Charles C. Selecman. (Ministry—Jud. Adm.)

No. 281. Oklahoma Conference by Charles H. Nixon on Bishop Charles C. Selecman. (Ministry—Jud. Adm.)

No. 282. Oklahoma Conference by Walter M. Armstrong on Bishop Charles C. Selecman. (Ministry—Jud. Adm.)

No. 283. Southern Asia Conference by E. M. Moffatt on Bishop B. T. Badley. (Ministry—Jud. Adm.)

No. 284. Oklahoma Conference by W. B. Glook on Bishop Charles C. Selecman. (Ministry—Jud. Adm.)

No. 285. Oklahoma Conference by R. T. Blackburn on Bishop Charles C. Selecman. (Ministry—Jud. Adm.)

No. 286. Erie Conference by David J. Blasdell on Bishop Adna Wright Leonard. (Ministry—Jud. Adm.)

No. 287. Erie Conference by David J. Blasdell on Boundaries. (Conferences.)

No. 288. Executive Commission Conference by G. Bromley Oxnam on Enabling Act. (Education.)

No. 289. By W. E. Blackstock on Episcopal Residence. (Ministry—Jud. Adm.)

No. 290. Nebraska Conference by Roy N. Spooner on Bishop G. Bromley Oxnam. (Ministry—Jud. Adm.)

No. 291. Nebraska Conference by W. H. Stephens on Bishop G. Bromley Oxnam. (Ministry—Jud. Adm.)

No. 292. Nebraska Conference by B. O. Lyle on Bishop G. Bromley Oxnam. (Ministry—Jud. Adm.)

No. 293. Nebraska Conference by A. A. Brooks on Bishop G. Bromley Oxnam. (Ministry—Jud. Adm.)

No. 294. Upper Iowa Conference by E. A. Sabin on Board of Hospitals. (Missions.)

No. 295. Northwest Iowa Conference by M. D. Bush on Board of Hospitals. (Missions.)

No. 296. On Classification of Schools. (Education.)

No. 297. Switzerland Conference by Ferdinand Sigg on Bishop Nuelsen. (Ministry—Jud. Adm.)

No. 298. St. Louis on Boundaries. (Conferences.)

No. 299. National Youth Council by Ellen Lund on Youth Representation. (Membership—Temp. Econ.)

No. 300. By Ernest S. Lyons on Pensions. (Superannuate.)

No. 301. North Indiana Conference by B. D. Beck on Board Woman's Work. (Missions.)

No. 302. Missouri Conference by Joseph W. Thompson on Boundaries. (Conferences.)

No. 303. By Leroy G. White on Self-Perpetuating. (Membership—Temp. Econ.)

No. 304. Erie Conference by Lee Ralph Phipps on Missionary Literature. (Education.)

No. 305. Africa Conference by Edward Irving Everett on Episcopal Residence. (Missions.)

No. 306. By A. G. Williamson on Bishop Charles C. Selecman. (Ministry—Jud. Adm.)

No. 307. Newark Conference by Norman P. Champlin on Bishop Francis J. McConnell. (Ministry—Jud. Adm.)

No. 308. Northwest Kansas Conference by C. A. Kemp on Boundaries. (Conferences.)

No. 309. Eastern Asia Central Conference by Bessie A. Hollows on Unified Mission Program. (Missions.)

No. 310. Chattanooga Conference by C. P. Hardin on Boundaries. (Conferences.)

No. 311. Chattanooga Conference by Henry J. Boss on Boundaries. (Conferences.)

No. 312. Baltimore Conference by William H. Best on Christian Sabbath. (Education.)

No. 313. Rock River Conference by Nettie Needen Bagg on Women's Organizations. (Membership—Temp. Econ.)

No. 314. West Virginia Conference by U. I. Jenkins on Prospectus. (Membership—Temp. Econ.)

No. 315. By Mrs. Julia Foster on Un-Christian Conduct. (Membership—Temp. Econ.)

No. 316. By Madge Hussey on Praying Bands. (Education.)

No. 317. Southern Asia Central Conference by William Dye on Financial Administration. (Education.)

No. 318. Eastern Asia Central Conference by Bessie A. Hollows on Shanghai Meeting. (Missions.)

No. 319. Southern Asia Central Conference by William Dye on B. F. M. and W. F. M. S. (Missions.)

No. 320. Detroit Missions by W. Clyde Donald on Board of Education. (Education.)

No. 321. New York East Conference by Mrs. J. W. Potter on Missionary Society. (Missions.)

No. 322. Rock River Conference by Mrs. James Glover on Bishop E. L. Waldorf. (Ministry—Jud. Adm.)

No. 323. Memphis Conference by Warren G. Barbour on Boundaries. (Conferences.)

No. 324. On Young People's Work. (Education.)

No. 325. Rock River Conference by Mrs. Nellie R. Pierce on Missionary Society. (Missions.)

No. 326. Northern Minnesota Conference by Allen E. Dripps on Bishop J. Ralph Magee. (Ministry—Jud. Adm.)

No. 327. Wyoming Conference by Enoch W. Clark on Boundaries. (Conferences.)

No. 328. Utah Mission by Albert E. Ennis on Boundaries. (Conferences.)

ᐧNo. 329. ᐧBy Rae Lawton on Deaconess Organization.
(Missions.)

No. 330. Minnesota Conference by R. Jay Wilson on
Bishop J. Ralph Magee. (Ministry—Jud. Adm.)

No. 331. Minnesota Conference by R. Jay Wilson on
Outside Service. (Ministry—Jud. Adm.)

No. 332. Nebraska Conference by Roy N. Spooner on
Bishop G. Bromley Oxnam. (Ministry—Jud. Adm.)

No. 333. New Jersey Conference by Leon Chamberlain
on Bishop E. G. Richardson. (Ministry—Jud. Adm.)

No. 334. Central Northwest Conference by S. W. Matt-
son on Bishop Ernest L. Waldorf. (Ministry—Jud. Adm.)

No. 335. Switzerland Conference by Ferdinand Sigg on
Bishop Nuelsen. (Ministry—Jud. Adm.)

No. 336. Colorado Conference by W. E. Blackstock on
Pension Supply Pastors. (Superannuate.)

No. 337. By Henry Stehl on Tenure Central Bishops.
(Ministry—Jud. Adm.)

No. 338. Northeast Ohio Conference by Virgil E. Turner
on Hospitals and Homes. (Missions.)

No. 339. By Eva N. Burch on Hospitals and Homes.
(Missions.)

No. 340. By A. Lincoln Shute on Decisions by Bishops.
(Ministry—Jud. Adm.)

No. 341. By R. H. Garrison on Ministers. (Ministry—
Jud. Adm.)

No. 342. Colorado Conference by C. E. Schofield on Wyoming State. (Ministry—Jud. Adm.)

No. 343. Sweden Conference by Theodore Arvidson on
Central Conferences. (Conferences.)

No. 344. By Joint Committee Conference on Foreign
Education. (Missions.)

No. 345. Ohio Conference by R. V. Johnson on Hospitals
and Homes. (Missions.)

No. 346. Joint Committee Conference on Foreign Education. ᐧ(Missions.)

No. 347. Wisconsin Conference by Alida M. Jacobson on
Hospitals and Homes. (Missions.)

No. 348. Iowa Methodist Hospital Conference by R. A.
Nettleton on Hospitals and Homes. (Missions.)

No. 349. By T. O. Cunningham on Hospitals and Homes.
(Missions.)

No. 350. Holston Conference by R. Luke Wright on
Boundaries. (Conferences.)

No. 351. By Nettie W. Bagg on Women's Organization.
(Membership—Temp. Econ.)

No. 352. On Service of Worship. (Ritual.)

No. 353. Central Conference by E. M. Moffatt on Tenure of Bishops.   (Ministry—Jud. Adm.)

No. 354. Virginia Conference by Mrs. Lee Britt on Boundaries (Conferences).

No. 355. By M. S. Davage on Bishops for Jurisdictions. (Ministry—Jud. Adm.)

No. 356. Nebraska Conference by Byron E. Nelson on Bishop G. Bromley Oxnam.   (Ministry—Jud. Adm.)

No. 357. Nebraska Conference by Paul M. Hillman on Bishop G. Bromley Oxnam.   (Ministry—Jud. Adm.)

No. 358. By Walter J. Coleman on Uniting Day.   (Superannuate.)

No. 359. St. Louis Conference by Rev. Fred M. Bailey on Episcopal Residence.   (Ministry—Jud. Adm.)

No. 360. Pittsburgh Conference by Sanford W. Caicasano on Bishop Adna Wright Leonard.   (Ministry—Jud. Adm.)

No. 361. Central Northwest Conference by T. J. Westerberg on Enabling Act.   (Conferences.)

No. 362. Joint Committees by Wade Crawford Barclay on Administration Education.   (Education.)

No. 303. By Lee Ralph Phipps on Publication Matter. (Education.)

No. 364. By A. A. Perkins on Women Ministers.   (Conferences.)

No. 365. By Ernest S. Lyons on Bilingual Situations. (Membership.)

No. 366. By Ernest S. Lyons on Annual Mission Meeting.   (Conferences.)

No. 367. Joint Committee Conference on Missions and Education.   (Missions.)

No. 368. Maine Conference by Louis S. Seaples on Bishop Herbert Welch.   (Ministry—Jud. Adm.)

No. 369. Montana Conference by Mrs. Reynold Platt, Jr., on Unemployment.   (Membership—Temp. Econ.)

No. 370. Colorado Conference by C. E. Schofield on Bishop Ralph S. Cushman.   (Ministry—Jud. Adm.)

No. 371. California Conference by Walter C. Buckner on Enabling Act.   (Conferences.)

No. 372. St. Louis Conference by Hugh O. Isbell on Episcopal Residence.   (Conferences.)

No. 373. By Mrs. Beniah Ivy on Women Ministers. (Conferences.)

No. 374. By Nettie W. Bagg on Women's Organizations. (Membership—Temp. Econ.)

No. 375. New York Conference by Carl H. Fowler on Council of Churches.   (Conferences.)

No. 376. Baltimore Conference by Bessy B. Beall on Bishop Edwin Holt Hughes. (Ministry—Jud. Adm.)

No. 377. By M. N. English on China Civilian Relief. (Missions.)

No. 378. West Virginia Conference by M. S. Collins on Bishop Adna W. Leonard. (Ministry—Jud. Adm.)

No. 379. Kentucky Conference by James T. Cannon on Episcopal Area. (Conferences.)

No. 380. Pacific Northwest Conference by Mrs. Ed. Redford on Missionary Society. (Missions.)

No. 381. By Mrs. Hanry Hoag Frost on Women's Organizations. (Membership—Temp. Econ.)

No. 382. Newark Conference by Norman P. Chapman on Equitable Salary Basis. (Membership—Temp. Econ.)

No. 383. By Eva C. Fields on Evangelism. (Missions.)

No. 384. Pittsburgh Conference by Carl E. Chapman on Spiritual Welfare. (Missions.)

No. 385. By Umphrey Lee on Permanent Funds. (Membership—Temp. Econ.)

No. 386. By U. B. Jardine on Women Ministers. (Ministry—Jud. Adm.)

No. 387. Northwest Indiana Conference by Mrs. E. R. Bartlett on Women's Organizations. (Missions.)

No. 388. Nebraska Conference by W. B. Zimmerman on Bishop G. Bromley Oxnam. (Ministry—Jud. Adm.)

No. 389. Oregon Conference by Ernest W. Peterson on Dr. Clarence True Wilson. (Missions.)

No. 390. California Conference by Correll M. Julian on Annual Conference Question. (Conferences.)

No. 391. Iowa-Missouri Conference by Rev. W. H. Betz on Women Ministers. (Ministry—Jud. Adm.)

No. 392. Ohio Conference by Mrs. John Haas on Women Ministers. (Ministry—Jud. Adm.)

No. 393. By Rev. E. P. Spurlock on Women Ministers. (Ministry—Jud. Adm.)

No. 394. Miss Tressie Border on Women Ministers. (Ministry—Jud. Adm.)

PREACHING ASSIGNMENTS FOR APRIL 30
METHODIST EPISCOPAL CHURCHES

Agnes Avenue .... Bishop John Gowdy
Broadway .... Dr. G. C. Bond
Central (K. C., K.) .... Bishop Charles W. Flint
Central Avenue . . . . Dr. A. Smith
Country Club .... Dr. Merton S. Rice
Grand Avenue .... Dr. J. M. M. Gray

Independence Avenue   Bishop Edwin Holt Hughes
Linwood Boulevard . . .   . Bishop Ivan Lee Holt
London Heights (K. C., K.) . Bishop Ralph S. Cushman
Oakhurst . . . . Dr. Samson Ding
Oakley . . . .   Bishop James C. Baker
Paseo . . . . Dr. W. Kendall
Phoenix Park . . . .   .   Bishop Robert E. Jones
Quayle (North K. C.)   Bishop Titus Lowe
Quayle Memorial (K. C., K.)   . . . Bishop Edwin Lee
Raymore . . . . Dr. T. P. Potter
Washington Avenue (K.C., K.) . . Bishop Ernest L. Waldorf
Wesley . . . . Dr. H. A. Smith

SOUTHERN METHODIST CHURCHES

Brookside . . . . Bishop W. T. Watkins
Central . . . . Bishop F. J. McConnell
Epworth . . .   . .Bishop A. Frank Smith
Institutional . .   . . Dr. Gilbert T. Rowe
Melrose . . . . Dr. Lynn Harold Hough
Mount Washington . . . . Dr. A. Norman Evans
South Prospect . .   .   . .Dr. Costen J. Harrell
Swope Park. . .   . . .Rt. Hon. Isaac Foot
Troost Avenue   . . . . Dr. Z. T. Kaung
Westport. .   . Dr. J. C. Broomfield
White Avenue   . . . .   Dr. John C. Glenn

METHODIST PROTESTANT CHURCHES

Gordon Place . .   .   . Dr. C. E. Forlines
Jackson Avenue . .   .   . . Dr. Kenneth Copeland
Queens Garden   `. .   . . Dr. Clarence A. Sutton
Stephens Memorial   . . . . Dr. J. S. Eddins
Westheight . . . . Dr. J. C. Williams

OTHER DENOMINATIONS

Broadway Baptist .   .   . Bishop J. Waskom Pickett
Central Christian . . . . Dr. Leonard Oechsli
Community Church   .   . . .   Dr. Jacob S. Payton
Country Club Christian   .   . Bishop Raymond J. Wade
First Baptist   . . . . Dr. G. Ray Jordan
First Baptist (K. C., K.)   . . . .   Dr. A. R. Corn
Linwood Boulevard Presbyterian . Bishop Charles L. Mead
Second Presbyterian   . . . . Dr. Harold Paul Sloan
Van Brunt Presbyterian. . . . . : . . . . Dr. E. D. Soper
Westminster Congregational . . . . . Dr. R. E. Diffendorfer
Westport Presbyterian . . . . Dr. Loren M. Edwards

OUT-OF-TOWN METHODIST

Belton, Mo.	Dr. R. W. Goodloe
Blue Springs, Mo.	Bishop Clare Purcell
Bonner Springs, Kans.	Dr. R. L. Archer
Bucyrus, Kans.	H. P. Clark
Chillicothe, Mo.	Bishop William W. Peele
Cleveland, Mo.	Dr. T. P. Potter
Independence, Mo.	Dr. L. L. Evans
Lawrence, Kans.	Bishop Paul B. Kern
Lees Summit	Bishop Herbert C. Welch
Liberty, Mo.	Dr. Forney Hutchinson
Malta Bend, Mo.	Dr. J. S. K. Patel
Oak Grove, Mo. (evening)	Dr. Harry Denman
Olathe, Kans.	Dr. Richard T. Baker
Ottawa, Kans.	Dr. John B. Magee
Plattsburg, Mo.	Dr. Henry H. Jones
Sedalia, Mo.	Dr. Harry Denman
Shawnee Mission, Kans.	Bishop Ralph Ward
Smithton, Mo.	Dr. Tully C. Knoles
Topeka, Kans. (First Church)	Dr. Paul Quillian
Topeka, Kans. (Lowman Memorial).	
	Bishop Brenton T. Badley
Warrensburg, Mo.	Dr. M. C. Miles

PREACHING ASSIGNMENTS FOR MAY 7
METHODIST EPISCOPAL

Agnes Avenue	Frank F. Cartwright
Broadway	{ Mrs. J. M. Springer
	{ Dr. Daniel L. Marsh
Central (K. C., Kans.)	Arlo Brown
Central Avenue (K. C., Kans.)	Bishop James H. Straughn
Country Club	Dr. J. R. N. Score
Grand Avenue Temple	Bishop Francis J. McConnell
Independence Avenue	Dr. Lynn H. Hough
Indiana Avenue	Bishop John L. Nuelsen
Linwood Boulevard	Bishop Ernest Lynn Waldorf
London Heights	Bishop Titus Lowe
Mason Memorial (K. C., Kans.)	Bishop Robert E. Jones
Mount Washington	Dr. E. R. Stribling
Oakhurst	Dr. Thomas B. Mather
Oakley	Bishop James C. Baker
Paseo	Dr. E. E. Pierce
Phoenix Park	Dr. J. W. Surles
Quayle Memorial (K. C., Kans.)	Dr. Harold Paul Sloan
Quayle (No. K. C., Mo.)	Rev. Ezra Cox
Roanoke	Bishop Herbert Welch

Rosedale, Kans. . . . . .Rev. D. S. Bullock
Shawnee, Kans. . . . . .Mr. Edgar T. Welch
Trinity . . . . .Bishop Ivan Lee Holt
Washington Avenue (K. C., Kans.).
                            Bishop Edwin Holt Hughes
Watson Memorial (Independence, Mo.).
                            Bishop H. Lester Smith
Wesley. . . . .   Bishop Ralph A. Ward
Wesley (K. C., Kans.) .   . . . .Dr. E. M. Rugg

METHODIST EPISCOPAL, SOUTH

Blue Ridge . . . .   Dr. E. R. Stafford
Brookside. . . . . .Bishop Adna Wright Leonard
Central . . . . .Bishop William T. Watkins
Cleveland Avenue . . . .   Dr. Frank A. Lindhorst
Epworth . . . .   .Dr. Z. T. Kaung
First Methodist (Independence, Mo.)   Bishop Clare Purcell
Institutional   . .   . . Dr. J. M. Ormond
Melrose .   . . . .Dr. Ralph Sockman
Seventh Street (K. C., Kans.) . . . .Dr. John C. McPheeters
South Prospect   .   .   .   Dr. J. S. K. Patel
Swope Park . . . . .Bishop J. Ralph Magee
Trinity . . . . Dr. Walter L. Barr
Troost Avenue . . . . .Bishop Ralph S. Cushman
Westport . . . . Bishop U. V. W. Darlington
White Avenue   . . .   . .Dr. R. C. Holliday

METHODIST PROTESTANT

Gordon Place   .   . . Dr. J. C. Williams
Jackson Avenue   Dr. Frank W. Stephenson
Queens Garden. . . . .   .Rev. C. W. Walton
Stevens Memorial . . . . Dr. J. N. Link
Westheight   { Mrs. J. W. Shell
                                      { Rev. F. L. Gibbs

OTHER DENOMINATIONS

Country Club Congregational   Bishop Alexander P. Shaw
Covenant Evangelical . . . .   B. M. Mitchell
First Presbyterian (K. C., Kans.) . . Dr. Marshall R. Reed
Linwood Boulevard Presbyterian.
                            Bishop Brenton T. Badley
North Kansas City Baptist. .   . . . Dr. Earl A. Roadman
Oak Park Christian . . . .   Dr. H. H. Jones
Roanoke Baptist. . . . . .Bishop Roberto Elphick
Roanoke Presbyterian . . . . .Bishop J. C. Broomfield
St. Mark's Lutheran (Frost and Harrison St.).
                       Rev. Dr. Frank Willard Court

Second Presbyterian   Dr. E. D. Kohlstedt
Swope Park Baptist .   .   . Dr. Robert Smith
Unitarian ....Dr. Charles O. Ransford
Westminister Congregational   .   . Bishop Edgar Blake

OUT OF THE CITY

Belton, Mo. (Methodist, South)   Dr. Fred H. Peeples
Bethany, Mo. (Methodist) .   Bishop Paul B. Kern
Boonville, Mo. (Methodist) ·   Dr. Robert W. Goodloe
Butler, Mo. (Methodist) .   .   .. Dr. E. C. Dewey
Cameron, Mo. (Methodist) . ..   . . Bishop John Gowdy
Carthage, Mo. (First Methodist) . Bishop Charles L. Mead
Chillicothe, Mo. (Methodist)   .. .Bishop Edwin F. Lee
Cleveland, Mo. (First Methodist) . . Dr. A. T. McIlwain
Excelsior Springs, Mo. (Methodist) . Rev. R. D. Swinney
Indianola, Iowa .... Bishop J. M. Springer
Joplin, Mo. (Methodist)   . Dr. Ralph E. Diffendorfer
Lawrence, Kans. (First Methodist).
                          Bishop William C. Martin
Leavenworth, Kans. (First Methodist) . .W. M. Coleman
Lees Summit, Mo. (Methodist) . . Bishop L. Lloyd Decell
Liberty, Mo. (Methodist, South, Evening).
                                Dr. Ralph Sockman
Maryville, Mo. (Methodist)   ..   ..   J. A. Rinkel
Ottawa, Kans. (First Methodist) ..... Dr. W. E. J. Gratz
Parkville, Mo. (Park College)   .   Dr. E. D. Soper
Plattsburg, Mo. (Methodist) ..   Dr. Charles C. Jarrell
Pleasanton, Kans. (Methodist) ....Rev. E. P. Blamires
Raymore, Mo. (Methodist Protestant).Dr. John R. Kennedy
St. Joseph, Mo. (Trinity)·........Bishop F. H. Otto Melle
St. Louis, Mo. (Dr. Fry Memorial· Methodist).
                                Dr. Joseph E. Bartak
Savannah, Mo. (Methodist)   Bishop Charles C. Selecman
Sedalia, Mo. (First Methodist) .....   Rev. R. L. Archer
Smithville, Mo. (Methodist)   .... Dr. Clem Baker
Tonganoxie, Kans. (Methodist) ......Dr. V. M. McCombs
Topeka, Kans. (First Methodist) .. .. Dr. Roy L. Smith
Topeka, Kans. (Methodist, Kansas Avenue).
                                Rev. Kyugogo Obata
Tulsa, Okla. (St. Paul's)   Bishop Jashwant R. Chitambar
Warrensburg, Mo. (Methodist, South).Dr. Gilbert T. Rowe
Wellington, Mo. (Methodist) ..... . Dr. Eugene B. Hawk
Wichita, Kans. (First Methodist).
                                Bishop Charles W. Flint

REPORT OF TREASURERS OF JOINT UNITING CONFERENCE EXPENSE FUNDS

RECEIPTS AND DISBURSEMENTS—JULY 31, 1939

RECEIPTS

	Appropriation Publicity	Daily Advocate
Methodist Episcopal Church.... ....$ 8,800 00	$ 250 00	$ 6,956 70
Methodist Episcopal Church, South 8,800 00	250 00	2,288 16
Methodist Protestant Church........... 2,200 00	62 50	....
Daily Advocate Receipts—Kansas City	....	4,327 52
$19,800 00	$ 562 50	$13,572 38

	$33,934 88
Handbooks Sold......	15 00
Episcopal Address Sold	2 00
	$33,951 88

DISBURSEMENTS

Commissions on Interdenominational Relations and Church Union .$	993 93
Commission on Entertainment...................................	2,438 26
Committee on Publicity....	576 30
Committee on Legal Counsel...................................	794 55
Committee on Rules of Order...................................	410 30
Committee on Program..	198 71
Daily Advocate.....	16,274 49
Horne and Shull, Stenographers..............................	2,247 05
Prospectus of the Discipline (Net)...................	1,819 90
Handbook for Delegates......................................	896 40
Bishops' Address.	119 63
Consecration Certificates and Programs......................	245 85
Declaration of Union Service	177 41
Fraternal Messengers..	350 10
Honorarium for Secretary....................................	500 00
Secretary's Expense..	605 39
Treasurers' Expense	15 64
General Committees Expense.	32 70
Joint Meeting of Bishops......	12 10
	28,708 71

Balance on Deposit in Commerce Trust Co., Kansas City, Mo ... .$ 5,243 17

LIABILITIES

Printing of Journal and Distributing same to Bishops, Official Delegates, Schools, and Colleges.

O. GRANT MARKHAM, *Treas.;*
WHITMORE & SMITH, *Treas.;*
H. C. STALEY, *Treas.*

REPORT OF TREASURERS OF UNITING CONFERENCE EXPENSE FUND, METHODIST EPISCOPAL CHURCH, SOUTH

JULY 31, 1939

RECEIPTS

From Annual Conferences $69,462 66

DISBURSEMENTS

Interest........... . ...$	260 55
Commission on Interdenominational Relations and Church Union ...	3,070 41
Committee on Conferences.....................................	260 83
Committee on Education.......................................	518 96
Committee on Ministry..	635 44
Committee on Missions..	1,116 96
Committee on Publishing Interests.............................	441 91
Committee on Ritual..	367 74

```
Committee on Superannuate Support. ...........  ...........  $      72 25
Committee on Temporal Economy ......  ......  .   ..       388 98
Committee on Arrangements.................................       1,138 00
Cost of Kansas City Conference ................ ... .. ....      57,500 40
Commission on Budget  ...................................        605 02
Arranging Discipline....  ................................       1,949 63
Foster and Parkes, Printing Checks .. ...  .............. ...      24 75
Honorarium, H. E. Woolever.................. ....  ...... ...     150 00
Stenographer  ......... .. ........, .... .. .... .. ....           4 25
Postage............................................... :...        33 70
```

$ 68,539 78

Balance on Deposit in Third National Bank, Nashville, Tenn. .... $ 922 88

WHITMORE AND SMITH, *Treas.*

APPORTIONMENTS AND RECEIPTS
BY ANNUAL CONFERENCES

RECEIPTS

	Amount Assessed	Amount Paid	Assessment Unpaid
Alabama Conference...................................$	2,338 27	$ 2,084 28	$ 253 99
Arizona Conference................................	169 99	169 99	....
Baltimore Conference..............................	2,688 59	2,688 59	....
Belgium Conference................................	15 94	15 94	....
Central Texas Conference..........................	2,552 65	2,241 45	311 20
China Conference... .. ..,.....,	204 52	204 52	....
Cuba Conference.................................	91 19	....	91 19
Czechoslovakia Conference.....................:..	40 54	40 54	....
Florida Conference	2,211 12	2,060 94	150 18
Holston Conference	3,022 56	2,875 39	147 17
Illinois Conference................................	191 02	208 20	17 18*
Kentucky Conference..............................	1,181 38	1,137 30	44 08
Little Rock Conference	1,738 04	1,738 04	....
Louisiana Conference..............................	1,895 58	1,866 55	29 03
Louisville Conference..............................	1,775 99	1,706 98	69 01
Memphis Conference	2,408 44	2,403 82	4 62
Mississippi Conference............................	1,976 08	1,907 25	68 83
Missouri Conference..............................	1,287 58	1,300 69	13 11*
New Mexico Conference...........................	742 03	742 03	....
North Alabama Conference	3,502 87	2,951 06	551 31
North Arkansas Conference.......................	1,969 06	1,962 91	6 15
North Carolina Conference.................	3,324 64	3,324 00	64
North Georgia Conference.........	3,804 95	2,246 45	1,558 50
North Mississippi Conference.....	1,887 77	915 85	971 92
North Texas Conference........	2,326 97	2,326 97	....
Northwest Conference.....	114 77	126 89	12 12*
Northwest Texas Conference...................`	2,135 48	2,051 35	84 13
Oklahoma Conference.....	2,543 18	2,506 00	37 18
Pacific Conference............................. .	708 08	708 08	....
St. Louis Conference.....	1,318 93	1,315 50	3 43
South Carolina Conference.....	1,807 60	1,081 42	726 18
South Georgia Conference.........................	2,871 43	2,141 49	729 94
Southwest Missouri Conference	1,142 24	1,142 24	....
Tennessee Conference. ....:.	2,290 82	2,287 00	3 82
Texas Conference..	3,269 45	3,141 06	128 39
Texas Mexican Conference...	80 64	54 30	26 34
Upper South Carolina Conference..................	2,102 94	1,991 17	111 77
Virginia Conference. ....`.. ...	4,365 79	4,401 59	35 80*
West Texas Conference.....	1,946 05	1,836 83	109 22
Western Mexican Conference.`..................	41 36	41 36	....
Western North Carolina Conference ....:..	4,169 09	4,169 09	....
Western Virginia Conference.......	1,344 88	1,347 55	2 67*

| | $75,600 00 | $69,462 66 | $ 6,137 34 |

*Overpaid.

REPORT OF THE TREASURER OF THE UNITING CONFERENCE EXPENSE FUND OF THE METHODIST EPISCOPAL CHURCH

STATEMENT OF INCOME AND EXPENDITURES STATED ON A CASH BASIS
FOR THE PERIOD FROM JULY 27, 1938, TO JULY 15, 1939, INCLUSIVE

INCOME

From Annual Conferences in the United States............................$68,963 91

EXPENSES AND CONTRIBUTIONS

Expenses and allowances of Delegates of the Uniting Conference............$43,348 72
Expenses of Commissions on:
Interdenominational Relations $5,057 76		
Entertainment. 710 16	5,767 92	

Expenses of Committees on:
Conferences....... ....$ 707 36		
Education...............................,...................... 893 61		
Membership. 623 32		
Ministry and Judicial Administration 563 07		
Missions in all Fields 678 66		
Pensions 160 48		
Publishing Interests....................................... 660 87		
Ritual....... .... 171 53	4,458 90	

Expenses of General Conference Secretary's office:
Clerical services........................... ....$ 340 00		
Rent, moving, etc 40 00		
Postage, printing, and stationery... .... 86 55		
Office Supplies and equipment 22 53		
Telephone, telegraph, and messenger service.. . ... 46 04		
Travel expense 93 65	628 77	

Expenses of Treasurer's office:
Rent and services.. ....$1,005 16		
Postage, printing, and stationery... .... 491 15		
Travel expense.. 473 29		
Miscellaneous...................................... 74 92	2,044 52	

Payments made to The Joint Uniting Conference Expense Fund 9,050 00

$65,298 83

Cash balance in the Fund, July 15, 1939, on deposit as follows:
Corn Exchange Bank Trust Company, New York, N. Y.........$ 502 94		
Commerce Trust Company, Kansas City, Mo................... 3,162 14	$ 3,665 08	

AUDITOR'S CERTIFICATE

We have examined the accounts of Dr. O. Grant Markham, Treasurer of the Uniting Conference Expense Fund of the Methodist Episcopal Church for the period from July 27, 1938, to July 15, 1939, inclusive. We made tests of selected recorded collections by examining duplicate copies of receipts issued and comparing the total recorded receipts with the amounts deposited in banks. All recorded disbursements were supported by paid checks and/or bank charge slips with the exception of five items, representing outstanding checks at July 15, 1939, which were supported by vouchers on file. The cash on deposit as shown by bank statements was reconciled with the balances shown in the cash book as at July 15, 1939. Confirmations of the balances on deposit as shown by the bank statements as at July 15, 1939, were received directly from the depositaries.

In our opinion, based upon such examination, the annexed statement of income and expenditures, stated on a cash basis, for the period from July 27, 1938, to July 15, 1939, inclusive, summarizes the transactions recorded in the books of account for the period stated.

LYBRAND, ROSS BROS. & MONTGOMERY.

New York, July 26, 1939.

TREASURER'S NOTE

The above report includes payment of all expenses of the Uniting Conference as obligations of the Methodist Episcopal Church, so far as known, except some further contribution to the Joint Uniting Conference Expense, to meet the expense of printing the Journal of the Uniting Conference, and related expenses.

APPORTIONMENTS AND PAYMENTS

JULY 15, 1938, TO JULY 15, 1939

The 1936 General Conference of the Methodist Episcopal Church ordered that the Book Committee shall estimate the amount of approximate expense of the Uniting Conference and shall have authority to send to the Conferences and Churches such apportionments as may appear necessary for meeting our quota of the financial obligations. An equitable apportionment of this total estimate was sent to the District Superintendents of each Annual Conference. Herewith is the statement of these apportionments and the payments made.

ANNUAL CONFERENCES IN THE UNITED STATES

Conference and Districts	Apportionment	Paid
ALABAMA		
Birmingham ....$	39 00	$ 39 00
Boaz..........	37 00	37 00
Gulf	10 00	10 00
	$ 86 00	$ 86 00
ATLANTA		
Atlanta........$	39 00	$ 39 00
Atlanta East....	27 00	27 00
Rome	23 00	23 00
	$ 89 00	$ 89 00
BALTIMORE		
Baltimore East. $	525 00	$ 546 00
Baltimore West	518 00	500 00
Frederick.......	337 00	340 00
Washington	537 00	551 00
	$ 1,917 00	$ 1,937 00
BLUE RIDGE-ATLANTIC		
Asheville........$	64 00	$ 66 25
Statesville.	71 00	77 77
	$ 135 00	$ 144 02
CALIFORNIA		
Nevada Mission .$	75 00	$ 33 00
Oakland	311 00	379 50
Redwood-Shasta.	223 00	135 00
Sacramento......	164 00	129 00
San Francisco....	314 00	226 00
	$ 1,087 00	$ 902 50
CENTRAL ALABAMA		
Birmingham.....$	39 00	$ 22 00
Huntsville	34 00	21 50
Montgomery. ..	26 00	26 00
Opelika.........	26 00	26 00
	$ 125 00	$ 95 50

Conference and Districts	Apportionment	Paid
CENTRAL NEW YORK		
Elmira. ...... $	366 00	$ 133 77
Geneva . .	303 00	139 00
Syracuse East...	374 00	165 15
Syracuse West ..	153 00	126 00
	$ 1,196 00	$ 563 92
CENTRAL NORTHWEST		
Chicago .. ....$	114 00	$ 101 80
Galesburg ...	46 00	39 50
Jamestown.... .	32 00	32 00
Omaha.........	70 00	41 50
St. Paul	97 00	88 80
	$ 359 00	$ 303 60
CENTRAL PENNSYLVANIA		
Altoona. ... . $	483 00	$ 494 00
Harrisburg . .	496 00	489 00
Sunbury . ..	430 00	371 00
Williamsport	444 00	454 15
	$ 1,853 00	$ 1,808 15
CENTRAL TENNESSEE		
Baxter-Lawrenceburg ..... $	52 00	$ 52 00
CENTRAL WEST		
Kansas City . $	52 00	$ 52 00
St. Louis........	59 00	59 00
Sedalia	39 00	39 00
Topeka.........	43 00	43 00
	$ 193 00	$ 193 00
COLORADO		
Colorado Springs-Pueblo.... $	285 00	$ 149 00
Denver-Grand Junction... .	287 00	94 00
Greeley.	285 00	195 50
	$ 857 00	$ 438 50

Conference and Districts	Apportionment	Paid
DAKOTA		
Northern.........$	215 00	$ 121 51
Southern...... .	242 00	147 43
Western	121 00	78 50
	$ 578 00	$ 347 44
DELAWARE		
Dover.........$	127 00	$ 127 00
Easton.........	134 00	72 95
Philadelphia ..	147 00	113 75
Salisbury.... .	137 00	121 42
Wilmington.. ..	151 00	122 00
	$ 696 00	$ 557 12
DETROIT		
Ann Arbor.. ...$	402 00	$ 285 88
Detroit.........	638 00	555 00
Flint...........	424 00	166 00
Marquette......	253 00	128 00
Port Huron.....	362 00	348 75
Saginaw........	341 00	172 34
	$ 2,420 00	$ 1,655 97
EAST GERMAN		
Central........$	58 00	$ 42 00
East...........	75 00	36 00
South.	71 00	72 00
	$ 204 00	$ 150 00
EAST TENNESSEE		
Bluefield.. .....$	49 00	$ 49 00
Bristol	41 00	41 50
Chattanooga	32 00	32 50
	$ 122 00	$ 123 00
EASTERN SWEDISH		
New England....$	75 00	$ 76 00
New York.......	69 00	69 75
	$ 144 00	$ 145 75
ERIE		
Brookville .. ...$	346 00	$ 355 00
Grove City.. . .	349 00	358 00
Jamestown......	371 00	308 10
Meadville.......	356 00	334 50
	$ 1,422 00	$ 1,355 60
FLORIDA		
Gainesville-Ocala.$	21 00	$ 21 00
Jacksonville.....	38 00	38 00
	$ 59 00	$ 59 00
GENESEE		
Buffalo . ...$	504 00	$ 403 65
Hornell	328 00	106 78
Olean.	326 00	289 95
Rochester.......	449 00	249 15
	$ 1,607 00	$ 1,049 53
GEORGIA		
Atlanta... ....$	25 00	$ 25 00
Blue Ridge......	26 00	26 00
	$ 51 00	$ 51 00
HOLSTON		
Bristol..........$	68 00	$ 29 00
Chattanooga.....	147 00	113 00
Harriman	98 00	102 75
Johnson City....	139 00	142 50
Knoxville.......	177 00	140 00
	$ 629 00	$ 527 25
IDAHO		
Eastern ....$	137 00	$ 129 40
Western..	128 00	134 20
	$ 265 00	$ 263 60

Conference and Districts	Apportionment	Paid
ILLINOIS		
Bloomington.... $	411 00	$ 289 88
Champaign......	428 00	438 23
Decatur	359 00	377 50
Galesburg... ..	427 00	372 60
Jacksonville	316 00	333 48
Peoria	427 00	428 25
Springfield......	386 00	359 25
	$ 2,754 00	$ 2,599 19
INDIANA		
Bloomington.....$	192 00	$ 162 50
Evansville	306 00	306 00
Indianapolis.....	444 00	458 00
New Albany.....	214 00	205 00
Rushville........	235 00	231 00
Seymour........	245 00	197 25
Vincennes	202 00	179 00
	$ 1,838 00	$ 1,738 75
IOWA-DES MOINES		
Boone.........$	319 00	$ 230 28
Burlington.. ...	311 00	218 00
Council Bluffs...	275 00	213 00
Creston	226 00	201 00
Des Moines ...	325 00	327 25
Ottumwa........	302 00	239 00
	$ 1,758 00	$ 1,428 53
KANSAS		
Emporia . ....$	284 00	$ 243 30
Kansas City.....	313 00	268 70
Manhattan......	252 00	255 85
Parsons........	304 00	297 23
Topeka...	305 00	241 08
	$ 1,458 00	$ 1,306 16
KENTUCKY		
Ashland.........$	122 00	$ 115 50
Barbourville.....	102 00	92 00
Covington.......	135 00	135 00
Louisville.,.....	127 00	41 26
	$ 486 00	$ 383 76
LEXINGTON		
Chicago-Detroit-Indianapolis ..$	114 00	$ 114 00
Cincinnati-Lexington ...	84 00	84 00
Cleveland-Columbus. ..	99 00	99 00
Evansville-Louisville ...	63 00	63 00
	$ 360 00	$ 360 00
LOUISIANA		
Alexandria.. ...$	27 00	$ 27 00
Baton Rouge ...	29 00	29 00
Lake Charles ...	41 00	30 00
North New Orleans.........	44 00	21 00
South New Orleans	51 00	51 00
Shreveport	34 00	34 00
	$ 226 00	$ 192 00
MAINE		
Augusta...... $	303 00	$ 121 00
Bangor....	288 00	99 00
Portland	317 00	215 50
	$ 908 00	$ 435 50
MICHIGAN		
Albion-Lansing...$	343 00	$ 271 50
Big Rapids.. ...	222 00	137 50
Grand Rapids...	265 00	129 10
Grand Traverse .	152 00	110 00
Kalamazoo.. ..	306 00	221 30
	$ 1,288 00	$ 869 40

Conference and Districts	Appor- tionment	Paid
MINNESOTA		
Mankato........$	285 00	$ 223 55
St. Paul.........	276 00	267 95
Winona	284 00	196 85
	$ 845 00	$ 688 35
MISSISSIPPI		
Brookhaven.....$	34 00	$ 34 00
Gulfside.........	34 00	34 00
Hattiesburg.....	46 00	46 00
Jackson.........	51 00	51 00
Meridian	49 00	25 00
	$ 214 00	$ 190 00
MISSOURI		
Arkansas........$	68 00	$ 39 00
Carthage...	158 00	94 00
Kansas City.....	225 00	221 50
Kirksville......	206 00	137 30
St. Joseph.......	198 00	86 40
St. Louis........	259 00	272 00
Sedalia..........	170 00	174 00
Springfield	177 00	189 00
	$ 1,461 00	$ 1,213 20
MONTANA STATE		
Glacier Park.....$	125 00	$ 120 92
Rocky Mountain.	140 00	114 75
Yellowstone.....	141 00	116 85
	$ 406 00	$ 352 52
NEBRASKA		
Beatrice........$	245 00	$ 188 73
Hastings	218 00	157 50
Holdredge.......	244 00	70 00
Kearney........	260 00	225 75
Lincoln	254 00	222 00
Norfolk.........	243 00	124 60
Northwest.......	186 00	152 00
Omaha..........	254 00	119 00
	$ 1,904 00	$ 1,259 58
NEW ENGLAND		
Boston..........$	491 00	$ 301 00
Lynn............	573 00	470 46
Springfield......	253 00	125 00
Worcester	328 00	237 00
	$ 1,645 00	$ 1,133 46
NEW ENGLAND SOUTHERN		
New Bedford....$	342 00	$ 295 65
Norwich........	242 00	117 10
Providence......	387 00	258 00
	$ 971 00	$ 670 75
NEW HAMPSHIRE		
Northern........$	287 00	$ 220 95
Southern........	264 00	147 25
	$ 551 00	$ 368 20
NEW JERSEY		
Bridgeton.......$	485 00	$ 343 25
Camden.........	520 00	490 73
New Brunswick..	521 00	374 30
Trenton.........	473 00	413 43
	$ 1,999 00	$ 1,621 71
NEW YORK		
Kingston........$	297 00	$ 119 90
Newburgh.......	440 00	277 50
New York.......	717 00	532 25
Poughkeepsie.:..	295 00	194 00
	$ 1,749 00	$ 1,123 65

Conference and Districts	Appor- tionment	Paid
NEW YORK EAST		
Brooklyn North..$	652 00	$ 538 23
Brooklyn South..	664 00	588 00
New Haven... .	550 00	336 50
New York.......	512 00	406 03
	$ 2,378 00	$ 1,868 76
NEWARK		
Jersey City .... $	606 00	$ 417 00
Newark.........	864 00	688 00
Paterson........	591 00	286 00
	$ 2,061 00	$ 1,391 00
NORTH CAROLINA		
Greensboro ....$	70 00	$ 50 25
Laurinburg......	59 00	18 00
Western········	58 00	57 00
Winston	60 00	26 00
	$ 247 00	$ 151 25
NORTH DAKOTA		
Eastern .. ..$	172 00	$ 122 50
Northwestern...	131 00	92 00
Southwestern ...	133 00	83 50
	$ 436 00	$ 298 00
NORTH INDIANA		
Fort Wayne....$	285 00	$ 236 00
Kokomo	263 00	273 00
Muncie	288 00	291 00
Richmond...... .	265 00	261 00
Wabash...	287 00	279 00
Warsaw	288 00	298 75
	$ 1,676 00	$ 1,638 75
NORTHEAST OHIO		
Akron ... .$	388 00	$ 246 28
Cambridge- Barnesville ..	384 00	332 68
Canton	407 00	377 35
Cleveland	517 00	439 25
Mansfield.......	488 00	394 87
Norwalk........	348 00	262 25
Steubenville.....	407 00	372 89
Youngstown.....	429 00	431 00
	$ 3,318 00	$ 2,856 57
NORTHERN MINNESOTA		
Duluth.........$	209 00	$ 126 00
Fergus Falls	175 00	124 00
Litchfield	274 00	209 00
Minneapolis.....	355 00	391 05
	$ 1,013 00	$ 850 05
NORTHERN NEW YORK		
Black River ....$	263 00	$ 234 42
Mohawk........	271 00	242 50
Ontario..	277 00	47 50
St. Lawrence ..	271 00	256 45
	$ 1,082 00	$ 780 87
NORTHWEST INDIANA		
Crawfordsville...$	197 00	$ 179 25
Greencastle......	240 00	202 60
Lafayette	242 00	253 00
South Bend.....	380 00	266 00
	$ 1,059 00	$ 900 85
NORTHWEST IOWA		
Algona.. .....$	274 00	$ 192 75
Fort Dodge.... .	261 00	146 20
Sheldon	266 00	152 75
Sioux City.	251 00	62 76
	$ 1,052 00	$ 554 46

Conference and Districts	Appor- tionment	Paid
NORTHWEST KANSAS		
Cobly. .... $	158 00	$ 134 15
Concordia.......	163 00	100 00
Salina	187 00	166 00
	$ 508 00	$ 400 15
NORWEGIAN AND DANISH		
Chicago $	98 00	$ 22 00
Eastern	63 00	42 00
Minneapolis	59 00	59 00
Red River Valley.	32 00	29 50
	$ 252 00	$ 152 50
OHIO		
Chillicothe.. . .$	365 00	$ 370 00
Cincinnati.... .	492 00	425 00
Columbus.......	443 00	352 02
Dayton........	370 00	288 91
Defiance........	335 00	157 30
Lima....... . .	345 00	310 00
Portsmouth.. ..	339 00	287 45
Springfield.... .	396 00	325 95
Toledo........	370 00	307 95
Wilmington. ..	311 00	318 00
Zanesville	345 00	266 40
	$ 4,111 00	$ 3,408 98
OKLAHOMA		
Alva ....$	164 00	$. 115 50
El Reno........	186 00	138 00
Enid	224 00	162 75
Oklahoma City...	258 00	254 00
Tulsa	273 00	218 00
	$ 1,105 00	$ 888 25
OREGON		
Cascade . .....$	159 00	$ 160 90
Portland..	253 00	236 25
Salem	218 00	196 90
	$ 630 00	$ 594 05
PACIFIC NORTHWEST		
Alaska.. . .$	22 00	$ 5 00
Puget Sound . .	188 00	144 00
Seattle-Tacoma .	267 00	275 50
Spokane	245 00	256 00
Vancouver......	179 00	171 50
Walla Walla	221 00	196 00
	$ 1,122 00	$ 1,048 00
PHILADELPHIA		
North... .. $	792 00	$ 631 35
Northwest	692 00	574 66
South. . .	755 00	634 50
West...	629 00	528 01
	$ 2,868 00	$ 2,368 52
PITTSBURGH		
Allegheny ....$	469 00	$ 469 00
Blairsville.......	508 00	508 00
Monongahela....	498 00	498 00
Pittsburgh....	752 00	752 00
	$ 2,227 00	$ 2,227 00
ROCK RIVER		
Chicago Northern$	574 00	$ 397 00
Chicago Southern	568 00	852 00
Chicago Western	567 00	347 00
Joliet-Dixon.....	449 00	217 45
Rockford	405 00	183 50
	$ 2,563 00	$ 1,496 95
ST. JOHNS RIVER		
Jacksonville . $	185 00	$ 159 55
Miami	162 00	152 00
	$ 347 00	$ 311 55

Conference and Districts	Appor- tionment	Paid
SAVANNAH		
La Grange..... $	19 00	$ 19 00
Savannah.....	23 00	23 00
Waynesboro.....	18 00	18 00
	$ 60 00	$ 60 00
SOUTH CAROLINA		
Beaufort.. ... $	51 00	$ 51 00
Bennettsville....	60 00	60 00
Charleston......	60 00	60 00
Florence...... .	83 00	83 00
Greenville.... .	49 00	49 00
Orangeburg......	49 00	52 00
Spartanburg.....	52 00	52 00
Sumter........	72 00	72 00
	$ 476 00	$ 479 00
SOUTH FLORIDA		
Atlantic ....$	24 00	$ 24 00
Gulf...	19 00	19 00
	$ 43 00	$ 43 00
SOUTHERN		
Lake Charles ...$	163 00	$ 117 00
San Antonio.....	165 00	98 40
	$ 328 00	$ 215 40
SOUTHERN CALIFORNIA		
Fresno-Glendale..$	389 00	$ 227 00
Long Beach	457 00	285 00
Los Angeles ...	576 00	447 00
Pasadena-Arizona	464 00	425 00
San Diego-Phoenix	426 00	412 00
	$ 2,312 00	$ 1,896 00
SOUTHERN ILLINOIS		
Carbondale . ....$	296 00	$ 152 63
Centralia	292 00	298 50
East St. Louis...	282 00	212 50
Olney . ..	267 00	225 50
	$ 1,107 00	$ 889 13
SOUTHWEST		
Fort Smith.... $	30 00	$ 30 00
Little Rock......	41 00	41 00
Oklahoma.. ..	21 00	21 00
	$ 92 00	$ 92 00
SOUTHWEST KANSAS		
Dodge City ... .$	257 00	$ 270 00
Hutchinson.... .	309 00	302 75
Liberal	163 00	109 00
Wichita	352 00	254 00
Winfield	214 00	185 50
	$ 1,295 00	$ 1,121 25
TENNESSEE		
Memphis .. . $	25 00	$ 25 00
Murfreesboro ...	21 00	21 00
Nashville	45 00	45 00
	$ 91 00	$ 91 00
TEXAS		
Beaumont .....$	40 00	$ 37 00
Houston . .	94 00	94 00
Marshall	41 00	41 00
Navasota.	19 00	19 00
Palestine... .	29 00	29 00
	$ 223 00	$ 220 00
TROY		
Albany . ....$	606 00	$ 570 00
Plattsburg	432 00	299 52
Troy..	520 00	342 50
	$ 1,558 00	$ 1,212 02

Conference and Districts	Appor-tionment	Paid
UPPER IOWA		
Cedar Rapids...	$ 256 00	$ 222 60
Davenport....	260 00	232 00
Dubuque........	282 00	288 00
Waterloo........	314 00	322 00
	$ 1,112 00	$ 1,064 60
UPPER MISSISSIPPI		
Aberdeen..... ..	$ 39 00	....
Clarksdale......	23 00	$ 20 00
Holly Springs...	39 00	38 00
Starkville..	32 00	....
Winona........	35 00	12 00
	$ 168 00	$ 70 00
VERMONT		
Montpelier	$ 361 00	$ 323 35
WASHINGTON		
Alexandria......	$ 122 00	$ 37 00
Charleston	96 00	56 00
North Baltimore.	144 00	144 00
South Baltimore..	124 00	91 00
Washington ...	166 00	166 00
	$ 652 00	$ 494 00
WEST TEXAS		
Austin	$ 23 00	$ 23 00
Dallas	42 00	30 50
San Angelo.....	12 00	12 00
San Antonio....	51 00	51 00
Victoria....	21 00	21 00
Waco..........	28 00	28 00
	$ 177 00	$ 165 50
WEST VIRGINIA		
Buckhannon.. ..	$ 236 00	$ 202 00
Charleston	279 00	197 50
Huntington-Parkersburg ..	259 00	187 90
Morgantown. ...	282 00	203 00
Wheeling.......	324 00	317 52
	$ 1,380 00	$ 1,107 92

Conference and Districts	Appor-tionment	Paid
WEST WISCONSIN		
Eau Claire... ..	$ 207 00	$ 151 00
La Crosse.......	254 00	137 00
Madison-Platteville.....	238 00	257 98
Superior........	153 00	51 00
	$ 852 00	$ 596 98
WESTERN NORWEGIAN-DANISH		
California	$ 28 00	$ 26 00
Pacific Northwest	38 00	22 00
	$ 66 00	$ 48 00
WILMINGTON		
Dover........ ...	$ 397 00	$ 327 91
Salisbury...... .	420 00	420 75
Wilmington.....	426 00	430 13
Miscellaneous ...	....	6 00
	$ 1,243 00	$ 1,184 79
WISCONSIN		
Appleton........	$ 362 00	$ 362 50
Milwaukee	393 00	370 50
Watertown	376 00	367 50
	$ 1,131 00	$ 1,100 50
WYOMING		
Binghamton . .	$ 416 00	$ 335 80
Oneonta.. . .	300 00	198 65
Scranton...... .	431 00	340 75
Wilkes Barre. ..	466 00	356 25
	$ 1,613 00	$ 1,231 45
WYOMING STATE		
Cheyenne-Sheridan. . ..	$ 173 00	$ 176 00
COLUMBUS AREA (Miscellaneous receipt)	.....	$ 1 00
	$85,565 00	$68,902 56

Missions

NEW MEXICO.. ....$		10 50
UTAH...		50 85
	$	61 35

Total Apportionment to Annual Conferences in the United States $85,565 00

Amount Paid by Annual Conferences in the United States..... . ...$68,902 56

Percentage of payment—80.53%

Amount Paid by Missions... ....   61 35

Total Amount Received to July 15, 1939. . ...$68,963 91

INDEX

To the Journal of the Uniting Conference, 1939

PREPARED BY CURTIS B. HALEY